THE CENTURY PSYCHOLOGY SERIES

Richard M. Elliott, Gardner Lindzey & Kenneth MacCorquodale

Editors

BASIC PSYCHOLOGY

Howard H. Kendler

UNIVERSITY OF CALIFORNIA,
SANTA BARBARA

BASIC PSYCHOLOGY

APPLETON-CENTURY-CROFTS

DIVISION OF MEREDITH PUBLISHING COMPANY

PRINTED IN THE UNITED STATES OF AMERICA

E 50310

To Tracy

PREFACE

The large number of introductory psychology textbooks forces the author of a new one to justify his efforts—if only to himself. This demand can best be met by a description of the two related aims that governed the writing of *Basic Psychology*. One was to provide a realistic and clear picture of contemporary psychology. The other was to meet the educational needs of introductory psychology courses.

In my opinion, both aims have to be met by an integrated text that not only covers the length and breadth of psychological knowledge but also provides some depth of understanding. Psychology—a discipline that is hurtling toward scientific maturity—possesses an intrinsic structure that demands three-dimensional treatment. In an effort to reveal this structure I have emphasized in this book the core of psychological knowledge. This core has, I believe, two components: basic psychological processes and complex psychological processes. In the former category are the facts and theories that emerge from the experimental analysis of sensation, conditioning, perception, and motivation. They reveal how fundamental principles of behavior operate in isolation. How these principles interact can be seen most clearly in the study of such complex psychological processes as learning and forgetting, verbal behavior and problem solving, and frustration and conflict. The other areas of psychology like personality and social behavior can be best understood in terms of how they radiate from the inner core of psychology.

The structure of knowledge is not the only consideration in preparing an introductory psychology text. Educational goals must also be weighed. Introductory courses must obviously be tailored to meet the needs of the terminal student—the student who will not take advanced courses—but it is shortsighted to consider his needs as the only ones. The introductory course is a showcase for the science of psychology. If it is not sufficiently interesting and challenging, it will not attract psychology's fair share of scientifically talented students. We all agree that research is psychology's lifeblood, but we sometimes forget that unless we recruit potentially creative scientists, psychology's growth is bound to be stunted.

It might be argued that we need two kinds of introductory courses—one for majors, the other for nonmajors. I question such a solution. It has been my experience, in teaching introductory psychology for over 15 years, that many students decide to major in psychology, or give up the idea, only after completing an introductory course. In addition, we have to consider pedagogical principles. Psychology is psychology regardless of the student's program of study; and all students should be taught psychology in an integrated, systematic fashion. Although this approach challenges the teacher more than a two-dimensional survey course, its success is more rewarding to the teacher himself, to his students, and to the science of psychology.

No one can write an introductory psychology textbook alone. An author needs help, both intellectual and technical, from many others. I want to acknowledge the assistance I have received.

I am obviously indebted to many psychologists whose research I have described and whose ideas I have freely borrowed. Those who read the following pages will recognize the special debt owed to Neal Miller, B. F. Skinner, and Kenneth W. Spence (in alphabetical order). I am also indebted to my teachers at Brooklyn College and the State University of Iowa, and to my former fellow graduate students who provided intellectual stimulation and friendship. Professor Karl Muenzinger, whose memory I will always cherish, encouraged me to undertake this project because he believed that writing an introductory textbook is the best way to learn psychology. He may have been right—but there must be easier ways.

During the time this book was under way I profited from discussions with Charles Cofer, Mike D'Amato, Dottie Hurvich, Leo Postman, and Bob Silverman. Leo Hurvich and Ben McKeever offered many helpful suggestions to improve some chapters they read. The contributions of my graduate students and teaching assistants in the introductory psychology course must also be acknowledged. My greatest intellectual debt is to my teacher, mentor, and friend, Kenneth W. Spence, whose demands for clarity and organization of ideas served as ideals, which I knew I could not achieve but, nevertheless, tried to approach.

To Mike Elliott and Ken MacCorquodale I owe a debt of gratitude about which only I know, since they are too generous to acknowledge it. Gardner Lindzey offered many important suggestions, and in a manner that I will never forget. Although the members of the editorial staff at Appleton-Century-Crofts were just doing their jobs in preparing this book, I feel compelled to express my appreciation for the way they did it.

Many different secretaries worked on this project. The major contribution was made by Anne Zeidberg, whose involvement in this book could not have been any greater if it had been her very own.

To complete my list of obligations, I must mention the members of my family. My mother, under most trying circumstances, made it possible for me to attend college and graduate school. My two sons, Joel and Kenneth, passed from childhood to early adolescence during the time this book was being written. They tried to learn not to disturb me when I was writing, and I tried to learn not to join them when they were playing. All in all, our combined efforts at self-discipline postponed the publication of this book by no more than two years.

And finally, I turn my attention to the person to whom I dedicate this book. Tracy Kendler's contribution cannot be measured by her invaluable suggestions and criticisms, or by the length of time she spent in reading, rereading, and proofreading. Her ability to execute a variety of roles with distinction—wife, companion, mother, research colleague, housekeeper, and some others—made this book possible and life enjoyable.

H. H. K.

TO THE TEACHER

A book designed to present psychology in a unified fashion cannot be used as flexibly as one designed to present a general overview. The chapters in *Basic Psychology* cannot be arranged in a wide variety of sequences without confusing the reader. Nevertheless, some options are available to teachers using this book.

The greatest freedom of choice is at the beginning. Every instructor in an introductory psychology course faces a major dilemma. Shall the student be *prepared* to study psychology, or shall he start with fundamental facts and theories? Many students bring erroneous ideas and attitudes to their first psychology course. Would it not be better for them to unlearn their misconceptions before they start to learn about psychology? Section I, consisting of two brief chapters, is designed to do this. It describes the nature of scientific method and relates it to the study of psychology.

Providing some methodological sophistication is not the only preparation that the beginning student can be offered. Some teachers believe that the student who knows something about psychology's origins and contemporary status will find it easier to understand its facts and theories. Others believe that knowledge about statistics is helpful, and there are still others who insist that an elementary understanding of physiology is essential. Section II, containing short chapters on each of these three topics, offers such preparation.

Sections I and II can be handled by the instructor in a number of different ways. One radical solution would be to eliminate them completely. Naturally, I do not favor such an alternative. I would not have written these sections if I did. But I can appreciate a teacher's concern with getting his class onto the content of psychology as rapidly as possible. Another choice is to assign Section I, and eliminate all or part of Section II, with little or no lecturing and classroom discussion. I have never subscribed to the view that a teacher must lecture about everything he requires the student to read. The important consideration is whether reading all or part of the first two sections, with or without lectures and discussion, will assist the student in understanding and integrating psychological knowledge. I believe they do, but am well aware that many instructors who agree with me about the aims of an introductory psychology course may not share this opinion.

Whereas Sections I and II offer several options, Sections III and IV provide practically none. They are the backbone of this book, and the topics they cover are, in my opinion, the essential ingredients of an introductory course in the science of behavior. Section III (Chapters 6 through 9) offers a treatment of basic psychological processes (sensation, conditioning, perception, and motivation), and Section IV (Chapters 10 through 12) describes complex psychological processes (learning and forgetting, verbal behavior and problem solving, and frustration and conflict). Section III must precede Section IV, although within each section the position of some chapters may be shifted: perception might be taught before conditioning, frustration and conflict might precede verbal behavior and problem solving.

The sequence that begins with the description of simple forms of behavior (Section III) is brought to its conclusion in Section V (Chapters 13 through 15), which discusses in order the psychology of personality, behavior pathology, and social behavior. Chapters 13 and 14 must be taught one after the other, and the student would benefit from reading Chapter 15 after he completes the previous two.

The major problem with Section VI is whether there will be sufficient time in a semester course to cover both chapters. To my mind an introductory student's education would be incomplete if he failed to have contact with the topics psychological testing and intelligence, both of which form the subject matter of Chapter 16. Chapter 17, which reviews three areas of applied psychology (human engineering, the technology of learning, and vocational guidance), can be more easily dispensed with, unless some overriding reason demands its inclusion at the expense of another chapter.

More as a result of the nature of the subject matter than by design, I have placed most of the discussion of physiological variables at the end of each chapter. This is true also of the theoretical discussions. Although in neither case is the segregation of these topics complete, the instructor could eliminate most, if not all, of these sections if he wished.

TO THE STUDENT

Psychology is an extremely popular subject because it deals with such fascinating topics as how personalities are formed—and sometimes malformed. However, many of those who express an interest in the subject are really interested only in its more sensational and superficial aspects; they are unwilling to give the time and effort necessary to understand psychology fully.

It has been claimed, and rightly so, that psychology is too popular for its own good. People are so eager to understand themselves and others that they gobble up information without considering its source. Self-styled psychological experts who offer advice to anyone, anywhere, at any time after seeing two psychiatric movies and reading one book by Freud are all too common. Such presumption would simply be amusing if it did not cause mischief. Naive psychological advice can be harmful, but possibly more dangerous in the long run are the misconceptions about psychology which these self-styled psychologists give the public. Psychology plays an important role in our society; it would be unfortunate if its potential value were compromised by the misinformation offered by those more eager to borrow its name than its principles or methods.

Blame for these misconceptions belongs not only to those who pose as psychologists, but also, and even more, to those who are willing—almost eager—to accept superficial answers to complex questions. Many of these same people would be suspicious immediately if they were given simple explanations of how an automobile or an earth satellite functions; they would know at once that both of these are complicated mechanisms. Yet they will swallow simple explanations of human behavior. Human behavior, or even the behavior of laboratory rats, is far more complicated than the working of an automobile or an earth satellite. If you want to understand how automobiles or satellites work, you have to give them intensive study. So, if you genuinely want to understand psychology, you must accept right away the idea that you are going to have to expend a good deal of effort and thought.

Some students, electing to take a psychology course, may hope that the study will begin with a discussion of individuals who behave strangely. But scientific psychology does not begin with the study of the surprising, the bizarre, or even the unusual. In psychology, as in other sciences, a student must understand simple or basic things before he can appreciate what is complex. Before you can have any valuable insight into pathological behavior, you must have some understanding of how we see and hear, how we learn and perceive, why we want things, and why we sometimes persist in going after them. After you acquire this basic knowledge you will be better prepared to understand complex psychological processes like forgetting, verbal behavior, problem solving, frustration, and conflict. And finally, you will be ready to study personality, the pathology of behavior, social behavior, psychological tests, human engineering, programmed learning, and vocational guidance.

You must realize that learning about psychology depends more on you than on anybody else. This statement is not made to disclaim any responsibility the writer or your instructor has for your education. Instead, it is made to highlight the fact that the student is not a receptacle into which knowledge is poured. He does not passively absorb the information from textbooks and lectures. Learning is an active process, as you will discover, if you have not already, when we discuss the facts and theories of the psychology of learning. You cannot, if you desire to learn, read this text as if it were a light novel. You must read it with real effort. You must pay attention. You must interpret what you read and relate it to what you already know. You must select important ideas by underlining appropriate passages. You must take meaningful notes, preferably *in your own words*. When you come to a new concept or fact you should rehearse it to yourself so that you will remember it better. If you don't understand something, do not proceed to the next section. Reread the section that gives you difficulty and see whether you cannot improve your comprehension. Only by such active participation in reading can you hope to organize and understand the information this book contains.

Now that your job has been described, let us turn our attention to how this book was designed to help you. It was written with the intention of providing the student with optimal conditions for learning.

The book contains six sections, each consisting of a group of related chapters. Each section is preceded by a short introduction which provides an overview of the material to be presented. This should help you organize your thoughts so that you will be prepared for what follows. Each chapter concludes with a summary that presents the essence of the material in capsule form. If any part of the summary does not strike a familiar chord, you should return to the appropriate section in the chapter and review the material. Some students will find it helpful to read the summary before the chapter, so that they will have some idea of its organization and high points.

Because psychology is something new, you will be required to learn many technical terms. When an important term is introduced it appears in boldface and is defined. A list of important terms is defined in the Glossary at the end of the book. It is essential that you know the definition of these terms. Do not, however, be fooled into believing that knowing their definitions is sufficient. Psychological knowledge consists of more than that. You must learn the relationships between each technical term and a host of other terms. One other warning. Do not assume that if a term is familiar to you (intelligence, motivation, attitude), you know its technical meaning. The definition of such psychological concepts is quite different from their vague everyday meaning.

Scientific knowledge can often be presented most clearly and precisely in graphical and tabular form. Graphs and tables appear throughout the book. Don't just glance at them. Study them and discover what information they convey. Also, pay attention to photographs. Very often they clarify a complicated point.

A *Study Guide* has been written to accompany *Basic Psychology*. It provides a number of different kinds of exercises that will help you to learn, and to prepare for examinations. They will also help you determine how well you know your subject matter.

At the end of each chapter are Suggestions for Further Reading. The reader who is interested in learning more about any topic can refer to these sources. He should also confer with his instructor for additional suggestions.

Psychology, like any other science, is a sum total of the efforts of individual scientists. It is proper that their work be acknowledged when reference is made to it. This is done by the conventional method of citing within parentheses the author and the year of the publication. The complete citation is given in the list of references at the end of the book. This list is also a useful reference for those students who wish to expand their knowledge of psychology.

CONTENTS

BASIC PSYCHOLOGY

GENERAL ORIENTATION

I

Everyone likes to think of himself as something of a psychologist. In a way, everyone is. Most of us want to—and need to—understand our own behavior as well as the behavior of others. Sometimes, we think we do, judging by the interpretations we confidently offer: "I am not really lazy," "Bill is insecure," "Betty is weak-willed," "Jack is frustrated," "Jim has a bad heredity," and so on.

This book is about behavior, and in this sense, reflects the general interest in what people do. However, I have deliberately restricted myself to one general method in describing, systematizing, and explaining the facts of behavior—the *scientific method*. It is an exacting and completely different method from the informal ways of common sense, or from theological, literary, and esthetic interpretations of the behavior of men and animals. Therefore, we should not be surprised if a drastically different picture of behavior emerges from scientific inquiry than from these other disciplines.

Scientific method has its rules and regulations. To fully understand its results, whether in physics, biology, or psychology, we must first gain some familiarity with its basic principles. This is not a forbidding task—or even a dull one. In fact, it is rather simple, interesting, and often, extremely useful. Though relatively few of you will become scientists, many occasions shall arise when you will know the advantages of thinking and acting scientifically.

A little reflection will convince you of the need to acquire a better understanding of science. Although you would probably say you are "for" science, can you describe just what science is? What do *truth, reality, objective* and *explanation* mean? We often use such concepts in describing scientific method.

1

Science students are not the only ones who would have difficulty answering these questions. Less highly trained science teachers may also experience similar difficulty. Some scientists too, though quite at home among the facts of their discipline, do not fully appreciate the nature of scientific method. In this scientific age, the teaching of science as such, in the abstract, has been sadly neglected.

To help you understand psychology, the first two chapters will instruct you in the nature of science. From a deeper appreciation of the facts and theories in psychology you will be better able to apply it in a sensible way to everyday problems.

SCIENTIFIC METHOD

1

THE DEFINITION OF PSYCHOLOGY

It is customary to begin an introductory text by defining its subject. Following this convention, we state at once that *psychology* is the *science* of *behavior*. This statement, flatly made, means only that contemporary psychologists elected, for reasons that will become clearer later in this book, to direct their investigations to the scientific study of behavior.

THE NATURE OF SCIENCE

If we were limited to one adjective to describe the uniqueness of our contemporary civilization, most of us would choose the word *scientific*. And yet, if we are asked to specify the meaning of this term, we discover that it is not at once clear to us. Our educational system offers many courses in physics, chemistry, and other sciences, but fails to provide adequate instruction in *science itself*. The result is that from courses in science we learn a great many facts (or what we believe are facts) and some theories (or what we believe are theories). We rarely learn, however, how to discriminate between facts and pseudo facts, or between theories and pseudo theories. This is an especially serious handicap in anyone who wishes to study psychology.

Practically everyone has some preconceived notions or theories about psychological matters. Perhaps we believe that a person's intelligence is determined by the kind of environment he has been brought up in, that insanity is caused by heredity, or that reading aloud slowly is the best method of studying for an examination. Unless we are trained to evaluate such statements critically, and especially to demand

4

the evidence required to support or refute such statements, we will not be able to understand the science of psychology, or to profit from its many practical implications.

And, it should be added, the need to understand the nature of science goes beyond the requirements of an introductory psychology course. We live in an age in which the findings and technology of science pose important problems that demand solution. Dr. James B. Conant, a famous chemist and former president of Harvard University, puts it this way:

We need a widespread understanding of science in this country, for only thus can science be assimilated into our secular pattern. When that has been achieved, we shall be one step nearer the goal which we now desire so earnestly, a unified, coherent culture suitable for our American democracy in this new age of machines and experts (1947, p. 3).

Scientists are often looked upon as a race apart who explore nature with the aid of a mysterious, hard-to-understand technique known as scientific method. This view should not exist. Scientists are human beings, and the general nature of their method is comprehensible to every college student.

Science may be compared to a game of chess. There are certain fixed rules that must be obeyed in order to play this game. In a similar sense there are fixed rules in science—how terms are to be defined, how events are to be explained, and many others. Some people learn to play chess well. They learn various types of "openings" (an opening is a more or less fixed sequence of moves at the beginning of the game); they adopt a certain strategy which determines their various moves; and finally they learn how to win a game after they have achieved an advantage. To "play" well at science, one must also learn adequate "openings" in the sense of learning how to ask meaningful and important

questions. One must also adopt a research strategy that will lead to experimentation capable of answering these questions. Once the facts are obtained, the scientist must interpret them reasonably in the light of much else that is known, in order to fully realize their implications. There are three stages or steps in a single "game" of science, usually called an experiment: (1) forming a conjecture, i.e., a hypothesis, (2) investigation, or experimentation proper, and (3) interpretation. Moreover, just as there is no sharp division between the opening, middle, and end of a chess game, so there is no sharp division between the stages of conjecture, experimentation, and interpretation. Of course, in chess, as well as in science, there are those individuals who are never satisfied to stop when one game or one experiment is concluded. That is how experts in chess and science begin to develop.

A similar analogy between science and such games as football, baseball, Scrabble, or poker can be made. These analogies, however, suffer somewhat from oversimplification. First, there is no universally accepted book of formal rules in science such as there is in checkers or football. What has actually happened is that some individual scientist, or perhaps philosopher, has attempted to analyze what scientists actually do and has formulated the principles underlying these procedures—or, in terms of our analogy, the rules of the game of science. This formulation has been done with special thoroughness since the beginning of our century, and a whole field, the philosophy of science, has developed. Its task has been to make a systematic analysis of the structure of scientific knowledge. These specialists in the philosophy of science (many of whom have also been scientists) have provided us with a more sophisticated formulation of scientific method, one that was necessary before many difficult problems could be attacked.

The second manner in which science differs from sports and games is that it is a much more serious undertaking. The history of science is studded with the names of illustrious scientists who have made great sacrifices to maintain their scientific integrity and freedom of inquiry. Unfortunately history records numerous incidents of groups or governments attempting to interfere with science because they feared that their own interests and preconceived ideas were threatened by the searching techniques and inherent honesty of scientific inquiry. To the scientist, however, one of the most gratifying trends in the history of our civilization is the gradual but persistent liberation of scientific inquiry from those forces which seek to shackle it. In the sense that games demand certain rules of conduct, science is a game; but in the sense that a game is an amusing diversion, science is certainly not a game—but rather one of the most serious and taxing of human undertakings.

THE FUNCTION OF SCIENCE

When we turn from thinking in general terms of the role of science—the search for verifiable truth, the advancement of civilization, control of the forces of nature, etc.—what science is actually engaged in doing can be described simply and prosaically. It is the job of scientific inquiry to discover those conditions or factors that bring about, determine, or cause the occurrence of a particular event. Different scientists concern themselves with the causes of different events: a physicist with the rate at which bodies fall, a chemist with explosives, an economist with price changes, a psychologist with the development of fears. They are all interested in different events, but their basic task is similar: to discover those factors or conditions—scientists usually call them variables—which are effective in bringing about the occurrence of an event. This task can be clearly and simply expressed by the following formula:

$$Y = f(X_1, X_2, X_3 \ldots X_n)$$

In this formula Y represents an event, the conditions of which the scientist wishes to discover; f represents the phrase "function of," in the sense of "is causally dependent upon"; while the X's represent those factors or variables upon which the occurrence of the Y event depends.

Once he has decided to investigate a particular phenomenon, the task of the scientist in psychology, as well as in the other sciences, is to *fill in* the above formula—to discover those variables which determine the occurrence of that phenomenon. This is a time-consuming task which requires, in addition to much thought and planning, extensive experimentation. One experiment usually provides information about one variable only (perhaps X_1 in the above formula).

For example, a question that has interested many people, including psychologists, is: Can learning occur during sleep? That is, can sleep be one of several X's in the above formula when Y represents learning? Or does sleep prevent learning, so that learning (Y) can never occur during (is not a function of) sleep (X).

At first glance the question as stated seems to be a simple one. Actually it is rather complex. The reason for its complexity is that, contrary to popular opinion, it is not easy to know whether a person is awake or asleep. There is no sharp and clear separation between wakefulness and sleep. As you fall asleep, what usually happens is that you proceed by a gradual transition from complete wakefulness to deep sleep. Initially you become drowsy, but are still aware of nearby noises and conversation. Gradually you become less

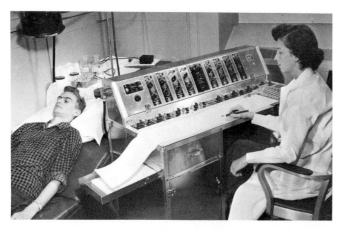

FIGURE 1.1 How EEG Records Are Obtained. Electrodes are mounted on the scalp and the spontaneous electrical activity of the brain is amplified and then recorded (National Institute of Health).

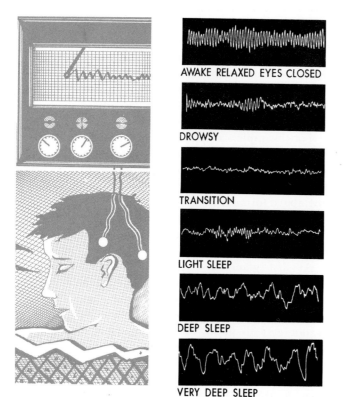

AWAKE RELAXED EYES CLOSED

DROWSY

TRANSITION

LIGHT SLEEP

DEEP SLEEP

VERY DEEP SLEEP

FIGURE 1.2 Characteristic EEG Patterns Appearing During Different Stages of Waking and Sleep (After Simon & Emmons, 1956, with permission of *The American Journal of Psychology*).

aware of your immediate environment. You pass into a light sleep during which you are insensitive to all sounds except those that are sufficiently intense to awaken you. Then you proceed into a deeper and deeper sleep. The deeper the sleep, the more intense is the stimulation required to awaken you. The course one takes in falling asleep varies from individual to individual and from time to time in the same individual. Some people can shift rapidly from alert wakefulness to deep sleep, while others are not so fortunate. It may take them a long time to fall asleep, and they may be incapable of achieving the deepest levels of sleep.

If you wish to know whether a person can learn during sleep, you must have a foolproof method of knowing whether he is asleep and how deep is his sleep. Is he just drowsy or is he fast asleep? You cannot ask him because if he does not answer it may be due either to his drowsiness or to his deep sleep.

Fortunately, depth of sleep can be measured without the cooperation of the sleeping person. This is accomplished by measuring a phenomenon of which you are probably unaware. Your brain constantly generates electrical activity. This electrical activity is very weak, but by attaching electrodes to the scalp (see Figure 1.1) these electrical currents can be amplified and recorded. The resulting record, examples of which are shown in Figure 1.2, is known as an **electroencephalogram** (abbreviated to EEG and literally meaning electrical-brain-record). The pattern of the EEG record changes as a person falls asleep. Thus it is possible to distinguish a drowsy state from one of deep sleep.

Several years ago an experiment (Simon & Emmons, 1956) was conducted upon a group of 21 men selected to serve as subjects, which threw much light upon the question whether learning could occur during sleep. The design of the experiment was to have these young men hear a series of 96 questions and answers while they were supposedly asleep. One such question-answer combination was: Question, "In what kind of store did Ulysses S. Grant work before the war?" Answer, "Before the war Ulysses S. Grant worked in a hardware store." In order to estimate exactly what was learned during the sleep period, the researchers gave the young men, before they lay down, a test consisting of the 96 questions, which they were required to answer if they could. Each man's performance on this test provided a score from which the amount he learned later during the sleep period could be determined.

Following the initial test, the men were permitted to sleep in comfortable beds for a period of eight hours. During this period their EEG's were taken continuously while every five minutes one of the 96 question-answer combinations was broadcast through a loudspeaker at a normal conversational level. At the end of the eight-hour period the men were awakened (if they were not already awake) and permitted to wash and dress. Then they were tested. They were asked the very same questions they had been asked before and during the eight-hour sleep period. Since the experimenter had found out how many questions each subject could answer before the sleep-training period, he could determine what each subject had learned during that period. In addition the experimenter could estimate from the EEG records the depth of sleep of each subject at the very time he was acquiring any new piece of information. The results provided no support to the idea that learning can take place during sleep. When the EEG records revealed that the subjects were awake, or were simply relaxed with their eyes closed, they learned about 80 per cent of the information broadcast to them. However, when they were asleep, as defined by the patterns of the EEG record, there was no evidence of learning. Consequently we must conclude that devices which purport to teach during sleep fail in their purpose. At best these gadgets, instead of teaching during sleep, keep people awake so that learning can take place.

THE RULES OF THE GAME

Let us now return to our original task, the understanding of science. However, we will refer occasionally to the sleep-learning experiment in order to clarify some abstract idea with a concrete example.

Perhaps there is no more important rule in the game of science, even if it is sometimes overlooked, than that it is founded in what is given in sensory experience. This simple point, otherwise stated—and although simple, having profound implications—is that the basis of all science is *observation*. By observation we mean the sensory experience of a scientist noting that a given event occurs. In this way the raw data (Latin plural for *datum,* meaning "something given") of all sciences are of one sort: they are given to an observer. The knowledge that you obtain from any scientific book—whether in physics, chemistry, biology, or psychology—stems ultimately from *the observations of the scientist,* although the observations may sometimes be made, to be sure, with the aid of exceedingly complex instruments.

In order to clarify this point, let us consider the following question: Is there any essential *difference* between the physicist reporting his observations of the movements of a pointer on a pressure gauge, or the chemist reporting his observation of a change in color produced by adding a chemical to some mixture, or a psychologist reporting his observation that a young man does not know where Ulysses S. Grant worked before the war? My point is that *there is no essential difference.* The basic data of all sciences are the same. The "925-lb. pressure" which the physicist records, or the word *red* which the chemist writes in his data book, or the checkmark which the psychologist records indicating a subject's "I don't know," all refer to the same kind of thing: an observation made by a human being. The raw materials of science must have passed through the sense organs of the observing scientist. Hence they must be *public,* i.e., freely observable by any properly equipped and trained observer.

It follows that the conventional division of science into areas of study such as physics, biology, and psychology constitutes a *convenient division of labor,* and does not reflect any *basic difference* between these various areas. In support of this statement we might point to the breakdown that has occurred in recent decades of the borders separating our conventional divisions of scientific research; today we have such fields as biophysics, biochemistry, social psychology, and physiological psychology. If each "science" involved a unique type of observation, the merging of various fields would not—and could not—have occurred.

It is possible you still feel that there must be a basic difference between two such seemingly different areas as physics and psychology. "Isn't physics a more exact science than psychology?" you ask. It certainly is! But this does not necessarily imply that the two areas of study are qualitatively different. A man is taller and stronger than a boy, but that does not mean he is an altogether different animal. Moreover, you should remember that the greater exactness of physics results in part from the fact that it is a relatively mature science. Psychology, on the other hand, is an exceedingly young science; the first laboratory labeled "psychological" was founded at the University of Leipzig in 1879 (some Harvard men deny this, insisting that Harvard had a psychology laboratory even before the University of Leipzig). Physics was once

at the same developmental stage at which psychology is now—striving both to develop experimental techniques from which basic data could be obtained and to formulate meaningful and answerable questions. And, it might also be added, before that time physics was less of an exact science than psychology is today.

You may still be unconvinced, holding to the idea of a basic difference between psychology and physics. Physics deals with inanimate phenomena, and is capable of predicting them, whereas psychology, you suppose, can never predict the behavior of human beings, who are so complex and inscrutable that adequate predictions are impossible. But a moment's reflection will reveal that much of human behavior is predictable. You are constantly willing to risk your very life on predictions of the behavior of others. You predict that the driver coming the opposite way will not swerve in front of you; you predict that both pilot and copilot of the airliner will not fall asleep; you predict that the farmer and groceryman can safely distinguish between an edible mushroom and a poisonous toadstool; you predict that the pharmacist will not make a fatal mistake in putting up your prescription—in fact, your being alive today is testimony to the fact that human behavior can be highly predictable.

Of course, it may be that even after centuries psychology will not achieve the high degree of predictability of which contemporary physics is capable. But the important point is that behavior is predictable, and as you will see, psychologists are constantly devising newer and better methods and theories to render psychological predictions more and more accurate.

If any reader remains unconvinced about the unity of all sciences, I can only urge him that for the present he examine tolerantly and thoughtfully the ideas he will encounter in this book. Perhaps the remainder of the book will achieve what this brief introduction to scientific method is unable to do. Ultimately he should realize that the right to be considered a science is not inherent in any particular area of investigation; nor is it dependent upon any particular degree of precision in predicting events in that area. Rather scientific status is earned by the *methods of investigation* brought to bear upon a group of problems. Hence, instead of continuing to debate whether psychology is really a science, it will be wiser for us to examine the methods of study used in contemporary psychology and to discover whether they meet the requirements of scientific method. This we will do throughout this book.

Now let us return to the problem of the foundation of science. The fact that the data of every science are obtained by the observation of some experimenter (or observer) is both a basic and an important point. However, a common reaction of some students will be a cynical "so what?" We can best answer the "so what" attitude by citing an important implication of the observational basis of scientific knowledge. Frequently questions are raised that are not reducible to any set of observations and hence, in a scientific sense, remain unanswerable. Some questions cannot be answered, not because they are profound, but rather because they are *meaningless*. Nobody today can take seriously the question, "How many angels can dance on the head of a pin?" If we remember that science is based on observations, then this question is scientifically meaningless because angels can be neither observed nor counted. There are also questions in psychology which cannot be answered because they are wrongly asked. As we shall discover, whether intelligence is determined by heredity *or* by environment is, if asked in this form, quite without meaning. You have probably seriously considered questions which you thought were about psychology but which you will discover are meaningless because they fail to contain any reference to an observational component by which they could be answered.

THE RULES OF LANGUAGE

Up to now we have been referring to science within its laboratory setting. We have stated that science begins with observations, and that in order for any question to have scientific meaning it must have a reference to variables that can be observed. We know, however, that scientific method consists of more than making observations. Science may begin with the observations of the scientist, but it certainly does not end there. Not only must observations be made, but they must also be communicated to other scientists, and there is great danger that during this process of communication misunderstanding and confusion may arise. In order to minimize these dangers certain precautions in language usage are necessary.

This brings us to the problem of how statements (or propositions) are to be made in science, what these statements and the terms in them mean, a problem crucial both to science and to society. Our concern, for the present, will be restricted to the problem of the meaning of *scientific terms* and *scientific statements,* but as you read on you may realize that the implications of this analysis are relevant to problems of everyday life.

There are two types of meaning, and the failure to distinguish sharply and clearly between them has been a source of great confusion. The first type of meaning is **operational meaning,** and it has to do with the definition of terms or what are sometimes called concepts. The second type is **factual meaning,** and it has to do with the truth or falsity of scientific statements. Let us consider operational meaning first.

Operational Meaning

If you were to undertake an extensive research project on the factors that make women beautiful, your first problem would be to define beauty. The term at present is vague, since there are individuals who would be called beautiful by some judges and not by others. Are they beautiful? This question can best be examined by referring to another question. How would you settle a dispute whether a certain table is more or less than three feet long? The answer is simple. You take a ruler and measure it. The difference between the terms is that *foot* has a clear operational definition whereas *beauty* does not, that is, there are explicit operations accepted by all, which can be performed to measure the length of a table, but none to measure beauty. Does this mean, therefore, that research on beauty cannot be initiated? Certainly not! At one time everyone was not in agreement as to what operations they should use to measure length. The length of an individual's foot or the width of his hand was used, but as we know, the size of these varies appreciably from individual to individual. With the development of cooperative projects, it became necessary to have standards of measurement which were precise and easily communicable. Just consider what would happen if four men, who were each to build one of the four sides of the *same* house, were to use the width of their own hands as the unit of measurement. Science is just as much, if not more, of a cooperative venture as building a house and therefore requires agreement as to the meaning of terms. Since length is an important dimension in physics, the demand for the invention of a scale of length was great, and consequently precise and fruitful operational definitions of length were formulated. Psychology is at that stage in its development where it, too, needs precise

definitions of basic dimensions. Many have been developed, but many more will be required.

We may now state that the operational meaning of a term or concept is defined by those operations or manipulations made by the scientist when his work involves that term or concept. For example, the operational definition of length is given in the specifications of the procedure used in measurement: the successive superimposing of the ruler on the thing to be measured. Or, to use an example from psychology, the operational definition of intelligence is given in the description of the technique of intelligence testing.

The significance of the operational definition is twofold. First, it facilitates communication by reducing vague meaning. The problem of understanding the meaning of a term is reduced to the problem of knowing what operations the research scientist performed. For example, if you wish to understand the use of the concept of sleep in the sleep-learning experiment, you need only know those operations used to define it, i.e., measurement of the EEG patterns.

The second important feature of operational definitions is that they discourage scientifically meaningless questions. If we insist that scientific terms possess operational definitions, it becomes easier to detect those questions which cannot be answered by experimentation or controlled observation. "Can you change human nature?" is such a question. What are the techniques by which we measure human nature? How would we know if it changed? In short, what is the operational definition of human nature? Questions involving concepts for which no operational definitions exist, or none are suggested, can obviously not be subjected to experimental investigation. By insisting on operational definitions, we can save ourselves much time and effort, for in the history of all fields of science certain questions, considered important at one time, were discovered to be essentially meaningless at a later date. The terms, indeed the very things these questions were about, lacked any operational definition.

Factual Meaning

Scientific work does not end with the formulation of adequate operational definitions, but is only just ready to get under way. You may recall that it has been stated that the function of science is to discover those factors which determine the occurrence of an event. In order to do this, operational definitions of both the event and the factor or factors assumed to be related to its occurrence are required. For example, before the question whether learning could occur during sleep could be answered, operational definitions of both

learning and sleep were needed. Learning was operationally defined by a *very common* criterion: the ability of subjects to answer correctly questions they were unable to answer before. Sleep was operationally defined by EEG patterns.

The results of the sleep-learning experiment establish factual meaning involving the concepts of learning and sleep; they indicate how the two are related. Figure 1.3 is designed to clarify the distinction between operational meaning and factual meaning by using the sleep-learning study as a model.

You note that the two concepts are represented within circles connected by straight lines to squares which represent all the observations associated with use of these concepts. For the purposes of communication these squares are labeled only with the

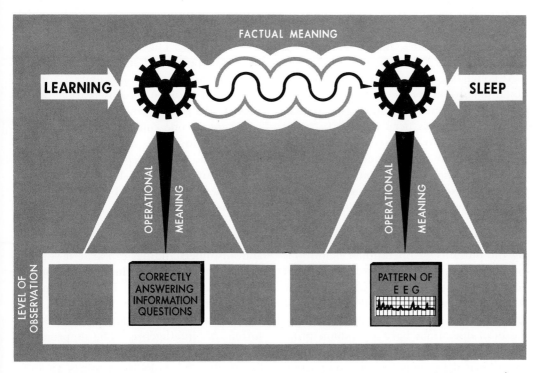

FIGURE 1.3 A Schematic Representation of the Distinction Between Operational Meaning and Factual Meaning. Operational definitions link concepts to observations while factual meaning states the relationship between concepts.

dominant set of observations linked to the concepts. It should be remembered, however, that the operational definitions refer to all the operations made by the scientist in his use of the concept. Scientific concepts are nothing more than name tags for sets of operations.

You will note that in the diagram three lines stemming from the concepts are "connected" to the level of observation. This indicates that there is *not only one* operational definition for these concepts. We will discover later that learning is defined in many different ways in many different situations. For example, learning is sometimes defined in terms of how rapidly rats depress a bar and other times by the ability of humans to acquire abstract concepts. That is, the concept of learning in contemporary psychology refers to a *class* of sets of operations rather than just one set of operations. This situation is analogous to that existing in physics, where many different operational definitions exist for the concept of atoms, and in biology, for heredity.

Although we do not have many operational definitions for sleep, there is no reason why new ones cannot be formulated. Depth of sleep has been defined in terms of insensitivity to a series of noises, and perhaps someday it may be defined in terms of level of muscular tension. It is likely that future research involving sleep will provide new operational definitions of sleep.

To grasp the important point concerning the plurality of operational definitions for many concepts, such as learning and sleep, one must realize that implied in use of the same label for different classes of operations is the assumption that these classes of operations have a common property. In the case of learning, all the various operational definitions refer to some situation in which an organism acquires new modes of behaving as a result of practice,

and the common property of the various operational definitions of sleep would be a certain physiological state of the organism.

We come now to the heart of scientific method: the problem of factual meaning which is schematically represented in Figure 1.3 by the wavy solid line connecting the two concepts. The first point to realize is that factual meaning refers to the *results of experimentation* (or its equivalent in *controlled observation,* such as occurs in the science of astronomy). For example, learning, defined in terms of acquiring information, did not occur during sleep, defined in terms of an EEG pattern. Such a finding is referred to as an empirical relationship (*empirical* means based on observation), or more commonly, as a fact. The second point to realize is that before this factual meaning could be established, the concepts (learning and sleep) under consideration had to be *operationally defined.* The operational definitions were the tools by which the empirical law involving the concepts was obtained. The distinction, therefore, between operational meaning and factual meaning, as illustrated in Figure 1.3, is the distinction between the observations which *identify* the concept and those observations which *relate* one concept to another.

This distinction is an extremely important one and will be repeatedly emphasized throughout this book. It is a very sharp distinction which must be maintained at all times. Frequently you will think of— or be asked—such a question as, "What is the meaning of intelligence?" Confusions and misunderstandings can arise if you fail to distinguish between the two components of this single question. The question can be interpreted in either of two ways. The first is as a demand for the operational definition of intelligence. The appropriate answer, then, will describe the operations by which a psychologist measures an individual's intelligence. The second interpretation would be as a request for information about how intelligence is related to other concepts, i.e., the empirical relationships of the concept of intelligence. The required answer will involve a description of how intelligence is functionally related to such concepts as education, socioeconomic level, or sex. The important point is to understand whether the questioner is seeking the operational meaning of a concept, or its factual (empirical) meaning, or both.

The distinction between the two types of meaning is shown clearly by two questions formulated by a philosopher of science (Feigl, 1949) in his attempt to describe simply the nature of scientific method. These two questions are, "What do you mean?" and, "How do you know?" The first is a demand for operational meaning; the second is a demand for factual meaning. If you were asked these two questions about the concepts involved in the following statement as well as the statement itself, "Learning fails to occur during sleep," *you* should now be able to answer them, so far as this particular instance goes.

In closing this section, let me urge you to ask these questions frequently of yourself and your teachers in psychology as well as in other fields. You will discover that these questions have an amazing ability to sift fact from fiction.

UNDERSTANDING, EXPLANATION, AND THEORY

Scientific workers in all fields have naturally always been eager to *understand* the phenomena with which they deal. This desire for understanding is, of course, not the exclusive property of the scientist, for practically everyone wishes to understand the phenomena which he encounters. At present, however, our concern will only be with the problem of knowing what is meant when a certain phenomenon is said to be *scientifically understood,* that is, we will again restrict our discussion to the realm of science.

There are many current ways of defining *understanding.* Many of them are purely verbal: "Understanding occurs when we become acquainted with the nature of reality," or "We understand an event when we know what causes it." If you have learned your lesson, however, you will not accept any such definition uncritically, but rather you will inquire about the operational definition of the concept *understanding.* That is, you will want to know what procedures a scientist follows when he claims that he has achieved understanding.

Understanding an event is achieved when the event is explained. Obviously, such a statement shifts interest from the term *understanding* to the concept **explanation.**

As you will recall, the function of science is to discover those factors which determine the occurrence of an event. This is essentially what explanation is—the specification of those factors or conditions related to the occurrence of an event. The statement that information was not learned when the brain generated a certain pattern of electrical activity is at least a part of an explanation of why learning does not occur during sleep.

You may be critical of this conclusion. Fine. We hope that this book will encourage a critical attitude. Your objection probably goes something like this: "Well, if you say that you explain an event by merely stating the factors related to that event, then you can explain the rapid evaporation of a water puddle by stating that the sun was shining on it, or you can explain the happiness of a coed by stating that her engagement has just been announced. Why, that is nothing more than *describing* what is going on, rather than explaining it."

This line of reasoning is basically sound except for the implication that there is a fundamental difference between description and explanation. We will attempt to demonstrate that this is not so; even a description of an event is essentially a low-level explanation. Description refers to the specification of the variables surrounding the occurrence of a *single event,* whereas higher order explanations consist of more general statements that apply to many different events that have some feature or features in common.

Consider the history of physics. Everybody observed that apples fell and stones that were thrown up ultimately came down and that the waters of the seas periodically rose and fell. Some people also noted that the time taken for any particular pendulum to swing back and forth was the same, regardless of whether the arc of its swing was large or small, and that planets followed certain paths in their trips around the sun. It was possible to offer an individual explanation for each of these events, and this is what actually happened first. However, theoretical physicists, like Galileo and Newton, did not perceive these facts as isolated events. Instead they saw a basic similarity among them. The theory of gravitation (the attraction that masses of matter have for each other) was formulated and from it all these various facts could logically be deduced.

Theoretical scientists indulge in a never-ending search for more and more general statements capable of explaining more and more individual facts. As you have probably already guessed from the direction of our analysis, a theory is a statement, or a group of statements, the purpose of which is to explain a group of events.

The theory of gravitation, like all scientific theories, serves two major functions. First, it *integrates* existing data. Instead of each fact being isolated and unrelated, a theory unifies them into an integrated and coherent body of knowledge. Second, it *predicts* new events. The theory of gravitation has helped astronomers chart our universe. It was noted that the planet Uranus followed a peculiar and variable path around the sun. Astronomers deduced from the theory of gravitation that some unknown body must be exerting a gravitational pull on Uranus. The location of this unknown planetary body was predicted from the theory of gravitation. The prediction was confirmed with the discovery of the planet Neptune.

Psychology has its theories too. The theory of reinforcement assumes that certain events are necessary for people and animals to learn. Hungry dogs learn to salivate to a tone if food is given them while the tone is sounding. Thirsty pigeons learn to peck at a round circle if water is given to them for doing this. Rats learn to jump over a hurdle in order to escape from a box in which they were previously shocked. Children learn to choose a black cup instead of a white cup if the black cup always contains an attractive token. The theory of reinforcement attempts to integrate the various phenomena by specifying the nature of the events that made learning possible.

Psychological theories are not as precisely formulated as are physical theories. Nor can they explain such a variety of separate events. But psychological theories are similar to physical theories in that they serve a common function: to integrate existing facts and predict new ones.

Figure 1.4 will assist you in understanding some of the distinctions we have made. The lowest level of the diagram is the level of observation. The concept level is tied by operational definitions to the level of observation. When two concepts are factually related, like learning and sleep, or time and a pendulum's arc, then an empirical relationship exists. This is the descriptive level. Theoretical level 1 contains theories that integrate several empirical relationships. In Figure 1.4 theory *A* integrates events 1 and 2, while theory *B* explains two different events, 3 and 4. In terms of our illustra-

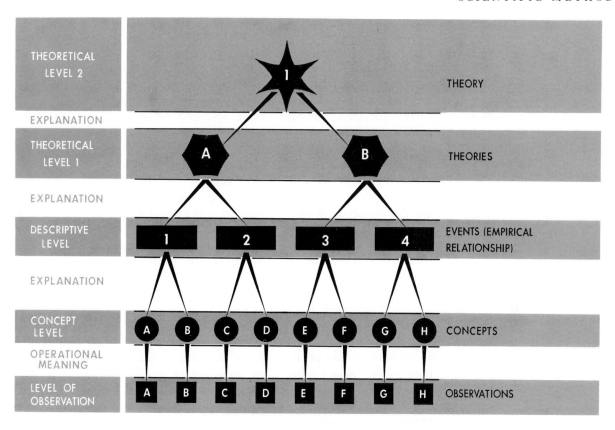

FIGURE 1.4 A Schematic Representation of the Nature of Theory and Explanation.

tions from physics, theory *A* could be conceived of as a set of theoretical statements capable of explaining tides and falling objects, and theory *B* would represent a theory capable of explaining swinging pendulums and planetary orbits. Similarly theory *A* could be considered as one psychological theory capable of explaining why learning occurs with food or water rewards, and theory *B* might represent a theory explaining why learning occurs with token rewards or with escape from situations in which pain previously occurred. Finally, theoretical level 2 represents a higher order theory. As contrasted with theories *A* or *B,* theory I is broader; it explains four facts instead of two. The theories of gravitation and reinforcement, in terms of our examples, would belong on theoretical level 2.

You must remember the obvious limitations of Figure 1.4. In actual practice, there are many more events than the four represented on the descriptive level. There can also be many more theoretical levels than are represented in the figure. But the essential idea is there—that explanation consists in specifying the factors related to the occurrence of an event. This can be accomplished by offering general statements whose implications are relevant to a specific event.

It is possible to think of theoretical formulations as pyramids. A high-order theory would be a tall pyramid with a broad base representing the large number of facts integrated by the theoretical propositions contained at its top. Low-order theories would be small pyramids because the amount of knowledge they encompass is rather limited. A feature of our analogy that must be remembered is that the apex of a pyramid is always connected to its base. The rules governing the nature of the connection between the theoretical formulation at the apex and the facts at the base are the rules of deductive logic which simply tell how to get from the theory back down to the data. In more advanced sciences the connection is expressed mathematically, whereas in less developed sciences the connection is maintained by rigorous and logical use of language. Psychology is at that stage of development in which mathematics is used in some areas but not in others.

Physicists have been very successful in formulating higher order theories. The theory of gravitation is one such example. Another is Maxwell's electromagnetic wave theory. This general theory is relevant to many different optical phenomena such as reflection, refraction, dispersion, and polarization. At one time these various phenomena were explained by independent theories. Psychology is at present mainly concerned with obtaining small bodies of systematic knowledge in various areas. This is the reason, as you will see, why psychology is at present divided into what appear to be so many different fields of study, such as learning, motivation, sensation, perception, social psychology, and personality. But there are, and we will try to show you, certain general theoretical patterns emerging which appear to underly many different psychological phenomena. Perhaps we have reached that point in the history of psychology where somewhat more general theories will be attained, capable of breaking down some of the barriers separating psychology into different fields. If this is so, the next few decades will witness great strides forward in the science of behavior.

In concluding this chapter it is helpful to recall its major theme. There is a foundation underlying all of psychology as well as all the rest of science. That foundation is the scientific method. By understanding the structure of this foundation, you will be better able to appreciate and to understand the knowledge which it supports.

SUMMARY

Psychology is the science of behavior. Science is best thought of as a method that aims to discover the variables responsible for the occurrence of an event. All sciences share a common scientific method. They differ only in the kinds of events in which they are interested.

One important characteristic of scientific knowledge is that it is based upon observations. When entertaining any scientific question one must know whether observations can be made to answer it. Sometimes apparently meaningful questions are impossible to answer simply because no appropriate observations can be made.

In analyzing scientific knowledge, one must distinguish between operational meaning and factual meaning. The operational meaning of a concept is defined by the operations the scientist makes in using the concept. Operational definitions help reduce vagueness of meaning and discourage the raising of scientifically meaningless problems. Factual meaning is concerned with the relationship between two or more operationally defined concepts.

The scientific enterprise does not end with the discovery of empirical relationships. Scientists seek to understand them. They do this by formulating theories. Theories are general statements that apply to specific events. They unify facts into an integrated body of knowledge and help predict new events by deducing their occurrences from theoretical assumptions.

SUGGESTIONS FOR FURTHER READING

COHEN, M. R., & NAGEL, E. *An introduction to logic and scientific method.* New York: Harcourt, Brace, 1934.

A textbook written for undergraduate courses in logic and the philosophy of science. Although the book is old, its clear and simple presentation recommends it to the beginning student who desires to increase his knowledge about the scientific method.

CONANT, J. B. *On understanding science.* New Haven, Conn.: Yale Univer. Press, 1947.

In this brief, readable book, a noted scientist and educator discusses individual cases in the history of science, and thus enables the reader to see how the scientific method works in practice.

NAGEL, E. *The structure of science.* New York: Harcourt, Brace, & World, 1961.

A lengthy and detailed treatise on the nature of science by one of the leading American philosophers of science.

TOULMIN, S. *The philosophy of science.* London: Hutchinson Univer. Library, 1953.

A fairly short book, extremely well written, that illustrates the distinctive characteristics of science.

THE SCIENCE OF BEHAVIOR

2

SCIENTIFIC METHOD AND PSYCHOLOGY

In this chapter you will see how scientific method applies to psychology. Our discussion will of necessity deal with abstract principles. Therefore, a bit of reassurance may be in order. Abstract principles are always somewhat challenging, particularly when they are new. What seems complicated now will become clear in later chapters when you read what facts psychologists have discovered and what theories they have proposed. One fact they did not have to work hard to discover is that a complex idea is not always understood immediately. You yourself have, no doubt, found that sometimes understanding develops gradually. Therefore, give yourself a chance to develop an understanding of scientific psychology.

In the first chapter of this book you were introduced to the idea, possibly new to you, that the method of investigating psychological phenomena, as well as of formulating theories of behavior, is basically identical with the method used in physics, chemistry, and other sciences. The differences between these fields of study and psychology lie not in fundamental methods used, but rather in what is being observed.

The physicist deals with observations relating to energy and matter. The chemist makes observations of changes in matter due especially to interacting atoms and molecules. Of course, the observations of the physicist and chemist are not uniquely different. The great amount of work done in the area known as physical chemistry demonstrates that no hard-and-fast boundary can be established between these two fields. The fact that much scientific work stretches over two different fields makes it clear that the arbitrary classification of science into areas of study is merely a *convenience*. Like those in physics and chemistry, the psychologist's observations are shared by neighboring sciences, especially biology, sociology, and anthropology.

BEHAVIOR OF ORGANISMS

The basic observations made by psychologists are observations of the behavior of organisms. The term **behavior** covers a wide range of phenomena: from the behavior of rats to the misbehavior of human adults, from the rate of saliva flow in dogs to the rapidity with which a group of humans can solve a problem requiring their cooperation, from breathing rates to muscle twitches. This wide diversity is apparent in the following titles, selected more or less randomly from a list of papers presented by psychologists at a recent meeting of the American Psychological Association:

Adolescent dependence and rebelliousness

Self-body recognition in schizophrenia

Vision during voluntary saccadic eye movements

The allegiance pattern of unionized professionals

All-numeral telephone dialing

Effects of alcohol and sodium amytal on learning and extinction

A group approach to the study of independence and conformity

Punishment during fixed-interval reinforcement

A cerebral electrographic response directly correlated with behavioral inhibition induced by stimulation of the caudate nucleus

What is the justification for including these seemingly diverse topics in the field of psychology? In spite of their apparent diversity there is a unity within the list. Various as they may at first seem, reflection shows that all of them refer to the behavior of organisms.

What is behavior? This is a "What do you mean?" type of question. We define behavior as the observable responses of the organism. The term *observable* is important to remember. The study of psychology can become vague, confusing, and mystical if we forget the all-important rule that the basis of scientific knowledge is to be sought in the observations of the scientists.

All psychologists, in some way, are trying to render intelligible some aspect of behavior. Behavior, then, is the Y variable in the general formula, $Y = f(X_1, X_2, X_3 \ldots X_n)$. Psychologists attempt to fill in the formula by discovering what variables are related to behavior. In a more formal manner this idea can be summarized by saying that behavior is the **dependent variable** in psychology. The dependent variable in scientific work is the event that the scientist seeks to understand. For convenience, psychologists use the letter R, representing the term **response,** to stand for the dependent variable, and refer to it as the **response variable.** We will use this term and symbol when referring to any particular instance of behavior, such as a response to the question, "In what kind of store did Ulysses S. Grant work before the war?"

THE DEPENDENT VARIABLE

We have identified the dependent variable in psychology as the response variable, but in order to understand the dependent variable completely, we must do more than merely identify it. Consider a particular case. Suppose somebody were given the task of reporting his observation of your behavior at the present time. Would the statement be complete if he said that you were reading? Certainly not! There are many aspects of your behavior which fail to be conveyed by the simple report that you are reading. Are your legs crossed? Are you scratching your head? Is your blood pressure high or low? Do you understand what you are reading? Are you reading continuously or do you sometimes lapse into daydreaming? Are you tense? How rapidly are you reading? Your behavior while reading these words has an indefinitely large number of components.

For this reason psychologists do not report—or even attempt to report, which may surprise you—a complete picture of behavior. One obvious reason is that it just cannot be done. Behavior is both continuous and complex. A psychologist finds it practically impossible to report every activity of every part—down to each individual muscle and gland—of the organism. But what is more important, such a complete description *is unnecessary*.

In every science the scientist must analyze the phenomena with which he deals and abstract from the totality of possible observations those events that he considers important to his task. If a psychologist is interested in discovering how rapidly male undergraduates read as compared with female undergraduates, he does not need to know their blood pressures when reading. If, however, a psychologist is concerned with changes in blood pressure of subjects reading textbooks as compared with mystery stories, he will not have to record the reading rate.

The psychologist's purpose in doing his research dictates what part of his subject's behavior he pays attention to and what part he ignores. He tries to select a response which will prove fruitful. A fruitful response is one that will lead to hypotheses with broad implications. You will recall that theoretical explanations consist of general statements that apply to many specific events. It is difficult to know beforehand whether a particular response will lead to significant theoretical constructions. In psychology, as in other sciences, certain measures of the dependent variable have been exceptionally fruitful, while others have led to isolated findings lacking all general implications. Investigation of the amount of

salivation of dogs, for example, has proved to be a fruitful response measure. The findings obtained with it have been applicable to a wide variety of other responses. It has also led to an understanding of certain aspects of the learning process. However, for each instance of such a fruitful response a large number of sterile measures could be mentioned. The theoretical psychologist essentially plays a hunch when he decides to direct his efforts toward a particular class of response measures. Sometimes his hunch pays off, sometimes it does not. There are many different ways in which science is experimental in nature. Naturally, in this book we will take up the response measures that have proved especially fruitful.

Methods of Measuring Behavior

How does the psychologist measure behavior? What sort of observations does he make? Sometimes he measures physiological activity directly—the contraction of a muscle, the secretions of a gland. At other times he measures behavior by its effect—a child breaks a doll, a man returns home. In the former case, which we shall call a direct measure, the psychologist describes how the response is performed, whereas in the latter case, the indirect measure, he describes what the response accomplishes.

A very popular technique for investigating animal learning makes use of a device called the Skinner box, after its inventor, B. F. Skinner. It is an enclosed compartment with a metal bar extended from the side of one of the walls. When this bar is pushed down a short distance, a pellet of food is mechanically delivered into the box. A hungry rat is placed in this box and his behavior in learning to press the bar and obtain food observed. The rat's behavior in this case is typically measured in terms of what he accomplishes, whether the bar is depressed or not. No attention is paid to the rat's muscular activity—

 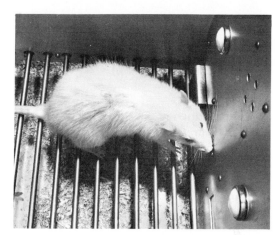

FIGURE 2.1 A Rat's Behavior in a Skinner Box. In the first photograph (upper left) the rat approaches the bar; in the second (upper right) he presses it; in the third (lower left) he approaches the food pellet; and in the last (lower right) he eats the pellet (Dr. Larry Stein).

whether he presses the bar heavily or lightly, with his left foreleg, right foreleg, or both forelegs; only the results of the bar-pressing get attention. The bar-pressing behavior of a rat need not always be measured indirectly. With appropriate electrical recording instruments, it would also be possible to measure what muscular contractions were involved in the bar-pressing act.

An example of an indirect measure of behavior in human problem solving is the time it would take you to connect the nine dots in Figure 2.2 by drawing four straight lines without retracing and without removing your pencil from the paper. If you had the necessary electrical equipment, you could obtain a direct measure of muscular activity in your lips, tongue, and larynx. It has been reported that problem solving is frequently accompanied by slight muscular activity in these organs. You see, therefore, that in the very same situation your behavior can be measured directly or indirectly. By the way, don't spend too much time on the problem of the line through the dots. The answer is on page 680.

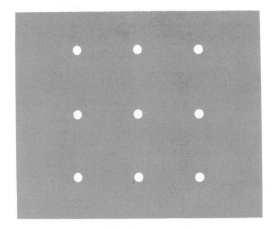

FIGURE 2.2 Connect these nine dots by drawing four successive straight lines without removing your pencil from the paper.

The distinction between direct and indirect measures of behavior is made merely to show you the general techniques which psychologists use to describe their dependent variables. Almost immediately after he learns the distinction, the student will ask, "Which is the better method—the direct or indirect?" Answering a question like this depends on our definition of *better*. If we accept the pragmatic view—which type of measurement leads to more fruitful relationships—then we must hedge in our answer. In some areas of psychology direct measures of behavior have been more fruitful than indirect measures; in other areas indirect measures have proved more useful than direct measures. At the present time there is no reason to believe that one type of measure is intrinsically better than the other. This book will report both types.

INDEPENDENT VARIABLES

The dependent variable in psychology has been described and identified as the response variable. To continue with our description of the science of psychology, it now becomes necessary to discuss the factors responsible for the occurrence of responses. These factors are called **independent variables.** They are the X's in the $Y = f(X_1, X_2, X_3 \ldots X_n)$ formula. The independent variables are the factors investigated by the experimenter to discover their effect on the dependent variable. In the sleep-learning experiment different degrees of sleep were selected to determine their influence on learning. Sleep was the independent variable, learning the dependent variable. If you were to investigate how rapidly a subject was able to read under different intensities of illumination, the levels of illumination would be the independent variable, while reading rate would be the dependent variable. Literally then, the dependent variable (reading rate) is dependent on the independent variable (levels of illumination).

Now our task will be to describe the independent variables in the science of psychology. When this has been done, the skeleton formula $Y = f(X_1, X_2, X_3 \ldots X_n)$ will have sufficient substance to provide you with an impression, albeit an incomplete one, of the science of psychology.

Psychologists have investigated how behavior is modified by a large number of independent variables. If we were to list all the individual independent variables that have been used in psychological research, the listing itself would exceed many times the size of this volume. Not only would this be a huge and awkward volume, but the listing itself would be of little use in conveying an over-all picture of the independent variables in psychology. We will instead attempt a systematic description. The independent variables used in psychological experimentation can be divided conveniently into three groups: (1) stimulus variables, (2) organismic variables, and (3) response variables. Each of them will be described and analyzed, and then the nature of the empirical laws (see page 5) relating them to behavior will be discussed.

Stimulus Variables

In Chapter 1 we saw how an experiment was designed to discover whether learning was possible during sleep. Basically the experiment consisted of arranging a sequence of environmental situations in which the subjects were placed. Initially they were asked a series of questions to determine how much they knew about a certain topic. Then they were instructed to sleep and were exposed to bits of information transmitted by a loudspeaker. Finally, they were once again tested with the original series of questions. The purpose of the experiment was to determine whether the subjects' exposure to information during sleep benefited their later performance.

Much of this book will deal with how the environment, past and present, affects the behavior of organisms in a wide variety of experimental situations. Unlike the sleep-learning experiment, most of the experiments cited in this book will report instances when environmental stimulation did exert an influence, rather than none, on behavior. Traditionally in psychology, the term *stimulus* has been applied to environmental variables. We shall define a **stimulus** as any property (any thing, element, characteristic, or change) of the environment. The bits of information transmitted to the subjects when supposedly asleep are stimuli. When you are driving, a red traffic light is a stimulus. The words of these sentences are stimuli. The words of the last chapter were stimuli.

Organismic Variables

Whereas stimulus variables include features of the environment, organismic variables denote characteristics of the subject. That is, the differences among the subjects themselves may become the focal point of the experimenter's attention. In such experiments the subjects, differing in such physiological characteristics as sex, blood chemistry, or nervous system, receive identical treatment in the same environmental situation. Any differences in behavior may then be attributed to different physiological characteristics of the subjects. We shall label these distinctive characteristics **organismic variables.**

For the sake of convenience, we can divide organismic variables into two major categories: characteristics of species and characteristics of individuals. A whole area of psychology is given to the study of species differences. This field is called comparative psychology and its task is to discover how the differences between different species of organisms affect behavior. Typical research in the field of comparative psychology might involve comparing the sexual behavior of rats, monkeys, and humans.

Individual organisms vary not only in terms of the characteristics of the species to which they belong, but also in terms of features that distinguish them from other members of their own species. In spite of the fact that the combination of these individual features sets you off as a unique individual, you can, nevertheless, be grouped with others on the basis of similarities in certain of these characteristics. You can be classified in terms of age, sex, height, weight, color of hair, eyes, skin, blood pressure, metabolism, or a combination of these features.

Why should psychologists be interested in classifying people in these various ways? Because such characteristics *may* be related to behavior. This idea has long intrigued man and, incidentally, has resulted in some bizarre aberrations having nothing to do with the main story of psychology. Palmists and phrenologists, for example, have sought to relate certain behavioral characteristics to the lines in a person's hand or to the contours of his skull. And although their theories have never been scientifically proved, and have often been scientifically disproved, these charlatans have continued to peddle their wares to a gullible public under the guise of science.

Organismic variables range from those which stay fixed throughout the life of the organism, such as sex and species, to those whose onset is sudden and which remain permanently thereafter, such as the altered structure of the brain following destruction of some of its parts, to those which remain more or less constant for a limited period of time, such as height and weight, and finally to essentially temporary conditions, such as pregnancy or the effects of drugs.

Response Variables

It may surprise you to discover that behavior, which is the dependent variable in psychology, can also serve as an independent variable. But it is quite obvious that one set of responses can be related to another set of responses. Consider the track coach who is lucky enough to have at one time seven crack quarter-milers on his squad and must select a relay team of four for an important track meet. Usually the coach will conduct a tryout race and select the first four runners for the mile relay team. He has no guarantee that the runners who placed fifth, sixth, or seventh in the tryout race would not turn in a performance during the relay race superior to one of the runners who has been selected. But from years of experience coaches have learned that those runners who perform best in track meets are the ones who performed best in practice. That is, coaches have learned that behavior is related to previous behavior.

Over and over again our own acts are based on the assumption that we can predict the future behavior of individuals by knowing how they behave now. We select people as friends, confident that the behavior we like and enjoy now is indicative of their future behavior. In an exceedingly impulsive and, as it turns out, sometimes disastrously haphazard manner, people choose a mate on the assumption that future behavior is predictable from behavior during courtship. Psychologists, going far beyond these everyday examples, have developed many complex techniques by which they relate a dependent response variable with an independent response variable. The techniques will be described later. For the time being we need only emphasize that a response, whether it be a dependent or an independent variable, has similar properties. Consequently, our analysis of the response variable, when we described it as a dependent variable, is applicable to the present section.

EMPIRICAL RELATIONSHIPS IN PSYCHOLOGY

You will recall that the generalized formula stating that an event is functionally related to certain variables is: $Y = f(X_1, X_2, X_3 \ldots X_n)$. We are now in the process of giving substance to this basic formula of science as it operates in psychology.

The Y or dependent variable in psychology is the behavior of an organism or organisms. It is conventionally referred to as a response variable. The X's or independent variables will be some set of stimulus, organismic, and response variables. Behavior, even of the most elementary sort, is some function of a set of independent variables rather than of one individual independent variable. Typically, an experiment involves the *variation* of only one independent variable in order to determine how different values, amounts, degrees, or intensities of that particular independent variable affect behavior (e.g., how age differences influence problem solving). But it should always be remembered that those factors that have a *constant* (non-fluctuating) value are also responsible for the resultant behavior. Behavior is a function of a large number of variables and the interaction between them. This point will become more and more obvious to you as you learn more about psychology.

From our analysis of the three types of independent variables, it follows that there are three fundamental types of empirical relationships in the science of psychology. Each of these involves the combination of the dependent response variable with one of the three independent variables and is represented by one of the following relationships in which S and R, as is the custom, stand for stimulus and response and O represents the organismic variable.

$$R = f(S)$$
$$R = f(O)$$
$$R = f(R)$$

These are the fundamental types of relationships. Later in the book we shall frequently deal with complex relationships involving a combination of several types of independent variables.

You have now been acquainted for the first time with the three types of independent variables which psychologists relate to behavior. It must be added that in each case these independent variables are related to behavior in one of two ways: historical or concurrent. A **historical relationship** exists when an organism's response can be traced to a past event, and a **concurrent relationship** exists when the response can be traced to an event occurring at the same time.

In order to clarify this distinction, let us consider a form of behavior that unfortunately is far too prevalent, juvenile delinquency. Many studies have reported that economic deprivation characterizes the majority of families of juvenile delinquents. It may be stated, therefore, that criminal responses among juveniles are due to economically deprived environments. This relationship is a historical one. The delin-

quent behavior is a function of the environmental situation in which the offenders have been reared. To conclude, however, that a juvenile commits a crime because he spent his childhood years in a slum is both incomplete and misleading. We know perfectly well that not all underprivileged children become juvenile delinquents. Delinquency and crime can be adequately understood only when it is clearly recognized that historical factors by themselves are not sufficient to account fully for such behavior.

We must understand the concurrent factors that trigger antisocial responses. In the case of a fifteen-year-old slum-reared child who joins a gang dedicated to petty thieving and acts of violence, what were the factors responsible for his saying "Yes" instead of "No" to the invitation to become a member of the gang? In order to answer this we must know how all the social, parental, and religious pressures acting upon him simultaneously were resolved by his accepting rather than rejecting the invitation. Similarly, why do some gang members change their minds at the moment they are about to commit a crime, while others feel compelled to go through with the previous decision? These are problems in concurrent psychological relationships. In order to understand juvenile delinquency, as well as all forms of behavior, we must understand how psychological variables acting upon an organism simultaneously converge to initiate certain responses.

In your study of psychology you will come into contact with both historical and concurrent relationships. Psychologists must investigate both kinds of relationships.

Our analysis has revealed that there are three fundamental types of relationships between a dependent variable and an independent variable, and that each of these three types can take either the form of a historical or concurrent relationship. This results in six kinds of empirical relationships. A response can be a function of a stimulus, organismic, or response variable which occurs coincidentally with the dependent response variable itself (concurrent relationship), or a response can be a function of a stimulus, organismic, or response variable which precedes the occurrence of the dependent response variable (historical relationship). In order to clarify the distinction between these six kinds of relationships, let us consider some examples of each.

Concurrent Relationships

$R = f(S)$. Your behavior at present illustrates a concurrent $R = f(S)$ relationship. It is likely that your behavior would be somewhat different if you were reading another book. No doubt you would read faster or slower and be more or less interested depending on whether you were reading a calculus text or *Life* magazine. An example of a concurrent $R = f(S)$ relationship in an experimental situation, one with which you are probably familiar, occurs when visual acuity is measured. A subject, confronted with a chart containing sets of letters of different size at a standard distance, is instructed to identify the various letters. His ability to identify the letters will depend on the amount of available light, as well as on his eyesight. That is, visual acuity is a function of level of illumination. In this example, as well as the first one, the response and the environmental factors related to it occur simultaneously.

$R = f(O)$. A simple example of a concurrent $R = f(O)$ kind of relationship could be demonstrated with some puppies, kittens, and a piece of string. If you dangled the string in front of these animals, you would observe that the puppies' pattern of response differs from the kittens' pattern of response. These differences are attributable to differences in the anatomical and physiological characteristics of the two

species. Another example of this kind of relationship is that the sound produced by certain dog whistles can be heard by dogs but not by humans. This is due to differences in the structure of the auditory organs of men and dogs. A concurrent $R = f(O)$ type of relationship does not, however, always involve species comparisons. It would be possible to develop a whistle that could be heard by young adults but not by old men, for as man grows older he loses his ability to hear certain high-pitched sounds. The distinguishing feature of a concurrent $R = f(O)$ relationship is that the physiological make-up of an organism is related to its behavior.

$R = f(R)$. Considering that a concurrent relationship involves factors related to the response at the time that the response is being made, you might legitimately ask how an organism can give two responses simultaneously. The answer to this question is that, of course, there are many facets to the behavior occurring at any given moment. Moreover, it is possible to measure several features of behavior occurring simultaneously. The well-publicized "lie detector" involves the simultaneous recording of several physiological responses. Typically, a person is asked a question, and while he answers, his respiration rate, blood pressure, pulse, and galvanic skin response (the latter due to the secretion of the sweat glands in the palms of the hands) are recorded. The content of his answer (and incidentally the time it takes him to start his reply) is then considered in the light of his constellation of concomitant physiological responses, and from this concurrent $R = f(R)$ relationship the truth or falsity of his answer is *inferred* by the examiner.

The concurrent $R = f(R)$ is a relationship frequently investigated in the study of personality. Some tests of personality provide several numerical scores, each representing a different feature of personality. Such tests make it possible to note how certain simultaneous personality responses tend to be related to each other. For example, such tests permit you to answer the question whether dominant people tend to be more self-sufficient than nondominant people. And thus, knowing *only* that an individual is dominant, you may determine whether he is likely also to be self-sufficient.

Historical Relationships

$R = f(S)$. In a Skinner box situation, as described on page 20, an animal's response will be dependent on his past experience in the apparatus. A hungry rat that has pressed the bar 50 times with each response being rewarded with food will press the bar much more readily than a rat who has no previous bar-pressing experience. This is an example of a historical $R = f(S)$ relationship because it relates present behavior to a past environmental situation.

Another obvious example can be drawn from education, which is based on the idea that an individual's future behavior is capable of being modified by the educational situations in which he is placed. Final examinations are devices which in practice measure the influence past exposures to educational situations have upon test behavior. In historical relationships of this sort an organism's response is related to an experience that organism underwent in some past environmental situation.

$R = f(O)$. In recent years psychological research involving drugs has become both popular and important. An organism is injected with a drug and, after a specified amount of time, his behavior measured. This is an example of a historical $R = f(O)$ type of relationship; behavior at one time is related to a change induced at a previous time in an organism's physiological condition.

Other examples of $R = f(O)$ type relationships are represented by the following questions: Is an adult's personality at all related to whether he was thin or fat as a child? Can a person's intelligence be lowered by an extended illness with high fever? Or can a retarded child's intelligence be raised by drug injections?

The difference between a concurrent and a historical $R = f(O)$ relationship rests upon the point in time at which the experimenter measures the independent organismic variable. If he measures the variable at the same time that he measures the response, then it is a concurrent relationship. If, however, the organismic variable is, for example, some surgical destruction which took place prior to the time he measures the response, then the relationship becomes a historical one. Quite often in psychological research involving drugs (psychopharmacological research) both concurrent and historical $R = f(O)$ relationships are obtained. The behavior might be related both to a simultaneous blood sample and to a previous drug injection.

$R = f(R)$. Our society assumes the historical $R = f(R)$ type of relationship in applying some of its legal restraints: those who repeatedly commit crimes of the gravest order may be considered incorrigible and receive a sentence of life imprisonment. This practice is supported by records which indicate a relationship between criminal acts and previous criminal behavior. Another historical $R = f(R)$ relationship is the one medical and other professional schools have discovered between scholastic performance in professional school and previous scholarship in the undergraduate years. Hence, scholastic records are used in selecting students in order to reduce as much as possible their chances of failure once they have been admitted.

Common observation has always revealed what psychologists have repeatedly confirmed more technically and in more complex situations: that an individual's behavior at a given time is related to his previous behavior. This information has the greatest practical usefulness because it permits us under some circumstances to predict an individual's future behavior accurately by examining his present behavior. The principle of a historical $R = f(R)$ is simple to grasp, but the successful formulation and utilization of an important historical $R = f(R)$ type of relationship demands a great deal of technical skill.

Comments on Empirical Knowledge in Psychology

We have analyzed the basic formulas of the science of psychology in terms of the variables involved and the nature of the empirical relationships between them. Our purpose has been to throw light on some features of psychological science. Lest such an attempt invite misconception, certain qualifications should be added.

First, it should be understood that any experimental situation has the *potentiality* of yielding historical or concurrent relationships involving any one of the three types of independent variables. The very nature of a scientific task, however, requires the scientist to simplify phenomena to some extent, rather than to deal with them in all their complexity. Consequently, in his research work a psychologist customarily focuses his attention on only one, or perhaps a very few, of the large number of possible relationships that might be investigated in any one experimental situation. Thus, while you should always remember that the demands of the scientific method force research to be analytic, you must never conclude that any given behavior phenomenon is solely and exclusively a function of any one given independent variable. In other words, multiple causation is the rule in the science of psychology.

The second point to remember is that our analysis is a somewhat idealized representation of empirical knowledge in psychology. Any piece of psychological research does not necessarily fall neatly into one of the six slots (three concurrent and three historical). Although many psychological problems can be identified in terms of whether they report historical or concurrent relationships or whether they involve as their independent variable a stimulus, organismic, or response variable, you will also come across research which includes a combination of some of these factors. In our discussion of historical relationships involving a response variable as the independent variable, we noted that behavior at a given time is related to previous behavior. Psychologists have discovered that their predictions about behavior can be improved if they consider not only what previous response was made, but also the stimulus situation in which it occurred. This is not surprising, if we refer again to our example of the selection of students for admission into medical school. The selection could, at its simplest, be based on the applicant's undergraduate grade average without any reference to the courses he took or the particular college he attended. But although it is clear that grade averages of this sort are related to scholastic success in medical school, much more accurate predictions of the applicant's probable success can be made if his past behavior is measured in relation to *known conditions of stimulation*. In predicting success in medical school, psychologists also measure the applicant's behavior in a medical aptitude test. This test measures behavior in response to an environmental situation composed of a series of test items. Students who score high on these tests tend to have higher grades in medical school and fewer of them fail than is true of those with low scores. In other words, scores on a medical aptitude test predict success in medical school more accurately than does a simple grade point average. That is, scholastic behavior in medical school is more highly related to an R measure in conjunction with an S measure than to an R measure alone.

THEORETICAL CONSTRUCTS AND PSYCHOLOGICAL THEORY

The structure of the science of psychology could be more easily described if it were possible to restrict the analysis to historical and concurrent $R = f(S)$, $R = f(O)$, and $R = f(R)$ relationships. But such a description would be incomplete. To discover empirical relationships is the basic task of psychology, as of every science, but it is not the only one. Scientists go on to develop theories so that already discovered facts can be understood and new facts predicted.

In our description of scientific theories we noted that theories contain general statements from which individual facts can be deduced. We proposed the analogy of a pyramid, at the base of which are the individual facts and at the apex, a small number of theoretical propositions. The apex is "connected" to the base by the rules of deductive logic, which in certain advanced areas of scientific inquiry can be expressed mathematically, while in less developed areas they are expressed by precisely used language.

This analysis emphasizes a point which is often misunderstood. Theory is not a substitute for facts. The very existence of scientific theories depends upon the prior availability of facts. Every theoretical structure rests upon a foundation of facts. Facts and theories must be thought of as complementary rather than antagonistic.

Let us now turn our attention to the ingredient of scientific theories which distinguishes them from scientific facts—the theoretical proposition. We will begin by defining a theoretical proposition as a statement containing a **theoretical construct**. In order to clarify the abstract notion of a theoretical construct, let us refer

back to the example of the hungry rat pressing a bar in a Skinner box. The rat will continue to press the bar if he continues to receive some food or water immediately afterwards.

The term usually applied to the learning which takes place in such experiments is the one that refers to the concept of *habit*. It would be quite appropriate to state that because his bar-pressing response is rewarded, the rat develops a habit of pressing the bar. Used in this context the term *habit* is a theoretical construct representing a relationship between a stimulus situation (the bar in the Skinner box) and a particular response (bar pressing). As a function of training, rats acquire a tendency to press a bar. The strength of this tendency will vary according to the conditions of training. Animals with 100 rewarded bar-pressing experiences will have a stronger habit than those with only five rewarded bar-pressing experiences.

You will grasp the meaning of a theoretical construct if you understand that it represents a relationship between directly observable variables, such as a stimulus situation and a response. Much of the research in the psychology of learning has been devoted to the discovery of variables related to the formation and strengthening of habits. The concept of habit is just one of a large number of theoretical constructs used by psychologists. We shall refer to this concept frequently when we report the findings of psychology, but for the present our interest is solely in the features which distinguish it as a theoretical construct, so that you will become adept at recognizing and even evaluting the adequacy of numerous theoretical constructs.

A theoretical construct is not observable directly but is in a sense observable *indirectly*. More commonly stated, it is *inferred* from observable events. Suppose you went into an animal behavior laboratory in which there were animals that had had extensive training in bar pressing and other animals that had none. If all the animals were in their home cages, would you be able to identify, by appearance alone, those rats that had formed bar-pressing habits from those rats that had not? Certainly not, for there are no distinguishing characteristics in the appearance of bar-pressing rats. If, however, you examined the research records of each rat, you could easily *infer* which rats would press the bar readily in the Skinner box and which would not. You would then be in a position to predict their behavior.

It should be recognized that it is not necessary to use the term *habit* in reporting the results obtained in the Skinner box. In fact, if you recall, the term was not used in describing a historical $R = f(S)$ relationship. It was noted that rats which have pressed the bar 50 times and been rewarded will press the bar much more readily than rats with no previous experience. No reference was made to the concept of *habit*. The obvious question now is: What is the virtue of the theoretical construct of *habit* in reporting the results of a Skinner-box study? The answer is that without theoretical constructs experimental facts remain isolated events. Scientists are interested in discovering uniformities among the phenomena with which they deal, and are especially interested in discovering higher-order explanations that apply to *many different* situations. They may do this by using theoretical constructs such as habit, the implications of which are relevant to more than one specific experimental situation and to a wide variety of responses. You will see later how the theoretical construct of *habit* can be applied to an immense variety of situations and behaviors and, thus, assist in establishing uniformity among very different psychological phenomena.

Because theoretical constructs are applicable to many situations, we can say that at the same time they both summarize the data collected and make predictions about data not yet obtained. There is, of course,

no guarantee that such predictions will be confirmed, but the important point for you to keep in mind now is that a proposition containing a theoretical construct integrates data already obtained and on the basis of these data permits predictions about further data not yet obtained.

In your study of psychology you will come across a large number of theoretical constructs. Some of them will be like the concept of habit which relates stimulus and response variables. Some will refer to historical or concurrent relationships between two response variables; others will refer to relationships between a response variable and an organismic variable. Still others will relate a response variable or a group of response variables with a combination of independent variables. It should not be surprising that the types of theoretical constructs are similar to types of empirical relationships, since one function of theoretical propositions is to summarize prevailing data.

Now that we have examined theoretical constructs, we can systematize their features. First, a theoretical construct, such as habit, is not directly observable but rather is inferred. Second, a theoretical construct incorporates a relationship between two or more experimental variables. Third, a theoretical construct functions to summarize economically the data on hand and to predict the nature of experimental results yet to be obtained.

Theoretical constructs are not unique to psychology. They are essential ingredients of scientific theory in *all sciences*. There are no differences in principle between theoretical constructs in psychology and those in physics. However, the theoretical constructs in psychology tend to apply precisely to a rather restricted range of phenomena, whereas the theoretical constructs in physics, such as atom, proton, neutron, and electron apply to a vast range of phenomena with an amazing degree of exactness.

Lest you think that the process of formulating theoretical constructs is a simple task, let me add some words of caution. Our analysis of theoretical constructs and of scientific theory has been at a most elementary level—so elementary, indeed, that its significance may have appeared to be trivial. There are, however, many problems associated with theoretical construction which are exceedingly technical and complex and go far beyond the scope of problems properly belonging in a course in introductory psychology. It would be difficult to point to any human effort more demanding both in terms of sheer intellectual ability and ingenuity than the task of creating adequate scientific theories.

As we proceed and examine some of the formulations offered to explain behavior, you will want to recall this analysis of the science of psychology so that you may judge their adequacy. For in order to clarify some of the important theories of behavior, we will not restrict our attention to those theories formulated by professional psychologists, but at times will discuss certain "common-sense" theories frequently invoked in our society. You shall then be in a position to test whether the claims made for common sense are always justified.

SUMMARY

Behavior, or what is technically known as a response, is the dependent variable in the science of psychology. Psychologists measure a response in one of two ways: in terms of physiological activity (e.g., contraction of a muscle), or by its effect (e.g., depression of a lever).

Responses are related to three kinds of independent variables: stimulus (property of the environment), organismic (characteristic of the subject), and response (measure of behavior). From the analysis of the dependent and independent variables, empirical laws in psychology can be classified into three fundamental types: $R = f(S)$, $R = f(O)$, and $R = f(R)$. Each of these can be expressed in either a historical or concurrent fashion, depending on whether the independent variable is a past or current event.

In order to explain the facts of psychology, theoretical constructs are postulated that represent a relationship between behavior and a set of independent variables. These theoretical constructs serve to integrate existing data and make predictions about future data.

SUGGESTIONS FOR FURTHER READING

MANDLER, G., & KESSEN, W. *The language of psychology.* New York: Wiley, 1959.

A systematic analysis of language and theory in psychology.

MARX, M. H. *Psychological theory.* New York: Macmillan, 1951.

A collection of papers written by outstanding psychologists about problems of scientific method in psychology.

PRATT, C. C. *The logic of modern psychology.* New York: Macmillan, 1939.

A discussion of the basic assumptions underlying the science of psychology.

UNDERWOOD, B. J. *Psychological research.* New York, Appleton-Century-Crofts, 1958.

An analysis and evaluation of various methods of doing research.

TOOLS FOR THE STUDY
OF PSYCHOLOGY

II

Even though you are now taking an *introductory* course in psychology, you need some preparation. Present-day psychology is insulated neither from other fields nor from its own history. Your task of understanding the facts and theories of psychology will be made easier if you became acquainted—at a very elementary level—with the history of psychology, with statistics, and with physiology.

Practically everyone shares the desire to understand the world we live in. In fact, we have become so sophisticated about physical science that we are no longer surprised at new discoveries. But the science of behavior is another matter. Some people actually think it is wrong to try to understand behavior; others believe it impossible. Yet in spite of these attitudes, men have persistently sought to explain behavior. A review of the various attempts should prove both interesting and instructive. By familiarizing yourself with psychology's past, you will be prepared to understand contemporary psychology.

One of the most obvious things about behavior is that it differs from individual to individual. There is no dispute about the fact that in every situation, whether it is social dancing or intellectual communication, individuals behave differently. Since this is so, how is it ever possible to understand behavior? The answer is that an individual's behavior is not a unique event totally independent of and different from that of others. With the help of statistics and its mathematical techniques we can discover those characteristics common to the behavior of all individuals. In addition, statistics serves another important function —that becomes obvious about election time. It permits us to predict the behavior of large groups of individuals from samples of the behavior of certain small groups. This predictive power has made important contributions to psychology.

Finally, to understand behavior we must have some familiarity with physiological processes. After all, behavior is a substantial event, and if we want to understand it, we must know something about its physiological components.

THE ORIGINS AND STATUS
OF MODERN PSYCHOLOGY

3

THE PRESENT AND ITS PAST

It has been said that psychology has a long past but only a short history. In order to understand this paradox, one must remember that although a dominant theme in recorded history is man's great interest in his own behavior, the first scientific laboratory for its study was not established until 1879. Psychologists think of this as the birth date of their science, because it marked their first real independence from other disciplines. Prior to that the study of behavior had been the concern of philosophers, theologians, and physiologists.

Although psychologists consider 1879 as a date of special significance, they are, none the less, interested in earlier interpretations of behavior. The definitive historical

treatments of psychology begin with a description and evaluation of the Greek philosophical systems and their conceptions of the "why" of human behavior. This is no mere concession to scholarly convention. Knowledge of the past has many uses. Like ideas in general, scientific discoveries are usually as much a result of the historical setting in which they occur as of a particular scientist's creative inspiration. If we are to appreciate and understand fully any scientific contribution, we must have some conception of how it came about, of ideas and events which led up to it.

It will be helpful to take a look at some of the attempts to explain behavior prior to scientific psychology. After you understand the reasons for their inadequacies, you will be in a better position to appreciate the scientific approach. Further, his-

36

tory does not restrict itself to reporting successful undertakings, for there is much to learn from failures. You will, no doubt, recognize the similarity between the errors committed by past generations in their interpretation of behavior and mistaken nonscientific formulations widely held today. Some of these similarities will be pointed out and analyzed.

PRESCIENTIFIC SPECULATIONS

The use of scientific method requires evidence in the form of data obtained from observations. The distinctive features of prescientific speculation about behavior were that it was based upon both inadequate evidence and inadequate techniques of interpretation.

Instead of attempting to trace the numerous prescientific ways of looking at behavior in any historical manner, we will limit ourselves to two classes of speculations that embody the essential features of most of these formulations.

Mystical Speculations

The earliest formulations put forward to explain behavior involved the assumption that mystical forces, agents, or spirits, independent and separate from the body, were responsible. Differences in behavior among individuals were consequently attributed to differences in the spirits inhabiting their bodies.

People would state, for example, that an individual who committed murder was possessed by an evil spirit. Or, in the language of scientific method as we formulated it earlier, a certain relationship existed between the act of murder and the possession of an evil spirit.

Now, what is wrong with such an explanation? Let us look closely and compare the relationship between the act of murder and possession by an evil spirit with the relationship, in Figure 1.3, page 11, between learning and sleep. Note that in Figure 1.3 learning has an operational definition distinct from the operational definition of sleep. Consider whether there is this independence between the operational definitions of the concepts of murder and evil spirit. How does one know whether a person possesses an evil spirit impelling him to murder? If he commits murder. But why does he commit murder? Because he possesses an evil spirit. But how do you know whether he possesses an evil spirit to murder? When he commits murder. This sort of merry-go-round, questions-and-answer sequence could go on indefinitely. It is circular reasoning because the concepts of murder and of evil spirit have the *same* operational definition. Note that in Figure 3.1 the relationship between murder and evil spirit is represented in the same manner as the relationship between learning and sleep in Figure 1.3 (see page 11). Upon examination we discover that the statement that people murder because they possess evil spirits is a tautology which, when reduced to its intrinsic meaning by operational analysis, states no more than "an act of murder is related to an act of murder." Such a statement does not provide any information about which factors might be responsible for an individual's committing murder. Worse, it suppresses and discourages any attempt to find them. The relationship between learning and sleep differs from the pseudo relationship between murder and an evil spirit in a manner that points to a crucial feature of scientific knowledge. Factual meaning, or what is conventionally called an empirical law, requires that the relationship be between two or more *independently* defined concepts, such as learning and sleep in our example. The pseudo knowledge that results from mystical speculation does not fulfill this

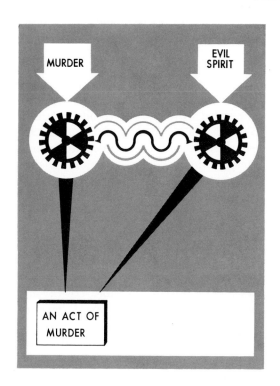

FIGURE 3.1 An analysis of the Proposition That an Individual Who Commits Murder Possesses an Evil Spirit. Note that both the concepts of *murder* and *evil spirit* have the same operational definition.

requirement because the concept, spirit, introduced to explain the phenomenon, murder, is defined in terms of the phenomenon itself. Mystical speculation, although it may give the appearance of saying something, says nothing.

No doubt most if not all of you are convinced of the inadequacies of the "spirit theory" of behavior. You may be muttering something like "Why is it necessary to beat a dead horse?" Well, true it is that the spirit theory is more-or-less obsolete in Western civilization, but what about other so-called common-sense theories? One frequently hears that it is human nature to be selfish, or that it is human nature to be competitive or to engage in international wars. Sometimes one even hears that human na-

ture is basically peaceful, and it is other conditions that produce war. In any case, when such a concept as human nature is used this way, does it differ from the concept of spirit as we have used it? An operational analysis reveals that it does not, because the definition of the concept of human nature is *no different* from the behavior it seeks to explain.

Armchair Speculation

The phrase *armchair speculation,* as we use it in this book, denotes any system of ideas that seeks to understand behavior by *rational,* or purely logical, processes *alone.* These terms are not used derisively so much as they are used to capture the quality of formulations which are products of reason alone and, as Webster's dictionary puts it, "comfortably remote" from the work of active investigation.

Ethical Interpretations. Some analyses of behavior have been made because they accord with ethical precepts. Adherents of ethical systems that condone or encourage polygamy defend their point of view by stating that polygamy is more consistent with the true nature of man than monogamy. The evidence that a large part of the world practices monogamy does not seem to perturb them.

As you can see, different ethical systems result in different conceptions of the true nature of behavior. These assertions are based solely on consistency with a larger philosophical system and are not likely to meet the chief requirements of scientific method—consistency with experimental evidence. It is not surprising, then, that interpretations arising from ethical systems may not agree with those resulting from scientific investigation, since the two methods of formulation have such different objectives. In science there is complete rejection of all authority except that of facts.

38

Reasonable Interpretations. Closer to scientific psychology are speculations of those philosophers who departed sufficiently from their principle that pure reason is capable of generating an understanding of behavior to make sound observations of their own behavior and the behavior of others. Aristotle might be considered one of the first of these philosophers who supplemented

FIGURE 3.2   Aristotle, 384-322 B.C.

the purely rational method by observations. He pointed the way for a scientific psychology by concluding that our behavior is a product of our bodily processes.

A reasonable philosophical interpretation of behavior was developed by a group of philosophers known as the British Empiricists, who included John Locke, David Hume, Jeremy Bentham, James Mill, and John Stuart Mill. They held that all knowledge is derived from sense experience, thus emphasizing the role of past experience in determining behavior. By their scepticism and belief that it is the duty of all thinkers to investigate ideas for themselves rather than accept the authority of others, they

encouraged the development of scientific psychology.

In another sense the methods of the British Empiricists were not consistent with scientific method, for although they expressed admiration for scientific method, they failed to see how it could be utilized to test their own interpretations of behavior. Instead, they tended to evaluate interpretations by the criterion of their reasonableness, that is, their logical consistency and agreement with "good sense." (This term, paradoxically known sometimes as "horse sense" or "common sense," commands a lot of respect in our society, probably because everyone thinks he has a large store of it and is therefore willing to proclaim its merits.) A more critical attitude toward good sense would have revealed its severe limitations. The history of physics is filled with examples of ideas that initially appeared eminently reasonable, but were later proven false by the facts of scientific observation. Good sense dictated that the earth was flat and that heavier objects must fall more rapidly than light objects. But men like Galileo were not willing to accept reasonableness as the ultimate criterion of truth and demanded empirical evidence. When they obtained facts that were inconsistent with reasonable assumptions, they did not ignore them, but instead, rejected the reasonable assumptions.

We must have the same reverence for facts in the science of behavior. Students frequently enter introductory psychology courses with preconceived notions about behavior that are similar both in origin and in kind to what we have described as armchair speculation.

Armchair speculation about behavior is one of the most widely played parlor games in our society. Typically, the behavior of an individual or perhaps even the whole human race is subjected to the scrutiny of a group. Individuals offer opinions which seek to explain the behavior under consideration on the basis of sets of principles which appear self-evident to those who propose them. But more often than not, members of the group accept different sets of basic principles, and an impasse to any agreement is reached. Sometimes, in order to convince the group that a particular interpretation is correct, a participant will appeal to an outside authority—"Modern psychology says . . . ," "Freud says. . . ." Sometimes the appeal is, "It is obviously reasonable to assume. . . ." Such appeals are easy to make, but one should realize that the mere mention of an authority does not by itself validate any particular interpretation of behavior. More often than not, the opinions and conclusions people ascribe to modern psychology and Freud are not actually asserted by these authorities, and the confidence individuals place in what appears to be reasonable can, as the history of science has repeatedly demonstrated, often be misplaced. What is important, from the scientific point of view, is that interpretations of behavior, no matter how sensible they may sound and no matter how many authorities may support them, require evidence from controlled observations. In science empirical evidence is the only standard by which the adequacy of any interpretation of behavior may be measured.

THE BEGINNING OF THE SCIENCE OF PSYCHOLOGY

The science of psychology did not spring up overnight, even though psychologists identify its beginning with the establishment of the first laboratory in Leipzig in 1879. In the nineteenth century, certain physiologists were forerunners to the experimental psychologists. Johannes Müller, an experimental physiologist, integrated what knowledge of physiology there was at that date in an exhaustive treatise entitled *Handbook of Human Physiology*. His topics included the nature of neural events and of muscular movements and the physiological factors underlying sight, hearing, and other sensory experience. He even attempted to explain the physiological basis of such complex psychological activities as memory, imagination, feeling, passion, and sleep.

FIGURE 3.3   Johannes Müller, 1801-1858 (Bettman Archive)

Müller's lasting contribution was his analysis of how the human physiological system functions as a mechanism. His analysis was strikingly similar in its gross features to contemporary physiological knowledge. Metaphorically speaking, by filling the body up with so much physiological material, he helped to dislodge the spirits which people had commonly supposed did the work. Basing his conclusions on experimental evidence wherever possible, and considering general observations when it was not, Müller laid the groundwork for an experimental psychology.

His student, Hermann von Helmholtz,

destined to become one of the most versatile geniuses in the whole history of science, pushed further the work that interested Müller. Helmholtz was primarily a physicist and secondarily a physiologist, but this combination of interests forced him to consider problems of a psychological nature. His two works, one on vision and one on hearing, are still among the classics of psychology. With the use of experimental techniques from physics and physiology, he discovered some of the physical and physiological factors responsible for our visual and auditory experiences. His methods of investigation into these subjects were both rigorous and imaginative, and superimposed upon his experimental findings were brilliant theoretical formulations.

About the same time that Müller and Helmholtz were laying the groundwork for a scientific psychology, Gustav T. Fechner, in pursuit of an experimental solution to a philosophical problem, hit upon techniques by which he demonstrated that scientific measurement could be used in the study of behavior. Thinking that he was in some manner showing how the "ethereal mind" was related to the "material body," Fechner experimented upon the ability of human beings to discriminate between stimuli of different physical intensities. Although Fechner's philosophical conclusions concerning the "ethereal mind" have been ignored, his general methods are still used in experimental investigation of the relationships between stimuli and responses, and have served as starting points in developing techniques of measurement of intelligence, attitudes, traits of personality, and many other topics of interest to psychologists.

The Establishment of Psychology as an Independent Science

The name of Wilhelm Wundt, another German, is most closely linked with the establishment of psychology as an independent science. It has been said that before Wundt there had been plenty of psychology, but no psychologists. Müller was a physiologist, Helmholtz was a physicist and physiologist, and Fechner, initially a physicist, became a philosopher while engaged in his pioneer experiments in psychological measurement. Wundt studied with both Müller and Helmholtz and was well trained in physiology, physics, and philosophy. But he, more than his predecessors, concentrated squarely on the problems of psychology, and it was he who established the first psychological laboratory in Leipzig, in 1879.

Wundt's influence on the history of psychology was profound. In addition to establishing the first laboratory, he founded a psychological journal which served as a medium for the dissemination of both experimental and theoretical articles. He was also personally responsible for training a large number of psychologists, most of

FIGURE 3.4   Hermann von Helmholtz, 1821-1894

FIGURE 3.5 Wilhelm Wundt, 1832-1920 (Bettman Archive)

whom later played important roles in the development of scientific psychology both in Germany and in the United States.

It is difficult for present-day American students to appreciate the significance of Wundt's system of psychology because its goal was so narrowly conceived that ultimately the whole enterprise was abandoned as sterile. Despite its limitations, however, its rigorously disciplined scientific method exerted a powerful influence on the growth of psychology. As such it demands our attention.

Wundt saw the task of psychology as the analysis of "conscious experience" into its basic elements, much as the chemist analyzes a chemical compound into its constituent elements. This view assumes that complex experiences are compounded out of these elementary experiences. His basic position derived from the philosophic distinction between mind and body, which

had received its most explicit early exposition in the writings of Descartes. According to Descartes, man is uniquely different from other animals. Whereas other animals have only bodies, man has also a mind. This belief in the existence of mind gave Wundt the rationale for establishing an independent science of psychology. Psychology, of all the sciences, he said, has the unique task of studying mind, the conscious experience of human beings.

But how can conscious experience be investigated? Wundt found his answer to this question in a method of self-observation, or technically, the method of **introspection.** For example, a stimulus such as a patch of color is presented under controlled conditions to a subject. The subject reports exactly what he experiences, describing what he immediately perceives not in terms of its physical qualities, but rather in terms of its elementary, sensory qualities. The introspective report is supposed to mirror faithfully conscious experience, to describe the experience as such.

We shall consider a very oversimplified example in an attempt to convey Wundt's basic approach to psychological problems and to point up its limitations. Look at the series of color patches in Figure 3.6 (see color plate 1 between pages 126 and 127) and analyze each one into its basic sensory elements. To do this in a manner consistent with the principles and practices of Wundt's introspective psychology, you would have to become sophisticated by long training in the techniques of observing experience. Psychology is no different from physics or chemistry, thought Wundt, in requiring extensive technical training of the individual who conducts experiments.

Let us assume that you are a trained introspectionist and that you have analyzed each patch. You conclude that the only elementary color experiences to be had from this series of patches are the six basic colors—black, white, red, yellow, green, and blue. Let us assume that another trained introspectionist decides, after his analysis, that only five elementary color experiences are induced by the series of patches. The second introspectionist might conclude, as some have actually done, that green is not a unique color experience, but one merely compounded of the elementary blue and yellow experiences. He actually *sees* green as a yellow blue, just as you see orange as a yellow red. Who would be right?

It was this sort of disagreement which finally led to the abandonment of introspective psychology and its goal of analyzing conscious experience into basic sensory elements. The introspective method was not a technique capable of discriminating elementary sensory experiences from those compounded or built up out of elementary experiences. Whereas chemistry possessed an objective method which could sort basic chemical elements from chemical compounds, psychology had none, and so psychologists frequently disagreed among themselves as to what constituted the basic elements of conscious experience.

We have dealt with only a small part of Wundt's psychology and have ignored many variations of his systematic position. But our purpose is not to give anything like a complete history of psychology, but merely to describe the dominant trends. Wundt established the first independent system of psychology based upon scientific method. Its failure was not due to any inadequacy of scientific method, but rather to the nature of the questions he sought to answer. Conscious experience, as used by Wundt, was at best a vague and unreliable concept that stemmed from a philosophical postion (distinction between mind and body) incompatible with an empirical science. This is not to say that Wundtian psychology was a waste of time. It was not. It established psychology as an independent science, although it misinterpreted its role. Moreover, Wundt and his contemporaries

were concerned with some problems that are still considered important. For example, the ability of human organisms to discriminate between stimuli having different physical properties—an example of a concurrent stimulus-response relationship — interests contemporary psychologists, who continue to utilize and refine many of the techniques originated by the introspective psychologists.

James McKeen Cattell, an American who studied in Germany with Wundt, provided a different slant to a research project which Wundt had assigned him to. The project involved the description of an individual's conscious experience when he is suddenly exposed to a visual stimulus. Cattell asked, Why not measure the time required for his subjects to respond to the light? Such an investigation is conventionally referred to as a *reaction-time* experiment. Many everyday situations involve reaction time; the time it takes a driver to step on the brake when the red light appears or the time it takes the sprinter to start when the starter fires the gun are but two examples. The importance of Cattell's experiment was that he sought to discover how individuals (organismic variable) differ in speed of response (response variable) to the sudden appearance of a light stimulus (stimulus variable). No reference to the conscious experience of the subject was needed. It was thus proved possible to do psychological research without considering the experiences of the subjects.

At about the same time that Cattell was doing his reaction-time studies, Hermann Ebbinghaus, an independent and hardworking scholar, sought to demonstrate that memory (one of the so-called higher mental processes) was susceptible to experimental investigation. Ebbinghaus, who was not attached to any university, became interested in this problem after reading Fechner's book, which he had picked up in a secondhand bookstore. Ebbinghaus

FIGURE 3.7 James McKeen Cattell, 1860-1944 (Brown Brothers)

decided to see whether the technique of scientific measurement which Fechner had applied to sensory discrimination could also be applied to the memory process.

To conduct his investigation he invented the **nonsense syllable,** consisting of two consonants and a vowel selected at random to form syllables like *tav* and *xat*. Such syllables, reasoned Ebbinghaus, would be freer of contaminating associations than words whose familiarity or strangeness might make them particularly easy or difficult for people to memorize. Using himself as a subject, he systematically investigated how his ability to recall a series of nonsense syllables was influenced by the number of times he read them. Thus Ebbinghaus, in a most straightforward and uncomplicated manner, objectively investigated the relationship between ability to remember and amount of practice.

A related problem, forgetting, Ebbinghaus measured as a function of time. Figure

3.8 shows the classical forgetting curve reported by Ebbinghaus in 1885.

Breaking the barrier to the study of the so-called higher mental processes was an important accomplishment. The pattern of research Ebbinghaus initiated in the field of memory and forgetting is still used today, and many of his observations and conclusions have been confirmed by other investigators who repeated his work with large numbers of subjects.

Like Cattell, Ebbinghaus conducted his research without being primarily interested in the conscious experience of his subjects. Although both these investigators did not oppose Wundt's interpretation of the function of psychology, they more-or-less unconsciously departed from his line of inquiry. In a simple, nonphilosophical manner, Cattell and Ebbinghaus studied the relationship of behavior to organismic and stimulus variables. In this respect both were precursors of the American school of psychology called **Functionalism.**

Unlike the Wundtian psychologists, who attempted to discover the *elements* of con-

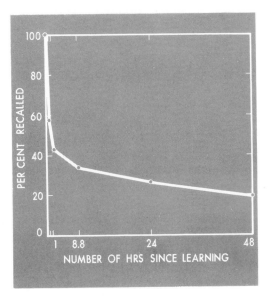

FIGURE 3.8 The Classical Curve of Forgetting Based Upon Data Collected by Ebbinghaus.

sciousness, the Functionalists attempted to discover the *operations* and *functions* of consciousness. The American Functionalists were influenced by Darwin's biological theory of evolution, which emphasized the role of adaptation in the behavior of organisms to their environment. Functional psychology had its beginnings at the University of Chicago under the guidance of the philosopher John Dewey. Many of the early leaders of American psychology received their training there, and partly as a result, there has always been a strong Functionalist tradition in American psychology.

The Functionalists' concern with the functions of the mind, rather than with its elementary experiences, prompted them to investigate new kinds of phenomena. Their interest in the adaptive function of behavior led them to trace the development of organisms under controlled environmental conditions. They carried out studies of the behavior of children and animals. And since they were Americans concerned with practical problems, the Functionalists continued some of Cattell's work and developed so-called mental tests which, when applied to various situations, particularly educational ones, provided measures of behavior serving both to evaluate the effects of previous training and to predict future behavior.

One might describe the history of psychology from Wundt to the Functionalists as the transition from the study of consciousness to the study of behavior. But this transition was not smooth, nor was it clearly recognized until in 1912 a vigorous and aggressive psychologist by the name of John B. Watson noted the inconsistencies and contradictions within psychology. He saw that Wundt's psychology was based on the philosophical premise of a distinction between man's conscious experience and his body. Descartes had assumed that man was different from other animals because he alone possessed a mind. Darwin,

on the other hand, essentially denied that any absolute difference between animals and man could be demonstrated. His theory of evolution was based upon the continuity of species, rather than upon any discontinuity as assumed by Descartes. Functionalism seemed to Watson to be embracing both positions, and he sought to demonstrate that this was impossible.

FIGURE 3.9 John B. Watson, 1878-1958 (Brown Brothers)

Watson believed that the assumption that man is made up of two separate entities, a physical body and a psychic mind, was not confirmed by scientific observation. He had established an animal laboratory at the University of Chicago, and his experience in animal research led him to defend a position he called **behaviorism.** He found he was able to conduct research with animals without any reference to consciousness, by merely studying the relation between the behavior of the organisms and the variables he could manipulate in an experiment. For example, if he was trying to find out whether rats could tell the difference between the two grays appearing in Figure 3.10, he used a discrimination apparatus, the design of which is shown in Figure 3.11.

In an apparatus such as this, the animal is always fed when he approaches one of the two grays and never fed when he approaches the other gray. If the animal

FIGURE 3.10 Can a rat discriminate between these two grays?

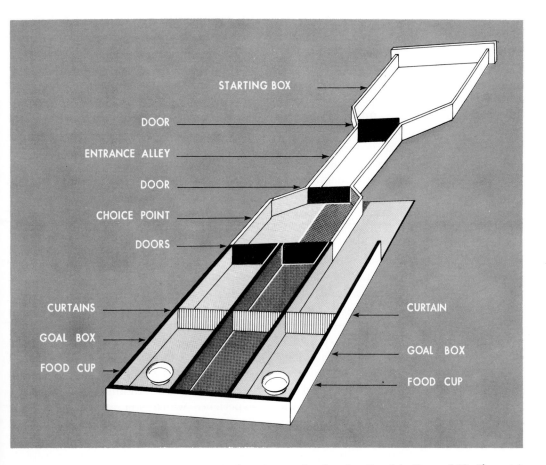

FIGURE 3.11 A Discrimination Apparatus Used to Answer the Question Posed in Figure 3.10. The rat is placed in the starting box from which he can proceed, after the experimenter raises the appropriate doors to the choice point. At this point he chooses, by turning slightly, the light gray or the dark gray stimulus alley. He is rewarded with food if he selects the correct one but receives no food if he selects the other. Although there are three alleys in the apparatus, only two, one dark gray and one light gray, are visible to the rat on any one trial. The alleys are so arranged that they can be moved at right angles to the entrance alley, thus reversing the spatial position of light and dark gray alleys. This guarantees that if the rat chooses the correct stimulus consistently he is responding to the brightness of the stimulus rather than to its location on the right or left side.

learns to consistently choose the gray which leads to his being fed, the observer concludes that the animal can discriminate between the two grays. If he cannot consistently choose the correct gray, the observer concludes that the animal cannot discriminate between the two grays.

As you can see, these observations make no reference to the conscious experience of the rat. The nature of the problem, to Watson, was whether the animal could respond differently (i.e., approach or avoid) to the two different stimuli. Watson asked why the same method used so clearly and simply with rats could not be applied to the study of human behavior.

Watson's position was essentially to deny —or for all scientific purposes to ignore— the assumption of the introspective psychologists that psychology had a unique subject matter: mental processes as contrasted with physical processes. Rather, he asserted, the basic data with which the psychologist deals are similar to those of the physical scientist, being simply the observations of the scientist. The prime requirement of scientific data, argued Watson, is that they be objective—objective in the sense of "public," open and accessible to any observer properly trained and equipped. In introspective psychology the one introspecting is the only person capable of observing his own conscious experience. Watson insisted that the basic data of psychology must be such that they are accessible to all. He therefore substituted behavior for conscious experience as the subject matter of psychology.

The debate between behaviorism and introspective psychology continued over a span of years, with overtones which excited the debaters, but need not concern us here. The major result of this debate was the victory of behavioristic methodology and the gradual abandonment of the attempt to analyze conscious experience into its elements. This does not mean that all the empirical problems which concerned the introspectionists were forgotten. As we have already mentioned, their inquiry into the nature of sensory experience can easily be reformulated into objective behavioristic terms. For example, the subject's introspective analysis of conscious sensory experience can become an investigation of the objective responses an organism makes between stimuli of various physical attributes.

As frequently happens in heated debates, Watson and other behaviorists at times took extreme positions in their attacks upon the introspective psychologists. In their zeal to rule out the concepts of mind and conscious experience, they stated that the technique of introspection in any form whatever should be discarded. Modern psychologists are freed from the polemics of their predecessors, and in many experimental situations subjects are encouraged to give introspective reports. The difference is that now these verbal reports are considered as just another type of behavior, rather than as full evidence of the nature of the mind.

Although the "behavioristic revolution" has been most influential in the development of psychology, it is by no means the only influential systematic position. **Gestalt psychology,** a system of psychology originating in Germany, emphasizes the organization, the quality of wholeness, that inheres in both behavior and experience. For example, in Figure 3.12 there are 12 dots, but more likely you will first perceive them as the corners of three squares, rather than as 12 separate dots. Another example is an experience which you are probably very familiar with but have not analyzed. When you are watching a movie or a television screen, you are actually seeing a rapidly presented series of still pictures in which all objects and people are stationary. Despite this, you see movement when you look at the screen. Why do you organize the 12 dots into three squares, and why do you see movement when none actually exists? These are the kinds of questions raised by the Gestalt psychologists. They have taught us much about the organized nature of behavior in sensation and perception, and have investigated similar problems in learning, thinking, personality, and social psychology.

The systematic position adopted by the Gestalt psychologists also arose in opposition to Wundt's introspective psychology. Unlike the behaviorists, they did not protest against the concept of conscious experience and introspection in any form. Instead they objected to the idea of "mental chemistry," that complex conscious experience could be broken down by introspective observation into its elementary components.

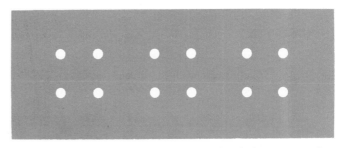

FIGURE 3.12 Do you perceive twelve isolated dots, or are they organized into three squares?

THE INFLUENCE OF PRACTICAL PROBLEMS ON THE GROWTH OF PSYCHOLOGY

One can draw an analogy between the course of a river and the history of psychology. For like the tributaries which flow into a river, many developments outside the psychological laboratory have widened and modified the course of psychology. In this respect the history of psychology seems at times unique among sciences, certainly different from the science of physics. The problems which concerned the early physicists were almost entirely those generated by their own experiments. Only after a basic core of physical knowledge was obtained did the practical problems of applying this knowledge become important. Psychology, on the other hand, has never been free from society's insistent demands that it do something about practical problems of controlling human behavior. These demands, antedating the beginnings of experimental psychology by centuries, have had a powerful influence upon the direction in which psychology has developed. It is difficult to decide whether this influence

has been for better or worse. Certainly it has broadened the interest of psychologists and led them to consider problems they would otherwise have overlooked. In some instances, the resulting experimental techniques and theories have had a beneficial influence on psychology as a pure science. On the other hand, the young science of psychology has undoubtedly been—and still often is—asked to deal with questions for which it was not ready. It is also certain that time and effort have been lost which might have been better spent in building the foundations of a fundamental experimental science from which applied techniques could later be derived. But it is difficult, if not impossible, to know exactly the influence which the concern with practical problems has had upon the growth of psychology. All we can do is discuss some of them and indicate how they have shaped the course of psychology.

The Deviant Individual

Deviant individuals incapable of adjusting to the demands of their physical and social environment have always been a problem for society. The behavior of some of these deviants seems so strange and unpredictable that it is often necessary to confine them for their own good and to protect other members of society from their possibly violent outbursts. These individuals, legally committed as insane and medically classified as psychotic, were formerly thought to be wicked persons possessed by

48

devils. Hence society for a long time felt no responsibility to help them and did not even attempt to cure them. Instead, they were confined with criminals or in lunatic asylums. Care was purely custodial and the techniques of treatment that were evolved, including the physical weakening of the inmates, were intended to make supervision easier.

FIGURE 3.13 Phillipe Pinel, 1745-1826 (Bettman Archive)

A change in society's attitude toward psychotics developed after the French Revolution. Partly as a result of more enlightened political ethics and an emphasis upon the brotherhood of man, and partly as a result of the personal efforts of a French physician, Phillipe Pinel, the treatment of psychotics became more humane. Pinel, sometimes considered the father of psychiatry (a branch of medicine devoted to the study and treatment of behavior disorders), rejected the idea that psychosis was due to supernatural influence. He saw that the insane were suffering from illness and should be treated with the same consideration as other sick persons. When he was placed in charge of an asylum in Paris, Pinel enacted reforms in line with his views. He freed his patients from dungeons and their chains, treated them more humanely, and was able to restore many to society. Pinel's program for the improvement of conditions in institutions was developed step by step by others and today is being pushed ahead more vigorously than ever before. The care of psychotics has a fascinating history in which science and humane feelings have won out all too slowly over superstition, ignorance, and callousness.

Once "mental abnormalities" began to be considered as illness, it became obvious that some individuals suffered from conditions such as senile deterioration, alcoholism, and brain injury, whereas others had no discernible physiological disorder. Such patients were considered to have some **functional** disorder, as contrasted with an **organic** condition responsible for aberrant behavior. Psychiatrists then began to see that those individuals with no apparent physical defects were functioning in an abnormal way due to confused habits of feeling and thinking, which were in turn the outcome of inadequate personal and social adjustment.

This focus upon faulty habit systems and on personal and social development that had taken undesirable directions provided a field for study where the psychiatrist and the psychologist could meet. The psychiatrist was a medically trained individual whose primary aim was to diagnose and treat "mental disorders," whereas the psychologist was a trained research scientist whose aim was to discover by experimentation whatever he could about both normal and abnormal behavior. The psychiatrist saw that an understanding of the behavior of psychologically healthy individuals would throw light upon the behavior of the psychologically disturbed. Comparisons of the two should highlight the principal mechanisms of behavior disorders. The psychologist, on the other hand, naturally took an interest in aberrant behavior, since the science of psychology is concerned with all behavior. Psychologists also felt that aberrant behavior might reflect with special clarity some of the principles at work in all behavior. This community of interests between the psychiatrist and psychologist developed into an exchange of points of view and a joint attempt in many cases to clarify the problems of behavior disorders.

It is not surprising that the study of behavior disorders, initially attributed to the influence of supernatural powers, has many terms and concepts without clear operational definitions. The term *insanity* itself has been a source of great confusion. Its correct contemporary usage is solely as a legal term applied to the condition of those who have been adjudged by a court not responsible for their actions and are therefore placed under such restraints as confinement in an institution. No doubt you have read about murder trials in which disagreements arose over the question of the defendant's sanity at the time he committed the crime. In such cases experts called in to testify sometimes give opposing views. The reason for this disagreement lies in the nature of the term *insanity,* itself. Formerly it meant severe unsoundness of mind which makes it impossible for a person to evaluate rationally the consequences of his behavior. We have already noted the impasse to progress in experimental psychology which the concept of mind constituted. This concept is ambiguous; it lacks a clear and reliable operational definition. Experimental psychologists therefore concluded that it would be best to dispense with the vague concept of mind and to use instead a term which stands for something that can be directly dealt with

—*behavior*. Psychiatry has not experienced a behavioristic revolution directly, and consequently, many whose primary concern is the care and treatment of those who suffer from behavior disorders were slow to appreciate the inadequacy of the concept of mind and the advantage of dealing directly with behavior.

Except in its legal context, professional psychiatrists and psychologists today do not use the term *insane* because of its confusing connotations. A severe behavior disorder is referred to as a **psychosis.** The use of this term does not, however, solve all the problems. The term is inexact, and there remains the question, "When is a person psychotic?" Until the past few decades, it was customary for psychiatrists in clinics and institutions to interview patients briefly and determine whether they were psychotic simply by listening to their talk. The method was plainly unreliable, and it was possible for an individual patient to be considered psychotic by some, mildly disturbed by others, and normal, but unconventional, by others.

Psychologists who had a strong tradition of studying behavior under *known* and *controlled* conditions of stimulation developed tests for diagnosing psychological disorders much more reliably. The concept of test reliability will be discussed more fully later on. Suffice it to say, for the present, that reliability refers to the relationship between successive measures of the same thing by the same test. Physical measurement of length is a highly reliable technique. Measure the length of your desk several times and you will discover that each measure provides approximately the same result. The techniques of measuring or testing for psychosis are not as reliable as those for measuring length, but great progress has been made in the development of tests designed to measure the kind and severity of behavior disorders. As a result, the diagnosis of a psychosis has become more reliable.

50

A professional team composed of a psychiatrist, a clinical psychologist (psychologists who deal with people suffering from behavior disorders), and a psychiatric social worker often share in the study and treatment of behavior disorders. In order that the services of such a team may be improved, there must be constant efforts to try out and evaluate new techniques of diagnosis and treatment. Since psychologists are required to demonstrate research ability and competence to qualify for a Ph.D. degree, it is usually the clinical psychologist who designs and executes the necessary research projects in the field of behavior disorders.

In addition to the interests psychologists and psychiatrists have in common, these two professional groups have been brought closer by the revolutionary influence of one outstandingly important figure in the history of both their fields, Sigmund Freud. It is difficult to treat Freud's influence briefly because it is both profound and exceedingly complex. Freud was a Viennese physician who, as everyone knows, developed the methods of personality analysis and treatment known as psychoanalysis.

Freud took the first steps in the development of psychoanalysis as a result of what he discovered about **neurotic** behavior disorders. These disorders manifest themselves in a large number of symptoms, ranging from bodily aches and pains without any apparent organic disfunction to generally inadequate modes of behaving. These disorders rarely require hospitalization. Freud was impressed by the fact that many of his patients under hypnosis were able to report desires and experiences which they were unaware of during normal waking life, and he developed the concept of the **unconscious** to designate the repository of these **repressed** elements of experience. He believed that under certain conditions, these feelings were responsible for behavioral disorders.

Psychoanalysis developed from the methods of treatment he designed to make people aware of their unconscious desires and memories. Both the free, uninhibited motives of the patients and the reports they gave of dreams proved to be important clues in laying bare a patient's unconscious. The aim of psychoanalysis was to make the patient aware of his repressed and unconscious desires, so that through their understanding and acceptance they could be controlled.

FIGURE 3.14   Sigmund Freud, 1856-1939 (Bettman Archive)

The reactions to Freud's ideas were varied, ranging from wholehearted acceptance to complete rejection. Our review and evaluation of psychoanalytic theory and method will have to be postponed until we have studied the psychology of personality. It may, however, be of interest to note here that American psychology, particularly that branch devoted to the study of learning, viewed Freud's efforts in an unexpectedly sympathetic fashion, considering that his formulations were based not upon experimentally controlled data but upon observations in clinical situations where the variables influencing the course of behavior could not be easily or conveniently isolated. This favorable reception of Freud's ideas was due partly to the fact that they were not concerned with behavior disorders only but were applicable to the whole field of personality and particularly to child psychology, the development of which was encouraged by the Functionalists and the Behaviorists. In addition, Freud emphasized the role of past experience in human behavior. The psychology of learning was primarily devoted to the study of this temporal relationship, and some psychologists working in this field perceived points of agreement between their formulations and those of Freud.

Not only were the strands of interest shared by psychiatry and psychology drawn together by Freud's ideas and hypotheses, which could be applied by the professionals of both fields, but the atmosphere surrounding the problems of behavior disorders was changed. Prior to Freud, the study of behavior disorders was largely restricted to the practical problems of diagnosis, care, and treatment of disturbed individuals. Although he did not abandon these problems, Freud was able through the breadth of his imaginative ideas to spotlight the broad theoretical implications that underlie the disorders of behavior. By his inspiring example he attracted research workers interested in theoretical problems to the study of aberrant behavior. As a result there has been a merging of research efforts by experimental psychology and clinical psychology in many areas. Clinical psychiatrists and psychologists have thus been brought to consider theoretical problems which would otherwise have seemed too abstract or too far afield, and experimental psychologists have come to grips with problems which they had not known existed.

Psychological Testing

We turn now to another field where the challenge of a practical problem touched off developments that have greatly influenced the growth of psychology.

FIGURE 3.15 Alfred Binet, 1857-1911 (Culver Pictures)

In 1904 the French Minister of Public Instruction appointed a commission of leading citizens to study how children unable to cope successfully with the regular work in the elementary schools should be taught. The commission consulted Alfred Binet, a psychologist, and Théophile Simon, a physician, both of whom felt that before this question could be answered, a technique for identifying intellectually retarded children had to be found.

An obvious solution was to ask the classroom teachers to identify their slow students. This would, however, raise basic diagnostic problems similar to those encountered in identifying individuals suffering from behavior disorders by means of a simple interview. The opinions of teachers could hardly be sufficiently reliable when, for example, a pupil that one teacher considered stupid, might be considered excessively shy by another teacher. You are probably aware, from your own long experience as a student, that a large number of nonintellectual factors can enter into a teacher's evaluation of a student's intellectual ability. Looks, clothes, manners, cleanliness, and conduct are but a few of the things which sometimes influence a teacher's estimate of a pupil's brightness.

Binet and Simon together designed an ingenious test which provided an objective and reliable estimate of a child's intellectual ability. Binet had proposed the idea of measuring a child's intelligence in relation to the intellectual performance of children of different ages. By using a series of tests ranging from very easy to very difficult with large groups of children of various ages, Binet and Simon discovered the average performance at each age level. With such specific information it was then possible to ascertain the intellectual ability of any child in a fairly exact manner. For example, after testing a four-year-old child with the test devised by Binet and Simon, one could characterize that child's performance as being equivalent to the average performance of a particular age group. Most four-year-olds perform at a level equivalent to the average four-year-old, but some perform at a lower level (e.g., that of two-year-olds) and some at a higher level (e.g., that of six-year-olds).

The superiority of Binet's **age-standard method** over the common practice of labeling a child "bright," "average," or "dull" should be apparent at once. Such vague terms mean different things to different people. A child who appears bright to one person may appear average to another. With Binet's method it was possible to characterize a child's intelligence by objective and quantitative standards, and to develop an operational definition of intelligence.

Of course, Binet's method of evaluating intellectual ability might appear today to be a rather simple and obvious technique. At the time it was proposed, however, it was a brilliant innovation, and ranks as one of the great practical inventions in the history of psychology. As the result of this test, the educator is able to discover, in most cases, whether a student's poor performance is due to intellectual deficiency or to nonintellectual factors.

Consider the case of an eight-year-old girl who is doing very poorly in the second grade. An intelligence test reveals that her intellectual performance is equivalent to the average nine-year-old's. Obviously her difficulty is not inadequate intelligence. The difficulty lies elsewhere, perhaps in motivation. Perhaps she does not like school and does not try to do her best. In other cases, of course, the test might reveal that poor academic performance was indeed a result of low intelligence. You can see, therefore, how such a test as Binet and Simon devised would be a tremendous help to the educator in identifying students who were incapable of profiting from a normal course of study and needed special educational programs set up for them.

The uses of intelligence tests are, of course, not limited to the identification of slow-learners. The unusually bright may also be identified, and this is probably even more important to society, provided something constructive is done about their ability. Once the intelligence test has permitted us to pick out the child whose intellectual ability is well above that of his own age group, we may give this gifted child an educational program to stimulate and train him in a manner consistent with his unusual ability.

The intelligence testing movement, which grew out of the specific problem of dealing with the intellectually defective child, has developed and spread into many other areas and has contributed to the solution of a large number of practical problems. Various revisions of the initial Binet-Simon test have been made, and other tests of intelligence have been designed for certain groups (adults, illiterates, etc.). In certain jobs, both in industry and the armed services, the intelligence levels required have been ascertained so that individuals can be selected and assigned to jobs suited to their abilities. Such policies of selection and placement contribute to the efficiency of any organization, and increase job satisfaction of the worker as well. Psychologists have applied the techniques of intelligence testing to the development of tests designed to measure other behavioral characteristics (e.g., special aptitudes, interests) found to be related to successful performance in a variety of situations.

The implications of intelligence testing and other types of psychological testing have not been restricted to the solution of practical problems. The testing of intelligence and other psychological characteristics and capacities raises problems relevant to all areas of psychology, and the history of psychology has witnessed a constant interaction between the development of traditional experimental methods originated in Wundt's laboratory and the more applied approach of psychologists like Binet, whose primary objective has been to measure particular psychological abilities. Each tradition has contributed to the development of the other. As the science of psychology matures, the interaction between its various sections increases.

Industrial Psychology

The main stream of experimental psychology has been broadened also by what has happened in our complex industrial age, with problems that no previous culture has had to face. Efficiency in machine operation requires quantitative knowledge of the capacities of men and women, so that machines can be designed to suit human capabilities. Look at Figure 3.16. It is a diagram of the conventional three-pointer altimeter of a decade ago. The correct reading of this altimeter is an altitude of 13,960 feet. However, research has shown that even experienced pilots make mistakes. In fact, the reading of the dial in Figure 3.16 is often mistaken for 14,960. Imagine what

FIGURE 3.16 A Three-Pointer Altimeter. The shortest pointer indicates altitude in units of 10,000 feet; the medium length pointer, in units of 1,000 feet; and the longest pointer, units of 100 feet. What altitude is represented by this setting? (After Grether, 1948)

can happen when a plane is flying toward a mountain peak 14,000 feet above sea level and a pilot mistakes a 13,960 feet altimeter reading for one of 14,960 feet.

By his research methods, the psychologist can evaluate the readability of dial faces and recommend those which pilots can read accurately and quickly. Joint efforts of this kind between psychologists and engineers are what has come to be known as **human engineering.** Not many years ago the only criterion for a machine or any of its parts was that it be mechanically perfect. But World War II repeatedly demonstrated

54

that mechanical perfection is not sufficient. The following verbatim account of a pilot's experiences during World War II illustrates this fact dramatically:

It was an extremely dark night. My co-pilot was at the controls. I gave him instructions to take the ship, a B-25, into the traffic pattern and land. He began letting down from an altitude of 4,000 feet. At 1,000 feet above the ground, I expected him to level off. Instead, he kept right on letting down until I finally had to take over. His trouble was that he had misread the altimeter by 1,000 feet. This incident might seem extremely stupid, but it was not the first time that I have seen it happen. Pilots are pushing up plenty of daisies today because they read their altimeter wrong while letting down on a dark night (Fitts & Jones, 1961, p. 368).

The application of psychology to industrial problems actually has its roots in the experimental work of two of Wundt's students. We have already referred to Cattell's interest in how people differ. His research work was primarily concerned with the study of individual differences: how people vary in speed of reaction to the sudden appearance of a stimulus such as a light or sound, or how they differ in their ability to see, hear, or smell. His work led naturally to research designed to improve techniques of selecting workers for different jobs. Since different jobs require different abilities, the psychologist's task was to devise tests capable of selecting people with the abilities necessary for various types of jobs. Hugo Münsterberg, another student of Wundt's, but not greatly influenced by him, was the first to see what industrial psychology might accomplish, and at the end of his career, he made the earliest contributions to the solution of specific industrial problems, such as the qualifications needed for driving streetcars. This type of work has been greatly expanded, and its methods perfected to the point where they now have far-reaching applications.

Social Psychology

Any systematic attempt to arrive at a basic understanding of human behavior must sooner or later deal with the influence of social factors. People grow up in social as

FIGURE 3.17 Hugo Münsterberg, 1863-1916 (Brown Brothers)

well as in physical environments, and their behavior in most situations is due in great part to the character of their society. Most psychologists from Wundt on have recognized this obvious truth, but the early psychologists felt compelled to deal with laboratory problems with a limited number of variables to control, situations somewhat simpler than the interaction between a person and his society.

However, social psychology was not entirely ignored even then. Wundt himself wrote several volumes in the field, but what he had to say lacked the experimental foundation of his writings in other areas. G. Stanley Hall, an American student of Wundt's, criticized the aims of the introspective psychologists, feeling that psychology should come closer to real life. He was particularly interested in the social problems of children and adolescents.

Social psychology achieved something like real status when William McDougall, an English psychologist who spent his later years at Harvard and Duke University, published a text on *Social Psychology*. McDougall emphasized the importance of instincts as the driving forces in social behavior, a topic that will demand our critical attention later on, and his vigorous inquiries into man's behavior in social situations created a great deal of interest in the subject.

Perhaps the most important role in establishing social psychology as a branch of experimental psychology was played by Kurt Lewin and his associates, for they observed social interaction under controlled

FIGURE 3.18 Kurt Lewin (1890-1947)

experimental situations. One of the pioneer American investigations was a doctoral thesis under Lewin's sponsorship by Ronald Lippitt. Lippitt investigated the behavior of groups of five ten-year-old boys. These boys were encouraged to form clubs ostensibly for the purpose of making theatrical masks. The experimental variable was the behavior of the leaders. In some groups the leader was coached to behave "democratically," to be friendly and to encourage group discussion and decisions, while in others the leader was to be "authoritarian," to deliberately dictate the group's policies and actions. Discussion of the empirical results of this experiment belongs to another section of this book. Their major significance, however, was as a ground-breaking demonstration of the feasibility of adjusting the "social environment" experimentally and measuring group behavior within that environment objectively. This was an important contribution; the advancement of any science has been highly correlated with the ability to investigate phenomena in a controlled experimental situation.

In recent years the problems of social psychology have become crucially important. World War II, with the invention of the A-bomb and the H-bomb, has made us terribly aware that social forces will ultimately decide whether mankind survives. We constantly hear that our knowledge of physics and chemistry has outstripped our understanding of how to use it constructively. Many of us look to the social scientist for the knowledge that will enable society to profit sensibly from the advance of the physical sciences. Whether the social scientist can ultimately help our world to survive is a question that only the future can decide. Meanwhile some social psychologists and social scientists in related fields are making efforts at least to get more light on the crucial social issues of our time, and thus, it may be hoped, to move nearer to their solution.

THE METHOD OF MODERN PSYCHOLOGY

We have sketched the history of psychology from its prescientific origins to the present primarily in terms of its methods. We are able only to give a bare outline, to reflect the most general trends in the development of a science of behavior. Because so many influences have shaped psychology as it is today, it would be difficult to describe its current method simply. In essence, however, modern psychology is largely behavioristic in methodology, but this is a neo-behaviorism appreciably broader and more tolerant than that first advocated by Watson. In fact, as several psychologists have suggested, there would be less chance of misunderstanding if contemporary psychology were described as **objective psychology.** For today psychologists hold that any behavior publicly observable or capable of being recorded in a form such that it can be re-recorded from repeated observation, if necessary, can serve as a dependent variable in research. This requirement does not exclude all private experience as a suitable object of investigation. For example, people's verbal reports about the content of their dreams can serve as the dependent variable in research on dreams. And with the development of new physiological and electronic techniques, it is possible that what are now private experiences will someday be public events. You will see later that the requirement that behavior be publicly observable in order to be investigated does not seriously prevent psychologists from studying a wide range of behavior. Rather it insures that such investigations will yield tangible results of known reliability.

SUMMARY

Since the beginning of recorded time man has sought to understand his own behavior. Only recently has he tried to do this scientifically.

The initial efforts to investigate behavior in an experimental manner were made by physiologists, physicists, and philosophers. Then Wilhelm Wundt established psychology as an independent science by founding the first laboratory in Leipzig, Germany, in 1879. Wundt perceived the task of psychology as ·that of analyzing conscious experience into fundamental elements, just as the chemist analyzes compounds into their basic elements. Gradually but persistently psychologists began to attend more to overt behavior and less to conscious experience. This trend culminated in the behaviorist approach. John B. Watson, the founder of behaviorism, insisted that observable behavior and not private conscious experience was the proper subject matter of psychology.

The growth of the science of psychology has been influenced greatly by pressures to consider a wide variety of practical problems. The need for caring for, diagnosing, and treating people suffering from "abnormal" behavior have led to the field of clinical psychology. Clinical psychologists and psychiatrists have been brought closer together by the teachings of Sigmund Freud, who formulated a revolutionary theory of personality, as well as a technique for treating pathological behavior. Psychologists have also responded to the need of schools to measure the intelligence of their students. From their efforts, and especially those of the French psychologist, Alfred Binet, have emerged a number of widely used intelligence tests, as well as techniques for the construction of tests to measure other behavioral characteristics. Psychologists have contributed to industrial efficiency by helping to design machines suited to the men who run them and by developing tests that help to select the right person for the right job. Most recently psychologists have turned their attention to problems of social psychology. They have demonstrated, among other things, that it is possible to investigate social behavior with experimental techniques.

Today contemporary psychology is objective psychology. It seeks to investigate all forms of behavior with methods that are publicly observable.

SUGGESTIONS FOR FURTHER READING

BORING, E. G. *A history of experimental psychology.* (Rev. ed.) New York: Appleton-Century-Crofts, 1950.

A classic which describes in both a thorough and interesting manner how psychology became an experimental science.

CHAPLIN, J. P., & KRAWIEC, T. S. *Systems and theories of psychology.* New York: Holt, Rinehart, & Winston, 1960.

A recent book that discusses the history of psychology in relation to the development of important problems and concepts in modern psychology.

DENNIS, W. *Readings in the history of psychology.* New York: Appleton-Century-Crofts, 1948.

Excerpts from writings of philosophers, physicists, physiologists, and psychologists who have played important roles in the history of psychology.

HEIDBREDER, E. *Seven psychologies.* New York: Appleton-Century-Crofts, 1933.

An excellent analysis of seven systematic positions in the history of psychology.

KELLER, F. S. *The definition of psychology.* New York: Appleton-Century-Crofts, 1937.

A brief (less than 100 pages) overview of the history of psychology.

MURPHY, G. *Historical introduction to modern psychology.* (Rev. ed.) New York: Harcourt, Brace, 1949.

An interestingly written history that provides a good picture of the background of contemporary psychology.

WOODWORTH, R. S. *Contemporary schools of psychology.* (Rev. ed.) New York: Ronald, 1948.

A brief but penetrating analysis of various systematic positions in psychology.

STATISTICS—THE DESCRIPTION AND INTERPRETATION OF SCIENTIFIC DATA

4

THE NEED FOR STATISTICS

Statistics is one of the major tools of scientific method. Essentially it is the use of mathematics in collecting, ordering, and interpreting—a set of empirical data.

Consider for the moment a few of the problems that arise when the national census is taken once every ten years. A large number of questions are asked which apply to each adult and child in the country. These data, collected by the census-taker, are initially recorded on a questionnaire blank. In this form the total number of items of information obtained and their sheer physical bulk stagger the imagination. How can this vast amount of data be summarized and made intelligible, so that an overall picture of whatever information is desired may be obtained? Statisticians have developed techniques capable of embodying vast amounts of information in a few simple numerical indices. Without

such techniques we should have only incoherent masses of numbers.

Consider for a moment one simple situation which points to the need for interpreting data. Suppose you tossed a quarter and a dime four times each, and that three out of the four tosses with the quarter produced heads, while only one out of four with the dime produced a head. Would it be correct to say that that quarter would always produce more heads than would that dime? You can understand why such a conclusion would be unwarranted. The difference between the number of heads resulting from tosses of the quarter and of the dime might be due to chance and not to any inherent difference between the coins. To test this hypothesis you would need only to toss the quarter and dime repeatedly. If on some sets of four tosses, the dime landed heads more often than the quarter, while on other sets the reverse was true, or if there was no difference between the coins, then you would very likely be justified in concluding that the initial superiority of the quarter in producing heads was merely a matter of chance.

Although people are ready to recognize the operation of chance in coin tossing, they usually are reluctant to consider this possibility when interpreting results of other investigations. Suppose someone tested the effectiveness of a pill containing vaccine in preventing infantile paralysis in a group of 500 youngsters, and that at the end of the trial period not one of the children had been stricken with polio. Would that demonstrate that the pill was effective in preventing this dreaded disease? No, it would not. Because paralytic polio is so relatively infrequent, it is possible that the children who composed the sample would never have contracted it in the first place. That is, the apparent findings of this hypothetical experiment might have been due to chance rather than to the effects of the experimental pill. Therefore, it was necessary to use thousands of children in testing the effectiveness of the Salk vaccine.

Statisticians have developed techniques which permit them to determine whether they should attribute experimental results to significant effects of experimental variables or to chance factors. In the hypothetical cases of tossing the coins or testing the effects of a polio vaccine, the results could reasonably be attributed to chance occurrences. When we reach such a conclusion, we say that the experimental results are *not significant*. Of course, most of the results reported in this book will be **significant,** since they demonstrably cannot, on the basis of statistical tests, be reasonably attributed to the operations of chance. But at present it is important for you to realize that experimental findings cannot be accepted solely at face value. We must always question whether these findings could reasonably be attributed to chance. This requirement is not unique to psychological research; it is part of all scientific work where masses of data must be interpreted. Statistical technique provides the means to evaluate the significance of experimental results.

This chapter does not pretend to train you as a statistician. However, it does attempt to describe on an elementary level various fundamental statistical techniques and to make clear *the logic underlying their use*. These techniques are simpler, much more interesting, and more practical than students think they are. The greatest difficulty in understanding them stems from preconceived fears about numbers, rather than from any inherent difficulty in the subject matter. Don't let a few statistics panic you. Keep a clear head and you will find that difficulties vanish.

The statistical understanding you will gain will be essential to you in acquiring a fundamental knowledge of the science of psychology. It will, moreover, have other uses. We are all constantly faced with the task of interpreting statistical statements—when we listen to politicians or TV hucksters, when we read the sports pages or news of business, whenever we are confronted with information expressed in averages and percentages. H. G. Wells foresaw this development many years ago when he wrote: "Statistical thinking will one day be as necessary for efficient citizenship as the ability to read and write."

There are two main uses of statistics: for description and for sampling. Descriptive statistics summarize large masses of data; sampling statistics interpret and forecast events.

DESCRIPTIVE STATISTICS

By arranging and grouping data it is possible to describe a large population of findings in a simple manner. To comprehend fully what these simpler representations mean, it is necessary to understand the techniques used to obtain them.

Figure 4.1 shows ten cartoons from the famous English humor magazine *Punch*. Which of them do you think are funny?

"Better not use up all the bandages before the fight."

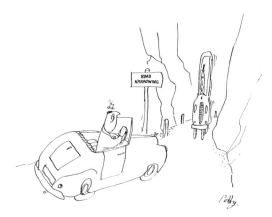

FIGURE 4.1 Which of these cartoons do you judge to be funny? (© *Punch*, London)

"We'll have to stop meeting like this. My insurance company's getting suspicious."

To answer you must sort these cartoons into two categories: funny or not funny. Such a sorting will result in a response measure which can be used to describe the humorousness of *this set* of cartoons.

Suppose that 100 students in a class judged the cartoons. The number of cartoons judged funny by each student was as follows:

5; 8; 2; 0; 6; 2; 3; 1; 8; 2; 2; 7; 1; 6; 3;
4; 3; 5; 0; 4; 6; 2; 3; 7; 1; 2; 8; 6; 7; 1;
6; 3; 9; 2; 5; 4; 8; 9; 4; 6; 2; 7; 9; 1; 6;
4; 7; 3; 6; 4; 8; 7; 5; 5; 6; 3; 7; 5; 3; 9;
5; 5; 3; 3; 8; 5; 7; 4; 5; 4; 10; 5; 2; 4; 3;
8; 5; 5; 4; 6; 5; 7; 5; 4; 7; 5; 2; 5; 5; 8;
4; 10; 5; 3; 6; 9; 5; 8; 4; 1.

How would you answer someone who asked you to describe the group's reaction to this series of cartoons? You could report the score for each student, just as has been done here. Although there is nothing intrinsically wrong with this method, it is cumbersome and fails to provide us with a concise description that can be readily assimilated, understood, and used to compare the judgments of this group of students with those of another group.

Frequency Distribution

Another way of treating the data would be to tally the scores and arrange them in a **frequency distribution.** To begin with, you would select the lowest and highest scores obtained. In our example, they are 0 and 10. You would order these scores and the ones falling between them in a vertical column, and then tally each occurrence of the 11 possible scores and determine their total frequency. You can see how this is done in Table 4.1.

You can see how it got its name. By grouping the scores of one class it is possible first to count the *frequency* of scores

in each class, and then to see how the frequencies are *distributed* among the various classes.

The frequency distribution in Table 4.1 can be graphically represented in a **histogram** and in a **frequency polygon.** In both

TABLE 4.1   Frequency Distribution

RANGE OF SCORES	FREQUENCY OF OCCURENCE
0	2
1	6
2	10
3	12
4	13
5	20
6	11
7	10
8	9
9	5
10	2

kinds of graphical representation the scores are arranged along the horizontal axis (abscissa) of a graph, and the frequency of scores is indicated along the vertical axis (ordinate). In the histogram the frequency of scores in each class is represented by the height of a bar or line. In a frequency polygon the points of the frequency of each score are connected to form one continuous line representing the distribution of frequencies.

The frequency distribution can be plotted in terms of the number of subjects or in terms of the per cent of subjects obtaining a specific score. Since there were 100 subjects in our example, the frequency of occurrence represents both the actual number and the per cent of subjects obtaining each score.

Quite often, there are many different scores in a frequency distribution with the extremes differing by a large amount. For the sake of convenience, therefore, it is necessary to group such data into class intervals. Each point on the abscissa then represents a class of scores rather than one

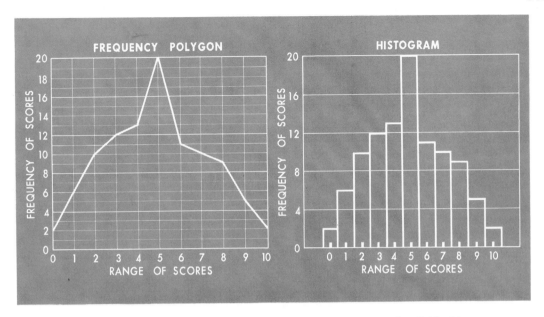

FIGURE 4.2   Histogram and Frequency Polygon of Data Reported in Table 4.1.

particular score. Figure 4.3 is an example of a frequency distribution representing the per cent of children with various levels of intelligence (defined in terms of intelligence quotient obtained on the Stanford-Binet Intelligence Test) in a sample of 2,904 children. The range of IQ (intelligence quotient) is so wide that the results are more conveniently represented in class intervals of ten IQ points.

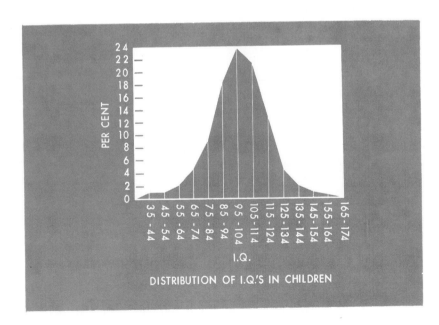

FIGURE 4.3   Distribution of IQ's of 2904 Children (After L. M. Terman & M. A. Merrill, *Measuring Intelligence,* 1937, p. 37).

Shapes of Frequency Distributions. Frequency distributions can have a variety of forms. Figure 4.4 shows six of the infinite number of possible forms they can take.

Consider for a moment the hypothetical rectangular frequency distribution in Figure 4.4. For the sake of convenience, we will refer to it as an *R distribution,* and shall use it to clarify certain principles underlying the logic of statistics. Assume that you have a test consisting of four questions and that out of a total sample of 1,000 students you discover that 200 fail to answer any of the questions correctly,

200 answer one question correctly, 200 answer two questions correctly, 200 answer three questions correctly, and the remaining 200 students answer all four questions correctly. This *R* distribution can easily be described by stating that it consists of five possible scores and that the frequency of occurrence of each score is the same, 20 per cent of the total.

Another type of distribution, the **normal probability curve,** has properties different from the *R* distribution. A normal probability curve is the most important type of frequency distribution because much of sampling statistics is based upon its characteristics, some of which you will study later on. For the present note that a frequency distribution curve of chance occurrences approximates a normal probability curve. If 20 pennies are tossed simultaneously 1,000 times, the frequency distribution curve of the number of heads on each toss would have essentially the shape of a normal probability curve. This is why this curve is sometimes referred to as a chance distribution.

Measures of Central Tendency

Distributions of scores have certain distinctive features. In order to compare various distributions, statisticians have developed measures which seek to describe economically the center of a distribution. These are called measures of central tendency.

The need for some measure of central tendency was eloquently revealed by a sports story appearing in a newspaper near the end of a baseball season several years ago. It dealt with the number of home runs hit off various major league pitchers. The story reported that more home runs had been hit off Robin Roberts, then in his prime as star pitcher of the Philadelphia Phillies, than off any other pitcher in the major leagues, and concluded that Roberts would wind up with the title of "Gopher Ball Leader." The facts behind the story were

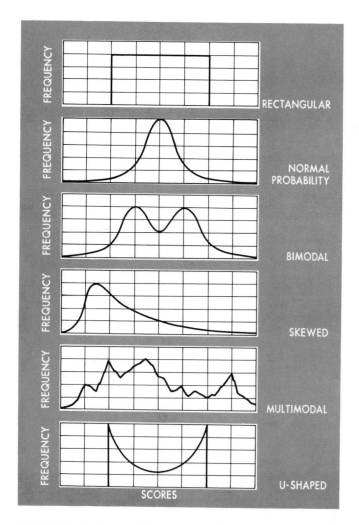

FIGURE 4.4   Six Types of Frequency Distribution.

that 30 home runs had been hit off Roberts, while the two pitchers nearest him in this respect had each pitched 28 home-run balls. There is no denying the fact that Roberts did pitch the most "gopher balls." But that fact, by itself, does not tell the whole story, and it would be unjustified to conclude that a player stood a better chance of hitting a home run off Robin Roberts than off these other pitchers. Further data, which appeared in the news story but were not taken into account, showed that Robin Roberts pitched the equivalent of 31 complete games (nine innings being considered a complete game), while his two nearest competitors for the dubious title of "Gopher Ball Leader" pitched 15 and 24 complete games respectively. If we divide the number of home runs by the number of complete games pitched, we get the average or **mean** number of home runs hit off each pitcher during each complete game. The computations show that whereas Roberts averaged 0.97 home runs per game, the two other pitchers averaged 1.87 and 1.17 home runs per game. Actually the impression given by the story that Roberts was the pitcher most likely to pitch a "gopher ball" was entirely misleading; Roberts pitched fewer home-run balls per game than most other major league pitchers that year. So, in spite of the fact that he pitched the most home-run balls, he was one of the most difficult pitchers to hit a home run off.

In our analysis of the baseball data a numerical index was used to describe the records of a group of pitchers. The measure used, the mean, represented the typical performance of a pitcher in terms of his propensity to hurl "gopher balls." Two other measures of central tendency are the **mode** and the **median.** We shall now discuss these measures of central tendency formally. However, the point made with the baseball example is one that bears repetition. When comparing the behavior of individuals, it is often necessary to obtain a single measure that typifies their performance. Measures of central tendency serve this function.

A measure of central tendency is a **single** number representing the "center" of a distribution. There are three such "centers," and it is necessary to distinguish among them if one is to avoid confusion and misrepresentation.

The Mode. The mode is the most frequent score. In Figure 4.4 on page 64, the mode is represented by the score occurring with the highest frequency. In the R distribution there is no single mode, since all scores have equal frequencies. The normal probability curve has a mode in the center of its range of scores, whereas the bimodal distribution has two modes represented by the two "peaks" in the frequency polygon. In the other frequency distributions in Figure 4.4, as in any distribution, one can ascertain the mode by inspection.

The Median. The median is the score that falls in the middle of the distribution. If the scores are arranged in rank order, from highest to lowest, half of them are greater than the median, and half of them are less than the median. To find the median of a distribution involving an odd number of scores, one simply picks the middlemost score: for example, the median of scores 5, 8, 9, 20, and 30 is 9. In distributions with an even number of scores, the point halfway between the two middlemost scores is selected: the median of scores 2, 5, 8, 9, 20, and 30 is 8.5. The median of the frequency distribution of cartoon ratings appearing on page 62 is 5.

The Mean. The mean, which has already been used to compute the average number of home-run balls pitched by Robin Roberts and two other pitchers, is the most commonly used measure of central tendency. Its formula is

$$M = \frac{\Sigma X}{N}$$

where ΣX represents the sum of all the scores (with Σ, the Greek capital letter *sigma,* representing the phrase "the sum of," while X stands for an individual score), and N refers to the number of scores. The mean, therefore, is the sum of all the scores divided by the number of scores.

At this point, you may wonder why there are three measures of central tendency? The reason is that they provide different information. In order to interpret uses of the measures intelligently, it is necessary merely to understand how they are computed.

In distributions approaching the normal probability curve, there is no problem in interpreting the meaning of a central tendency because the mode, median, and mean are approximately equivalent. However, in distributions where the scores tend to pile up at one end, as they do in distributions of yearly income because there is a preponderance of small incomes, the values of the mode, median, and mean fall some distance apart. Take the simple example of five individuals who have yearly incomes of $2,500, $2,500, $4,000, $11,000, and $100,000. The mode income would be $2,500, the median income would be $4,000, and the mean income would be $24,000.

In the arena of national politics critics of the party in power prefer to cite the mode or median as representative of the income of the nation, while the defenders of the party in power are more inclined to use the mean income as representative, because it is higher and makes people seem more prosperous. If the type of measure used is specified, then by knowing the meaning of the three measures of central tendency, you can avoid being misled. If, however, a figure is cited without an indication of what measure of central tendency it represents, the alert reader or listener will be on his guard to detect possible statistical shenanigans.

One other example of the need for caution in evaluating averages comes from a news story which appeared several years ago. It gave the impressive information that the average Yale man, class of '36, had an annual income of $50,536. Such information would seem likely to motivate naive parents to send their sons to Yale (and their daughters to schools near Yale). If, however, they read between the statistical lines, they would be more cautious. For the figure might represent a mean greatly influenced by a few extremely high incomes. But what is more important, the statement fails to specify the precise population from which the mean was obtained. Such figures usually result from mail surveys, and only those alumni whose addresses are known are included in the results. The Yale alumnus of the class of '36 who became a beachcomber or an itinerant soda jerk would in all likelihood not be included among the mailed returns. Neither would those alumni whose addresses were known but who, embarrassed by failure, threw the questionnaire in the wastebasket. If it were accurate, the news story would have read: "Mean income reported by Yale men of the class of '36, whose addresses are known and who answered a questionnaire, is $50,-536 a year." Going to Yale, fortunately or not, is no *guarantee* of a sizable future yearly income. Many Yale men could testify to this. The important point for you, however, assuming you are not at Yale, is that a correct interpretation of such figures requires an understanding of the three different measures of central tendency and a knowledge of the data on which any particular one is based.

Measures of Variability

Frequency distributions differ not only in average scores, but also in their variability. Figure 4.5 shows three distributions having the same means, modes, and medians, but varying in the extent to which the scores *within* a distribution differ from each other.

The concept of variability is exceedingly important, as you will discover when the techniques of sampling statistics are discussed. Its importance can be simply stated by referring to the age-old custom of tossing a pair of dice. If a properly constructed pair of dice is thrown many times, the mean, mode, and median "point" per toss would be approximately 7. A pair of dice that would produce average scores of 7 would not, however, necessarily be a properly constructed pair of dice. Anyone with a little knowledge of physical laws can make a pair of dice produce means, modes, and medians of 7 for a long series of tosses by simply loading the dice. The difference between the loaded dice that produce 7 on every toss and the properly constructed dice that produce *average* scores of 7, is in variability of results. With loaded dice, all tosses result in 7 and hence no variability exists; with properly constructed dice the scores vary from 2 to 12, with a mean of 7.

Range. A simple measure of variability is the **range** between the highest and lowest score. It is easily computed by subtracting the lowest score from the highest score. The range shows the spread between the extreme scores, but fails to show how the rest of the scores are distributed. Figure 4.6 shows three distributions having the same mean score and range, but varying in their distribution about the mean.

Standard Deviation. By far the most common and most useful measure of variability is the **standard deviation.** Although you need not become proficient in computing standard deviations, you should know how the standard deviation is obtained if you are to understand fully this measure of variability.

The formula is

$$S.D. = \sqrt{\frac{\Sigma d^2}{N}}$$

where *S.D.* is the abbreviation for standard deviation, Σ again stands for "the sum of," while d represents the deviation or difference between an individual score and the mean, and N represents the number of cases

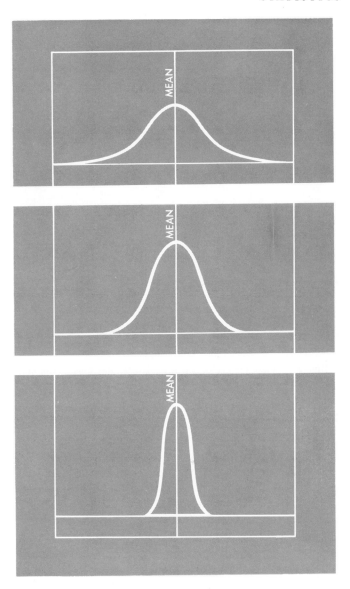

FIGURE 4.5   Three Frequency Distributions With the Same Measures of Central Tendency but Differing in Variability.

in the frequency distribution. Taking the very simple case of a distribution involving five scores of 5, 9, 10, 11, and 15, the *S.D.* is computed by first obtaining the mean, which in this case is 10, and then computing the deviation of each score from the mean. For example, the score 5 would have a deviation of 5, the score 9 would have a

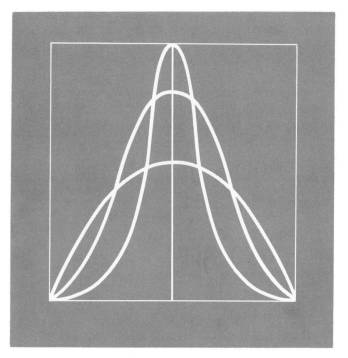

FIGURE 4.6 Three Frequency Distributions With the Same Mean and Range but Differing in the Dispersion of Scores About the Mean.

deviation of 1, etc. Each deviation is then squared and the sum of the squared deviations is divided by the number of scores. The square root of the result is then obtained, giving the value of the standard deviation. Table 4.2 shows the complete set of computations and the value of the standard deviation, which in this example is 3:23.

If the scores were 5, 5, 10, 15, and 15, the distributions would have a standard deviation of 4.47. These two distributions have the same range, 10; the difference in

TABLE 4.2 The Computation of the Standard Deviation of a Distribution of Scores of 5, 9, 10, 11, and 15

SCORES	d	d^2
5	—5	25
9	—1	1
10	0	0
11	+1	1
15	+5	25
$\Sigma X = 50$		$\Sigma d^2 = 52$

$$M = \frac{50}{5} = 10 \quad \text{S.D.} = \sqrt{\frac{52}{5}} = \sqrt{10.4} = 3.23$$

the standard deviations of the two distributions results from the *dispersion* of the scores. In the first distribution, the scores, except for the two extremes, tend to be grouped closely around the mean. In the second distribution only two scores differ in value, but these two scores are at the extremes rather than near the mean and this explains the difference between the standard deviations of these distributions. The standard deviation, therefore, is a numerical index that indicates the degree of dispersion of the data. The smaller the standard deviation, the more closely are the scores grouped around the mean. The larger the standard deviation, the farther away are the scores from the mean.

The Dispersion of Scores in a Normal Distribution. Recall our description of the R distribution. It is a hypothetical distribution which we are using solely for pedagogical purposes. We described it as being rectangular in shape, with the scores ranging from 0 to 4, each having 20 per cent of the total frequency. Twenty per cent of the scores had the mean value (2), 60 per cent ranged from one score below the mean to one score above the mean (from 1-3), and 100 per cent ranged from two scores below the mean to two scores above the mean (from 0-4). As you see, the R distribution can be described in terms of how the five possible scores are dispersed from the mean.

A normal distribution can be similarly described, but with it the standard deviation serves as the unit to indicate how the scores are dispersed. In a normal frequency distribution, 68.3 per cent of the cases will fall within the range of one standard deviation unit on either side of the mean, 95.4 per cent will fall within the range of two standard deviation units, and 99.7 per cent, within the range of three units. Figure 4.7 shows these relationships for both the R distribution and the normal distribution. Later, when we are discussing sampling statistics, you will see how knowledge in terms of standard deviation units of the dispersion of scores in a normal distribution assists in interpreting the data and in predicting something about them.

Correlation

Up to this point we have been concerned with describing data that vary along a *single dimension,* such as the numbers of cartoons judged humorous by members of a class or the number of "gopher balls" pitched by several pitchers. You have learned about numerical indices which represent the central tendency or variability of a particular distribution of scores.

It is often desirable to know the relationship between two sets of measures. For example, we are all aware that there is some degree of relationship between an individual's height and his weight. Tall people *tend* to be heavier than short people. Yet, this is not always true; it is *not* a universal, or what will be called a *perfect,* relationship, because some short people weigh more than some taller people. A tabular representation of a hypothetical perfect relationship is, however, provided in Table 4.3. It ranks the scores five individuals received on two tests, X and Y.

TABLE 4.3 Scores Obtained by Five Students in Mathematics Midterm and Final Examinations

MIDTERM EXAMINATION	STUDENT	FINAL EXAMINATION
100%	A	100%
90	B	90
80	C	80
70	D	70
50	E	50

You can observe the two scores of each individual and see the relationship between them. You will note that each individual's performance has the same rank on the first and on the second test. In other words, there is a perfect relationship between performance on the two tests; if you knew only the rank of an individual's score on one

test, you would be in a position to state exactly what his relative performance would be on the other test.

Perfect relationships such as this rarely occur in nature. But there frequently are

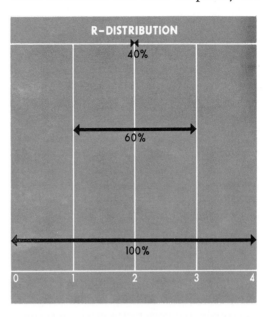

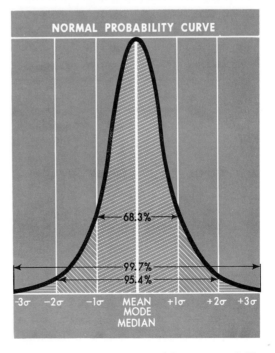

FIGURE 4.7 The Dispersion of Scores in an *R* Distribution and a Normal Distribution.

relationships with some degree of correspondence, as illustrated by the height and weight example above or by the cases of similar scores made by the same individual on midterm and on final examinations. In order to express the degree of relationship existing between two sets of scores, statisticians have developed a single numerical index called the **coefficient of correlation.** The possible range of the coefficient of correlation is from +1.00 to −1.00. The perfect relationship illustrated in Table 4.3 would have a coefficient of correlation of +1.00. Table 4.4 shows a hypothetical relationship having a coefficient of correlation of −1.00. The individuals who got the low scores in one test got the high scores in the other test and vice versa. The two scores of each individual are inversely related. A coefficient of correlation of −1.00 is another example of a perfect relationship since, where it is found, knowledge of an individual's score on one test enables us to say exactly what his score is on the other. The predictive power of a negative correlation of 1.00 is equal to that of a positive correlation of 1.00. When dealing with some *degree* of relationship, the size of the coefficient of correlation is the important factor, not the sign, plus or minus.

TABLE 4.4 Scores Obtained by Five Students on Psychological Tests Designed to Measure Sociability and Suspiciousness

TEST OF SOCIABILITY	STUDENT	TEST OF SUSPICIOUSNESS
100%	A	0%
90	B	10
80	C	20
50	D	50
0	E	100

Relationships which occur more frequently than the two described are pictured in Figure 4.8. Shown first is a positive but not perfect relationship in which high scores in one test tend to correspond with high scores in the other. With this relation-

ship you could not make a perfect prediction of a person's relative score on one test with only the knowledge of how well he did on the other test, but your prediction of his relative score would be better than if you knew nothing at all about him. The second relationship in Figure 4.8 represents a coefficient of correlation of .00, zero correspondence between the two sets of test scores. The chances that an individual having a low score on one test will make a high score on the second test are just as good as the chances that an individual having a high score on the first test will make another high score. The third relationship in Figure 4.8 is a negative relationship which, in one sense, is similar to the first relationship, but is exactly its opposite in sign. In this case a high score in one test tends to be associated with a low score in the other.

One important but obvious point to remember is that in order to correlate two sets of data, it is necessary that they be obtained either from the same groups of individuals, or from two groups related to each other in some way such as fathers and sons. We could not describe the relationship between height and weight if we had the weight measures of one group of 100 individuals and the height measures of an entirely different group of 100 individuals. In order to compute the coefficient of correlation, we must have both weight and height measures of the same individuals or of related pairs of individuals, such as fathers and sons. If we were interested in discovering the correlation between the intelligence of husbands and wives, for example, we would have to get the intelligence test scores of married pairs.

Computation of Coefficient of Correlation. This discussion has attempted to explain the logical principles underlying the correlational technique. So far it has not been concerned with the actual computational procedures; their mastery is likely to be

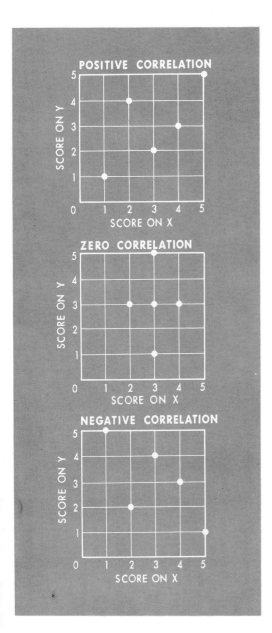

FIGURE 4.8 Examples of Positive, Zero, and Negative Correlations. The graphs, which are scatter diagrams, show the performance of five individuals on two separate tests (X and Y). Each dot represents one individual's performance on both tests. In the positive correlation scatter diagram, the dot in the lower left-hand corner represents the performance of an individual receiving a score of 1 on both the X and Y tests.

achieved only in a statistics course. But in order to make concrete the notion of a correlation, one computational technique will be described. The most common technique, the *product-moment correlation,* is customarily used when the number of items is large and the frequency distribution of each set of scores approximates the normal distribution. The formula is

$$r = \frac{\Sigma d_x d_y}{N \sigma_x \sigma_y}$$

where r is the coefficient of correlation, and $\Sigma d_x d_y$ represents the sum of the products of the deviations of the individual scores. For example, if one individual scored 60 and 80 on two tests, both of which had mean scores of 70, then his deviations would be —10 and +10 respectively. The product of both deviations $(d_x d_y)$ would then be —100. In computing a coefficient of correlation, the product of the two deviations is obtained for each individual and then all the products are added. The sum is represented in the formula by $\Sigma d_x d_y$. The denominator in the formula is the product of the number of cases multiplied by the standard deviations (represented by the Greek letter σ) of each distribution of scores for the two tests. You can see that the greater the sum of the products of the deviations $(\Sigma d_x d_y)$, the higher will be the coefficient of correlation. If most of the individuals who get extreme scores in one distribution get extreme scores in the other distribution, the correlation will be high. In such cases the coefficient will be positive if the individuals who get high scores in one test also get high scores in the other test, and those who achieve low scores in one test also get low scores in the other test. The correlation will be negative if high scores in one test are accompanied by low scores in the other test. Students usually ask how is it possible to know that such a formula will result in coefficients of correlation not exceeding +1.00 or —1.00. That it will not can be proven mathematically, but if your curiosity is aroused, try inventing some hypothetical distributions and see whether you can obtain a coefficient of correlation exceeding the above range.

Interpreting Correlations. Interpreting a coefficient of correlation is tricky business. There is great danger that a person who is not careful will read too much into a coefficient, supposing it tells him more than it does.

The higher the coefficient, the closer the relationship between two sets of scores. Another way of saying this is that the higher the correlation, the better one can predict a person's relative score on one test from knowledge of his score on the other test. Thus, a correlation of + or −.70 indicates a closer relationship than one of + or −.35. But it does *not* indicate a relationship twice as close. The major concern should be whether the coefficient of correlation between two sets of scores is significantly (see page 59) greater than zero, whether a relationship really exists at all.

The second and greater danger in interpreting correlations lies in believing that a high correlation between two variables means that one causes the other. If you always remember the essential steps in computing a coefficient of correlation, you will not be tempted to think this. Correlations merely reflect the degree of relationship between two sets of scores. They involve no experimental manipulations to determine how one variable is influenced by systematic changes in the other.

During a period of several years a positive correlation was noted in a Swiss town between the number of human births and the number of storks that nested there in a given season. Such data would not shake sophisticated people's conviction in the facts of life. What did the positive correlation between the number of storks and the number of births actually mean? It meant nothing more than that as one increased the other also tended to increase.

We can speculate about factors underlying this relationship, but without additional evidence we cannot be certain of the accuracy of any particular hypothesis. We can guess that the correspondence between the two variables was due to agricultural conditions. Good crops might attract storks and at the same time produce the sense of economic well-being that encourages parents to have more children. Or this relationship between storks and a high birth rate might be due to something else.

Another interesting example is the set of correlations reported many years ago showing positive relationships between the amount of milk consumed and the incidence of cancer. Places such as the American dairy states and countries like Switzerland, where milk consumption was high, showed a high and increasing incidence of cancer. The incidence of cancer in milk-drinking English women was 18 times higher than in Japanese women, who rarely drank milk. Such a relationship sounded significant and frightening to milk drinkers. Critical examination of this relationship merely revealed that in areas where the life span was long, the incidence of cancer was high. Cancer is predominantly a disease of middle age and later life and is not frequent in areas where people die young. The correlations just mentioned represent an *indirect relationship* between milk consumption and incidence of cancer. A high correlation can, however, result from events that are *directly* related. The amount of damage to a car hitting a telephone pole will correlate highly with the speed at which the car was traveling.

In summary then, the coefficient of correlation reveals the degree two sets of measures (the scores made by the same individuals on two tests) vary in relation to each other. Sometimes the correlation is a sign of an indirect relationship, as in the case of cancer and milk drinking, and sometimes of a direct relationship, as in the case of the amounts of damage automobiles sustain when they hit telephone poles at various speeds. Whether a significant positive or negative correlation indicates a direct or indirect relationship can only be determined by outside evidence, perhaps experimental. But whether the significant correlation is directly or indirectly determined, the coefficient of correlation has great practical importance, because on the basis of one set of findings, other findings can be predicted.

SAMPLING STATISTICS

Psychologists seek to discover how people think, how children acquire fears, how people learn to be well adjusted and happy. They seek to learn how people and other organisms behave. But when psychologists experiment, they do not observe the behavior of people in general or of rats in general, but rather they observe the behavior of individual persons and individual rats. How can we generalize from observations of individuals? The answer lies in the understanding of sampling statistics.

Population and Sample

Most people first meet the idea of sampling statistics when they read about public opinion polls. Hence, let us use them to clarify the distinction between two concepts, a **population** and a **sample.**

In 1936 the *Literary Digest,* a popular magazine of that period, conducted a poll in order to predict the winner of the upcoming presidential contest between Franklin D. Roosevelt and Alfred M. Landon. The magazine sent out several million "ballots" asking the recipients to indicate the candidate they would vote for. Twice as many people "voted" for Landon as "voted" for Roosevelt. From such evidence the *Literary Digest* predicted an overwhelming victory for Landon. Unfortunately for them, Roosevelt won the election with a total

popular vote of approximately 28 million, compared to 17 million for Landon. Only Maine and Vermont gave a plurality to Landon, and so the political slogan "As Maine goes, so goes the nation," was changed to "As Maine goes, so goes Vermont."

How could there be such a discrepancy between the results of the poll and of the election? Did the *Literary Digest* fake their results? Not at all, although many people must have thought so because the magazine, once very popular, suspended publication the following year. The truth of the matter was that the people who conducted the *Literary Digest* poll failed to appreciate fully the difference between a sample and a population.

The sample in this case was made up of the people who returned the mailed ballots, and the population was the total number of voters. Mathematicians have demonstrated that fairly accurate predictions about a population can be made if we have a **random** sample drawn from that population—a sample is said to be random if each individual in the population has in principle the same chance of being selected for the sample as any other individual—but the sample in the *Literary Digest* poll was biased. It failed to represent the total population of voters, because the magazine's mailing lists were made up of individuals mainly in the upper income brackets; the names were drawn from lists of automobile owners, telephone subscribers, and the like. In 1936, when the great depression had not yet run its course, being on such lists correlated highly with high yearly income. You can see, therefore, what little chance there was for a voter from a low income group to participate in the *Literary Digest* poll. The sample was biased by being, on the whole, wealthier than the total population whose behavior it sought to predict. Furthermore, in 1936, economic factors appeared to have played an important role in the presidential election. The *Literary*

Digest poll may have been a good sample for predicting the voting behavior of the higher income group, but as it turned out, it was a biased sample for predicting the behavior of the entire voting population.

The problem thus is to develop techniques which insure that one has a random sample, so that the characteristics of a larger population may be inferred from it. This is a task much more complex than appears at first glance. In terms of the presidential election, it requires a knowledge not only of the variables which determine a person's preference for one candidate, but also an understanding of the factors responsible for a person's going to the polls, staying at home, or going hunting on election day. As we understand the psychology of voting better, the polls will predict election results with greater precision. The poll-takers will understand better the techniques of selecting samples which reflect more accurately the behavior of the population they wish to predict. Actually, during the past 25 years, public opinion polls have greatly improved in the accuracy of their predictions. They are very accurate these days, except in very close elections.

Now that the distinction between a sample and a population has been made, a specific example may be used to demonstrate how the statistician can generalize from the characteristics of the sample to those of the population. Suppose you were interested in estimating the mean height of the male undergraduates at your school. You decided to measure 101 students and use them as your sample. Which 101 students should you measure? One possibility would be for you to stand outside a building, say the gymnasium, and measure the first 101 male undergraduates who passed by. This would be a very poor technique, almost certain to result in a biased sample. Every undergraduate does not spend an equal amount of time near the gym. Suppose you were standing outside the gym when the football or basketball squad was

reporting for practice. The discrepancy between the mean height of your sample and the entire male undergraduate body would certainly be great.

How, then, can you obtain a random sample? A safe, though not the only or the most simple, way to obtain a random sample, would be to place the name of each male undergraduate in a capsule, put all the capsules in a large drum, and after thoroughly mixing the contents of the drum, draw 101 capsules. The names in these capsules would designate the members of your sample. You would then measure the heights of these 101 undergraduates and compute the mean height. What conclusions could you then draw? If the sample had a mean height of 5 feet 9 inches, would it be correct to say that the mean height of the entire population of male undergraduates was also 5 feet 9 inches? Another question will suggest the answer. If you selected another random sample of 101 undergraduates, would their mean height also be 5 feet 9 inches? No, it would most likely not. The second sample would consist of different individuals, although some individuals might be members of both samples. If you took 100 samples, you would note that the means of successive samples would vary somewhat from sample to sample. The mean height of any given sample would probably be somewhat different from the mean height of the population, because by chance a taller or shorter group had been selected.

What good, then, is an individual sample? It begins to look as if the only information a sample provides is information about itself. This is not so. The importance of an individual sample stems from three statistical principles: (1) A series of successive samples from the same population yields the *normal distribution* of the *means of those samples*. The distribution of these means of the samples is called the **sampling distribution.** (2) The standard deviation of this sampling distribution can be estimated from the standard deviation of the single sample. (3) The mean of the sampling distribution comes closer and closer to the mean of the population as more and more samples are taken.

These statistical principles serve as a bridge between the characteristics of the sample, which can be *known,* and the characteristics of the population, which can most often only be *inferred.* If you know the standard deviation of the sampling distribution, you may evaluate the *reasonableness* of any hypothesis about the true mean of the population. Let us see how this is done.

The formula for the standard deviation of the sampling distribution, conventionally referred to as the *standard error of the mean* (σ_m), is

$$\sigma_m = \frac{\sigma\ sample}{\sqrt{N\text{-}1}}$$

The standard deviation (represented by the Greek letter σ) of the sampling distribution is simply derived by dividing the standard deviation of the sample by the square root of one less than the number of individuals in the sample. In our example, suppose that the data from the sample of 101 students which provided a mean of 5 feet 9 inches also provided a standard deviation of 3 inches. To estimate the standard deviation of the sampling distribution, you would divide the 3 inches by 10, which is the square root of 100, or 101 minus 1. The result would be .33 inches.

The importance of estimating the standard deviation of the sampling distribution has been emphasized, because in a normal distribution the standard deviation indicates how the various scores are distributed. Figure 4.7 sought to depict this distribution by showing that 68.3 per cent of the scores fall within one standard deviation unit of the mean, 95.4 per cent of the scores fall within two standard deviation units of the mean, and 99.7 per cent of the scores fall between three standard

deviation units of the mean. Stated otherwise, the chances of obtaining a score greater or less than the mean by one standard deviation unit would be 31.7 in a hundred; the chances of obtaining a score exceeding the mean by two or three standard deviation units would be 4.6 in a hundred and .3 in a hundred, respectively. These figures, you no doubt noticed, were obtained by subtracting the first set of figures from 100. If 68.3 per cent of all cases fall within one standard deviation unit of a mean, then 31.7 per cent of all cases fall beyond one standard deviation unit of the mean. These relationships are shown in Figure 4.9.

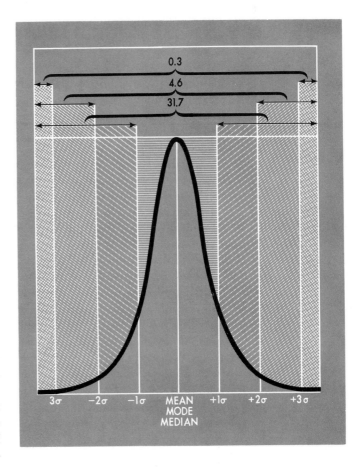

FIGURE 4.9 The Probability of Obtaining Scores That Differ From the Mean by 1, 2, and 3 Standard Deviation Units.

If each score of any normal distribution is placed in an individual capsule, the chances of picking a score greater or less than three standard deviations from the mean is less than one in a hundred.

We now have all the necessary information to interpret the sample mean of 5 feet 9 inches. After having obtained this mean, suppose you asked two friends to estimate the mean height of the male undergraduates. Let us say, one guessed 5 feet 10 inches, while the other guessed 5 feet 8⅔ inches. To decide which is the better guess you would ask yourself: If the true mean were 5 feet 10 inches, what would be the probability of obtaining such a sample as we did, with a mean which differed from the true mean by one inch or more? You could answer this question because you would have an accurate estimate of the standard deviation of the sampling distribution. The answer is that a sample which deviated from the true mean by one inch or more would be obtained less than 1 per cent of the time. If the true mean were 5 feet 8⅔ inches, the chances of obtaining a sample mean of 5 feet 9 inches would be much greater. The chances of obtaining a score one standard deviation unit or greater from the mean is 31.7 per cent. Consequently, in evaluating these two estimates, or hypotheses, the statistician would tend to reject the hypothesis that the true mean of the population was 5 feet 10 inches. If that were so, it would be *highly improbable* (less than one chance in a hundred) that a sample with a mean which differed from the true mean by three or more standard deviation units would be obtained. The statistician would not, however, reject the hypothesis that the true mean was 5 feet 8⅔ inches. He would say that this was a tenable hypothesis because it would *not be a highly improbable event* for a population with a true mean of 5 feet 8⅔ inches to yield a sample which differed from the true mean by one standard deviation unit.

Our hypothetical example has been concerned with estimating the mean score of a particular population. We have discussed a statistical technique by which hypotheses about the true mean could be evaluated. Experimenters frequently are confronted with somewhat different problems than the estimation of one mean of a population. A common problem is to evaluate the difference between two means. For example, if you wished to evaluate the difference in the heights of the male undergraduates in a western and eastern college, say for example, the University of Washington and the University of Connecticut, you might take a random sample of 200 students from each institution. After the means of the two samples had been computed, you would have to decide whether the difference (assuming there is one, which would be most likely) is reliable. Would additional samples produce essentially similar results? Would further sampling still reveal a difference, or perhaps, even reverse the direction of the difference?

The Null Hypothesis. We answer these questions by applying the **null hypothesis,** which assumes that the difference between two means is zero, and that any observed differences are merely due to sampling. This hypothesis is evaluated by a technique similar to that used in obtaining the single mean of the height of male students in your college. Successive samples of the mean height of male undergraduates at the Universities of Washington and Connecticut would be taken. For each sample a difference score would be obtained representing the difference between the mean heights of the students of the two schools. For example, difference scores of + 1 inch, + .5 inch, and −.25 inch could mean that in the first two samples, the Washington students were taller than the Connecticut students by 1 inch and .5 inch, whereas in the third sample, the Connecticut students were taller by

.25 inch. It has been demonstrated that such difference scores between means of successive samples distribute themselves normally.

Again, it would obviously be cumbersome to take successive samples to determine the standard deviation of the sampling distribution of difference scores. But from *one* sample involving both schools, you could *estimate* the standard deviation of the sampling distribution of difference scores. When this standard deviation is estimated, it is possible to determine the chances of obtaining differences of various magnitudes. For example, if the estimated standard deviation of the sampling distribution were .25 inch and the obtained difference were one inch, the experimenter would reject the null hypothesis. If the true difference were zero, the chances of getting a difference score as large or larger than one inch would be much less than one in a hundred.

The null hypothesis is frequently used in election polls. In a typical contest involving two candidates, the preference of a sample of voters is recorded. The pollster then applies the null hypothesis, which asserts that there is no difference between the two candidates—each will poll 50 per cent of the vote. Once he has accepted (provisionally of course) this hypothesis, he is in a position to interpret the results of an actual sample. He would reject the null hypothesis if the obtained sample could not reasonably have come from a population in which the votes were equally distributed between the two candidates. He would not reject the null hypothesis if the sample could reasonably have come from a population in which the votes were equally distributed between the two candidates. Polls which fail to provide evidence justifying rejection of the null hypothesis are a source of headaches to pollsters. Frequently they are not frank enough to tell their readers that the evidence their samples provide cannot suggest the winner with a fair degree of confidence.

Statistical evaluations of studies involving a coefficient of correlation employ techniques similar to those just described. If a psychologist wishes to find the correlation between college students' interest in biology and success in medical school, he first collects two sets of scores from the same sample of students, and then entertains the hypothesis that the true coefficient of correlation was .00. By appropriate statistical techniques, the psychologist would be in a position to reject or accept this hypothesis.

What are the exact rules for rejecting a statistical hypothesis? Consider the null hypothesis, which assumes that the means of two populations are the same. Is the null hypothesis rejected only when the difference between the sample means could occur by chance less than 1 per cent of the time? Actually no hard-and-fast rules apply. Suppose an industrial psychologist wishes to evaluate a new type of training program for mechanics in a large industrial organization. He conducts an experiment comparing the performance of a sample of mechanics trained under the new training program with a sample trained under the old method. The results indicate that the graduates of the new program are better than those of the old training program. The industrial psychologist must then decide whether this difference is due to chance (i.e., by some chance more mechanically inclined men got into the group that was to be trained under the new method), or whether it reflects a genuine superiority of the new method. By statistical methods he evaluates the difference between the means from the two samples. He discovers that the chances of getting the obtained difference, assuming that the null hypothesis be true, is 5 in 100. Should the industrial psychologist accept or reject the null hypothesis? Should he recommend that the new training program be instituted? Such a decision will depend on several factors. If the old training program appeared to be functioning adequately and the cost of instituting a new training program were very high, then the industrial psychologist would want to be almost certain that the new program will be an improvement. Under these circumstances he may decide to reject the null hypothesis only if the difference between the means could be attributed to chance in one out of 100 cases. Consequently he would not recommend that the new training method be instituted. If, however, there were many complaints against the old training method and the cost of instituting a new training method for mechanics were low, then the industrial psychologist might be willing to reject the null hypothesis with evidence that could be due to chance in five cases out of 100.

There is a possibility that the industrial psychologist may make the wrong decision. He may not reject the null hypothesis when in reality the new method is superior. Or he may reject the null hypothesis when in reality there is no difference between the effectiveness of the two methods. He has to consider these two possibilities and make his decision accordingly. In the first situation as we have just described it, the industrial psychologist was overcautious because he knew that rejection of the null hypothesis, if it were really true, would be a costly mistake. In the second situation he was not very cautious because the error of rejecting the null hypothesis would not be so costly.

Scientists tend to be cautious. When psychologists do fundamental research designed to clarify an important theoretical problem, they want to be almost certain that their results are not due to chance. They usually do not reject a hypothesis unless it can be attributed to chance no more often than one in 100 times. Moreover, as in other sciences, psychological experiments are repeated to determine whether essentially the same results are obtained.

STATISTICS AND SCIENCE

The emphasis in this chapter on averages and statistical probabilities might be interpreted by some as confirmation of the belief that psychology is an inexact science. Such a viewpoint can only be the product of a misunderstanding of procedures in other sciences. Students sometimes believe that it is possible to predict to a fraction of a second when a solar eclipse will occur at a particular place, or that all water will boil at precisely 212 degrees Fahrenheit at sea level. These "facts," however, are not 100 per cent invariant, but merely represent statistical averages. All facts, whether they be physical, biological, or psychological, have a probabilistic component. Since this realization has not diminished the accomplishments of scientists, it should not be disconcerting to you. It is merely a "fact" of science.

SUMMARY

Statistics is an essential tool of scientific method. It helps us describe and interpret data.

Descriptive statistics helps represent large masses of data in a simple, efficient way. A frequency distribution organizes scores into class intervals so that the frequency of each interval is readily apparent. Frequency distributions assume a variety of forms, the most common of which is the distribution of chance events known as the normal probability curve. In addition to its form a frequency distribution has two other characteristics: its central tendency and its variability.

There are three measures of central tendency. The mode is the score of the greatest frequency, the median is the middlemost score, and the mean is computed by dividing the sum of all scores by the number of scores.

The simplest measure of variability is the range, which is the difference between the highest and lowest scores. The most useful measure of variability is the standard deviation, which is a sensitive measure of the dispersion of all the scores from the mean.

The relationships between two sets of measures obtained from related pairs of individuals can be expressed by a coefficient of correlation. Correlation coefficients range from + 1.00 through .00 to − 1.00. A posi-

tive correlation indicates that as one measure increases so does the other related measure, for example, intelligence and school grades. A negative correlation indicates that as one measure increases the other decreases, for example, the number of absences and school grades. A zero correlation, indicates that there is no correspondence between two sets of scores. The closer the coefficient of correlation is to unity (that is, + 1.00 or − 1.00), the greater the relationship between the two sets of scores.

Sampling statistics helps make valid generalizations from specific individuals to groups of individuals. We do this by discovering certain characteristics of a random sample of a population, and then, with appropriate statistical techniques, determining the probability that these characteristics exist for the entire population.

SUGGESTIONS FOR FURTHER READING

Because statistical methods are so important in psychology, numerous textbooks have been written specifically for the student of psychology. The following list of books represents only a small sample of all that have been published. If you are interested in doing some supplementary reading in the area of statistics consultation with your instructor would be advisable.

BLOMMERS, P., & LINDQUIST, E. F. *Elementary statistical methods.* Boston: Houghton Mifflin, 1960.

EDWARDS, A. L. *Experimental design in psychological research.* (Rev. ed.) New York: Holt, Rinehart, & Winston, 1960.

HAMMOND, K. R., & HOUSEHOLDER, J. E. *Introduction to the statistical method.* New York: Knopf, 1962.

McNEMAR, Q. *Psychological statistics.* (3rd ed.) New York: Wiley, 1962.

SMITH, G. M. *A simplified guide to statistics.* (3rd ed.) New York: Holt, Rinehart, & Winston, 1962.

UNDERWOOD, B. J., DUNCAN, C. P., TAYLOR, J. A., & COTTON, J. W. *Elementary statistics.* New York: Appleton-Century-Crofts, 1954.

WALKER, H. M., & LEV, J. *Elementary statistical methods.* (Rev. ed.) New York: Holt, Rinehart, & Winston, 1958.

THE BIOLOGICAL FOUNDATIONS
OF BEHAVIOR

5

PHYSIOLOGY AND PSYCHOLOGY

All sciences are related. They all begin with observation, which is accurate noting of what occurs, whether in nature or in an experimental situation, and they all use a basically similar method. In certain cases more than one science may even deal with the same phenomenon. For example, the action of digestive juices on food is of interest to both biologists and chemists. How a group of orderly people can change into a howling mob concerns both psychologists and sociologists. Radioactivity engages the attention of physicists, geologists, chemists, and biologists. There are also cases where a discovery in one science can be explained by a theory developed in another. In recent decades many kinds of chemical phenomena have been shown to dovetail perfectly with physical theories, and it is commonplace to find explanations for biological phenomena by chemical analysis.

Physiology and psychology share both data and theories. Both study the living organism, though commonly with somewhat differing orientations. The physiologist aims to find out how the individual organs of the body function, whereas the psychologist focuses on the behavior, which is, after all, but an aggregate of organ systems. In spite of a difference in general orientation, the two fields overlap; either of them may inquire, for example, into the role of certain brain centers, or glands, involved in a given kind of behavior.

The interests of a particular psychologist determine how closely, if at all, his work parallels that of the physiologist. Binet's pioneer work in intelligence testing, for example, makes it quite clear that psychological work can be entirely independent of physiology. At the same time, in much of psychology, including the field of intellectual behavior, the work of the psychologist and physiologist go hand in hand.

Although the professional psychologist engaged in research must make a choice whether or not to consider psychological phenomena in relation to physiological processes, no such choice exists for the student who wishes to obtain a basic understanding of psychology. Many basic psychological facts and theories demand that you acquire some understanding of physiological processes. This chapter will help you to understand them.

THE PHYSIOLOGICAL FOUNDATION OF BEHAVIOR

The physiological basis of behavior can be divided conveniently into three functions, each having its basis in different bodily structures, or mechanisms:

    Receiving mechanisms: **receptors**
    Connecting mechanisms: **nerve cells**
    Reacting mechanisms: **effectors**

An example of how these three kinds of mechanisms cooperate to produce a simple **sensory-motor reflex** is diagrammed in Figure 5.1. If you accidentally prick your finger while working, your hand gives a sudden twitch of withdrawal from the source of painful stimulation.

The first stage in this protective reflex is that the pin's entering the skin activates some tiny sensitive receiving mechanisms called receptors. Neural activity is then transmitted through the connecting mechanisms to the spinal cord and thence to the reacting mechanisms (a group of effectors), in this case, muscles of the arm. As a consequence of these contractions the hand is abruptly withdrawn from the noxious stimulation. All this activity takes place within a fraction of a second.

A word of caution! Do not think that the physiological basis of *all* behavior is as simple as our example implies. Even the

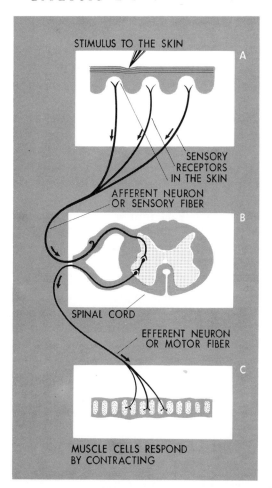

FIGURE 5.1 A Sensory-Motor Reflex Initiated by a Pinprick. Neural impulses travel to the spinal cord and then to the muscles whose contractions produce hand withdrawal.

protective reflex just described is not really so isolated an action as our brief description suggests. It is actually imbedded in a much larger and more complex sequence of physiological events, especially of the neurological sort. Our present aim is to provide only a schematic, simplified, and overall picture of the functioning of the physiological structures involved in behavior, which will be expanded and filled in later on. But some reference to these complications is necessary even here.

You may recall, from your experience with pinpricks or other sudden painful stimulation, that there is more to your be-

82

havior than a single act of rapid avoidance. Your sensation of pain, curiously enough, usually occurs very shortly after the withdrawal of the affected body part from the source of stimulation. This sensation of pain involves neural activity other than the simple connection between the receptors in the skin and the contraction of the muscle in the arm. It depends on neural impulses that go to the brain, and even the simplest neural event involving the brain is of fantastic complexity. For one thing, there are approximately 14 billion individual nerve cells in the brain. For another most of us can, if we have to or want to, inhibit (i.e., suppress) a protective reflex to a pinprick. This may be what happens when a nurse pricks one of your fingers to draw blood. Although you feel the pain, you reduce or eliminate the impulse to withdraw from it. Like the sensation of pain, this inhibition is also a product of brain function. In spite of these complicating factors, the reflex serves well the function of a simplified model whose purpose is to identify the various physiological components underlying behavior.

The Scope of This Chapter

This chapter will include a description of (1) some simple reacting mechanisms, (2) the sensory and neural mechanisms involved in the production of responses, and (3) hereditary mechanisms. This third topic is included because the inherited physiological systems of an organism determine in large measure the behavior it is capable of. This is one of the reasons why the behavior differs among species. In order to understand how and why organisms develop their distinctive physiological systems, the psychologist must have some knowledge of genetics and the interactions of heredity and environment in the development of behavior.

Only those physiological processes upon which behavior clearly depends will be described. Any process that primarily contributes to body maintenance, such as breathing, circulation, or digestion, will be ignored. This is not to say, of course, that behavior cannot be influenced by such processes. Severe dysfunctioning of any of these processes can demonstrate dramatically that they do influence behavior. But normally, and in most kinds of behavior, their influence is slight and indirect, and for that reason they will not be treated here.

For the present, too, the anatomy of various sense organs, such as our eyes and ears will not be described. Their structures are so intimately tied up with our behavior when we are looking or listening—sensory behavior in general—that it will be more efficient to describe them in connection with the topic of sensation.

THE REACTING MECHANISMS

The dependent variable in psychology is behavior. Behavior—what an organism is observed to be doing—consists of the actions of muscles and glands. To most people muscular and glandular activity as such appears to be far removed from the kind of behavior that is of interest to them and is the central interest of psychologists. However, muscular and glandular activities are not really alien to everyday behavior: physical tasks are accomplished by contractions of various sets of muscles; fear involves excessive secretions of the sweat and other glands; and tears are the secretions of the tear glands. Common behavior is composed of these elementary physiological processes organized into complex patterns. So at the outset, we turn our attention to certain of these basic physiological activities.

Muscles

Skeletal Muscles. Your body can make thousands of movements ranging from lifting a suitcase to raising your eyebrow, from threading a needle to pushing a piano, from doing calisthenics to expressing happiness, sadness, or boredom. In spite of their apparent dissimilarity, such responses are alike in one important way. They all result from contractions of **skeletal muscles.**

Skeletal muscles are made of a kind of living cells which work in this way: they contract, that is, they tighten up and get shorter, and they relax again. There are nearly 700 skeletal muscles in the human body. They are called skeletal muscles because they are attached by means of tendons (tough bands of connective tissue) to the bones of the skeleton, which move as the muscles contract.

Figure 5.2 shows two diagrams, one of the bones and muscles of an arm and one of sticks and strings. Arm bones are like two sticks hinged together, and muscles function like two cords. When cord 1 is pulled the bottom stick moves up; when cord 2 is pulled the bottom stick moves down. When the biceps gets shorter the bones of the forearm are raised; when the triceps gets shorter the forearm is lowered. This arrangement of bones and muscles is not unique to the arm. The leg, with the knee acting as the hinge, functions in a similar manner.

In other parts of the body the mechanical system is constructed somewhat differently. The neck, for example, has more than two muscles and the hinge is more complex, permitting head movements in many more directions than the elbow permits to the forearm. In spite of the differences in types of bodily movements, the physiological principle governing the action of skeletal muscles is the same throughout the body. The contraction of muscles, attached as they are by means of tendons to the mechanical system of the skeleton, produces bodily movements.

Skeletal muscles are made up of muscle fibers which are long and thin. The individual fibers of each skeletal muscle are largely anatomically independent of each other, and thus permit independent func-

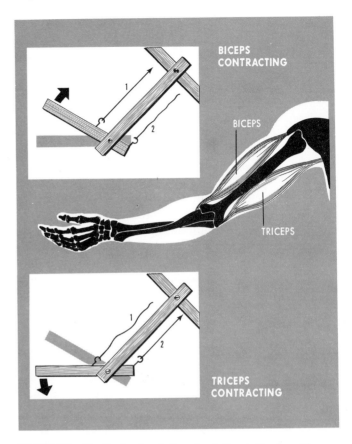

FIGURE 5.2 The Mechanics of Muscular Action in the Arm. The arm bones are like two hinged sticks, and the muscles function as two cords attached to them. When one cord is pulled the bottom stick moves up; when the other cord is pulled it moves down.

tioning. The activity pattern of a skeletal muscle as a whole can range—depending upon how many individual fibers contract—from slight gradual movements to sudden violent contractions.

Smooth Muscles. There is another group of muscles in the body that are not connected to the skeleton and hence do not control the visible movements of the limbs, trunk, and head. These **smooth muscles** are found especially in the linings of the soft visceral organs in the body and in the walls of the blood vessels.

After food is swallowed it is pushed along to the stomach by wave-like contractions of smooth muscles in the lining of the esophagus. Smooth muscles in the walls of blood vessels, through their contractions and relaxations, control the diameter of the blood vessels and hence determine to some extent the pressure and amount of blood circulating through the body. The size of the pupil of the eye is also controlled by the actions of the smooth muscles that make up the iris. There are other examples also, too many to enumerate.

The actual functioning of smooth muscles is similar to that of skeletal muscles: they contract and relax, but they do this at an appreciably slower rate than the skeletal muscles. A single contraction of a skeletal muscle fiber requires less than one-tenth of a second, whereas a contraction of a smooth muscle may require several seconds.

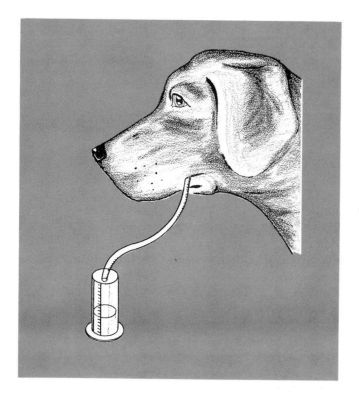

FIGURE 5.3 The Salivary Response Used by Pavlov in His Famous Conditioning Experiments. The amount of salivation is measured in a graduated cylinder at the end of a tube connected to one of the salivary glands.

Glands

Like muscular contractions, gland secretions are responses. Glands are composed of cells that specialize in secreting highly complex chemical substances. Many experimental studies in psychology use as their dependent variable some direct or indirect measures of the amount of secretion from a particular gland or group of glands.

There are two major classes of glands: **duct glands** and **ductless glands.** Ductless glands are also known as **endocrine glands** or the glands of internal secretion.

Duct glands. As their name indicates, these glands are distinguished by having channels through which their chemical secretions flow.

The salivary glands in the mouth which secrete digestive juices that soften and produce chemical changes in the food are duct glands. The salivary response was what Pavlov, the Russian physiologist, used as the dependent variable in his famous conditioning experiments. In these experiments, he made a simple surgical incision in a dog's cheek and inserted a tube into the duct of one of the salivary glands. When the dog secreted saliva, it passed through the tube and was collected in a graduated container that measured the response very precisely, in units as fine as one tenth of a drop. With this technique of defining his dependent variable, Pavlov was able to conduct a systematic research program to discover the influence of a large number of independent variables on this simple behavior measure.

Other duct glands that play a role in the digestive process are the gastric glands in the walls of the stomach, the intestinal glands, certain portions of the pancreas, and the liver. Another group of duct glands have as their primary function the elimination of wastes from the body. This group includes the kidneys, which remove waste products from the blood and secrete them into the bladder, from which they are eventually expelled, and the sweat and sebaceous (oily) glands which eliminate waste products in fluid form through the pores of the skin. The tear glands furnish fluid to keep the eyeballs moist, while the sex glands secrete either sperm cells or eggs that serve the function of reproduction.

Endocrine Glands. What goes on inside an organism is obviously an important determinant of his behavior. In creatures built as we are, the amount of oxygen and water, the temperature, and the chemical balance of our bodies can only vary slightly if life is to continue. Therefore the endocrine system plays a crucial role in maintaining the constancy of this internal environment. The endocrine or ductless glands, depicted in Figure 5.4, secrete minute amounts of chemical substances known as **hormones** directly into the blood or lymph streams. The bulk of these secretions is fantastically small, considering how unbelievably great is their influence.

The pituitary gland, which is about the size of a kernel of corn, is located in the skull beneath the brain and above the nasal passages. It has been called the master gland because in addition to secreting hormones that act directly on many parts of the body, it secretes hormones which affect the activities of other endocrine glands.

Marked physiological changes can result from the malfunctioning of the pituitary gland. The giant and the midget in Figure 5.5 were produced by excessive and deficient secretions respectively of that component of the pituitary secretion which has an effect on growth. In some cases after maturity is reached and growth has stopped, the pituitary resumes its secretion of its growth-inducing chemical producing a condition known as acromegaly. The major symptoms of this disorder are the enlarge-

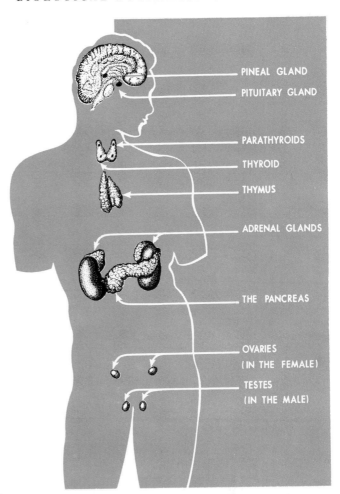

FIGURE 5.4 The Endocrine Glands and Their Location in the Body.

ment of the bones of the face, nose, chin, hands, and feet, and increased size of the tongue and lips. The appearance of the person afflicted with this disorder can change drastically in a relatively short time; so much so that a separation of several months can make a person afflicted with acromegaly unrecognizable even to a close friend. Fortunately, the progress of this disorder can now be terminated by injections which inhibit this particular activity of the pituitary gland.

The endocrine glands do not play the same kind of role in psychology that the muscles and duct glands play. Although they are reacting mechanisms, they are rarely used as a dependent variable in psychological research because their activity can not be measured as directly or as simply as the activity of muscles and duct glands. They may, however, have an important indirect influence on personality, for their malfunctioning at times produces dramatic behavioral changes. Therefore, this discussion of the endocrine system will be resumed later.

THE CONNECTING MECHANISMS

The Nervous System

An act, like tying your shoelace, is made possible by the activities of many reacting mechanisms. These mechanisms are not self-activating, for without the nervous system, which literally connects the reacting mechanisms with the sources of stimulation, the response mechanisms would not operate. The nervous system is the trigger that determines if, when, and, in part, how a reacting mechanism will respond.

The nervous system is without doubt the most complex and elaborate system of structures in the human body. A thoroughgoing account of it would involve an endless maze of detail and raise a large number of unanswered questions. Although it is possible to trace in detail the major neurological events active in a protective reflex to a pinprick, to describe the neurological mechanisms underlying the act of adding two and two is far beyond our present knowledge. And we are indefinitely far from understanding the physiological (especially neural) processes underlying a person's behavior in solving the nine-dot problem on page 22, or from understanding Einstein's genius in developing the world-shaking theory based on the formula $E = MC^2$.

FIGURE 5.5 A Giant and a Midget, Both Caused by Defective Functioning of the Pituitary Gland (Ewing Galloway).

In spite of these limitations in present-day knowledge, we do know certain fundamental things about the functioning of the nervous system relevant to our aim of understanding behavior. First, in order for you to grasp these fundamentals, certain structural and functional features of the nervous system must be pointed out.

On the most general level we distinguish, for the sake of convenience, between the **central nervous system** and the **peripheral nervous system.** The central nervous system has as its main components the brain and the spinal cord. The peripheral nervous system is composed of the group of sensory or **afferent nerves** (from two Latin words: *ad,* meaning "toward," and *ferre,* meaning "to carry") that extend from the receiving mechanisms (sense organs) to the central nervous system, and another group of motor or **efferent nerves** (*ex* and *ferre,*

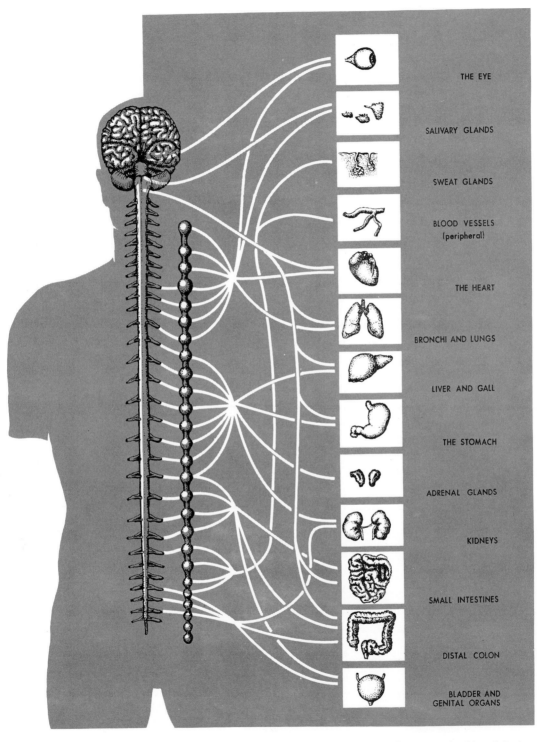

THE EYE

SALIVARY GLANDS

SWEAT GLANDS

BLOOD VESSELS
(peripheral)

THE HEART

BRONCHI AND LUNGS

LIVER AND GALL

THE STOMACH

ADRENAL GLANDS

KIDNEYS

SMALL INTESTINES

DISTAL COLON

BLADDER AND
GENITAL ORGANS

FIGURE 5.6 A Schematic Representation of the Autonomic Nervous System Illustrating the Neural Pathways to the Smooth Muscles and the Glands.

meaning "to carry away") running from the central nervous system to the reacting mechanisms, the muscles and glands.

Also within the peripheral nervous system is a group of structures known as the **autonomic nervous system,** which is mainly responsible for the activation of the smooth muscles, the glands, and in part, the heart muscle. The autonomic nervous system, largely a motor system, consists mostly of motor nerves that lead from the central nervous system through masses of nerve cells (called ganglia) outside the spinal cord to smooth muscles and glands.

The Neuron

The structural unit of the nervous system is the **neuron.** It is a single nerve cell possessing all the characteristics of living cells in general—being made up of protoplasm (living substance) surrounded by a thin membrane. Neurons have cell bodies, but unlike other cells, they also have slender extensions called **nerve fibers.** Nerve fibers are of two sorts. At the receiving end of a neuron are the **dendrites;** at the delivery, or transmitting, end is the **axon.** The dendrites usually have several short branches, but axons most commonly possess ·

one long branch which divides at its terminal into small **end brushes.**

Neurons transmit **neural impulses,** energy changes electro-chemical in nature. We know this because as an impulse travels wave-like along a nerve fiber, changes in polarization occur and oxygen is consumed while carbon dioxide is released.

The nerve impulse travels along a nerve fiber much as a spark sweeps along the fuse of a firecracker. This analogy applies to the initiation of a neural impulse as well. The spark that travels along a fuse will be the same whether it is ignited by a blowtorch or by a match. A certain amount of heat is needed to ignite the fuse; greater amounts do not have any effect on the size or speed of the spark. Neurons seem to behave in the same all-or-none fashion: if there is sufficient energy to initiate a neural impulse, the nerve fiber will respond; if there is insufficient energy, the fiber will not respond and no impulse will be transmitted. Another way of stating this law of the initiation of a neural impulse is that stimulation either excites a neuron completely or does not excite it at all; when it does excite the neuron, the strength of the impulse is not a product of the intensity of stimulation, but rather a function of the characteristics of the fiber excited.

We must add that as a result of the tremendous strides being made in neurology today, the supposed *generality* of the **all-or-none law** of the initiation of neural impulses, along with some other widely held conceptions, has been questioned. Here is another illustration of the fact that science does not rest upon the sanctity of any particular proclaimed fact but upon its methods, and these are, in the long run and if developed far enough, self-correcting.

The speed of a neural impulse varies with the fiber involved. Some nerve impulses travel as slowly as one yard per second, or at a rate equivalent to a normal walking pace. Other impulses attain the speed of 100 yards per second, or the

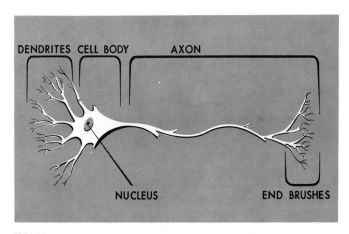

FIGURE 5.7 The Anatomy of a Neuron.

DENDRITES CELL BODY AXON

NUCLEUS END BRUSHES

speed of a plane going 200 miles per hour.

Nerve fibers are excited by the activity of receptor organs (e.g., structures in the eyes or ears) or by neural impulses coming from other nerves. The amount of energy capable of initiating a neural impulse varies from fiber to fiber. Weak stimulation is sufficient to arouse neural impulses in some nerve fibers, while other fibers require strong stimulation. The amount of energy required to produce stimulation in any nerve fiber is known as that fiber's **threshold of excitation.**

Unlike the fuse of a firecracker, the nerve fiber recharges itself. Whereas the fuse is consumed by the spark, the nerve fiber is, after a period of time, once again capable of transmitting a neural impulse. But the recharging process takes time, so that for a short period after the transmission of one impulse, the nerve fiber is completely unresponsive to stimulation. This period is called the **absolute refractory phase,** and lasts from one-thousandth to three-thousandths of a second. It is followed by a **relative refractory phase** lasting about eight-thousandths of a second longer. During this phase the nerve fiber is partially refractory, since only stimulation *above* the threshold of excitation can set it off.

In the normal functioning of nerve tissue which is being continuously excited, individual fibers transmit a volley of impulses. Intense stimulation may produce as many as 1,000 impulses per second, while moderate stimulation of the same fiber will produce only 100 impulses during the same period of one second. This difference in the rate of transmission is due to the fact that intense stimulation can initiate neural impulses during the relative refractory phase, a time when moderate stimulation would be incapable of doing so.

Neural Pathways

Behavioral activity of even the simplest kind involves more than one neuron. So let us now go beyond the single nerve cell and examine more closely a reflex such as the protective reflex to a pinprick briefly described on page 81. It can be represented as consisting of three neurons. The **sensory neuron** has at one end dendrites sensitive to stimulation from the external environment. When these endings are stimulated, a neural impulse travels along the nerve fiber until it reaches the end brushes of the axon which are located in the spinal cord close to **association neurons.**

These neurons, located throughout the central nervous system, "associate," or functionally connect, sensory neurons with motor neurons. They do not physically connect because the end brushes of the axon of the sensory neuron lie alongside the dendrites of the association neuron without actually touching them. This point of functional connection between two neurons is called a **synapse.** The neural impulse cannot cross the synapse. If the neural impulse in the axon is sufficiently

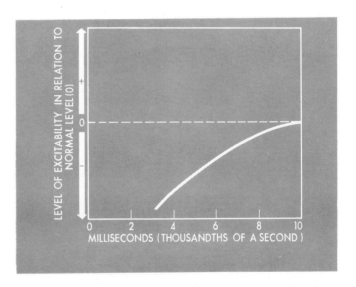

FIGURE 5.8 Changes in the Excitability of a Nerve Fiber Following the Passage of an Impulse. Immediately afterwards, during the absolute refractory phase, the fiber is unresponsive. Gradually, during the relative refractory phase, it regains the normal level of excitability. The actual length of these two phases varies widely for different fibers.

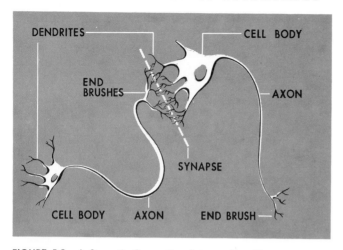

FIGURE 5.9   A Synaptic Connection Between Two Neurons.

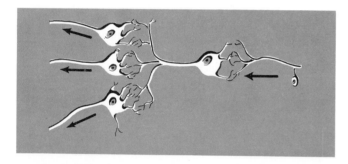

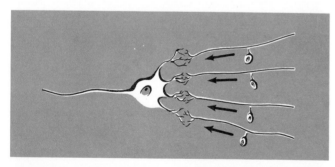

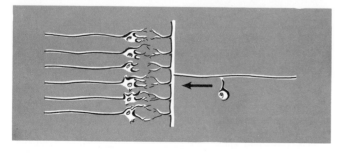

FIGURE 5.10   Some Examples of Possible Synaptic Connections.

strong it will stimulate the adjacent dendrite and initiate a new impulse there. In this way neural impulses are transmitted from sensory to association neurons. If the impulse travelling through the sensory neuron is not sufficiently powerful, the association neuron will not be activated.

However, to continue the neural travelogue of a simple sensory-motor reflex, once the neural impulse is transmitted to the association neuron it is conducted to the synapse between the axon of the association neuron and the dendrite of the motor neuron. If it has sufficient energy to activate the motor neuron a neural impulse will be directed to the reacting mechanism, where it can initiate a muscular or glandular response.

In principle, the response of an individual muscle or gland cell can be thought of as occurring after a neural impulse has been transmitted through a series of three neurons: a sensory neuron, an association neuron, and finally the **motor neuron** (a few reflexes can be represented as consisting only of a sensory and motor neuron). But gross behavior of the sort involved in the withdrawal of an entire limb from noxious stimulation plus concomitant responses involves vastly more neurons than three. There are several reasons for this. First, neurons are usually strung along parallel to each other, the whole collection forming a **nerve.** The smallest nerve in our body contains hundreds of neurons, and the optic nerve, which connects the eye to the brain, consists of about one-half million neurons. Second, successive neurons in a sensory-motor arc are not linked individually to each other. As you can see from the structure of a neuron, it is capable of forming synaptic connections with many other neurons simultaneously. An axon of one neuron can form synaptic connections with dendrites of many other neurons, and dendrites of one neuron can have synaptic connections with axons of many other neurons. Third, when the neural impulse reaches the central nervous system it is usually transmitted in several directions simultaneously. In addition to being directed to a motor neuron, the neural impulse is usually transmitted to other association neurons in the spinal cord, which direct the impulse up through the spinal cord to the brain and down again to various levels of the spinal cord, where many motor neurons connected to reacting mechanisms may be activated.

Because of this complexity, there are many potentially different neural pathways which may be activated by the same physical stimulation. This is particularly true when the brain is involved. The association neurons in the brain are so numerous and so closely packed that there is a tremendous amount of overlapping between them. And to add to the complexity, recent evidence suggests that nonsynaptic neural transmission can take place in the brain. A neuron lying parallel to one that is transmitting an impulse may be excited into activity.

An analogy between a telephone system and the nervous system has frequently been made. In some ways the analogy is a good one, but is excessively oversimplified. It is true that in both telephone and nervous systems there is no simple, direct connection between the two ends: the speaker and the listener, the receptor and the effector. The "messages" in both systems have to be transmitted through a central network, which in both cases is sufficiently complex to preclude simple description. But further comparison of the two systems dramatically emphasizes that the nervous system is vastly more complex. The number of telephones that can be connected simultaneously, even considering such complications as party lines, extensions, and wire-tapping, is well within the range of human imagination. This is not so with the human nervous system.

We have already stated that each neuron runs alongside many other neurons, the

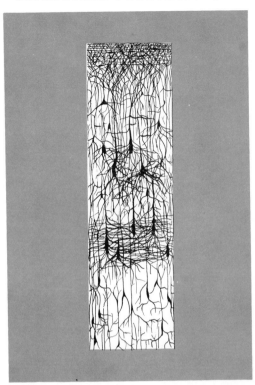

FIGURE 5.11 A Drawing of a Highly Magnified Section of the Cortex.

whole collection forming a nerve. In a similar way telephone wires are bound together to form cables. There are, however, no synapses in a telephone system; wires of the same telephone route make direct physical contact with each other by means of splices, jacks, and other mechanical devices. As a result the messages going through a telephone system stick to a route and do not leak into other routes. However, in the nervous system impulses that start simultaneously in neighboring fibers of the same nerve often terminate in entirely different effectors, and within one nerve any particular impulse may take an incredibly large number of possible routes. Figure 5.10 shows some of the possible synaptic connections.

The exact pathway that a nerve impulse will follow at its synaptic points depends on its energy level, the thresholds of excitation of the neurons that lie within its path,

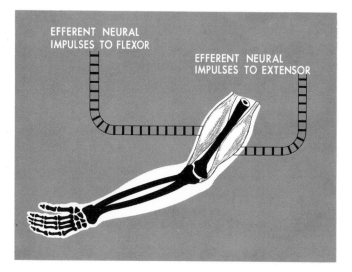

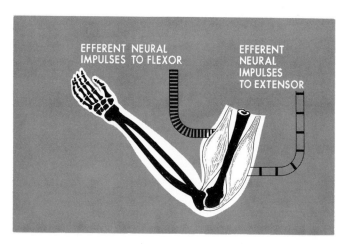

FIGURE 5.12 An Example of Reciprocal Innervation of the Flexor (biceps) and Extensor (triceps) Muscles of the Arm. The top drawing shows both muscles in their normal state of contraction. Painful stimulation to the hand produces an increase in the nerve impulses to the flexor with a simultaneous decrease (inhibition) to the extensor. The frequency of neural impulses is indicated by the density of the black lines along the neural pathways.

preceding neurons in the same pathway. Whereas the connections in the telephone system are rigidly fixed, those in the nervous system are flexible.

Another shortcoming of the analogy is that the intricacy of the central telephone switchboard does not approach that of the spinal cord and the brain. It has been estimated that if the nerve connections of the brain alone were duplicated by an electronic machine, it would have to be housed in a room many thousands of times larger than the human body.

Nevertheless, certain built-in controls within the nervous system are similar in their function to some safeguards in a telephone system. But our purpose is not to describe each analogue, especially if to do so would take us too far afield into the science of electronics. We therefore will drop the analogy and proceed with our description of neurological pathways and some of the mechanisms involved when they are activated.

You will recall that most of the skeletal muscles are coupled into antagonistic pairs, one extending and the other bending a given joint. What would happen if the pair of arm muscles both contracted at once? Fortunately for our bodily integrity, the nervous system functions to prevent such a deadlock. Each of the muscles controlling the activity of the elbow receives different patterns of neural stimulation; the stimulation of the muscle producing flexion of the arm is always accompanied by the *inhibition* of neural stimulation to the muscle producing extension. In the same way contraction of the muscle producing extension is always accompanied by inhibition of neural stimulation to the muscle producing flexion. This **reciprocal innervation** results in coordinated activity of antagonistic muscle groups. Its mechanism is illustrated in Figure 5.12. You may recall that in Figure 5.2 on page 83 arm movements were likened to the movement of hinged sticks. Following this analogy reciprocal innervation

and their temporary condition. The stronger the impulse, the more neurons it will stimulate. Any neuron in an absolute refractory phase will have to be bypassed if the impulse is to get through to an effector, and a neuron in its relative refractory phase will require a higher than usual amount of energy to be stimulated. Hence, the neurons in any particular neural pathway will not automatically be excited by means that only one string can be pulled at a time.

In the case of the protective reflex, contraction of the arm muscle and resulting hand withdrawal is not all that happens. We have already referred to the neural impulses that go to the brain with results beyond mere hand withdrawal. As the muscle in the arm contracts, new neural stimulation is produced, for there are receptors imbedded in muscles and tendons which are stimulated by muscular movements. This type of sensitivity, called **kinesthesis,** operates in a manner similar to the thermostatic control of a heating system. When the temperature in a room falls below a certain point, it activates the thermostat, which starts the furnace. Again when the temperature in the room rises to a predetermined point, the thermostat is activated and the furnace turned off. This self-regulating system is commonly called a **feedback system**—a *feedback* is a general term used to describe any system which uses information from an event in the system to control the course of related subsequent events. Kinesthetic sensitivity is an example of a feedback system, since it is the basis of the body's ability to regulate its own movements. When you are walking, muscular movements in your legs initiate neural impulses that proceed to the central nervous system and supply cues (stimuli) as to where your legs are, so that by knowing their position you can then make the next appropriate leg movements in a smooth, harmonious manner. Actually, of course, walking ordinarily proceeds without voluntary guidance, once it is begun.

This automatic looped connection between the central nervous system and the muscles is a feedback mechanism that is essential for all types of muscular skills. We are so accustomed to our kinesthetic sensitivity that most of us are unaware of it. We are impressed with its importance when we observe someone who, because of defective kinesthetic sensitivity, can only walk in a halting, unsure gait while looking at his feet.

It should now be apparent that the neurological basis of even the simplest behavior is much more than a simple one-two-three process in which stimulation from the external environment is converted to neural impulses and transmitted to an effector where it terminates in some response.

The Human Brain

The brain is that portion of the central nervous system which is encased in the skull. It has been aptly described by Sir Charles Sherrington, the famous English physiologist, as "the great ravelled knot." Physically, it resembles a knot because the **cortex,** its outer layer, grows so large that it is forced to fold in on itself in order

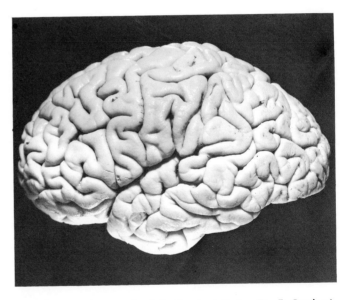

FIGURE 5.13 Photograph of the Cerebral Cortex (Dr. E. Gardner).

to fit into the confining walls of the skull. Figuratively also, the brain is a knot, for the problems of its functioning are nowhere near untangled.

The brain consists of approximately 14 billion neurons woven into an incredibly intricate pattern. The nerve cells are so tightly packed together that one cell is probably never active without influencing some of its neighboring cells. The activity pattern of the brain may involve a tremendous number of different combinations of individual brain cells; the number of different combinations, taking only five cells of the total number of brain cells at a time, would exceed by far a trillion trillion—a number that staggers the imagination. Such a number would, however, underestimate the number of actual combinations of neurons that the human brain is capable of forming. For, of course, combinations of brain cells are far from limited to groups of only five cells.

The brain does not operate independently of other parts of the body. Such essentials as food and oxygen required to maintain its high rate of activity are conveyed to the brain by the blood. Interruption of the blood supply for more than a few seconds will stop brain activity. This is what happens when a person faints, not enough blood reaches the brain to keep the brain cells operating.

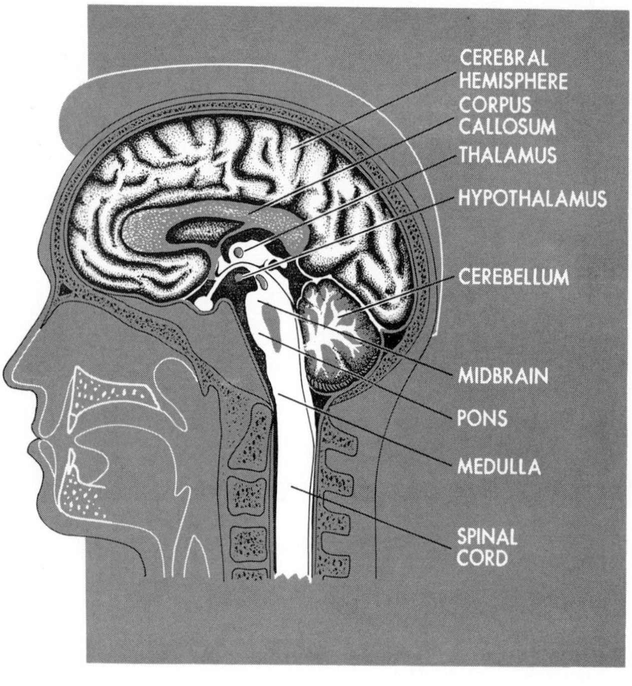

Viewed from above, the brain is a large spherical organ divided into partially separated halves, or hemispheres. These hemispheres hide the numerous structural units that lie lower down between themselves and the spinal cord.

There is no sharp separation between the spinal cord and the brain; they are continuous both structurally and functionally. As the spinal cord proceeds upward it swells into the lower portion of the brain stem. Figure 5.14 shows a vertical section of the human brain in its place in the skull. The brain stem contains large numbers of association neurons that connect the upper portion of the brain with the spinal system below. The brain stem functions not only as a communication center; it also plays a vital role in the activities of the autonomic nervous system, which we will describe later. The major structural units of the brain stem are the **medulla, pons, midbrain, hypothalamus,** and **thalamus.** Although their specific functions are many and detailed, they will concern us only when their functioning is intimately tied to some response that demands special attention.

Situated back of and above the medulla are the two hemispheres of the **cerebellum.** These hemispheres contain large masses of nerve tissue which are connected to various other parts of the brain. The cerebellum plays an important role in controlling the tonicity of the skeletal muscles and in maintaining bodily posture and equilibrium. Birds with normal wing structure and musculature cannot fly if their cerebellar hemispheres are seriously damaged. Even slight damage to the human cerebellum from injury or disease can interfere seriously with

FIGURE 5.14   A Vertical Section of the Human Brain in Its Position in the Skull.

walking and other activities requiring coordination. The importance of the cerebellum can be simply demonstrated: Close your eyes, extend your arm, and then touch the tip of your nose with your index finger. You can do this without difficulty. A patient suffering from damage to part of his cerebellum would find this difficult, if not impossible.

Above the cerebellum and other structures of the lower brain lies the **cerebrum,** the structure in which the human brain differs most markedly from the brains of other mammals; it is the structure most responsible for civilization. During the evolution of the vertebrate nervous system, it has been the cerebrum that has grown the most both in size and in complexity, and has established dominance over other parts of the nervous system. In contrast, the cerebrum of the fish is but a small part of the entire brain, and it functions primarily in the detection of odors (receptors in the nasal cavity enable fish to respond to different chemicals in the water).

The cerebrum is divided into two halves, the left and right cerebral hemispheres.

Separated by a deep groove, or what is technically called the **longitudinal fissure,** they are nonetheless connected by a large tract of fibers, the **corpus callosum.** A shallow layer consisting mainly of cell bodies of neurons covers the whole outer surface of the cerebrum and forms a gray mantle one-eighth to one-quarter inch thick called the cerebral bark or cortex. The cortex is corrugated into a complex pattern of convolutions, which greatly increase its surface area. The pattern's complexity varies in mammals from species to species, is very striking in monkeys and apes, and particularly so in humans. In man more of the cortex lies out of sight within the fissures (folds) than can be seen on the external surface.

Each hemisphere has four parts, which are represented in Figure 5.15. The **fissure of Rolando** (or central fissure) runs almost vertically, dividing the **frontal lobe** from the **parietal lobe.** The increased development of the cortex of man as compared with lower animals is particularly evident in the development of the frontal lobes. For example, even allowing for difference

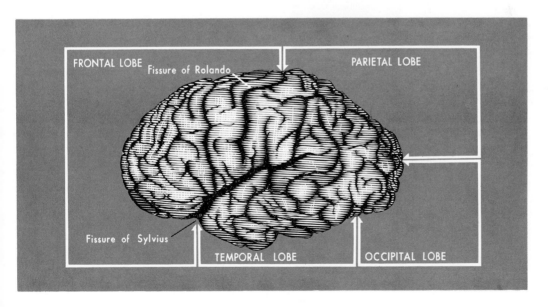

FIGURE 5.15 The Lobes of Each Cerebral Hemisphere.

in the sizes of the brains, man has eight times as much cortex in this forward part of his brain as has the cat. The forehead profiles of cats and men slope differently, supplying indirect evidence of this anatomical difference. Another major fissure is the **fissure of Sylvius** (or lateral fissure). It runs diagonally separating the **temporal lobe** below it from the frontal and parietal lobes above it. The **occipital lobe** lies at the back of each hemisphere.

The human cortex undergoes important structural changes during the early stages of its development. At first the cortex of the unborn child is smooth. Its convolution

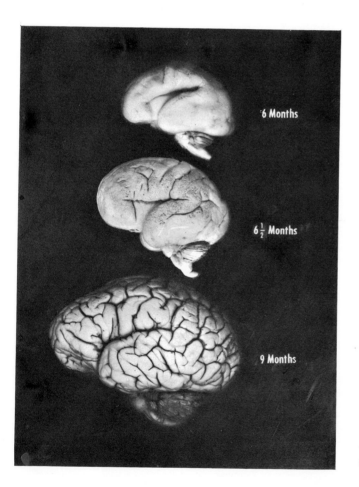

FIGURE 5.16 The Growth of the Brain During Fetal Life (The Smithsonian Institution).

begins only during the terminal period of pregnancy when the number of brain cells of the fetus multiply very rapidly. At birth the child possesses as many brain cells as he ever will. Following birth the major gross change in the child's nervous system is the increase in size and length of the neurons throughout the body.

Beneath the cortex lies the remainder of the cerebrum, consisting mainly of nerve fibers covered by a white **myelin** sheath, which distinguishes this part from the gray matter of the cortex. The subcortical cells in the cerebral hemispheres provide connections between various parts of the nervous system. Some connect areas of the cortex to other areas within the same hemisphere; others connect areas of separate hemispheres. Still others serve to connect the cerebral cortex with some of the lower centers in the brain stem or spinal cord.

By using electrical techniques, physiologists have been able to discover something about how various parts of the brain function. One type of research has been to trace neural pathways from sense organs to the brain. When we see a light or hear a sound, the first thing that happens in the brain is that a large number of neural impulses arrive. All these impulses, whether they are initiated in the eyes or ears, are much alike. So far as is known, they all involve the same type of electrochemical process and differ only in their destination. The individual impulses from the eyes are channeled to the back of the brain (occipital lobes); those from the ears go to its sides (temporal lobes). When these impulses arrive at their destinations we see or hear. If they are blocked just prior to reaching their final destinations, we do not see or hear. The obvious statement that we see with our eyes and hear with our ears is not completely correct; it fails to tell the whole story.

Electrical prospecting methods have also been used to trace neurological events leading from the brain to the reacting mechanisms. As long ago as 1870 two German scientists, Fritsch and Hitzig, applied weak electrical currents to the exposed cortex of dogs. When the stimulation was applied to a certain portion in the rear of the frontal region of the dog's right hemisphere, muscular movements occurred in the left leg. Similarly, stimulation of the same region of the dog's left hemisphere produced muscular movements in the right leg. These responses occurred because the electrical currents in the cortex initiated neural impulses which traveled along nerve paths from that particular area of the cortex to the effectors in the legs.

Research of this sort has led to the conclusion that the effector activity for all skeletal muscles of dogs and other animals is represented in particular areas of the cortex. Certain parts of the cortex control the activities of the muscles of a leg, while other areas control tongue movement, and so forth. The parts of the human body are not represented on the cortex by areas proportional to their size; they are represented by areas proportional to the variety and precision of movement of which the body parts are capable. The brain surface associated with the movement of the hands and fingers is much larger than the area associated with the movement of the feet and toes. The part controlling tongue and lip movements occupies an area approximately as large as that for the rest of the face. The two together, that is, the whole face including the tongue, requires a cortical area of relatively Gargantuan proportions. Figure 5.17 is the drawing of a man that would be made if the artist drew the parts of the body in proportion to the areas of the brain controlling them (as revealed by electrical stimulation of the motor areas of the cortex). If the artist made such drawings of animals down the evolutionary scale, this grotesque distortion would decrease until he reached the rat, where the bodily representation on the cortex is a reasonable facsimile of the anatomical structure.

Three fourths of the human cortex consists of association areas as opposed to sensory and motor areas. These areas play a vital role in such high-level processes as learning, thinking, and remembering. Around the visual areas in the occipital lobes are association neurons which connect the visual areas with the frontal lobes.

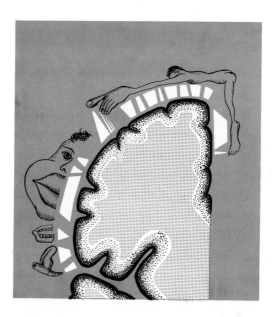

FIGURE 5.17 A Motor Homunculus. It represents an area of the cerebral cortex, called the motor area, which controls different muscular activities. A relatively large proportion of cerebral tissue is given over to the control of the hand and face.

If the visual cortical areas in both hemispheres are destroyed, a person is blind. If, however, only a part of the association areas surrounding the visual areas in the occipital lobes and containing association neurons connected to the frontal lobes is destroyed, the person can see, but his memory based upon visual cues may be impaired. In **agnosia**, a condition due to damage of visual association neurons through injury or disease, the patient can see but cannot identify objects on the basis of visual cues alone. If he is shown a bunch of keys, he may fail to name it even though

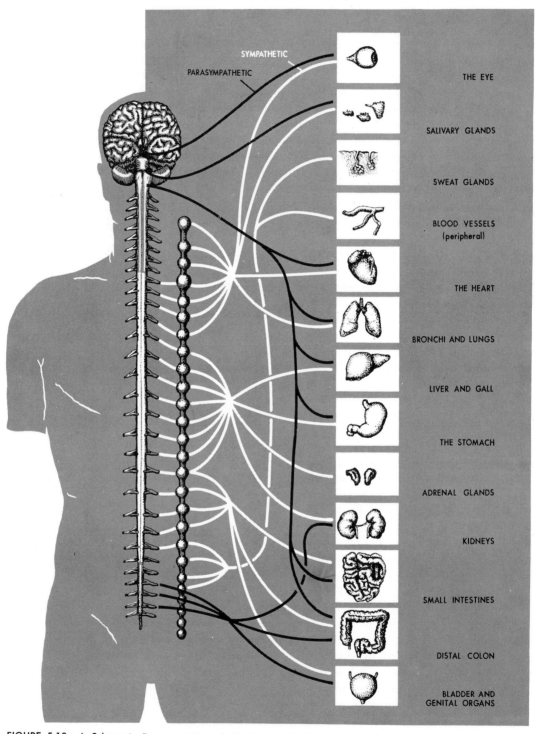

FIGURE 5.18 A Schematic Representation of the Autonomic Nervous System. The black lines represent the parasympathetic and the white lines the sympathetic division of the autonomic nervous system.

he can see it, as demonstrated by his ability to point at and touch it. If, however, the keys are jingled, he will perhaps be able to say what they are. Presumably the jingling stimulates the auditory area, which in turn initiates impulses via association neurons to the frontal lobes, resulting in recognition.

The Autonomic Nervous System

The portion of the nervous system involving the reactions of the skeletal muscles has up to now been our primary concern. Skeletal muscular reactions relate an organism to its external environment. The maintenance of the internal environment, on the other hand, is largely the responsibility of the glands, smooth muscles, and heart muscles. The activities of these effectors are controlled by the **autonomic nervous system.**

The autonomic nervous system has two components that operate somewhat antagonistically to each other. One is called the **sympathetic division** and the other is known as the **parasympathetic division.** Figure 5.18 provides a schematic drawing of the autonomic nervous system, showing the two sets of connections to each of the effector organs. The sympathetic and parasympathetic divisions are separated for clarity in showing how they function.

The sympathetic division gains dominance during moments of stress, such as anticipation of a dentist's drill, a very important final examination, or the sight of an impending car crash. In such stressful situations the body reacts with a widespread pattern of physiological responses produced through the sympathetic division of the autonomic nervous system. The heart beats faster and more strongly, blood pressure rises, salivary secretion is inhibited, perspiration is increased. At the same time, the pupils of the eyes dilate, blood sugar is released from the liver, and adrenalin is released from the adrenal gland of the endocrine system. In short, the sympathetic division mobilizes the energies of the body for an emergency.

The parasympathetic division operates in a way opposite to that of the sympathetic division. It slows the heart beat and reduces blood pressure, producing the typical visceral responses during periods of rest and relaxation. In short, the parasympathetic division usually conserves the resources of the body.

HEREDITY

The continuity of this chapter may seem to be rudely broken by the sudden transition here. Actually this transition follows logically. You saw that because the structure of an organism determines the general form of its behavior, the student of psychology requires some knowledge of physiology. That you cannot fly and a canary cannot read is a difference in behavior due, in the first place, to the differences between your gross anatomy and, above all, your nervous system and those of a canary. But how did these structural differences arise? Why does man develop a convoluted cerebral cortex instead of the smooth cortex of a canary? Why does a canary develop wings instead of arms with dexterous hands? The obvious answer is "heredity." But this answer is useful only if you properly understand what is meant by heredity.

We do not inherit anatomical characteristics as we may inherit money. Transmission by heredity is neither so direct nor so simple as that, although it is common enough. Look at Figure 5.19. It shows four types of embryos, one of which is human. They are all quite similar; the human embryo appears just as inhuman as the other three. At this early stage, it does not have a convoluted cortex or even arms with hands; it has only the *potentialities* for them.

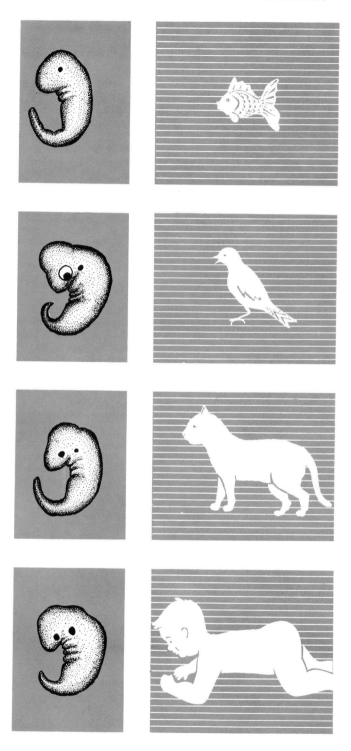

FIGURE 5.19 The early embryos of all vertebrates are very similar during the early stages of their development.

If a human embryo initially has no convoluted cortex, how does it acquire one? The answer to this question takes us straight to the way heredity works. In the cells of the human embryo are agents or substances that control the biochemical activities responsible for physiological growth and development. At the embryonic stage these agents control the growth of brain cells, so that out of primitive beginnings a human convoluted cortex will develop with time. In the same way agents within the cells of the canary control the development, so that certain characteristic structures will result. What actually is inherited, then, are agents that control the immensely complex processes of organ building. For example, strictly speaking, you did not inherit the color of your eyes; you inherited agents that controlled the development of particular eye pigments.

The question of *what* is inherited is an important one, especially when you consider the respective contributions that heredity and environment make in determining various kinds of responses. In everyday usage the meaning of the term *heredity* is so cloudy that it tends to confuse issues rather than to clarify them. Our task for the time being will be to clarify the term by describing the underlying mechanism responsible for hereditary transmission from generation to generation. The science dealing with this subject is **genetics.**

Genetic Determination

Every person begins life as a single fertilized cell a few thousandths of an inch in diameter. This single cell is a result of the union of a sperm cell from the father with an egg cell from the mother.

The key to hereditary transmission is contained within the sperm and egg cells. These cells, like all living cells, contain a nucleus surrounded by cytoplasm. Within the nucleus are structures known as **chromosomes** which contain the unitary agents of inheritance called **genes.**

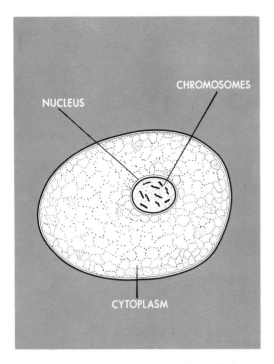

FIGURE 5.20 Schematic Diagram of a Cell

In humans there is a key gene responsible for determining the color of the eyes. It exists in two forms. One form, *B,* will influence development so that brown eyes will result. The other form, *b,* is responsible for the development of blue eyes. Each reproductive cell, sperm or egg, contains one eye color gene. When the two reproductive cells unite the resulting offspring possesses two eye color genes, one from the sperm and the other from the egg. The nature of this combination will determine the eye pigment of the offspring. If the offspring has received two *B* genes his eyes will be brown, whereas if he has received two *b* genes his eyes will be blue. If there is a combination of one *B* gene from either a sperm or egg cell and a *b* gene from the other reproductive cell, the offspring will develop brown eyes. The *B* gene dominates or masks the effect of the *b* gene. Therefore, *B* is said to be a *dominant* genetic characteristic, and *b* is said to be *recessive.*

It would seem, then, a simple matter to predict accurately the color of an offspring's eyes if you knew what kind of eye color genes his parents had. But individual genes cannot as yet be identified directly, and therefore, geneticists are forced to infer their characteristics. They would assume a person to have received a *B* gene from each of his parents if only brown-eyed individuals had appeared in their families for some time. Such a person would be an offspring from a *pure eye strain.* In human genetics it is difficult to know for sure whether a strain is pure for any given characteristic, because human breeding, unlike that of animals in the laboratory, cannot be controlled. Besides, only a limited number of generations is available for study. Geneticists avoid these difficulties by studying subhuman organisms whose reproductive activities are carefully controlled and whose evolutionary development is very rapid. In the evolution of generations, a thousand years for man may be equivalent to a few weeks for the fruit fly and to only a few days for bacteria. With such species it is possible to infer an organism's genetic constitution with a high degree of confidence.

Perhaps it is a good idea to make clear that although the genes for eye color produce brown or blue eyes, they themselves are not assumed to be colored. Nor is it true that the genes themselves develop into brown or blue eyes. What is assumed is that an individual's development is controlled by the chemistry of the genes. One of the major differences between embryos pictured in Figure 5.19 is that each has a different set of genes. By initiating different biochemical reactions, these genes influence the growth of the organism so that different characteristics develop.

The Gene and Its Environment

Up to now we have considered genes as the units of inheritance that control physical

102

development. But what controls the activities of the genes? Are they completely insulated from all other physiological activities? They are not. Genes reside within the chromosomes within the nucleus, which in turn is located within the cell. Events occurring in the chromosomes, in the nucleus, in the cytoplasm of the cell, or even outside the cell itself, can influence the operation of the genes.

It is believed that genes are molecular structures and are therefore subject to change like all molecules. Some of these changes can occur in the normal course of events; others can be produced artificially, as a result of physical forces from the outside. H. J. Muller, a Nobel prize winner, found that he was able to produce structural changes in some of the offspring of fruit flies if he exposed them to a blast of x-rays just short of a death-dealing dose. These structural changes persisted in following generations, and consequently, Muller concluded that the x-rays permanently altered certain of the genes' structure-determining potentialities. Note that this environmental influence was exerted *prior to* fertilization of the cell.

The cellular environment that surround genes can also influence their expression, that is, it can have an effect on what they bring about during development of the organism. Experiments with sea urchins, small marine organisms, demonstrate that cells containing identical genes but different cytoplasm will develop differently. Recent investigations using a high-powered electron microscope on slices of frog's eggs one-millionth of an inch thick, have revealed slender fibers that connect the nucleus with the cytoplasm. These threads may be the structural units by which the genes within the nucleus are influenced by events within the cytoplasm.

The kind of external environment in which an embryo develops can also influence the course of genetic determination.

The larvae of certain fish, if raised in a specific chemical solution, will develop one eye instead of two. Environmental influence on genetic determination can also take place after birth. In summer the snowshoe rabbit is the same color as his brownish environment. But when autumn comes and the weather gets colder, the snowshoe rabbit starts to change color, until in winter with snow covering the ground, he is entirely white. In the case of the snowshoe rabbit, it appears that some condition characteristic of the environment during the cold months (low temperature, short days) can determine the expression of the genes.

What bearing do these facts have on psychology? Clearly, genes do not rigidly fix the structural destiny of an organism beyond any possibility of deviation. Genes determine the course of physiological development by controlling certain biochemical reactions of the cells. But the activities of the genes themselves are influenced by their surroundings. This evidence of interaction between the agents of heredity and environment refutes the general notion of a sharp and distinct cleavage between the effects of heredity and environment. Actually no such distinct cleavage of effects can be discovered. Is the fur color of the snowshoe rabbit produced by hereditary *or* environmental factors? To put it boldly, such a question *cannot* be answered because we know that the fur color is determined by the interaction between hereditary and environmental factors. Genes are always in some sort of environment and their influence on development has to be considered in relation to this. With the realization of this point comes the redefinition of the problem of heredity and environment. Instead of considering them as separate and opposed forces, we must accept the fact that they are inextricably interdependent and then seek to understand the nature of their reciprocal influences.

Maturation

An organism is influenced by the effects of genetic determination throughout its life. Its physiological system changes continuously according to developmental patterns governed by biochemical reactions. These reactions are initiated by the genes and influenced by the organism's environment. You have already seen how the brain grows from conception to maturity. The other portions of the nervous system, as well as our receptors and effectors, also follow an orderly sequence of growth.

The structural unit of the nervous system, the neuron, develops gradually. Initially a motor neuron in a chick embryo has no axon. But with time the neuron spins out a long axon that finally terminates in some muscle fiber. Until this happens the embryo will be incapable of a reflex response involving contraction of that muscle fiber.

This maturational development of a neuron is constantly influenced by environmental factors. Its destiny is not irrevocably determined at an early stage. A small piece of prospective nerve tissue transplanted from its original site to a new site may develop into nerve tissue altered to conform with its new environment. Brain tissue of a chick embryo has even been transplanted to the eye, where it developed into normal eye tissue. The rate of growth of a neuron can also be modified by the injection of certain chemicals. Snake venom, which contains a growth agent, injected in a chick embryo causes an exuberant growth of spinal nerve fibers.

Maturational development is not restricted to growth; it involves decay as well. Nerve cells do not escape the ravages of time; an old neuron undergoes structural changes which are responsible for some of the senile behavior that an older organism may display.

The rate and other characteristics of the growth of a nervous system place limits on the behavior that it makes possible. Compare, for example, the rate of motor development of the Macaque rhesus monkey with that of man. The average rhesus monkey can, at the age of three days, visually follow a moving object by turning his head and eyes. A human infant is not able to do this until he is two to three months old. Similarly the monkey grasps at objects he can see when he is five days old, whereas the human reaches the same stage of development only after he is five or six months old. A monkey can pick up a pellet with apposing thumb and fingers when he is six weeks old; the average human infant is not capable of doing this until he is ten months old. In spite of the more rapid motor development of monkeys, we know that human beings ultimately reach a stage of much more refined development. No monkey can achieve the manual dexterity required to be a watchmaker, nor can the monkey ever make all the precise lip and tongue movements necessary for human speech.

The growth pattern, then, places certain limits on behavior. We cannot train a human infant to do what a monkey can as early in his life, nor can we train a monkey to do everything man can do in later life. The physiological systems of monkeys and men place limits on their behavior at each stage of development. This is true not only of members of different species but also of different members of the same species. For example, a newborn infant cannot read, and you cannot respond with a Babinski reflex to light stroking of the sole of your foot. Many neonates (newborn babies) respond to such stroking by extending the big toe and fanning out the other toes. This Babinski reflex disappears as the child grows older. The nervous system of the newborn infant is structurally capable of producing this reflex, and your nervous system no longer is. The various parts of your physiological system can respond in the highly integrated fashion necessary for reading. But, of course, no matter how intensively you might try to train an infant, you could not teach him to read. In short, members of the same species behave differently at different stages of development.

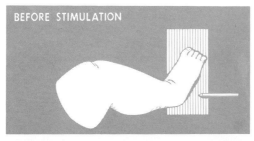

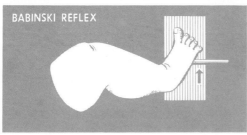

FIGURE 5.21 The Babinski Reflex. The upper drawing shows the normal position of the infant's foot. When the sole of his foot is stroked, his big toe is extended and the other toes fan out.

A behavior difference nowhere near as great as the one between a Babinski reflex and reading is the one between sitting and walking. Infants are able to sit up before they can walk; walking, a more complex activity, requires a more mature physiological system. As infants grow their physiological systems develop enabling them to acquire new forms of behavior. A typical six-month-old child can sit but cannot walk, and no matter how much training he may receive from his doting and ambitious parents, his walking will have to be postponed.

Maturation is the name applied to the

sequence of changes in behavior that are due not to learning but primarily to physiological growth. In an experimental demonstration of the importance of the maturational process, Carmichael (1927) showed how the development of swimming responses in frog and salamander tadpoles was due to growth and not to practice. Carmichael divided newly hatched tadpoles of frogs and salamanders into two groups. One group, the control group, was permitted to develop in clear water, while the experimental group was raised in water containing chloretone. This solution, although not interfering with normal growth processes, inhibited all muscular activity, thus preventing the subjects from swimming.

The tadpoles in the control group developed normally and began to swim at the expected time. After the control subjects had been swimming for about five days, the group of tadpoles constituting the experimental subjects were placed in clear water. After a period of thirty minutes the swimming responses of the experimental subjects were indistinguishable from those of the control subjects.

One possible interpretation of this experiment is that thirty minutes of practice by the experimental subjects was equivalent to five days of practice by the control subjects. Another interpretation is that the experimental subjects needed thirty minutes for the drug to wear off. This second interpretation would mean that these tadpoles did not need practice before they could swim. Swimming is automatic when the physiological system of the tadpole is sufficiently mature. In order to evaluate these two interpretations, Carmichael placed another group of tadpoles that had been swimming normally into a chloretone solution. When removed from the solution they also needed a thirty-minute period before they could swim freely. Thus Carmichael's results suggest that the swimming response in tadpoles occurs automatically when the animal is physiologically ready.

Responses resulting from maturation cannot always be separated so neatly from those due to training. This is particularly true when we deal with such complicated behavior as reading. Most children of two cannot profit from an attempt to train them to read. They are not sufficiently developed to make the necessary visual discrimination between words. The average child of six, however, is sufficiently mature. But appropriate reading responses will not emerge spontaneously when the average child reaches the age of six, as was the case with the swimming responses of the tadpoles. Training is necessary before a child will acquire reading skills. In other words, it is maturation that provides the foundation upon which learning to read takes place.

How behavior changes as organisms develop has been an area of great interest to psychologists. The many observations they have made have great practical as well as theoretical value. All parents should know something about the maturational sequence of children's behavior. Too often they eagerly but prematurely institute training to read, toilet training, or training in some other activity for which their child is not sufficiently developed. Failure can only result and sometimes can have unhealthy psychological influences on the child.

The study of maturation is a natural outgrowth of what we have learned of physiology and genetics. The genes determine how and at what rate organisms develop; the genes steer the maturation process. It should be emphasized, however, that in the study of maturation, as in genetics, environmental influences can never be completely ignored. For example, when the tadpoles were kept in a chloretone solution for over 13 days, their swimming behavior was definitely retarded (Matthews & Detwiler, 1926). Obviously, then, their swimming response is not insulated against all environmental influence.

Maturation should not be conceived as occurring in opposition to learning in the way that hereditary influences are commonly, but wrongly, contrasted with environmental influences. We tried to redefine the latter problem by demonstrating the reciprocal influences between heredity and environment. We will try to do the same thing when we discuss maturational and learning problems in various portions of this book.

Our discussion of heredity and environment does not provide the simple answers to complex questions that are offered by those who mistakenly assume a completely isolated and independent relationship between the two. But you will discover that in spite of its somewhat greater complexity, our analysis is intellectually sounder simply because it fits the facts.

SUMMARY

Three kinds of physiological structures are related to behavior: (1) receiving mechanisms (receptors), (2) connecting mechanisms (nerve cells), and (3) reacting mechanisms (effectors). In a sensory-motor reflex following the stimulation of a receptor, neural activity is initiated in the connecting nerve cells, and an effector is activated.

Reacting mechanisms are either muscles or glands. There are two kinds of muscles: skeletal and smooth. Skeletal muscles are attached to the skeleton and initiate all body movements. Smooth muscles are responsible for the activity of many vital functions within the body, such as the movement of food along the esophagus and the contracting and enlarging of the iris. Glands secret complex chemical substances, which control numerous body functions.

Duct glands, such as the salivary gland, secrete their fluids through tube-like structures. Ductless glands, known more commonly as endocrine glands, secrete hormones directly into the blood or lymph streams.

If there was no nervous system the reacting mechanisms would not respond. The nervous system is composed of a central and a peripheral component. The main components of the central nervous system are the brain and the spinal cord. The peripheral nervous system includes sensory (afferent) and motor (efferent) nerves, as well as the autonomic system, which controls the action of the smooth muscles and glands.

The neuron, the elementary structural unit of the nervous system, is a single cell containing two kinds of hairlike extensions: dendrites and axons. Neural impulses, electrochemical in nature, travel in the direction from dendrites to axons. Neural impulses are transmitted from a sensory neuron across a synapse to an association neuron and then across another synapse to a motor neuron which activates an effector. Typically, many more neurons than three are involved in any reflex, because: (1) neurons are bunched together to form nerves; (2) each neuron forms synapses with many other neurons; and (3) nerve impulses after reaching the central nervous system are transmitted up and down the spinal cord as well as across to motor neurons.

As it proceeds upward the spinal cord swells into the brain stem, which in addition to other functions, regulates the activities of the autonomic nervous system and serves as a communication center between the higher centers of the brain and the spinal cord. Back of the brain stem is the cerebellum, which functions to maintain both the tonicity of the skeletal muscles and bodily equilibrium. The human cerebrum, which envelops the brain stem from above, is divided into the right and left cerebral hemispheres. Their outer layer, or cortex, consists of four main lobes. It contains both sensory and motor areas, but the largest portion of it consists of association neurons that connect various sections of the cortex.

The autonomic nervous system consists of the sympathetic and parasympathetic divisions. The former helps mobilize the body for action in times of stress; the latter usually helps conserve the resources of the body during periods of rest.

The development of an organism's physiological system is governed by biochemical actions controlled by genes, the units of heredity. Genes, however, do not rigidly fix physiological development beyond any possibility of modification. Genes are molecular structures that can be modified by their environment. Thus heredity and environment are not independent of each other.

The sequence of behavioral changes that organisms typically pass through is known as maturation. Regardless of the amount of training, certain kinds of behavior cannot be acquired until the organism's physiological system has matured sufficiently.

SUGGESTIONS FOR FURTHER READING

BEACH, F. A. *Hormones and behavior.* New York: Hoeber-Harper, 1948.

A review of experimental studies showing the effects of hormones on behavior.

BEST, C. H., & TAYLOR, N. B. *The living body.* (4th ed.) New York: Holt, Rinehart, & Winston, 1958.

A well-illustrated and interestingly written book on human physiology.

FULLER, J. L., & THOMPSON, W. R. *Behavior genetics.* New York: Wiley, 1960.

An excellent survey of genetic concepts and experimental findings in the important and rapidly expanding field of behavior genetics.

GARDNER, E. *Fundamentals of neurology.* (3rd ed.) Philadelphia: Saunders, 1958.
An elementary treatment of the nervous system.

MORGAN, C. T., & STELLAR, E. *Physiological psychology.* (2nd ed.) New York: McGraw-Hill, 1950.
One of the most popular textbooks on the physiological mechanisms of behavior.

WENGER, M. A., JONES, F. N., & JONES, M. H. *Physiological psychology.* New York: Holt, Rinehart, & Winston, 1956.
An elementary textbook that briefly describes the physiological correlates of behavior.

BASIC PSYCHOLOGICAL
PROCESSES
III

Now that you are equipped with the basic tools to study psychology, the problem becomes where in the science of behavior to begin. Consider your present behavior. What are the factors responsible for it? There are many. You must be able to see the black marks on the white page; you must have learned to organize these marks into words and understand their meaning; you must have decided to read this book instead of doing something else; you must remember previous portions of the book, or at least previous parts of your present assignment; you must have chosen to go to college; you must be bright enough to have gotten admitted into college; you must be sufficiently conscientious to read your assignments. We could add to this list almost indefinitely. If nothing else, it shows that behavior is a function of a large number of factors operating simultaneously. It also suggests that in trying to understand behavior there are innumerable places to begin. The question is whether they are all equally good. The history of science suggests that there are advantages in beginning the study of empirical phenomena by examining them in their simplest form. It seems reasonable to try the same approach when studying psychology, to first understand simple behavior before progressing to more complicated behavior. This is the plan that we will follow.

Although simple in conception, the plan is difficult to execute. Behavior is a complex ongoing activity that resists divisions into nice, neat categories. It becomes necessary to analyze behavior and abstract from it those processes that are fundamental. We will divide the study of basic psychological processes into four major divisions: sensation, learning, perception, and motivation.

Sensation deals with factors responsible for the reception of elementary forms of stimulation. We possess several kinds of receptors which provide us with information about the world around us as well as within us. How physical events in our external world are translated into visual and auditory sensation will be the main topics of our treatment of the psychology of sensation.

When you are reading a book or listening to music, you do more than sense light or sound. These sensations are somehow organized into a pattern. For example, when you read you do not merely see black marks on a white background. You perceive words. You do not hear a series of discrete tones. You perceive a melody. How you organize and interpret a pattern of stimuli is the subject matter of the psychology of perception.

The psychology of learning is concerned with the acquisition of new modes of behavior. Before learning to read, a child must be able to see and organize letters into words. But that is not enough. He must learn to associate the nouns he reads with their referents and to understand the functions and meanings of the other parts of speech.

Motivation is perhaps the most dramatic topic, but it is the one we know least about. The psychology of motivation is concerned with arousal of such drives as hunger, thirst, and sex. It is also concerned with how we become fearful of people and things, as well as how social and cultural factors mold our drives.

It will become apparent as you read the following chapters that although different processes are emphasized when studying sensation, perception, learning, and motivation, the dividing lines between these areas are not sharp and clear. Sensation tends to merge into perception, and the interaction between perception and learning is sometimes so great that it is necessary to apply the term *perceptual learning* to some phenomena. Finally, you will discover that although we are born with several motivations, we *learn* new ones. So do not be too surprised when studying these four processes that they are to some extent interrelated.

The order in which these topics should be studied is to a large extent arbitrary. For matters of convenience you will study initially sensation, then learning and perception, and finally motivation.

SENSATION—THE RECEPTION OF STIMULATION

6

SENSITIVITY

We are surrounded by a crowded, changing world. Sounds, lights, pressures constantly bombard us. In order to protect ourselves and maintain life, we must detect many of these changes. So common an action as crossing a busy traffic intersection safely depends upon our sensing a multitude of sounds and sights.

The frequent changes that take place in our bodies also demand our attention. Hunger pangs indicate that we need nourishment; pain signals threats of bodily damage. Occasionally children are born without the normal sensitivity to pain. They constantly injure themselves because they can suffer severe bodily damage with no signs of distress. Such a child may hold a piece of red-hot metal and burn himself seriously before he puts it down. For these unfortunate children pain would be a blessing.

The psychology of sensation is concerned with an organism's ability to detect stimuli. When we have the capacity to react to a stimulus, we are said to be **sensitive** to that stimulus. Right now your eyes are sensitive to the black markings on this white page. You may simultaneously be sensitive to other stimuli. Perhaps you hear the conversation in the adjoining room or feel the pressure of your clothing or the dryness in your mouth. You are, however, not sensitive to everything. You are not sensitive to the radio or TV waves or to the cosmic rays that are streaming through space about you. Nor are you sensitive to the secreting of your endocrine glands which is constantly going on.

Many great inventions of the last century have compensated for our sensory limitations. Radio and television sets and x-ray machines convert energy which we are insensitive to into stimuli that we can hear or see. The telescope and microscope enlarge the range of our visual receptors so that we can detect stimulation that would ordinarily be too faint for us to see.

The Investigation of Sensitivity

How is it possible to investigate an organism's sensitivity to its environment? It is quite simple. Let us briefly consider two nontechnical examples which demonstrate the basic principles of research in sensory psychology.

Are you sensitive to the ticking of a watch when it is 15 inches from your ear? You can answer this question scientifically by performing a simple experiment. Close your eyes or blindfold yourself, and have a friend give you a series of tests in which he either holds a watch fifteen inches from your ear or buries it under a pillow and he asks you whether or not you hear the ticking. If you are consistently able to detect the presence or absence of the watch, then you can conclude that you are sensitive to the ticking of that particular watch when it is 15 inches away. If you try this on other people, you will discover that some are more sensitive than others, and that many are not equally sensitive in both ears.

Are you sensitive to the difference between the same musical note as played on a clarinet and on an oboe? In order to answer this question you must be exposed to a series of pairs of equally loud tones, sometimes both played on the same instrument and other times one of the two played on a clarinet and the other on an oboe. After hearing each pair you will have to indicate whether the two tones sound the same or different.

If your hearing is normal, you can "tell" the difference between the two instruments. That is, when the two tones are produced by the same instrument you respond "Same," but when they are produced by different instruments you respond "Different." From this ability to respond dif-

ferently to the two instruments the psychologist concludes that you had different sensations when hearing the tones each produced. Thus the concept of a sensation is based upon the ability of an organism to discriminate between different stimuli.

These two examples serve as simple models of some of the research in sensory psychology. The key to a clear understanding of sensory psychology is to realize that an organism can serve as a measuring instrument. Consider the problem of discovering which of two objects is heavier. This problem can be solved simply by placing the objects on the platforms of a balance scale. The object that raises the other one is heavier. Thus it may be said that the scale is sensitive to differences in weight. In a typical experiment in sensory psychology, the subject plays the role of the scale by discriminating between the sensory characteristics of two stimuli, much as the scale discriminates between the weights of two objects. The discriminative response (e.g., "Same" or "Different") of the subject is equivalent to the pointer reading of the scale.

Empirical Relationships in Sensory Psychology

There is obviously more to sensory psychology than we have suggested by our two simple examples. Research in sensory psychology begins with the concept of sensitivity but does not end there. Why an organism is sensitive to some stimuli and not to others must also be investigated. This problem has been approached in two general ways.

In an attempt to understand an organism's sensitivity to certain physical stimuli, psychologists have sought to discover the attribute of the stimulus that enables the organism to respond to it. In the case of the ability to discriminate between an oboe and clarinet, they have discovered that the instruments differ in the pattern of sound waves each produces. (What this pattern is will be discussed later in this chapter.) Thus it is possible to relate the discriminative response to some physical feature of the stimulus. That is, you recall, an example of a $R = f(S)$ type of relationship. Usually the $R = f(S)$ laws in the field of sensory psychology are of the concurrent type because the organism makes his discriminative response at the time he is being stimulated. The term **psychophysical** has been used to describe this kind of relationship. It is a good term because it neatly summarizes the relationship between a psychological response of discrimination and the physical characteristics of stimuli.

In studying sensation, psychologists are also interested in discovering **psychophysiological** relationships. Once the attribute of the physical stimulus that enables us to discriminate between an oboe and clarinet is known, the next question is, What physiological mechanism enables us to respond to this physical attribute? This problem you will recognize as an example of a $R = f(O)$ type of relationship.

You see, then, the psychology of sensation is an orderly and methodical field of study. Its problems can be distinctly stated and solutions to them can usually be found. The primary concern of sensory psychology is to understand how and why organisms respond to various modes and intensities of stimulation. To accomplish this it is necessary to analyze the source of stimulation as well as the physiological mechanisms that enable an organism to respond to it.

The Scope of This Chapter

It is the aim of this chapter to review the basic facts and theories of human visual and auditory behavior. Of course, seeing and hearing are not our only senses; we possess receptors that enable us to respond to smells, tastes, touch, pain, warmth, cold, and the position of our bodies and limbs.

But to discuss all these senses in anything but the most superficial manner would require an entire book. Therefore this discussion of sensation will be restricted to vision and hearing, the two sense modalities we know most about and the two that are on the whole, the most interesting.

In this chapter the physical stimulus effective in initiating receptor activity will be described first; then the structure and functioning of the receptor will be taken up. The discussion of each sense will conclude with a description of the major phenomena and the major theories that explain them.

VISION

Although visual sensations are normally initiated by light, they are not always. Someone who has been punched in the eye will probably tell you that he saw "stars." You can have somewhat the same sensation without hurting yourself if you close your eyes and gently press one eyelid. As the pressure increases you will experience a sensation of brightness. These visual sensations are obviously not initiated by light since your eyes are closed. They result from the pressure on the eyeball initiating neural activity in the optic nerve that connects the eyeball and the brain. When this neural activity is transmitted to the visual sensory area of the brain (see page 97), a visual sensation occurs. Sensory experience depends on appropriate brain activity and not necessarily on customary stimulation; that is, we can have visual sensations without light waves.

Dramatic proof of this comes from recent research on restoring vision to the blind. The researchers were able to initiate visual sensations in a woman whose optic nerve had been destroyed 18 years earlier and who had been totally blind ever since. They implanted thin wires in the occipital lobes

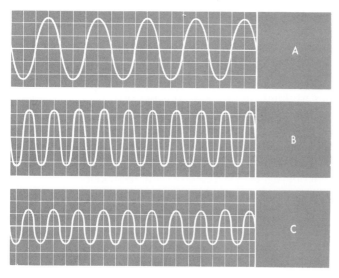

FIGURE 6.1 A Schematic Representation of Three Different Light Waves (electromagnetic radiation). Light waves A and B differ in wave length but not in intensity. Light waves B and C differ in intensity but not in wave length.

of her brain and attached them to a transistor amplifier, which was connected to a photocell capable of generating an electrical signal in response to light. The patient, in a dark room, saw flashes of light when a light was turned on. The photocell served as a crude eye, while the amplifier changed the electrical impulses from the photocell into a form that aroused neural activities in the occipital lobes. Here is evidence that sensory experience can occur in the absence of both the usual receptor activity and normal neural transmission to the brain. The one essential condition for sensory experience is neurological activity in the appropriate sensory area of the brain.

Now, of course, visual sensations resulting from pressure on the eyeball or direct cerebral stimulation are rare exceptions rather than the rule. Most of the time our

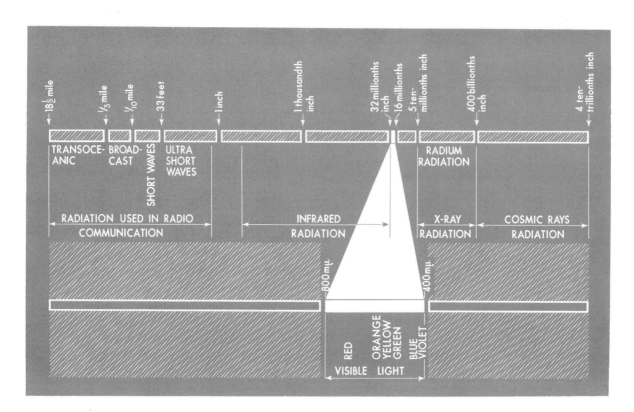

FIGURE 6.2 The Range of Electromagnetic Radiations. The visible portion is shown enlarged. The wave length of electromagnetic radiation in the visible spectrum determines what color we see.

visual sensations are initiated by light stimulation, and it is these that psychologists have usually studied.

Light

Theoretical physicists, it may surprise you to hear, are not in complete agreement about the nature of light. For our purposes we can conceive of light as electromagnetic radiations traveling through space at the unimaginable speed of 186,000 miles per second. It is convenient to think of these radiations as moving like waves. As the distance between the crests of successive waves rolling in at the seashore varies, so do the **wave lengths** of different electromagnetic radiations. The wave length (distance between crests of successive waves) of electromagetic radiations varies over a stupendous range—from ten trillionths of an inch to many miles in length.

We cannot see all these radiations. In fact, we see only a very small proportion of them. Under normal conditions of illumination our eyes are sensitive to radiations ranging between 16 and 32 millionths of an inch, or in the more conventional scientific terminology, between 400 and 800 millimicrons (abbreviated as $m\mu$ and defined as a millionth of a millimeter). Under optimal conditions the range of sensitivity (the visible spectrum) is even broader, extending from 320 to 1000 $m\mu$ (Judd, 1951). Exposure to these extremes, which are those of ultraviolet and infrared radiations can, however, result in injury to the eye.

Most light that reaches our eyes consists of more than a single wave length. Sunlight is an example. Isaac Newton in 1666 passed a beam of sunlight through a glass prism and noted how it separated into a rainbow-like spectrum of colors (see Figure 6.3 on color plate 1 between page 126 and 127). Newton rightly concluded that sunlight ("white" light) was physically complex, being composed of many wave lengths. In contrast, light of a single color—or what is technically described as **spectrally homogeneous light**—consists of radiations that are on the same wave length (actually of a very narrow band of slightly differing wave lengths). We refer to the assortment of wave lengths composing any beam of light as its **composition.** Theoretically the composition of visible light can vary from a single wave length to a mixture of all the wave lengths that can be seen.

So far we have described two different physical properties of light: wave length and composition. A third property that concerns us is the **intensity** of light, which is its energy level. It is represented in Figure 6.1 by the height, or amplitude, of the light waves; the greater the height of a light wave, the greater the intensity of the light.

The Eye

The Eye and the Camera. The eye resembles a camera. Both admit light through an adjustable diaphragm. Both have lenses through which the light passes and by which an image is focused on a sensitive surface. When a photographer takes a picture in a dim light, he opens the iris of his camera so that more light passes through the lens. In bright light he makes the opening smaller. Similarly the pupil of the eye enlarges in dim light and becomes smaller in bright light. In the human eye the area of the widest opening is approximately seventeen times greater than the smallest.

The surface inside the camera that is sensitive to light is of course, the film. Its analogue in the eye is the retina. The grain of the film consists of chemicals sensitive to light. Similarly, the retina, which is about the size of the bowl of a teaspoon, contains receptor cells sensitive to light. The light-sensitive elements of photographic film are distributed evenly over its entire surface, whereas the light-sensitive elements (receptor cells) of the retina are distributed in an intricate design, that will be described below.

The similarities between the eye and a camera are so great that in the nineteenth century a professor of physiology concluded that it would be possible to take a picture with a living eye, and he finally demonstrated his point by a process which he named optography. He placed an albino rabbit in a stock so that the animal's head was facing a barred window seen against a gray, clouded sky. A black hood covered the rabbit's head. Some time later he lifted the hood briefly exposing the rabbit to the light. The animal was then killed and the retina removed and placed in a chemical solution of alum. Gradually the retina developed a clear picture—or what was called an optogram—of the window with its bars.

Rods and Cones. Imbedded in the retina are two different types of light-sensitive structures or receptors, called **rods** and **cones** because of their shapes. The inner portions of both are similar to ordinary nerve cells.

One difference between these two kinds of visual sensory cells is much like the difference between fast and slow film. Fast film contains chemicals sensitive to light of low intensity. You can take a good picture at sundown with fast film. Slow film is sensitive only to light of high intensity. If you use it to take a picture at sundown, the print will be dark and blurry. Rods are analogous to fast film; they are more sensitive to light than cones are. In starlight, and in moonlight except at its very brightest, our vision is mediated solely by rods. When the light is more intense the cones operate. They activate at a level of illumination approximately one thousand times greater than the minimum required for the stimulation of rods.

The fineness of detail in a photograph depends on the distribution of light-sensitive chemicals on the film. Similarly, the fineness of detail of our visual sensations depends on the number and distribution of light-sensitive receptors on the retina. The normal human retina contains about 100 million rods and six and one-half million cones. They are, however, not evenly distributed. The cones are tightly packed together in the **fovea,** which is in the center of the retina and somewhat indented. Their density sharply decreases with increasing distance from the fovea. The rods, however, have their greatest density about 20

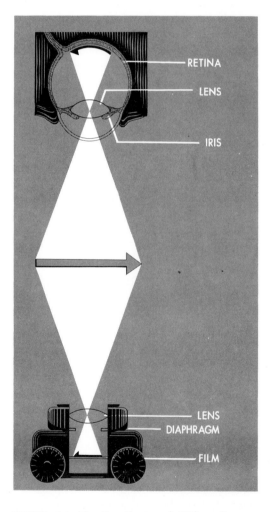

FIGURE 6.4 The Eye Compared With a Camera. Each has (1) an adjustable opening to regulate the amount of light coming in, (2) a lens for focusing, and (3) a sensitive surface upon which the image falls. In both the eye and the camera the image that is focused on the sensitive surface is upside down and reversed.

degrees from the fovea; there are no rods at all in the fovea itself.

Slightly below the fovea and to the nasal side of it is the blind spot. All the individual nerve fibers from the retina converge here to form the optic nerve. There are no receptors in the blind spot; hence, as its name indicates, the area is insensitive to light stimulation. The existence of the blind spot was known at least as far back as the seventeenth century. It is said to have afforded Charles II of England some macabre amusement. He used a demonstration of the blind spot to show his court attendants how they would look after their heads were chopped off! Figure 6.7 shows how he was able to do this.

Pathways of the Optic Nerve. As the optic nerves from each eye proceed toward the occipital lobes of the brain they converge at the optic chiasma. At this point half of the fibers from each nerve cross over and travel to the side of the brain opposite the

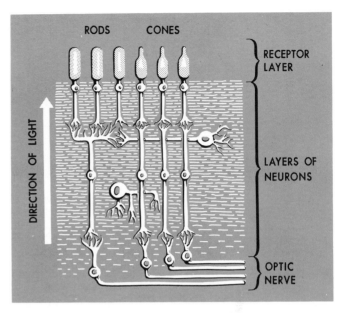

FIGURE 6.5 A Schematic Representation of the Cells of the Human Retina. The rods and cones convert light energy into neural impulses which are transmitted through several layers of neurons before they reach the optic nerve. The diagram merely hints at the complex interconnections among the various nerve cells within the retina. The arrow indicates the direction the light travels as it goes through the diffuse network of neurons to reach the receptors in the retina.

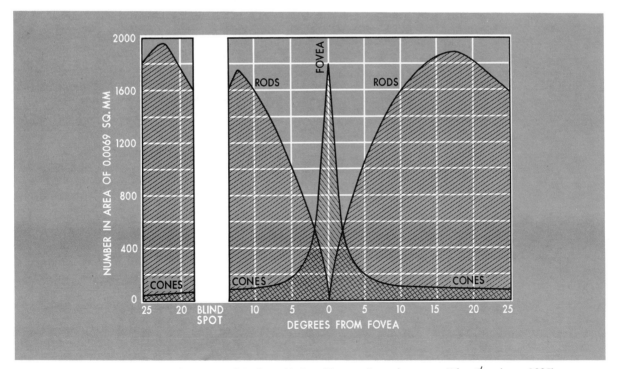

FIGURE 6.6 Number of Cones and Rods at Various Distance From the Fovea (After Østerberg, 1935).

FIGURE 6.7 The Blind Spot. Close your left eye and look directly at the cross with your right eye. Hold the book at a distance of fourteen inches. If you still see the head of the person to the right of the cross then move the book slightly closer or farther away until the head disappears. You cannot see it because the light from the head is striking your blind spot.

eye from which they originated. Thus, if the optic nerve on the left side of the head is severed between the optic chiasma and the brain, the person will not be blind in his left eye but will instead be blind in the *left half of each eye.* You can experience how a person with such an injury would see by placing a piece of cardboard over the left half of each eye. Of course, if the left

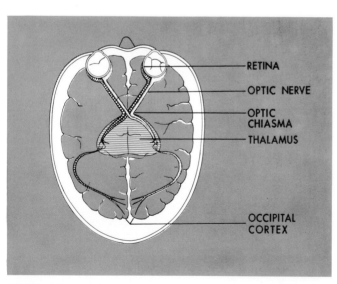

FIGURE 6.8 A Schematic Drawing of the Pathways of the Optic Nerves as They Proceed From the Retina to the Thalamus and Then to the Occipital Cortex. The dark portion of each optic nerve consists of fibers mediating vision in the left half of each eye, while the light portion contains fibers mediating vision in the right half of each eye.

optic nerve is severed before it reaches the optic chiasma, the entire left eye will be blinded.

THE PSYCHOLOGY OF VISION

Visibility

As you well know, you cannot see any object in a completely dark room. In the absence of light your visual receptors, rods and cones, remain unstimulated. How much light do you need to start seeing? This is a problem of **visibility,** the ability to detect the presence of a point of light.

Visibility as a Function of the Part of the Retina Stimulated. In one of several studies conducted to determine how visibility is a function of the part of the retina stimulated, a narrow beam of "white" light was projected through the subject's pupil onto a small area of the retina for one thousandth (0.001) of a second. The intensity of the light beam varied, and the subject was instructed to report after each exposure whether or not he saw the light flash.

The results of this experiment, represented in Figure 6.9, reveal the relationship between a physical measure of the intensity of the light and a psychological measure of sensitivity, the subject's ability to detect the light. Increasing values of light intensity are represented along the ordinate, and the various portions of the retina are indicated along the abscissa. Zero degrees represents the fovea, at the center of the retina. The other numbers represent parts of the retina at various distances to the left and right of the fovea. The line in the graph represents the weakest light that can be seen when different parts of the retina are stimulated. In the language of psychology, this line represents the **absolute stimulus threshold** of seeing for each portion of the retina.

As you can see, there is no one absolute threshold for the whole eye; it depends upon what portion of the retina is being stimulated. It may at first surprise you to hear that the eye is *not* most sensitive to faint light at its center (fovea), but instead at about 20 degrees from the fovea. You will remember, however, that this is consistent with the physiological and anatomical facts already mentioned, that rods are more sensitive than cones and have their greatest density at approximately 20 degrees from the fovea (see page 116).

What do these findings mean in terms of our ability to detect very dim lights? It means that we can see a dim light best by looking a little to one side of it. This way the light will strike the more sensitive receptors. You can demonstrate this phenomenon to yourself if you go out on a clear, moonless night, away from artificial lights, and scan the sky for one of the dimmest stars you can see. If you look off to one side of it, you will see it quite clearly, but if you look at it directly, its image will either become faint or disappear entirely. During World War II this technique was of tremendous importance to night-time spotters watching for enemy aircraft.

Visibility as a Function of Wave Length. The visibility function described in Figure 6.9 was obtained with a "white" light, a

light composed of wave lengths from almost the entire spectral range. Our eyes, however, are not equally sensitive to all wave lengths. This is clearly shown in Figure 6.10, which reports the intensity of light required at different wave lengths to initiate a visual sensation.

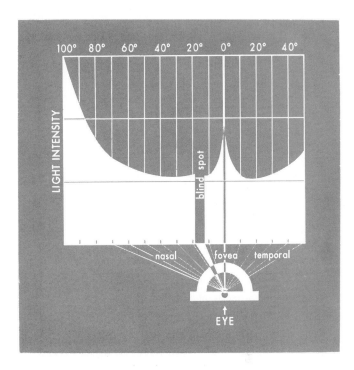

FIGURE 6.9   The Sensitivity of Different Parts of the Eye (After Sloan, 1947).

You will note that there are two visibility curves (known technically as **spectral luminosity functions** because spectrally homogeneous lights are used) in this figure: one for cones and the other for rods. Vision mediated by cones is technically known as **photopic vision,** and that mediated by rods is **scotopic vision.**

If cones and rods were each equally sensitive to all wave lengths, their threshold curves would be represented by straight lines parallel to the abscissa of the graph. But as you see, the sensitivity of rods and of cones varies according to the wave length of the light they are exposed to. Rod vision

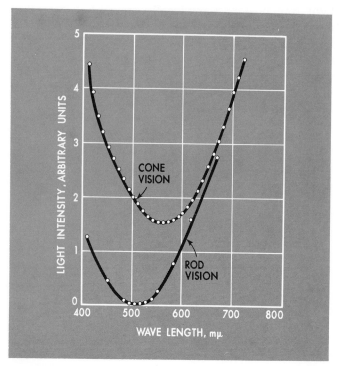

FIGURE 6.10 Photopic (cone) and Scotopic (rod) Visibility (spectral luminosity) Curves Compared. Each point on each curve represents the minimum amount of light of a given wave length that can be detected (After Chapanis, 1949. Courtesy of the National Research Council, National Academy of Sciences, and the author).

Visibility as a Function of Dark Adaptation. The eye's sensitivity to lights of various intensities is drastically affected by the intensity of the light in the eye's most recent environment. When you go from bright sunlight into a dark movie theater, you probably have difficulty finding your way to an empty seat and trip over the legs of the people you cannot see. But after you have been there awhile, the heads of the audience begin to emerge from the blackness of the surroundings. Later, when you are leaving the theater, you have no difficulty detecting the legs and bodies between you and the aisle. Why has the visibility improved? The answer is that your eyes have become more sensitive as a result of an increased concentration of a photochemical substance, **rhodopsin,** in the rods. Hence you can see objects distinctly that at first you could not see at all. This phenomenon is known as dark adaptation.

Dark adaptation follows a very definite course which we can chart by discovering the weakest light a subject can see after he has been in the dark for various periods of time. Figure 6.11 shows how the visibility of dim lights increases with time. Note that the curve drops continuously during a 30-minute period. This means that after the eye goes into darkness its sensitivity continues to improve for a considerable time. Complete dark adaptation takes about one hour, although the added improvement following the first 30 minutes is very slight.

The curve of dark adaptation is not smooth. It has two sections. In the first section it drops steeply and levels off, under standard experimental conditions, after five minutes. The second section drops almost as sharply at the beginning, then levels off and drops very slowly for a long period of time. The two sections, as you might have guessed, result from the difference in functioning of rods and cones. Cones recover their sensitivity more rapidly in the dark

is maximally sensitive to lights having a wave length of 511 mμ, and less sensitive to lights with shorter or longer wave lengths. This means that it is possible for us to see only one of two lights of equal intensity. If, for example, you were exposed to a 511 mμ light at its absolute threshold intensity level and then to a 600 mμ light at the same physical intensity, you would see the first light but not the second. Visibility is then not simply a function of light intensity.

The maximal sensitivity of cones (see Figure 6.10) occurs at wave lengths of 555 mμ. Note also that the threshold of cone visibility is higher than the corresponding curve for rods. As we said before, rods are more sensitive than cones, and a less intense light will stimulate them.

than rods, but the extent of the rods' adaptation is greater. The first section of the dark adaptation curve in Figure 6.11 represents cone adaptation; the second, rod adaptation.

During the course of dark adaptation, both cones and rods become sensitive to lights that were at first too weak to stimulate them. If you glance at the end of the first section, you will see that when cones are fully dark adapted, after about five minutes, they are sensitive to lights hundreds of times weaker than the lights they could respond to initially. The change in sensitivity of the rods is even greater. After dark adaptation is complete the rods are sensitive to lights 10,000 times weaker in intensity than those to which they were initially sensitive. At the end of the dark adaptation process the eye is amazingly sensitive; assuming normal vision it can see the flame of a match ten miles away on a perfectly clear, moonless night.

Problems associated with dark adaptation challenged military psychologists during World War II. Fighter pilots defending cities and military installations often received sudden commands to fight off enemy bomber attacks at night. If they had to run from a well-lit room into the darkness and immediately take off in their planes to engage the enemy, they would be at a terrible and perhaps fatal disadvantage. Not having sufficient time to dark adapt, they would not be able to see as well as the enemy. Obviously fighter pilots could not wait 30 minutes to become dark adapted. Nor was it sensible to have them wait in the dark, unable to do anything but build up tension, for the signal of combat. Fortunately for our fighters, Walter R. Miles, a psychologist, had a simple but brilliant idea. The germ of his idea is contained in Figure 6.10. Look at that figure closely. Note that lights with wave lengths just below 700 mμ, at the red end of the spectrum, barely stimulate the rods, although they do stimulate the cones. Thus, if light of only these wave

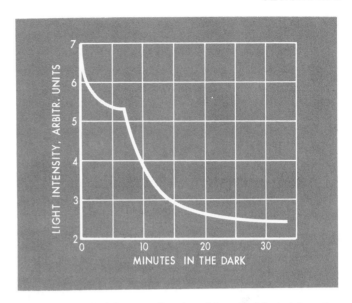

FIGURE 6.11 Visibility as a Function of Length of Dark Adaptation. The curve is obtained by placing a subject, who has been in normal illumination for some time, in a dark room where he is repeatedly tested to determine the weakest light he can see.

lengths stimulates the eye, the *rods* stay in a constant state of dark adaptation. This was accomplished by having the pilots wear goggles with red lenses that transmitted only light of wave lengths above 620 mμ while waiting for an enemy attack. They were permitted to wear these goggles in rooms with ordinary illumination, so that they could see well enough with their cones to read, write, play cards, or "shoot pool." When the alarm for combat rang, a pilot would dash into the darkness, remove his goggles, and in a very short time attain the same level of dark adaptation that remaining in the dark for a period of 30 minutes could give him. Our fighter pilots were thus able to engage the enemy on even terms.

Visual Acuity

Our discussion of visibility has been concerned with some of the factors responsible for the detection of the presence of light. **Visual acuity,** on the other hand, is a matter of ability to distinguish fine detail. If

121

122

you recall your last eye examination you will find it easy to understand the difference. On the bottom line of the eye chart there were letters that you were probably unable to recognize although you could see them. They appeared as black, fuzzy figures against a white background. These figures were visible (you could see them), but they were unrecognizable (you could not identify them).

What makes a visible stimulus recognizable? Since a complete answer to this question would take an entire book, we shall only go into a few of the most significant facts of visual acuity.

Angle of Retinal Stimulation. We have already noted that the fineness of detail in a photograph depends, among other factors, on how the light-sensitive chemical

elements are distributed on the film. Film with a very fine grain produces photographs so finely detailed that the lines around a person's eyes show. Coarse grain film cannot do this.

In a good photograph the details are sharp everywhere: at the center, the sides, and the corners. The human eye does not function as well, at least in this respect. In daylight vision details of objects straight ahead are very sharp, but they very rapidly become less clear proceeding out from the center. Objects straight ahead cast an image on the fovea. An object that is only 20 degrees off center can be seen about one-tenth as well as one seen straight ahead. You can demonstrate how visual acuity is influenced by the angle of retinal stimulation. Stare directly at a letter on this page. You will have great difficulty in recognizing letters two inches to either side, if you do not move your eyes.

This phenomenon has important implications for the placement of road signs. When you drive a car you cannot read a sign on the side of the road and look ahead simultaneously. You must turn your eyes and thus look away from traffic ahead of you. One obvious way of improving safety conditions is to put essential highway signs above the road so that the driver need not take his eyes off the road.

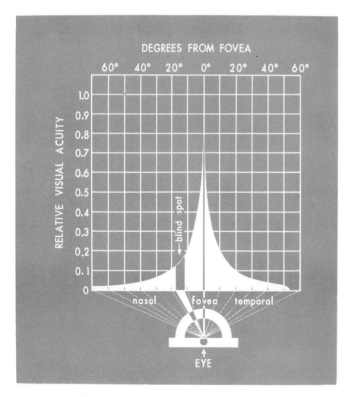

FIGURE 6.12 Daylight Visual Acuity for Different Parts of the Eye. The fovea, located in the center of the retina, has the best acuity (After Wertheim, 1894).

Light Intensity. There is no one level of light intensity that produces the clearest vision. A light sufficient for you to identify the words in this book would not be sufficient if you were repairing a watch. Up to a point, visual acuity usually can be improved by increasing illumination. Although you may be able to recognize all the words in this book under a 10 watt bulb, your speed of recognition would increase if you were using a 100 watt bulb. Of course, the relationship between visual acuity and light intensity depends on the angle of illumination. To produce the

FIGURE 6.13 An Illustration Showing the Advantage of Placing Traffic Signs Over the Road Instead of to the Side. Fixate on the car in front and see which of the two signs is clearer.

maximal amount of visual acuity the source of light must not be directed into the observer's eyes, but toward what he is looking at.

Visual acuity decreases at night. The lower the illumination, the poorer the visual acuity. Cone vision produces superior visual acuity because cones have a better supply of nerve connections than do rods. But we are able to compensate for lower levels of illumination. For example, after sundown you may not be able to see the shape of your friend's nose, but you are likely to recognize him by the outline of his body. In nighttime combat, during World War II and the Korean War, pilots were advised to pursue other aircraft by flying above or below their sterns rather than directly astern, so that they could see a more complete silhouette of the other plane. Pilots who did this were in a better position to recognize the other plane and to pursue it if necessary.

Other Factors Determining Visual Acuity. A common test of vision demonstrates that distance influences visual acuity. If you prop your book against some support and gradually walk backwards, you can demonstrate to yourself that visual acuity decreases with increasing distance. But in the nearer range, visual acuity can be reduced by decreasing distance. If you gradually move your book toward your eyes from its normal reading distance, you will reach a point where the letters begin to blur and become unrecognizable.

The longer you look at an object, the more likely you can identify it. This is why speed is so essential in the tricks of a magician. Visual acuity also increases with sharpened contrast between an object and its background. A black letter can be more easily identified against a white background than against a gray background, and even more easily against a yellow one.

From our brief discussion of visual acuity it should be clear that we cannot state unequivocally whether or not a given stimulus will be recognized if we describe only one of its features. Can the letter *A*, for example, be identified if it is only 1/32 of an inch high? The answer to this depends upon, among many other factors, how long the observer is permitted to look, the degree of contrast between the letter and its background, the intensity of light falling upon the letter, how far the observer is from the letter, and what part of his retina is being stimulated. Thus visual acuity, like many psychological phenomena, is a function of several variables and the interaction among them.

Brightness

Up to this point what we have said about the psychology of vision has been restricted to visual sensitivity and acuity. Another interesting subject is how we respond discriminatively to the intensity of a light. Look at Figure 6.14, which contains five gray patches. Without knowing just how intense they are compared to other patches or lights, we can rank them in order of **brightness.** Patch *B* is the brightest, Patch *D* next brightest, and so forth. Figure 6.15 shows them in order from brightest to darkest.

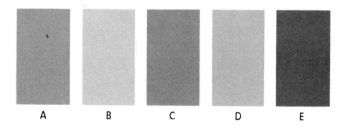

| A | B | C | D | E |

FIGURE 6.14 Rank these five patches of gray from brightest to darkest.

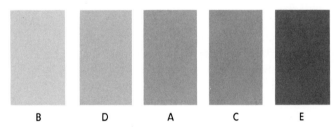

| B | D | A | C | E |

FIGURE 6.15 The Patches of Gray From Figure 6.14 Ranked in Descending Order of Brightness.

FIGURE 6.16 The sensation of brightness is not determined only by the intensity of light. If it were, then the two gray circles, which are of equal light intensity, would appear equally bright. Do they?

Brightness is a psychological dimension. When you ranked these five gray patches, you made a complex series of discriminative responses. For each pair of stimuli, you judged which possessed the *higher* or *lower* brightness value.

Brightness is a function of both light intensity and stimulus context. Students are quick to point out that the ordering of these patches on the basis of psychological brightness is identical with the ordering based upon physical intensity. Then they jump to the conclusion that psychological brightness and physical light intensity are one and the same thing. They are *not!*

There are two reasons for this. First, the operational definitions of brightness and light intensity differ. The former is measured by the discriminative response of an organism, the latter by some such instrument as a light meter. Second, stimuli possessing the same light intensity values do not necessarily appear equally bright. Look at Figure 6.16 and compare the brightness of the two circles. The circle imbedded in the black is brighter, but the light intensity of the two circles is equal. Figures 6.14 and 6.15 demonstrate that brightness is related to light intensity, whereas Figure 6.16 demonstrates that the brightness of a stimulus object can be influenced by its context, i.e., its surroundings. If the contrast effects produced by the surroundings were eliminated, the two circles would appear equally bright. You can demonstrate this to yourself by blotting out the frames in Figure 6.15. Brightness is solely a function of light intensity only when the influence of differing contexts is eliminated.

Brightness as a Function of Wave Length. Lights of the same intensity but of different wave lengths are not equally bright. When illumination is low—approximately at the level of twilight—and the human eye is exposed to equally intense lights from various portions of the visible spectrum, some wave lengths appear brighter than others.

Under dim illumination the brightest part of the spectrum is light with a wave length of 511 mμ with light of 462 mμ and 555 mμ appearing approximately half as bright. Figure 6.17 shows this relationship. It represents the relative brightness curve for rods (scotopic vision), since they are the receptors operating in dim light.

A similar relationship holds for cones. In bright daylight equally intense lights

different colors. The physical correlates of the colors we see, generally speaking, are the different wave lengths of light. When these different wave lengths are received by the cones, the receptors for color vision, they produce different color sensations.

Figure 6.18 shows that in daylight equally intense lights of different wave lengths are not equally bright: a yellow-green of exactly the same intensity as an orange or a

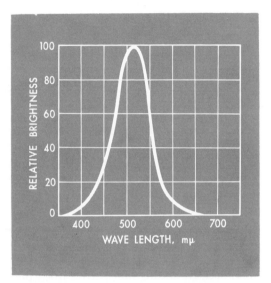

FIGURE 6.17 This curve shows the relative brightness of equally intense lights of different wave lengths under conditions of scotopic vision. Notice that the brightest light has a wave length of about 511 mμ.

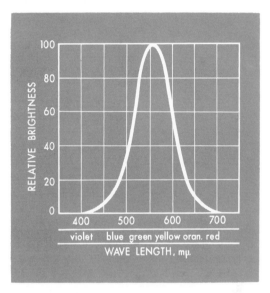

FIGURE 6.18 This curve shows the relative brightness of equally intense lights of different wave lengths under conditions of photopic vision. Notice that the brightest light has a wave length of about 555 mμ.

will also not appear equally bright, but the point of maximal brightness is 555 mμ (yellow-green) and not 511 mμ (blue-green) as was the case for rods.

So that you will appreciate fully the implications of the relative brightness curves of rod and cone vision for our everyday visual sensations, we have to make another reference to the phenomenon of color vision, a topic that we will treat in detail in the next section. As we mentioned briefly on page 115 and as is apparent in Figure 6.3, when white light is broken down into its component wave lengths we see many

green will be brighter; an orange or green will be brighter than a red or blue of equal intensity.

If you compare Figures 6.17 and 6.18, it will be apparent that the relative brightness of light shifts down the spectrum when a transition is made from cone to rod vision, the point of maximal brightness shifting from 555 mμ to 511 mμ. You experience this shift practically every day, when as the afternoon light becomes dimmer, you make the gradual transition from cone to rod vision. As a result, greens, blues, and violets gain in *relative brightness* when compared with the reds, oranges, and yellows. If you look repeatedly at a rose bush as night falls, you will notice that at a certain point the green leaves appear brighter than the red rose, or if you look at equally bright pieces of red and green paper in daylight and then again under dim illumination, the green paper will be brighter. Under very dim illumination both papers will have lost their color, because vision is then mediated solely by the rods. The red and green papers will appear gray, the red being darker.

The fact that colors at the red end of the spectrum drop rapidly to black as twilight approaches, while those at the violet end of the spectrum lose brightness much more gradually, is known as the Purkinje phenomenon, after the Bohemian physiologist who discovered it. You may have noted that the Purkinje phenomenon is closely related to visibility (refer to Figure 6.10, with accompanying discussion). The wave lengths (511 mμ and 555 mμ) to which rods and cones respectively are most sensitive are also the wave lengths that appear brightest.

Color Vision

The ability to see colors is perhaps the most amazing of our visual capacities. Yet we take it so much for granted that we fail to appreciate its importance. Only when we can compare visual experiences with and without color are we able to fully appreciate the wonders of color vision. A black-and-white photograph of a sunset or of tropical birds cannot reproduce the gorgeous beauty of the originals. Imagine what would be lost if the cathedrals of Europe had no windows of colored glass.

Color plays a major role in our surroundings—in clothes, home decoration, entertainment and art, the finest outdoor scenery. No wonder artists, engineers, and designers are all interested in the question: How and

why do we see colors? We took the first step in answering this question, when we pointed to the roles of the physical stimulus (wave length of light) and the receptors (cones) in making color vision possible. Now we must analyze our color sensations more closely.

The human being is normally capable of distinguishing 7,500,000 different colors. Since it would be confusing and really impossible to name them all, a simple method of classifying them is used.

Colors can be ordered by a human observer along three dimensions; **hue, brightness,** and **saturation,** just as every box can be described in terms of its length, width, and height.

Hue. Hue, or what commonly gives a color its name, refers to that characteristic or dimension of visual sensations that results from stimulation by lights of different wave lengths. Hue can be represented on a circle with the colors in the same order as in the spectrum (see Figure 6.3 on color plate 1). The spectrum of sunlight runs from reds through oranges, yellows, greens, and blues to violets. By adding nonspectral hues, purples and magentas, the series can be bent into a band. This hoop of hues is shown in Figure 6.19 (see color plate 2).

Brightness. This is the dimension commonly spoken of as light to dark, but a scale of brightness is not solely whites, grays, and blacks; hues also have a brightness dimension. Figure 6.20 (see color plate 2) shows two series, one of blues and one of grays. Note that both series vary in essentially the same way, from brightest to darkest. Since this sensory dimension of brightness exists for the blues as well as the grays, we conclude that in addition to possessing hue every color also possesses brightness. The physical correlate of the brightness of a spectral hue is the amplitude of the light wave. A dim and a bright blue light wave have the same wave lengths; they dif-

FIGURE 3.6 What elementary color experiences can account for the sensations produced by the center column of seven colors? Do the five colors on the right or the six colors on the left generate the necessary elementary color experiences?

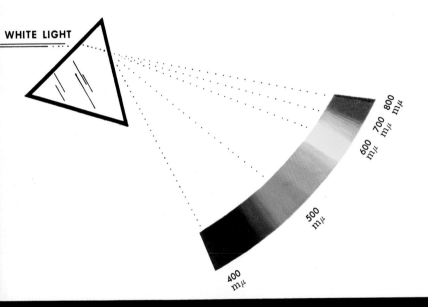

WHITE LIGHT

800 mμ
700 mμ
600 mμ
500 mμ
400 mμ

FIGURE 6.3 How Newton Showed That a White Light (Sunlight) Was Composed of Many Different Colors. By passing a beam of white light through a prism the various components are separated to produce the visible spectrum ranging from red at one end through the various hues to violet at the other end. Below to the left is an actual photograph of the visible spectrum and to the right is a prepared diagram, similiar to Figure 6.2, showing the position of the visible rays (between about 400 and 800 millimicrons) in the range of electromagnetic radiations.

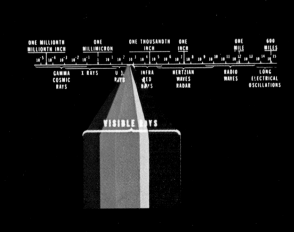

FIGURE 6.19 A Color Circle.
This circle consists of spectral and
nonspectral hues. The diameters of
the circle connect complementary
hues, which when mixed,
produce gray.

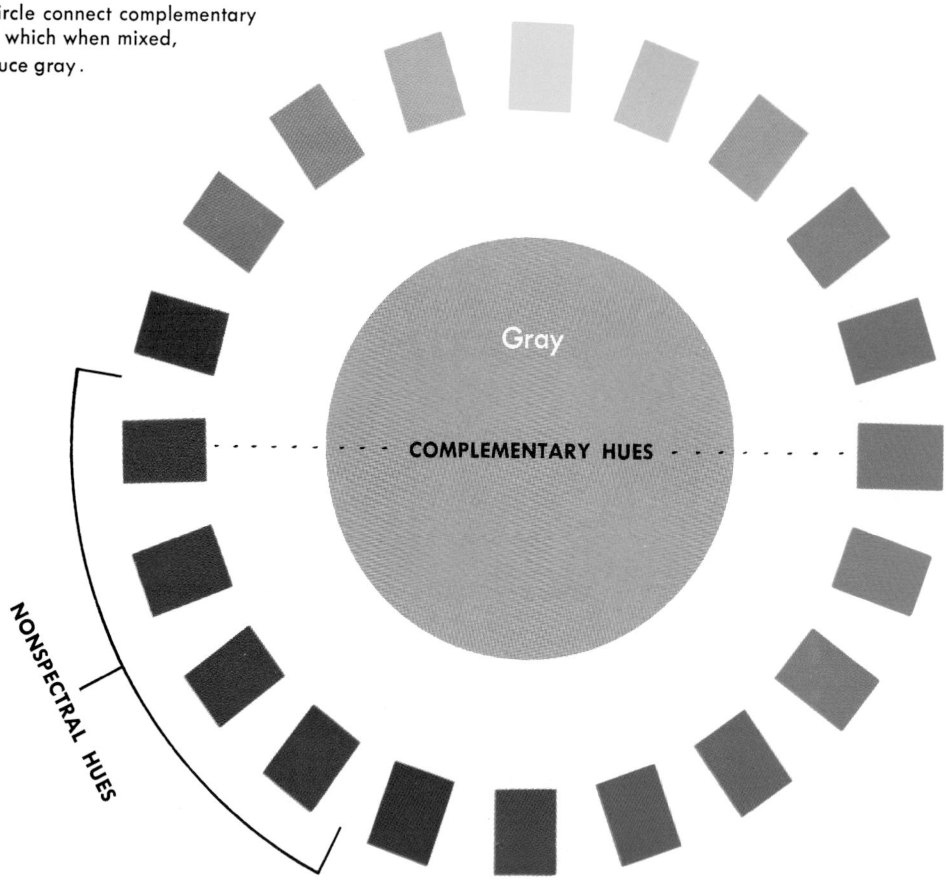

Gray

COMPLEMENTARY HUES

NONSPECTRAL HUES

FIGURE 6.20 A Series of Blues and Grays That Vary in Degree of Brightness.

FIGURE 6.21 A Series of Reds that Vary in Degree of Saturation.

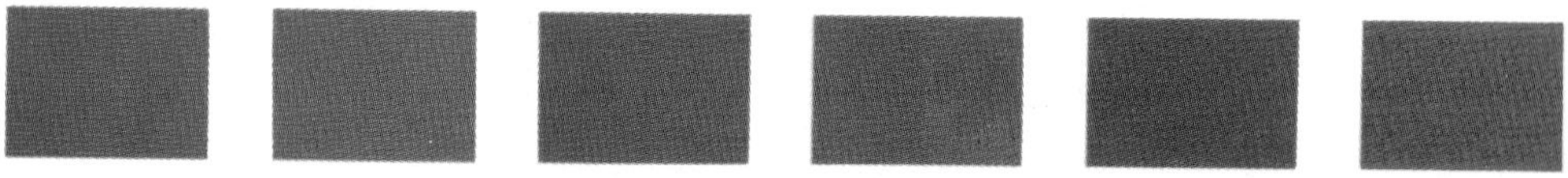

FIGURE 6.23 A Color Solid Showing the Three Dimensions of Color Sensitivity. In this illustration the gradual change in brightness from black to white along the center axis is not indicated.

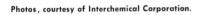

FIGURE 6.24 A Vertical Slice of a Color Solid Showing Differences in Brightness and Saturation. of a Single Hue.

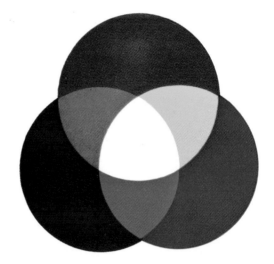

FIGURE 6.26 Color Mixture Resulting From Projecting Red, Green, and Blue Lights on a White Surface. The eye integrates into one color the areas where the colors overlap.

Photo, courtesy of Interchemical Corporation.

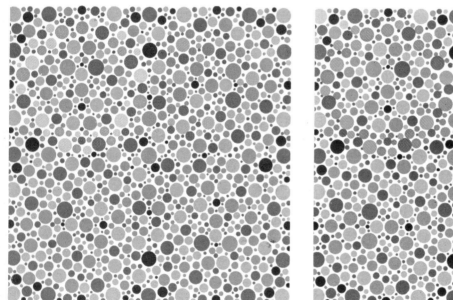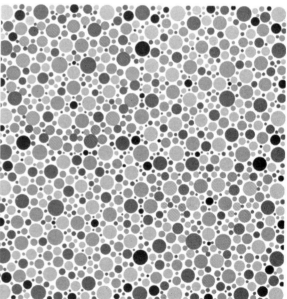

FIGURE 6.29 Two Plates From the AO H-R-R Pseudoisochromatic Test for Detecting, Classifying, and Estimating the Degree of Defective Color Vision. A person with normal color vision will be able to locate the circle and triangle in both plates. Defective red-green vision of medium intensity will prevent a person from seeing one or both of the two symbols in the left-hand plate but will not interfere with his recognizing both symbols in the plate on the right. A person with defective red-green vision of strong intensity will be unable to identify both symbols in the left-hand plates and one or both symbols in the right-hand plates.

fer in amplitude, or wave height (see Figure 6.1 on page 114).

Saturation. Two colors, the same in hue *and* equal in brightness, may differ in another dimension, their saturation. A rose might have the same distinctive hue as a brick and be precisely equal to it in brightness, but the two would still differ, in the purity or saturation of their redness. The rose, though no brighter, would be a redder red, that is, would be more highly saturated. The reddest red is the most saturated red. Figure 6.21 (see color plate 2) shows a series of reds that vary in degree of saturation. Notice how the color becomes grayer as it becomes less saturated. The major physical correlate of saturation is the composition of the light wave. A light wave of only one or a very few wave lengths will produce the highest possible degree of saturation, the purest color. As the composition of light includes more and more different wave lengths, its color becomes more neutral as to hue, more and more gray.

The Color Solid. All three dimensions of our color sensitivity can be represented simultaneously in a simplified manner by a geometrical solid in the shape of a double cone. Figure 6.22 is a line drawing of such a solid, while Figure 6.23 (see color plate 3) shows the color solid itself.

Brightness in the color solid is represented by the central axis connecting the apices of the double cone. On this axis is a series of grays ranging from highest brightness, "snow white," to lowest brightness, "pitch black." Radii extend at right angles from the central axis to the surface of the solid. Degree of saturation is represented along these radii. Zero saturation—the absence of any hue—is located where the radius meets the central (brightness) axis; the highest degree of saturation, where the radius meets the surface. Here are the reddest red, the yellowest yellow, etc. If you were to cut a vertical slice of the color solid

(see Figure 6.24 on color plate 3), all the colors would be of the same hue, but would vary in brightness and saturation.

Because of the characteristics of our color

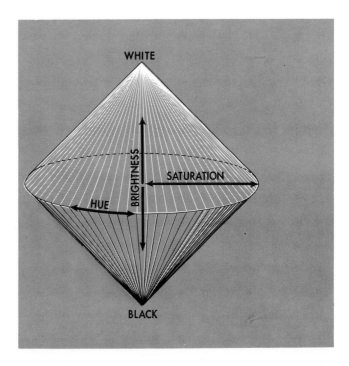

FIGURE 6.22 A Line Drawing of the Color Solid. A person makes his discrimination between two colors on the basis of one or more of the three characteristics of color: hue, brightness, and saturation. The dimension of hue is represented by points along the circumference; brightness, by points along the vertical axis; and saturation, by points along the radius.

sensations, the color solid tapers to a point at the top and bottom. The most highly saturated colors are generally of medium brightness. When their brightness is increased or decreased, colors lose some of their saturation. Consequently, colors vary over a more restricted range of saturation as their brightness tends toward the extremes. Finally, at the terminal points of the brightness axis there is no variation in saturation because there is no hue. White and black are by definition without hue and therefore of zero saturation.

The Eye as an Integrator. Rarely, and then only in a laboratory, does the eye see spectrally homogeneous lights (see page 115). A lemon skin reflects a great many wave lengths, including some that by themselves are the basis of blue, green, yellow, orange, and red. The eye, however, sees the lemon as yellow. It integrates a collection of various wave lengths, it does not analyze them. If the eye analyzed light we would not see a white light; we would see all the spectral hues simultaneously.

Because the eye is an integrator it is possible for combinations of different wave lengths to produce the same visual sensations. Figure 6.25 shows five combinations of different wave lengths that mix to produce the same "off-white" in the normal human eye.

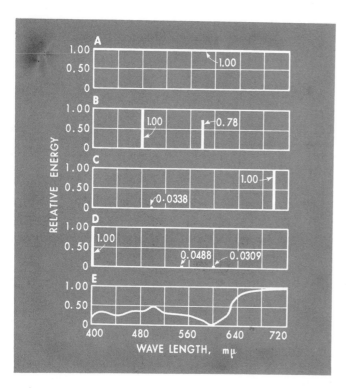

FIGURE 6.25 All the combinations of wave lengths represented in the five graphs look alike (an off-white) to the human eye. This indicates that the eye is an integrating mechanism (After Moon, 1936).

Color Mixture. Since the eye is an integrator, lights of various wave lengths can be projected simultaneously on the surface of the retina and be mixed (integrated) there to form different colors. One of the most important, as well as one of the oldest, laws of color vision is that every hue of the spectrum can be created by a mixture of properly selected colored lights of different wave lengths. One possible combination consists of lights of 650 (yellowish-red), 540 (yellowish-green), and 460 (reddish-blue) mμ. Yellow is produced by combining the first two, and purple results when the first and third are mixed. When all three are combined (see Figure 6.26 on color plate 4) white results.

Color mixture can be accomplished by casting overlapping beams of light on a white screen, and by fitting together disks of colored papers and rotating them rapidly (see Figure 6.27). The color solid helps us to predict the hue resulting from this method of color mixing. For every hue there is another hue which when mixed with the first will produce a gray. Two such hues are known as complementary colors, and appear opposite each other on the color circle (see Figure 6.19). Thus any two hues that are connected by the diameter of the color circle (see any horizontal cross section of the color solid) will produce a gray when mixed. Examples of such complementary pairs are yellow and blue, red and blue-green, and orange and green-blue.

If complementary hues have the same brightness their mixture will be of the same brightness. If however, two complementary colors differ in brightness, the resultant gray will have a brightness approximately halfway between that of each color. A bright red and a dark blue-green will produce a gray of medium brightness. A line drawn between two complementary hues of different brightnesses will intersect the brightness axis of the color solid at the

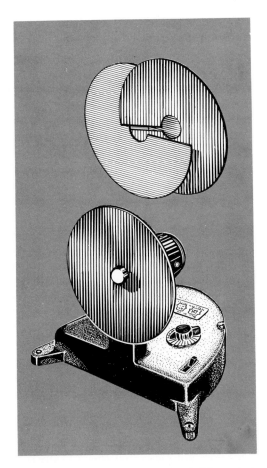

FIGURE 6.27 A Color Mixer. Disks of different colored paper are interlocked and fastened to the shaft of a small electric motor. When the disks are rotated rapidly, the two colors appear to merge and are seen as one.

point equal to the brightness of the gray produced by the mixture.

Another law of color mixture applies to noncomplementary colors. When noncomplementary colors are mixed in appropriate proportions, the hue of the resulting mixture will fall somewhere between them on the color circle. A mixture of red and blue will produce a red-blue, or what is commonly called a purple. A mixture of red and yellow will produce an orange, and a combination of blue and green will result in a blue-green.

The brightness of the mixture of noncomplementary colors will fall between the brightness of the two component hues, while the saturation of the mixture will depend upon the distance between the component hues. If they are close together, like two shades of highly saturated yellow, the saturation of the mixture will be high. If they are far apart, however, the saturation of the mixture will be low. A highly saturated purple when mixed with a highly saturated yellow-green will produce a grayish mixture with only a slight bluish-green tint. Of course, when colors of the greatest possible distance apart are mixed, like complementary colors, the mixture will have zero saturation.

This discussion of the principles governing color mixture may have surprised some readers, those who have had experience mixing paints. They know that when they mix blue and yellow pigments a green is produced. Yet according to our exposition, yellow and blue are complementary colors and when mixed produce a gray. How is this discrepancy explained? Mixing lights and mixing pigments are two different processes. When we mix a beam of yellow and a beam of blue light, our eyes receive a mixture involving the *addition* of blue and yellow lights. When we mix yellow and blue pigments, however, some of the light waves are physically eliminated at the stimulus source. Pigments are not "pure"; they do not reflect light of only one hue. When a white light hits yellow paint most wave lengths are absorbed except for yellow and green, which are reflected. Blue pigment absorbs most wave lengths except those for blue and green. But when blue and yellow pigments are mixed, the blue and yellow lights are eliminated, leaving only light waves that produce a green sensation. Pigment mixture in which colors eliminate each other is therefore appropriately described *subtractive*. Since color mixture of lights and of pigments produce different light waves, it is not surprising then to discover that they can produce different color sensations.

Color Blindness and Color Weakness. In 1777 an article (Huddart) appeared in a philosophical magazine which reported the behavior of people who were unable to distinguish colors. One such person, "having by accident found in the street a child's stocking, . . . carried it to a neighboring house to inquire for the owner; he observed that the people called it a red stocking, though he did not understand why they gave it that denomination, as he himself thought it completely described by being called a stocking."

Those extremely rare people who are *completely* **color-blind** see the visible spectrum (see Figure 6.3 on color plate 1) as a series of grays. They can discriminate between different wave lengths only on the basis of brightness. If two paints are of equal brightness, the completely color-blind person cannot tell them apart; he receives the same visual sensation from both.

It would seem that something must be wrong with the cones of the totally color-blind individual. Moreover, when he is examining something, the completely color-blind individual keeps shifting his gaze so that the image does not fall upon the fovea, which in the normal eye contains only cones. This behavior is called *nystagmus* and indicates that a totally color-blind person is blind in this area. In addition, the spectral luminosity curve of a completely color-blind person resembles the rod visibility function of the normal eye (see Figure 6.10, on page 120); a totally color-blind person is maximally sensitive to lights having a wave length of 511 mμ. These facts suggest that he either lacks cones, or that those he has do not function properly. At present we do not know which of these hypotheses is correct, or whether both of them are correct in different cases.

Color defects less severe than complete color blindness are quite common. Some people are color-blind for only two colors. The form of this defect most frequently encountered is red-green blindness. Approximately 8 per cent of the male population have a considerable degree of this visual anomaly. It is a sex-linked trait almost always transmitted from a male grandparent through his daughter (who is herself very rarely color-blind) to her son. If you are a male who is red-green color-blind, your maternal grandfather is to be "blamed." The red-green color-blind individual sees red and green as poorly saturated yellows or browns. He is not too badly off, for he sees yellow and blue as well as those who have normal vision, and his visual acuity is normal. This suggests that the red-green blind, unlike the totally color-blind, has a complete set of light receptors. The cones of the red-green blind operate, but they operate differently from those of people with complete color vision.

Red-green color-blind people often use the words *red* and *green* freely. They refer to "red brick walls" and "green grass." This does not mean that they can discriminate between red and green stimuli as such; it merely indicates that they have learned to describe their environment as others do. Typically a red-green color-blind male does not have any great difficulty with traffic lights. He may have learned that the red light is above the green and is not as bright (see Figure 6.28). Today a green traffic light usually has a bluish cast, while the red light actually is a rather yellowish-red. Thus the red-green color-blind person has several different cues, including color, which permit him to make the all-important discrimination between red and green traffic lights.

People seem to vary widely in sensitivity to color. This is even true of those who presumably have "normal" color vision. Some people may have superior color-dis-

FIGURE 6.28 A Black-and-White Photograph of a Red (top) and Green (bottom) Traffic Light. Notice how the two lights differ in brightness (Ralph Morse, *Life,* © 1957, Time, Inc.).

crimination because they have had extensive practice, such as painters and interior decorators. Other people's color-discriminating abilities seem to be inherently weak. Under low degrees of illumination they may confuse red and green, although under optimal conditions they have no difficulty. In some such cases we have reason to believe that genetic factors play a role. Hence, we may also entertain the hypothesis that the ability of some people to make very fine color discriminations depends in part on their being born with a high degree of color sensitivity.

Testing for Color Blindness. It is very important to know how well certain individuals, such as airplane pilots, can discriminate between colors. When radios do not function planes are given landing signals by means of red-green semaphore lights;

failure to see a red roof against a field of grass during an emergency landing might cause a disaster. During the war years young men who enlisted for pilot training had to be tested for color vision. Many were surprised to learn for the first time that they had color vision defects. One soldier had complete red-green blindness in his right eye and a mild degree of red-green weakness in his left eye. A light that appeared blue-green to his left eye was a bluish-gray to the other eye. What was reddish-brown to the left eye was simply brown to the right. Oddly enough, this fellow was completely unaware that the color sensations produced by his two eyes differed.

There are several different color vision tests. One commonly used is the AO H-R-R Pseudoisochromatic test. In each plate of this test the person has simply to identify any symbol he can see. The main principle of the test is easy to understand. Look at Figure 6.29 (see color plate 4). The symbols in both plates are approximately equal to their background in brightness. If a person can respond to the hue of the symbol he will identify it. Otherwise it will blend into the background and remain undetected, as it does for a person with defective red-green vision.

The Duplexity Theory of Vision

For a long time many facts about our visual sensations were reported without much attempt to organize them into a theory. You will recall that a theory has been described (see page 14) as consisting of general statements that apply to, or subsume, many specific events. An example of such a theory having to do with vision is the duplexity theory and it consists of the following three general statements:

1. There are two kinds of visual receptors —rods and cones.
2. Rods operate at low intensities of light and initiate colorless sensations of vari-

ous degrees of brightness; cones react at higher intensities and instigate sensations of color.

3. Rods and cones are distributed differently over the retina.

Let us review the facts that are consistent with these theoretical statements. First, there is the anatomical evidence for the two kinds of receptor cells with different distribution patterns on the retina. Second, many behavioral facts that we have already stated are consistent with the claims of the duplexity theory:

1. The absolute threshold of vision depends upon what part of the retina is stimulated.
2. The spectral luminosity curves of daylight (photopic) and nighttime vision (scotopic) are different.
3. A graph of the time required to achieve dark adaptation to lights of known intensity has two distinct sections.
4. The wearing of red goggles in the light will reduce the time required for dark adaptation.
5. Visual acuity varies, depending upon what region of the retina is stimulated.
6. The relative brightness of any particular light wave differs with low and high illumination.
7. The Purkinje phenomenon.
8. The typical totally color-blind person suffers from a more or less constant nystagmus (slight, jerking movements of the eyes), suggesting that the fovea is being avoided when the retina is stimulated by light waves.
9. The spectral luminosity function of the completely color-blind person resembles the scotopic spectral luminosity function of the normal eye.

The duplexity theory is a good example of a psychological theory based on physiological facts. It states that our visual behavior is a function of different kinds of receptors imbedded in the retina. As such the duplexity theory is an example of an $R = f(O)$ type of formulation. The facts it explains, however, are mainly of the $R = f(S)$ type of relationship: how behavior, an organism's discriminative response, is related to the environmental situation, the intensity of a light wave.

We have stated the duplexity theory in a somewhat simplified manner, so that we could convey the gist of it while ignoring many of its more complicated features. But the truth is that the duplexity theory does not explain all visual phenomena. Many facts of color vision have not been integrated into it. Every scientific theory embraces a limited set of facts. Quite often, when more information is obtained, a theory must be broadened, modified, or supplemented. With the aid of new discoveries yet to be made concerning the chemical changes that take place in the rods and cones, and with increased understanding of the neurological events in the visual area of the cortex, the duplexity theory may someday cover a broader range of psychological events.

It should be noted that not all psychological theories include any reference to physiological mechanisms. This will become clearer as we proceed. Physiological theories are numerous in sensory psychology simply because psychologists and physiologists have been successful in relating the forms of behavior that are the immediate consequences of the stimuli that impinge upon us to underlying physiological events.

One last point. Some physiologists and psychologists object to using the term *theory* to describe the duplexity thesis, because its major statements have more the status of facts than hypotheses. The writer prefers the word *theory* because the duplexity formulation is a set of statements that summarize a variety of independent facts in a consistent way. Regardless of the definition of *theory* one prefers, the duplexity formulation does systematize knowledge.

Closely related to the duplexity theory are theories of color vision. These have been concerned with the operation of cones. Many different theories have been proposed; none has gained universal acceptance. One, however, has dominated the field, being accepted by a large number of research workers and stimulating much experimental investigation. This theory was first formulated by Thomas Young (1773-1829) over 160 years ago, and was later elaborated by Helmholtz (see page 40) and others. It is based on the fact that every hue can be described in terms of the relative amounts of red, blue, and green light (called primary colors) required to produce it. According to the **Young-Helmholtz theory,** there are three types of cones and they respond differently to various light waves. One type of cone is maximally responsive to light waves in the red region of the visible spectrum, another type, to blue light, and the third is most sensitive to green light. All sensations of color are considered to be compounded out of varying amounts of excitation of these three kinds of cones. The sensation of white arises from equal and simultaneous excitation of all three, and yellow, for example, from equal red and green excitations.

The Young-Helmholtz theory works admirably in predicting many of the facts of color mixture. But there are certain findings that its adherents have found difficult, and sometimes impossible, to fit into their theory. The sensation of yellow is a great stumbling block for the Young-Helmholtz formulation, for there are certain areas of the retina sensitive to yellow, but not to red and green. If the sensation of yellow stems from the stimulation of receptors maximally sensitive to red and green, how is it possible for the eye to see yellow where it cannot see red or green? Another failure of the Young-Helmholtz theory lies in the apparent link between pairs of colors. Several visual phenomena demonstrate that in some way the sensations of red and green,

yellow and blue, and black and white are paired. For instance, when color vision is impaired as the result of a congenital anomaly or disease, defects are likely to be paired; red and green sensations suffer together and so do yellow and blue sensations.

During the last century Ewald Hering (1834-1918), a German physiologist and psychologist, formulated an opponent-process theory of color vision, which recently has been extended and clarified by a husband-and-wife team of psychologists who publish under the names of Leo Hurvich and Dorothea Jameson. The Hering theory is like the Young-Helmholtz theory in that three different visual processes are postulated. In the Hering theory, however, three *opponent pairs* of visual systems are assumed: yellow-blue, red-green, and white-black. Each system is capable of two modes of reaction that are incompatible with each other. That is, when the yellow-blue receptors are stimulated, they can react in only a yellow *or* a blue manner; they cannot react in both ways simultaneously. That is why, according to this theory, it is impossible to see a yellow-blue or a red-green, whereas it is possible to see a yellow-green and a red-blue. Without any stimulation the visual system is assumed to be in a state of equilibrium in which the subject, after a long stay in darkness, sees a neutral gray representing the "halfway" point between these opponent processes.

For the most part, theories of vision have been concerned primarily with the structure and the function of receptors. But obviously color sensation involves more than this. Chemical reactions, neurological pathways, and the terminal brain events are also important. An adequate theory of color vision will have to deal with these processes also. The Hering-Hurvich-Jameson formulation attempts to do this, but for the present it can best be thought of as a ". . . fruitful working hypothesis . . . [which brings] . . . a systematic coherence to the mass of isolated color phenomena that have been reported and subjected to quantitative experiment throughout the years." (Hurvich & Jameson, 1957, page 402). Whether this formulation, a still newer modification of the Young-Helmholtz view, or an entirely new formulation will prevail is something for future research to decide.

AUDITION

Hearing, like vision, helps us to keep in touch with what is happening in our environment. However, in many ways audition is not as precise as vision. We can locate objects in the visual world much more accurately than we can locate sounds in the auditory world. The superiority of vision is evident when you drive a car in heavy traffic; it is easy to locate an ambulance or fire engine exactly when you see it, but it can be terribly confusing if you just hear the screeching of the siren. Even though hearing may be a less effective sense modality than vision in this respect, it plays a most vital role. It helps us organize our environment, especially in situations where we cannot see well. It makes the art of music possible. But surely, most important, our auditory sensitivity enables us to converse with our fellows. Talking and listening are cornerstones of social behavior.

We will discuss audition in the same topical order as vision, first describing the effective stimuli, then the structure and function of the auditory receptors, and finally the major auditory phenomena.

The effective stimuli for most auditory sensations are sound waves. Auditory sensations are, however, quite often reported in the absence of sound. People sometimes suffer from a constant "ringing in the ears." Somewhat more dramatic are the cases of psychologically disturbed individuals suffering from auditory hallucinations; they hear voices in the absence of any physical sound. Nevertheless, this discussion of audition will emphasize situations involving physical stimulation, as did the discussion of vision.

Sound

Sound, unlike light, requires a medium through which to travel. If a bell inside a glass jar is struck, you can hear it as well as see it struck. If the air is then pumped out of the jar, you can still see the little hammer vibrating against the bell, but you can no longer hear it. Sounds are vibrations transmitted through a material medium. In a vacuum there is nothing to vibrate. There is no medium for sound propagation in outer space. Space travelers, if they are to communicate with each other by sound, will require some artificial medium.

When you pluck a violin string it vibrates back and forth. When it moves to the right it compresses the molecules in the air, cre-

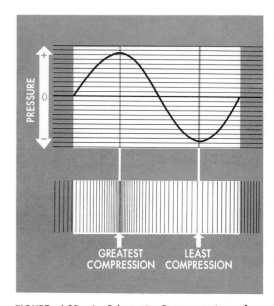

FIGURE 6.30 A Schematic Representation of a Sound Wave and Its Pattern of Pressure. The crest of the wave represents greatest compression of molecules, whereas the trough indicates the point of least compression.

ating a positive pressure in that direction. When it moves to the left the opposite occurs; the molecules are spread thin so that a so-called "negative pressure" is directed toward the right. Sound is essentially waves of positive and negative pressure and can be represented in the simple wavelike form pictured in Figure 6.30. The crests of the waves are the points of greatest compression, while the troughs are the points of minimal pressure.

Sound moves through air at a speed of about 760 miles per hour at sea level. It travels about four times as fast in water and much faster than that in solids such as steel. You can hear a train much sooner if you put your ear to the track than if you wait for its sound to travel by air. Do not suppose that the molecules moved by the vibrating body travel at these speeds. The molecules of air affected by a violin

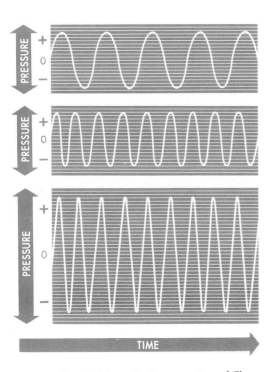

FIGURE 6.31 A Schematic Representation of Three Sound Waves Differing in Frequency and Intensity. The upper two curves differ in their frequencies but not in their intensities. The lower two curves have the same frequency but different intensities.

string actually move a very short distance. What does move are the pressure waves, and they move much as the waves in the ocean do. When you see a crest of a wave sweeping toward shore, you have to remind yourself that the water on the crest moves only slightly, if at all, toward shore. It is the wave-form that moves.

The Physical Attributes of Sound. Sound waves vary in a number of ways. One way they vary is in their **frequency.** Violin or piano strings differ in the number of complete waves or cycles produced (from crest to trough and back to the crest) during each second they are vibrating. Tone can be described physically in terms of these cycles per second (c.p.s.). The two top representations of sound waves in Figure 6.31 differ in frequency; the time interval between the successive points of maximal compression is greater for the upper wave.

Note that the wave in the lower curve in Figure 6.31 has the same frequency as the curve above it, but the distance between the points of highest and lowest pressures is greater in the lower curve. This is a difference in amount of pressure or what is commonly called **intensity** of the sound. The common measure of sound intensity is the **bel,** named after Alexander Graham Bell, the inventor of the telephone, and intensity is usually given in terms of decibels (db), a one-tenth of a bel. Some familiar sounds and their decibel readings are shown in Figure 6.32.

Up to now we have described sound as if it consisted only of pure tones. Pure tones are the result of sound waves of only one frequency, but except under laboratory conditions a pure tone rarely ever reaches our ears. When we listen to a musical instrument we are hearing notes that consist of several different frequencies of sound wave. Such notes are called complex tones. The wave-form of the sound emitted by a piano when the key of C (one octave below middle C) is struck is represented in Figure

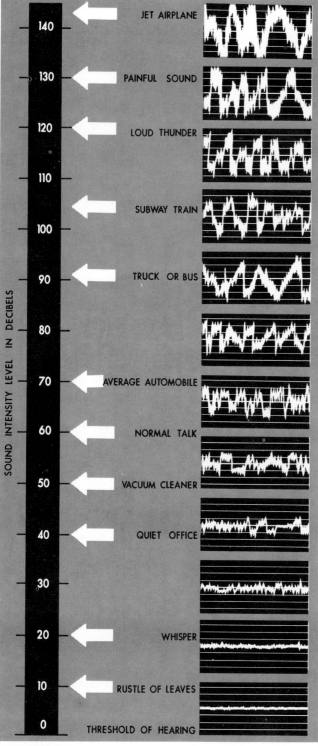

FIGURE 6.32   The Intensity Level of Various Familiar Sounds Near Their Sources.

6.33. It is possible to analyze such a complex note into its simple components. Figure 6.34 shows the results of such an analysis. The largest contribution is made by a tone of 128 c.p.s., but there are 15 other tones contributing to this complex tone.

The wave-form of a complex tone is repetitive, as indicated in Figure 6.33; the same complex wave-form repeats itself over and over again for an appreciable time. There are many sounds that do not have any repetitive pattern and contain a greater conglomeration of tones than complex tones. Such sounds we classify as noises. The clanging of a garbage-pail cover on a sidewalk and hand-clapping are noises. A "white" noise is a noise that contains all frequencies in the same way that a white light contains all frequencies of the visible spectrum. A jet generates a white noise. There is no sharp distinction between a noise and a complex tone. The banging of two hardwood sticks together produces noise, but if it is possible to sustain such a noise, as with a xylophone, the sound takes on the characteristics of a complex tone.

The Ear

The Ear and the Microphone. When you speak into the mouthpiece of a telephone you can be heard quite clearly, for the mouthpiece acts as a microphone; it receives your speech sounds and transmits them in an electrical form to their destination. The ear functions in an analogous way. Two psychologists, Weaver and Bray, demonstrated this in 1930 when they used a cat's ear as a microphone. They anesthetized a cat and attached electrodes to its auditory nerve, connecting the ear to the brain. The wires from the electrodes went through an amplifying system and then were connected to a telephone earpiece. When one of the experimenters spoke into the cat's ear, the experimenter who was in another room listening to the telephone earpiece heard his co-worker's voice clearly.

136

How was this possible? How does the ear transmit physical sound? And how is physical sound transformed into an auditory sensation? To answer these questions it is necessary to know something about the ear, its structure and functioning.

In order to be seen light must stimulate rods or cones. In order to be heard sound must stimulate the **organ of Corti** (named after its discoverer). It is a group of hair cells located in a bony cavity in the inner ear.

Sound waves travel a complicated path to reach the organ of Corti. Initially, they pass through the channel of the external ear, which is rather like a funnel. The outer rim of the funnel is the external ear, which has very little function other than to hold up our eyeglasses or suspend earrings from. The tube in the funnel is equivalent to the auditory canal, which you can feel by putting your finger gently into your ear. The auditory canal funnels sound waves toward a tightly stretched membrane at its inner end. This membrane, commonly referred to as the eardrum and technically known as the **tympanic membrane,** vibrates when stimulated.

If hearing is to take place these vibrations must be transmitted by a group of three small bones known as the **ossicles** which are located behind the eardrum. An enlarged photograph of the ossicles is shown in Figure 6.35. The first bone, called the *malleus* (because that is the Latin word for hammer), is attached to the eardrum and moves when it vibrates. The vibrations of the malleus set in motion another small bone, the *incus* (anvil), which in turn moves a third bone, the *stapes* (stirrup). The stapes sends the vibrations against a small membranous patch (the oval "window") on an organ the size of a pea, the **cochlea.** The cochlea resembles a tiny snail shell, its spiral making two and one half turns.

In 1777 it was discovered that the cochlea was filled with fluid. When the cochlea of a cat was opened under water, no air

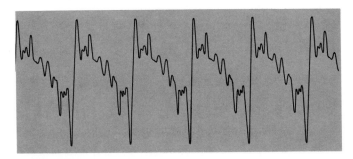

FIGURE 6.33 The Wave Form of the Sound Emitted by a Piano Playing C (one octave below middle C) (After Fletcher's *Speech and Hearing,* Copyright 1953, D. Van Nostrand Company, Inc., Princeton, N. J.).

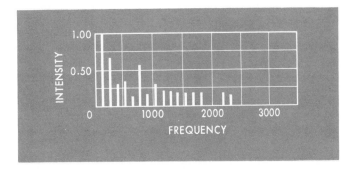

FIGURE 6.34 The Various Components of a Complex Sound Produced by a Piano Playing C (one octave below middle C). The vertical lines indicate each of the various components and their relative intensities (After Fletcher's *Speech and Hearing,* Copyright 1953, D. Van Nostrand Company, Inc., Princeton, N. J.).

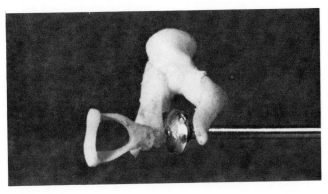

FIGURE 6.35 The Ossicles of an Adult Male Shown in Relation to the Head of an Ordinary Straight Pin. Clearly depicted are the stapes (stirrup-shaped structure), the incus, and the malleus. These bones connect with the eardrum and transmit vibrations from it to the sensory mechanism of the internal ear (Myron R. Kirsch).

137

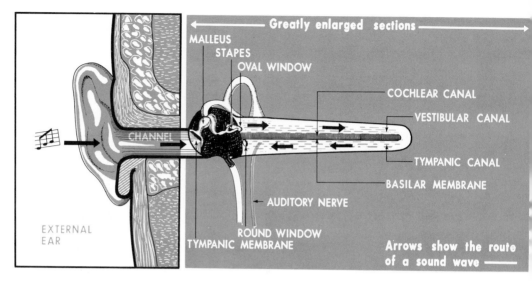

FIGURE 6.36   A Schematic Cross Section of the Ear. The various portions of the cochlea are greatly enlarged so that the route of a sound wave can be easily traced (After Bekesy, 1956, with permission of *Science*).

bubbles came to the surface of the water, proving that the cochlea contained a liquid. Later three liquid-filled canals (*vestibular,* *tympanic,* and *cochlear* canals) were discovered within the cavity of the cochlea.

When the stapes delivers the vibrations

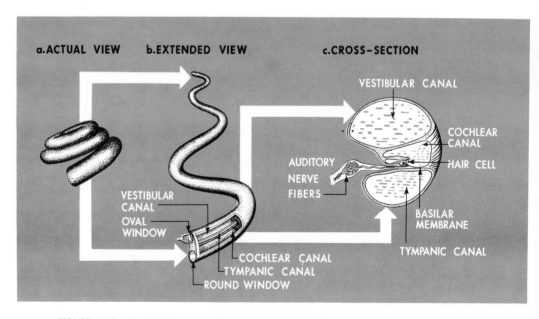

FIGURE 6.37   The Cochlea. (A) The cochlea as it is coiled within the ear. (B) The cochlea as it would appear if extended and sectioned. (C) A cross section of the cochlea showing the hair cells (After N. H. Munn. *Psychology* (3rd ed.) Boston: Houghton Mifflin, 1951).

to the oval window at the base of the cochlea, waves travel up the liquid-filled vestibular canal to the apex of the cochlea. At this point the vestibular canal joins the tympanic canal, and the sound waves turn around and travel down the tympanic canal causing its roof to bulge. The roof of the tympanic canal is the **basilar membrane,** and it separates the tympanic canal from the third and narrowest canal, the cochlear canal. Attached to the basilar membrane, within the cochlear canal, is the organ of Corti. There are about 23,000 of these hair cells which move when the basilar membrane bulges and initiate neural impulses in the nerve fibers to which they are connected. These nerve fibers join together to form the auditory nerve that travels to the brain.

Auditory sensations can be aroused in two other ways. Vibrations of the eardrum can produce waves of air pressure that ultimately stimulate the organ of Corti, and it can be stimulated by vibrations within the bony mass that encases the ear. These two forms of stimulation are, however, of secondary importance. Only when something goes wrong with the mechanical transmission involving the ossicles (malleus, incus, and stapes) do these secondary forms of sound transmission become important. In such cases hearing aids are frequently used to amplify sound waves, so that these secondary forms of sound transmission become more effective.

The Pathways of the Auditory Nerves. The pathways of the auditory nerves resemble those of the optic nerves (see Figure 6.8 on page 118). Nerve fibers from each ear travel to both cerebral hemispheres (see Figure 6.38). They go first to the thalamus and from there to the temporal lobes. Since each ear is connected to both temporal lobes, the complete destruction of one temporal lobe will not cause complete deafness in either ear.

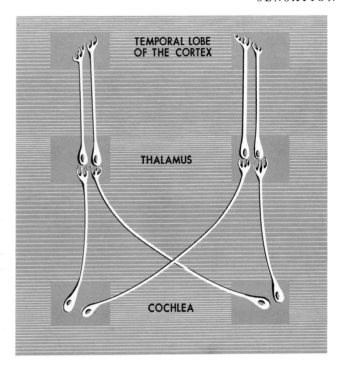

FIGURE 6.38   The Pathways of the Auditory Nerves.

THE PSYCHOLOGY OF HEARING

Audibility

Just as the problem of visibility was to determine the minimal intensity of light necessary to instigate a visual sensation, so the problem of audibility is to discover the intensity of a sound wave needed to initiate an auditory sensation.

Normal hearing is amazingly sensitive! We are fortunate that it is not more so, for if our hearing were any better we would hear the blood rushing through our veins and arteries and the air molecules striking our eardrums even in "still" air. As it is, any microscopic movement of the eardrum will cause an auditory sensation, since even the finest movements of the basilar membrane will arouse an auditory sensation. It has been estimated that when the basilar

140

membrane moves a distance equal to one per cent of the diameter of a hydrogen molecule, a tonal sensation will result.

The absolute threshold of hearing is represented in Figure 6.39. Intensity of sound is represented on the ordinate and its frequency is indicated on the abscissa. The lower curve shows the intensity level of the minimal sounds that can be detected for the different frequencies. A tone at any point below this curve would not be heard. If we were equally sensitive to all frequencies, the line representing the absolute threshold of hearing would be straight and parallel to the abscissa. All frequencies, however, are not equally audible. We are most sensitive to tones between 2,000 and 4,000 cycles per second. If it is to be heard, a tone of 500 cycles or 10,000 must exert more pressure on the eardrum than any tone between 2,000 and 4,000 cycles.

The curve of the absolute threshold of hearing should help you understand why hi-fi addicts play their sets loudly. A hi-fi

radio or record player is capable of reproducing sounds closely resembling the original. At a symphony or jazz concert you will hear sounds within the range of approximately 20 to 20,000 cycles, if your hearing is good, but an ordinary radio or record player cannot reproduce such a wide range of sounds, since it typically has a sound range between 70 to 7,500 cycles. In contrast, a good hi-fi in a fairly large room can reproduce sound waves between 40 and 17,000 cycles. But in order for you to hear tones extremely low or high in frequency, their intensity must be fairly high, and so you must play a hi-fi set rather loudly to enjoy its full reproduction power, unless you have automatic compensators.

The upper curve of Figure 6.39, which is approximately parallel to the abscissa, represents the threshold above which sounds are felt as well as heard. Low frequency tones above this level of intensity (approximately 130 db) produce vibratory pressures, while tones of high frequency produce an itchy, burning, pricking sensation, or some other form of sensory annoyance. It is fortunate we get these sensations because they serve as a warning signal. Although it is possible to hear sounds above the threshold of feeling, such intense stimulation can cause tissue damage in the auditory mechanism.

Unfortunately, many of our modern machines do generate noises above the threshold of feeling. Some jet planes produce noises up to 160 or 170 db. The catapults of aircraft carriers produce a noise of about 140 db when a plane is launched. These machine-generated noises can damage a man's ears, and it is necessary to try to reduce the intensity of these noises or at least to provide men who are exposed to them with some protective device.

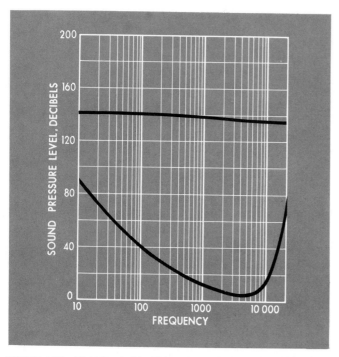

FIGURE 6.39 The Threshold of Hearing and the Threshold of Feeling.

Audibility as a Function of Age. Our auditory sensitivity changes as we grow older. Most of us can expect to suffer, with aging, a progressive hearing loss for tones of 500

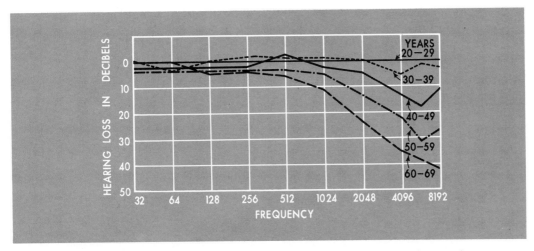

FIGURE 6.40 The Average Audiograms for Different Age Groups (After Bunch, 1929).

cycles and above. Figure 6.40 shows the mean audibility curves for different age groups. A tone of 4,096 cycles must be 20 db more intense if it is to be heard by the average 55-year-old than it would have to be to be heard by the average 25-year-old. However, you cannot estimate very accurately how great your own hearing loss will be as you grow older, for the hearing ability of individuals of the same age differs widely. Some suffer no loss in hearing as they grow older; others require a hearing aid before they reach 40. Men and women are affected differently: men tend to show greater losses for tones above 2,000 cycles, and women, for tones within the range of 500 to 2,000 cycles.

It has been estimated that over 10,000,000 Americans suffer various degrees of hearing loss. About half of them are sufficiently impaired to be called deaf. One type of deafness, called **nerve deafness,** is due to impairment of the auditory nerve as a result of injury or disease. Another type, **conduction deafness,** is due to failure in the transmission of sound waves to the cochlea and thence to the auditory nerve. One of the most common types of conduction deafness is due to a bonelike growth that immobilizes the stapes. If the stapes is un-

able to vibrate, then the sound waves cannot be transmitted from the eardrum through the ossicles to the cochlea. Patients suffering from the immobilization of their stapes can sometimes hear with the help of hearing aids. Sometimes their hearing loss can be eliminated by a relatively simple surgical operation in which the bone tissue that immobilizes the stapes is scraped off. Once the stapes is able to vibrate, normal hearing is restored.

Auditory Sensations

You are capable of making several kinds of discriminations when responding to visual stimuli. You can reliably judge the hue, brightness, and saturation of visual stimuli. Similarly you can reliably judge the **pitch, loudness,** and **timbre** of tonal stimuli.

Pitch. If you judge which of two tones is higher you are discriminating between them in terms of their pitch. Pitch, strictly speaking, is a psychological characteristic of sound waves and it is largely, but not exclusively, a function of the frequency of the vibrations producing the tone.

As the frequency of a tone increases, so does its pitch. But equal increments in frequency do not produce equal increments

142

in pitch. If they did Figure 6.41 would be a straight line. Instead Figure 6.41, which shows how pitch changes with frequency, indicates that pitch rises slowly as frequency increases from 20 cycles to about 1,000, but from then on pitch rises much more rapidly.

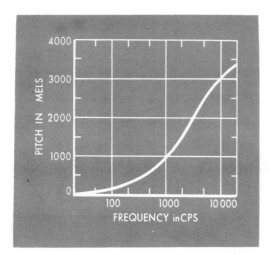

FIGURE 6.41 The Relationship Between the Psychological Measure of Pitch and the Physical Measure of Frequency. The unit of measure for pitch is the *mel* which is obtained by having human observers judge a series of tones in terms of their relative pitch (After Stevens & Volkmann, 1940, with permission of *The American Journal of Psychology*).

To some extent pitch is also dependent upon tonal intensity. As the intensity of a tone below 500 cycles is increased, its pitch becomes lower. The opposite holds for tones above 3,000 cycles, that is, pitch rises with increasing intensity. This relationship between pitch and intensity stated here holds only for pure tones, not for complex tones. This is most fortunate. If the intensity of a complex tone influenced its pitch, playing an instrument such as a trumpet would become extremely difficult for the musician. Pitch would change, depending upon whether he blew hard or gently. But trumpets emit complex tones. So when the trumpet player blows harder or softer, the loudness of his notes changes but their pitch stays the same. On the other hand, a soprano whose tones are purer may sound flat to the people in the balcony when she sings louder.

Loudness. A scale of loudness can be constructed in somewhat the same manner as a scale of pitch. Human subjects were asked to judge tones in terms of loudness and it is their responses that serve as the basis for the scale of loudness shown in Figure 6.42.

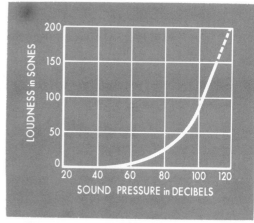

FIGURE 6.42 The Relationship Between the Psychological Measure of Loudness and the Physical Measure of Intensity. The unit of measure for loudness is the *sone* which is obtained by having human observers judge a series of tones in terms of their relative loudness (After Boring, Langfeld, & Weld, 1948).

You might expect loudness to increase directly in proportion to the amplitude of the sound wave, but this is not so. The gain in loudness is relatively small as intensity increases from 0 to 80 db. Above 80 db small increases in intensity produce large increases in loudness.

Like pitch, loudness is not exclusively a function of one physical dimension; it is also somewhat dependent on frequency. This relationship is demonstrated in Figure 6.39 on page 140. All the tones represented on the absolute threshold curve are equally loud—or perhaps we should say equally soft because all of them can barely be heard —but note that in order to be heard a tone of 100 cycles must be much more intense than a tone of 1,000 cycles. Figure 6.43 shows more fully the relationship between loudness and frequency. This figure shows a series of **equal-loudness contours** expressed in a measure of loudness known as a *sone*. These contours or curves represent all tones ranging from 100 to 10,000 cycles that appear equally loud. The zero sone curve is the same as the absolute threshold curve in Figure 6.39. Note that in all the contours tones of 10,000 cycles have to be more intense to equal in loudness tones of between 1,000 and 2,000 cycles.

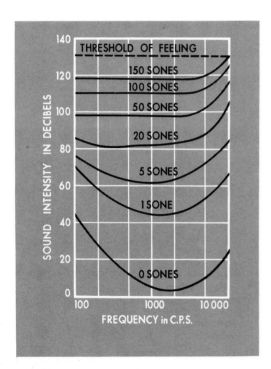

FIGURE 6.43 Equal Loudness Contours. Tones corresponding to the points along each curve are judged equally loud (After Boring, Langfeld, & Weld, 1948).

Timbre. Tones emitted by different musical instruments have certain unique characteristics. If you hear the same note on the musical scale played with equal loudness on a violin, a piano, and a clarinet, you can tell that they sound different. What is the physical feature of the sound that enables you to make this discrimination? It is its timbre, which depends upon the composition of the sound waves.

When a taut wire, such as a violin string, is plucked it emits several tones at the same time. The *fundamental tone* is produced by the wire vibrating as a whole. The wire also vibrates in sections—in halves, thirds, quarters, fifths, tenths, and so on, and each of these sectional vibrations produces a so-called *partial* tone known as an *overtone*. The fundamental tone and the various overtones differ both in pitch and loudness. Figure 6.33 on page 137 shows the various tones emitted by a piano string whose fundamental tone (C below middle C) has a frequency of 128 cycles. The first overtone, produced by the string vibrating in halves, has a frequency of 256 cycles. Naturally, because of its higher frequency the first overtone would have a higher pitch than the fundamental tone, but the intensity level, and consequently the loudness of the first overtone, is less than the fundamental tone. Note that in Figure 6.33 the intensity, and therefore the loudness, of successive overtones does not continuously decrease. The first overtone is the loudest but the fifth overtone is the next most prominent.

Different musical instruments emit different patterns of overtones. The clarinet, for example, differs from the oboe because in its low register (tones of low pitch) the third overtone is the most prominent, whereas the fifth overtone is the most prominent for the oboe. The saxophone has very weak and hazy overtones, possibly the reason it is a good jazz instrument and a poor symphonic one.

Moreover, individual instruments of the same type may differ in their pattern of overtones. Figure 6.44 shows the overtones of a particular violin playing a note of 400 cycles. Another violin may emit a somewhat different pattern, all its overtones

144

being less loud. Subtle differences of this sort are what make a Stradivarius sound superior to an ordinary fiddle.

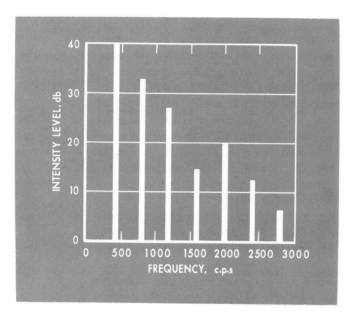

FIGURE 6.44 A Spectrum Analysis of a Tone From a Violin Playing a Note at 400 Cycles Per Second (After Chapanis, Garner, & Morgan, 1949).

The qualities we call timbre, then, come from the different patterns of overtones. It follows from this analysis that if it were possible to eliminate all overtones from the different instruments playing the same tone, it would be impossible to tell them apart. This is exactly what happens when an electronic sound filter is used to eliminate all the overtones produced by such different instruments as a French horn and violin. Except for fundamental pitch, women's and men's voices would also sound much the same if the overtones produced in speech were eliminated.

Theories of Hearing

If all differences in the intensity and frequency of pure tones which we can respond to are counted, we find that we can discriminate 340,000 tones. How this is possible is a question that has fascinated and challenged psychologists and physiologists for generations.

Auditory theory bears a striking resemblance to visual theory. A little is known about the functioning of the optic and auditory nerves. Much less is known about the visual and auditory centers of the cerebral cortex. As a result theories of seeing and hearing have been largely based upon what we know of the functioning of receptors. We remind you that the receptors for hearing are the hair cells of the organ of Corti, and that they are stimulated only when moved by vibrations of the basilar membrane.

Resonance Theory. Helmholtz (see page 40) was one of the first scientists who advanced a hypothesis as to how the basilar membrane vibrates. He assumed that it behaved as a series of resonators. When a sound wave sets up vibrations in an object, the object is said to resonate, in sympathy as it were. By striking the correct pitch, a strong-voiced singer can make a thin waterglass vibrate (or resonate) until it shatters.

Knowing that the width of the basilar membrane changes continuously from one end to the other, Helmholtz assumed that the fibers of the basilar membrane behave like a set of resonators tuned to different pitches from one end of the instrument to the other, like the strings of a harp or piano.

Helmholtz, it turns out, was in error in believing that the basilar membrane consisted of a series of separate resonators. We now know that when the tip of a needle is pressed perpendicularly against the surface of the basilar membrane of a partially anesthetized mammal, the resulting deformation is circular (Békésy, 1956). This is also true with man and some other vertebrates. Helmholtz' resonance theory postulated a basilar membrane divided into a series of almost independent strands, much like a harp. When a single string of a harp is depressed, however, the two adjacent strings remain unmoved. In short, Helmholtz' theory has been disproved by anatomical evidence.

Place Theory. Helmholtz' resonance theory, although incorrect, was on the right track. According to his hypothesis, sensations of pitch depended on which particular place in the basilar membrane was set in motion. Actually, when the ear is stimulated by tones, a wavelike motion is produced in the basilar membrane. The location of the maximal amplitude of vibration on the basilar membrane does differ for tones of different frequencies and it can serve as an important cue in pitch discrimination. Thus the place theory of hearing, historically an outgrowth of Helmholtz' resonance theory, holds that a particular sensation of pitch is determined by what part of the basilar membrane is maximally stimulated at the time.

It has been demonstrated by electronic techniques that the portion of the basilar membrane near the base of the cochlea responds maximally to sounds of high pitch, and the portion of the basilar membrane near the apex of the cochlea, to tones of low pitch. There is additional support for this from the results of some experiments with animals. Guinea pigs were experimentally exposed to high frequency tones of great intensity. Post-mortem examination revealed that the portion of basilar membrane near the base of the cochlea had been destroyed.

The mechanisms responsible for sensations differing in loudness or in timbre have not been completely worked out in the place theory. Loudness is apparently correlated with the total amount of the basilar membrane that vibrates from tonal stimulation. Two tones of the same frequency, but different in amplitude, would maximally stimulate the same place in the basilar membrane, but the more intense tone would activate the entire membrane more strongly.

Differences in timbre are assumed to arise from different patterns of activation occurring over the entire basilar membrane. When two or more tonal frequencies (fundamental tones and overtones) reach the basilar membrane simultaneously, different areas of the membrane will vibrate maximally. The specific pattern of vibration, according to the place theory, will determine the timbre that is heard.

Frequency Theory. A rival theory that has been advanced to explain the facts of hearing is known as the frequency theory. Unlike the place theory, which stresses the role of the basilar membrane in determining what we hear, the frequency theory emphasizes the contributions of the neural impulses in the auditory nerve.

The frequency theory conceives of the ear as operating in much the same way as a telephone. When you speak into the mouthpiece of your telephone the vibration of your voice sets the diaphragm vibrating with the same frequencies that occur in your speech. These vibrations are converted into electrical impulses and transmitted at the same frequencies as the original sound. Specifically, then, according to the frequency theory, when a tone of 1,000 cycles per second strikes the ear, neural impulses at the frequency of 1,000 per second are set up in the auditory nerve, which transmits them to the brain. Thus the frequency theory holds that the pitch of an auditory sensation is determined by the frequency at which neural impulses reach the auditory area of the brain.

The frequency theory runs into difficulties in explaining the upper levels of pitch. We know that the maximum number of impulses that a single nerve fiber can transmit in one second is only about 1,000. We can, however, hear tones of almost 20,000 cycles. How can the frequency theory explain this? It cannot. But it can, with the volley principle, explain reception of tonal stimulation as high as 5,000 cycles.

According to the volley principle, the nerve fibers within the auditory nerve operate in squads. An analogy will help to make clear what this means. You may have seen smart children or college students use the volley principle in a large-scale snowball fight. By dividing their forces into several squads they can deliver a steady bombardment at a faster rate than unorganized individuals can. Four squads, synchronized so that each fires every fourth second, could throw a barrage of snowballs *every* second. While one squad is grabbing snow, the second is shaping snowballs, the third is aiming, and the fourth throwing. One second later each squad is at the next stage in the sequence. In this way the frequency theory, plus the hypothesis of nerve fibers operating in squads on the additional volley principle, might explain neural transmission at rates beyond the capability of any single nerve fiber.

The Place-Frequency Theory. We must conclude, however, that as formulated today neither the place nor the frequency theory can explain all the facts of pitch discrimination. Tones of very low frequencies appear to stimulate extensive regions of the basilar membrane maximally, rather than any single restricted region, as the place theory maintains. The frequency theory cannot explain sensitivity to tones above 5,000 cycles. Since the assumptions of both theories are not incompatible, it has been suggested that by combining the principal features of each theory a better theory would result. Such a theory is known as the place-frequency theory. It assumes that our auditory sensitivity is both a function of the place on the basilar membrane which is maximally stimulated and the frequency of neural impulses in the auditory nerve. Beyond this there is no complete agreement about the details of such a combined theory. It has been suggested that the place mechanism plays a role in the reception of tones above 400 cycles, while the frequency mechanism, involving the volley principle, operates with tones lower than 5,000 cycles. Both mechanisms operate in a complementary manner within the range 400 to 5,000 cycles. It is likely, however, that theories concerning what happens near the boundaries between the operation of the place and frequency mechanisms will be appreciably modified as more knowledge is obtained. It is also extremely likely that the theoretical interpretation of auditory sensitivity will be markedly altered when the functioning of the auditory cortex is more clearly understood.

SOME CONCLUDING REMARKS ON SENSORY PSYCHOLOGY

The facts and theories of hearing appear to be quite similar in form to those of vision. The facts in both cases relate kinds of stimulation to our different forms of sensitivity, while the theories which are advanced to explain these facts consist of hypotheses concerning the physiological mechanisms responsible for the relationship between stimuli and responses.

This pattern of knowledge involving stimulation and response and the underlying physiological mechanism has been worked out in most detail for the senses of vision and audition. The pattern is the same, however, for all of sensory psychology.

For example, in studying sensations of taste the first problem is to discover the stimuli to which we are sensitive. It appears that there are four major dimensions of taste: salt, sweet, sour, and bitter. Each of these sensations of taste is produced by a different group of chemicals. The receptors for taste are special cells grouped together in taste buds. They are distributed mainly on the upper surface of the tongue, but are also found on the underside of the tongue as well as on the palate, the cheeks, and the floor of the mouth. Some of these taste buds are more sensitive to one kind of chemical stimulation than to others. For example, the tip of the tongue is particularly sensitive to the complex organic compounds, of which the sugars are a main example. We cannot proceed much further in the explanation of taste; theories of the physiological processes involved in producing different tastes are decidedly conjectural.

It should be kept in mind that although sensory psychology is of interest in its own right, it also has relevance to all behavior. Since it deals with an organism's capacity to respond to his internal and external environments it is, in a certain sense, the starting point of much of his behavior. This will become apparent as we proceed in the next chapter.

SUMMARY

An organism is sensitive to a stimulus when he can respond to it, that is, when he can discriminate it from other stimuli. From the viewpoint of the psychology of sensation the organism operates as a measuring instrument. Sensory psychologists are interested in both psychophysical, $R = f(S)$, and psychophysiological, $R = f(O)$, laws.

Visual sensations are usually, although not necessarily, initiated by light waves. Under optimal conditions humans are sensitive to light waves that vary in length from approximately 320 to 1,000 millimicrons. Most of the light that reaches our eyes is composed of many different wave lengths; only in the laboratory are we stimulated by a narrow band of wave lengths (spectrally homogeneous light). In addition to their frequency and composition, light waves vary in intensity.

The eye resembles a camera in that it has an adjustable diaphragm (iris), a lens through which light passes, and a light-sensitive surface (retina), on which an image can be focused. Imbedded in the retina are two kinds of receptors, rods and cones. They vary in sensitivity and in the way they are distributed in the retina.

Visibility, the ability to sense a light, is not only influenced by the intensity of light, but it is also a function of the wave length of the light, the part of the retina that is being stimulated, and the degree of dark adaptation of the eye. Visual acuity, the ability to sense fine detail, is a function of the retinal angle of stimulation, light intensity, distance between the eye and the stimulus, and the contrast between the stimulus and its background.

Human observers can order light in terms of brightness. Although brightness is primarily related to light intensity, it is also influenced by the wave length of the visual stimulus and its context.

Color vision is mediated by the cone receptors in the retina. Colors can be discriminated in terms of their hue, brightness, and saturation. The major physical correlates of these three sensations are respectively, wave length, light intensity, and wave composition.

Some people's ability to discriminate among colors is poorer than others. Completely color-blind individuals are unable to sense any colors; the visible spectrum is to them a series of grays. Some individuals have difficulty only in discriminating between two colors, most commonly between red and green. These people are said to be red-green blind, and see both colors as poorly saturated yellow or brown. Other individuals are merely color-weak; their ability to discriminate among certain colors is poorer than the average.

The duplexity theory of vision, which describes the functioning and distribution of rods and cones, explains many facts of vision, but not those of color discrimination. The Young-Helmholtz theory and the Hurvich-Jameson reformulation of the Hering theory each attempt to explain color vision by postulating that there are three different kinds of cones, each of which functions in a characteristic way.

The structure of our knowledge about hearing resembles in many ways our knowledge about seeing. The physical stimuli responsible for most of our auditory sensations are sound waves. Sound waves vary in terms of three characteristics: frequency, intensity, and wave-form. The receptors of hearing are the organ of Corti, tiny hair cells attached to the basilar membrane in the cochlea. The organ of Corti is connected to nerve cells which join together to form the auditory nerve which travels to the brain.

Audibility, the ability to sense sound, is a function of the intensity and frequency of sound waves and the age of the observer.

The sensation of pitch is primarily, although not exclusively, related to frequency. Similarly loudness is mainly related to sound intensity. Timbre, the characteristic sensation produced by complex tones, is a function of the composition of the sound wave.

Auditory theory, for the most part, is concerned with the functioning of the organ of Corti. The place theory postulates that pitch depends on the particular place in the basilar membrane which is set in motion. The frequency theory assumes that pitch is a function of the frequency at which neural impulses reach the brain. Since neither the place nor frequency theory can explain all the facts of pitch discrimination, they have been combined into a place-frequency formulation. This theory assumes that the place mechanism operates with tones above 400 cycles, while the frequency mechanism, involving a volley principle, acts with tones below 5,000 cycles. Both mechanisms function in the range between 400 and 5,000 cycles.

SUGGESTIONS FOR FURTHER READING

BÉKÉSY, G. VON. *Experiments in hearing.* New York: McGraw-Hill, 1960.

A report by the recipient of the Nobel prize in 1961 of his experiments on the physiological basis of hearing.

CHAPANIS, A., GARNER, W. R., & MORGAN, C. T. *Applied experimental psychology.* New York: Wiley, 1949.

A textbook that contains chapters on vision and hearing and illustrates how knowledge about these senses has been applied to practical problems.

GELDARD, F. A. *The human senses.* New York: Wiley, 1953.

An informative and well-written introduction to the psychology of vision, hearing, and other senses.

STEVENS, S. S. (Ed.) *Handbook of experimental psychology.* New York: Wiley, 1951.

An authoritative reference book containing several chapters written by experts on different topics in the field of sensation.

WOODWORTH, R. S., & SCHLOSBERG, H. *Experimental psychology.* (Rev. ed.) New York: Holt, Rinehart, & Winston, 1954.

A standard text in psychology that contains several chapters on various senses.

CONDITIONING—THE SIMPLEST FORM OF LEARNING

7

THE IMPORTANCE OF LEARNING

Most of you are aware that your ability to learn new modes of behavior has exerted a profound influence on your lives. You have learned a language that enables you to communicate with others. You have acquired a large number of skills, as diverse as tying your shoelaces and driving a car. You have learned some sports: to ski, to swim, to play ping-pong, or tennis. You have somehow learned to like or dislike certain novels, TV comedians, or styles of clothing. You have learned how to study and prepare for examinations, to love certain people and, perhaps, to hate others. You have learned that certain kinds of behavior are good, others bad. And last, you have learned, for the most part, your particular style of being tense or relaxed, happy or unhappy.

The enormous influence learning has had on your everyday living would be demonstrated dramatically if it were possible to eliminate miraculously right now all that you have ever learned. What would happen to you in such an event? You could not continue to read. Indeed, you would not even be able to act like a decently civilized person. You would be helpless. Your survival, like a newborn's, would depend on the care of others. The results of learning, however, are not always useful. We just reminded you that people can learn to be unhappy. This is one reason why our society is confronted with a serious mental health problem. That people learn to hate those with a different culture or ancestry is one reason the goal of international harmony remains so remote. In our own country, grave social problems have arisen because members of one religious or racial group have learned negative attitudes toward members of other groups.

You can also learn to do things the wrong way. For example, you may have learned to hold your tennis racket incorrectly, so that on your backhand the ball hits the face of the racket at an angle and, more often than not, goes into the net or out of the court. Or you may have learned to breathe the wrong way while swimming, so that your supply of oxygen is never sufficient to allow you to swim smoothly for a long period of time. Or you may have learned such poor reading habits that you find it difficult to understand any but the simplest ideas in your textbooks.

So you see the psychology of learning plays a central role in human behavior. What we learn can help us—or hinder us—in adjusting to the world we live in.

HOW THE PSYCHOLOGY OF LEARNING IS STUDIED

Since learning is crucially important and ubiquitous, it is altogether appropriate that it has been studied in many different ways. One group of learning experts has investigated the acquisition of specific skills. Educators have tested the effectiveness of different methods of teaching reading, writing, arithmetic, and other subjects. Our armed services are constantly trying to improve their methods of training men and women to perform jobs ranging from baking bread to flying jets. Sports instructors are always seeking the most effective training methods. Each year, thousands of books are published offering bits of advice supposed to chop strokes off your golf score or accelerate your tennis serve. Probably less well known are the training techniques developed by athletic coaches who are largely responsible for the spectacular records made in track and swimming in recent decades. Dog trainers, whether they train trick dogs, show dogs, or hunting dogs, have

always shown a keen interest in the learning process. The dramatic performances of their dogs testify to the effectiveness of their training methods.

Some psychologists have investigated the psychology of learning from an entirely different perspective. Unlike those who are interested primarily in discovering how specific skills, such as reading or flying planes, are acquired, they are interested in the learning process itself and, particularly, in discovering its basic principles.

Such learning psychologists, as they are called because of their interest in the learning process in general, must always study learning in some specific situation, for it cannot be studied in a vacuum. What, then, is the best learning situation to use if they wish to investigate the basic laws of learning? Learning to fly a plane? Learning to read? Learning mathematics? After having given this question much thought, many learning psychologists have come up with the same answer: Let us study learning in its simplest form! The rationale of this answer is easy to grasp. It rests mainly on the belief that certain principles of learning operate in all learning situations. Studying such complex acts as learning to fly a jet or learning to read will force them to deal with problems unique to these skills, and not fundamental to *all learning situations.* Why should they complicate the study of learning by dealing at the outset with unnecessarily complex situations when they might begin nearer the bare essentials of learning itself?

Studying a phenomenon in its simplest form is a research strategy adopted in all science. It has frequently paid off handsomely. Much of our understanding of the movements of celestial bodies stems from observations of the movement of pendulums and of balls rolling down inclined planes. What we know of the laws of human heredity is based, in part, on studies of simple examples of genetic determination in plants and fruit flies. And conditioning in psychology, as you will see, has provided us with penetrating insights into the psychology of learning.

We shall, then, begin with **conditioning,** the simplest form of learning. And what is learning? Defined generally, **learning** *is a change in behavior resulting from practice.* Hence *conditioning, the simplest form of learning, deals with the formation, strengthening, and weakening of S-R associations resulting from practice.*

It is likely that these two rather abstract definitions do not "mesh" for you. You may ask, How can conditioning, a simple form of learning, require what seems the more complex definition? The relationship between these two definitions, as well as their more concrete meanings, will become clear after you have learned more about each of them.

CLASSICAL CONDITIONING

At the turn of the twentieth century Ivan Pavlov (1849-1936), a Russian physiologist, reported the results of experiments on conditioning, which were to change the course of psychology. The experimental method invented by Pavlov is known as **classical conditioning.** To understand both conditioning and learning you must have an intimate acquaintance with the experimental procedures used in classical conditioning.

Figure 7.1 illustrates the experimental situation designed by Pavlov. A hungry dog is led into a soundproof room and placed on a table top in a comfortable harness and frame which prevents him from sitting down and making other gross movements. In the dog's cheek a small opening has been made through which a tube is inserted and attached to one of his salivary glands. When the dog salivates the saliva from this gland flows through the tube and is collected in a graduated glass cylinder. The

experimenter can then tell whether the dog has salivated and, if so, how much.

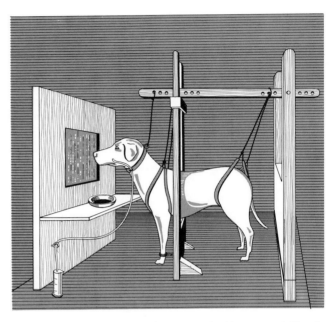

FIGURE 7.1 The Position of the Dog in the Experimental Situation Used to Investigate Conditioning.

Before the conditioning procedure is begun some preliminary testing is necessary. First a stimulus, such as a tone, is sounded. Typically the dog does not salivate to it. When some powdered food which he is accustomed to is moved within his sight, however, the dog begins to salivate. Psychologists represent these events in the following "shorthand" manner:

$$S_{tone}$$
$$S_{food} \underline{\hspace{5cm}} R_{salivation}$$

The tone does not have the tendency to evoke salivation but the food does. The stimulus *tone* is therefore not connected to the response, *salivation,* whereas the stimulus *food* is.

Now that these preliminary tests have been carried out, the main portion of the classical conditioning procedure can begin.

The tone is sounded and a fraction of a second later food is given the dog. If the paired presentations of the tone and the food are repeated from 10 to 20 times, the presentation of the *tone alone* will evoke a salivary response. The tone, which initially lacked the power to evoke the salivary response, has now, because it has been paired with the food, acquired the tendency to evoke the salivary response. A broken line between the tone and the salivary response is added to the diagram to represent the *new association* that has been formed.

The salivary response to food is called the **unconditioned response** because it occurred before the conditioning procedure

began. The food then is known as the **unconditioned stimulus.** Since the tone becomes conditioned to the salivary response it is known as the **conditioned stimulus.** When the salivary response is evoked by the conditioned stimulus (tone) it becomes a **conditioned response.** Each paired presentation of the conditioned and unconditioned stimulus is called a **trial.** Thus a trial is a unitary exposure to the stimulus situation beginning when tone and food are presented and ending when these stimuli are removed.

The period during which the dog learns the new association between the conditioned stimulus and conditioned response is known as the **acquisition stage** of classical conditioning. The course of the acquisition of a conditioned response is graphically represented in Figure 7.2. Note that the *amount* (sometimes referred to as **amplitude**) of salivation gradually increases with successive combined presentations of the conditioned and unconditioned stimuli until a limit is reached.

The amount is not the only aspect of the conditioned response that is undergoing change during the acquisition stage of conditioning. The **latency** of the conditioned response is decreasing. Latency of a conditioned response refers to the time elapsing between the beginning of the tone and the beginning of the salivary response. At first the latency of the conditioned response is about 18 seconds, but later on the dog begins to salivate one or two seconds after the tone has been sounded. Figure 7.3 shows a typical conditioning curve in which the dependent variable (see page 19) is the latency of the conditioned response. When latency is used as a measure of conditioning the curve of conditioning takes a downward course.

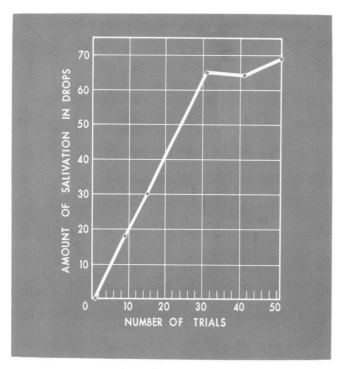

FIGURE 7.2 The Acquisition Stage of a Classical Conditioned Response. The graph shows changes in amplitude (amount) of conditioned response as a function of the number of paired presentations of conditioned and unconditioned stimuli (After data in Anrep, 1920).

Three Essential Features of Classical Conditioning. We can now list the three essential features of the classical conditioning procedure (Hilgard & Marquis, 1940).

1. An unconditioned stimulus that evokes an unconditioned response.
2. A conditioned stimulus that does not initially evoke the unconditioned response.
3. Paired presentations of the conditioned and unconditioned stimuli.

Why is each of these features essential? (1) If the unconditioned stimulus did not evoke the unconditioned response, the conditioned stimulus would not have the opportunity to become associated with the unconditioned response. (2) If the conditioned stimulus initially evoked the unconditioned response, there would be no way of knowing whether conditioning took place. (3) Conditioning depends upon the close temporal pairing of the conditioned stimulus and the unconditioned stimulus. If these two stimuli are presented in an unrelated and haphazard manner, so that the conditioned stimulus is not closely followed by the unconditioned stimulus, conditioning will not take place.

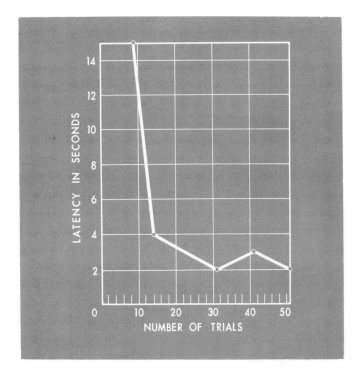

FIGURE 7.3 The Acquisition Stage of a Classical Conditioned Response. The graph shows changes in the latency of the conditioned response as a function of the number of paired presentations of the conditioned and unconditioned stimuli (After data in Anrep, 1920).

Examples of Classical Conditioning

Classical conditioning can occur in a variety of situations with a variety of subjects and conditioned stimuli. One of the most thoroughly investigated conditioning procedures in America uses the eyelid response, the reflex closing of the lid (unconditioned response) when a puff of air (unconditioned stimulus) is blown into the subject's eye. A *weak* light is typically used as a conditioned stimulus in this procedure. The **eyelid conditioning** procedure has been used successfully with dogs, monkeys, and college students, and interesting to note, the course of conditioning is quite similar with all three kinds of subjects. Figure 7.4 has three sample records obtained at different stages of conditioning. The top record represents the first trial, the second record shows the conditioned response beginning

to take effect, and the third record shows a conditioned response when it has become well established.

Notice that each record consists of four horizontal lines, the top line indicating the passing of time. The distance between each vertical cross bar on the time line represents a time interval of .05 seconds. The white portion of the next line indicates that the light (conditioned stimulus) is on. The third line represents the activity of the eyelid. An upward excursion indicates that it is closing. The lowest line records the occurrence of the air puff (unconditioned stimulus). In the top record the eyelid responds following the onset of the air puff (unconditioned stimulus). Consequently it is an unconditioned response. In the next record there are two distinct eyelid responses. The first and smaller one begins

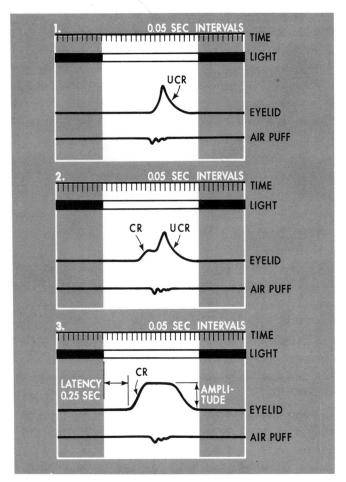

FIGURE 7.4 Sample Records Obtained at Three Stages of Eyelid Conditioning (Suggested by Hilgard, 1936).

It is common practice in eyelid conditioning to measure the acquisition of the conditioned response in terms of the percentage of conditioned responses for successive blocks of trials. Figure 7.5 shows such a graph. Only 20 per cent of the first ten trials produced conditioned responses. This percentage gradually increased until at the sixth block of trials (trials 51-60) almost 90 per cent of the trials produced conditioned responses.

It will no doubt surprise you to discover how wide a variety of stimuli and responses can be used in establishing conditioned responses. Russian psychologists, who are exceptionally well trained in surgical and physiological techniques, have recently reported (Razran, 1961) many dramatic examples of conditioning. They have developed techniques in which pressure or heat as the conditioned stimulus can be delivered directly to the internal walls of such organs as the intestine, uterus, and stomach. They have conditioned these stimuli, and others, to such responses as breathing rates, stomach contractions, and the urge to urinate.

One such study made use of three hospital patients with urinary bladder fistulas through which liquids could be poured directly into their bladders. The unconditioned response was the patient's expression of an urge to urinate. The unconditioned stimulus for this response was pressure in the bladder, which could be controlled by the experimenter who poured in varying amounts of liquid. Dials placed conspicuously in front of the patient served as conditioned stimuli. During training these dials indicated the actual bladder pressure. The patients' urges to urinate, as was expected, were highly correlated with the amount of pressure. Later on, however, the dials were disconnected and their readings were controlled by the experimenter independently of the actual bladder pressure. Conditioning to these sham readings occurred in all cases. The patients began to

to occur after the onset of the light (conditioned stimulus) but before the occurrence of the air puff. It is therefore a conditioned response. The second, larger eyelid response is an unconditioned response because it follows the air puff. In the lowest record the conditioned response and unconditioned response merge together into one large response. That portion of the eyelid response which anticipates the air puff can be considered the conditioned response. Comparing the conditioned response of the second and third record, you will note that the conditioned response of the third record has a shorter latency and a greater amplitude.

154

report intense urination urges when the dial readings were high, even though very little or no liquid had been poured into the bladder. On the other hand, low or zero readings failed to produce the urinary urge, even when the inflow of liquids was considerably greater than the amount which under normal conditions produced the need to urinate.

Another dramatic experiment in conditioning with human subjects, done in the United States, involved constriction of the blood vessels (*vasoconstriction*) in the hands (Menzies, 1937). Unconditioned vasoconstriction can be produced either by electric shock or by submerging a subject's hand in ice water. That is, both shock and ice water can serve as an unconditioned stimulus to evoke the response of vasoconstriction. When a buzzer immediately preceded either of these unconditioned stimuli in the experiment, the buzzer, after a series of paired presentations, was able to produce vasoconstriction.

An interesting variation of the conditioning of a vasomotor response consists of using a spoken nonsense syllable (see page 43) instead of a buzzer as the conditioned stimulus (Roessler & Brogden, 1943). The procedure involving the use of a syllable as a conditioned stimulus can be carried a step further. Instead of having the subject say the syllable (conditioned stimulus) out loud, he may be instructed merely to "think" the syllable. Conditioning will again be successfully executed.

These examples of conditioning have

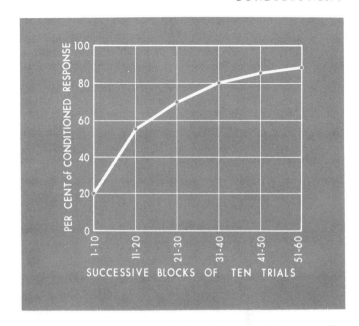

FIGURE 7.5 The Acquisition of a Conditioned Eyelid Response. The graph shows changes in the percentage of conditioned responses in successive blocks of ten trials (After *Principles of General Psychology* by Gregory A. Kimble, Copyright 1956, The Ronald Press Co.)

important theoretical implications. They demonstrate that an organism's response (e.g., saying or thinking a word) can serve

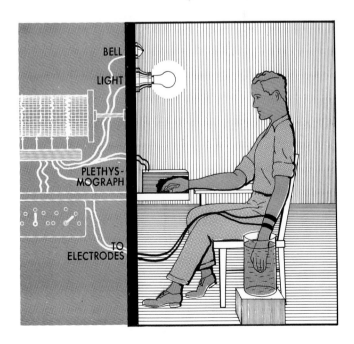

FIGURE 7.6 Schematic Representation of Apparatus Used to Investigate the Conditioning of the Vasoconstriction Response. Electrodes are attached to the subject's left wrist (or his left hand is plunged into cold water) while his right hand is in an air plethysmograph. This instrument measures the changes in the volume of the hand caused by changes in the amount of blood. The buzzer serves as the conditioned stimulus. Onset and termination of the conditioned and unconditioned stimuli, as well as the recording of the subject's responses, are controlled by the equipment behind the screen.

155

as a conditioned stimulus. The organism can thus generate his own stimulus to serve as a cue for his own subsequent behavior. Psychologists refer to such self-evoked stimuli as **response-produced cues.** They play an extremely important role in complex forms of behavior, as you will discover later.

This demonstration of how a vasomotor response may be conditioned also has implications for everyday living. Take the example of the child who has been beaten by the school bully. Since pain stimulation produces vasoconstriction, the school bully becomes for the child a conditioned stimulus to evoke vasoconstriction—which is the cause of paling, or "turning white as a sheet," in an extreme instance. According to what you have just learned about the conditioning of vasoconstriction responses, you would expect the victim to become pale at the sound of the bully's name or even at the thought of him, as indeed he does.

Blushing behavior can be analyzed in much the same way. Paling is due to vasoconstriction, blushing to vasodilation. Both are vasomoter responses controlled by the autonomic nervous system. Individuals differ greatly in their vasomotor responses in social situations. Some people become pale or blush intensely and frequently, others pale or blush rarely. Presumably in their past histories they have had differing exposure to the unconditioned stimuli that evoke vasomotor responses and to the stimuli that condition these responses.

Extinction of a Conditioned Response

Conditioning does not produce a permanent, unmodifiable change in behavior. A conditioned response can be weakened or gradually eliminated by a process known as **experimental extinction.** Experimental extinction involves the presentation of the conditioned stimulus alone, without the unconditioned stimulus. Using an animal in which a conditioned salivary response to a tone had been well established, Pavlov repeatedly presented the tone alone. It was observed that the salivary response gradually decreased in amount and increased in latency, until finally the animal no longer salivated to the sound of the tone. The conditioned salivary response had been experimentally extinguished. All classical conditioned responses can be experimentally extinguished by the experimenter simply failing to follow a conditioned stimulus with its unconditioned stimulus for a series of trials. A trial during experimental extinction differs from a trial during acquisition in that only the conditioned stimulus is presented.

THE PRINCIPLE OF REINFORCEMENT

Why does an organism acquire a conditioned response? Why does the conditioned response disappear when the unconditioned stimulus is repeatedly withheld? To answer these questions psychologists direct our attention to the theoretical principle which they call **reinforcement.** The principle is intended to be sufficiently broad to summarize a host of facts in the field of conditioning.

The principle of reinforcement is invoked to explain the fact that certain events are capable of strengthening the tendency of a conditioned stimulus to evoke a conditioned response. The absence of these events (i.e., the absence of reinforcement) weakens the tendency of the conditioned stimulus to evoke a conditioned response. From what you have just learned about classical conditioning, you have probably guessed what event controls the reinforcement process. Reinforcement must, in some way, depend upon the unconditioned stimulus. The conditioned response is acquired when the unconditioned stimulus is operative; it tends to be extinguished when the unconditioned stimulus is absent. The unconditioned stimulus, therefore, is said to serve as a reinforcer in classical conditioning—it reinforces or strengthens the tendency for a conditioned stimulus to evoke a conditioned response.

Positive and Negative Reinforcers

It is helpful to distinguish between two types of reinforcers. A **positive reinforcer,** such as food, strengthens an association between a stimulus and response by virtue of its presentation. A **negative reinforcer,** such as a puff of air or an electric shock, strengthens an association by its termination.

What is reinforcing about a reinforcer, whether positive or negative? Otherwise stated, Why is the presence of food or the termination of the air puff necessary to produce conditioning of the kind we have been talking about? This is a straightforward question. Unfortunately, psychology at the present time is unable to give a straightforward reply.

Some psychologists believe that the reinforcing properties of positive and negative reinforcers stem from their functioning as rewards. Others disagree, believing that the primary function of reinforcers is to provide an organism with information about its environment. Still others believe that the reinforcing quality of the unconditioned stimulus in classical conditioning stems from its ability to evoke the unconditioned response. To complicate the picture still more, there are those psychologists who believe reinforcers operate in one way in classical conditioning but in another way in other learning situations. And there are still other psychologists who feel that a good deal more information is needed before this question can be answered.

This controversy over a theoretical issue in psychology should not disturb you. There is comparable controversy over the-oretical questions in physics and other sciences. The important point for you to understand is that behavior can be modified by the experimental operations that psychologists conveniently label *reinforcing* or *nonreinforcing.* A conditioned response can be acquired or extinguished by presenting or withholding the unconditioned stimulus. The facts themselves are not in controversy.

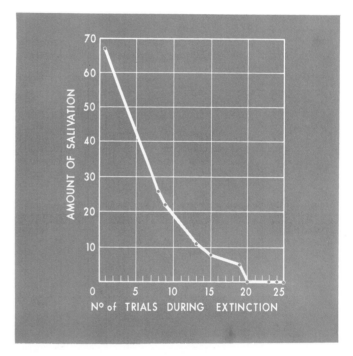

FIGURE 7.7 The Experimental Extinction of a Classical Conditioned Response. The graph shows changes in the amount of the conditioned salivary response as a function of successive presentations of the conditioned stimulus *without* the unconditioned stimulus (After data in Anrep, 1920).

That psychologists do not fully understand the reinforcing process does not prevent them from using what knowledge they do have to control and predict behavior. An analogy may be helpful here. It is doubtful whether you *fully understand* all the minute details of how pressing the accelerator increases the speed of a car or depressing

158 the brake pedal stops the car. Yet this does not prevent you from using the accelerator or brake pedal effectively.

That we are able to use in a straightforward, practical way what we now know about conditioning techniques in no way stops us from trying to achieve a more penetrating theoretical understanding of the reinforcing process. In the future someone will surely formulate a theory of learning capable of providing a fully acceptable explanation of the reinforcing properties of reinforcers.

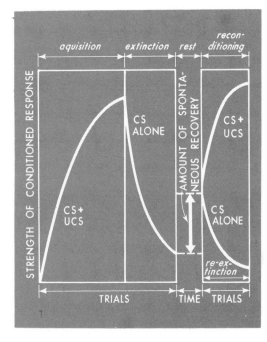

FIGURE 7.8 Changes in the Strength of a Conditioned Response During Various Experimental Conditions. At the left is depicted the acquisition stage when the conditioned and unconditioned stimuli are both presented. During extinction the conditioned stimulus is presented alone. After a rest interval the conditioned response spontaneously recovers some of its strength. In the last panel on the right, changes in the conditioned response are shown if the conditioned and unconditioned stimuli are once again paired (reconditioning) or if the conditioned stimulus is presented alone (re-extinction) (After *Principles of General Psychology* by Gregory A. Kimble, Copyright 1956, The Ronald Press Co.).

BASIC PHENOMENA IN CLASSICAL CONDITIONING

Spontaneous Recovery

Pavlov (1927) discovered that the effects of experimental extinction are only temporary. He found that although he had apparently extinguished a dog's salivary response to a conditioned stimulus, after a half-hour rest period the dog would once again salivate to the conditioned stimulus. Pavlov aptly described this phenomenon as **spontaneous recovery.**

However, spontaneous recovery is not complete. This is shown in Figure 7.8. The strength of the response, although greater after the rest interval than before it, is appreciably less than it was before experimental extinction was initiated. The effects of experimental extinction in weakening the strength of the association cannot be completely erased by rest alone; only additional reinforcements can bring the association back to its former strength.

You will wonder whether it is ever possible to extinguish a conditioned response permanently and completely. After spontaneous recovery has occurred, the conditioned response can be extinguished again by further unreinforced conditioned stimulation. After several such re-extinction sessions, interspersed with rest intervals, the conditioned response will disappear completely.

Spontaneous recovery has an important practical implication. We like to think that when we are trying to correct some bad habit, such as slicing a golf ball or consistently typing *hte* for *the*, we have succeeded when the habit fails to appear a few times. Unfortunately, this is not so. A response that is eliminated once can recur, as the phenomenon of spontaneous recovery shows.

Stimulus Generalization

Suppose that an animal has been conditioned to salivate to a tone of 1,000 cycles. What will happen if a tone of 900 cycles is substituted for the tone of 1,000 cycles? Will the animal salivate? Yes, but the amount of salivation will be smaller. This is an example of the phenomenon known as **stimulus generalization.** In stimulus generalization conditioning occurs to a class of stimuli rather than to one specific conditioned stimulus. Many experiments have demonstrated the phenomenon, but perhaps the best known (Hovland, 1937a) involved the human **galvanic skin response** (abbreviated to GSR). The GSR is a change in electric resistance of the skin caused by the activity of the sweat glands. The GSR can easily be evoked by an electric shock of moderate intensity.

In this experiment a shock served as an unconditioned stimulus, and a pure tone of a specific frequency was the conditioned stimulus. After the GSR was conditioned, the amplitude of the conditioned response to each of a series of tones, differing in frequencies (pitch) from the original conditioned stimulus was measured. Figure 7.9 shows the results of this experiment. Tone 1 was the tone used during the acquisition trials (i.e., the conditioned stimulus). The remaining tones differed from Tone 1 in frequency, Tone 2 being the most similar and Tone 4 most dissimilar.

The results of this experiment, represented in Figure 7.9, illustrate an important psychological law: the greater the similarity between stimuli, the greater the degree of generalization. Otherwise stated, the more similar a stimulus is to the conditioned stimulus, the greater will be the response it evokes; the less similar, the smaller the response.

A curve of generalization does not always have the same shape as the one illustrated in Figure 7.9, but may vary from experiment to experiment. Sometimes the sides of a curve of generalization are straight, sometimes convex. In general, however, the curve of generalization descends on both sides from the point representing a characteristic such as frequency or intensity of the original conditioned stimulus. Sometimes there is stimulus generalization over a wide range of stimulus differences, at other times over only a restricted range. Figure 7.10 shows a hypothetical example in which an organism is responding to a generalized stimulus quite unlike the original stimulus. Figure 7.11 shows an actual case in which the difference between the two stimuli, although still great, is somewhat less than that represented in Figure 7.10.

The conclusions that can be drawn from these experimental studies of generalization are first, that when conditioning occurs it is not to a single, precise stimulus but to a class of stimuli, and second, that the strength of the response (its amplitude) evoked by a generalized stimulus will depend on how similar it is to the conditioned stimulus.

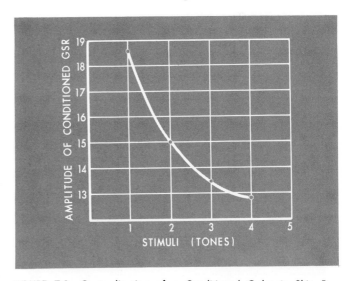

FIGURE 7.9 Generalization of a Conditioned Galvanic Skin Response (GSR). Tone 1 represents the conditioned stimulus while Tones 2, 3, and 4 are tones of decreasing similarity to Tone 1 (After Hovland, 1937b).

FIGURE 7.10 A Hypothetical Example of an Organism Responding to a Generalized Stimulus (Drawing by Whitney Darrow, Jr., © 1953, The New Yorker Magazine, Inc.).

Experimental extinction can have an influence on stimulus generalization. In an experimental situation similar to the one just described, a GSR was established to each of four tones of different intensities (Hovland, 1937b). The amplitude of the conditioned GSR was approximately the same for all stimuli. Then the conditioned response to the tone with the highest frequency was extinguished. Generalization of extinction effects was measured by the amount of reduction of the conditioned response to the other frequencies. Figure 7.12 shows the results of the experiment. The upper broken line represents the amplitude of the conditioned GSR before extinction trials were initiated for the tone with the highest frequency (Tone 4). The lower solid line shows the conditioned responses after extinction to Tone 4 was completed. The results indicate that the generalization of extinction effects is related to stimulus similarity. The greatest amount of generalization occurs between stimuli that are most similar.

We can thus conclude that experimental extinction occurs to a class of stimuli just as experimental conditioning does. When the tendency of a conditioned stimulus to evoke a response is weakened, the tendency for similar stimuli to elicit the same response is also weakened. The amount of weakening will depend on the similarity between the two stimuli.

Conditioned Discrimination

Stimulus generalization can facilitate learning. The hunting dog trained to track wild fowl will probably not receive exactly the same bird scent when he hunts again. Yet the odors will be sufficiently similar to permit him to make the pointing response.

FIGURE 7.11 The duck on the left was reported to be courting the white duck for three months. The white duck is a concrete lawn ornament (Wide World Photo).

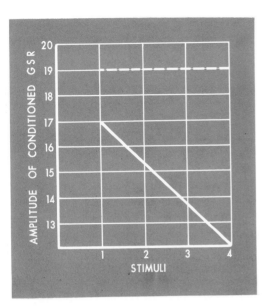

FIGURE 7.12 The Generalization of Extinction Effects. The upper broken line indicates the amplitude of the conditioned response to each of the four tones. The solid line shows the amplitude of the four responses after the conditioned response to Tone 4 was extinguished (After Hovland, 1937b).

Stimulus generalization can, in other situations, interfere with learning. The infant beginning to talk receives agitated approval when he responds to the sight of his father with the vocalization "Da-Da." What often happens next, however, is that he calls other men "Da-Da," to the amusement of many and perhaps the embarrassment of some. Since other men are physically similar to his father, it is difficult for the infant to learn to call only his own father "Da-Da." The response generalizes to stimuli (other men) similiar to the conditioned stimulus (his father).

How can the effects of stimulus generalization be overcome? How can the infant who uses "Da-Da" indiscriminately learn to apply it properly? Pavlov and his associates discovered the procedure for doing this. They trained a dog to salivate to a tone of specific frequency. As expected, the dog also salivated to a neighboring tone (generalized stimulus). Then a series of trials was given

in which sometimes the conditioned stimulus, sometimes the generalized stimulus appeared. The conditioned stimulus was always followed by the unconditioned stimulus; the generalized stimulus never was. As a result the conditioned salivary response to the conditioned stimulus was strengthened, and the conditioned response to the generalized stimulus was weakened. Eventually the dog learned to salivate to the conditioned stimulus and not to the generalized stimulus. This procedure is appropriately called **conditioned discrimination.** It combines the technique used in both the acquisition and extinction of conditioned responses; the conditioned response to the conditioned stimulus receives reinforcement, as in acquisition trials, while the conditioned response to the generalized stimulus never receives reinforcement, as in experimental extinction. If approval is withheld from the infant when he generalizes the "Da-Da" response to all men and if he continues to receive approval for uttering these sounds in the presence of his father, then he, like Pavlov's subjects, will learn to discriminate between similar stimuli.

Not all conditioned discriminations are easily accomplished. Dogs in Pavlov's laboratory were conditioned to discriminate between a circle and an ellipse. The ellipse was then gradually changed so that it became more and more like a circle. Finally, when the axes of the ellipse differed only in the ratio of 9:8 (see Figure 7.13) the animal had difficulty in discriminating between it and the circle; he frequently salivated to the wrong stimulus. On continued exposure to this difficult discrimination the animal's ability to discriminate a circle from an ellipse actually became worse and finally disappeared. He could no longer respond differentially even to the original circle and to the ellipse. Along with the deterioration in the dog's ability to discriminate, there were other changes in his behavior. Before he encountered the difficult discrimination

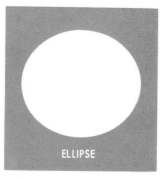

FIGURE 7.13 The Stimuli Used in Conditioned Discrimination. Pavlov's dog was unable to discriminate between the stimuli. Upon continued exposure to this problem the dog developed neurotic symptoms.

the dog was a quiet, pleasant animal. Now he was inclined to squeal and bite his restraining straps. Pavlov described the dog as exhibiting "neurotic symptoms."

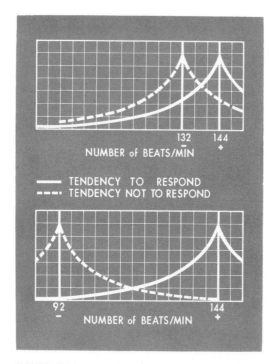

FIGURE 7.14 How Stimulus Generalization Influences Conditioned Discrimination. In an easy discrimination the generalization curves barely overlap, while in a difficult discrimination the amount of overlap is relatively great.

Similar results were obtained with a child. A six-year-old child was conditioned to discriminate between two different rates of a metronome. The child had no difficulty in discriminating 144 beats per minute from rates of 92 and 108 beats per minute. But when closer discrimination was required, for example between 144 and 132 beats per minute, he became aggressive and disobedient.

The effects of stimulus generalization are fundamental to the difficulty organisms have in acquiring fine discriminations. Consider the example of the child who is being trained to discriminate between the metronome beating at 144 and at 132. When he is reinforced for responding to the rate of 144 the tendency to respond to the rate of 132 is also strengthened. When the child is not reinforced for responding to the rate of 132 the tendency to respond to the rate of 144 is also weakened. The more similar the two stimuli, the more difficult will be the discrimination. Figure 7.14 shows schematically why this is so.

In an easy discrimination the curves of generalization of conditioning and extinction barely overlap. Reinforcement of the response to the conditioned stimulus, therefore, strengthens only slightly the tendency for the generalized stimulus to evoke the conditioned response. Similarly nonreinforcement of the response to the generalized stimulus scarcely weakens the tendency for the conditioned stimulus to evoke the conditioned response. The situation is different for the difficult (close) discrimination. Both the generalization curves of conditioning and extinction overlap so much that the tendency of the conditioned stimulus to evoke the conditioned response is greatly weakened, whereas the tendency for the generalized stimulus to evoke the conditioned response is greatly strengthened.

The difficulty of establishing fine conditioned discriminations and the disturbed behavior it sometimes produces have interesting implications. Consider for a moment the fine social discriminations we often require of children. Take a child who has been brought up to be both honest and polite. When his wealthy aunt, who squeezes him too tightly or teases him too much, asks "Do you love your auntie?" the child honestly answers "No!" His parents are shocked and punish him for not being polite. It is fair to ask whether the discrimination between honesty and politeness here is not as difficult, if not more difficult, as the discrimination between metronomes beating 132 and 144 per minute.

Higher-Order Conditioning

Another important phenomenon that Pavlov reported was what he called **higher-order conditioning.** Higher-order conditioning demonstrates that a conditioned stimulus can function in much the same way as an unconditioned stimulus. Initially a first-order conditioned response was established by pairing the sound of a metronome (conditioned stimulus) with food (unconditioned stimulus). Then a second-order conditioned response was established by pairing a black square with the metronome, the conditioned stimulus of the first-order conditioned response. Since the metronome had acquired the capacity to evoke the salivary response, it was possible to use it as a reinforcer in place of an unconditioned stimulus. Pavlov found that after a series of paired presentations of the black square with the metronome, the black square by itself elicited a salivary response.

The second-order conditioned response was appreciably weaker than the first-order conditioned response. This was to be expected. During the second-order conditioning the capacity of the metronome to evoke a salivary response is undergoing experimental extinction. Pavlov found it impossible to establish a third-order conditioned response. The ability of the black square (conditioned stimulus of the second-order

conditioned response) to evoke a salivary response was so weak that it could not function as an unconditioned stimulus.

Higher-order conditioning demonstrates a psychological process of vast practical and theoretical importance. It shows how a stimulus such as the sound of a metronome can acquire the capacity to strengthen stimulus-response associations. That is, a neutral stimulus can acquire reinforcing properties. When a stimulus *acquires* reinforcing properties we refer to it as a **secondary reinforcement.**

INSTRUMENTAL CONDITIONING

During the acquisition stage of classical conditioning the tone was consistently followed by food. The dog learned to anticipate the food by salivating to the tone.

There is another kind of conditioning called **instrumental conditioning.** Here, instead of *anticipating* events in its environment, as in classical conditioning, the organism, *changes* its environment. Let us see how this is done.

Instrumental Reward Conditioning

The most widely used instrumental conditioning apparatus is the **Skinner box,** named after the psychologist, B. F. Skinner, who designed it. There are many shapes and sizes of Skinner boxes, depending on the animals they are designed for. A Skinner box for rats is small and has bare walls except for a protruding bar. Below or to the side of the bar is an opening from which pellets of food can be ejected. A hungry rat in a Skinner box for the first time will wander around sniffing in corners and indulging in other casual behavior. Sooner or later, by mere chance, he will put some of his weight on the bar, and pressing it, receive a small pellet of food, delivered by a mechanical gadget through the opening below the bar. The rat will sniff and eventually eat the food. In contrast to classical conditioning situations where food is delivered regardless of the animal's behavior, the animal here has, by pressing the bar, effectively produced food in its environment.

Psychologists use the following notation to represent instrumental conditioning:

$$S_1 — R \rightarrow S_2$$

In the example just described, S_1 represents the Skinner box which evokes a bar-pressing response (R), which in turn produces $(\rightarrow)$ food (S_2).

A Skinner box can be constructed so that the bar can be withdrawn or inserted, mak-

ing it possible to observe how a rat's behavior changes on successive trials. A trial is defined as the period during which the bar is available to the rat, beginning with its insertion into the box and ending with its withdrawal.

When an animal receives a series of successive trials in the Skinner box the sequence of behavior involving pressing the bar and then eating the food repeats itself. Important changes, however, do take place. The time it takes the rat to press the bar gradually decreases. So does the time taken to pick up the food and consume it. For any one rat this improvement in behavior will not always be steady. On a few trials he will respond more slowly than on previous trials. However, if a sufficiently large group of rats is used in such an experiment, the mean latency of their responses (time elapsing between the insertion of the bar and the animal pressing it) will decrease consistently on successive trials until a point where further improvement is limited. Figure 7.16 shows the typical instrumental conditioning curves of both an individual rat and a group of rats.

Latency of response is not the only characteristic of an organism's behavior that provides a measure of the strength of instrumental conditioning. Frequently the duration of experimental extinction is used as a measure. One study varied the number of trials in which the rat pressed the bar and consumed the food. During the acquisition stage, each such trial is known as a reinforced trial. After an animal had received his allotted number of reinforced trials, his bar-pressing response was experimentally extinguished. The food delivery mechanism was simply disconnected from the bar so that the pressing response would no longer produce food, and the number of times the rat pressed the bar without receiving food was counted. When he stopped for a given period of time his bar-pressing response was considered to be experimentally extinguished. The results of the experi-

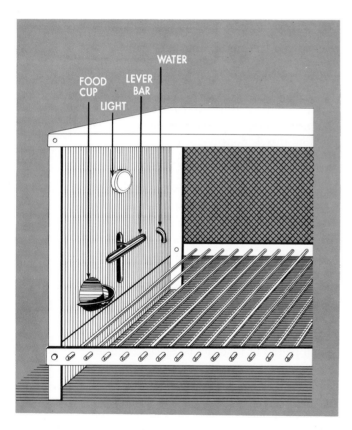

FIGURE 7.15 A Skinner Box. When the bar is pressed food pellets drop into the tray (Dr. Larry Stein).

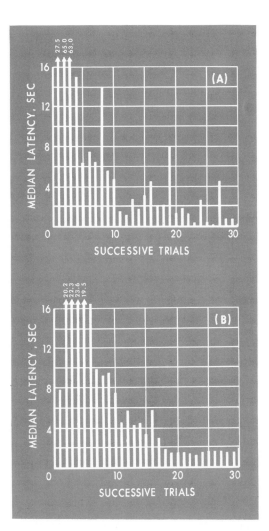

FIGURE 7.16 The Course of Instrumental Conditioning as Measured by Changes in the Latency of the
Response. The results were obtained in a study in
which a bar was inserted into a Skinner box and
the time required by the rat to press it was recorded.
Graph A shows the record of one rat, while Graph B
represents the median performance of a group of
45 animals.

Similar results were obtained in a comparable experiment (Siegel & Foshee, 1953)
with children ranging in age from about
three to six years old. The child stood in
front of a box with a projecting steel bar
and a tray beneath it. When he pressed the
bar a pellet of candy fell into the tray, but
the number of reinforcements with candy
varied for each of four groups. The results
are reported in Figure 7.18. As you see, they
are similar to those obtained with rats.
With both organisms the number of trials
to reach extinction is proportional to the
number of reinforced trials during acquisition. A psychological law does not necessarily apply to humans just because it
applies to lower animals, but often the
same empirical law does hold for both.

These experiments demonstrate an
important psychological principle. The
strength of an association between a stimulus and a response is a function of the

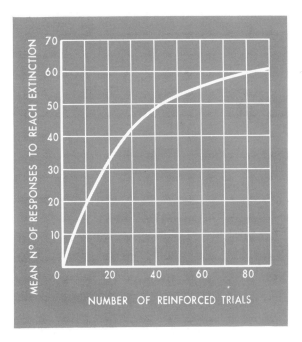

FIGURE 7.17 The Relationship Between the Number
of Reinforced Trials During Acquisition of the Response and the Number of Responses Made During
Experimental Extinction. These data were obtained
with rats (Perin, 1942).

ment indicated a positive relationship
between the number of reinforced trials
during acquisition and the number of responses made during experimental extinction. The greater the number of reinforcements during acquisition, the greater the
number of responses made during extinction (see Figure 7.17).

166

number of times that the association has been reinforced. Suppose a child cries when he is refused candy. And suppose also that the mother gives in, as often happens in such cases, and lets the child have a piece of candy. After several similar experiences, the mother finally realizes that she has been

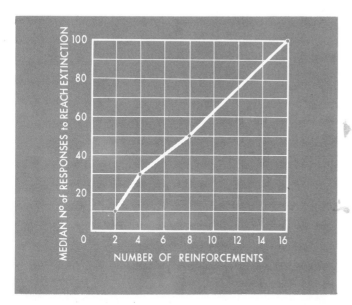

FIGURE 7.18 The Relationship Between the Number of Reinforced Trials During Acquisition of the Response and the Number of Responses Made During Experimental Extinction. These data were obtained with children (Siegel & Foshee, 1953).

encouraging an undesirable habit, and decides to be firm. She refuses the child candy no matter how long or how vigorously he cries. How long will it take to extinguish the crying response? The crying response is, of course, equivalent to the bar-pressing response in the two experiments just reported. It is instrumental in obtaining candy in the same sense that the bar-pressing response was instrumental in obtaining food or candy. The difficulty the mother will have in extinguishing the crying habit will depend to an important degree on how often she had previously submitted to his demands.

Instrumental Conditioning with Secondary Reinforcement

The phenomenon of secondary reinforcement operates in instrumental conditioning much as it did in classical conditioning. By being closely related to a **primary reinforcer** such as food, a neutral stimulus can become a secondary reinforcing agent. One such demonstration of this phenomenon was obtained in a study with a Skinner box (Bugelski, 1938). In this experiment the bar pressing was always accompanied by a click of the food delivery mechanism. During extinction the subjects were divided into two groups. For one group, the bar-pressing response produced a click just as it did during acquisition. For the other group, the click as well as the food was eliminated. Which group should extinguish more rapidly? Consider this question with the following principle in mind. In higher-order conditioning a conditioned stimulus closely and consistently followed by an unconditioned stimulus acquires secondary reinforcing properties, which serve in the formation and strengthening of a new association, the second-order conditioned response. In this instrumental conditioning situation the click was closely and consistently followed by the primary reinforcing agent, food. Consequently, it should acquire reinforcing properties, and the click group should be receiving secondary reinforcement during extinction although no longer receiving food. The click (secondary reinforcement) would work against the effects of extinction because it would strengthen the animal's tendency to press the bar, and the absence of primary food reinforcement would weaken this tendency. Hence the bar-pressing response of the no-click group would not be strengthened during extinction. According to this analysis then, the no-click group should extinguish more rapidly, and this is exactly what happened. The no-click group extinguished more rapidly than the click group. However, the click group was ultimately extinguished because the click lost its reinforcing properties by not being followed by food. In line with the facts of higher-order conditioning, this experiment suggests the principle that stimuli closely and frequently preceding primary reinforcers acquire reinforcing properties.

In the study just described the click was followed during acquisition by only one kind of primary reinforcement, food. Some stimuli are consistently followed by a large variety of reinforcers. His mother is to the infant a sign for food, water, warmth, cleanliness, and many other primary reinforcers. Money although it cannot buy everything, can be traded for many different kinds of reinforcers. Stimuli that precede a large number of primary reinforcers, and therefore acquire their own reinforcing properties, are called **generalized secondary reinforcers.** They play a very important role in social behavior, as you know.

Instrumental Escape and Avoidance Conditioning

Negative reinforcers (see page 157) can function in instrumental conditioning as well as in classical conditioning situations. One instrumental technique uses a Skinner box with an electric grid on the floor. The grid delivers a shock to the paws of a rat placed inside, and it is terminated only when the rat presses the bar. Placed in such a box a naive rat will eventually learn to press the bar whenever he is shocked, but when he is shocked for the first time he will exhibit a wide variety of behavior, usually including crouching, leaping, squealing, urinating, and defecating. In the course of this behavior the rat will accidentally press the bar and terminate the shock. He learns to escape shock in much the way that he learns to press the bar for food, except that he learns at a more rapid rate. This kind of instrumental conditioning is known as **escape conditioning** because the bar-pressing response is instrumental in bringing about escape from the noxious stimulus.

Avoidance conditioning is very similar to escape conditioning. It differs, however, in one important respect. A signal precedes the onset of the shock. This means that if the tone is sounded one second prior to the shock, during the initial trials the rat will learn to press the bar when he is shocked, and soon after he will learn also to press the bar in response to the tone so that he will avoid shock. In escape conditioning the rat gets shocked on all trials, and the bar-pressing response is instrumental only to *escaping* the shock. In avoidance conditioning he is in a somewhat more fortunate situation. By making the appropriate response prior to the shock, the rat can completely *avoid* it.

Escape and avoidance conditioning occur quite often in everyday life. If you are in the dentist's chair and the drilling becomes unbearable, you will probably wince or even groan a little, and if the dentist is considerate, he will give you a short rest. In the future, you will be even more likely to wince or groan because you have learned that these are instrumental responses which help you escape the pain, at least for a time.

Instrumental avoidance conditioning has recently been applied in a novel way (Smith & Geis, 1956); psychologists suggested its use after solving the puzzling case of the missing trout. The State of Michigan spent several hundred thousand dollars a year raising trout in fish hatcheries. When the trout reached a length of about eight inches they were put in streams, but much to everyone's chagrin, most of them disappeared within a few days. The mystery of the trout's disappearance was solved by psychologists who investigated the responses the fish learned to make during their early life. In the hatchery food was thrown to the trout, making small splashes on the surface of the water. Therefore, the trout learned to swim up to the splashes. In the streams, which the trout were transferred to, the splashes had, however, a different meaning, since they were usually caused by predatory otters, blue herons, or fishermen's flies. A positive response here could be, and usually was, fatal to the young trout.

In order to lengthen the life of the trout, a new training program was instituted in the hatchery. The young fish that rose at a splash were given a mild electric shock instead of food. Soon they learned to avoid splashes and wait for their food to settle. When they were transferred to the streams, they were able to survive a much longer time than their predecessors.

CLASSICAL AND INSTRUMENTAL CONDITIONING COMPARED

In classical conditioning, so named because it was the first form to be tried, the experimenter decides when reinforcement is to be given. During the acquisition stage of Pavlovian conditioning, the dog is given food whether or not he salivates to the tone. In contrast, the rat in the Skinner box gets food only if he makes the appropriate response. This is why the term *instrumental* is used to describe conditioning situations of the Skinner-box variety. If a functionally descriptive term is needed to characterize classical conditioning, *preparatory* or *anticipatory* would be appropriate. The classical conditioned response prepares for or anticipates the unconditioned stimulus.

Is it necessary, you may ask, to introduce different theoretical principles to account for the facts of classical and instrumental conditioning? Here again we find a theoretical disagreement among psychologists. Perhaps your instructor has a viewpoint which he will explain and attempt to defend against whatever arguments you think up. This book, however, will avoid taking

sides. One point which is not subject to dispute, however, is that many experimental variables produce the same effects upon conditioning, whether of the classical or instrumental variety. We must examine these relationships because they are important to all psychology.

VARIABLES THAT INFLUENCE CONDITIONING

Since psychologists are interested in discovering variables that influence behavior, conditioning has proved a fertile field for psychological research. On the one hand there are a host of independent variables (see page 22); on the other hand there are objective measures of behavior (dependent variables). How does variation of the first affect the second? This is the question we shall now consider.

Amount of Reinforced Practice

We have already stated that the strength of the response increases with the amount of reinforced practice. The results reported in Figures 7.2, 7.3, 7.5, and 7.18 are consistent with this generalization. These data do not necessarily confirm the old adage, practice makes perfect. True, conditioning does improve with practice but only under certain conditions. Reinforcement must be present. Without reinforcement, as in experimental extinction, the conditioned response weakens and fades away.

Time Interval Between the Conditioned Stimulus and the Unconditioned Stimulus

In classical conditioning the tendency for a conditioned stimulus to evoke a conditioned response is influenced by the length of the interval between presentation of the conditioned and unconditioned stimuli. Figure 7.19 is a composite curve from several studies showing the general form of the empirical relationship. This figure shows that the strongest associations between the conditioned stimulus and the conditioned response in eyelid conditioning are formed when the unconditioned stimulus follows the conditioned stimulus with a lapse of a little less than one-half second (approximately .4 seconds). Figure 7.19 also shows that the simultaneous presentation of the conditioned and unconditioned stimuli produces very weak conditioned responses. It also seems that **backward conditioning,** the presentation of the unconditioned stimulus prior to the conditioned stimulus, is at best ineffective. Indeed, there is reason to believe that no organism except man is capable of forming a habit by backward conditioning. In classical conditioning, we may conclude, the formation of a conditioned response is retarded, and even prevented, when the time intervals between the conditioned and unconditioned stimuli are unsuitable.

Conditions of Reinforcement

The importance of reinforcement in conditioning suggests that the amount and the manner in which the reinforcing agent is presented will affect conditioning. There are hundreds of experiments to demonstrate this fact.

Amount of Reinforcement. In order to discover how the amount of reinforcement influences conditioning, an experiment was conducted with two groups of rats each receiving a different amount of reinforcement following their performance of a simple instrumental act (Zeaman, 1949). One group was reinforced with a .05 gram piece of cheese; the other with a larger piece (2.4 grams). After 20 trials the group receiving the larger reinforcement responded much more rapidly than the other group. The latency of responses for the

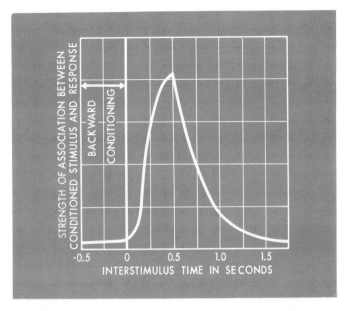

FIGURE 7.19 Strength of Conditioning As a Function of the Time Between the Conditioned and Unconditioned Stimulus (After *Principles of General Psychology* by Gregory A. Kimble, Copyright 1956, The Ronald Press Co.).

2.4 gram group was less than a second (.8 seconds), while the latency for the 0.5 gram group was more than two seconds (2.3 seconds), on the average. From this we can conclude that an instrumental response built by giving an organism a large reinforcement will be stronger than one based on a small reinforcement.

The difference between the efficacy of a large reinforcement and a small one was even more clearly revealed when the sizes of the reinforcements were reversed for the two groups, on the twentieth trial and for eight trials thereafter. The groups quickly traded places in speed of response: the group previously reinforced with a small piece of cheese and now reinforced with a large one soon responded more quickly than did the group previously reinforced with the large piece and now reinforced with the small one. Figure 7.20 shows this change.

If an experimenter were interested in training a group of animals to make a very

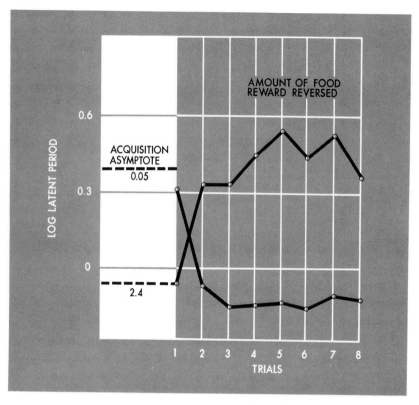

FIGURE 7.20 The Influence of the Amount of Reinforcement on the Latency of an Instrumental Response. The left-hand section of the graph shows that after the rats had reached the limit of their performance (acquisition asymptote), the rats with the larger incentive responded more rapidly. The change in the amount of incentive produced an immediate shift in behavior (After Zeaman, 1949).

rapid instrumental response, he would not, however, have to use a large reinforcement throughout the training period. Instead, he could use a small reward for the initial trials and substitute a larger reward later on. In the experiment just described, the substitution of a large reinforcement for a small one produced an immediate change in behavior, and more recent studies (Spence, 1956) have shown that animals extensively trained with a small reinforcement require only several additional trials with larger reinforcement before they can match animals trained on a large reinforcement from the very beginning.

Quality of Reinforcement. The relationship between conditioning and quality of reinforcement appears to be the same as the relationship between conditioning and amount of reinforcement. The quality of reinforcement will determine the level at which an instrumental response is performed. Rats will press a bar much more readily for sweet than for sour food (Hutt, 1954), and an individual rat's level of performance can be raised and lowered by changing the sweetness of the liquid reward he receives. The sweeter it is the more readily he will respond (Guttman, 1953), Again you see that behavior can be changed by modifying the conditions of reinforcement.

Delay of Reinforcement. In the Skinner box (see page 163), the bar-pressing response is immediately followed by delivery

170

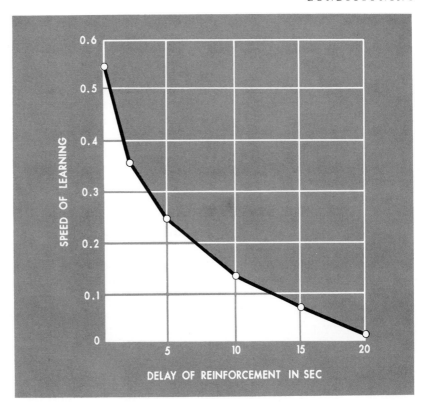

FIGURE 7.21   The Speed of Learning As a Function of Delay of Reinforcement (After *Principles of General Psychology* by Gregory A. Kimble, Copyright 1956, The Ronald Press Company, from data in Perin, 1942).

of a food pellet. But in our everyday lives immediate reinforcement is the exception rather than the rule. After making an instrumental response we usually have to wait a while before reinforcement. Time usually elapses between bidding a bridge hand and discovering whether the bid was the right one; an even longer time sometimes passes between ordering a meal in a restaurant and eating it; and many years intervene between studying hard in college and earning the rewards of a distinguished career.

What is the effect on conditioning of delayed reinforcement? One experiment (Perin, 1942) to discover its effect employed a Skinner box equipped with a mechanism for controlling the lapse of time between pressing the bar and delivery of the food. Six different experimental groups were used, each having a different length of reinforcement delay, varying from 0 to 30 seconds. The speed with which the animals acquired the response can be seen in Figure 7.21. The shorter the delay the faster the animals were conditioned. The data on speed of response for the 30 seconds group is missing from the graph, because almost half the animals in this group failed to acquire the response. This will not surprise you if you consider that a long delay of reinforcement may function as experimental extinction, for experimental extinction is essentially an infinite delay of reinforcement.

People are often unaware of this when they attempt to train their pets or children. Too often, rewards for appropriate behavior are given at a time when they have no effect. Giving an infant a toy for being

171

good two days ago or a dog a bone in the evening because he performed a trick well in the morning, is both ineffective and wasteful of something that might have been put to good use. To obtain the maximum beneficial effects from a reinforcing agent you must give it to the subject immediately after he makes the response.

The data just cited do not mean that instrumental responses cannot be learned when the primary reinforcement follows them by more than 30 seconds. Results have been obtained indicating that rats are capable of learning responses even when the delay of food reinforcement is as long as 20 minutes. Under such conditions it appears that the mechanism of secondary reinforcement makes learning possible. Stimuli followed closely and consistently by primary reinforcement acquire secondary reinforcing properties, and if the time gap between a response and a primary reinforcing agent is consistently filled by some appropriate secondary reinforcing stimulus, learning will occur because that stimulus will serve as the reinforcing agent.

One experiment (Grice, 1948) attempted to separate the effects of primary reinforcement on the white rat from those of secondary reinforcement. The results suggested that delay of primary reinforcement beyond two seconds will prevent rats from acquiring an instrumental conditioned response if that interval contains no secondary reinforcers. But whatever the exact time duration, the important psychological principles to remember are first, that increasing delays of reinforcement produce increasingly poor performance in conditioning, and second, that conditioning will not occur if delays of reinforcement are too long.

If an instrumental response is acquired under a relatively long delay of reinforcement, will it improve rapidly when a shorter delay is substituted? And will a response acquired under a short delay decline when a longer delay is substituted? Experimental data (Spence, 1956) suggest

that the answers to both these questions are affirmative.

It would appear that the performance of instrumental responses can be fairly rapidly improved or impaired by modifying the amount, quality, or delay of reinforcement. This general relationship between the performance of a conditioned response and the characteristics of the reinforcing conditions are not only important for conditioning, but as you will see, for the psychology of motivation as well.

Variables That Retard Conditioning

Up to now we have been talking mostly about variables that can improve the performance of a conditioned response. There is also a group of variables that have the opposite effect. They can weaken or eliminate the performance of a conditioned response.

Nonreinforcement. We have already reviewed the facts of experimental extinction. They demonstrate that both instrumental and classical conditioned responses can be weakened or eliminated by continued nonreinforcement. Nonreinforcement operates in a manner opposite to that of reinforcement.

Effort. The amount of effort required of a subject in making a response has proved very potent in its effects upon conditioning. In one experiment (Mowrer & Jones, 1943) a Skinner box was fixed so that the amount of pressure required to depress the bar could be controlled. During acquisition the latency (delay) of the rats' responses when 5 grams pressure were required to depress the bar was significantly less than when 80 grams were needed. This difference was even more noticeable during extinction. Figure 7.22 shows how many responses were made during extinction by three groups, each of which had to exert a different amount of pressure to press the bar.

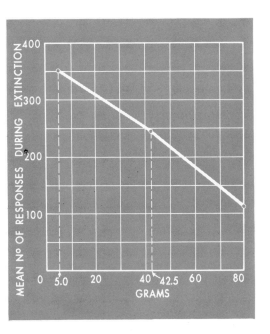

FIGURE 7.22 How Extinction Is Influenced by the Amount of Effort Needed To Perform the Task (After Mowrer & Jones, 1943).

tion requires fewer trials when the inter-trial intervals are short. One explanation is that massing the trials (small intertrial intervals) functions in the same manner that increasing effort does. When trials are crowded together the organism becomes fatigued, with the result that acquisition is retarded and extinction accelerated.

A THEORY OF CONDITIONING

Now that we have reviewed many facts concerning conditioning, we can turn our attention to its theoretical interpretations. Several theories of conditioning are current. Some are similar in fundamentals and differ only in their fine points. Others have extensive areas of disagreement. Nevertheless, all these theories have one aim in common. They seek to order the data of conditioning

These results suggest that extinction can be facilitated by making the instrumental response more difficult.

Massing of Trials. In both classical and instrumental conditioning the time between successive trials, **intertrial interval,** can be varied. In classical conditioning the intertrial interval refers to the time elapsing between one trial (conditioned stimulus followed by the unconditioned) and the next. In instrumental conditioning the intertrial interval refers to the time elapsing between the successive opportunities an organism has to make the instrumental response. For example, spacing of trials in the Skinner box can be manipulated by varying the time interval between the successive insertions of the bar into the box.

In general, when the time interval is brief, conditioning tends to be retarded. In addition, some studies show that extinc-

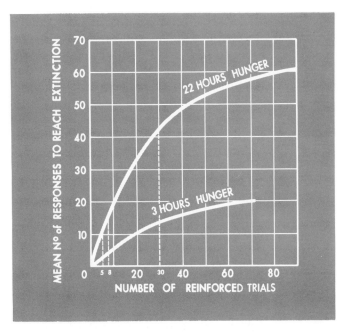

FIGURE 7.23 The Relationship Between the Number of Reinforced Trials During Acquisition of the Response and the Number of Responses Made During Experimental Extinction Under Two Levels of Hunger (Perin, 1942).

and to develop from them an integrated, consistent whole.

An introductory textbook in psychology is obviously not the place to review and evaluate all modern theories of conditioning. But this does not mean that we can ignore the topic completely. An abridged theory of conditioning will not only give you a general idea of what such a theory is like, but it will also pull together some of the experimental data we have been talking about. You must understand, however, that the theoretical formulation that follows is greatly simplified.

The Learning-Performance Distinction

We must begin our sketch of a theory of conditioning by citing still another experiment or two. You know already that the conditioned response improves with increasing amounts of reinforced practice (see Figures 7.2, 7.3, 7.5, and 7.18). But in spite of what seems the obvious validity of this statement, it is possible for two animals with the same amount of reinforced practice to *perform* at different levels. Animals with less reinforced practice can even demonstrate stronger instrumental and conditioned responses than animals with more reinforced practice. How is this possible?

This can be explained if we refer to an experiment (Perin, 1942) with groups of rats who received different numbers of food-reinforced trials during the acquisition of an instrumental bar-pressing response. The number of reinforced trials varied from 5 to 90, and they were given after the animals had been deprived of food for about 24 hours. When the bar-pressing response was to be extinguished the animals were divided into two major groups: one group had been deprived of food for 22 hours when the process of extinction began; the second group had been deprived of food for only 3 hours. If an animal failed to press the bar during a 5-minute period,

his bar-pressing response was considered extinguished. The results are shown in Figure 7.23.

The upper curve represents the performance of the animals who had been deprived of food for 22 hours; the lower curve reports the behavior of the animals deprived of food for 3 hours. Look at the points on each curve showing the performance of animals that had been originally given 5 reinforcements. Although all these animals had the *same amount of practice,* the hungrier group demonstrated a greater resistance to extinction. The less hungry animals made practically no responses. The same relationship holds for the animals who had 8 reinforcements: it took longer to extinguish the instrumental responses of the hungrier animals. Now if we compare the 22-hour animals who had 8 reinforcements with the 3-hour animals who had 30 reinforcements, we discover that the rats with *less* practice performed *more* bar-pressing responses during extinction.

The results of this experiment make it clear that *both* the number of reinforcements during acquisition and the number of hours of food deprivation during extinction are important variables in determining an animal's resistance to experimental extinction.

Would it be correct to state that the animals with 30 reinforcements in the 3-hour group learned less about bar pressing than the 22-hour animals with 8 reinforcements? No, this would not be true, even though it took more trials to extinguish the conditioning of the latter group. For if hunger were *equated* in both groups, it would take more trials to extinguish the responses of the animals with 30 reinforcements than of those with 8 reinforcements.

Obviously performance does not necessarily mirror the amount of learning that has taken place. This experiment shows the necessity of distinguishing between an organism's *performance* and what he has *learned.* From your own experience you are probably familiar with such a distinction. Confronted with an examination grade not as high as you expected, you may have remarked, "I could have done better than that!" What you meant is that for some reason your performance did not measure up to your knowledge, to how much you had learned. When there are guests to dinner and their children are behaving atrociously at the table, mothers sometimes remark, "His table manners are really not that bad." Such a remark, if it is justified, as it often is, simply means that the child has learned proper table manners but for some reason is not utilizing his learning.

Habit and Drive

In order to account for the data proving that the bar-pressing response during extinction is a function both of number of past reinforcements and of amount of food deprivation, psychologists distinguish between the two theoretical concepts, **habit** and **drive**. These concepts also explain why in many situations an organism's performance fails to measure up to his past training.

Habit refers to the tendency of a stimulus situation to evoke a response. Pavlov studied the habit of salivating to a tone. Skinner studied the habit of pressing a bar in a Skinner box. Both investigators found that other things being equal the strength of a habit increases in orderly fashion with increased amounts of reinforced practice. But the behavior of an organism is not determined by habits alone. Habits, acquired response readinesses, must be activated to show up as behavior. At this moment most of your habits are inactive. You can walk, you can drive a car, and you can whistle, but you are probably doing none of these. Your reading habits, however, are activated.

In the study reported in Figure 7.23, the bar-pressing habit was activated by food deprivation or, to put it more directly, by a hunger drive. Habit, in other words,

determines *what* is done; drive determines *whether* it is done. We will discuss drive more extensively in the chapter on motivation, but because conditioning involves motivational variables, we must make some further reference to the psychology of motivation now.

Interaction Between Habit and Drive. We can describe the way habits are activated by drives most simply by doing some multiplication. Assume, purely for pedagogical reasons, that numerical values can be assigned to the concepts habit and drive. Further, assume that the strength of a bar-pressing habit after eight food reinforcements is 5, and that the strength of a hunger drive after three hours is 1 and after 22 hours is 4. Now multiply the habit values by the drive values. The product of eight reinforcements and three hours hunger (5×1) is 5, whereas the product of the same number of reinforcements and the greater 22-hour drive (5×4) is 20.

The products obtained by multiplying strength of drive by strength of habit represent the *behavior* of the organism. The larger the product, the greater the value of the dependent variable, and in the experiment we have described, the dependent variable is the number of responses that occur before extinction is reached. A simple algebraic formula represents the interaction between habit and drive:

$$R = H \times D$$

R being the response, H the habit, and D the drive.

Of course, the numbers used in our exposition are arbitrary. They merely furnish a concrete instance of the psychological principle that the theoretical relationship between habit and drive is *multiplicative*. In other words, we can say that the drive energizes the habit.

According to this formula, if the amount of drive is zero, the performance should also be zero. One experiment (Koch &

Daniels, 1945) tested the validity of this prediction. A group of hungry rats was given 70 reinforcements of bar pressing, and immediately prior to extinction they were fed as much food as they wanted. The mean number of bar-pressing responses they made was less than one each. Their performance was essentially the same as that of rats with no previous training in bar pressing.

Similarly if the number of reinforcements is zero and the hunger drive is strong, the behavior should also be zero. This prediction is also confirmed. Naive hungry rats placed for the first time in a Skinner box and exposed to the bar for a short period of time will make few or no responses. One or two animals may, in making random movements, accidentally press the bar, but since there is no reinforcement, they will not continue.

You may now ask, Why is the relationship multiplicative? Why do drives energize behavior? Modern learning theorists have advanced several answers. They range from postulating certain underlying physiological events to assigning complex mathematical properties to the conditioning process. The relative merits of these explanations are now being explored in many different research projects under way in university laboratories.

It is important for us to understand and remember that both drive and habit are theoretical constructs. Theoretical constructs, you may recall (see page 29), are abstractions; they are not directly observable but are inferred from data. The constructs of habit and drive are inferred from the relationships that exist between sets of independent and dependent variables in conditioning. Habit is inferred from the relationships between reinforced practice and performance. Drive is inferred from the relationships between an organism's schedule of food or water deprivation and its performance. Both constructs summarize economically a vast amount of conditioning data and at the same time aid in the prediction of new findings.

The Learning and Performance of Habits

Habit refers to the strength of an association between a stimulus and a response. In order for a habit to be transformed into behavior it must be activated by a drive. It is necessary for the psychologist who desires to formulate a theory of conditioning to know what variables influence the learning of a habit, and what variables influence its performance. Because of their complexity, these questions cannot be answered fully, but some of the important variables can be mentioned.

The Learning of a Habit. We have frequently cited the amount of reinforced practice as a variable influencing the growth of a habit. Figures 7.2, 7.3, and 7.5 represent the performance of animals who are under a constant strength of drive. These curves presumably mirror the growth of habit. If you examine them you will note that habits gain more strength during the initial stages of practice than during the later stages. The increments in performance resulting from early reinforced trials are much greater than those resulting from later reinforced trials. That is, as training proceeds, less and less improvement is made. You can observe this pattern of improvement when you learn simple skills. For example, you improve rapidly when you first learn to throw darts at a target or to "shoot pool," but your improvement decreases sharply with increasing practice until you reach a point where for even slight improvement you need extensive practice.

The Performance of a Habit. The performance of an instrumental or conditioned response can be abruptly raised or lowered by changing the intensity of the drive. If an animal has been trained until his habit of bar-pressing to obtain food has been thoroughly learned (extinction would occur only after a long time), his bar-pressing performance will depend on his hunger. After a long period of food deprivation he will press the bar rapidly; after a short period he will respond slowly or not at all.

Performance of a habit can also be changed abruptly by changing the reinforcing agent. You will recall (see page 169) that when a large amount of food was substituted for a small amount, the performance of the instrumental response improved immediately. Similarly when the amount of reinforcement was reduced the performance decreased rapidly. The same kinds of changes occurred when the quality or delay of reinforcement was modified.

Thus you see performance of a habit can be suddenly raised or lowered either by modifying the deprivation schedule or by changing the reinforcing agent in some respect, that is, by changing its amount, quality, or delay. We are, therefore, forced to conclude that the amount, quality, or delay of reinforcement functions in a manner similar to the length of the deprivation period. That is to say, reinforcing agents have some of the properties of a drive. They can energize habits into different levels of performance.

An example from everyday life may help to make this clear to you. You go into a restaurant, not feeling particularly hungry. A waiter passes you carrying a sizzling, juicy steak or a thick piece of apple pie. All of a sudden your mouth begins to water. The sight of a reinforcing agent, food, has increased your hunger drive.

Advertisers make use of the drive-strengthening properties of reinforcing agents all the time. By attractively displaying their products they strengthen the consumer's drive to buy them.

Habit, Drive, and Inhibition

In our analysis of conditioning, we have discussed three different components of the conditioning process. The first was habit. It represents an association between a stimulus and a response. The tendency for the stimulus to evoke the response can increase or decrease as a function of reinforced or nonreinforced practice. The second was drive. It stands for an energizing mechanism that activates a habit. The same habit produces different levels of performance, depending on the strength of the drive. The third was inhibition. Although this has been discussed it has not been named. You will recall that certain variables retard the course of conditioning. The performance of a conditioned response will diminish if the response is not reinforced (nonreinforcement), if the effort involved is increased, or if the trials are bunched up, massed. The negative influences these variables have on conditioning are illustrative of inhibition. So to the two theoretical constructs of habit and drive we first introduced you, we now add **inhibition.**

Following is a general formula summarizing the manner in which these three theoretical constructs interact:

$$R = f(H \times D) - I$$

R refers, of course, to the response which in conditioning can be measured in one of several ways (e.g., latency of response, number of trials to reach extinction). H represents the strength of the habit, D, the strength of the drive. Habit is activated by drive, so that an organism's response in a conditioning situation will be some multiplicative function of both its habit and drive. But the product of the habit multiplied by the drive will not alone determine an animal's behavior. From this product must be subtracted the amount of momentary inhibition produced by such conditions as nonreinforcement, increased effort, or the massing of trials.

This is, of course, a skeletonized version of conditioning theory, and it should not be taken as a final and complete theory. We think, however, that it is sufficiently inclusive to serve as a systematic summary of the facts of conditioning, but your instructor may feel that he must expand the formula or modify it in some way. If so, he will give you reasons which you will surely find challenging.

When making use of this formula do not overlook the facts of stimulus generalization: the more similar a stimulus is to the conditioned stimulus, the greater will be the response it evokes; the less similar, the smaller the response. This means that even though a conditioned response is acquired under optimal conditions, its performance level may be low in a stimulus situation markedly different from the one in which it was acquired. Just as habits may remain inactive because drive is lacking, they may remain inactive because the stimulus situation in which they were learned has been drastically changed.

This principle also applies to the highly complex behavior involved in championship tennis. Some of the world's top-ranking tennis players have difficulty when they compete in American championship matches, because they are played on grass courts. Italians, for example, have no grass courts in their country on which to learn the speed and angle at which a tennis ball rises from a grass court. Since these are quite different on grass and on clay, a player accustomed to clay courts must respond to a different stimulus situation on grass, and inevitably there is a slump in his game.

ORGANISMIC VARIABLES IN CONDITIONING

Up to now the facts and theories of conditioning have been presented with practically no references to the action of organismic variables. One reason for this is that organismic variables have not received the same amount of attention in experiments on conditioning that environmental (stimulus) variables have. The bulk of conditioning research has involved rela-

tionships between the behavior of animals and their present and past environments (e.g., the intensity of a conditioned stimulus, the number of reinforced trials). But organismic variables have not been ignored completely. Many psychologists and physiologists are interested in such questions as: What neurophysiological processes, after all, go on inside an animal when conditioning takes place? What parts of the nervous system of an animal are involved in the formation of conditioned responses? Let us begin what little we shall say on this topic with this last question.

Neurophysiological Correlates of Conditioning

Typically in classical conditioning an unconditioned stimulus activates a receptor which in turn initiates neural impulses that travel through sensory pathways to the central nervous system and finally to effectors via motor pathways. A similar sequence of events is triggered by the conditioned stimulus, except that its influence on effector activity during the early stages of conditioning is less obvious than that of the unconditioned stimulus.

Many investigators have attempted to eliminate portions of these neurophysiological sequences to see whether conditioning can take place in the absence of certain segments. For example, one study (Crisler, 1930) attempted to answer the question whether an animal incapable of *responding* to an unconditioned stimulus could nevertheless acquire a conditioned response. The subjects were given a drug that prevented them from salivating. During the time the drug was effective the conditioned and unconditioned stimuli were paired for a series of acquisition trials. After the effects of the drug had worn off, it was found that the conditioned stimulus was capable of evoking the conditioned response. Obviously then, a salivary conditioned response can be *learned* during the time when the salivary response cannot be *performed*.

There have been a number of other ingenious studies in which conditioned and unconditioned stimuli were paired in the absence of certain neural events. In one study (Loucks & Gantt, 1938) the sensory mechanism and the particular region of the central nervous system which the unconditioned stimulus would normally arouse were bypassed by directly stimulating the motor nerve, and yet conditioning occurred. In another study (Loucks, 1938) the sensory portion of the conditioned stimulus was bypassed and the sensory region of the cortex stimulated directly. Again, conditioning occurred. Hence, we conclude conditioning can take place when receptor and effector activities as well as peripheral sensory and motor pathways are absent. Conditioning, however—and this is not surprising—cannot occur in the absence of all neural activity in the central nervous system. We must continue to look for the physiological locus of conditioning somewhere in the central nervous system.

Pavlov thought that the most highly developed part of the brain, the cerebral hemispheres with their outer cortical layer, was necessary for the formation of conditioned responses. But later research proved him wrong. Several investigators have successfully conditioned animals whose cerebral hemispheres have been completely removed.

The fact that higher brain centers are not required for conditioning is not too surprising when you realize that organisms as low in the evolutionary scale as the marine worm have been conditioned. These organisms have practically no brain at all, just a collection of synapses in their head segment. Yet in spite of this, they can be trained to approach a light that did not originally evoke their approach. Marine worms will approach a region where clam juice is diffused (unconditioned stimulus). By pairing a light (conditioned stimulus) with clam juice, the worm can be conditioned to go toward the light.

We must, however, be careful in interpreting the relationship between neural structures and conditionability. We must keep the differences between species constantly in mind. The lack of a cerebrum has a more drastic effect upon the behavior of higher forms of animals than upon lower forms. Birds and fish can balance and move around as efficiently without a cerebrum as with one. Decerebrated rats, cats, and dogs have their posture impaired, although they can stand and walk. A decerebrated monkey, however, cannot walk at all. The progressive shifting of behavior functions, such as walking, to higher centers of the central nervous system as one ascends the evolutionary scale, is known as encephalization. Because of encephalization, we cannot conclude that if a dog without cerebral hemispheres can be conditioned, the same must be true of man. Much evidence suggests that the cerebral hemispheres play a more important role in conditioning as one ascends the evolutionary scale.

The Brain and Reinforcement

One of the most dramatic findings in recent decades is that a mild electric shock to certain portions of the brain serves as a positive reinforcement (Olds & Milner, 1954). This discovery of positive reinforcement effects of brain stimulation was made with rats that had electrodes implanted in their brains. Figure 7.24 shows an X-ray of such a rat. The two antennae which spring from the rat's head are connected to the electrode implanted in his brain. When the rat is placed in a Skinner box, the antennae are attached to an electrical source so that when he presses the bar he receives a shock through the implanted electrode.

The frequency of the rat's bar pressing depends upon the location of the implanted electrode. One rat who had the electrode placed in the posterior hypothalamic region of his brain responded so enthusiastically that he made as many as 5,000 bar-pressing

180

responses per hour (Olds, 1958), and when his response no longer produced brain stimulation, because the electric current had been cut off, he soon stopped making it. Some other areas of the brain produce fewer responses, still others none at all. Rats with electrodes in brain areas with no reinforcing properties do not acquire the bar-pressing response.

Negative reinforcing centers in the brain have also been found (Miller, 1957). Electrical stimulation of certain parts of the brain stem function as do aversive stimuli in escape and avoidance conditioning. The instrumental responses to escape or avoid shock are exactly the same as those which terminate brain stimulation.

Fragmentary reports (Sem-Jacobsen, 1958) suggest that pleasurable experiences are generated by stimulating positively reinforcing centers in the brain of man. In the language of objective psychology, it would seem that portions of the brain contain "reinforcing structures." When these structures are stimulated, the organism's response at that time is reinforced. In other words, habits are formed and strengthened when appropriate areas of the brain are electrically stimulated.

These findings raise fascinating questions. If there are unique structures in the brain which when stimulated have the effect of reinforcement, what and where are they and what methods can be used to control their activities? Do positive and negative reinforcing centers function in the same way? When we can answer these questions, it is likely that we shall have achieved a major breakthrough in the science of psychology.

Neurophysiological Changes in Conditioning

It seems reasonable to assume that as conditioning takes place some changes in the nervous system occur. If behavior changes,

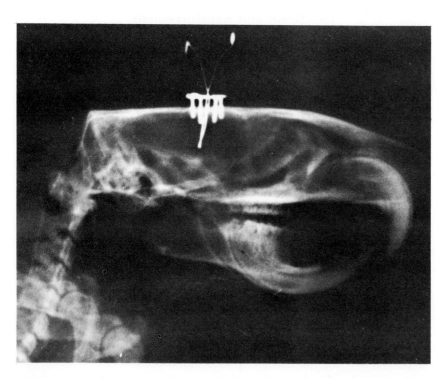

FIGURE 7.24   X-ray Photograph of a Rat With Imbedded Electrodes (Dr. James Olds).

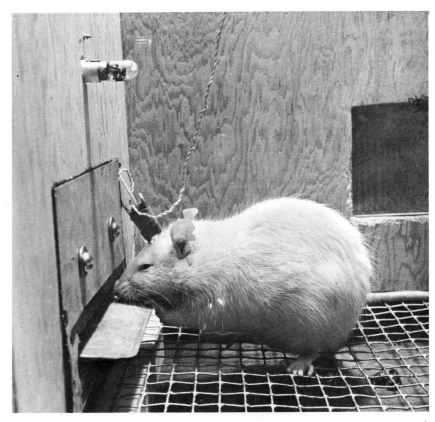

FIGURE 7.25 Rat with Electrodes Implanted in His Brain. An electric shock is delivered to the brain every time the bar is pressed (Dr. James Olds).

shouldn't there be some trace of this change in the nervous system? Although it would indeed be difficult to justify a negative answer, unfortunately, no one has been able to locate any changing of processes in the nervous system as conditioning progresses.

The basic problem is one of observation. The brain, even of a rat, is so complex that with our most advanced techniques of observation we are incapable of isolating neural pathways, much less detecting changes in them. Perhaps we have studied the wrong organisms. The squid, for example, a relative of the octopus, has a comparatively simple nervous system and, what is equally important, giant-sized nerves. It has a nerve fiber one millimeter (.04 inch) in diameter, which is 50 times larger than a nerve cell of man. The feeding reactions

of the squid can be conditioned, and it may be that observation of neural changes taking place in the squid as conditioning progresses would be feasible.

Nevertheless, a number of speculations have been advanced about the nature of neurophysiological changes which accompany conditioning. One persistent notion has been that conditioning results from structural changes in the nerve cells, and a specific hypothesis is that the structural changes that do occur consist in a tendency for the end knobs at synaptic junctions to swell when a nerve impulse passes through. This swelling makes it easier for impulses to pass through in the future and in turn to produce more swelling. The reciprocal influence between the facilitation of transmission of neural impulses and knoblike growths at the synaptic junction is assumed to be the neurophysiological basis of conditioning.

However, many physiological psychologists now believe that the search for changes in the structure of the brain occurring during conditioning may prove fruitless. Their opinion is based on the fact that it is now known definitely that neural transmission is accompanied by chemical changes. They suggest that chemical changes in the brain are responsible for learning also. If this were so we could hardly expect simple microscopic observation to detect the neurophysiological correlates of conditioning; others methods of observation would be needed.

But such structural and chemical hypotheses do not exhaust all the possibilities requiring investigation. Some researchers incline toward the idea that electrical changes in the brain are responsible for conditioning. Actually, there is no reason to believe that only one kind of neurophysiological change occurs during conditioning. It may well be that a combination of neurophysiological modifications are responsible for conditioning and learning. But until techniques are developed to prove the validity of the hypotheses offered, they can only be considered as interesting speculations. The future will decide whether these surmises have substance.

SUMMARY

Psychologists interested in the phenomenon of learning have sought to discover an experimental method capable of revealing fundamental principles of learning. Classical and instrumental conditioning are two methods that have provided information about the formation, strengthening, and weakening of S-R associations.

In classical conditioning a conditioned stimulus (e.g., tone) is paired with an unconditioned stimulus (e.g., food) that evokes an unconditioned response (e.g., salivation). After repeated pairings of the two stimuli, the conditioned stimulus is by itself capable of evoking the response evoked by the unconditioned stimulus (e.g., salivation).

A conditioned response can be extinguished by presenting the conditioned stimulus in the absence of the unconditioned stimulus. The unconditioned stimulus functions as a reinforcement in classical conditioning; its presence strengthens the tendency for the conditioned stimulus to evoke the unconditioned response, its absence weakens this tendency.

Basic phenomena in classical conditioning are spontaneous recovery (the reappearance of an extinguished conditioned response after a passage of time), stimulus generalization (the ability of stimuli similar to the conditioned stimulus to evoke the conditioned response), conditioned discrimination (the application of acquisition and extinction methods to training an organism to respond to one stimulus but not to a similar one), and higher-order conditioning (the acquisition of reinforcing properties by a previously neutral stimulus).

In instrumental conditioning reinforcement occurs only after the subject makes an appropriate response (e.g., presses the bar). The main kinds of instrumental conditioning are reward (with primary or secondary reinforcement), escape, and avoidance.

Practice and conditions (amount, quality, and delay) of reinforcement are important variables in both classical and instrumental conditioning. Variables that retard conditioning are nonreinforcement, effort, and massing of trials (brief intertrial intervals).

An analysis of the facts of conditioning suggests that there are three major components of both classical and instrumental conditioning: habit, drive, and inhibition.

A recent study which promises to provide insights into the neurophysiological basis of reinforcement indicates that electrical stimulation of certain brain centers is reinforcing.

SUGGESTIONS FOR FURTHER READING

HULL, C. L. *Principles of behavior.* New York: Appleton-Century-Crofts, 1943.

An historically important attempt to formulate some fundamental principles of behavior from the facts of conditioning. This book served to stimulate a tremendous amount of research and theorizing.

KELLER, F. S., & SCHOENFELD, W. N. *Principles of psychology.* New York: Appleton-Century-Crofts, 1950.

An introductory textbook in psychology that analyzes behavior in terms of principles of conditioning.

KIMBLE, G. A. *Hilgard and Marquis' conditioning and learning.* (2nd ed.) New York: Appleton-Century-Crofts, 1961.

An integrated review of the more recent work in the field of conditioning and learning.

PAVLOV, I. P. *Conditioned reflexes.* London: Oxford Univer. Press, 1927.

A brilliantly reasoned and written book which is now acknowledged to be a classic in the history of psychology.

SKINNER, B. F. *The behavior of organisms.* New York: Appleton-Century-Crofts, 1938.

The original effort of one of today's most influential psychologists to describe behavior with concepts from the conditioning laboratory.

SKINNER, B. F. *Cumulative record.* New York: Appleton-Century-Crofts, 1959.

A stimulating series of papers which reviews various facets of Skinner's research program in the field of instrumental conditioning.

Spence, K. W. *Behavior theory and conditioning.* New Haven, Conn.: Yale Univer. Press, 1956.

A modern theoretical analysis of the facts of conditioning. Spence's formulation is historically related to Hull's.

PERCEPTION—HOW WE ORGANIZE OUR WORLD

8

PERCEPTION AND PSYCHOLOGY

Look at Figure 8.1. It contains 49 small black squares. However, you do not see simply 49 separate and distinct squares. You almost certainly perceive all of them together, as falling into some sort of organized pattern. At first you may perceive the figure as consisting of seven rows or seven columns of black squares. Then you may perceive them as being organized into larger squares, each consisting of four or nine black squares. Or again, you may see the central lines of squares standing out as a large cross.

You have just demonstrated to yourself the major feature of perception. When we perceive complex forms of stimulation we automatically organize their features in

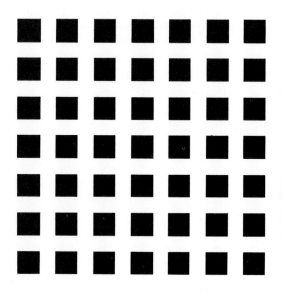

FIGURE 8.1 Forty-Nine Black Squares. Do you perceive them in some order?

some way. How we organize and arrange such complex forms of stimulation is the subject matter of the psychology of perception.

Sensation, Perception, and Learning

The study of sensation deals primarily with our reaction to some relatively simple form of stimulation, as when we see orange when viewing a light wave of 650 mμ. The study of perception, on the other hand, usually relates behavior to *complex* patterns of stimuli (such as the 49 black squares in Figure 8.1) rather than to an individual stimulus element. Of course, no sharp line can be drawn between simple and complex forms of stimulation. Visual acuity, fineness of visual discrimination, which we discussed under the heading of sensation, would be considered by some psychologists an example of a perceptual process. Depth perception, a topic to be discussed in this chapter, is considered by others as essentially a sensory process. Such distinctions are largely matters of convenience.

The relation between perception and learning is somewhat different. Conditioning, with its emphasis on practice, involves historical relationships. Perception, on the other hand, deals more with concurrent relationships such as an organism's responses in organizing a whole complex of stimuli all at once. This does not mean that learning fails to play a role in perception. It does. How we perceive the moon, for example, partly depends upon what we have learned in our culture. You were probably taught as a child to see a "man in the moon." If you were raised in another culture, you might see the head of a hare, or the profile of a woman, a donkey, or a man carrying a load of wood. The moon is a complex, ambiguous stimulus, and how anyone sees its depends mostly on how he was trained to perceive it.

The way you perceive Figure 8.2 also depends on your past experience. What seems to be happening in that picture? Compare your reactions with some of your fellow students'. You will be surprised to discover how differently you perceive the same picture. Learning is very influential in slanting perception.

FIGURE 8.2　How do you perceive this picture? (Reprinted by permission of the publishers from Henry A. Murray, Thematic Apperception Test, Cambridge, Mass.: Harvard University Press, Copyright, 1943, by the President and Fellows of Harvard College.)

Now that we have located perception against the background of the study of behavior, we can turn to our analysis of the perceptual process.

PERCEPTUAL ORGANIZATION

Figure and Ground

A famous Gestalt psychologist (see page 46) once raised a simple question that would never occur to most people. Why,

186 he asked, do we see the *things* and not the holes, that is, the spaces between them?

Raise your hand above your head and look at it with the fingers spread out. It stands out from the more formless background of the ceiling. Psychologists refer to this kind of perception as embodying a **figure-ground** relationship. The hand is a definite figure standing out against an amorphous background. Figure 8.3 illustrates another kind of figure-ground perception. Although you have never seen this ink spot before, you at once perceive it as a definite, blocked out, cohesive figure standing out against a formless gray background.

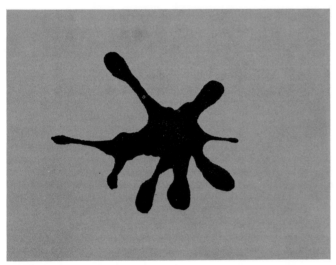

FIGURE 8.3   An Inkspot That Evokes a Figure-Ground Perception.

A figure-ground perceptual response possesses two major characteristics:

The figure is perceived to have a form, while the ground is relatively formless.

The figure is perceived to stand out against the background.

These characteristics of a figure-ground perceptual response are clearly demonstrated by designs capable of evoking a reversible figure-ground perception. Figure 8.4, an example of such a design, can be perceived as either a vase or two profiles. When you perceive it as a vase, the white portion has form while the gray appears

FIGURE 8.4   Is it a vase or two faces in profile?

formless. The white vase also appears to come forward while the gray recedes as the background. The reverse is true when you perceive the figure as two profiles; the white loses its form, recedes, and becomes background, while the gray profiles take on form and come forward.

The figure-ground way of perceiving things has been described as fundamental because it appears to develop independent of practice. Support for this claim comes from the experience of adults, blind from birth, whose cataracts were surgically removed (Senden, 1960). When they had recovered, they were shown various objects (spheres and cubes) against a homogeneous background. They reported a figure-ground perception; what they saw was some shape against a ground. In other words, human subjects, blind throughout their lives, *spontaneously* and without previous experience organized their perceptions into a figure-ground relationship.

Although figure-ground perception is fundamental, shape perception itself appears not to be. When blind, these same patients were able to feel the difference between spheres and cubes and to name them correctly (touch perception). Yet seeing these objects for the first time after surgery, they were unable to tell the spheres from the cubes. Even when a sphere was beside a cube, the patients could not tell them apart. They required extensive training before they were able to make what appears to be an absurdly simple discrimination. Thus it would seem that visual shape perception requires training, whereas the figure-ground perception occurs spontaneously.

A figure-ground perception is fundamental in another sense. When you look at a stimulus pattern, the figure-ground property emerges prior to other perceptual features. By means of an apparatus known as a tachistoscope, experimental subjects can be shown stimulus patterns for brief periods of time, shorter than one-thousandth of a second, if necessary. When a subject is shown a pattern just long enough for a quick look, the thing he sees is a figure and a ground (Flavell & Draguns, 1957). He can-

not identify the form; he can merely report some kind of figure against a background. But when the exposure time is lengthened other perceptual features, such as form, emerge.

Figure-ground perceptions are not restricted to vision. A melody from a symphony has a perceptual property similar to that of the inkblot in Figure 8.3. The melody stands out from the background.

Laws of Perceptual Grouping

Closely related to spontaneous figure-ground perceptions are **perceptual grouping** responses. The checkerboard pattern of Figure 8.1 initiates a variety of these responses. At one time you may perceive a particular black square as belonging with other black squares in a row. Seconds later you may group the same square with others to form a different perceptual organization (group of four squares).

The fluctuating perceptual organization of Figure 8.1 is due, in part, to the physical arrangement of the squares. By changing this arrangement it is possible to modify the resulting perceptual organization. If 13 empty circles are substituted for 13 of the solid black squares, the perceptual response shifts from one that permits alternate perceptual organizations to one that produces a single permanent perceptual grouping (see Figure 8.6). No matter how hard you try you probably cannot perceive Figure 8.6 as seven rows or seven columns. You are forced to perceive Figure 8.6 as a cross of circles surrounded by groups of black squares.

There appear to be certain underlying uniformities in our perceptual responses to relatively simple constellations of stimuli. Different patterns of stimuli do not produce unique perceptual organizations. Rather, we tend to organize various stimulus patterns according to a few basic principles of perceptual grouping.

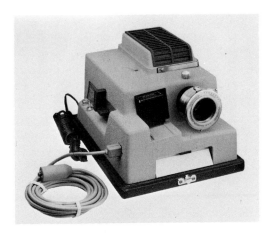

FIGURE 8.5 A Projection Tachistoscope. This projector is equipped with a camera shutter so that visual material can be projected on a screen for a brief time (Lafayette Instrument Co.).

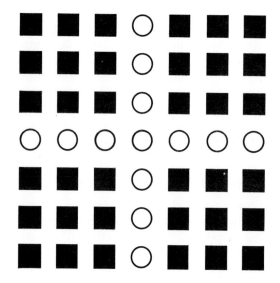

FIGURE 8.6 How Perceptual Organization Can Be Modified When Part of the Physical Stimulus Pattern Is Changed. Compare your reaction to this figure with your reaction to Figure 8.1 on page 184.

Principle of Nearness. Stimulus elements that are close together tend to be perceived as belonging together. Both the eight vertical lines and eight dots in Figure 8.7 are usually perceived in four groups of two. The first and second, the third and fourth, the fifth and sixth, and the seventh and eighth lines are perceived as belonging together. It is practically impossible to perceive the second and third lines or the fourth and fifth as being members of the same perceptual pair. The same pattern of perceptual grouping holds true for the dots.

It is also possible to demonstrate the principle of nearness for auditory stimuli. Tap a pencil on a tabletop so that the time interval between the even and odd taps (second and third) is appreciably longer than the time interval between the odd and even taps (first and second). You will perceive the odd and even taps as being paired because they are nearer together in time.

Principle of Similarity. The principle of nearness does not hold for all stimulus constellations. In some situations other factors operate to override the influence. Figure 8.8 demonstrates this. Each black square is nearer a circle than it is to another black square, yet the black squares are perceived as being grouped with other black squares instead of with their neighboring circles. This perceptual phenomenon illustrates the principle of similarity.

The similarity principle may be stated as follows: the greater the similarity among stimuli, the more likely they will be perceived as part of a common group. That the cross in Figure 8.6 is seen immediately as a unified whole is another example of the operation of stimulus similarity in visual perception.

Principle of Continuity. Stimulus elements part of a continuous sequence, such as the dots appearing in Figure 8.9, tend to be grouped together.

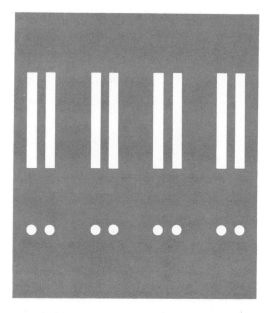

FIGURE 8.7 A Stimulus Pattern Illustrating the Principle of Nearness. You tend to organize the dots and lines in groups of two.

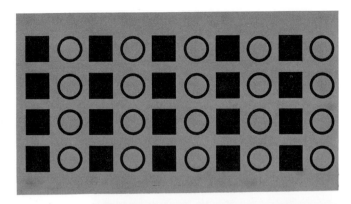

FIGURE 8.8 A Stimulus Pattern Illustrating the Principle of Similarity.
You tend to perceive the pattern as
a group of columns, not rows.

You perceive this pattern of dots as·being organized into two lines, one straight and one curved. The straight line intersects with the curved line where they share a common dot. Why didn't you at first see the curved line become suddenly straight at this junction, instead of continuing as a curved line? Considering only the principle of nearness and similarity, you should just as readily perceive two lines, each with a curved and straight portion, as perceive straight and curved lines. But you do not, and consequently the principle of contin-uity has to be advanced to explain this kind of a perceptual response.

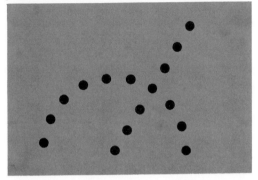

FIGURE 8.9 A Stimulus Pattern Illustrating the Prin-ciple of Continuity. You tend to perceive a straight and a curved line instead of two lines each with a straight and a curved portion.

The principle of continuity also explains how we fill in gaps when stimulation is incomplete. Instead of seeing a curved line and a disjointed straight line in Figure 8.10, we see a circle and a rectangle. In saying what is physically there, you cannot say that the lines form a circle or a square. However the perceptual principle of con-tinuity operates to induce the perceiver to see continuous lines and thus, completed figures.

Perceptual Illusions

The perceptual process organizes physical stimulation. Sometimes it organizes phys-ical stimulation erroneously. When this happens we perceive our physical environ-ment in a way that does not correspond with reality. Such false perceptions are called **illusions.**

FIGURE 8.10 Illustrations of the Principle of Con-tinuity. You tend to perceive a completed figure where none exists.

Illusions of Shape and Size. In Figure 8.11 there are a perfect circle and a perfect square, yet you do not perceive either of them as perfect. The circle appears flattened at one end and the sides of the square bent inwards. Even after you have measured the two shapes and discovered their geometric perfection, you are the victim of this illusion.

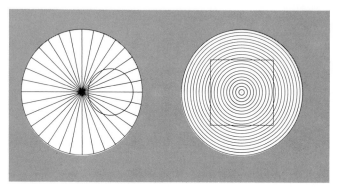

FIGURE 8.11 Two Illusions of Shape. The inner figure on the left is a perfect circle while the one on the right is a perfect square (Orbison, 1939, with permission of *The American Journal of Psychology*).

An illusion can be conceived of as representing a discrepancy between physical and psychological measurement. The most widely known visual illusion is shown in Figure 8.12. When you compare the two vertical lines in Figure 8.12 by actually measuring them with a ruler, they are equal in length. However, when you compare them perceptually, by measuring them psychologically, as it were, you judge the lines to be unequal. Even chickens have been proved to be the dupes of this illusion!

Another illusion, one that has fascinated man at least since the time of the Greeks, is the moon illusion. Near the horizon the moon appears much larger than it does high in the sky. Actually, of course, it is not. The area of the retina stimulated is the same in both cases. Why, then, do we perceive the horizon moon as larger? This question is currently a matter of much controversy among psychologists.

For several decades it was accepted that the moon illusion was due to the angle of vision at which you perceive the moon at the horizon and at its zenith. When you look at the moon at the zenith you raise your eyes, and this, in some unknown manner, makes it seem smaller than it does when you look at it straight ahead on the horizon. The implication of this eye-elevation hypothesis is that if you were to look upwards at the horizon moon its apparent size would decrease. And according to some reports (Holway & Boring, 1940), this is exactly what happens. The next time the moon appears big on the horizon and you are sufficiently curious to know why, lie down on your back and stretch you neck over a log (or somebody's limb) so that you are looking at the moon with your head hanging down backward. The horizon moon, enormous before, should now appear smaller, according to the eye-elevation hypothesis, because when you look at the

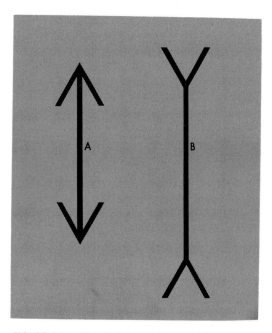

FIGURE 8.12 The Muller-Lyer Illusion. Which vertical line looks longer? Which is longer?

horizon moon with your head upside down, you must "raise" your eyes toward your forehead in order to see it. The raising of the eyes is presumably responsible for dispelling the moon illusion.

The experimental evidence in favor of the eye-level hypothesis was obtained with subjects who were strapped to a board which could be rotated from a horizontal to a vertical position. When the board was rotated so that the subject always looked straight ahead at the moon without raising his eyes, the moon did not appear to change in size as it rose from the horizon to the zenith. When, however, the board was rotated so that the subject was always supine with his head hanging down backward as he looked at the moon, it appeared small at the horizon and larger as it ascended. In this position, the subject had to "lower" his eyes toward his chin in order to follow the moon.

Recently the eye-elevation hypothesis has been attacked by two investigators (Kaufman & Rock, 1962) who have offered evidence to support the apparent-distance hypothesis originally proposed by Ptolemy, the Greek astronomer. The essence of this interpretation is that you see the horizon moon in relation to cues of the terrain— behind trees, houses, and hills—and thus it appears further away than the zenith moon which you see against the empty sky. Because of this, you automatically apply the rule that when two objects form retinal images of equal size and one is more distant than the other, the more distant one must actually be larger. Hence you judge the horizon moon to be larger and see it in that way.

Findings in support of the apparent-distance hypothesis show that the size of the horizon moon decreases when the landscape is masked, and that the size of the zenith moon increases when, by means of mirrors, it is perceived immediately above the terrain.

The data in support of these two hypotheses come from radically different experimental techniques, and quite obviously more research has to be done before this controversy is resolved. Possibly both hypotheses are to some extent true. Recent evidence (Baird, Gulick, & Smith, 1962) from the laboratory does suggest that visual size estimation is influenced by the angle of the eye position, and there is much evidence that of two objects projecting retinal images of equal size the one further away is perceived as larger.

Illusions of Brightness. Figure 8.13 shows two illusions involving brightness. In the right-hand figure the white bars separating the black square are pure white throughout, though you do not perceive it that way. You see gray at every intersection except the one you are focusing on. In the left-hand figure you perceive a gray circle, half against a black background and half against a white background. The circle appears to be, as it truly is, uniform in respect to light intensity. Now, place a pencil or pen on top of the line that separates the black half from the white half. Suddenly the gray portion against the black background appears brighter. The illusory change in brightness can be extended by slowly moving the divider across the figure. If you move it to the right the brighter gray extends into the white portion of the figure. If you move it to the left the darker gray is pulled into the black portion of the figure.

Illusions of Movement. We also perceive movement when no physical movement occurs. On both motion picture and television screens a series of still pictures are projected separately for a small fraction of a second. Yet instead of seeing a series of discrete still pictures, we perceive smooth-flowing movement. A famous sign on New York's Broadway represents an eagle in flight. The sign contains a number of fixed outlines, each with the bird's wings in a

FIGURE 8.13 Two Illusions of Brightness (Osgood, 1953).

different position. Turning the lights on and off so that these outlines are lit in sequence produces the illusion of a bird in flight. The movement is apparent, not real.

In 1912 the German psychologist Max Wertheimer (1880-1943), founder of the Gestalt school of psychology, discovered some of the stimulus conditions responsible for the perception of apparent movement, which he named the **phi-phenomenon.** He projected two short parallel lines, one centimeter apart, at reading distance from the subject. The lines were flashed on the screen one after the other. The length of the interval between the successive flashes determined what the subject perceived. If the interval between the exposure of each line was longer than .03 seconds, the subject perceived only what actually existed: two stationary lines, first one and then the other. However, if the duration of the interval was .002 seconds or less, the two lines appeared to be projected simultaneously. When the time interval was between .03 and .002 seconds, the observer perceived a flashing movement, with the first line seemingly to move from its own position to the second position. This is the phi-phenomenon, an apparent movement where in fact none occurs.

You can demonstrate the basis of apparent movement to yourself. Place the index finger of one of your hands about three inches in front of your nose, and wink your eyes rapidly one after the other. Your finger will appear to move from one position to another. Apparent movement depends upon the perception of successive stimulations appropriately separated in time and space.

Perception, the Nervous System, and Learning

Up to this point the perceptual responses we have described (figure-ground, perceptual grouping) are evoked by relatively simple patterns of stimuli. Why do we perceive these simple stimulus configurations as we do? This question can be answered directly, although incompletely, with figure-ground perceptions. Since they are independent of the organism's past training and occur spontaneously at the first opportunity, the conclusion is inevitable that certain stimulus conditions (e.g., Figure 8.3) initiate neural activities which produce a figure-ground perception. In an important sense however, the conclusion is incomplete. It tells you where to look to understand the figure-ground perception, but it does not tell you what to look for. It fails to specify the actual processes within the nervous system involved in the production of the figure-ground perception. A more complete understanding of fundamental perceptual responses, such as figure-ground, will have to await a more complete understanding of cerebral functioning.

We cannot be equally sure that innate physiological mechanisms are primarily responsible for such other phenomena as perceptual grouping and illusions. To demonstrate whether a specific perceptual response is generated by innate neural structures is most difficult. Newborn babes can hardly see and, of course, cannot communicate. With age vision improves and language habits develop. But with age also comes experience. Obviously, then, it is very difficult to unravel the influences of innate neural mechanisms from those of training. Only with the help of ingenious experiments or unusual events (humans having their first visual experience when adults) are we able to assess the relative contribution of innate physiological mechanisms and of training to perceptual phenomena. Some evidence does suggest that the perceptual groupings and illusions described above are largely, if not exclusively, independent of experience. For example, the Mueller-Lyer illusion is more effective with children than with adults (Seashore & Williams, 1900), and if training were responsible for this illusion, one would expect the opposite relationship. Hence the fact that the Mueller-Lyer effect decreases with age suggests that the illusion occurs spontaneously in the first place. Training enters only to lessen the extent to which the illusion is observed.

Once again we must emphasize an obvious point. The fact that psychologists try to find out whether a given perceptual response is spontaneous and therefore attributed to innate neurological mechanisms, does not mean that all perceptual responses can be attributed either to training or to maturational factors. Training and maturational factors can, and often do, interact. The neurological system we are born with provides a foundation for many perceptual responses which are then modified by experience. We now turn to examples of such perceptual phenomena.

VISUAL SPACE PERCEPTION

Only in laboratory situations is it possible to restrict an organism's environment to simple patterns of stimuli, but in our everyday world we must respond to exceedingly complex forms of stimulation. Many basic psychological problems are raised by our everyday perceptions. Perhaps the most persistently challenging of these has been to explain how we perceive a world possessing three dimensions: height, width, and depth. You perceive the location of an object in a room three-dimensionally; that is, you perceive that it is on the floor, near the wall with windows, and midway between the walls on either side. Again, you perceive that a book has length, width, and thickness. Well, you ask, what is so amazing about locating an object in relation to the three dimensions of a room, or perceiving the three dimensions of a book? Why should anyone be surprised to discover that things as we perceive them agree with physical realities? Well, for one thing, it is amazing that our three-dimensional perception is generated on a two-dimensional surface. The retina has but two dimensions, height and width, and no depth. Remember that when you look at two objects that are at different distances from you, the image on the retina of the farther object is not physically behind the image of the nearer. It cannot be, since the retina is flat. The retinal image of one object can only be to the left or right, above or below the retinal image of another object. Since all our visual images are projected on a two-dimensional surface, how can we possibly perceive a three-dimensional world? This

194

is the problem of visual space perception, and psychologists have offered two complementary sets of solutions.

One set consists of specifying the environmental cues that initiate a perception of three-dimensional space—it is an $R = f(S)$ type relationship. The second set specifies the physiological mechanisms that are re-

sponsible for depth perception—it is an $R = f(O)$ type relationship. Both these sets of answers must now be described.

Visual Depth Perception and Stimulus Variables

Depth perception does not always depend on perceiving a three-dimensional object, as Figure 8.14 demonstrates. Movies, especially those like Cinerama, that use a wide, curved screen also demonstrate this phenomenon. This makes depth perception seem even more of a puzzle. In Figure 8.14 the stimulus and the retinal image it initiates are both two-dimensional. Yet the perception is three-dimensional. There are stimulus cues, we conclude, in a two-dimensional picture that evoke a three-dimensional perceptual response. What are they?

Linear Perspective. Linear perspective is the technical term for the arrangement of lines in a drawing or painting to produce a representation of depth. Artists discovered quite early that they could create the impression of distance on a flat surface by making the objects supposed to be distant smaller and by gradually decreasing toward the top of the picture the size of one object or a group of similar objects. This way they could evoke a depth perception in the viewer. When an artist wants to represent one person as being farther away than another, he paints the first person smaller. When he paints a road that recedes into the distance, he makes the two lines representing the edges of the road converge as they approach the horizon. The larger representation, whether it is the size of the figure or the distance between the edges of the road, appears nearer to the viewer.

Interposition. When two objects are in the same line of vision, the nearer one conceals at least part of the farther one. Figure 8.16 shows how this helps us perceive depth in a two dimensional picture. The technical term for this cue to perceiving depth,

FIGURE 8.14 A Two-Dimensional Stimulus That Evokes a Three-Dimensional Perceptual Response.

FIGURE 8.15 An Example of Linear Perspective. This drawing of a highway scene shows how relative size and position contribute to our perception of depth.

FIGURE 8.16 A Photograph in Which the Perception of Depth Is Aided by Interposition (S. C. Johnson & Sons).

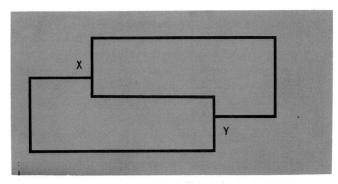

FIGURE 8.17 The Outline of an Object Functions as the Interpositional Cue. Observe that the relative positions of the two rectangles change when you shift your gaze from X to Y (After Ratoosh, 1949).

where one object partially blots out another, is **interposition.**

Since the stimulus cues responsible for interposition are the outlines of objects, the positions with respect to each other of the two rectangles in Figure 8.17 are ambiguous. At X the upper rectangle appears closer, whereas at Y the lower rectangle appears closer.

Light and Shadow. By distributing lights and shadows appropriately, one can give a two-dimensional drawing a three-dimensional look. Figure 8.18 shows how a simple geometrical surface can be transformed into a solid by the addition of shadows. Note that these shadows essentially indicate what happens when a light shines on a solid. The surface of the solid nearest the light source is the brightest and hence without shadows. As the surface recedes from the light it becomes less and less bright and more and more darkly shadowed.

Shadows can produce tricky effects. In Figure 8.19 you perceive several large dents in a steel plate in addition to the regularly placed rivets that appear as bumps. Turn the book upside down and look at the picture again. The dents have become bumps and the bumps have become dents. Why?

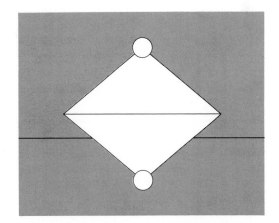

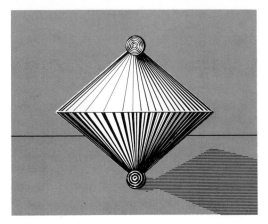

FIGURE 8.18 Lights and Shadows Can Provide a Two-Dimensional Figure With a Three-Dimensional Appearance.

FIGURE 8.19 How Lights and Shadows Determine Depth Perception. Look at this picture with the book turned upside down (C. H. Stoelting Co.).

The answer is to be found in the shadows. You have lived for years in a world in which sunlight and most other sources of light come from above. Under these circumstances the top part of a dent is normally in shadow while the bottom is in light. The reverse is true of bumps. When the picture is turned upside down the position of the lights and shadows is reversed, and hence, you immediately see the dents as bumps and the bumps as dents.

Clearness. Generally the nearer we are to an object the clearer its details; a person's face becomes less distinct the farther away

he is. Since clearness serves as a cue for distance perception, we can easily be deceived by shifting conditions of clearness. The city dweller, accustomed to seeing objects through haze and smog, makes poor judgments about the distance of the mountains in Colorado. Since the mountains stand out so clearly, the observer judges them to be nearby, when in reality they are many miles away. Figure 8.20 shows how mountains look closer in a clear atmosphere than they do in a hazy atmosphere. Stage designers create the illusion of depth on a relatively shallow stage by interposing layers of netting with bits of scenery.

Movements. The speed of an object as it travels through space can serve as a cue to its distance. A plane that zooms by is automatically judged closer than one that appears to be lazily drifting. A stationary observer tends to recognize faster-moving objects as being closer than slow-moving objects. However, an observer who is himself moving judges the distance of an object by the direction of its movement. When you are riding in a train or car, the distant hills or moon appear to move with you, but the nearby telegraph poles snap back in the opposite direction as you pass them. These are examples of what is technically known as **motion parallax,** the change in the apparent direction of an object as a result of a change in the observer's position in space.

Gradients. Two similar checker-board patterns are shown in Figure 8.21. They differ in the spacing of the horizontal lines; in the upper section the lines are equally spaced, while in the lower section they get gradually closer. Unlike the upper half, which appears flat, the lower half gives the impression of depth. The reason is that it has a texture gradient. When we look at any flat surface with regular markings (the lines of the boards in a floor) or texture (the clods of earth in Figure 8.22), the

FIGURE 8.20 Clearness of Detail Serves as a Cue for Depth Perception. The mountains seem nearer when they are not obscured by haze.

FIGURE 8.22 A Photograph of Clods of Earth That Demonstrates How a Texture Gradient Can Serve as a Cue for the Perception of Distance (J. J. Gibson. *The perception of the visual world,* Boston: Houghton Mifflin, 1950).

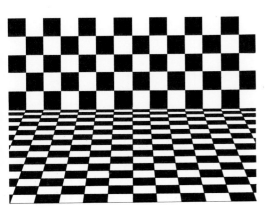

FIGURE 8.21 A Texture Gradient Can Give the Impression of Depth. Compare your perception of the upper half of the above drawing with the lower half.

markings become denser as distance increases. Such a gradient of texture provides us with a good cue to physical distance.

Visual Depth Perception and Organismic Variables

Cues to depth perception are not found exclusively in the environment. The structure of our visual receptors provides us with additional cues that help us estimate the position of objects in the three-dimensional world. We shall mention several of these aids.

Accommodation. When a photographer takes successive pictures of objects at different distances from him, he must adjust the distance of the lens from the film each time, to get a sharp image. The human eye acts on the same principle but in a somewhat different way. So that the retina will receive a sharp image, the lens bulges when we look at a nearby object; it flattens out when we look at more distant objects. This change in lens shape is called **accommodation,** and is accomplished by muscles and ligaments acting upon a somewhat elastic lens. Kinesthetic receptors (see page 93) are imbedded in these muscles and ligaments, and consequently are stimulated by their action. Stimulated differently when the eye looks at a nearby object from when it looks at a more distant object, the kinesthetic receptors supply cues for depth perception. However, it has been estimated that accommodation-produced cues are helpful in estimating distance only within about four feet of the eyes. Beyond this point there is no appreciable increase in the flattening of the lens. For most of us, then, accommodation is probably not a very important cue in depth perception, but for the lathe operator or watch repairman who must make precise estimates of close distances, accommodation can be of valuable assistance.

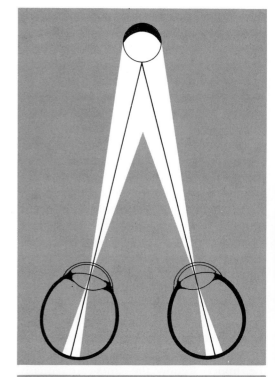

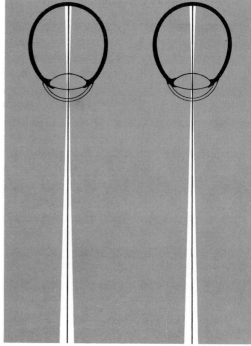

FIGURE 8.23   The Lines of Vision for Near and Distant Objects.

Convergence. When you look at a distant object the lines of vision of your eyes are parallel. As the object is brought nearer than 50 feet the lines of vision converge. Figure 8.23 shows this difference.

The amount of convergence is controlled by skeletal muscles attached to the eyeball. When the position of the eyes is adjusted by these skeletal muscles, kinesthetic nerve impulses are generated. These serve as distance cues. You may not be aware that you depend upon these convergence cues, as you probably were not aware of the cues of accommodation. Nevertheless, both can aid you in estimating distance.

Retinal Disparity. The most important physiological cue to distance is a result of the fact that we have two eyes set about two and one-half inches apart, and because of this, each eye receives a somewhat different view of the same object. To demonstrate this to yourself, take a common wooden lead pencil with printing on one of its sides. Hold the pencil about six inches in front of your nose, and close your left eye. While looking at the pencil with your right eye, turn it so that the printing becomes barely visible on the right side. Now close your right eye and look at the pencil with your left. You will no longer be able to see the printing. Obviously each eye receives a different picture of the same pencil.

The fact that different images are received by each eye is appropriately termed **retinal disparity.** Its effectiveness as a distance cue is apparent to everyone who has viewed a picture taken by a stereo camera through a Viewmaster or comparable device. A stereo camera is a double camera. Its two lenses are separated by a distance equivalent to the space between two eyes, so that you take two pictures simultaneously, one from the position of each eye. When you see these two pictures in a stereo viewer your left eye sees the left picture while your right eye sees the right picture. These two separate views are fused in your brain so that the one picture you perceive possesses a strikingly real depth effect.

The principle of retinal disparity has been applied in many ways. You may have once seen 3-D comics or drawings printed in both red and blue ink, with the two sets of colored lines alongside each other. When you look at such drawings without glasses you receive a double-image impression, but when you look at them through 3-D spectacles with one red and one blue lens, you see a single picture with realistic depth. This is because the red lens eliminates the red lines of the picture so that only the blue lines are visible; likewise, the blue lens eliminates the blue lines so that only the red lines are visible. Since each eye sees a slightly different picture, the viewer gets a perception of depth.

The Combined Operation of Stimulus and Physiological Depth Perception Cues

Several variables responsible for our perception of depth and distance have just been described one by one, and this may have suggested to you that each variable operates in isolation. This is not true. Typically we perceive depth as a result of the simultaneous operation of several different variables.

Sometimes space perception cues conflict with each other; some cues evoke a three-dimensional perceptual response, while others simultaneously suggest a two-dimensional surface. Figure 8:24 contains such a conflicting set of cues. Several stimulus cues (linear perspective, interposition) elicit a perception of depth. At the same time, similar retinal images are produced in both eyes, retinal similarity being a cue for a two-dimensional perceptual response. Because of this conflict, Figure 8.24 produces a relatively weak depth perception response. Although you perceive depth when you look at the photograph, the depth effect is appreciably less than what you would

FIGURE 8.24 Can you name all the stimulus variables in this picture that elicit a perception of depth?

perceive if you were looking at the real scene. This conflict between the space perception cues would be eliminated if the photograph of the scene in Figure 8.24 has been taken with a stereo camera and you were viewing it in a Viewmaster. Then instead of conflicting, as they now do, the space perception cues would be mutually supportive.

You can increase the impression of depth in Figure 8.24 by looking at it through a rolled-up paper tube. This will eliminate the frame of the picture, which serves as a two-dimensional cue. When we look at the world about us we do not perceive a frame around our view, and therefore we associate frames with two-dimensional objects such as pictures. You may have noticed in viewing Cinerama, or some other projection technique using a large, curved screen, that the depth perception effect is greater when you are sitting up front. By sitting close you avoid seeing the frame of the screen.

AUDITORY SPACE PERCEPTION

The Perception of Obstacles by the Blind

The sense of hearing also helps us perceive a three-dimensional world. This is dramatically demonstrated by the apparently magical feats of the blind.

For centuries people have wondered how blind men are able to avoid colliding with silent obstacles like walls. The blind are even able to avoid obstacles which they have never confronted before. How can they do this? The answer was revealed in the results of a cleverly designed experiment (Supa, Cotzin, & Dallenbach, 1944). Human subjects were placed blindfolded at a predetermined distance from a stonewall or masonite panel. They were instructed to walk toward the obstacle and approach as close to it as possible without touching it, but to stop as soon as they first perceived it. Some of the subjects had been blind all their lives, the remainder had normal vision. The blind subjects were far superior to the normal subjects in their performance. They walked unhesitantly toward the wall and stopped in time to avoid a collision. The subjects with normal vision had much difficulty; their forward progress was hesitant and they collided with the wall repeatedly.

The blind subjects obviously possessed an ability to perceive distance superior to that of blindfolded subjects. But this decreased after the normal subjects had an opportunity to practice, suggesting that the ability to avoid silent obstacles can be learned to some extent. The next problem was to determine the basis of this ability.

One possibility was that the sense of hearing contributed to the ability to avoid obstacles. During the experiment just described, both the blind and normal subjects wore shoes and walked on a wooden floor. In order to eliminate the sound produced by their footsteps, they were required to walk on a carpeted floor in their stocking feet. The accuracy of both groups in avoiding obstacles decreased markedly, and the hypothesis that ability to avoid silent obstacles depends in some manner on the sense of hearing received support.

FIGURE 8.25 Tests Determining That the Sense of Hearing is Used in Avoiding Silent Obstacles. In the upper drawing the subject, walking on a hardwood floor with his shoes on, approaches the masonite screen. In the lower drawing the subject, in stocking feet, approaches the obstacle on a carpet.

A blind subject with earphones was then seated in a soundproof room. The experimenter, carrying a high fidelity microphone, walked in his shoes on a hardwood floor toward the obstacle. The blind subject, sensing when the experimenter was approaching the obstacle, warned him to stop at the right time. Again the evidence suggested that the sense of hearing was responsible for the ability to avoid obstacles. The final proof came when it was found (Worchel & Dallenbach, 1947) that blind subjects who were completely deaf were incapable of avoiding obstacles in their path.

How can the sense of hearing help a person avoid a silent obstacle? The answer is that when the subjects approached a wall the sounds of their footsteps traveled forward, hit the wall, and were reflected backwards. The blind subjects, and later the normal subjects with training, responded to these reflected sounds (echoes). When the experimental situation was modified to eliminate the echoes from the footsteps, the appropriate avoidance behavior deteriorated.

You may have seen blind people tapping their canes in front of them as they walk down a street. Their purpose is not only to feel out obstacles, but also to send out sound waves which will reflect back from obstacles beyond reach of the cane. Bats are known to operate in much the same manner (Griffin & Galambos, 1941). When flying in the dark through forest foliage or winding caves, they emit short bursts of very high frequency sound, varying from 30,000 to 70,000 cycles per second. These ultrasonic sounds (above the upper human threshold), like the taps from the blind man's cane, echo back from obstacles and provide nonvisual cues that help the bat to avoid collisions. When the bat's ears are plugged, he loses this ability to fly blind, and flies head on into trees or walls of caves.

You may have wondered whether the research into how the blind subjects avoid silent obstacles was really necessary. Would it not have been sufficient to ask them how they did this? The truth is that when asked, blind subjects did not agree about the basis of their unusual skill. Some of them attributed their skill to an unknown sense or to sensations of pressure on the face. But, as the experimental evidence indicated, the true reason for their capacity to avoid obstacles was their ability to respond to reflected sound. This will not be the last time that we shall mention behavior in which humans respond to a cue they cannot identify.

The ability of the blind to detect silent obstacles demonstrates that the sense of hearing can aid an individual by orienting to three-dimensional space. People with normal vision do not usually respond to such subtle auditory cues as reflected sound, but they do respond to more obvious auditory cues. When you are in a large room and somebody calls your name, you wheel around and more than likely find that you are looking directly at the caller. You probably never stop to appreciate the accuracy of your response or wonder how it was possible. Similarly, when driving a car, you can usually, although certainly not all the time, locate the automobile whose horn is blowing.

Just as it was possible for us to analyze visual space perception, it is possible to analyze auditory space perception in terms of stimulus and organismic (physiological) variables. The stimulus variables are those attributes of sound itself which provide cues for space perception. The organismic variables are the structural features of the physiological system which mediate our ability to locate sounds in space.

Stimulus Variables

The intensity of sound decreases with distance. Therefore, the nearer we are to the source of a sound, the louder it is; the farther away, the less loud. If the sound is familiar, as of a friend's voice, we can usually judge its distance from its loudness.

With increased distance sounds become less complex. A clarinet and an oboe that sound strikingly different to a nearby observer, will be indistinguishable to a distant observer. The timbre of a sound can thus serve as an auditory cue for distance perception. It is a particularly helpful cue in judging the distance of a plane at night. The sound of an airplane motor is highly complex, and since this complexity decreases rapidly with distance, at a great distance you hear only a low hum.

Organismic Variables

It is possible to respond to the stimulus variables of auditory depth perception with only one ear. If one ear is deaf, or deliberately plugged, a person can still estimate the distance of a sound fairly well. However, the ability to localize a sound, to determine its *direction* as well as its distance, depends on our hearing it with both ears. The fact that we have two receptors for auditory as well as for visual stimuli helps us immensely in adjusting to a three-dimensional world.

If you ask someone to talk to you while your eyes are shut, you will have no difficulty in determining whether he is on your left or on your right. You can do this because you receive three different **binaural** cues (the term *binaural* refers to the use of two ears). When your friend speaks from your left side, the sound (1) reaches your left ear sooner than the right because it has to travel a shorter distance, (2) is stronger for the left ear than for the right ear because its intensity decreases with distance, and (3) is different in phase when it reaches the left ear than it is when it reaches the right.

The effectiveness of the first two cues is easy to understand, the third needs some explanation. Of the three, differences in the phase of sound striking the ear are the most subtle and, except in the case of tones of low frequency, usually the least effective auditory cues. You recall that a sound wave (see page 135) consists of a succession of greater and lesser pressures, of periods of condensation and rarefaction. With tones of low frequency, one ear may be stimulated by a condensed period at the moment the other ear is stimulated by a rarefied period. When sound is represented in transverse wave form, differences in phase are represented by differences in the portion of the sound wave that strikes the ear. In Figure 8.26 arrows point to the portions of the sound wave that might strike each ear and produce phase differences.

If binaural cues enable us to localize bodies that emit sounds in three-dimensional space, then the absence or confusion of these cues should reduce or eliminate our localizing ability. This is exactly what

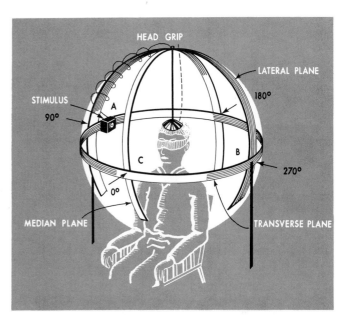

FIGURE 8.27 An Experimental Apparatus Used to Investigate Auditory Localization. The stimulus is placed in different positions, and after the subject hears it, he indicates its position of origin.

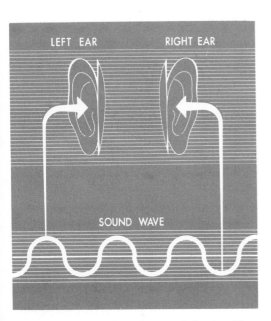

FIGURE 8.26 The Physical Basis of Sensing Phase Differences. When sound comes from the side, the sound wave stimulates the left ear at the point indicated by the first arrow, and stimulates the right ear at the point indicated by the second arrow.

happens. In a conventional sound-localizing experiment the subject is placed in the domed frame represented in Figure 8.27.

By remote control, the experimenter produces a definite, sharp click at various locations within the dome. The subject is instructed to tell where the click comes from. The subject with normal hearing has no difficulty locating clicks when they emanate from either the right or left side, but if the click comes from the median plane, the subject is usually unable to locate its exact position. A sound from any point on the median plane strikes both ears at the same time, with the same intensity, and in the same phase. Its failure to provide any time, intensity, or phase differences serves to notify the observer that the click came from a point equidistant from both ears, but there is no cue to suggest from what position on the median plane the click came. A click from the front of the median plane is just as likely to be located as coming from the rear or from above, as from the front. You can demonstrate this phenomenon by having a friend sit in a chair with his eyes closed. Click two quarters together at different positions around his head. If you do the experiment properly, you will discover that your friend is able to locate the sound as long as it does not emanate from the median plane.

If it were possible for a sound emanating from a subject's left side to strike his right ear before the left and be louder there, you would expect the subject to be tricked into believing that the sound came from the right. This expectation is confirmed by a pseudophone, pictured in Figure 8.28. This device, invented by psychologist Paul T. Young, consists of two curved tubes, one opening on the left side but connected to the right ear, and the other opening on the right side but connected to the left ear. When he is wearing such a device and has his eyes closed, a subject locates a sound as coming from the side opposite to its origin. He has, however, no more difficulty in locating a tone that originates in the median plane than a person with normal binaural

hearing has. With or without the pseudophone, sounds from the median plane strike both ears at the same time with the same intensity and at the same phase, and so the subject receives no cues to help him locate the sound within the median plane.

Learning, of course, plays an important role in our ability to locate sounds. We have learned to look up at the sound of an airplane and down when shoes squeak. We have also learned to integrate auditory with visual cues. We hear a car's horn and look down the street to locate its exact position. But sometimes vision can upset our auditory localizations. We seem to hear sound coming from the mouth of a dummy because we see his mouth moving and not the ventriloquist's. We also seem to hear a voice in a movie coming from the appropriate actor's mouth, although it may actually come from a loudspeaker at the side of the screen.

PERCEPTUAL CONSTANCY

Size Constancy. In many instances our perceptions of objects remain unexpectedly stable, in view of the variety of physical stimuli that reach our receptors. Consider for a moment the size of a quarter. First hold it about a foot away from your eyes; then extend your arm full length so that the distance between your eyes and the coin will be about doubled. Does the quarter really seem to get smaller as you move it away? No, if you are honest with yourself, you perceive it as being constant in size regardless of the distance. Yet on your retina the image of the coin at one foot is four times as large as it is at double that distance (see Figure 8.29). The resistance of a visually perceived object to change in size as its retinal image changes in size is known as (visual) **size constancy.**

Is it because we are familiar with the size of a quarter that we perceive it as having

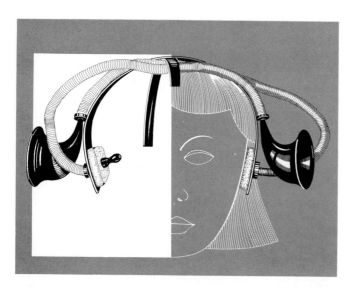

FIGURE 8.28   A Pseudophone Invented by Dr. Paul T. Young. A tube transmits to the right ear sound waves which would normally stimulate the left ear. Another tube sends to the left ear sound waves which would normally stimulate the right ear (After Young, 1928).

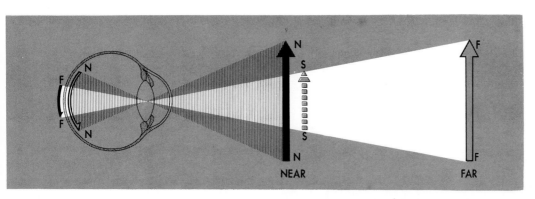

FIGURE 8.29 The Relationship Between the Physical Size of an Object, its Distance From the Eye, and the Size of the Image It Casts Upon the Retina. The near arrow, which is the same size as the far arrow, throws a larger image on the retina. Note that the smaller image *F-F* may be projected either by the short arrow (*S-S*) at the near distance or by the large arrow at the far distance.

a constant size no matter how far away it is? Suppose, instead, you are asked to judge the size at various distances of an unfamiliar circular disk? The general outcome of experiments of this kind (Holway & Boring, 1941; Lichten & Lurie, 1950) is that perception of the size of an unfamiliar object is dependent solely upon the customary cues in space perception.

To go into detail: when unrestricted binocular or monocular vision was permitted, disks at different distances were judged to be approximately the size they actually were. The size of the object, not the size of the retinal image it projected, proved to be the important variable. When some of the depth cues were eliminated by requiring the subject to peer monocularly through an artificial pupil (a hole 1.8 millimeters in diameter), disks were judged smaller the farther away they were. Under these conditions the perception of size produced a compromise between an object's actual physical size and the size of its retinal image. Finally, when a heavy black cloth known as a reduction tunnel was added, eliminating all cues except the disks themselves, no trace of size constancy remained. The size of the retinal image determined perceived size.

These results clearly demonstrate that size constancy does not operate under all conditions. Familiarity with the object and the presence of cues (both stimulus and organismic) that assist in depth perception favor size constancy. Reduction or elimination of these factors tends to keep estimates of size more in line with the size of the retinal image.

Shape Constancy. Size is not the only characteristic of perceived objects which remains stable. The shape of a familiar object is perceived as constant in spite of the fact that the retinal image it projects varies widely according to the angle it is viewed from. Think how rarely a common dinner plate projects a perfectly circular image on your retina. It does so only when your line of vision falls perpendicularly on the center of the surface of the dinner plate. At other times the retinal image of a round plate is oval, sometimes very much elongated. Yet you regularly perceive the plate as round. In the same way, a door rarely projects a rectangular image on the retina, but, as Figure 8.30 shows, it always looks the same.

There is some degree of shape constancy even with unfamiliar objects. Subjects were asked to draw the shape of cardboard circles and squares placed at different distances from them. Their drawings show that their

FIGURE 8.30 Examples of Shape Constancy. The shape of the retinal images projected by each of the three drawings is different. Nevertheless you perceive each of the three doors as having the same shape (After Gibson, 1950).

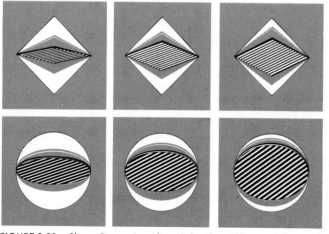

FIGURE 8.31 Shape Perception of an Unfamiliar Object as Influenced by Its Physical Shape and the Retinal Image It Projects. The outside line represents the physical shape of the cardboard disk, whereas the striped figure indicates the shape of the retinal image. The in-between gray figure is the subject's perception as indicated by his drawing (After Thouless, 1931).

perceptions were a kind of compromise between the shape of the retinal image and the physical shape of the object. Figure 8.31 represents the results of such an experiment.

Brightness Constancy. Whether you place a sheet of white paper in deep shadow or bright light, it looks white, so white, indeed, even in dim moonlight, that you will be surprised when you first notice it. It retains its whiteness regardless of the amount of light it reflects. Brightness constancy also holds for a sheet of gray paper. If a sheet of gray paper is placed in sunlight and a sheet of white paper is placed in deep shadow, the white paper will look brighter even though it will actually reflect less light!

The phenomenon of brightness constancy may appear at first glance to be inconsistent with what you know about the psychological dimension of brightness. Brightness, you will recall (see page 123), is primarily a function of light intensity. Yet white paper which is reflecting less light than gray paper is seen as brighter. The reason for this apparent discrepancy lies in the conditions of illumination. When the same light shines on both gray and white paper, the latter will naturally reflect more light. However, when different stimulus objects (white and gray sheets of paper) are perceived under different conditions of illumination, the phenomenon of brightness constancy applies.

When light falls on the surface of a sheet of paper, some of the light is reflected and the remainder absorbed. A white paper reflects about 90 per cent of the light shining on it. This percentage of light reflected is constant in all illuminations; whether the sun or a flashlight is shining on a sheet of white paper, it will reflect about 90 per cent of the light. When placed on a dull brown table top the sheet's relative brightness will be the same regardless of the amount of illumination. When illuminated by sunlight or flashlight both the white paper and the table top will reflect the same percentage of available light. This percentage is a measure of what is technically known as the **albedo** of a surface. Thus we see that the *sensation of brightness* is primarily a function of light intensity, while *brightness constancy* is due to the albedos of a surface and its surround.

Color Constancy. Colors also maintain a degree of constancy under a variety of conditions. After you have spent a moment adjusting to colored sunglasses, you· find that in general things assume their normal colors. For example, the hood of a red convertible still looks red, even though the light reaching your eyes has changed markedly in passing through the sunglasses. A sheet of white paper under a red light appears white. But if you look at a piece of it through a tube, it becomes reddish. The tube eliminates all environmental cues, so that your perception is dependent solely on retinal stimulation. Without the tube, you see, in addition to the surface of the paper, the entire environment including the source of illumination, the outline of the paper, and other familiar objects. When you perceive all these cues together, your psychological perception (e.g., perception of the paper as white) is of the world as you know it to be, with sizes, shapes, and colors preserved by the constancy principle. Under a variety of conditions our perceptual system integrates all relevant information so that our perception remains consistent with physical reality.

The Nature of Perceptual Constancy

Perceptual constancy is a useful talent, for it keeps us in touch with things as they really are. Without it our perceptual world would be chaotic. Suppose our friends appeared to be midgets at a distance and then became giants as we approached them. A baby in arms would be perceived as larger than an adult several feet away. The mechanic who had to select a bolt or nut of the proper size from a wide variety at varying distances from him would face a hopeless task. As he moved about, the perceived sizes and shapes of objects would change and make it impossible for him to rely on what he saw in interpreting reality.

How do perceptual constancies operate? It is a common misconception to assume that our ability to perceive an object in its true size is possible because we disregard the cue provided by the size of the retinal image. This is not so. Perceptual constancy does not result from ignoring any particular cue; it results from responding to *patterns* of cues. The retinal image of the object whose size remains constant is one cue along with other cues. Just as the retinal image of a distant object decreases in size as its distance from the observer increases, so do the sizes of the retinal images of nearby objects. Our retinal image of a child decreases as he rides away on his bicycle, but so do the retinal images of the bicycle, the width of the road, and the trees lining the road. Thus it is that the absolute size of any retinal image decreases, but not its *relative* size. The relative size serves as the important cue for size constancy. You will recall that in the artificial situation of the laboratory when unfamiliar objects were used alone so that the subject was unable to perceive relative size, he did not experience perfect size constancy. Under such conditions the size perceived tended to vary directly with distance.

The next question is, How do perceptual constancies develop? Are these responses to patterns of cues independent of learning, as the figure-ground perception appears to be? Or do perceptual constancies result from practice, as do conditioned responses?

No general answer to this question can be given. Actually it is not a single problem with a single answer; instead, it is a group of problems, each requiring its own experimental analysis and identification of the relevant cue or cues (e.g., albedo in brightness constancy).

Practice does seem to play an important role in the size constancy responses of humans. For example, before a certain age, children do not know that the size of an object remains constant as its position changes. Piaget, a Swiss psychologist, demonstrated that when two blocks of equal length are placed one above the other (see Figure 8.32), preschool children judge them to be equal in length. When, however, one block is shifted to the right, that block is judged to be longer. The child must learn, as all of us have, that the size of an object remains constant regardless of its position.

Their judgments of brightness and shape also improve with age. As they grow older they improve in ability to integrate the pattern of perceptual cues necessary for perceiving, under varying conditions, an object's true physical characteristics.

PERCEPTUAL LEARNING

Figure 8.33 shows how learning can play a role in perception. When you look at this photograph you probably see swirling flames in the branches of a tree. But it is not a photograph of a tree in flames. It is an aerial photograph of the Colorado River as it forces its way through bright sands forming a delta. What you saw when you first looked at it was what you have been trained to perceive. Since more than

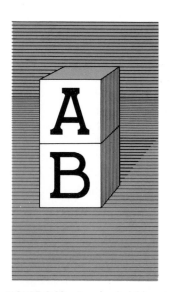 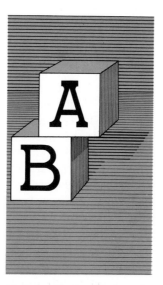

FIGURE 8.32 Preschool children tend to judge the two blocks to be equal in length. However, when the top block is pushed to the right it is judged to be longer (Suggested by Piaget, 1953).

FIGURE 8.33 What do you see? See the text to discover what the subject of this photograph is (Fairchild Aerial Surveys).

Another line of evidence suggesting that size constancies are learned comes from experiments with children of different ages (Osgood, 1953). Children up to ten years of age become more and more accurate in judging the physical size of objects.

likely your experience with aerial views is limited, you automatically interpreted the pattern of stimulation in Figure 8.33 in a manner consistent with your past experience, in this case, of flames and trees.

Your learning can also distort your perception of simple English phrase. Have a look at the triangles in Figure 8.34 and read aloud what they say. Did you, like most others, read one triangle as "Paris in the Spring"? Look again! It reads "Paris in the *the* Spring." The other triangle also repeats a word unnecessarily. These triangles illustrate the point that we tend to organize what we perceive in line with what past experiences have taught us to expect.

Because perceptions can be influenced by past experience, psychologists find it convenient to speak of **perceptual learning.** They might with equal propriety speak of *learning perceptions.*

Figure 8.35 is an ambiguous figure. It can be perceived either as an attractive young lady or an old hag (Leeper, 1935*b*). Psychologists like to call this picture the wife and mother-in-law. About 60 per cent of the people who are shown this figure for the first time see the attractive young woman (the wife) first. The remaining 40 per cent see the mother-in-law. These percentages can be radically altered by training. In one experiment two groups of subjects were each shown one of the two unambiguous figures in Figure 8.36. Afterwards, when these subjects were shown the ambiguous figure, all of those who had been shown the wife, saw the wife. Ninety-five per cent of the subjects who had seen the mother-in-law earlier saw her first in the ambiguous picture. Because the perception of a picture can depend upon past experience, clinical psychologists often try to find out how their patients perceive certain pictures (see Figure 8.2 on page 185) which come from specially selected groups, or tests, in order to secure important clues to the patients' past experiences, as well as their present interests.

Perhaps the most dramatic demonstration of the influence of learning on perception comes from a series of exhibits, named after their designer, the Ames demonstrations (Ittleson, 1952). Figure 8.37 is a good example of the series. This photograph demonstrates a most compelling illusion. In the top photograph you perceive the man on the right as being much larger than

the man on the left. But from the reversed positions of the same two men in the bottom photograph, you know this can't be true. The larger man appears smaller and the smaller man appears larger.

FIGURE 8.34 What do the triangles say?

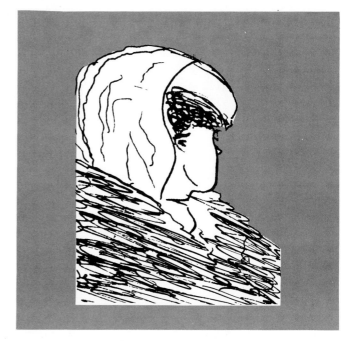

FIGURE 8.35 An Ambiguous Drawing Which Can Be Seen as "a Wife" or "Mother-in-law" (Leeper, 1935).

FIGURE 8.36   An Unambiguous "Wife" and an Unambiguous "Mother-in-law" (Leeper, 1935).

FIGURE 8.37   Who is really larger? The two men in both photographs are actually the same size (Institute for International Social Research).

The figure contains two examples of sets of perceptual cues apparently in conflict. Each example shows two men whom you know to be similar in size, but the retinal image of the man on the left is smaller, and therefore he should be perceived as being farther away. Yet he does not appear farther away because both men are standing in the opposite corners of a room and at the same distance from the camera.

At least, it seems that they are the same distance away, because in your experience four-sided rooms have always been rectangular. But they need not be! Figure 8.38 is a model of the room shown in Figure 8.37. The room is distorted so that the left corner is farther away than the right corner. The floor and ceilings are slanted in opposite directions, so that the distance between floor and ceiling at the left corner is much greater than that at the right corner. The distorted room in Figure 8.37 was constructed so that when viewed through an artificial pupil (see page 205) with one eye (thus eliminating many depth perception cues), it appears to be a normal rectangular room. Consequently a person tall enough to fill the entire distance between ceiling and floor in one corner is seen as much taller than a person only reaching up about half the distance between floor and ceiling in the neighboring corner.

Here, then, is conflict between two perceptions. Either the room or the man must be perceived as distorted (the height either of one corner of the room or of one man must appear very much smaller than the other). Most observers resolve this conflict at once and automatically by accepting the man as smaller. If, however, the observer had had extensive experiences with lopsided rooms of this sort, he would almost certainly have perceived the men in Figure 8.37 as equal in size. This assumption is supported by evidence that the striking perceptual illusion of Figure 8.37 can be modified by experience. One quick way to do this is to step inside the room. You immediately perceive that the room is distorted and the two men equal in size. In short, you perceive both the room and the men as they really are. Another way of overcoming the illusion is to undergo extensive training in perceiving objects in different locations in the distorted room. If, for example, you look through an artificial pupil at a pack of cigarettes drawn across the rear wall from left to right, the pack will appear to get progressively larger. When the pack is in the same position as the "small" man in Figure 8.37 it will be seen at its smallest, and as it travels across the back toward the "large" man, it will appear to get bigger and bigger. After a varied and intensive training program of this sort, during which you see the pack of cigarettes move across the room in various directions or see a yardstick in various positions in the room, you will "catch on," that is, size constancy will take control, the apparently magical change in size of the pack of cigarettes will cease, and you will perceive the room in its true distorted shape (Weiner, 1956).

If after learning to perceive the shape

FIGURE 8.38 A Model of the Room Shown in Figure 8.37 (Institute for International Social Research).

of this distorted room, you are asked to look at another room distorted in the opposite direction (the right corner being higher and farther away), you will quickly learn in what way it was distorted. The perceptual learning that had already occurred in one distorted room would speed your progress in learning to make correct perceptions in a differently distorted room.

It is interesting to note that when a human observer perceives a pack of cigarettes moving across the back wall of a distorted room through an artificial pupil, his perceptions are consistent; they hang together. They tend to perceive this ambiguous situation in one of two ways: either the pack of cigarettes changes size in a normal room, or the size of the pack remains constant in a distorted room. The naive observer perceives the pack of cigarettes as changing size, while for the observer trained to perceive the distortion of the room, the pack of cigarettes keeps a constant size.

One final example of how learning can influence perception. When looking at Figure 8.39 you will discover that the apparent

212

distance of the ball depends upon how you perceive it. If you perceive the ball as a ping-pong ball it appears at about the same distance as the nearest face. If you see it as a beach ball it seems to move back and become located on the same plane as one of the more distant faces. You have learned the real sizes of ping-pong and beach balls, and human heads. You know that a ping-pong ball is much smaller than a person's head, while a beach ball is larger. When you look at Figure 8.39 you have no choice but to perceive the apparent distance of the ball in terms of what you have learned about its size.

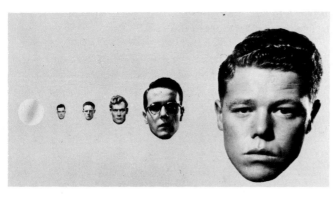

FIGURE 8.39 The apparent distance of the ball depends on how you perceive it. If you see it as a beach ball, it appears farther away than if it is perceived as a ping-pong ball (Eric Schaal, *Life*, © 1950, Time, Inc.).

MOTIVATION AND PERCEPTION

Once again it is necessary to anticipate what we shall have to say on the topic of motivation. You may recall that the description of conditioning included references to such motivational variables as drive and incentives (see page 176). Perception, like conditioning, is a topic that cannot be discussed adequately without bringing in the psychology of motivation, and consequently we must say something now about the influence of motivational variables on perceptual processes.

If it were possible for a person to be completely honest with himself, he would quickly realize how often his perceptions are influenced by his motives and desires. When you root enthusiastically for your college's football team, do you somehow never seem to see the pass defenders on your own team interfering with the receiver, even when the referee, surely unfairly or mistakenly, rules that they have? Do you complain that the referee cannot see as clearly as you the numerous infractions of the rules the opposing team commits? Similarly, in baseball, do the close plays, as you see them, almost always go in favor of your team, and if the umpire rules otherwise, do you question his eyesight?

The influence of motivation on perception is found everywhere in daily life. When an attractive coed walks across the campus, a clothes-conscious friend will notice how smartly she is dressed, while an ever-susceptible male student will appraise her attractive figure. Other examples will occur by the dozen to anyone who looks for them. In themselves such instances do not prove the influence of motivation on perception. Science requires that the relationship between motivation and perception be investigated under experimentally controlled settings. We proceed to describe a few such experiments.

Value as a Factor in Perceived Size

It has been discovered that the perception of an object's size can be influenced by the value the perceiver attaches to it. One experiment demonstrated this by hypnosis, a state that can usually be induced in any person capable of concentrating and willing to assent to the hypnotist's suggestions. It is not a strange, mystical process; the subject under hypnosis is in   dreamlike state of heightened suggestibility, and accepts any of the hypnotist's suggestions readily, as if they accorded with reality.

The college students who acted as subjects were hypnotized individually on two separate occasions. On each occasion the subject was told that he would remember nothing of his former life except his name, and since this was so, the experimenter would relate his past history to him. On one occasion the subject was told a history of being "poor":

He had been born of poor parents and his childhood had been spent in poverty; his father had never had an adequate income and consequently could not afford many of life's necessities; his clothes had been rags, his diet meager, his allowance negligible; he could not go to high school because he had to help support his family; he was still very poor; he had no regular job; what money he did earn was used to help support his family and to pay some of his many debts (Ashley, Harper, & Runyon, 1951, p. 566).

On the other occasion a history of being rich was related:

He had been born of very wealthy parents; he lived in a large mansion in the best and wealthiest neighborhood; he had attended the very best schools; he had always had a large allowance and never had to wish for anything; his father had given him a car and a large expense account when he had entered high school; his clothes had always been of the best quality and very expensive; he had never had any financial worries; at present he had an extremely large income that was further supplemented by his father (Ashley, Harper, & Runyon, 1951, pp. 566-567).

After each of these two financial conditions was hypnotically suggested, the subject was asked to adjust a variable light spot so that it would successively be equal in diameter to that of four different coins (cent, nickel, dime, and quarter) placed two feet away. Figure 8.40 reports the re-

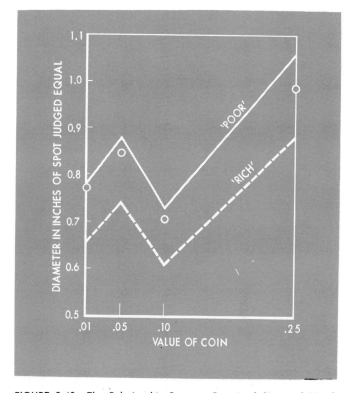

FIGURE 8.40 The Relationship Between Perceived Size and Need. When the subjects were told under hypnosis that they were poor, they judged the size of the four coins to be greater than they did when they were told they were rich. The circles indicate the physical size of the coins (After Ashley, Harper, & Runyon, 1951, with permission of *The American Journal of Psychology*).

sults of the experiment. Measurements of the coin sizes, as the subjects estimated them, showed that when "poor" the subjects judged the sizes of all four coins to be larger than when "rich." If we make the reasonable assumption that people who are poor have a greater need for money than rich people, the results support the idea that perceptions vary according to one's needs.

Similar results were obtained using a somewhat different experimental procedure. In both the "rich" and "poor" states the subjects were shown a grayish metal slug and told it was made of a different metal—either lead, silver, white gold, or platinum. They were instructed to adjust the spot of light until it appeared to be the size of the slug. Figure 8.41 shows that the light spot the subjects set to equal the size of the slug increased with the suggested value of the slug. In addition the slug, at any suggested value, was perceived as larger when the subject was "poor." Again the data suggest that how we perceive things is in part due to motivational variables.

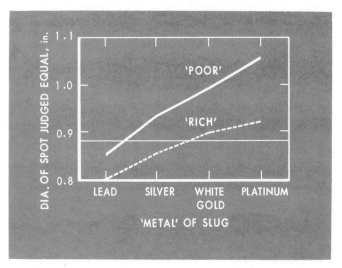

FIGURE 8.41 The Relationship Between Perceived Size and Suggested Value. The subjects judged the size of the metal slug to be larger when its apparent value increased. However, subjects told under hypnosis that they were poor judged the size of the slug at all suggested values to be larger than subjects who were told they were rich. The horizontal line indicates the actual size of the slug (After Ashley, Harper, & Runyon, 1951, with permission of *The American Journal of Psychology*).

Although these studies suggest that an individual's need will influence his perception, they may leave you wondering why valuable objects should be perceived as larger instead of smaller. Very commonly in our society we associate bigness with value. With many commodities, ranging from chocolate bars to cars and diamonds, there exists a high positive correlation (see page 69) between the value and size. It is more than likely, then, that we learn this relationship between value and size and thereafter perceive valuable objects as

larger. Presumably, if there was a society in which small objects were consistently valued more than large objects, such experiments as we have described would have exactly reversed outcomes.

We will describe one last experiment in this field, in which nursery school children were used as subjects (Lambert, Solomon, & Watson, 1949). After two groups of children had shown that they both estimated a poker chip to be the same size, they were treated in different ways. One group (the experimental group) had to turn the crank of a machine to obtain poker chips which they could then use to get candy from a vending machine. The other group (the control group) had simply to turn the crank of the machine and receive candy directly. After a while both groups were again asked to estimate the size of the poker chips.

Since the poker chips were paired with candy for the subjects in the experimental group, one would expect that the value they placed on the chips had increased, that, consequently, their second estimate of size had increased over the first estimate, and that, therefore, the experimental group's second estimate of the size of the chips would be larger than the control group's. This expectation was confirmed.

ATTENTION AND PERCEPTION

Perhaps some readers have been wondering why we have not yet discussed the topic of attention. Isn't it true, they might ask, that we pay attention to the figure and ignore the ground? Don't we first pay attention to one figure, in a reversible figure-ground pattern, and then to the other? Doesn't brightness constancy result from attending to the relationship between the brightness of a given object and the brightness of its surroundings?

The difficulty in answering such questions in a straightforward manner lies in the ambiguity of the term *attention*. In everyday speech the word *attention* means very different things to different people. But science cannot tolerate such ambiguities. The concept of **attention** in the technical vocabulary of psychology refers to the selectivity of the perceptual processes. We do not respond equally to all stimuli that impinge on our receptors. Instead we focus upon some stimuli while de-emphasizing or ignoring others. Recall your experiences in a classroom. Sometimes you listen attentively to the lecturer so that you clearly perceive his words and the ideas they express. At other times, especially in the midst of a daydream, the sounds of his words, stripped of all meaning, barely reach your ears. In both instances your physical environment is essentially the same and the sound waves of the lecturer's speech bombard your ears.

Attention, then, is an integral part of the study of perception. But whereas the general problem of perception is how patterns of stimuli become organized, attention is concerned with the special problem of *emphasis,* why certain elements in the total pattern stand out. For our purposes we may divide the variables that are likely to produce emphasis or influence attention into two main categories: (1) stimulus variables and (2) motivational and learning variables.

Attention and Stimulus Variables

Perceptual Satiation. In responding to many stimulus patterns we are able to attend to one detail while ignoring another. This problem was encountered in Figure 8.4 on page 186, where the same stimulus situation can evoke different perceptual responses, sometimes a vase, sometimes two profiles. The shifting of attention from one impression to another occurs because the

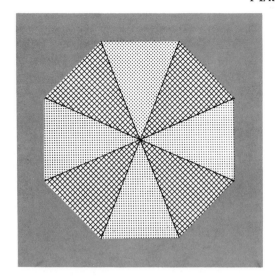

FIGURE 8.42 A Reversible Cross. Fixate your vision at the center of the figure. You will note that your perception will constantly shift between seeing a + and a × (After Boring, Langfeld, & Weld, 1948).

stimulus pattern allows two possible perceptual organizations, and certain momentary conditions favor one perceptual organization over the other. One important condition is known as **perceptual satiation.** It is easy to demonstrate how it works.

Look at Figure 8.42, another reversible figure-ground stimulus pattern. If you gaze steadily at the center of the figure you will find it impossible to perceive only an × or only a +. The figure will spontaneously reverse. No matter how intently you try to hold your perception of one of the two crosses, you will find yourself looking at the other.

The mechanism responsible for this fluctuation of perceptual responses is suggested by the following experiment. Gaze steadily at the center of one of the figures in Figure 8.43. Count slowly to 30. Quickly turn back to Figure 8.42 on this page and note whether you see an × or a +. Now rest a minute or so and gaze steadily at the other figure in Figure 8.43. Gaze steadily at it for a period of approximately 30 seconds and then return to Figure 8.42.

You will discover that after looking steadily at one of the two figures in Figure 8.43 you perceive the other figure when you look at the reversible cross (Figure 8.42). This demonstrates that your perception of

a figure weakens after you have looked at it for a while. This perceptual weakening process is called satiation, and its effects are usually not noticed because most stimulus patterns elicit only one figure response. A reversible figure-ground pattern, however, provides a sensitive measure of satiation. As soon as one figural percept (impression) is satiated, the observer will find himself perceiving the other. In other words, the satiation effects produced by continued perception are responsible for the shifting perceptual organization in stimulus patterns such as Figures 8.1, 8.36, and 8.45.

The facts of satiation suggest that the perceptual mechanism does not function like a mirror that simply reflects a pattern of stimulation. Instead the perceptual process appears to be undergoing change as it is perceiving.

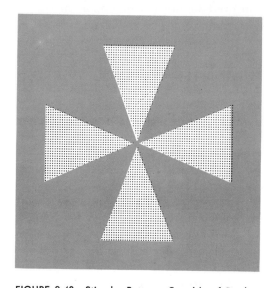

FIGURE 8.43 Stimulus Patterns Capable of Producing Satiation Effects. Gaze steadily at the center of one of the two figures for about 30 seconds and then immediately look at the center of Figure 8.42. Repeat the experiment with the other cross (After Boring, Langfeld, & Weld, 1948).

Intensity. Stimulus patterns can be arranged so that one stimulus feature "stands out." It is the perennial task of advertisers to discover those stimulus characteristics that catch and hold the attention of the perceiver. The most commonly used attention-getting stimulus characteristics are **intensity, contrast,** and **movement.**

We tend to pay more attention to whatever is intensely stimulating. Trade names on billboards must be printed in large, bright letters so that passing motorists will perceive at least the product's name. Television commercials, in order to keep the viewer's attention, tend to be louder and more glaring than the noncommercial portion of the program.

Contrast. Stimulus contrast operates in a similar manner. Stimuli that stand out in contrast with the background get attention. The audience tends to watch the star dancer whose costume as well as skill is more striking than anything in the chorus. The letters of a stop sign are usually painted in black on yellow or white on red. The word *stop* in black letters against a gray background would not be as effective in catching a driver's attention.

Movement. Movement attracts and maintains attention. Animated cartoons are widely used in TV commercials because of the extensive amount of movement they permit. If you want to demonstrate the attention-getting power of moving objects, compare an infant's reaction to a pencil held still and one that moves. Every parent knows that you can gain and maintain an infant's attention more easily with a moving object.

Attention and Motivational and Learning Variables

Perceptual Set. The sprinter waiting for the race to begin is ready to start at the crack of the starter's gun. A shoe salesman is set to notice a person's shoes, a tie salesman his customer's neckwear. **Perceptual set** is the term applied to the tendency for an organism to pay attention to certain features of a stimulus pattern.

Perceptual sets can be created by training, as in the experiment (see page 209) using the ambiguous drawing of the wife and mother-in-law. Continual repetition is a method used by advertisers to establish perceptual sets. "Messages" aimed to stimulate sales (e.g., cigarette jingles) are played over and over again, and if we can trust sales figures, the repetition of advertising jingles seems to be effective. Recalling, however, that repetition by itself does not produce learning, we may reasonably conclude that the effectiveness of repetition in advertising is largely due to the reinforcement (discussed in Chapter 7) a listener

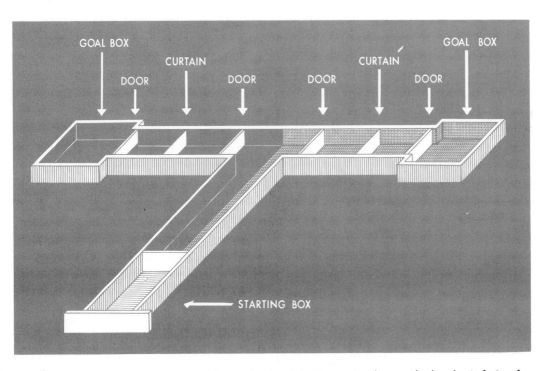

FIGURE 8.44 A Drawing of a T Maze. The rat is placed in the starting box, and when he is facing forward, the door is raised. After he has gone either right or left at the choice point, the door is lowered to prevent him from returning. Once he enters the goal box a door is lowered to keep him there for a certain length of time or until he consumes the incentive. The curtains in front of each goal box prevent the rat from seeing the contents of each goal box at the choice point.

may get from the pleasing content of the jingle heard in a situation where he is resting comfortably and enjoying the program.

We pay attention to a new stimulus, whether a new appetizing smell emanating from the kitchen or a new-fashioned dispenser for toothpaste. This is another example of how training can establish a perceptual set. It may appear odd to assign the attention-getting power of new stimuli to learning, but a moment's reflection will show why this is so. We become accustomed to our daily environments. We learn what to expect. When a new stimulus appears, a new sound or sight, we immediately notice it. It can only be new, however, to someone who has learned what to expect in his environment. New model cars are new only to the person who is familiar with the design of older cars. In short, a perceptual set for novelty can result from training.

An experiment (Kendler, 1947) with rats as subjects suggests how perception can be selectively focused by the combined action of motivational and learning variables. Two groups of rats received the same experience in a T maze, the floor plan of which is shown in Figure 8.44. The motivated group was deprived of both food and water for 21 hours. The satiated group was permitted to eat and drink as much as they wanted immediately before their experimental session. Food was present in a goal box at one end of the T maze, and water was present at the other end. The training experiences were so arranged that for a period of seven days each rat had two daily runs from the starting box to the food goal box and two daily runs from the starting box to the water goal box. Because they were hungry and thirsty, the motivated group consumed some of the incentives (food and water) in each goal box. The satiated animals, although they did not consume either food or water, did come into physical contact with both incentives. After the training series was completed,

the motivational conditions of both groups were changed: some days the subjects in each group were hungry but not thirsty, and other days they were thirsty but not hungry. Thus it was possible to evaluate the influence the difference in the animal's motivation during training had upon the learning of the location of the food and water. During the test trials, when the subjects were either hungry or thirsty, the animals previously motivated made significantly more appropriate responses, chose the food side when hungry or the water side when thirsty, than did the previously satiated group.

An organism, when motivated and allowed to consume the appropriate incentives (e.g., food and water) learns to attend to those features of his environment that will satisfy his prevailing motivational conditions. A satiated animal does not establish such a perceptual set. In short, a hungry and thirsty animal is reinforced more for attending to food and water than is a satiated animal.

THEORETICAL PROBLEMS IN PERCEPTION

There are two general approaches to the problem of formulating a theory of perception. One is to state the principles that govern the stimulus-response relationships in perception. The second is to discover the physiological mechanisms that underlie the psychology of perception. Although these two orientations are not always separate, it is useful to keep them separate here.

Stimulus-Response Relationships in Perception

In the previous sections of this chapter many relationships between complex patterns of stimuli and the perceptual responses they evoke were reported. These relationships should not be considered as isolated, unrelated facts. A certain similarity appears to underlie many of them. A theory is needed if we are to conceptualize this similarity in a way that will integrate and organize the facts as far as possible, and the theoretical construct, **perceptual tendency,** will be useful for this purpose. You will recall that the theoretical construct of habit (see page 29) was used to integrate the relationships between stimulus and response variables in conditioning experiments. Similarly, the theoretical construct of perceptual tendency systematizes stimulus-response relationships in perception. Perceptual tendencies influence perceptual responses. Their influence is expressed in terms of the (1) organization, (2) emphasis, and (3) consistency of the perceptual response. Let us review these properties of perceptual responses once again.

Discrete stimulus elements of a complex pattern of stimuli are not perceived as separate and independent. Instead organisms tend to perceive stimulus elements as part of an *organized* pattern. Organisms, when perceiving patterns of stimuli, do not pay equal attention to all stimulus elements. Some features of the stimulus patterns are *emphasized,* others are barely noticed, and still others are ignored. Their perceptual tendencies operate to make perceptual responses *consistent,* so that the various parts of a stimulus pattern tend to be perceived in harmony with each other.

Consistency, this third property of a perceptual tendency, can be better understood if we refer to the results of a study (Bruner & Postman, 1949) involving a tachistoscope and a deck of ordinary playing cards supplemented by some specially prepared cards. Subjects were exposed to individual playing cards for brief periods of time. At the beginning only common playing cards were presented, each briefly. Then a red four of spades would appear among them. Twenty-seven of the 28 adult subjects perceived this incongruous card as either a red four of hearts or a black four of spades. That is, their perceptions showed a marked tendency to preserve the traditional and familiar consistency between the color and form of ordinary playing cards.

These three properties (organization, emphasis, and consistency) of a perceptual tendency do not always operate all at once. Studies (Flavell & Draguns, 1957) with tachistoscopic exposures suggest that a perceptual response develops temporally, that when a stimulus pattern is presented for gradually lengthening time periods, the observer's perception develops from a diffuse response to a specific one. Brief exposures are sufficient for the operation of tendencies to simple perceptual organizations such as figure and ground. As the exposure time is lengthened, more intricate forms of perceptual organizations, such as simple geometrical shapes, become possible. When still more time is available certain portions of the stimulus pattern become perceptually emphasized. And eventually exposure is long enough for the observer to see a consistent, integrated percept. According to this analysis the three basic properties of a perceptual tendency operate in sequence and then finally in unison. The longer a perceiver is permitted to observe a stimulus pattern, the greater is the opportunity for the tendencies of perceptual emphasis and consistency to operate.

We admit that at best this analysis represents a first approximation to a satisfactory theoretical analysis of the stimulus-response relationships in perception. More facts are needed. When additional data become available, no doubt this analysis will have to be modified and expanded.

Variables That Influence Perceptual Tendencies

With this much understanding of the concept of a perceptual tendency, our problem becomes one of specifying the factors that influence the operation of a perceptual

220

tendency. We must answer such questions as: What makes a perceptual response organized? Why are some stimuli perceptually emphasized? What causes perceptual consistency? At best, only partial answers can be given. There is, however, no doubt that three major sets of variables influence a perceptual tendency: the particular stimulus pattern that initiates a perceptual response, the organism's past experience, and his prevailing motivation at the time. In most situations all three sets of variables operate simultaneously.

Perceptual organizing responses often occur spontaneously. Figure-ground (see Figure 8.3 on page 186) and perceptual grouping (see Figures 8.7, 8.8, and 8.9 on pages 188-189) responses are examples of this. If the perceptual tendency for these simple organizing responses is independent of practice, the explanation of these phenomena must lie in the interaction between the stimulus pattern and the perceiving organism. One is forced to conclude that just as a liquid assumes the shape of the vessel into which it is poured, simple patterns of stimulation are organized by the innate structure of the organism's nervous system.

The degree of perceptual organization will vary for different patterns of stimuli. Figure 8.45 shows three patterns of 20 dots that produce different degrees of perceptual organization.

The fact that we perceive patterns of stimuli in terms of the innate capabilities of our nervous system does not mean, however, that perceptual organizing tendencies cannot be modified. It is true that training and motivational variables do not seem to modify to any appreciable extent simple perceptual figure-ground and grouping responses, but they do modify more complex stimulus patterns. This was demonstrated in our discussion of perceptual learning and the influence of motivation on perception.

You can probably draw on your own experiences to demonstrate how the perceptual organization of complex patterns of stimuli can be influenced by training and motivational variables. Consider a scene from a football game in which a quarterback is fading back to pass after faking a handoff to the fullback, who is plunging through to the opposing line. You can imagine the difference such a scene would produce in the perceptual organization of a sophisticated football fan and in that of an English princess viewing her first (and probably last) game of American football. You can also imagine how motivational factors would influence perceptual organization. What the fathers of the quarterback, fullback, and opposing tackle would see would certainly be different, even if all three were experienced football fans.

The tendency for certain portions of a stimulus pattern to be perceptually emphasized must also occur spontaneously. Organisms spontaneously pay more attention to figures than to grounds. But attention can be strongly influenced by learning and motivational variables. An organism can be forced to attend to specific aspects of his environment in the same way that a rat can be conditioned to respond to a stimulus. Just as bar-pressing responses can be reinforced, so can the response of attention. For example, in solving the problem posed by Figure 8.46 there are a large number of details on which you may focus, but some of your perceptual responses will be reinforced, and others will not be. You will

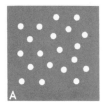 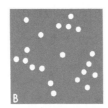 

FIGURE 8.45 How Perceptual Organization Can Vary Under Different Patterns of Stimulation.

eventually attend to details that distinguish one drawing from another while you ignore those that do not.

Attention responses can be strengthened and weakened in the very same way that classical and instrumental conditioned responses are. In brief, habits to attend can be formed, strengthened, and weakened. It appears that the same variables (see page 168) influencing classical and instrumental conditioned responses also influence simple habits of attention.

The tendency to perceive separate elements of a stimulus pattern in a consistent way results from the combined effects of learning and motivation. In one study (Siipola, 1935) a series of short words was flashed one at a time on a screen for one-tenth of a second. One group of subjects was told that the words they would see had to do with animals or birds; another group was instructed that they would see words related to travel or transportation. After seeing the word briefly flashed on the screen the subjects in both groups were instructed to record the word they thought they saw. Among the words were six nonsense words: *chack, sael, wharl, pasrort, dack,* and *pengion.* The perceptual responses of the two groups to the nonsense words were markedly different. The majority of the group instructed to expect animals or birds perceived the nonsense words as meaningful names of some animal or bird: *chick, seal, whale, parrot, duck,* and *penguin.* By contrast the other group tended to perceive the same nonsense words as *check, sail, wharf, passport, deck,* and *pension.* In short, the subjects perceived the letters of nonsense words in a manner consistent with the perceptual set they had received.

Perhaps the most dramatic examples of perceptual consistency come from clinical case records. It is characteristic in cases of paranoia (a form of psychiatric disturbance) for the patient to be convinced that he is being persecuted. His perceptions are

FIGURE 8.46 Which two men are exactly alike?

dominated by this belief. Consequently, he perceives various events in a manner consistent with his delusion (false belief) that he is being persecuted. The following case history demonstrates this.

The patient is a middle-aged male. According to him, his difficulties came on suddenly following a quarrel over a racing bet placed with "bookies." After the race he claimed to have put his money on the winning horse, while the bookies insisted he had not. After a few drinks elsewhere, he returned to the scene and got into a noisy altercation with the "bookies" in which he insulted them, threatened them, and invited them out into the street. After he had returned to the hotel where he lived, he began thinking it over. He remembered stories of nationwide gangster protection given to "bookies," and the more he thought about it the more dangerous his attack upon them seemed to him. He looked about the hotel lobby next day and noticed some strangers watching him closely. They seemed to be making signs to each other. During the morning an automobile full of men stopped in front of the hotel door and he became convinced he was about to be kidnapped, tortured, and killed. Now he began to notice strangers and loiterers everywhere, and they all seemed to be keeping track of him. He was a "marked man." He barricaded himself in his room and told a relative over the telephone about it. That night he fled across the country in his car; but incidents en route made him realize he was being followed and spurred him on. In one city, for instance, he saw a policeman examining his auto license. Under the circumstances that could only mean the police were in league with the gangsters. In a shoeshining parlor the attendant eyed him narrowly; "the grapevine system was catching up." Finally he equipped himself for suicide; but by this time he had joined relatives who suspected as much and guarded him. They persuaded him to come to a psychiatric clinic.

In the clinic he felt for some time secure. . . . He made frequent allusions to things in his past that he would like to get cleared up; but he could bring himself only to go over some unethical business procedures. He persuaded a new physician to let him ask a local pastor by telephone to visit him at the clinic; and to the pastor he told the story of his recent difficulties and made an appointment to talk about other things without consulting his physician. The more the patient thought about it, after the pastor had gone, the more he suspected that he had been unwise to confide so much. He reflected that the pastor was somewhat dark-skinned and foreign-looking; and then he realized that his telephone call had probably been intercepted by the gang who had sent a confederate around pretending to be a minister of the gospel. There was a violent resurgence of fear, which he kept to himself, and another suicidal plan that was nearly successful . . ." (Cameron, 1943, pp. 227-228).

Practically everything that happened in the visual environment of this patient was integrated into a consistent, if completely false, picture of persecution. You will recall the behavior of the subjects who were exposed briefly to nonsense words after having been given a set to perceive words related to animals or transportation. Although the behavior is in many ways different from that of the paranoid individual just described, there is a basic similarity between them. Both the normal subjects and the paranoid individual manifest a tendency to order the separate details of their visual environments into a consistent perceptual response.

The future development of theories designed to explain the stimulus-response relationships in perception will depend on the ability of psychologists to develop quantitative measures of both stimulus and response variables. When this is accomplished, more precise theoretical propositions can be offered.

PERCEPTION AND THE NERVOUS SYSTEM

We have repeatedly mentioned the importance of brain mechanisms in perception. From a better understanding of how the brain functions, we shall surely derive a better understanding of perceptual processes.

Three basic questions must be answered if a clearer understanding of the relationship between perception and physiology is to be achieved. (1) What specific mechanisms enable the brain to integrate and organize patterns of stimuli? For example, how does the brain function so that the discrete dots and dashes in Figure 8.47 are perceived as organized shapes? (2) What are the physiological correlates of attention? Why can you sometimes hear someone calling your name although his voice is faint, and not hear him at all when his voice is louder? (3) What are the physiological mechanisms that enable some event in the past to influence the perception of the present? Why do we perceive a burning tree in the aerial view of a river delta (see Figure 8.33 on page 208)?

The Physiology of Perceptual Organization

Of these three questions the first is the most difficult to answer. There have been many attempts to explain physiologically the tendency for patterns of discrete stimuli to initiate integrated and organized perceptions. None has attained general acceptance. But one physiological fact has been clearly established. When we perceive four dots at the corner of an imaginary square, the sensory neural events initiated by the dots do not reach four separate and distinct areas of the brain. The nerve cells in one spot of the brain are intertwined with nerve cells in adjacent locations. Also the brain is continually active electrically and electrical activity generated at one spot spreads to other areas. Consequently a specific area of the brain is both structurally and functionally connected to other areas. Within this structural and functional interdependence of various brain areas lies the key to the understanding of the physiology of perceptual organization.

The Physiology of Attention

A large step forward has recently been made in comprehending the physiological basis of attention. It has been demonstrated that the brain in some manner "edits" in-

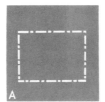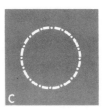

FIGURE 8.47 Discrete Dots and Dashes That Are Perceived as Organized Shapes.

coming sensory stimulation. This conclusion comes from a study (Hernández-Peón, Scherrer, & Jouvet, 1956) in which the electrical activity in the auditory (sensory) nerve of an unanesthetized, unrestrained cat was studied. When a click was sounded there appeared a concomitant increase in the electrical activity in the auditory nerve. This increase, produced by the click, was practically abolished when mice in a glass jar were brought within view of the cat. When the mice were removed and the click was once again sounded, the increase in electrical activity in the auditory nerve reappeared. Figure 8.48 summarizes the results of this experimental demonstration.

The click response in the auditory nerve was similarly blocked by other attention-getting stimuli. The click was sounded while the cat was sniffing odors of fish, and there was practically no increase in electrical activity in the auditory nerve. This simply means that while the cat was attending to the mice or to the odor of fish, the neural impulses initiated by the click were partially, if not completely, blocked from reaching the brain. According to this line of evidence, a child who is immersed in reading a book and does not answer his mother's call is not really ignoring her, but actually does not hear her.

It would appear that on the physiological level, attention involves the selective screening-out of certain sensory impulses. There is evidence that this screening-out process can result also from continuous exposure to the same stimulus. A tone that is sounded will initially produce an increase in electri-

224 cal activity in the auditory nerve, but with prolonged exposure to the same tone the neural activity decreases until it practically disappears. No doubt you have had the

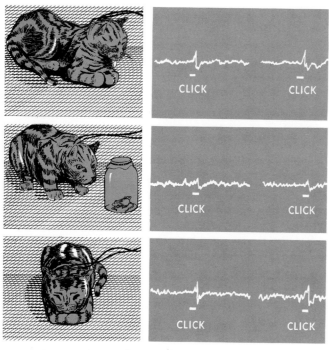

FIGURE 8.48 Electrical Activity in the Auditory Nerve of a Cat. The top picture shows the sharp increase in electrical activity initiated by the click. This increase was eliminated when mice in a glass jar were placed in front of the cat. After they were removed the click once again produced an increase in electrical activity (After Hernández-Peón, Scherrer, & Jouvet, 1956, with the permission of *Science*).

experience of driving a car with an irritating squeak which annoyed you for a mile or two, but soon you no longer noticed it. The squeak was still there but your nervous system was filtering it out, and if you started attending to it again, you would hear it as plainly as before.

All stimuli that impinge upon our receptors do not succeed in getting through to the brain. In some manner the nervous system is able to set up a selective screening device which permits some afferent neural impulses to reach it and simultaneously blocks others.

Now that we know some sort of physiological screening device operates, our next step is to determine how it operates. When we have done this, we may find that such phenomena as perceptual satiation and attention, and perhaps even experimental extinction, result from similar, if not identical, physiological events.

The Physiology of Perceptual Learning. The fact that our past experiences can influence our present perceptions means that, in some way, our neurophysiological system can store records of past events. Where this storehouse is and how it functions are puzzles that psychologists and physiologists wish desperately to solve. The answer is sure to be found in processes going on in the brain, an organ weighing about 50 ounces and occupying a volume of space equivalent to about one and a half quarts.

Dr. Wilder Penfield, a Canadian brain surgeon, has reported that he was able to produce vivid memories in some of his patients by stimulating certain areas of the temporal lobes with weak electric currents. One patient reported hearing a song; in his words, ". . . it was not as though I were imagining the tune to myself. I actually heard it." Other patients suddenly relived long-forgotten childhood experiences. Stimulation of the same cerebral area always produced the same episode.

It is likely that these cerebral records of past events function to influence our present perceptions. The perception of a long-forgotten tune may activate in some manner the cerebral residue of previous experience with that tune, and because of this the perceiver hears not a new tune but a familiar tune. He has interpreted his perception of the tune in terms of a similar past experience.

The reports we have been able to give you of theoretical developments in the field of perception are modest in nature and scope, but some order is beginning to emerge in them and this promises a better understanding of the stimulus-response relationships in the field of perception and of the physiological mechanisms underlying them. The ingenuity and persistence now being expended in the investigation of perception cannot fail to yield new facts and better theories that will not only clarify the study of perception, but will also throw light on much of the rest of psychology.

SUMMARY

The psychology of perception deals with the means by which complex forms of stimulation are organized and arranged by the perceiver. In a figure-ground perception, such as seeing an inkblot on a white piece of paper, you perceive something as having a form that stands out from the formless background. When you perceive a group of discrete stimuli you tend to organize them according to the principles of perceptual grouping: nearness, similarity, and continuity. You may even organize stimuli in a manner that fails to correspond with reality and thus experience a perceptual illusion, such as seeing movement when a series of still pictures are projected in succession (the phi-phenomenon). The figure-ground perception appears to be independent of previous training, and it is assumed to result from innate physiological mechanisms. These mechanisms play important roles in our perception of patterns of discrete stimuli as well as in many perceptual illusions.

The visual perception of three-dimensional space is due to two main classes of variables, stimulus and organismic (physiological). Such stimulus features as linear perspective, interposition, light and shadow, clearness, movements, and gradients help us perceive depth. So do the physiological mechanisms of accommodation, convergence, and retinal disparity. Auditory space perception results also from a combination of stimulus and organismic variables. With increasing distance the intensity of sounds decreases and their timbre becomes less distinctive. The fact that when we listen to one sound we usually hear somewhat different sounds in each ear also helps us localize sound in space.

A round plate looks round to us even when it is viewed at angles that would project a decidedly elliptical image on our retina. This is an example of perceptual constancy. There are many variables that encourage perceptual constancy. Familiarity of objects causes us to perceive them as possessing constant perceptual characteristics under widely varying conditions. The relationship of an object with its surroundings also helps us to achieve perceptual constancy. The perceived size of a man does not decrease as he walks away because as the retinal image of him becomes smaller so do the retinal images of objects surrounding him. Size constancy of an unfamiliar object is dependent entirely upon the presence of the customary cues of space perception, and when they are eliminated, the size of the object is closely related to its retinal image.

We can learn to perceive stimulus patterns in distinctive ways. This phenomenon is known as perceptual learning. Sometimes because of learning we are confronted with situations in which there is a conflict between different ways of perceiving the same things, as in the case of the two men in the corners of a distorted room. In such cases we tend to perceive the environment in a consistent fashion; we see either the men as different in height or the room as distorted.

The term *attention* refers to the fact that the perceptual process is selective; all stimulus features of the environment are not perceived with equal clearness. Attention has been found to be a function of stimulus, motivation, and learning variables.

Theories of perception have generally been approached in two ways. One is the specification of principles that govern the stimulus-response relationships in perception. As a first approximation it has been suggested that perceptual tendencies pos-sess three main properties: organization, emphasis, and consistency. The other approach is to discover the underlying physiological mechanisms of perception. A particularly important discovery in this line is that when an organism attends to certain stimuli, other stimuli that impinge on the receptors are blocked from reaching the central nervous system.

SUGGESTIONS FOR FURTHER READING

BARTLEY, S. H. *Principles of perception.* New York: Harper & Row, 1958.

A textbook devoted to the fields of sensation and perception.

DEMBER, W. N. *Psychology of perception.* Holt, Rinehart, & Winston, 1960.

A textbook on perception that reviews and integrates important facts and theories.

GIBSON, J. J. *The perception of the visual world.* Boston: Houghton Mifflin, 1950.

An interesting account of visual space perception.

KÖHLER, W. *Gestalt psychology.* (2nd ed.) New York: Liveright, 1947.

An analysis of perceptual and other phenomena by one of the most important and creative Gestalt psychologists.

OSGOOD, C. E. *Method and theory in experimental psychology.* New York: Oxford Univer. Press, 1953.

An advanced textbook in experimental psychology that includes three stimulating chapters on perception.

WOODWORTH, R. S. & SCHLOSBERG, H. *Experimental psychology.* (Rev. ed.) New York: Holt, Rinehart, & Winston, 1954.

A standard text in psychology that contains chapters on perception and attention.

MOTIVATION—THE ENERGIZER OF BEHAVIOR

9

GOAL-DIRECTED BEHAVIOR

Behavior can be, and usually is, orderly. There seem to be reasons for most behavior. The infant cries to get food or to escape from pain. The dog runs to his master to be petted or away from him to avoid punishment. You are now reading this book to satisfy your curiosity about psychology (or at least to pass your psychology course). Even the helter-skelter behavior of infants and puppies has direction; mammals need activity in order to maintain their muscles in a healthy state. In short, there is motivation in behavior and much of it is goal-oriented.

The psychology of motivation deals with the variables that activate and direct behavior. Why do we get hungry? When hungry, why is our behavior directed toward ham and eggs or steak and potatoes, instead of snails in garlic sauce or roasted grasshoppers? How do fears develop and function? These are but a few of the questions we shall discuss in this chapter.

A Misconception About Motivation

At the outset one point needs to be made crystal clear. Common-sense interpretations of behavior sometimes invoke motivation as the *sole cause* of behavior. A child cries because he wants candy. Sometimes a male adolescent avoids girls because he is fearful. Such statements as these are at best incomplete. Consider the very simple situation of a rat in a T maze.

A T maze (see Figure 9.1) is a piece of experimental apparatus slightly more complicated than the one used in classical or simple instrumental conditioning. It is

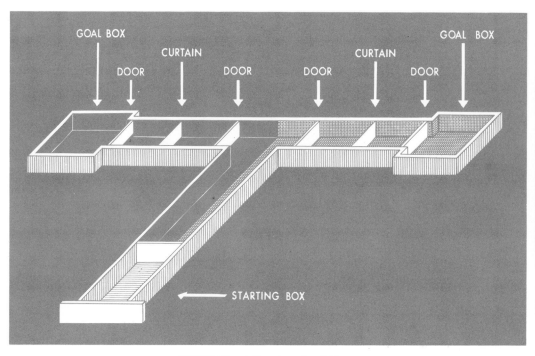

FIGURE 9.1 A Drawing of a T Maze.

made up of three boxes opening into each other and arranged in the shape of a T. An animal (usually a white rat) placed in such a maze can make one of two major responses; he can either turn to the right or left. A piece of food is usually placed in one of the arms of the T. Suppose food has been placed in the left arm and a rat who has been deprived of food for a day is placed at the starting point, the base of the T. Sooner or later this rat will reach the choice point and make a turn. If he turns left he will reach the baited end and eat the food. If he turns right he will reach the empty end and receive nothing for his efforts. In a typical learning experiment involving a T maze, an animal is given a group of trials each day for several days. Figure 9.2 shows the results of one experiment. Note that on the first trial approximately 50 per cent of the rats chose the left (correct) side. As the number of trials increased their percentage of correct choices increased. Finally on trial 20 every rat made

a correct choice. Why were they able to do this? Was it just because they were motivated (hungry)? Obviously not. On the first trial they were hungry, but they were able to respond correctly only by chance, being wrong as often as they were right. If motivation is not the cause of their correct choices on the twentieth trial, what is? Did all the rats make a correct choice on the twentieth trial because a left-turning response had been rewarded on previous occasions? As it stands this question must also get a negative answer. If prior reinforcements were the sole cause of the correct choices on trial 20, then even if the animals were not hungry they would all make correct choices on the twentieth trial. But rats who were satiated with food immediately prior to trial 20 would not all turn left. Some would turn left, some right, and some would stay in the starting box. The only possible conclusion is that the correct choices of the rats on the twentieth trial, as depicted in Figure 9.2, were due both to hunger and to reinforced practice. Both are necessary for perfect performance. You will recall that this conclusion is identical to the one in our analysis of how amount of food deprivation and amount of training influenced the extinction scores of an instrumental bar-pressing response (see page 173).

This point can be stated more generally. The task of science is represented by the formula $Y = f(X_1, X_2, X_3, \ldots X_n)$. In psychology Y represents behavior. The study of motivation does not embrace all of the independent variables from X_1 to X_n. Instead, motivation, like sensation, learning, and perception, includes some, but not all, of the independent variables that can affect behavior. Understanding behavior depends on understanding the influence of sensory, perceptual, and learning variables as well as motivational variables. That is, motivation is but a part of psychology and cannot be the sole cause of any psychological event.

The Motivational Sequence

You probably have noted that behavior often possesses a sequential character. The baby eats, thus reducing or eliminating his hunger. After an interval during which his body consumes the nourishment, a tissue deficit gradually develops. The baby then becomes restless and starts making responses (crying) that previously led to getting food. When he is presented with food, he makes other responses (suckling and salivating) which are reinforced by food in his mouth

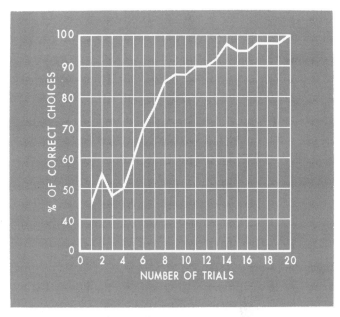

FIGURE 9.2 The Choice Behavior of a Group of Hungry Rats in a T Maze in Which There Was Food at the End of the Left Arm. The percentage of left choices gradually increases on successive trials.

and stomach. With food comes hunger reduction once more.

Psychologists characterize the sequence of events just described as consisting of a hunger *drive* created during a passage of time, which in turn initiates an *instrumental response* that leads to an *incentive* which reduces or eliminates the *drive*. There is a similar sequence in the case of other drives, such as thirst and the need for sleep.

In many cases the motivational sequence repeats itself with only short intervals between. Parents become painfully aware of

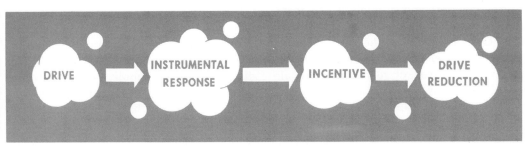

FIGURE 9.3 The Motivational Sequence.

the cyclical property of their infant's drive for food. Almost as soon as the hunger drive is satisfied the sequence begins anew, until it is once again terminated by food consumption. Not all motivational sequences are cyclical. Having a speck of dirt removed from your eye terminates the drive to escape from pain, and as long as the eye is kept free of foreign bodies, the same motivational sequence will not recur.

Motivational Concepts

Now that the motivated behavior has been characterized in terms of the motivational sequence, it is necessary to define some essential concepts. A few of these will be familiar, since they are used in everyday conversation. It will be helpful, however, to scrutinize and define them with more care than is customary.

Drive. A **drive** refers to a condition or state in which behavior is activated and directed. Psychologists speak of drives when they wish to integrate and systematize a great many independent facts. In short, a drive is a theoretical construct used to help explain behavior. Therefore, do not suppose that a drive must be something as concrete, tangible, and easily perceived as a pencil.

In addition to drives activating behavior, as hunger activates the bar-pressing response of rats trained in a Skinner box (see page 163), drive conditions can also exert a steering function on behavior. The meaning of this statement can be conveyed best by describing an experiment (Leeper, 1935a) with a group of rats and a single-choice maze similar to the T maze described on page 228. On any one day the animals were either hungry or thirsty. On some days the rats were deprived of food, but were allowed to have water; on other days they were deprived of water, but were allowed to have food. On the days the rats were hungry, food was available in the box at the right end. When they were thirsty, water was available in the box at the left end. As training progressed the animals chose the right side more and more frequently when hungry, and the left side more and more often when thirsty. Finally, the rats almost always turned right on hungry days and left on thirsty days.

Although these results are not surprising, we must make sure we understand just what has happened. Recall that in classical conditioning the conditioned stimulus served as a cue for the subject to make a conditioned response. In the experiment just described, what was the cue for the subject to turn left on thirsty days and right on hungry days? The choice point in the maze was the same on both days. The end boxes were hidden from the view of the rats by curtains; hence the incentive could not have operated as a cue. The cue must have been within the organism. The hunger drive must produce an internal cue distinctively different from the cue produced by the thirst drive. It is this internal cue, or what is known as a **drive stimulus,** that enables rats to respond appropriately to their needs. The left-turning response became associated with a pattern of stimuli including the thirst-drive stimulus, whereas the right-turning response became associated with a pattern of stimuli including the hunger-drive stimulus. Hunger, in addition to possessing drive properties, possesses cue properties.

The strength of a drive such as hunger can serve as a cue. Rats have been trained to turn right in a T maze under both a relatively weak hunger drive (12 hours of food deprivation) and a strong hunger drive (48 hours of food deprivation). This finding (Jenkins & Hanratty, 1949) indicates that distinctive drive stimuli are produced by different intensities of the same drive. You, yourself, probably have learned different responses to weak and strong hunger-drive stimuli. When you are only slightly hungry you may respond by eating a candy bar, but a strong hunger-drive stimulus is associated with responses involved in getting a large meal.

Incentive. Another term requiring definition is **incentive** or **goal.** An incentive, or goal, is a commodity or condition capable of reducing or eliminating a drive. Thus food constitutes an incentive for the hunger drive. Rest is an incentive for the tired worker; a high grade is an incentive for the student studying for an examination; money is an incentive for the boy mowing a lawn.

Instrumental Response. When you have a need for food you are driven to find something edible, which is the incentive. Drives, alone and by themselves, do not make incentives appear. An incentive is something that is achieved, a goal that is reached, only after an appropriate response or sequence of responses is made. To satisfy your hunger drive you may have to go to the refrigerator and prepare a sandwich or go to a restaurant and order some food. Even when your mother prepares a meal and calls you to the dinner table, you have to lift the food from the plate, put it in your mouth, and chew it. Some effort has to be expended, though it may be minimal, to obtain reinforcement—a term which we may as well point out now, can often be used interchangeably with incentive or goal. It is exceedingly important to distinguish between the hunger drive on one hand and the behavior directed toward satisfying it. To emphasize this distinction, psychologists refer to the behavior that leads to the reduction of a drive as an **instrumental response.** This term, you will remember, is the same as that used in conditioning experiments where an animal's response was instrumental in achieving reinforcement (see page 163).

The Psychology and the Physiology of Motivation

It may have occurred to you that some of our drives are closely correlated with physiological conditions. As you well know, our bodies need to maintain a physiological balance both to survive and to function. When our physiological condition has diverged to some extent from this optimal balance, an **organic need** is said to exist. Sometimes the need takes the form of a deficit, such as lack of food, oxygen, or vitamin A. At other times the need is the result of injury to tissues produced by noxious stimulation. When such conditions of physiological imbalance arise the animal often restores the physiological equilibrium by appropriate action. When hungry he gets food; when being burnt he escapes the noxious stimulation. **Homeostasis** is the overall term for all the equilibrium-preserving tendencies within an organism by which an optimal physiological condition is maintained.

Although it is quite obvious that some drives, such as hunger and thirst, are related to homeostatic conditions, one should not conclude that *all* drives are so based or that *all* organic needs produce a drive. Psychologists distinguish between physiological (primary) and learned (secondary) drives. A **physiological** or **primary drive** is directly related to a homeostatic condition. A **learned** or **secondary drive** is not. It is a product of learning. The student who is driven to excel in school, or the child who fears dogs, both illustrate behavior that is the product of learning.

Sometimes an organic need exists without a drive. Suffocation resulting from inhaling excessive amounts of carbon monoxide is a tragic example that illustrates this point. The unfortunate person who allows the motor of his car to run in a closed garage is not driven to action by his need for oxygen. The carbon monoxide produces a need for oxygen, but not a drive; the organic need fails to serve as an impetus to action.

It should be quite obvious by now that the relationship between the psychology and the physiology of motivation is not a simple one. Since our main interest is the psychology of motivation, we will naturally consider *drive* as a central topic. This does not mean that we will ignore the physiology of motivation. We cannot, since we are interested in discovering the physiological correlates of motivated behavior.

PHYSIOLOGICAL DRIVES

Up to this point the study of motivation seems fairly simple and straightforward— a drive develops, the organism responds appropriately, an incentive is obtained, and the drive disappears. But within this apparently simple sequence of events lie many complex problems. One of them is to discover the physiological correlates of our drives. Why, for example, do we get hungry?

Hunger

A famous physiologist (Cannon, 1934) once sought to discover the physiological correlates of the hunger drive. Quite naturally he supposed the stomach must be involved. Knowing that the stomach is a rather thick-walled muscular sac, he decided to find out whether its muscular contractions were related to the sensation of hunger, and so he had human subjects swallow a balloon (not as torturous an experience as it sounds). The balloon was inflated and attached to a recording mechanism. As the stomach muscles contracted, pressure was exerted on the balloon and the resulting changes in air pressure were recorded. The subject was instructed to press a telegraph key when-

ever he felt hungry. A high positive correlation (see page 70) was found to exist between the sensation of hunger and stomach contractions.

The story of hunger does not stop with stomach contractions. What initiates stomach contractions? A clue to the right answer is contained in the results of two dramatic studies (Luckhardt & Carlson, 1915; Templeton & Quigley, 1930). When blood from a hungry dog was transfused into a satiated dog, contractions began in the stomach of the satiated dog. When blood from a satiated dog was transfused into a starving dog, the stomach contractions in the starving dog ceased. If the initiation and cessation of stomach contractions can be controlled by blood transfusions, then obviously there is some link between the chemical condition of the blood and stomach contractions. What could this condition be? One hypothesis is that it is the amount of blood sugar in the blood. Another suggestion is that some hormonal condition is responsible. But whatever the answer, one can be sure that some other question will be raised. The attempt to discover *the* underlying chemistry of food deprivation—which, incidentally, is not strictly a psychological problem—is a never-ending search. The answer to one question immediately raises another.

Hunger cannot be described in terms of a simple causal chain with each link (stomach contractions) responsible for another event (sensation of hunger) and caused by a different event (blood chemistry). No such simple causal linking exists even among the facts that we have discussed so far. Stomach contractions, for example, are not essential to the hunger drive. Humans who have had their stomachs removed because of injury or disease have reported sensations of hunger. Rats without stomachs behave very much like rats with stomachs in learning problems that involve food reward. Obviously then, links in the chain of internal, physiological events related to the psychological effects of the hunger drive can be bypassed.

Research has shown that the brain must also be considered in any systematic attempt to understand the physiological correlates of the hunger drive (Stellar, 1954). Stomach contractions can be evoked by direct electrical stimulation of certain portions of the hypothalamus, one of the major structural units of the brain stem (see page 94). Stimulation of other parts of the hypothalamus can stop hunger contractions. The drive to eat would therefore appear to be intimately tied to the functioning of the hypothalamus. Additional support for this conclusion comes from studies involving surgical lesions in a rat's hypothalamus. The destruction of small areas in certain parts of the rat's hypothalamus can produce enormous increases in the rat's eating rates, so much so that an animal may double its weight in two months (Miller, 1957). Conversely, small lesions in a different part of the hypothalamus can eliminate eating behavior. It would seem that the hypothalamus contains neural centers capable of turning on and turning off the hunger drive. Obviously then, the chain of events we have described (sensation of hunger, stomach contractions, blood chemistry, etc.) is not insulated from other bodily processes, particularly those occurring in the hypothalamus.

Specific Hungers. Because we have been discussing it in such general terms, we may have created the impression that hunger is a unitary drive. But consider your own experience. Often you do not crave simply food; you crave certain kinds of food. Although bread is cheap and would suffice to stop your stomach contractions, you will on occasion expend much effort, time, and money to get a T-bone steak.

Thus it is often more appropriate to speak of one or more specific hungers rather than a general hunger for food. At such times food-seeking behavior is directed to-

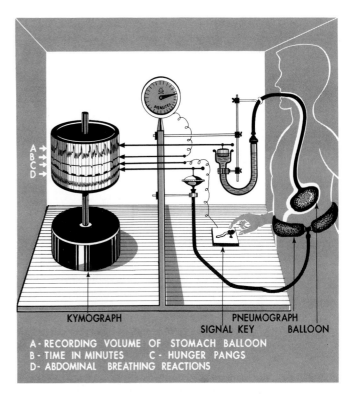

KYMOGRAPH   PNEUMOGRAPH

SIGNAL KEY   BALLOON

A - RECORDING VOLUME OF STOMACH BALLOON
B - TIME IN MINUTES   C - HUNGER PANGS
D - ABDOMINAL BREATHING REACTIONS

FIGURE 9.4   The Apparatus Used to Discover Whether Hunger Pangs Are Correlated With Stomach Contractions. A record of stomach contractions, passage of time, hunger pangs, and abdominal breathing reactions is registered on a slowly rotating drum (kymograph). Observe that the hunger pangs coincide with stomach contractions but are independent of abdominal breathing (After Cannon, 1934).

ward particular kinds of reinforcements. There are several reasons for this. Before discussing them, we should examine some of the relevant facts.

Rats who have been fed a sugar-free diet will exhibit a definite preference for sugar when given a choice among sugar, wheat, and fat. Their preference for sugar is not simply a result of their having a "sweet tooth." Rats who have been fed on a fat-free diet will, when given the same choice, demonstrate a marked preference for fat. Similarly rats who have been deprived of wheat will prefer wheat (Young, 1940). It has been shown that rats have the capacity to demonstrate a preference for sugar, fat, salt, sodium, calcium, phosphorus, thiamine, and riboflavin when they have been deprived of these essential food substances. Rats are obviously not trained nutrition experts, yet they behave as though they were. They are able to choose from a wide variety of foods those they need for a balanced diet.

Cafeteria-feeding experiments have been carried out with a number of farm animals (Young, 1933). These experiments are so named because, as in a cafeteria, the organism is free to choose from a large number of foods. Pigs, cows, and chickens in such free-choice situations have been able to select a balanced diet. In fact, the growth records of pigs in a cafeteria-feeding situation compare favorably with pigs raised on a scientifically balanced commercial feed. (The expense and trouble of cafeteria-feeding techniques prohibit their commercial use.) One experiment conducted by Davis (1928) in a hospital setting and lasting over a full year showed that human babies were able to select, from a variety of natural raw and cooked foods, a balanced diet that enabled them to develop just as well as other babies whose food was scientifically chosen for them. Some babies in the experiment went in heavily at times for certain foods (e.g., banana, liver)—they went on regular food jags. One child who was suffering from rickets, a vitamin D deficiency, when he was admitted into the experiment voluntarily selected cod-liver oil.

Such experiments prove that organisms have specific hunger needs each requiring its own food as reinforcement. Also, that in some manner organisms are able to select foods that satisfy these specific hungers. If organisms are capable of selecting adequate diets, why do they not always do so? Many citizens of the United States, a country with an abundant and sufficiently diversified food supply, are undernourished or suffer from vitamin deficiencies.

Inadequate diets result from three different causes. The first is that not every specific dietary need produces a specific drive. Although fat-starved rats will prefer foods containing fat, rats deprived of vitamin A do not similarly prefer food rich in vitamin A (Wilder, 1937). Some protein-deprived rats are incapable of selecting the right foods to make up the deficiency even though such foods are available. Unfortunately, self-regulating mechanisms that prompt animals to select needed foods do not operate for all dietary needs.

Social customs or training can also interfere with the selection of properly balanced and adequate diets. Asiatics frequently suffer from a deficiency of vitamin B_1 severe enough to cause the disease known as beriberi. Their diet consists mainly of polished rice. During the polishing process the outer layers surrounding the kernel of rice are removed and with them a vital source of vitamin B_1. Also, people can be harmed by developing strong preferences for or aversions to particular foods. The person who has an intense hunger for candy or a strong aversion to cereals or vegetables is liable to become undernourished. Even rats can be trained to select an inadequate food in preference to a balanced diet.

The third reason why an inadequate diet may be selected is that organisms may develop an appetite for foods they do not need. Rats will learn and practice instrumental acts rewarded by saccharin, which is sweet tasting but nonnutritive (Sheffield & Roby, 1950). Many humans in various parts of the world consume alcoholic beverages in preference to more nourishing beverages.

Eating is obviously complexly determined. Instead of having one hunger need, we have many. We have physiological, self-regulating mechanisms that enable us to select foods that satisfy some, but not all, of our specific hungers. And finally, we can learn eating responses that go counter to the needs of our bodies.

Although hunger develops within the body, environmental conditions may have a strong influence on eating. Chickens will eat more from a large heap of food than from a small one, even when both heaps are so large that neither is entirely consumed (Bayer, 1929). This fact is consistent with the finding previously reported (see page 169) that relatively stronger instrumental responses will occur in a conditioning situation involving a large food reward. Eating behavior is an instrumental response, and therefore it is not surprising to discover that a variable such as amount of food available has an effect upon it. When you enter a restaurant intending to get "a bite to eat" but happen to see someone else devouring steak and French fries, you may suddenly order the same. External stimuli can influence the intensity of a hunger drive.

Eating can take unusual forms as a result of strong drives or intensive training. The writer once borrowed some white rats from a colony maintained by the chemistry department of his university. He was distressed to find that all the animals had one or more legs missing. Only stumps remained where complete legs should have been. It was discovered that their laboratory food was deficient in calcium. The mother rats, being totally without the sentiments celebrated on Mother's Day cards, had compensated for their calcium deficiency by chewing off some of the legs of their offspring. The cannibalistic inclinations of some Australian aborigines can supposedly be attributed, in part, to the extremely low level of fats in their normal diet. Even in a culture such as ours, the intense aversion to human flesh has at times been overcome in situations of desperate food deprivation. Though some of a group of prospectors trapped by snow in the mountains on their way to the California gold rush resorted to cannibalism to avoid starvation, a threat of starvation cannot force other men to abandon their moral and religious beliefs. During the tragic famines that have scourged India, people have died of starvation rather than molest the sacred Brahman cattle.

Thirst

Although humans are capable of surviving for several weeks without food, they cannot live more than a few days without water. Our bodies demand a minimum water level, below which death results. Dryness of the mouth and throat tissue plays much the same role in the thirst drive as stomach contractions do in the hunger drive. Although dryness of the mouth and throat tissue serves as a primary cue for the sensation of thirst, it is in turn controlled by a host of other variables.

As the water supply in the body lowers, and the throat and mouth become dry, tiny nerve endings imbedded in the tissue are stimulated. The organism then has a sensation of thirst and in turn a drive for the relief of thirst is initiated. Wetting the dry tissues by drinking water or some other beverage reduces the sensation of thirst.

The degree of dryness of the tissues in the oral cavity does not of itself determine the strength of the thirst drive. If it did we should expect that the removal of the salivary glands, which keep the tissues in the mouth moist, would increase water consumption. This has been found to be untrue. Dogs with their salivary glands removed drink no more water than dogs with intact salivary glands (Montgomery, 1931).

Nor does the dryness of the throat and mouth determine how much water you will drink. The first mouthful of water is sufficient to wet the mouth and throat tissues. Yet sometimes, particularly after strenuous exercise, you may drink several glasses of water; at other times your thirst drive will be eliminated by a few sips of water. Obviously some physiological mechanism enables you to make a rather precise estimate of your body's need for water.

This point was made dramatically clear in a study (Bellows, 1939) in which a dog's esophagus, the tube that runs between the throat and the stomach, was severed and both ends were brought through the skin to the outside of the body. When a dog drank, water poured out of the opened upper end of the severed esophagus. The animal was kept alive by injecting food and water into the opening of the lower half of the esophagus leading to the stomach. These surgically treated dogs were deprived of liquids for various periods of time. After each period of deprivation they were offered water, which they proceeded to drink in amounts proportional to the water lost during the deprivation period. The dogs were able to gauge the extent of their water needs even though the water they drank never reached their stomachs, but poured out through the severed esophagus. This finding provides additional confirmation of the existence of some physiological mechanism that regulates the amount of liquid drunk in accordance with the current need of the body for water. This regulating mechanism must operate independently of the water entering the stomach. Water did not enter the stomachs of the surgically treated dogs after they drank it, yet they were able to drink appropriate amounts.

The physiological factors responsible for the maintenance of the proper water level in body tissue appear to be localized in the brain and the blood. Located in the hypothalamus are cells that are extremely sensitive to water loss. Direct dehydration of the cells of the hypothalamus by an injection of a salt solution results in excessive drinking. It is likely that the water level of these water-sensitive cells in the hypothalamus is controlled by the chemical and hormonal condition of the blood. When the blood stream of an animal is loaded with salt, the animal reacts by drinking. Like hunger, thirst is not simply a function of a single physiological event; it is complexly determined by several physiological variables and the interaction among them.

We noted that many different incentives can reduce the hunger drive. The same is true, although to a lesser extent, for the thirst drive. Water is by no means the only thirst-quenching beverage. There are people who proudly claim that they have not touched a drop of plain water most of their lives. People learn to consume some beverage other than water, such as wine, milk, soda pop, or coconut milk, to satisfy their need for fluids. In water-scarce countries people turn to plants and fruits with high water content.

Sex

There are several respects in which the sex drive resembles the hunger and thirst drives: all three are based upon physiological mechanisms; each possesses a range of incentives; each requires instrumental acts before drive reduction can be achieved.

Nevertheless, there are important differences between the sex drive and the hunger and thirst drives. First, survival does not depend on sexual satisfaction. Complete food and water deprivation will result in death, but sexual abstinence has been practiced by many people for religious, moral, or other reasons without apparent harm or shortening of the life span. Second, in our society no strong social taboos block the satisfaction of hunger and thirst. A wide diversity of incentives is tolerated. Eating spaghetti and meatballs is just as moral as eating steak and potatoes. In contrast, strong moral and legal pressures dictate where, when, how, and with whom sexual satisfaction shall be obtained. Because of these two differences, sexual behavior is psychologically much more complicated than eating and drinking behavior. But it is possible, if one is able to maintain a detached scientific attitude, to understand sexual behavior.

The Physiology of Sex. Stomach contractions and a parched mouth initiate hunger and thirst sensations. Is the sex drive associated with comparable local sensations? Yes, although the sensations are not as strictly localized.

In the male heightened sex drive is indicated when the penis becomes enlarged and erect. Ejaculations, resulting usually, but not always, from touch and pressure stimulation of sensitive receptors located on the surface of the penis, leads to reduction of the sex drive. Ejaculation in the human male is accompanied by the sensation of an orgasm, a sharp reduction in the tension accompanying the peak of sexual excitement occurring immediately before ejaculation. Other physiological indicators of orgasm in the male, in addition to ejaculation, are a sharp and sudden lowering of heart rate and blood pressure.

The feminine counterpart of the penis is the relatively small clitoris located above the entrance to the vagina. Like the penis it is very sensitive and has the capacity for erection. But nothing comparable to the male ejaculation occurs in the female. Human females report sensations of orgasm (sometimes referred to as "climax"), but their physiological and psychological basis is much more obscure than in the case of the male. During sexual intercourse (coitus) the female's physiological reactions, resulting from clitoral and vaginal stimulation, consist of a general state of arousal that does not include any climactic physiological event followed immediately by a sudden reduction. Typically her state of arousal both develops and subsides more gradually than the male's. Changes in heart rate and blood pressure do occur, but their intensity is not usually comparable to those accompanying the male's ejaculation.

The sex organs are not the only parts of the anatomy which, when stimulated, generate sexual excitement. The lips, nipples, and other areas of the body, depending on the individual and the culture from which he comes, can serve as erotic zones. Thus the sensations associated with the sex drive are neither as uniform nor as localized as those related to the hunger and thirst drives.

What has been described up to now are some of the terminal physiological events in the motivational sequence that begins with sexual arousal and ends with sexual gratification. Something must now be added about other physiological events that are involved.

Sex Hormones. When at puberty the sex glands of human beings become mature, there is a sharp increase in the secretion of sex hormones by the ovaries of the female and the testes of the male. The onset of puberty is itself controlled by secretions from the pituitary gland. When the pituitary gland of lower animals is removed prior to puberty, mature sexual characteristics fail to develop. In contrast, when animals are injected with pituitary extract prior to puberty, the development of sexual maturity is accelerated. After receiving injections of pituitary extract, male chicks only a few days old crow like roosters, grow combs, and make sexual advances toward females (Ford & Beach, 1952).

Injection of the sex hormones of one sex into a member of the other sex may produce behavior that is characteristic of the opposite sex. Unscrupulous exporters of foreign birds to this country have been known to inject female canaries with male hormones, because only male canaries sing, and except for breeding purposes, female canaries are commercially worthless. A few weeks after female birds have been injected, they start singing a song indistinguishable from a male's, and during this time they can be sold to customers who, like most people, are unable to distinguish male from female canaries. Unfortunately, after the effects of the hormone injection have worn off several weeks later, the birds stop singing. Some dealers received so many com-

238

plaints that they stopped handling imported birds (Herrick & Harris, 1957).

Secretions from the endocrine system exert powerful control over the sexual behavior of lower animals. Consider the sexual behavior of the psychologist's favorite laboratory animal—the white rat. After sexual maturity is attained the female rat is periodically in heat—technically, in **estrus.** At such time the ovaries secrete relatively large amounts of female sex hormone (estrogen) into the blood stream, and at the height of estrus, which occurs every fourth or fifth day, the ovaries release the *ovum,* or egg.

At the height of the estrus cycle the female rat, in addition to being physically active, is sexually receptive. In the presence of a male she will assume a sexually receptive posture that enables the male to mount and copulate. When not in estrus, the female rat is sexually unresponsive and will not assume the sexually receptive posture. Prior to sexual maturity a female white rat will never assume a sexually receptive posture in the presence of a male rat.

During the period when the female rat is in estrus her activity level increases enormously. Figure 9.5 shows a typical record of a female rat placed in an activity wheel, in which each revolution of the cylindrical cage was recorded, furnishing a cumulative measure of the total amount of the rat's activity during a given time period. Peaks of activity prove to be associated with peaks of the estrus cycle.

If the ovaries of a female rat are removed by a surgical technique known as an ovariectomy, the pattern of activity depicted in Figure 9.5 disappears and is replaced by one that shows only minor fluctuations from day to day and averages less than 2,000 daily revolutions. She will no longer assume a sexually receptive posture and hence will not engage in copulation. If, however, the ovariectomized female is injected with ovarian hormones (estrogen), she will once again become sexually responsive and engage in coitus. It is also important to note, for reasons that will soon become apparent, that rats who have been ovariectomized prior to maturity will also exhibit mating responses for the first time when injected with estrogen. These facts show that the sexual behavior of the female rat is controlled by ovarian hormones. When estrogen is present, sexual behavior occurs; when estrogen is absent, sexual behavior fails to appear. The same relation between ovarian hormones and sexual behavior is found in females of other mammals such as mice, cats, dogs, and cows.

The hormonal control of the male rat's behavior is less rigid than the female's, as two sets of facts show (Beach, 1947). First, immature male rats have been observed to mount receptive females and indulge in copulatory behavior even though they are

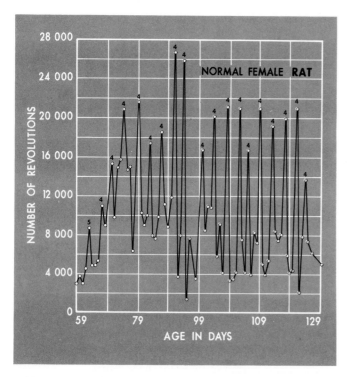

FIGURE 9.5 A Typical Record of a Female Rat's Activity During Different Portions of the Estrus Cycle. The peaks of activity are correlated with ovarian secretions. Each peak indicates the number of days from the last day of high activity (After Richter, 1932).

incapable of ejaculating. Second, when the testes of a sexually experienced male rat are removed, he will continue to copulate, with declining frequency, for a period of approximately six months thereafter. With these two exceptions, there is a close and intimate relationship between the sexual behavior of the male rat and testicular hormonal secretions. At the onset of maturity there is a sudden increase in the male's sexual behavior, together with the capacity for ejaculation. Sexual behavior gradually disappears following castration, the removal of the testes. Copulatory behavior can be reinstituted after castration by injections of the male hormones.

The male rat's sexual behavior follows no periodic cycle as does the female's. But, as with the female, removal of the sex glands (testes) produces a marked decrease in the general activity level of the male rat.

The sexual behavior of male and female white rats is obviously under the control of hormonal secretions. With the female rat the control is complete. The hormonal control of sexual behavior of the male rat is not as complete, but it is still fairly strict. Prior to puberty and for a short period after castration, the male rat engages in some sexual behavior. At other times such behavior is intimately related to presence of hormonal secretions in the blood stream.

The higher up on the evolutionary scale we go the more signs we find that sexual behavior has become emancipated from hormonal control. Whereas the female white rat assumes a sexually receptive posture only at the time of estrus, the sexual responses of some monkeys and primates (e.g., chimpanzees) are not similarly restricted. A female chimpanzee may accept a male when she is not in estrus and therefore not fertile. The sexual behavior of the human female is even more liberated from hormonal control. The ovaries secrete an egg approximately halfway between successive menstruations. At the same time maximal amounts of estrogenic hormones are secreted into the blood stream. If hormonal secretions controlled the sex responses of the human female more strictly, sex desire would be at its greatest at the time of ovulation. Various investigators (Davis, 1929; Terman, 1938) who have questioned large numbers of married women found that this is not so. With most women sexual desire does not reach a peak at the time of ovulation; willingness to indulge in sexual relations appears to be evenly distributed throughout the month, except for a sharp increase in sexual desire immediately before and after menstruation. In our society, which in this respect is like other societies, a woman is usually deprived of sexual satisfaction during menstruation. It is possible that the increase in sexual desire prior to menstruation reflects anticipated deprivation. Similarly the postmenstrual peak in sexual desire may be attributable to enforced sexual deprivation.

The differences in effect upon behavior of removing ovaries from rats and from still higher organisms are striking. Whereas ovariectomy abolishes the sexual behavior of a rat, an ovariectomized chimpanzee will occasionally indulge in copulation, and many human females who undergo an ovariectomy for medical reasons report no loss in sexual desire.

The higher a species is on the evolutionary scale, the more the sexual behavior of its males appears to be freed from hormonal control. Rats, you will recall, lost their ability to copulate approximately six months after castration. Some male dogs who have been castrated in adulthood show no decline in their copulatory behavior for a period as long as two years after the operation. The effects of castration in humans vary widely from one individual to another. Some men report no decrease in sexual desire and potency, but in many cases there is a gradual decrease in both desire and capacity.

In mammals other than man the effect of castration depends on whether the opera-

240

tion occurs before or after puberty. If it occurs before puberty, animals such as rats and dogs never develop adult sexual responses. The same is true for most higher animals, including human males. However, there is a record of one chimpanzee castrated in infancy who, when mature, was able to copulate but apparently without ejaculation.

If nothing else, the facts we have cited should make it clear how complex the sex drive is. But the facts do more than that. They show the influence sex hormones have upon sexual behavior in general, and they show that this control becomes progressively less as one ascends the evolutionary scale. The data also suggest that in each of the mentioned species, with the possible exception of humans, the hormonal control of sexual behavior is greater among females than among males.

The Brain and Sexual Behavior. We do not usually associate brain functioning with sexual behavior, but nevertheless, there is a definite link between the two, especially among higher mammals.

The cerebral cortex (see page 93) constitutes a much larger portion of the human brain than of the rat's brain. In lower animals, such as rats, the entire cerebral cortex can be removed without fatal results. When this is done the sexual behavior of the male is abolished, but not of the female. Decorticated female rats display typical mating behavior when in heat (Beach, 1944). Similar differences have been found in cats and dogs. Among lower animals, brain damage interferes more with the male's sexual behavior than with the female's.

There is even some suggestion that specific kinds of brain destruction will increase the frequency of female sexual behavior. When the temporal lobes (see page 96) of a female rhesus monkey were removed, the animal demonstrated an increased readiness to copulate (Klüver &

Bucy, 1939). Similar kinds of cerebral destruction in the male monkey will decrease or abolish sexual behavior.

The difference in the effect of cerebral destruction on the sexual responses of male and female animals points to the importance of instrumental acts in sexual behavior. In the sexual behavior of lower animals the female responses are much less complex than those of the male. A sexually receptive female rat is merely required to assume an appropriate posture. In contrast, the sexually aroused male rat has to perform a sequence of intricate responses when he is approaching and mounting the female. These active movements of the male are more dependent on the cerebral cortex than is the passive sexual response of the female. When, for example, the brains of male cats were severely damaged, it was discovered that the animals were capable of sexual excitement but incapable of performing the sequence of acts necessary for approaching and mounting the female. These brain-damaged cats did not respond normally to a sexually receptive female cat when she was at a distance, although when placed directly on the female such a brain-damaged male was able to copulate and ejaculate (Beach, 1947). These findings suggest that the various acts involved in the sexual behavior of the cat, beginning with sexual arousal, then approach and mounting behavior, and finally copulation and ejaculation, do not all depend on the same brain area. If they did, specific brain damage would eliminate all or none of them.

There is very little direct evidence relating brain functioning to the sexual behavior of primates and humans. The limited evidence available suggests that the cerebral cortex plays a larger part in the sexual behavior of animals higher in the evolutionary scale. That there is indirect support for this conclusion will be shown when we discuss the relationship between sex behavior and learning.

Pain

The last drive to be treated here in any detail is pain. It differs from the drives that have already been discussed in one important characteristic. Hunger, thirst, and sex are *approach* or **appetitive** drives. In order to satisfy them an organism must approach a goal and make appropriate consummatory responses (eating, drinking, or sexual responses). The pain drive, on the other hand, is an *avoidance* drive or an **aversive** drive. In order to eliminate pain, an organism moves away from the source of noxious stimulation. The organism is not required to make consummatory responses with respect to an incentive, as he did for approach drives. Instead he merely escapes from the painful stimulation. We dealt with this distinction when we explained the difference between positive and negative reinforcers (see page 157). A positive reinforcer, such as food, water, or a mate, strengthens the association between the stimulus and response by its presentation. Approach or appetitive drives have positive reinforcers. Negative reinforcers, such as an electric shock, strengthen an association by their removal. Avoidance or aversive drives have negative reinforcers.

Pain is a sensation as well as a drive. Reference was made to this fact when we noted earlier that some children constantly injure themselves because they are born without the normal sensitivity to pain. Receptors for pain are free nerve endings widely distributed throughout the skin, muscles, blood vessels, and internal organs. These free nerve endings can be stimulated by a wide variety of encounters with the environment: excessive pressures, burns, cuts, electric shocks. Pain receptors are usually stimulated by tissue damage, but not always. A mild electric shock which does not destroy any tissue is painful. Tissue damage may also occur in the absence of any immediate pain sensation. The first sun bath of the season may cause rather extensive tissue damage without producing any immediate sensation of pain.

Pain receptors vary in their anatomy, and different forms of stimulation are required to initiate activity in different receptors. Burns or cuts will stimulate pain receptors in the skin, but certain internal organs, such as the intestines, can be cut or burned without evoking any painful sensation. The pain receptors in the intestines, however, respond vigorously to stretching.

The sensation of pain also varies. Pain produced by a hypodermic needle puncturing the skin is different from a muscle ache, which in turn is different from a headache or stomach ache. Moreover, the same injury can produce different kinds of pain. If something very heavy has ever fallen on your toes, probably you felt first a sharp localized pain that disappeared fairly rapidly and was followed by a dull, throbbing pain that spread from the toes through the entire foot. These two kinds of pain reflect two kinds of neural transmission: "fast" pain is carried by relatively large, myeli-

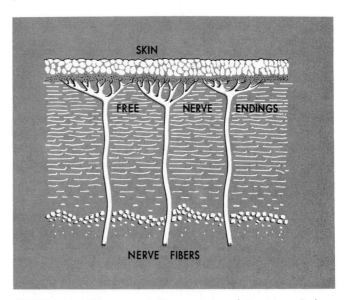

FIGURE 9.6 A Diagrammatic Representation of Free Nerve Endings in the Skin. Stimulation of these nerve endings produces sensations of pain.

nated (sheathed) fibers, while "slow" pain is transmitted by small fibers with little or no covering.

The sensation of pain is not, however, simply a matter of which receptors are stimulated and which fibers transmit the neural impulses. As with other sensory experiences, what is happening in the brain is important. This is why it is sometimes necessary to sever the connections between nerve receptors and the brain in order to terminate the intense and continuing pain known technically as *intractable pain.*

Numerous facts, support the idea that what we feel as pain can be influenced by learning and perceptual processes. In our culture, for example, women are taught that childbirth is painful, whereas in certain other cultures it is treated casually. The result is that childbirth is felt as more painful in our culture. One explanation offered for this difference is that fear increases the amount of pain sensed. Having been brought up to believe that childbirth is painful, American women fear it. During World War II it was observed that only about one out of every three severely wounded soldiers complained of enough pain to require morphine while being moved from the combat zone to the hospital. In sharp contrast, four out of five civilian patients with similar wounds need morphine to relieve their intense pain. One reasonable explanation of this difference is that a wounded soldier is often relieved, in spite of his wounds, to escape from combat, whereas in the case of a civilian major surgery induces instead of reduces fear (Melzack, 1961).

Pain-producing stimuli will not generate the distress they usually produce if they are followed by positive reinforcement. Dogs normally react violently to a shock to the paw. Pavlov found, however, that if they are consistently fed food after being shocked, they react to the noxious stimulation with salivation and tail-wagging.

Attention can either reduce or increase pain. Prize fighters and football players deeply engrossed in competition often sustain severe injuries without sensing any pain. Even more surprising is the ability of a patient whose attention is concentrated solely on the suggestions of a hypnotist to withstand pinpricks and even surgery, without experiencing pain. Normally, however, when a patient's attention is directed toward noxious stimulation, his sensation of pain will increase.

In addition to providing sensations, pain functions as a drive, for organisms are motivated to eliminate or relieve the pain that they feel. In some instances the body possesses an automatic mechanism for doing this. A cough, which is a reflex (see page 81) can sometimes eliminate discomfort in the throat. Similarly a pain produced by a cinder in the eye can sometimes be reflexively eliminated by eye-blinking and tears. Pain is liable to persist, and when it does, the organism is stirred into action until it finds a response which eliminates the pain, if this is possible. The rat in the Skinner box learns to press the bar when it leads to escape from an electric shock. Bar pressing is an instrumental act that eliminates the pain. The incentive to press the bar is provided by the *termination* of the noxious stimulus.

Organisms can learn a wide variety of responses that help eliminate painful drive states. Of particular interest is the response associated with other drives which can become instrumental in avoiding noxious stimulation. In one experiment (Williams & Teitelbaum, 1956) a group of rats was shocked unless they performed the instrumental response of drinking a liquid consisting of milk, sugar, and other nutritious ingredients. Needless to say, these animals consumed huge quantities of this liquid, which resulted in extreme obesity, the weight of a rat practically doubling within a short period of time.

It may strike you that with man painful drive states are relatively unimportant.

After all, most of us encounter physical pain infrequently, and when we do it is only for brief periods of time. In spite of this you will discover that painful drive states are psychologically important, since they provide a basis for learning other forms of motivation.

Other Physiological Drives

Hunger, thirst, sex, and pain do not exhaust the list of physiological drives, but space is not available for a discussion of such physiological drives as the need for air, maintenance of a constant body temperature, and sleep. These drives operate in a manner similar to those we have examined. Each depends upon physiological mechanisms, but in many instances not enough is known about their precise nature.

For example, consider sleep. One young man sought to prove that sleep was a waste of time. In an effort to stay awake, he forced himself to punch a clock every ten minutes. After doing this for seven consecutive days and nights, during which time he began taking catnaps during some ten-minute periods, the experiment had to be terminated because his behavior became very disturbed. He vehemently denied taking the catnaps and became extremely suspicious that someone was tampering with his clock (Katz & Landis, 1935). Soldiers in combat, or those unfortunate prisoners who are "brainwashed," report the gradual but definite breakdown of normal behavior during prolonged periods of sleep deprivation.

We do not completely understand the physiological basis of sleep, but as far as we can discover, the need for sleep is not related to any particular chemical condition of the blood. Transfusing blood from a sleeping dog into one that is awake does not cause him to sleep. Moreover, the individual heads of a two-headed baby that survived for a few months did not sleep simultaneously. Since such a baby has a common circulatory system, the physiological locus of sleep must lie elsewhere. The best guess is that it is located in the brain.

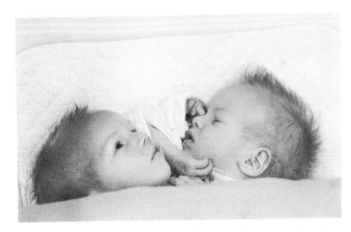

FIGURE 9.7 A Two-Headed Baby. While one head sleeps, the other remains awake (Yale Joel, *Life*, © 1960, Time, Inc.).

Drives and Instrumental Acts

It is appropriate to conclude our discussion of physiological drives by returning to a problem briefly touched upon at the beginning of this chapter (see page 231), the relationship between physiological drives and instrumental acts.

Organisms are capable of learning many different instrumental acts to reduce or eliminate their drive states. The American child learns to eat by means of a relatively complex series of movements, usually of the right hand holding a fork or spoon which delivers bits of food into his mouth. These, of course, are not the only instrumental acts that can lead to the satisfaction of the hunger drive. The European child learns to put food, at the end of a fork, into his mouth with his left hand. Other children, depending on their culture, learn to convey food to their mouths with chopsticks, knives, forks, spoons, or just plain fingers. The final consummatory responses of chewing and swallowing foods may be quite similar, although certainly not identical, among different peoples of the world. But the responses utilized in obtaining and preparing food, as well as inserting food into the mouth, vary tremendously from one culture to another and even differ among members of the same culture. Obviously then, the reduction of the hunger drive does not depend on a single uniform set of instrumental acts. The same is true of the thirst drive; a wide variety of instrumental acts is capable of quenching thirst, but individual organisms utilize only a few. The difference between drives and instrumental acts can be pinpointed by referring to the behavior of rats in a laboratory situation. You can train rats to achieve food reinforcement when hungry by pressing a bar, by turning right in a T maze, or by any of a wide variety of other hunger-reducing instrumental acts. It is also true that a given response may be strengthened by nearly any incentive. You reinforce a child you want to be "good" by candy, money, toys, praise, affection.

It is especially important that we maintain the distinction between instrumental acts and drives in discussing sex behavior. Any discussion of sex behavior not maintaining this distinction will be both confusing and misleading.

The sex drive of the rat is closely related, you recall, to endocrine secretion. When a rat matures, the appropriate mating responses (instrumental acts) occur spontaneously. These instrumental responses are not acquired in the same way as responses to press a bar or to turn right in a T maze. Experiments have shown that male and female rats, after being raised to maturity in isolation and therefore with no previous opportunity to observe the mating of other rats, will themselves, on their first opportunity, perform appropriate mating responses that are indistinguishable from those of experienced rats (Beach, 1942; Stone, 1926). The instrumental mating re-

sponses of the chimpanzee, however, do not occur spontaneously (Yerkes & Elder, 1936). When a sexually mature but inexperienced male is placed near a receptive female, he becomes sexually aroused but is unable to copulate immediately because he is inexperienced in making the appropriate instrumental responses. Practice is necessary before the male chimpanzee becomes adept at mating. In contrast, a sexually naive female chimpanzee will usually respond appropriately, when receptive, to the advances of a sexually experienced male. Presumably, sexually naive male and female chimpanzees would find it difficult to mate when initially brought together. Again it should be recalled that the instrumental acts of a male chimpanzee are much more complicated than those of a female.

It is quite obvious that in the human species appropriate copulatory behavior does not occur spontaneously. If it did, the large number of books that describe, frankly or suggestively, patterns of copulatory behavior would not be so much in demand. Human sexual behavior includes instrumental responses ranging from general courting behavior to specific acts that produce orgasm. The orgasm itself is reflexive; erection and ejaculation can occur without involvement of the brain. Male paraplegics, whose lower spinal cord has been severed and thus detached from the brain, have nocturnal erections and ejaculations. The fact that the human male orgasm can occur reflexively does not mean, however, that the response is not influenced by learning. We have already noted (see page 93) that spinal reflexes are not isolated from other activities of the nervous system. Orgasm is the terminal response in a long sequence of instrumental responses. The behavior which leads up to and makes possible the orgasm depends in humans on learning. This conclusion is supported by a vast amount of evidence obtained from surveys of sexual behavior in different cultures, including our own.

In all human societies heterosexual mating behavior (the achievement of sexual gratification with a partner of the opposite sex) is encouraged over other methods of achieving sexual satisfaction. A society that failed to do this would, of course, have difficulty in surviving. But the attitudes of different societies about when, where, and how heterosexual mating behavior should occur vary. Some societies permit free sexual activity prior to marriage; others, like our own, frown on premarital mating behavior, but in varying degrees. Monogamy, the marriage of one man to one woman, is not universally insisted upon. In some societies various forms of polygamy (having more than one mate) are sanctioned. Polygyny, a marital relationship involving one man and several women, occurs more frequently than polyandry (the marital relationship involving one woman and two or more men). A few societies approve group mateships involving several men and several women.

The instrumental acts associated with the expression of romantic interests differ among different societies. In general it is the man who makes the initial romantic overture. Exceptions to this rule may be noted in other societies and sometimes in our own. Supposedly in our society a man courts a girl by dating her, giving her presents, and declaring his desire to marry her. Among the Goajiros, an Indian tribe of South America, the woman expresses her romantic interest by tripping the man of her choice during a ceremonial dance.

The sexual act itself is performed in a variety of ways. Societies differ in the forms of heterosexual relations they encourage as well as in those they disapprove. As a result individuals learn to varying degrees to adopt the forms of coital behavior sanctioned or encouraged in their society. For example, in some societies a woman is encouraged to display passionate responses during sexual intercourse, while in other cultures the code demands that the female be completely passive. Some societies encourage aggressive behavior during coitus. The Sirionos in Central America emerge from love making with scars resulting from biting and scratching, considered to be expressions of true affection. The Sirionos are proud of such "love scars" except when they provide evidence of infidelity.

Sexually gratifying acts are not restricted to heterosexual behavior. Self-stimulation, or what is more commonly known as masturbation, has been observed in a large number of lower animals even when heterosexual mating opportunities are available, and it occurs more frequently among males than among females. Masturbation is very common among human males. It has been estimated that approximately 90 per cent of American males have experienced orgasm by self-stimulation (Kinsey, Pomeroy, & Martin, 1948). This form of achieving sexual satisfaction is the most common sexual instrumental act during adolescence. Although the incidence of masturbation decreases with age, it may be practiced on occasion by married men. Masturbation occurs among females in our society, but to a lesser degree than in the male. Most societies disapprove of masturbation. It is believed to occur with less frequency in other societies than our own. In a few societies masturbation by adolescents is not frowned upon.

Homosexual behavior (the achievement of sexual gratification with a partner of the same sex) is common among lower animals, particularly monkeys. Like masturbation, it is much less common among females than males. Although our society strongly disapproves of homosexual behavior, it occurs with greater frequency than is commonly realized, as the investigations of Kinsey and his coworkers, who interviewed more than 5,000 American men, have shown. Some societies approve homosexual behavior and encourage its development by deliberately rearing male children to occupy a female role. Other societies approve of men having both homosexual and heterosexual affairs.

These brief references to the sexual behavior of subhuman mammals and humans make it clear that a variety of instrumental sexual responses occur. Although heterosexual coitus is the most common mode of sexual behavior, it is by no means the only one that leads to sexual gratification. These facts show that it is necessary to distinguish between the physiological basis of the sex drives and the drive-reducing behavior.

INSTINCT

Many readers feel inclined to break into any discussion of the facts of sexual behavior with the blunt question, "But isn't sex instinctive?" This is a question that cannot be answered with a simple yes or no. It is the kind of question that first demands a clarification of terms, and in particular, of the term **instinct.**

What do you think *instinct* means? Whatever the answer, you can be sure that instinct does not have the same meaning for everybody. The concept of instinct was, and still is, widely used. The Greeks used it 2,500 years ago. The early psychologists used it especially freely. William James (1842-1910) said man had more instincts than any other animal. Among them he included shyness, cleanliness, fear of dark, and many others. In 1924 a compilation of various lists of purported instincts disclosed a total of 6,000 different ones.

Now, you may be disappointed, at least temporarily, if instead of attempting straightway to define the term *instinct,* we first review some of the sort of observations that have been responsible for the frequency with which the word is employed. Female loggerhead turtles, found on the eastern coast of Florida, dig small holes in a sandy beach in which they deposit their eggs (from 50 to 200). The eggs hatch after an incubation period of about 50 days. The infant turtles spend from three to five days in the nest and then crawl out, head straight for the sea, and swim out. It is therefore said that the loggerhead turtle has an instinct to go to sea.

Soon after the eggs of a goose hatch, the young goslings begin following her wherever she goes. Hence, young goslings are said to follow their mother instinctively.

Some crows that live in the western part of North America migrate in the fall from Alberta, Canada, to Kansas. In the spring they head north again. These crows are said to have an instinct to migrate.

During pregnancy female laboratory rats build a nest of wood shavings or other available material. The mother rat, after her young are born, will usually take good care of them. She will suckle them and, if they stray from the nest, will retrieve them by carrying them gently in her mouth.

Female ringdoves also exhibit maternal behavior. The mother dove sits on her eggs and after hatching feeds her young squabs by regurgitating "crop-milk" (dead tissue from the internal walls of her crop) into their open beaks.

What are the characteristics of the **instinctive behavior** just described? At least four features are outstanding. (1) The behavior is complex. It is not like a simple knee jerk reflex in which one form of stimulation evokes a single response. The seagoing behavior of the loggerhead turtle includes such acts as climbing out of the nest, orienting toward the sea, crawling down the beach, entering the water, and swimming out to sea. (2) Instinctive behavior is rather rigidly patterned. There is not much variability among turtles in their ways of doing these things. (3) The behavior is not learned. Young goslings do not require any preliminary practice in following; from the time they can walk they take off after their mother. Certainly there is no training, such as in necessary if they are to acquire a conditioned response. (4) Instinctive behavior is found in all members of the species. Little difference exists in the way crows migrate, or how mother doves care for their young.

After we have described—and thereby defined—instinctive behavior to include these characteristics, can we claim that we have explained it? No, we cannot! Nothing has been asserted about the factors responsible for the development of maternal behavior in the white rat when we state that "female rats have a maternal instinct." By attaching a common label to similar kinds of behavior we point up evidence that requires explanation, but in no sense can applying the name, no matter how scientific it may sound, be said to fully explain the behavior. At best the term *instinct* describes the behavior, but the description of a thing cannot be said to identify its causes.

Psychologists and biologists are dissatisfied with just labeling a certain kind of behavior *instinctive,* and they have sought to discover the variables responsible for it. Knowing that responses are usually made to stimuli, they have asked, what are the cues that evoke instinctive behavior? For example, what cues the young loggerhead turtle's responses when he journeys to the sea? Is it the sound of the sea? Is it the smell? Or what? Attempts to answer these questions have shown that infant turtles migrate to the ocean on moonlit nights. Since the sea reflects more moonlight than the sand, it is on such nights the brightest portion of the turtle's environment. The hypothesis that the turtles might be responding to light was confirmed by a number of different tests (Daniel & Smith, 1947). A black hood over a young turtle's head as he journeyed toward the water effectively prevented him from reaching his destination. Infant turtles removed from their nests on moonless nights crawled haphazardly about, but they pursued a beam of light flashed in front of them even when it led away from the sea. By lining up a group of cars with their headlights shining on the landward side of the beach, it was possible to direct the infant turtles away from the sea.

The migratory behavior of crows can also be modified (Rowan, 1931). A large number of crows captured in Canada during the early fall were divided into two groups. One group, the control group, was placed in an aviary. Here they were exposed to the normal daily *decreases* in illumination that results when autumn days become progressively shorter. The experimental group was placed in an artificially lit environment in which regular *increases* in the daily illumination took place. The birds were banded and released during November. Among the crows that were subsequently shot or trapped by hunters a significantly larger percentage of control birds was found to the south. Not one control bird was found to the north of the place from which they were released. In contrast, several of the experimental birds were killed north of it, and there were persistent reports during the subsequent months that others were observed to the north. These results suggest that the normal migration of crows is at least in part a response to the change in daily illumination. If the day becomes progressively shorter, the crows will fly south. If, however, the daily illumination can be progressively increased, as it was for the experimental crows, then the crows will exhibit a tendency to fly north.

So you see that so-called instinctive behavior does not emerge independently of environmental stimulation. Instinctive behavior is the result of an organism's response to appropriate cues. Specifically, there is some external control over instinctive behavior.

You have now learned how the seaward migration of young loggerhead turtles and the southward migration of crows in the autumn are in part responses to certain light stimuli. If the cues that elicit an animal's instinctive behavior can be identified, it may sometimes be modified by controlling the manner in which the cues are presented. Figure 9.8 shows how the substitution of an unusual cue for a common one can have startling results. Goslings and many other birds, soon after hatching, follow any moving object. In their natural environments that moving object is usually their mother. But the goslings shown in Figure 9.8 had been raised in an incubator, and after they had hatched, the first large moving object they saw was Dr. Konrad Lorenz, a famous European biologist. They followed him and continued to do so. This kind of phenomenon, where the response of a very young organism is triggered either by the natural stimulus or by an experi-

mentally substituted one, is known as **imprinting.** The first sizable moving object to which a newly hatched gosling is exposed is "imprinted" in such a decisive way that henceforth it becomes the only stimulus capable of eliciting the instinctive reaction.

Figure 9.9 is a diagram of an apparatus used to study imprinting. In this apparatus it was demonstrated that newly hatched New Hampshire Red chicks would follow a mechanically moving green cardboard cube if they were exposed to it in their first 54 hours of life (Jaynes, 1956; 1957). Ten days later they were still following it, although not so frequently or persistently. Chicks exposed to the same moving cube for the first time when they were 11 or 12 days old would not pursue it. Thus it appears that imprinting depends on the birds' being exposed to a moving object during a critical early period, which in the case of New Hampshire Red chicks had to be less than 54 hours after hatching. In this experiment the emergence of a form of instinctive behavior was shown to depend, at least partly, upon the presence of an appropriate stimulus object in the environment.

Now that we have illustrated that instinctive behavior is to some extent under external control, we need to cite other cases in which experiences influence instinctive behavior. Although one of the distinctive attributes of instinctive behavior is that it occurs without prior practice, this does not mean that such a response is uninfluenced by past events. That it is influenced by past events is a point clearly supported by the results of one study of the maternal behavior of the laboratory rat (Birch, 1956). It has often been noticed that pregnant rats lick the undersurface of their bodies profusely, a form of behavior which, surprisingly enough, has proved to be intimately related to the behavior the same rats exhibited toward their offspring. In the experiment in question, pregnant rats were fitted with rubber collars that effectively prevented them from licking themselves.

FIGURE 9.8 An Example of How Instinctive Behavior Can Be Modified. After hatching, goslings follow the first large moving object they encounter, which is usually their mother. The goslings shown in this picture were hatched in an incubator and saw Dr. Lorenz soon thereafter. As a result they follow him (Tom McAvoy, *Life*, © 1955, Time, Inc.).

After giving birth to their offspring the collars were removed, but the mothers failed to demonstrate the customary maternal behavior. Instead, they proceeded to eat most of their young, and the few young that were not eaten died of starvation because they got inadequate nursing care. Another experiment (Riess, 1950) showed that female rats who had never had access to material that could be carried, failed to build nests during pregnancy, even though nest-building material was available to them then. Apparently the normal maternal behavior of building nests and caring for the offspring emerges only if a mother rat has had previous experience in carrying material and being permitted the usual opportunities to lick herself. Since building nests involves positive responses to carrying material, it is easy to see the bearing of such experiences on nest building. But why should maternal behavior depend on a female rat licking herself during pregnancy? One suggested answer is that the pregnant mother's responses of licking herself generalize to her responses with newborn pups. It is as if the mother rat has to learn that something resembling her undersurface (the flesh of her young is at first without hair) must be licked, not bitten. Another suggestion is that some dietary factor is involved.

Laboratory investigations of the maternal behavior of ringdoves have also contributed in an interesting way to what has been learned about instinctive behavior (Lehrman, 1956). The pituitary glands of most birds secrete the hormone *prolactin* during the time eggs are incubated and when the young are born. When a female ringdove who has laid and hatched eggs at least once is injected with prolactin, she will feed young squabs which are not her own by regurgitating her crop-milk into their open beaks, but she will behave quite differently toward squabs if she has not been injected with prolactin. She will then either attack or court the squabs. One explanation of

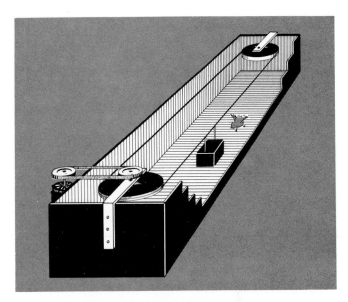

FIGURE 9.9 An Apparatus to Study Imprinting in Birds. In the diagram the recently hatched chick is being imprinted to follow a cardboard cube (After Jaynes, 1956).

this difference is that the crop-milk produced by the prolactin is a source of noxious stimulation. A female bird who has had maternal experiences has learned to eliminate the irritation by regurgitating the crop-milk into the mouths of squabs. If this hypothesis is correct, then we could predict that when prolactin is injected into a female bird who has had no previous breeding experience, she will not feed the squabs. This prediction has been confirmed. We could also expect that if the feeding of squabs by regurgitating crop-milk is an instrumental act that female ringdoves learn as a way to eliminate this noxious stimulation, then an experienced female whose crop had been anesthetized and the irritation thereby eliminated would not feed the squabs presented to her even when she was injected with prolactin. Again the prediction was confirmed.

It has also been suggested that the instinct of birds to sit on their eggs is an instrumental act which reduces noxious stimulation. At the time that eggs are laid, the female ringdove develops on her under-surface an incubation patch that is de-feathered and swollen. When she sits on her eggs she presses the incubation patch against them, and this suggests the hypoth-esis that the incubation patch is a source of irritation which can be reduced by con-tact with the smooth, cool surface of the eggs. This hypothesis receives some support from the observation that female birds will sit on cool, smooth stones placed in their nests.

The similarity between the maternal sit-ting and feeding responses of the ringdove and the bar-pressing response of a white rat in a Skinner box with an electrically charged grid should be obvious. Both or-ganisms are subject to painful drive states, and it is not surprising that both should perform an act which reduces or eliminates the noxious stimulation.

Instincts, Environment, and Heredity

In the preceding section we set forth the identifying characteristics of the kind of behavior considered instinctive. Because instinct has always been a rather vague concept and has been saddled with a multi-plicity of meanings, we also provided it with a clear definition. In order to do this, we first gave examples of the behavior of lower animals correctly labeled as in-stinctive. We then showed that such be-havior has four main characteristics; it is complex, rigidly patterned, unlearned, and universal among the members of a species (or at least among all individuals of the same sex). Our analysis of experiments de-signed to investigate variables influencing instinctive behavior shows that it does not spontaneously emerge *regardless* of environ-mental and historical influences. Hence, the popular notion that instinctive behav-ior always emerges full-blown from nowhere and that it is unmodifiable must itself be

modified. More generally, our review demonstrates once again the futility of try-ing to interpret any pattern of behavior as caused exclusively by either hereditary *or* environmental factors. To argue that in-stinctive behavior is exclusively a function of hereditary factors would be as foolish as to attribute conditioning exclusively to environmental influences. We know that an organism's physiological system, which is largely genetically determined, plays an important role in the acquisition of con-ditioned responses. Asking whether en-vironmental or hereditary factors deter-mine the character of behavior is like ask-ing whether the length or the height of a rectangle determines its area. Both dimen-sions are obviously involved in making the area of a rectangle what it is. Similarly both environmental and hereditary variables are essential determiners of behavior, whether the behavior is instinctive or learned. If we accept this, we can then undertake ex-perimental investigations to determine the respective contributions of each to any par-ticular instance of behavior we wish to understand.

Instincts, Drives, and Instrumental Acts

Our analysis suggests the necessity of distin-guishing between two components of in-stinctive behavior: the drive component and the instrumental act component. The newly hatched loggerhead turtle has a drive to move toward light in the same way that a hungry rat has a drive for food. This drive is reduced in the turtle's natural environ-ment by his crawling to the sea in the moonlight. Instrumental acts other than crawling to the sea can reduce the drive for light, as was demonstrated when the baby turtles followed the beam of a flashlight.

The physiological basis of the newly hatched loggerhead turtle's drive for light is not known No matter what it is, the important point is that under certain environmental situations (e.g., lights on the landward side of a beach) the turtles will crawl away from the sea instead of toward it. It might even be possible to restrict the movements of a young turtle drastically by placing it in the center of a brightly lit circle surrounded by darkness.

Much the same account can be made for other forms of instinctive behavior. The physiological mechanism responsible for causing a newly hatched New Hampshire Red chick to follow a moving object is not known. Whatever it is, *following* is reinforced, and just what object is followed depends upon what the chick has encountered in its early environment.

Instinctive behavior does not, of course, always have to be an expression of an approach, or positive, drive. Some instinctive behavior is directed toward avoidance of noxious stimulation. It has already been suggested that mother doves sit on eggs and feed their young because this behavior reduces or eliminates sources of irritation. Young salmon in the rivers of the Northwest migrate downstream because as they mature they lose skin pigmentation. This results in exposure of the light-sensitive cells which lie immediately beneath the pigment layer of the skin. The illumination of ordinary daylight becomes so irritating that young salmon are driven to deeper water downstream.

Although the physiological basis of the drives connected with instinctive behavior is not understood fully, it is easy to see how instinctive behavior has become so firmly entrenched in many species. Suppose that some loggerhead turtles were born with a weak drive or none at all to approach light. Such turtles would probably not reach the sea and would starve to death on land. Or suppose that some mother doves did not develop irritating brood patches or that some goslings were born with no drive to follow a moving object during their early days of life. The mother doves would probably not hatch whatever eggs they had laid, and the goslings would probably either fail to find food or fall prey to predators. The drives connected to instincts have survival value. Organisms with weaker instinctive drives associated with instinctive behavior or with none have less chance to survive and to reproduce. Assuming that these drives are genetically determined, it is easy to understand how, by natural selection, instinctive behavior has become universal in certain species. In this respect it is interesting to note that domestic fowl are not as easily imprinted as wild birds. The value of imprinting as an aid to survival in wild fowl who must be cared for by their parents, is obviously much greater than it is for pampered domestic birds who begin their lives in brooders that supply food and water and in sheltered pens where there are no enemies.

It should be pointed out that our analysis has not attempted to deal with complete sequences of instinctive behavior. In discussing the instinctive behavior of the loggerhead turtle, the nest-building behavior of the mother turtle was ignored, as was the behavior of the young turtle after he reached the sea. Presumably such components of a species' instinctive behavior pattern could be identified by experimentation similar to that used in investigating the infant turtle's crawling toward the sea. Our analysis of the seagoing behavior of young turtles is scientifically more meaningful and, it is hoped, intellectually more satisfying, than the assumption that young loggerhead turtles are endowed with an "instinctive longing for the sea," which seems about equivalent to saying, "They go to the sea because they go to the sea."

There are psychologists who would prefer to discard the term *instinct* because it has been used so vaguely and loosely in everyday language. Their judgment deserves respect. The history of science is full of instances where vague terms thoughtlessly taken over from common usage have had to be replaced by newly coined, precisely defined technical terms. On the other hand, there is value in refining the term *instinct* for contemporary use. Most students of psychology have definite preconceptions about instincts, and it is just as worthwhile for an introductory psychology course to clarify misunderstandings about behavior as it is to impart a new outlook and new ideas. But you must keep firmly in mind that when the term *instinct* is used here, it does not mean whatever it may mean in common parlance. *Instinct,* as we use it, exemplifies the four characteristics of instinctive behavior that we discussed earlier. We also made a clear and important distinction between drives associated with instincts (e.g., the approach drive of the loggerhead turtle to light) and the instrumental acts which reduce or eliminate them.

Instincts and Human Behavior

Now that the importance of the operational definition of instinct has been properly emphasized, the relationship between the instinctive behavior as it is found in the lower animals and in humans can be considered. Instinctive behavior is complex, rigidly patterned, not dependent on training, and universal for all members of the species. What sort of human behavior can fulfill these specifications?

Is there a human maternal instinct comparable to the maternal behavior exhibited by white rats (when raised on an adequate diet and without rubber collars)? In our society, we know that many expectant mothers are so ignorant about the care of infants that they must take courses on the subject or at least read a book. Moreover, there is a tremendous variety in infant care among different societies, and among mothers in the same society. A Balinese mother may be moving about while her baby suckles in a sling hung from her neck.

An American mother customarily sits or lies when nursing her baby. However, more than half of the babies in the United States are bottle fed. Most American infants have been weaned before they are 16 months old; children in the Chenchu tribe in India are not weaned until they are five or six years old. Human maternal behavior cannot be classified as instinctive, since it is not independent of training, nor is one kind of maternal behavior practiced universally. The supreme evidence for this conclusion is that in many primitive societies living precariously on the edge of want, infanticide is encouraged and practiced. And even in this country an occasional mother abandons her baby as soon as she can.

The obvious next question is, Do women have an instinctive drive to have children? If they do, how are we going to account for the married women in our society who, although healthy and physically capable of bearing children, decide not to have them? Or the fact that even those who do have children vary in their attitudes toward maternity. Several surveys have reported that a relatively large proportion, sometimes exceeding 50 per cent, of expectant mothers express regret over their impending motherhood.

Human sex behavior, like human maternal behavior, falls outside the classification of instinctive behavior. It is not independent of training, as is, for example, that of the rat, nor is it as stereotyped. The detailed pattern of sexually satisfying behavior typical in one society may rarely or never occur in another society.

As long as we adhere to the specifications for instinctive behavior we have insisted upon, it is impossible to discover any complex adult human behavior pattern that can qualify as instinct. This is not surprising, considering that our nervous systems, and especially the cortex, are so much more complex than those of the organisms where instinctive behavior is found in its most complex and rigid forms. Human behavior is more variable and more easily and profoundly affected by learning than the behavior of lower organisms. Whereas the survival of lower organisms depends on rigid instinctive patterns of behavior, the survival of the human race has rested upon its ability to mold its behavior so as to adapt and control a wide range of environments. In addition, man is a unique animal able to create complex moral and legal codes that powerfully influence the manner in which physiological drives are satisfied. The result of all these differences is that rigid, uniform instinctive behavior of the type we find in lower animals has no counterpart in human behavior.

You would not, however, be justified in concluding that all the forms of drive-satisfying behavior in humans occur with equal ease; humans develop some patterns of behavior more easily than others. Not all nutritious foods have the same chance of being consumed by humans. What we eat and can be nourished by is determined in great part by the physiology and chemistry of our digestive systems. This is one especially good reason why we prefer peas and string beans to grass. Similarly, of course, human sexual behavior is influenced by the structure of our bodies and nervous systems, and as a consequence some forms of sexual behavior occur much more frequently than others. However, the important point is that the human body with its complicated nervous system is not limited to a single pattern of behavior to satisfy the nutritional, sexual, and other drives which are generated by basic physiochemical processes.

LEARNED DRIVES

The physiochemical bases of much of what we—and the race—need merely to survive have been frequently mentioned. The hunger, thirst, and sex drives (with such other drives as the need for sleep, oxygen, and constant body temperature) are classified as physiological or primary drives because they are expressions of fundamental physiochemical processes. In contrast to the primary drives are the learned or secondary drives. Learned drives are distinguishable from primary drives by their dependence on a particular organism's individual experience instead of, as with primary drives, on its basic physiochemical processes. The need for nourishing food is a primary drive, but an individual's passion for organ music or modern art is a learned drive. He can survive, of course, without either. In spite of this, some people have learned to enjoy organ music or modern art so much that they will gladly allot much time, energy, and money in order to be able to do so. Many young men who read this book may wish to be physicians; others may prefer to be businessmen, teachers, engineers, athletes, or entertainers; and some may prefer to get by without doing much of anything. The women also probably have diverse vocational ambitions. Some are like men in being strongly career-minded, whereas others aspire to be wives and mothers. But no matter what your motivation toward a vocation is, the important point is that it operates as a drive. Striving to be a doctor influences the behavior of the premedical student in somewhat the same way that hunger influences him to eat. Both drives provide behavior with a direction and an incentive (an M.D. degree in one case, food in the other).

Such drives as vocational ambitions are learned. But how are they learned? This is a difficult question to answer, and for the moment we must be content with describing some relatively simple experimental situations from which psychologists hope to obtain findings that will give them important insights into the more complex forms of learned drives.

Fear

In one experiment on learned drives, Neal Miller (1948*a*) used the apparatus illustrated in Figure 9.10. It consists of two compartments, one painted white, the other black. A small door, painted with horizontal white and black stripes, separates the two compartments. Before the main part of the experiment began, Miller tested the animals in the apparatus for any symptoms

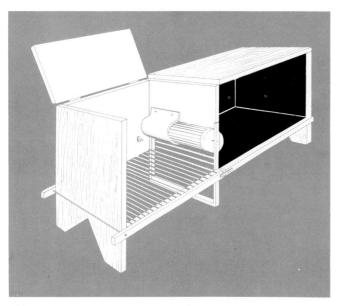

FIGURE 9.10 The Apparatus Used by Miller to Study the Learning of Fear. The left compartment is painted white, the right, black. The striped black and white door can be raised so the rat can go from the white into the black compartment, and a shock can be administered through the floor of the white compartment (After Miller, 1948a).

of fear. Fear is operationally defined in rats in terms of the following indices: tenseness, crouching, excessive urination and defecation. None of these occurred. The rats were then given a series of brief electric shocks through the metal bars of the electric grid in the white compartment. After this experience the rats showed agitated, fearful behavior in the white compartment. This fear was obviously learned,

since it had not been manifested prior to the series of shocks.

After demonstrating that fear could be learned, Miller tried to discover whether a learned fear response operated in the same way as does a primary drive such as hunger. We know, that is, that primary drives in conjunction with an appropriate situation can produce learning; but can a learned fear response also mediate learning? To answer this question the apparatus depicted in Figure 9.11 was arranged so that the door separating the white from the black compartment could be opened by turning a wheel above the door. Under these conditions rats previously shocked in the white compartment and now returned to it made a series of responses until, by chance, they finally turned the wheel. The door opened and the rats raced out of the fear-provoking white compartment. If learned fear operates as a drive, we would expect that the rats would learn to turn the wheel whenever they were placed in the white compartment. This is exactly what happened. Figure 9.11 shows that the fearful rats learned to turn the wheel more rapidly on each successive trial; that is, the latency of the wheel-turning response decreased on successive trials.

If learned fear is comparable to the primary drive of hunger, what is equivalent to food? The answer would seem to be escape from the white compartment. Psychologists refer to such an escape as fear-reduction. Thus Miller demonstrated that a simple instrumental act would be learned when rats are motivated by fear and reinforced by fear-reduction.

If escape from the fear-provoking white compartment acts as a reinforcer, then we should expect that delay in escape, and thus in fear-reduction, should depress performance in the same way that delay in food reinforcement depresses the performance of an instrumental response (see page 170). One experiment (Mowrer & Lamoreaux, 1942) demonstrated that the performance of an instrumental response was depressed when fear-reduction was delayed, and this contrasted with the situation in which fear-reduction occurred immediately after the performance of an instrumental response.

Miller's experiment is so important to our understanding of personality and behavior pathology as well as of the psychology of motivation, that it demands careful examination on three points: (1) During the learning of the wheel-turning response the rats *never* received an electric shock. That is, the animals learned the wheel-turning response in the complete absence of the primary drive to escape pain. (2) The acquisition of fear was similar to the acquisition of a classical conditioned response. The white compartment served as a conditioned stimulus. The unconditioned stimulus was shock and the unconditioned response was the agitated, fearful behavior the shock produced. The conditioned stimulus (white compartment) became associated with the response the shock produced. Fear is essentially a conditioned response to painful stimulation. (3) The conditioned fear response has drive properties. Organisms are motivated to make responses that reduce or eliminate the fear-provoking stimulus. In short, fear enabled Miller's subjects to learn a new response.

Responses learned under fear motivation differ in one important respect from those learned under such an appetitive drive as hunger. It is fairly easy to extinguish an instrumental response that has consistently led to food reinforcement; you have merely to eliminate food so that the instrumental response will no longer be reinforced (see page 164). But fear, unlike hunger, has a built-in reinforcement mechanism. If the animal escapes from the fear-provoking situation, reinforcement (fear-reduction) is automatic; the response itself insures its own reinforcement. As a result, a habit based on fear tends to persist in the absence of any primary reinforcement. Figure 9.12 shows the performance curves of three rats

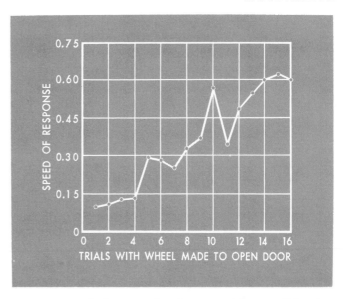

FIGURE 9.11 The Learning of an Instrumental Response When Rats Are Motivated by Fear and Reinforced by Fear Reduction (After Miller, 1948a).

that learned an instrumental response to escape from a fear-provoking situation. During a run of 100 trials all the animals responded rapidly. One animal stopped responding after making more than 300 responses, while the other two animals were

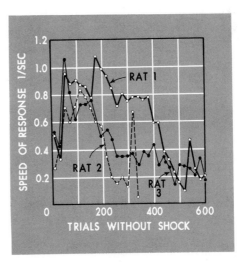

FIGURE 9.12 The Resistance to Extinction of a Habit Based on Fear. The graph shows the speed with which three rats made an instrumental response to escape a fear-provoking situation (After Miller, 1951).

still responding after the six hundredth trial. It is important to emphasize once again that shock was *never* present in any of these trials.

Once acquired, fear leads the organism to make strong and persistent responses to avoid the fear-arousing situation. The child who has been knocked down and suffered pain by the surf at the seashore may invent all kinds of excuses to avoid returning to the water. These excuses and any other responses that are successful in keeping him out of the water are reinforced by fear-reduction. They serve the same function as the wheel-turning responses of Miller's rats. Perhaps if you are frank with yourself you will discover that you, too, have learned to make fear-reducing responses. Are you aware of any?

Fears can be of any intensity from strong to mild. One study (Miller, 1951) duplicating Miller's experimental technique, showed how it was possible to control the intensity of a learned fear drive. This was accomplished by varying the intensity of the shock the rats experienced in the white compartment at the beginning of the experiment. Three different intensities were used. The rats who received the fear-conditioning trials with the strong shock acquired the wheel-turning response most rapidly. The stronger the fear, the faster were the fear-reducing responses learned. The animals who received the medium shock learned the fear-reducing instrumental act (wheel turning) but the weakly shocked animals did not. Learning to fear the white compartment required an amount of noxious stimulation greater than that provided by the weak shock.

Generalizing from these results to the case of the boy who comes to grief in the waves, you would expect that the greater the pain he suffered the more intense his fear and the faster he would learn to avoid the water. It is appropriate to mention here that although the present discussion is restricted to the acquisition of learned

drives, you should not conclude that once a fear is learned it cannot be modified or eliminated. Every child knocked down in the surf is not predestined to spend the remainder of his life avoiding surf bathing. How fears can be modified and eliminated will be discussed later.

The intensity of a fear can be increased by repeated experiences. Knowing that the intensity of a conditioned response (e.g., conditioned salivary response) increases with repetition, you should not find it difficult to imagine how a fear can be increased in intensity. In an experimental situation similar to the one used by Miller (Kalish, 1954), different groups of rats received different numbers of fear-conditioning trials, with the shock on each trial having the same intensity. The groups received respectively 1, 3, 9, or 27 fear-conditioning trials. After these trials the animals were tested to determine how rapidly they could learn an instrumental response that led to escape from the fear-provoking stimulus. As expected, the results indicated that the greater the number of fear-conditioning trials, the faster was the learning of fear-reducing responses.

Fear responses can become attached to a wide variety of stimuli. In one experiment (Watson & Raynor, 1920) which sought to demonstrate that fears are learned, a child was exposed to noxious stimulation (a loud, unexpected sound) in the presence of a white rat. Prior to this experience the child had shown no fear of rats. But following the pairing of a white rat with noxious stimulation the child had learned to fear the rat, and through the mechanism of stimulus generalization, other furry animals as well. In another experiment (Hayward, 1957) baby male albino rats were shocked when they were placed near female rats in heat. As a result, a female rat in heat became a cue to evoke fear responses. When these male rats reached maturity they approached receptive females much less often than did male rats who had not been so trained. Since it was fear-reducing, avoiding receptive females became reinforcing.

If we can judge by the behavior of organisms, learned fear can be worse than pain itself. When given a choice in the presence of a fear-provoking cue between taking the shock immediately or postponing it, both college students (D'Amato & Gumenik, 1960) and rats (Sidman & Boren, 1957) will take the shock and escape from the fear-inducing stimulus rather than prolong the fear. The behavior exhibited in these studies is analogous to the reactions of many patients who have appointments with a dentist. Most people would prefer going directly into the dentist chair instead of anticipating the worst in the waiting room.

Other Learned Drives

Most of the research on learned drives has used fear-producing situations. There are two reasons for this. First, it is easy to produce a learned fear, and as a result many variables that influence the development of learned fears have been investigated. Second, and more important, the learned drive of fear, with the cues that evoke it as well as the responses that reduce it, plays a vital role in personality development. Although fear is not the only learned drive, it is certainly one of the most important.

In much the same way that distinctive cues can be conditioned to arouse the fear drive, so can they be conditioned to arouse hunger and sex drives. One study (Danziger, 1951) reported that satiated rats who had refused to eat more in their home cages would consume more food when it was offered to them in the situation in which they had been trained to feed. It would appear that the cues which had been consistently associated with the primary hunger drive were able to acquire drive-arousing properties themselves. Consistent with this principle is the common observation that a person who disclaims any sensation of hunger may, if exposed to an exceptionally delectable food, suddenly experience a compelling appetite. Even with animals the manner in which food is presented will influence their eating. Hens will eat more food if, after they have stopped eating, what grain is left is swept away and a new pile is placed in front of them (Bayer, 1929). After this "removal-replacement" technique was repeated eight consecutive times, it was discovered that the hens on the average had eaten as much as 67 per cent more than they had after they stopped the first time. Clearly, a new pile of grain suffices to energize their eating response.

Stimuli initially not related to the sex drive can become sexually arousing through conditioning. By being paired with sex behavior, perfume and lingerie may come to elicit or heighten sex responses. The operation of this principle is by no means restricted to human behavior. Male rats and rabbits who have had extensive copulating experiences with receptive females in mating cages will, when confronted with a nonreceptive female *in the same cage,* approach and mount her. The male rats and rabbits may even attempt, in such a sexually arousing environment, to mount males and animals of other species (Beach, 1939; Brooks, 1937).

Learned Drives and Primary Drives

We started out talking about the physiological basis of several primary drives. Then we showed how, through a process resembling classical conditioning, environmental stimuli become capable of evoking some component of such primary drives as escape from pain, hunger, and sex. Learned drives, therefore, are considered to be outgrowths of primary drives. Without the primary drive to escape pain there would be no learned fear drive. Without the primary sex drive, external and remote cues would be ineffective in inducing sexual arousal. The primary drives have their roots in the healthy physiological functioning of an organism. The learned (secondary) drives have their roots both in the primary drives and in the experiences of the organism.

Why is it necessary to invent the category of learned drives? If learned drives are acquired merely through classical conditioning, why can't we conceive of them simply as conditioned responses and thus dispense with the category of learned drives? There are some psychologists who favor this simple view. Other psychologists, notably Miller, consider the concept of learned drive to be essential to the understanding of behavior. Although learned drives result from a conditioning process, the important point, they argue, is that learned drives play the same functional role in behavior that primary drives do. They mediate new learning just as primary drives do, and they energize behavior. The notion that fear operates as an energizer is implicit in the widely accepted belief that fearful persons are capable of performing superhuman feats of strength or speed. To support this idea is experimental evidence (Brown, 1961) that fearful animals do in fact behave with more vigor and speed than nonfearful ones.

Actually what we have said so far about learned drives is only an introduction to the subject. Many of the most important human motives (sociability, prestige) are learned drives, but discussion of them must be postponed until we reach such topics as personality and social behavior.

STIMULUS-INDUCED MOTIVATIONS

Can all primary drives be traced to tissue deficits and physiochemical conditions? In other words, are they in some manner connected to homeostatic processes? If only such drives as hunger, thirst, and sex are considered, these questions must be answered affirmatively. But are there not sources of motivation that are independent of any life-maintaining or life-reproducing physiological mechanism? Everyday observations suggest that there are.

Curiosity. Children are known for their curiosity and their love of play. They will play with puzzles and toys for hours. In recent years a number of studies have been reported which show that animals will learn a wide variety of responses seemingly without involvement of any primary physiological drives. Rats whose hunger and thirst drives have been satiated will, when placed in a new environment, spontaneously explore it (Berlyne, 1955). They will explore situations in which they encounter numerous and complex stimuli more thoroughly than simpler environments. From such observations it has been concluded that rats have a curiosity drive that is automatically aroused by novel situations. P. T. Barnum, the famous showman of the last century, skillfully traded on people's curiosity in many ways. He even got them to leave a crowded circus sideshow and make room for new customers by simply posting a sign "To the Egress" over the exit door.

Manipulation. One series of studies (Harlow, Blazek, & McClearn, 1956) has shown that monkeys will solve over and again a mechanical puzzle similar to the one shown in Figure 9.13. The monkey's manipulatory responses continue in the absence of any apparent incentive from internal drive systems such as hunger or thirst. This manipulatory behavior is found to increase in amount and efficiency with age, thus suggesting that it is self-sustaining, that it provides its own reinforcement. These data seem to justify the claim that monkeys have a manipulatory drive.

FIGURE 9.13 A Mechanical Puzzle That Monkeys Persist in Solving Repeatedly in the Absence of an Incentive. The puzzle consists of a hasp restrained by a hook which is held in place by a pin attached to a chain.

Although it appears that the manipulatory behavior is not directly dependent upon the satisfaction of such appetitive drives as hunger and thirst, the possibility that manipulatory behavior is a learned drive has to be carefully considered. Conceivably monkeys might have learned the manipulatory drive during infantile suckling experiences. This is only a possibility and cannot be considered a fact without confirming evidence.

The suggestion that the manipulatory drive might be a learned drive points to the difficulty of classifying those drives that appear to be independent of both learning and homeostatic regulation. To classify such a drive reliably, we must establish the truth of one of two possible sets of facts. If the manipulatory drive really is a learned drive, then we should be able to show how it is learned. If the manipulatory drive, for example, is learned during infantile suckling experiences, then monkeys raised in the absence of such experiences should not demonstrate manipulatory behavior. If,

however, the manipulatory drive is a primary drive, then we should be able to discover the physiological mechanism mediating its expression. Until one of these alternatives has been satisfied, we cannot make any final classification.

There is, of course, no reason to exclude the possibility that manipulatory behavior and curiosity are expressions of truly primary drives in the sense that they are independent of learning. When we examine our own behavior, we discover that we are motivated by a multiplicity of incentives: the appeal of music, the excitement of speeding in a sports car, the pleasure of talking to a friend, or attaining prestige, or artistic expression, and many others. Are the drives underlying such incentives simply transformations of homeostatic (primary) drives? Can all such drives eventually be traced back to the interaction between a homeostatic drive and an individual's developmental history? Some psychologists feel rather strongly that the weight of the evidence favors the view that the homeostatic drives, including the sex drive, cannot serve as the basis for all human motivation. Others disagree, believing that the capacity for learning is so great among humans that a group of primary drives can serve as the foundation from which a multiplicity of human drives can spring. Controversy thrives at the frontiers of knowledge. And knowledge thrives on controversy, for the need of evidence to support one's side stimulates research.

ACTIVATION AND MOTIVATION

Several psychologists whose primary interest is in correlating physiological processes with behavior hold that behavior can be considered as varying over a dimension of activation or arousal. Near one end of this dimension is the minimal state of activation that exists during deep sleep. At the other extreme is the maximal state of arousal such as intense rage or a violent temper tantrum. Midway between are the moderate degrees of activation occurring when a person is alert and responds to the demands of a specific task—such as reading and understanding a textbook in psychology.

The terms **activation** and **arousal** do not apply to behavior alone. They are used also to describe what happens to the physiological processes that underlie the behavior of a person who is aroused from deep sleep and then becomes extremely active. An electroencephalograph (EEG) is a record of the wavelike electrical activity of the brain made by attaching electrodes to the skull. When a man is asleep his cerebral cortex is relatively inactive; his brain waves are slow; the sympathetic division of his autonomic nervous system (see page 99)

is inactive; and his skeletal muscles are relaxed. As the man awakens his physiological processes become more active; the rate of his brain waves becomes faster; his autonomic system activates the adrenal glands, which in turn secrete an energizing hormone; his skeletal muscles become more tense and as they do so feed neural impulses back into the central nervous system. Of great importance is the transmission of neural impulses through the brain stem (see page 94) to the cerebral cortex. All this physiological activity results in greater alertness and responsiveness of the person. But of course the upper limits of physiological arousal are not reached when a person simply wakens. Intense reactions like rage and the fighting it may lead to are correlated with maximal increases in physiological activity in the autonomic system, in hormonal secretion, in prodigious muscular activity, in a flood of neural im-

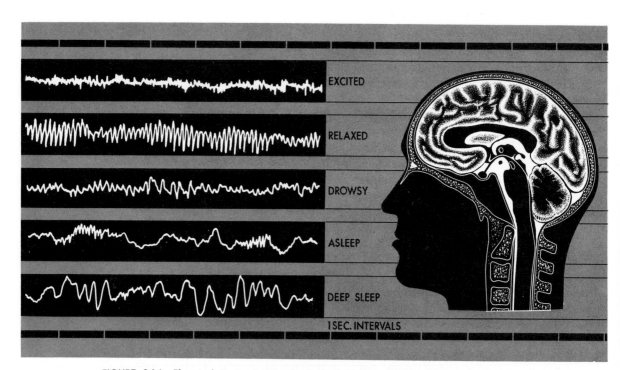

FIGURE 9.14 Electrical Brain Activity Typical of Various Stages of Arousal. Note the changes in the frequency of the waves as the person goes from deep sleep to excitement (After Jasper, 1941).

pulses upward through the brain stem into the cerebral cortex, and in a very fast rhythm of electrical activity in the brain.

It would seem, therefore, that there is a general physiological system, consisting of neural, glandular, and muscular activities, that sustains and energizes concurrent behavior that is related to what is going on in the environment. An interesting example of the energizing influence of an increased activation level comes from an experiment (Fuster, 1958) in which monkeys were trained to choose one of two geometrical objects (e.g., a 12-sided pyramid or a cone) by rewarding them with food when they selected the arbitrarily "correct" object. After some training each animal was subjected to several series of trials, during which the same geometrical objects were exposed in a tachistoscope for times varying from 10 to 40 milliseconds (a millisecond is one-thousandth of a second).

Electrodes had been implanted in the monkey's **reticular formation,** a small collection of neurons in the brain stem which functions to influence neural activity in the cerebral cortex. When a certain portion of the reticular formation known as the **reticular activating system** is electrically stimulated, a sleeping or relaxed animal suddenly becomes aroused, as is demonstrated both by his behavior and by the brain-wave activity that accompanies it (Moruzzi & Magoun, 1949). When a large region of the reticular activating system is destroyed, an animal goes into a coma, becoming insensitive to his environment (French & Magoun, 1952).

It was found that when a mild electrical stimulus was administered to the reticular activating system for a short period of time before the monkey was given an opportunity to choose one of the two stimuli, he was able to make more correct choices than he was in the control situation where no such stimulation occurred. Figure 9.16 reports the major results. Under mild electrical stimulation of the reticular activating

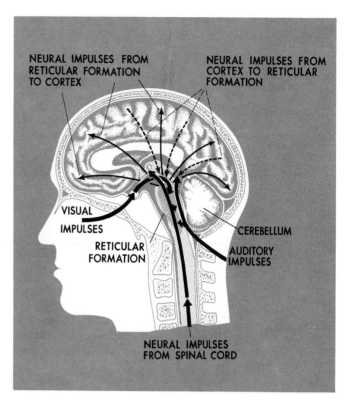

FIGURE 9.15 A Schematic Representation of the Reticular Formation in Man. The reticular formation is a core of nerve cells in the brain stem that influences, and is influenced by, the general activity in the brain above and in the spinal cord below. What we see and hear is determined by the influence the reticular formation exerts on visual and auditory impulses passing through it.

system more of the monkeys' choices were correct, and the longer the duration of the stimulation, the larger the percentage of correct responses. Of equal importance, as shown in the second graph of Figure 9.16, was the demonstrated increase in the speed of the response when the monkey was under the influence of electrical stimulation. It would seem that stimulation of the reticular activating system in some way energizes the S-R association between the test stimulus and the correct response.

It will be recalled that drives also energize S-R habits. This similarity between activation and motivation may be only superficial or it may stem from a common source. It is likely that the energizing effect

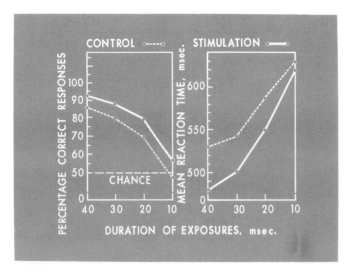

FIGURE 9.16 Effects of Stimulation of the Reticular Formation on the Discrimination Behavior of Monkeys. The first graph shows that brain stimulation increases the percentage of correct choices, and the second graph shows that it increases the speed of the animals' responses (After Fuster, 1958, with permission of *Science*).

of stimulation of the reticular formation results from a process of sensory facilitation. That is, stimulation of the reticular formation facilitates the transmission of sensory impulses from the monkeys' eyes to their brains. This helps the monkeys select the correct one of the two stimuli tachistoscopically presented and also makes their choice reaction time faster.

Little is known about why drives energize behavior. Perhaps they, too, produce sensory facilitation effects. Only future research can decide whether the concepts of motivation and activation possess common roots.

Some facts can be mustered in support of a basic similarity between activation and motivation. Increases in drives are usually accompanied by increases in physiological activation. Positive correlations have been obtained between the overall action of the autonomic nervous system and fear of being shocked (i.e., the stronger the fear, the greater the activation). It has been found that muscular tension is positively correlated with amount of motivation

(Bartoshuk, 1955). The muscular tension of young men who were performing a simple task increased with increasing amounts of money reward. Even the composition of blood reflects the correlation between motivation and activation. During a difficult examination the leucocyte (white blood cell) count increases, and during relaxation it decreases (Halmosh, 1953).

Further examination of this correlation between drive and activation suggests that both have some of their roots in the central nervous system—particularly in the activity of the hypothalamus and other brainstem centers (Stellar, 1954). Rage in cats, induced by pinching their tails or exposing them to dogs, is largely dependent upon the hypothalamus. When the hypothalamus is removed or partially destroyed the rage response is virtually eliminated. The hypothalamus appears to play an equally important role in the motivated behavior of cats. When a specific portion of the cat's hypothalamus is electrically stimulated, he will indulge in vast amounts of overeating. This area of the hypothalamus is considered to be an excitatory center for eating. When it is surgically removed, the animal never eats again. Similar excitatory centers have been found for sleep and the sex drive. In addition to centers that excite the hunger and sleep drives, there are centers that inhibit them. These inhibitory centers, which operate in opposition to the excitatory centers, are also located in the hypothalamus. If the inhibitory center of the hunger drive is removed an animal will overeat, and if the inhibitory center for wakefulness is removed the animal will stay awake indefinitely. It would seem that the excitatory centers in the hypothalamus are responsible for drive arousal, whereas the activity of inhibitory centers is correlated with drive satiation.

To all statements about the functions of specific portions of the nervous system must be added the qualification that no part of the nervous system is independent of the rest of the body. The hypothalamus is no exception to this rule. Since it has connections with receptors, the activities that occur within the excitatory and inhibitory centers of the hypothalamus can be initiated and sustained by external stimulation. The hypothalamus is also connected to the cortex and other portions of the central nervous system. The effects this structural linkage has upon behavior are shown in the numerous studies involving learned fears. Also, since many blood vessels pass through the hypothalamus, conditions of the blood, including its hormone content, can influence hypothalamic activity, and the latter in turn may influence the motivational component of behavior.

Some readers may wonder why we have not referred to fear and rage as emotions, as we do in everyday usage. The answer is that the term *emotion* is so vague and has acquired so many slippery connotations that many psychologists, including the author, consider it no longer useful in scientific writing. But it is both interesting and important to note that rage and fear, which the layman unhesitatingly considers emotion, have some of their physiological basis in the hypothalamus, as do many motivational states. This common locus would seem to justify the use of the common Latin root *mot,* meaning to move, in both the words *emotion* and *motivation.*

MOTIVATIONAL THEORY

No major topic in psychology has inspired more theory than motivation. In fact, theories of motivation are so varied and so mutually contradictory that it is impossible either to summarize or to integrate them. The review of a few important theories of motivation—notably the one we owe to Freud—will be postponed until we take up the subjects of personality and social behavior. For the time being we shall restrict ourselves to an attempt to describe the problems with which any adequate theory of motivation must strive to cope.

The Arousal of Drives

Where do drives come from? Drives seem to have two general sources of arousal. One source of drives is found within the body. Physiological changes, especially those that result from deficit conditions within it, initiate such drive states as hunger and thirst. The second source appears as an organism matures and learns—and particularly if it is capable of intricate learning as humans are—for external cues then play a more and more important role in drive arousal. It is impossible to state any overall principle of the relative importance of these two factors in the arousal of drives, that is, of internal physiological conditions on the one hand and external cues on the other. It is likely that as physiological deficit conditions become greater, external cues become less effective in drive arousal. An attractive piece of candy or cake, for example, may play an important role in the arousal of hunger in a person who has recently eaten dinner. In contrast, a hunger drive will certainly be aroused in a healthy person who has not eaten for 12 hours, whether or not any tempting food is in sight.

The Steering Function of Drives

Drives direct behavior in two ways. First, they direct behavior toward reducing or eliminating the drive. There are goals, that is, commodities or conditions that can reduce the strength of, or entirely eliminate, a drive. A deficit of food in the body can be eliminated by appropriate nourishment. Here the drive leads the organism to approach the incentive. Pain can be eliminated by escape from the source of noxious stimulation. In this case the drive encourages the organism to escape the pain.

In both cases it is the relation of a drive to its goals that helps determine what happens.

In addition to being directed in relation to certain goals, drives are also associated with certain forms of behavior. A rat may learn to go to the right side of a T maze for water and to the left for food. One child may learn to get candy by whimpering for it, while another child may learn to drink all his milk and eat his vegetables for the same incentive. Different organisms motivated by the identical drive may be cued to different kinds of behavior to obtain the same incentive.

The Persistence of Motivated Behavior

A very common observation is that motivated behavior varies in persistence. After being refused an ice cream cone one child will immediately abandon his attempts to obtain one; another child will persist for a very long time despite numerous refusals. What is the psychological basis of such differences in persistence? Again, in order to answer this question it is necessary for us to distinguish between the drive and the habit components of motivated behavior.

In the case of appetitive drives, such as hunger, the drive tends to increase the longer the period of deprivation. It has been estimated that the energizing component of the hunger drive will, in white rats, increase up to 60 hours after food was last eaten (Yamaguchi, 1951). If deprivation continues after 60 hours, the animals seem to be weakened by lack of nourishment, and as a result the rate of emission of food-seeking instrumental responses begins to decrease. In short, appetitive drives tend to persist either until the physiological imbalance is restored or until the animal weakens, or eventually dies. The primary pain-avoidance drive produced by such aversive stimuli as electric shock tends to persist as long as the organism is being stimulated. It terminates when the organism escapes from the shock. The persistence of secondary drives depends on how strongly they have been learned.

The peristsence of goal-oriented behavior in contrast to the drive itself depends on several motivational and learning factors. The stronger their drive, the longer animals will persist in making instrumental responses in the absence of reinforcement (see page 173). Likewise, the stronger their habit, motivation being constant, the longer animals will persist in their instrumental responses (see page 174) in the absence of reinforcement. A related condition that determines the persistence of goal-directed behavior is its consequence. The child whose parent usually gives in to his persistent demands will have his behavior reinforced, and hence will persevere in it. However, if the same persistent behavior is never again reinforced, after a time, its tendency to continue will weaken. It is quite possible, of course, that a child will be persistent in one kind of behavior and lack persistence in another. The "spoiled child" may be frightfully persistent in making demands for candy or ice cream, but will not persevere at a task in which he himself has to do the "work," keeping his room clean or finishing a jigsaw puzzle. In the first case the child has been reinforced to persist; in the second case he has not been reinforced to accomplish things by himself. The problems of persistent behavior will come up again when we discuss the complex psychological processes of frustration and conflict, and also when we discuss what are known as schedules of reinforcement.

The Energizing Function of Drives

Perhaps the most important function of drives is to energize behavior. And yet psychologists and physiologists cannot claim to understand how these energizing functions operate. Experimental data have been reported (see page 173) showing that different levels of drive activate habits so that different levels of performance result. These experiments have been interpreted as supporting the theoretical assumption that there is a multiplicative relationship between habits and drive (see page 174). It seems that the physiological basis of this multiplicative function lies somewhere in the central nervous system, doubtless with the hypothalamus and the reticular activating system playing particularly important roles.

Future research must discover how and in what manner these energizing influences develop and operate. Fortunately, however, it is not necessary to understand the physiological mechanisms underlying the energizing effects of drives any more than we now do in order to use them in the prediction and control of behavior. In this way our knowledge of the energizing properties of drives is similar to our knowledge of the effects produced by reinforcers. In both instances our knowledge is incomplete, but we have enough of it to set about constructing theories and to put what we do know to work in many practical ways.

Learned Drives

Drives can be generated by innate physiological mechanisms or can result from learning. Some learned drives seem to develop along the lines of conditioned responses. The learned drive of fear is the response to pain stimulation conditioned to some actually painless stimulus. Fear differs from an ordinary conditioned response in that it has drive properties; it energizes and steers behavior leading to escape and provides the basis for new learning. However, it has one of the most important attributes of learned drives in that it is primarily under external stimulus control.

Many problems in which learned drives are involved remain unsolved. First, it is

not at all clear whether such drives as curiosity belong to the category of a primary or a secondary drive. The uncertainty that surrounds the proper classification of the curiosity drive, along with such drives as the need for novelty and the manipulatory drive, should not in any way hide the fact that such drives do operate and play an important role in the behavior of animals and men. Second, it is not fully understood how organisms, and human beings in particular, learn such a large number of different drives. Are all drives learned independently of each other? Or do they spring from a common source? An interesting hypothesis (Brown, 1961) is that many, if not all, learned drives share a common component. For example, it is possible that all—or many—learned drives are based upon the tendency to be fearful in the absence of certain incentives. Thus, the absence of affection, or prestige, or success in a competitive situation initiates a fear response, which in turn serves as the motivation to attain the desired incentive. At present the hypothesis that fear serves as the basis for many learned drives should be considered as only one interesting speculation among a number of rivals. Much more research will be required before it can be properly evaluated.

The Relationship Between Motivation and Learning

You might think that the question of how motivation influences learning would be a simple one. Actually it is one of the most complex questions in all of psychology. It is commonly believed that increasing motivation will always speed up learning. This is not true. In the next chapter you will see how learning in some situations is retarded by increasing motivation. For the present, however, what we have to say about the influence of motivation on learning will be limited to reporting the general results of a few conditioning experiments.

In order to discover whether different degrees of the hunger drive influence the rate of learning of an instrumental response, different groups of rats were trained in an instrumental reward-conditioning situation after they had been deprived of food for different lengths of time (Strassburger, 1950). Each group received the same number of reinforcements, and during extinction the motivation of the various groups was equated. Thus, it was possible to discover whether different levels of drive *during acquisition* influenced the strength of a habit. Surprisingly, they did not. Animals that had been trained under different strengths of drive extinguished at the same rate. These results supported the conclusion that in a situation in which all factors are held constant, different levels of a drive, provided they are not below some minimum, do not produce different levels of conditioning.

But you should note that this conclusion is restricted, so far as available evidence goes, to situations involving such appetitive drives as hunger. Level of drive does influence the conditioning of aversive responses, as in the case of eyelid conditioning, where level is defined in terms of intensity of the air puff. Different levels of drive in eyelid conditioning appear to produce different amounts of conditioning, when the drive level is equated at the time of testing (Spence, 1953).

From evidence such as this, and from other findings, it is becoming apparent that there are important psychological differences between appetitive and aversive drives. At one time psychologists thought that all drives were essentially aversive. The hunger drive, for example, was conceived as escape from the noxious stimulation produced by food deprivation. More recent experiments seem to refute the hypothesis that all drives are basically aversive, for they have shown that electrical stimulation of the brain sometimes has positive and sometimes negative motivational effects. A rat will repeatedly press a bar which causes an electric shock to be delivered through electrodes planted in one area of the brain. However, if the electrodes are implanted in another area of the brain, rats will avoid pressing the same bar. Such a finding points to a neurologically based dualism of motivation: approach (appetitive) motivation on the one hand and aversive motivation on the other.

The experimental study of motivation is, in a sense, just beginning. For many years preconceived notions about motivation dominated the interpretation of motivated behavior. Then, with the development of experimental techniques for investigating motivation objectively, facts began to accumulate. Now scientists have been forced to abandon the idea that motivation can be considered a simple causal agent in behavior. The new look at motivation has revealed that it has several facets, each of which raises a different question demanding a different answer. Speculation does not explain motivated behavior. In short, adequate motivational theories depend upon a structure of experimental facts yet to be assembled.

SUMMARY

Behavior is often characterized by what is known as a motivational sequence: a drive, a condition that activates and directs behavior, followed by an instrumental response that leads to an incentive, which in turn reduces or eliminates the drive. The psychology of motivation studies how drives develop and influence behavior.

There are two main classes of drives. Physiological or primary drives are correlated to organic needs. Learned or secondary drives are acquired as a result of training.

The hunger drive is related to stomach contractions, chemistry of the blood, and activities within the central nervous system, particularly in the hypothalamus. The hunger drive is not a single unitary drive because organisms often develop hungers for specific foods necessary to maintain health.

Dryness of the mouth and throat stimulate tiny nerve endings which produce a sensation of thirst and a drive for the relief of the thirst. Conditions in the hypothalamus and in the blood are responsible for the maintenance of the level of moisture in bodily tissue.

Although there are sensations that initiate the sex drive, they are not as localized as those for the hunger and thirst drives. Sexual behavior is controlled to varying degrees by sex hormones. The higher an animal is on the evolutionary scale the less rigid is this control. With the possible exception of humans, the hormonal control of female mammalian sexual behavior seems to be greater than that of males in the same species.

Pain is both a sensation and a drive. The receptors for pain are free nerve endings distributed throughout the skin, muscles, blood vessels, and internal organs. Different forms of stimulation stimulate different pain receptors. Sensations of pain also vary depending upon the nature of the neural transmission. The brain plays a role in the sensation of pain as demonstrated by the fact that learning and perception can influence it. Pain functions as a drive because it activates organisms to acquire instrumental responses to avoid and escape from it.

Instinctive behavior possesses four main characteristics; it is complex, rigidly patterned, unlearned, and universal among the members of a species. An analysis of the instinctive behavior of lower animals shows that it is not unmodifiable; like any other behavior it is influenced by both hereditary and environmental events. With humans it is impossible to identify any behavior that fits the specifications of instinctive behavior.

Learned drives are distinguishable from physiological drives by the fact that they are dependent on an organism's individual experience. An organism can be trained, by a method similar to classical conditioning, to be fearful in response to stimuli that have been paired with shock. Fear, once learned, leads an organism to acquire responses that allow it to escape from the fear-provoking stimuli, that is, fear mediates new learning. A habit learned under the motivation of fear is difficult to extinguish because escape from fear is reinforcing.

The question of whether all learned drives can be ultimately traced to homeostatic processes has not been resolved. Several experiments have shown that animals will acquire a wide variety of responses seemingly without involvement of any physiological drives. This has led to the hypothesis that there are stimulus-induced motivations.

Both behavior and underlying neural, glandular, and muscular processes can be characterized as varying over a dimension from minimal activation during sleep to extreme activation during a rage. By stimulating the reticular activating system the activation level of an organism, both behaviorally and physiologically, can be increased. It has been suggested that the observed energizing influence of drives may be correlated with the level of physiological activation.

At present there is no widely accepted general theory of motivation. The problems a theory of motivation must explain are the arousal of drives, the steering function of drives, the persistence of motivated behavior, the energizing effect of drives, learned drives, and the relationship between motivation and learning.

SUGGESTIONS FOR FURTHER READING

BERLYNE, D. E. *Conflict arousal and curiosity.* New York: McGraw-Hill, 1960.

An analysis of the role of motivation in behavior, with particular emphasis on the curiosity and exploratory drives.

BINDRA, D. *Motivation: A systematic reinterpretation.* New York: Ronald, 1958.

A textbook that seeks to systematize the role of motivation in behavior.

BROWN, J. S. *The motivation of behavior.* New York: McGraw-Hill, 1961.

A textbook for the advanced undergraduate student that presents a systematic account of how motivation influences behavior.

FORD, C. S., & BEACH, F. A. *Patterns of sexual behavior.* New York: Hoeber-Harper, 1951.

An interesting and well-organized account of sexual behavior among different animals and human societies.

HALL, J. F. *Psychology of motivation.* Chicago: Lippincott, 1961.

A tightly organized textbook that reviews and systematizes the experimental findings in the field of motivation.

McCLELLAND, D. C. *Studies in motivation.* New York: Appleton-Century-Crofts, 1955.

A collection of important articles in the field of motivation.

YOUNG, P. T. *Motivation and emotion: A survey of determinants of human and animal activity.* New York: Wiley, 1961.

A textbook that attempts to review most of the important facts and concepts in the psychology of motivation. The emphasis is on animal and physiological studies.

COMPLEX PSYCHOLOGICAL
PROCESSES

IV

In the previous section we described four basic psychological processes in their purest form. We were concerned with phenomena which emerged from relatively simple experimental situations. Sensation was studied in relation to elementary forms of stimulation. Learning was analyzed in terms of the formation and strengthening of single stimulus-response associations. The perceptual process was investigated through relatively simple patterns of stimulation. And finally, the fundamental principles of motivation were extracted from studies in which individual variables were isolated.

In order to understand behavior in all its complexity and diversity, you must know how these basic processes operate and interact in complicated situations. The present section will be concerned with these problems.

We will begin the analysis of complex psychological processes with a study of the more complicated forms of learning. We will consider first how habits compete with each other and how they become integrated into chains of S-R associations. Then we will study the psychology of language and problem solving. You will discover that even though the skillful use of language enables humans to behave in a way that seems far removed from laboratory phenomena, verbal behavior has many of the properties of behavior already studied. Problem solving, or what is commonly called thinking or reasoning, is intimately related to verbal behavior, and like it, rests upon more fundamental processes even though its product seems unlike simple behavioral phenomena. Finally we will examine the psychology of frustration and conflict. Our study of frustration will be concerned with the consequences of blocking an organism from attaining a goal. The study of conflict, which is an outgrowth of habit competition, will consider the psychological consequences of evoking incompatible forms of behavior.

A suggestion to the reader is in order here. You are reaching the point in your study of psychology where what you have learned should begin to modify your perception of everyday behavior. If what you have studied in the classroom so far seems at times far removed from what happens outside, you should realize that you may still be examining everyday behavior in an unsophisticated way. You should try instead to *analyze* it as you do laboratory phenomena. If you adopt the same frame of reference, you will discover that what you have learned and what you are now going to learn will be useful in your attempt to understand the behavior in the world about you.

LEARNING AND FORGETTING

10

CONDITIONING AND LEARNING

Learning has been defined (see page 151) as a change in behavior resulting from practice. The simplest form of learning is conditioning. In conditioning, as you know, the probability that a stimulus will evoke a response increases with reinforced practice.

In certain ways conditioning as it is investigated in the psychology laboratory is like the vacuum investigated in physics. Both make it possible for the scientist to investigate important variables in isolation; both have contributed enormously to the fund of basic knowledge; and both are highly artificial situations. But because laboratory conditioning is such an artificial situation, inferences from it may be very misleading. If you know only the facts of conditioning, you may have a distorted, oversimplified view of the psychology of learning. Conditioning by itself fails to provide a clear picture of two important features of more complicated learning situations, namely **habit competition** and **habit chaining.**

Learning involves competition between habits. If you memorize Shakespeare's sonnet 151, which begins,

Love is too young to know what conscience is:
Yet who knows not conscience is born of love?

you have to learn that the word following *knows* in the second line is *not* instead of *conscience*. That is, following the word *knows* there is competition between the responses *not* and *conscience*. Learning the quotation correctly requires that the association between *knows* and *not* must prevail over the association between *knows* and *conscience*. A paradigm (a model) of this example of habit competition is shown in Figure 10.1.

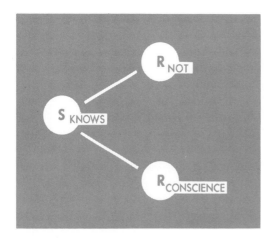

FIGURE 10.1 A Representation of Habit Competition. The stimulus *knows* has a tendency to evoke the responses *not* and *conscience*.

Everyone who has learned to typewrite has experienced habit competition. For example, after striking the last letter of one word one may experience competition between pressing the space bar and hitting the key for the first letter of the next word. Every error in typing is an instance of a correct habit failing to compete successfully with an incorrect habit. With an experienced typist correct habits are so much stronger than incorrect habits that she rarely makes errors. A beginning typist, on the other hand, experiences such keen competition between correct and incorrect habits that she makes frequent errors. As her learning progresses, however, correct habits become stronger until they achieve dominance over incorrect habits.

The problem of habit competition is actually found in laboratory conditioning, although there it is less frequent and more limited than it is in everyday life. During classical salivary conditioning the conditioned stimulus (tone) evokes two different responses. During the early stages of training the dog responds to the conditioned stimulus by turning his head toward the sound. This habit is weak. The salivary response quickly gains dominance over the

investigatory response, head turning. Similarly in instrumental conditioning, responses other than the instrumental response occur. The animal in a Skinner box may at first lean against one of the walls or stand on his haunches before he presses the bar. But such habits are relatively weak and disappear rapidly because they are never followed immediately by reinforcement. In other conditioning situations, however, the competition is strong. These will be described in this chapter because they afford the psychologist a good view of habit competition in action.

The principle of habit competition is illustrated in Figure 10.2. It shows that a

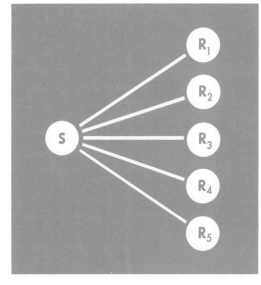

FIGURE 10.2 A Hierarchy of Responses to the Same Stimulus. The responses are ranked according to their tendency to be evoked by the stimulus (S). R_1 has a greater probability of being evoked than R_2, which in turn has a greater probability of being evoked than R_3, and so on.

stimulus can be associated with several responses. Some of these associations are stronger than others, so the responses associated with the stimulus are arranged in a hierarchy. The tendency for S to evoke R_1 is greater than the tendency for S to evoke R_2, which in turn is stronger than the tendency to evoke R_3, and so on. Depending on the problem, the correct response can in the beginning occupy any position on the scale of relative response strength. That is, its association with the stimulus can be relatively strong, of moderate strength, or relatively weak. Learning occurs when, as a result of practice, the correct response becomes dominant over the other responses. This usually involves a change in the position of the correct response in the hierarchy. Now let us turn our attention to habit chaining.

In classical conditioning a conditioned stimulus is presented and the conditioned response occurs. In instrumental conditioning the organism makes the instrumental response. In both situations an observer usually ignores any behavior that precedes and follows the response. As a result, the conditioned and instrumental responses appear to be frozen and isolated in time. But everyday behavior is not a series of separated stimulus-response associations; it is usually continuous. Walking, for example, is not a series of disjoined movements, each an isolated S-R association. Instead, walking is a smooth, continuous activity.

If conditioning is a basic form of learning, how can it explain this smoothly continuous sequence of behavior? In order to answer this question one has to analyze the behavior of a rat in a Skinner box closely. A major point is that the total stimulus situation the animal responds to is not restricted to stimuli from the Skinner box itself. As the animal moves, his body posture changes; his movements produce different patterns of kinesthetic stimulation (see page 93) which serve as cues for different responses.

Figure 10.3 shows how a sequence of S-R associations is chained together, permitting us to analyze behavior into S-R associations without ignoring its continuous quality. The top line indicates the passage of time. The first stimulus-response association represents a rat moving toward the lever. This locomoting response produces (represented by the curved line) distinctive kinesthetic cues. These response-produced cues, represented by s_1 (the small s is used to indicate response-produced cues, as contrasted with the large S, which represents an environmental stimulus) combine with the environmental stimulus of the bar to form a stimulus compound (a combination of two or more separate stimuli) which elicits the next response, the raising of the paws. This behavior produces its own distinctive response-produced cues (s_2) that serve as a part of the next stimulus-compound, which is associated with the pressing response. The pressing response causes a click. The click and the response-produced cues combine to form a stimulus compound, which is connected to the head-lowering response that enables the animal to perceive the food. Then the animal seizes the food and eats it.

The most important feature of Figure 10.3 is that every response after the initial response is attached to the cues which are received from the previous response. Response-produced cues serve to chain together a series of S-R associations so that the behavior is continuous. It should be mentioned that Figure 10.3, which schematically shows the underlying reason for the apparent continuity of behavior, is arbitrarily divided into five S-R associations. The figure could be made more detailed by dividing the pressing response, or any of the other responses, into smaller units of behavior. Conceivably the pressing response could be analyzed into four responses consisting of placing the paws on the bar, pressing, maintaining the pressure, and finally releasing the bar. Or, alternatively, the bar-pressing behavior of the rat could be described more grossly by eliminating some of the behavior segments now shown in Figure 10.3. In either case the analysis is based upon an important psychological principle: *S-R associations are integrated into smooth-flowing behavior*

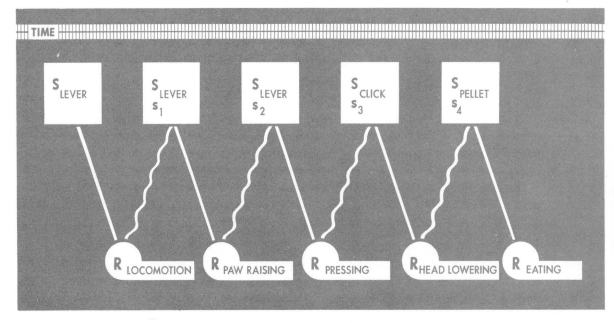

FIGURE 10.3 A Sequence of S-R Associations Which Represents the Behavior of a Rat in a Skinner Box. The separate S-R associations are chained together by the cues from one response being conditioned to the next response.

sequences because successive associations are linked together by response-produced cues.

HABIT COMPETITION

The simplest form of habit competition occurs when an organism is required to *select* one of two possible responses. Psychologists use many kinds of experimental apparatus to investigate learning in such a two-choice situation. A T maze is one example of an experimental situation in which an organism has to choose between two competing responses. A Skinner box fitted with two bars is another example of a **selective learning** situation. Still a third example is a discrimination apparatus, in which the subject is on each trial confronted with the choice of responding to one of two stimuli, such as black and white cards. Typically the apparatus is baited so that only by approaching one of these two

stimuli will the rat receive reinforcement, and the position of the positive cue (e.g., black) is shifted on successive trials randomly from side to side to prevent the subject from solving the problem by always going to one side. When the subject consistently chooses the positive stimulus, he is said to have learned to discriminate between the two stimuli.

Here is a question not entirely new to us. What are the factors responsible for one habit becoming dominant over a competing habit? We asked a similar question earlier in a somewhat different context. When we analyzed conditioning, we studied factors responsible for the strengthening and weakening of S-R associations. Rats who had 60 food reinforcements in a Skinner box (see page 163) were shown to have stronger bar-pressing habits than rats who had only five food reinforcements. This finding, however, concerns the relative strength of the same habit in *different* animals. The question we now ask is, What factors are responsible for the dominance of one habit over another, for its greater strength, in the *same* animal?

An apparently sensible hypothesis is that the principles which operate in the strengthening and weakening of the same habit in different animals operate in the strengthening and weakening of different habits in the same animal. Let us examine this hypothesis specifically, with reference to relative amounts of the two variables, reinforcement and motivation.

Reinforcement. One of the most powerful variables in determining the strength of a habit is the amount of reinforcement the subject has received. As we have already shown, the strength of a bar-pressing habit is a function of the number of reinforcements (see page 165). Since this is so, you would expect an animal who has to choose between two bars to press the one that has been reinforced more frequently. This ex-

pectation is confirmed in the case of the simple discrimination problem in which pressing one bar is always reinforced while pressing the other is never reinforced. In such a situation the animal soon learns to press the bar that leads to reinforcement. That is, he performs the stronger habit.

The competition between a reinforced and a nonreinforced habit is not the only kind of habit competition involving different amounts of reinforcement. Sometimes when competing habits are *both reinforced,* one habit receives a larger number of reinforcements. What happens in such a case? Since the strength of a habit increases, up to a point, with the increasing number of reinforcements, we would expect a subject to exhibit a preference for the more frequently reinforced bar. This expectation was confirmed in an experiment in which rats received twice as many reinforcements on one of two bars in a double-bar Skinner box (Spence, 1956).

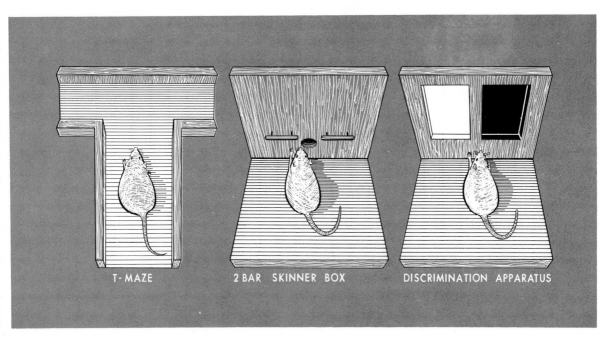

FIGURE 10.4 Three Selective Learning Situations in Which a Rat Has a Choice Between Two Responses. In the first he has to turn left or right in a T maze; in the second, to press one of two bars in a Skinner box; in the third, to choose either a black or a white card.

It is, however, extremely important to understand that the selection of one habit over another does not depend merely on the strength of the stronger association. It depends also on the strength of the weaker competing association. It is easier to learn a habit when it is competing with a weak association than when it is competing with a strong one. That is, any condition that increases the strength of an incorrect habit will make the choice of the correct response *less probable*. This principle was tested in an experiment (Ehrenfreund, 1949) in which rats were required to discriminate between a black and a white alley. Whenever they chose the white alley they re-

ceived a pellet of food in a cup. When they chose the black alley, they didn't receive any food. The animals were divided into two groups. After making an incorrect response, one group, the experimental group, found an empty food cup in the end box. The cup was identical to the one that contained food at the end of the correct white alley. Thus the experimental subjects received secondary reinforcement for their errors, since the sight or touch of the food cup had been closely and frequently followed by food (see page 166). The other group, the control group, received neither food *nor an empty food cup* after making an error.

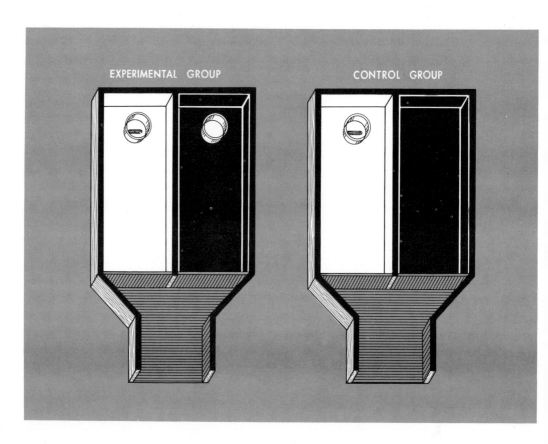

FIGURE 10.5 The Discrimination Problems Confronting the Experimental and the Control Groups in a Study Testing the Effect of Strength of the Weaker Association on Habit Competition. The subjects in both groups were reinforced with food for choosing the white alley. The rats in the experimental group found an empty food cup when they chose the wrong alley (black), but the control animals did not find anything in this alley (After Ehrenfreund, 1949).

Which of the two groups should learn the discrimination more rapidly? In order to answer this question, we have to recognize that the *incorrect responses* of the experimental group were reinforced but those of the control group were not. As a result, the difference between the strengths of the correct and incorrect associations was greater for the control group than it was for the experimental group. Another way of saying this is that the correct habit of the control group had less competition from the incorrect habit. Therefore, it was expected that the control subjects would master the discrimination problem more rapidly than the experimental subjects. This prediction was confirmed by the results of the experiment, depicted in Figure 10.6.

The reinforcement of incorrect responses is one of the major reasons why learning is often retarded. It may seem to you that a rat learning to discriminate between black and white is far removed from a human learning one of many complex tasks, but this is not the case. With respect to basic psychological principles, there is a similarity between a rat being reinforced for an incorrect response and a person being reinforced for doing something incorrectly. Consider two human activities, tennis playing and talking. Often a person is prevented from improving his tennis game because, for example, his weak backhand stroke manages to get the ball over the net. Although the shot is really a poor one, for his opponent has little difficulty in "putting it away" and winning the point, it is reinforced, since it at least gets the ball over the net and sometimes even wins a point. Because his ineffective stroke is reinforced, the player tends to repeat it. This habit impairs his game and if it persists may prevent him from improving. Similarly a four-year-old child who articulates his speech sounds so poorly that only his mother can understand him, may be seriously retarded in learning to speak clearly

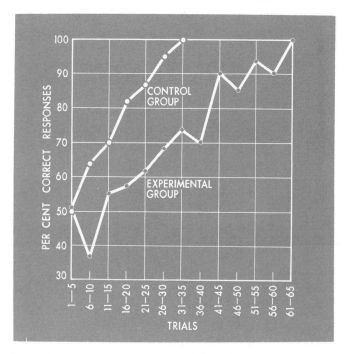

FIGURE 10.6 The Effect of Reinforcement of Incorrect Responses Upon Learning. The learning of the experimental group was retarded, because their errors led to secondary reinforcement, whereas the learning of the control group was not, because their incorrect responses did not lead to reinforcement of any kind (After Ehrenfreund, 1949).

if his mother consistently satisfies each of his verbal requests, no matter how poorly articulated they are. Such a mother is plainly retarding his speech development by reinforcing baby talk. Instead, she should try to reinforce only those of his speech sounds that are slightly better than usual. Then, because only better articulated sounds are reinforced, the child's speech will gradually improve. Inadequate or incorrect responses tend to persist as long as they are reinforced.

Motivation. Motivation is another important factor in selective learning. The performance of a response in instrumental conditioning is a joint function (or product) of the strength of the habit and the strength of the drive (see page 174). The same habit will produce a stronger response

278

(one that will have greater resistance to extinction) when it is energized by a strong drive than when it is energized by a weak drive. This suggests that strong drives will facilitate selective learning, but this is not always so. The influence of motivation in a simple two-choice selective learning situation depends on the relative strengths of the competing habits. There is evidence that in a two-choice situation, such as a T maze or discrimination apparatus, when the competing habits are equal at the beginning of training, learning will be facilitated by a relatively high level of motivation. Rats who have been deprived of water for twenty and one-half hours will learn to choose consistently the side of a T maze that leads to water in less than half the number of trials that subjects whose thirst is due to only one and one-half hours of water deprivation will require (Buchwald & Yamaguchi, 1955). Similarly rats will learn a black-white discrimination (Eisman, Asimow, & Maltzman, 1956) more rapidly under strong hunger (46 hours) deprivation than under weak hunger (4 hours) deprivation.

What will happen if the incorrect habit is stronger at the start of training? Will a strong drive then facilitate or retard learning? An experiment (Kendler & Lachman, 1958) was devised to answer these questions. Rats were trained to select the brighter of two lights. After learning, they were required to reverse their choice, to shift their preference from the bright to the dim light. During this reversal learning half of the subjects had a high level of drive, the other half, a low level. At the beginning of the reversal (see Figure 10.7) the curves of performance of both groups were well below the chance (50 per cent) level, because the subjects persisted in responding to the bright stimulus which had previously been reinforced. However, the performance curve of the low-drive group increased more rapidly than the curve of the other group and reached the 50 per cent level at an earlier stage. Thus in this portion of reversal learning, when the correct response is relatively weak, a strong drive retards learning. In essence this finding is similar to the one already reported (see page 173) where *experimental extinction occurred more rapidly under a low drive than under a high one*. Both groups, in order to reverse their preference, had to extinguish their initial habit, and the group with low drive accomplished this more rapidly.

The experiment reported in Figure 10.7 was terminated soon after the animals reached the 50 per cent line. Presumably, if the experiment had been continued beyond this point, a high drive would have had beneficial effects for reversal learning. Once the correct habit becomes dominant (stronger than the incorrect habit), the high drive enhances the preference for the stronger habit.

One final word of caution: the relation between level of motivation and selective learning has many complex features which cannot be touched on in this book. However complex, these phenomena are *orderly*,

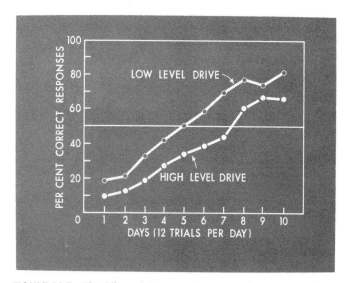

FIGURE 10.7 The Effect of Strength of Drive on Reversal Learning. The results show that a strong drive retards learning during the initial stage of reversal learning (After Kendler & Lachman, 1958).

and in general they follow from the simpler processes you already understand.

PUNISHMENT

Few psychological ideas are more widely used and less well understood than the one for which we use the term **punishment.** At one extreme we find self-appointed experts who warn parents against the evil consequences of any kind of punishment; at the other extreme, those who state indignantly that every form of delinquency results from the failure of parents and teachers to mete out sufficient punishment for each misdeed.

Is punishment good or bad? Although this sweeping question is frequently asked, especially when psychologists are around, it is an awkward one for two reasons. First, it may be taken to raise an ethical problem. The question whether punishment is *morally* good or bad, because it introduces values, is one that scientists in their role as scientists are not entitled to answer. Science as science is neutral. Second, the question is too general, too vague, and encompasses much too much to permit a single answer. When we come to the psychology of personality in a later chapter, we will show that the effect of punishment has to be considered in the context of who is punishing whom, for what reason, and with what sort of punishment. Hence, the question must promptly be recast and whittled down to answerable proportions, so that it becomes one that pinpoints the psychological problem of punishment: How does punishment affect behavior? Experimental findings on this question support two main points: (1) Punishment is less effective than experimental extinction in weakening and eliminating an undesirable habit. In fact, punishment seems only to suppress it. (2) When punishment *is* effective in changing behavior, it is mainly so because it forces an individual to select a desirable alternative habit leading to positive reinforcement.

One common view is that when behavior is punished it is less likely to be repeated. This is the idea that parents act on in punishing their children for misbehavior, and that society uses to rationalize its treatment of criminals. But does punishment actually *weaken* a habit? The correct answer, it turns out, is that it usually does not. This answer is supported by the results of several Skinner-box experiments. In one typical study (Estes, 1944), the experimenters trained two groups of rats to press a bar by reinforcing them with food. They then extinguished the response by withholding food. During the first portion of the extinction process the punished group of rats was shocked through the floor of the apparatus when they pressed the bar. The nonpunished group received no shocks during this period. Thereafter, the responses of both the punished and nonpunished groups were extinguished without shock, food was simply withheld. If punishment does in fact weaken a habit, you would expect the punished subjects to make fewer bar-pressing responses than the nonpunished subjects. This did not happen; the total number of responses made during extinction was the same for both groups. The rats of the punished group behaved differently from those in the other group only in the frequency with which they pressed the bar during the time they were being punished and shortly thereafter. During this short period they responded more slowly and therefore did not make as many bar-pressing responses. Afterwards they resumed their previous speed of response and eventually made as many bar-pressing responses during extinction as the nonpunished animals made.

From this experiment, then, it was concluded that punishment momentarily suppresses a habit, but does not weaken it. The **suppression** of the habit is demonstrated by less frequent response during and immediately after the period in which pun-

280

ishment was inflicted. The failure of punishment to weaken a habit is demonstrated by the fact that beginning shortly after punishment had ceased the punished animals went on to make as many responses during extinction as nonpunished subjects.

The strength and duration of the suppression effect varies with the intensity of punishment. If animals are given a relatively intense shock, they will stop responding to the bar completely. When the punishment is terminated and a sufficient time is permitted to elapse—sometimes months —the punished group will once again respond as rapidly as the nonpunished group. The strength of the suppression effect will also be determined by the duration of punishment. A prolonged period of punishment will lengthen the time during which the punished response is suppressed, that is, not practiced, or practiced at a slower rate.

This suppression of a response can be maintained only as long as punishment is inflicted whenever the animal presses the bar. If he is permitted to press the bar for a stretch without punishment, he will once again perform the bar-pressing response. The mother who has tried to stop her child from nail-biting simply by punishing him when she catches him doing it is painfully aware of this fact. She usually finds that when she lets up on her punishment, the child rapidly returns to nail-biting.

This experiment shows that punishment is not a substitute for experimental extinction. Whereas experimental extinction weakens and ultimately eliminates a habit, punishment only temporarily suppresses it.

Some of you will have noted a similarity between the studies on effect of punishment and those on learned fear. This similarity suggests the basis for the suppression effect. You recall that stimuli present at the time a shock is administered acquire the power to evoke fear, and that this fear response can be weakened if it is practiced repeatedly in the absence of punishment. In the punishment study that we have

just reviewed, the subjects could not completely escape from the fear-provoking bar, but they could stay away from it. Presumably, staying away from the bar reduced the animal's fear, and so the bar-pressing response was suppressed. But at the same time the subjects were constantly exposed to the fear-provoking stimulus without receiving any more shocks. Under such conditions the fear response gradually extinguished, and finally reached a point where it became so weak that the bar-pressing response recurred. The time taken for the fear response to weaken depends on the intensity and frequency of the shock experiences, and these are the same variables that determine how long a previously punished response is suppressed.

It would seem from the facts we have so far reported that punishment is a poor method for eliminating undesirable behavior. Punishment seems effective only when it is continuously applied. We must, however, consider the results of another experiment. This study used a single-choice maze, the floor plan of which appears in Figure 10.8. This maze had two alternative pathways to the goal box, one short and one long. At the beginning of training the rats received food when they reached the goal box regardless of the path they selected. Soon all subjects selected the shorter path. This was to be expected, because the response to the shorter pathway involved a shorter delay of reinforcement (see page 170).

Once the habit to select the shorter path became dominant, the subjects were trained to reverse their preference. Three methods of doing this were used. One group of rats (extinction group) was no longer rewarded for choosing the shorter path. They received food in the goal box only after selecting the longer path. Another group (barrier group) was confronted with an impassable barrier in the middle of the short path. Therefore the only possible route to the baited goal box was the

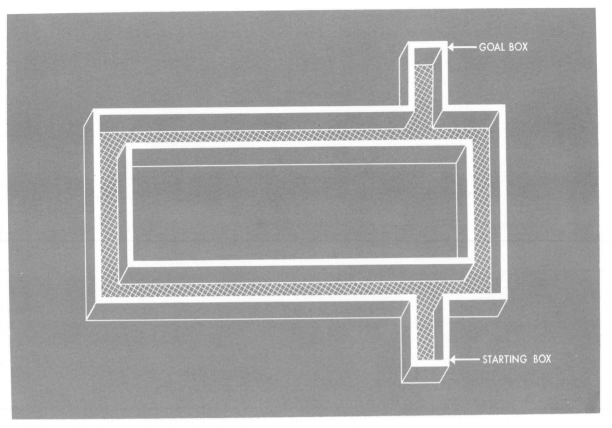

FIGURE 10.8 The Maze Plan Used in Studying the Effects of Different Methods of Habit Elimination. Initially the rats learned to select the shorter path to the goal box. Later they learned to select the longer path because of nonreinforcement, a barrier in the shorter path, or punishment (After Whiting & Mowrer, 1943).

longer path. The third group (punished group) received an electric shock halfway through the short path. This shock could of course be avoided when the subjects choose the longer path.

The subjects in all three groups were trained until they consistently chose the longer path. The number of errors, choices of the short path, was recorded. It was found that the shocked group learned to choose the long path more quickly than the barrier group, which in turn did better than the extinction group. The differences in mean scores are most interesting. The shocked group had a mean of six errors, while the barrier and extinction groups had means of 82 and 230 respectively. In

terms of error scores, punishment was 38 times more effective than nonreinforcement in training an organism to abandon one habit and adopt another.

The findings of this study may appear at first glance to be inconsistent with the findings of the Skinner box experiments. This apparent inconsistency disappears, however, when the differences in experimental procedure are examined closely. In the Skinner box studies positive reinforcement was obtainable only by bar pressing; in the maze study a competing nonpunished response that led to positive reinforcement was available to the subjects. When the punished habit was being suppressed, the subjects had an opportunity to practice another habit, the selection of the longer pathway, which was positively reinforced. Punishment is highly effective in breaking a habit if, and only if, another habit that leads to positive reinforcement is available *and is reinforced.*

Now you see that if we are to attempt an overall evaluation of the effectiveness of punishment, we will have to examine further certain conditions under which it occurs. The effectiveness of punishment depends on what it makes an organism do. If punishment forces an animal to select a desirable alternative habit that leads to reinforcement, then punishment serves as an effective method of modifying behavior. However, if punishment fails to provide an organism with the opportunity to form a new habit, then it will have little effect, and the punished response will not be eliminated. Punishment is often ineffective in that it does not insure the substitution of a desirable response for the punished one.

Why the discussion of punishment was preceded by an analysis of habit competition should now be clear. The psychological effects of punishment depend on what habits are available to the punished organism. This important psychological principle is too often ignored by parents who wish to modify the behavior of their children. Frequently children are punished for undesirable behavior without at the same time being given an opportunity for practicing and being reinforced for a more desirable habit. Punishing a child for his poor table manners or for failing to keep himself clean is useless if the punishment does not lead to active, and reinforced, practice of better habits. Too often children hear, "Don't do this!" or "Don't do that!" without ever being praised for doing *what they should do.* If punishment is to be used effectively, it must be combined with positive reinforcement of desirable habits.

Some additional points need to be made. Punishment is much more effective if it is applied at the time the undesirable habit is being performed, rather than sometime later. Punishment given much afterwards may suppress whatever behavior immediately precedes it, instead of the undesirable habit itself. The writer remembers the vain attempts of a psychologically naive friend to eliminate an unfortunate habit in his new ten-month-old dog. Several times this dog came home, his head held high, his tail wagging, one of the neighbor's chickens in his mouth, and the neighbor puffing in red-faced pursuit. Each time the dog was roundly scolded but did not mend his ways. The neighbor became more and more annoyed and made a point of cleaning his shotgun in plain view of the dog's owner. Once more it happened, and in desperation, without thinking what he was punishing, the owner whipped the dog unmercifully as the animal proudly laid the prize at his feet. What behavior was he punishing the dog for? Not stealing the chicken, which the dog had done several minutes before. He was punishing the dog for bringing the chicken home. This was very apparent when the dog went right on catching chickens but stopped bringing them home.

Punishment can stop dogs from stealing chickens. But if it is to do so it has to be applied at the time the dog chases or grabs the chicken. More specifically, the dog should be placed somewhere near chickens and punished whenever he approaches them, and reinforced when he lets them alone.

A similar problem is faced by owners of dogs who pursue automobiles. Dogs should be punished while they are running after the car, not when they return from doing it. You may think that such advice is sensible only for dog owners who are track stars as well. But you can rig up a situation in which punishment is applied at the appropriate time if you have a friend drive you slowly by so that you can douse the dog at the moment he is actually chasing the car.

Similar problems are met, in still more complicated form, with children. A mother often believes she is punishing an undesirable form of behavior when actually she is punishing a desirable act. A child admits to breaking a window and is punished. This may train him to lie instead of stopping him from breaking windows.

One must apply punishment with extreme care if one wants to prevent it from becoming a reward for an undesirable act. You recall that in both classical and instrumental conditioning learning takes place with shock serving as a reinforcer. The *termination* of punishment is a reinforcer. When a mother stops spanking her child because he is emitting terrifying screams, she is training him to utter such sounds. He will learn rapidly that blood-curdling shrieks will terminate his ordeal. This is a more or less unavoidable dilemma for those who insist on spanking. It would be better for them to consider what behavior they wish to encourage, rather than what behavior they wish to punish.

CHAINING

Our analysis of learning has dealt primarily with isolated segments of behavior known as experimental trials. A trial begins when the subject is exposed to a stimulus and ends when he makes a response. Figure 10.3 earlier in this chapter (page 274) showed how segments of behavior are chained together to produce smooth-flowing sequences of behavior. Now we must find out how behavior sequences of this sort operate. In order to do this, we must first describe a special experimental technique in which a chain consisting of sequences of the same responses is formed and practiced. By confining our interest to the recurrence of a single instrumental response, it is possible to observe clearly the influence of one of the most important variables in chained behavior, the schedule of reinforcement. How reinforcements are distributed throughout the various segments of the entire chain will determine how the chain of responses will be performed.

Instrumental Conditioning in Free-Responding Situations

In psychological experiments involving discrete trials, the subject's responses must await the presence of the appropriate stimulus. A bar must be present before it can be pressed. It is possible, however, to arrange a Skinner box so that the bar is always available. Such an arrangement, known as **free-responding conditioning,** and often referred to as **operant conditioning,** allows the subject to press the bar whenever he is so inclined. In free-responding conditioning, behavior is measured in terms of the **rate of responding.** Consider a simple situation. One rat presses the bar 60 times during a period of 30 seconds. During the same period of time another rat presses the bar only 15 times. The first rat is obviously responding more frequently, that is, at a higher rate. Rate of responding is computed by dividing the number of responses by a constant unit of time.

$$\text{rate of responding} = \frac{\text{number of responses}}{\text{unit of time}}$$

Using 30 seconds as the unit of time, the first rat has a rate of 2, and the second rat's rate is .5.

The rate of responding can also be represented graphically if recording equipment is connected to a Skinner box in such a way that each bar-pressing response is indicated on a constantly moving sheet of paper. Whenever the bar is pressed the pen moves upward, causing the line to be raised a notch. Figure 10.9 shows three sample records of **cumulative response curves** obtained from such recording techniques. The total number of responses is shown by height on the ordinate, while the abscissa

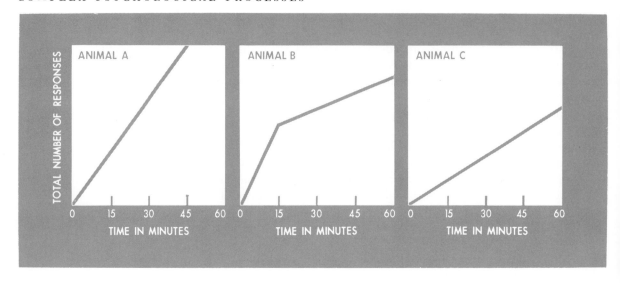

FIGURE 10.9   Different Rates of Responding as Shown by Cumulative Response Curves. The three curves represent the performances of three animals during a one-hour period in a free-responding, Skinner box situation.

indicates the passage of time. Each curve records the bar-pressing behavior of an individual animal during a one-hour period. Note that at the end of the hour the heights of the three curves differ, the curve made by animal *A* reaching the highest point on the ordinate. Animal *A* made a larger total number of responses than did the other two animals. The fact that the curves of animals *A* and *C* are essentially straight for the entire period of one hour means that these animals were responding at a constant rate. Animal *B* behaved differently. Its rate was higher during the first 15 minutes. This is indicated by the difference in the steepness of the curve for the two sections of the curve. The steeper the curve, the higher is the rate of responding.

Schedules of Reinforcement

What determines the rate of responding? Why will one organism make the same instrumental response more frequently than another of the same species? One important variable is the **schedule of reinforcement.**

Schedule of reinforcement, as the name implies, refers to a program of successive reinforcements and nonreinforcements. Up to now only two different schedules of reinforcement have been discussed, continuous reinforcement (acquisition) and continuous nonreinforcement (extinction). By *continuous* we mean that the animal is consistently reinforced every time he makes the appropriate response. These two alternatives do not exhaust all possible schedules of reinforcement.

Continuous reinforcement or continuous nonreinforcement is the exception rather than the rule in the world of everyday life. Reinforcements and nonreinforcements usually occur intermittently. Even in such automatic yet fallible devices as gum vending machines the instrumental response of inserting a coin is not always followed by a reinforcement. In games of chance, such as poker and dice throwing, behavior is unfortunately reinforced only intermittently. The same is true of going to the movies. Sometimes the movie is reinforcing, but at other times it is not. Cooks, with the possible exception of one's mother, are notorious purveyors of intermittent reinforcements. On some occasions what they have created is reinforcing; on other occasions it borders on punishment. And there are situations where reinforcements occur much less frequently than nonreinforcements. The fisherman's casting of his lure or bait is infrequently reinforced by hooking and landing a fish.

What is the psychological consequence of an intermittent reinforcement schedule? The major consequence is that it creates greater resistance to extinction. This generalization is true for both the discrete trial and the free-responding situation. In an experiment (Kendler, Pliskoff, D'Amato, & Katz, 1957) involving the discrete trial procedure the subjects in one group (Group 100%) received reinforcement by food after each one of 40 successive instrumental responses. Another group (Group 50%) received a reinforcement on only half of these trials, the reinforced trials being distributed randomly throughout the 40 trials. The intermittently reinforced group (Group 50%) made more responses during extinction than did the consistently reinforced group. The mean number of trials for Group 50% was 38, while the mean for Group 100% was 12, even though the latter group had received twice as many reinforced trials during the 40 training trials.

Figure 10.10 shows extinction curves of continuous and intermittent reinforcement schedules in a free-responding situation. The dropping off of responses is indicated by the flattening out of the cumulative response curve as its course becomes parallel to the abscissa. In Figure 10.10 the curve of the intermittently reinforced subject rises to a higher level and begins to flatten out later than does the curve of the consistently reinforced subject. This means that during extinction the intermittently reinforced subject makes more responses over a longer period of time.

Do these results go counter to the psychological law which states that the greater the number of reinforced training trials, the greater the number of responses made during extinction? No, they do not. The em-

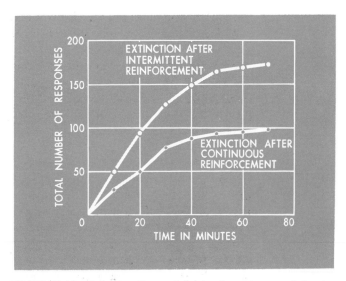

FIGURE 10.10 Extinction Curves Following Intermittent and Continuous Reinforcement Schedules. An intermittent reinforcement schedule produces the greater resistance to extinction.

pirical law asserting the relationship between number of reinforcements and number of responses made during extinction (see page 164) was obtained in a situation involving only *one* schedule of reinforcement. All groups operated on a 100 per cent schedule of reinforcement; each one of their responses was reinforced. The empirical law relating number of reinforced training trials to number of responses during extinction holds true with respect to any *one* reinforcement schedule. One hundred trials with a 50 per cent schedule of reinforcement will produce greater resistance to extinction than will 40 trials with the same schedule of reinforcement. Or again, under the same schedule of reinforcement 50 reinforced trials will produce greater resistance to extinction than will 20 trials.

It may seem paradoxical that an intermittent reinforcement schedule creates greater resistance to experimental extinction than a consistent schedule of reinforcement. Why can you make an organism respond more by reinforcing him less? The answer is not simple and is somewhat different for the discrete trial and for the free-

285

responding situation. But the main factor in both situations is that the subject in the intermittent reinforcement schedule learns *to continue* to respond when his previous instrumental responses have been reinforced only a fraction of the time. Consequently, when extinction begins, the intermittently reinforced subject continues to respond because *he has learned to respond in the absence of previous reinforcements.* The consistently reinforced subject has not learned this and hence he extinguishes more rapidly. Another way of stating this is to say that during acquisition the intermittently reinforced subjects learn to respond to cues produced by nonreinforcement, whereas the consistently reinforced subjects do not. Since nonreinforcement is the rule during extinction, and it acts as a cue for the instrumental responses of the intermittently reinforced subjects, but not for the consistently reinforced subjects.

Gambling machines are built so as to take advantage of an intermittent reinforcement schedule. Since they reinforce the risk-taking responses intermittently, risk taking is not likely to be extinguished quickly; it tends to go on and on. This point was demonstrated in an experiment (Lewis & Duncan, 1956) in which college students were given money to use in a gambling device nicknamed the "one arm bandit." Although the subjects did not know it, the machine was rigged to "pay off" the members of a consistently reinforced group every time they played it, but to pay off an intermittently reinforced group only half of the time. After a series of training trials the machine was rigged again so that it would never pay anybody anything at any time. Which group should persist in playing the gambling device in the complete absence of payoffs? If the principles discovered in the animal studies just described apply to human behavior, then you would expect that during this extinction series the intermittently reinforced subjects would persist in playing the one

arm bandit longer than the consistently reinforced subjects. This is in fact· what happened. Intermittently reinforced subjects took longer to extinguish than did consistently reinforced subjects. The intermittently reinforced subjects had learned to respond in the absence of previous reinforcements.

You can now understand why gambling behavior can be so persistent even in the face of big losses. The gambler's persistence is not solely the result of his previous winnings; it is due equally, if not more, to the fact that he has frequently lost! We can observe the same persistence in spite of nonreinforcement among fishermen, hunters, and many others whose behavior is intermittently reinforced. These people actually learn to persist in the absence of reinforcement, since only by persisting have they previously been reinforced.

Different Schedules of Intermittent Reinforcements

Intermittent reinforcements can be scheduled in a variety of ways. Skinner and his coworkers have investigated the behavioral consequences of many different intermittent reinforcement schedules in free-responding situations. In most of this work pigeons are used as the experimental subjects. Each pigeon is placed individually in a Skinner box with a small circular disk on one of its walls (see Figure 10.11). When the pigeon pecks the disk, he closes an electric circuit that records the response and also controls the food delivery mechanism.

Skinner distinguishes between two main classes of intermittent reinforcement schedules: interval schedules and ratio schedules.

Interval Reinforcement Schedule. In a **fixed interval schedule,** which we shall take up first, reinforcements are given after predetermined time intervals, and food is not available except after these intervals. An apparatus including a clock is arranged so that the first response (the pigeon's pecking) which occurs after a given lapse of time will be reinforced. Thereafter the animal is reinforced for every response he makes after an interval of the same length. Figure 10.12 shows the cumulative response curves of animals under fixed interval schedules. The first curves report data obtained during single one-hour sessions. The steepest of these is the three-minute curve. The first responses this animal made after successive three-minute periods were reinforced. No other responses were reinforced. Under this schedule the animal emitted about 420 responses during the hour, or 21 every three minutes, but only 20 of these were reinforced. A six-minute fixed interval schedule produced slightly less than half as many responses as a three-minute schedule, while the nine and twelve-minute schedules produced proportionally fewer still. The data for repeated one-hour periods, also given in Figure 10.12, are similar to those for single one-hour periods. They

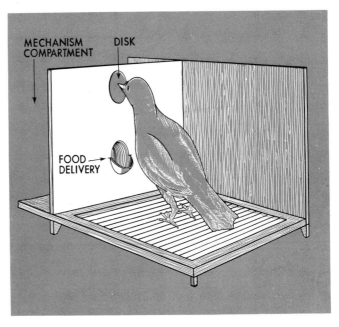

FIGURE 10.11 An Operant Conditioning Situation Used to Investigate the Effects Different Schedules of Reinforcement Have Upon Behavior. The pigeon's pecking the disk closes an electric circuit that records the response and controls the food delivery mechanism (After Ferster & Skinner, 1957).

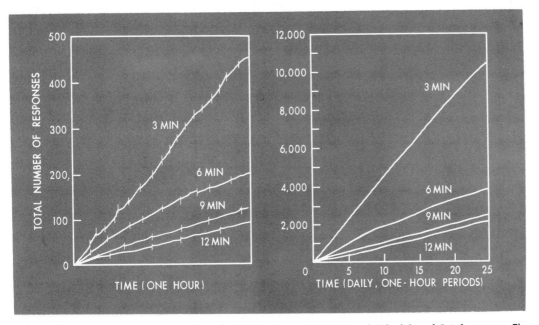

FIGURE 10.12 Cumulative Response Records of Animals on Fixed Interval Schedules of Reinforcement. The curves on the left represent behavior obtained in single one-hour sessions. The vertical lines indicate individual reinforcements. The curves on the right report behavior during repeated sessions on fixed interval reinforcement schedules (After Skinner, 1938).

are included to show the remarkable stability of the animal's behavior, as it emits responses with almost machine-like precision.

An organism will adjust to a fixed interval schedule of reinforcement by responding at a fairly constant rate. The shorter the interval, the higher will be the rate. This is true not only of instrumental responses emitted by rats and pigeons, but also those of chimpanzees and children.

If you are interested in influencing or controlling someone else's behavior—and every parent is—then you can put to practical use the knowledge that the rate of responding is altered by the length of the interval between reinforcements. A parent whose child is just beginning music lessons is wise to reinforce the child's efforts at short intervals rather than to withhold approval and complimentary remarks until the close of a practice session. When reinforcements come at short intervals they sustain more persistent effort.

Figure 10.13 is an enlarged portion of a record similar to those in Figure 10.12. Notice the scallops between successive reinforcements (indicated by the short vertical lines). The scalloping indicates that the rate of responding is very low for the period immediately following reinforcement but it rises rapidly as the time for the next reinforcement approaches. Small children behave in the same way before Christmas; their angelic responses become more and more frequent as the holiday approaches. The low rate of responding immediately after reinforcement in a fixed interval schedule indicates, of course, that the animal has learned one reinforcement is never immediately followed by another.

This decline in rate of responding in a fixed interval schedule does not appear in a **variable interval schedule,** the other form of an interval schedule. Here the subject is reinforced after intervals which vary in length. For example, in a variable five-minute schedule the response is reinforced

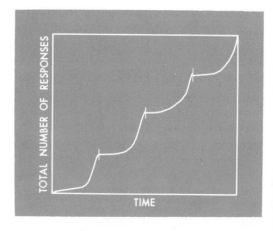

FIGURE 10.13 An Enlarged Portion of a Cumulative Response Record Obtained From an Animal Operating on a Fixed Interval Schedule of Reinforcement. Each vertical line indicates a single reinforcement.

once every five minutes *on the average,* the interval intervening between successive reinforcements being perhaps as long as ten minutes or as short as a few seconds. If a response is occasionally reinforced again immediately after a preceding reinforcement, the animal learns not to slow down after each reinforcement. Figure 10.14 shows a typical cumulative response curve obtained with a variable interval schedule. The scalloping effect of the fixed interval schedule does not appear.

The performance of an instrumental response, such as the pecking response of a pigeon, is remarkably uniform under a variable interval schedule. Pigeons reinforced on a variable interval schedule averaging five minutes between successive reinforcements have responded at a rate of approximately two responses *per second* for a period as long as 15 hours without at any time pausing for more than 20 seconds (Skinner, 1953). In one demonstration (Skinner, 1950) of the effectiveness of a variable interval schedule, a pigeon made 20,000 responses in three hours although he received a total of only 36 reinforcements during the entire period!

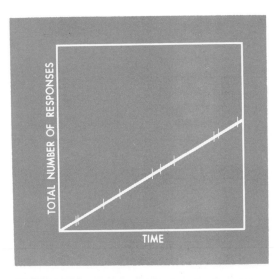

FIGURE 10.14 An Enlarged Portion of a Cumulative Response Record Obtained From an Animal Operating on a Variable Interval Schedule of Reinforcement. Each vertical line indicates a single reinforcement. Note that the scalloping effect which appears in Figure 10.13 is absent.

Referring again to the parent whose youngster is practicing a musical instrument and who wishes him to do his best as much of the time as possible, we would advise him to praise his youngster on a variable interval schedule rather than on a fixed interval schedule. Reinforcements at fixed intervals might result in the child's letting down in his efforts shortly after each compliment.

As you would expect, responses acquired under a variable interval schedule are extremely difficult to extinguish. A pigeon has given as many as 10,000 unreinforced pecking responses in extinction following a variable interval reinforcement schedule.

Ratio Reinforcement Schedule. An entirely different way to schedule intermittent reinforcements is to use a ratio schedule. In both the fixed and variable interval schedules it is the lapse of time since reinforcement that determines when the next reinforcement will come. In contrast to this, reinforcement in a ratio schedule depends solely on the behavior of the organism, since the reinforcement is arranged to occur immediately after the organism has made a fixed number of responses. The animal, for example, may receive a reinforcement after every fifth time he responds, or after every one hundred responses. Because the subject must make a certain number of responses before receiving a reinforcement, a ratio schedule encourages rapid responding.

The ratio of nonreinforced responses to reinforced responses can become exceedingly high without decreasing the rate of responding. In one study (Skinner, 1938) rats received only one reinforcement for every 192 responses they made. In spite of what seems to an observer to be discouragingly infrequent reinforcement, bar pressing occurred at a very high rate. It is important to note, however, that the bar-pressing response could not be learned with such a high ratio of nonreinforcements. Even if the rat's first response was reinforced, extinction would occur before the rat had made the required additional responses, 192 of them, to get a second reinforcement. In order to train animals to respond steadily at high ratios of nonreinforcements, the high ratio must be worked up to gradually. At the beginning of training, reinforcements are arranged to come frequently, and then the number of nonreinforced responses between successive reinforced responses is gradually increased until the high ratio of nonreinforcements has been reached.

In one experiment food pellets were delivered to different animals after 16, 24, 32, 48, 64, 96, or 192 responses, respectively. Each of these ratios, especially the higher ones, had to be approached gradually. Figure 10.15 shows the results of this study in terms of cumulative response curves for the three highest ratios, which were obtained after extensive training. The 48:1 animal made about 600 responses during an hour and was reinforced 13 times. The 192:1

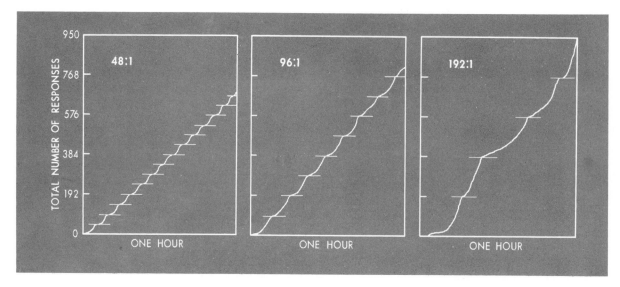

FIGURE 10.15 Cumulative Response Records of Animals Behaving Under Different Fixed Ratio Schedules of Reinforcement. The horizontal lines indicate single reinforcements (After Skinner, 1938).

animal, with only four reinforcements, made 960 responses during the same time period. These results show that the less frequent the reinforcement in a ratio schedule, the more numerous will be the number of responses in a given length of time.

The **fixed ratio schedule** is similar to the principle behind certain uses of the practice of piecework in the garment industry. A shirtmaker, for example, may be paid according to the number of buttons she sews on and is in this way reinforced to increase her productivity. This sounds fair enough. However, as the productivity of the worker increases and her pay goes up, some employers shift the ratio upward and demand more work for the same pay. This puts her under constant pressure to increase her productivity in order to maintain her income. This form of pay schedule encourages high rates of responding, but unions, of course, object to the long, hard hours of work that it also encourages, which they maintain are injurious to the workers' health.

Under high fixed ratios of reinforcement the rate of responding tends to slow down immediately after a reinforcement (see Figure 10.15). As with the fixed interval schedule, the organism learns that one reinforcement is not soon followed by another. If the ratio is very high, the animal may suddenly stop responding after a reinforcement. Laboratory studies of fixed ratio schedules suggest that each organism has its limit, beyond which the ratio fails to sustain a high rate of responding. When this limit is reached, long periods of inactivity follow each reinforcement, until finally the animal quits altogether.

This low rate of responding following a reinforcement common under a high fixed ratio schedule is also typical of the piecework practice mentioned above. Writers, too, report a marked drop in their ability to work just after they have completed a book. The reason for this is plain: they have so much work to do before they can receive the next reinforcement—publication of a book. College students also experience a marked letdown after completing an important term paper or their final examinations.

The pauses in responding that occur in a fixed ratio schedule can be eliminated in much the same way as they are eliminated in a fixed interval schedule. In a **variable ratio schedule** the ratios can be varied over a considerable range, while the average ratio is kept constant. In a 48:1 fixed ratio schedule 48 nonreinforced responses must intervene between successive reinforcements. In a 48:1 variable ratio schedule the number of nonreinforced responses intervening between successive reinforced responses may vary from zero to a couple of hundred. As a result, responses that occur soon after a reinforced response will sometimes be reinforced, which they never are in a fixed ratio schedule.

Variable ratio schedules produce fantastically high rates of sustained, no-pause responding. Pigeons have been trained with a variable ratio schedule to peck five times per second for several hours. This is at the same rate as the ticks of a fine wrist watch.

Most forms of gambling are governed by a variable ratio reinforcement schedule. Winning, which is a reinforcement, depends on a gambler's having made an instrumental response, such as placing a bet on the right horse, the winning poker hand, or the right number on the roulette wheel. Reinforcements occur intermittently and in an unpredictable fashion, but if the gambler makes a large number of responses, he is practically assured of winning sooner or later. As a result, gambling usually generates a very high rate of responding. The chronic gambler, like the pigeon pecking five times per second for many hours, is a victim of a variable ratio schedule. At Las Vegas some addicts keep two slot machines going at once, because one machine is too slow to accommodate their rate of responding.

But you must not think that intermittent reinforcement schedules sustain only questionable behavior such as gambling. Students who apply themselves vigorously and writers or artists who always strive to write or paint at their best, maintained their behavior on a notoriously intermittent reinforcement schedule. Not every day's effort, or even every month's, can bring rewards, that is, be reinforced.

We have now finished our discussion of schedules of reinforcement, at least for the time being. One last point must be made, however. What we now know about how long chains of behavior, made up of repetitions of the same response, can be acquired and maintained by appropriate scheduling of reinforcements constitutes one of the most useful and important discoveries of modern psychology. The principles we have discussed, as they operate with rats, pigeons, and children, have important implications for other kinds of behavior which we will describe later.

SHAPING BEHAVIOR

The principles that operate in habit competition and chaining both function in a psychological technique known as shaping behavior or, for short, just **shaping.** As the name implies, this is a technique by which the behavior of an organism is molded much as clay is molded by a sculptor.

Suppose it is your aim to shape the behavior of an untrained pigeon in a Skinner box so that he will rapidly learn to make a particular instrumental response, such as pecking at a circular disk. You would accomplish this shaping process through a series of successive approximations. Instead of waiting until the pigeon makes a full and correct pecking response (which he would probably not make for a long time) and then reinforcing this response, you would reinforce some bit of the pigeon's behavior that forms part of a chain, the terminal link of which is the disk-pecking act. So at first you would give the naive pigeon reinforcement when he merely turned slightly in the direction of the disk. As a result, competition between turning toward or away from it would be weighted in favor of turning toward it. Once a definite tendency to turn toward the disk had been established, you would withhold further reinforcement until the pigeon made a definite approach movement toward the disk. By reinforcing those responses that make the pigeon come closer and closer to the disk and then those that bring his beak near it, you would be sure finally to induce the pigeon to peck the disk, and you would, of course, reinforce this behavior. With this shaping technique, a naive but hungry pigeon can usually be made to peck at the disk within a period of about three minutes; if left alone he might not have pecked the disk and obtained his first reinforcement until after several hours had elapsed.

After the first successful peck the pigeon would be reinforced for additional pecks. If he failed to peck again you would reinstitute the shaping process at the point where it had broken down. Once the chain of responses leading to pecking was emitted fairly regularly, then the pecking response could be placed on one of several different schedules of reinforcement.

Three important psychological principles are involved in successful shaping. First is the principle of *response generalization*. Although a response has been reinforced, it may not be repeated in exactly the same way the next time it is made. For example, when a pigeon is reinforced for approaching the disk, the next time he may go even closer to the disk or he may not go as close. In other words, response generalization refers to the fact that when responses are repeated, they are likely to vary over a range of more or less similar acts. It is important that response generalization does occur, for if it did not, shaping would be impossible. If the pigeon could only rigidly repeat his previously reinforced response, in exactly the same form, he would never get closer to the disk. Indeed, what we call *skill* would be impossible. But among the responses possible under the principle of

response generalization is the one that allows him to get somewhat nearer. This closer approach is then reinforced and the groundwork laid for response generalization to get the pigeon even closer later on.

The second essential principle in shaping is *successful habit competition*. At each point in the chain the correct habit must attain dominance over competing habits. This is accomplished by reinforcing the correct habit and not reinforcing the incorrect one.

The third essential principle is that *each segment in the chain must be linked to the succeeding segment*. That is, cues produced by making one response must be closely connected to the next response. To make this clear, we will take another example of shaping behavior. A pigeon may be trained to turn around in a circle. This is done by reinforcing the pigeon for making even a slight movement in the direction of turning around. After this habit is thus strengthened, other responses that are part of the chain of responses required to turn around are successively reinforced. By this shaping technique the response chain of spinning around, one that a pigeon would normally rarely make, can be made to occur over and over again at a high rate of frequency; in a very short time you can have him literally spinning like a top.

Secondary reinforcements are more effective in shaping behavior than primary reinforcements. If food had to be used as a reinforcement for each segment of a chain of responses, the pigeon's stopping to eat would interfere with his development of a smooth-flowing sequence of responses. The movements made in eating would confuse the association between the cues produced by one response and the succeeding response. This interference can be avoided if a strong secondary reinforcing agent is introduced. For example, a buzzer may be sounded whenever the desired response is made. As a secondary reinforcing agent the buzzer has an advantage in that it does not instigate strong orienting movements that would interfere with the desired chain of responses. Whenever the animal makes the appropriate response the buzzer is sounded, and so his tendency to make the response is strengthened without interfering with his tendency to make the next response.

If you want to take advantage of the psychological technique of shaping in training your dog, your first task is to develop a strong secondary reinforcing agent, perhaps a clicker or whistle. At the outset you sound this stimulus only when the animal is fed; on each separate training trial, following the sound you offer the dog a biscuit. After a while you introduce an intermittent reinforcement schedule, the sound is not always followed by food. Gradually you increase the proportion of nonreinforced to reinforced trials (Zimmerman, 1957). You are then in a position to use the sound effectively in shaping the dog's behavior. Thus, if you want the dog to heel (follow you closely as you walk), you reinforce him with the sound when his response is in the direction of following you. By successively reinforcing responses that bring the dog nearer and nearer to you as you walk, you soon make him respond appropriately. You may hasten the training by putting him on a leash so that his heeling behavior is forced to occur early in the training.

There are obvious disadvantages in having the dog heel at all times—especially when you are getting into bed! A better plan is to train him to heel on certain occasions but not on others. If you want the dog to follow you only when you command him to "Heel," then you reinforce him only when you give the command. The command "Heel" is the stimulus that controls the dog's behavior, for he makes the response only when it has been spoken, not in its absence. The rotating behavior of the pigeon described above might also be put under such a stimulus control. If the turning behavior is reinforced when a light is on and never in its absence, the pigeon will soon turn only when the light is on.

The stimulus "Heel" elicits heeling behavior, and the light, rotating behavior, much as a conditioned stimulus evokes a conditioned response. A conditioned stimulus is sometimes called an *evoking* or *eliciting* stimulus. However, in our examples the command and the light do more. They not only evoke the desired response but serve to *maintain* it. A stimulus that has the dual function of evoking and maintaining behavior has been called a **discriminative stimulus,** and it is essentially one that indicates the proper occasion for the response, because it has been a distinctive part of the occasions on which the response was reinforced. An example of a discriminative stimulus in everyday life is the one particular chair in the particular room that a student finds essential if he is to get down seriously to concentrated study. The particular chair in the particular room functions as a discriminative stimulus for studying. Incidentally, this is not a bad habit to form. Only remember, never do anything but study in that chair—no loafing, no chattering with your roommate, no letter writing.

Shaping technique can induce animals to do odd tricks. The photographs in Figure 10.16 illustrate a complete chain of responses a rat acquired by shaping techniques. Barnabus, a male rat in the psychological laboratory of a women's college, has been trained to perform a series of intricate responses in a large aluminum and glass cage. When a light flashes at the lower left-hand side of the cage, Barnabus scampers to a rising circular mesh pathway and runs up (1) to a first landing, where he crosses a moat (2) to the bottom of a 16-step ladder. He climbs the ladder (3) to the second platform. There with his teeth and paws he hauls in a chain that is attached to a small red car. Having brought the car to him, Barnabus climbs in and pedals away (4).

When the car reaches the bottom of a stairway he gets out, runs upstairs (5) to reach a third platform, and squeezes through a glass tube 17 inches long (6). Barnabus then enters an elevator, and as it descends, he yanks with his front paws and teeth a chain that raises the flag of his university (7). (The students at this point often stand at attention, some with moist eyes.) When he reaches the bottom of the cage, Barnabus presses a bar. A buzzer sounds and he is free to eat all the food he can during a one-minute period (8). Hail the powers of reinforcement!

Make no mistake, shaping an intricate chain of behavior like Barnabus' is a diffi-

cult task and requires much preliminary experience. One needs skill to know exactly when to reinforce and when not to reinforce a particular bit of behavior, and how to integrate the various segments of the chain of responses. At one time, naturally, Barnabus had to be reinforced after completing each separate act of the entire chain. Then this reinforcement was gradually withdrawn, forcing him to do more for each reinforcement.

Some psychologists have become so successful in shaping the behavior of animals that they have created new vocational opportunities for themselves. They are employed by famous animal shows, where they

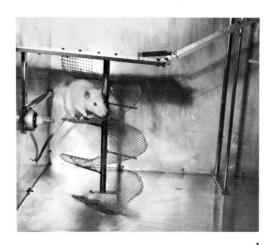

1

3

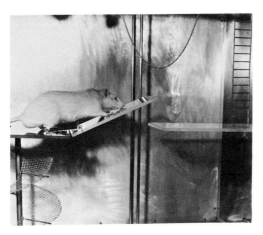

2

FIGURE 10.16 A Demonstration of Shaping With a White Rat. Barnabus, the rat in these photographs, is able to execute this complex chain of responses in less than two minutes (Drs. R. Pierrel and J. G. Sherman; *The New York Times* and Meyer Hiebowitz).

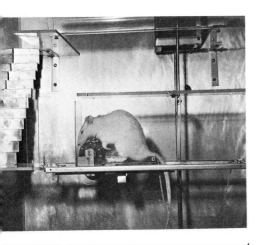

4

5

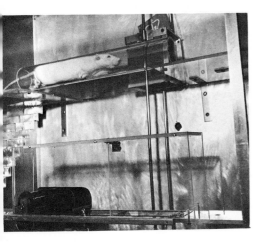

6

7

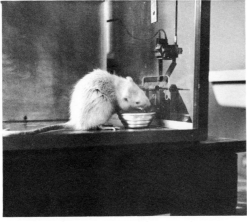

8

teach animals ranging from porpoises to chimpanzees to perform startling stunts that delight audiences and have strong box-office appeal. And as you will see in the last chapter of this book, the technique of shaping has been put to important use in making education more effective in schools throughout the country.

"Superstitious" Behavior

In order to illustrate superstitious behavior, we will take a simple experimental situation. To begin with, a pigeon is placed in a box which has in one corner a mechanism that delivers food. Every once in a while, in a more or less irregular order, a light blinks, indicating that food is available. The light blinks regardless of what the pigeon is doing. More concisely and technically, the reinforcement is *not contingent* on the behavior of the pigeon; it is a **noncontingent reinforcement.**

What kind of behavior would you expect the pigeon to exhibit in this situation? Some act would surely gain dominance, but it is difficult, if not impossible, to specify which response it would be. This prediction is based on the reinforcement principle. According to that principle, *any* act that happens to occur at the time of reinforcement is going to be strengthened *whether the act is responsible for producing the reinforcement or not.* Consequently, when a noncontingent reinforcement occurs, some kind of behavior is strengthened, and the probability that this behavior will occur on the next occasion of a noncontingent reinforcement is thereby increased. If it does not occur some other act will, and thereby increase the probability of *its* recurrence. If a sufficient number of noncontingent reinforcements is given, some behavior will attain dominance simply because it occurs frequently at the time of the noncontingent reinforcements. Several noncontingent reinforcements, for example, may follow the head-raising response of one

pigeon, while the head-lowering response may be reinforced in another pigeon. As a result, the first pigeon will tend to strut around with his head held high, while the second pigeon will keep his head low.

This sort of behavior has been called *superstitious* because it reflects the same psychological mechanisms that operate in human beings who have learned to do certain things because they are in some way associated with good luck. The writer, who plays poker infrequently (actually on a fixed interval schedule of once a year), has noticed that his method of sorting his chips depends upon how successful he is at the time. If he has a winning streak when his chips happen to be separated into neat red, blue, and white piles, then he continues to sort them, but if he begins to win when his chips are disarranged, then he doesn't dare sort them. Now, the writer believes he is sufficiently sophisticated to know that the manner in which he sorts his chips can have no possible influence on his winning or losing. Yet the way he sorts them is part of the chain of responses that terminates in winning or losing. When he wins, all segments of the chain are strengthened, even those responses that he admits can have no effect in producing the reinforcement, winning.

Of course, the author's superstition is minor compared to that of the fly fisherman convinced that his homemade fly will catch the gamiest trout. You need not accept his tall tales of success in order to understand how he became so convinced of its efficacy. He probably had a relatively high proportion of successful casts when he first used the fly, and although on most of his casts since then, he has not caught a fish or even got a bite, he has persisted in using his pet fly because its use has been intermittently reinforced. Even though he has run into streaks of bad luck (series of casts, none of them reinforced), his tendency to use the fly has not been extinguished because its use has been reinforced on a variable ratio schedule. Fishermen are not scientists; or if they are, they do not behave like scientists when they fish. A scientist would naturally ask whether another fly would not be just as effective, and whether, if the other fly had been used first, it would not now occupy the favored position. Also, he might suggest that the fish's hunger may be as important, if not more so, than the attractiveness of the fly. Perhaps when his hunger is strong many different flies are equally attractive to the fish.

Gamblers (who are the psychological relatives of fishermen) develop even more flagrant superstitious habits. They may pull an ear lobe or cross their fingers every time they place a bet. If they bet often enough, such responses are bound to be reinforced from time to time on a variable ratio schedule and will therefore become resistant to extinction.

Superstitious behavior, which results from noncontingent reinforcements, can become intertwined in a chain of behavior with responses that really are instrumental in achieving reinforcements. To be a leading batter in major league baseball, a player's skill must be shaped to near perfection. If his chain of responses deviates even slightly from those required to make the bat connect solidly with the ball, he will in all probability not get a hit. The major league batter must practice his swing to such an extent that it does not vary appreciably from one time to the next. Figure 10.17 shows two photographs of Ted Williams, one of the greatest batters of all time, on two different occasions. His batting form appears identical. This is the result of years and years of intensive training.

If you watch baseball on TV you will notice that not only does the batting form of a topnotch player remain practically constant, but so do his other responses. One batter may always tug at his cap's peak when stepping up to the plate; another will pull at his sleeve; still another will press the bridge of his nose. These responses have

no instrumental value, but they occur about as regularly as the essential bat-swinging responses. The point is that some behavior must occur when the batter steps up to the plate, and such responses get built into the total behavior pattern becoming almost as stereotyped as the batting behavior itself. Any inveterate baseball fan

FIGURE 10.17 Ted Williams Getting His 2,000th Hit in the First Inning and 2,001st Hit in the Fifth Inning of a Game Played in the Yankee Stadium on August 11, 1955 (*The New York Times* and Patrick A. Burns).

can identify a batter solely from the way he steps up to the plate. Some players are superstitious about such behavior; they claim, or will admit at least, that their "prebatting" behavior brings them luck. Other batters may be completely unaware that their prebatting responses have become so rigidly shaped.

One last point about superstitious behavior. It is always necessary to warn introductory psychology students to proceed cautiously in interpreting behavior. The fact that we have considered superstitious behavior as a function of noncontingent reinforcement does not mean that it is soley accounted for by that variable. Some fishermen, gamblers, and baseball players are more superstitious than others, even though the schedules of reinforcement they have been subjected to are similar. Obviously, then, there must be other factors that play a role in fixating superstitious behavior, such as the attitude a person has learned to take toward superstitions in general. Our conclusion at present is that noncontingent reinforcements are an important variable in superstitious behavior, but not necessarily the only one.

Differential Reinforcement

Shaping behavior depends on differential reinforcement. The behavior that is reinforced becomes part of the final chain of responses, whereas the responses that do not lead to reinforcement drop out. However, as we have already mentioned, in situations involving competition between habits, inappropriate habits can be learned. Similarly, behavior can often be shaped in an undesirable manner. Parents are shaping their children's behavior all the time without always being aware that they are doing so and, in the process, sometimes encourage the acquisition of undesirable response sequences. The mother whose child cries a great deal usually bemoans her lot, and yet she is often responsible for the habit. She may ignore the child quite consistently whenever he calls out to her, but once he cries she is all attention. In this way, crying becomes a habit because it is consistently reinforced, whereas calling to the mother, without crying, is extinguished. The mother saves time in the long run if she responds when he calls her name and at the same time shapes his behavior in the direction of independence, by teaching him the little tasks he can perform to receive reinforcements.

In shaping human behavior the major problem is to understand and control the reinforcing mechanisms. Up to now we have only discussed relatively simple and obvious reinforcements, but human behavior can be tied to a wide range of secondary reinforcing agents. Where one child will get reinforcement by pleasing his parents, another child will get his reinforcement by annoying them. In both instances a certain kind of behavior has become instrumental in getting the parents' attention which is a powerful secondary reinforcing agent for children, since the satisfaction of their physiological drives is usually preceded by parental attention. If a certain kind of behavior has become persistently annoying, the parents must devise some technique to reshape it. Sometimes the assistance of a trained psychiatrist or clinical psychologist is needed; at other times parents can modify a child's behavior by attending to his wants when his behavior is acceptable, and ignoring it, and thus withholding reinforcement, when it is annoying.

MOTOR AND VERBAL LEARNING

For many years psychologists have employed a distinction which they themselves do not fully accept, the distinction between motor and verbal learning in humans.

Much of human learning involves language. Learning the meaning of a new word or trying to discover Plato's political philosophy are examples of behavior consisting primarily of language habits. Such learning is customarily referred to as **verbal learning.** From some forms of learning, language seems to be absent. We learn to play ping-pong primarily by playing ping-pong, not by reading or hearing somebody talk about it. Similarly, a child learns to tie his shoelace by tying it, perhaps after watching somebody else do it. This kind of learning is known as **motor learning.** Yet this distinction between verbal and motor learning is obviously not a hard-and-fast one; they often occur together. Such verbal instructions as, "Grasp the ping-pong racket as if you are shaking hands with it," "Always watch the ball," "Follow through on your stroke after completing it," can be helpful to a novice at the game.

It is inaccurate to pigeonhole any human learning activity as exclusively either verbal or motor. At best we can only point out certain verbal and motor features of a total learning process. For example, if a person is to learn to speak a language fluently, he must not only learn the meaning of a large number of words, along with the basic structure of the language, but also learn muscular responses in the throat and mouth in order to enunciate properly what he wishes to say and make it understandable.

The learning activities of lower animals involve predominantly motor learning. For this reason we shall discuss it first. Afterwards, we will take up simple verbal learning, in preparation for a more extensive discussion of verbal behavior in the following chapter.

Motor Skills

Psychologists have designed several kinds of apparatus for the investigation of human motor learning in which verbal processes seem to play a very minor role. Two widely used forms of apparatus are the pursuit rotor (Figure 10.18) and the mirror-drawing task (Figure 10.19). The subject in a pursuit rotor task tries to keep the tip of a hinged stylus in contact with a metal disk imbedded in a rotating turntable. In mirror-drawing the subject traces the outlines of a geometrical shape, such as a star, which he sees only as a mirror image. Because the

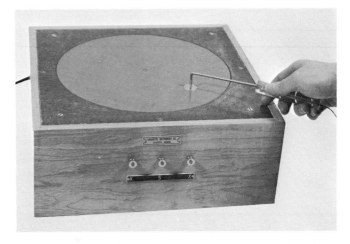

FIGURE 10.18 A Pursuit Rotor. As the turntable rotates the subject attempts to keep the tip of a stylus in contact with the metal disk. A clock connected to the apparatus records the amount of time the subject keeps in contact with the target (Lafayette Instrument Co.).

FIGURE 10.19 A Mirror-Drawing Apparatus. The subject must trace the outlines of a star which she sees only as a mirror image.

300

mirror image reverses the right-left relationships, the subject must learn new eye-hand coordinations.

One motor task that does not require any apparatus is printing the alphabet in reverse. In this task the subject is required to print the alphabet upside down and backwards, thus:

ſ I H Ɔ Ⅎ Ǝ ◖ Ɔ Ᏸ ∀

A subject's score is the number of letters he prints correctly in a certain length of time.

Although the pursuit rotor, mirror-drawing, and reverse alphabet printing tasks are conveniently referred to as motor tasks, you will very quickly discover, if you try to do any one of them, that some verbal behavior ("talking to oneself") is unavoidable.

Some psychologists recommend use of the longer and more correct term **sensorimotor skill,** in place of the simpler **motor skill,** to prevent anyone from being misled into believing that such skills involve only a pattern of movements. In the pursuit rotor

task the subject must watch the moving disk, but all the while kinesthetic cues (see page 93) are arising from movements of his arms and hands, and these serve, from instant to instant, to guide what he is doing as he keeps the stylus as closely as possible on the moving target. A person with defective kinesthetic sensitivity would be hopelessly handicapped in the performance of a pursuit rotor task.

Distribution of Practice

When someone is learning a motor task, he can either practice almost continuously or take frequent periods of rest between periods of practice. Continuous learning is known as **massed practice;** learning with rests between is called **spaced practice.** In general, spaced practice is much more efficient. Figure 10.20 reports the results of an experiment designed to investigate the influence of different distributions of practice on the performance of a mirror-drawing task. The ordinate of the curve represents the average amount of time a group of subjects required to trace a figure, while the abscissa indicates their successive attempts (trials). The subjects whose training was massed (20 trials without any rest) did least well. The best performance was by subjects who were also given 20 trials, but at the rate of only one trial per day, with 24 hours of rest intervening between successive trials. Slightly poorer was the performance of another spaced group, who were allowed a one-minute rest between successive trials. In short, both these schedules of spaced practice proved superior to massed training. This result is consistent, you may recall, with those obtained (see page 172) in cases where classical and instrumental conditioning occurred more rapidly when practice was spaced than when it was massed.

In massed practice there are longer practice periods and much shorter rest intervals

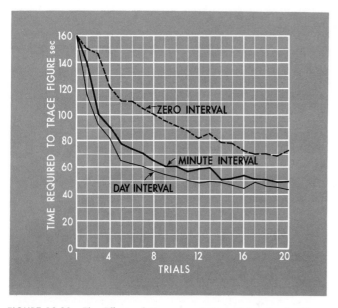

FIGURE 10.20 The Effects of Massed and Spaced Practice in Mirror Drawing. The best performance was exhibited by subjects who had a 24-hour interval between successive trials (After Lorge, 1930).

than in spaced practice. Is the superiority of spaced practice, we may inquire, due to the longer rest periods or to the shorter practice sessions? It turns out that both contribute. The question of what happens when the practice periods are of equal length but are separated by rest periods of unequal length, was answered by an experiment in which college students received a series of one-minute trials in reverse alphabet printing. The rest intervals between successive trials varied for different groups from zero seconds (massed training) to seven days. The results of the tenth trial (Figure 10.21) show a rest interval of up to approximately 45 seconds has beneficial effects.

Now we may ask, what happens when the rest intervals are of the same length but the practice periods vary in length? The results of the study reported in Figure 10.22 demonstrate that relatively short practice periods result in better performance of a simple motor task. In this experiment all trials were separated by 30-second intervals; only the length of the practice trial varied. The average performance of subjects whose practice trials were ten seconds long was superior to those who had 30-second practice sessions.

No simple rule can tell us the optimal length of practice period and rest interval for a particular task. In general, practice periods should be short, though long enough to get the learner over an initial inefficient period called the "warm-up" (see page 304). Unless fatigue is a factor, increasing the length of a rest interval appreciably does not usually influence performance very much, if at all. These are merely guiding principles, however, and to find out what is best in a particular case usually requires an empirical investigation. In part this is because the optimal distribution of practice varies with the task. It has been found (Young, 1954) that college students practicing archery profit most from having lessons four days a week. Badminton, on

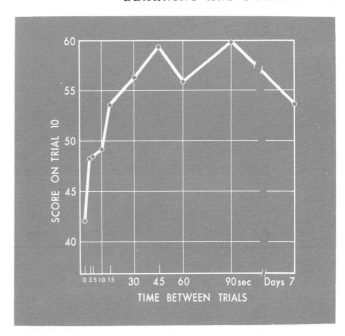

FIGURE 10.21 Performance in the Reverse Alphabet Printing Task as a Function of the Time Between Successive Trials. This graph shows the performance on the tenth trial and indicates that with spaced trials performance is superior to what it is with massed practice (After Kientzle, 1946).

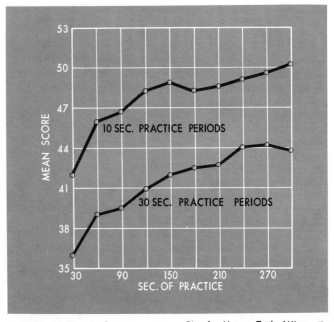

FIGURE 10.22 Performance on a Simple Motor Task When the Length of the Practice Trials Was Varied (10 or 30 seconds) but the Time Between Them Was Kept Constant (30 seconds). The shorter practice trials led to superior performance (After Kimble & Bilodeau, 1949).

the other hand, is learned best when practice periods are spaced further apart. Two periods a week seem to produce optimal results.

Although some forms of spaced practice are more effective than others, it is not always feasible to use them. In mirror-drawing (see Figure 10.20), one-day rest intervals proved superior to one-minute rest intervals. But if a person has to meet an early deadline in learning mirror-drawing—say, within one day—no one is going to recommend that he use a one-day rest interval, which would allow him exactly two practice trials. According to Figure 10.20, the average time required to trace a figure in the mirror after two trials separated by one day is approximately two minutes. In contrast, approximately 50 seconds are needed to do the same thing after 20 trials separated by one-minute intervals. The total time required with such a learning schedule is less than one hour, as compared to a whole day when the most efficient kind of spaced practice is permitted. In short, massed practice often proves more feasible than spaced practice, even though in principle it is less economical.

Clearly, if you wish to benefit from the principle of spaced practice you must plan ahead. Even when learning motor skills (and many verbal skills, as you will see) you will find some form of spaced practice advisable, and you are fortunate if you are not in a rush to get the learning done so quickly that you must adopt something less than the optimal form of spaced practice. However, in studying a subject in school, you must resist pressures to speed up very firmly. A wise student distributes the study time he is able and willing to allot to a given subject over the entire semester. Sadly, some students postpone serious study until the night before an examination. The writer will never forget one student who pathetically complained to him that he had failed the final examination in a course although, he solemnly

explained, he had faithfully utilized the principle of spaced practice. What he had done was to space his practice evenly—the night before the examination—first studying and then resting from 7 P.M. until midnight!

Work Inhibition

Earlier we discussed the concept of inhibition (see page 176), a negative process that retarded the course of conditioning. Since conditioning is a form of motor learning, especially in lower animals when there is no question of a verbal component, it should not surprise you to discover that a concept related to inhibition, namely, **work inhibition,** can be invoked to explain some of the effects of massed practice. As practice continues this negative process operates to inhibit *performance*, that is, weaken the response rather than the habit.

Two lines of evidence support the idea that there is such a thing as work inhibition. The first of these is the greater effectiveness of distributed practice. Continuous or uninterrupted practice should in principle, and actually does, produce the greatest amount of inhibition and therefore interferes most with performance.

But why, referring again to Figure 10.20, are some forms of spaced practice superior to others? It is reasonable to answer that the work inhibition resulting from practice gradually dissipates during a rest interval, and when a rest interval is too brief not all of the work inhibition has time to dissipate. Figure 10.21 suggests that a rest interval of approximately 45 seconds is needed for the complete dissipation of work inhibition following 60 seconds of practice on reverse alphabet printing. Shorter rest intervals allow some, but not all of the work inhibition to dissipate. The nearer the rest interval to the optimal 45 seconds, the greater is the opportunity for work inhibition to dissipate, and hence the better the performance.

Thus the curve in Figure 10.21 rises gradually from the point representing continuous practice to the point representing the rest interval (45 seconds) that allows the complete dissipation of work inhibition.

The same line of reasoning can be applied to Figure 10.22. Longer practice sessions develop greater amounts of work inhibition. The complete dissipation of greater amounts of work inhibition requires longer rest intervals.

A second line of support for the concept of work inhibition may be referred to under the term *reminiscence.* First let us describe the phenomenon itself, and then define it. If work inhibition develops during practice and dissipates during rest, then we would expect the introduction of a rest interval following massed practice to produce a sudden and marked improvement in performance after the rest. The reason for expecting this is simply that rest intervals provide the opportunity for the work inhibition that had been accumulated during practice to dissipate. Figure 10.23 supplies evidence consistent with this expectation. The performance of a massed practice group in a pursuit rotor task is shown to be appreciably poorer than that of a spaced group. However, immediately after a rest period the performance of the massed practice subjects improves sharply and becomes equal to that of the spaced group. The sudden improvement in performance resulting from a rest period with no intervening practice is known as **reminiscence.**

The improvement in performance resulting from reminiscence does not always enable a massed practice group to catch up with a spaced group. In Figure 10.23, it is true, the performance of the massed practice group did suddenly become equal to the performance of the spaced training group, but a rest interval will enable a massed practice group to catch up with a spaced training group only if it is introduced fairly soon after training begins. If

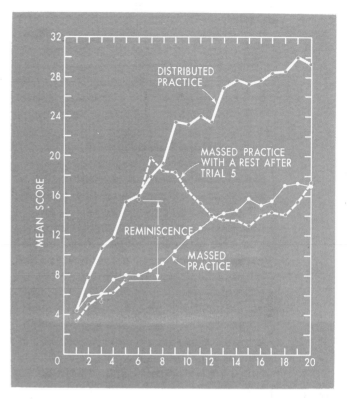

FIGURE 10.23 A Graphic Representation of Reminiscence. The performance of the spaced practice group on a pursuit rotor task was initially superior to that of the massed practice group. Immediately after a rest period, following the fifth trial, the performance of the massed group equaled that of the spaced practice group. The jump in performance resulting from a rest period is known as reminiscence (After Gregory A. Kimble, *Principles of General Psychology,* Copyright 1956, The Ronald Press Company. From data of Marcia H. Graves).

it is introduced after extensive amounts of continuous practice, the performance curve of the massed group will fail to jump to the level achieved by the spaced group. Figure 10.24 shows the amount of reminiscence occurring when the rest interval is introduced later in training. Although there is still evidence of reminiscence, the amount of improvement resulting from it is not large enough to permit the subjects whose practice has been massed to equal the performance of those whose practice has been distributed.

The phenomenon of reminiscence should remind you of the distinction between learning and performance. Although

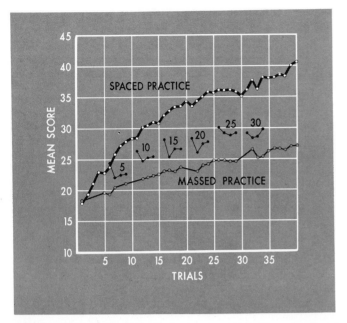

FIGURE 10.24 The Amount of Reminiscence at Different Stages of Learning the Reverse Alphabet Printing Task. The upper curve represents the performance of a spaced practice group having 30-second trials and 30-second intertrial intervals. The lower curve represents the performance of a massed practice group. The intermediate curves show the performance of massed practice groups following 10-minute rest intervals after different numbers of massed training trials. Reminiscence occurred at all stages of learning but only after five trials was it sufficiently great to allow the performance of the massed practice group to equal that of the spaced practice group (After Kimble, 1949).

massed practice results in performance inferior to that produced by spaced practice, it does not always produce poorer learning. If, as Figure 10.23 shows, a sufficiently long rest interval is allowed a subject who had received massed training, his performance after the rest period can attain the same level as that resulting from spaced practice, indicating that the learning of a massed practice subject is equal to that of the spaced learner. But if more massed training follows the rest interval, the subject will be unable to catch up with the spaced practice group even though he is allowed an additional rest period.

We are forced to conclude, therefore, that the advantage of spaced practice over massed practice in learning is not as great as performance curves indicate. In fact, the difference in performance can sometimes be completely misleading, as the considerable reminiscence produced by a rest interval testifies. But this is not by any means a refutation of the general principle we have been defending: that extensive amounts of massed training, or for that matter, spaced training, with very brief intervening rest periods, will in the long run result in poorer learning. In short, both training that is prolonged continuously and insufficient amounts of rest have a tendency to produce less effective learning.

Warm-up

There is another kind of sudden and sharp rise in the level of performance of a motor skill. Very often marked improvement in performance takes place during a practice period immediately after a long rest interval. This rapid improvement is appropriately known as the **warm-up** effect. Athletes often take advantage of this phenomenon. Before the batter strides up to the plate he may swing his bat a few times. The sprinter practices a few starts and brief runs. The golfer waggles his club before hitting the ball. The musician plays a few bars of music softly before the concert begins. The operatic soprano warbles some enchanting tones, while the jazz singer belts out a sample of her raucous notes before singing in earnest. These age-old practices of warming up receive solid support from the results of experiments. Figure 10.25 illustrates the improved performance on the pursuit rotor that results from warm-up.

Patterns of Movement

The *way* in which a motor skill is practiced is on the whole more important than when it is practiced. Unfortunately, laboratory scientists have largely overlooked this important variable. But it is not surprising that industrial psychologists and engineers, as well as athletic coaches, have devoted much attention to the effect that patterns of movement have in determining how well a motor skill will be performed.

Industrial psychologists and engineers have long been interested in the most economical way of performing a routine task, one that is repeated over and over. For practical reasons they try to discover what sequence of movements by a man or woman on the job will accomplish the greatest amount of work in the shortest time and with the least effort. About a half-century ago Frank Gilbreth (1911), who became famous as one of the early industrial "efficiency experts," showed how it was possible, by improving his pattern of movements, to increase the number of bricks a bricklayer could lay in an hour from 120 to 350, with no increase in fatigue. This early time-and-motion study and its strikingly practical results paved the way for other studies, such as how to operate a machine on an assembly line in such a way as to raise output dramatically.

In the field events of a track meet there are brilliant illustrations of how performance can be improved by introducing new patterns of movement. Over twenty years ago a couple of Americans participating in a track meet in Copenhagen noted the word *baseball* in the otherwise completely Danish program. It appeared there was to be a baseball-throwing event, so they decided to enter. The Danish contestants one and all ran up to the line and threw the baseball by swinging the whole arm stiffly and releasing the ball. Each throw was duly measured and recorded by the officials. Then one of the Americans threw the ball in the way he had learned as an American outfielder. It landed outside the stadium. That ended the event.

A few years ago a Basque by the name of Felix Erauzquin invented a new method of throwing the javelin. Until then this spearlike instrument was typically thrown by a running contestant who whipped it

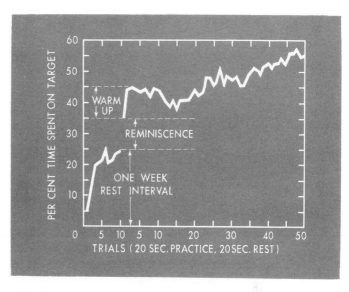

FIGURE 10.25 Improved Performance on a Pursuit Rotor Task Resulting From Warm-Up. A marked improvement occurred after the first trial following a rest interval of one week. The graph also shows the reminiscence phenomenon, an increase in the level of performance following a rest period with no intervening practice (After Pomeroy, 1944).

forward over his shoulder. The world record for this old-fashioned method was at the time approximately 275 feet. Erauzquin developed an entirely different pattern of movements. He first soaped his throwing hand, then grasped the javelin behind him and whirled it around three times as he ran forward to release it. With this method a throw of over 300 feet was not uncommon. The innovation, however, had one great shortcoming. The athlete had very little control over the direction in which his javelin would travel. So, for fear of skewering a spectator, the new method had to be outlawed.

Other novel patterns of movement can smash world records without endangering life and limb. Old-time shot-putters cradled the shot in the hand, skipped to the front of a restraining circle, and thrust the shot forward. The best put was about 53 feet. Then along came Jim Fuchs of Yale. By crouching lower and making a half turn he made greater use of leverage and momentum. He had no difficulty in putting

305

FIGURE 10.26 Felix Erauzquin Demonstrating His Method of Throwing the Javelin. He grasped the spear behind him and whirled it three times before releasing it. This method of throwing a javelin produced a number of throws over 300 feet. At the time the world record was about 275 feet (Wide World Photo).

the shot 58 feet. A successor, Parry O'Brien, then exaggerated everything Fuchs did. He increased his turn and crouched still lower. He finally raised the world record to 62 feet 6½ inches, which has since been excelled.

The facts of increased industrial productivity and broken athletic records show clearly how important is the pattern of movement involved in the execution of motor skills. Practicing the old-fashioned shot-putting method under optimal conditions of spaced practice and everything else could not possibly result in a performance equalling what was achieved by the Fuchs technique. No stress on the value of properly distributing practice should make us forget the extreme importance of how a skill is performed.

Verbal Learning

The term *verbal learning* covers a wide range of behavior. At one end of the range is a word functioning as a conditioned stimulus (see page 342). At the other extreme are highly abstract ideas creatively manipulated in order to solve the most formidable philosophical and scientific problems.

When the sound of a simple word operates as a conditioned stimulus, as in vasomotor conditioning (see page 155), the word is an isolated stimulus occurring alone. But most verbal behavior involves more than a single, isolated word because words are usually chained together, as in this sentence. In an attempt to discover some of the elementary principles that govern the linking together of words, psychologists have investigated two simple forms of verbal learning: the learning of paired associates and serial learning.

In studying both these kinds of learning

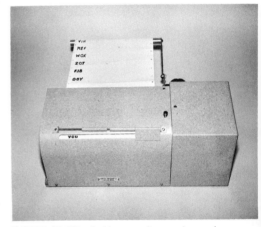

FIGURE 10.27 A Memory Drum. A word or nonsense syllable appears in the window. In paired-associate learning the subject learns to anticipate the response that is paired with a given stimulus term. In serial learning, which is illustrated here, the subject must learn to anticipate the next term in the list (Lafayette Instrument Co.).

a memory drum is commonly used. It is an electrically rotated drum with a sheet of printed material, which permits nonsense syllables (a three-letter syllable that is not a meaningful word, such as *rul*) or words to be exposed successively, each for a limited period of time. As the drum rotates, one item of the material to be memorized appears at a time in an open slit or window in front of which the subject sits, while the remainder of the material is hidden.

In the method of paired-associate learning, the subject must learn to associate one syllable or word with another. Typically these pairs of items are presented on a memory drum so that the first, or stimulus, member is exposed alone, followed after a short time interval by the second, or response, member. The subject's task is to react to the stimulus word by pronouncing or spelling the response syllable or word before it appears. The list of paired associates is presented in a different order on each successive trial. Table 10.1 shows a list of paired adjectives and the order in which it might appear on our successive trials.

Note that although the pairs are the same on each trial, they do not appear in the same order. The order is shifted on purpose to prevent the subject from simply memorizing the list of response words as they follow one another, and ignoring the stimulus words. On the first trial, when each stimulus word appears, the subject does not know what its associate may be. On the second and successive trials, the subject's task is to anticipate the response word when he sees the stimulus word. The subject is said to have "learned" the list when he meets some predetermined criterion such as being able to anticipate correctly, on two successive trials, all the response words.

Paired-associate learning is what you do in learning the vocabulary of a foreign language. In learning to read French you must at a very early stage respond to the stimulus word *le livre* with the response *the book*. Or when translating English into German you must respond to the stimulus word *the book* with the response word *das Buch*. Learning a radio code is another real-life situation that involves paired-asso-

TABLE 10.1 Lists of Eight Paired Adjectives Used in Paired Associate Learning. The pairs of adjectives are presented in different orders on successive trials to prevent the subjects from learning only a list of response terms without attending to the stimulus terms.

ORDER 1		ORDER 2	
Stimulus —	*Response*	*Stimulus* —	*Response*
merry —	hot	major —	various
safe —	green	first —	new
wild —	soft	many —	keen
many —	keen	happy —	late
major —	various	direct —	proper
happy —	late	merry —	hot
first —	new	wild —	soft
direct —	proper	safe —	green

ORDER 3		ORDER 4	
Stimulus —	*Response*	*Stimulus* —	*Response*
many —	keen	happy —	late
direct —	proper	many —	keen
safe —	green	merry —	hot
major —	various	direct —	proper
merry —	hot	wild —	soft
first —	new	major —	various
happy —	late	safe —	green
wild —	soft	first —	new

ciate learning. In receiving radio code it is necessary to respond to a very brief dot-sounding stimulus with the letter *e*. When sending radio code the response to the stimulus *e* is an abrupt pressure on a telegraph key.

Serial learning differs from paired-associate learning in that more than two words are chained together. A series of nonsense syllables, like the one in Table 10.2, is typically presented one at a time for as many runs as are necessary until the subject is able to recite the entire list in correct order. This kind of learning resembles the memorizing of prose or poetry. It requires learning not only the terms but also their correct order.

Simple verbal learning of the sort just described (sometimes referred to as **rote**

TABLE 10.2 List of Nonsense Syllables Used in Serial Learning Task. The syllables are presented one at a time in succession, and the subject's task is to anticipate each syllable before it appears in the window. Some symbol, an asterisk here, appears at the beginning of the list, and when the subject sees this, he must respond with the syllable *BEW*. When *BEW* then appears, it evokes the response *ZUR*. This in turn evokes the next response, and so on.

*

BEW

ZUR

VOD

JEK

NAX

TEP

DOY

KIB

ZOT

WOX

MEF

YIN

learning) resembles conditioning and simple motor learning in that the same variables operate. Practice is vitally important. Increasing practice in paired-associate or serial learning usually increases the amount learned. But a very important point to understand is that this is true only in those situations in which the learner is motivated to remember.

Many years ago a psychologist came across an interesting case in an experiment in which subjects were instructed to read aloud a series of eight syllables time after time until they felt they had memorized the list. At the forty-sixth repetition one subject still had failed to master the list. The psychologist was astonished, stopped the memory drum, and asked the subject whether he could recite the series. "What! Am I to learn the syllables by heart?" was the reply. He could not recite them and needed six more trials before he could. The subject had obviously misunderstood the instructions. The important point is that

in the absence of motivation—in this case the intention to recite the syllables without prompting—observing and repeating them were not sufficient to ensure learning (McGeoch & Irion, 1952).

Although students will claim that they fully understand the importance of motivation and practice in learning, they frequently forget how essential they are for doing well in school work. If a student slouches in his chair and doodles or daydreams during his professor's lecture, he is not justified in complaining bitterly over his failure to learn anything. Similarly, if he glances in a leisurely and passive way at the pages of his texts, he should not wonder later why his grades do not reflect the amount of time he thinks he has spent "studying." The reasons for his lack of academic success are obvious. He may suppose that he was listening and studying, because he knows at least that he was not doing anything else he enjoyed. Nevertheless, all this time he was not putting any real effort into what he was doing. He was not actively listening, taking meaningful notes, interpreting, comparing, recalling, relating, asking himself questions and digging up answers to them. These are the essentials of learning.

A student will be better off if he can keep from pretending that he is studying when actually he is unmotivated to do so. What he is really doing then is learning poor study habits—habits that are exceedingly difficult to break later on. The unmotivated student, in short, is doing something worse than squandering time. In fairness to students, we should admit, of course, that some lecturers and textbook writers are at fault in their poor presentation of material, but this is not nearly as often the case as easy-going, glibly rationalizing students would like us to believe.

That active study is necessary for learning to take place receives support from the fact that complete relaxation is not conducive to learning. A *slight* amount of skeletal muscular tension seems to be actually helpful in studying. When they were required to squeeze a hand dynamometer (an instrument for measuring the strength of grip) while learning lists of nonsense syllables students learned them more rapidly than they did at other times (Bills, 1927). The added muscular tension probably helped to maintain a higher level of activation (see page 259). Students should be warned against studying in ultracomfortable lounging chairs. Taking it easy and learning do not mix.

Different Types of Verbal Associations

We may draw on simple verbal learning to illustrate the highly integrated character of more complex forms of verbal behavior. When the subject learns a list of paired associates or a series of nonsense syllables, he is also forming many associations other than those he is required to learn. This is illustrated by both backward associations and remote associations.

Backward Associations. In learning paired associates the subject has been instructed to learn the association between each stimulus term and the response term paired with it. For example, if one pair is *ordinary-fragrant,* the subject learns to respond to the stimulus term *ordinary* with the response term *fragrant.* But there is a lot of experimental evidence to show that when a subject learns such an association between a preceding and following term he also tends to learn a backward association between the following term and the preceding one. Specifically, he learns to respond to *fragrant* with *ordinary.* Such an association is called a **backward association.**

In an experiment which illustrates this phenomenon, subjects required to learn a second list of paired associates in which the former stimulus and response terms were reversed (*A-B* are paired in that order in the original list, and *B-A* in the second list), learned the second list much more

rapidly than subjects who had not previously learned the first list (Murdock, 1956). This is evidence that backward associations (*B-A*) were also being formed while the forward associations (*A-B*) were being learned. In short, learning an *A-B* association facilitates the learning of a *B-A* association. Backward associations, then, it may have occurred to you, can interfere with the correct recall of something you have learned. In trying to recall even a familiar phone number you may become confused about the order of the numbers. Is it 643-9437 or 643-9473? Your fumbling and uncertainty demonstrate that forward and backward associations are competing.

Remote Associations. Experiments in serial learning have also provided evidence of the formation of associations other than those between adjacent words. In serial learning the subject often responds with the right syllable in the wrong place. For example, if he is learning the list of syllables in Table 10.2 he may respond to the second term *zur* with the fifth term *nax.* Such an error is known as an **anticipatory error.** Sometimes, but not nearly as often, the subject makes a **perseverative error;** he responds with a word that in an earlier place would have been correct. For example, in the place where the seventh syllable would be correct, he comes out with the third.

Both anticipatory and perseverative errors, sometimes referred to as **intrusion errors,** indicate that **remote associations** are being formed during serial learning. The subject associates an item not only with its subsequent item, as he has been instructed to do, but also to some extent with all other items in the list. Since not all remote associations occur as intrusions equally often, we may conclude that they are not all of the same strength. The strength of a remote association, as revealed by the likelihood that it will intrude, is proportional to its degree of remoteness. A syllable that is correct two items later is more likely to occur than one that is correct three or more items later. Using the material in Table 10.2 for example, when the syllable *vod* is in the window of the memory drum, the subject is more likely to make the mistake of responding with *nax* than with *tep* or *zot*. Or in recalling the phone number 643-9437, a person is more likely to dial 643-9473 than 743-9436.

The tendency to form remote associations makes serial learning more difficult. At each point in the list the correct association must compete successfully with all the remote associations. That erroneous responses are made testifies to the fact that the conflict between competing responses is not always resolved without error. Remote associations do not reveal themselves only in actual intrusion errors. Sometimes a subject is incapable of responding out loud at all because the competition between the correct association and one or more that are remote and incorrect is so balanced that he is for a time speechless.

Remote associations make their appearance in everyday activities. When we are typing we often omit words because we tend to make anticipatory errors. Or phrases are frequently repeated, that is, they perseverate. The school child is a victim of his remote associations when he leaves out a section of the poem he is reciting.

PROBABILITY LEARNING

In recent years psychologists have been very interested in a new kind of learning experiment. In **probability learning** the subject is confronted with a simple choice between two alternatives on any one trial. For example, simply by guessing, he must pull either a red or black lever. If he makes the "correct" response a light flashes, and that constitutes reinforcement. The sub-

ject's job is to make as many correct responses as possible.

The experimenter has arranged the situation so that each lever is correct only a certain percentage of the time. If within a given setting of the machine the red lever is correct for 70 per cent of the trials, then the black lever will be correct for the remaining 30 per cent. The trials for which the red lever is correct and the ones for which the black lever is correct are randomized, that is, distributed in no fixed order. On any one trial the subject has no cue to indicate which of the two levers will be correct, although he does believe some pattern governs the sequence of correct choices.

The reason that probability learning has captured the interest of psychologists is that a mathematical theory has been proposed to predict the behavior of subjects in such a situation. The mathematical theory, largely statistical in nature, is not very complex, although it is a little too advanced for a first course in psychology. We shall therefore skip the details of the theory and concentrate upon its major predictions.

The theory predicts that after *prolonged* training with a given setting of the machine the subject will choose a given lever on the same percentage of trials that has arbitrarily been made correct by the experimenter. This means that in the setting we have mentioned he will select the red lever on 70 per cent of the trials, the black lever on 30 per cent. And this turns out to be essentially what happens. A large number of studies have shown that in such a learning situation, the subject will choose one of the two alternatives approximately the same percentage of times that that response has been reinforced. Nevertheless, this pattern of responding is not the smartest he might adopt. Consider that if the subject should choose the red lever 100 per cent of the time he would be correct on 70 per cent of the trials. When, however, he chooses the red lever only 70 per cent of the time and the black lever the remaining 30 per cent, his total percentage of correct responses will turn out to be appreciably less than 70 per cent. This follows from simple probability theory. When he chooses the red lever he is going to be correct on the average seven out of ten times. Thus 70 choices of the red lever will produce approximately 49 correct choices. When he chooses the black lever he is going to be correct three out of ten times, so 30 choices of the black lever will produce on the average nine correct responses. Consequently, during a series of 100 trials, subjects will make on the average 58 correct responses. This is an appreciably poorer score than the 70 correct responses that would result if he adopted the strategy of always choosing the lever that is correct a majority of the times.

In addition to predicting the percentage of responses to each lever when the choices have become stabilized after long training, the mathematical theory predicts how the percentage of responses will change if training is continued still longer but with a new distribution of reinforcements. Figure 10.28 shows the percentage of choices of the red lever made by a group of students for whom the red lever was initially correct for 85 per cent of the trials and then correct for only 30 per cent of the trials. The ordinate represents percentages of the choice of the red lever and the abscissa represents the number of trials. The small circles indicate the results of the experiment, and the continuous line indicates the theoretical predictions at various stages of training. As you can see, the mathematical theory predicts with considerable accuracy both the trend of change in the subjects' choices and the final level of preference attained. Probability learning, a fascinating topic in its own right, has proved to be a source of fruitful hypotheses for psychologists, such as W. K. Estes (1959), who formulate mathematical theories that apply to the facts of conditioning and other learning phenom-

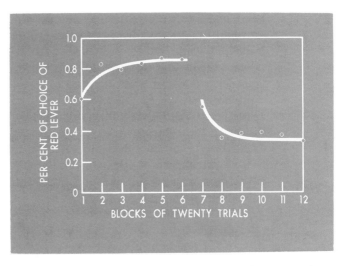

FIGURE 10.28 The Accuracy of a Mathematical Theory in Predicting Behavior in Probability Learning. The dots represent the obtained results, whereas the continuous line indicates the theoretical predictions. The theory obviously predicts the results very closely (After Estes & Straughan, 1954).

ena. Their work is an especially good illustration of how mathematics has become an important tool in psychology, just as it has in other sciences.

TRANSFER OF TRAINING

Up to this point we have been examining the behavior of organisms in a more or less unchanging environment. The conditioned stimulus in classical conditioning remains constant from trial to trial; the bar in the Skinner box stays in the same position; the same list of nonsense syllables is repeated over and over again in simple verbal learning. But most animal organisms, and human beings especially, move about from one situation to another in their everyday lives. The child goes from his home, where his mother tells him what to do, to the classroom, where his teacher tells him what to do. You listen, we assume, to your psychology instructor during one period and then go to hear another instructor expound perhaps differential calculus, perhaps anthropology. Meanwhile, the professor, after concluding his lecture, goes home and lectures his wife and children (or vice versa?). Now, if we ask whether anyone's behavior in one situation is completely insulated from his behavior in other situations or whether the consequences of his learning something are confined to the situation in which he learned it, the answer to both questions is going to be an unequivocal "No!"

What we learn in a particular environment tends to transfer to other situations. In learning to multiply, the child who has learned to add numbers enjoys a considerable advantage over the child who knows nothing about addition. The person who has exchanged his old automobile license plate for a new one has more difficulty remembering the new number than a person who has just gotten his first license plate. The former will tend to confuse the old number with the new, whereas the latter will not be handicapped by such habit competition.

Transfer of training refers to the influence which learning one task may have upon the subsequent learning or performance of another task. The following example, purposely uncomplicated by distracting details, illustrates the principle involved in three different kinds of transfer. Suppose a group of college students is required to learn Task B. They are able to do this, on the average, in ten trials. However, another group of students who had previously learned Task A is able to accomplish the same feat in five trials. This is evidence that learning Task A has influenced the learning of Task B, making it easier. **Positive transfer** of training is said to have taken place. Since the normal number of trials required to learn Task B was shown to be ten and this number was cut to five by the prior learning of Task A, the transfer from Task A to Task B is said to be positive, that is, it has aided in learning

the second task ($10 - 5 = +5$). In short, positive transfer occurs when the learning of one task is facilitated by the prior learning of another task.

But sometimes transfer is in the opposite direction. If Task A is such that subjects who have previously learned it need 15 trials to learn Task B, whereas they require only ten trials when they have had no previous experience with Task A, then **negative transfer** ($10 - 15 = -5$) is said to have taken place. Another way of referring to negative transfer is to say that the learning of A interferes with or retards the learning of B.

The amount of transfer of training between two different tasks is often minimal, and may even be zero. If the learning of Task B with or without the previous training on A requires ten trials, then the amount of transfer between Tasks A and B is zero ($10 - 10 = 0$). Although, understandably, no one has yet been foolish enough to try to prove it, the amount of transfer between learning to tie a bow tie and learning how to bake a cake is doubtless zero.

The concept of transfer of training is introduced here by name for the first time, but its principle should be familiar to you. Stimulus generalization (see page 159) may be considered an example of transfer of training. An association formed between a conditioned stimulus and a conditioned response will transfer to stimuli similar to the conditioned stimulus. In short, an organism can be rapidly trained to respond to a stimulus if he has previously been trained to make the same response to a similar stimulus.

Are there general principles involved in transfer of training that apply to many different kinds of tasks, or is each case of transfer unique and due to some particular psychological mechanism? Or, to ask a closely related question, is there any general theory to account for transfer of training when it does occur? The answers to these questions will appear as we review some of the more important facts of transfer.

Stimulus and Response Similarity

The method of paired associates is a form of learning well adapted to investigate the influence of stimulus and response similarity upon transfer of training. Subjects can be trained to learn two successive lists of paired associates in which either or both the stimulus and the response terms are varied. In this way we can determine how changes in stimuli or in responses affect transfer of training.

Stimulus Similarity. Higher than any degree of similarity is identity; nothing could be more like the nonsense syllable *req* than the nonsense syllable *req*. When subjects learn two successive lists of paired associates in which the stimulus elements are the same but the response terms are changed (*req-kiv* in list *A, req-zam* in list *B*), negative transfer results. The reason for the negative transfer is obvious. When a subject encounters the stimulus syllable (*req*) while he is learning the second list, he has a strong tendency to respond with the response syllable (*kiv*) that was previously correct but no longer is. If he was learning the second list without having learned the first he would not be so handicapped. He would have only to learn the new association and not to unlearn (extinguish) the old one as well. In short, his learning would not be retarded by **associative interference,** an old association interfering with the learning of a new one (Bruce, 1933; Porter & Duncan, 1953).

The next question is, What sort of transfer results when the response terms are different and the stimulus elements are similar, but not identical? After learning *req-kiv*, would the learning of *rec-zam* be easier or more difficult? It would, of course, be definitely more difficult. The principle

that operates in such situations is that the greater the similarity in stimulus elements when the response items change, the greater the amount of negative transfer. The greatest amount of negative transfer occurs when the stimulus items are identical. As they become less similar, the amount of negative transfer decreases until there is no similarity and zero transfer.

Negative transfer is a common everyday occurrence. We frequently find ourselves in situations which may be similar to or even identical to ones we have experienced previously, but in which new responses are required. In many cars the hand brake is to the left of the steering wheel, but in some it is to the right. A person driving one of these cars for the first time will probably automatically reach in the wrong place for the hand brake. Changing the place where you carry your wallet or purse will also result in associative interference. If you now decide to place your wallet in your jacket instead of in your hip pocket, or your purse in the left side of your handbag instead of the right, you will be very likely to fumble around when you want it.

Negative transfer is not just a matter of inconvenience. During World War II, with our industrial capacity straining at the seams and war planes being produced at many different factories throughout the country, little attention was paid to standardizing the arrangement of the instrument dials in the cockpit. One fighter pilot reports what we would call an experience of negative transfer in these words.

We had an alert one morning, because about 35 Japanese planes had been picked up on the radar screen. In the mad scramble for planes, the one I had happened to pick out was a brand-new ship which had arrived about two days previously. I climbed in, and it seemed that the whole cockpit was rearranged. Finally, I got it started, but the Japs hit about that time. The rest of the gang had gotten off and were climbing up to altitude. I took a look at that instrument panel and viewed the gauges around me, sweat falling off my brow. The first bomb dropped just about 100 yards from operations. I figured then and there I wasn't going to take it off, but I sure could run it on the ground. That's exactly what I did—ran it all around the field, up and down the runway, during the attack (Fitts & Jones, 1961, p. 387).

Less serious cases of negative transfer may still be of great importance. The child whose mother has done everything for him is at a loss when he is put in a schoolroom with 20 other active children and has to learn to do for himself all the little things that the teacher will not and cannot help him with at every moment. When such a dependent child is abruptly put in this situation, he is likely to feel helpless and neglected and is bound to create trouble for himself and everyone else with his demands and misbehavior. It may take the skill of a clinical psychologist or a psychiatrist to overcome the negative transfer effects of his overindulgence at home and to establish a clear-cut discrimination between the home situation and school.

Associative interference can operate in marriage. The boy whose mother slaved to maintain a clean and orderly household may suffer rudely from the effects of negative transfer, when he marries a woman (probably a college graduate?) who does not share his mother's high standards of neatness or skill in running a household. He will be shocked by the changed environment he must adjust to. Having been trained to expect a neatly made bed, shiny dishes, dusted furniture, and unburned food, he will be sullen and resentful at unmade beds, dirty dishes stacked in the sink, dust everywhere, and charcoal toast for breakfast. Although discussions of future housekeeping techniques usually do not intrude upon the bliss of courtship, marriage counselors (many are clinical psychologists) will testify that learned differences about what constitutes good housekeeping can get a marriage off to a dismal start.

Response Similarity. The learning of paired associates, which is a particularly suitable method of investigating the effects of stimulus similarity on transfer of training, is equally appropriate for studying the influence of *response similarity*. Two lists of paired nonsense syllables can be arranged with a different stimulus item in each pair but with identical response terms (*zam-req* in list *A*, *kiv-req* in list *B*). When a subject learns lists of items of this sort successively, he experiences positive transfer. Having learned a response to one stimulus, he finds it easier to associate the same response to a new stimulus. The amount of positive transfer is positively correlated (see page 70) with the degree of similarity between the new and the old response terms.

Why are there positive transfer effects when the same response is appropriate in two different situations? This is not an easy question to answer; psychologists do not as yet fully understand the nature of response similarity. It does seem, however, that a basic factor is that responses themselves have to be learned. Before *req* can be associated with any stimulus, it must first be learned. That is, paired associate learning involves two processes: first, learning the response term, and second, learning when to perform it. Positive transfer occurs when the response terms are identical in two successive lists, because the first of the two learning processes is completed before the second list begins to be learned.

It is also easier to learn a second motor task when it involves responses similar to those in the first task. For example, the skill learned in pouring a liquid from one vessel to another transfers to a variety of similar situations. Pouring is a complex skill involving a chain of appropriate movements. In order to learn this task, one must form associations between response-produced cues and subsequent movements. Once the sequence of movements is learned, one can transfer the response easily from one situation to another, from pouring milk from a bottle into a glass to pouring coffee from a percolator into a cup. Or, less obviously because less similarity is involved, once a child has learned to say "Dada," he may find it easier to say "Mama," though to an entirely different stimulus, because both vocalizations involve partly identical muscular movements in the throat and mouth.

Other Forms of Transfer

All cases of transfer cannot be categorized as simple examples of either stimulus or response similarity. Sometimes both of these factors interact to produce transfer between tasks that are apparently dissimilar.

Mediated Transfer. In **mediated transfer** (sometimes called mediated generalization) an organism learns to make a new response to an old stimulus with relative ease because he has previously learned an intermediate response which functions as a cue to mediate transfer from the first situation to the second. In one study (Gagné & Baker, 1950), representative of a number of others, college students first learned to respond to each of four different light stimuli by saying a different letter (*J, V, S,* or *M*). Following this the subjects were required to respond to each of the same four light stimuli by pressing one of four switches. The speed with which the subjects learned this second task was highly related to how well they had learned the association between the lights and the verbal stimuli. This would seem to contradict the generalization that learning new responses to old stimuli produces negative transfer. Here, however, the subjects found it easier to make a particular motor response to each of the lights because they had already learned to make a particular verbal re-

sponse to each of them. The first verbal responses served as cues which enhanced the difference between the four lights and helped the subjects make the motor discrimination.

Learning How to Learn. If you were required to learn successive lists of dissimilar nonsense syllables, the ease with which you could learn the later lists would increase. Figure 10.29 shows the results of an experiment in which the same subjects learned consecutively 16 lists of 12 nonsense syllables each. Their score continually improved, until they were able to learn the later lists in less than half the number of trials they required to learn the first one. This positive transfer occurred even though there was no marked similarity among the items of the 16 lists. The subjects, it would seem, learned not only specific lists of nonsense syllables, but also a general technique of learning that improved their performance on successive lists.

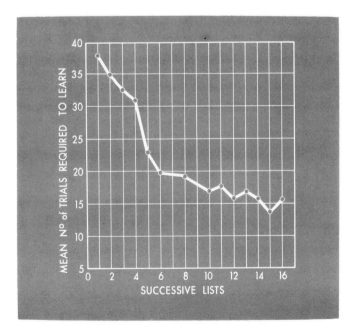

FIGURE 10.29 The Mean Number of Trials Required for a Subject to Learn 16 Successive Lists of Nonsense Syllables (After Ward, 1937).

316   Perhaps the most extensive work on learning to learn has been carried out with monkeys. These particular monkeys learned more than 300 discrimination problems in succession. In each of them the monkeys attempted to select one of two stimulus objects that contained food (see Figure

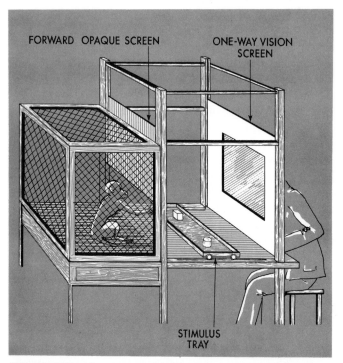

FORWARD OPAQUE SCREEN   ONE-WAY VISION SCREEN

STIMULUS TRAY

FIGURE 10.30   The Wisconsin General Test Apparatus for Presenting Discrimination Problems to Monkeys. A tray on which there are two stimulus objects, one of which (the positive stimulus) covers a piece of food, is pushed within the monkey's reach and withdrawn immediately after he has made a choice (After Harlow, 1949).

10.30). The positive (reinforced) and negative (nonreinforced) stimuli were small objects of great variety. In one problem which consisted of a series of trials, the subject had to discriminate between an aspirin tin and a small jar. The next problem required discrimination between two entirely different objects. Because each task was different you might think that the learning in each successive problem would have to start afresh. The monkeys, however, improved their performance on successive

tasks. This was clearly revealed by the kind of choices they made on the second trial of each problem. There could, of course, be no cue to indicate the correct stimulus on the first trial. If the subject guessed correctly on the first trial, then on the second trial he would only have to choose the same stimulus to be correct thereafter; if he made an error on the first trial, then the other stimulus would automatically be the one he should choose next. The responses made on the second trial of the first few problems were correct approximately half of the time. After 25 tasks had been mastered, the subjects made 70 per cent correct choices on the second trial of each task. This percentage increased to 80 per cent after the learning of 100 tasks, to 88 per cent after 200 tasks, and finally to 95 per cent after 300. If, for example, the three hundred and first discrimination in the series was between a Coca-Cola bottle cap (positive stimulus) and a soap dish (negative stimulus), 95 per cent of the subjects would choose the cap on the second trial and continue to choose the cap thereafter, regardless of whether their very first choice had been right or wrong. Thus, after a long series of separate tasks, all of the same type, the first trial usually provided sufficient information for the animal to continue solving the problem correctly.

Since each of the successive discrimination problems was different, what was it that actually transferred, that could account for what may seem an amazing degree of success? In discrimination problems such as the kind the monkeys had to solve, there was much to learn besides the correct stimulus. The subjects had to learn to pay attention to an area of their environment limited to the objects on the stimulus tray. They also had to learn to abandon any preference they might, and usually did have at first for the object on either the left or right (the correct stimulus was shifted from side to side in a random sequence). They also had to learn that one stimulus was consistently right, while the other was consistently wrong. Although these habits alone would not serve to identify the correct stimulus in a new discrimination problem, they help the subject to locate it very rapidly. For, with the help of these habits, the subjects finally learned to respond appropriately after having received the cue provided by the first trial of a new problem. After encountering 300 such discriminations the subjects had learned to select on 95 per cent of the second trials any stimulus cue that led to reinforcement and to shift away from one that did not.

Interesting variations of the "learning how to learn," or what are sometimes called **learning sets,** experiments have been introduced with a technique known as **reversal learning.** In this kind of experiment the animal subject first learns a simple discrimination, to choose black in a black-white discrimination or to go left in a T maze. After the subject has learned this, he is trained to reverse his choice, to choose white or to go right. This proves to be a very difficult problem even for higher animals to solve, for they persist in responding to the stimulus that was originally correct, just as they persist in making a conditioned response during experimental extinction. But finally, the previously correct association becomes weaker and the animal begins to make the competing response that is now correct more frequently. Slowly the percentage of correct responses increases until finally the subject reaches the criterion of learning. However, after the animal has been given a series of reversal learning problems, he requires an appreciably shorter time for any one such reversal. With extended training some animals can learn to make the reversal shift (shift from correct black to correct white) in one trial, that is, after only one "extinction" experience with black. After a stimulus has been consistently rewarded one nonreinforcement provides the cue for such an animal to shift his response to the other stimulus.

The speed with which a given species of animal can be taught to make a reversal of this kind seems to be closely related to its place in evolutionary development. Humans, possessing language, can solve even a first reversal learning problem with great rapidity (Kendler & Kendler, 1962). Monkeys can learn to perform equally well after a series of reversal learning tasks (Harlow, 1949), but isopods, a small relative of the crab and shrimp with a very primitive brain, do not improve their performance at all during a series of reversal learning tasks (Thompson, 1957). This collection of data has been interpreted as suggesting that the ease of positive transfer in a reversal learning task may be intimately related to the ability of an organism to respond to his own response-produced cues. As we ascend the evolutionary scale we seem to find a greater and greater degree of this ability.

Cross Education. Of importance in a discussion of the concept of response similarity are the facts of **cross education:** the positive transfer of a skill acquired by one part of the body to another part. Some biology teachers have the knack of drawing simultaneously with their right and left hands the two symmetrical though reversed halves of a cross-section diagram. Originally they learned to draw the whole diagram with their preferred hand, and then the skill was transferred from the preferred hand to the other. A number of motor skills such as ball tossing, mirror-drawing (see page 299), and dart throwing have been used by psychologists to demonstrate the phenomenon of **bilateral transfer**—a special class of cross education involving the transfer of a skill from one limb to its opposite member. Transfer has even been shown to occur between a hand and a foot (Cook, 1934). After human subjects had learned to move a stylus by hand along a winding groove which they could not see, they were fitted with a sandal with a stylus attached to the

318

sole, and they proceeded to trace the groove with their feet much more efficiently than did other subjects who had had no previous training with their hands. Similar results were obtained when the initial training involved the foot and the test for transfer, the hand.

The facts of cross education raise an interesting theoretical problem. Since the same muscles are not involved in the action of different limbs, positive transfer cannot be attributed simply to common muscular movements. The answer is that transfer in general, and cross education in particular, depends upon certain controlling brain centers from which motor pathways lead to different groups of muscles.

Transposition. A phenomenon known as **transposition** and somewhat akin to stimulus generalization is illustrated by the following experiment. First, chickens were trained by consistent reinforcement to discriminate between two grays differing in brightness by making a response to the brighter gray. Following training the sub-

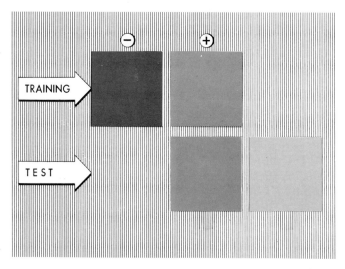

FIGURE 10.31 The Phenomenon of Transposition. First, subjects learn to choose a medium gray in preference to a darker gray. After learning this discrimination, they are confronted with the same medium gray and a brighter gray. Transposition is made when they choose the brighter gray.

jects were confronted with a single test trial involving the bright gray they had learned to choose and another still brighter gray. Which one did they choose? The same bright stimulus which they had learned to respond to because it had hitherto been reinforced or the new brighter stimulus? A majority of chickens chose the new brighter stimulus. In short, the subjects *transposed* their positive response to the brighter of two stimuli from one pair to another, even though this required them to avoid the stimulus identical to the one they had previously responded positively to.

Psychologists are not agreed upon the correct interpretation of such a transposition experiment. Some believe that transposition is evidence that in a discrimination problem an animal learns to respond to the relationship (in this case relative brightness) between the two stimuli rather than to the positive stimulus alone (Kohler, 1929). Others find this explanation inadequate. It fails to explain why in the test trial just described some animals chose the stimulus that was now the darker of the two, but had been the brighter in the training series. Moreover, additional experimentation has shown that the tendency to transpose varies with different test stimuli. In general, it decreases as the difference between the test pair of stimuli and the original training pair increases (Kendler, 1950; Alberts & Ehrenfreund, 1951). Obviously, something different from a simple relational response must have been learned. One hypothesis is that transposition can be explained on principles derived from conditioning, most notably stimulus generalization (Spence, 1937). A related theory (Riley, 1958), based upon our knowledge that the brightness of an object is influenced by its surroundings (see Figure 6.16 on page 124), suggests that both perceptual and conditioning principles must be used in explaining transposition.

Regardless of its underlying mechanisms, transposition is important because it shows that a reaction to a relationship can be transferred from one situation to another.

Education and Transfer of Training

Over 50 years ago it was common for a high school to require all students to study both Latin and mathematics. One of the reasons given for this curricular requirement was that intellectual abilities (*then* more often called *faculties*), like muscles, could be strengthened through exercise. Many people believed that Latin and mathematics would "discipline the mind" by strengthening the ability to reason, to grasp relationships, to infer correct principles, etc., etc. These educational assumptions, lumped together and known as the theory of *formal discipline,* received a terrible jolt when they were subjected to experimental test. In 1924 Edward L. Thorndike, a famous educational psychologist, compared the reasoning ability of students who had studied mathematics with those who had not. Since no appreciable difference was discovered, this upset the assumption of positive transfer between studying mathematics and the ability to reason in general. Studies of this sort were cited by educators as justification for abandoning the requirement that all high school students take the traditional courses in languages, mathematics, and science. Unless a student is going to need such subjects for his future life work, the argument went, there is no need for him to study them.

Today, psychologists and educators are taking a second look at this policy. They are not reopening the old issue of formal discipline and searching for some way in which the learning of Latin can be shown to benefit automatically the intellectual processes in general. But they see that Latin, like any other school subject, can be taught in a variety of ways, and when Latin is taught, as one study proved, with special attention to word derivation, the students'

gain in English vocabulary is twice as great as when Latin is taught by conventional methods (Haskell, 1923). They are now attempting to teach arithmetic in a manner that will increase its transfer to the study of algebra. Arithmetic and algebra, after all, have many principles in common. If it is possible to teach students the principles that govern both of these branches of mathematics, one may confidently expect that the study of arithmetic will speed the mastery of algebra. Similarly, new methods of teaching science are coming to the fore. No longer is emphasis upon clean white laboratory coats, precise work habits, sharp pencils, memorized lists of impressive technical terms, and neat notes thought to teach the essence of scientific method. However desirable such things may be in themselves, emphasis upon them alone does not produce scientists. Today educators believe that if a student grasps the basic principles of experimental method in his courses in physics, chemistry, biology, or psychology, this should, through positive transfer, accelerate his progress in any science.

How the teaching of principles can produce positive transfer has been demonstrated by a neat and simple experiment (Hendrickson & Schroeder, 1941). Two groups of boys shot with rifles at a target submerged in water. After both groups were able to hit the target fairly consistently, the depth of the water was changed. One group was then taught the principles of light refraction, so they understood what the consequences of changing the depth of the water would be and could adjust their aiming to the new situation. The other group was taught nothing. The group that had learned how light is refracted by passing through water performed significantly better in a second session of target shooting. Their greater skill resulted from understanding the principles that underlie the two different situations and can thus be attributed to mediated transfer.

320

The principles, operating in the same way that a response-produced cue does, bridged the two physically dissimilar situations and enabled the first group of boys to use their marksman's skill in both.

FORGETTING

It may seem odd to include the topic of forgetting in a chapter on learning. Isn't forgetting, you ask, the opposite of learning? Since we learn by practicing, don't we forget by failing to practice? The answer,

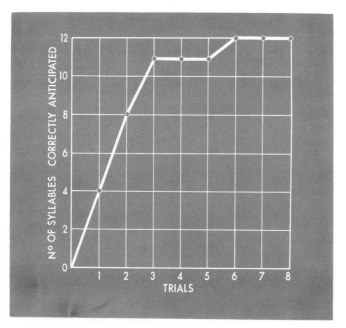

FIGURE 10.32 The Performance of a Subject Learning a List of 12 Nonsense Syllables. The number of syllables correctly anticipated increases in successive trials.

surprisingly, is "No." Forgetting is primarily the result either of failure to learn or learning to forget. But before we explain this seemingly paradoxical statement, we must introduce some new terms and their meanings, which will be needed in describ-

ing what is measured in experiments on forgetting.

Recall, Forgetting, and Retention. Learning and forgetting are intimately related in experimental work. Figure 10.32 shows the trial-by-trial scores of a subject learning a list of 12 nonsense syllables. On the first trial, not having met the list before, he made no correct responses. On the second trial four of his responses were correct, which means that he anticipated—that is, **recalled**—four syllables as a result of his one previous exposure to the list. On the third trial he recalled eight syllables. Since he recalled only four syllables on the second trial and by the third he was able to recall eight syllables, we infer that he learned four more. Learning in this instance is inferred from the greater number of correctly recalled items; it increases in proportion to increases in the recall score. Although Figure 10.32 is conventionally referred to as a learning curve, it could have just as appropriately been called a curve of recalling.

Now we will explain the difference in meaning between **forgetting** and **retention**. If you have learned a list of 12 nonsense syllables, that is, are able to recall all 12, but two hours later are able to recall only four, you are said to have retained four and forgotten eight, or in terms of percentages, you have retained 33 per cent of the material and forgotten 67 per cent. Or if you have learned the English equivalents of one thousand German words and one year later can recall 800, you have retained 80 per cent and have forgotten 20 per cent. In a test for recall the sum of the amount retained and amount forgotten must equal 100 per cent. Figure 10.33 shows a curve of forgetting based upon data gathered by Ebbinghaus (see page 43). It shows the percentage retained after the lapse of different lengths of time following learning. As the percentage forgotten increases, the amount of retention decreases.

Forgetting Due to Failure to Learn

It is of course incorrect to speak of forgetting anything that one had not previously learned. Forgetting is measured by inability to recall *after learning has taken place,* but in everyday life failure really to have learned something is probably the most common reason for so-called lapses of memory. A person who complains about his inability to remember names has usually failed to learn those names in the first place. When he is introduced to Mr. Reldnek, for example, he says, "Hello" or "Glad to meet you," and grasps Mr. Reldnek's outstretched hand. Soon they part and when they meet again he fails to recall Mr. Reldnek's name or possibly even to recognize his face. Similar behavior in learning paired associates would mean the subject had neither looked at the stimulus word nor recited the response term, a procedure guaranteed to produce zero recall. If this person was really interested in remembering Mr. Reldnek's name, he should have taken the opportunity when they first met to practice the association between Mr. Reldnek's face and his name. He should have used the name as much as he felt was decent, saying: "I'm glad to meet you, Mr. Reldnek"; "I have heard a good deal about you, Mr. Reldnek," while he was talking to him and looking directly at him. And he might have ended with, "I hope to see you again soon, Mr. Reldnek." If he had followed this routine he would have remembered Mr. Reldnek's name—although both of them might wish that he could forget it.

Failure to learn is also one of the most common reasons why students are unable to recall the correct answer to an examination question. "Professor, I read the textbook and read my notes several times before the exams. I don't see why my grade should be so low unless the test isn't fair."

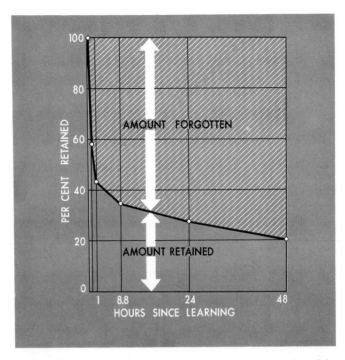

FIGURE 10.33 A Curve of Forgetting Based on Data Obtained by Ebbinghaus (1913). This curve shows the relation between retention and forgetting; as one increases the other decreases.

But a passive reading of your notes, or the textbook (see page 308), is not a guarantee that you are learning anything. Learning requires active rehearsal of what is to be learned; it means recalling relevant information, grasping principles that underlie details, memorizing key facts, asking questions and answering them—in short, studying. In one experiment—which used simplified material and thus does not illustrate all the principles of active study—five groups of students were required to memorize a series of nonsense syllables (Gates, 1917). One group spent the entire time allotted to the experiment silently reading and rereading the list of syllables. The other groups divided the same amount of time between straight reading and active recitation, with each group devoting to rehearsal a fixed percentage of time ranging from 20 per cent to 80 per cent. All the groups were tested for recall four hours after exposure to the material. Figure 10.34 shows the results of the test. The amount the students learned in the same length of time increased progressively with the percentage of time spent in recital. The group that recited during 80 per cent of their study time recalled more than three times as much as the group that read silently the entire time, even though this 0 per cent rehearsal group had been instructed to concentrate on learning and not to gaze emptily at the assignment while dreaming of other things, as some students who imagine they are studying do.

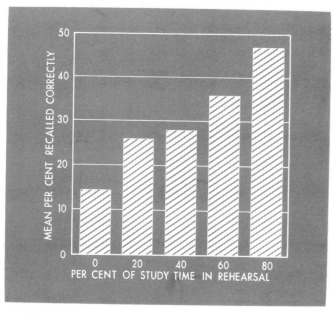

FIGURE 10.34 The Effect of Rehearsal on Retention. All groups spent the same amount of time memorizing a list of nonsense syllables, but they differed in the percentage of time they rehearsed actively (After Gates, 1917).

Learning to Forget

Most nonpsychologists believe that merely the passage of time produces forgetting. This widely held idea, which claims that failing to practice what has once been learned will of itself result in progressive forgetting as time passes, is called the **theory of disuse.** Basic to it is an assumption that learning leaves a trace in the nervous system which automatically fades or dissipates with time. The experimental data reported in Figure 10.33 on page 321 would on the surface appear to be consistent with the theory of disuse, since the amount of forgetting increases with time. But although it is reasonable and there are data that seem to support it, there are certain other facts that require us to reconsider the theory. First, if the claim that disuse alone operates to produce inability to recall, *any* length of time that elapses should produce some loss in memory. The facts of reminiscence (see page 303) deny this; retention actually improves following a brief time interval of no practice.

Second, if the theory of disuse is correct, we would expect additional practice always to result in improved retention. The facts of experimental extinction contradict this expectation. Responses are eliminated when they are practiced *in the absence of reinforcement.*

Third, instances of excellent retention following the passage of long time intervals are numerous. During a period of one year a person may forget many things, but not how to skate or swim or ski. People are often surprised to discover how well they can play ping-pong or bowl or drive a car although they have done none of these things for many years. Some skills appear to be capable of resisting the so-called dissipating effects of time. Dogs have retained conditioned responses over a period of two years, during which time no practice occurred (Wendt, 1937). A pigeon has been known to peck readily at a circular disk after six years had elapsed since the last reinforcement of this particular response (Skinner, 1953), even though six years are more than half of a pigeon's normal life span. Why doesn't disuse operate in these instances?

The three lines of evidence that seem inconsistent with the theory of disuse direct our attention to another factor that may play an important role in forgetting. Perhaps it is not time itself but rather what happens between learning and recall that is the important factor. A famous experiment (Jenkins & Dallenbach, 1924) shows the importance of intervening activity on the ability to remember. Two Cornell University undergraduates dedicated a two-month period of their lives to serving as subjects in an experiment designed to discover whether forgetting occurred more readily during sleep or during wakefulness. The subjects learned lists of nonsense syllables and then were tested for recall one, two, four, *or* eight hours after. Sometimes the subjects slept during the time that intervened between learning and recall; at other times they stayed awake and went about the daily activities of college undergraduates. The results are reported in Figure 10.35. It is quite clear that more forgetting occurs during waking hours. For each of the time intervals that intervened between learning and recall, retention was greater when the subject spent it asleep. It is also interesting to note that after the first two hours of sleep there was no additional loss in retention; the subjects recalled approximately the same number of syllables after two, four, or eight hours of sleep. From this study we must conclude that differences in intervening activities are responsible for differences in amount of forgetting.

The beneficial effects of inactivity on recall have also been demonstrated with the lowly cockroach (Minami & Dallenbach, 1946). A number of cockroaches were taught to avoid darkness by pairing darkness with an electric shock. After this avoidance conditioning some of them were immobilized by placing them in a small tube lined with soft paper (a cockroach placed in such a tube will remain inactive for hours), while others were allowed to remain active in a cage. When tested for retention of their conditioning against darkness, it was found that the inactive cockroaches had practically perfect retention, whereas the active cockroaches gave evidence of considerable forgetting.

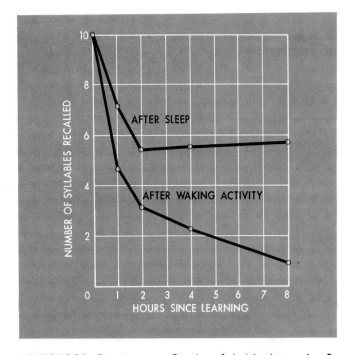

FIGURE 10.35 Retention as a Function of Activity Intervening Between Learning and Recall. This graph shows the relative effects of sleep and waking activity on recall of nonsense syllables (After Jenkins & Dallenbach, 1924).

The relation between intervening activities and retention has been systematically investigated in a transfer-of-training type of experiment that demonstrates what is technically known as **retroactive inhibition.** In the common transfer-of-training experiment the subject learns one task (*B*) to see how this affects the learning of another task (*A*). In a study of retroactive inhibition the subject learns *B* to determine how it influences the *retention* of *previously* learned *A*. The design of such an experiment is represented in Figure 10.36. Both the ex-

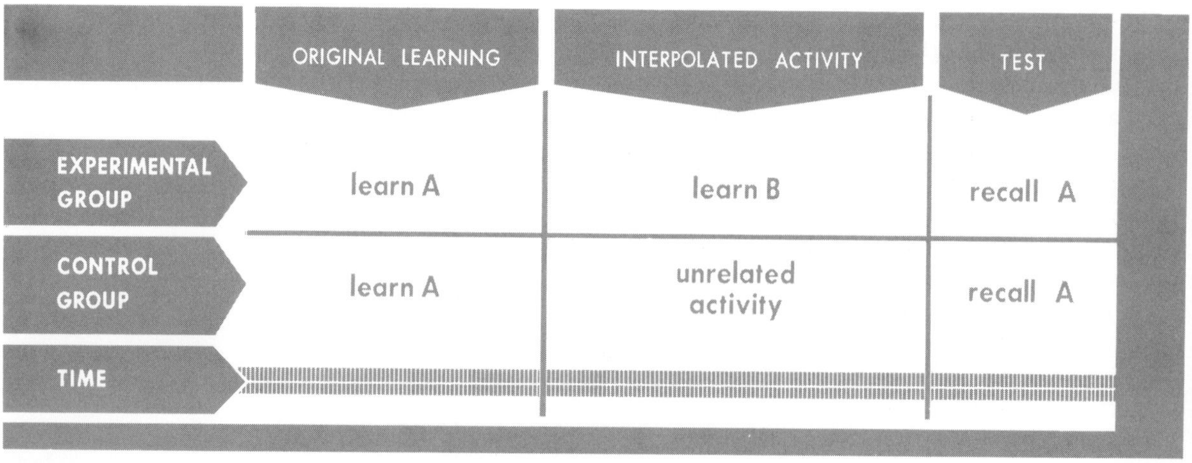

	ORIGINAL LEARNING	INTERPOLATED ACTIVITY	TEST
EXPERIMENTAL GROUP	learn A	learn B	recall A
CONTROL GROUP	learn A	unrelated activity	recall A
TIME			

FIGURE 10.36 The Experimental Design for Studying Retroactive Inhibition.

perimental and control groups learn *A* (a list of words) and are tested for recall of *A* after a specified time interval. The groups differ in what they do in the interval. The experimental group performs an activity; they are required to learn *B*. The control group has no such task; they can relax by looking at some cartoons, or they can indulge in various mild activities to prevent them from rehearsing *A*. Thus, if the two groups differ in their ability to recall *A,* the difference must be attributed to the effect of learning *B* in the interval before the test. Note that the time interval between learning *A* and the test for recall of *A* is exactly the same for both groups and therefore differences in recall cannot possibly be attributed merely to the passage of time.

The results of numerous studies of retroactive inhibition show that typically the experimental group is poorer in recall of *A*. An interpolated activity, particularly a similar one such as memorizing a second list of adjectives, interferes with the recall of the first list. In one study (McGeoch & McDonald, 1931) the degree of similarity between tasks *A* and *B* varied; the experimental subjects learned the list of adjectives (*A*) and then learned different kinds of material (*B*) in the interval. The control group spent the time between learning *A*

and the test for recall of *A* in reading jokes. The results showed that the more similar the interpolated activity (*B*) is to the original learning (*A*), the less the amount recalled (the greater, the retroactive inhibition).

An experimental design for demonstrating **proactive inhibition,** a phenomenon related to retroactive inhibition, is represented in Figure 10.37. This experimental design differs from the one used in investigating retroactive inhibition in that the experimental group learns *B* before, instead of after learning *A*. Whereas *B* was a task interpolated between the learning and the recall of *A* in the retroactive inhibition study, *B* is a task *preceding* the learning of *A* in the proactive inhibition study. To evaluate the effects upon the experimental group of learning *B* prior to *A,* the control group relaxes during the time the experimental group is learning *B*.

The results of these experiments in proactive inhibition are similar to those obtained in the experiments with retroactive inhibition. In the former experiment, the control group's recall of *A* is better than the experimental group's, the amount of superiority depending on the degree of similarity between *A* and *B*. Proactive inhibition, however, produces appreciably less forgetting of *A* than does retroactive

324

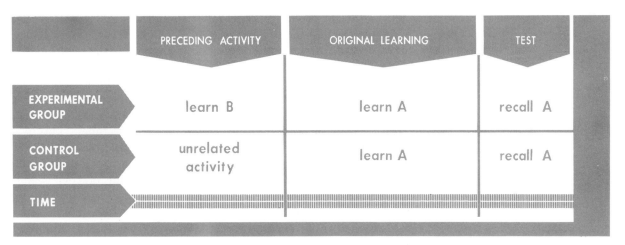

	PRECEDING ACTIVITY	ORIGINAL LEARNING	TEST
EXPERIMENTAL GROUP	learn B	learn A	recall A
CONTROL GROUP	unrelated activity	learn A	recall A
TIME			

FIGURE 10.37   The Experimental Design for Studying Proactive Inhibition.

inhibition. When the material used in each experiment is identical, the superiority of the control group over the experimental group in the recall of *A* is much greater when the inhibition is retroactive than when it is proactive.

In spite of this, however, an analysis (Underwood, 1957) of a large body of experimental data as well as recent studies (e.g., Postman, 1962*b*) suggests that the forgetting we experience in everyday living is largely, but not exclusively, the result of processes similar to proactive inhibition. Our ability to recall what we learn is reduced primarily by the things we have learned previously (proactive inhibition) and to a much lesser extent by what we learn later (retroactive inhibition). The more influential role played by proactive inhibition in everyday living would seem to explain the phenomenal memories children often have. They are young and have not had time to learn very much, so they have fewer memories to interfere with new learning. Elderly people, because of their wealth of previous learning, are particularly susceptible to the effects of proactive inhibition.

Forgetting, then, seems to be primarily the result of interference, or of what may be called habit competition. Two studies (Steinberg & Summerfield, 1957; Summer-field & Steinberg, 1957) that used the drug nitrous oxide, which functions to depress the activity of the central nervous system, have provided a neat confirmation of this hypothesis. In the first study it was shown that the administration of nitrous oxide impairs the formation of associations in a rote-learning task. Therefore, the administration of nitrous oxide immediately after learning should enhance retention, it should help prevent the formation of associations that would interfere with the recall of what had been originally learned. It turned out that nitrous oxide administered after learning improved recall, thereby giving additional confirmation of the interference theory of forgetting.

Improving Retention

The facts of proactive and retroactive inhibition seem to paint a bleak picture for those who count on being able to remember what they learn. For, unlike the cockroach, we cannot stay in suspended animation, nor can we insure ourselves against interference with what we have learned by constantly taking nitrous oxide. It remains true that we invite forgetting by staying awake and active. But the situa-

325

tion is not hopeless. Although we cannot eliminate forgetting completely, we can take steps to lessen it where retention is important.

Amount of Learning. Retention is greater when material is well learned. In a study (McGeoch, 1929) of retroactive inhibition a list of nonsense syllables was presented to different groups of subjects respectively 6, 11, 16, 21, and 26 times. Each group then was required to learn a second (i.e., interpolated) list presented 11 times. Figure 10.38 shows the results. Retroactive inhibition proved to be less effective as the num-

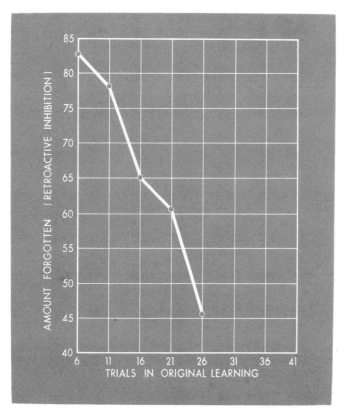

FIGURE 10.38 The Amount of Retroactive Inhibition as a Function of the Amount of Original Learning (After McGeoch, 1929).

ber of presentations of the original list increased. In other words, the better something is learned, the greater are its chances

of survival despite interference due to learning other material.

The results reported in Figure 10.38 point to an important fact frequently overlooked by students. Note that those subjects whose recall was best (who showed the least effect of retroactive inhibition) had been shown the list 26 times. This was more than enough times to repeat the original list once without error; these subjects were required to continue practicing after they had mastered their task. **Overlearning** is the term used to describe practice that continues after a perfect recall has been scored. For example, take the case of a student who must learn the French equivalents of 100 English words. He writes each English word on one side of a card and its French counterpart on the other. Often he dutifully studies the cards until he goes through the whole set without making an error, and, feeling he has learned them, he stops studying. However, if he would continue practicing even after he is able to say them once without error, he would remember his lesson better. This conclusion is supported by data obtained in the following experiment (Krueger, 1929) designed specifically to investigate what effects different amounts of overlearning have on retention.

Three groups of subjects learned a list of nouns in order. One group, called the 0 per cent overlearning group, practiced until they were able to recall the list just once without error. Another group (the 50 per cent overlearning group) continued to practice until they had had half again as many trials as they required for the first recall without an error. This means that a subject in this group who had required 10 trials before he could recall the list without error would continue to practice for a total of 15 trials. The third group, the 100 per cent overlearning group, had double the number of trials they needed first to say the list. Several tests of retention were given a week later, and it was demonstrated that overlearning paid off. The 100 per cent overlearning group proved superior to the 50 per cent overlearning group, which in turn was better than the group that had no overlearning.

By how much, then, should one overlearn? The answer depends to some extent on the difficulty of the material to be learned. The experiment on overlearning just reported indicated that the superiority of the 50 per cent group over the 0 per cent group was *greater than* that of the 100 per cent group over the 50 per cent, a result that suggests diminishing returns from overlearning beyond a certain point. In this experiment, however, the lists were difficult to memorize because of powerful interference from proactive inhibition. Another more recent experiment (Postman, 1962a) in which strong proactive interference was absent, showed that the superiority of the 50 per cent group over the 0 per cent was *less than* that of the 100 per cent group over the 50 per cent group, indicating that doubling the amount of overlearning resulted in proportionately better retention.

Thus, the general question of how much one should overlearn remains unanswered, simply because there can be no one answer. Conceivably, one could practice the French equivalents of 100 English words for months, or even years. That is to say, overlearning might be extended to a thousand or a million per cent, and even beyond. However, in every case of overlearning a point will be reached after which additional amounts of overlearning will yield diminishing returns. This does not mean that overlearning after this point is not worthwhile, since additional amounts of overlearning may still produce some increment in retention, even though it is very small. The final decision about how much time and effort you should be willing to spend for the added assurance overlearning provides depends on how important it is and for how long you wish to remember

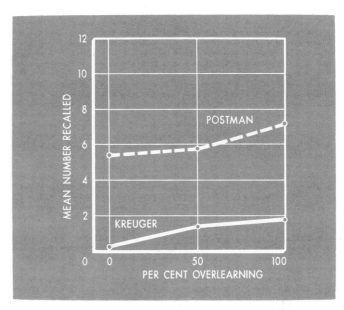

FIGURE 10.39 The Results of Two Experiments on the Effect of Different Amounts of Overlearning on Retention (After Postman, 1962a).

what you are learning. If you are studying for a weekly quiz in a course you are doing well in and thinking only of the mark you will get in that one quiz, a small amount of overlearning might suffice. If, however, you are competing in a nationwide examination, with a prize of spending the summer in France at stake, you would do well to overlearn your material to a considerable degree. But in any case, when you want to remember something, it is inadvisable to stop studying before some overlearning has taken place.

Retention and Meaningfulness. *Lov* and *zyw* are nonsense syllables, but most people have an easier time learning and remembering the first. *Lov* sounds like *love*, a word that is part of our vocabulary. Instead of just trying to remember three isolated letter *zyw*, the person required to recall *lov* can remember that it is the three-letter syllable that sounds like the word that "makes the world go round," or the central theme of most modern songs, or what one seeks, or many other possible associations.

Nonsense syllables, even though they are chosen so far as possible to avoid the problem of meaningfulness, do nevertheless often have "meaning." The *meaningfulness* or **association value** of a so-called nonsense syllable arises from its tendency to remind people of a real word, or words. A nonsense syllable such as *lov* with nearly 100 per cent association is one that calls forth a word from practically every subject, whereas a nonsense syllable with 0 per cent association (perhaps *zyw*) fails to remind anybody of any word. In an experiment (McGeoch, 1930) designed to test the influence of meaningfulness on retention, each of four groups of subjects studied a different 10-item list for two minutes with the aim of reproducing it. One group learned three-letter *words* (cat, far), while the other three groups all learned nonsense syllables which an experimental tryout had already proved possessed different association values (0 per cent, 53 per cent, and 100 per cent). The results confirmed the experimenter's expectation (see Table 10.3). The real words were retained best, and the number of nonsense syllables recalled correlated positively with their association value.

TABLE 10.3 The Effect of Meaningfulness on Retention (McGeoch, 1930).

MATERIAL MEMORIZED IN TEN-ITEM LISTS	NUMBER OF ITEMS RECALLED AFTER TWO MINUTE'S STUDY
Three-letter words	9.1
Nonsense syllables	
High association value (100%)	7.4
Medium association value (53%)	6.4
Low association value (0%)	5.1

The effect of meaningfulness on retention becomes still more striking when a comparison is made between learning a list of isolated nonsense syllables and learning a sequence of words organized into meaningful prose and poetry. Figure 10.40 shows the curves of retention of these three kinds of materials.

Obviously, then, if material is to be retained, there are advantages in making it meaningful. The number 1248163264 could be learned with difficulty as a series of 10 unrelated digits, or learned with ease as a sequence of seven numbers in which the first number is 1 and each number thereafter is twice the sum of the preceding one (1, 2, 4, 8, 16, 32, 64). Although this is a trick example, it is still true that much of the material we learn can be made meaningful, and should be, if we desire to speed learning or strengthen retention. Proofs of mathematical theorems should be learned in the most meaningful manner possible— by grasping the principles that underlie the particular sequence of steps leading up to the proof. A good teacher of mathematics knows how to make these meaningful relationships clear. A mathematical proof learned mechanically as if it were a series of isolated nonsense syllables is sure not to be retained very long.

Actually we are sometimes required to learn material that comes close to being meaningless. In such instances it may be useful to use mnemonic devices to assist us. Grade school children are aided in remembering the notes corresponding to the lines and spaces of the staff by recalling that the lines are the first letters of "*every good boy does fine*" and that the spaces spell "*face*." However, many so-called memory experts who teach courses designed to improve memory recommend elaborate mnemonic devices which bring order and meaning into the material to be learned, but which may be too clumsy in themselves to be worthwhile, and if resorted to, often become overweighted with a mass of conflicting associations.

Why is meaningful material easier to retain? Is it, perhaps, not meaning as such, but some inextricable part of meaning that strengthens retention? You have already seen that additional learning improves retention. Meaningful words, because they are familiar in a way that nonsense syllables are not, are by virtue of that fact already better learned. The unfamiliar nonsense syllable *zyw*, difficult for most people to remember, would be easy for a person whose initials are Z.Y.W. Having overlearned his own initials, he would have no difficulty in recalling them in the form of a nonsense syllable.

Two recent studies lend support to the hypothesis that amount of previous learning of meaningful material is really responsible for the relative ease with which that meaningful material is retained. In one experiment (Underwood & Richardson, 1956) lists of nonsense syllables of different levels of meaningfulness were used. One list consisted of syllables which suggested familiar words to most people: *bes, sel, bil,* and *doz;* the other lists were made up of syllables less easily associated with meanings: *gyk, gah, tou,* and *cef.* As expected, the subjects found it easier to learn the meaningful list. But when the two lists were learned equally well (this required more practice with the less meaningful list), they proved equally accessible to recall. When stripped of the advantage of being better learned, the meaningful material was not retained any better than the less meaningful syllables.

If the amount of prior learning of meaningful material is responsible for its better retention, then it should be possible to remember words better when they are organized into more meaningful contexts. We have more experience with meaningful combinations than with ones without meaning. This interpretation was supported by a study (Miller & Selfridge, 1950) which used a rather unusual method of controlling the level of meaningfulness.

A passage of 50 words was constructed, in which each word was dependent only on the previous word. This was done by

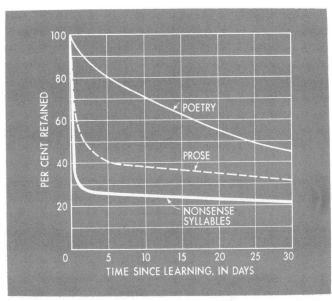

FIGURE 10.40 The Effect of Meaningfulness on Retention (After Guilford's *General Psychology,* Copyright 1939, D. Van Nostrand, Inc., Princeton, New Jersey).

asking one individual to compose a sentence with the word *you* in it. The word following *you* in his sentence was then incorporated into the passage. If, for example, it had been *come,* then the next person was requested to construct a sentence with *come* included. The word following *come* would then be added to the passage. By this procedure the following passage resulted, in which each word served as the cue for *only* the following one:

You come through my appetite is that game since he lives in school is jumping and wanted help call him well and substance was a piano is a mistake on this is warm glow in and girl went to write four turtledoves in my book is fine appearance of the

Another passage was constructed which was similar, except that each new word was given in response to the preceding *six* words. The passage looked like this:

Then go ahead and do it if possible while I make an appointment I want to skip very much around the tree and back home again to eat dinner after the movie early so that we could get lunch because we like her method for sewing blouses and skirts is

In this passage a person responded with the word *if* when told to complete a sentence including the six-word phrase *then go ahead and do it.* Similarly, the phrase *go ahead and do it if* evoked the word *possible.*

Which passage would you remember better? Both contain 50 words, and if the meaningfulness of the individual words were the important factor, then they would be remembered equally well. But if the important factor were the meaningfulness of associations between words, then the second passage would be remembered better. And that is what happened. The second passage with the more meaningful associations was easier to recall.

Perception and Retention

Things are not always recalled or events remembered as they really happened. The manner in which we perceive them influences our recall. No matter how many common failings they may have had, our childhood heroes or sweethearts seem now to have been nearly perfect. In the remarkable Japanese movie *Rashomon,* the same incident was recalled by three different people who participated in it: the husband, his wife, and a bandit. Since each of them perceived the original experience differently, their memories of it were bound to vary. Testimony in court is commonly different, perhaps widely so, for witnesses who supposedly had an equal opportunity to observe the event. This does not necessarily mean that any one of them is deliberately lying. More often than not the reports differ because their perceptions of the same event differ.

In an experimental demonstration of the influence that perception exerts on memory, each stimulus appearing in Figure 10.41 was presented along with a word

describing it. Different subjects were shown the same outlined figures, each of them coupled with a different word. Later the subjects were asked to draw from memory the figures they had been shown. Their drawings tended to be distorted in the direction of being more like the objects whose names the figures had been paired with.

Motivation and Forgetting

Remembering can be considered an instrumental act. You obtain reinforcement when you can remember the answer to an examination question, just as a pigeon obtains reinforcement when he pecks a disk. What most people have not noticed is that a person can obtain reinforcement for forgetting. That is, forgetting can function as an instrumental act.

The writer has an acquaintance who is blessed with an unusually good memory. He does, however, tend to forget one regular monthly appointment—with his doctor, who gives him an allergy shot. Sometimes these shots are painful and by forgetting the appointment, this person avoids the pain and escapes the anxiety aroused whenever he thinks of the injections.

Sigmund Freud (see page 50) was the first person to emphasize the influence of motives upon retention. He used the term **repression** to describe the tendency to avoid remembering anything associated with fear or unpleasantness of any kind. When we describe disordered personalities in Chapter 14, you will discover that there are more extreme kinds of forgetting than forgetting an appointment with your doctor, but for the time being we will merely refer to a common kind of repression which the writer observed as a clinical psychologist in the United States Army during World War II. A few men returning from active fighting at the front suffered from what is technically called **amnesia,** loss of memory of some experience so vivid that

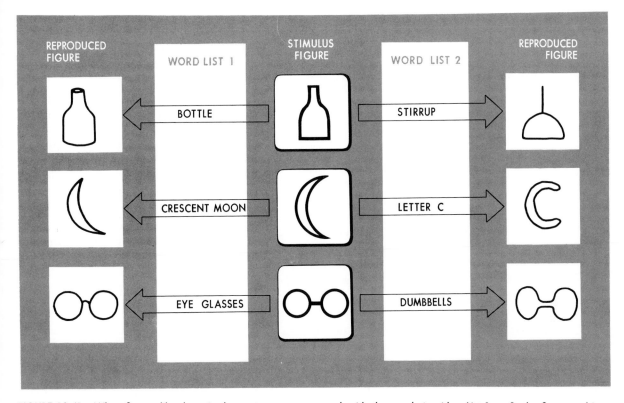

FIGURE 10.41 When figures like those in the center were presented with the words in either List 1 or 2, the figures subjects reproduced tended to be distorted in the direction of the name assigned to them (After Carmichael, Hogan, & Walter, 1932).

the memory loss could not be attributed to ordinary forgetting. They had not forgotten who they were, nor the name of their home town, the number of their regiment, or any other of the kind of events that a normal person can usually recall with ease. Their forgetting was sharply selective; they were unable to recall any detail of certain combat experiences. Here their memories were blanks. Under the influence of hypnosis or of drugs that induced a state similar to hypnosis, these men could relive their battle experiences, including reconstruction of the forgotten (actually repressed) events. It often turned out that the experiences the soldiers had forgotten were ones they were ashamed of. Perhaps they felt they had behaved like cowards or had in some way let "their buddies down." By forgetting (which is to say, by unintentionally suppressing memories of) such incidents, these

soldiers escaped the intense distress and humiliation that recalling them would have brought.

There are obvious difficulties in investigating repression in the laboratory. Psychologists are unable, or altogether unwilling, to force upon their subjects experiences comparable to those they would meet in combat. And even if they were not so scrupulous, where would they find cooperative subjects? Consequently, repression has been studied in the laboratory by techniques that are, for the most part, insufficiently powerful in their effects to produce striking instances of repression. In one of these experiments (Zeller, 1950) two groups of college students were first required to learn a list of nonsense syllables. Soon thereafter they were subjects in another memory task which appeared easy but actually was rather difficult, namely, to reproduce a complex pattern of taps. Each subject in one group, the experimental group, was told he had failed miserably, while those in the control group were informed that they had done quite well. When both groups were tested for retention of the nonsense syllables, the control group's performance was much superior. The interpretation of this difference is that the experimental subjects had repressed their memory of the syllables because that test was closely associated with the later test which had involved embarrassment and humiliation. This interpretation gains support from the fact that later on, when the experimental subjects had another opportunity to perform the tapping task and were told they succeeded, their tested recall of the nonsense syllables was much better this time. Removing the grounds for repression improved retention.

Another set of experiments showing how motivation can influence retention compares the recall of completed and incompleted tasks. Subjects (Zeigarnik, 1927) were required to work at a series of interesting tasks such as solving a Chinese puzzle and modeling clay. They were allowed to complete some of the tasks, but were forced to abandon others just when they had been most absorbed in them, perhaps when they had finally got the hang of things and felt success was near. At the end of the experimental session the subjects were asked to list each task that they had worked on. They could recall more incompleted tasks than completed ones, in spite of the fact that they had spent a longer total time on completed tasks. The obvious explanation of such a finding is that although the subjects reported that all the tasks were challenging and fascinating to work on, their motivation had been satisfied in the case of the completed tasks, and not in the case of the incompleted ones. The attraction of those they were unable to finish remained. This difference was reflected in a higher percentage of recall of the incompleted tasks.

PHYSIOLOGY AND COMPLEX LEARNING PHENOMENA

For a good reason, not much progress has been made in discovering the physiological, and especially the neurological, bases of complex learning phenomena. In this area, more progress has naturally been made with the simpler forms of learning, for physiological functions are more easily correlated to conditioned behavior than to complex learned behavior, but important and promising research in the latter field is under way.

Maze Learning and the Cerebral Cortex

In one experiment (Lashley, 1929), parts of the cortex of rats were destroyed. After the wounds healed the animals were required to learn a maze. Finally the subjects were killed so that the experimenters could ascertain exactly how much of the cortex and which particular regions had been destroyed. It was found that the greater the *amount* of cortical damage, the longer it had taken the animal to learn the maze. But the loss in learning ability seemed unrelated to the *location* of the cortical damage, or lesion. This finding encouraged researchers to support the hypothesis that all parts of a rat's cortex are equipotential, equally important for learning. Such a conclusion is open to question. A more reasonable explanation is that in a complex learning situation many different cues (visual, auditory, tactual, kinesthetic) help guide a rat through a maze. Also, many different muscular movements as well as S-R associations are involved in learning. Because maze learning involves so many *different* sensory, motor, and association areas, the total amount of cortical destruction is highly correlated with the rat's loss in learning ability. Specific areas of the cortex are, however, of prime importance for specific learning tasks. Destroying the visual area of a rat's cortex (see page 97) will prevent him from ever learning to discriminate between two different patterns of light. Electrical stimulation of certain portions of the brain (see page 180) will operate as a reinforcer in instrumental conditioning, while stimulation of other areas will not. One must conclude that different parts of the brain, including the cortex, are not of equal importance for all kinds, or perhaps all aspects, of learning, even though in *some* complex learning problems all appear to be equally involved.

Added to the difficulty of assessing the contributions of different portions of the cortex to learning, are the facts that the higher an animal is in the evolutionary scale, the more intricate his cortex appears to be and the more complex are the tasks he can master. These factors complicate the problem of formulating any overall principle that suffices to describe the functioning of the cortex in complex learning situations.

Transfer of Training and the Cerebral Hemispheres

You recall that there are two cerebral hemispheres (see page 94), each a mirror image of the other, one on each side of the brain. Normally these two sections are in direct communication with each other through a massive system of neural fibers known as the *corpus callosum* (see Figure 5.14). Surprisingly, when these strategically located tracts of fiber are severed, no clear-cut change in behavior occurs. Clinical cases of destruction of the corpus callosum in human beings and experimental studies with animals both seem to support this conclusion. Organisms with their cerebral hemispheres separated by this destruction apparently perceive, learn, and remember as well as normal animals.

The reason is that each cerebral hemisphere has the capacity to function as a separate and independent brain. This conclusion is supported by experiments (Sperry, 1961) with animals in which the corpus callosum is bisected making it possible for the sensory information each hemisphere receives to be separately controlled. Such cats were trained to discriminate between the feel of two different pedals in the absence of any visual sensation (see Figure 10.42). The sensory pathways from the left paw go to the right cerebral hem-

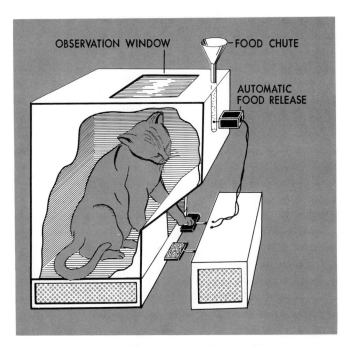

FIGURE 10.42 A Simplified Diagram of the Pedal-Pressing Apparatus Used for Training in Tactual Discrimination. The animal is restricted to using only one paw (After Sperry, 1961, with permission of *Science*).

isphere, while those from the right paw go to the left hemisphere. There was no transfer of training from one hemisphere to the other. The learning of diametrically opposed discriminations was carried out simultaneously with absolutely no evidence of negative transfer. Though the animal had learned to press with his right paw a pedal with raised horizontal lines in preference to one with raised vertical lines, he showed no difficulty in learning to make the opposite discrimination with his left paw. A normal cat whose corpus callosum was intact would find it very difficult to learn these two opposed discriminations simultaneously because of negative transfer; the pedal-pushing responses would transfer readily from one paw to the other. There is also no evidence of positive transfer in the "split-brain" animal. Learning to make one discrimination with one paw does not facilitate learning to make the same discrimination with the other paw. The changes produced by the training are not transferred from one hemisphere to the other.

This and other evidence suggest that in an intact animal the corpus callosum functions to transfer the learning that occurs in one hemisphere to the other. To prove this some animals were taught a discrimination in which the sensory information was directed to only one hemisphere. Afterwards the corpus callosum was severed. The discrimination previously learned by one hemisphere was "remembered" by the other, proving that it had transferred through the corpus callosum.

Thus there are two main reasons why the bisection of the corpus callosum fails to produce any appreciable disturbance in behavior. Everything that has been learned has already been transferred to both hemispheres, and therefore no loss of memory attends bisection. Secondly, current learning and perception are not usually impaired because they generally depend upon sensory information that has been transmitted directly to both hemispheres. When, for example, a visual discrimination is learned, the information transmitted through both eyes reaches both hemispheres. The sectioning of the corpus callosum creates a problem only when sensory input is restricted to one of the two hemispheres.

The "split-brain" technique has already provided important information regarding the neurological basis of transfer of training, particularly the kind described as *cross education* (see page 317). However, research of this kind holds even greater promise for the future; it provides endless possibilities for investigating how behavior can be modified by controlling the perceptual and learning experiences of each hemisphere independently.

SUMMARY

Conditioning consists primarily of habit formation and habit strengthening. For more complicated learning situations, we must add the processes of habit competition and habit chaining. In habit competition, responses arranged in a hierarchy of strength compete with each other. In habit chaining, S-R associations are integrated into a sequence of successive associations primarily through the operation of response-produced cues.

The principles of habit competition suggest that the same factors (reinforcement, motivation, etc.) responsible for the strengthening and weakening of a conditioned response also operate to make one habit dominant over a competing one.

Punishment is less effective than experimental extinction in weakening and eliminating an undesirable habit. Its main effect is that of temporarily suppressing a habit. Nevertheless, punishment can help break an undesirable habit if it forces an organism to select a new response that leads to positive reinforcement.

Chaining has been studied most thoroughly in a free-responding (operant) conditioning situation where the same response is repeated over and over again. The major variable that determines the rate of responding is the schedule of reinforcement. In an intermittent schedule, reinforcements occur only after some responses but not after others. One consequence of an intermittent schedule is that it creates greater resistance to extinction than consistent reinforcement does.

In a fixed interval schedule of reinforcement the first response after a certain period of time is reinforced, and the shorter the interval the higher is the rate of responding. Immediately after a reinforcement in a fixed interval schedule the rate of response tends to decrease. This "scalloping effect" can be eliminated by a variable interval schedule in which reinforcements occur after intervals that vary in length. In a fixed ratio schedule a specified number of responses have to occur before reinforcement is given. Once a fixed ratio schedule is established, the higher the ratio the more responses will be emitted in a given time period. Under high fixed ratio schedules the rate of responding also tends to decrease immediately after a reinforcement. This low rate of responding following a reinforcement can be eliminated by a variable ratio schedule in which reinforcements occur after varying numbers of responses.

Behavior can be shaped into new forms by reinforcement of successive approximations of the desired responses. The three principles utilized in shaping are response generalization, habit competition, and habit chaining.

Psychologists distinguish between motor and verbal learning realizing that the categories are not mutually exclusive. The acquisition of a motor skill, more appropriately described as a sensorimotor skill, is influenced by the way the practice is distributed. In general, some form of spaced practice is more effective because it allows work inhibition to be dissipated. Warm-up and the pattern of movements are also important variables in the learning and performance of motor skills.

Two simple forms of verbal learning are paired associate and serial learning. In paired associate learning a syllable or word is associated with another. In serial learning a series of words or nonsense syllables are chained together. When a subject learns a list of paired associates or a series of nonsense syllables, he learns, in addition to the correct associations, backward and remote associations.

In probability learning a subject must guess which of two randomly occurring events will occur. His choices, usually highly correlated with the probability of the occurrence of each event, have served as the basis for the formulation of mathematical theories of learning.

Transfer of training refers to the influence the learning of one task has upon the subsequent learning of another. In paired associate learning, when a new response has to be learned to a stimulus identical or similar to an old one, negative transfer occurs. When a response identical or similar to an old response has to be associated with a new stimulus, positive transfer occurs. Mediated transfer occurs when a response to a stimulus serves as the cue for the acquisition of a new response. Positive transfer has been exhibited in a series of successive discrimination problems which are different from each other. Presumably the subject is learning how to learn that certain responses are appropriate to all the different problems. Cross education, transposition, and transfer of principles are additional examples of positive transfer.

The experimental analysis of forgetting suggests that it is primarily the effects of interference between competing habits instead of the mere passage of time. Although retroactive inhibition usually produces greater amounts of forgetting than proactive inhibition, it is likely that the latter plays a more important role in the forgetting that occurs in everyday living.

Retention can be improved by overlearning, and by making what is learned more meaningful. Retention is influenced by both perception and motivation, as illustrated by the fact that we tend to remember events in terms of how we perceived them and by forgetting events which arouse fear.

There is no simple relationship between complex learning phenomena and the underlying physiology for the simple reason that many different neurological events interact depending upon the nature of the task. It has been demonstrated by the "split-brain" technique that each cerebral hemisphere has the capacity to function as a separate and independent brain.

SUGGESTIONS FOR FURTHER READING

Since conditioning and learning are such interrelated topics the suggested readings listed at the end of Chapter 7 (page 181) are also appropriate for this chapter. This is particularly true for G. A. Kimble's *Hilgard and Marquis' Conditioning and Learning* (2nd ed.), which surveys both the fields of conditioning and learning. Additional supplementary sources follow.

BUGELSKI, B. R. *The psychology of learning.* New York: Holt, Rinehart, & Winston, 1956.

An introductory textbook that attempts to summarize and systematize the major phenomena of learning.

BUSH, R. R., & ESTES, W. K. (Eds.) *Studies in mathematical learning theory.* Stanford, Calif.: Stanford Univer. Press, 1959.

A collection of papers that interpret learning as a mathematical process.

DEESE, J. *The psychology of learning.* (2nd ed.) New York: McGraw-Hill, 1958.

An elementary treatment of the psychology of learning. Introductory chapters cover the basic problems of conditioning and learning, and subsequent chapters deal with the topics of discrimination learning, chaining, transfer of training, retention, and problem solving.

ESTES, W. K. The statistical approach to learning theory. In S. Koch (Ed.), *Psychology: A study of a science.* Vol. 2. New York: McGraw-Hill, 1959. Pp. 380-491.

A sophisticated analysis for the advanced student of the mathematical approach to theoretical problems in learning.

GUTHRIE, E. R. *The psychology of learning.* New York: Harper & Row, 1952.

A simple and clever analysis of the psychology of learning. Guthrie shows how instances of everyday behavior are related to phenomena observed in the laboratory.

HILGARD, E. R. *Theories of learning.* (Rev. ed.) New York: Appleton-Century-Crofts, 1956.

A textbook for advanced students that both summarizes and evaluates the major theories of learning.

LAWSON, R. *Learning and behavior.* New York: Macmillan, 1960.

A systematic treatment of simple and complex forms of learning.

McGEOCH, J. A., & IRION, A. L. *Psychology of human learning.* (2nd ed.) New York: David McKay, 1952.

A comprehensive textbook that reviews the major experimental phenomena of human learning and forgetting.

SKINNER, B. F. *Science and human behavior.* New York: Macmillan, 1953.

One of the most influential books in contemporary psychology. Starting from his research in operant conditioning, Professor Skinner draws implications that are relevant to complex forms of learning and behavior observed in the laboratory and in society.

WOODWORTH, R. S., & SCHLOSBERG, H. *Experimental psychology.* (Rev. ed.) New York: Holt, Rinehart, & Winston, 1954.

An excellent textbook that contains eight chapters on various aspects of learning.

VERBAL BEHAVIOR AND PROBLEM SOLVING

11

INTRODUCTION

Benjamin Whorf, a chemical engineer who studied the structure and function of language as a hobby, reported (Whorf, 1956) an interesting incident from his experience as a fire insurance investigator. Whorf's job was to find out the causes of fires and explosions in industrial plants, in order to help prevent future catastrophes. Reporting upon physical conditions that led to one such disaster, such as defective wiring and lack of air space between a metal flue and woodwork, Whorf soon learned that physical conditions alone were not responsible. Equally important, if not more so, was the behavior of the industrial workers. Whorf noted that workers were cautious near a storage room labeled "Gasoline Drums," but around a room labeled "Empty Gasoline Drums," they behaved

negligently, not hesitating to smoke and toss cigarette butts away. Yet empty gasoline tanks contain explosive vapor, and are, in truth, more dangerous than full ones.

Why did the workers behave differently in the two situations? The difference, Whorf discovered, was due to the workers' reaction to the word *empty*. *Empty* meant something more to them than the absence of liquid gasoline; they associated it with *nothing*. And how could *nothing* be dangerous? Consequently they were careless in a situation that demanded extreme care. Thus Whorf discovered that the cause of a disastrous fire lay not only with the physically empty gasoline drums, but also with the common psychological responses to the word *empty*.

This anecdote illustrates—in the workers' reaction to *empty* and Whorf's discovery of the origin of the fire—two of the most important and complicated forms of human behavior: verbal behavior and problem solving. Language and problem solving emerge from the more basic psychological processes: sensation, learning, perception, and motivation. This chapter will try to help you understand some of the important things about language and problem solving that psychologists have discovered.

VERBAL BEHAVIOR

Man is impressed with his superior standing in the animal kingdom. He often looks upon his behavior, and most especially his language ability, as having no parallel among lower animals. One can, however, question whether verbal behavior is as unique to man as he would like to believe.

Animals do respond to verbal cues from man. Dogs can be trained to behave appropriately to a large variety of commands. Some animals can even produce humanoid noises. Parrots and parakeets, for example, can acquire a rich, if limited, repertory of speech sounds. Other animals obviously communicate with each other. Consider the howler monkeys, who travel in packs. They appoint lookouts who screech warnings whenever they sight predatory beasts so that the entire pack can escape. The Adélie penguin can recognize its mate's voice in a densely crowded nesting area after months of absence. Even bees can communicate information to their hive mates. An Austrian zoologist, Von Frisch (1950), noticed that when a bee has discovered a large source of food, he returns to the hive and performs a "dance." The movements of this "dance" function as cues that enable other bees to go directly to the food. Von Frisch studied the behavior of the bees and learned their "language." He demonstrated his understanding by his ability to interpret the "dance" of bees returning from food his assistant had hidden and to tell where the source was located. He could tell this from the speed, pattern, direction, and duration of the bees' movements.

But can animals deal with abstract concepts? In our vocabulary words such as *apple* or *triangle* refer not only to specific items but also to collections of items having common features. We can identify a particular fruit as an apple. Some of the fruits we call apples are red, others are yellow or green; some are large, others small. Yet we identify in all these fruits the common quality of being an apple. Does not this ability, so clearly indicated in our language behavior, distinguish us from lower animals? Not completely. The rat can be trained to choose a triangle in preference to other geometrical shapes even when the position and size of the triangle changes from trial to trial (Fields, 1932). This suggests that the rat can consistently choose a stimulus pattern that maintains the properties of a triangle. In short, the rat can abstract from the features of particular triangles something common to them all. The chimpanzee has demonstrated an ability to acquire the concept of threeness (Kelleher, 1958). Confronted by a bank of nine lights, he can learn to make an instrumental lever-pressing response to different patterns of three lights, and not to respond to a greater or smaller number.

Finally, to demonstrate that verbal behavior is not unique to man, we shall describe the case of Viki (Hayes, 1951), a chimpanzee reared by a married couple, both of whom were psychologists. They wanted to know if a chimpanzee raised like a human child would learn to speak. After three years Viki could say and use three words: *Mama, Papa,* and *cup*. In short, Viki acquired a language consisting of a three-word vocabulary; her behavior, in this respect, was equal to the average one-year-old human child.

This discussion is not designed to deflate the reader (or compliment him, if he hap-

340

pens to be a chimpanzee), but to show that human verbal behavior is not an isolated phenomenon. In many ways our verbal behavior is on a continuum with the behavior of lower animals and, therefore, should not be thought of as a unique psychological problem.

While recognizing the similarity between human verbal behavior and its primitive counterparts on the subhuman level, one should not forget the important differences. Whereas dogs can be trained to respond to a few verbal commands and parrots and parakeets can enunciate a limited number of words, a highly literate person can handle a vocabulary of about 200,000 words (Miller, 1951). And this vocabulary consists not only of simple nouns with direct sensory referents, such as *Mama, Papa,* and *cup,* but of nouns so abstract that whole books may be written about them, such as *life, patriotism, love, honesty, matter, energy,* and *psychology.* All these are part of an educated person's vocabulary. Whereas an animal can learn a simple abstraction, we can deal with abstractions of abstractions. *Fruit,* for example, is a more abstract concept than *apple,* since it refers to qualities possessed not only by apples but also by pears. *Plant* is more abstract than *fruit,* and *living matter* is still more abstract.

Moreover, we do not often use words singly, but in a practically infinite number of possible combinations. Perhaps the most impressive feature of our verbal behavior is our ability to use words like *is. Is* and words such as *some, all, and, if, true,* and *false* are known as logical words, since they state relationships among other words.

The importance of these logical words can be illustrated in the following way: suppose you learn that all *melchers* are *reldniks* and that all *reldniks flim.* You then know that all *melchers flim.* The fact that you have no idea what *melchers, reldniks,* and *flim* are does not prevent you from drawing the correct conclusion.

FIGURE 11.1 Viki, the "Talking Chimpanzee." After being taught to make a sound like "ahhh," Viki's lips were shaped so that it began to sound like "Mama." (From *The Ape in our House* by Cathy Hayes; copyright 1951 by Catherine Hayes. Reprinted with the permission of Harper & Row, Publishers, Inc. Photograph by Dr. Keith J. Hayes).

You have been able to deduce the correct conclusion according to the rules governing the use of logical words. In this connection we might mention that logicians have been described as men who never know what they are talking about.

Thus, one must conclude that the verbal behavior of human beings is continuous with its counterpart among lower animals, but is nevertheless vastly more complex.

The Development of Language

Vocal behavior begins with the birth cry. When the umbilical cord which transports blood from the mother to her child is severed, the infant's prenatal source of oxygen is cut off. The carbon dioxide content of his own blood builds up quickly and produces a reflexive expansion of the lung cavity, causing air to be rapidly sucked in and drawn over the vocal cords of the larynx. From this birth cry develops the variety of sounds that make up spoken language.

It is commonly thought that as the infant matures he learns to make the sounds necessary to speak. This is not strictly true. Sounds an infant made during his first year of life were recorded (Osgood, 1955). Surprisingly, during his early months he made all the sounds that the human voice can produce, including German gutturals and French trills. In the beginning a child is able to make any sound required for any spoken language. This may surprise and frustrate the foreign-language student who is trying unsuccessfully to reproduce a weirdly unfamiliar sound, but the fact remains that during his early years he would probably not have had any difficulty in making that sound. What happens is that our speech becomes shaped (see page 291).

A growing child's speech sounds are shaped much as a rat's behavior is shaped in a Skinner box. Initially the rat makes a wide variety of muscular movements, but after his behavior is shaped by reinforcement, he makes, for the most part, those responses that are part of the behavior chain: approaching and pressing the bar, getting and consuming food. Human infants also make, to begin with, a very wide variety of muscular movements in the lips, mouth, throat, and chest. Infants of different races emit the same speech sounds. However, the shaping process begins early. The child is, in a sense, shaped by his environment. He is reinforced when he utters sounds that occur in his native tongue and not reinforced when he makes other sounds. As early as six months, the sounds of the infant begin to resemble those his parents make, and at 30 months the resemblance between the infant's sounds and his parents' is marked.

The shaping of speech sounds goes on for many years. A ten-year-old Hungarian immigrant would find it easier to learn to speak English without an accent than a 30-year-old immigrant—for two reasons. First, the sounds which occur in English and not in Hungarian but are made by Hungarian infants, nevertheless, would be nearer complete extinction in the adult's speech than in the child's. Second, the habits of making the sounds which occur in Hungarian and not in English would be stronger in the adult and hence more difficult to extinguish. In short, the adult immigrant would have more to learn and more to extinguish.

Of course, verbal behavior does not consist only of making certain speech sounds. The sounds must be used appropriately, and to be used appropriately they must acquire meaning. They acquire meaning by a process similar to classical conditioning (see page 151). When the child says *Da-da* in the presence of his father he is reinforced. He is not reinforced when he makes the same response to similar stimuli. Thus he learns to use the word appropriately. As he matures the speech sound representing the father changes to comply with social custom. *Da-da* becomes *Daddy* or *Dad*. Many words also acquire meaning by a combination of classical conditioning and imitation. Children sometimes repeat sounds they hear and are reinforced for doing so; parents are delighted when babies imitate their speech. A mother, for example, holds up a doll and says *doll*. Her word, operating as an imitative model for the child's response *dah,* becomes conditioned to the sight of the doll (the conditioned stimulus). In this way sounds such as *shoe, spoon,* and other names of objects acquire meaning.

To the child the association he learns between the word and the object is so strong that the name becomes just as important an attribute of the object as its physical properties. The word *dog* is just as much part of the animal as its fur and its four legs. The child simply does not conceive of a word as a convenient but arbitrary way of designating an object.

342

Anyone who has ever tried to convince a child that a dog could just as well be called a *shoe,* and a shoe, a *dog,* will understand this all too well.

Eventually, out of simple name-calling, the child develops, through learning, the complex verbal behavior involved in reading and conversing on an adult level.

STIMULUS AND RESPONSE PROPERTIES OF VERBAL BEHAVIOR

Verbal behavior can be conveniently analyzed in terms of its stimulus and response properties. In short, words possess a dual function. They act as stimuli. The word STOP in the sign at the side of the road, for example, functions as does a red light. Both are stimuli to evoke the response, stepping on the brake. Words can also be responses. "Water, please" may get you a drink just as effectively as turning the knob of a drinking fountain. The stimulus and response characteristics of words, however, go much beyond these two simple examples.

Stimulus Properties of Words

Words can function as conditioned stimuli. We have already noted in Chapter 7 how a word served as a conditioned stimulus for the vasoconstriction response (see page 155). Pavlov could just as well have used a word as a bell when he conditioned the salivary response of the dog.

Semantic Generalization. Words, like physical stimuli, generalize. **Semantic generalization** is the term used to describe this phenomenon, and there are several kinds of semantic generalization. Generalization can occur between an object and a word. If a conditioned response is established to the sound of a metronome in an English-speaking adult, then it will also be elicited by the word *metronome.* Semantic generalization also operates in the other direction. That is, if the response is originally conditioned to the word *metronome,* then the sound of the metronome will evoke the conditioned response. This kind of semantic generalization (from the word to the object) is widely used to control a soldier's behavior. In World War II the feelings of hatred aroused by the word *Nazi* among American soldiers were expected to generalize to the German soldiers they met in battle.

The most interesting, and perhaps the most important kind of semantic generalization occurs between words, either presented alone or in sentences. In one experiment (Riess, 1946) the galvanic skin response was conditioned to the stimulus word, *won.* Three test words, *one, lost,* and *beat,* related to the original conditioned stimulus in different ways, were then shown to the subject separately. *One* is a homonym to *won,* alike in sound but different in meaning. *Lost,* an antonym, has an opposite meaning, while *beat,* a synonym, has a similar meaning. The amount of generalization occurring between *won* and these three test words depended on the age of the subjects. The youngest group, whose mean age was just short of eight years, showed the greatest amount of generalization to the homonym (*one*), and least to the synonym (*beat*). At approximately 11 years of age the antonym (*lost*) produced the greatest amount of generalization, with the homonym and synonym evoking about the same amounts. With the two oldest groups (14 and 18 and a half years of age) the order changed, the synonym demonstrating the largest amount of generalization, followed by the antonym, with the homonym last. At all age groups synonyms, antonyms, and homonyms all evoked some degree of generalization.

This study shows that generalization occurs between physically similar words (they sound alike), but that this kind of generalization decreases with age. In contrast, semantic generalization based on meaning increases with age, although accompanied by a shift in direction. With younger children there is greater generalization between antonyms, with older ones, between synonyms.

Age, however, is not the important variable. Level of intelligence is. In a Russian study (Razran, 1961) of semantic generalization, school children of normal intelligence were compared with feeble-minded children of approximately the same age (13 to 17 years). After the children were conditioned to the word *koshka* (cat), a large number of words related either in a meaningful or a similar sounding way were presented to them. Examples of the former were *zhivotnoye* (animal) and *sobaka* (dog); of the latter, *kroska* (crumb) and *okoshko* (window). There were clearcut differences in response between the two groups of children. The children of average intelligence gave generalized conditioned responses only to words with related meaning; the children with a moderate degree of intellectual deficiency gave responses to both kinds of words; and the severely retarded children gave generalized responses only to similar sounding words.

There is also semantic generalization from a sentence to its various components. If, for example, a conditioned response is established to the simple sentence, "She wants to buy a gray purse," the individual words will be capable of evoking the conditioned response. The amount of generalization will vary as a function of the part of speech each word represents, verbs (*buy*) and direct objects (*purse*) eliciting a relatively strong generalized response, subjects (*she*) and adjectives (*gray*) evoking weak ones.

Discrimination and Semantic Generalization. Does semantic generalization influence the course of discrimination learning

as stimulus generalization does? You recall (see page 160) that it is easier for an animal, such as a rat to discriminate between black and white than between two grays, because there is more stimulus generalization between the grays. If the same principle holds for verbal behavior, then a discrimination involving similar words should be more difficult than one involving different words. This prediction was tested in a study (Dietze, 1955) with two groups of preschool children who were required to discriminate among three different kinds of odd-shaped geometrical objects. For one group the names *jod, daf,* and *meep* were assigned to the three kinds of objects. The other group was required to call the same objects *beem, meem,* and *peem.* After learning the assigned names for the three kinds of objects, the subjects were required to learn to supply the names to additional objects which belonged to the same three categories. If the original discrimination was learned only on the basis of the physical shapes of the objects, then both groups should master the new task at the same rate. If, however, the names of the objects served as part of the stimulus pattern the subjects were responding to, then the learning of the group whose objects had the names *beem, meem,* and *peem* should be retarded. The greater the generalization among the three sets of objects, the greater would be the confusion and, hence, the slower the discrimination. The results of the study confirmed the prediction. The similar sounding names *beem, meem,* and *peem* produced poorer learning than did the distinctively different *jod, daf,* and *meep.*

Response Properties of Words

Verbal behavior often functions as an instrumental response does. Objects can be obtained by asking for them. The spoken request, "May I please have the book?" is equivalent to the correct response an animal makes in an instrumental conditioning situation; both act upon the environment to produce a desired object. They differ in that the animal's response acts upon an inanimate object, such as a lever, whereas the person's verbal response controls the behavior of another individual. Both responses, however, can be reinforced.

If verbal behavior is like an instrumental response, then it should possess some of its psychological properties. Organisms repeat instrumental responses that are reinforced. Is this true of verbal behavior? In recent years a large number of experiments (Krasner, 1958) has shown that reinforced verbal responses are repeated.

Experiments of this sort, although they vary widely in particulars, make use of two shared features: a distinctive kind of verbal response and a reinforcing agent. In one experiment the subject is reinforced whenever he utters a plural noun (horses, books); in others, when he uses a first person pronoun (I, we), when he refers to *mother* or to a form of behavior involving movement (running), or when he expresses certain kinds of attitudes or opinions (for or against capital punishment). In short, a wide variety of verbal responses have been selected for consistent reinforcement in different experiments. The experimenter in these studies reinforces the appropriate response by saying *good* or *fine* or just by nodding his head and smiling encouragement. These experiments have shown that when a particular verbal response is consistently reinforced, it begins to occur more frequently. This is what we would expect from our knowledge of instrumental conditioning.

In one of the earlier experiments (Greenspoon, 1955), college students were instructed to say a series of individual words. Whenever a subject said a plural noun the experimenter said "mmm-hmmm." Subjects in a control group were given the identical instructions, but in their case the experimenter remained silent when they said

plural nouns. When the performances of the two groups were compared, it was discovered that where the experimenter had said "mmm-hmmm" after plural nouns they had increased in frequency. In other words, "mmm-hmmm" was a reinforcer. When experimental extinction was instituted (the "mmm-hmmm," previously given, was eliminated), the plural noun responses of the experimental group dropped off to the level of those emitted by the members of the control group. In this manner, the experiment demonstrated that a verbal response functions as an instrumental response does; its frequency increases when it is followed by reinforcement and decreases when not followed by reinforcement.

An interesting variation of this experiment was conducted outside the psychological laboratory (Verplanck, 1955). Seventeen students taking an advanced psychology course served as experimenters. For about half an hour they carried on informal conversations with their friends, who were unaware that they were participating in a psychological experiment. The experimenter *agreed with* (reinforced) any sentence beginning with "I think . . . ," "I believe . . . ," "It seems to me . . . ," "I feel . . . ," or the like by saying, "You're right," "I agree," "That's so," or something similar and nodding or just smiling if he did not want to interrupt. The opinions expressed ranged over many topics from dates to Marxism, from religion, to TV stars. During the first ten minutes of each conversation, when there was no reinforcement, the rate at which the subjects expressed opinions beginning, "I think . . . ," "I believe . . . ," etc., was measured so that the effects of reinforcement could be estimated later. During the next ten minutes the experimenter reinforced the subject's opinions by agreeing with them. The last ten minutes were spent in extinction, that is, the experimenter abstained from commenting on any opinion. The results were similar to those obtained in the plural noun study. The reinforcement of sentences expressing opinions increased the frequency with which opinions were given. The absence of reinforcement reduced their frequency. So you see, not only does the uttering of individual words obey the principles of instrumental conditioned responses, but so also does the college student's expression of an opinion about a complex issue of life.

Combined Stimulus-Response Properties of Words

Up to now the stimulus and response properties of words have been treated separately. Quite often, especially when we are speaking or writing, our words function simultaneously as stimuli and responses. The phrase "Will you please give me a glass of" is not only a response but also a stimulus for the word *water*—or the name of some other beverage.

We are not usually aware, in conversation, of the effect of what has been said upon what will be said, but the cue property of past speech is clearly illustrated by a fiendish modification of a tape recorder. The subject speaks into the microphone and his comments are recorded on tape. This is played back to him through the earphone, with a very brief time lapse, while he is still talking. As a result, the subject hears not what he is saying but what he has just said. The following example describes this confused situation. The subject says into the microphone, "Will you please give me . . . ," and because of the built-in lag he hears only "Will you" as he says the word "me." This situation creates intense habit competition. If he responds to the muscle sensations of what he has just *said* he will say "a glass of water"; if he responds to what he has just *heard himself say*, he will say, "please give me. . . ." As a consequence of this habit competition, the subject's speech pattern breaks down. When the delay in hearing what he has

just said is about .2 seconds, he begins to stammer and finally becomes so confused that he becomes literally speechless.

The concept of a response-produced cue has already been described. You have learned how a person's response can serve as the cue for his own conditioned response. You have also seen how the cue resulting from a slight muscle movement can help in perceiving our three-dimensional world. And recently you have read how response-produced cues enable us to integrate long chains of responses. The cue properties of verbal responses function in a manner similar to other response-produced cues. The major difference is that any one word is usually linked to a fantastically large number of other verbal responses. Consider, for example, the many different words you have used to follow the preposition *of*, each of which has, therefore, to some slight extent, become linked with it in paired associate fashion.

The complicated network of associations involved in language behavior is clearly revealed by a comparison between the primary generalization of animals and the semantic generalization of humans. After conditioning a dog to salivate to a tone, Pavlov found that a similar tone would also elicit the salivary response. This kind of generalization is known as **primary generalization** since the stimulus, being on the same physical dimension as the original conditioned stimulus, directly evokes the response, as in the following notation:

$$S\text{————————}R$$
similar tone   salivation

You recall that when a person's galvanic skin response was conditioned to the written word *won*, the word *beat* became capable of evoking the same response. Although this behavior was also labeled generalization, the mechanism responsible for it is somewhat different from that underlying primary generalization. The

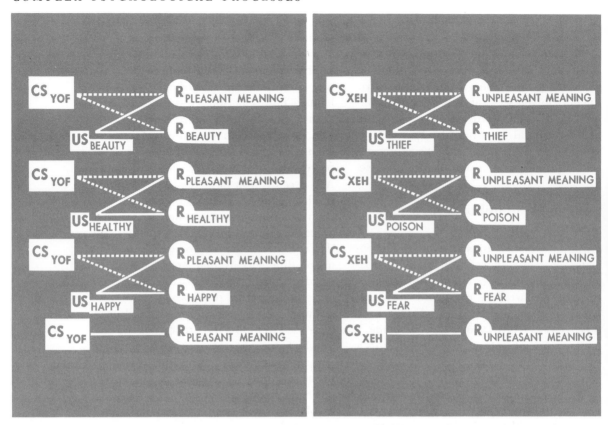

FIGURE 11.2 How Meaning Was Conditioned to a Nonsense Syllable. By being paired with a series of pleasant words (beauty, healthy, happy), the nonsense syllable *yof* acquired a pleasant meaning. The nonsense syllable functioned as a conditioned stimulus (CS), while the pleasant words functioned as unconditioned stimuli (US). Similarly, another nonsense syllable, *xeh*, was conditioned to words with unpleasant meanings. At the end of training, *yof*, by itself, evoked a pleasant association, while *xeh* elicited an unpleasant association (After Staats & Staats, 1957).

generalization of a response from the word *won* to *beat* is based upon their common meaning. This makes the generalization possible. In an attempt to explain semantic generalization it has been hypothesized that meaning is actually a response which serves, in turn, as a cue. The galvanic skin response is first conditioned to the written word *won*. The subject is then exposed to the word *beat*, which already has the tendency to evoke the response *won* because of previous learning which established them as synonyms. The response *won* serves as the stimulus cue to evoke the galvanic skin response. In other words, *beat* is not directly linked to the galvanic skin response; its capacity to evoke such a response is medi-

ated by the ability of *beat* to elicit *won*. This example of semantic or mediated generalization can be represented by the following notation:

$$S\underset{\text{beat}}{\rule{2cm}{0.4pt}}r\underset{\text{won}}{\rule{2cm}{0.4pt}}s\underset{\text{won}}{\rule{2cm}{0.4pt}}R\;\underset{\text{GSR}}{}$$

The response *won* and its resultant cue are represented by small letters to indicate that they are implicit, that the experimenter does not observe this mediated response but merely infers it. Neither are the subjects aware of making any mediating responses. Again we may note, as we did in the case of space perception (see page 201), that people are not always able to identify the cues to which they respond.

Words, of course, have several meanings. They possess general as well as specific meanings. Although the words *beauty, gift, honest, love,* and *happy* mean different things, they all possess a common pleasant connotation. In contrast, the meanings of the words *ugly, sad, dirty, insane* and *evil,* each of which possesses an individual meaning, all signify something unpleasant. Would it be possible to condition the pleasant or unpleasant meanings of these two sets of words directly to some neutral cue? In order to answer this question the following experiment (Staats & Staats, 1957) was conducted. College students were instructed to learn a series of 108 paired associates in which the stimulus member was one of six nonsense syllables and the response member was one of 108 words, that is, each response word appeared only once. One of the six nonsense syllables was consistently associated with a word having a pleasant connotation, while another syllable was linked only with unpleasant words. The remaining four nonsense syllables were paired with words having no common meaning.

This experimental procedure is similar to classical conditioning. Each nonsense syllable functions as a conditioned stimulus with the pleasant and unpleasant words operating as unconditioned stimuli. If the analogy is appropriate, the nonsense syllable (conditioned stimulus) should acquire some of the meaning responses of the words (unconditioned stimuli) they are paired with. This is exactly what happened. At the end of the experiment the subjects judged the nonsense syllable that was paired with pleasant words to be pleasant and nonsense syllable paired with the unpleasant words to be unpleasant. In short, the nonsense syllables acquired some of the meaning of the words they were associated with. The amount of pleasant or unpleasant meaning acquired, as a later study (Staats & Staats, 1958) showed, depended on the number of times each nonsense syllable

was paired with a different pleasant or unpleasant word. In this respect conditioned meaning resembles other forms of conditioning: the strength of the conditioned association is a function of the amount of training.

This experiment with conditioned meaning has its parallel in many real-life situations. For example, we expect the names of the drugs we buy to sound medically appropriate. Names like *terramycin* and *tetracyn* not only identify the drug but also impart a conditioned meaning of scientific respectability. We would certainly be reluctant to purchase drugs with names resembling perfumes, like *Passion, Desire,* or *Love.* Realizing that commercial success depends on the "scientific meaning" of the names of its products, one drug firm uses an electronic machine to coin new names for drugs. The machine is programmed to devise names by combining two syllable prefixes with one and two syllable endings, the prefixes and endings having been selected as suitable sounding after an examination of medical literature in several languages. The machine has spewed out such impressive drug names as *abemycin, byulamycin, platuphyl,* and *cliohacyn.* Wouldn't you have confidence in drugs with such names? The positive evaluative meaning that has been conditioned to proven drugs generalizes to these newly coined names. Now the drug firm has to develop drugs whose medicinal properties are as impressive as these names!

The conditioned meanings of words influence the names we give things. Although we would happily accept an invitation to a dinner of the finest filet mignon, we would think at least twice before agreeing to dine on a first-class piece of dead steer. Both phrases refer to the same thing, but we react differently to them because they evoke different connotations. It is common practice today to refer to the white and dark meat of a chicken, because in Victorian times the words *breast* and *leg* could,

348

only with difficulty, be separated from their sexual connotations and hence were barred from polite dinner table conversation. Today, because of the negative connotations of the word *butcher,* butchers prefer to be called meat cutters (or at least, meat cutters dislike being called butchers). And because *quart* and *pound* are more strongly conditioned to largeness than *pint* or *ounce,* advertisers label a can of beer a half-quart instead of a pint and a candy bar, one-eighth of a pound instead of two ounces.

The stimulus and response qualities of a word are shaped by the context in which the word appears. What response does this stimulus evoke?

square

Its meaning, that is, the response it evokes, differs from reader to reader. But the same word presented in several similar verbal contexts evokes essentially similar meanings.

> The table is *square.*
> A *square* is a form of a rectangle.
> The room is *square.*

Conversely, the same stimulus word elicits different responses when it is in different verbal contexts.

> It is a *square*-cut diamond.
> He is a *square.*
> That store is on the *square.*
> This information does not *square* with that.

In language behavior one cannot predict which of several possible responses a stimulus word or phrase will produce unless one knows the context in which it occurs.

Words are not imbedded in a verbal context in any haphazard order. "May I please have a glass of . . . ?" is a question that can be finished in a number of ways, but obviously, some words are more probable than others. You would not be surprised to hear this phrase end with a word like *water, beer,* or *soda,* but you would be startled to hear *snakes* or *clouds* instead. Words have different probabilities of being associated with other words. For example, names of beverages have relatively high probabilities of finishing the question, "May I please have a glass of . . . ?" and the words *snakes* or *clouds* have very low probabilities, but not zero probability. Perhaps in some zoology laboratory small snakes are placed in glass receptacles, and there somebody could conceivably say, "May I please have a glass of snakes?" "May I please have a glass of clouds?" could easily serve as the first line of a modern poem or the last line of a joke, or as an example of some *unlikely* verbal chain.

THE STRUCTURE AND USE OF LANGUAGE

The meanings of words and the various associations among them, as well as their probabilities of occurrence, make up the *structure of the language.* The structure of a language determines to a large extent how the language will be used, just as the shape of a tool will determine its use.

Extensional and Intensional Meaning

Language provides us with two kinds of meaning. **Extensional meaning** refers to the object a word stands for. The question, "What is a kettledrum?" can be answered by pointing to a kettledrum, the word's external referent. Infants usually learn new words this way. A kettledrum can, however, be defined another way. It can be described by words as a musical instrument consisting of a brass hemispherical shell with a parchment head. Such a description or definition can help someone identify a kettledrum even though he has never seen one. He can do this because some of the words used in the definition have extensional meanings. The meaning conveyed by the verbal description of a word is known as its **intensional meaning.**

Names can aid in discriminations (see page 343). Preschool children who are taught distinctive names for similar objects learn to discriminate among them more rapidly than children who have learned no names (Cantor, 1955). The ability to respond with distinctive names counteracts the effects of stimulus generalization and thereby facilitates discrimination.

Since all people live in the same world, we might expect them all to devise words, though different ones, for the same physical referents. Snow is snow, no matter what you call it, and each group which speaks a different language and experiences snow should have a word for it. But it is not as simple as that. Names help us all to discriminate among different events, but not all societies have to discriminate among the same events. Consider how important snow is to the Eskimo. For this reason, he needs to make very fine distinctions among the different kinds of snow (Pruitt, 1960). He has to know what kinds of snow are suitable for traveling by toboggan, what kinds require snowshoes, and what kind to build igloos from. Consequently, Eskimos have different names for different kinds of snow: *qali,* snow that collects on trees; *pukak,* deep snow; *upsik,* wind-beaten snow; *siqóq,* drifting snow; *kimoaqruk,* snowdrift. Unlike the Eskimos, we are not reinforced for noting these differences; snow is not usually so important for our survival. Hence our language has only one word for snow. But to the Eskimos, snow is not a single thing, it is a group of things.

On the other hand, in our society automobiles are highly important, and so our language contains words that allow for many fine distinctions: *sports car, hot rod, convertible, station wagon, hard-top, jalopy,* *sedan, coupé, limousine,* as well as the brand names—*Caddy, Ford,* etc.—which are sometimes used to describe a particular car. And if we are to judge by the more than 6,000 words Arabs have to describe a camel and its trappings, we can conclude that the camel in Arab countries is as important to them, if not more so, as the American automobile is to us.

In our society we tend to make fine discriminations among different colors. This is true particularly of those people (interior decorators, clothes designers) whose livelihood depends upon making precise color discriminations. In contrast, the Zuni Indians, in their native language, employ a single term for both orange and yellow. The difference between these colors obviously does not play a role in their everyday lives. Interestingly, Zunis who do not know English often confuse these two colors (Lenneberg & Roberts, 1953).

Although we all live in the same world, we do not describe it in the same way. Our language directs attention to some features while it permits us to ignore others.

The intensional meaning of a word can be found in a dictionary. This does not mean, however, that the word is used in only one way. The intensional meaning of a particular word may, and usually does, vary from person to person. Ask your classmates what they mean by the terms *liberal* and *conservative.* Or ask them to which category they would assign Nelson A. Rockefeller and John F. Kennedy? You will surely receive different answers simply because the intensional meanings of these words vary from person to person.

The fact that the same word may have a number of intensional meanings has unfortunate consequences. Controversies, some crucial to our very existence, cannot be resolved because different intensional meanings have been attached to key words. International harmony will be difficult to achieve as long as nations differ in their understanding of words like *aggression,*

350

freedom, and *democracy.* The confusions caused by different intensional meanings have led scientists to emphasize the extensional meanings of terms. This is why operational definitions (see page 9) are stressed in this book.

Verbal Habits

Closely related to the variations of the intensional meaning of words are differences in verbal habits. Words differ in the strength of their associations with other words. These differences are clearly revealed in the **word-association test.** In this test a person responds with the first word that occurs to him upon seeing or hearing a given stimulus word. What is the first word that occurs to you when you see the word *mother?* Your response, which will surely differ from the responses of many others, will be a word which you strongly associate with *mother,* at least at the moment.

Sir Francis Galton (1822-1911), a cousin of Charles Darwin and an outstanding scientist, first used the word-association test. He served as his own subject and refused to publish his reactions because, "They lay bare the foundations of a man's thoughts with curious distinctness, and exhibit his mental anatomy with more vividness and truth than he would probably care to publish to the world."

The word-association test is naturally of special interest to students of behavior. Carl G. Jung (1875-1961), a noted psychiatrist you will hear more about later, held that the word-association test is a powerful tool in diagnosing a person's difficulties. He concluded that a stimulus word which produced either an unusual or an excessively delayed response was associated with some personal emotional problem. But one cannot determine which response is unusual without first discovering which are the common responses. In 1910 (Kent & Rosanoff) a systematic study was carried out.

TABLE 11.1 Frequency of Word Associations in 1000 Men and Women, (Kent and Rosanoff, 1910)

STIMULUS—**chair**

191	table
127	seat
107	sit
83	furniture
56	sitting
49	wood
45	rest
38	stool
21	comfort
17	rocker
15	rocking
13	bench
12	cushion
11	legs
10	floor
9	desk, room
8	comfortable
7	ease, leg
6	easy, sofa, wooden
5	couch, hard, Morris, seated, soft
4	arm, article, brown, high
3	cane, convenience, house, large, lounge, low, mahogany, person, resting, rung, settee, useful
2	broken, hickory, home, necessity, oak, rounds, seating, use
1	back, beauty, bed, book, boy, bureau, caning, careful, carpet, cart, color, crooked, cushions, feet, foot, footstool, form, Governor Winthrop, hair, idleness, implement, joiner, lunch, massive, mission, myself, object, occupy, office, people, place, placed, plant, platform, pleasant, pleasure, posture, reading, rubber, size, spooning, stand, stoop, study, support, tables, talk, teacher, timber, tool, upholstered, upholstery, white

In it 1,000 men and women of different ages, occupations, and education were instructed to give "the first word that occurs to you other than the stimulus word." A list of 100 stimulus words was read to them and the subject's responses to each word were noted.

The results showed that the verbal habits

of individuals do indeed vary, but that in spite of these individual variations certain associations are quite common. Almost 20 per cent of the subjects gave the response *table* to the stimulus word *chair,* while slightly more than 10 per cent each gave the responses *seat* and *sit.* Thus, 40 per cent of the subjects responded to *table* with one of three words. Table 11.1 shows the frequency of the different responses to the word *chair.* Other words differed in the percentage of common responses they evoked. For example, 65 per cent of the subjects gave *light* as the response to the stimulus word *lamp.*

What determines these verbal habits? Several different variables are responsible. For one thing, as we mature our verbal habits change. Table 11.2 compares the common responses of children with those of two different groups of adults. Children tend to respond to stimulus words in a

TABLE 11.3 Similarity in Responses of Mother and Daughter (Jung, 1918)

STIMULUS WORD	RESPONSE WORDS	
	Mother	*Daughter*
Angel	Innocent	Innocent
Naughty	Bad boy	Bad boy
Stalk	Leek's stalk	Stalks for soup
Dance	Couple	Man and lady
Lake	Much water	Great
Threaten	Father	Father
Lamp	Burns bright	Gives light
Rich	King	King
New	Dress	Dress
Tooth	Biting	Pains
Take care	Industrious pupil	Pupil
Pencil	Long	Black
Law	God's command	Moses
Love	Child	Father and mother

TABLE 11.2 Word Associations from Different Groups of People (Woodworth, 1938)

STIMULUS	RESPONSE	1000 CHILDREN	1000 MEN AND WOMEN	1000 MEN IN INDUSTRY
Table	Eat	358	63	40
	Chair	24	274	333
Dark	Night	421	221	162
	Light	38	427	626
Man	Work	168	17	8
	Woman	8	394	561
Deep	Hole	257	32	20
	Shallow	6	180	296
Soft	Pillow	138	53	42
	Hard	27	365	548
Mountain ..	High	390	246	171
	Hill	91	184	364

word-association test with **syntagmatic associates,** that is, with words that would be next to them in a sentence (*dark-night, deep-hole*). Adults are not restricted in their associations to words that could be used in the same sentence. They favor **paradigmatic associates,** words which bear some logical relationship to the stimulus word. Words that contrast (*dark-light*) or that represent a similar class of objects (*table-chair*) are common adult responses. This change in verbal habits indicates that as a person matures he develops an understanding of more complicated interrelationships among words (Ervin, 1961).

Another important factor that influences verbal associations is the individual's background. Members of the same profession share common verbal habits (Foley & Macmillan, 1943). Lawyers respond more like other lawyers than like doctors. Members of the same family have been shown to have even greater correspondence among their word associations. Table 11.3 reports the similarity in the responses of a mother and daughter observed by Jung in 1918. This similarity is not surprising when you consider that most of the first words a child hears are those of his parents. Since small children are around their mother more often than their father, one would expect their verbal habits to be more like their mother's. This expectation has been confirmed, with the added observation—not unexpected since sons are encouraged to imitate their fathers—that father's and son's responses are more similar than father's and daughter's. The results of these observations can be summarized by the following principle: the more experiences people share, the more similar are their verbal habits.

Not only does the language behavior of an individual change with time, but so do the conventional verbal responses of an entire society. New words are invented, old ones become archaic, and associations between words change. The same word-association test was given to students at the University of Minnesota in 1927 and 1952 (Jenkins & Russell, 1960). The responses of the two different groups were similar in some ways but different in others. The most common response given to 71 of the 100 stimulus words remained the same. Of the 29 most common responses that were new in 1952, 22 had either been the second or third most popular responses in 1927. Thus, we may conclude that there was a fair degree of consistency in the popularity of certain responses to a set of stimulus words for a 25-year period. The absolute frequency, however, of the most common responses increased significantly. In 1927 the most common response was given by an average of 29 per cent of the subjects. This figure jumped to 38 per cent in 1952, suggesting greater conformity in the verbal habits of these college students. Perhaps this change reflects the greater impact of the mass media of television and radio; exposure to programs with a distinctive language pattern encourages a higher communality of word associations. Perhaps our school systems have become more standardized, so that a greater percentage of students learn the most common word associations. Or perhaps it is because more people

are going to college today that the use of common word associations has increased. In 1927 approximately 11 per cent of the high school graduates actually went to college, whereas in 1952 this percentage had increased to 22.

Another interesting trend appeared when the word associations of the two groups were compared. The 1927 students tended to respond more abstractly. They gave more superordinate responses, that is, words that represent a higher classification than the stimulus word (*spinach-vegetable, dog-animal, butterfly-insect*). In addition, the 1927 students responded more with synonyms (*swift-fast, blossom-flower*). In contrast the 1952 students responded more concretely by naming some property of the stimulus word (*room-dark*) or by naming a coordinate term (*apple-peach, dog-cat*). In short, it appears that the 1952 students behaved somewhat more immaturely when it came to word associations, in that their responses, as compared to those of the 1927 students, were more concrete.

Implicit Verbal Chains

Verbal habits are very powerful—so powerful that we are often unable to inhibit them. When the subjects in a word-association test were instructed to respond quickly with *un*associated words, it was found, nevertheless, that common associations were likely to guide their replies (Atherton & Washburn, 1912). For example, the stimulus word *sheep* evoked *cotton*, a response resulting from a mediated association in which *sheep* elicited an implicit response of *wool*, which in turn served as the cue for *cotton*. This is an example of an implicit verbal chain with the first word evoking an implicit response that serves as the cue for the overt verbal response.

These implicit verbal chains have been shown to facilitate simple paired associate learning. Common word associations are essentially pre-existing language habits.

Therefore, paired-associates connected by intervening common word associations should be relatively easy to learn. Let us see how this hypothesis was confirmed.

First, college students learned (Russell & Storms, 1955) a list of paired-associates in which the stimulus was a nonsense syllable and the response, a real word (*cef-stem*). Then they were trained to associate the old stimulus (*cef*) with a new response. Half the new response words were related to the old ones as members of the same verbal chain. For example, some subjects were required to pair *smell* with *cef;* others had to pair *joy* with *cef*. The former was easier to do because *smell* is the final member of a three-item verbal chain that begins with *stem*. The most common word association given to *stem* is *flower,* and the most common word association to *flower* is *smell*. That is, *stem* evokes *flower,* which in turn has a tendency to elicit *smell*. Thus, after learning *cef-stem* it was easier to learn *cef-smell* than to learn *cef-joy,* because the former was facilitated by an already learned implicit verbal chain.

This study was done with a group of subjects. A single individual who generally associates *glassware* with *stem* would probably not profit from having learned *cef-stem* in learning *cef-smell*. If we could know exactly what verbal habits a given person has and how strong each is, we could predict with great accuracy the course of his verbal learning. So far this is not possible. But an attempt is being made to understand the effects of the kinds of verbal associations different individuals have. One study (Peterson & Jenkins, 1957) shows that a person's verbal habits are not isolated parts of his total behavior pattern. The behavior of a college student whose word associations were similar to the average responses of the student body was compared with the behavior of an individual student who had uncommon verbal habits. The comparison revealed that the social and intellectual behavior of the former resem-bled that of other students more than did that of the latter. This would suggest that the more a person's verbal associations resemble those of others, the more conventional will his behavior be.

The Sentence

Up to now our discussion of language behavior has been largely restricted to simple word responses. The meaning of single words and their capacity to evoke other single words have been our major concern. These two topics, however, do not by any means exhaust all the psychological characteristics of verbal behavior. Far from it. Probably our most important verbal ability is combining words into meaningful sentences.

As a matter of fact, we rarely communicate in single words. Even when we do, other words are usually implied. The command "Stop!" means to the person commanded, "You stop what you are doing." The infant's babbled "bottle" (or something close to it) probably means, "I want a bottle, now."

When he begins to speak, a baby uses only such one-word sentences. Not until he is approximately 24 months old does he delight his parents by combining two words, usually nouns, into a rudimentary sentence. "Ken-toy" might mean "Ken has a toy" or "Ken took my toy." Verbs are usually absent from these two-word sentences, so that the listener has to infer the intended relationship between the words. When he is three years of age, verbs, adjectives, and other parts of speech appear in the child's sentences. Thus, in terms of the developmental pattern, nouns are the simplest kind of words. This agrees with the observation that nouns were the only words a chimpanzee was able to learn to use appropriately (see page 339).

This important ability to combine words into sentences is much more difficult to analyze than the association between one word and another which we dealt with before. Nevertheless, some attempts have been made to understand how words are linked together to form sentences. These endeavors have been largely restricted, however, to simple present-tense sentences that equate a subject with a complement (Mr. Jones is a thief).

The function that the verb plays in this simple sentence is to equate Jones with a thief (Mowrer, 1954), placing him in a class of persons to which we have learned definite responses. The negative reactions we have to the concept of thief thus become attached to Mr. Jones. Since we avoid or are suspicious of thieves, we will now avoid or be suspicious of Mr. Jones. In this way, a simple statement like "Mr. Jones is a thief" can help us save the time and property that we might lose if we had to learn about Mr. Jones' unpleasant inclinations by ourselves. This transfer of meaning resembles a simple case of classical conditioning in some respects. *Thief* acts like an unconditioned stimulus that evokes a negative response. *Mr. Jones* functions like a conditioned stimulus. Just as the salivary response was transferred from the food (unconditioned stimulus) to the tone (conditioned stimulus), so the negative reaction to *thief* (unconditioned stimulus) is transferred to *Mr. Jones* (conditioned stimulus).

Some students may ask why the meaning is not transferred from Mr. Jones to the word *thief?* Sometimes it is. Suppose Mr. Jones is a friend whom you like and respect, and suppose there were extenuating circumstances to his theft. In this case some of the positive feelings you would have for Mr. Jones could easily be transferred to all thieves, so that you would realize that they also might not be entirely responsible for their misdeeds.

An interesting example of how a response to a negative word can be modified comes from an experiment (Staats, Staats & Biggs, 1958), designed like the one in which non-sense syllables acquired meaning (see page 347). The unpleasant words *unfair* and *awful* were paired with one of two sets of words. One set had been rated pleasant, the other unpleasant. The negative evaluative meanings of *unfair* and *awful* were found to be modified, depending upon whether they were paired with pleasant or unpleasant words. When paired with pleasant words their evaluative meaning was much more positive than when paired with unpleasant words.

Attempts to transfer meaning from one word to another often occur in political debate. By insidious repetition politicians try to make the electorate adopt syllogisms such as the following:

War is bad.
Wars during the twentieth century have occurred under Democratic administrations.
Therefore, the Democratic Party is bad.

Depressions are bad.
The Great Depression of 1929 started during a Republican administration.
Therefore, the Republican Party is bad.

Although the validity, as well as the logic, of such arguments is open to question, voters have nevertheless at times proved to be susceptible to such political appeals.

Our discussion of language behavior suggests that it has much in common with simpler forms of behavior. The acquisition of the extensional meaning of a word, as well as the transfer of meaning that occurs in a simple declarative sentence, resembles conditioning in important respects. Psychologists have only just begun to understand verbal behavior, but you will find that even the limited insights we have had space for here will be useful to you in enlarging your understanding of some more complex forms of behavior we shall discuss later in the book.

PROBLEM SOLVING

Consider this problem. Two trains traveling toward each other are 100 miles apart. The train going east is speeding along at 60 miles an hour. The westbound train travels at a rate of 40 miles an hour. A bird flying east at a speed of 80 miles per hour starts from the front of one train and heads directly toward the other. When the bird reaches the other train he turns around and immediately flies back westward without losing any speed or time in turning. The bird continues to fly back and forth between the two trains as they approach each other. How many miles will the bird travel before the two trains reach each other?

How do you solve such a problem? The problem itself is clear, but not the method of solving it. A common reaction to this problem is first to determine the number of miles the bird will fly on his initial eastbound trip, then to determine the number on each of his successive trips between the approaching trains, and finally to add all the distances and obtain the answer. This method requires, however, the kind of complex figuring that only a competent mathematician can do. If you have difficulty trying to find the solution to the problem using this method, you might try to solve it another way. Since the trains are 100 miles apart and since they are traveling directly toward each other at 40 and 60 miles per hour, respectively, they will meet in one hour. The bird is traveling at 80 miles per hour. Hence, he will have traveled exactly 80 miles before the two trains meet.

This problem and the behavior required for its solution throw light on some of the basic characteristics of problem solving. First, in a problem-solving situation the correct response is not immediately forthcoming. If it were, there would be no prob-lem. There is a psychological gap between the problem and its solution that can be filled only by discovering the correct response. Second, human problem-solving behavior consists largely of covert responses. Confronted with the problem above, you may have started "talking to yourself" about various ways of solving it. But no one would know what method you were using until you started making some overt responses, such as whispering or writing numbers on a paper, that to some extent would expose your problem-solving method to others. That is to say, much of the underlying processes of solving a problem are hidden from immediate observation. Third, the correct solution often occurs suddenly, after a period of little or no apparent progress. Problem solvers frequently feel that they are making no headway, and then suddenly, they get a flash of *insight* that enables them to solve the problem.

Our task, however, is not merely to describe features of problem solving; we must try to make you understand it. In order to do this, we must first give you a picture of problem solving in relation to the whole field of psychology.

THE PSYCHOLOGY OF PROBLEM SOLVING

In our discussion we have differentiated complex learning from conditioning by noting the different psychological processes each emphasizes. With conditioning our major emphasis was upon the formation and strengthening of a single S-R association. In discussing complex learning situations in turn, we emphasized how S-R associations are linked together (chaining) and how they compete with each other (habit competition). Problem solving also involves chaining and habit competition, but to a much greater degree. The chains are longer and the habit competition is more frequent. And to make analysis more difficult, the longer chains and subtler habit competition are usually not directly observable.

When you were confronted with the bird and train problem, you could have made one of several different responses: you could have tried to determine the distance traveled by the bird on its first trip; you could have tried to discover the amount of time the bird would have to fly before the trains crossed; you might have come up with some other solution. The point, however, is that several responses were available, and only one of them could occur first. In short, habit competition was operating. In addition, when one habit was activated it led to a sequence of responses. Determining the distance traveled by the bird on its first trip led to an attempt to discover the distance it traveled on its second trip, and so on. Each attempt to solve the problem consisted of a chain of responses, some of which extended over a long period of time.

It is impossible to draw a line separating problem solving from other kinds of learning. The difference appears to be one of degree. There is covert behavior in conditioning as well as in complex learning tasks, but there is a great deal more covert behavior involved in problem solving. The same holds for such processes as habit chaining and habit competition. It would seem, then, that as the learning process becomes more complex, it merges into problem solving.

To many people the most distinctive feature of problem solving is that it involves original behavior. In solving the bird and train problem for the first time you have to make an original response, one you have never made before. The originality of problem-solving behavior is, of course, illustrated most forcefully by the strikingly unique behavior of Darwin or Einstein in formulating their revolutionary theories.

No man had previously formulated, at least with such convincing brilliance, their respective theories of natural selection in evolution and of general relativity.

Originality, however, is not as distinctive to problem solving as you may think. Original behavior emerges in many learning situations. Consider, for example, the shaping behavior described in the preceding chapter (see page 291). With appropriate reinforcement, pigeons can be made to exhibit such original behavior as whirling rapidly around in circles.

It is important to understand that original behavior does not emerge from a vacuum, but is as dependent on the subject's past experience as is a conditioned response. Solving the bird and train problem requires an original response, but this response is dependent on familiarity with the concepts of speed and numbers. Darwin had to acquire a vast acquaintance with different animal species and their environments before he could formulate his theory of evolution. Einstein had to master intricate mathematical techniques and accumulate a profound knowledge of physics before he was ready to develop his theory of relativity. Certainly it was no accident that it was Darwin who formulated the theory of evolution and Einstein who formulated the theory of relativity and not the other way around. Both these original scientific theories had roots going far back into the experience of their authors.

Because problem solving is not sharply separated from learning, the reader approaches the topic with some preparation. Again, an understanding of simple forms of behavior will be useful in comprehending its more complicated forms.

Before we begin to sketch the general outlines of the topic, we must formulate a working definition of problem solving. For our purposes it can be said that problem solving deals with an organism's behavior in discovering a correct response to a new situation. Our interest will be in factors that influence this activity, beginning with symbolic behavior.

Symbolic Behavior

One question that has intrigued psychologists is whether or not animals are capable of symbolic behavior. Obviously, the answer depends on our definition of symbolic behavior. If we define symbolic behavior as a response to a cue that represents something else (the word *apple* represents the object *apple*), then we are forced to conclude that animals are capable of symbolic behavior. The dogs in Pavlov's classical conditioning experiments learned to react to the tone as they did to food. The tone became a symbol of food to come. But all mammals prove easy to condition, and so we still must answer the question, how different are the capacities of different

mammals to respond to symbolic cues? In order to answer this question psychologists devised two experimental techniques: the **delayed reaction method** and the **double alternation method.**

Delayed Reaction Method. In a delayed reaction experiment the animal is placed in a wire mesh enclosure at one side of a large box (see Figure 11.3). At each of the three remaining sides there is a compartment with a light over the door. The floor of the box contains an electrified wire grid that can shock the rat's paws when the current is on. At first, the animal receives food when he chooses the compartment with the light turned on, but he receives a shock when he chooses either of the two unlighted compartments. The compartment that is lighted varies from trial to trial to insure that the animal is responding to the light

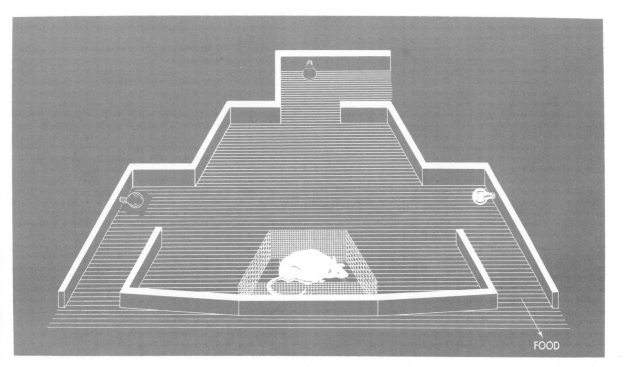

FIGURE 11.3 A Delayed Reaction Box. The subject is placed in a wire mesh enclosure that serves as a starting box. After learning to choose the lighted compartment, the animal must learn to choose the compartment which *had been lighted* but is dark at the time he must make the choice (After Hunter, 1913).

and not just to a particular position.

After the animal has learned to select the lighted compartment, the delayed reaction feature is introduced. The light over one compartment is turned on and turned off *before* the animal is released from the wire mesh enclosure (delayed chamber).

The results (Munn, 1950) differed widely among different species. Rats could make correct responses only if the delay did not exceed 10 seconds. Dogs could respond after delays up to 3 minutes, whereas five-year-old children were able to make correct responses after delay periods of more than 20 minutes.

Of greater importance than the duration of the delay period was the behavior of the animals between the time the light went off and their release from the delay chamber. In the first delayed reaction experiment (Hunter, 1913), rats were able to respond correctly only if they kept their heads and bodies oriented toward the correct compartment during the entire period of delay. If they turned away from the correct compartment they lost their ability to respond appropriately. In short, their choice behavior depended on their maintaining an appropriate posture. This would suggest that kinesthetic cues (see page 93) were responsible for their symbolic behavior.

The symbolic behavior of higher-order animals was not limited to the maintenance of an appropriate posture. A raccoon, for example, had no need for maintaining a fixed bodily orientation during the delay period. For periods up to 15 seconds, he could turn from side to side in the delay chamber and then go directly to the correct compartment after being released. Young children could delay successfully for much longer periods of time without maintaining any fixed bodily orientation. The symbolic behavior of raccoons and young children, unlike that of the rats, obviously did not depend on kinesthetic cues. There

is one important conclusion to be drawn from this and related studies: different species have different capacities to generate covert or implicit responses that function as symbolic cues.

Double Alternation Method. The double alternation method constitutes a more demanding test of symbolic behavior than the delayed reaction method. In the delayed reaction experiment the relevant cue is initially an external stimulus. The animals first learn to respond to a light and later develop an internal cue to symbolize the light. In a double alternation experiment the animal must, even at the very beginning, generate the relevant symbolic cue himself.

Figure 11.4 shows the floor plan of a maze used in a double alternation experiment. From the starting point in the center alley of this maze the animal must make a sequence of different responses to the same stimulus situation, the choice point. In the double alternation response sequence the subject makes two successive turning responses in one direction, followed by two successive turning responses in the opposite direction (right, right, left, left). After making the first correct response (right turn), he must return to the starting point by way of the outside alley where he will make the second correct response, and so on. The reward is withheld until he makes the correct sequence of responses.

The double alternation (RRLL) response sequence cannot be learned simply on the basis of kinesthetic cues from the last response. Since a right response has to be followed by a right response the first time and by a left response the next time, the cues from the right response cannot always serve as the stimulus for the next response.

Rats do very poorly in double alternation experiments. With extensive practice a few rats have learned to make the first four turns of a double alternation se-

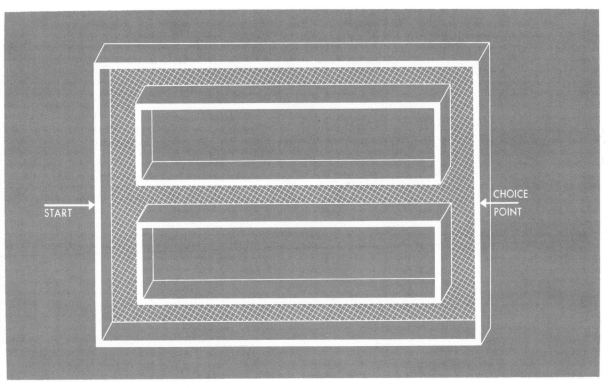

FIGURE 11.4 The Floor Plan of a Double Alternation Maze. In order to solve the problem the subject must make two successive turning responses in one direction followed by two successive turning responses in the opposite direction (right, right, left, left). No external cue is available to guide his behavior.

quence, but even these animals have not been able to extend the sequence farther (Hunter & Nagge, 1931). Raccoons (Hunter, 1928) can learn an RRLLRR sequence, and monkeys can do several additional turns (Gellerman, 1931). Human beings, with the aid of their language ability, can extend the double alternation sequence indefinitely.

The delayed reaction and double alternation experiments demonstrate that animals, in varying degrees, can behave symbolically. To do so they require extensive training. Literally hundreds and sometimes thousands of training trials are required before animals can generate cues that consistently represent past events (the light in the delayed reaction experiment or the sequence of turns in the double alternation study). In contrast, language ability

allows humans to solve the same problems, as well as much more complex ones, with ease.

Reversal and Nonreversal Shifts in Discrimination Learning. The difference between the capacity of animals and men to react to symbolic cues is clearly revealed by their ability to transfer what is learned in one discrimination problem to another. Consider for a moment a relatively simple discrimination task. Subjects must discover which of two different squares, varying both in size (large and small) and brightness (black and white), is correct. For choosing only one of the four stimulus elements (large, small, black, and white), the subject is consistently reinforced. If, for example, the large cue is correct, then the subject must select it regardless of whether the

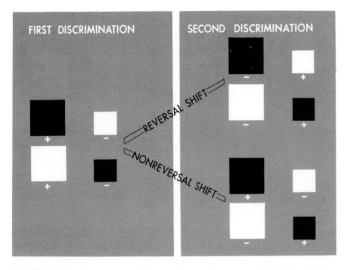

FIGURE 11.5 Examples of Reversal and Nonreversal Shifts in Discrimination Learning. In a reversal shift, after learning to select the large stimuli in the first discrimination, the subject is reinforced for selecting the small stimuli in the second discrimination. In a nonreversal shift, he is required to respond to another dimension (brightness) in the second discrimination (After Kendler & Kendler, 1962).

square is black or white. In this discrimination problem size is the *relevant* dimension because the subject must attend to it; brightness is *irrelevant* and must be ignored.

After learning such a discrimination, the subject can be shifted to a new problem. He can be trained to choose small instead of large. This transfer problem is known as a **reversal shift,** since the subject must learn to make a response opposite to the one he had previously learned. In another kind of transfer problem, a **nonreversal shift,** the subject is required to respond to a different dimension, to shift his preference from large to black (or white). That is, in a reversal shift the subject must respond to the same dimension but reverse his preference within that dimension; in a nonreversal shift the subject must learn to respond to a dimension which he had learned to ignore previously.

Reversal and nonreversal shifts can be arranged for discrimination problems of various levels of difficulty. Some are sufficiently easy for rats to solve: others tax the

problem-solving ability of human adults. Thus, we can compare the ability of different species to execute reversal and non-reversal shifts. In doing so we have noted a striking difference between humans and animals. Human adults accomplish a reversal shift much more rapidly than they can accomplish a nonreversal shift (Kendler & Kendler, 1962a), whereas rats find a non-reversal shift somewhat easier to make (Kelleher, 1956). The explanation for this lies in the manner in which rats and humans solve discrimination problems. Rats learn simple habits. Initially they learn to approach the black object and avoid the white one. A reversal shift is terribly difficult for them because they have to extinguish completely a habit that has been continuously reinforced, and then develop a new habit, which has never previously been reinforced. Human adults, on the other hand, find a reversal shift easy to make because they do not simply associate their choice response directly to the relevant stimuli but make instead an implicit response which functions as a cue for their choice. For example, if the correct stimulus is black, the human generates a symbolic response (e.g., the "darker" or "black but not white") which serves as the cue for the selection of the correct alternative. Since a similar kind of symbolic response is appropriate in a reversal shift, because the relevant dimension remains the same, this kind of shift is easy for humans to accomplish. In a nonreversal shift, however, the human subject must learn an entirely new symbolic response (e.g. from "darker" to "larger" or "smaller"), and therefore he finds it more difficult than a reversal shift. Figure 11.6 schematizes the different psychological processes of rats and of humans in executing reversal and nonreversal shifts.

This difference in the relative speeds with which rats and humans execute reversal and nonreversal shifts reflects the importance of symbolic behavior in prob-

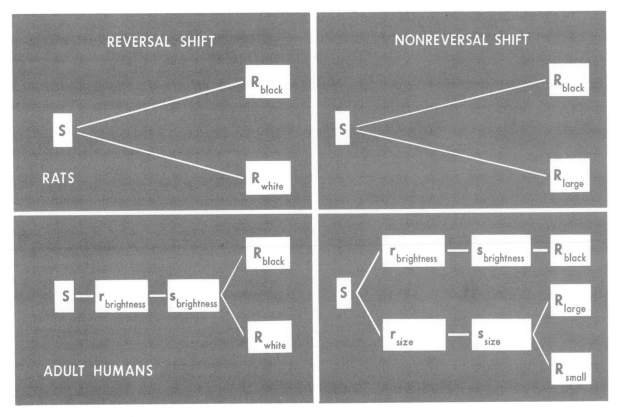

FIGURE 11.6 A Schematic Representation of the Differences Between Behavior of Rats and of Adult Humans in Executing Reversal and Nonreversal Shifts (After Kendler & Kendler, 1962).

lem solving. The ability to make appropriate implicit responses transforms a difficult reversal shift into an easy task. A study (Kendler & Kendler, 1959) with kindergarten children strongly suggests that a reversal shift is easy for children who have acquired verbal responses appropriate to the problem, but very difficult for those who have not.

Habit Integration

Some problems can be solved by combining separate and distinct habits. Two examples of habit integration come from studies designed to examine reasoning and insight.

Reasoning. In one experiment in reasoning (Kendler & Kendler, 1962*b*) two groups of

children, one of kindergarten age and the other in the third grade, were trained to use an apparatus (see Figure 11.7) with three distinctively colored panels. In the center of each of the side panels was a button and an opening. When the button on the left panel was pressed, a steel ball bearing dropped out of the opening; when the button on the right panel was pressed a glass marble appeared. After the children had learned this difference, their attention was shifted to the center panel, in which there was a circular opening. Into this opening they could insert either the ball bearing or the marble. If the ball bearing were inserted, a gold-colored charm dropped into a trough near the bottom of the panel, whereas if the marble were inserted nothing appeared.

361

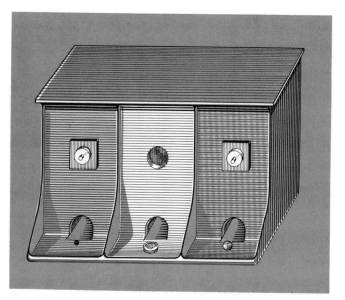

FIGURE 11.7 The Design of the Apparatus Used to Investigate Reasoning. The button on the left delivers a ball bearing, whereas the button on the right releases a marble. If the ball bearing is inserted into the circular opening of the center panel, a charm is delivered into the trough near the bottom of the panel.

After the children had become accustomed to the apparatus and understood how it worked, the test of their reasoning began. They were instructed to get a charm. The correct solution to this problem is obviously not very difficult; it involves only two steps. The subjects have merely to press the button on the left panel, take the ball bearing, and drop it into the opening in the center panel. In spite of its apparent simplicity, kindergartners find this a most difficult problem. Only a very small proportion of them, about 5 per cent, solved the problem without making an incorrect response, like pressing the button that delivered the marble. The third graders discovered the correct procedure much more easily, half of them solving the problem directly.

Some readers may question whether such behavior should be labeled *reasoning*. The behavior exhibited they will say, may be a succession of two *distinct* habits. After the first habit is executed (pressing the button

on the left panel), the child finds himself in a situation that contains the stimuli (the ball bearing and the center panel) that elicit the second habit (inserting the ball bearing into the opening of the middle panel). But there is experimental evidence to show that this behavior is really reasoned behavior, not merely the successive evocation of two separate habits. On some of the test trials for some of the subjects, the apparatus was so arranged that when the button on the right panel was pressed, the ball bearing dropped into the trough, instead of the marble that had appeared during training. If the subject's behavior were in this case based on two distinct habits, approximately the same percentage of subjects who got the ball bearing from the right panel as got it from the left panel would insert it into the opening in the center panel. This is not what happened. A significantly (see page 59) larger percentage of subjects who made the initially correct response (pressing the button on the left panel) made the second correct response (dropping the ball bearing into the opening of the center panel). In short, the evidence suggested that the chain of two habits involved in this **reasoning** sequence was integrated; the occurrence of the second habit depended on the occurrence of the first. In other words, the second habit became conditioned to the response-produced cues of the first habit.

Insight. At the outbreak of World War I, Wolfgang Köhler, a German psychologist, was studying anthropoid apes on an island off the coast of Africa. Prevented from returning to his native land, Köhler decided to investigate the problem-solving ability of chimpanzees rather than become a beachcomber on the tropical island. In one of the problems Köhler devised to investigate this ability, a chimpanzee was shown a banana suspended from the top of the cage out of his reach. At the other end of the cage there was a box which he could use to stand on and grasp the food if he moved it under the banana. Typically, the animal jumped for the food repeatedly without success. Eventually these futile jumping responses were extinguished, giving way to restless pacing. Then usually, the animal suddenly stopped pacing in front of the box, pushed it to a position below the banana, climbed on top, and grabbed the fruit.

Köhler used the term **insight** to describe the behavior of these chimpanzees. He assumed that insight resulted from a sudden change in the chimpanzee's perception of the problem. Instead of seeing the box and banana as isolated objects, the chimpanzee suddenly perceived them as related parts of a problem-solving sequence. As a result of this new perception he was able to solve the problem. Of course, Köhler did not observe the insight process directly, but inferred it from the behavior of the animals.

At first glance it seems that insight is not dependent on past experience, that it is unlearned. Such a conclusion, however, does not agree with the results of another experiment (Birch, 1945), in which young chimpanzees were confronted with food just beyond their reach outside their cages. Within reach, however, was a stick they could use to gather in the food. Only one of the six animals solved the problem, and he was the only one who previously had extensive experience playing with sticks. The five other animals were then given sticks to play with for a three-day period. During this time they were never observed using the sticks as rakes; they used them to poke the other chimpanzees or the experimenter. Yet when these five animals were retested they solved the problem with ease. Their experience with the sticks enabled the chimpanzees to use them as rakes in solving the problem. In short, insight is dependent on the transfer of previous responses to the problem situation. There is no evidence for unlearned insight.

These experiments in insight resemble the studies in reasoning in that both processes depend on the integration of previously learned habits. The specific symbolic responses in such integrating behavior are difficult to identify, and for the time being we can only remind you that symbolic responses are not different from other forms of behavior. Symbolic behavior is simply another example of a response serving as a cue. It is a kind of mediated behavior. Mediated behavior has many forms. It can be relatively simple, as in convergence (see page 199), where the stimulation produced by movement of eye muscles serves as a cue for depth perception. Or, it can be relatively complex, as in problem-solving behavior, where the organism is required to generate a series of mediated responses that provide the cues for an implicit behavior chain leading to solution of the problem. Although these two examples of behavior differ widely in their complexity, they both reflect the common psychological process that underlies all mediated behavior: covert responses provide cues for subsequent behavior.

Habit Competition and Problem Solving

Problems are often difficult to solve because the incorrect responses persist and thus prevent one from making the correct one. The solution is delayed or even prevented, not because the subject is incapable of making the correct response, but rather because he cannot avoid making the incorrect response. This point is clearly demonstrated in the following cases.

Detour Problems. Organisms learn to go directly to goal objects if they can. A dog, at supper time, approaches his food in a straight line rather than in a roundabout manner. By taking a direct route he experiences less delay in obtaining reinforcement (see page 170).

364

Sometimes, however, organisms are confronted with problems in which the goal object is in sight, but a direct approach is blocked. Figure 11.8 illustrates such a problem. The child cannot reach directly for the doll because an obstacle blocks her way. She must take a roundabout approach,

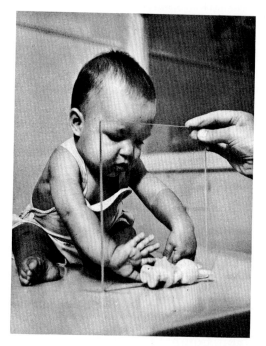

FIGURE 11.8 A Detour Problem. The child cannot get the doll by going directly toward it. In order to get the incentive, she must learn to move her hand away from it before approaching it (Houghton Mifflin).

actually moving her hand away from the doll in order to reach it. This sort of task has been described appropriately as a *detour* or *Umweg* (from the German, meaning *roundabout*) problem, since its solution demands an indirect approach.

Detour problems involve habit competition. The habit of going directly toward a goal object competes with the habit of going farther away from it. Only if the latter habit competes successfully with the former will the subject solve the problem. Whether or not he solves a detour problem

depends on the relative strengths of the competing habits. If the habit to go directly toward an incentive is very strong, then it will be difficult for him to adopt a roundabout response to avoid the obstacle. In other words, the stronger the direct approach habit, the more difficult it is to solve the problem.

The closer an animal is to food, the stronger is his tendency to approach it and, we can predict, the greater his difficulty in surmounting any obstacle blocking his direct approach. One observation (Köhler, 1925) of the behavior of a chimpanzee seems to support this prediction. When the chimpanzee was standing behind a wire fence and food was thrown some distance away on the other side, he had no difficulty in going around the fence to get the food. However, when the food was placed just on the opposite side, the animal seemed helpless. The very nearness of the food, with its tendency to evoke a strong approach response, prevented him from taking any other step toward solving the problem. Another observation (Lewin, 1935) supporting this principle is that children have more difficulty solving an *Umweg* problem when they are highly motivated. The greater their drive, the stronger their tendency to go straight toward the goal object, and this in turn makes it difficult for them to adopt a roundabout approach.

Observations on the behavior of one chimpanzee, or even of several children, do not establish the validity of a general scientific principle. They are, nevertheless, of interest in suggesting underlying principles which may be confirmed by further investigation. The detour problems do show that complex behavior can be analyzed in terms of principles that apply to simpler forms of behavior.

The habit competition between a direct and a roundabout approach is greater for certain subjects than for others. The child in Figure 11.8 was eight months old and intellectually advanced for her age, but she was unable to solve the problem. Older children have no difficulty when confronted with a similar detour problem. They learn by experience that when an obstacle bars the way, they can attain the incentive only by going, in some sense, away from it at first.

Functional Fixedness. Another phenomenon that underlines the importance of habit competition in problem solving is functional fixedness. **Functional fixedness** refers to the difficulty an organism has in using an object in a manner different from that he is accustomed to. The psychological root of this difficulty is the great strength of the "wrong habit."

You can understand the meaning of functional fixedness best if we describe an actual experiment. College students were instructed to tie together two strings hanging from the ceiling. The distance between the strings was too great for the subjects to be able to reach one string while holding on to the other. They could solve the problem only by tying a weight to the end of one string and converting it into a pendulum, which could be set swinging. When it reached the top of its swing, they could catch it while they held on to the other string (see Figure 11.9).

In one experiment (Birch & Rabinowitz, 1951) involving this two-string problem, only two objects were available to be used as weights: an electric switch and an electrical relay. The subjects were divided into different groups and were given different experiences before they were confronted with the central problem. Group *S* was asked to complete an electrical circuit by installing a *switch*; Group *R* had to install a *relay* to complete the circuit. Shortly afterward they were asked to solve the two-string problem by using either the relay or the switch, both of which were lying on the table.

Which of the two objects did either group of subjects use as a weight? To

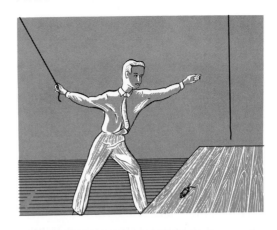

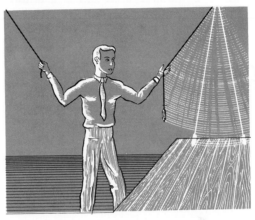

FIGURE 11.9 The Two-String Problem. The problem is to tie the two strings together when they are too far apart to hold one while grasping the other.

answer this question, you must remember that in each case there was competition between the habits to use one of the objects as an electrical item or merely as a weight. Each group's experience in using that object to complete the electrical circuit strengthened the habit of using it in its electrical function. After using a switch as a switch or a relay as a relay the groups were less likely to use them as weights. From this analysis you would predict that the subjects in Group *R* (relay group) would tend to use the switch as a weight in solving the two-string problem, whereas subjects in Group *S* would prefer to use the relay in that capacity. This prediction was confirmed.

366

The term *functional fixedness* is particularly appropriate to this phenomenon. The traditional function of an object becomes so fixed that its user cannot use it in a different manner. That is, when a habit to respond in a particular way to a given object has become very strong, it is difficult, if not impossible, for us to respond to it in another way. It is nearly impossible to see a printed word as a black-on-white design. It is a *word* and not a *design*.

Another experiment in functional fixedness confirms these last statements (Adamson, 1952). Subjects were shown a number of different objects, including three candles, lying on a table. They were instructed to mount each of the three candles vertically on a wooden screen. Among the objects available to them were (see Figure 11.10) three cardboard boxes, some matches, and thumbtacks. The subjects could solve the problem by dripping melted candle wax

on the outside end of each box, sticking the base of each candle in the wax, and tacking the boxes with the candles to the screen.

The problem was presented differently to each of two groups of college students. For one group the candles, tacks, and matches were placed *in* the three boxes, so that the subjects were encouraged to respond to the boxes as containers. For the second group the boxes were empty and the objects were lying loose on the table. Which group demonstrated better problem-solving ability? The important point is whether one group of subjects was more inclined than the other group to use the boxes as shelves for the candles. Since the first group was encouraged to respond to the boxes as containers, they would be less inclined to respond to them as shelves than the second group. The results confirmed this analysis. Forty-one per cent of

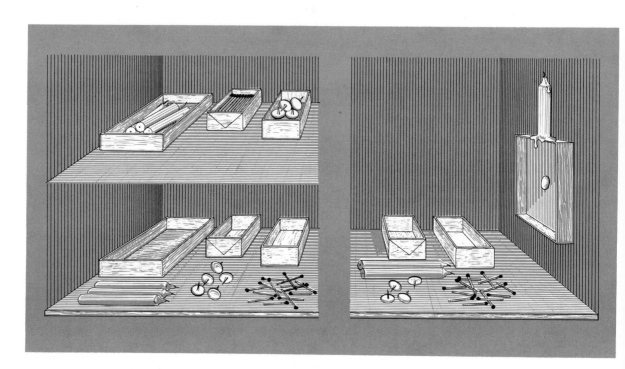

FIGURE 11.10 A Problem Used to Investigate Functional Fixedness. The subjects are instructed to mount each of the three candles vertically on a wooden screen using only the objects shown above. The problem is much more difficult to solve when it is presented with the boxes filled with the other objects.

the first group of subjects were able to solve the problem in less than 20 minutes. In contrast, 86 per cent of the subjects in the second group solved the problem within the same time.

One variation (Glucksberg, 1962) of this functional fixedness experiment illustrates how different levels of motivation facilitate or hamper problem solving, depending upon whether the correct habit is weak or strong to begin with. You may recall that strong motivation retarded reversal learning (see page 278). Because the correct habit is initially very weak in reversal learning, a strong drive has the effect of increasing the time needed to extinguish the previously correct but now incorrect habit. If the same principle applies to problem-solving behavior, then we would expect that when the correct response is very weak and the incorrect response strong, high motivation would retard problem solving. This hypothesis led to the experiment in which two groups of college students were given the difficult task of mounting candles vertically on wooden screens when the matches, thumbtacks, and candles were placed in the boxes that had to serve as shelves. One group was motivated by the promise of, what was under the circumstances, a large sum of money if they solved the problem quickly. The other was merely instructed to solve the problem. The performance of the group with the weaker drive was superior to the group with the stronger drive.

Another portion of the same study demonstrated that it was not low motivation *per se* that facilitated the problem solving. When the problem was made very easy so that the correct response was dominant, a high drive was more effective for problem solving than a low drive. In this part of the experiment the boxes were empty and the instructions subtly suggested the correct response.

So you see, the relationship between motivation and problem solving is not sim-ple. Some motivation is needed, but motivation by itself is not sufficient. Appropriate habits are also necessary. Moreover, the particular level of motivation suitable to a given problem depends upon the relative strength of the correct habit. If it is very weak, a strong drive can actually retard or even prevent problem solution.

Set. In both the detour and functional fixedness problems a correct response has difficulty competing successfully with an incorrect response. This is also true of problems involving a **set** or *Einstellung* (the German word meaning *mental set*). An organism learns a set in a situation and then finds it difficult or impossible to shift to a more appropriate response.

A response becomes a set simply by continuous reinforcement. Consider the following series of problems, each of which you must solve by obtaining a prescribed volume of water. For example, if you have a 29-pint jar, a 3-pint jar, and an unlimited supply of water, how do you measure out exactly 20 pints of water? You fill the 29-pint vessel and then pour 9 pints from it by filling the 3-pint container three times: $29 - 3 - 3 - 3 = 20$. Now solve the first of the following six problems.

	CAPACITIES OF JARS IN PINTS			PINTS TO OBTAIN
1.	21	127	3	100
2.	14	163	25	99
3.	18	43	10	5
4.	10	41	8	15
5.	18	41	8	7
6.	23	49	3	20

You can solve the first problem easily. You fill the 127-pint jar and from it fill the 21-pint jar once and the 3-pint jar twice. After these operations the 127-pint jar will contain exactly 100 pints of water: $127 - 21 - 3 - 3 = 100$. Now do the remaining five problems.

Typical subjects who do not know about the phenomenon of set solve the sixth prob-

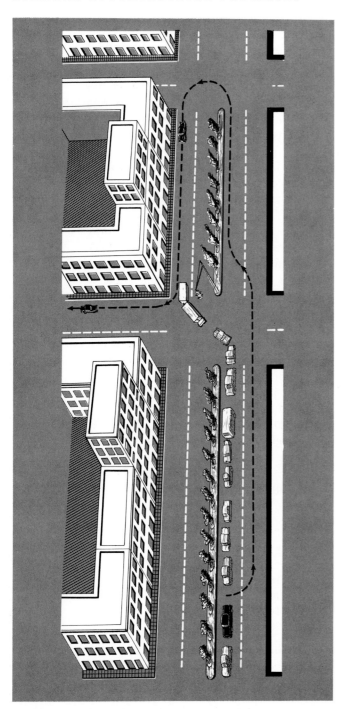

FIGURE 11.11 Breaking a Set Response. The driver in the black car wants to turn left at the intersection, but a stop light and heavy traffic slow his progress. Instead of staying in the left lane, he pulls into the right and follows the path shown by the arrows (From *Personality and Psychotherapy* by J. Dollard & N. E. Miller, copyright 1950, McGraw-Hill Book Company, Inc. Used by permission.)

lem by filling the 49-pint jar and from it filling the 23-pint jar once and the 3-pint jar twice: $49 - 23 - 3 - 3 = 20$. But the problem can be solved much more simply. After filling the 23-pint jar, you can pour 3 pints off into the 3-pint jar, leaving 20 pints $(23 - 3 = 20)$. Most people solve the sixth problem in the less direct manner, because they have solved the first five problems in the only possible way, by filling the middle container and from it filling the container on the left once and the container on the right twice. This method works for these problems and is therefore reinforced. As a result the subject learns to respond to all such problems in the set manner, even to the problem which can be solved more directly. If the sixth problem is presented before the five set-building problems, subjects solve it directly $(23 - 3 = 20)$. Thus, practice can interfere with efficient problem solving if it strengthens inappropriate habits (Luchins, 1942).

In problems of this sort set responses can lead to absurd solutions. In a variation of the experiment just described, the subject, after solving several problems in the set manner, is required to obtain five pints of water with containers of 10-, 25-, and 5-pint capacities. If he maintains the set he solves the problem in the $25 - 10 - 5 - 5 = 5$ manner, and a sizable percentage of subjects do this. Others, thinking they are clever and quick to catch on, solve the problem by the $10 - 5 = 5$ method. But why don't they simply fill the 5-pint container!

A strong set response can even prevent the solution to such problems. After learning the set response, some subjects find it impossible to obtain 25 pints of water with three containers of 28-, 76-, and 3-pint capacities. The set response is so strong that they are prevented from using the $28 - 3 = 25$ solution. If they had not been exposed to the set-building problems they would have no difficulty with this problem.

We are often victims of inappropriate sets without being aware of their insidious influence. Take the case of someone who has to make a left turn at an intersection, but traffic in his lane is backed-up halfway down the street, moving only inches closer to the intersection with each green light. Traffic in the other direction is moderately light. Clearly, it would take him considerable time to make a left turn in the set manner. A more efficient procedure would be for him to pull into the right lane (see Figure 11.11), pass the intersection, make a U-turn at the next intersection where there is no traffic light, if this is legal, and finally make a right turn at the intersection where the left turn is still being blocked. A response of this sort obviously depends on one's ability to overcome one's habitual set to make left turns.

Sets often corrupt logical reasoning. Experiments (Woodworth & Sells, 1935) in the so-called atmosphere effect have shown that the conclusion drawn from two statements is not determined solely by logical considerations, but also by the nature of the set established by the premises. Is the conclusion of the following syllogism correct?

> All A is B.
> All C is B.
> Therefore, all A is C.

This conclusion is illogical, but it would be judged correct by many students, particularly those who are not acquainted with the rules of logic. Look at Figure 11.12 and you will see why the conclusion is false. Although both the smaller circles A and C are part of the larger circle B (i.e., all A is B and all C is B), A and C nevertheless are separate and distinct. Translated into a concrete example, the abstract syllogism would run as follows:

All members of the football team (A) are students (B).
All sorority sisters (C) are students (B).

Therefore, all members of the football team (A) are sorority sisters (C).

But do people erroneously accept the *therefore, all A is C* conclusion of the abstract syllogism solely because it is abstract? Consider the following syllogism:

> All socialists are Marxists.
> All communists are Marxists.
> Therefore, all socialists are communists.

Many people would accept this conclusion as true. The form of the syllogism, however, is the same as the previous two: socialists are A, Marxists are B, and communists are C. One reason this kind of syllogism encourages illogical conclusions is that the premises are stated in a positive universal (all) manner. This creates a positive universal set that increases the chances for a positive universal conclusion to be accepted, even though it may be false. Similarly, when the premises of a syllogism are stated in a particular (some) or negative (no) manner, the likelihood that

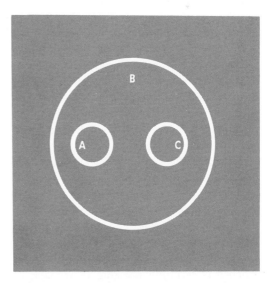

FIGURE 11.12 A Simple Demonstration of Why the Following Syllogism Is Incorrect: All A Is B; All C Is B; Therefore, All A Is C. Although all portions of A and C are part of B, A and C are separate and distinct.

370

a conclusion of the same form will be accepted is increased. Obviously, logical reasoning is not insulated against the effects of set.

Practically everyone can be trapped into error if he is given a strong set. For instance, *folk* is pronounced *foke* with the *l* silent, and *polk* is pronounced *poke,* also with the silent *l,* and the white of an egg is pronounced . . . . . ? It is a rare person who on his first exposure to this question fails to answer *yoke.* The *white* of an egg, however, is not the *yolk,* but the *albumen.*

You should not conclude that set responses are bad or necessarily ineffective. Any series of problems that requires a common method of solution can be handled more efficiently if one uses a set approach, rather than solving each problem separately.

But when problems change, as the water jar problems did, sets can become very inappropriate. One must conclude that sets do not by themselves possess any inherent advantage or disadvantage. Their usefulness, or lack of it, depends upon the problems themselves. If a series of problems requires a common problem-solving technique, then a set response will be efficient. If, however, new kinds of problems are likely to be introduced suddenly, the set response can retard or prevent problem solution. The important psychological law to remember is that the repetition of any reinforced response will strengthen its tendency to be evoked. This is as true for a complex problem-solving set as it is for a simple conditioned response.

Perception and Habit Competition. Some readers may wonder why the concept of perception has been absent almost entirely from our discussion of problem solving. Its absence is certainly not due to its lack of importance. Perception plays a vital role in problem solving, but its role is not clearly distinguishable from that of learning (see page 208). Consider the results of

the functional fixedness experiment in which subjects were required to mount three candles on a vertical screen. Their difficulty in solving the problem by using as shelves boxes that held candles to begin with was said to be due to habit competition. Knowing that the boxes were containers interfered with their learning to use them as shelves. The same problem can be analyzed in a somewhat different manner. It is difficult to *perceive* of a box containing candles as a shelf because the shelf function is obscured when it is perceived as a container.

Of course, it is largely a matter of semantics (the meaning of words) whether functional fixedness is described in terms of learning or of perceptual processes. The important consideration is that problem solution is retarded or prevented when inappropriate behavior interferes. Sometimes, however, perceptual processes actually dominate problem-solving behavior. The very way a problem is presented elicits perceptual responses that retard problem solution. Do you remember the nine-dot problem in the second chapter? The subject (see Figure 11.13) is required to connect the nine dots by drawing four straight lines without retracing and without removing his pencil from the paper.

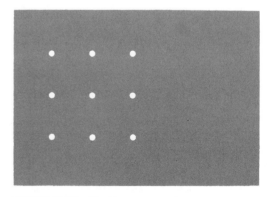

FIGURE 11.13 The Nine Dot Problem. The nine dots are to be connected by four successive straight lines drawn without retracing or removing the pencil from the paper.

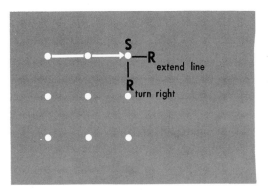

FIGURE 11.14 Why the Nine Dot Problem Is Difficult to Solve. The pattern of dots are perceived as a square, and the subject tends to draw his lines within the confines of the square.

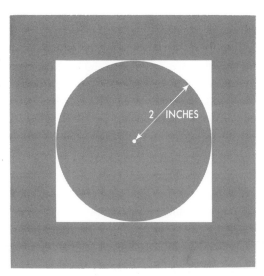

FIGURE 11.15 The Square Enclosing the Circle. The radius of the circle is two inches. What is the area of the square?

This is a very difficult problem. Many people cannot solve it, and those that do usually require a lot of time. Why is this problem so difficult? One reason is that the dots are perceptually grouped together (see page 187) to form a square. As a result the subject's tendency to extend his lines beyond the limits of the square is very weak. A subject who is trying to solve the problem will draw a line connecting the dots on one side of the square (see Figure 11.14). At this point, two habits compete to direct him: to turn in the direction of the square or to extend the line beyond the final dot on one side. The latter response might lead to problem solution, but the former will not. Nevertheless, his tendency to extend the straight line is likely to be much weaker than his tendency to change directions and draw a line connecting the dots on the adjacent side of the "square." Perceiving the dots as a square makes him respond to them as a square. In short, the manner in which we perceive a problem determines the relative strengths of different response tendencies. When our perceptions direct us toward making the correct response, problem solution is hastened. When our perceptions increase our tendency to make inappropriate responses, then problem solution is retarded.

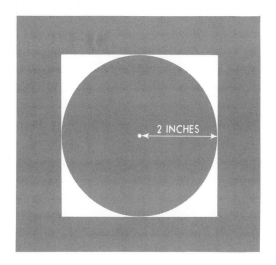

FIGURE 11.16 What is the area of this square? No more information is provided in this figure than is provided in Figure 11.15, yet it is easier to solve. The radius in this drawing is readily perceived as one-half the length of the side of the square.

The following problem shows how perceptual processes can influence problem solution. What is the area of the square which encloses the circle in Figure 11.15? You would probably solve this problem more easily if it had been originally presented as it appears in Figure 11.16. Both figures (11.15 and 11.16) provide exactly the same information, but in Figure 11.16 you perceive the radius of the circle as "part of" the square, and thus it is simple to determine that the side of the square is four inches and its area sixteen inches. In contrast, in Figure 11.15 you perceive the radius only in its relation to the circle; it is therefore necessary to infer that the radius is one-half the length of the side of the square. This is a very simple demonstration of the fact that the difficulty of a problem depends upon how it is perceived.

CONCEPTS

Our world is filled with objects which possess some common quality that sets them off from other objects. When an organism learns to respond only to this common quality and to ignore differences, he has learned a concept. The child, for example, learns the concept of redness when he is able to select a *red* wagon or a *red* lollypop or a *red* balloon from similar objects of different colors. When he makes this conceptual response he is discriminating among different properties of the same object. He is separating the *redness,* for example, from the structural properties of the object or from its weight. Similarly, when he responds to wagons regardless of their color, he is abstracting the common features of all wagons.

Language is not needed to form concepts. Animals can abstract a common feature from a number of different stimuli. Rats have been taught to discriminate on the basis of triangularity, which is a concept. If they are reinforced for choosing triangles of various sizes and shapes in preference to other kinds of geometrical objects, they soon learn to respond consistently to triangles, and since the size and shape of the triangles they are exposed to vary from trial to trial, we must conclude that they have learned the concept of triangularity. Monkeys have been taught the concept of *oddity*. They learn (Moon & Harlow, 1955) to choose the odd stimulus from a group of three ·novel stimuli, two of which are alike and one different. Since the odd stimulus changes from trial to trial, the monkey is obviously not responding to any specific object, such as a square or circle, but is learning to abstract a common property, oddity, from a continuously changing situation.

Two important psychological processes operate in learning concepts: generalization and discrimination. When the rat learns the concept of triangularity, the response of choosing a triangle initially generalizes to other geometrical objects such as rectangles and circles. These responses, however, are not reinforced and so extinguish. As a result the rat gradually learns to discriminate triangles from these other geometrical shapes. If responses to similar but different stimuli are not reinforced the effects of generalization are restricted, and thereby, the subjects are enabled to form concepts.

Concepts are usually not learned all at once. A child may be able to discriminate consistently between a dog and a horse, but at the same time become confused about the differences between a dog and a cat. Although he has learned that the range of sizes of dogs excludes animals the size of a horse, he has failed to learn those stimulus features that differentiate dogs from cats. His concept of dog is incomplete and must be developed further. He must abstract properties other than size that are characteristic of dogs if he is to use the concept *dog* appropriately. Children sometimes have similar problems in learning the concept of gender. Even very young children commonly make quite adequate discriminations between males and females of the human species, until they are confronted by a woman with a mannish hairstyle or a man from another culture who wears his hair long. Then it becomes apparent that their concepts of male and female are based on aspects of the stimulus situation that cannot always be relied upon.

Concept Learning

Although lower animals can acquire concepts, humans learn them more rapidly. And what is more important, they can acquire concepts with degrees of abstraction well beyond the capacities of lower animals. But even these more abstract concepts are based upon the psychological mechanisms of generalization and discrimination.

One of the earliest studies (Hull, 1920) of concept formation utilized the paired-associate learning technique. College students were required to associate Chinese characters with sounds. A total of 36 characters served as stimulus items. These characters belonged to one of six groups, each of which had a common part known as a radical. The response term for each character was a sound which was the same for all the characters having the same radical. For example, the following characters 肀乑辰牠 were associated with the sound *oo*, whereas the characters 組孤參夗 were associated with the sound *yer*. All the *oo* characters contained the common radical 亻; the *yer* characters contained the common radical 彡.

The subjects were under the impression that their task was just to memorize the paired associates. After a subject was able to give the correct response for all 36 characters, he was tested with an entirely new set of characters, but ones which had the same radicals. Thus it was possible to discover whether the subject's learning resulted from his having learned to respond to the common element, or from his having learned the appropriate response to each of the 36 characters. If he had learned to respond to the common element, he should now respond appropriately to all the new characters which had that common element. If, however, he had only learned a response to each complete character, he would be unable to identify the new characters.

The results indicated that the subjects as a group behaved in a manner that falls somewhere between these two extremes. On the very first trial they made 27 per cent correct responses, which suggests that they had learned, to some extent, to respond to the common element. Although there was some abstracting, it was far from complete.

Learning improved gradually after the first trial. The number of correct responses was 38 per cent on the second trial, and this figure rose to 56 per cent on the sixth trial. All in all, the course of concept learning resembled that of simpler discrimination learning. Erroneous responses dropped out and correct responses took their place.

An interesting side result was that several subjects who responded correctly to the new characters were unable to identify the common element. Although they were responding to this element, they were not aware of the relation between the radical and their own responses. This behavior is not unusual. In our daily lives, we often respond to things or people as being alike, even though we may be unable to specify what they have in common. Even in humans, concepts are not always dependent on language.

Factors that encourage discrimination facilitate concept formation. For example, in the experiment just described, it was found that the most effective method of teaching the six Chinese character concepts was to present each series of characters with the common element drawn in red. In this way the relevant portion of each character functioned as a perceptual figure, with the irrelevant portion serving as the ground (see page 185), and facilitated the discrimination between the *essential cues*.

If the essential cues of one concept are not made clearly different from those of another, concepts are difficult to learn. Consider the problem of teaching a child that a whale is a mammal and not a fish. He has probably learned the clearly different but incomplete concepts that fish live in water and mammals on land. A whale, then, is to the child a fish because he dwells in the sea. In making such an error the child is discriminating, but discriminating wrongly.

A good example of the importance of the discrimination process in concept learning comes from an experiment (Kendler & Karasik, 1958) in which college students had to select from lists words which had a common property. For example, the words *platter, derby, moon,* and *bracelet* appeared with different groups of four other words. For some students these four words for objects which have the common property of roundness were shown with the words *chalk, milk, snow,* and *teeth;* for other subjects the same four "round" words were presented with *blush, dagger, eel,* and *sugar.* After the subjects had an opportunity to look at all eight words (the four "round" and four "nonround" words) for 15 seconds, they were handed a card with the word *platter* on it and instructed to select the three words from the remaining seven that possessed a common property with platter. Which group of words—*chalk, milk, snow,* and *teeth* or *blush, dagger, eel,* and *sugar*—would make it easier for them to select the three appropriate words—*derby, moon,* and *bracelet?* If concept learning depended only on grouping the four relevant "round" words together, then the kind of irrelevant words they were presented with would not matter. If, however, concept learning depended on actively *discriminating the relevant from the irrelevant* words, then the kind of irrelevant words and their difference from the relevant words would matter very much. Since the irrelevant words *chalk,*

milk, snow, and *teeth* have a strong tendency to evoke the response "white," it should be easier to discriminate "round" words from them than from words that have no obvious common property (*blush, dagger, eel,* and *sugar*). The results confirmed this expectation, suggesting that the speed of concept learning varies directly with the ease of discrimination.

In an earlier section of this chapter (see page 343) a similar result was reported. Learning to discriminate between differently shaped objects was influenced by the nonsense syllable names assigned to the objects. Dissimilar names (*jod, daf,* and *meep*) produced faster discrimination learning than did similar names (*beem, meem,* and *peem*). Concept formation was facilitated by increasing the degree of difference between the responses that a subject was expected to make to the stimuli belonging to various concepts.

PROBLEM SOLVING AND VERBAL BEHAVIOR

Although problem solving and verbal behavior are taken up in separate sections of this chapter, it is obvious that we cannot maintain a strict division between them. They are intimately related in human behavior. Without language the scientist would be unable to solve the problems posed by the world he lives in. Our ability to abstract similarities from diverse objects and apply names to the abstractions enables us to solve problems far beyond the reach of nonarticulate organisms.

Language is involved in problem solving in many different ways. Our analysis will be limited to three kinds of relationships between them: (1) the linguistic form in which a problem is described; (2) language as a response to a problem, and (3) verbal associations involved in problem solving.

Language as a Vehicle for Formulating Problems

The verbal statement of a problem will have an influence on how, if at all, it is solved. The powerful set produced by the series of water jar problems (see page 367) can sometimes be broken down if the verbal warning, "Don't be blind!" is given immediately before the critical sixth problem. The warning may initiate responses to the problem that are non-set, or at odds with the previous set.

Another example of how the verbal presentation can influence problem solving comes from the study demonstrating an "atmosphere effect" in syllogistic reasoning (see page 369). Premises stated in a positive manner encourage one to accept a positive conclusion, even when the conclusion is a non sequitur.

Consider the problem (on page 355) of estimating the distance a bird would fly before two trains, traveling toward each other, would meet. If the problem is stated so that certain features, such as the route of the bird flying back and forth between the approaching trains are emphasized, finding the solution is made difficult. If the problem is stated so that other features, such as the speeds of the bird and the two trains, are emphasized, presumably its solution would be easier. Although the experiment has not been carried out (perhaps the reader would like to try it), it is likely that the ease with which subjects reach solutions to the problem will depend on which of the two ways the problem is stated.

The verbal formulation of a problem determines in great part how it is perceived. In any verbal description certain features of the problem tend to gain the subject's attention, while others tend to be ignored. That is, some features operate to become perceptual figures, while others play the role of perceptual ground. If the verbal perceptual figures encourage behavior that leads to solution, then the description will hasten problem solving. If, however, factors that encourage inappropriate behavior are highlighted, then the description will retard or prevent problem solving.

Verbal Responses to Problems

The verbal reactions a person makes to a problem can influence his problem solving in two important ways. First, it can determine how rapidly, if at all, he solves a particular problem. Second, it can influence the amount of transfer that takes place between this problem and any problem he encounters in the future.

To illustrate how verbal responses determine speed in solving a problem, we cite the results of a study (Liublinskaya, 1957) in which children were shown pictures of butterfly wings and instructed to match them to similar ones in a large sample. In order to match correctly, they had to match the patterns of markings. The children found this task perplexing because they had difficulty separating the pattern from the color of the wings. An experimental group was then given words (*spots* or *stripes*) to describe the various patterns; the control group was not given any verbal labels. After the patterns had been denoted by names, the matching performance of the experimental group improved markedly. Even the younger members of the experimental group outperformed the older children of the control group. Another experiment (Kendler & Vineberg, 1954) in which college students served as subjects showed that when the subjects had words to describe certain physical features of colored designs, it was easy for them to form concepts. In the absence of adequate verbal labeling the task was difficult for some and impossible for others.

Often the solution to a problem can be achieved in any one of a number of ways. The method by which a problem is solved is often as important, if not more so, than the solution itself.

Max Wertheimer (1880-1943), the founder of Gestalt psychology (see page 46), made some interesting observations of children who were learning to compute the area of a rectangle (Wertheimer, 1959). These illustrate how verbal reactions influence the amount of transfer that will take place. Sometimes children are taught to compute the area of a rectangle by simply multiplying its length by its width. Essentially they learn a simple verbal rule, "The area of a rectangle is equal to the product of two adjacent sides." In contrast, other children learn the identical arithmetical operation, but understand the reasons for its use. They learn that the length is multiplied by the width because area refers to the amount of surface enclosed within the boundaries of a geometric figure. They are taught that if one divides the surface within a rectangle into small squares (see Figure 11.17), one may compute the area simply by counting up the number of squares. They are taught further that when one realizes that all the rows contain the same number of squares, as do all the columns, then a simpler procedure than counting is available. The area can be computed by multiplying the number of squares on one side by the number of squares on the adjacent side.

You might ask why it matters whether one understands the reasons for using a rule? Isn't the important thing to get the correct answer? True, both methods lead to the same answer when it is only the area of a particular rectangle that must be computed. But they do not necessarily lead to the same answer in the case of a similar but slightly different problem. In short, the two methods lead to different kinds of transfer (see page 311). The child who has memorized only the rule that the area of a rectangle equals the product of two adjacent sides tends to apply the very same rule to computing the area of any parallelogram. This procedure will lead him to the wrong answer, unless the parallelogram is a rectangle. On the other hand, the child who has learned the reasons for multiplying two sides of a rectangle to obtain its area, will probably be puzzled when he is first confronted with the problem of computing the area of a parallelogram. Soon, however, he will realize that the difficulty of solving the problem lies in the parallelogram's two lopsided ends, and awareness of this difficulty will probably lead him to discover that a parallelogram

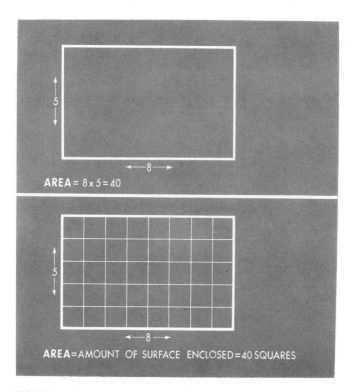

FIGURE 11.17 The Two Ways in Which a Child Can Learn to Compute the Area of a Rectangle. He can learn either simply to apply the rule of multiplying the length of one side by the length of its adjacent side or to perform the same operation by understanding the principle underlying this rule. The principle can be taught by making the child comprehend that area refers to the amount of surface enclosed and that it can be computed by counting the number of squares, or more simply, by obtaining the product of the length of adjacent sides.

is basically a rectangle. By removing one lopsided end and attaching it to the other lopsided end (see Figure 11.18), he can change the parallelogram into a rectangle. Once he realizes this, he can state the rule for computing the area of a rectangle: multiply the length of any side by the length of a perpendicular erected from that side to the side opposite.

The role which verbal responses play in problem solving has important implications for education. The *method of arriving* at the correct answer to a problem is of more lasting importance than the answer itself. Teachers must try to teach their students verbal responses that will aid them in transferring their knowledge to other problems. Memorizing rules often leads to isolated bits of knowledge without relevance to anything else.

Verbal Associations Involved in Problem Solving. If a solution to a problem is dependent on verbal responses, then it should be possible to direct the course of problem solution by controlling the subject's verbalizations. A simple word game was used to test this hypothesis (Judson & Cofer, 1956). Subjects were shown the following four words with the instructions to select the one that was unrelated to the other three:

ANGLE RECTANGLE SQUARE CIRCLE

A large majority of the subjects chose *circle* as the unrelated word. When the same four words were presented in this order:

CIRCLE RECTANGLE SQUARE ANGLE

the results were different. *Angle* was chosen by many of the subjects. Since the meanings of the words had not changed, although their position had shifted, what could possibly account for the different results? The answer to this question lies in the fact that these four words can be divided

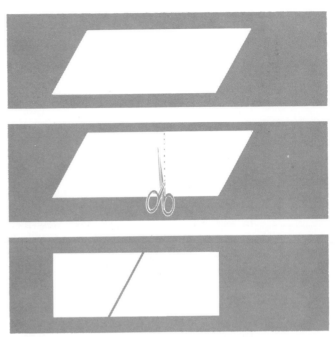

FIGURE 11.18 How a Parallelogram Can Be Converted Into a Rectangle. Cutting the parallelogram in half and then fitting the lopsided ends together produces a rectangle.

readily into two groups of related words: an *angle,* a *rectangle,* and a *square* are all made by drawing straight lines; a *circle,* a *rectangle,* and a *square* are all enclosed geometric figures. A person confronted with this problem cannot read all the words simultaneously; he has to read them in order one after another. Depending on the order he reads them in, certain kinds of verbal associations are encouraged. The word *angle* followed by *rectangle* and *square* initiates a chain of verbal responses associated with straight lines, whereas the word *circle* preceding *rectangle* and *square* initiates verbal associations connected with enclosed geometric figures. Thus the very same problem may be solved differently, depending upon the verbal habit that is activated.

A variation of this experiment showed how a person's attitudes can influence problem solving by controlling the kind of verbal associations he makes. The problem consisted of eliminating the unlike one from among *skyscraper, temple, cathedral,* and *prayer,* and it was found that strongly religious subjects had a greater tendency to include *prayer* and eliminate *skyscraper* than subjects with weak religious interests. When the strongly religious person perceived these four words, religious associations dominated and he grouped the words accordingly.

One more experiment (Judson, Cofer, & Gelfand, 1956) showing how verbal associations influence problem-solving should be described. Several groups of subjects had to perform the two-string task described on page 365). One group of male subjects was, however, taught a series of verbal associations pertinent to the solution of the problem; they were required to memorize several short lists of words, one of which contained *rope, swing,* and *pendulum.* In this group there was a higher percentage of solutions than there was in other groups who did not have the opportunity to learn to associate *rope, swing,* and *pendulum.*

Problem solving usually consists of chains of verbal associations much more complex than these, which involve only three words. The above experiments merely demonstrate that verbal associations can affect problem solving. However, the extent to which we can at present control problem solving is limited, because our knowledge of verbal associations is far from complete. Superior control will result when we know more about how such verbal associations are organized.

PHYSIOLOGY, LANGUAGE BEHAVIOR, AND PROBLEM SOLVING

We finally come to discussing the relationship between physiology and language and problem-solving behavior. We have already noted that as one progresses from simple to complex behavior, the relationship between behavior and physiology becomes less and less completely understood. One reason is that our understanding of simple behavior, such as seeing and hearing, is enhanced by what we know about how the eye and ear work. Language and problem-solving behavior, on the other hand, are not functions of any single receptor. Stimulation from many different internal and external sources initiates such behavior. Moreover, it involves the simultaneous activation of many portions of the central nervous system, the most complicated parts of our bodies. However, although the obstacles to our understanding the physiology of language and problem-solving behavior are formidable, they are not insurmountable. A body of knowledge, far from complete, is already available to provide some understanding of the role physiological processes play in the kinds of behavior we are now discussing. And there is no doubt that this understanding will increase with time.

Aphasia

Aphasia is the technical name applied to disordered language behavior resulting from damage to the brain. It is a misleading term because although the suffix *phasia,* of Greek origin, denotes "speech," while the prefix *a* means "without," most people suffering from aphasia retain some portion of their language behavior. Typically their ability to speak or understand language is impaired rather than eliminated. A more appropriate term would be *dysphasia,* which emphasizes the disturbance rather than the absence of verbal behavior. But more important than the term are the facts and their implications for the physiology of language behavior.

The information about aphasia comes from clinical patients who have suffered damage to brain tissue from injuries (war wounds, automobile accidents) or tumors.

The amount and kind of disturbance in language function is first determined and then an attempt is made to correlate this with the location and amount of cortical destruction. Technical problems make this a very difficult task. Nevertheless, from thousands and thousands of clinical cases it has been possible to piece together some principles that describe the activity of the brain in language behavior.

Cerebral Dominance. The effects that destruction of cerebral tissue has upon verbal behavior depend to a large extent on which of the two cerebral hemispheres suffers the damage. You know (see page 95) that the part of the brain known as the cerebrum is divided into two halves, the left and right cerebral hemispheres. One hemisphere plays a more important role in language behavior than the other, even when the corpus callosum (see page 95) is intact. The hemisphere that is usually dominant is on the side opposite the favored hand. Typically the left cerebral hemisphere is the dominant hemisphere for the right-handed person, whereas the right hemisphere is dominant for the left-handed person.

This principle of dominance is illustrated by the following case history. A right-handed woman was admitted into a hospital, complaining that her memory was getting progressively worse. She was having great difficulty in reading because she was unable to understand words which she had previously understood. The neurologists concluded that something was wrong with her *left* cerebral hemisphere. Their hypothesis was confirmed when surgery revealed a large growing tumor in the occipital lobe of the *left* cerebral hemisphere.

In contrast to this, but also illustrating the principle of dominance, are those cases in which little, if any, disturbance resulted from tumors. A left-handed man had his entire left frontal lobe removed because of a tumor, but he failed to develop any speech disorders. If he had been right-handed his speech most certainly would have been disturbed.

Cerebral Localization. It was once thought that the center for language behavior was localized in one small specific part of the cortex. This hypothesis was proposed to account for an interesting medical case of the nineteenth century. In 1831, a patient whose principal symptom was an inability to talk was admitted to a state institution near Paris. This patient could communicate rather effectively by means of signs and in general appeared intellectually competent. He remained in the institution until 1861 when, because of an infection, he was placed under the care of Paul Broca, a noted surgeon. Broca carefully examined the patient and became convinced that both his vocal and intellectual equipment were adequate for normal speech. Why, then, was the patient unable to speak? This question was answered when the patient died. The autopsy revealed in the frontal lobe of the left cerebral hemisphere a localized lesion (injury) above the fissure of Sylvius (see Figure 11.19 on page 380). Broca concluded that the lesion was responsible for the patient's inability to talk. He also assumed, as did others, that every psychological function could be localized in a small area of the cortex. This assumption, although containing a kernel of truth, was in general misleading.

Lesions in exactly the same area of the brains of right-handed individuals do not always produce the same psychological effect. Whereas the lesion in Broca's patient eliminated his ability to speak, similar lesions in other patients may produce less severe speech difficulties, or perhaps none at all. One reason for this discrepancy is that the brains of different individuals are never exactly alike. Just as bodies differ in structure, so do brains. Another reason is that an individual's experiences influence how his brain functions. A specific brain injury has been known to eliminate a person's ability to speak or understand a foreign language, but not his ability in his native tongue. Obviously, no brain injury can produce this effect on an individual who knows only one language.

Although our speech function is not precisely localized, there appears to be a general area on the lateral frontal side of the cortex (see Figure 11.19) where it is usually

fissure of Rolando). Lesions in Broca's area have the effect of separating the parts of the brain that control speech movement from those association areas that mediate language habits.

The writer once had a patient who was misdiagnosed as feeble-minded because he was unable to respond to many of the questions on an intelligence test given to him in a station hospital back of the combat zone. His examiner did not know it but

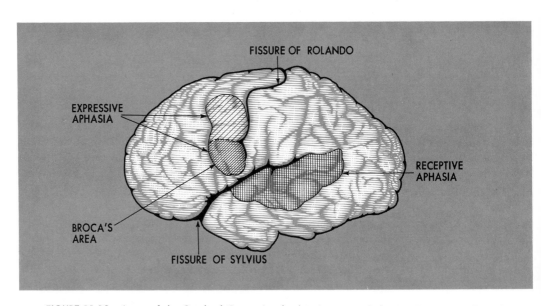

FIGURE 11.19 Areas of the Cerebral Cortex Involved in Language Behavior. Damage to Broca's area interferes with the coordination of muscles of speech. Lesions in the area immediately above have been found in cases where the patient is unable to express his ideas in writing. Damage to the area below the fissure of Sylvius can result in receptive aphasia.

located. Broca's patient suffered a lesion in a part of this general area now referred to as **Broca's area.** A lesion in this location usually produces symptoms of **expressive aphasia.** The patient has difficulty talking. Although he usually knows what he wants to say and can even point to the one of several sentences that expresses his ideas, he just cannot say it. Broca's area is probably connected to the motor areas of the cortex that control the movements of the jaw and tongue (located just before the

he had suffered a scalp wound which probably produced a blood clot that interfered with the functioning of the cells in his motor speech area. His educational records, not available to his first examiner, later revealed that he had been graduated valedictorian from his high school class. Actually, he knew most of the answers to the questions on the test, but was unable to express them. He was not, as expressive aphasics sometimes are, completely inarticulate. When angry he cursed eloquently.

But the verbal associations essential for expressing ideas were absent. Aphasia is often temporary. The author's patient ultimately regained all his speech abilities and the blood clot probably disappeared with time. His recovery was hastened by training in forming words and using them appropriately.

The task of teaching an aphasic to speak normally depends upon the extent of his injury. In less severe cases the patient re-learns to talk instead of learning to talk anew. This point is illustrated by the case (Teuber, 1951) of a Southerner who was treated by a speech teacher from New England. The treatment proved successful, and moreover, when the patient regained his speech, he spoke with his original Southern drawl. He had completely relearned his old language habits. In more severe cases the patient must learn to talk from the beginning. His task is as arduous, if not more so, as that of an infant who is learning to talk. In such cases cerebral tissue containing the association fibers responsible for speech has presumably been damaged beyond repair. As a result, new learning, involving entirely different association fibers, must take place in order for the patient to speak again.

In another form of expressive aphasia the patient is unable to write, although he usually can speak. In such cases lesions in a region above the motor speech area (see Figure 11.19) have usually been found. The behavior of these patients is essentially similar to that of patients suffering from lesions in Broca's area, except that their difficulties are in writing rather than in speaking.

Difficulty in understanding characterizes those patients suffering from **receptive aphasia.** They may be able to hear speech sounds but the words are as incomprehensible to them as if they were learning a strange language. Patients with this defect usually have lesions in the speech recognition areas located near the auditory area of the temporal lobe. There are also other kinds of receptive aphasia: Some patients are unable to read; they see words but fail to recognize them. Still others are unable to recognize objects when they see them (see Figure 11.19).

In one case (Goldstein, 1942) of receptive aphasia, the patient could neither read nor recognize objects. The damage to his brain presumably covered not only the reading area but the visual recognition area as well. Consequently this patient was required to begin over again the long, arduous process of learning to read. However, since his tactual recognition ability was apparently intact, he was trained to trace letters with his fingers while following them with his eyes, a technique that proved successful in teaching him to read again.

It must be emphasized that these localizations of centers for language behavior, which are represented in Figure 11.19, are approximate at best. The regions as well as their boundaries have been estimated from the observations in many clinical cases. But as we have already noted, the brains of individuals differ and therefore Figure 11.19 may best be conceived as a composite of many human brains, rather than representing some model that holds for *every* brain.

The study of aphasia and other kinds of brain injury demonstrates that complex psychological functions such as language behavior are not localized in any minute region of the cortex. There is, however, some division of labor. Such functions as reading and writing are located in fairly well-defined, general areas. But these areas do not have exclusive control over any particular function. If they did, their destruction would result in permanent loss of the psychological function localized in them. However, when a reading area is destroyed, it is sometimes possible for a patient to relearn reading by special training. Presumably what happens in such cases is that neighboring regions of the brain take over the functions of the destroyed areas.

Cerebral Localization of Problem Solving

You will recall (see page 332) that the maze-learning ability of rats did not seem to be localized in any particular area of their brain. Loss in maze-learning ability was found to depend on the amount but not the location of cortical damage. In primates (man, apes, and monkeys), however, there is a connection between fairly definite cerebral locations and more complex behavior. The locus of brain damage is related to the kinds of difficulty monkeys exhibit in solving problems. This conclusion received support from the results of a study (Harlow, 1952) of two groups of brain-injured monkeys and one normal (control) group. One brain-injured group had lesions in their frontal association area, whereas the second group suffered damage to their posterior association area (see Figure 11.20). All three groups of monkeys were confronted with a delayed-reaction test and with an oddity problem. In the delayed-reaction problem a monkey was allowed to watch the experimenter place food under one of two cups. The cups were then hidden from the subject's view for several seconds, and after this he was tested to see whether he could select the cup with food under it. Consistent selection of the correct cup would indicate that a monkey was able to maintain some kind of symbolic representation of the baited cup during the delay period.

In the oddity problem the monkey was required to select the odd object in a group of three. For example, he had to choose the round object when the other two were square, or the square object when the other two were round. The monkey could not solve this problem by selecting one particular object over and over because the objects varied from trial to trial. A successful solution to such an oddity problem depends on the subject's response to the relationship between the three objects. That is, the monkey had to abstract the feature of oddity if he was to respond successfully.

The brain-injured monkeys were unable to solve either problem as rapidly as the animals with intact brains. However, the *locus* of the brain injury influenced the animal's performance on the delayed-reaction problem alone. In this problem the monkeys who had their posterior association area damaged made only slightly more errors than did the control subjects, but the monkeys with damaged frontal association areas made many more errors, performing at a level only slightly better than chance. In the oddity problem there was no difference between the frontal and posterior subjects, both of whom performed at a much poorer level than did the normals.

The important conclusion to be drawn from this study is that different kinds of problem-solving ability are differentially impaired by lesions in the frontal and posterior association areas, but that neither association area is completely responsible for the problem-solving behavior of monkeys. This is demonstrated by the brain-injured animals' ability to do some problem solving in both the delayed-reaction and oddity problems. In short, it would seem that although the problem-solving ability of the monkey is localized to some degree, this localization is not completely specific.

For obvious reasons we do not have such nice, neat experimental data on the cerebral localization of human problem-solving ability. However, the evidence from clinical cases of human brain injury suggests that there is some degree of localized problem-solving ability in the human cortex also. There is, however, a difference of opinion as to the exact nature of this localization. Some neurologists believe that the frontal lobes play the most important role in problem solving, a hypothesis consistent with the results just discussed. Lesions in the frontal association areas of the monkeys produced the greatest decrement in their solution of the delayed-response problems, initially designed to test symbolic functioning (see page 357). Although other neurologists believe it is too early to draw exact conclusions about cortical involvement in human problem-solving behavior, there is no doubt that some areas play more important roles than others, as our study of aphasia revealed. In relating brain physiology to problem solving, one must always consider the nature of the problem. Our review of aphasia emphasized this point. Obviously a person who cannot understand language cannot solve a verbal problem. Such a person, however, might be able to solve jigsaw puzzles with little difficulty. Different problems challenge different problem-solving abilities, which in turn may depend on different regions of the cerebral cortex. It is certain, therefore, that no one specific and limited region of the brain will be found responsible for all human problem-solving behavior.

Muscular Activity and Problem Solving

A child, assuming he knows something about his body, would probably answer the question, "What part of the body do we think with?" by saying, "the brain." Most adults would agree, but such an answer does not tell the whole story.

The science of electronics allows us to observe muscular activity too slight to see, by recording the changes in electrical potential associated with faint muscular movements. These changes can be amplified and made to appear in wavelike forms on the screen of an oscilloscope. Several studies (Jacobson, 1932) have shown that when we are thinking our muscles are active. Subjects who were instructed to *imagine* counting, while the neural and muscular activi-

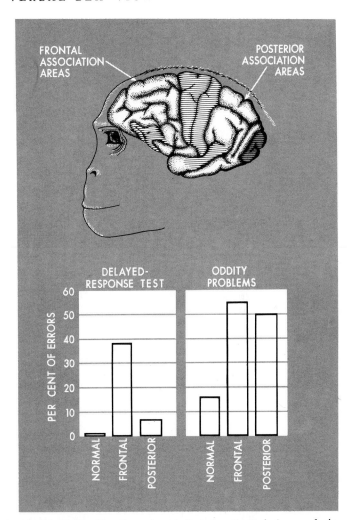

FIGURE 11.20 The Frontal and Posterior Cortical Areas of the Monkey. Damage to these areas reduces the ability of the monkey to solve a problem, with the amount of impairment determined by the nature of the problem.

ties of their tongue and lips were recorded, appeared to be talking subvocally. The importance of muscular activity in the speech mechanisms during problem solving was .cleverly demonstrated by research with deaf mutes who had learned to "speak" with their hands. In one study (Max, 1937) deaf mutes were instructed to multiply and divide numbers "in their heads." Eighty per cent of them exhibited slight muscular activity in their hands, and with some subjects the hand movements were sufficiently large to be seen by the naked eye. When

384

subjects with normal hearing were placed in the same experimental situation, only 30 per cent of them gave any sign of hand movements, and the magnitude of their hand movements was approximately only one-fourth as great as those of the deaf mutes. But why should subjects with normal hearing exhibit any hand movements at all during thought? Probably because they often write their calculations when doing problems in arithmetic. The important result of this study, however, is that problem-solving behavior seems to be accompanied by muscular movements, and particularly with those associated with speech.

Many other studies have provided evidence of the interaction between brain and muscles when a person is thinking. After subjects had been trained to relax, they were instructed to *imagine* lifting a ten-pound weight with their right forearms. Doing this produced recordable muscular activity in the right forearm. When subjects were told to imagine different kinds of objects, their eye movements resembled those they would have made if they were actually examining the object (Totten, 1935). Also, when subjects recalled verbal material, the pattern of their eye movements resembled the pattern of movements they made when they read the material originally (Ewert, 1933).

These facts show that the brain does not operate in physiological isolation. Muscular activity, normally too small to be seen with the naked eye, is usually involved in such intellectual tasks as problem solving, imagination, and thought.

Although our physiological techniques are not sufficiently developed to identify the exact nature of the interplay between cortical and muscular activities, it is likely that there is true interaction; the muscles respond to the neural stimulation from the brain and also initiate neural impulses which return to the brain and influence its activities.

PROBLEM-SOLVING THEORY

Problem solving is not a unitary psychological process. Such basic psychological processes as learning, perception, and motivation play important roles in the solving of problems. Sensation also enters in, although its psychological importance is often overlooked. If our receptors are not attuned to the outside world, we may not solve a problem simply because we are not aware of it. The mechanic who is hard-of-hearing may not repair an engine which is not running properly because he does not hear that something is wrong. Or a child may not solve a jigsaw puzzle because he cannot discriminate among the subtle color differences of the various pieces.

Because problem solving involves the interaction of several basic psychological processes, there is really no independent theory of problem solving. To understand problem solving, one must understand behavior itself, not any single segment of it. A theory of problem solving, in short, must be a theory of behavior.

Nevertheless, there have been several attempts to arrange the facts of problem solving into an organized system. One such attempt makes use of introspective reports. Subjects have often been asked to report what they experience while solving problems. Creative scientists and mathematicians have also been asked to describe their experiences at the moment they made some great discovery. Although the reports vary considerably, a certain pattern that applies to most of the introspective reports does emerge. This pattern suggests that problem-solving behavior occurs in four successive stages: (1) *preparation,* (2) *incubation,* (3) *illumination,* and (4) *verification.*

Poincaré, a famous French mathematician, described an episode associated with one of his great mathematical discoveries that illustrates these different stages. After he had worked unsuccessfully on a mathematical problem for some time, he decided to go on a vacation. Traveling from his home to another town, he completely forgot about his mathematical problem until he arrived at his destination and boarded a bus. At the moment he put his foot on the bus the solution to the problem that had plagued him for weeks suddenly became clear. He did not have an opportunity to check his solution immediately, but verified it later in his study. This anecdote nicely illustrates the four successive stages of problem solving. First there was the period of *preparation* during which Poincaré acquired the necessary basic and special skills for solving mathematical problems and eventually became aware of the particular problem itself and set himself the task of solving it. The time, during his trip, that he seemingly forgot about the particular problem can be conceived as the *incubation* period. His sudden insight into the problem as he boarded the bus was the period of *illumination*. The period of *verification* came when he was back in his study.

The writer experienced a similar sequence of events when he was attempting to design an experiment to test a particular hypothesis. He thought about the problem for several days, but could not solve it. One night, when he was almost convinced that there was no solution, he had a dream that suggested how the hypothesis could be tested. The next morning he was able to design an appropriate experiment.

The observation that problem solving tends to occur in four successive stages is of great interest. It does not, however, provide an explanation of problem solving; rather it raises an important question. Why are there these four successive stages? At this time we can only hazard a guess about the correct answer.

Preparation facilitates problem solving in at least three ways. First, it raises the prob-

lem. Awareness that there is a problem is often the first step toward solving it. Possibly the greatest help the Russians had toward developing the atom bomb was the positive proof that such a bomb could be produced. Second, preparation provides the problem-solver with the habits (techniques) necessary to solve the problem. Without his mathematical skills Poincaré could not have made his original contributions. Third, preparation gives the problem-solver an opportunity to weaken (extinguish) incorrect habits of responding. Poincaré attempted to solve his problem in several different ways. Although none of these attempts led directly to its solution, they served an important psychological function nevertheless. They weakened the incorrect habits and thereby provided the correct habits more opportunity to become dominant.

The major function of the period of incubation is to provide a new stimulus situation. The stimulus situation during preparation was generating incorrect solutions, and in some manner not yet specified, the conditions during incubation are able to evoke the correct responses. Many educators and psychologists have emphasized the importance of getting away for a while from a problem that resists solution. Some students take this advice too literally. A period of incubation is useful only when it is preceded by a period of preparation. Beachcombers are notoriously unproductive, even though they are masters at "incubating" ideas. Problem solving, especially the kind that goes into scientific creativity, is hard work, and incubation leads to illumination only after persistent efforts (preparation) at problem solution have already taken place. Illumination, or what is commonly thought of as the problem-solving act itself, is not an accidental phenomenon but is imbedded in the past experiences of the problem-solver.

The importance of verification in problem solving should not be overlooked. People often believe that they have solved a problem when they have merely failed to check a solution. After he has replaced some part of the engine, the mechanic is often convinced that he has repaired the car, but this illusion is quickly dispelled when the car comes sputtering back with the angry owner inside. Verification is usually a simple task. The solution is tried to determine whether it really solves the problem. If it does not, the problem must once again be considered and the attack on the solution renewed.

Some psychologists view the study of problem solving as an extension of the psychology of learning. This does not mean that problem-solving behavior is as simple as conditioning or other elementary forms of learning. Nor does it mean that an adequate theory of learning will automatically explain the facts of problem-solving behavior. What it does mean is that the psychological processes which operate in learning also operate in problem solving.

The importance of the role that learning plays in problem solving should not blind us to the roles of other basic processes. The analysis of functional fixedness (on page 365) showed how motivation and perception influence problem solving. Ample evidence compels us to emphasize once again that our perception of a problem influences our ability to solve it and the method we employ. Psychologists do differ in how they conceptualize this relationship between perception and problem solving. Some, like the author, analyze the role of perception in terms of its influence on habit competition. They are the ones who view the study of problem solving as primarily an extension of the psychology of learning. Other psy-

chologists view habit competition as the result of conflicting perceptual tendencies. They view the study of problem solving as primarily an extension of the psychology of perception. In a sense the difference in views, with the emphasis either on perception or on learning, is more a matter of difference of habits of expression than of facts.

The influence of learning on problem solving has been expressed largely in terms of habit competition and habit chaining. We have already noted how these two processes operate in complex learning problems. The manner in which they operate in learning and problem solving is essentially the same, the difference being only one of degree. However, symbolic processes play a greater role in problem solving than they do in complex learning. In problem solving, habit competition often takes place between symbolic habits, such as different verbal associations. Similarly, the behavior chains in problem-solving behavior are largely composed of symbolic habits. The problem-solving theorists must now discover the rules that govern the competition and chaining of these implicit symbolic habits.

The wide range of topics discussed in this chapter testifies to the progress that has been made in the study of verbal behavior and problem solving. Much remains to be learned, but more and more psychologists are devoting their research efforts to the understanding of language and problem-solving behavior. This suggests that the construction of problem-solving theory in particular, and behavior theory in general, is advancing at an accelerated rate.

SUMMARY

Although similar to some forms of behavior exhibited by lower animals, human verbal behavior is vastly more complex.

Human speech originates in the spontaneous babbling of infants and is thereafter shaped into appropriate speech sounds. These sounds acquire meaning by a process resembling classical conditioning.

Words have both stimulus and response properties. In speech and in writing, a word, in addition to being a response, functions as a stimulus for subsequent words. Semantic generalization occurs between words having similar meanings or sounds. A verbal response, like an instrumental response, tends to be repeated if it is reinforced.

An experimental analysis of verbal behavior supports the following conclusions: (a) The assignment of different names to similar objects facilitates discrimination among them; (b) Verbal habits change with age and experience; (c) In a simple declarative sentence with a copulative verb, the meaning associated with one noun is conditioned to the other noun.

If symbolic behavior may be defined as a response to a cue that represents something else, then the results of delayed reaction and double alternation experiments indicate that some lower animals can behave symbolically. Man, with his language ability, exhibits the greatest amount as well as the most complicated forms of symbolic behavior.

Organisms are capable of spontaneously integrating (chaining) separate habits to solve a problem (e.g., reasoning and insight). Habit competition in problem solving is illustrated in detour problems, functional fixedness, set, and competition between perceptual habits. All of these phenomena emphasize the point that problem solution can be retarded or prevented by the persistence of an incorrect habit.

The principles of generalization and discrimination play an important role in concept learning. Variables that reduce the effect of generalization and encourage discrimination facilitate concept formation.

Verbal behavior and problem solving are highly interrelated phenomena. Human problem solving is influenced by the verbal description of the problem and the verbal reactions and associations it elicits.

Many portions of the central nervous system are involved in verbal behavior and problem solving. In disordered verbal behavior which results from brain damage, the particular impairment depends on the locus of the damage, whether the dominant hemisphere is involved, and the previous experiences of the patient. The neurological correlates of problem solving depend on the nature of the problem. For some problems one part of the cortex will play an important role but for another problem it will have no influence. Muscular activity has been demonstrated to be related to problem solving.

SUGGESTIONS FOR FURTHER READING

BROWN, R. W. *Words and things.* New York: Crowell-Collier, 1958.

An interesting analysis of the relation between verbal behavior and thought. The book attempts to draw together facts and ideas from the fields of psychology, speech, anthropology, sociology, and comparative linguistics.

BRUNER, J. S., GOODNOW, J. J., & AUSTIN, G. A. *A study of thinking.* New York: Wiley, 1956.

A review of the authors' research on concept formation.

INHELDER, B., & PIAGET, J. *The growth of logical thinking from childhood to adolescence.* New York: Basic, 1958.

A review of experiments conducted by the authors, both Swiss psychologists, that aims to understand how a child's conception of natural events changes as he grows older.

JOHNSON, D. M. *The psychology of thought and judgment.* New York: Harper & Row, 1955.

A text that reviews the experimental findings in the fields of thinking and problem solving.

388

MILLER, G. A. *Language and communication.* New York: McGraw-Hill, 1951.

A stimulating review and analysis of language behavior.

THOMSON, R. *The psychology of thinking.* Baltimore, Md.: Penguin, 1959.

An interesting presentation on a fairly elementary level of some of the recent work in problem solving, concept learning, and verbal behavior.

VINACKE, W. E. *The psychology of thinking.* New York: McGraw-Hill, 1952.

A summary of experimental data on thinking and problem solving.

WERTHEIMER, M. *Productive thinking.* (Rev. ed.) New York: Harper & Row, 1959.

An analysis of problem solving in terms of the principles of Gestalt psychology.

WHORF, B. L. *Language, thought and reality.* New York: Wiley, 1956.

A series of interesting papers that expound the idea that a person's verbal habits determine both how he perceives the world and how he solves problems.

WOODWORTH, R. S., & SCHLOSBERG, H. *Experimental psychology.* (Rev. ed.) New York: Holt, Rinehart, & Winston, 1954.

A comprehensive textbook that contains a chapter on problem solving.

FRUSTRATION AND CONFLICT

12

THE MEANING OF FRUSTRATION AND CONFLICT

Frustration and conflict are forbidding words; we tend to associate them with the threatening and gloomy side of life. However, psychological analysis shows that although they are present in much of behavior, their consequences are not necessarily undesirable. At times, of course, they lead to unhappiness and despair; at other times they prove to be constructive and beneficial. The outcome, as you will learn, depends on how we respond to them rather than on their mere occurrence.

Although we have not explicitly mentioned either frustration or conflict until now, they have not been completely ignored. For example, the concept of frustration was implicit in the description of experimental extinction (see page 156). In this process a subject is suddenly deprived of an incentive (food) he has learned to expect. Since being prevented from reaching a goal is the essence of frustration, we can consider experimental extinction an example of frustration.

Again, a conditioned discrimination, which we discussed on page 160, illustrated one form of conflict. In this experiment Pavlov trained dogs to discriminate between a circle and an ellipse by responding positively to the circle and not to the ellipse. As the two figures were made more and more alike the dogs developed strong conflicts, for each stimulus now evoked two tendencies simultaneously: to respond and not to respond.

Everyday language is a poor vehicle for scientific communication. If we are to go deeper into the psychology of frustration and conflict, we must clarify the meaning of both terms by stripping away the confusing connotations they have developed in common speech. There must remain only meanings that apply to observable events, events which can be measured scientifically.

In studying motivation we were concerned with the goal-directed behavior of organisms. We saw how they acquire, that is, learn, those responses that lead to reinforcement. In studying frustration we will be concerned with *the psychological consequences of blocked goal-achievement*. What happens when an organism finds it impossible to reach a goal object? This is the basic question for the study of frustration.

Frustration and conflict are related because each may be the consequence of the other. A boy asks a girl for a date and is turned down. Should he call her again or should he give up? What was at first frustration develops into conflict. The reverse occurs when a student entertains the conflicting alternatives of whether to study for tomorrow's examination or go to the movies. If he studies, his desire to see the movie will be frustrated. If he sees the movie, his desire to do well in his exams will be frustrated. A conflict of this sort must produce some frustration because he cannot satisfy both motivations simultaneously.

It is useful to distinguish between two kinds of conflicts: those having their origin in incompatible motivational systems, as in the case of the student torn between studying and going to the movies, and those based on incompatible habit systems, as in the case of the hungry dog who must learn to salivate to a circle and not to an ellipse. Conflict, generally speaking, can best be conceived as the arousal of incompatible tendencies to behavior. When the conflict stems from rival motivations it is labeled **motivational conflict.** When the conflict is restricted solely to competing habits under one and the same drive, the terms **habit conflict** or **habit competition** are most appropriate.

AN ANALYSIS OF FRUSTRATION

Frustration is an easy term to use but a difficult one to make precise. We all think we know what we mean when we say,

"Jack acted badly because he was frustrated, because he couldn't have his way." But such simple analyses as this seem to attribute most of the ills of the world to the pernicious effects of frustration, of people not getting what they want. A moment's contemplation will reveal the stark inadequacies of this formula. We are all frustrated much of the time. If you are thirsty, even the distance between you and the drinking fountain is a source of frustration because it blocks the immediate satisfaction of your thirst. But obviously you don't let this *frustrating situation* upset you. You simply go to the fountain and drink. Clearly, then, all frustration does not produce disturbed behavior.

Moreover, people also respond differently to frustrating situations. One young man who has been refused a date will get angry and say something nasty. Another will behave like a good sport and immediately get in touch with another prospect.

In order to understand the concept of frustration we must reduce it to three components: (1) a **frustrating situation;** (2) a **state of frustration** within the organism, and (3) the overt **response to frustration.** The first and third components are easy to define. For a frustrating situation to exist there must be (*a*) an incentive that an organism is motivated to obtain and (*b*) an obstacle that blocks him from obtaining it. An organism's reaction to such a situation is his response to frustration, and if everybody responded the same way to each kind of frustrating situation, there would be no need to introduce the concept of a state of frustration. But as we have already indicated, people *do* behave differently in similar frustrating situations. In order to explain why, psychologists have assumed that a frustrating situation generates a state of frustration within the organism which influences its resulting behavior. The differences in states of frustration are assumed to account, in part, for the differences in reactions to frustrating situations.

Some psychologists think of this theoretical concept, state of frustration, or what we shall refer to simply as frustration, as a special case of the more general concept, habit. According to this view, people form different habits of responding to frustration. Other psychologists believe that frustration is more like drive, and still others consider it to have components of both habit and drive. Our concern will be to try to understand why essentially the same frustrating situation produces different responses. Or, in other words, how is the organism's state of frustration influenced by the frustrating situation, and how does it in turn influence the overt response. In order to come to grips with this problem, let us analyze various situations that produce frustration.

Sources of Frustration

There is an almost infinite variety of obstacles to goal achievement, ranging from simple physical ones to complex personal inadequacies. It is helpful to distinguish three main sources of frustration: (1) the physical environment; (2) the social environment, and (3) the organism itself.

The Physical Environment. Quite often the source of our frustration is in some physical fact of our environment. The child cannot play with his ball because it has bounced over the fence into the neighbor's yard, and he is too young to go and fetch it. The dog cannot gnaw his bone because it has been thrown beyond the reach of his restraining leash.

Another aspect of our physical environment which often causes us frustration is time. The college student, eager to graduate, must wait for commencement no matter how good his grades. The cancer victim who has just been operated on must wait months, perhaps years, to find out whether his operation has been successful. The professional golfer who thinks he did

well in the tournament must wait until all the competitors have completed their rounds before he can be sure he is the winner and not just a runner-up.

We can surmount many obstacles in our physical environment by adopting new forms of behavior. The child can learn to climb fences or the dog can learn to howl until food is brought within his reach. But there remain many obstacles we must learn to live with. We cannot make time move faster; we can, however, learn to tolerate delay.

The Social Environment. Just as something in our physical environment can prevent us from attaining some goal, so can something in our social environment. The successful businessman may not join a particular country club because its members find his race or religion unacceptable. The child entering in the middle of the school year is prevented from making many friends by the barriers of established friendships and cliques. The father who lets it appear that he is pathetically eager to be pals with his son is inviting frustration, because the boy will probably find it impossible to share intimate feelings with a father he has been brought up to respect.

Such barriers, roughly classified as social, are as real and powerful as physical restraints. And quite often their consequences are much more profound. The obstacles confronting the new child in school day after day are more frustrating and formidable than any facing the child whose ball has just gone over the fence.

Personal Factors. We are often frustrated because of our personal inadequacies. The young man who wants to make a good impression on his date at the prom will probably fail if he dances poorly and is a dull conversationalist. The fat, clumsy boy whose father is coaching him to become a star player in Little League baseball is destined to frustration because his physical

392

equipment is utterly inadequate for such a role. The child whose intellectual ability is below average faces disappointment if he develops the ambition to be a doctor or lawyer. Stuttering, skin blemishes, excess fat, poor eyesight or hearing, very short stature, and other physical handicaps are all sources of frustration because they make it difficult or impossible to achieve certain goals.

This breakdown of sources of frustration into three major categories does not mean that these categories are mutually exclusive. Take for example the child who cannot reach the ball on the other side of the fence. Is the fence the source of the frustration? Or is it the person who built the fence because his neighbor's children sometimes strayed over the property line? Or is it the child's own inability to climb over the fence? In a very real sense the frustration is the result of a combination of physical and social factors, and of personal factors as well. But the distinction among the three kinds of frustration remains useful. The child's response to the frustrating situation will depend upon what he considers to be its source. If he is young and has not learned to use more complex ideas, he is likely to see the fence as the source of his frustration, especially if it had been there a long time. But let us take a more complex instance. An Oriental is refused membership in a swank country club because of his race. His reaction to this disappointment will depend on how he has learned to perceive such discrimination. He may see social tradition as the obstacle, in which case his anger will be directed at society. Or he may put the primary blame on his racial background, resenting this bitterly. What he cannot do is attribute his frustration to the physical obstacle of a closed door at the club. In any case, he has a choice of several alternatives on which to blame his predicament. Or he may blame it on a com-

bination of alternatives. In a situation of this kind it is not uncommon for the frustrated person to resent not only the prevalent social prejudice but also the fact that he belongs to a minority group.

Responses to Frustration

The response to a frustration is not like a reaction to a blow on the knee; frustration does not elicit a single reflex response. Responses vary in character, depending partly on the obstacle, but more on the make-up and past experience of the organism thwarted.

We may analyze behavior resulting from frustration by means of three criteria: (1) how successful or unsuccessful it is in surmounting the obstacle; (2) whether it tends to persist, in some form, as long as frustration continues, and (3) what new forms of behavior continued frustration elicit. Since it would be confusing to examine all these points simultaneously, we shall analyze them separately.

Success or Failure in Surmounting the Obstacle. In one sense, a limited one, there are only two possible consequences of frustration. The organism may succeed in removing the obstacle to his goal, or he may fail.

Because people are interested in the dramatic aspects of frustrated behavior, they fail to note how frequently the reaction to frustration is increased effort followed by success in overcoming the source of frustration. The child finds a stick, inserts it below the fence, and retrieves his ball, or he gets help from someone on the other side of the fence. In such common cases, whether the problem is to bypass a fence or to solve a mathematical equation, problem solving is one way of dealing with a frustrating situation.

As long as the obstacle continues to block goal achievement effectively, the organism's behavior can be said to fail. However, failure itself leads to different reactions in different individuals. A child who abandons his attempts to retrieve his ball from the other side of the fence may turn to some other form of play and soon be as happy as before. Another child may persist in his attempts to get to the other side. He may get so steamed up that by sheer strength he manages to squeeze under the fence and get his ball, although he may then be too exhausted and scratched to enjoy his triumph.

Obviously, then, an account of how people react to frustration told in terms of their successes and failures does not give the whole story of their behavior. This is particularly true if it does not take time into account. What may seem to be success initially, may turn to failure, and *vice versa*. The college student bent on gaining admission into some social organization may succeed at first primarily because he is aggressive. But this very characteristic may create so much ill feeling against him that he will eventually be ostracized. In contrast, the more retiring student with similar social ambitions may be frustrated initially. With time, however, his positive qualities may win him as much recognition as he could desire. Success comes to many people partly because they have the ability to tolerate frustration for a long time without discouragement, bitterness, or self-reproach.

It is for such reasons that any description of frustrated behavior in terms of its immediate success or failure is incomplete and superficial. Quite often the attainment of success or its denial proves in the end to be the least important feature of the person's behavior.

Persistence. We have already seen how a response that leads to frustration tends to persist during experimental extinction, the number of repetitions before extinction

depending on the strength of the habit and drive. We have also seen how a response that has been intermittently reinforced will persist longer after the complete withdrawal of reinforcement than one that has been consistently reinforced (see page 285).

Besides strength of drive, strength of habit, and schedules of reinforcement, another variable that affects the persistence of a response is the point in a behavior chain at which it is blocked. In several experiments (Williams & Williams, 1943; Lambert & Solomon, 1952) barriers preventing rats from reaching the goals were placed at different points in the runways for different groups of animals. The results showed clearly that the closer the frustration point was to the goal, the more resistant to extinction the running response. As is so often the case with variables that influence behavior, what is found to be true of animal behavior is also true of human behavior. In one experiment (Adelman & Rosenbaum, 1954) college students were required to learn a maze pattern. Their performance, they were told, would be compared with the performance of students all over the country, and those lagging far behind the country-wide average would be stopped and required to begin again. Actually all the subjects were stopped (frustrated)—some near the beginning of the maze, others at the middle, still others near the end. The frustration was repeated until each subject gave up and admitted he could not make what he believed was an average score. As Figure 12.1 shows, the different groups varied markedly in the length of time they persisted in the face of this prearranged frustration. But just as in the experiment with the rats, those college students who persisted the longest were stopped closer to the goal.

These experimental findings are borne out by everyday experience. A child fitting a difficult jigsaw puzzle together (a task involving repeated frustration) is less likely

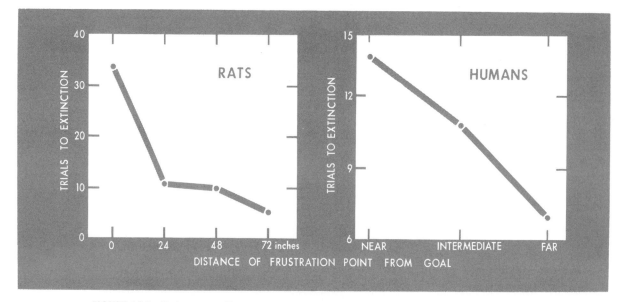

FIGURE 12.1 Resistance to Extinction as a Function of the Distance of the Point of Frustration From the Goal. The closer to the goal the barrier was placed, the more responses the subjects made before extinguishing. The graph on the left represents the behavior of rats (After Lambert & Solomon, 1952), the one at the right summarizes the behavior of college students (After Adelman & Rosenbaum, 1954).

to quit near the end of his task than he was at the beginning. The nearer a suitor believes he is to persuading his girl to say "yes," the more likely he is to continue his pursuit. Or, as men believe is more often true, the girl will be more persistent in trying to catch her beau the nearer she thinks she is to marriage. The same principle undoubtedly holds over a wide range of behavior.

An interesting observation made independently by a number of investigators is that responses become more vigorous when frustrated. For example, rats who have been consistently reinforced for bar pressing will often, during the initial stages of extinction, press the bar with more force than they did during acquisition. One reason for this, some psychologists believe, is that frustration has drive properties that can energize a habit (see page 264).

Evidence in support of the notion of a "frustration drive" comes from a study in which rats were trained to traverse a two-section runway in which they received a

pellet at the end of each section. When the pellet at the end of one section was withheld, the rats ran faster than usual in the other (Amsel & Roussel, 1952). Their frustration energized their running habit. Frustration also seems to make an avoidance response stronger. In one experiment, after the subjects had learned an avoidance response, they were for a time prevented from making it. Thereafter, as soon as it was permitted again, it became a more vigorous response than before (Bernstein, 1957).

We often see this increase in vigor that frustration produces in everyday life. People are always shaking vending machines that don't deliver and rattling coin-return buttons on pay telephones that are out of order. In fact, the energizing effect of frustration provides one of the most important themes of slapstick comedy. We have all seen—and probably even laughed at—the comedy about a persistently frustrated character whose reactions become more and more vigorous until he goes out of control altogether.

FRUSTRATION-PRODUCED BEHAVIOR

An acute observer of behavior—and we hope the reader is close to being one by now—is aware that frustration often generates new forms of behavior. A child attacks the playmate who has appropriated his toy. A premedical student who finds he cannot cope with the rigors of laboratory science develops an intense interest in the humanities, and eventually attains real distinction in his new field. Another student who is doing badly reacts by convincing himself and others that his teachers "have it in for him."

As these examples show, frustration often leads to forms of behavior other than those that existed prior to it. There are many kinds of these frustration-produced responses, and we can put them into some kind of order if we sort them out not only by description but also by causes. Before we continue, however, we must remember two points. First, there is no *natural* or *inevitable* response to frustration. Responses are determined by a constellation of learned, perceptual, and motivational, as well as organismic variables. As the constellation varies, so will the response. Second, although these different kinds of responses to frustration may occur separately, they can—and often do—occur in combination.

Aggression

Aggression, by which we mean attack on a person or object, is one of the most common responses to frustration. It can be expressed in a great variety of ways, ranging from gross physical attack to slurring, hostile remarks.

A few decades ago a group of psychologists at Yale (Dollard, Doob, Miller, Mowrer, Sears, Ford, Hovland, & Sollenberger, 1939) conducted a number of experiments that showed how common it is for aggressive behavior to be the consequence of frustration. This frustration-aggression relation agrees with what we often see: dogs growl and bite when their bones are taken away; people make aggressive verbal insults when they are offended.

In one experiment (Zander, 1944), fifth- and sixth-grade children were put to solving a problem which was in fact insolvable. They were supposed to memorize long lists of digits, but these were changed by the experimenter, without the subject's knowing it, and thus every attempt to learn them was frustrated. Many of the children became aggressive in the experimental situation and later outside of it. One boy, who had never before shown any aggressive behavior in the classroom, returned from the experimental room and immediately started a fight. The experimenter, even though he never admitted he was responsible for their frustration, became extremely unpopular. To quote him: "Individual cases of hitting the writer, making faces at him, calling names, aggressive remarks, and even kicking him were frequent during the weeks of the study, happening at least once a day as he passed through the classroom or the hall" (Zander, 1944, p. 26).

In other similar experiment (Sears, Hovland, & Miller, 1940) a group of college students were kept awake all night on the pretense that they were serving as subjects in an experiment to measure the effects of fatigue. They were also forbidden to smoke and were interrupted, with a command to be silent whenever they started to talk. In addition, games and food which had been promised were deliberately withheld. To this frustrating situation the subjects responded with direct aggression, by making nasty remarks about the experiment and questioning the sanity of the psychologists who supervised it. One subject with crude artistic talents drew a sketch of mutilated

FIGURE 12.2 Displacement of Aggression. The rat learns to strike another rat, and when the other rat is removed, this aggressive response generalizes to an "innocent" doll (Dr. N. E. Miller).

and bleeding bodies. Asked what the pictures represented, he replied at once, "psychologists."

Although in these experiments the aggression that developed was directed against the source of the frustration, this is not always the case. Aggression is sometimes **displaced,** that is, directed against an innocent object or person not in any way responsible for the frustration.

Displacement of aggression is often an example of stimulus generalization, as the following experiment illustrates (Miller, 1948). Two rats were placed in a box with an electric grid on the floor. The experimenter trained them to be aggressive toward each other by reinforcing whatever tendencies to fighting they showed. He cut off the electric current in the floor grid only when the animals attacked each other. After the two rats had developed the habit of fighting each other, a celluloid doll was placed in the box with them. The rats ignored it and continued to fight. However, when one rat was removed from the box,

the remaining rat attacked the doll. This was a clear instance of displaced aggression, for the doll had obviously done nothing to provoke the rat. The aggressive response simply generalized from the rat to the doll (see Figure 12.2).

We see more complicated examples of displaced aggression in everyday life: The husband who has been severely criticized by his boss comes home and abuses his wife and children for no apparent reason; the child who has been spanked pulls the tail of his pet; the student who has failed an examination picks a senseless argument with his roommate.

In one interesting study (Miller & Bugelski, 1948) it was shown that frustration, by provoking aggression, could modify racial attitudes. Workers at a summer camp were given a questionnaire which measured their attitudes toward Mexicans and Japanese. Later they were subjected to a series of frustrating circumstances. They were forced to take several tests which were impossible to pass and lasted far longer than they had been led to expect. Consequently, they missed their weekly movie at the local theatre. This was particularly frustrating because the week before one of them had won the lottery at the movie and they all hoped to win this week. After they had experienced these frustrations the workers' attitudes toward Mexicans and Japanese were measured once again. They turned out to be less favorable than before. It was concluded that the aggression induced by the experimental frustration was to some extent displaced onto the two racial groups which had nothing whatever to do with the frustration.

This example of displaced aggression has its counterpart in a statistical study covering the years 1882 to 1930 in the South. In this there was found to be a negative correlation between the annual per acre value of cotton in regions and the number of lynchings that took place in them. The lower the price of cotton the higher was the number of lynchings. That is, the more severe a man's economic frustration, the more likely he was to take it out on Negroes even though they were not responsible for the depressed prices.

We are fairly sure that displaced aggression operates throughout an entire nation during times of extreme deprivation and frustration. As a consequence of their defeat in World War I the people of Germany were forced to endure much suffering and humiliation; they lost standing in the community of nations and were subjected to economic hardships of all sorts: undernourishment, unemployment, and so on. Adolf Hitler rose to power partly through his ability to organize the aggressions of the German people and displace them onto Jews, and onto the people of those nations that had once conquered Germany. Hence, after World War II the United States spent enormous sums building up the economies of the defeated nations, in order to prevent a repetition of the tragedy.

Displaced aggression sometimes directs the turn of a person's fantasies, the flights of his imagination. One study (Bellak, 1944) sought evidence that frustration produces aggression in responses to the Thematic Apperception Test (see Figure 8.2 on page 185). This test makes use of pictures, each of which represent a rather dramatic but somewhat ambiguous situation (a girl running along a beach, the head of a young woman with a very wrinkled old woman behind her). Subjects are instructed to make up a story for each picture. Since the pictures themselves have no single meaning, the stories are not determined by them alone. Everyone responds to them differently and projects something of his own needs and interests into the stories. This particular experiment was planned to discover whether or not the subjects' responses were influenced by recent frustrating experiences.

The subjects were handed a series of pictures from the TAT and asked to make up a story for each. Then they were told— and this is how frustration was induced— that their stories were just about the worst the experimenter had ever heard, he certainly couldn't be bothered with such trash, and they must try again. Following this the subjects were shown a different series of pictures for which they made up stories. The stories were then analyzed for aggressive content. The analysis revealed that the mean number of aggressive words used in the stories *before* frustration was 12.6. *After* frustration this figure rose to 23.7. Thus it was shown that with frustration the amount of aggression present in the stories increased.

If we are to reach any conclusions about the hypothesis that frustration leads to aggression, we must recognize that overt aggression is sometimes inhibited. A person may not betray openly aggressive behavior, but we cannot therefore conclude that he harbors no aggressive feelings. An army private may appear to submit meekly to punishment by his sergeant, and actually be boiling with aggressive impulses that he cannot express for fear of retaliation. Later, safe among his buddies in the barracks, his aggressiveness will probably lead him to give a bitter and inspired characterization of the lousy sergeant.

The fact that aggressive behavior can be inhibited leads us to ask, What determines whether or not frustration will evoke overt aggression? In trying to answer this question, we must remember that frustration does not automatically instigate aggressive acts. Learning plays an important role in determining what sort of behavior will occur in response to frustration. If aggression as a response to frustration has been reinforced, then frustration will tend to produce aggression. For instance, the child who is being physically restrained may force his release by thrashing about or striking the person who is holding him. If he succeeds, and if the same sequence of events recurs several times, he will have learned an aggressive response. This behavior can be analyzed point by point: restraint increases the child's level of activation (see page 259). This in turn leads to agitated behavior. One component of the jumble of agitated behavior, striking out, becomes an instrumental response for release. Thus aggressive behavior is learned.

On the other hand, it need not be aggressive behavior that is learned in such a situation. Suppose the child is released only when he *refrains* from struggling. He may then learn to be quiet instead of aggressive. Such learning would probably be more difficult, because children probably have inborn tendencies to become agitated when suddenly restrained. The important point, however, is that a frustrated child can be trained to be quiet instead of aggressive.

Aggression is an instrumental response that can have many different consequences. When it can eliminate the source of frustration, or minimize its effects, it is reinforced and therefore tends to persist. Aggression can also be self-reinforcing. Because frustration often produces uncomfortable tension, venting one's aggressive feelings "lets off steam" so to speak and therefore reinforces itself. Under these circumstances aggression will recur even though it may not remove the source of frustration. But in some frustrating situations where aggression does not lead to any sort of reinforcement, it tends to disappear.

The behavior of subjects observed during experimental extinction testifies to the importance of experience in determining what response an organism will make to frustration. It has been frequently observed that some rats become aggressive during the early part of experimental extinction. They bite the bar or the opening of the food delivery mechanism. The instrumental conditioning situation, however, can be arranged so that the aggression that normally occurs during extinction is minimized or even avoided. When rats are given a series of sessions devoted *successively* to acquiring

and then extinguishing a response, the aggressive responses which appear during the initial extinction sessions subsequently disappear. It appears, then, that the aggressive responses themselves can be extinguished. Not being reinforced, they tend to drop out. In short, when repeatedly confronted with frustration, the rats learn to tolerate it without becoming aggressive.

Rats who have been conditioned on an intermittent reinforcement schedule (see page 286) do not exhibit aggressiveness when they are extinguished. During conditioning, nonreinforced trials were intermingled with reinforced ones, and so the rat's first frustrating experience came after only a few reinforced trials, when their instrumental habit was very weak. The tendency to react to frustration with aggression depends on the strength of the frustrated habit. If the habit is weak, little or no aggression occurs. In addition, organisms on intermittent reinforcement schedules learn that frustration leads eventually to reinforcement, and instead of learning to respond aggressively, they learn to respond to frustration by persisting in making the instrumental response. This is why instrumental responses learned on an intermittent reinforcement schedule take longer to extinguish than those of continuously reinforced animals.

Another instance of severe frustration met without aggression is seen in the behavior of cormorants (see Figure 12.3), diving birds who catch trout in their beaks. Japanese fishermen have found that they can use cormorants to catch trout for them, that in fact the birds are more efficient than any other method of catching trout. They do this by putting a tight collar around the bird's neck and controlling him with a leash. When a cormorant catches a fish he is pulled back and the fish snatched from his mouth—he has been unable to swallow it because of the tight collar. Imagine how you would respond to such frustration! The cormorants, unable to do anything better, have learned to tolerate the situation. Besides, in spite of repeated frustrations, they receive an ample daily ration of fish and can swallow all the fish that are too small to be obstructed by the tight collar. This arrangement constitutes for them an intermittent reinforcement schedule.

FIGURE 12.3   A Cormorant Being Fed (*The New York Times*).

As we have seen, one of the most important factors in determining the strength of aggression as a response to frustration is whether or not the organism has been reinforced for previous aggressions in response to frustration. The environments of many organisms (beasts of prey as well as civilized man) reinforce aggressive responses to frustrating situations. In such environments organisms tend to become aggressive when frustrated.

Assuming that an organism has learned to respond to frustration with aggression, what determines the intensity of his aggression? One important factor is the strength of the behavior being frustrated. A hungry dog will exhibit much stronger aggression when his food is taken away than a dog whose appetite is nearly satiated will. The frustration of a strong drive produces a stronger tendency to aggressive behavior than the frustration of a weak drive. Similarly, the frustration of a strong habit will increase the tendency to aggressive behavior more than the blocking of a weak habit. You are more likely to mutter aggressively when your top bureau drawer sticks than you are when the same thing happens to a drawer you rarely use. The tendency to be aggressive, in short, is proportional to the strength of the drive or the habit, or a combination of both, that is being frustrated.

Another variable that determines the strength of the tendency to aggression is the intensity of the frustrating situation. College students served as experimenters for a study in which some of their classmates were required to sort a pack of cards within a stipulated time. The experimenters were coached to falsify the scores and tell the subjects that they failed. They were also expected to make derogatory remarks about the subjects' performances. The aggressive remarks the subjects made in reply were counted, and the number was found to be proportional to the intensity of the experimenter's disparaging remarks (McClelland & Apicella, 1945). The more derogatory the remarks, the more aggressive responses the subjects made.

Frustration can have cumulative effects. A father who had been looking forward to a pleasant, relaxed Sunday at home may react to a series of minor frustrations—relatives dropping in, children pestering him—without apparent effect. But let him have one more minor frustration—finding his Sunday paper scattered around the living room—and he will suddenly "blow his top." What happens is that successive bits of frustration accumulate until the last bit is the straw that breaks the camel's back. Suddenly his aggression becomes strong enough, as a result of the cumulative effects of frustration, to develop into overt hostility (Wilensky, 1952).

Thus far in our discussion the strength of aggression has been related to the (1) learning of aggressive responses to frustration; (2) strength of the drive and habit of the behavior that is being blocked; (3) intensity of the frustration, and (4) number of frustrations immediately preceding. A fifth factor—punishment of aggressive behavior—is not completely independent of the first four, but it is so important that it deserves separate treatment. Aggressive behavior, particularly physical violence, is not usually condoned in our society, and children who resort to it are often spanked or punished in some other way. Unfortunately, instead of reducing the tendency to aggression, punishment, it appears, often increases it. Consider the findings of a recent survey of child-rearing practices (Sears, Maccoby, & Levin, 1957) in the United States, in which 379 mothers were interviewed and divided into two main groups on the basis of how they handled their children's aggressive behavior toward themselves and their husbands. The mothers who were most severely punitive were shown to have the most aggressive children.

There is no single reason for this relationship. One contributing factor may be that children are often reinforced for imitating their parents' behavior. When they are punished they learn by example that aggression is an appropriate response to frustration. If they are spanked for frustrating their mother, why shouldn't they be aggressive when they themselves are frustrated? A parent who punishes his child physically has to remember that he is serving as a model for them to imitate. Another factor is that punishment encourages displaced aggression to a wide range of stimuli (see page 396). Here is one mother's report on a child who has been punished if she hit out at either parent:

She seldom turns around and is directly defiant. If she can't get what she wants or if she is angry about something, she'll walk by, and she'll probably fight the first person she comes in contact with. She doesn't usually turn around and defy us or take it out on us. Usually she'll go out and she'll fight with anybody she sees, or she'll turn around and she'll slap the dog on the leg. She seems to go to a certain extent—like she'll say, "No, I won't," or something; and she seems to watch your face, and when she finds she's gone past the limit, she just closes up, and that's the end of it. She seldom turns around and slings anything or does anything to let off steam in front of you. It's usually a walk past the dog, and she'll slap him like this on the way out, or something like that. It—I don't know—it's directed at us, but it's on someone else (Sears, Maccoby, & Levin, p. 232).

Such behavior in an aggressive child raises the question, What keeps aggression from becoming overt? When an organism has learned to respond to frustration with aggression, he will continue to be aggressive unless something interferes. One such factor—but certainly not the only one—is punishment.

The more a child fears being punished, the smaller the chance that he will commit overt aggression. A child is less likely to strike back at a parent who has spanked him if he has learned that such retaliatory behavior will be punished. At first glance this may appear to be inconsistent with the findings that the children who are punished most often for being aggressive are the most aggressive. But it is not. The study of child-rearing practices found that those children who were physically punished for aggressive behavior toward their parents were less likely to retaliate than those children who were punished and *allowed to retaliate*. One can assume that in this comparison the tendency to be aggressive was the same for both groups of children, since they were both frequent recipients of punishment. However, the children who had been punished for retaliating gave less evidence of actual aggressive behavior than those who had been permitted to strike back.

The same study reported that the smallest percentage of highly aggressive children came from homes in which parents not only discouraged aggressive behavior but used a minimal amount of physical punishment themselves. At a very early age these children were taught to respond in other than aggressive ways to frustration.

Another factor that influences the nature of aggressive behavior is the availability of persons or objects on whom it may be vented. For if a suitable target is not available, aggression can take the form of fantasy or turn inward. Although daydreams about beating enemies are common enough, the idea that aggression can be directed inwards (toward oneself) may surprise some. People rarely inflict pain on themselves, but self-directed aggression is not at all rare. People blame *themselves* for being frustrated, and thus think of themselves as inadequate (at times with little justification).

Aggression tends to increase the general level of activation (see page 395). When two pigeons are trained to peck at each other, their initial responses are simple, calm, thrusting movements of the neck and head. No evidence of excitement is apparent. But as learning progresses their behavior becomes livelier. The birds get excited; their chests swell and their feathers rise, indicating a higher level of activation. The first "aggressive" responses which are simple instrumental responses involving only a few muscles, finally develop into what seems to be a regular emotional outburst. We often observe the same transformation in the players of games involving bodily contact. At the beginning they are relatively calm, but at the end of the game, especially if it has been close, they may be savages.

In concluding this discussion of aggressive responses to frustration, we must emphasize that our analysis has, of necessity, been general in scope. It is essential for you to understand that aggressive responses can take many forms and that a variety of situations may produce frustration. The same boy might respond aggressively in one frustrating situation and not in another. He may fight with his playmate when frustrated because his parents condone such behavior, but he may tolerate frustration at home because he has been taught to. You must always take the specific stimulus-response conditions into account when you apply the principle of the frustration-aggression sequence.

You must always remember that aggression is not the only response to frustration. Our decision to take it up first in this chapter was based on several considerations. First, aggression is a common response to frustration, as we have seen. Second, it is a primary one in the sense that it is often the first response evoked by frustration, although others may follow. And last, because of the large amount of knowledge we have about the frustration-aggression sequence, it can serve well as a model for understanding other reactions to frustration.

We will now discuss several other methods of coping with frustration. The information about these reactions stems primarily from observations of psychiatrists and psychologists in clinical situations supplemented by experimental studies. Later we will discuss how some of these reactions to frustration, if consistently adopted, may shape the distinctive pattern of an individual's behavior, which we customarily refer to as his *personality*.

Apathy

An organism sometimes responds to a frustrating situation with apathy. **Apathy** is marked by extreme indifference to surroundings and general listlessness. We encountered something akin to apathy when we discussed schedules of reinforcement. You may remember that in a high fixed ratio schedule, animals become apathetic just after receiving a reinforcement (see page 290). They have learned that they have to make many responses before getting another reinforcement. Their frustration is so difficult to overcome that they give up.

Apathy was one of the dominant symptoms exhibited by inmates of Nazi concentration camps at the end of World War II. At first they were not at all apathetic: they tried to improve their living conditions; they planned escapes and vented their aggression toward their oppressors in various kinds of sabotage. But for most of the prisoners this was useless. Their living conditions were beastly and nothing could be done to improve them. Their acts of aggression and sabotage were detected and punished severely. There was practically no chance of escape. In short, there was no solution to their plight; torture and death loomed as their inevitable fate. To this persistent and insurmountable frustration the majority of prisoners finally responded with complete apathy. By not caring, so it seemed, they could minimize the horror of their existence. More analytically, we would say that apathy reduced the drive component of their behavior. With drive lowered, the effects of frustration were lessened.

As this example shows, persistent and insurmountable frustration breeds apathy. In America today, we are all witnessing, and many of us experiencing, genuine apathy in our preparation for civilian defense against possible atomic warfare. It seems so likely that an enemy attack would cause complete annihilation or incredible destruction that the precautions recommended by civil defense authorities appear utterly futile. Such apathy can be overcome only if people become convinced that the time, effort, and money spent on civil defense would actually avail against the threat by possible enemy attack.

Rationalization

The fox in Aesop's fable provides the classical example of **rationalization.** Unable to reach the bunch of juicy grapes, he decided that he didn't really want them because they would probably be sour. He met the frustration neither by surmounting the obstacle nor by realistically accepting failure. Instead he denied his failure, he rationalized.

An interesting kind of rationalization often results from posthypnotic suggestion. In a typical instance, a subject under hypnosis is told that after he wakes up he is to raise the window whenever he sees the hypnotist remove a handkerchief from his pocket, and that he is to forget he was instructed to do so. So, after he is aroused from his hypnotic trance, even while he is conversing with others, the subject watches the hypnotist furtively. When the hypnotist removes the handkerchief from his pocket the subject steps toward the window, then perhaps hesitates. He doesn't understand his desire to open it, but wanting to behave rationally, exclaims, "Isn't it a little stuffy in here?" Having offered a plausible reason for what he is about to do, he opens the window.

The major point of this demonstration is that the hypnotized person rationalizes his behavior by offering a sensible, self-convincing, but nevertheless incorrect explanation for it. Why does he fool himself? Because for one thing, like the rest of us, he feels compelled to give a rational explanation for everything he does. Considering the very early age at which children in our society learn that they are expected to "behave rationally," this is not surprising. It is not uncommon to hear mothers demand that their three-year-olds answer such complicated questions as "Why are you teasing your brother?" or "Why did you break your toy?" In the demonstration of the posthypnotic suggestion, the subject is not aware of his real motive and consequently must invent a reason in order to appear rational, at least to himself.

We sometimes rationalize our behavior because a true explanation of it would create fear and anxiety. Consider the child who has been taught to succeed, but has failed in school. Failure means that he is either dull or lazy, and these are qualities he has learned to look down on and avoid. So when he fails, he has to convince himself that the examination was unfair. This rationalization permits him to avoid making a negative self-evaluation. Rationalization, in short, functions as an instrumental response that brings reinforcement because it shields the rationalizer from something noxious.

Fantasy

Frustration often generates **fantasy** or, as it is usually called, daydreaming, because it can be overcome more easily in imagination than in reality. The belief that daydreaming occurs infrequently and is always harmful is unjustified. People are confused about daydreaming because they are more interested in evaluating it than in understanding the conditions responsible for it.

Table 12.1 reports the results of a questionnaire administered to groups of undergraduate and graduate students. The questionnaire was answered anonymously, so we can safely conclude that the answers were given without fear of embarrassment. The only factual information required of each respondent was sex, age, and year in college. From a variety of daydreams described to them, the students were asked to indicate which kinds they had experienced in the last 30 days. The results showed that daydreaming is frequent, with the median number at five; only 3 per cent of the entire sample reported that they had none. There was practically no differ-

TABLE 12.1 Frequency of Occurrence of Different Types of Daydreams in Two Groups of Students During a 30-Day Period (L. F. Shaffer & E. J. Shoben, Jr. *The psychology of adjustment.* 2nd ed. Boston: Houghton Mifflin, 1956).

| | UNDERGRADUATE | | GRADUATE | |
	Men	Women	Men	Women
1. Physical feat	30	3	13	2
2. Physical attractiveness	34	63	17	56
3. Mental feat	48	42	47	61
4. Vocational success	81	69	78	64
5. Money or possessions	69	66	51	52
6. Display	22	16	19	19
7. Saving	14	5	14	8
8. Grandeur	11	7	6	0
9. Homage	16	13	24	18
10. Sexual	74	73	63	71
11. Death or destruction	9	9	10	9
12. Martyr	9	15	10	12
13. Worry	45	56	49	50
14. Other types	30	20	24	23

ence between the fantasy behavior of the undergraduate and graduate students. The main differences between the sexes was that a higher percentage of women had fantasies about their physical attractiveness, while men daydreamed more about outstanding physical exploits. Presumably these differences reflect reactions to culturally imposed frustrations. Although many men wish to be physically attractive, this attribute is of much greater importance to women. In contrast, almost all men want to be heroic and strong, qualities which the vast majority of girls do not aspire to. We know that such learned drives are often frustrated and if daydreaming is a response that overcomes frustration, then we would expect men and women to have different daydreams.

Daydreams mirror the change in motives that comes with age. Themes dominating the daydreams of young children are the acquisition of desired toys and the enjoyment of favorite kinds of amusement. As they grow older their daydreams become more socially oriented; they dream of being heroes and of receiving praise. In the daydreams of adolescents dominant themes are winning the affection of members of the opposite sex and achieving social position and wealth. Adults also daydream of sexual conquests, success in work, wealth and power, and other goals society has taught them to strive for.

The finding that most students daydream suggests that daydreaming is not of itself evidence of a psychological disorder. All of us are constantly subjected to frustrations of one kind or another that we cannot immediately surmount. The aspiring medical student has to leap many a hurdle before he can hope to have his own practice. Daydreaming of the rewards he will someday enjoy can lessen his present frustration. In addition, daydreams allow humans to tolerate the inevitable frustrations of living. This is particularly true for children who, because they are small and weak, are persistently frustrated. By identifying themselves with such glorious characters as Cinderella, Jack-the-giant-killer, Superman, and the "fastest-draw-in-the-west," they escape, through fantasy, from the harsh reality of their inadequacies.

We are forced to conclude that it is neither possible nor proper to give an overall evaluation of the psychological consequences of daydreaming. The important consideration is whether daydreaming contributes to the solution of the problem posed by the frustrating situation. Daydreams can help us overcome obstacles. They have been called "the nursery of great accomplishment." The premedical student's fantasies can motivate him to study harder and increase his chances of admission to a first-rate medical school. Or his fantasies may help him plan his future career by encouraging him to specialize in one area of medicine. He may dream for example, of studying with a great surgeon and successfully performing rare operations. Such daydreams serve the useful function of assisting him to see and master his problems. On the other hand, daydreams can hinder problem solution if they become substitutes for realistic attempts to surmount the obstacles. The premedical student who night after night, while he is supposed to be studying, imagines himself a great surgeon saving countless lives, may flunk out. He could not be cited as one who benefitted from his daydreams.

To sum up then, daydreams are often generated by frustration, and if they can help us tolerate it without interfering with or retarding problem solution, we must conclude that the psychological effects are beneficial. It is likely that a large percentage of the daydreams college students indulge in fall into this category. But daydreams can do more than help us simply tolerate frustration. They can help or hinder us in overcoming it.

Compensation

Compensation is one of the psychological expedients individuals adopt to make up for (compensate for) their deficiencies. A simple example comes from the behavior of a group of college students (Overton & Brown, 1957) who were unaware of their weak color vision (see page 130). Asked whether the red or green traffic light was on top, they gave quicker and more correct answers than students who had normal color vision. By learning the position of the lights they had compensated, to some degree, for their physiological defect.

We often encounter insurmountable obstacles that threaten us with enduring or even permanent frustration. No matter how much some boys practice they can never excel as athletes, and no matter how they preen and fuss some girls will never turn into Hollywood beauties. Such personal handicaps and inadequacies are too great to overcome, and those who have them may respond to the frustration by striving to excel in some other way, by compensating for the deficiency. The frustrated athlete may shift his interest from sports to sports writing, where he has the ability to excel. The frustrated movie star may become a clothes designer and achieve a degree of success that her original aspiration could never lead her to.

Behind the mechanism of compensation lies the fact that our motives are not as simple as they may seem. When a boy longs for a career as a major league baseball player he wants to be an outstanding person, not just an excellent ballplayer. What is important is for him to *excel* at something. Hence, the boy who becomes a successful sports writer and the girl who becomes a topnotch dress designer are to some extent satisfying the motivation which directed them initially toward other pursuits.

As was true for daydreaming, the psychological consequences of compensation cannot be stated simply. They depend upon a constellation of factors. The person who compensates for failing to become a physician by becoming a dentist is solving his career problem, if his new profession brings him satisfaction and contentment. If it does not and he detests his work, then his compensatory behavior has not solved his career problem. Compensation, like daydreaming, can be useful and helpful in overcoming frustration, or it can leave the frustration unresolved and even make it worse.

Some psychologists have found it useful to distinguish among several different forms of compensation. One kind, known as **overcompensation,** results from trying to excel

where one is weakest. Demosthenes, the greatest orator of ancient Greece, was a stutterer, but his drive to compensate for this defect was so great that he became an eloquent speaker. Teddy Roosevelt is said to have overcompensated for his childhood physical weakness by rigorous physical training. His overcompensation was so successful that he was able to be a military hero during the Spanish-American War and a big game hunter.

A form of behavior similar to compensation is known as **sublimation.** Noting that the sexual drive often led to behavior running counter to society's moral codes, Freud pointed out that it could be—and frequently is—sublimated, that is, redirected into socially acceptable activities. He saw much of artistic creation as sublimated sexual drive. There is much evidence that other kinds of antisocial drives can be redirected into socially acceptable forms. One can point to several recent prize-fighting champions who had records as juvenile delinquents. Once they had the opportunity to fight in a socially approved manner, they were able to channel their intense aggression into acceptable modes of behavior.

Regression

Regression can also result from frustration. Let us define this term by citing a specific example. When they are placed in a Skinner box some rats rub their faces with their paws at first. They soon discard this response in favor of the bar-pressing response which is reinforced. But during experimental extinction, when the bar-pressing habit is weakened, this "face washing" behavior often reappears. **Regression** can thus be defined as the reappearance of a previously abandoned habit.

Regression sometimes results from frustration induced by punishment. In one experiment (Mowrer, 1940) rats were placed in a box with an electrified grid in the floor. The intensity of the shock they received from the grid was minimized when the animals sat on their haunches, a response they all quickly learned. Later, a lever which would terminate the shock when it was pressed was inserted in the box. The rats soon stopped sitting on their haunches and learned to make this new response. After a while conditions were changed once again; the bar was electrified and the bar-pressing habit frustrated. As a result, most of the subjects regressed to sitting on their haunches, that is, the previously abandoned habit reappeared.

Another interesting example of regression occurred as part of an experiment (Barker, Dembo, & Lewin, 1941) when some highly attractive toys were taken away from a group of preschool children who were playing with them. At the beginning of this experiment the children were observed while they played with some moderately attractive toys and were rated on the constructiveness of their play. Constructiveness was defined in terms of the imaginativeness and organization shown. Highly constructive play with a boat and paper would be pretending to go on an extensive boat trip and using the paper as the ocean. Less constructive play would be pushing the boat back and forth repetitively. After the children's level of play was evaluated with the moderately attractive toys, they were allowed to enjoy new and more fascinating toys in a part of the room previously closed off. Then they were returned to their regular play area where only the moderately interesting toys were available, and a wire screen was put between them and the more attractive toys. The effects of frustration were determined by comparing the level of constructiveness of play before and after frustration. Over three-quarters of the children, in the face of frustration, regressed to a less constructive level. Presumably less constructive forms of play occur at earlier ages, and thus when a child goes from a more advanced to a less advanced level of play he is regressing, an

earlier mode of response is reappearing.

Clinical psychologists and psychiatrists frequently observe cases of regression to more immature forms of behavior. A common example is the child who regresses to more immature forms of behavior after the birth of a younger sibling. He may begin to cry more often and become more demanding and dependent, or even return to such infantile behavior as bed-wetting and thumb-sucking. An analysis of this kind of regressive behavior suggests that the infantile forms reappear because the more mature habits are extinguished by lack of reinforcement. One very important kind of reinforcement for the child is the attention his parents give him. As a result, his behavior is shaped (see page 291) to attract attention. With the birth of the second child, the parents, particularly the mother, no longer have the same amount of time for the older child, or they may have become more interested in the new baby. As a result, many of the older child's attention-getting responses ("Will you play with me, Mommy?") are no longer effective and are extinguished. Just as subjects revert to older habits during experimental extinction, the child returns to earlier forms of attention-getting behavior. These earlier habits are usually reinforced because they practically force the parents to pay attention. Consequently, regressive forms of behavior are particularly difficult to eliminate. The parents seem to be caught on the horns of a dilemma. If they ignore the immature behavior, the older child may regress to even more undesirable behavior. If they pay attention to the regressive responses, then the behavior will be reinforced and will tend to persist.

Is such a problem insolvable? Can psychologists or psychiatrists offer any advice to parents struggling with this problem? They can, although they usually find it easier to tell people how to prevent or minimize the onset of a psychological difficulty than to tell them how to solve one.

To *prevent* his regression after the birth of a younger child, parents should make sure that the older child has been trained to be just as independent as his age permits. Before the baby is born he should be given tasks that will encourage him to solve problems by himself. In this way he will learn to depend on, and to be confident of, his own abilities. The more independent a child is, the less likely he is to regress at the birth of a younger sibling. In addition, the parents should try to avoid giving him much less attention than they gave him before the new child was born. Newborn infants sleep about 20 hours a day and actually do not require much personal attention. If the mother can free herself from some of her time-consuming household chores, she should be able to devote sufficient time to the older child to soften the frustration of having a rival in the household.

Once regressive behavior occurs, however, there is no simple remedy. Some important principles and hints to possible procedures are highlighted in the following clinical case:

A girl five-and-a-half years old began wetting her bed soon after a little brother was born. The parents loved their daughter very much, and in many ways she was a model child. They had, however, been very eager to have a son and were thrilled when he was born. Everyone gave the baby a great deal of attention including the father's parents, who were overjoyed that the family name would now be perpetuated (their name was Brown). Shortly thereafter, the girl began wetting her bed. The father surmised that this might be due to her loss of attention, and it occurred to him that, if this were so, the problem could be solved by giving her more attention. He deliberately began to do just this, but unfortunately, he chose to do it in the wrong way. He paid attention to her problem. He did not scold her, but he discussed it at length with her and promised her attractive toys if she could control herself during the night. Every morning bed-wetting was the dominant topic of conversation. The result of all this fuss and bother was that the girl continued to wet her bed about once every three nights. The parents persisted in their attempts to stop her from wetting her bed, but they were unsuccessful. Finally, they brought their troubles to a clinical psychologist.

A medical examination showed that no organic condition was responsible for the enuresis (the medical term for bed-wetting). Moreover, both the parents and the child, except for her symptom of enuresis, appeared to be what is commonly described as well adjusted. In essence the psychologist's hypothesis about the child's difficulty agreed with her father's: the regressive symptom began as a reaction to her loss of attention after the birth of her baby brother. But he felt that the kind of attention the parents were giving, instead of discouraging the bed-wetting, was actually maintaining it. The girl was being reinforced by parental attention to her bed-wetting. The psychologist's advice was simple. Ignore the bed-wetting completely and pay more attention to the girl.

Before his son was born the father had often taken his daughter on visits to the zoo. He began to do this again. The parents thought up other parent-child activities, which they encouraged. But they never mentioned the bed-wetting. If the child wet her bed the sheets were changed, and that was all. If she did not wet her bed no congratulations or rewards were offered. Since bed-wetting no longer attracted attention it gradually decreased. In about three months it ceased altogether.

This case, because it was not complicated by other factors, proved easy to solve. The girl had regressed to a previous habit because she was frustrated by being deprived of her parents' attention. The regressive behavior was instrumental in achieving their attention and thus persisted. When reinforcement was removed the regressive responses were extinguished.

Clinical evidence of this sort is not offered as proof that regression had occurred. Rigorous proof is usually the product of controlled experimentation. Such a case history does, however, *illustrate* how basic psychological processes operate in the lives of individuals.

Fixation

If an organism is repeatedly confronted with the same frustrating situation he may finally learn to make the same response over and over again. Such a stereotyped reaction is called a **fixation.** You can see how a fixated response can develop from the following experiment:

At the beginning of the experiment rats are trained to jump toward one of two cards in a discrimination apparatus (see Figure 12.4). When the rat jumps toward the correct card (e.g., the black circle on the white background), it gives way, providing him direct access to food in back of it. If the rat jumps toward the incorrect card (e.g., the white circle on the black background), it fails to give way and he tumbles into a net below.

After he has learned to do this, the rat is then frustrated by an impossible task. There is no longer a consistently correct or incorrect card. Each card is now correct only half the time. Therefore, as long as the rat continues to jump he is bound to experience a number of punishments in the form of striking a rigid wall and falling into the net. Moreover, he cannot stop jumping and escape punishment because

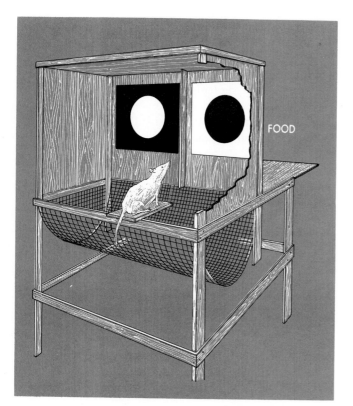

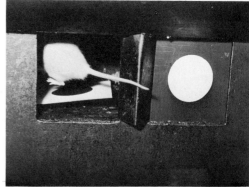

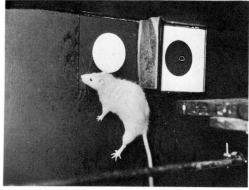

FIGURE 12.4 A Diagram of a Discrimination Apparatus and Photographs of Correct and Incorrect Choices (Bernard Hoffman, *Life,* © 1939, Time, Inc.)

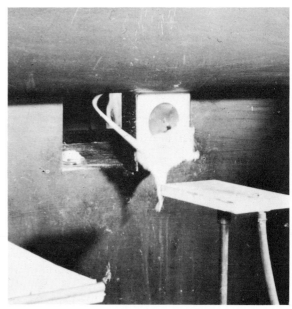

FIGURE 12.5 A Case of Fixation. This rat has adopted the stereotyped response of jumping toward a card locked in place even though food would be available if he jumped to the other side (Dr. N. R. F. Maier).

a noxious blast of air is directed at him until he jumps. To this insolvable problem, from which there is no escape, the rat adopts a stereotyped response. He jumps repeatedly to the left or right side, regardless of the card on that side. As a result of this "position habit" the rat is reinforced for about half his responses and punished for the rest.

Once this stereotyped habit is adopted it is so resistant to change that it has been labeled an "abnormal" fixation. This description is appropriate considering the results of the next stage of the experiment. The card opposite the one on which the rat's responses are fixated is removed and the food is left in plain view. A card on which his responses are fixated is locked into position. The rat then has a choice between a response that will lead to punishment and one that will lead to reinforcement. Yet he persists in his abnormally fixated habit even though it is now punished 100 per cent of the time. This rigidly stereotyped behavior lasts for as many as

200 successive trials (Maier, Glaser, & Klee, 1940).

Such fixated behavior develops from frustration (insolvable problem) from which the organism cannot escape. The fixated behavior actually does serve a function. It helps the animal to minimize the punishment by anticipating it. Instead of jumping point-blank at the locked card, the rat learns to turn sideways in flight, and thus reduce the effect of the impact as well as prepare for the landing in the net below. One reason, then, that the fixated jumping habit is so persistent is that it minimizes the effect of punishment and thereby reduces the fear.

Some psychologists (e.g., Maier, 1949) believe that the punishment-minimizing and fear-reducing qualities of fixated behavior cannot alone explain its persistence. There is something unique about frustration, they believe, that must also be considered. Regardless of the final explanation, the important point for you to remember is that when an organism is forced to deal with an insolvable problem, behavior extremely resistant to change can develop.

It may seem like a big leap to go from abnormal fixation in rats to the behavior problems of children, but there are striking similarities here. Consider the child whose mother behaves erratically and unpredictably toward his immature speech patterns. Sometimes she reinforces his baby talk by cuddling him and calling him her cute "itty-bitty-babee." At other times, when she is exasperated by his poor articulation, she scolds and nags him and may even strike him. What can the child do? He is in the same predicament as the rat in the insolvable problem. It is not unusual for such a child to develop a form of persistent stereotyped behavior, a speech defect. It is a sort of compromise between the baby talk that is intermittently reinforced and punished and the correct speech pattern the child aspires to but cannot yet achieve. Inadequate speech patterns of this kind are very resistant to change and usually require the assistance of a speech therapist.

It is important to point out that in a case like this, the child would find it difficult to escape from the frustration since he is more or less forced to talk in some way. Many of the reinforcements required in everyday life are obtained by speech. Nevertheless, there are rare cases where children develop *mutism,* and remain silent. Presumably mutism is a response that avoids the punishment and fear that speaking produces.

An interesting demonstration of the fear-reducing quality of fixated responses comes from an experiment (Farber, 1948) with rats who were trained in a T maze. For the first 40 trials the rats were reinforced with food for choosing the right side. For the next 60 trials the rats received an electric shock at the point where the choice had to be made (see Figure 12.6). They persisted in making their initial response (they were forced to the choice point), because it not only got them food but also allowed

them to escape the shock. After this phase of the experiment was completed, an attempt was made to reverse the subject's habit. Food was placed at the left side of the maze and the rats were not shocked. For an average of 61 trials they persisted in running to the side that had no food (the one that was initially correct). Two rats persisted for as long as 250 trials without receiving any apparent reinforcement.

Is this an example of fixated behavior? The answer is provided by the behavior of a control group of rats who were trained to choose one side of the same T maze for 100 trials. Differing from the fixated rats only in that they never received any shock, they required an average of only ten trials to reverse their choice when food was shifted to the other arm.

Why did the shock produce fixated behavior? One explanation is that, because of the shock, the cues at the choice point became conditioned to evoke fear. The animals escaped from these fear-provoking cues by making their usual turn and running to the end box. When food reinforcement was withdrawn, the subjects nevertheless persisted in their habit because it was still reinforced by fear reduction.

If fear provided the motivation, then eliminating fear should reduce the fixation. This hypothesis was tested by feeding rats at the choice point where they had previously been shocked. It was assumed that eating produced internal responses (e.g., relaxation) incompatible with the fear reaction. These rats, as predicted, showed no signs of fixation and reversed their responses as rapidly as the control animals who were not shocked.

The more general implications of the last portion of this experiment should not be overlooked. What we see are subjects ready to adopt a fixated habit. The experimenter prevented them from doing so by reducing their fear. In a certain sense this is an example of psychological treatment, a topic discussed in Chapter 14.

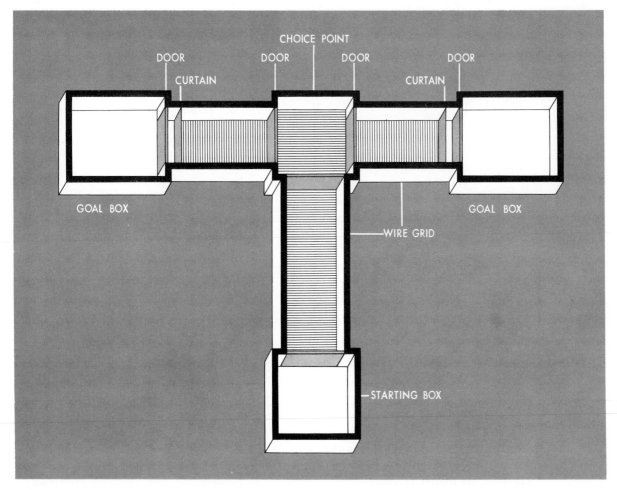

FIGURE 12.6 The Maze Used to Investigate Fixation Resulting From the Persistence of a Fear-Reducing Response. The rats learned to go to one side of the maze to escape shock and obtain food. When both were eliminated, the rats continued to make the same choice because the response led to the escape from the fear-arousing cues (After Farber, 1948).

CONFLICT

From their birth, organisms are likely to find themselves in situations where incompatible response tendencies are aroused. Sometimes these conflicts are resolved easily; at other times they are not. Some conflicts, persisting for long periods, can interfere with an organism's behavior and even seriously disrupt it.

The psychology of conflict has its roots in habit competition and frustration. It is an organism's ability to respond in different ways to the same situation that allows him to suffer conflict. If men and women were able to behave in only one way in every situation, they would not experience conflict. Our very versatility sometimes proves to be our undoing. If we possess two or more competing habits only one of which can be performed at a time, frustration is the inevitable consequence.

It is somewhat surprising that a topic as important as conflict has received little

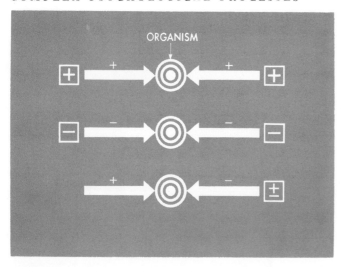

ORGANISM

FIGURE 12.7 A Threefold Classification of Conflict. In each conflict situation the organism is subjected to two incompatible response tendencies, indicated by the direction of the arrows. The upper diagram illustrates an approach-approach conflict, where the organism is between two attracting (positive) incentives. The middle diagram illustrates an avoidance-avoidance conflict, where the organism is between two repelling (negative) situations. The lower diagram shows an approach-avoidance gradient, where the organism is both attracted and repelled by the same situation (After Lewin, 1935).

scientific attention until recent years. The pages of literature and history are filled with accounts of personal conflicts (e.g., Hamlet and Abraham Lincoln) that have not only fascinated generations of readers, but have also exerted profound effects on our cultural traditions and systems of value. Not until the twentieth century, however, did man seriously begin to analyze conflict as a psychological problem, a problem that so often dominates his very existence.

Two great men stand out in the early history of the psychology of conflict. One is Freud, the other Pavlov. Freud, the clinician who sought to help his psychologically disturbed patients, saw clearly the profound effect that conflict could have upon behavior. He concluded that conflict is the basis of all the disturbances which he called neurotic. Pavlov, the experimentalist, discovered that a dog, if continuously subjected to a difficult discrimination (see

page 161), will break down and begin to exhibit symptoms which, in some respects, are similar to those displayed by neurotic individuals. The importance of Pavlov's contribution to the understanding of conflict was threefold. He showed: (1) that the conflict produced by a difficult discrimination is capable of producing neurotic symptoms; (2) that conflict behavior is essentially continuous with such ordinary, "normal" behavior as discrimination learning, and (3) that the study of the psychology of conflict need not be restricted to clinical situations; it may also be investigated in the laboratory.

With the basic foundation laid for an experimental investigation of conflict behavior, it was not long before other scientists turned their attention to this new field of research. One of them, Kurt Lewin (1935), a follower of the Gestalt tradition (see page 46), made a simple and widely influential analysis of conflict behavior. He saw that all conflicts may be described as effects of two polar opposites in an organism's environment: its attracting (+) and repelling (—) aspects. This analysis resulted in a threefold classification of conflicts (see Figure 12.7): approach-approach, avoidance-avoidance, and approach-avoidance.

In an **approach-approach** conflict the organism is caught between two attracting (positive) goal objects. The ancient fable of the donkey caught midway between two bales of hay typifies the approach-approach conflict. The fable relates that the donkey starved to death because he could not resolve his conflict. Such an outcome, however dramatic, is very unlikely, as you will see. Ordinary approach-approach conflicts usually present no great difficulty. Shall I get a coke at the drugstore or the restaurant? Which seat shall I occupy in the movie? Typically, such conflicts are easily resolved.

In an **avoidance-avoidance** conflict an organism is caught between two repelling or negative situations, both of which he seeks to avoid. Shall I get my tooth pulled, or shall I have it filled? Shall I take the test for which I am not prepared or cut the test and suffer whatever penalty my professor imposes? In both examples no complete escape is possible. The person must either remain in conflict or choose an alternative.

The **approach-avoidance** conflict probably occurs most frequently. Psychologically it is the most important of the three kinds of conflict situations. The person in an approach-avoidance conflict is both attracted and repelled by the same thing. Shall I go swimming in the cold water? Shall I take this well-paid job under the obnoxious boss? Shall I go to the party without a date? In all these examples the person is in conflict because the goal object has both desirable and undesirable features, positive and negative reinforcing characteristics.

The basic mechanisms involved in these three forms of conflict, as well as their behavioral consequences, have been greatly clarified by a series of experiments conducted by Neal Miller (1959) and his co-workers. These experiments are of interest not only because they cast light upon the psychology of conflict, but also because they represent one of the most interesting and fruitful examples of psychological theorizing.

Miller's work has been successful for a number of reasons. He made some straight-forward assumptions and used simple experimental situations to test them in. In addition, he and his associates have been extremely perceptive in seeing the implications of their results for a wide range of behavior.

Miller formulated several principles to describe and explain conflict behavior. His first principle, dealing with the *approach gradient,* states that *the nearer a subject is to a goal, the stronger is his tendency to approach it.* Miller devised an experimental situation in which everything involved in

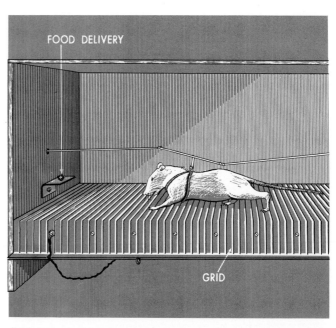

FIGURE 12.8 The Technique Used to Measure the Strength of the Tendencies to Approach or Avoid in a Conflict Situation. The rat is placed in a harness so that when he is restrained briefly the amount of pull he exerts may be measured and recorded (After Brown, 1946).

this principle was given clear operational definition. In Miller's experiments, rats learned to run down a straight alley 200 centimeters in length toward one end where there was a dish of food. *Nearness* could, therefore, be measured spatially. A *goal* was defined as the part of the alley where the food was. The strength of the *tendency to approach* was measured by an ingenious strength-of-pull technique. The rat was put in a light harness connected to a spring, a device which permitted the experimenter to restrain the rat briefly as he ran through the alley (Brown, 1948). The amount of pull he exerted when he was momentarily restrained was measured in grams.

Figure 12.9 shows the results of one study which established the validity of the principle, the nearer the goal, the stronger tendency to approach it. After being trained to run down the alley to get food, the rats were restrained in one of two locations, one near (30 cm.) the goal and one far (170 cm.) from it. The rats pulled harder

413

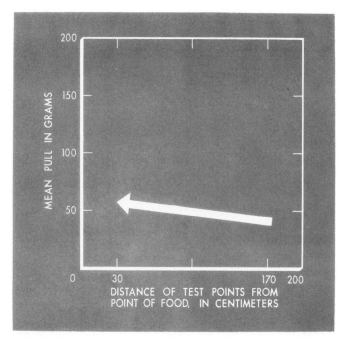

FIGURE 12.9   The Approach Gradient Obtained by the Strength-of-Pull Technique. The closer rats were to the goal, the stronger their pull toward it (After Brown, 1948).

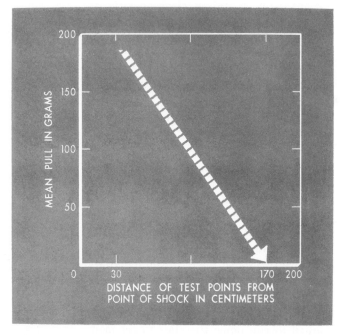

FIGURE 12.10   The Avoidance Gradient Obtained by the Strength-of-Pull Technique. The closer the rats were to the place they had been shocked, the stronger their pull away from it (After Brown, 1948).

when they were nearer the goal than when they were farther away. But you should not overlook a very important finding in Figure 12.9. The approach gradient slopes very gradually. Although the rats did pull harder when they were closer to the goal, the difference between their pulls at the far and near points was slight.

A second principle, dealing with the *avoidance gradient,* states that *the nearer a subject is to a feared stimulus, the stronger is his tendency to avoid it.* This assumption was tested in an experimental study by having a group of rats shocked at one end of the alley. Since a stimulus associated with shock acquires the ability to evoke fear, the end compartment would become a *feared stimulus.* The results of the experiment are shown in Figure 12.10. When the animals were released from that end of the alley where they had been shocked, they ran toward the other end, exerting more pull when restrained near the feared stimulus than when restrained farther away. Thus the second assumption was also confirmed. Note that the difference between the strengths of pulls at these two locations is great, making the avoidance gradient steep.

The third principle stems from the difference in steepness of slope in the approach and the avoidance gradients. It states that the avoidance gradient changes with distance more rapidly than the approach gradient, in other words that *the slope of the avoidance gradient is steeper than the slope of the approach gradient.* The difference between Figures 12.9 and 12.10 is, of course, consistent with this principle.

Psychologists have speculated about why the avoidance gradient is steeper. One hypothesis is that there is greater stimulus generalization between the nearest and farthest points of the approach gradient than there is between the nearest and farthest points of the avoidance gradient. The reason for this is that hunger is largely dependent on internal physiological cues. Thus the amount of generalization between the near and far end of the alley is large, because these internal physiological cues (the hunger drive stimulus) are common to both situations. Fear, however, is a learned drive and more dependent on situational (i.e., external) cues, namely, the stimuli of the shock situation. Since it is based primarily on external stimulus situations, there is less generalization between the near and far end of the alley. Consequently the slope of the avoidance gradient should be steeper than the approach gradient.

The fourth principle of Miller's analysis of conflict behavior is that *the strength of the tendencies to approach or to avoid varies directly with the strength of the drive involved.* This principle was easy to test. Approach gradients were obtained for animals operating under two different drive conditions: a 46-hour hunger drive and a one-hour hunger drive. Figure 12.11 shows the results. The subjects with the more intense hunger drive exhibited stronger tendencies to approach. Those with a drive level of one hour failed to exert any pull at the far end of the alley, and at the near end their response was extremely weak.

The results (see Figure 12.12) relating drive level to height of avoidance gradient were also found to be consistent with the fourth principle. Two groups of rats received different strengths of shock. The subjects given the more intense shocks, and therefore experiencing the greater fear (see page 256), exhibited stronger avoidance tendencies than those whose fear was derived from weak shocks.

The fifth principle states that *increasing the number of reinforced trials will up to a point (i.e., the limit or asymptote of learning) increase the tendency to approach or avoid.* This means that a group of animals who have had a great deal of training to go to the end of the experimental alley to get

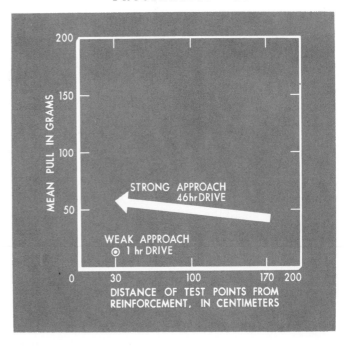

FIGURE 12.11 The Results of an Experiment Designed to Test the Validity of the Principle That the Height of the Approach Gradient Varies With the Strength of the Drive. Animals deprived of food for 46 hours exhibited a stronger tendency to approach than those who had been deprived of food for only one hour. The animals with a weak hunger drive failed to exert any pull toward the goal when they were placed at the far end of the alley (After Brown, 1948).

food will exert a greater pull when restrained than another group of animals who have had less training, even though their hunger is equally strong. Another implication of this principle is that the more fear-learning trials a subject has received, the stronger his avoidance tendency will be. If he receives a number of shocks of a given intensity, he will produce a higher avoidance gradient than he would if he received one or two. In general, the experimental evidence appears to be consistent with both predictions.

The sixth principle brings us directly to the problem of conflict. It states that *when two incompatible response tendencies (e.g., approach and avoid) are in conflict, the one that is stronger will prevail.* We must examine the numerous ramifications of this principle systematically in terms of three main kinds of conflict.

Approach-Approach Conflict

An approach-approach conflict can be established easily with Miller's experimental technique. An animal fed an equal number of times at both ends of the alley will develop incompatible approach tendencies of approximately equal strengths (see Figure 12.13). If he is placed in the middle of the alley, to which end will he go? According to the sixth principle, when two incompatible response tendencies are in conflict, the stronger will prevail. But in this situation the tendencies are equal. Will the rat therefore remain immobilized and starve to death? No, because any change, however slight, in the animal's position will resolve the conflict.

An analogy from physics will illustrate this. The approach-approach conflict is like an *unstable equilibrium*. Suppose a

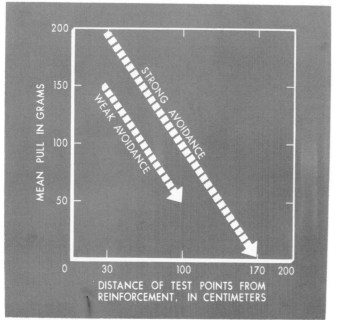

FIGURE 12.12 The Results of an Experiment Designed to Test the Validity of the Principle That the Height of the Avoidance Gradient Varies With the Strength of the Drive. Subjects receiving more intense shocks exhibited stronger avoidance behavior (After Brown, 1948).

marble is placed exactly and delicately in balance on top of an inverted round bowl. It will remain there if it is in perfect equilibrium, but any slight air current will push it off dead center. Once its equilibrium is upset, the marble will gather momentum and roll off the bowl.

The equilibrium of an animal in the center of an approach-approach conflict is also unstable. Even if it were possible to place an animal at the exact point where the two opposed approach tendencies were equal (where they intersect), his slightest movement would upset the equilibrium. If, for example, he turned slightly to the right, then he would be at a point where the approach gradient to the right would be slightly stronger than the one to the left. As a result he would probably move on farther to the right. The more he went toward the right, the greater would be the difference in strength between the two competing tendencies. He would finally reach the goal at the right end. Just as the marble gathered momentum after going slightly off center, so would the rat. Hence, when they are placed in the center of the runway, rats who have been trained to go to both ends start quickly toward one end. The only evidence of conflict is that some animals vacillate in the center before darting toward one of the goals.

We are often confronted with approach-approach conflicts which we resolve so rapidly that we fail to notice the momentary conflict. Someone passes you a box of chocolate candy. You like chocolate-covered cherries best, and you can see that there are two, at opposite corners of the box, but you do not hesitate long before choosing (even when they are equally large). With little vacillation or forethought you select one.

Avoidance-Avoidance Conflict

The avoidance-avoidance conflict is an example of a *stable equilibrium*. A marble inside a cup will stay at the bottom and will *return to this position* when it is moved. If it is pushed in one direction up the side of the cup, it will roll back down past the center, oscillate back and forth, and finally return to its original position.

The behavior of the marble resembles that of a rat in an avoidance-avoidance conflict. When he is shocked at both ends of the alley, he develops the incompatible avoidance tendencies depicted in Figure 12.14. Placed in the center of the alley he tends to remain there. If, for example, he turns toward the right he will not continue in that direction, as he would in the approach-approach conflict. For once the rat goes slightly to the right, his avoidance tendency for the right side becomes greater than that for the left. As a result, he is forced back toward the center. The nearer the rat gets toward either end, the stronger is his tendency to return toward the center.

We must add one qualification to this analysis. The rat can avoid both ends if he can escape altogether from the alley. Many rats attempt to climb over the walls at the center of the alley. But if the alley is covered by wire mesh, his attempts to escape are frustrated. The rat finally returns to the center, where the fear of both ends is as near the minimum as possible.

We do not often experience avoidance-avoidance conflicts in our lives, because, unlike the laboratory rats, we can usually escape from the situation. We do not often have to choose between two unpleasant dinner companions; fortunately, we can usually eat alone if we prefer. But when a child has to select one of two equally unpleasant tasting medicines, his behavior

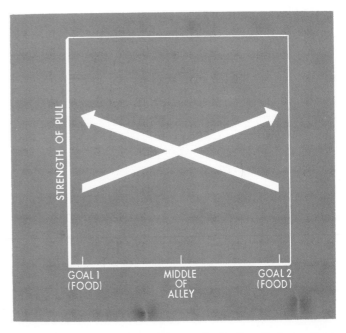

FIGURE 12.13 An Approach-Approach Conflict. Each approach gradient has an arrow indicating the direction in which the animal is attracted. At all points the animal has a stronger tendency to approach the goal that he is nearest to than to approach the one he is farthest from. Hence, if he gets slightly to one side of the middle, his conflict will be resolved (After Miller, 1944).

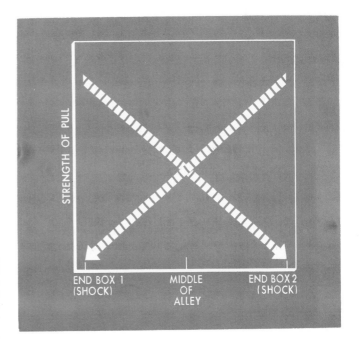

FIGURE 12.14 An Avoidance-Avoidance Conflict. Each avoidance gradient has an arrow indicating the direction in which the animal is forced. The nearer he gets to either end of the alley, the stronger his tendency to go in the opposite direction. As a result, he is forced back to the center where he tends to remain (After Miller, 1944).

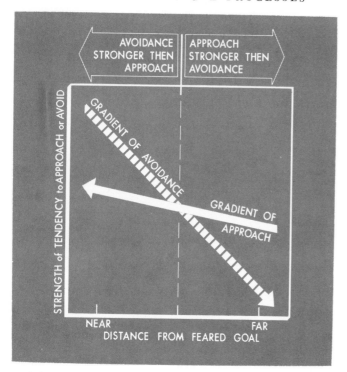

FIGURE 12.15 An Approach-Avoidance Conflict. The rat is simultaneously attracted toward and repelled by the feared goal. When he is far from it, his tendency to approach is stronger than his tendency to avoid, but when he is near the feared goal, his tendency to avoid is stronger than his tendency to approach (After Miller, 1944).

resembles a rat's in an avoidance-avoidance conflict. He finds it difficult to reach a decision, and like the rat he may even try to escape from the situation by feigning health or by hiding. Only when his parents force him to swallow one medicine by threatening him with even greater punishment, or by helping him reach a decision through reasonable arguments, will his conflict be resolved.

Another example of an avoidance-avoidance conflict comes from a recent news story. A young man stole several thousand dollars from a store his father managed. Knowing perfectly well who took the money, his father avoided reporting the theft, but he also recognized that the shortage would soon be discovered and that he himself would be suspected, and he wanted to avoid this possibility also. After vacil-

lating several days, he decided to report the crime. His wish to avoid the blame for a crime his son committed was stronger than his wish to keep his son from being caught.

Approach-Avoidance Conflict

We can establish an approach-avoidance conflict by alternately feeding and shocking a rat at the same end of the runway. As a result, the rat acquires incompatible response tendencies to approach and to avoid one end of the alley. Figure 12.15 shows the psychological consequences of this kind of conflict. If the animal is placed at the far end of the alley, he will begin to move toward the point where he was previously fed and shocked. At the beginning of the alley the approach gradient is stronger than the avoidance gradient. But after approaching for some distance the rat will arrive at the point where the two gradients intersect. If he overshoots this point the avoidance gradient will be higher than the approach gradient, and this will force him back to the place where the two gradients are of equal strength. From Miller's set of assumptions the prediction is that the animal, if placed at the far end of the alley, should approach part way toward the goal and then stop. This is exactly what happens. Similarly, if he is placed near the goal, he should run part of the way toward the other end and then stop. This prediction has also been confirmed.

An approach-avoidance conflict is another example of a stable equilibrium. Like the marble in the bottom of the cup, the rat in an approach-avoidance conflict is forced to stay where the gradients intersect. If he strays toward the goal, the avoidance gradient forces him back; if he goes away from it, the approach gradient pushes him back.

The psychological importance of the approach-avoidance conflict stems from the fact that (1) it is not easily resolved, and (2) the subject remains a captive of it. In an approach-avoidance conflict, the animal does not try to escape, as he does in an avoidance-avoidance conflict. Although he wants to avoid he also *wants to approach*. This keeps him in the situation and makes him truly a prisoner of his conflict.

Many human problems that we shall discuss in the topics on personality and the pathology of behavior will illustrate approach-avoidance conflicts. A parent's desire to have his children become independent, and at the same time to have them remain dependent on him, is an example of such a conflict. So are the approach-avoidance conflicts engendered by the maturing of sex drives of adolescents. As they become aware of their strong approach tendencies toward sexual behavior, they are also moved by strong avoidance responses built into them by moral codes, social customs, the fear of undesirable consequences, and so forth.

For the moment you will be wise to ignore such complex approach-avoidance conflicts. If you restrict your attention to a rat caught in a simple approach-avoidance conflict, you will obtain a deeper insight into the basic principles of the psychology of conflict. We often achieve clarity of conception best by focusing on simple cases, and therefore freedom from complexity is frequently the hallmark of scientific progress.

Up to now the approach-avoidance conflict has been viewed as a single approach gradient interacting with a single avoidance gradient. By enlarging upon this analysis, we can help you to understand how approach-avoidance gradients, once created, can be resolved. Consider the influence of *different* levels of avoidance gradient on an approach gradient of a given strength. Figure 12.16, representing such an example, shows that the weaker the avoidance gradient, the closer the animal gets to the goal. When the avoidance gra-

dient is very weak, the animal actually reaches the goal because the incompatible gradients do not intersect; at all points throughout the alley the tendency to approach is stronger than the tendency to avoid. From this we get our first clue as to how an approach-avoidance gradient can be resolved. If the avoidance gradient can be lowered in some way, the rat, instead of being caught in the middle of the alley, will run to the end.

Figure 12.17, showing several approach gradients of different strength and a single avoidance gradient, suggests another way an approach-avoidance conflict can be resolved. If we check the points at which each approach gradient intersects with the avoidance gradient, we can predict that the stronger the approach gradient, the closer the animal will come to the goal. If an approach gradient is stronger than the avoidance gradient throughout the

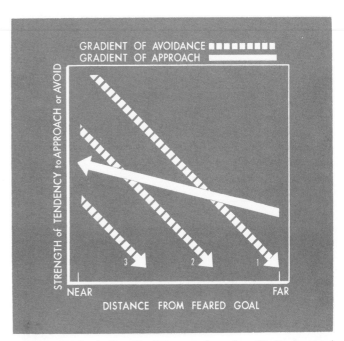

FIGURE 12.16 A Graphic Representation of a Single Approach Gradient and Three Avoidance Gradients of Different Strengths. The weaker the avoidance gradient, the closer will the subject approach the goal.

length of the alley, then he will reach the goal. Thus an approach-avoidance conflict can also be resolved by increasing the strength of the approach tendency.

The implications of both Figures 12.16 and 12.17 have been tested. The experimenters controlled the heights of incompatible gradients in one of two ways: by manipulating the intensity of the hunger or the fear drive or by varying the amount of training. The first technique employed shocks of varying intensities and food deprivation for differing periods. The rats, as predicted, stopped nearer the goal both when the experimenter decreased the strength of the electric shock and when he increased the strength of hunger. If the shock was sufficiently weak or the hunger sufficiently strong, the rat would resolve the conflict and reach the goal. Essentially the same results were obtained when the heights of the gradients were manipulated by controlling the amount of training. When the number of shocked trials was decreased (Miller, 1959) or the number of

food-reward trials increased (Kaufman & Miller, 1949), the rats went closer to the goal.

Although it is possible to resolve an approach-avoidance conflict either by raising the approach gradient or by lowering the avoidance gradient, the psychological consequences are different. The reason for this is that the avoidance gradient is a *gradient of fear*. The closer an organism gets to the point where he received the shock, the greater his fear will be. This is understandable if you remember that the origin of the avoidance gradient is painful stimulation, which is also the basis of fear.

Figure 12.18, which is similar to the preceding figure, includes the fear component of the avoidance gradient. It shows that when the approach gradient in an approach-avoidance conflict is increased, the animal will go closer to the goal but he will also exhibit more fear.

Consider the child who yearns to swim but fears the water. His parents may encourage him to get into the water for a swimming lesson by promising him a toy and thus increasing his approach gradient. But this technique often backfires, for the child who had shown some fear in the water may become panic-stricken when his swimming lessons begin. Trying to get him to do a "deadman's float," with all the frightening associations aroused by the name, will merely increase his fear to such an extent that he will be unable to profit from any instructions. What, then, should be done?

Instead of trying to increase the approach gradient, the parents will find it more effective to reduce the avoidance gradient. This will usually require more time but it will pay off in the end. By playing with the child in the water where he has

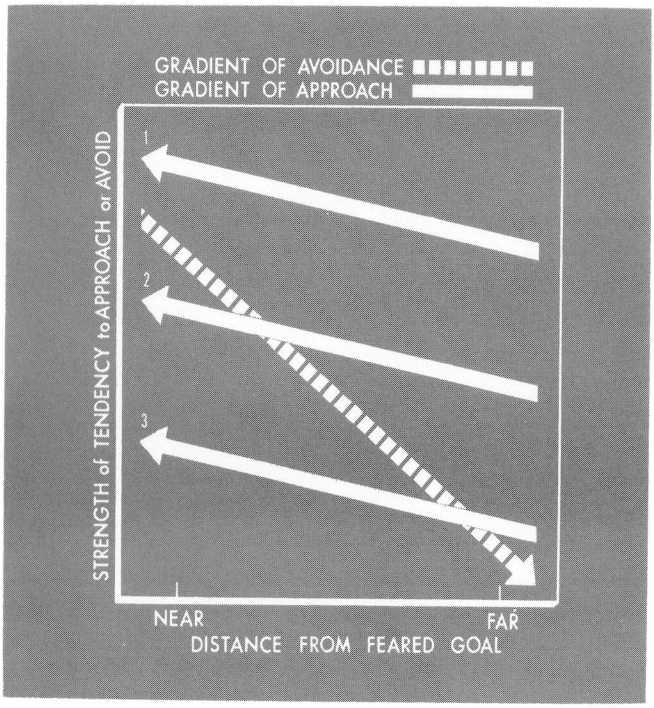

FIGURE 12.17 A Graphic Representation of a Single Avoidance Gradient and Three Approach Gradients of Different Strengths. The stronger the approach gradient, the closer will the subject approach the goal.

firm footing, they will not teach him any of the necessary swimming skills, but it will eventually be more effective than trying at first to teach him to float with his head in the water. Once his fear response is markedly reduced, or eliminated, he can profit from the swimming instructions. For the less his fear, the more a child can learn. With each new skill, his fear decreases and he is that much more ready for further learning. To push training in the face of overwhelming fear is usually ineffective. Even when such a method leads to some success—and stories of children thrown into deep water to "sink or swim" try to suggest that it does—the child may learn to swim at the price of disliking swimming for the rest of his life.

We cannot offer a step-by-step procedure for reducing the fear response to water because the desire to avoid water can result from different fears. One child may fear getting his head under water. It may be best to teach him the side stroke first, since it does not require him to put his head in the water. After he has learned this stroke, his fear will be so much less (the avoidance gradient will be lowered) that he can experiment with getting his face under water. Another child may be afraid of losing his support, although not of submerging his head. Such a child will have his fear reduced if he can hold on to a kickboard or his instructor while getting accustomed to the water. Once his fear is reduced he can begin learning the crawl. The important point is that you may resolve approach-avoidance conflicts of the sort generated when a child sets out to learn to swim more effectively by lowering the avoidance gradient than by raising the approach gradient. Most modern techniques of psychotherapy, discussed in Chapter 14, are based upon the premise that strategies which reduce fear are more effective than those which urge or force a person to go ahead and do something he fears.

Some experiments on approach-avoid-

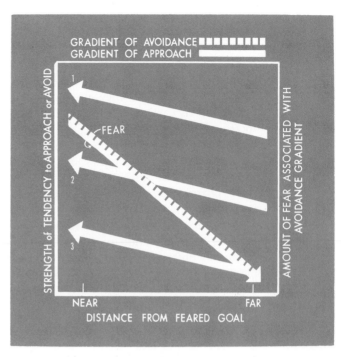

FIGURE 12.18 A Graphic Representation of a Single Avoidance Gradient and Three Approach Gradients of Different Strengths. This graph is the same as Figure 12.17 except that it also illustrates the fear component of the avoidance gradient. The stronger the approach gradient the closer will the subject approach the goal *and* the more fearful he will become.

ance conflicts have supplied interesting insights into the effect of alcohol on behavior. In one study (Conger, 1951) an approach-avoidance conflict was set up in rats, one that prevented them from going to the end of an alley. They were then injected with a dose of alcohol and soon thereafter staggered to the end of the alley. Thus we conclude that alcohol can dissipate fear.

We can also see alcohol's effect in dissipating fear when it retards, or prevents, the learning of an instrumental avoidance response. An injection of alcohol markedly reduces the strength of pull a rat exerts in avoiding the region where he has been shocked. This is not due simply to the debilitating effects of alcohol, for alcohol reduces the pull to approach much less than it reduces the pull to avoid. More evidence supporting the idea that alcohol reduces fear comes from a study (Clark &

Polish, 1960) in which monkeys were given avoidance training over long stretches of time. In avoidance conditioning, you will recall, animals are confronted by a feared stimulus to which they must make an instrumental response if they are to avoid a shock. In this particular study the monkeys increased their consumption of alcohol, which was freely available to them during the avoidance conditioning sessions. In fact, they consumed so much alcohol during the early phases that they became obviously intoxicated.

The conclusion that alcohol reduces fear suggests an explanation of the differences commonly observed in the behavior of people under its influence. Some get amorous; others get aggressive; still others get depressed. The experiments just cited suggest that these different reactions may all result from one psychological cause. Under the influence of alcohol, people do more freely what they are at other times usually afraid to do.

Presumably the middle-aged man who after several drinks starts flirting with all the young girls would like to make amorous advances toward them when sober but is afraid to. Alcohol reduces his fear and permits his amorous approach responses to gain dominance. Similarly, the mild-mannered man who becomes aggressive and self-assertive when drunk betrays a conflict within him. When he is sober he is afraid to be aggressive, although he would like to be. Alcohol dissipates this fear and reveals his inhibited aggression. The man who is ashamed to appear depressed, because social codes require him to respond stoically to adversity, becomes the drunk who "cries in his beer." He never complains or bemoans his fate except when he is under the influence of alcohol. Just as it allows others to become amorous or aggressive, alcohol allows him to behave in a way he is normally afraid to.

Again it is necessary to add some qualifications. The principle we have been illustrating applies primarily to those who have drunk so much that they have lost control. However, the effects alcohol has upon behavior may often be traced simply to social customs. The gaiety of a cocktail party should not be taken as a sign that under normal conditions people are afraid to be gay. Alcohol may encourage some hilarity by eliminating inhibitions on free discussion, but a good deal of the gaiety stems from social expectations about the nature of cocktail parties, rather than from removal of fears.

Another qualification we must add is that drinking can, and often does, simultaneously encourage and prevent a person from doing what he fears. Remember the example of the rat who gets closer to the goal because the avoidance gradient is lowered, and then because he is nearer to the goal develops more fear. Similarly, the person who has had some drinks and is on the point of behaving in a way he is normally afraid to may suddenly leave the party or stop drinking. Because he is getting psychologically close to feared behavior, his fears suddenly dominate his actions.

Certain drugs have a psychological effect similar to that of alcohol. Sodium amytal, which belongs to the family of barbiturates, aids in resolving approach-avoidance conflicts. In one experiment, following an injection of this drug, cats were willing to eat where they had previously been shocked (Baily & Miller, 1952). This finding suggests the effectiveness of sodium amytal and similar drugs in assisting soldiers to recall their repressed experiences in combat (see page 330). These drugs reduce the fear associated with the repressed memory. If their fear and the feelings of guilt for being afraid are reduced, many patients can overcome the serious psychological difficulties they suffered as a result of their combat experiences.

Temporal Conflicts

In the studies cited, approach and avoidance gradients are measured against distance (spatial conflicts). Quite often the decisive dimension in an approach-avoidance conflict is time. The reader has more than once, no doubt, accepted a social invitation primarily out of politeness. Although you do not particularly like the people who sent the invitation, you lacked sufficient courage to refuse it. In short, your approach gradient was at that moment stronger than your avoidance gradient. But as the time for the party gets nearer, your reluctance to go becomes greater; the avoidance gradient becomes the stronger. Perhaps it becomes so strong that you pretend you are ill or discover some other excuse that you can use to escape from a situation which ten days earlier did not seem intolerable. We must conclude that an undesirable invitation is more likely to be refused if it is received immediately before the party than if it arrives a couple of weeks earlier.

Figure 12.19 represents a simple approach-avoidance conflict plotted against the dimension of time. In this temporal approach-avoidance conflict the further away in time the person is from the goal, the more attractive it appears. As time approaches the negative aspects become dominant. This kind of temporal approach-avoidance conflict is common in engagements. Under a full moon the ardent suitor proposes marriage. Marital bliss for all time seems to outweigh by far loss of a few freedoms and assumption of some financial responsibilities. But the closer the marriage ceremony approaches, the larger do the negative features of marriage loom. Fortunately, in most cases, the approach and avoidance gradients do not intersect and the couple marry, despite the doubts and reservations. On rare occasions the avoidance gradient becomes so great at the last moment before the ceremony that a bride, and sometimes even a groom, is left waiting at the altar.

Discrimination Conflict

The principles of an approach-avoidance spatial conflict extend also to the discrimi-

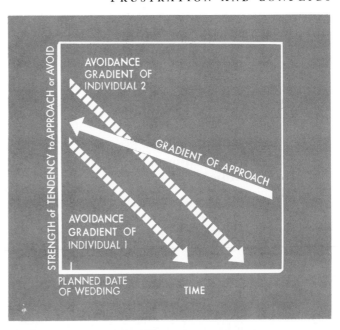

FIGURE 12.19 An Approach-Avoidance Conflict Interpretation of Reactions Toward Impending Marriage. Although individual 1 has reservations, he will go through with the marriage, since his approach and avoidance gradients do not intersect. Individual 2 will back out before the ceremony.

nation conflict (see page 161) Pavlov discovered. In one of Pavlov's studies a child was forced to discriminate between two different rates at which a metronome was beating. He found it easy to make the conditioned response to 144 beats per minute and not to 92 or 108 beats. He failed, however, to discriminate between rates of 144 and 132. In the easy discrimination the gradients to make (approach) or not to make (avoid) the response to the positive (144) or negative stimulus (92 or 108) did not intersect. When the finer discrimination was required the two gradients intersected; the positive stimulus (144) evoked a tendency both to respond and not to respond, and so did the negative stimulus (132). Because the stimuli had the capacity to evoke two incompatible responses, the child developed a conflict, which was expressed in temper tantrums.

Thus you see that discrimination, temporal, and spatial approach-avoidance conflicts emerge as the result of a common psychological process. They are all generated by a stimulus situation that evokes incompatible responses. The vacillation and indecision that such conflicts produce are most pronounced when the incompatible response tendencies are approximately of equal strength.

Double Approach-Avoidance Conflicts

Some readers may have had reservations about the claim that approach-approach conflicts are easily resolved. No doubt they recalled some personal experience with an exceedingly difficult choice between two attractive alternatives. Shall I become engaged to Joel or Montgomery? Should I take a premedical or a prelaw course? Shall I order pie *à la mode* or a hot-fudge sundae? All of these questions require a choice between appealing alternatives, and at first sight may appear to be examples of approach-approach conflicts. But usually they are not, because the choice of one alternative *eliminates the other*. Each choice, therefore, represents an example of an approach-avoidance conflict. Assuming you are a typical undergraduate with a normal appetite and average financial resources, your choice between two equally appealing desserts may be difficult because choosing one means that you cannot have the other. The choice of pie *à la mode* generates both approach and avoidance tendencies. The approach tendency comes from desiring it; the avoidance tendency comes from the knowledge that by ordering it, you forfeit the hot-fudge sundae. In the same manner the hot-fudge sundae has an approach and an avoidance component. This kind of conflict would not exist for the person with a huge appetite and plenty of money. He would have little difficulty choosing one dessert if, after he had finished it, he could have the other. In his case the choice would more accurately fall in the category of an approach-approach conflict.

Most of us do not become seriously conflicted over choices of food because we usually have a preference, or one is cheaper than the other, and moreover, the choice of one does not exclude the future choice of the other. The person who finds it easy to choose between pie *à la mode* or a hot-fudge sundae for dessert tonight would experience a really difficult conflict if by choosing one alternative he had to forfeit the other forever. This is the sort of conflict involved in becoming engaged to one of two attractive suitors, or choosing between two professional careers. These are examples of **double approach-avoidance** conflicts.

It has been shown experimentally (Goodbeer, 1940) that a double approach-avoidance conflict is more difficult to resolve than a simple approach-approach conflict. Children given a choice between two attractive beverages demonstrated this. One group (approach-approach), after drinking one beverage, was allowed to consume the other. They made the choice of which to drink first easily. The other group (double approach-avoidance) was not so fortunate; if they chose one drink, they could not have the other. Their choice was more difficult, and they took a longer time to reach a decision.

A double approach-avoidance conflict is rather complicated to analyze, since it involves four independent gradients. Figure 12.20 depicts one such conflict. The closer the organism gets to one alternative, the stronger becomes the avoidance tendency based upon the loss of the other alternative. It bears a similarity to an avoidance-avoidance conflict in that near each goal the avoidance tendencies dominate. As a result, the organism is thrown back into the region of unresolved choice. He does not try to escape, as he does when he faces an avoidance-avoidance conflict, because the approach tendencies keep him in a stable equilibrium within the region of the conflict. A double approach-avoidance conflict can therefore remain unresolved for a long period of time. The conflict disappears when one of the two alternatives is eliminated (e.g., when one of the two suitors becomes exasperated and withdraws his proposal, or when the student is refused admission to medical school but not law school).

Transfer of Training and Conflict Behavior

Just as learning transfers, so does conflict. A child who experiences an approach-avoidance conflict over his aggressive feelings toward his father may strike his grandfather for no apparent reason. What has happened is that his hostility to his father has generalized to his grandfather, but the fear of expressing this hostility has not extended to his grandfather, since he is more indulgent than the parent. An unresolved conflict, involving inhibited aggression, is transferred (displaced) to a situation where the hostility becomes overt.

It is extremely important for clinical psychologists and psychiatrists to know how conflicts are transferred. Many of their patients suffer from the effects of conflicts. Since the therapists, the psychiatrists and psychologists, are not able to treat these psychological problems when they develop, they must treat them indirectly, by dealing with the conflict in the form it assumes as it transfers to the clinical situation. This, however, is not always a disadvantage, as you will see later, but for the moment, we must go back to basic principles and see what happens in an experimental instance.

One of the first experiments dealing with the transfer of conflict behavior investigated the generalization of individual approach and avoidance gradients (Murray & Miller, 1952). When an approach or avoidance response has been established in one alley, it will generalize to similar situations. For example, an animal trained to approach food in a wide white alley will also

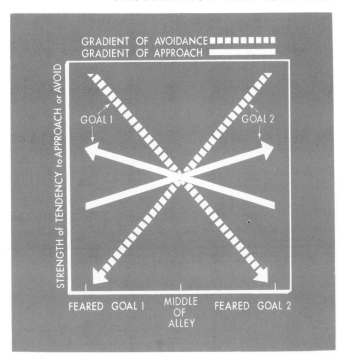

FIGURE 12.20 A Double Approach-Avoidance Conflict. The subject has a tendency to approach and avoid both ends of the alley (After Miller, 1944).

exert a measurable pull in a narrow black alley. The amount of pull he exerts is related to the degree of similarity existing between the alley in which he is now being tested and the alley in which he acquired the original tendency. The rat will exert the greatest pull in the wide white alley and less pull in the narrow black alley. The same kind of generalized response will also occur in the case of an avoidance tendency. The greater the similarity between the test alley and the original alley where the shock took place, the stronger will be the pull exerted by the rat.

The most important finding of this study was obtained when the shapes of the curves of generalization of both approach and avoidance tendencies were compared. The avoidance generalization curve proved to be steeper, meaning that the avoidance habit is weakened more by generalization than the approach habit (see Figure 12.21). This finding had been expected. It agrees

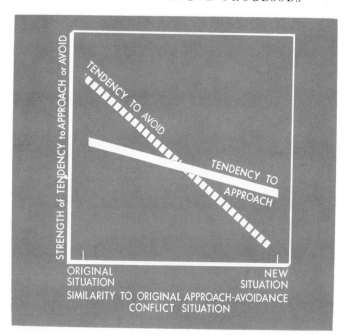

FIGURE 12.21 The Transfer of an Approach-Avoidance Conflict to a New Situation. In the original situation, the avoidance tendency was stronger than the approach tendency. Hence, the subject was unable to resolve the conflict and obtain the goal. In the new situation, because an avoidance tendency loses more of its strength through generalization than does an approach tendency, the tendency to approach is stronger than the tendency to avoid. The conflict can therefore be resolved.

with the implications of Miller's third principle (see page 414) that the slope of the avoidance gradient is steeper than that of the approach gradient. The greater steepness of the avoidance gradient simply means that generalization weakens the avoidance habit more than the approach habit.

There is a very interesting implication to this. An approach-avoidance conflict established in one alley (e.g., a wide white one) should be resolved more easily in another alley (e.g., a narrow black one). The reasons for this should be obvious. Because the avoidance tendency loses more of its strength through generalization than the approach response does, the rat should be able to go closer to the goal in the new alley. This prediction was confirmed (Mil-

ler & Kraeling, 1952; Murray & Berkun, 1955). An approach-avoidance conflict was established in one alley and observed in other alleys. The greater the difference from the original alley, the larger the number of rats that reached the goal and the nearer, on the average, did they approach the food.

This finding, and the theory behind it, have wide applications in the practice of clinical psychology. The writer recalls the case of a mild-mannered young married woman who, for no reasons the physicians could discover, suffered from headaches and stomach trouble, as well as from sleeplessness, general nervousness, and depressions. Interviewed by psychiatrists, she could give no explanation for her numerous physical complaints and her overall unhappiness. She was then given the Thematic Apperception Test, a projective technique clinical psychologists often use to uncover a patient's psychological problems (see page 185). One common theme that ran through many of her stories was the extreme hostility women felt toward men. With the aid of this clue she was found to harbor intense aggressions toward her husband. Her hiding of these aggressions was not conscious because she was not aware of them. Having been taught a wife ought to be loving and dutiful, she was unable to admit to herself that she harbored aggressive feelings and repressed them to avoid the fear and guilt they would otherwise have generated. But that did not keep them from influencing her behavior. Her marriage could not be called tragically unhappy, but neither was it happy. Because of her frustrated aggressiveness, her behavior could be characterized as having the properties of an approach-avoidance conflict. She intensely wished to be aggressive but could not let herself go. The aggression generalized to the story-telling situation and became overt because, in comparison to the tendency to approach it, the tendency to *avoid* aggression suffered a greater loss from stimulus generalization. Once the trouble, which revolved about sexual problems, was brought into the open, it became treatable. She was made aware of her feelings and helped to understand them, and she also discovered that her difficulty was not unique, but was shared by many other wives. The source of the difficulty was discussed with both the wife and the husband, first individually and then jointly. The difficulty was overcome and soon thereafter the wife's symptoms disappeared.

This case history is just one example of the application of the conflict theory to clinical problems. Obviously Miller's theory is not restricted to the behavior of rats in a runway; its implications apply to a wide range of behavior, including the kinds of behavior exhibited by those taking psychological tests. The full usefulness of this theory has yet to be realized. Most needed at present is a technique for measuring the degree of similarity between situations in which conflicts arise and the situations to which they transfer.

HABIT BREAKING

Everybody has acquired some undesirable habits he would be better off without. Hence, the topic, **habit breaking** is of wide interest. We have, of course, already touched upon the problem of eliminating habits. Experimental extinction is one method of doing this; if reinforcement is withdrawn from a habit it becomes weaker and may finally disappear. Punishment can also help break a habit; by suppressing one habit, punishment permits another to take its place. The present section is in some ways a continuation of the previous discussion of experimental extinction and punishment; it will be concerned with the elimination of one form of behavior and the substitution of another.

Habit breaking is a topic closely allied with the psychology of conflict. Both involve the competition between habits, and in the final analysis both the resolution of a conflict and the breaking of a habit depend on one habit gaining dominance over another.

The various techniques of habit breaking we shall describe are all examples of the **incompatible response method.** As its name implies, the method calls for breaking an undesirable habit by substituting an incompatible response for it. This may be done in several different ways.

Substitution Method. In the **substitution method** one tries to prevent an undesirable habit and simultaneously to replace it with another response. A practical joke from the era of the horse and buggy illustrates this method perfectly. In those days, boys would sometimes hitch a horse to a surrey, and while one boy held a tight rein and yelled "Whoa!" another would jab the animal's rump with a pitchfork. After repeated trials the horse would learn to substitute a lurch forward for his former reaction of stopping when he heard the command "Whoa." Then the boys would hide, and when the owner went out for a drive they would jump out and frighten the horse. He would, of course, start to run away, but when the driver shouted "Whoa," would lurch forward instead of stopping. Needless to say, this would frighten the driver and convulse the boys.

Anyone who objects to our using this anecdote as an example of a "good" habit being substituted for an "undesirable" one should remember that the use of such evaluative terms depends on where your sympathy lies, with the boys or with the driver of the surrey. What is important is that the stunt is based entirely on the principle of the substitution method: an unwanted habit is eliminated and another one put in its place.

Take another example. Since all golfers are passionately interested in the success of each shot, they have a tendency, very difficult to curb in beginners and not unknown among seasoned players, to raise their heads for a look at the ball's flight even before their club has hit it. Naturally this plays havoc with the stroke, for in order to hit a ball precisely right, a golfer must be looking directly at it at the moment of contact. Golf instructors sometimes break their students of this habit of lifting the eyes prematurely by making them keep their eyes on the place where the ball rested even after it has been hit. Golfers are usually reinforced for following these instructions, because their shots improve. With more practice, they learn that there is still enough time after they have hit the ball to lift their eyes and watch its flight.

Exhaustion Method. One of the most interesting, and least practiced, methods of habit breaking is the **exhaustion method.** It consists of forcing the subject to repeat the undesirable response until he becomes so fatigued that he can no longer respond to the cues that normally evoke it. Obviously this technique rests heavily on the effects of experimental extinction.

Interesting accounts of two applications of this technique have appeared in psychological literature. One was published many years ago by a psychologist (Dunlap, 1932) who suggested using this method, which he called **negative practice,** to eliminate repetitive typing errors: For example, a person who repeatedly typed *hte* for *the* was urged to deliberately practice typing *hte* over and over. This negative practice helped him eliminate the undesirable habit because, for one thing, he built up inhibition (see page 323) as he repeatedly typed the wrong spelling. In short, he got tired of making the error. Negative practice also helped him break the incorrect habit by exaggerating the difference between it and the correct habit, facilitating the discrimination between them.

Perhaps a more clear-cut example of the exhaustion method is the technique used to treat a 25-year-old woman who suffered from a tic originating from a traumatic experience ten years earlier (Yates, 1958). While she was being put under anesthesia she had become terrified that she was going to suffocate and die. She struggled madly until the anesthetic took effect. From that time on she could not tolerate having any object placed over her face. She also developed a tic, a short, nasal explosion; a sudden, forceful expiration of air through the nose.

A reasonable explanation of this tic was that it originated in an attempt to cope with the threat of suffocation; she made the nasal explosion originally to resist inhaling the anesthesia, although it was actually ineffective. It also operated as a conditioned avoidance response that served to reduce fear, and so on subsequent occasions, through the process of stimulus generalization, the arousal of fear encouraged the performance of the fear-reducing tic, which finally became a powerful habit.

A psychologist was called in to treat this woman. Since other methods of treatment had failed, he decided to try the exhaustion method. Knowing that massed practice builds up inhibition, he reasoned that if the patient were forced to repeat the tic over and over and over again she would become so fatigued that she would be unable to continue. The nasal explosion would then fail to occur, even when the cues that had previously evoked it were present. As a result, the incompatible habit of not making the tic would become associated with the cues that previously had been associated with making it.

The patient was instructed to give herself *hundreds of sessions* of massed practice in which she voluntarily emitted the tic without pause. The dramatic results of this therapeutic technique can be best summarized by quoting from the report of the patient: the nasal tic "has almost vanished. It returns occasionally . . . every now and then . . . but most definitely it does not plague me every few minutes as before. It is absent for days on end."

Here the reader must be cautioned against accepting this interpretation of the reported improvement without reservation. One goal of this book is to encourage the kind of critical attitude that makes one skeptical about generalizations from a single instance. The validity and effectiveness of the exhaustion method of treating tics cannot be established by the report of one clinical case. The success of the treatment, which, you remember, was not complete, might have been due wholly or partly to other factors, such as the large amount of time the therapist spent with the patient. At best the exhaustion method of treating a tic is promising. But much more experimental and clinical data are needed to justify its wide use.

Toleration Method. The **toleration method** consists in the gradual substitution of a desirable habit for an undesirable one. The stimulus evoking the undesirable response is introduced so gradually that by the time it occurs in full force the undesirable habit has been extinguished. The toleration method is especially effective in treating fears. A child who is afraid of dogs may be given a very small puppy that elicits no fear. As the puppy grows, the child's positive reactions toward it will generalize to other dogs. Finally, by the time the dog is full grown the child will have entirely lost his earlier fear of dogs. In this case an avoidance response toward dogs has gradually been replaced by an approach response.

The toleration method was used effectively to rid a three-year-old boy of his fear of rabbits (Jones, 1924). While he was involved in pleasant activities, the child was gradually exposed more and more closely to a rabbit. For example, on the first day, while the boy was eating, an adult held the rabbit in a corner of the room where it did not arouse any fear. Then, each day the rabbit was brought a little closer to the child without ever frightening him until the rabbit became part of the pattern of comforting stimuli: food, trusted adults, and so on. Instead of responding with fear, the child gradually learned to relax in the presence of the rabbit, to tolerate him. At the end of the treatment, he had no qualms about petting the animal.

The efficiency of the toleration method was also shown in the elimination of a conditioned avoidance response to a *bright* light (Kimble & Kendall, 1953). The conventional method would be to extinguish the response by not presenting the unconditioned stimulus following the conditioned stimulus. But experimental extinction of avoidance conditioning takes a long time (see page 280). In an attempt to short-cut this process, a group of rats were given a series of "toleration" trials in which the light was kept dim at first and later turned on to its full intensity. The idea was that the dim light would evoke little, if any, avoidance behavior because of the loss due to stimulus generalization. Nonavoidance as the dominant response to the dim light would generalize to the brighter lights until finally the animals would tolerate the bright conditioned stimulus. It was predicted that such toleration trials would hasten extinction and the prediction was confirmed.

Change-of-Cue Method. One of the most widely practiced, and in many cases least effective, methods of breaking an undesirable habit is to remove the organism from the situation where the habit developed and to place him in an entirely new one.

The business executive who worries excessively is encouraged to go on vacation. Even if the change of scene helps him to stop worrying, which it usually does not, he is likely to start worrying again as soon as he returns.

If a habit which is evoked in a particular situation is to be broken, then the *stimuli that make up the situation* must acquire the capacity to evoke a new and incompatible response, or at least lose their capacity to evoke the undesirable habit. An incompatible response developed in a *new* situation is not at all guaranteed to generalize to the *old* situation. Many parents have learned this lesson bitterly. With high hopes they send their problem child to a summer camp noted for its excellent discipline. When they visit the camp, they note with surprise and relief how polite and responsible he is. But their pleasure is short-lived, for when he returns home he soon becomes his obnoxious self once more. The reason is that the good behavior fails to generalize from the camp to the home environment. To be sure, the child has learned to respond in a new way at camp, but the **change-of-cue technique** has failed because his polite and considerate behavior has not been substituted for unruly behavior *in either the home or a situation similar to it.*

In spite of its limitations, the change-of-cue technique can be effective if it is used as a starting point for habit breaking. The writer recalls the case of a colleague who wished to break her smoking habit. She had noted that she smoked most heavily in those situations in which she became somewhat tense (yes, even psychologists get tense!): at professional meetings in which she reported the results of her research, even during run-of-the-mill conversations with her colleagues about professional matters. On vacations she smoked much less. She assumed this was because she felt more relaxed then, and decided that a vacation was the time to begin a serious attempt to break her smoking habit. For encouragement, she paid herself by adding to her clothing allowance the cost of one package of cigarettes every day she did not smoke. By the end of the summer she had completely stopped smoking and had the positive reinforcement of being able to purchase a pair of shoes, which would ordinarily be far too expensive for her. With this reward for not smoking and the knowledge that she was capable of breaking the habit, she was able to withstand the temptation to smoke in situations that previously elicited the habit. Today, several years later, she still does not smoke and is perhaps one of the best-dressed women academics in the country.

The change-of-cue technique was used in treating soldiers who developed incapacitating fears during combat, men who had to be sent back behind the lines because their ineffectiveness constituted a threat to their comrades as well as to themselves. At the beginning of World War II such men were removed far behind the line of action where their fears, in most cases, subsided. It was soon discovered, however, that this expedient did not help many of the soldiers return to active combat, for as soon as they returned their fears were immediately aroused again and they became incapacitated once more. A new technique of treating demoralizing fear had to be evolved. A frightened soldier removed from combat was placed in a hospital not too far behind the lines, where his fear subsided but where he could still hear the noise of combat. As a result, his fear was reduced in a situation where he could still perceive some of the cues of combat. A much higher percentage of soldiers treated this way were able to return to combat.

The change-of-cue technique may also be effective when the individual does not need to return to the situation in which the undesirable behavior occurs. The parents of a sensitive, meek boy who dislikes his rough-and-tough schoolmates and is unable to contend with them may decide to transfer him to a school where the students are more subdued. In the new environment the boy's shyness may decrease appreciably and no longer cause him the embarrassment it previously did. If this happens, the parents are justified in removing their son from a problem situation he could not solve. If, in a more sympathetic environment, he develops into a happy and creative individual, then the change is for the good, even though he may never succeed in measuring up to conventional standards of "tough" masculinity. If, however, he is not able to get along with his peers any better in the new environment, and his parents have to keep moving him from one school to another, then the change-of-cue technique has probably done more harm than good. It has probably encouraged the boy to run away from his problems instead of trying to solve them.

In summary, the change-of-cue technique can be effective when an organism does not have to return to the environment in which the undesirable habit originated or when the responses in the new environment generalize to the old. In other cases the change of environment appears to be helpful in eliminating undesirable habits only when it is supplemented by specific training or by the drive to acquire a new, desirable habit to supplant the old one.

Maturation and Habit Breaking

The importance of maturation in eliminating many undesirable habits should never be overlooked. The mother who has given her three-year-old child a crayon and some typewriter-paper to keep him busy, is wrong to be angry when she discovers that he has extended his creative masterpiece beyond the edges of the paper and onto the tablecloth. The child has not really misbehaved. A three-year-old child regularly makes large, gross motions when he moves his hands. If he is expected to occupy himself by drawing and is given a thick crayon, he will need a very large piece of drawing paper. Only then can the mother reasonably expect him to limit his drawing to the paper. Training a three-year-old to keep within the confines of an 8 by 11 inch piece of paper is about as difficult as training him to fly. His neural and muscular organization has not matured sufficiently to enable him to confine his drawing to a small piece of paper.

Parents also ask something impossible of their children when they expect them to remain quiet for long periods of time, particularly on car trips. Sometimes you hear parents ask, "How can I break my child of his incessant restlessness in the car?" The fact is that a child's activity level is much greater than an adult's, and they cannot be expected to remain quiet and inactive for long periods of time. As far as possible parents should not undertake long trips with young children. If they are necessary, frequent stops should be made and the idea of covering 400 to 500 miles a day given up. There are many other examples of the importance of considering maturational variables in breaking undesirable habits in children. Toilet training, table manners, speech habits are but a few areas in which parents must delay corrective training until the proper stage of development. Many behavior problems originate because parents are insensitive to maturational limitations. You have to remember that the child does not simply have bad, childish habits that must be broken, but that he is as yet incapable of the good habits he can learn when the appropriate time comes.

STRESS

Stress is a word we use frequently today to describe the effect upon contemporary man of many of the disturbing and difficult situations in which he finds himself. We speak of the stress produced when he must make decisions upon which success or failure depend; when he must work for long periods; when he engages in competitive sports; and even when he takes college examinations. The list could be extended indefinitely.

Although stress seems to be a familiar and pervasive ingredient of modern life, the concept of stress creates difficulty for the psychologist. Part of the difficulty stems from the fact that the term, as commonly used, covers too much territory. Hence its meaning has become vague, as often happens with the "psychological" vocabulary of everyday speech. Three separate components of the idea of stress may be discriminated: the stressful situation, the physiological changes produced by stress, and the resulting behavior. To understand each of these aspects is a large order, and psychologists and physiologists have not been completely successful in doing so. Nevertheless, some features have been brought into focus, in considerable part through the efforts of Hans Selye (1956), a noted endocrinologist.

Selye has developed the concept of a **general adaptation syndrome** which refers to the physiological processes that develop when an organism is exposed to a stressful situation. He assumes that the body reacts to stress in three successive stages: an alarm reaction, a stage of resistance, and finally, a stage of exhaustion.

Stressors, or stress-provoking agents, arise from two main sources: from physical conditions that damage the body, such as starvation or physical injury, or from psychological problems, such as intense, persistent fear or prolonged, unresolved conflict. Two important features of stressors must be kept in mind. First, although stressors differ in their origins, they produce a common physiological reaction. Second, something that constitutes a stressor to one person (e.g., fear of sex) is not necessarily a stressor to another. Stress, particularly of

the psychological kind, is a personal matter.

Whenever a stressor acts upon the body, an **alarm reaction** takes place. This consists of a complicated pattern of physiological and chemical changes. One component of this general reaction is the hypothalamic stimulation of the pituitary gland. This gland releases various hormones (chemical substances), one of which, ACTH (adreno-corticotrophin), stimulates the adrenal cortex (the outer layer of the adrenal gland) to secrete *cortin,* a chemically complex hormone. A component of cortin, *cortisone,* much publicized for its success in the treatment of some forms of arthritis as well as other diseases, helps the body to cope with the damage produced by the illness. In essentially the same way, the physiological changes resulting from the alarm reaction help the body to cope with the damage caused by a variety of other stressors.

During the **stage of resistance** the bodily reactions to stress increase. This often has the effect, especially with not-too-severe physical injuries, of eliminating the source of stress. Sometimes the stress persists, as when an infection cannot be controlled or a conflict resolved. The body's reaction can then become too intense. Cortin, for example, may be secreted at such a high rate that its supply becomes depleted. When this happens the **stage of exhaustion** begins, when the body is without the necessary resources to deal with the stressor.

Stressful situations, as we have already indicated, do not necessarily lead to exhaustion. Usually the stress ends or is removed before this stage is reached. But in those situations where the stage of exhaustion is reached, the consequences can be disastrous. Several years ago, a young couple was lost on Mount Washington on a summer night. The temperature was well above zero, yet they both perished. Many people have survived in worse situations for longer periods of time, but a situation can produce quite different physiological reactions in different people. Presumably this couple reacted with intense fear and literally exhausted their bodies' capacity to deal with the stress of exposure to a difficult and threatening environment.

It has been suggested that physical aging is due in part to the fact that the body has expended its ability to adapt. It is as if the body starts life with a certain reservoir of capability to adapt to stress-induced crises. This reservoir is gradually depleted in combat with illness, injuries, and psychological disturbances, until finally the reservoir is exhausted. Thus, the same disease may have quite different effects on younger and older animals. The older animals are more vulnerable, less able to adapt to stressors.

An interesting and somewhat disturbing example of the consequence of stress comes from a study (Brady, Porter, Conrad, & Mason, 1958) involving four pairs of monkeys in a relatively lengthy avoidance conditioning problem. Figure 12.22 shows the main features of the experimental setup. The monkeys were subjected to their experimental ordeals in pairs. Restrained in a chair, each monkey received a brief electric shock in his feet every 20 seconds, unless one of the monkeys, known as the "executive" animal, pressed a lever which would delay the shock another 20 seconds for *both* animals. The pairs of monkeys underwent six-hour shock-or-avoidance sessions followed by six-hour "off periods" during which they received no shocks. A red light plainly in view of both animals was turned on to indicate when a shock-or-avoidance period was in progress.

During the avoidance periods, the executive monkey learned to avoid the shock by pressing the lever every 15 to 20 seconds. His instrumental responses effectively prevented all but an occasional shock averaging less then one per hour for both animals. In spite of this, the results were catastrophic for the subjects who served as executive animals. One died after 23 days, during the course of one 6-hour shock-or-avoidance

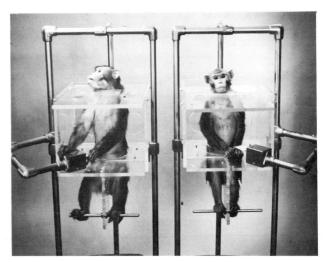

FIGURE 12.22 Experimental Situation to Study the Effects of Prolonged Avoidance Conditioning. The monkey on the left ("executive" animal) must press a lever every 20 seconds if he and the monkey on the right are to avoid an electric shock to their feet (Dr. J. V. Brady).

period. Another died 25 days after the start of the experiment, also during an avoidance period. The death of the third executive monkey during an avoidance period terminated the experiment on the ninth day. All of these deaths were related to extensive lesions with ulcerations that developed in the monkeys' stomachs and intestines. Only the fourth executive survived, withstanding 48 days of the experimental procedure. But he, too, suffered severe gastroduodenal ulcers. Although he survived, he obviously did not escape unscathed from the experimental stress. In dramatic contrast was the *absence* of effects produced by the experimental procedure upon the control animals. Not one showed any indications of gastrointestinal complications.

Obviously the shocks were not responsible for the ulcers and the deaths of three of the four executive animals; the control animal experienced every shock his executive partner did. Apparently the key to the difference in the consequences of the experimental situation upon the executive and control animals lies in the *ability to control the shock*. For we may assume that the executive animal was subjected to the greater stress, which in turn produced the violent physiological reactions. It was he who had to pay attention, for six hours at a stretch, to the subtle time relationship between his last response and the impending shock. It was he who had to make the shock-avoiding response. It seems likely, therefore, that the experimental situation generated much greater fear in him. The control subject, although he experienced shocks of the same intensity and number, which after all were few, did not have to attend to the fear-provoking cues. Consequently his fear was neither as great nor as sustained as the executive subject's.

The underlying physiological changes linking the executive animals' sustained fear with gastroduodenal ulcers are unclear. Evidence suggests that the ulcers began to develop during the six-hour "off periods." The sudden shift from avoidance responding to relative quiescence set off physiological changes that, in some unknown manner, produced the ulcers.

If we are to incorporate these results into Selye's analysis, we need more information on the physiological changes, and particularly on the adrenal cortical activity, that occurred during the "on" and "off periods" in the executive and the control animals. So we must admit that the conception of a general adaptation syndrome (perhaps more appropriately described as a general *over*adaptation syndrome) is at the stage of orientation rather than finished theory. It seems that the body reacts to stressors in three successive stages and that the consequences of stress depend on what stage is reached. We have still to discover all the physiological processes that operate during these stages.

In discussing stress one variable that obviously demands attention is the individual reacting to it. That the individual is important was shown in an experiment (Lazarus & Eriksen, 1952) in which the performance of two groups of college students, equated for intelligence, on a task of the intelligence-test type was compared. Both groups had previously taken a test similar to the task. One group was placed under stress by being told that their earlier performances were very poor and that it was extremely important for them to improve. The other group was treated more gently. They were told they had done well before, but that it was necessary for them to take another similar test. The most interesting finding was that although the average scores of the two groups were the same, the stress group demonstrated much greater variability (the standard deviation of their scores was larger than that of the control group). In short, the same stressful situation had the effect of increasing some students' efficiency while decreasing that of others.

Perhaps the results of this experiment strike a familiar chord. We have all known the fierce competitor whose performance improves when the going gets tough and the individual whose performance deteriorates in moments of stress. There is no simple explanation for this difference. Learning, no doubt, plays a role (Miller, 1960). The star athlete has had extensive training in stressful competitive situations. Motivational variables also play a role. Fear of failure or of losing may cause a person to avoid stressful situations and thus keep him from acquiring the skills necessary to cope with them. In addition, fear itself, can generate behavior (such as tenseness and worry) that interferes with efficient performance in a stressful situation.

Are there basic physiological differences in the persons who respond differently to stress? There would seem to be. In one study (King & Henry, 1955) a stress situation caused some subjects to react predominantly with fear. These subjects expressed anger toward themselves for being afraid. Other subjects reacted to the situation with anger directed outward, toward whatever had made them afraid.

The groups exhibiting these different responses scored differently on a variety of physiological measures (e.g., blood pressure).

In addition to discovering that the "anger-inward" and "anger-outward" subjects had different physiological reactions, the study also found that these reactions seemed to be related to influences in the subjects' past. The "anger-outward" subjects tended to have strict fathers who played a major role in their discipline. In contrast, the "anger-inward" subjects had mild fathers who left most of the disciplinary problems to the mother. These results show that specific physiological reactions to stress can be learned. This is not surprising, considering our repeated demonstrations that responses controlled by the autonomic nervous system can be conditioned.

Many basic questions about the physiology of stress remain to be answered. We need to know, for example, whether physiological stress consists of a unitary pattern of biochemical changes, or whether it should be conceived of as a family of different physiological reactions that somehow combine to operate in a similar manner. This is certainly one crucial question, but it is far from being the only one. Physiological stress, no matter what its ultimate biochemical structure proves to be, must be considered in relation both to the conditions that generate it and to the behavior that accompanies it. Another way of expressing this idea is to say that stress must be considered in terms of stimulus and response variables as well as organismic (physiological) variables.

Although at this point we must leave our brief discussion of stress, we will return to the subject later.

SUMMARY

Frustration occurs when goal achievement is blocked; a conflict is created when incompatible response tendencies are aroused.

To make an analysis of frustration meaningful it is useful to break it down into three components: (1) the frustration situation, (2) the state of frustration, and (3) the overt response to frustration.

Aggression, the most thoroughly investigated of responses to frustration, can be directed at the source of frustration or can be displaced. The strength of the aggressive response to frustration depends on its previous reinforcements and punishments, the strength of the habit and drive being blocked, the intensity of the frustration, the number of immediately preceding frustrations, and the availability of a target for aggressive behavior. Other responses to frustration are apathy, rationalization, fantasy, compensation, regression, and fixation. Like aggression, these responses tend to persist in the face of frustration if they are reinforced and extinguish if they are not.

Conflict can be profitably analyzed in terms of the attracting (+) and repelling (−) features of the environment. This leads to a threefold classification of conflicts: approach - approach, avoidance - avoidance, and approach-avoidance. Conflict behavior can be understood according to six principles: the gradient of approach, the gradient of avoidance, the greater steepness of the avoidance gradient, the heightening of the approach or avoidance gradient with increased motivation, the heightening of the approach or avoidance gradient with increased training, and the tendency for the stronger of the two incompatible responses to occur.

Because the approach-approach tendency is unstable, it is easily resolved. The avoid-

436

ance-avoidance and approach-avoidance conflicts are examples of a stable equilibrium. The organism in the avoidance-avoidance conflict attempts to escape while in the approach-avoidance conflict he remains a captive of it. Approach-avoidance gradients can be resolved by either lowering the avoidance gradient or increasing the approach gradient. They can sometimes be resolved by placing an organism in a situation similar to the one in which the conflict is aroused, since the avoidance habit is weakened more by generalization than the approach habit.

In addition to eliminating habits by experimental extinction and temporarily suppressing them by punishment, habits can be broken by the substitution of an incompatible response. The several techniques used to accomplish this are known as the methods of substitution, exhaustion, toleration, and change-of-cue.

Organisms tend to respond to stressful situations in three successive stages: an alarm stage, a stage of resistance, and finally, if the stressful reaction continues, a stage of exhaustion.

SUGGESTIONS FOR FURTHER READING

Buss, A. H. *The psychology of aggression.* New York: Wiley, 1961.

The author presents a systematic view of the experimental work on aggressive behavior and attempts to integrate the results.

Dollard, J., Doob, L. W., Miller, N. E., Mowrer, O. H., Sears, R. R., Ford, C. S., Hovland, C. I., & Sollenberg, R. I. *Frustration and aggression.* New Haven, Conn.: Yale Univer. Press, 1939.

An analysis of evidence supporting the principle that frustration generates aggressive behavior.

Maier, N. R. F. *Frustration: the study of behavior without a goal.* New York: McGraw-Hill, 1949.

An analysis and theoretical interpretation of research on frustration.

Miller, N. E. Experimental studies of conflict. In J. McV. Hunt (Ed.), *Personality and the behavior disorders.* Vol. 1. New York: Ronald, 1944. Pp. 431-465.

A clear exposition of the author's pioneering experimental investigations of conflict behavior.

Miller, N. E. Liberalization of basic S-R concepts: Extension to conflict behavior, motivation, and social learning. In S. Koch (Ed.), *Psychology: A study of a science.* Vol. 2. New York: McGraw-Hill, 1959. Pp. 196-292.

The first part of this paper presents a detailed treatment for the advanced student, of approach-avoidance conflict behavior.

Selye, H. *The stress of life.* New York: McGraw-Hill, 1956.

A statement of the author's interpretation of stress and its role in disease.

PERSONALITY AND
SOCIAL BEHAVIOR

V

We have now come to the end of our plan to analyze behavior from its simplest to its most complex forms. Our major concern in this section will be behavior that falls under the classification of *personality and social behavior*.

A person tends to behave consistently from time to time and place to place. Personality refers to those organized response systems (e.g., being aggressive) that occur in a variety of situations.

Our study of personality will begin with an analysis of the relationship between personality and the rest of psychology. You will be introduced to some of the major formulations that have been offered to describe the development of personality, and then you will learn how psychologists measure personality. A discussion of pathological forms of behavior will follow, and this section of the book will be concluded by an analysis of how groups influence individual behavior and how individuals behave in groups.

The topics of personality, behavior pathology, and social behavior should reveal to you the tremendous scope of the subject matter of psychology. It should also emphasize the great challenges which are constantly confronting psychologists. In responding to these challenges you will see that psychologists have invented ingenious research techniques and have accumulated much basic information. But many unrealized goals still exist. Whether they are achieved will depend upon the creativeness and persistence of future generations of psychologists.

13

PERSONALITY AND PSYCHOLOGY

Some students enrolling in introductory psychology courses hope that **personality,** the topic dealing with an individual's general patterns of behavior, will be discussed first. A few even believe that it will be the only topic. Obviously, the previous chapters have shown this to be a misconception. But there is another misconception about personality and its place in psychology that we must correct: the belief that the study of personality is sharply separated both in method and content from the areas of psychology already reviewed. At its root lie two related ideas: (1) that the test of a theory of personality lies in its ability to predict the behavior of *an individual* in real-life situations and (2) that personality cannot be studied in the laboratory. We must discuss these ideas before proceeding, because they can make the study of personality both confusing and misleading.

The study of personality highlights two somewhat separate components of scientific work. Basic scientific work is concerned with *discovering* the principles governing fundamental phenomena. Applied work has to do with *applying* knowledge for practical purposes. In the field of personality this distinction is reflected in the work of some psychologists, the personality theorists, who seek to discover the principles of personality development, whereas others, the clinical psychologists, try to help people who suffer from what are called personality difficulties. The personality theorist is interested in identifying the uniformities in the behavior of all people; the clinical psychologist is primarily interested in predicting how particular individuals will behave in real-life situations.

This distinction is made in other sciences as well. In biology and its branches, physiology and biochemistry, laboratory work has led to the understanding of disease-borne infection. The physician with the techniques of his profession applies such knowledge to the treatment of his patients. Similarly in physics principles underlying the nature and operation of physical loads and forces as well as stresses and strains have been discovered. The engineer with his professional skills applies some of this knowledge to the design and construction of bridges.

When a bridge is planned the stress and strains that will result from its maximum load are estimated. Although physics is an "exact science," no engineer would dare recommend that a bridge be constructed to bear only its maximum load, even if it were possible to guarantee that it would never be exceeded. Because the load-bearing ability of a bridge is a function of so many interacting variables it is impossible to estimate the maximum load precisely. To compensate for this lack of precision engineers introduce a safety factor into their plans. They build bridges to support loads much greater than their estimated maxima. Similarly engineers who apply physical principles to the construction of airplanes add a safety factor. Airplanes are made to withstand stresses many times greater than they usually meet.

Uncertainty seems to be the rule when we try to predict complexly determined individual events. Recently a car manufacturer bought back a car it had sold to a taxi company, because the car had run over a half-million miles without any major repair. The corporation wanted to find out why this particular car held up so well (in order, according to the cynics, to prevent it from ever happening again). They knew that engineers could not have predicted that car's unusual performance as it came off the assembly line. The future of individual cars, even if they are likely to receive the same handling, is impossible to predict with accuracy. The same is true of violins. Although they are both made in the same way, one violin may have an excellent tone, while another is but a mediocre instrument.

The problem of predicting individual events comes into sharpest focus when one analyzes the task of that much-maligned figure, the weatherman. The public complains constantly about inaccurate weather reports without appreciating the problem of weather prediction. Weather is determined by a constellation of interacting variables. Subtle changes in the constellation can produce marked changes in the weather. Hence the weatherman's prediction of "fair and warmer" may be followed by cloudy and cold weather, because he is unable to estimate exactly how several variables will interact.

Because weather prediction depends so much on estimating the effects of complex and subtle interactions, many weathermen have abandoned categorical predictions such as "rain today, tonight, and tomorrow." Predicting in terms of probabilities—probability of rain today 40 per cent, tonight 80 per cent, and tomorrow 30 per cent—has become more common. Such a probability prediction means that in the past, when the same weather pattern has prevailed, rain occurred 40 per cent of the time during the day, 80 per cent during the night, and 30 per cent of the time on the following day. Although probability predictions fail to satisfy peoples' yearning for exactness, they are nevertheless more appropriate because they reflect multiple causation. The statistical predictions of the weatherman are somewhat like the engineer's safety factor; they both compensate for inability to predict exactly the consequences of many interacting variables.

A suspension bridge collapsed in the Northwest some years ago; jet airliners have been known to explode in flight; weather predictors often err; automobile factories sometimes produce "lemons"; and modern technology is unable to duplicate the mellow and brilliant sounding violins of the seventeenth and eighteenth centuries. Such failures do not, however, shake our confidence in the science of physics. We make allowance for miscalculations where such complex events are concerned. Many people do not, however, make this kind of allowance for psychology. If a clinical psychologist's prediction about one person's behavior goes awry, they question the scientific validity of all psychology immediately. It hardly seems fair to expect psychology to outperform physics.

On the contrary, psychology should be treated in the same way the other sciences are. There are two components of the psychology of personality, just as there are of the other sciences, and different frames of references must be used in considering basic principles and in considering applied psychology. The principles of personality are one matter; how these principles are applied is another.

To illustrate this point we must describe a case history in which the principle of extinction was applied in an attempt to eliminate the temper tantrums of a 21-month-old infant boy (Williams, 1959). The child's tantrums grew indirectly out of a serious illness he suffered during his first 18 months of life. After he was put to bed, he would scream and fuss if his parents left his room. Reluctant to upset him during his illness, they gave in to his tantrum by returning to his room and staying with him until he fell asleep.

When the child had completely recovered, the parents felt they could begin to cure him of these tyrannical tantrums. They decided to extinguish them by eliminating the reinforcement of re-entering his bedroom after they had left it. They put their son to bed in a relaxed manner, and after saying "good-night" they left, closing the door. As expected, the boy screamed and raged, but his parents firmly refused to return.

The results of this application of the extinction principle are presented in Figure 13.1. As you can see the child cried for 45 minutes during the first extinction trial. He did not cry at all the second time, but

screamed and fussed for about ten minutes during the third extinction trial. Thereafter the amount he cried gradually decreased until on the tenth night he fell asleep immediately after his parents left the room.

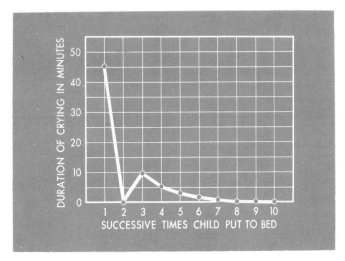

FIGURE 13.1 Length of Crying on Successive Days in an Application of the Extinction Principle to the Elimination of a Child's Bedtime Tantrum. The graph shows the results of the first extinction series, during which the parents refused to re-enter the bedroom in response to the child's crying (After Williams, 1959).

About a week after the boy's tantrum behavior disappeared, his aunt put him to bed and he screamed and fussed. She reinforced this tantrum by returning to the room and staying with him until he fell asleep. Once again the parents tried experimental extinction. Figure 13.2 shows the results of the second extinction series. With removal of reinforcement the tantrum behavior once again subsided and gradually disappeared, never to reappear again.

Although the principle of experimental extinction has been repeatedly validated in well-controlled laboratory experiments, one must be cautious in interpreting its apparently successful application here. The success of the treatment may not have resulted simply, if at all, from the extinction procedure. After all, there was only one

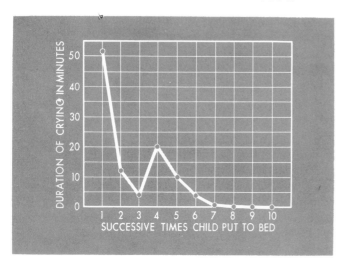

FIGURE 13.2 Length of Crying at Bedtime During the Second Extinction Series (After Williams, 1959).

subject in this demonstration. Perhaps something unknown to the parents was operating to cause this change in the child's behavior, and perhaps, the tantrums would have disappeared just as rapidly if the extinction procedure had never been instituted. Or perhaps the treatment combined with some special factors related to the child and his parents produced the successful results. In other words, the same treatment with another child might not have been effective. The point is that although it is *likely* that the extinction technique was responsible for the child's abandoning his tantrums, one cannot be absolutely *certain*.

The validity of the extinction principle, as well as other psychological principles, rests upon facts obtained in rigorously controlled experimental situations and not upon their successful application. Many other factors besides a principle's inherent validity are involved in its successful application. If, for example, in another instance the extinction technique failed to eliminate a child's tantrum, one would not reject the extinction principle. Rather, one would

assume either that factors were operating to counteract the effects of extinction or that the technique of withholding reinforcement was ineffective. In short, the validity of a general principle cannot be properly evaluated by a single, complexly determined event.

The case of the child's tantrums redirects our attention to the issues of whether personality can be studied in the laboratory and whether the validity of personality theory should rest on its ability to predict *individual* behavior. In commenting on the first, we must point out that many of the psychological principles relevant to the study of personality have been discovered in situations which appear to be far removed from personality behavior. For example, the salivary response of a dog is unlike the temper tantrum of an infant. Nevertheless, the psychological principle of experimental extinction obtained with dogs is applied to the behavior of children. This is not merely an isolated example. The psychology of personality is always closely related to the behavior we have been studying up to now. The psychology of personality and its important application in clinical psychology depend on basic experimental analyses of behavior, just as medicine depends on fundamental research in biochemistry, physiology, and pharmacology. Do not, therefore, be surprised that you will not learn a host of new principles in your study of personality. Instead, be prepared to extend previously learned principles to new areas of behavior.

The second issue implied in the case of the child's tantrums has, as we said, to do with the ticklish problem of predicting and explaining an individual's behavior. The author is often asked to explain or predict somebody's behavior. "Why is my Aunt Ruth so aggressive?" "Will my younger brother outgrow his stuttering?" If you recall the complex problems associated with interpreting the behavior of the child who had temper tantrums, you will understand why we are limited to answering such questions, if we answer them at all, with many qualifications. Questions of this sort are not concerned with the effect of one or a few variables. They cannot be answered by performing a simple experiment which will provide an unequivocal answer. Instead, these questions are directed at the psychological effects of a fantastically large number of variables. Unless we know what these factors are and how they influence the behavior involved, it is simply impossible to give any valid and meaningful answers. To make a reasonable prediction about whether a child will stop stuttering, for example, a psychologist must know many things: how long he has been stuttering; how severe his stuttering is; under what conditions it began; how he and his parents reacted to the stuttering, and many other bits of information. In addition, he needs to know what sort of environment the child is going to face from now on, whether he will receive any speech therapy, and if so, what kind.

The accuracy of our predictions of individual behavior can be increased. And it has been, just as the accuracy of weather prediction has been increased by the discovery of additional variables that control the occurrence of a given phenomenon, and by an understanding of how they interact with other variables.

The realization that exact predictions of an individual's behavior are almost impossible because a huge number of variables are interacting should stop the reader, once and for all, from indulging in the common practice of attributing to human behavior a single cause. We shall never be able to deal effectively with human problems if we persist in oversimplifying them. No matter how much we may long for simple explanations, we must recognize and accept the fact that the behavior of a human being in his everyday environment is complexly determined.

THE CONCEPT OF PERSONALITY

Personality has been described as the general pattern of behavior exhibited by an individual. Although this description is misleading in its simplicity, it can serve for a time as a working definition, because it does convey the broad outlines of this chapter's subject matter.

The concept of personality has its origin in the consistency one observes in an individual's behavior over a period of time as well as in different situations. The shy, retiring high school coed tends to become the bashful college student; and the energetic, aggressive college student develops into the forceful, assertive business man. Figure 13.3 is a perfect illustration of behavior acquired in one situation extending to another. His military personality is not shed when the British guards' officer takes off his uniform and puts on civilian clothes.

Behavioral consistency can be conceived as an example of transfer of training. People tend to behave consistently because the numerous situations they find themselves in are not unlike each other. What they learn in one situation transfers to another. That is, a person acquires a unified system of responses. The concept of personality essentially represents habits, both instrumental and perceptual, and drives that make a person respond in a similar way to markedly different situations.

It is not, however, true that an individual's personality is as fixed and unchanging as his name. Since habits and drives change, personality also changes with time and experience. A shy child may even develop into a gregarious adult. Moreover, personality is influenced by situational variables, as any keen observer knows. Many of us know the polite, considerate gentleman

FIGURE 13.3 A British Guards Regiment in Civilian Clothes. The two photographs show them out of uniform at a memorial service. Although no order was given, they behaved in military fashion (Photos from European).

who assumes the role of an aggressive, unreasonable maniac when he gets behind the wheel of his car. And there is the dear old Japanese lady who kneels before a visitor in her home, and yet is willing to break a stranger's instep in order to get ahead of him in a movie line.

The failure of people to behave with complete consistency was demonstrated in a television show several years ago. A moving-picture camera was hidden in a small cleaning establishment and in a pay-phone booth so that the audience could observe people's reactions to various opportunities to be dishonest. In one test a twenty-dollar bill was planted in a pocket of each of several suits that were to be called for. In every case the money was returned by the owner of the suit. In marked contrast were the results of another test, in which a fat handful of coins was placed in the slot of the pay phone. In this situation every individual proceeded to pocket the money that did not belong to him.

Inconsistency of behavior was demonstrated in a study (Hartshorne & May, 1928) in which a group of children were given an opportunity to cheat in a number of different situations. The major finding of the study was that the children as a whole failed to be consistently honest. Honest in one situation, they cheated in another.

This may seem to be a contradiction of what we said originally. To begin with, we offered the concept of personality to help account for the consistent pattern of behavior exhibited by individuals; we now point out that people are not always completely consistent. Actually there is no contradiction. If behavior is not completely consistent, neither is it entirely erratic. Consistent behavior is the rule rather than the exception, and when there is an exception the reason for it is usually fairly evident. A used-car salesman may be completely honest with his family because such behavior is reinforced with pleasant and rewarding personal relations, and at the same time be forced to utter distortions of the truth, if not outright lies, when he is at work in order to receive monetary reinforcement.

In summary, then, the concept of personality can be defined as the organization of behavior patterns which characterize a person as an individual in a variety of situations.

The Study of Personality

There is no *single* right way to investigate personality. Characteristically, the psychologists have approached the topic in one of two ways, thus reflecting the two major tasks associated with understanding personality. One is to discover how personality develops; the other is to develop methods of measuring personality. It may be argued that before we can understand how personality develops we must first have methods of measuring the changes that do occur. At the same time, before we can measure personality we have to know something more about it, especially how it develops, and about how it changes with experience. Although these two strategies of investigating personality need not, and probably should not, be mutually exclusive, they have, for the most part, been so.

Attempts to formulate theories about personality development have, historically, preceded efforts to measure personality. We shall discuss them in the same order. After a discussion of personality development and personality assessment, we shall touch upon the constancy of personality, and finally, describe certain organismic variables which have effects upon personality.

No one should be surprised to discover that several different interpretations of how personality develops have been offered by different psychologists. Although it is impossible to take up all such interpretations in an introductory textbook, we shall nev-

ertheless attempt to review a few of the formulations that have been most influential.

THE PSYCHOANALYTIC INTERPRETATION OF PERSONALITY

Freud was one of the first, and in many ways, the most influential of those who have attempted to give a systematic account of the growth of personality. It would, however, be quite impossible to undertake an exposition of Freudian ideas within a single framework. Freud was an intellectual giant whose ideas have had a profound effect upon our culture at many points. His influence on writers and artists must be judged against the background of literary and art criticism—areas which this writer dares not invade. Our discussion of Freud will be limited—as it should be—to his effect upon the science of psychology.

But even here Freud's contributions cannot be treated as a single set of ideas. It is necessary to distinguish among three components of his scientific work: (1) the observations he made about human personality, (2) the theory of personality he formulated, and (3) the treatment, known as **psychoanalysis** (the analysis of the *psyche*, "mind"), which he fashioned. Freud was a clinician who treated patients suffering from psychological problems. From his clinical experience he observed certain relationships between his patients' present difficulties and their reports of their past. Freud, however, was not satisfied merely to report these relationships. He also sought to explain them by formulating his theory of personality development. And this theory served, in part, as the basis of Freud's therapeutic technique (psychoanalysis).

It is quite possible, for example, that Freud's clinical observations may be valid, but the theory designed to explain them, inadequate. It would be unwise to reject the former due to the shortcomings of the latter. Similarly, psychoanalytic therapy must be considered apart from both the clinical observations and the theory. It, too, can have assets and limitations independent of the assets and limitations of the observations and the theory. With these qualifications we may now proceed with an analysis of Freud's contributions to the science of behavior.

Freudian Theory of Personality Development

Freud's theory of personality is complicated. It contains many new concepts, the meanings of which are often strange and unclear. In addition, the relationships assumed to exist among these concepts are rather complex. Moreover, Freud was capable of changing his theory when new facts, as he saw them, required this—an ability that is often commendable. Nevertheless, these changes do complicate further an already complicated picture. Even among adherents of Freudian theory there is not unanimous agreement about all the facets of his complex formulation.

Nevertheless, the psychology student who wishes to get the flavor and some of the fundamentals of Freudian theory does not have an impossible task. You do not have to master all the details of Freud's theory before you can understand some of its general principles.

In his formulations Freud used the concept of the *mind* freely without being aware of its limitations and the confusions it engenders (see page 41). He likened the mind to an iceberg whose great bulk is concealed and described it as consisting of three "parts," the **conscious, preconscious,** and **unconscious.** The conscious portion is similar to the small part of the iceberg above water; the preconscious is equivalent to that section that rises above and falls

below the water line with the sea's motion; the unconscious, is the largest mass hidden below the water. The conscious content of the mind is what a person is *momentarily aware* of. The conscious content of the reader's mind, if he is paying attention, is the Freudian concept of consciousness. The preconscious content is those events not in a person's consciousness at the moment but which he can become aware of without difficulty. What did you do last Saturday night? Before we asked this question your consciousness did not contain memories of that night. But once you read the question, you probably had little difficulty in bringing the appropriate memories into consciousness. The unconscious of a person's mind is what he is unaware of. One of Freud's major assumptions is that all kinds of drives, conflicts, and experiences may affect our behavior although we are unconscious of them. These psychological events he assumed to exist in the largest and most influential area of the mind—the unconscious. The unconscious was not a figment of Freud's imagination; it was suggested by the phenomenon of post-hypnotic suggestion (see page 402) and the behavior of his patients.

Personality, according to Freud, is made up of three major systems: the **id, ego,** and **superego.** The id is entirely unconscious; the ego and superego exist at all three levels. Essentially the id consists of the animal (biological) drives, whereas the superego is comprised of the ethical and moral principles that have a profound effect upon the behavior of civilized man. The ego, representing reason, attempts to reconcile these conflicting forces.

Freud assumed that everybody is born with a predetermined amount of psychological energy, the **libido,** that drives him to seek pleasure, especially erotic pleasure. Psychosexual development occurs as a succession of stages, each characterized by a dominant mode of achieving libidinal satisfaction. If all goes well, the individual passes through this sequence of **psychosexual stages** to its terminus, a mature heterosexual relationship. However, an individual may be arrested in his development at any one of the stages.

The first stage of psychological development is the **oral-erotic** and is especially characteristic of the first year of life. During this period the infant is bent upon securing libidinal satisfaction through sucking, nursing, and other oral activities. The **anal-erotic** is the next stage and it lasts up to about two or three years of age. The eliminative functions become the focus of the child's libidinal activities, and he receives intense pleasure from the expulsion and retention of feces. Next comes the **phallic stage,** which may last for a few years. It is during this stage that the child discovers the pleasure-giving qualities of the sexual organs and indulges in self-stimulating play.

Up to and including the early portions of the phallic stage the child's libido is directed toward himself. His pleasures are *auto-erotic*. At the end of the phallic stage an important change takes place. The child begins to direct his libido to love objects external to himself. Freud hypothesized that the libido of the male child begins to be directed toward the mother, resulting in what he called the **Oedipus complex,** named after the young man in the Greek myth who unknowingly slew his father and married his mother. According to Freud the libidinal desires of the son toward his mother are totally unconscious. Although they do influence his behavior, he is unaware of them. As the desire becomes stronger the child unconsciously competes with his father for the affection of his mother, and becomes hostile toward his father. This brings on another complex—the **castration complex**—in which the boy fears that his father will retaliate by injuring him, particularly by harming his genitals. However, this fear helps the boy resolve his Oedipus complex; because of it

he renounces his libidinal desires for his mother and therefore escapes from the castration threat. At the same time the boy *identifies* with his father, whose pleasures and accomplishments he regards as his own, thus indirectly satisfying his libidinal desires for his mother.

The personality development of a girl follows along somewhat the same lines. Suffice it to say she, too, develops an Oedipus complex (sometimes called an **Electra complex**). She develops hostility toward her parent of the same sex, her mother, her libidinal desires being directed toward her father. However, the resolution of this complex is not brought to an abrupt close by a sudden intense fear similar to the castration complex. Instead, it is resolved slowly, and when it ends successfully, the girl identifies with her mother and **sublimates** (makes more socially acceptable) her feelings toward her father.

Following the Oedipal period, which occurs at the end of the phallic stage, the child enters the **latency period,** during which the libido or sexual drive remains in a quiescent state. The increased activity of the genital glands at puberty increases libidinal urges. If the Oedipus complex has been resolved successfully, the individual transfers his libidinal energy to some person outside the family and proceeds to a mature heterosexual adjustment. If, however, the Oedipus complex is not resolved, personality difficulties arise.

One of the major consequences of psychosexual development is the change that takes place in the id, ego, and superego. At birth the ego is relatively weak. Infantile behavior is determined primarily by the action of the id, which demands immediate and total satisfaction of its impulses. As the child passes through the successive stages of psychosexual development, his ego becomes stronger. This comes about by the experiences it gains controlling the id during the time the child is weaned, and later, toilet trained. The ego's task is not to frustrate the id, but to keep it in line with the demands of reality, that is, to make it satisfy the biological drives in a socially acceptable way. In this task the ego has the assistance of the superego. Freud assumed that the infant had inherited a sense of morality, albeit a weak one, and that, in addition, he acquires moral values from his experiences. Resolution of the Oedipus complex results when the child, identifying with the parent of the same sex, is encouraged to accept that parent's moral code.

The alliance between the superego and ego does not always run smoothly. Actually, the ego must curb the superego as well as the id. If the psychological development of an individual progresses through its normal course, the ego becomes strong enough to reconcile the demands of the conflicting id and superego. Many of the forms of psychological disorders Freud attributed to the ego's failure to become strong enough to keep both the id and superego in line. If the id dominates behavior, the individual gets in trouble with society because of his failure to check and inhibit his antisocial impulses. If the superego becomes too powerful, the individual becomes too fearful to satisfy his biological drives.

An Evaluation of Freud's Contribution

Only the barest skeleton of Freud's formulation has been reported. It does, however, offer a basis for some degree of critical evaluation. For some students the first reaction to Freudian theory is unbridled amazement. Some find it distasteful and distressing; others find it fascinating and exciting. Science, however, is supposed to supply a means of evaluation other than emotional reactions. If one can assume a detached and dispassionate view, it becomes possible to assess Freud, not in any overall manner, but in relation to specific points and ideas. The evaluation of his

psychoanalytic technique of treating psychologically disturbed individuals will be postponed until the next chapter. At present our attention will be directed toward appraising the importance of his clinical observations and theoretical formulation.

Before beginning our analysis we must remind the reader once again that the preceding description of Freud's theory—which may seem bizarre—describes the *normal* development of personality. Psychological disturbances do not result from infantile sexuality, but from the child's failure to progress through the various stages of it. For example, Freud assumed that if a person failed to advance through the later phase of the anal-erotic stage, when libidinal pleasure was obtained by retention of feces, he would exhibit signs of avarice, obstinacy, and suspiciousness as an adult.

Freud was an exceedingly acute observer of human behavior. It is in this area of his work that there has been the greatest acceptance of his contributions. These may be categorized as follows: (1) psychological determinism; (2) unconscious determinants of behavior; (3) the prevalence of conflict in human behavior; (4) emphasis on instrumental responses that reduce anxiety or minimize conflicts; and (5) emphasis on the importance of motivation in human behavior. Many of these points were not original with Freud, but it was he who compelled behavior scientists to consider them by his forceful presentation.

Psychological Determinism. That an individual's present behavior is related to his past experiences, may seem very obvious to you, but this was not always seen so clearly. Even during Freud's lifetime it was commonly believed that an individual acquired his personality in a kind of haphazard manner. Although people were willing to accept determinism (causality) in the physical sciences, they were reluctant to accept it as a principle in psychology. It was

Freud who drove home the point that adult personality emerged from early experiences. His theory of psychosexual development, in its broadest sense, is an attempt to identify those early experiences that shape an individual's adult behavior.

Freud insisted that all behavior is causally determined, even what seems to be accidental. Thus he was opposed to the notion that some of our everyday behavior is fortuitous. He would say that the young lady who writes a note to her handsome postman and addresses him as "Dear Mr. Maleman" is not just misspelling a word, but is revealing her motivation. Freud repeatedly emphasized that such slips-of-the-tongue have their causes.

Another area in which Freud placed strong emphasis on psychological determinism was in his treatment of dreams. Formerly dreams had been considered to be fortuitous events, and their contents to bear no relationship to the personality of the dreamer. "Not so!" said Freud. Like any other form of behavior they had their origin. Moreover, Freud believed that by discovering their causes he could obtain interesting and important insights into an individual's personality.

Unconscious Determinants of Personality. Western man had for so many centuries stressed his uniqueness as a *rational* animal that he was very loath to accept the idea that after all he might not always be aware of why or how he was behaving. Many historians and scientists would now assert that Freud's emphasis on unconscious and irrational determinants of behavior was his greatest single contribution to psychology and to contemporary thought in general.

The idea behind the concept of the unconscious receives support not only from clinical observations but from many experimental findings. Subjects who have learned a concept (see page 373) are sometimes unable to specify the relevant stimuli. Indeed, human beings are very often unaware of the stimuli they are responding to, or of the responses they are making, and certainly of the motivations that impel them. In one experiment (Hefferline, Keenan, & Hanford, 1959) subjects were trained to avoid an obnoxious noise by executing an invisible thumb-twitch, which was recorded electronically. The rate of this minute response increased when it served to terminate the obnoxious noise, and then decreased during experimental extinction. The subjects were completely unaware of what was happening. The same is true of subjects who were trained to repeat certain words or phrases in verbal conditioning experiments. They were completely unaware that their verbal behavior was controlled by the schedule of reinforcement (see page 344).

The writer also recalls the conduct of a young man who was the epitome of kindness and consideration to everybody except the girl to whom he was engaged. He would criticize her unmercifully even before others, his sarcasm so intense that it made everybody except himself uncomfortable. Much to his surprise, the girl wisely broke the engagement. When his hostile behavior was mentioned as a cause, he was amazed for he was actually unaware of it. Similarly the student who is hostile towards his professor may not realize that his behavior is in part due to the aggressive feelings he has for his father which have now generalized to almost anyone in authority.

Freud emphasized unconscious processes mostly in relation to motivation. He saw that psychological difficulties developed because people were unaware of their own true motivation. That a person can be unaware of his own motivation is demonstrated in the phenomenon of post-hypnotic suggestion (see page 402). In everyday life we often observe examples of unconscious motivation: intense competition, even among members of the same family, sometimes expresses hidden hostility; a husband's forgetting of a wife's birthday or a wife's neglect of her husband's food preferences are sometimes examples of unconscious aggression.

The Prevalence of Conflict Behavior. If you ask a child whether he likes one of the neighborhood children he will probably give an unqualified response: "I like him" or "I hate him." Adults also believe that they harbor consistent positive or negative feelings toward others. They love their children and hate one of their coworkers. Freud doubted whether such unequivocal attitudes could validly describe interpersonal relationships, particularly close ones. People's reactions toward others are often **ambivalent,** that is, they feel affection and hostility simultaneously.

Ambivalence is essentially an expression of an approach-avoidance conflict. A rat is ambivalent toward the end of the runway where he has been both fed and shocked and exhibits this ambivalence by his tendencies to approach and to avoid. People exhibit similar conflicts in their behavior toward each other. The writer recalls an incident involving his younger son which clearly illustrates this. The relationship between his son and a neighbor boy had been marked by numerous ups and downs. They would play together and be great friends one day, then quarrel, come to blows, and consider each other mortal enemies the next. One afternoon his son started across the lawn to the neighbors. As he got closer to their house his pace slackened. He stopped, turned, and started back toward his own house, where he suddenly wheeled around and walked straight toward his "friendly enemy's" house. Once more he stopped and seemed puzzled about what to do. His conflict was finally resolved when another boy appeared and invited him to play football. His ambivalent behavior, however charmingly human, resembled that of conflicted rats.

Freud emphasized the importance of ambivalent attitudes in close relationships, such as those between parents and their children. In such relationships positive feelings are almost invariably accompanied by some negative attitudes. This should surprise no one. The child is often a source of frustration to his parents. He restricts their freedom; his behavior is naughty and exasperating, and so on. But the parents in turn frustrate the child. They punish him, withhold toys from him, force him to comply with customs he doesn't understand, and so on. As a result ambivalent reactions inevitably creep into the relationship between parents and child.

Defense Mechanisms. In the last chapter we discussed such reactions to frustration as displacement, rationalization, and regression. Freud was the first to observe these reactions which he referred to as **defense mechanisms** and to explain and elaborate the dynamics of their functioning, and this testifies again to his genius as an observer of human behavior. He saw that people adopt these interesting forms of behavior in varying situations of stress and interpreted them as techniques to control the violent impulses of the id. We can conceive of them as instrumental responses that can yield reinforcement by helping the subject to avoid or escape fear-provoking stimuli.

Freud considered **repression** that most basic of all defense mechanisms. A child who feels both affection and hostility toward his sibling may repress the negative attitude. Through repression he forgets the hostility and escapes from the guilt and fear he has learned to feel when he fails to act in ways that are socially approved.

Most of the experimental studies of repression (e.g., Shaw, 1944; Eriksen & Kuethe, 1956) have demonstrated how anxiety-producing events tend to be forgotten. Forgetting is, however, only half the mechanism of repression. According to Freud, not only is the unpleasant event forgotten, but it continues to exert an insidious effect on behavior. The evidence in support of this aspect of repression comes largely from clinical cases. Two such cases, which the writer came across when he was serving as an army clinical psychologist during World War II follow:

Frank J. was a major in the Army Medical Corps and a well-thought-of surgeon. He did not exhibit any obvious signs of psychological disturbance, but had a problem that came to the writer's attention when they both were driving together to New York City on a weekend pass from the hospital they both were stationed at. As they approached the Holland Tunnel (an underwater route that connects New Jersey with New York City), Frank tried to persuade the writer to change his route and go by way of the George Washington Bridge, arguing that it would take less time. This was obviously false, for it would have taken at least an hour longer. Therefore the writer ignored Frank's suggestion. But the closer they came to the tunnel, the more upset Frank became, and finally admitted that he was "scared as hell" about going through a tunnel. The writer then abruptly switched routes in order to go over the bridge. On the return journey to the hospital they discussed the major's **phobia** (an excessive fear in the absence of any real danger). He had had this fear "since he was a kid" and would travel any distance to avoid going through a tunnel under a river. His phobia was not incapacitating because he usually traveled by air, and did not seem to possess any other irrational fears. Knowing that the psychiatric section of the hospital was working with hypnotic techniques, the major inquired whether his fear could be eliminated in this way. He eventually decided to try this method.

During the third hypnotic session the major was able to recall an experience he had when he was about seven years old. Driving with his father through the Holland Tunnel, he became frightened at the thought that the tunnel was entirely surrounded by water (a misconception, since the tunnel is built under the river bed and is entirely surrounded by rock). He imagined that if the walls of the tunnel suddenly sprang a leak, he and his father would surely drown, and asked his father how leaks were prevented. His father, who was probably teasing him, responded that the builders tried to make the tunnel as watertight as possible but leaks sometimes did occur, and added, "When they do, you'd better not be here!" His father then depressed the accelerator and they sped out of the tunnel. Frank never again discussed the tunnel problem with his father, probably because, "He didn't like me to be scared." He also recalled under hypnosis that he had once persuaded an uncle to go by an alternative route rather than the Holland Tunnel. Following the hypnotic session the major's intense fear of tunnels was discussed with him. He readily understood that this experience could be responsible for his phobia and decided that on his next trip to New York he would "risk the tunnel." This he did with great trepidation but nothing approaching panic. Thereafter, when traveling by car, he has felt no need to take a roundabout route in order to avoid a tunnel under a river.

Patricia S., a young, attractive married woman, came to the psychiatric section seeking help about a "marital problem." Although, as she described it, her recent marriage to a lieutenant was "exceedingly happy," her husband had persuaded her to seek some professional help. She admitted she was very much in love with her husband, but that "making love" was becoming more and more unpleasant for her, and as a result she was inventing excuses to avoid sexual relations. She was very disappointed in the sexual component of marriage, which she had expected to be "a wonderful experience, but instead it has turned into a nightmare." She said she did not achieve sexual satisfaction in their love-making and this in itself aggravated the situation. She feared that she was frigid and that her unsuitability as a sexual partner would soon force her husband to seek a divorce. The therapist explained to Mrs. S. that her problem was not uncommon, and that her marriage was not in any immediate danger, since she and her husband were obviously still very much in love. It was decided that she should be subjected to several hypnotic sessions to discover whether any earlier traumatic experience was responsible for her difficulties. While hypnotized she recalled under great stress an incident that occurred when she was 12. Her widowed mother had married a man who had a 19-year-old son. One night when her mother and stepfather were out and she was in bed, she was awakened by her stepbrother, who was making sexual advances. She screamed in terror, and the boy stopped but threatened her with bodily harm if she dared to tell their parents about the episode. Even without this threat, she declared, she would have kept quiet because the affair was "so embarrassing, so horrible and disgusting." The episode was then discussed with the patient in her normal state. The therapist explained to her that an unfortunate event such as that, even though forgotten, could influence her present behavior because of the fear and tension about sexual matters it would generate. He told her that now she was aware of the cause of her fear, it would gradually subside and she would in all likelihood be able to enjoy sexual relations. The recall of the previously repressed event seemed to help her. Her fear subsided and in about six months she and her husband reported an adequate sexual adjustment.

The basis of such "irrational fears" is not always, and perhaps not often, as easily discovered as it was with these two patients. Nevertheless, both cases do illustrate the point that repressed memories can influence present behavior. They operate, as do conditioned avoidance responses, to keep an organism away from a feared situation. One other lesson can be learned from these two cases. Repression can occur in people who, for the most part, are psychologically healthy and sound.

The Importance of Motivation in Human Behavior. Originally psychologists were principally interested in understanding sensory experience. They paid little attention to the influence of motivational variables. Even the early work in learning was slanted much more toward how habits were formed and strengthened than toward the role of motivation in learning. It was Freud who hammered home the importance of motivation, particularly sexual, in human behavior. The emphasis on the sex drive was one reason that Freud's theory encountered so much opposition, particularly during his lifetime, when frank discussion of sex was frowned upon much more than it is today. It was not uncommon then, nor is it today, for Freud's theory to be critcized, on the ground that he himself must have a pathological interest in sex to perceive it as such a dominant force in human behavior. This accusation is both unfair and inaccurate. Freud was led to emphasize sex because many of his patients suffered from sexual maladjustments; the role he assigned to it had roots in clinical observations. However, regardless of whether or not he was justified in emphasizing the role of sex in personality, that view encouraged psychologists to pay attention to all forms of motivation.

The Evaluation of Freud's Theory of Personality Development

What was Freud's aim in formulating his theory of personality development? It was to understand why men act as they do.

If we ask was he successful, we have to choose some frame of reference before we can answer. The Constitution serves as a guide when justices of the Supreme Court decide whether a given law is constitutional; the judges in a dog show have definite standards for the various breeds available to guide them in making their awards; and in science we judge a theory not by how appealing or offensive it may sound, but by the criteria of an acceptable scientific theory, whether it is constructed logically and whether its implications agree with the data. Naturally disagreements over whether certain standards have been met arise sometimes. This is why Supreme Court justices, as well as dog show judges, may differ in their opinions. Psychologists also disagree. And in this instance, their disagreement prevents any definitive evaluation of Freudian theory. There is, however, general agreement that Freud's theory suffers from one great defect. It is so vaguely stated that almost any kind of behavior will appear compatible with it. Theories ought, in principle, to be so stated that they can be proven wrong as well as proven right. This means simply that a scientific hypothesis must be in such a form that it can be tested, and its implications demonstrated to be true *or false*. Freudian theory is not formulated in this manner. It does not consist of a logically interrelated set of assumptions from which determinate consequences can be predicted. Rather, it is a disorderly array of principles stated somewhat ambiguously and applied in a rather arbitrary and not strictly logical manner to a given kind of behavior.

One reason for this vagueness is that Freud assumes the operation of a large number of antagonistic processes (the id versus superego, unconscious versus conscious), whose strengths in a given instance cannot be ascertained before the behavior occurs. Consider some examples. In one of his later formulations Freud assumes people to have what he calls life and death instincts. Life instincts are directed toward love and pleasure, whereas death instincts are directed toward destruction and death. Any aggressive, destructive behavior Freud attributes to the operation of the death instinct. The life instinct he holds responsible for all pleasure-seeking responses. In this way he is able to account for the behavior *after* it occurs, but the problem for any psychological theory is to specify the conditions that will lead to a certain kind of behavior *before* it occurs, that is, to predict it. If Freudian theory were to meet this requirement it would have to be modified so that the strengths of such antagonistic processes as the life and death instincts could be measured independently of the behavior they produce, thus permitting us to predict the probability of pleasure-seeking or of hostile behavior. Another example of the ambiguity inherent in Freudian theory comes from his very profound insight concerning the prevalence of ambivalent attitudes in close relationships. This observation has obviously had a deep influence on our thought, but if it is to be truly meaningful scientifically, we should be able to measure separately the amounts of hostility and affection individuals possess, and to predict what kind of behavior will occur. Otherwise, any and every form of behavior a child exhibits toward his father or mother can be arbitrarily attributed to the dominance of one of these two antagonistic motivations. It was this inherent ambiguity in Freud's theory that led a well-known philosopher of science to conclude, following an analysis of the scientific structure of Freudian theory: "But on the Freudian theory itself, as a body of doctrine for which factual validity can be reasonably claimed, I can only echo the Scottish verdict: Not proven" (Nagel, 1959, p. 55).

In rebuttal to the criticism of ambiguity two arguments can be offered. One is that a precise, logically organized theory does not usually emerge full-blown. A formulation often undergoes several revisions before it meets the exacting standards of

454

science. The second is that Freud undertook a most difficult task in his attempt to predict individual behavior in real-life situations (see page 440). His lack of complete success must be considered in relation to his enormous endeavor.

Has Freudian theory, in fact, served as a "first approximation" out of which a more adequate theory of personality has developed? The answer to this question depends on the particular "Freudian-influenced" theory examined. Freud has impressed a group of psychologists who are, as he was, engaged primarily in trying to assist people to overcome their personality difficulties. The theories proposed by this psychoanalytic group, of which Freud is the leading figure, have their roots in clinical observations. Freud has also stimulated other psychologists who are convinced that a theory of personality must be anchored in experimental facts. Freud's influence on these two groups has been different, as you will see.

Theories proposed by members of the psychoanalytic group are in large part modifications of Freudian theory. Most of the psychoanalytic theorists were themselves associated with Freud at one time, but then broke away from him because of what they considered to be basic mistakes in his formulations. Our attention will be directed briefly toward two important variations of Freudian theory.

Alfred Adler (1870-1937), one of Freud's early disciples, came to the conclusion that Freud's emphasis on infantile sexuality as a powerful determiner of adult personality was an exaggerated and distorted interpretation. According to Adler, the fundamental driving force of human behavior is a self-assertive drive. Adler perceives the newborn child as being constantly frustrated because he is weak and inadequate. Seeking power to overcome his own inadequacy, he **compensates** (see page 404) for his inferiorities by learning techniques that enable him to dominate his parents. The

child's personality, therefore, is an outgrowth of the behavior patterns he learns in such efforts to dominate. In short, Adler substitutes primarily social motivations for the biological drives Freud believes responsible. Adler says that personality is shaped more by our society than by our biology. An extension of this principle is Adler's conviction that men and women do not develop psychologically in distinctive ways simply because of their different physiological systems. It is the social order that determines masculine and feminine behavior. The kinds of behavior men and women exhibit are products of the methods by which they have learned to achieve power and get their way in the world.

Carl Jung (1875-1961) was a Swiss psychiatrist who was at one time closely associated with Freud. Then differences sprang up between them, and their professional association and friendship cooled and finally ended. Jung, like Adler, could not accept Freud's emphasis on sex. Although he adheres to the concept of libido, he does not restrict it to sexual pleasures. As a person develops, the libido changes. In infancy the libido is directed toward nourishment; in childhood, toward play; after puberty, toward heterosexual relationships; and still later, toward spiritual values. Jung also expands the realm of the unconscious to include the **collective unconscious,** inherited from past generations. The collective unconscious predisposes the individual to think and feel and act as have countless generations of humanity before him. Individual behavior, for Jung, has its roots in the history of mankind.

Besides the views of Adler and Jung, there are several other important variations of psychoanalytic theory, but their subtleties and complexities would fill many a volume. However, this brief and very inadequate reference to only two of these variations highlights the theoretical problems of psychoanalytic formulations, which a half-century after their birth are no nearer resolution. The theories of Adler and Jung, like Freud's, are stated in such an equivocal manner that their validity cannot be evaluated objectively. It is impossible to discover whether Freud's conception of the libido is more adequate than Jung's. Nor has it been possible to ascertain whether the self-assertive drive is more basic than the sexual drive.

Once again it is necessary to warn the reader that positive contributions to the growth of a science can be made in spite of theoretical inadequacies. Both Adler and Jung, and Freud above all, have given tremendous impetus to the study of personality. Freud was the revolutionary pioneer. Adler pointed to the social factors that shape human personality, whereas Jung has directed our attention to the complex nature of human motivation, and especially to how it changes with age.

PERSONALITY AND LEARNING

Freud saw the adult's behavior as the outgrowth of his childhood experiences. The child, as the old saying goes, is father to the man. Psychologists who study learning naturally emphasize the role past experience plays in current behavior. It is not surprising, therefore, that Freud's ideas have proved to be a source of stimulation to psychologists who seek to apply the principles of learning to the understanding of human personality. The actual impact of Freudian ideas varies considerably from one learning psychologist to another. For some, Freudian ideas play a central role in their thinking; for others, the influence is peripheral.

The best-known attempt to combine psychoanalytic ideas with those of learning theory is the collaborative undertaking of John Dollard and Neal Miller. John Dollard, trained as a sociologist, has been sufficiently versatile to obtain academic appointments in anthropology, sociology, and psychology. Neal Miller is a distinguished experimental psychologist whose work on fear and conflict we have already reviewed. Both Dollard and Miller were stimulated by Freudian ideas during early stages of their careers, especially while studying psychoanalysis in Europe. At Yale University, where they both hold appointments now, they came under the influence of Clark Hull, who successfully applied natural science methods to the study of learning. Hull himself, in turn, had been influenced greatly by both the experimental methodology and the theoretical formulations of Pavlov. So Dollard and Miller (1950) represent the merging of two separate streams of thought in psychology: the psychoanalytic movement and the experimental investigation of learning.

Dollard and Miller, unlike Freud, do not conceive of personality as evolving from the operation of a basic libidinal drive through a predetermined sequence of developmental stages. Their conception is that the child, as he matures, learns important habits which mold his personality. These are the habits he acquires when he encounters the frustrations imposed by authority, or when he learns to be affectionate or aggressive. He acquires them during feeding experiences, toilet training, and social situations in which his parents and siblings play major roles. The importance of any one learning experience varies from child to child, depending on what he learns and what is transferred to other situations. One child may learn important habits from his feeding experiences; another may acquire basic habits in his relations with his siblings. With still another child a variety of situations may be equally important. The fundamental point is that if you can discover how the basic processes of learning and motivation operate as a child matures, you will be able to understand how his personality develops.

456

Dollard and Miller do not believe it is possible, as the orthodox Freudians do, to provide a blow-by-blow account of personality development. According to the "learning theory approach" the formation of personality is not rigidly determined by any particular sequence of situations or events. Instead, we must be content with showing how some of the critical problems infants and children face may shape their personalities. We will now do this, with particular, although not exclusive, reference to the contributions of Dollard and Miller.

The Feeding Situation

The human infant, possessing a limited array of behavioral equipment and a few primary drives, is completely helpless. His survival depends upon the cooperation of others. Moreover, he is motivated by intense drives and suffers severe frustrations. It is difficult for us to imagine the intensity of an infant's hunger drive and the discomfort it produces. Most adults find it unbearable when their dinner is delayed a few hours. The infant, with a limited space for storing food and a tremendous need for nourishment created by his rapid growth, often finds himself literally starving. Look at a baby screaming for milk, and notice his extreme tenseness and generally high level of activation (see page 259). Perhaps then you will realize the intensity of his hunger.

Because of this strong drive, because of the reinforcing power of food, and because of its frequency, the feeding situation provides optimal conditions for learning to take place. It challenges the child with one of the first problems he himself can learn to solve. Assuming that his parents are willing to cooperate, if he can learn to communicate his hunger need (by crying) and get food, he has taken the first step in controlling his environment. In contrast, the child whose cries go unheeded and is allowed to cry himself out may learn to be apathetic. Nothing he can do is going to help solve his problems. A child who is fed under variable conditions (sometimes immediately after beginning to cry, at other times after crying for long periods of time) may learn to be persistent in the face of frustration.

Feeding experiences can be a source of strong conflict. For example, infants can develop colic because they overeat. They must then regurgitate some of the food and let out the gases that digestion produces. Once they have done this, they are often hungry again and demand further feeding. If they are fed again the sequence of feeding and vomiting may repeat itself. This can be so vexing to the mother that she will punish the child, making him afraid of vomiting. Rather than risk punishment, he may learn to inhibit vomiting and endure his gastric distress. On the other hand, if the child is punished for demanding food after regurgitating, he may learn to be afraid of being hungry. In either case, the child is hindered in learning the difficult discrimination of eating proper amounts of food.

The infant learns his first social response when he is feeding. If his feeding experience is satisfactory, the mother herself becomes a stimulus for relaxing. However, if she provides insufficient food or something goes wrong, the mother can become a cue for continued tension and frustration.

The feeding situation is very much like a learning experiment. One trial occurs every time the infant gets hungry, and how he responds and what reinforcements he gets determine what he learns. If what he learns generalizes to other situations—if, for example, the relaxed reaction to his mother generalizes to other people—then the feeding experiences will play an important role in his personality development.

Cleanliness Training

Adults are well aware of the virtues of sanitary practices. Infants are not. They neither abhor excretions nor appreciate the need for sanitations. Nevertheless, they must be toilet trained, and parents see to it that they are. Infants typically find toilet training difficult to learn, but parents often find it more difficult to understand why. They fail to appreciate the difficult discriminations a child must learn to make in toilet training.

When he is learning appropriate habits of cleanliness a child is confronted with a built-in approach-avoidance conflict. Instead of defecating or urinating immediately to all pressures in the bowel or bladder, he must learn to inhibit these powerful response tendencies in all situations except the appropriate ones. And he has to learn this discrimination when he has limited verbal responses to help him.

American mothers are usually anxious to toilet train their children early, because they want to avoid both the messy cleaning-up and extensive laundering. Probably more important to some mothers, is the prestige they get for training their children young.

In order to train their children some mothers punish the children's lapses. Unfortunately, punishment can have unexpected consequences (see page 279). A child can learn to fear the cues resulting from pressure in his bowels, and if he cannot learn when it is safe to defecate, he may learn to avoid punishment by not defecating, that is, by becoming constipated. As a result the mother is confronted with a much more difficult training problem than she had at first. In addition, the mother who uses harsh toilet-training techniques runs the risk of increasing the probability that her child will develop a personality disorder, such as a behavior or speech problem, or a pathological fear, later on. Case histories of children referred to child guidance clinics suggest that the majority suffered harsh toilet training (Mussen & Conger, 1956). Such evidence, we must point out, suffers from a limitation common to clinical data—the lack of adequate controls. We need to know whether a group of children who developed without giving signs of psychological difficulties did in fact undergo appreciably less harsh toilet training. Most practicing clinical psychologists and psychiatrists believe this is so, but if we demand of psychology the same rules of evidence that we demand of the older sciences, we cannot be satisfied with expert opinion alone.

Sex Training

Problems associated with the development of sexual behavior are frequently cited as responsible for adult personality difficulties. We have suggested (see page 236) that this may not be because sex is the most powerful of all human drives, but because it is the drive most often frustrated.

Dollard and Miller analyze sex behavior, also, by generalizing from the facts and theories of learning and conflict. They hold, as do most authorities today, that sex behavior begins in infancy. Infants fondle their genitalia presumably because they receive pleasurable sensations when they do. To infants such behavior is no different from other positive reinforcing activities; to many parents the sight of their child indulging in masturbatory behavior is frightening, disgusting, or otherwise upsetting. So they punish the child, or if he is old enough to understand, try to frighten him by telling him that if his behavior continues, something terrible will happen to him. In either case the child develops an approach-avoidance sex conflict in which he is simultaneously motivated to indulge and not to induge in self-manipulatory acts.

The ultimate effect of such a conflict depends on the intensity of the fear and the situations to which it is transferred. An intense fear reaction to masturbatory behavior may generalize to adult sex behavior and hinder the development of mature social behavior in general. The early conflict would, in this case, play a central role in personality formation. On the other hand, a weak fear which fails to transfer to other areas of sexual behavior would have little effect.

Closely related to a parent's reaction to masturbatory behavior are his attitudes about his child's sexual curiosity. The child who is made to feel shameful or embarrassed each time he asks about sex may acquire a disturbing approach-avoidance conflict that will interfere with his subsequent adjustment. The fear response which has its origin in his own verbal behavior may generalize to his later adult sex behavior. Parents can handle the problem of sex education in a straightforward and realistic manner that will minimize the fear and shame so often associated with sex. The following advice to parents is both simple and sensible.

When the child becomes interested in the problems pertaining to sex and birth, his questions should be answered frankly, truthfully, and without embarrassment as they come up. That is not so difficult a job as one might think because children need and want very little information at any one time. If children ask where they come from, and they are told that babies grow within the mother's body, that answer will satisfy most children for that particular day and, perhaps, for several weeks or months to come. They just do not get around to asking any more until something in connection with their play with other children or some event in the home life comes up which prompts a question for additional information. Very often parents make a problem for themselves by the feeling that when the child asks the first question about sex, they are obligated to tell him everything that has been written in a twelve-volume treatise on sexuality. Obviously this is

neither necessary nor advisable. Any parent who will put himself at ease on the subject of sex, not try to show how much he knows or be afraid of how little he knows, not be flustered with embarrassment but just answer what the child asks, will manage sex education in a very satisfactory manner (English & Pearson, 1945, p. 72).

Another important area of sex training is *sex-typing*. Although boys and girls are different physiologically, their behavior sometimes fails to coincide with this difference. A "tom-boyish" girl is often more masculine than many boys, and some boys are more feminine than many girls.

We begin to "sex-type" our children at a very early age—often before two years. Boys are reinforced for being masculine, "like daddy," and girls, for being feminine. Sex-typing is usually achieved without difficulty in a household where both parents consistently reinforce the appropriate behavior. Where there is disharmony between husband and wife, the task of sex-typing is often more difficult. A mother who resents her husband and does not get along well with him will not usually reinforce her son for being just like his father. In fact, she often encourages him to be like herself. If she succeeds the child is likely to be taunted by his father for being a sissy, which will probably not make him any less of one.

According to this analysis the like-sexed parent in a congenial household serves as the model for a child to imitate, and when the household is not congenial or in the absence of such a parent, sex-typing becomes more difficult. This point was demonstrated in a study (Sears, Pintler, & Sears, 1946) comparing the behavior of children (3 to 5 years of age) raised in households where the father was present with children in households where the father was absent. Boys raised away from their fathers were found to be less masculine than boys who lived with their fathers. In contrast, girls raised by their mothers with and without fathers did not differ in their femininity.

There are no universally applicable levels of masculinity and femininity that should be considered optimal. Thus, it would be silly to advise parents as to the precise goals they should aim for in training children. Besides, it is naive to believe that any child can be trained to acquire a particular pattern of masculine or feminine behavior, since genetic factors probably play some role. Fortunately, society accepts a considerable range of behavior as appropriate for both men and women. Difficulty is encountered only when individuals with a certain level of masculinity or femininity find themselves in situations where their particular behavior is disapproved. A dress designer who behaved like a truck driver would doubtless be shunned, and vice versa. Probably the most sensible approach for a parent is to encourage his child to acquire behavior patterns appropriate to his or her sex, and at the same time not insist on too specific kinds of behavior ("My son is going to be the toughest kid on the block!").

Aggression

Aggressive behavior is a troublesome training problem for parents of most children. They are likely to encourage boys, and sometimes girls at younger ages, to fight in defense of their rights but not to start the fights. But the history of international tensions testifies to the difficulty people have in discriminating between aggression and defense. How can children be expected to learn a discrimination that is usually beyond the powers of their elders?

Nevertheless, most children learn to control their aggression, at least to the extent of not breaking the law. Sometimes, however, this learning is too effective, and a child loses his capacity to become angry and aggressive. This can happen if he is consistently and severely punished for any sign of aggressive behavior. The child who

fears punishment avoids getting angry. He learns to be excessively meek, and often becomes unable to resist being exploited. Some people who feel incapacitated by their excessive meekness finally seek the help of a psychotherapist (see page 523). In such cases, the main goal of treatment is to extinguish the patient's undue fear that he will become angry.

At the other extreme is the child who never learns to inhibit his aggression. He, too, has a problem. Although his parents may tolerate—even fear—his aggressions, society will not, especially when these aggressions take on an antisocial character. Thus the child has to learn to inhibit his aggression to some degree. The amount of overt aggression he will be allowed to express depends on the situations he encounters. Just as there is no one optimal level of masculinity or femininity, neither is there one appropriate standard of aggressiveness. Some situations call for more willingness to show fight than others. The clergyman learns to "turn the other cheek," but the professional football player knows he must "fight back."

The Self

Although we are all aware that as a child matures he is forming judgments about others, we forget that he is also learning attitudes toward himself. The concept of **the self** refers to these attitudes.

Learning about oneself is a gradual affair. The infant must first learn that he exists as an individual separate and distinct from everybody and everything around him. He has to learn, for example, that when he pinches himself he causes himself pain, but that when he pinches his toy he does not. Reacting to his bodily sensations is only the beginning of reacting to himself. Later, when the child learns reactions to the behavior of others, he learns also to respond to his own behavior. He perceives his mother as kind and gentle and his father as strong and competent. It is a truism to add that how he perceives himself becomes *his* self.

Self-evaluating reactions vary as a child matures; he learns new dimensions in judging himself. One especially important dimension concerns his own competence, or as it is often technically labelled, his **self-esteem.** A related dimension is the evaluation of his own goodness or badness. You frequently hear a child say, "I'm a good boy (or girl)" or "I'm bad." Although the specific reaction and the meaning may change, self-evaluations persist throughout life. The reader is aware, though nobody else may be, of how competent he believes he is at anything, and how generally "good" or "bad."

The reader will not be surprised to learn that people differ in their self-concepts. But most of us are not aware of how vast are the differences among individuals in their reactions toward themselves or of how wide a discrepancy often exists between individuals' reactions toward themselves and others' reactions toward them. Some individuals have great confidence in themselves; others are convinced that they are hopelessly inadequate. The people at these two extremes of self-perception may be equal in ability, or the one whose self-esteem is low may actually be the more competent. There are these discrepancies between self-evaluation and performance in all sorts of activities. For example, an individual may think he is socially popular when, in fact, others consider him a bore, and the opposite can be true.

The self-concept emerges from an individual's experience and in turn influences his behavior. A bright child placed in difficult problem situations (given toys which are too "old" for him) by overambitious parents eager to demonstrate his superiority, may fail so often that he develops low self-esteem. He cannot know that the problem situations he faces are beyond what he can reasonably be expected to cope with.

Another child, less talented than he, may be raised in an environment where he can cope with any situation that arises, and thus become self-assured and confident of his abilities. Later, when these children are confronted with similar problems, the less competent but more confident child will do better than the one whose level of performance has been lowered by his doubts and fears.

A person's concept of himself functions as a response-produced cue, and it can be the most important stimulus to which he responds. A child who is constantly told how bad or incompetent he is begins to accept this picture of himself as true and to behave accordingly. An interesting example of this process comes from the observations of a psychologist on the Gold Coast of Africa (Jahoda, 1954). When the natives told him that the day of the week on which a person is born determines his character, the psychologist was naturally but politely skeptical. However, his examination of the records of the juvenile courts revealed some basis for this belief: those born on Wednesday were by far most frequently in trouble, whereas those born on Monday had the best records.

Quite surprising at first, this finding became understandable when Jahoda discovered that each child was given one name which corresponded to the day of the week on which he was born. Each day-name indicated that a particular spirit had entered the body of the baby and endowed him with a disposition to behave a certain way. A *Kwadwo* (Monday) child was believed to be quiet, retiring, and peaceful. In contrast a *Kwaku* (Wednesday) child was held to be quick-tempered, aggressive, and trouble-making. These children lived in a society where such superstitions were firmly and almost universally believed. Like children in general, they got their ideas about themselves from what they heard others assert, and once they began to believe these assertions, they acted according to them.

Of course, our self-concepts may change in some respects at different times or in different situations. A man may be serenely confident in his role as head of a family, but feel miserably incompetent as the administrator of a small business organization. A woman may think herself a good mother but a bad daughter. A college coed may perceive herself as intellectually competent but socially inept. Each of us is forced to play many different roles in life, and it is not surprising that we acquire different ways of reacting to our various performances. These reactions are elicited by the distinctive stimulus features of the environments in which the different roles are played. Nevertheless, we do carry around with us certain fairly stable conceptions of ourselves that we may—but usually do not—put into words. It is this core of abiding evaluations that lies at the center of the concept of personality. Largely because of it we cannot, in a certain sense, escape from ourselves. And because we do not escape we are ourselves.

Family Relations and Social Behavior

We have already mentioned that the child learns his reactions to others from important training experiences. This learning plays an important role in the development of his social behavior. A child also learns much about interpersonal relations from the numerous and varied experiences he has with members of his family.

At one time psychologists believed that the close and intimate relationship that commonly develops between a mother and her baby has its roots in the mother's devotion and the child's need for nourishment. Research with infant macaque monkeys, whose behavior during infancy resembles that of human children, suggests that the motivational base of infant behavior is much more complex (Harlow, 1958).

Harlow, a psychologist who observed the behavior of infant monkeys separated from their mothers several hours after birth, maintains that they have a need for "contact-comfort." His monkeys exhibited a strong attachment to the folded gauze diapers that covered the wire floors of their cages, clinging to them and resisted attempts to remove them. Their devotion was very like that frequently exhibited by human infants for soft blankets, pillows, and stuffed toys.

FIGURE 13.4 A One-Day-Old Monkey's Response to a Soft Cloth (Dr. H. F. Harlow).

These observations led Harlow to study the affectional responses of infant monkeys to artificial, inanimate "mothers." He constructed two mother surrogates, (substitutes for the real mother), each with essentially the same body shape and each capable of holding in its chest region a bottle from which the infant could nurse. One mother surrogate was made out of a block of wood padded with a layer of sponge rubber covered by terry cloth. A second was designed to provide as little comfort as possible to any monkey who had contact with it; it was made of wire mesh. Both were warmed by radiant heat, and each provided the same postural support for feeding.

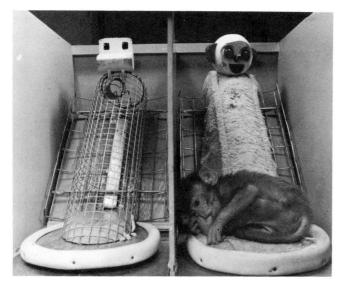

FIGURE 13.5 Wire Mother Surrogate and Cloth-Covered Mother Surrogate (Dr. H. F. Harlow).

An experiment was conducted to see which of the two substitute mothers the infant monkeys preferred. Each mother surrogate was placed in a cubicle adjoining the cage in which an infant monkey lived. Half the subjects could get milk, that is,

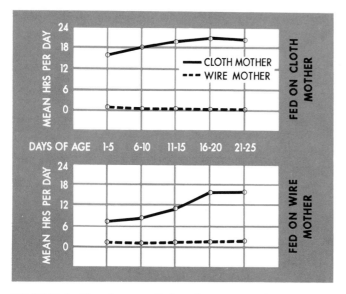

FIGURE 13.6 Time Spent on Cloth and on Wire Mother Surrogates by Infant Monkeys Fed on the Cloth Mother and Infant Monkeys Fed on the Wire Mother (After Harlow, 1958).

be "nursed," only by the cloth mother, whereas the other half could get nourishment only from the wire mother.

If the affectional, or hugging, response depends on secondary reinforcement, we would expect each group of monkeys to learn to hug the "mother" who fed him. If, however, it requires a "mother" who is soft and cuddly, then the infants would choose the cloth mother, regardless of who nursed them. The results support the second alternative. Figure 13.6, the total time in hours spent daily on each of the two mothers, shows that both groups preferred the cloth mother surrogate. Nursing seems to be much less important than contact-comfort in determining the affectional response.

In addition to providing comfort, the cloth mother surrogate serves the important psychological function of providing a haven of safety in time of fear and danger. When a monkey is confronted with a fear-producing stimulus he tends to clutch the soft "mother," regardless of which one had nursed him. When he is placed in a strange environment he rushes to the cloth mother surrogate and hugs her. Afterwards he gathers enough courage to explore the new environment, but returns frequently to the security of his "mother." The infant monkeys behave much less confidently when the cloth mother is absent. They don't explore as much, and they frequently freeze in a crouched position (see Figure 13.8), cry, and give other signs of emotionality.

This study dramatically demonstrates that the motivational system of the infant macaque monkey is not restricted to drives for such obvious biological necessities as nourishment and warmth. He has need for contact-comfort. It is likely that the same need exists among other mammalian infants, including human babies.

Like all good scientific research, Harlow's studies raise many new and important questions. What are the basic sensory qualities underlying this need? You may recall that

462

the tendency of the infant loggerhead turtle to crawl to the sea (see page 246) was based on the positive reinforcing value of light. Do the infant monkeys respond to the softness, to the texture, or to both? Do they avoid the wire mother? How long does this need exist? What experiences, if any, can modify its strength? Harlow reports that monkeys who are separated from their mothers soon after birth and are first exposed to the surrogate mothers when they are 250 days old exhibit behavior similar to the animals raised with the mother surrogates from birth (see Figure 13.6), except that the amount of "affectional" response seems to be less. But obviously more information is needed, especially about human infants, before we fully understand infantile affection.

From the viewpoint of personality development, probably the most important aspect of Harlow's work is the observations on the reactions of the baby monkey in strange and fear-producing situations. Although we do not know exactly how the presence or absence of a comforting mother or mother surrogate in such circumstances influences later personality development, from our knowledge of the psychology of learning, it would seem reasonable to suppose that the influence is great. The infant who can explore strange situations with the help of a comforting mother is learning different habits than the child who is thrust alone and afraid into a new environment. According to Harlow's data, the infant who lacks the support of a mother does not learn to explore his environment, but learns instead to assume frozen postures and to exhibit signs of fear.

You would misinterpret these findings badly if you concluded that a child's interests would be best served by providing him at all times with an abundance of cuddling, affection, and attention. Parents who do this can create severe psychological problems for their children, as did the mother of the eight-year-old boy described

FIGURE 13.7 A Typical Response of an Infant Monkey to a Fear-Producing Stimulus in the Presence of the Cloth Mother Surrogate. The monkey will hug the cloth mother regardless of which of the two mother surrogates he was fed on (Dr. H. F. Harlow).

(Levy, 1943) in the following brief case history:

The mother had excessive contact with the child. She breast fed him much longer than was common (13 months). She tried not to leave him

FIGURE 13.8 A Typical Fear Response of an Infant Monkey in a Strange Environment (Dr. H. F. Harlow).

alone for an instant, and worried if he ever got out of her sight. She sleeps with him at night when he calls her even though he is now eight years of age. When walking in the street she holds his hand. The mother dresses him every day and takes him to and from the school, and also arranges for special lunches. She refuses to let him help in housework for fear he might hurt himself.

The boy has only one friend to whom his mother takes him every two weeks. The mother always gives in to him and does everything for him. She in turn is dominated by him. When mad the boy strikes his mother and sometimes spits at her.

This case illustrates one important feature of what is technically termed **maternal overprotection.** The mother's overprotective behavior did more than amply satisfy this child's need for contact-comfort. It effectively prevented him from developing independence. An analogous condition would arise in Harlow's experiment if the infant monkey were prevented from exploring a strange environment by being restrained in some way by the cloth "mother." In this way an overprotective mother might have the same effect as no mother at all. Both conditions would effectively prevent the child from exploring new situations and thus developing some ability to do things on his own, without timid hesitation or retreat.

Most people who have had at least one brother or sister look back on their relationship with those siblings as one of the most important social influences in their development. In fact, siblings are considered so important that many parents feel it is both unfair and unhealthy for a child to be raised without one. Yet there is no solid evidence to suggest that being an "only child" is a psychological handicap. After all, the effect of "onlyness" depends on how parental behavior is influenced by it. Some parents so overindulge an only child that he develops into an egocentric, con-

ceited, and generally unpopular individual. Other parents, raise an only child with such wise care and concern, that he turns out to be a more mature, courteous, and dependable person than the average child.

Although there is no evidence that an only child suffers from an insurmountable psychological handicap, recent findings do suggest that the order in which a child is born in a family (first, second, third) exerts some influence on his later social behavior. In one experiment (Schachter, 1959), young adults were placed in a stressful situation. It was found that a larger percentage of those who were first-born children showed greater need of social companionship than of those who were second-born and later children. They wanted someone to be near when they faced difficulty. One possible explanation of this finding is that first-borns receive more attention from their parents when they are in trouble. Their parents are inexperienced and insecure and rush to help them whenever they get into difficulty. By the time a second child comes along, the parents have learned that children do not need as much attention as they originally thought. They become more relaxed and respond less quickly—sometimes not at all—to every loud cry from their new baby. Consequently, the younger child is encouraged to learn to cope with problems by himself.

The relationship a child has with his brothers and sisters (80 per cent of American children have siblings) is often a trying one. Although there is no fixed pattern in the development of a sibling relationship, there is usually some degree of **sibling rivalry.** This term has been invented to describe the competitive struggle that develops between siblings for the affection of their parents. One pattern that *sometimes* develops is that the older child, deprived of some of the affection and attention he formerly received from his parents, reacts aggressively toward the "intruder." Because the younger child is weaker and cannot respond in kind, he competes for his parents' affection by being cute and even by inciting his older sibling to get into trouble. If the aggressive behavior of the older child irritates the parents and the cuteness of the younger charms them, the older one may "lose out" to the younger. As a result, the older child may begin to lose self-confidence and to withdraw socially in order to avoid additional defeats.

Sibling rivalry need not lead to such severe consequences. Although there is no sure-fire way of avoiding it, its harmful effects can be minimized. Parents should use the sibling relationship to reinforce cooperation, loyalty, and helpfulness, being careful not to reinforce the behavior of either child if it directly or indirectly harms the other.

Stress in Infancy

Several decades ago it was observed that "gentled" rats—that is, rats which have been stroked and petted—seem to survive surgery better than rats that have not been handled. The gentling experience in some manner prepares the rat's physiological system to cope more effectively with such a stress-provoking situation as surgery.

A clue to the meaning of this finding comes from a number of recent studies showing that brief exposures to mildly stressful situations, during infancy prepares the organism to cope with stressors (stress-provoking agents) later in life. One experimenter (Levine, 1960)—reasoning in a common-sense sort of way—assumed that if rats were given a series of mild electric shocks during infancy they would become more emotional. He used an experimental group which he placed in a shock cage to receive the series of shocks and two control groups to estimate the effects of the shocks. One control group was handled and placed in the shock cage but did not receive any

shocks. The second control group was simply left in their home cages without being handled. When they had grown to adulthood, all three groups of rats were tested in several different ways for signs of behavioral disturbance. In one test, their behavior in a large, unfamiliar box was observed. Unexpectedly, the animals who were not handled at all during infancy (the second control group) showed signs of disturbance. They spent most of their time crouching in the corners or creeping timidly about. They also defecated and urinated more frequently. In marked contrast was the behavior of the other two groups who had been exposed to mild forms of stress (weak shocks or handling). They freely explored the space of the unfamiliar box without showing any persistent signs of emotionality.

How can we explain these results? One possible analysis suggests that exposure to mild stresses early in life prepares the animals to cope with the stressful situations they meet later on, whereas failure to encounter stress in infancy may cause the body to *overreact* to stressors later in life. Overreacting soon depletes the chemical resources (hormones) needed for dealing with the stresses, causing the inexperienced animals to reach the *stage of exhaustion* quickly (see page 431). This hypothesis has received support from experiments (Weininger, 1954) in which differences have been found between the physiological structures (e.g., adrenal glands) of animals handled and those not handled during infancy. This finding may explain why many wild animals in zoos (otters, mink, cheetahs) have died suddenly after being moved from one cage to another or after being exposed to the disturbance of building operations in cages adjoining theirs (Richter, 1959). A similar phenomenon has also been reported with wild pigeons. One investigator developed a special method of weighing birds which required their being immobilized.

466

Not one of the many thousands of tame pigeons showed any ill effect from being weighed this way. In marked contrast three out of five wild pigeons died while they were being put on the scales. Presumably they expired because their response to the stressful situation was hyperactive, one condition of such a response probably being adrenal exhaustion.

We have to take two precautions in interpreting these results. First, we must not conclude that any and every amount of stress during infancy will have a healthy effect upon the organism's future capacity to adjust. This is obviously not true, since some investigations have shown that meeting situations in infancy that are too stressful *increases* later emotionality. We still have to discover what are the optimal amounts of stress in infancy for the development of adaptive reactions to stress in later life. No doubt many variables will be found to influence this. It has already been shown that the exact age of the animal at the time of early stressful experiences is an important factor; the advantages of having been handled fail to show up when the handling took place either before or after a certain age. Other variables sure to be found important are the species of animal used as subjects and the type of stressful situation (shock, handling, immersion in cold water, etc.).

The second precaution we must take is not to infer that mild stressful experiences in infancy are advantageous because they encourage organisms to react to stressors in a more relaxed manner. Reacting this way can be as maladaptive as overreacting. The adult animal that has been exposed to an appropriate amount of stress during infancy responds to a stressor efficiently for he is able to mobilize his chemical resources quickly to cope with the stressor. An inexperienced animal responds more slowly but then reaches his stage of exhaustion rapidly.

CHILD TRAINING AND PERSONALITY

Our discussion of how personality may be molded by events that occur during the critical stages of development leads directly into one of the most widely discussed topics —child-rearing practices. Lord Chesterfield is reputed to have said, "Before I got married I had six theories of bringing up children; now I have six children and no theories." In spite of the failures of his theories—and those of many others—the persistent search for *the* proper method of raising children goes on. Books that espouse specific child-rearing practices pour from the presses. Almost all of them are based on the commonly accepted premise that a single proper method does, in fact, exist, and our task is simply to discover it.

Fortunately or not, the problem that faces parents and all of us who are responsible for training children is not that simple. For one thing, and this is a basic point which is frequently overlooked in discussions of child raising, we have to decide what we should set as our goals in child rearing. What kind of adults do we want our children to become? What responses should we train them to acquire? Should boys be trained to fight when they are pushed around, or should they be taught to avoid physical violence? Many boys in America are taught to defend their rights as soon as they are threatened, but American-Chinese children raised in the traditional ways of their ancestors are taught that the person who strikes the first blow is weak because he resorts to violence when words fail him. Should children be trained to seek material possessions and to aspire to careers associated with high social prestige? Most American children are now taught this. But not all. Typically, children of certain American Indian tribes are taught to ignore wealth and position and are encouraged to respect generosity, sagacity, and loyalty. Obviously, then, some disagreement exists about what are desirable personality characteristics.

What does all this mean? It means two things: First, the effectiveness of any child-rearing method must be judged against some approved set of personality characteristics. In order to judge a method, you must have a clear idea of the kind of personality you want to develop. Second, the selection of desirable personality traits is, in a certain sense, a matter of personal taste. In America, opinion differs widely as to the most desirable amounts of such traits as competitiveness, sociability, dominance, independence, and social conformity in the total personality. It is not the responsibility of the psychologist to decide on the qualifications of the ideal personality but a task for the entire society. The psychologist can, however, serve an important function by suggesting the best methods for training children. He can also be helpful in describing the full consequences of training children to certain approved modes of behavior; he can point out that other forms of behavior are likely to be produced along with the approved ones. When this is true, it is very important to point it out, for societies often approve one form of behavior while disapproving another highly correlated with it. For example, in our society we encourage competition, but we do not wish to encourage it so much that it leads to dishonest and vicious practices, as it can. We must decide how much competition, whether in sports or in business, we wish to encourage. The psychologist can do much by showing how competition can produce undesirable behavior. But in the last analysis, society in general, and parents in particular, must decide what behavior is desirable.

The point we wish to make, which admittedly has strong philosophical overtones, can be elucidated by a simple experimental analogue. Suppose we had a Skinner box whose bar could be pressed either up or down, right or left. If we were interested in training a rat to make only one of these four possible responses, we would provide reinforcement only when the rat made that particular response. If we wanted the rat to make one response persistently in the absence of reinforcement, we would train him under an intermittent reinforcement schedule. And if for some reason we wanted the rat to respond at an increasingly faster rate, we would place him on a fixed-interval reinforcement schedule. Similarly, for any other forms of behavior we wanted the rat to exhibit, we would alter our training methods appropriately. In the very same manner, although it is obviously a more complex process, the psychologist can offer advice on shaping personality. But he can only do it once the decision is made about the kinds of behavior which are to be encouraged.

It should now be clear that a discussion of child-training methods cannot simply be reduced to a listing of do's and don'ts. Any such lists depend upon an agreement as to what constitutes desirable behavior.

One reason that many child-training specialists espouse a single method is that they commonly believe an invariant and unmodifiable relationship exists between a specific experience and a particular kind of personality. For example, a child psychoanalyst (Ribble, 1943) once maintained that a mother was risking the future psychological health of her baby if she failed to breast feed him. Other child psychiatrists and pediatricians claim, not quite so dramatically, that breast feeding is preferable because it permits intimate physical contact between the mother and child and thus cements the love relationship. Yet when all the data from various studies on breast versus bottle feeding are evaluated, one is forced to conclude that *"there are as yet no demonstrably consistent effects on later behavior of breast versus bottle feeding in infancy"* (Sears, Maccoby, & Levin, 1957, p. 100). This conclusion is not surprising considering that breast and bottle feeding operate in conjunction with many other variables not exclusively associated with only one of the two feeding practices. Many children who are bottle fed are as warmly caressed during feeding as any breast-fed infant. Both kinds of feeding may at times frustrate the need for nourishment, for a mother's milk may, like a formula, be nutritionally inadequate. Individual circumstances can also influence each feeding practice. A mother who breast feeds her infant on the advice of her pediatrician in spite of her personal aversion to it may frustrate the child by terminating many feeding sessions before he is satiated. The feeding experience of the same child would have been more satisfying if the mother had obeyed her own feelings instead of attempting to overcome them.

What has been said about the effects of breast and bottle feeding can be applied with equal validity to other training procedures. There do not seem to be single proper training methods simply because all training experiences involve a constellation of variables. Therefore, the assumption that an individual's personality structure is formed by certain specific childhood experiences, although attractive in its simplicity, must be rejected on the evidence. The more reasonable assumption, favored by Dollard and Miller and other specialists in the psychology of learning, is that as a child develops, his personality is shaped by numerous experiences in a variety of situations. Some experiences are very influential, others may exert little or no effect. Although the critical training situations we have reviewed usually have important effects on personality, other situations may for some individuals have even more important effects. Moreover, personality is often formed by a slow, gradual accumulation of experiences in many kinds of situations. For example, in our society, parents are taught to think of their children first. As a result, children very often grow up thinking of themselves first. This extreme egocentricity, which interferes with adequate social adjustment later on, is not typically a result of a few critical training experiences, but of gradual development over the years.

THE MEASUREMENT OF PERSONALITY

It is clear that an individual's personality is not revealed by any single characteristic like facial expression, or the way he talks, walks, or dances. Personality is multidimensional. To obtain an adequate picture of an individual's personality, we must make many different kinds of observations of his behavior.

There are almost 18,000 words in English that refer to characteristics that may appear in people's behavior, words such as *dominating, courageous, affectionate,* and *alert.* Psychologists do not require 18,000 dimensions along which to describe personality. They do, however, need a good many. They find it necessary to break personality down into more basic components—what we will call **personality characteristics.** For example, to be highly dominant in many situations may be characteristic of one person. Whether he is at home, in the office, or with his friends, he tends to dictate, to assume leadership over, to try to control the behavior of the group. He tries to be the one who makes the major decisions. Another person may behave in just the opposite manner. His dominance level is low and he tends to be submissive, easy-going, passive.

The job of understanding an individual's personality does not end with the discovery of a number of its basic characteristics. The question of how they interreact still remains. Two people can be equally aggressive, and yet differ markedly in their behavior. The manner in which the aggression expresses itself will be influenced by other personality characteristics. A timid child may express his aggression by slyly damaging his enemy's bicycle, whereas an equally aggressive, but fearless child would step up and punch his enemy on the nose. In order to deal with the problem of describing the various characteristics and how they interact, the concept of **personality structure** has been devised. It refers to the way personality characteristics are organized and how the pattern is revealed in behavior.

Now that some of the major problems of personality assessment have been mentioned, we shall describe several methods of observing and measuring personality.

Interview Method

Perhaps the most widely used method of assessing an individual's personality is to interview him and ask him a number of questions.

The interview method as normally practiced has severe limitations. It is not very reliable. Two interviewers interviewing the same set of applicants for a job often come up with widely different recommendations. There are many reasons for this. They may be asking different questions, and therefore basing their judgment on different information. But even when they are asking the same questions, interviewers get different answers. One interviewer may gain the confidence of an applicant and encourage him to respond frankly; another interviewer may put the same applicant on his guard. Moreover, interviewers may reach different conclusions when they are confronted with essentially the same information, since the responses from an interview do not automatically provide a clear-cut description of the personality

characteristics of an individual. The results of an interview must be interpreted before recommendations can be made. Personal judgments enter interpretation, and constitute another source of unreliability.

From what we have said it may appear that the interview method is of little value in assessing personality. This is not really true. Improved techniques of interviewing have been developed that increase its reliability. Interviews can be conducted according to a preconceived plan so that all pertinent information is collected. Interviewers can also be trained to be adept at making the interviewee feel at ease and thereby increase their chances of obtaining honest responses. But one great shortcoming tends to remain in the standard interview. It typically results in a general, or global, impression of the interviewee. In order to overcome this limitation interviewers are sometimes required to translate their general impressions into quantitative ratings.

Rating Scales

A quantitative scale that permits judgment of the relative amount of some behavioral characteristic is known as a **rating scale.** Such scales are often used in personality assessment. A simple example of one, which seeks to evaluate a person's ability to cooperate with others, follows.

The person making the rating would estimate another individual's degree of co-

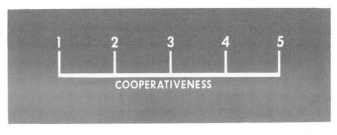

FIGURE 13.9 A Numerical Rating Scale. The rater checks the point on the dimension of cooperativeness which best describes the behavior of the person being judged.

operativeness, using 1 to represent the lowest amount, 5 to represent the highest amount, and 3 to represent the midpoint. In order to understand the rating process, the reader might try to evaluate his acquaintances with a scale of this sort.

The task of rating is made easier and more reliable if the behavior associated with various points of the scale is described. Figure 13.10 shows how the same rating scale is improved by descriptive statements added at the midpoint and two extreme points. The more informative these descriptions are, the greater the agreement among different raters.

Rating scales become more dependable when the judgments of several raters are averaged. For example, when a single army officer attempted to judge the intelligence of his fellow officers, the correlation be-

tween his judgments and their scores on an intelligence test was low. But when the rating of *several* judges were averaged, the correlation increased markedly. In short, the pooled (averaged) ratings were more *valid* than the judgments of an individual rater, since their correlation with the criterion (intelligence test scores) was higher. **Validity,** then, refers to the ability of a scale to measure what it intends to measure. Typically a scale's validity is measured by how well it correlates with some criterion.

Because rating scales usually consist of several items, each of which is designed to measure a certain facet of an individual's personality, ratings in some characteristics tend to be influenced by ratings in others. This error that can creep into ratings is called the **halo effect.** For example, a pretty girl with lots of charm might get higher ratings in personality characteristics than she deserves because of the "halo effect" produced by her good looks and charming manner. Similarly a person whose speech habits struck the rater unfavorably might receive unjustifiably low ratings in conscientiousness and dependability. The halo effect can be reduced if the rater is trained to judge each personality characteristic independently.

How good are rating scales? They do have many virtues, not the least of which is their adaptability to practically any situation. They are easily constructed and ratings, such as they are, are not difficult to assign. One cannot, however, assume that ratings automatically produce reliable and valid results. The proper evaluation of any rating scale requires that its worth be demonstrated objectively. In the Air Force rating scales where shown to be useful in selecting good teachers, but a demonstration that one rating scale works well does not mean that other rating scales work equally well. All in all, however, rating scales, when used with care, have shown their use as instruments for evaluating personalities and predicting future behavior.

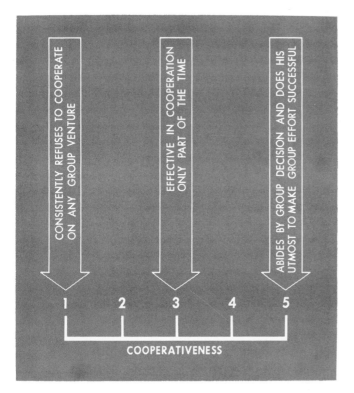

FIGURE 13.10 A Descriptive Rating Scale Similar to the Numerical Rating Scale in Figure 13.9. Descriptions of behavior associated with the two extreme points and the midpoint have been added.

Personality Inventory

Although rating scales have many advantages, they have the limitation of being dependent upon subjective scoring judgments. Scientists of all kinds strive to measure the phenomena they study as objectively as possible. Hence, personality measurements based on data observable to all and free from the contamination of personal interpretation are obviously to be preferred to subjective judgments. In an attempt to reduce the subjectivity inherent in interviews and rating scales, psychologists have designed a sort of formalized interview which at least introduces objectivity in scoring. This technique, known as the **personality inventory,** is essentially a questionnaire to which an individual responds by supplying information about various facets of his own behavior.

Robert S. Woodworth, a noted experimental psychologist at Columbia University, developed one of the first personality inventories during World War I (Woodworth, 1919). At that time a need was felt for an efficient instrument which could detect individuals who would crack under the stress of army life and combat. With the collaboration of other psychologists, Woodworth formulated 116 questions about possible personality difficulties. Some of them are:

1. Do you make friends easily?
2. Did you have a happy childhood?
3. Do you ever feel an awful pressure in or about your head?
4. Do you feel like jumping off when you are on high places?

From the psychological point of view each question has a favorable or an unfavorable answer. A "no" to the first two questions or a "yes" response to the last two is considered unfavorable, since it suggests the presence of a symptom often exhibited by psychologically disturbed individuals. Social aloofness (question 1), developmental difficulties (question 2), bodily complaints (question 3), and obsessive ideas (question 4) may be symptoms of behavior problems. One unfavorable answer by itself, however, would certainly not indicate a personality disorder. The answers to all the questions must be considered before any conclusions can be drawn. The score on the inventory is computed by counting the number of unfavorable responses. One study revealed that a group of psychologically healthy individuals gave an average of ten unfavorable answers, whereas the score of a group of persons suffering from personality difficulties averaged 36. Such a finding indicates that the questionnaire has some validity because it can discriminate between psychologically disturbed and healthy individuals. In World War I it proved useful in weeding out for closer examination many soldiers who were later diagnosed as suffering from some personality disorder.

This inventory has, however, one severe limitation. Anyone can see which are the "good" answers and which the "bad." A man who wanted to avoid being drafted into the armed services could deliberately "roll up" a very unfavorable score. Similarly, a psychologically disturbed person, required to complete a similar questionnaire for a job, would have no difficulty faking a favorable score. In short, this inventory, and others like it, are transparent; those who for one reason or another wish to avoid answering truthfully can lie with ease.

Many tests attempting to overcome this shortcoming have been devised, but one of the most successful is the Minnesota Multiphasic Personality Inventory (Hathaway & McKinley, 1943), commonly referred to by its initials, MMPI. In addition to providing scores on several personality characteristics, the inventory is so devised that it supplies clues on whether the score a

472 person obtains is intentionally or otherwise distorted.

The inventory consists of 550 statements, each printed on a card which the respondent must place in one of three categories: "True," "False," or "Cannot Say." Typical items are, "I am entirely self-confident," "I tire easily," and "One should never trust even his friends too much."

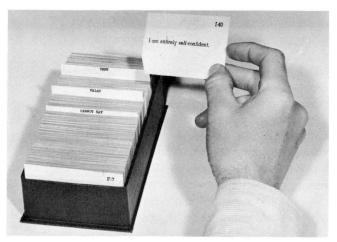

FIGURE 13.11 The Minnesota Multiphasic Personality Inventory (MMPI). The subject is required to sort each statement in the *True, False,* or *Cannot Say* categories. The subject in the photograph is deciding on the category in which he should place the statement, "I am entirely self-confident" (N. L. Munn. *Psychology.* [4th ed.] Boston: Houghton Mifflin, 1961).

Among the 550 items are several which ask the same questions in different ways and afford a check on how consistently the the subject is responding. Inconsistent responses may indicate carelessness, failure to take the test seriously or deliberate lying. Other items are designed to identify subjects who falsify their answers out of a desire to make a good impression. "I sometimes put off until tomorrow what I should do today" is a statement that applies to practically everyone. If a person classifies that and similar statements as false, the scorer concludes that the respondent is trying to create a favorable impression. Consequently the score he obtains on the entire inventory is discounted. The scoring

of the inventory contains several other checks—on ability to understand the questions, for example. As a result the expert who interprets the scores is provided with several clues to help him decide whether the inventory for a particular person constitutes a valid picture of his personality.

The MMPI is decidedly psychiatric in orientation. It was designed, in the first place, to discriminate between persons who suffer from somewhat severe psychological disturbances (psychiatric patients) and those who do not (normals). But as you will learn, there is no sharp dividing line between the two; much of the behavior of disturbed individuals is an exaggerated form of the behavior of normal people. For example, many normal individuals are suspicious, but the *paranoid* patient suffers from extreme suspiciousness. His suspiciousness is pathological. The continuity between normal and pathological behavior is also demonstrated by the scores obtained on the MMPI. Disturbed subjects obtain more extreme scores than normals, but if the scores from both groups are placed in the same frequency distribution (see page 62), they will be found to range continuously from high to low with no gap between the scores of the normals and disturbed persons.

The MMPI measures nine characteristics or dimensions of personality; its 550 statements are organized into nine subtests, each of which is commonly called a *scale.* A brief and superficial description of each scale runs as follows:

1. *Hypochondriasis*—exaggerated concern with bodily health.
2. *Depression*—tendency to despondency.
3. *Hysteria*—physical disabilities in the absence of justifying physiological causes (e.g., inability to move a limb without any detectable neurological or other pathology).
4. *Psychopathic Deviation*—disregard for ethical standards of conduct.

5. *Masculinity-Femininity*—behavior characteristic of men or of women.
6. *Paranoia*—extreme suspiciousness.
7. *Psychasthenia*—obsessive (recurring irrational thoughts) and compulsive (performing apparently meaningless acts) behavior.
8. *Schizophrenia*—pathological withdrawal from social contacts, eccentricities of thinking and manner.
9. *Hypomania*—excessive elation and excitement.

These terms, at their strongest, describe the top extremes that can be reached on each personality scale. A high score on the hypochondriasis scale indicates extreme and unwarranted concern for one's health. An average score indicates, however, that a person is behaving like most other people. He is neither indifferent to his health, nor is he overconcerned about it.

The scores on each of the nine scales are based upon the responses to that portion of the 550 items relevant to that particular scale. An individual who gets a high or abnormal score on a particular scale, as compared to one who obtains an average score, has responded to more of the relevant questions in a manner indicating the presence of that particular personality characteristic. Like any personality inventory, the response to *one item* by itself is not of great importance. People with average scores often make the same responses to several items as a person who obtains an abnormal score. It is the *sum* of the responses to *all* of the relevant items that determines the score on a particular scale.

The items in each scale were selected to insure the scale's validity. For example, the scale measuring schizophrenia was constructed so that people institutionalized with that disorder would obtain much higher scores than normals. All the scales were constructed on essentially the same principle: to discriminate between groups

which do and do not exhibit that particular personality characteristic to a pathological degree. Figure 13.12 is a graph showing the average scores obtained by one group of normal persons and two different psychiatric groups. A similar graph constructed to represent an individual's test performance is called a personality

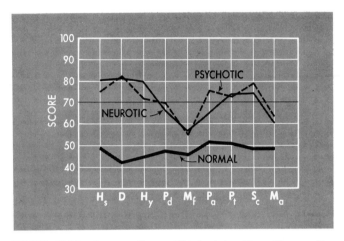

FIGURE 13.12 Average Scores Obtained by Three Groups, Two Psychiatric and One Normal, on the Minnesota Multiphasic Personality Inventory. The symbols below the graph represent the nine scales of the MMPI: H_s (Hypochondriasis), D (Depression), H_y (Hysteria), P_d (Psychopathic Deviation), M_f (Masculinity-Feminity), P_a (Paranoia), P_t (Psychasthenia), S_c (Schizophrenia), and M_a (Hypomania). Scores above 70 are abnormal (After Schmidt, 1945).

profile. It indicates in outline a profile, or pattern, of the particular characteristics of his behavior.

Another well-known personality inventory is the Allport-Vernon-Lindzey Study of Values (1960). It explores certain facets of a person's motivational system by measuring the strength of his interests in the following six areas: theoretical, economic, aesthetic, social, political, and religious.

The first part of the questionnaire consists of a series of statements, to each of which the subject must give a "yes" or "no" answer. Examples are:

Are our modern industrial and scientific developments signs of a greater degree of civilization than those attained by any previous society, the Greeks, for example?

The main object of scientific research should be the discovery of pure truth rather than its practical application.

An affirmative answer to the first question contributes a point to one's score on economic values, whereas a negative response adds a point to the score for aesthetic values. One's reaction to the second statement is relevant to both his theoretical and his economic scores, with a "yes" answer indicating theoretical interests and a "no" response suggesting an economic orientation.

In the second part of the inventory the subject must answer multiple-choice questions like the following:

Do you think that a good government should aim chiefly at——

a. More aid for the poor, sick, and old?
b. The development of manufacturing and trade?

c. Introducing more ethical principles into its policies and diplomacy?
d. Establishing a position of prestige and respect among nations?

The subject is required to rank these four alternatives in order of his agreement with them, from high to low. You should be able to figure out which of the six values is indicated by a high rank on each of these alternatives.

As in the MMPI, a profile can be made of a person's scores on the Allport-Vernon-Lindzey Inventory. Figure 13.13 reproduces an example.

The validity of the Allport-Vernon-Lindzey Inventory has been demonstrated by its ability to differentiate between different professional groups. Students of business administration obtain significantly different profiles than students of law or theology. Results of such a questionnaire are, therefore, useful in guiding a student in selecting a career. A boy who is thinking of going into business, for example, should seriously consider other career alternatives if he gets low economic scores.

A very large number of personality inventories have been constructed, too many to describe here. We will attempt only to acquaint the reader with the purpose and basic principles of these personality measures.

Frequently newspapers or magazines run what they call personality inventories which consist of a very few items, a catchy heading, and a simple method of scoring. These cannot be taken seriously. They have been concocted out of the blue to amuse readers. If a personality inventory is to be useful the scores obtained on it must be shown to be related to something outside themselves, to some criterion that is a guarantee of the inventory's significance, its validity. For example, people known by other techniques to be psychologically disturbed have been shown to respond differently than normal people to

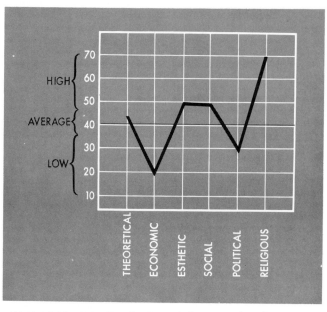

FIGURE 13.13 A Profile of a Person's Scores on the Allport-Vernon-Lindzey Study of Values.

the MMPI; members of different professions obtain significant and different profiles on the Allport-Vernon-Lindzey Inventory. But the score obtained on a magazine's personality inventory is typically not related to anything else; its factual meaning (see page 11) is unknown. Thus, a high submissive score on a typical magazine personality inventory reveals nothing more than a high score on an inventory which was constructed and scored in a purely arbitrary way, by guesswork. One cannot justifiably generalize from the subject's behavior on the inventory to his behavior in other situations. Such a score on scientifically constructed and validated personality inventories might, on the other hand, be quite significant. It could be compared with scores obtained by other people and interpreted in terms of how the responses on the inventory are related to behavior in other situations.

The Concept of Trait

An extremely important and useful concept has emerged from the research of personality inventories and rating scales, the concept of **trait.** A trait may be defined as some persisting characteristic of personality which, in principle at least, can be measured.

Literally hundreds of traits have been distinguished in the large number of rating scales and personality inventories now in use. And the one persistent question psychologists ask themselves is, Are all these traits needed for an adequate description of personality? In an attempt to answer this question a group of psychologists well versed in statistical techniques have sought to identify what they call **primary traits.** Their interest is in traits which are relatively *independent* of each other. Let us see what they mean by this.

Many different traits have been found to correlate with each other. If the scores obtained by the same group of subjects on

two different trait scales should correlate perfectly (produce coefficients of correlation of $+1.00$ or -1.00), the scales would obviously be measuring the same personality characteristic, even though different trait names had been originally assigned to them. There would be no sense in continuing to use two such scales, since one could do the work of both.

Although in practice perfect correlations between different tests never occur, highly significant positive (or negative) correlations do. For example, the traits *aggressiveness* and *assertiveness* correlate highly with each other. We must conclude, therefore, that to a considerable extent they measure the same personality characteristic, the degree of their similarity indicated by the size of the coefficient of correlation.

A rather complicated statistical technique known as **factor analysis** has been used to isolate primary traits. To explain the principle underlying this technique, let us consider the following hypothetical situation. Suppose we have a personality inventory measuring seven different traits: *A, B, C, D, E, F,* and *G.* This inventory is taken by a large number of subjects and the correlations between each trait and every other trait computed. The results indicate that traits *A, B,* and *C* correlate highly among themselves, but have little or no correlation with the remaining four traits, which in turn are highly correlated with each other. It would seem that there is a common factor underlying each set of intercorrelated traits. We would have to conclude that our inventory, instead of consisting, as it appeared to, of seven different traits, actually measures only two *primary* traits.

Factor analysis has been applied to several investigations of personality. In one early, important study (Cattell, 1946) 172 traits were finally reduced to 12 primary traits. That is, only 12 dimensions of personality were required to describe an individual's pattern of behavior. In Table

13.1 you will see that each of the 12 dimensions is described by opposed qualities which represent the two extremes of each. However, the terms describing qualities which are given in the list provide at best only a general impression of one of these primary traits. In order to gain a more meaningful and precise understanding of a trait, you must examine the test items.

One might suppose that the discovery of a set of primary personality traits would solve the problem of personality measurement. Unfortunately, the problem is not that simple. The composition of any set of primary factors is dependent on the specific personality inventories, rating scales, and interviews used, as well as on the sample of people who provide the raw data upon which the factor analysis is based. In short, an entirely different set of primary traits can be arrived at if different measures of behavior and different samples of subjects are used in the first place. And this is exactly what has happened when other investigators have tried to consolidate behavior into primary personality traits. One factor analysis of self-inventories (Thurstone, 1947) reported seven primary traits. Translated into adjectives they are *friendly, emotionally stable, reflective, impulsive, active, ascendant,* and *masculine.* Another investigator (Guilford, 1957) concluded that there were 14 primary personality traits.

The fact that different studies produce varying sets of primary traits does not invalidate the factor analytical techniques, nor does it suggest that one set of basic traits is as good as any other. We must remember that although primary traits are obtained to provide a reliable and efficient method of measuring personality, measuring personality is not an end in itself. You will recall (see page 11) that the scientist is interested in establishing factual meaning, that is, in discovering how one concept is related to another. Hence, the

TABLE 13.1 A Set of Primary Traits of Personality Resulting from Factor Analysis (Adapted from Cattell, 1946).

1. CYCLOTHYMIA emotionally expressive	*vs.*	SCHIZOTHYMIA withdrawn
2. INTELLEC- TUALLY EFFICIENT intelligent painstaking	*vs.*	INTELLEC- TUALLY DEFICIENT stupid slipshod
3. EMOTIONALLY STABLE realistic calm	*vs.*	EMOTIONALLY UNSTABLE unrealistic excitable
4. DOMINANCE assertive aggressive	*vs.*	SUBMISSIVENESS complaisant gentle
5. SURGENCY joyous cheerful sociable	*vs.*	DESURGENCY unhappy depressed aloof
6. SENSITIVE idealistic grateful	*vs.*	TOUGH cynical thankless

7. SOCIALIZED
poised
socially
  sensitive
	vs.	BOORISH
		awkward
		socially
		  insensitive

8. MATURE loyal persevering	*vs.*	IMMATURE irresponsible fickle
9. COOPERATIVE genial frank	*vs.*	OBSTRUCTIVE secretive withdrawn
10. MEEK weak unrealistic	*vs.*	FORCEFUL assertive practical
11. HYPERSENSITIVE self-pitying demanding	*vs.*	FRUSTRATION TOLERANT adjusting calm
12. FRIENDLY enthusiastic trustful	*vs.*	HOSTILE suspicious jealous

psychologist's ultimate aim in studying traits is to discover how they develop and how they influence behavior. It would be both interesting and important to be able to answer such questions as: Can the behavior of children be analyzed in terms of the same set of primary traits that apply to adults? Do the primary traits of adults emerge from a smaller set of traits in children? Does the same set of primary traits found in one culture exist in other cultures? How are primary traits influenced by hereditary factors? In what situations can we predict a person's behavior, knowing his scores on a test of primary traits?

We could list many others, but our purpose is not to cover all the important questions involving primary personality traits, but to direct your attention to the problem of evaluating a given set of primary traits. Up to now psychologists using factor analysis have concentrated on analyzing behavior into basic components to make the problems of measurement and research easier. Their efforts have been fruitful, but the ultimate worth of their analyses will depend on whether they can be used to gather and order the facts of behavior.

Projective Techniques

A different approach to personality measurement is that embodied in the use of the **projective techniques.** Rating scales and personality inventories, with the help of factor analysis, are attempts to analyze the global concept of personality into basic and more manageable units. To use an analogy, the concept primary trait resembles somewhat the concept basic chemical element, and just as a chemical compound can be broken down into its elements, a personality can be analyzed into its component traits. But the question has been raised, particularly by clinical psychologists, whether in the process of dissecting

personality into basic traits the overall organization of the traits has not been ignored.

The projective techniques have been developed for precisely that purpose, to get at the fundamental organization of personality. There are many such techniques, but they all possess a common feature: they present the subject with a relatively complex pattern of stimuli and permit a wide variety of different responses. The basic assumption is that the subject reveals his personality in the particular responses he makes.

The Rorschach Test. The Rorschach test, named after the Swiss psychiatrist who invented it (Rorschach, 1942), consists of ten inkblots. Rorschach selected these ten after extensive tryouts from many hundreds, because he believed that they were particularly helpful in uncovering important features of an individual's personality.

An example of an inkblot similar to those used in the Rorschach test is shown in Figure 13.14. It is just an inkblot, but if you are asked, "What do you see?" you will be able to find in it a likeness of something. One subject's response was, "Two clowns dancing on beach balls." He then turned the inkblot around and reported, "Two women gossiping and their neighbors throwing stones down at them." A nine-year-old boy did not perceive anything until he turned the inkblot upside down. He then saw "Two eyes with a moustache." An adult woman, who ignored the circular blots at the bottom perceived "Two elves sticking their tongues out at each other."

The subject is encouraged to perceive as many things as he can. His percepts do not have to involve the entire inkblot. He can respond to one part of it, as the woman who saw the two elves did. A response to another part would be "Two balloons floating in air." The subject can even respond to a small portion of the outline

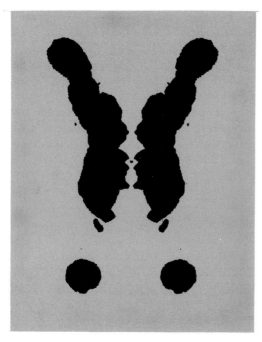

FIGURE 13.14 An Inkblot Similar to Those Used in the Rorschach Test.

("A woman's face") or to the shading ("An X-ray of the chest").

To score and interpret a Rorschach test record is exceedingly complicated and certainly no task for an amateur. Typically the person who administers the test has had extensive training and experience with it. At the outset, he analyzes a Rorschach test record by scoring each response in terms of four features:

1. LOCATION: Is this subject's response based on the entire inkblot, a large portion, a small detail, or on the white spaces?
2. DETERMINANT: Is the subject's percept suggested by the form, color (half the inkblots are colored), texture, or shading of the inkblot? Does the subject perceive movement in progress (e.g., two clowns dancing)?
3. CONTENT: What is perceived? An animal, human being, inanimate object, etc.?

4. ORIGINALITY: Is the percept an unusual one, or is it one many subjects make?

These scoring categories are said to reveal important characteristics of an individual's personality. For example, the perception of the blot as a whole suggests an ability to organize and think abstractly; the tendency to respond to small details, an overconcern with trivial matters. The perception of movement indicates a capacity for fantasy and creativeness, reaction to color is a sign of emotional behavior, and a large number of common responses (the same as those given by other subjects) suggests social conformity.

None of these four categories should be interpreted singly, however; each must be considered in relation to the others. For example, how the psychologist interprets the record of a subject whose response is frequently to the entire inkblot (whole responses) will also depend on the *quality* of the subject's responses. If he perceives all of the blots as different examples of birds and insects, he may simply have a low intelligence. A bright and imaginative person would be likely to give a number of whole responses of much higher quality. They would be more original, more closely related to the actual form of the inkblot, and probably involve more movement. The number of whole responses by itself has limited diagnostic meaning.

It is not surprising that the interpretation of a Rorschach record has been compared to the diagnosis of a confusing medical case. The physician must synthesize a great deal of information (symptoms, history, laboratory tests, etc.) to arrive at his diagnosis, and there are no set rules to help him. The same is true of a Rorschach record. The various measures have to be integrated and interpreted in the absence of any strict set of rules.

Customarily the interpretations of a Rorschach record are expressed not in a concise technical or statistical manner, but in rich descriptive prose. A small excerpt from one lengthy interpretation follows:

Although subject gives signs that he is of superior intelligence, he distorts his content much, on a personal basis. In this he evidences a self-centered kind of judgment. He is creative but does not adequately guide this activity by realistic thinking—an imbalance of ominous possibility. He suffers from inferiority feelings and from anxious moods. A potentially good psychic equipment is burning itself out wastefully (Beck, 1945, pp. 316-317).

How valuable is the Rorschach test? Those who are skilled in the test claim that it is a highly useful and revealing test of personality. They have not, however, succeeded in convincing all psychologists for two main reasons. First, the Rorschach test is not highly reliable. Different testers, confronted with the same set of responses, often arrive at different descriptions of the subject's personality. Obviously, in psychology as in the other sciences, we must expect and require that our measuring instruments be independent of the personal opinions of the measurer. Second, the research cited to support the validity of the Rorschach test often has not been at the level of the soundest and most rigorous psychological investigations (Cronbach, 1949). One reason for its deficiencies is that much of this research has been done in clinical situations where it is difficult and often impossible to control all the variables. But in spite of these objections, we do not mean to completely discount the Rorschach test. It is commonly accepted as a useful instrument in diagnosing psychiatric patients. We may hope that its present limitations will be overcome by continued research and, especially, by efforts to improve its reliability.

The Thematic Apperception Test (TAT). Another projective test that makes use of fantasy behavior is the *Thematic Apperception Test* (see page 185). The most widely used form of the test consists of 20 pictures (Murray, 1938), each representing a different situation (see Figure 8.2 on page 185). The subject is instructed to invent a story based on each picture, including an account of the events that led up to the scene in the picture, an interpretation of the present situation, and of its ultimate outcome. The name, Thematic Apperception Test, was chosen because it indicates that the test usually reveals certain basic *themes* which recur in a subject's stories because he *perceives* events most readily in a way characteristic of him.

The scoring and interpretation of the TAT, like the Rorschach, is not simple. Often the first step in interpretation is to discover which character in a story comes closest to representing the subject himself. The examiner then tries to understand the needs of this character by analyzing the role he plays in the story. According to Murray, the creator of the TAT, these needs represent states of tension which exist as long as some motive remains unsatisfied. Consider a simple example of how such an interpretation is made.

One picture shows two men, one apparently young, the other older. A common reaction to the picture is that it is a scene involving a conversation between a father and his son. A young man telling such a story will usually "identify" with the young man. A story in which the father solves a problem for his boy can be interpreted as revealing the subject's need for help, his need to be dependent on someone stronger or more competent. However, a story in which the son makes his own decision may reveal that the storyteller is more self-assured and prefers to work things out by himself.

The final interpretation of the subject's personality is based on his responses to the entire set of pictures. A conclusion that an individual has a strong dependency need, or any other, is justified only if related themes appear repeatedly.

The usefulness of the TAT, like any other personality test, is judged by how closely individuals' reactions to the test relate to the behavior they exhibit in other situations. The two following studies (McClelland, Atkinson, Clark, & Lowell, 1953) illustrate the ability of TAT scores to predict behavior.

In the first experiment a student was placed in a group whose members were secretly instructed to disagree with him deliberately and insistently in an attempt to change his opinion. The examiners found that a subject's performance on the TAT enabled them to predict his ability to resist group pressure of this kind. Those who had given dependency-revealing themes to the pictures were more likely to be pressured into agreement.

In the second study, a test similar to the TAT was used to evaluate the strength of student subjects' *need to achieve*. Subjects were shown pictures including one of a boy in a classroom sitting with his head in his hand over some open books on his desk. Responses to this picture and the others were scored in terms of how strongly they reflected the individual's drive to achieve. Here are two sample responses to the picture described:

STORY A

A student in a classroom is listening to a teacher explain the contents of a book which lies before the student. He is very interested in the subject. He passed through all preceding school years, and is an intelligent boy. He entered the classroom with his fellows and now is listening to the teacher. He is trying to understand the subject which is new to him. The teacher also is trying his best to make the students understand. The student will understand the subject and will go out of the class, happy about his success about grasping it. He will be a success in life (McClelland *et al.,* 1953, p. 357).

STORY B

This has all the markings of an examination, but the presence of the opened book suggests otherwise. The boy is about 16, and is having difficulty in following the instructions of the teacher. The boy hasn't been too punctual in his home assignments. He is tired. It is about 11:17 A.M. He is hungry. He is thinking about spring and all its manifestations. He wants to get the class over with. He is bored. The subject is dry, disinteresting. The class will finally end. The students will close their books and get out of here as fast as possible (McClelland *et al.*, 1953, pp. 358-359).

Which of these two stories reflects a stronger achievement motive? Definitely Story *A* does. Measuring the strength of the achievement drive by this method has proven to be quite reliable. The agreement among different scorers is high.

The measurement of the achievement motive correlates with other relevant measures of performance and is therefore valid (Henry & Farley, 1959). Students obtaining high achievement scores have been shown to be more persistent in laboratory tests involving sustained effort. High-achievement subjects work harder at solving anagrams and are more productive than low-achievement subjects. High achievers also come from families where achievement is encouraged.

The obvious usefulness of the TAT type of test in measuring the achievement drive suggests that perhaps this kind of test can measure other drives as well. But as with all measuring instruments, this ability cannot be taken on faith. It must first be demonstrated.

Sentence Completion Test. This is a form of projective technique which requires the subject to complete such sentences as:

I like . . . .
My greatest fear . . . .
I wish . . . .
My father . . . .

These items are selected from one (Rotter & Rafferty, 1950) of several different sentence completion tests which were designed to uncover the significant features of an individual's personality in a simple and convenient manner. To increase the reliability of this test, a scoring technique that makes use of ratings has been developed (Rotter, 1954). It gives the examiner a great many examples of possible responses each scored on a seven-point scale, going from positive to negative. If his patient makes a response that appears on this list, as he is likely to, the examiner can easily rate it for its positive or negative quality. For example, when a patient completes the item "My father . . ." with a negative statement, he gets a high rating, a six or a seven, depending on how negative his remark is; when he completes it positively, he gets a one or a two, or if his remark is very positive, a zero.

A rating scale provides an objective frame of reference for scoring answers and reduces the distortion due to personal judgments. Techniques of this kind help to make tests useful in clinical situations and provide research tools for investigating the development of personality.

Situational Tests. The major aim of a test of personality is to predict what a person's behavior will be in other situations. Essentially this is a problem of transfer, of the relationship between behavior in one situation (the test situation) and another. Experiments have shown that the amount of transfer depends on the degree of similarity between the two situations (see page 311). These findings justify the so-called **situational tests** of personality, which seek to predict future behavior in real-life situations from behavior in test situations believed to have something in common with the real-life situations.

The best-known situational test was developed by the Office of Strategic Services (OSS) during World War II (Office of Strategic Services, Assessment Staff, 1948).

This organization was interested in selecting men who could function successfully as secret agents behind enemy lines. Psychologists associated with the OSS developed a number of ingenious situations to test a subject's ability to cope quickly and resourcefully with many different problems. For example, one problem required a candidate to build a real bridge across a real stream strong enough to support a heavy load. No plans for building the bridge were supplied, but the subject did have a group of workers assigned to him. In this way his ingenuity and his ability to function as a leader were put to test. Moreover, the test was sometimes modified to reveal how the candidate would tolerate frustration. Two of his workers would be secretly coached to sabotage his efforts in every possible way. In this fiendish situation, some candidates were driven to tears.

The validity of any such test has to be demonstrated. That is to say it must be proved that the individual who "passes" the test actually performs better in a similar real-life situation than those who do not "pass." Because this particular situational test was tried out in wartime, the OSS did not have time to satisfy this requirement. But the basic idea of a situational test is sound, for it rests upon the well-demonstrated principles of transfer of training. Although it is impossible to give any overall evaluation of situational tests, they do hold the promise of developing into valid techniques for measuring personality.

THE CONSTANCY OF PERSONALITY

William James, one of the giants of psychology's early history, once wrote:

Already at the age of twenty-five you see the professional mannerism settling down on the young commercial traveler, on the young doctor, on the young minister, on the young counsellor-at-law. You see the little lines of cleavage running through the character, the tricks of thought, the prejudices, the ways of the "shop," in a word, from which the man can by-and-by no more escape than his coat-sleeve can suddenly fall into a new set of folds. On the whole, it is best he should not escape. It is well for the world that in most of us, by the age of thirty, the character has set like plaster, and will never soften again (James, 1950, p. 121).

Freud agreed with James but set the date for the fixing of fundamental traits much earlier. He believed that much of an individual's personality was molded by the end of his childhood, a view that is probably shared by most people and evidenced by such common remarks as, "Good old Bob is the same man he was twenty years ago. He'll always be the same!"

Is an adult's personality as unalterable as these views imply? It should now be obvious to the reader that this question is not as simple as it appears to people ignorant of the methods of scientific psychology. An answer to it requires objective measures of personality obtained from the same sample of subjects over a span of years. Studies like these are rare because they are difficult to design and expensive to carry through. One such test reported several years ago (Kelly, 1955) suggested that the constancy of personality is not as great as we generally believe. The evidence of change came from retests of several hundred adults on tests they had taken twenty years previously. Many of the changes in test scores were small, but others were rather large. The Allport-Vernon Scale of Values, for example, revealed marked increases in the value both men and women attached to religion as they grew older. This change was necessarily accomplished at the expense of other areas of interest. The women scored less high on aesthetic values (e.g., music and art), whereas the men's scores on theoretical values (e.g., pure science) dropped. As they matured, both men and women became more masculine

and exhibited marked changes in attitudes toward political parties, social movements, and even in such apparently trivial things as the kind of soap they preferred.

These results demand a cautious interpretation. They may reflect general principles of personality change, or they may be due to specific experimental conditions. It seems plausible to assume that as a person enters middle age and approaches the autumn of life religious experiences attain greater value. But it is also possible that their increased interest in religion might be due to a general religious renascence during the period the study was in progress. Similarly, the increase in masculinity observed in women might be due to changes associated with aging, or it might be due to their learning to cope with the new electrical gadgets that have become expected fixtures in the American kitchen.

Whatever the correct interpretation of these findings, they do suggest that some marked changes take place. Knowledge of the extent of these personality changes as well as of their causes will have to await further studies of a similar kind. The responses of individuals at one time will be correlated to their behavior later on (an $R = f(R)$ kind of relationship).

PERSONALITY AND ORGANISMIC VARIABLES

The fact that learning is vastly important in forming our personalities may sometimes lead us to shut our eyes to the influence of organismic variables. Such blindness leads to very one-sided conclusions. Behavior of every kind has a physiological base. This is as true of personality traits as it is of sensation.

Psychologists and physiologists have sought to discover the ties between personality and organismic variables in a number of ways. We shall turn first to the influence of genetic and chemical variables, and then to the question of whether a person's body build is somehow correlated with his kind of personality.

Psychogenetics

The question of whether we inherit personality traits can be interpreted in one of two ways. Do we inherit our personality as we inherit the color of our eyes? That is, is there a *direct causal* relation between our genetic constitution and, say, our self-esteem, aggressiveness, sociability, or co-operativeness? The answer is "No." No available evidence suggests a rigid link between genetic determinants and such traits of the adult human personality as these.

This does not mean, however, that heredity is without influence upon personality. We behave with our bodies, and the structure and functioning of our bodies are both influenced by genetic factors. Thus, if we rephrase our original question and ask, How do inherited physiological structures influence behavior? we shall be in a better position to understand how heredity can influence personality.

For obvious reasons it is difficult to carry out psychogenetic studies with humans. Lower animals can be used advantageously because their life span is appreciably shorter than ours and their matings can be controlled. Although we must exercise caution in generalizing from the animal to the human level, it is possible for us to see in the following studies the implications for the genetic determinants of personality.

In one study rats were bred selectively for physical activity (Rundquist, 1953). In each generation the experimenter selected highly active male and female rats for mating. Similarly, inactive rats were mated with each other. In the twelfth generation the active strain of rats ran on the average 8,200 daily revolutions in an activity wheel, whereas the inactive strain had a mean of only 400.

In another study (Hall, 1938) rats were bred selectively for emotionality. The ex-perimenter measured emotionality (see page 465) in terms of the rats' reactions in a brightly lighted circular enclosure. Susceptibility to emotional upsets was found to be definitely influenced by genetic factors, for strains of rats were bred who differed markedly in their reactions to the test situation. One strain reacted to it highly emotionally; another appeared to be relatively calm.

How are these differences in activity and emotionality produced? They seem to be linked to certain physiological character-istics of the endocrine system. Active strains of rats exhibit a higher metabolic rate than less active strains; emotional strains of rats have heavier thyroid glands than nonemo-tional rats. It is most likely that these differences are due, in part, to the action of genes which control the growth and activity of the endocrine system.

It may seem at first that activity level and susceptibility to emotional upsets in rats is a far cry from the complexities of human personality. This is not so. Many of the complex differences in humans are based on organismic differences. For an example of this, we have again to turn to an experiment with rats, but as you remem-ber, their behavior may be used to derive principles that apply to human behavior. This experiment (Farber, 1948), which has already been described in part (page 410), shows that an organism's susceptibil-ity to self-perpetuating and ineffectual fixated responses is definitely influenced by his innate tendency to be emotional. In it, rats who had been trained to go to one side of a T maze by experiencing shock at the choice point and food in the appro-priate goal box, were given a reversal learn-ing task in which they received no shock and the food was shifted to the previously empty goal box in the other arm of the T maze. These rats exhibited a very strong tendency to persist in making the initially correct turning response because it had proved effective in helping them escape the feared choice point, and the strength of this fixation appeared to be intimately related to the animal's susceptibility to becoming emotionally aroused.

The experimenters inferred the differences in the rats' susceptibilities from the differences in the environments they had come from. One group came from a psychology laboratory where most of the experiments were in psychology of learning. Here an unplanned but nevertheless effective selective breeding process was apparently taking place, for rats exhibiting emotional responses which interfered with their learning were not chosen as breeding stock, and therefore a strain of relatively fearless rats had been produced. The other rats came from the laboratories of anatomy and pharmacology where no such selection took place, since it is just as easy to dissect or drug an emotional animal as a non-emotional one.

The more emotional rats from the anatomy and pharmacology laboratories would be expected to develop a stronger fear at the choice point of the maze where they had been shocked. Since learning to reverse the turning response depends upon a weakening of the fear response (see page 274), these rats should reverse less rapidly than the animals from the psychology laboratory. These expectations were confirmed by the results of the experiment. Whereas the rats from the psychology laboratory took an average of 28 trials to reverse, the others required 117 trials.

To generalize these results to human behavior would seem justified, since individual differences in autonomic-nervous-system functioning have been found to be genetically determined to some extent (Jost & Sontag, 1944). Because of genetic differences people have different tendencies to be fearful in the same situations. The soldier whose physiological system tends to generate a great deal of fear responds differently than his more phlegmatic comrades. He is more likely to learn responses, such as repression or rationalization, to help

him cope with his fear, than his comrades, for they have little need for these responses. In this way a difference in personality having its roots in heredity may develop.

A number of other behavior patterns have been traced to genetic influences (Fuller, 1960). Some strains of mice have stronger hunger drives than others. Aggressive and submissive strains of mice have been produced. Fish have been bred that exhibit different forms of mating responses. A genetic basis has been found for a rat's preference for either saccharin-sweetened or plain water (Nachman, 1959). Dogs of different breeds react differently when they are placed in new situations. Terriers, for example, respond more aggressively than poodles (Mahut, 1958). If you consider these genetic differences as part of the raw materials with which learning deals, then you will see clearly that they can exert powerful influences on what a particular organism will learn. Genetic differences can tip the scales in favor of certain kinds of behavior. Although aggressive behavior may be stepped up by reinforcement, the chances of developing aggressiveness is greater with animals in whom such responses occur readily, as in aggressive strains of mice and dogs.

In generalizing from the above studies to human personality, we must keep one strong reservation in mind. You recall that the sexual behavior of lower animals is much more rigidly controlled by hormonal secretions than that of humans (see page 237). This is true of other behavior as well. Humans, because of their superior brain, are capable of a greater variety of learning. For this reason, it is most likely that hereditary factors play a much larger role in the general behavior patterns of animals than of man. Nevertheless, our genetically influenced physiological differences do appear to play a definite role in shaping our personalities. From the moment of birth, children behave differently. Some respond sensitively to changes in light, sound, cold, and heat; others remain comparatively unaffected. Some infants struggle in their cribs to move about, whereas others accept their environment passively. These differences may persist throughout their lives.

One concluding point about psychogenetics. Eventually we may hope to trace any hereditary differences in behavior to the roles of specific genes or groups of genes. At present this is only possible with such simple organisms as fruit flies. For example, a single gene determines the inheritance of red or white eyes in the fruit fly, and the eye color, in turn, influences the fly's behavior by determining whether he will crawl toward or away from a weak light. Ultimately, when we can tie together the genetic pattern of higher organisms with their behavior, the role of genetic influences in personality development will become much clearer than it is today.

Chemistry and Behavior

Chemical changes which may produce behavioral changes can occur in two ways: (1) The physiological system itself is able to manufacture and secrete a wide variety of chemical agents; and (2) chemicals can be injected *into* the body.

Probably the most potent sources of chemicals which influence behavior are the glands of the endocrine system (see page 85). These numerous ductless glands secrete directly into the blood stream many kinds of hormones with far-reaching effects. For example, glands in the pancreas secrete *insulin,* a hormone that regulates sugar metabolism. Failure of the gland to secrete a sufficient quantity of this hormone produces an abnormally high concentration of sugar in the blood. This chemical imbalance, which occurs in diabetes (fortunately remediable by injections of insulin), triggers severe behavioral changes such as depression and confusion.

The thyroid gland, located in the base of the neck, normally secretes about one milligram of *thyroxin* every three days. Deficient amounts of this hormone (hypothyroidism) cause a low metabolic rate that produces sluggish behavior. Furthermore, if a baby is born with a severely underactive thyroid that remains uncorrected, he will become a **cretin,** developing a distinctive dwarfish appearance characterized by a puffy face, protruding abdomen, and short arms and legs. His physical development, particularly that of his skeletal and nervous systems, will be severely retarded. He will be listless, and because of his underdeveloped nervous system, intellectually retarded. If cretinism occurs during the first two years of life, when the brain is developing very rapidly, proper hormone treatment involving injections of thyroxin improves the condition but is not usually successful in preventing some permanent damage. If the disorder develops after the age of two, when the growth of the nervous system has slowed, then the hormone treatment is usually successful in avoiding permanent impairments, both physiological and behavioral.

When thyroid deficiency occurs late in life its effects depend upon its severity, but even mild cases can produce a general listlessness and lack of vitality. In marked contrast are the effects of a hyperactive thyroid. Because of the increased tempo of their bodily activity, people who have hyperactive thyroids are overactive and excitable and often have difficulty sleeping.

The delicate chemical balance of the body upon which much of our normal behavior depends can also be upset by a defective diet. Severe salt deficiency can produce marked irritability and depression, which fortunately disappear when the normal salt balance of the body is restored (Saphir, 1945). Similarly, vitamin deficiencies can produce intense irritability, depression, and confusion, which also disappear when the deficiency is eliminated. Moreover, starvation can produce dramatic

486

behavioral changes. On a semistarvation diet, individuals who previously showed no personality problems became apathetic, less sociable, more irritable, and suspicious. Some even exhibited the extremes of behavior usually seen only in psychiatric patients (Keys, Brozek, Henschel, Mickelsen, & Taylor, 1950). Even more dramatic are the reactions of mountaineers suffering from lack of oxygen (*anoxemia*) on the highest mountain peaks. This condition initiates a chain-reaction of chemical imbalances which sometimes lead to an irresponsibility totally foreign to these highly skilled and disciplined mountain climbers. They throw away their protective clothing, attempt impossible climbs, or behave in an otherwise foolhardy way. When they are once more able to obtain the proper amount of oxygen, they literally regain their senses.

Behavior can also be changed dramatically by the introduction into the body of chemicals that it does not itself manufacture. You recall our discussion of the psychological effects of alcohol (see page 421). Certain tendencies to approach, normally inhibited by timidity or fear, are released under the influence of alcohol. Other chemicals also have an effect on behavior. We are all too familiar with the problem of drug addiction. Drugs, like the opium derivatives, morphine and heroin, induce in some people a state of blissfulness and buoyancy that contrasts markedly with their normally tense and depressed condition. These drugs presumably allow them to escape from the harsh realities of existence, but the cost is very high—dependency upon drugs and eventual irreparable damage to the physiological system.

The psychological effects of drugs are difficult to assess. Personal reports are often contradictory. To understand the effects we needed a technique that provides objective measures of behavior before and after a drug is administered. Free-respond-

ing instrumental conditioning (operant conditioning) has been found to provide an extremely sensitive measure of the influence of drugs on behavior. As a result, a whole new area of research employing a sizable number of psychologists has mushroomed. In less than a decade the amount of information gathered has become so vast that no brief summary is possible. Nevertheless, you can understand the impact of these methods, as well as their ultimate contribution, from a description of how the psychological effect of a particular drug was evaluated.

Reserpine is one of the well-known tranquilizing drugs. Along with other tranquilizers, it has been used successfully with psychiatric patients suffering from certain behavior disorders, which will be described in the next chapter. The effects reserpine can exert upon instrumental responses are revealed in the following experiment:

Monkeys were trained initially to respond by pressing a lever to get sugared orange juice on a variable interval schedule (see page 288). When a monkey's lever-pressing rate had stabilized (see Figure 13.15), he was

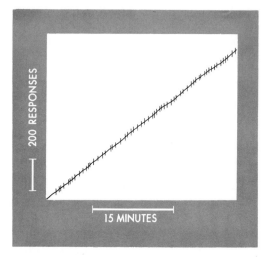

FIGURE 13.15 Sample Cumulative Response Curve of a Monkey on a Variable Interval Schedule. Each horizontal line, or "pip," denotes a reinforcement (sugared orange juice) (Brady, 1959).

subjected for a fixed period of time to a clicking noise which was terminated with a painful shock to his feet. Consequently the clicking sound became a cue for fear, and this fear kept the monkey from making the lever-pressing response. The fear-provoking sound effectively suppressed the response (see Figure 13.16); when the clicker was on

were given daily administrations of 0.75 milligrams of reserpine for each kilogram of weight. Figure 13.17 shows the results.

The reserpine had two major effects. It depressed the rate of responding and dissipated the fear. If you compare Figure 13.17 with Figures 13.15 and 13.16, you will see that when the clicker was *off* the overall lever-pressing rate under reserpine was depressed by over 50 per cent. The drug, then, markedly depresses the behavioral output of an organism. Moreover, the suppression effect of the clicking sound that is shown in Figure 13.16 virtually disappears in Figure 13.17. The monkeys continued to respond throughout the period in which the clicker was on *at the same rate* as they did when it was off. Reserpine, in short, practically eliminates fear at the expense of depressing overall behavioral output. It does not, however, permanently modify behavior. When the monkeys were taken off reserpine they reverted to their previous behavior; their rate of responding

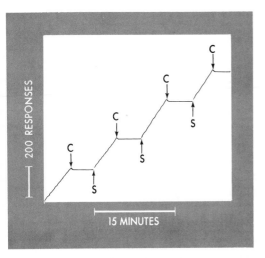

FIGURE 13.16 Sample Cumulative Response Curve of a Monkey Showing Complete Suppression of Lever-Pressing During the Period the Clicker, Which Was Terminated by a Shock, Was On. The onset of a clicker period is indicated by C, and S represents the shock. The conditioned fear evoked by the clicker suppressed the instrumental lever-pressing response (Brady, 1959).

he stopped responding. When it was off, however, he pressed the lever at the rate he had before the clicker-shock pairings.

After several sessions in which shock followed every presentation of the clicking sound, the subjects were shifted to a schedule in which the sound was paired only occasionally with the shock. Under this new schedule, the noise retained its ability to suppress the lever-pressing response, but not as consistently as before. In other words, the monkey sometimes pressed the lever while the clicker was on. It was at this point that the effect of reserpine on the monkeys' behavior was evaluated. They

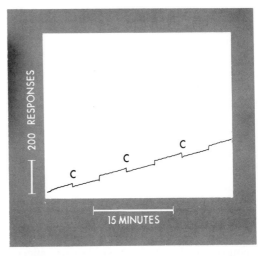

FIGURE 13.17 Sample Cumulative Response Curve Showing the Effect of Reserpine on the Conditioned Fear Response Which Had Suppressed the Lever-Pressing Response (see Figure 13.17). The repeated five-minute clicker periods are indicated by a slight lowering of the cumulative response curve. Reserpine eliminated the clicker's suppression effect but also reduced the overall response rate (Brady, 1959).

488

decreased when the clicker was on and increased when it was off.

Some drugs have an effect the opposite of reserpine. Amphetamine, a "pick-me-up" drug, produced an increase in the rate of lever pressing when the clicker was off, and a marked decrease when it was on. Amphetamine increases the behavioral output of an organism in the absence of a feared stimulus, but decreases it when the feared stimulus is present.

Drugs can have a delayed effect. Rats were trained to press a lever every 20 to 22 seconds. Responses which occurred either before or after the two-second "pay-off" period were not reinforced, and the next two-second pay-off period was postponed 20 seconds. After this fine temporal discrimination was established, the rats were injected with nicotine. At first their timing behavior was disrupted only slightly. However, pronounced effects occurred three to four days later, when their response rate increased so much that the number of reinforcements they obtained dropped to half their usual rate (Geller, 1960).

These examples of dramatic changes in behavior produced by alterations in the chemical conditions of the body should make one point clear: the unified system of responses, known as personality, is not independent of the physiological processes. Depending upon the chemical conditions of the body, an individual can behave in two entirely different ways in the very same situation.

In most of the examples we have cited an individual's behavior is restored to its "normal" functioning when the appropriate chemical balance is re-established. You should remember, however, that chemical changes in the body have lasting effects (such as the physiological deterioration resulting from prolonged addiction to morphine) that produce drastic personality changes. Chemical changes can also exert influences on the personality that are more subtle but just as great. An underactive

thyroid gland that makes an individual lethargic and reduces his stamina cannot help but shape his personality by influencing what he will learn. He cannot learn to be active and dominant simply because he cannot make these responses. Neither can a person suffering from an overactive thyroid learn to be relaxed and easygoing.

For the most part the studies using tranquilizers show that their effect disappears when their use is discontinued. However, the question still remains whether they may not exert a more permanent effect on an individual who takes them for long periods of time during his early life. In any case, the biochemical control of some form of behavior has been demonstrated. There is little doubt that the range of behavior that can be controlled will constantly be extended. Some biochemists and psychopharmacologists go so far as to maintain that all the problems of personality formation and change may some day be handled by appropriate prescriptions. Although this possibility cannot be rejected out of hand, it does not appear likely that such a goal—if it can be so described—will be realized in the near future.

Physique and Personality

The idea that personality varies with physique has been common for centuries. Shakespeare expressed it throughout his plays. For example, Julius Caesar voices an attitude about the relationship between physique and personality that is justified by later events in that tragedy.

Let me have men about me that are fat;
Sleek-headed men, and such as sleep o'nights:
Yon Cassius has a lean and hungry look;
He thinks too much: such men are dangerous.
Julius Caesar, Act 1, Scene 2

The idea persists today: the fat man is considered jolly and sociable; the thin man to be ambitious and seclusive. Your own experience more than likely contradicts this. Some thin people, you have probably noted, are sociable and pleasant, and fat people (who should be becoming rarer, because overweight is a health hazard) are often shy and retiring. The assumption of a relationship, or lack of it, between body build and personality cannot, however, be fairly judged on the basis of any one person's casual experiences. Is there any scientific evidence to support or refute this idea?

Kretchmer, a German psychiatrist of the nineteenth century, thought there was. He suggested that there were three basic body types: **pyknic, asthenic,** and **athletic.** The pyknic is characterized as stocky, with a relatively long torso and short legs. The asthenic is tall and thin, with a relatively short torso and long limbs. The athletic falls between the two; he has broad shoulders, a narrow waist, and is well muscled. Kretchmer concluded from his observations of psychiatric patients that pyknics are predominantly **extraverted**—sociable and outgoing. Asthenics, in contrast, are **introverted**—introspective and shy. The athletic type is aggressive and active.

The main evidence in support of this hypothesized relationship between body build and personality apparently came from schizophrenic and manic-depressive patients (see page 506) in psychiatric institutions. The former, who were for the most part socially seclusive, had asthenic and athletic physiques. Manic-depressive patients, who were predominantly extraverted, had pyknic physiques.

Although the evidence Kretchmer offered convinced many psychiatrists of his day, it soon became apparent that the data suffered from major defects. First, the descriptions of the three categories of body build do not allow reliable measurements. Judges do not always agree about an individual's physique. Second, a person's physique may change with age. As we get older most of us become heavier and are more likely to be judged pyknics. This observation of change in physique with increasing age proves particularly damaging to Kretch-

mer's theory, since schizophrenia is primarily a disorder of the adolescent and young adult, whereas manic-depressive psychosis occurs predominantly in middle age. Thus, at least one reason there are more pyknics among manic-depressives is that as people grow older they tend to become heavier. Any disorder that occurs in middle age is bound to afflict a higher proportion of pyknics than a disorder that occurs most frequently among younger age groups.

Further attempts to investigate Kretchmer's major claim for a relationship between personality and physique failed to provide encouraging results. It became obvious that many individuals do not fit neatly into one of the three body types described by Kretchmer. In addition, those whose body builds fitted one of Kretchmer's categories very often had personality characteristics inconsistent with the theory's expectations. One study (Burchard, 1936) involving normal subjects found that 50 per cent of those classified as pyknics were rated as extraverts and 30 per cent were rated as introverts. Although the direction of the results favor Kretchmer's hypothesis, the results themselves fail to suggest that body build of the sort that Kretchmer described plays a major role in personality.

Kretchmer's failure to prove his point did not rule out the possibility of some relationship between personality and physique. Perhaps if a reliable method of measuring body build were devised, one that is not influenced by age, the clear-cut relationship that Kretchmer believed existed could be obtained. Sheldon, who had both a Ph.D. in psychology and an M.D., pursued this possibility further.

Sheldon measured physiques along three dimensions: **endomorphy, mesomorphy,** and **ectomorphy.** The terms are derived from the names of the three layers of cells distinguishable in the early stages of the embryo. The inner layer of cells, the endoderm, is the one from which the digestive

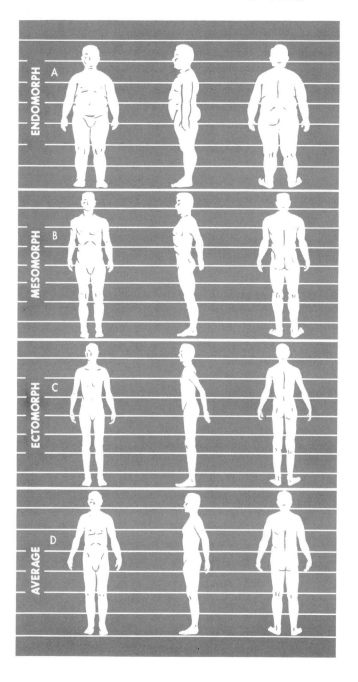

FIGURE 13.18 Four Examples of Different Somato-types. *A* is primarily an endomorph, with a somato-type of 7-1-1. *B,* whose somatotype is 1-7-1, is a mesomorph, and *C,* whose somatotype of 1-1-7, an ectomorph. *D* is an average individual, whose somato-type is 4-4-4 (W. H. Sheldon & S. S. Stevens. *The varieties of temperament.* New York: Harper, 1942).

and respiratory tracts develop. From the middle layer, the mesoderm, grow the muscles and the skeleton. The ectoderm, the outer layer, contains the cells that grow into the skin and nervous system.

According to Sheldon, physiques may be distinguished by degrees of development, ranging from 1 to 7, along these three dimensions. A very fat person with a prominent abdomen would be rated high in endomorphy, whereas a stocky, excessively muscular person would receive a rating of 7 in mesomorphy. A skinny individual would obtain a high rating in ectomorphy. By rating these three dimensions separately, one can express the **somatotype** (body build) of an individual quantitatively in terms of his relative amounts of endomorphy, mesomorphy, and ectomorphy. A person who was average in each dimension would be rated 4-4-4. A person who received the highest rating on endomorphy but the lowest ratings on mesomorphy and ectomorphy would have a somatotype of 7-1-1. Figure 13.18 shows the physiques of four persons who are predominantly endomorphic, mesomorphic, ectomorphic, and just average, respectively.

Sheldon's methods of measuring body types (Sheldon, Stevens, & Tucker, 1940) represent considerable improvement over those by Kretchmer. They have been found to be quite reliable when applied to a population of male undergraduates. Having developed a method of measuring physique, Sheldon's next step was to devise an appropriate method for measuring certain aspects of personality which he called **temperament**—that quality of personality pertaining to mood and general level of activity.

Sheldon and his associates concluded that temperament could be rated along three dimensions (Sheldon & Stevens, 1942): One dimension he designated **viscerotonia;** it refers to the desire for the so-called visceral comforts—relaxation, eating, sociability. **Somatotonia** is characterized by activity, aggressiveness, competitiveness. Finally, **cerebrotonia** is evidenced by traits like dominance of the cerebral processes—sensitivity, restraint, a liking for one's own company, and preoccupations.

The investigators found it feasible to represent each of these dimensions of temperament on a seven-point rating scale, comparable in form to the body build scale. For example, a person with extreme viscerotonia might be rated 7-1-1, whereas another person average in these three dimensions would receive an overall rating of 4-4-4.

Sheldon reported a very high correlation between the somatotypes and their temperaments. Students who were rated high in viscerotonia were found for the most part to have body builds high in endomorphy. Similarly, subjects high in somatotonia were found to be predominantly mesomorphs. And finally, ectomorphs were rated high in cerebrotonia.

Upon critical examination, these impressive findings, appear to be less convincing. Sheldon's research methods suffer from a major defect. An individual's somatotype and temperament were not measured independently; the same investigator rated both a person's body build and his temperament. The possibility that an investigator was influenced by a subject's physique when he rated him on temperament cannot be dismissed. Being interested in, and perhaps convinced of, the existence of a relationship between physique and temperament, the interviewer might have been swayed by what he could see of a particular person's body build, that is, cerebrotonic traits could be read into the obvious ectomorph, and so on. Thus, the high correlation found between temperament and physique may not necessarily reflect a true relationship, but may reveal a bias inherent in Sheldon's method. Remember, an empirical law states a relationship between two *independently* defined variables (see page 36). If physique and temperament

are not measured independently, if the measurement of one influences the measurement of the other, then the claimed relationship between them obviously cannot be considered proved. What is needed are experiments in which the measurement of personality and physique cannot influence each other. Several such experiments have been reported but their interpretations are debatable. One overall evaluation draws the following conclusion.

Thus, our belief is that an overall appraisal of the many studies conducted since Sheldon began his work will lead the reader to accept the existence of a significant and interesting relation between physique and personality, but will leave him unconvinced that the relation is so close as Sheldon seems to imply (Hall & Lindzey, 1957, p. 374).

Even if one accepts the conclusion that there is a low correlation between physique and personality, one must be careful in interpreting it. A correlation between two variables does not by itself indicate that a causal relation exists between them (see page 72). From the start, Sheldon has emphasized, like Kretchmer before him, his belief that the correlations between a mesomorphic build and somatonia or an ectomorphic build and cerebrotonia, for example, are constitutional, inborn, and traceable to inheritance. But such modest correlations as appear to exist between type of build and behavior may result from learning experiences. A strong, muscular boy (a mesomorph) scarcely has to be urged to become active and competitive in athletic skills where he is likely to excel. Once his accomplishments bring him the admiration of his fellows his behavior is reinforced. On the other hand, a delicate, skinny boy (an ectomorph) will have difficulty competing successfully in activities demanding physical strength and stamina. Thus he may seek the reinforcements that come from intellectual activities: from reading and doing well in school. And the fat boy (the endomorph), as an old saying goes, has to be easy-going and good-natured because he can neither fight nor run.

But finally, although it is reasonable to assume that learning is responsible for whatever modest correlation there is between physique and personality, the possi- bility that body build has some direct influence on personality cannot as yet be discarded. If such a relationship does exist, it should be possible someday to discover the physiological mechanism responsible for it.

SUMMARY

Individuals tend to behave consistently in a wide variety of situations. It is to this behavioral consistency that we apply the term *personality*. The two major problems associated with the investigation of personality are to understand how it develops and how it can be measured.

One of the most influential interpretations of the development of personality is the psychoanalytic formulation advanced by Freud. Freud postulated that personality develops as a result of an individual's experiences during a predetermined sequence of stages each of which is characterized by a dominant mode of achieving libidinal satisfaction. Freud's clinical observations led him to emphasize the importance of psychological determinism, unconscious determinants of behavior, conflict, defense mechanisms, and motivation in human behavior.

In contrast to the psychoanalytic interpretation of personality development is the interpretation that emphasizes principles of learning observed in the laboratory. According to this conception, mainly advanced by Dollard and Miller, each individual does not proceed through a predetermined sequence of developmental stages, but instead learns important habits in the various situations of his early life.

Particularly important are those he learns from feeding, cleanliness, and sex training experiences; aggressive behavior; reactions to himself and to other members of his family; and responses to stress.

Personality is measured by many methods: interviews, rating scales, personality inventories, projective techniques, and situational tests. Research, particularly with personality inventories, has suggested that personality can be considered as a group of traits (persisting characteristics of personality) that can be measured along a dimension. Factor analysis has attempted to reduce personality to a group of primary traits. Projective techniques, in contrast to personality inventories, attempt to measure the overall organization of personality, that is, its structure.

Personality is influenced by organismic variables. Research, mainly with lower animals, suggests that important characteristics of behavior like emotionality and aggressiveness can be genetically determined. Chemical changes initiated by hormonal secretions or by the introduction of chemicals into the body also exert powerful changes in behavior. Some evidence suggests that body build is related to temperament, but it is not known whether this influence is direct or indirect.

SUGGESTIONS FOR FURTHER READING

ANASTASI, A. *Psychological testing.* (2nd ed.) New York: Macmillan, 1961.

A section of this text is dedicated to a review and evaluation of various kinds of personality measurement.

CATTELL, R. *Personality and motivation structure and measurement.* New York: Harcourt, Brace, & World, 1957.

An analysis of personality based on the method of factor analysis.

CRONBACH, L. J. *Essentials of psychological testing.* (2nd ed.) New York: Harper & Row, 1960.

A survey of personality tests is contained in Chs. 15-19.

DOLLARD, J., & MILLER, N. E. *Personality and psychotherapy.* New York: McGraw-Hill, 1950.

An ingenious analysis of personality that integrates features of both Freudian and learning theory.

FREUD, S. *An outline of psychoanalysis.* New York: Norton, 1949.

A 127-page exposition of the author's interpretation of human behavior.

GUILFORD, J. P. *Personality.* New York: McGraw-Hill, 1959a.

A clear exposition of the analysis of personality into basic traits.

HALL, C. S. *A primer of Freudian psychology.* New York: New American Library (A Mentor Book), 1955.

A brief, clear exposition of Freudian interpretation of adjustment. This book is a paperback.

HALL, C. S., & LINDZEY, G. *Theories of personality.* New York: Wiley, 1957.

Compact yet comprehensive summaries of the major theoretical interpretations of personality.

LUNDIN, R. W. *Personality: an experimental approach.* New York: Macmillan, 1961.

An attempt to interpret personality in terms of principles of operant conditioning.

McCLELLAND, D. C. *Personality.* New York: Morrow, 1951.

A text by an active researcher in the field of personality.

NUNNALLY, J. C. *Tests and measurements: Assessment and prediction.* New York: McGraw-Hill, 1959.

A text covering both statistical methods and the measurement of personality.

RICHMAN, J. (Ed.) *A general selection from the works of Sigmund Freud.* New York: Liveright, 1951.

A selection of Freud's writings which is clearer than most of his interpreters. This book is available as a paperback.

STAGNER, R. *Psychology of personality.* (3rd ed.) New York: McGraw-Hill, 1961.

A popular text on personality.

WHITE, R. W. *Lives in progress: a study of the natural growth of personality.* New York: Holt, Rinehart, & Winston, 1952.

An interesting and readable analysis of personality that is illustrated by case histories of three individuals during the time they were in college and five to ten years later.

BEHAVIOR PATHOLOGY
14

THE SCOPE OF THE PROBLEM

One of every ten Americans now living will, at some time, require treatment for a psychological disturbance. If you are a student in a class of fifty, and if your class is representative of the entire population, five of your classmates will eventually succumb to a behavioral disturbance. This is a frightening idea at first glance, but on closer examination it is not so alarming. Not everyone, by any means, who falls victim to a psychological disorder is destined to spend the remainder of his life in a psychiatric institution. Many patients are discharged from institutions within less than a year after their admission and never return. And still others receive psychiatric help from their doctor at his office while they live what appears to everyone else a normal life.

But there is no denying that the high incidence of psychiatric disorders and their less serious counterparts in our society constitute a grave problem, whose tragic significance is reflected both in human suffering and in economic loss. It costs more than a billion dollars a year to care for the men and women who are behaviorally disturbed. Psychiatric patients occupy approximately 50 per cent of all hospital beds in the United States. People who are behaviorally ill—and many of them are skilled workers and professionals—are usually unproductive. Add to this the cost of the time and professional services rendered by psychiatrists, clinical psychologists, social workers, nurses, and others who help care for psychiatric patients, and the total is staggering. And finally, an estimate of the cost of psychiatric disturbances cannot ignore the incalculable suffering, not only of the patient, but of his family and friends.

All in all, psychological illness represents one of the great social problems of our times. This chapter is designed to provide the reader with information concerning the nature, origins, and treatment of these disorders.

PSYCHOLOGICAL HEALTH AND BEHAVIOR PATHOLOGY

An understanding of pathological behavior presupposes some conception of healthy behavior. Unfortunately, the distinction between the two is sometimes blurred. This is not surprising. Even in medical science, which is equipped with sensitive instruments to measure malfunction, the distinction between good health and ill health is not always clear. What is a healthy heartbeat? At what point does a person become overweight? What distinguishes a healthy metabolic rate from a pathological one? In short, where exactly is the slender boundary that separates bodily health from illness?

Psychologists and psychiatrists are similarly troubled when they try to state what they mean by the concept of **psychological health,** or what is more commonly called **mental health.** A definition of it in terms of what it *excludes,* although not completely satisfactory, is much easier to formulate than one in terms of what it *includes.* Defined in this negative way, psychological health is a condition from which pathological reactions are *absent.* Many clinical psychologists and psychiatrists prefer this kind of definition, because a patient, or former patient, who does not exhibit disturbed behavior can be given a clean bill of health. Others, however, insist that psychological health is something positive, that the distinguishing feature of the healthy person is not that he is free from pathological response, but that his behavior, including his ways of living and outlook on life, are healthy and good.

One psychologist (Maslow, 1950) describes a healthy person as one who *truly* realizes, that is, lives up to, his potentialities. In trying to isolate factors which produce psychological health he selected individuals, some of them well-known historical figures, who he believed exhibited a high degree of *self-actualization.* His list included Jefferson, Lincoln, Thoreau, as well as Einstein and Eleanor Roosevelt. He found that these self-actualizing people were efficient and spontaneous, accepted themselves and others, had a sense of humor, a love of mankind, and a democratic and philosophical outlook, as contrasted with an aggressive one. This analysis suggests a tentative definition of optimal mental health. But we may ask—and justifiably—whether such a conception of mental health does not depend too much upon the personal preferences of the psychologist interpreting the meaning of *self-actualization.* Individuals have many different potentialities. Is it defensible to say that one quality is basically superior to another? Would we not be justified in selecting as examples of self-actualizing individuals Alexander Hamilton, Elvis Presley, Jefferson Davis, Jayne Mansfield, or even Khrushchev? Different people would argue that certain of these exhibit optimal mental health.

The influence of personal and social biases on the concept of mental health is nowhere more apparent than in the reactions of different societies to the same behavior. In our culture a person who exhibited intense fear of snakes and of the dark would be diagnosed as suffering from a phobia. Yet almost all Menominee Indians are terrified of snakes and the dark; they believe that all but one species of snakes are inhabited by evil spirits, and that evil spirits, witches, and ghosts come out at night. The Zuni Indians encourage their men to be exceedingly mild and conventional, actually to avoid individualistic behavior. Similar behavior in an American often indicates extreme fearfulness. Even within various sections (subcultures) of American society we find different conceptions of behavior disorders. A perfect illustration of this is the case (Slotkin, 1955) of the man from an isolated mountain community who received revelations from God and a call to preach to his neighbors. He did so with success and achieved an honored position in his rural community. Subsequently he received a call to preach his message in a large city. Soon after he arrived, he was arrested for preaching on the street corner and later placed in a psychiatric institution because he was found to suffer from **delusions** of grandeur and **hallucinations** (false sensory impressions). Thus, the same behavior was considered healthy by a lower-class rural community and disturbed by a middle-class, urban subculture.

These varying conceptions of mental health seem to suggest that we define it in terms of **conformity** to some socially established standard of conduct. Such a definition would be equivalent to what is commonly meant by **adjustment.** If a person gets along in his society he is *adjusted;* if he doesn't, he is badly adjusted, or *maladjusted.*

At first glance it seems reasonable to equate mental health with social adjustment. But cannot an entire society, or a large segment of it, suffer from a behavior disorder? Most people catch colds and have cavities in their teeth, but neither is considered a sign of good health. Hitler, Goering, and many leaders of the Nazi party practiced and publicly condoned frankly **sadistic** behavior (cruelty was reinforcing). They also exhibited an intense suspiciousness, which led psychiatrists who examined them after World War II to diagnose many of them as **paranoids.** If behavior is to be judged only by what is acceptable or common in a society, then the actions of the Nazi leaders and their followers would have to be considered psychologically healthy. Therefore, a culturally oriented definition of mental health seems to be too limited. It fails to consider the possi-

bility that pathological processes could operate in an entire population.

Any contemporary positive formulation of what constitutes or characterizes mental health is likely to list several traits or dimensions of behavior, some of which will have a bearing upon social behavior. Following is such a list (Jahoda, 1958):

1. A realisitic understanding of oneself
2. The ability to become mature and to learn by experience
3. An integrated personality
4. Sufficient independence to enable one to make decisions and to act upon them
5. A realistic perception of one's social environment
6. The ability to control oneself and to some extent one's environment.

This conception of mental health, and similar ones, suffers from two major limitations. First, the problem of defining precisely and measuring these healthy traits has yet to be solved. Even if it proves possible some day to develop appropriate tests for them, the difficult task of establishing the boundary between sickness and health will remain. Second, the choice of these particular dimensions of health represents to some extent personal preferences, that is, value judgments. What is considered healthy by one person or one society may not appear healthy to another, as we said before.

Thus it seems that for now we have to conclude that a positive conception of psychological health cannot be freed from all value judgments. Nevertheless, we cannot put aside the problem of defining psychological health in a positive manner. For the more we learn about personality, the more we will be able to shape behavior, and we will have to reach some decision on how our fund of psychological knowledge is to be applied. Although psychologists can provide information to help make the alternatives clearer, the final decision as to what constitutes healthy reactions has in a democratic society to rest to some extent upon an informal consensus of its citizens, with due allowance for the democratic principle of "live and let live." The implications of this philosophical point will become clearer as you proceed through this chapter.

Now that we have described some of the difficulties of a positive conception of psychological health, we shall proceed in a general way to fill in the outlines of a negative conception. We shall deal primarily with different kinds of psychiatric disturbances, that is, with reactions that are rather seriously **disordered.** By disordered we mean responses that are either inappropriate to the external situation, or ineffective in achieving desired goals, or both. A paranoiac who believes totally without cause that a gang is planning to murder him and therefore disguises himself and flees (see page 221) is certainly behaving inappropriately and unrealistically. In psychiatric language, he is *out of contact with reality*. The case of the young married woman described on page 498 illustrates how ineffective a line of conduct can be. Although she is in contact with reality, this woman is behaving in a disordered manner. She desires a happy marriage, yet acts in a way that can only produce an unhappy one.

Before we proceed further, two possible sources of misunderstanding must be cleared up. The first, the belief that a person who is adjusted, that is, psychologically healthy, is altogether free from psychological problems, is simply untrue. He, too, may have unresolved conflicts, but unlike the disturbed individual he can tolerate them, even though he is unable to resolve them. For example, a married man often has incompatible demands made upon him by his wife and his mother. He is truly caught in the middle, for when he attempts to please both his wife and his mother he often antagonizes them both. If he is a fairly well-adjusted person, he is able to contain the conflict. It does not dominate

his existence and make him ineffective at work or in his roles as a father, friend, or particularly as husband and son. He is able to arrive at a reasonable compromise, which may not completely satisfy his wife or mother, but nevertheless does not destroy or even markedly disturb his relationship to both. On the other hand, a disturbed individual confronted with the same conflict would find no way to resolve the problem or to keep it within limits. The conflict would get him down, so that he would perform most of his roles badly. Instead of achieving a working compromise he would probably exacerbate the conflict and ruin his relationships with both his wife and his mother. His reactions would become more and more disordered until he reached the point where he required psychological help.

The second possible source of misunderstanding is the belief that conformity is basic to psychological health, that the person who toes the mark and obeys the conventions of his society avoids most of the problems the nonconformist meets. Again, this is simply not true. Many social reformers and unconventional artists and writers are adjusted by any accepted standards of mental health. The important consideration is not whether a person is conventional, but whether his conformity or nonconformity is an expression of a healthy adjustment or whether it can be traced to some psychological disturbance.

Having cleared up these misconceptions, we can point out more clearly what is meant by disordered behavior. Our plan will be to describe first the major diagnostic categories of behavior disorders and then the various kinds of therapies used in the treatment of psychiatric patients. Finally, we shall touch upon the prevention of psychiatric disorders.

But before we begin, we have to anticipate and clear up one more problem the reader may have. During their first years of study, medical students almost always become convinced that they themselves are afflicted with whatever disease they happen to be studying at the moment. Psychology students often react the same way. In case this happens to you, you should be reassured by the fact that most of the symptoms of disordered personalities are also exhibited to some degree by adjusted individuals. In disordered people, however, the symptoms are exaggerated and out of control. Thus, even though you may have some tendencies that resemble these symptoms, you should certainly not worry about having any fully developed mental illness.

NEUROSIS

Neurosis is a very broad term, covering a number of more-or-less distinct conditions. However, all neurotics have one common problem—they have failed to adjust to themselves and to the world. If you can persuade a neurotic to talk frankly, he is likely to admit to being unhappy. And what is even more decisive for a diagnosis, he cannot get at the roots of his troubles.

Dollard and Miller (1950), who have accomplished much in drawing behavior pathology and experimental psychology closer (see page 455), describe the neurotic as one ". . . who does not make use of the obvious opportunities for satisfaction which life offers him."

According to Dollard and Miller, neurotics can be distinguished by three common signs: (1) they are miserable; (2) they behave stupidly, that is, irrationally, because they have unresolved conflicts; and (3) they exhibit various symptoms. As an illustration of a neurosis, we report the following case and analyze it according to the Dollard and Miller definition of neurosis:

Mrs. *A.* was an attractive 23-year-old married woman whose husband worked in the office of an insurance company. She was obsessed by a number of fears, one of which was that her heart would stop beating unless she concentrated on counting the beats. These fears brought her to seek the help of a psychiatrist.

Her first symptom had appeared five months before when she was out shopping. She had felt faint and apprehensive of an impending disaster. Shortly afterwards she had had a conversation with an aunt, who complained of heart trouble. Thereafter Mrs. *A.*'s fear of fainting had ended and had been replaced by overconcern with her heart.

Mrs. *A.* was an orphan who had been born in the upper South. After spending the first few months of her life in an orphanage, she had been placed in a foster home. Her foster mother, who dominated the family, had been cruel, strict, and coarse. She had believed in a very strict and insensitive kind of sex training. As a result the patient had always thought of sex as evil and dirty. Also, because of her foster mother's domineering attitude, she never learned to think for herself.

Despite her repressive sex training Mrs. *A.* felt strong sexual desires. As a result she was in conflict about sex; she was attracted by its pleasures but simultaneously feared it because, to her, it was loathsome and unclean.

When she came to the psychiatrist Mrs. *A.* was in great distress and complained of all kinds of fears: fears of being alone, of going for a walk, that her heart would stop beating unless she paid constant attention to it. In addition she suffered from a vague, oppressive fear commonly referred to as **anxiety.** She felt utterly helpless. Her continuous complaints had alienated her friends and antagonized her husband, who threatened to divorce her. She did not get along with her foster mother and her mother-in-law disliked her. Having no one to talk to, she was confused and terrified by the thought that she was going crazy.

Now let us analyze this case in terms of Dollard and Miller's three signs of neurosis. First, Mrs. *A.* was obviously miserable. She was a victim of two unresolved approach-avoidance conflicts, the more damaging one over sex. The cues resulting from sexual excitement produced great anxiety, and because sexual behavior was revolting to her she had great difficulty in freely expressing her sexual drives with her husband. But this drive would not be denied. Without being aware of what she was doing, Mrs. *A.* had courted seduction. She had gone to bars unescorted and had hitch-hiked rides with truck drivers. This behavior is clearly characterized by the second sign of neurosis: it was dangerous and stupid, considering that Mrs. *A.* loved her husband and desperately wanted her marriage to continue. Her stupid behavior was clearly the consequence of her inability to understand her problem. She could not express the conflict in words or label it even to herself because she was unaware of its existence. In other words her conflict was repressed (see page 450).

However stupid the seduction-courting behavior was, it can be viewed as an attempt to reduce the anxieties that preceded sexual behavior. Because of her conflict, deciding to have sexual relations with her husband aroused anxiety. Her seduction-courting behavior aroused less anxiety, because in its case she did not have to admit her sexual desires to herself.

Her second conflict, between aggression and fear, involved her feelings toward her mother-in-law who did not approve of her son's marriage. Feeling that her son had married "below his class," she often slighted her daughter-in-law, made nasty remarks, and was generally hostile. Mrs. *A.* accepted these rebuffs meekly and continued to protest fondness for her mother-in-law. Actually Mrs. *A.* harbored aggression toward her unconsciously and was afraid to express it. The patient was unaware of this conflict, as she was of her sex-fear

conflict, and therefore could not act wisely in relation to it. Again her behavior was characterized by the second sign of neurosis; it was foolish. By "taking" all her mother-in-law's insults she encouraged them and even lost the little respect the mother-in-law initially had for her. Mrs. *A.* did not have to suffer this maltreatment; her husband did not demand that she tolerate it. If she had only "fought back" she would have improved the situation. After all, if the mother-in-law wanted to see her son and any future grandchildren, she would have to come to terms and behave decently toward Mrs. *A.*

Objectively the patient's situation should have provided much happiness. Her husband was attractive and still in love with her in spite of his obvious annoyance. And she loved him. Her sexual appetites could find satisfaction with her husband and her relations with her mother-in-law could be improved if she went about it the right way. But she was not likely to solve these problems easily because she was unaware of the conflicts that gave rise to them in the first place.

Mrs. *A.* also exhibited the third sign of neurosis: she had a number of symptoms. According to Dollard and Miller, these neurotic symptoms function as instrumental escape and avoidance responses (see page 167) to aversive stimuli. When Mrs. *A.* went alone to public places, she felt sexual temptations which generated anxiety. She could escape from this in the safety of her home, and so she was reinforced for not going out. Consequently, she began to stay at home more and more. The counting of her heartbeats served a similar avoidance function. It was after she had had sexual thoughts that she became preoccupied with the idea that her heart might stop. Since the counting was an all-consuming task, it eliminated the sexual thoughts and thereby reduced the fear.

It would not be fair to leave you with the impression that Dollard and Miller's analysis of neurosis is accepted universally, for this is not so. A Freudian-oriented psychiatrist or psychologist would have interpreted Mrs. *A.*'s case somewhat differently and in a way that could be specified only after many psychoanalytic sessions with her. He would probably emphasize certain influences in her "psychosexual" development, stressing conflicts between the ego and the id and superego (see page 446). Other psychologists would analyze such a case strictly in terms of the individual's avoidance behavior without recourse to such concepts as repression and fear. Perhaps your instructor has definite views about such matters.

Regardless of how neurosis is conceptualized, two points stand out. First, neurotic behavior is characterized by a punishing circularity. The neurotic repeats essentially the same behavior pattern over and over again, but instead of helping him solve his problems, this repetitive behavior usually increases them. Second, the conditions we have already described like conflict, frustration, avoidance and escape conditioning, and habit competition and interference, play basic roles in producing neurotic behavior.

Having completed an overview of neurosis we shall turn our attention to describing its various forms. Neuroses are classified by dominant symptoms. Although many neurotics exhibit symptoms from a variety of types of neuroses, in most cases one symptom stands out. Mrs. *A.*'s dominant symptom was her anxiety.

Anxiety Reactions

Anxiety is practically a household word today. Our age has been described as the "Age of Anxiety." When we leave a friend, we often say, "Take it easy!" instead of the old-fashioned "Goodbye." A psychological translation of this expression is, "Don't become anxious, don't get tense, don't break down under the strain of modern life!"

Anxiety is closely related to what we have for the most part called fear up to now. The fear response, you recall, can become associated with a neutral stimulus if it is paired with a noxious one (see page 254). The neutral stimulus is then said to evoke fear. Anxiety, too, is intimately related to instrumental avoidance conditioning. It differs from fear mainly in the specificity of the stimulus that evokes it. In avoidance conditioning the stimulus that evokes the fear is specific and obvious. This is also true in everyday life, where people fear fire, an approaching car, a power saw, and other dangerous things. Anxiety, however, is a more general reaction of being threatened which is not clearly and specifically attached to any apparent cue.

People suffering from **anxiety reaction** usually complain of a general nervousness and a high degree of tension. They act fearful but cannot point to specific reasons for their fear; they are unaware of the cue that arouses the anxiety.

The general apprehension and tension of the anxious individual are due, in part, to overactivity of the autonomic nervous system which produces such physical symptoms as irregular heart rhythm, gastric discomfort, bowel disturbances, visual difficulties, cold hands and feet, and tense muscles, particularly in the back of the neck and shoulders. Admonishing the patient to relax has no effect. Constantly tense, he physically exhausts himself and complains of fatigue and a failing memory. This memory loss is not real in the sense that any organic deterioration is responsible. It more often results from the patient's inability to pay attention because he is so distracted by the tension he is constantly under.

Free-floating anxiety is the term used to describe the general vague fear of the anxiety neurotic. It is very descriptive; the anxiety does appear to float from one situation to another because it is not generated by external happenings but within the patient himself.

The dividing line between fear and anxiety is obviously not sharp. Our analysis suggests that anxiety is a *blind* apprehension and fear; the anxious person is unable to say what it is he fears. Mrs. *A.* suffered from anxiety because she was not aware of what she was really afraid of: sex and aggression. Her anxiety stemmed from a fear of being unable to control her sexual desires and a fear of expressing aggression.

You should not think that all anxiety is harmful. An appropriate amount can be useful. The driver who is sufficiently anxious about the dangers of driving will have his brakes checked, will not drink before he drives, will not drive too fast, and will not take unnecessary chances. The driver who feels no anxiety whatever takes chance after chance and contributes heavily to the tragic death toll on the roads.

Although excellent descriptions of anxiety neurosis can be found in medical books written in the seventeenth century, many people today insist that anxiety results from the "pressures of modern life." Some clinicians even maintain that the complaint of anxiety and general tension has increased during the past decade. There are reasons for believing that this is true. For example, a person suffering from anxiety feels worse when he is not occupied. Work functions for him as counting heartbeats did for Mrs. *A.*; it supplants the anxiety reaction. Hence, the shortened work week and increased free time of the present day give the anxiety neurotic more opportunity to be victimized by his anxiety and tension. However, inadequate records and changing diagnostic procedures make the statement that anxiety has increased in the last decade impossible to prove or disprove.

Severe anxiety reactions can be caused by any number of problems. As you would expect, anxiety reactions are common among soldiers in wartime when they are under the constant threat of being maimed or killed. During World War II, many who finally succumbed to severe anxiety reactions and required hospitalization had excellent combat records. This suggests that every soldier has a breaking point depending on his past experiences and physiological functioning. For some the anxiety of leaving home was sufficient to initiate a severe reaction. For others incapacitating anxiety came only after months and even years of exposure to dangers which the average person could tolerate for only brief periods of time.

The origin of most anxiety reactions in unresolved conflicts has already been discussed (see page 498). However, we cannot overestimate the role of *guilt* in these conflicts. One of the things that distinguishes man from the lower animals in his *dread of breaking the rules of right conduct* that have been drilled into him since he was born. The author recalls a patient who exhibited a severe anxiety-tension reaction. The basis of his reaction was his belief that he had sinned badly. When he learned from his priest that his behavior was not sinful, his anxiety reactions subsided.

Although conflicts are usually linked to anxiety reactions, other factors contribute to the incidence of this disorder. People are made more susceptible to such reactions by learning to be tense in many situations. The overcareful parent who constantly warns his children, "Be careful!" "That's dangerous!" "Watch out!" teaches them to be tense and fearful. It is interesting to note that anxiety-tension reactions are rare among Southern Negroes and Indians who live on reservations. In contrast they are especially common among Italians and persons of the Jewish faith.

Phobic Reactions

A person suffering from an excessive fear in the absence of any real danger is said to have a **phobic reaction,** or a **phobia.** Common phobias are: *acrophobia,* fear of high places; *claustrophobia,* fear of closed places; *agoraphobia,* fear of open spaces; *mysophobia,* fear of dirt or contamination. At one time it was a popular pastime among medical writers to invent terms to describe all such morbid dreads. The task was fairly easy, since it merely required the attachment of the properly descriptive Greek prefix to the term *phobia.* From this practice came such terms as: *melissophobia,* a fear of bees; *homilophobia,* a fear of sermons; and *onomatophobia,* a fear of names —a fear these medical writers obviously did not have.

Although phobias are easy to name they are often difficult to account for in particular cases. Sometimes the phobia is simply the outcome of a frightening experience. In one famous case (Bagby, 1928) a woman complained of a terrible fear of running water, particularly when it made a splashing sound. It was discovered that her phobia had originated in a childhood experience. Once, when she was on a picnic with her aunt, she had gone wading in a stream which her parents had expressly forbidden her to wade in, and her disobedience had had a frightening consequence. She had been trapped by the strong current underneath a waterfall and had had to stand there for several minutes with water splashing all over her. When her aunt rescued her, she had pleaded with her not to tell her parents about the incident. Although the woman had herself repressed the incident, the association between running water and the fear response had been formed and had lasted ever since.

Sometimes phobias result from stimulus generalization. For example, a young girl who as a child was thrown into a panic by a dog may develop a generalized fear of cats or other furry animals. Later on, rather than admit such a fear, she may develop a phobic reaction to fur pieces. In other words, the fear generalizes and is finally displaced (see page 396) onto an object which merely resembles the one in the original traumatic situation.

A study (Diven, 1936) involving word associations makes clearer the role of language in the development of phobias. During the course of training the word *barn* was a signal for a shock. Thereafter *barn* evoked a strong galvanic skin response (see page 159), which generalized to words like *pasture* and *hay* and to other words with rural associations. The implication of this study is that fear can become attached to a word that is not *directly* involved in the fear conditioning itself.

Similarly, phobias to things or objects related to the originally feared stimulus by verbal associations can develop. A case in point is that of a nurse who had a phobia about snow. As soon as it began to snow, she would become uneasy and would soon be forced to go to her bedroom, pull down all the shades, and get into bed. During therapy her guilt about a juvenile sexual experience was discovered to be responsible for her phobia. Because she had been raised in a strongly religious environment, she had been obsessed with guilt after the experience. Her fear of snow resulted from this guilt in a strange and roundabout way, which appeared to be explained by her associations in a word-association test. Her first association to the word *snow* was *white;* to *white* she responded *collar,* and this word evoked the reaction *purity.* Her first two associations were not uncommon, but the reaction of *purity* to the word *collar* was. The explanation of this train of associations was that snow is white and white reminded her of the collar of her minister (who happened also to be her uncle), which reminded her of morality and what she was bothered by most—purity. The snow became frightening to her and she had to escape from it.

Obsessive-Compulsive Reactions

Obsessive-compulsive reactions are characterized by the persistent and ostensibly senseless repetition of some thought or act. This neurotic reaction occurs in three major forms: (1) **Obsessions** are thoughts that recur persistently, even though they may be both unwelcome and disturbing. A young man, for example, had an obsession about what his reaction to his father's death would be. Even though the thought was very unpleasant, he could not avoid thinking about it constantly. (2) **Compulsions** are stereotyped acts that an individual performs repeatedly without knowing why and often with a desire not to. Examples of compulsions are *kleptomania,* the compulsion to steal, and often to steal something for which the kleptomaniac has no use, and *pyromania,* the compulsion to set fires. (3) The third kind of obsessive-compulsive reactions are obsessive thoughts *coupled* with compulsive acts. For example, a person may be obsessed with the thought that he will become infected by germs and feel compelled to wash his hands not once but over and over again.

Obsessive-compulsive reactions bear some similarity to the recurring superstitious behavior that can be developed in instrumental avoidance conditioning (see page 167). Initially an animal is trained to fear a stimulus that precedes shock. If the fear stimulus is terminated independently of the animal's action, he will nevertheless learn some act which he made at the time the fear stimulus was removed. Although this superstitious act does not really terminate the aversive stimulus, it does nevertheless reduce the fear that the stimulus evokes. Similarly obsessive-compulsive behavior reduces or avoids anxiety and guilt.

Conversion Reactions

In **conversion reactions** a psychological conflict is presumably converted or transformed into a physical symptom. The patient may suddenly become blind, deaf, or paralyzed in one of his limbs, or he may develop an uncontrollable muscular tic or tremor. These symptoms have no organic pathology which medical examinations can discover.

Conversion reactions are customarily classified into one of three subcategories: **hysterical sensory disturbances, hysterical paralyses,** and **hysterical motor disturbances.** In the hysterical sensory disturbances the patient suffers a sensory defect like blindness or loss of the sense of touch or taste. In hysterical paralyses he suffers paralysis of a limb, part of the body, or complete loss of voice. Hysterical motor disturbances involve the loss of muscular control. The patient may exhibit a motor tic such as a sudden twisting of the neck or blinking of the eyes. No matter how much the patient wants to inhibit these motor reactions he is unable to.

Conversion reactions are sometimes observed in military service. A soldier may suddenly complain that he is unable to walk because his legs are paralyzed or shoot a rifle because his hand is paralyzed. Obviously with such handicaps combat becomes impossible. Frequently the soldier who exhibits these symptoms in the absence of any organic defect, is suspected of faking his illness. This is rarely true. In most cases the symptoms are as real to the patient as they would be if he were organically injured.

The author recalls the case of an infantryman who suffered complete sensory anesthesia (lack of sensation) and motor paralysis of his right hand. He was insensitive to any feeling in his hand; sticking him with a needle would draw blood but not cause pain. He could neither contract nor stretch any of his fingers. However, it was obvious that his difficulties were not due to any neural damage; the pattern of his symptoms did not fit the known distribution of the sensory and motor nerves in the hand. In treatment, it was discovered that, although he was strongly patriotic, religious training had given him a strong aversion to killing, even in defense of his country. A decision was then made to transfer him to the medical corps where he would not be required to carry arms. His symptoms subsequently disappeared and he showed no marked fear while preparing to go overseas for combat duty.

Psychologists are not always clear about how conversion symptoms develop, but it appears that they often serve the function of enabling the individual to avoid conflicts. The incapacitating symptoms of the soldier provided a solution that did not require him either to violate his religious convictions or to shirk his patriotic duty.

Concluding Remarks

Neurotic patients usually do not fall neatly into one of the four subcategories of neuroses. Mrs. *A.* exhibited symptoms typical of anxiety, phobic, and obsessive-compulsive reactions. Her predominant symptom was anxiety, and therefore she would probably be diagnosed as suffering from an anxiety reaction.

The four diagnostic categories of neuroses represent, to some extent, a dimension or scale of *overt* or **manifest anxiety.** Patients suffering from anxiety reaction exhibit the most anxiety and tension. Next come the phobic patients, who react with intense anxiety, but only when exposed to the stimuli they fear, and usually their phobia shields them from such stimuli. Obsessive-compulsive individuals exhibit even less manifest anxiety than do phobics. They are not tense about one overwhelming, threatening situation. Patients suffering from conversion reactions exhibit the least anxiety and tension, which have presumably been converted into bodily symptoms.

PSYCHOSOMATIC REACTIONS

In a **psychosomatic reaction,** as this term is most often used, there is both a neurosis and some organic disorder. The organic component of psychosomatic reactions is believed to be mediated by the autonomic nervous system, whereas the bodily symptoms of the conversion reactions are under the control of the central nervous system. Psychosomatic reactions demonstrate that behavior disorders may be linked with physiological processes in such a way as to produce physical illness or damage. In most of these cases the patient comes to his physician's office with a complaint such as stomach trouble or excessive fatigue. The physician discovers that his symptoms are based on genuine organic conditions, unlike the symptoms in cases of conversion reaction. There is an actual physical pathology. It may be that an ulcer is responsible for stomach distress, or that high blood pressure and hypertension are the causes of excessive fatigue. These somatic (bodily) complaints require medical treatment. Special diets and eventually surgery may be needed for the ulcer, or energizing drugs for the fatigue. However, the medical problem is not the only one; there is also a psychological problem. The somatic complaints are the end-products of psychological conflicts.

To the lay person psychosomatic disorders appear both mysterious and unbelievable, and the question of how a disturbance in the mind can cause damage to the body seems to him unanswerable. The difficulty, however, lies not in the answer but in the question itself. The separation between the psychological and the physiological, implied in the term *psychosomatic* (mind-body) is itself misleading, as the early history of psychology has shown (see page 39). If psychology is understood to be the science of behavior, and not of the mind, there will be no cleft between psychology and physiology. Underlying all behavior are physiological processes. Emotions like embarrassment and fear are not independent of bodily changes; we are embarrassed or fearful with our entire bodies. There is nothing mysterious in the fact that we blush when we are embarrassed or that our pulse rate increases when we become afraid or anxious, so why should there be anything more mysterious in the fact that physiological changes are involved in neurotic reactions?

Experiments (Sawrey & Weisz, 1956; Sawrey, Conger, & Turrell, 1956) have shown that rats develop ulcers when they are exposed to a continuous fear-hunger conflict. As you remember, monkeys also develop ulcers from long periods of avoidance training (see page 433). Even in man the physiological changes which lead to ulcers have been observed. Systematic observations (Wolff & Wolff, 1947) were made of a man who had cut into his stomach an artificial opening through which he was fed. He needed this gastric fistula because his esophagus had been closed in childhood by accidental scalding. When this man was fired from his job for reasons he believed were unjust, he became anxious and hostile. His stomach lining became engorged with blood and he complained of gastric pains. In this condition his stomach walls were easily damaged and minute ulcers began to appear. These healed when his reactions changed from hostility and anxiety to calmness and relaxation.

Not everyone who is anxious and hostile will develop gastric ulcers. If the intensity of his reactions reaches neurotic proportions, he may develop defensive neuroses that do not involve tissue damage. Or he may react with psychosomatic ailments not involving the gastrointestinal tract, such as hypertension, bronchial asthma, or a skin disorder.

There is no clear explanation of why one psychosomatic complaint develops rather than another. It would seem reasonable to assume that genetic factors play a role. Some people may inherit stomachs more susceptible to ulceration than others. This does not predestine them to stomach ulcers, but it does increase the probability of its happening if they are exposed to excessive anxiety or tension.

Environmental factors can also increase the probability that psychosomatic complaints will develop. Both Wall Street and Madison Avenue are sometimes called "Ulcer Alley" because the executives who work on them are constantly confronted with important decisions involving large amounts of money and therefore the incidence of ulcers is above average. The valid ity of the positive correlation between ulcers and tense business life is manifested by the greater frequency of ulcers among women in business than among women who spend their time largely in their homes.

The fact that psychosomatic disorders do occur should not lead us to conclude that anyone who develops ulcers, hypertension, asthma, or a skin ailment suffers from a personality disorder and requires psychiatric treatment. An ulcer can result from accidentally swallowing a piece of glass in one's food. The correct diagnosis of a psychosomatic ailment is not based solely upon bodily symptoms; there must also be positive evidence of a psychological disturbance.

PSYCHOSIS

The most extreme forms of pathological behavior are the **psychoses.** A psychosis is roughly similar but not identical to what is commonly called insanity (see page 49). Defining psychosis is difficult because the term covers so many different kinds of severely disordered reactions. A distinguishing feature of every psychosis, however, is that the psychotic's contact with reality is poor. In addition, his behavior, including his verbal behavior, is peculiar. He may become a danger to himself or to others. Usually he is unable to meet certain demands of society, like being able to take care of himself and get along with others. As a result, he may have to be institutionalized. When a person is legally committed to an institution because he can no longer be held responsible for his actions, he is declared to be insane. Insanity is, therefore, a legal term, not a psychological one.

It has been customary to distinguish between two main classes of psychoses: the *organic* and the *functional*. In an **organic psychosis** the abnormalities of behavior have a known physiological cause, as when brain damage sustained in an accident causes a previously well-adjusted individual to behave in a highly abnormal manner. A **functional psychosis** is one in which the disordered behavior appears to be the end result of years of poor adjustments and severe conflicts. Most kinds of schizophrenic reactions (the next topic in our discussion) are classified among the functional psychoses.

The distinction between functional and organic psychoses is, like many other distinctions, not to be considered absolute. Functional (learning) and organic (physiological) factors can interact. A person who has some disordered reactions may develop a full-blown psychosis after a brain injury. A better adjusted person may exhibit no marked deterioration in behavior after the same injury.

Nor must the distinction be taken to mean that although an organic psychosis results from physiological variables, a functional one is without a neurological basis. Ultimately physiological variables, and neurological ones especially, will be discovered for all psychotic behavior. The difference between organic and functional rests in the kinds of physiological changes responsible for the psychotic reactions. The organic disorders result from such physiological changes as those associated with injury, bodily disease, drugs, or aging. Functional disorders are *learned.* Although the physiological basis of such learning is not well understood (see page 180), there can be no doubt that it is connected with changes in underlying physiological processes. If and when they are discovered the physiological side of functional psychoses will be understood.

Schizophrenia

The form of psychosis that is most common and that constitutes the gravest problem for psychiatry is schizophrenia, a word derived from the Greek words *schizin* (to split) and *phren* (mind). The seriousness of the prob-lem was underlined by the decision of the Second International Congress of Psychiatry (held in Switzerland in 1957) to devote the entire meeting to the problem of schizophrenia. This meeting of leading psychiatrists from all over the world also demonstrated how much there is still to be learned about schizophrenia. No unanimous agreement prevailed on the care and treatment of schizophrenia, or for that matter, on its diagnosis. Some delegates maintain that the term *schizophrenia* represents not one but two disorders, and possibly more. Nevertheless the term is useful, at least for the present, because it refers to a general pattern of responses, or to a syndrome, as it is called in medicine.

As we have said, there are many definitions of schizophrenia, but one characterization that is sufficiently general and descriptive to serve our purposes runs as follows: **Schizophrenia** *is a psychotic reaction, usually beginning somewhere from the time of puberty to 40 years of age, characterized by disturbances in the patient's contact with reality and in his intellectual and affective* (emotional) *behavior. The schizophrenic becomes seclusive and exhibits inappropriate moods, odd verbal behavior, regressive* (see page 405) *intellectual functioning, and often hallucinations* (false sense impressions) *and delusions* (false beliefs).

Widespread use is made of a classificatory scheme which divides schizophrenia into four subcategories. There is much overlapping among the groups, and it is not uncommon for a patient's symptoms to shift from one subgroup to another during the course of the illness. Nevertheless such a classification is useful: it provides a fuller description of schizophrenia and sketches its course of development.

Simple Type. The simple schizophrenic is the opposite of the popular idea of the psychotic as a violent person: he is quiet and withdrawn. His isolation from his fellow men suggests a loss of interest in life and society. In some cases, but not all, this lack of interest is more apparent than real. The patient does not mix with people because he is unable to assert himself, to hold up his end of social contacts. He is so withdrawn that he has become incapable of making even the simple social overtures that precede forming friendships. In other cases of **simple schizophrenia** the patient is completely detached from society. He is suffering not from an extreme degree of shyness but rather from a complete lack of interest in other people.

In addition to being apathetic, the simple schizophrenic has disordered intellectual and emotional reactions. He seems unable to put things together in a way that will solve a problem. The following anecdote drawn from the writer's experience as a clinical psychologist illustrates this difficulty. A patient had been referred to him for diagnostic psychological testing to determine whether he was schizophrenic. The patient was given an intelligence test, because it is often an extremely sensitive instrument in uncovering schizophrenic thought processes. One question was: "What would you do if you were the first person in a crowded theatre to discover a fire?" The patient, a young man of 26, thought a while and then replied, "I would yell 'fire.' " Almost immediately he realized that "yelling fire" was the wrong answer, because it "would cause a panic." He had sufficient insight to see that the correct answer depended on informing someone without triggering a riot. The patient thought for several minutes, literally sweating in his efforts to find an answer. Finally he smiled shyly and commented, "I know the answer. I'd yell 'fire' in such a way that it would not cause a panic." When he was asked to show how he would do this, the patient rose to his feet slowly and whispered "fire."

You must realize that this patient was not stupid. He had graduated from high school with good grades. But in some slow, insidious manner his intellectual ability was deteriorating. He could not solve problems, particularly those requiring abstract symbolic processes, which previously had been easy for him.

The intellectual disorder had a counterpart in the patient's emotional reactions. He exhibited a *loss of affect* (loss of feeling), describing the recent death of his mother in the same colorless manner as he did the weather.

This simple form of schizophrenia almost never develops suddenly, as the other forms of schizophrenia sometimes do. In its early stages, when the disordered reactions are not severe, the onset of the illness often goes undetected. Sometimes the disorder does not progress beyond the incipient stages and the patient remains able to make some sort of an adjustment, although a poor one, outside of an institution. More often, however, his emotional and intellectual difficulties continue to increase, and on occasion he suffers from hallucinations and delusions, although they are difficult to detect because he usually does not tell anyone about them. Some simple schizophrenics wind up as hoboes and prostitutes, but more often, their inability to adjust leads them to be committed to a psychiatric institution, where many of them remain until they die of old age.

Paranoid Type. The distinctive feature of the **paranoid type** of schizophrenia is that the patient suffers from delusions, particularly delusions of persecution and self-reference. The paranoid schizophrenic is convinced that people are trying to harm him, deny him his rights, or even to kill him, and he tends to interpret almost everything that happens around him as evidence of his delusions. For example, an army sergeant, who was a patient of the institution the author was assigned to during World War II, suddenly became convinced that he was being persecuted by German agents, who were testing out a new weapon in order to make him their slave. As he and the author were walking along a hall in the hospital, he confided that the chief psychiatrist, who was standing nearby talking to a colleague, was in fact a German agent plotting at that moment to enslave him.

These patients often exhibit the aggressive attitude that would be natural in a person who was actually being victimized. At first they may be just bitter and suspicious, but as the disorder progresses they can become openly rebellious and violent and extremely dangerous to people around them as well as to themselves. They may attack "in self-defense," or attempt suicide in an effort to escape from persecution that threatens them with torture and suffering.

The disorder can flare up suddenly or develop gradually. In the beginning there is sometimes a perceptible link between the person's delusion and his motivation. It is not uncommon for a young male paranoid schizophrenic to believe that his father wishes to harm or even kill him, and in some of these cases there is a strong suggestion that the patient's fear is a form of projection. That is, he harbors hostile feelings toward his father which he projects outward and attributes to his father. But as the disorder progresses the delusions become so general and disorganized that it is difficult or impossible to discover how they originated.

Paranoid schizophrenics often experience auditory hallucinations and sometimes visual ones. They hear persecutory messages or voices announcing their fame and importance. Although delusions are the most dominant symptom of paranoid schizophrenia, the patient may also exhibit behavior similar to that seen in simple schizophrenia: disorders of affect and intelligence creep into his behavior. Many patients who begin as paranoids end up as deteriorated simple schizophrenics.

Hebephrenic Type. Like the paranoiac, the person with **hebephrenic schizophrenia** suffers from a delusional system, but it is a somewhat different one. His delusions are often concerned with bodily functions: he may believe that sand has gotten into his heart, that his bowels are filled with cement, or that his brain is melting. His delusional system is not as well organized as the paranoid's; it appears jumbled. The major symptoms of hebephrenia are silliness, inappropriate smiling and laughter; strange and disorganized ideas; and neologisms, the invention of new words. The following exchange between a psychiatrist and a Negro schizophrenic patient captures the peculiar quality of hebephrenia:

"How old are you?"
"Why, I am centuries old, sir."
"How long have you been here?"
"I have been now on this property on and off for a long time. I cannot say the exact time because we are absorbed by the air at night, and they bring black people. They kill up everything; they can make you lie; they can talk through your throat."
"Who is this?"
"Why, the air."
"What is the name of this place?"
"This place is called a star."
"Who is the doctor in charge of your ward?"
"A body just like yours, sir. They can make you black and white. I say 'good morning,' but he just comes through there. At first it was a colony. They said it was heaven. These buildings were not solid at the time, and I am positive this is the same place. They have others like it. People die, and all the microbes talk over there, and prestigitis you know is sending you from here to another world. . . . I was sent by the government to the United States to Washington to some star, and they had a pretty nice country there. Now you have a body like a young man who says he is of the prestigitis."
"Who was this prestigitis?"
"Why, you are yourself. You can be a prestigitis. They make you say bad things; they can read you; they bring back Negroes from the dead" (White, 1932, p. 228).

Catatonic Type. In **catatonic schizophrenia** motor disorders predominate. The patient may be overactive or impassive, excitable or stuporous.

One of the most dramatic symptoms in catatonia is **waxy flexibility.** The author

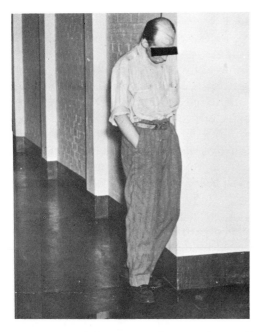

FIGURE 14.1 A Patient in a Catatonic Stupor. He was in this position for several hours (Dr. Ogden R. Lindsley).

remembers a neatly dressed sergeant who reported one day to the neuropsychiatric section of the army hospital. Since he complained in a vague way that people were after him, he was placed under observation: But at the end of the first day it was no longer possible to communicate with him; he sat on his bed and seemed completely insensitive to the world about him. At the end of the second day he was dishevelled and sat in the corner of the room in an odd position, one leg crossed over the other, one arm around his neck and the other across his chest. This posture could however, be molded. The psychiatrist moved the arm that lay across the patient's chest so that it extended straight out from his side, a position he maintained for several hours. In a state of waxy flexibility during a catatonic stupor, a patient's body can be molded into any odd posture. He may also assume a position and stay in it for weeks. In order to keep him alive, psychiatric aides have to feed him through a tube.

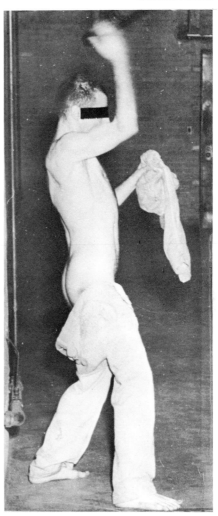

FIGURE 14.2 A Patient in a Hypermanic State (Dr. Ogden R. Lindsley).

Instead of exhibiting waxy flexibility some catatonics actively resist any change in their posture. Against strong resistance an arm can be stretched out straight by the doctor, but immediately it is released it snaps back to its former position.

A patient in a catatonic stupor appears to be unaware of what is happening about him. He is not; often patients can recall later all that went on while they were in a stuporous condition.

In contrast to the catatonic stupors are the less frequent catatonic excitements. These last for brief periods, because they require enormous physical energy. The pa-

510 tient is literally in a frenzied state that is sometimes governed by a delusion or hallucination, but at other times appears simply to be disorganized violence. During such episodes the danger that he may commit homicide or suicide is great.

Manic-depressive Psychosis

The second most common psychosis is the **manic-depressive reaction.** Its main symptom is a disturbance in mood. The manic-depressive psychotic has periods during which he is either exaggeratedly elated or depressed, and he may alternate between these. The mania is marked by flight of ideas, extreme elation, and overactivity. It varies in intensity. The less intense form, **hypomania** is characterized by a show of energy, enthusiasm, and optimism not un-like that of a mildly intoxicated person. It is not uncommon for a hypomanic individual to make what appears to be a reasonably good adjustment. His energy and enthusiasm may help him do his job unusually well, and his elation and optimism may make him well-liked, even though he is thought of as an "odd duck." Quite often, however, his symptoms like excessive talking and inability to concentrate, get him into difficulty. He bothers his neighbors by giving them unsolicited advice and becomes a general nuisance when his elation prevails over his social inhibitions and leads him to behave in an unacceptable way. Then complaints are usually made to the police, and as a result he is sooner or later given a psychiatric examination and his difficulties discovered. A patient with **hypermania,** the more intense form, behaves like a raving maniac. He is uncontrollably excitable and may lack almost every social inhibition, so that he becomes completely reckless about his own safety and that of others. His overactivity gives him the appearance of being superhuman.

The following case history describes a young soldier who exhibited at different times both hypomanic and hypermanic reactions:

He was a pleasant, friendly soldier who had an excellent record as an airplane mechanic. Over a period of a few months, however, his behavior gradually changed. He surprised his fellow soldiers and commanding officer by talking incessantly and telling everyone how to do his job. His own work began to deteriorate, since he was not giving it his customary attention. After work he would go out on parties and rarely get to bed before three o'clock in the morning.

One day he became more excitable. Instead of eating during lunchtime he performed, to the amusement of his coworkers, difficult gymnastic feats on top of a plane. Later, he suddenly became belligerent and socked another mechanic who wouldn't take his advice. The fight was broken up by a sergeant, who took the soldier to his commanding officer, where he started another argument and finally punched the officer. Four soldiers were required to subdue him. The officer, remembering his lessons from introductory psychology, decided that the offending soldier should be sent to the neuropsychiatric section instead of the guardhouse. However, the soldier broke away while he was being put in an ambulance and ran toward a bomber, shouting that he was going to end the war himself. Fortunately, he wasn't able to fly the plane, and after another struggle he was subdued and brought to the hospital under restraint. There uttering profanities he tried unsuccessfully to rip off a nurse's dress, but he did manage to rip a radiator from the wall, shouting, "I'm stronger than Superman." Again he was placed under restraint and given drugs to quiet him down.

This hypermanic episode lasted about two weeks, and then rather suddenly he started behaving in his former pleasant and friendly manner. His case history revealed that at 15 he had been institutionalized for a similar manic episode. When it was over he had returned home, resumed his schooling, and behaved normally until the mania recurred in the army.

FIGURE 14.3 A Patient in a Psychotically Depressed State (Ciba Pharmaceutical Co.).

lose weight, stopped socializing with his fellow officers, and spent all his spare time in his room, where he was known to have frequent crying spells. The day after an American military reverse, an incident that had no relation to anything he had done, he slashed his wrists. An orderly discovered him soon afterward and a physician was able to save his life.

The chief feature of his case, and one that is often true of other such cases, is that the patient suffered from tendencies to perceive himself as guilty of grave offenses and shortcomings. An extremely conscientious person, he suffered a sense of guilt so oppressive that he sought to escape from it by committing suicide.

Nearly all of us have mood swings. Some individuals alternate between exuberance and depression; others experience intermittent moods of either one. The mood swings of a manic-depressive psychotic are, however, much more extreme than those of a normal person, and they are not at all appropriate to the circumstances in which they occur.

As we have implied, not all people suffering from manic-depressive psychosis exhibit both phases of this disorder. The majority of them have only episodes of mania or of depression interspersed with periods of apparent normality. However, some do alternate between manic and depressed episodes (see Figure 14.4). It is not clear why they have these swings, but many clinicians agree that in spite of the apparent dissimilarity between mania and depression, they are psychologically akin. One plausible hypothesis is that mania constitutes an attempt to postpone and cover up fear of an impending depression. A similar kind of mechanism operates in the more normal individual who attempts to cope with feeling blue by going on a lark.

The prognosis, or the forecast of the course, of the disorder, is much better for manic-depressive psychosis than it is for

The depressed individual presents a picture quite the opposite of the manic. Instead of being overactive he is underactive. Instead of feeling fine and elated he feels utterly depressed and sad. Instead of feeling powerful he feels weak. Instead of feeling innocent of wrongdoing he is filled with guilt.

A case in point is that of a 40-year-old army major which follows:

He was returned from combat duty overseas because he attempted suicide during a severe depression. An extremely conscientious officer respected by his superiors and his men, his only failing seemed to be that he "took everything to heart," including military setbacks for which he was not responsible and over which he had no control.

The major became more and more depressed as the war went on. He began to

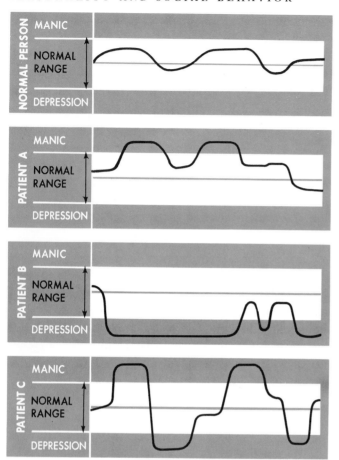

FIGURE 14.4 Mood Swings in Normal Persons and Manic-Depressive Psychotics. A healthy person's mood swings are within normal limits; a psychotic's exceed normal limits. A suffers from recurrent manic episodes, whereas patient B has recurrent depressions. Patient C alternates between manic and depressed periods.

schizophrenia. About 10 per cent of new admissions to psychiatric hospitals are diagnosed as manic-depressive psychotics. Because a very considerable proportion recover from this episode and never have another one, the resident population so diagnosed remains at about the 10 per cent level. The initial psychotic episode occurs with the greatest frequency in middle age, but it is not unusual for it to occur in the teens or the early twenties. There is a strong suggestion that those who eventually succumb to this psychosis are persons who have experienced definite mood swings earlier in their lives.

Involutional Melancholia

A disordered reaction somewhat similar to the depressive phase of the manic-depressive psychosis is **involutional melancholia.** This reaction occurs around the change-of-life period, ranging from 40 to 50 years of age in women and from 50 to 65 years in men, when marked physiological changes occur. Women experience the menopause, the termination of menstrual cycles, ovulation, and the ability to bear children. Men may also experience biochemical readjustments—although much less radical ones than women's—which result in lessened sexual activity and decreased ability to reproduce.

During this trying period some individuals succumb to the involutional melancholic reaction. They become depressed, agitated, or both, and sometimes suffer from delusions or persecution. Like the depressed psychotic, the involutional melancholic feels guilty, worthless, and unable to cope with the future. He may contemplate suicide and sometimes attempt it.

Since not everyone suffers from an involutional melancholic reaction in later middle-age, we cannot attribute this condition solely to physiological and endocrine changes. Other factors must contribute to the fully developed clinical picture, and some of them are not difficult to discover. As a person grows older and slows down physically, his position in society may change drastically. Because his economic worth is lessening he would find it difficult to change employment if he became dissatisfied with his job. Old age, and ultimately death, are closing in on him. And in a society like ours, where youth and sexual vigor are valued highly, he finds himself if not ignored, at least an object of sympathy or pity. In short, there is some justification in fact for his depression.

The prognosis for involutional melancholia is much better now than it was several decades ago. At that time a sizable number of people never recovered from their depressions and were forced to spend the rest of their days in psychiatric institutions. With new techniques of treatment, to be discussed later in this chapter, a large percentage of individuals who fall victim to involutional depressive states now recover rapidly.

Organic Psychoses

Organic psychoses are those directly attributable to damage to the brain or some other part of the central nervous system. About 40 per cent of first admissions into psychiatric institutions are patients with such disorders.

The symptoms vary markedly, depending on the location and the extent of the organic damage or deterioration. Patients with organic psychoses exhibit three major symptoms: (1) impairment of intellectual functions; (2) moderate to extreme mood swings; and (3) defective social behavior (irresponsible conduct, absence of concern for personal appearance, and antisocial actions).

The case of a 56-year-old woman who previously led a reasonably happy and productive existence illustrates the development of an organic psychosis (Goldstein & Katz, 1937).

She became disordered in ways that were innocuous enough, but for the fact that they were at great variance with her previous behavior. Always an exceedingly efficient housekeeper and dressmaker, she now became sloppy and surprised her husband by allowing food to burn on the stove. She began to neglect her dressmaking and spend her time reading magazines. She even read the same stories over and over again, apparently without realizing it. She had been a cheerful person, but now she suffered from spells of rather deep gloom.

It became obvious that she was behaving queerly when she began having hallucinations. A hallucination that her dead brother was walking around outside her house recurred repeatedly. Sometimes she would run out to talk to him, forgetting that she was not dressed. She became more and more confused and failed to recognize her friends and relatives, and even her husband. She saw a strange cat with legs all over his body, and concluded that it moved around by rolling instead of walking. Such bizarre forms of behavior convinced everybody that she should be institutionalized.

In the hospital, the patient first relapsed into a severe depression. After a while this gave way to a state of general cheerfulness, although her confusion, including the delusions and hallucinations remained. In spite of these disorders she was able to knit with skill and even solve simple arithmetic problems. However, on tests for higher level intellectual functioning requiring judgment and abstractions she did poorly.

Her behavior was found to be the result of a progressive brain disease known as Pick's Disease. The origin of this disorder is not known, but there is some suggestion that it has a genetic basis. It is a degenerative disorder that involves principally the cells of the frontal lobes of the cortex, postmortem examination of a victim shows that the cortex, especially the frontal lobes, has suffered decay. Pick's Disease has somewhat the same effect on behavior as aging, except that the symptoms are more extreme than those even in very old people. At present there is no known way of preventing or arresting the disorder.

Most organic psychoses can be classified by cause under one of four major categories: (1) disease, (2) injuries, (3) chemicals, and (4) aging.

Psychosis Due to Disease. The case of the woman suffering from **Pick's Disease** belongs to the first category. The category also includes the psychoses resulting from general paresis. The organic basis of general paresis is syphilitic damage to the brain. Only a small percentage of those who contract syphilis develop paresis. Even before the advent of the wonder drugs such as penicillin, which are extremely effective in destroying the microorganisms responsible for syphilis, only about 2 per cent of patients contracting this disease became paretic. The first symptoms, which may appear years after the initial syphilitic infection, are general sluggishness, sometimes including the complete loss of certain reflexes, particularly the pupillary reaction to light; difficulty in controlling lip and tongue movements, and consequently slurred speech; and incipient failure in intellectual ability, especially the memory of recent events. The paretic may also fall victim to mood swings as severe as those of the manic-depressive, or he may become relaxed and contented. Sometimes he develops the delusion that he is a great historical figure like Napoleon. If the disease is left untreated the disabilities become more and more severe until death occurs.

Psychosis Due to Injury. Since organic psychoses result from damage to the central nervous system, it is not surprising that brain injuries caused by automobile accidents and bullet wounds can lead to psychoses. This kind of brain damage usually fails to have a permanent effect, or it may cause only slight sensory and motor defects, depending upon the location of the injury. But on occasion full-blown psychoses with such symptoms as hallucinations, severe mood swings, and intellectual deficiencies follow injury to the brain. These symptoms cannot, however, be attributed entirely to the injury itself. The personality of the individual prior to the accident also plays a role. This is not difficult to understand. Although the patient's brain is damaged, he remains the same individual with many, if not all, of his previous habits. Evidence supports the idea that the behavioral symptoms following a brain injury are intimately related to the patient's previous behavior pattern. A person who becomes psychotically depressed is likely to be a person who was less severely depressed prior to the injury. Although the damage that finally results from these brain injuries cannot be repaired, the patients can sometimes profit from treatment if it is directed, as in other psychiatric cases, at substituting appropriate behavior for the disordered reactions.

Psychoses Due to Chemicals. At one time alcoholism, or excessive consumption of alcoholic beverages, was considered a moral problem. Today it is generally considered to be a form of illness. Approximately one-half of the population of the United States consumes alcoholic beverages in some form and amount and about five million of these people consume it to excess. The significant characteristic of excessive drinking is its compulsive character. The alcoholic cannot stop drinking after one or two drinks, no matter how strong his resolution. And if his usual source of liquor or wine has "dried up," his craving is so strong that he will drink hair tonic or almost any other liquid containing alcohol.

Compulsive drinking seems incomprehensible to the nonalcoholic, who tends to believe that the alcoholic suffers basically from a lack of moral fiber, that he could stop drinking if he would just make up his mind to do it. This is not true. Compulsive behavior, whether it is drinking to excess, an uncontrollable tic, obsessive thoughts, or a high rate of responding in a variable interval schedule of reinforcement, cannot be considered evidence of some vague lack of will power. It should be construed more positively, in terms of the conditions that combine to produce the recurring compulsive acts.

Several different explanations of alcoholism have been offered; all sound plausible but none are universally accepted. One explanation attributes alcoholism to a physiological or metabolic deficiency of some kind. Endocrine disturbances and nutritional abnormalities have all been advanced as root causes of alcoholism. Another hypothesis explains alcoholism as in some way an expression of a disordered personality. According to this interpretation, any accompanying physiological defects are the result, rather than the cause, of excessive drinking. Although popular at one time, this "disordered personality" view is nowadays held to be incomplete. Of course, no one would deny that unresolved conflicts exert a powerful influence upon behavior, as in neurotic reactions. However, we must not forget that in attributing disordered reactions to personal difficulties, we do not answer the important question, Why *this* particular disordered reaction? After all, not every person with an unresolved conflict becomes an alcoholic.

In the search for a more complete picture, three sets of variables have been emphasized: (1) the ability to drink; (2) a personality disorder; and (3) a suitable environment.

The first requirement may seem odd. But obviously people who cannot consume any sizable amount of alcohol without getting sick cannot become alcoholics, nor can people who cannot drink very much because the release from inhibitions they get after a drink or two raises too much fear for them to bear (see page 422).

The second condition for alcoholism is some psychological conflict within the personality. No one becomes an alcoholic simply from the enjoyment and relaxation of a cocktail or two. A conflicted personality is a prerequisite. In some cases alcoholism occurs after a psychosis has developed. More often, however, the alcoholic is a neurotic to begin with. He is hounded by fears, taut with tension, exhausted with fatigue, or perhaps all three. Unfortunately for him alcohol brings relief. After he has had a few drinks, fears, tension, and fatigue dissipate as rapidly as smoke in a cloudless sky. Of course, the old tortures return with a vengeance after the effects of alcohol wear off, and his problems are aggravated because drinking makes him less able and efficient in coping with them. Alcoholism ruins marriages, demolishes careers, and loses friends, but even these tragedies are blunted and then pushed into oblivion by drink.

The third cause for alcoholism is an environment that encourages the *excessive* use of alcohol. At one time people thought that the problem could be solved by creating strong public sentiment against drinking and by preventing the purchase of alcoholic beverages. The prohibition era in the United States proved this view to be naive. Moreover, personal histories of alcoholics show that many of them grow up in environments where strong prohibitions against drinking prevailed. Furthermore, many alcoholics accept, introject (see page 517) these anti-alcohol attitudes and firmly adhere to them even when they are drunk.

Of course, one can argue that if prohibition of the sale and consumption of alcoholic beverages was made effective, the problem of alcoholism would be solved simply because no one could get drunk. But even then the problems of existing alcoholics or potential alcoholics would not be solved. Many might turn to addiction to opium or codein, which also provides escape, however temporary, from the fears and stress of their conflicts. And those who did not acquire a different form of addiction might succumb to some psychiatric disturbance.

In a highly developed society like ours, where alcohol has many medicinal and industrial uses, it is terribly unrealistic to believe that any effective prohibition against its consumption can be enforced. The astonishing history of the prohibition era has shown us this. A more effective method of controlling alcoholism seems to be to train people to use alcoholic beverages sensibly. The value of this approach is suggested by the low incidence of alcoholism in this country among three cultural groups that sanction the use of alcohol—Jews, Italians, and Chinese. Each of these groups accepts the idea that alcoholic beverages exist and have a place in life, just as do food, carbonated beverages, and candy, but each has clear-cut ideas about where, when, and how much a person should drink. Drinking is acceptable at meals, at festive occasions, and for certain religious observances. Drinking alone, drinking to get drunk, or even frequenting a local bar because "you need a drink" are considered abuses of alcohol. In contrast, there is a relatively high incidence of alcoholism among cultural groups whose members do not learn a clear discrimination between acceptable and unacceptable drinking habits. When young people from these groups are exposed to the problem of drinking, as sooner or later most are in our society, they are more likely to drink frequently and excessively.

Basically, we can solve the problem of social influences on drinking by taking advantage of the phenomenon of habit competition. Learning to react to a stimulus with one response makes it difficult for people to react to it with another response. Thus learning to drink moderately within well-defined social situations helps prevent us from learning to drink excessively.

By itself alcoholism cannot properly be considered a psychosis. In the early stages of this disease the alcoholic, except during drunken stupors, is in contact with reality. He is able to meet the demands of his family and job, although not particularly well. But by continuing to drink excessively, he exposes himself increasingly to the risk of one of several psychotic reactions.

The most common of these reactions is **delirium tremens.** Typically only people who have been heavy drinkers for many years are susceptible. The delirium patient is both confused and insensitive to his enviroment. He is tortured by vivid hallucinations, usually of rats or snakes which crawl over him, and sometimes even attack him. His whole body trembles, he registers a high fever and a weak pulse, and sometimes he goes into convulsions.

The delirium lasts from three to seven days and is dangerous for two reasons. First, the patient is a suicide risk and must be watched carefully. Second, the delirium may, and often does, result in death. An attack of delirium tremens proves fatal to about 5 per cent of alcoholics in hospitals. The fatality rate for alcoholics who suffer an attack alone and unattended is considerably higher, estimated at from 20 to 25 per cent.

Some cases of delirium tremens are followed in a few days by a pattern of symptoms known as **Korsakow's syndrome,** named after the Russian psychiatrist who first described it. Its dominant symptom is loss of memory for recent events. In order to compensate for his memory lapses, the patient fills in his story by **confabulating** or improvising. For example, if the patient is asked what he ate at noon and cannot remember, he invents a fictitious menu. Sometimes memory lapses occur with unbelievable suddenness. Immediately after he has placed an emptied glass of milk on the table, the patient cannot remember that he just had a glass of milk. At the same time he may have perfect memory for events that occurred many years ago.

Korsakow's syndrome is caused by a vitamin deficiency. One vicious consequence of alcoholism is that the alcoholic drinks so much he does not eat properly. Alcohol, which is rich in calories, supplies him with enough energy, but with none of the essential proteins, minerals, and vitamins. Moreover, such a generous intake of calories in the form of alcohol increases abnormally the body's need for vitamins (especially B vitamins). Therefore, even if the alcoholic did have a normal diet, which would be unusual, he would still suffer from a vitamin deficiency.

Korsakow's syndrome, as you would expect, responds well to vigorous vitamin treatment. Some of the symptoms, such as polyneuritis—an inflammation of the nerves that causes a burning, prickly feeling in the hands and feet—disappear with heavy injections of vitamins. But complete cure of the memory defect is rare. Some permanent deterioration of the brain cells must occur, although at present we don't know the exact nature of this.

The chemically induced psychoses are not limited to those that result from the use of alcohol or drugs. The malfunction of certain endocrine glands can also produce psychotic reactions. An overactive thyroid gland, for example, may greatly accelerate a person's pulse and metabolic rate raising the activity level and making him irritable and anxious. If his condition is not treated, the hyperthyroid patient may suffer hallucinations. Because of this overactivity and hallucinatory behavior, a severe case of hyperthyroidism is quite commonly mistaken initially for a manic reaction.

Psychosis Due to Aging. Inevitably, as people grow older, they experience many kinds of physiological changes. However, physical aging does not proceed at the same rate for all people. In this respect individual differences are very great. Some people of 70 look and behave like the average 50-year-old; others appear excessively old even for 70.

A distressing form of behavioral change that overtakes a fair number of older people is **senile psychosis.** Typically the first symptoms of this disease are depression and irritability. Increasing egocentricity and conservatism ("the old way is the best way") are also characteristic, as well as a loss of efficiency and memory, particularly

memory of recent events. As the disorder progresses these symptoms increase in severity and sometimes new ones, such as paranoia, appear. The patient's judgment becomes poor and his attention begins to wander. Finally he may become so completely helpless and insensitive to his environment that nursing care is essential.

Not all senile psychotics reach this stage of helplessness and hopelessness. Many die before deterioration is far advanced; with others the symptoms are arrested before they reach a terminal stage. Even so, most cases constitute difficult and distressing problems to their families and society.

The physiological changes related to senile psychosis are the result of damage to or deterioration of brain tissue. With aging the walls of the blood vessels become harder and thicker, and this reduces the flow of blood to the brain. As a result, the cerebral tissues get less oxygen and begin to deteriorate. These changes are similar to but less drastic than, those that take place in Pick's Disease (see page 513).

Senile psychosis apparently cannot be attributed simply to different rates of physiological aging, for different individuals with what seem to be the same underlying physiological changes behave quite differently. One will adjust to old age fairly adequately, whereas another will become psychotic. Some of the psychological and social factors which play such an important role in involutional melancholia (see page 512) must also operate in senile psychosis.

CHARACTER DISORDERS

Character disorder is a diagnostic category with features common to both neurosis and psychosis, but it demands separate treatment. In the opinion of many clinicians, these disorders are markedly increasing in our society. The term *character disorder* is unfortunately vague, and it has been given different and sometimes contradictory definitions. We shall restrict it to a distinctive class of disorders in conduct. An individual with a character disorder commits antisocial acts because he failed, usually early in life, to learn or abide by the laws and customs of his society. His behavior is dominated by his own immediate needs, to the exclusion of the needs of others and of society.

A simple example that captures the quality of this kind of behavior comes from the case history of a 20-year-old soldier who had been arrested near midnight for stealing from a delicatessen. He described the incident as follows:

When I got out of the movies it was about eleven-thirty. I was really hungry. I walked around the square to find a restaurant open but in this hick town everything shuts down at eight o'clock. I passed a delicatessen and I noticed this luscious salami in the window. Boy, it made me hungry just to look at it. I looked around and saw nobody in sight, so I broke the window and grabbed the salami.

Obviously he did not "look around" very carefully because he failed to see some police officers parked in a car a block away.

This soldier knew he was doing wrong, but that did not bother him. He was hungry and his hunger dominated his behavior to the exclusion of all other considerations. In the same situation a person with a conscience would have gone to bed hungry if no food was available. This would not have been a very severe frustration for the soldier; he had eaten a large steak dinner several hours before. But he was unable to tolerate even that much frustration.

This soldier's history was dotted with incidents of getting into trouble because he couldn't tolerate the frustrations imposed on all of us by social laws and custom. In high school he had been arrested for stealing an automobile. It was not a premeditated crime. He had had a date with a pretty girl and on the way to meet

her he had passed a convertible. Thinking that the car would impress the girl and insure an enjoyable evening, he impulsively drove off with it. He had planned to return it but got caught by the police later the same evening. His employment and army record were no better. Working as an usher in a theatre, he had been discovered by the manager one evening "necking" with an usherette in the last row of the balcony. He had gone AWOL (absent without leave) twice in the army. On one occasion, when he was assigned to work in the kitchen ("kitchen police"), he had just left his post because he didn't feel like doing the work. On another occasion he had been having such a good time at a party that he had not returned to camp.

The explanation of this soldier's behavior seems to lie in his family background. His father had abandoned his mother when he was a child, and she had taken care of him in a very haphazard way. She was fond of playing with him and had given him all the toys he wanted, even though she could not afford them, but she treated him more like a cute pet than a child who would some day be a grown man. Moreover, she had several liaisons with men, none of whom she married, and she went off with them whenever she felt like it. The soldier remembered spending much of his boyhood alone. As he said, "Mom was always going away for a few days with some boyfriend and one of the neighbors would take care of me. I had a good time with them since I was successful in getting them to do what I wanted." He did not show any resentment toward his mother, but neither did he show any warm feeling for her. His attitude toward her was one of amused detachment.

In his several bouts with the law and his superiors, the soldier managed to escape punishment for the most part. A charming, extremely handsome young man, he conveyed a childlike innocence that made it difficult for people to dislike him, much less punish him. The owner of the convertible, who was a woman, was so taken with him that she persuaded the police to drop the charges against him; and the theatre owner who fired him helped him find another job. Even his commanding officer excused him for one of his AWOL's.

Psychologically the problem was not that he was simply fun-loving; it was much more serious. He was a person who had failed to introject socially acceptable standards from the adults who had shaped his early behavior. More specifically, he was incapable of exerting what is commonly referred to as self-control. He had not learned the responses which keep most people from committing antisocial acts or which make such acts aversive. Individuals without character disorders would have behaved quite differently in the stolen salami incident, for example, than our amiable "character" did. A person who believed stealing to be wrong might have wanted the salami just as much, but he would not have made any responses, even implicitly, that remotely suggested stealing as a way to get it. He would perhaps have planned to buy a salami the next day so that he would have some on hand the next time he wanted it so badly. Another person, perhaps less moral, might have thought of stealing it, but he would have been so anxious about being caught and punished that he would have immediately considered other safe and sensible alternatives.

The behavior of persons with character disorders ranges over the entire dimension of overt hostility. The soldier just described exhibited very little hostility simply because he himself was not very aggressive. He had no motivation to harm anybody and rarely did, even when he committed antisocial acts. All he wanted was to gratify whatever motive he had at the moment. Hermann Goering, second to Adolf Hitler in the Nazi party hierarchy, was a man with a character disorder who was de-

cidedly hostile. Examined by a psychologist (Gilbert, 1948) while awaiting trial as a war criminal, Goering reported that his earliest recollection was of bashing his mother's face when she tried to embrace him after she returned from a long absence. Throughout his life he was known for his physical aggressiveness, which was often openly sadistic. As a boy he enjoyed setting his dogs on helpless Jews. His mother, more prophetic than she probably realized, said of him, "Hermann will either be a great man or a great criminal."

Goering did not embrace the Nazi ideology from conviction as Hitler did, but merely from a desire to gratify his aspirations. He could probably have adopted, with equal ease, an ideology inconsistent with Nazism, if it had provided him with the same amount of social prestige, material reward, and outlet for his aggressiveness. An apt comment by a fellow Nazi describes Goering as ". . . a brutal egotist who doesn't give a damn about Germany as long as he can amount to something."

Thus Goering was psychologically similar to the soldier in that his behavior was not controlled by what is commonly known as a conscience, or what Freud called a superego (see page 446). The main difference between the two men, ability and intelligence aside, was their level of hostility. Goering was more aggressive than the soldier, but he was by no means as hostile as some individuals with character disorders. Goering recoiled at the mass executions of Jewish women and children and actually protested some of them. The excessively hostile person with a character disorder consistently commits aggressions against society.

The difference in amount of hostile behavior associated with character disorders has led some clinicians to differentiate two kinds of individuals with these disorders: the **psychopath** (or **psychopathic personality**) and the **sociopath** (or **sociopathic personality**). The psychopath, as the case of the amiable soldier illustrated, acts without regard for social laws and custom. The sociopath acts *against* society. The sociopath's behavior is in a sense governed by laws, but instead of obeying them he sets out to break them.

We have an example of a sociopath in a young man who had been hired by a rejected suitor to "beat up" his rival.

In carrying out the instructions, the young man was arrested. He was tried, convicted, and put in prison, where his case history was compiled. It was predominantly a list of antisocial acts. His father and mother, both immigrants, lived in a coal-mining town, where he had lived as a boy. The father was a brutal person who had often come home from work drunk and beaten his wife and any of the children who tried to interfere. In fact, violent beatings were the only discipline the prisoner had received as a boy. The mother, a woman of below-average intelligence, had had little contact with her son apart from preparing his meals and caring for the house he lived in. The other major social influence in his early life were the gangs of boys to which he belonged. He had achieved a great deal of prestige from these associations because he was strong, tough, and an effective fighter. At eight he had made money stealing hubcaps and selling them. He had continued this petty thievery until he was 14, when he had become a member of a gang which specialized in holding up gasoline stations. He vividly recalled that in his first hold-up he had helped to beat up an attendant. Later he had been caught, arrested, and convicted, and had served a two-year sentence in a prison for delinquent boys. Here his education as a criminal had progressed. He had joined a group that smuggled dope into the jail and had himself become addicted. He had participated in homosexual acts for payment, and had gotten into frequent fights—sometimes with knives. He boasted

of an episode in which he had stabbed a fellow prisoner and prevented him from seeking medical help by threatening him. After leaving the institution he had become a gangster and specialized in extorting money from small shopkeepers for "protection." If one of them failed to pay, he would be thrashed and his store damaged.

In an interview with the prison psychiatrist, the prisoner showed that he was very detached, expressing no shame or sense of guilt. He admitted he enjoyed attacking people, but expressed no hate for his victims. He did, however, express strong hostility toward his father, policemen, and other figures of authority in his responses to the Murray Thematic Apperception Test. To one picture of a fatherly figure, his comment included, "I would enjoy beating him up for nothing."

In spite of several differences, the similarities among these three cases of individuals with character disorders are striking. All are immature; they are preoccupied with their own needs and oblivious of the needs of others and of society. They are all incapable of forming a close and warm attachment to another person. None of them exhibits much self-control. And unlike most neurotics they give very few signs of anxiety and fear.

Two studies have been made of the characteristics of individuals with character disorders. In one study (Mischel, 1961), delinquent and nondelinquent boys 12 to 14 years of age were asked whether they preferred getting a small immediate reward or a larger delayed reward. The delinquent children exhibited a greater preference for the immediate reward. The other study (Lykken, 1957) showed that it was more difficult to establish a conditioned avoidance response in a group of prison subjects suffering from character disorders than in a group of normal subjects. Presumably the criminals could not generate as much fear and hence could not condition as well as the normal subject.

Although people with character disorders appear "sane" to society, their behavior sometimes becomes frankly psychotic. It is not uncommon for them, especially when they are under a great deal of stress, to have psychotic episodes during which they may even have hallucinations. But just as suddenly as they drift into these psychotic reactions, they return to "normality."

It is a mistake to think that all criminals have character disorders or, for that matter, that all people with character disorders are criminals. Individuals commit crimes for different reasons. A kleptomaniac steals because of a neurotic disorder. He may be extremely moral, but his morality is not strong enough to inhibit his compulsive behavior. A paranoid may murder because of delusions of persecution. And there are people who, like Jean Valjean in *Les Miserables,* steal not from moral weakness but from a strong sense of responsibility to others, a characteristic notably lacking in a true character disorder. There are people today who steal to pay medical debts or to finance vacations for an ailing spouse or child. On the other side of the coin, there are people with character disorders who never get into any real trouble with the law. Their consciences are no more developed than the consciences of criminal psychopaths or sociopaths, but they are more concerned with, and more clever at, avoiding arrest and jail sentence. They live near the fringe of the law, indulging in sharp business practices, lying, cheating, and generally disregarding the rights and interests of others.

You would expect individuals with character disorders to come from environments in which they received little or no training in moral behavior. Unfortunately, the problem is not so simple. Although many of those who have character disorders do come from slum environments where antisocial behavior is sometimes reinforced and moral behavior punished, some of them come from the kinds of backgrounds you would least suspect. Their parents were models of propriety, who conscientiously and devotedly tried to raise their children to be socially useful and responsible citizens. They gave their children the advantages of superior environment and education to attain these goals. Yet the children developed character disorders. This does not mean that social and economic conditions are not important variables in the development of character disorders; it does mean that they are not the only ones. Character disorders result from a constellation of variables. To understand their development fully we must go beyond the gross correlations between psychopathic and sociopathic behavior and socioeconomic level. The basic problem lies in the responses a child learns and how he perceives authority. Two brothers of conscientious, moral, loving parents might develop quite differently. One child might imitate his father and introject his moral code. The other child, for reasons that are sometimes difficult to discover, might learn to be negativistic. Instead of imitating his parents he might do exactly the opposite; he might be disobedient, untruthful, excessively aggressive, and generally antisocial. In order to understand how such children—and they may be the children of ministers, doctors, lawyers, and professors—develop character disorders, you must find out how and why their antisocial behavior got reinforced.

In any attempt to systematize the facts of character disorders, we must also consider physiological variables. Sometimes after an attack of **encephalitis** (a disease that damages brain tissue) a well-adjusted child will begin to behave in a delinquent manner. He becomes active, aggressive, and seems unable to adjust to the restraints of family and school. The same change in behavior can also result from a head injury. No one knows how and why this happens, but in view of these facts it is desirable to investigate the relationship between brain physiology and psychopathic and sociopathic behavior. At present we cannot tell whether there is any physiological factor common to both these physiologically based character disorders and to those we have described previously.

TREATMENT

The war against behavior disorders is waged on two fronts: their treatment once they have occurred and, perhaps more important, their prevention before they can occur.

Psychiatrists and psychologists are not the only ones engaged in these efforts. Social workers, nurses, hospital attendants, chemists, and many other groups participate, each in his own professional way. And in a broad sense all members of society are concerned. For it is within the power of citizens' groups to support the efforts of local, state, and the Federal governments and the numerous private agencies that are aiding the psychologically ill and doing the social thinking and planning that is necessary before we can reduce the proportion of persons who fall victims to these disorders.

Now that we have described the three main types of disordered reactions (neurosis, psychosis, and character disorders), we should add something about the most appropriate kinds of treatment for each. However, we cannot really do this. The failure of these diagnostic categories to suggest *highly curative* treatments, as medical diagnostic categories have been able to, has led some psychiatrists and psychologists to believe the categories have outlived their usefulness. If a diagnosis does not lead to definite treatment, what use is it? This is a valid question, but we must view the utility of psychiatric diagnosis in its historical perspective. These classifications were useful in caring for patients in psychiatric institutions, because they provided information about the course of their illnesses. They also highlighted certain causal processes: the neurotic's coping with anxiety, the psychotic's flight from reality, and the lack of a conscience in the person with a character disorder. These are the areas effective therapy must deal with. If nothing else, these diagnostic categories have given direction to the clinician and researcher interested in devising therapeutic techniques to help disordered personalities.

The goal of treatment is clear. The disordered reactions must be eliminated and healthy behavior substituted. Instead of drinking compulsively, the alcoholic must learn to avoid liquor, or better still, to find a solution to the conflict from which liquor provides temporary release. Instead of being constantly tense and apprehensive, the anxiety neurotic must learn to relax and be confident. Instead of being suspicious of everybody and seeing himself as threatened, the paranoiac must learn to perceive the world more as it is.

Methods of substituting one response for another do not constitute a new topic in this book. We have referred to them in our discussions of experimental extinction, perceptual learning, and discrimination learning. The treatment of disordered reactions can be conceived as being essentially similar to these methods of response substitution except that more complex behavior systems are involved. Instead of one simple habit being substituted for another, one complex habit system involving many different stimuli and complicated chains of response is substituted for another. There is also another difference between simple response substitution and treatment of behavior disorders. Practically all the methods of habit modification we have discussed have been worked out in the experimental laboratory, but most of the techniques used in modifying the behavior of disordered personalities have emerged from clinical practice. Only recently have therapeutic techniques devised in the laboratory been applied in clinical situations. In this respect the history of behavior therapy is beginning to resemble that of medical treatment. In the beginning of medicine most therapies were developed by clinical practitioners, but with increased knowledge in biology, biochemistry, and physiology, more and more were developed by researchers. If the author can read the signs of the future, the treatment of behavior disorders will evolve in the same way.

There are two major classes of behavior therapies. For want of better names they may be called **psychotherapy** and **somatotherapy.** Psychotherapy attempts to modify the patient's behavior by various communication techniques usually involving the patient and a therapist. Somatotherapy attempts to accomplish the change by direct intervention in the patient's physiological system. For example, the patient may be given drugs or an electric shock that induces convulsions. Psychotherapy and somatotherapy need not be used independently. In fact, it is becoming more and more common to use them jointly.

The Psychotherapies

Psychoanalysis. The most famous psychotherapeutic technique, and the one whose efficacy and value is perhaps most disputed, is psychoanalysis. It is the method that is related to Freud's theory of personality development (see page 446). There are many varieties of psychoanalysis, but for the time being only its traditional and most characteristic method will be described.

According to Freud the symptoms displayed by disordered personalities are caused by deeply buried conflicts which it is necessary to lay bare before the disorders can be treated. This requires prolonged probing into the patient's unconscious, so that he may learn either directly or with the aid of the analyst's interpretation how

his personality was shaped and why he is behaving as he does.

Psychoanalysis is a technique that allows the patient, with the help of his analyst, to become aware of memories and motives of which he had been unconscious. During psychoanalytical sessions, which take place several times a week over a long period, the patient lies on a couch with the analyst sitting behind him out of his sight. This arrangement helps the person to relax and minimizes the effect of any incidental distractions the analyst might create as he takes notes. The patient is encouraged to express his most personal thoughts and feelings without fear of embarrassment, criticism, or punishment.

Various methods are used for laying bare the unconscious, the most common being the method of **free association.** The patient is instructed to say aloud everything that he thinks of without any attempt to edit it, no matter how foolish, absurd, irrelevant, or indecent it may be. Since throughout our lives each of us has been trained to censor what we are about to say, this is extremely difficult to do. But the permissive nonjudgmental environment of the psychoanalytic session and the method itself enable both psychoanalyst and patient to go beneath the repressions and to peek into the patient's unconscious.

In his watchful attempts to bypass conscious censorship of unconscious material, the psychoanalyst is alert to analyze slips of the tongue and dreams. For example, if when asked what subject she majored in, a coed responded, "I'm a sex major," instead of "I'm a psych major," a psychoanalyst would not believe that her speech error could simply be attributed to an accidental confusion between *psych* and *sex*. He would want to know why she made that particular mistake. He would assume that it was an expression of some unconscious wish and by the method of free association attempt to discover its real origin.

In much the same way the analyst helps the patient to interpret his dreams. The content of dreams is not considered to be either mystical or dependent on chance, but instead as disguised expressions of something in the patient's unconscious. To illustrate, an unmarried man who suffered anxiety attacks and cared devotedly for his widowed mother reported a recurrent dream in which he was driving a truck which ran down and killed a woman. When he was asked to free associate about the dream, the patient, with great agitation, described the woman in his dream as being a little old lady whom he had never seen before. He mentioned spontaneously that she had black hair, unlike his mother, who had white hair, and stated emphatically that he did not recognize the woman. The analyst, in response, suggested that it seemed very important that the patient did not know who the woman was. The patient insisted that he could not identify her, but volunteered that he did not feel any remorse about killing her in the dream, although he did feel sick all over when he looked at her messy and bloody body. At this point he commented that his mother, the only old woman he knew well, was always so clean and neat.

As you have probably guessed by now, the psychoanalytic interpretation of this dream is that the old woman represented the patient's mother, but the death wish he harbored toward his mother was so anxiety-inducing that he repressed it. In the dream it came out in disguised form. Even here the mother's features had to be modified so that she was unrecognizable to him. But—and this would be important to the analyst—the patient spontaneously linked his mother with the woman in his dream. He associated the dream woman's black hair with his mother's white hair and the bloody and messy body reminded him of his mother, who was neat and orderly.

According to psychoanalytic theory, this patient could, with the help of his analyst, be made aware of his ambivalent feelings toward his mother. His feelings were not as shocking as the dream literally interpreted would imply. He did not really want to murder his mother. To maintain that he did would be as false in one way as to maintain that his devotion to her could only be described by the sweet sentiments expressed on a Mother's Day card would be false in the other. The truth is that the patient loved and resented his mother simultaneously. His devotion to her did not undo the fact that she made it difficult for him to marry and become independent, partly because he had to support her and partly because she was emotionally demanding. The unconscious hostility he felt toward her was responsible for his neurotic attacks of anxiety. According to psychoanalytic theory, if he could be made to understand and accept his ambivalence and its origin, the anxiety would disappear.

For several reasons, psychoanalysis is a long-drawn-out form of treatment, usually taking from two to five years. First the patient must learn the difficult technique of free association which, as we have indicated, goes counter to his early training to edit what he is about to say. Second, and more time-consuming, transference must be established between the patient and his analyst. **Transference,** in psychoanalysis, is the process in which the patient responds unconsciously, and usually emotionally, to the analyst, as he did to other important people in his early life, like his father or mother. For example, a patient might suddenly become hostile toward his analyst because he thought the analyst was trying to dominate him. When this hostility was analyzed, the patient might discover that the analyst reminded him of his father toward whom he harbored unconscious resentment. In essence, then, transference is a form of transfer of training; behavior in one situation is transferred to another. The interpretation of behavior resulting from transference is the core of the psychoanlytic process. It enables the patient to see how his present behavior has emerged from his early experiences, many of which he has repressed. It also permits the relationship between the analyst and patient to serve as a relearning experience. If the patient can learn to respond to the analyst as he did to his father then he can substitute new and appropriate responses for the old ones which were at the root of his present difficulty.

How successful is psychoanalysis? The simple truth is that we do not know, because psychologists and psychiatrists have failed to solve the persistent problem of measuring "mental health" in a reliable and objective way. In order to measure the effectiveness of any form of therapy, we must improve our methods of personality assessment.

Such evidence as has been offered to show the effectiveness of psychoanalysis has always suffered from some limitations. Many former patients testify with much emotion to its success. For them "life was not worth living" until they completed their analysis. Other former patients complain that their psychoanalysis was a waste of time and money (the analyst's fee is usually between $15 and $50 per hour). To them psychoanalysis meant disillusionment because it offered so much hope and produced so few results. Other patients believe that their condition was improved, but not as much as they had expected. One cannot place too much confidence in such personal judgments. People are not unusually adept at appraising their own psychological health. Furthermore, some people expect too much from psychotherapy. A shy, anxious person may expect to be completely relaxed and confident after analysis, and if his anxiety isn't erased entirely, although it is considerably reduced, he will think that his treatment has failed. Another may feel he has to rationalize the high cost of analysis by trying to convince himself and his friends that psychoanalysis has helped him, even though there is no discernible change in his behavior. He is like the man who buys an expensive car, and even though its performance is mediocre, or worse, praises it ecstatically for all its nonexistent virtues.

Psychoanalysts sometimes publish their own judgments of the effectiveness of treatment, not, of course, mentioning specific cases. Some of these reports claim that a high proportion of patients improve if they complete their analyses. But plainly, studies in which psychoanalysts estimate the value of their own work may be biased.

One of the difficulties in assessing the effectiveness of psychoanalysis, as well as other therapeutic techniques, is that there are often spontaneous improvements in the behavior of individuals with disordered personalities. It is not uncommon for a person with marked neurotic reactions to change without the help of psychoanalysis or any other form of therapy. The author has seen many anxious, overdependent, socially immature students in college who appeared ill-equipped for the rigors of adulthood, and yet when they returned to the college on visits several years later, they were confident and happy. Somehow they made the difficult transition between late adolescence and early adulthood successfully. Such healthy growth patterns occur in people at almost any period of life. Even patients in psychiatric institutions who are not being treated suddenly get better, no one is quite sure how. It appears that there are hidden sources of strength in many people which they can draw upon when they are in periods of stress, and that these resources, which have their origin in previously learned habits and motives, are sufficient to pull them through some difficult situations without the help of psychoanalysts or other therapists.

Obviously, then, all improvement which occurs during psychoanalysis cannot necessarily be attributed to the treatment itself. The question, What would have happened if the patient had not received any treatment? is always present. In order to judge the effectiveness of *any* form of therapy, we must compare the changes in a group of patients who received treatment with a similar group who did not. One famous survey (Eysenck, 1952) that did this reported that patients who received no treatment improved as much as patients who received psychoanalysis or other forms of psychotherapy. But because of serious defects, this study, too, is far from being definitive. For one thing, the experimenters did not use comparable groups of patients for the various kinds of treatment. For another, they used inadequate and inconsistent measures of psychological health.

Although there is no precise evaluation of psychoanalysis, we can draw certain conclusions about its effectiveness. It is not effective with certain kinds of patients. Even psychoanalysts admit that it is less effective with alcoholics, homosexuals, psychotics, and patients with character disorders than it is with neurotics. For the most part, psychoanalysts restrict their practice to patients whom they believe have the best chances of being helped, the neurotics with above-average intelligence. But even with these opinion differs as to how effective psychoanalysis is. Many analysts believe it is highly effective. At the other extreme is the following private evaluation of psychoanalysis by a dissenting analyst: *"If* what's troubling you isn't too serious, and *if* you're lucky enough to go to one of the few analysts who seem to be good at what they're doing, and *if* you're a good patient and work hard, then *maybe* analysis can help you" (Havemann, 1957, p. 90).

Such a skeptical evaluation may sound completely damning, and you may wonder why anyone undergoes psychoanalysis. But you must remember one thing. A neurotic does not have a choice between psychoanalysis and some ideal therapeutic technique guaranteed to be effective. His only alternatives to psychoanalysis are equally unsure therapeutic techniques, or enduring his misery. Hence, many neurotics understandably turn to psychoanalysis for help.

But for the scientist who wants to understand the problems of treating disordered personalities, psychoanalysis leaves many questions unanswered. No matter how reasonable it is to assume that psychoanalysis can help certain kinds of patients, this conclusion must ultimately be demonstrated. It would be very valuable for psychoanalysts to make a concerted move toward adopting that tradition of medical research in which the effectiveness of every therapy is expected to be demonstrated in an exhaustive and objective manner. For the most part, psychoanalysts have been remiss in meeting this responsibility. True, the task is difficult. They need the help of psychologists in devising methods and tests for measuring changes in psychological health. But equally important, a change of attitude is required, one that will bring the rest of the profession up to its most fair-minded and far-seeing psychoanalysts. The smug acceptance of psychoanalysis as an effective therapy must be replaced by a questioning and critical attitude.

The search to understand, and to improve, psychoanalysis will not end when, and if, its general effectiveness is demonstrated. We must then answer questions like: What kinds of patients is it effective with? What changes in behavior occur during a successful psychoanalysis? The author recalls a young lady who was in psychoanalysis. She was extremely bright but terribly sarcastic. Her witty and devastating remarks usually made her the center of attention at parties, but afterward she usually felt miserable because she knew she had embarrassed many people, and she would ask herself, "Why must I be so nasty?" After her analysis her behavior at parties was no different. She was still aggressively sarcastic. But she no longer felt guilty about it! Does psychoanalysis mainly change a person's reactions to his own undesirable form of behavior? Or can it induce more basic changes in a patient's overt behavior (in the present case reduce or eliminate the tendencies to overt hostility)?

The final question that will have to be answered is, How does psychoanalysis modify behavior? It would be wrong to conclude that a patient improves because important parts of his unconscious have been laid bare and he now understands his own psychological development. On the other hand, it is obvious that the patient is doing more than just relating his own history during psychoanalysis. Some therapists maintain that the theoretical concepts underlying a method of psychotherapy have no influence on the possible success of the treatment. According to this view analytic psychotherapy is effective because of its method, not because its theory is true. Adler's or Jung's theory—or anybody's theory, for that matter—can be applied to the process of the therapeutic session.

One possible answer is that psychoanalysis—and this may be true of some other kinds of psychotherapy—provides a situation in which certain conditioning principles can operate. It has been found (Pittes, 1957) that the galvanic skin responses which accompany embarrassing admissions are extinguished during therapy. The permissive and noncritical atmosphere of the therapeutic situation allows the patient to talk about personally embarrassing ideas and events. Unlike society, the therapist does not criticize or punish these responses, for to him these thoughts and events are everyday occurrences to be understood not judged. As a result the embarrassment —and with it the guilt and fear—extinguishes.

The heavy emphasis psychoanalysts place on the process of transference also fits into this explanation of the effects of psychoanalysis. If transference is successful, that is, if the patient can respond to the analyst as he did to those who were important in his early life, then he has an opportunity to

extinguish his maladjusted responses and to learn healthy ones. That the therapist influences a patient's behavior is supported by the results of a study (Colby, 1960) which found that male subjects gave different kinds of free associations when alone in a room speaking into a tape recorder than when an analyst, who remained silent, was present. With the analyst, subjects made many more references to male persons.

Verbal conditioning (see page 343) can also take place in psychotherapy. Unhealthy verbal reactions to guilt, anxiety, and low self-esteem are not reinforced and therefore disappear. Healthier verbal reactions are reinforced by the therapist and gain dominance.

There are other factors in the therapeutic situation which might possibly aid the patient in reducing his conflicts. Perhaps providing him with a definite conception of the nature and causes of his own behavior, regardless of whether it is right or wrong, is helpful. Or perhaps psychoanalysis is helpful because the patient hopes and believes that it will be helpful. In short, hope itself may be helpful. Or possibly, the salutary effects of psychoanalysis or other forms of psychotherapy are due to some unknown factor.

To some readers this picture of psychoanalysis may seem too sober, too critical, too bleak, but to others it should offer the hope that we will someday know a lot more. Meanwhile we can apply what we already know, remembering that medical research has often developed therapeutic techniques that yielded limited success at first, but blossomed into highly effective treatment later. Only the future will decide whether psychoanalysis, as it is practiced today, has been a step in the right direction.

Client-centered Therapy. The psychologist Carl Rogers has been the chief figure in the development of a method of psychotherapy that is in many ways strikingly

528

different from psychoanalysis. It is called **client-centered therapy** or **nondirective therapy** to emphasize its distinguishing features. It is *client-centered* because instead of suggesting a solution to the client's problem, the therapist deliberately leaves it up to him. It is *nondirective* because the therapist does not at any time intentionally encourage the client to discuss a particular topic (such as the client's relationship with his mother). Rather it is left completely up to the client to decide what he wants to discuss.

The client-centered therapist, unlike the psychoanalyst, does not attempt to uncover repressed drives and fears or to trace the development of the patient's personality from its earliest beginnings. He is simply interested in creating an understanding atmosphere that will at all times encourage the patient to clarify his *present* attitudes and feelings about any subject. The patient is regarded as an individual behaving in the present without regard to his past. In other words, concurrent relationships are considered of primary importance, not their historical antecedents (see page 25).

No one will deny that client-centered therapists have an intense desire and determination to investigate psychotherapy objectively. Interested in discovering exactly what goes on during psychotherapeutic sessions and in evaluating its effectiveness, they use recording devices extensively during psychotherapy sessions.

The following excerpts from the first and the last sessions of a course of interviews illustrate the major features of client-centered therapy. Notice that the therapist says very little, and meticulously avoids interpreting the patient's remarks. When he does speak, he tries to reflect the patient's words, and especially the patient's *feelings*. The basic assumption in client-centered therapy is that the patient has the power to solve his difficulties if he can only understand precisely what they are. The therapist considers that his task is not to explain or to interpret but to say only what will assist the patient in clarifying his own problem and his present situation.

EXCERPTS FROM THE FIRST INTERVIEW

P (patient). I hesitate to meet people—I hesitate to canvas for my photographic business. I feel a terrific aversion to any kind of activity, even dancing. I normally enjoy dancing very well. But when my inhibition, or whatever you wish to call it, is on me powerfully, it is an ordeal for me to dance. I notice a difference in my musical ability. On my good days I can harmonize with other people singing.

C (counselor). M-hm.

P. I have a good ear for harmony then. But when I'm blocked, I seem to lose that, as well as my dancing ability. I feel very awkward and stiff.

C. M-hm. So that both in your work and in your recreation you feel blocked.

P. I don't want to do anything. I just lie around. I get no gusto for any activity at all.

C. You just feel rather unable to do things, is that it? (Rogers, 1942, pp. 267-268).

* * * *

P. Well, it's just reached the point where it becomes unbearable. I'd rather be dead than live as I am now.

C. You'd rather be dead than live as you are now? Can you tell me a little more about that?

P. Well, I hope. Of course we always live on hope.

C. Yes.

P. But—no, I don't have any conscious suicidal urge or anything like that. It's just that—looking at it rationally, I feel that I'm—that I'm in the red now and I wouldn't want to keep on living in the red. (Pause)

C. Well, can you tell me in any more detailed way what—in what way it blocks you so much that you really feel sometimes that you'd be better off dead?

P. Well, I don't know if I can more accurately describe the sensation. It's just a—a very impressive and painful weight as if an axe were pressing on the whole abdomen, pressing down,

I can almost—I can almost sense the position and I feel that it's oppressing me very radically, that is, that it goes right down to the roots of my dynamic energy, so that no matter in what field I essay any sort of effort, I find the blocking (Rogers, 1942, pp. 272-273).

Excerpt From the Eighth and Final Interview

P. Well, I've been noticing something decidedly new. Rather than have fluctuations, I've been noticing a very gradual steady improvement. It's just as if I had become more stabilized and my growth had been one of the hard way and the sure way rather than the wavering and fluctuating way.

C. M-hm.

P. I go into situations, and even though it's an effort, why, I go ahead and make progress, and I find that when you sort of seize the bull by the horns, as it were, why it isn't so bad as if you sort of deliberate and perhaps—well, think too long about it, like I used to. I sort of say to myself, "Well, I know absolutely that avoiding the situation will leave me in the same old rut I've been taking," and I realize that I don't want to be in the same old rut, so I go ahead and go into the situation, and even when I have disappointments in the situation, I find that they don't bring me down as much as they used to.

C. That sounds like very real progress.

P. And what pleases me is that my feelings are on an even keel, steadily improving, which gives me much more of a feeling of security than if I had fluctuations. You see, fluctuations lead you from the peaks to the valleys, and you can't get as much self-confidence as when you're having gradual improvement.

C. M-hm.

P. So that the harder way is really the more satisfactory way.

C. Then you're really finding a step-by-step type of improvement that you hadn't found before.

P. That's right. I never—I'd always had a fluctuating thing before. I would either be all released or all inhibited. Well, I feel that this is something I'm earning rather than something that comes from my involuntary whim (Rogers, 1942, pp. 420-421).

A general evaluation of client-centered therapy is difficult to make because we lack a dependable, widely accepted, overall measure of psychological health. You will recall that we faced the same difficulty in evaluating psychoanalysis. But in client-centered therapy, this difficulty serves more as a challenge than as an obstacle, because client-centered therapists have conducted a number of studies using personality tests and clinical judgments to assess specific changes that take place during and after psychotherapy. They find that in successful psychotherapy, the patient's responses to himself, undergo major change. Patients become less critical of themselves and more realistic about their aspirations. They also become less defensive, behave more maturely, and feel more relaxed.

In discussing the variables essential for effective therapy, Rogers (1959) concludes that the therapist's ability to empathize with the client (share his feelings) may well be the most important factor. He also points to evidence that the therapists liking the patient and the patients belief that the therapist likes him also contribute to effective therapy.

Roger's conviction that "empathic understanding" is an invaluable ingredient of successful therapy is of particular interest in any attempt to understand psychotherapy. To some extent his belief is consistent with the heavy emphasis already laid on the importance of eliminating fear and anxiety responses. By allowing the patient to express his attitudes and feelings to a sympathetic and understanding therapist without exposing himself to the least threat of criticism or reproof, client-centered therapy does promote the extinction of fear responses. Once this occurs, the patient is in a position to acquire "healthier" responses. Thus we see that although psychoanalysis and client-centered therapy emerge from different theoretical orientations, their therapeutic techniques share a common property.

530

The major criticism of client-centered therapy is that its effective range is limited. A nondirective therapist can only function with a patient who wants to discuss his problems. But there are many who need psychological help who are unwilling or unable to relax sufficiently to discuss their problems. The delinquent, the prisoner, and even the neurotic who seeks out a therapist but avoids discussing the key problems with him are examples of patients who may not be able to discuss their problems spontaneously, and who are, therefore, in the eyes of the client-centered therapist, unable to achieve insights and move in the direction of a more effective adjustment. Although client-centered therapy has been attempted with psychotics (on a smaller scale than psychoanalysis), it is extremely difficult with some of them and impossible with others, because they cannot carry on any genuine social communication. These limitations have convinced some psychologists that client-centered therapy is most appropriate for mild forms of neurosis. Actually, it is mostly used with such cases. College counseling centers, mental hygiene clinics, child guidance clinics, and other organizations which treat mild cases of neurosis are usually staffed with some client-centered therapists. But like our judgments about the effectiveness of other forms of psychotherapy, our evaluation of client-centered therapy is tentative. Final judgments, if any, will depend upon evaluations still to be made.

Group Psychotherapy. Many patients believe that they alone suffer from disturbances that are really quite common. Guilt about sexual behavior, intense hostility toward parents, obsessive fear of being maimed, and fear of being a coward are but a few of these commonly shared reactions. These patients are helped when they learn that their problems are not unique, that others face similar difficulties. Realizing that their difficulties express their own humanity, they no longer respond to themselves as "sick" or "peculiar." As Shakespeare wrote, "One human failing makes the whole world akin."

Group psychotherapy attempts to exploit the benefits of treating a person's disordered reactions within a social setting. This seems very natural when you remember that one of the aims of psychotherapy is to help each patient achieve a more satisfactory relationship with other people. Not only can the patient learn that his troubles are not unique, even in his small world, but he may also learn to make progress in identifying with others and in giving and receiving help, and thus learn habits basic to social living. The following excerpt from a record of group psychotherapy conducted in a nondirective manner shows how the interaction between patients can work to the benefit of all:

MR. RAY: My brother got his medical degree when he was twenty-four. Before I went into the Navy, I figured out I'd graduate from college at such and such an age, and then have my doctorate ahead of me. I was very proud of that. (Pause) But, uh, now it no longer means very much to me.

MR. BERG: You think that your parents' attitudes fostered that feeling?

MR. RAY: My parents have never said, "You are not doing as well as *B*." (His brother.) They were satisfied when I just did average work. They never pushed me—to do better.

MR. BERG: When he went through, they were very pleased with him.

MR. RAY: Oh, definitely.

MR. BERG: And when you went through, do you think you might have felt somewhat rejected because there wasn't the same furor over your achievement. (Pause) I guess I'm projecting myself into it!

MR. RAY: Well, I didn't feel, well, uh, accepted as much as I would like to have. And I thought that my grades had a great deal to do with it. (Pause) But I just no longer feel that push to do better.

MR. HILL: You feel that the, uh, responsibility for the grades is your own, and that it won't matter to anyone else what you do. Is that the idea? Your motivation stems from yourself rather than trying to please somebody else.

MR. RAY: Yeah, I think that's it. I'm no longer so much concerned with showing my parents that I can do well. I still want to show it to myself, and, uh, I'm more satisfied, that's all. I don't feel the urge to rush.

MR. HILL: Sort of—seems to me it would be sort of a load off your shoulder.

MR. RAY: Oh, definitely. Not bucking up against something that you feel you can't overcome.

GROUP PSYCHOTHERAPIST: Makes you feel a good bit more independent—free.

MR. RAY: Definitely, in that I can satisfy myself and I don't have to worry about satisfying somebody else (Rogers, 1951, pp. 310-311).

Group psychotherapy is not necessarily conducted in a nondirective manner. In fact, most individual therapeutic orientations have been used in group practice. There are, besides, some special therapeutic techniques for which group participation is required. The most widely known and probably one of the most successful of these is the program of treatment conducted by *Alcoholics Anonymous,* an organization of ex-alcoholics that was founded in 1935 by two alcoholics who had helped each other give up drink. By 1960 its membership had grown to 200,000, all of them bent upon aiding each other to resist the temptation to drink. If a member is seized with a desire to drink at any hour of the day or night, he can call another AA member who will rush over and give him a kind of supportive therapy to strengthen his resistance to the temptation. Both participants benefit from the experience. The tempted person avoids drinking, an absolute necessity for any ex-alcoholic, and his protector's resistance to alcohol is increased by his active participation in an organization dedicated to breaking alcohol's grip on its victims. It has been said that being involved in this crusade is so important that if a member of Alcoholics Anonymous were deprived of

the opportunity to get up in the middle of the night to rush to the assistance of a fellow member, he would be driven to drink.

FIGURE 14.5 A Meeting of Alcoholics Anonymous.

In addition to giving mutual assistance, the members of each local chapter of Alcoholics Anonymous hold group meetings which are essentially group psychotherapy sessions. Here individual members discuss their experiences as well as the general problems of alcoholism. The alcoholic who attends these meetings is impressed and heartened by looking around the room and seeing many men and women who have proved that alcoholism can be licked. Firm faith in one's own ability to stop drinking is the first step in conquering or inhibiting the compulsion.

The program of Alcoholics Anonymous has been criticized by some professional psychiatrists and psychologists because it does not aim specifically at uncovering the root causes of each individual's alcoholism. Nevertheless, some observers report that the record of successes of Alcoholics Anonymous is better than most professional treatments.

Be that as it may, Alcoholics Anonymous has been unable to reach all alcoholics.

Some find it impossible to accept its religious orientation; others fail to identify closely enough with members of the organization; and still others drop out for no apparent reason after being active for some length of time.

A rather spectacular kind of group psychotherapy is **psychodrama** (Moreno, 1946). Its basic technique is a kind of spontaneous, *unrehearsed* play-acting that encourages the free expression of feelings. Psychodrama's technique is illustrated by a résumé of the case (Sarbin, 1943) of Harold, a 17-year-old high school boy, who was a hospital patient at the time.

Harold was excessively shy, although he pictured himself as very popular in his fantasies. He was originally invited to attend a psychodrama simply as a spectator. Later he was requested to prepare a short scene of his own. He gave a simple play in which he acted the role of a radio commentator. This was a safe, undemanding role, since there were no supporting characters and what he acted did not touch upon his problems in real life. At the next meeting Harold was called upon to play a minor role in a drama along with several other patients. In his role as buddy of a soldier who was abused by a tough sergeant, Harold did surprisingly well in the way he responded to his friend's difficulties. He was then called upon to prepare a scene of his own to be acted at the next session. This time he planned to include other actors, and he himself seemed to lose his self-consciousness for the first time. The next role Harold played, in another patient's drama, was that of a father. He became deeply absorbed in this role and did such a fine job that his acting dominated the drama. It was quite obvious that he was playing the father's role in a way that showed how he perceived his own father's attitude toward himself. In the next psychodrama which he planned, Harold, in line with his own fantasy, assumed the role of a popular high school boy.

Harold's acting seemed to produce an effect on his everyday behavior. Along with his freer expression in the psychodrama, his shyness disappeared and there was a noticeable increase in his socializing with other members of his group. It seems certain that the psychodrama aided him in behaving as he really wanted to. In the more technical language of psychology, his uninhibited behavior during the psychodrama was reinforced and generalized to situations in his real life.

There are many other forms of group therapy, some of which have not achieved formal status. For example, informal group psychotherapy goes on in summer camps where counselors deal with groups of children. The same sort of thing happens in scout organizations, in churches, and in social clubs. It would be desirable for behavior scientists to discover to what extent and in what way these social experiences effect changes in personality.

The effectiveness of group psychotherapy seems to depend to a large extent on the characteristics of the patients who need social reorientation. It was, for example, very effective with Harold, the 17-year-old high school student. Harold did not participate actively in socially constructive group activities prior to his therapy, but he was motivated to do so, although this motivation was not apparent at first. Persons with character disorders are not usually motivated in this direction. Indeed, this lack of motivation may constitute their chief difficulty. Many group therapists emphasize the importance of selecting for group psychotherapy patients who can not only be helped by the efforts of the group, but can contribute to them as well. Psychopaths and sociopaths can do much harm in group psychotherapy sessions. Their egocentricity and hostility lead them to be divisive forces instead of constructive group members. They usually touch off bickering and feuding that prevent the formation of cooperative attitudes and mutual respect so necessary if the members of the group are to successfully work out their problems together. Most psychotics and some neurotics can be equally destructive to group morale, and may therefore have to be kept out of group psychotherapy.

General Psychotherapy. The forms of psychotherapy which, taken together, are probably the most widely practiced, can be designated by the unspecific term **general psychotherapy.** Unlike the therapies we described before, general psychotherapy is not committed to any specific theory of behavior or technique of treatment. There is nothing distinctive about it except that its practitioners will use almost any technique or hypothesis which they think might be helpful. It is, in other words, an eclectic approach, one which seeks to select the best from all the different approaches and to reject what does not work.

Obviously it is impossible to describe any one method of general psychotherapy. Each effort at treatment depends on the specific patient and the specific therapist. The best we can do is to describe some of the techniques it uses most often.

If he is dealing with a patient who has an anxiety neurosis, the therapist will first obtain a general picture of the patient's symptoms and the history of his disorder. Then, if the patient has complained of his fear of going insane, a common symptom among anxiety neurotics, the psychotherapist will probably reassure him that nothing of the kind is happening. Although reassurance by itself will not cure the patient, it can reduce his fear while other techniques are being used to produce more basic changes in his behavior. If the patient has become convinced that his gastric discomfort, bowel disturbances, cold extremities, and general tenseness are due to some disease, the psychotherapist may explain to him that the autonomic nervous system, in the absence of any disease processes, can produce these symptoms.

In treating the anxiety neurotic, or any

other patient for that matter, the general psychotherapist tries to steer a course somewhere between the client-centered therapist's concern with concurrent relationships and the analyst's emphasis on the early history of the patient's development. He explores the patient's history whenever it appears to throw light on his present problem. But unlike the psychoanalyst, he feels no compulsion to dig far back into the patient's earliest memories.

The aim of general psychotherapy is to alter the patient's behavior so that he becomes more comfortable, more effective, and more capable of withstanding the adversities which normally crop up in anyone's life.

One way to make the anxiety neurotic more comfortable is to administer sedatives that help him relax. Psychoanalysts would oppose this, believing that the discomfort of anxiety serves to motivate the patient to give up his neurotic reactions. If it were not for the uncomfortable anxiety, they would maintain, the neurotic might be content to persist indefinitely in his maladaptive behavior. The general psychotherapist, on the other hand, treats the tension and anxiety partly as a problem in itself, not just as an expression of a deep-seated personal conflict. In addition to prescribing relaxing drugs he may even teach his patient how to relax. This might appear simple, but it is not. Since he has never been able to relax, the anxiety neurotic actually does not know what it feels like. He is like the golfer who continually slices his drives and never learns just what it is that he is doing wrong. The anxiety neurotic knows well-enough that he is tense, but he has not the slightest idea how to go about relaxing. Just as the professional trains the golfer to get the right feel for a good drive, the therapist trains his patient to relax. He has the patient drop his hands in a leisurely manner in order to sense the appropriate kind of response. From there he trains him to relax other parts of the body, particularly the posterior neck muscles, which are usually extremely tense in the anxiety neurotic.

The general therapist may also try to train the anxiety neurotic to be more effective in coping with all sorts of frustrations in everyday living. One way of doing this is to make him more realistic. No one can function as an effective member of a family or as a worker on a job if he has a distorted perception of his surroundings. The anxiety neurotic generally imagines his environment to be more threatening and dangerous than it really is. He may also set himself goals that he cannot reach. The therapist allows his patient to give vent to his fears, hostilities, and pent-up emotions in the hope that something of their origin will be discovered, for if the patient can understand his conflicts he will be able to perceive his environment more realistically and to formulate attainable goals.

No healthy person reacts to sizable adversities without being disturbed. The loss of someone he loved, serious illness, financial difficulties, are difficult even for the best adjusted person. However, the healthy person ultimately discovers an appropriate way of responding to his new situation, whereas the anxiety neurotic repeats the old nonadjustive responses. The general psychotherapist believes, however, that if the neurotic's anxiety can be reduced he may be led to abandon these fixated responses (see page 408) and to learn appropriate ones.

Many other kinds of treatment are used in general psychotherapy. One form that seems to be effective with young children is **play therapy.** Since a child's play almost always reflects something of his fantasy life, it can provide useful clues to his habits, motivations, and conflicts (see page 411). In play therapy children are provided with toys which bear some relation to their real world and are observed while they play with them. For example, a child may be given several clay dolls which are supposed to represent the members of his family. Since the child will not be punished for anything he does in play, he can symbolically release his hostilities toward any member of his family without fear of retaliation, providing the therapist with insight into his motivations. Play therapy has another advantage. It gives the child an opportunity to form a satisfactory relationship with an adult, the therapist. Once the child has made a beginning here, he may be able to improve his strained relationships with the members of his family. And finally, play therapy, with the help of the therapist's tactful suggestions and interpretations, can help the child to understand the things that bother him. If he can learn from the therapist's remarks to put his troubles into words, he will have a better chance of doing something about them.

The techniques of general psychotherapy as we have described them can be summarized in the vocabulary of basic psychology as involving three learning processes: extinction, counter-conditioning, and positive reinforcement. The ability to express in a permissive environment thoughts that provoke fear and guilt encourages these reactions to extinguish. Words and memory cues which are ordinarily associated with tension are counter-conditioned so that they evoke relaxation. Appropriate responses are positively reinforced by the social approval of the therapist and the relief this brings the patient.

Reinforcement Therapy. Experimental psychologists, who have observed how the appropriate application of reinforcement can control behavior, have sought to discover whether the same laboratory techniques can be applied to the behavior of disordered personalities. One recent study (Salzinger & Pisoni, 1956) demonstrated that the verbal conditioning procedure (see page 343) can work with schizophrenics. The plan of the experiment was to interview patients and reinforce every statement they made which contained a reference to their own affect, such as "I am a lonely person," "I was mad at him," "I'm happy."

The experimenter reinforced these utterances by responding with "Mmmm-hum," "I see," or "Yeah." The technique had the effect of increasing the rate at which the patient made statements containing self-referred affect. When reinforcement was deliberately withheld, in the second interview session, the rate, as conditioning principles would predict, decreased. The implication of this study for psychotherapy is obvious. If the verbal responses of a disordered personality can be controlled by reinforcement, then perhaps healthy responses can be substituted for unhealthy ones. We have already suggested that similar verbal conditioning operates informally in the more traditional psychotherapeutic techniques. Such techniques, however, might be made more effective if verbal conditioning were deliberately introduced.

An extremely interesting and dramatic extension of the shaping technique (see page 291), is provided in the following case report of a catatonic schizophrenic patient who had become completely mute almost immediately after he was institutionalized 19 years earlier. The case history reads as follows:

The S was brought to a group therapy session with other chronic schizophrenics (who were verbal), but he sat in the position in which he was placed and continued the withdrawal behaviors which characterized him. He remained impassive and stared ahead even when cigarettes, which other members accepted, were offered to him and were waved before his face. At one session, when E removed cigarettes from his pocket, a package of chewing gum accidentally fell out. The S's eyes moved toward the gum and then returned to their usual position. This response was chosen by E as one with which he would start to work, using the method of successive approximation. . . .

The S met individually with E three times a week. Group sessions also continued. The following sequence of procedures was introduced in the private sessions. Although the weeks are numbered consecutively, they did not follow at regular intervals since other duties kept E from S every week.

WEEKS 1, 2. A stick of gum was held before S's face, and E waited until S's eyes moved toward it. When this response occurred, E as a consequence gave him the gum. By the end of the second week, response probability in the presence of the gum was increased to such an extent that S's eyes moved toward the gum as soon as it was held up.

WEEKS 3, 4. The E now held the gum before S, waiting until he noticed movement in S's lips before giving it to him. Toward the end of the first session of the third week, a lip movement occurred spontaneously, which E promptly reinforced. By the end of this week, both lip movement and eye movement occurred when the gum was held up. The E then withheld giving S the gum until S spontaneously made a vocalization, at which time E gave S the gum. By the end of this week, holding up the gum readily occasioned eye movement toward it, lip movement, and a vocalization resembling a croak.

WEEKS 5, 6. The E held up the gum, and said, "Say gum, gum," repeating these words each time S vocalized. Giving S the gum was made contingent upon vocalizations increasingly approximating gum. At the sixth session (at the end of Week 6), when E said, "Say gum, gum," S suddenly said, "Gum, please." This response was accompanied by reinstatement of other responses, of this class, that is, S answered questions regarding his name and age.

Thereafter, he responded to questions by E both in individual sessions and in group sessions, but answered no one else. Responses to the discriminative stimuli of the room generalized to E on the ward; he greeted E on two occasions in the group room. He read from signs in E's office upon request by E.

Since the response now seemed to be under the strong stimulus control of E, the person, attempt was made to generalize the stimulus to other people. Accordingly, a nurse was brought into the private room; S smiled at her. After a month, he began answering her questions. Later, when he brought his coat to a volunteer worker on the ward, she interpreted the gesture as a desire to go outdoors and conducted him there. Upon informing E of the incident, she was instructed to obey S only as a consequence of explicit verbal requests by him. The S thereafter vocalized requests. These instructions have now been given to other hospital personnel, and

S regularly initiates verbal requests when non-verbal requests have no reinforcing conse-quences. Upon being taken to the commissary, he said, "ping pong," to the volunteer worker and played a game with her (Isaacs, Thomas, & Goldiamond, 1960, pp. 9-10).

The same soberly skeptical judgment must be used to appraise this remarkable demonstration as is used to appraise all other clinical cases. Although it seems likely that the shaping technique was responsible for the change in the patient's behavior, we cannot dismiss the hypothesis that some unknown factor may have been the cause. The shaping technique has achieved enough success, however, to support the recom-mendation that its possible therapeutic value in a number of different situations be explored. In one study (Lindsley, 1956) chronic schizophrenic adults who had been institutionalized for many years were placed on a fixed-ratio reinforcement sched-ule (see page 289). Their bizarre behavior, it was noted, appeared only during the pauses after reinforcement. During the time the patients were emitting the instrumental responses for which they received candy and cigarette reinforcements the psychotic behavior disappeared. A similar study was made with autistic children (Ferster & De-Myer, 1961). An **autistic child** typically has withdrawn completely from all social stim-ulation while exhibiting such bizarre be-havior patterns as muteness, destructive tantrums, long periods of idleness, and lack of bowel and bladder control. The simi-larity between their behavior and schizo-phrenia has led some psychiatrists to call the disorder *childhood schizophrenia,* al-though the relationship between the two disorders has never been clearly established.

The important point is that in these two demonstrations psychotics, whose chief symptoms were social isolation and aloof-ness, were trained to respond to their immediate environment by appropriate re-inforcement techniques. However, if rein-forcement therapy of this sort is to prove effective, a technique must be discovered which will cause the responsive behavior emitted in the laboratory to generalize to everyday social behavior.

The Somatotherapies

A good many psychiatrists and psycholo-gists have always assumed that the most effective ways of treating disordered reac-tions are the physiological or physical methods. Even Freud, who has influenced contemporary psychotherapy more than any other single person, predicted that one day the physician with a syringe filled with chemicals would take the place of the psy-choanalyst.

Today there is a greater interest in so-matotherapies than ever before, for three principal reasons. First, some somatothera-pies have proved highly successful. Vitamin treatment has reduced the behavioral dis-turbances caused by pellagra, and certain drugs have alleviated the symptoms of epilepsy. Second, psychotherapy is neither as effective nor as inexpensive as the mental health problem requires. None of the vari-ous psychotherapeutic techniques yields anything near 100 per cent success, and practically all are very slow processes. Hence, even if they were more effective, the mental health problem would still be grave, for there is a critical shortage of psychotherapists. The average psychoana-lyst is said to analyze about 150 patients during his entire professional career. Other therapists, using less time-consuming meth-ods, may see a larger number of patients. But the total number they treat is still a great deal less than the number who need help. And third, there are strong sugges-tions that many of the disorders which have been thought to be functional, that is, to result from a gradual acquisition of mal-adaptive habits, *may be* products of directly remediable internal biochemical changes.

The perfectly reasonable assumption that psychological disturbances originate in inadequate modes of adjustment to society's demands would lead one to expect the incidence and kind of disorder to vary in different societies. But we have some records of behavior disorders dating back more than one hundred years which reveal no sizable differences in the frequency or type of psychiatric disturbances in spite of the drastic social changes which have taken place. Furthermore, severe schizophrenic behavior develops in very young children who seemingly have not had time to learn such behavior. To some of those who work with these children, they almost appear to be a different species from ordinary children.

Evidence from a large number of studies suggests that internal biochemical conditions rather than learning play the major role in the production of some forms of psychoses. These studies show that the physiological systems of normals and schizophrenics differ in many ways, ranging from biochemical variations in the blood and urine to different concentrations of certain chemicals in the brain.

There is also evidence (Kallman, 1953) of a genetic basis for both schizophrenia and manic-depressive psychosis. A person with one schizophrenic parent is 16 times more likely to contract this disorder than the average person. And if one identical twin has schizophrenia, his twin also has it in 86 per cent of the cases studied. Whereas if one fraternal twin—whose heredity is, on the average, no more like his twin's than the hereditary of ordinary brothers is alike —is schizophrenic, the chance of his twin being schizophrenic is only 4 per cent. The case for the inheritance of manic-depressive psychosis is even stronger. When one identical twin has some form of this psychosis, the other twin has it in 96 per cent of the cases. Interestingly, no evidence has been found for the inheritance of involutional melancholia, although, so far as behavior goes, it closely resembles the depressed phase of manic-depressive psychosis.

And finally there is the evidence that psychotic behavior can be induced in normal individuals by certain chemical substances, which we might designate *neurochemicals*. Perhaps the oldest known neurochemicals are those in certain kinds of toxic mushrooms. One account of the psychotic behavior triggered by hallucinogenic mushrooms follows:

The patient, a middle-aged tavern keeper, picked some wild mushrooms and ate them at ten o'clock. . . . These mushrooms were later identified by the botany department as *Amanita muscaria*. Two hours after ingestion the patient had an explosive onset of diarrhea, profuse sweating, excessive salivation, and vertigo. He fell asleep and wakened at two A.M. completely disoriented, irrational and violent. . . . He was admitted to University Hospital. . . . Somnolence alternated with periods of excitement. He thought that he was in hell and identified the interne, nurses, and attending physicians as Christ, Satan, God, or angels. Nursing notes on admission indicated that he was thrashing about in bed, talking constantly and irrationally.

As the day wore on, the content of his hallucinatory and illusional output remained almost entirely religious. He constantly misidentified a tall resident physician as Christ. He kept referring to nurses and other attendants as God or angels. He felt he was in the Garden of Eden and then in hell. As evening came he cleared up mentally, lost his motor excitement, and felt relaxed. All laboratory tests were within normal limits. He appeared to be recovered on the following morning and was discharged (Fabing, 1956, p. 233).

A number of chemicals (bufotenine, mescaline) that have similar effects on behavior have been isolated. Their mode of operation is being studied in the hope that it may reveal something about the causes of schizophrenia.

However, none of the evidence we have presented can establish beyond any doubt that psychoses, such as schizophrenia, have an organic origin. Claims that physiological factors are responsible for schizophrenia rather than faulty learning and the neurological changes underlying habit formation are still unproved. And, moreover, they can be proved only when the exact physiological nature and locus of this condition is discovered. Nevertheless, for the time being, the somatic hypothesis must be judged a reasonable one for certain kinds of psychiatric disturbances which have long been assumed to result from learning seriously maladaptive modes of response.

Shock Therapy. One of the earliest forms of somatotherapy, and one that is still widely used, was accidentally discovered in 1928 by an Austrian physician, Manfred Sakel. Called upon to treat a famous actress who was both a diabetic and a narcotic addict and was also very confused Sakel prescribed insulin for her. Through some accident she was given an overdose, and Sakel was very surprised to discover a

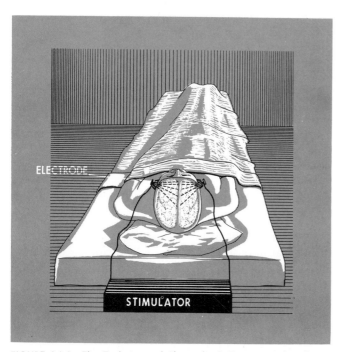

FIGURE 14.6 The Technique of Electroshock Treatment. An electric current is passed through the brain for a fraction of a second, producing convulsions, which are followed by a comatose period.

decided decrease in his patient's confusion. Being an alert and imaginative scientist, he did not ignore the implications of his discovery and resolved to try a massive dose of insulin on a schizophrenic. This was a dangerous gamble, for insulin in a large quantity can lead to death, but it paid off. The condition of the schizophrenic patient improved, and the era of **insulin shock therapy** began. The treatment was eagerly taken up by other psychiatrists, partly because so little else could be done, and in the flush of first enthusiasm, reports were published indicating that insulin shock therapy was extremely successful in treating schizophrenia. However, later reports have not been as favorable, particularly regarding the permanence of the beneficial changes that appear soon after the shock treatment. In general, extensive use of the method suggests that insulin shock therapy can help reduce the symptoms of schizophrenia, especially during the early stages of the disorder (Salzman, 1947), and some psychiatrists, including Sakel himself, believe that the immediate gains can be made to last longer if they are supplemented by appropriate psychotherapy.

For insulin shock treatment to be maximally effective, the insulin dosage must be great enough to initiate severe convulsions and a coma. The greater the intensity of this shock reaction, the better chance of success, but the greater the danger to the patient. During convulsions he may break his leg or his neck, or even die. Because the treatment takes several hours and involves great risks, the strain on the physicians and nursing staff responsible is almost unbearable. Many hospitals, therefore, would not use the treatment. But the degree of success obtained with it created an obvious need for a simpler and safer shock treatment.

Electroshock treatment, developed in Italy in 1938, seemed to meet this need. In this technique a controlled amount of shock is passed through a patient's brain for a few seconds by means of electrodes attached to his head. The patient loses consciousness and undergoes a brief and violent convulsion. When he awakens a little later his memory is hazy, but this impairment disappears in a short time. There is a minimum of risk in electroshock treatment and very little nursing care is needed. In fact, electroshock is so easy to administer that it is often used in office practice. The patient comes to the office, gets his shock, rests, and then returns home.

For some unknown reason electroshock is not as effective as insulin shock in the treatment of schizophrenics, but is quite effective with patients who are suffering from manic-depressive psychosis and involutional melancholia. The latter show the highest rate of improvement, and depressed psychotics do somewhat better than manics. Many psychiatrists believe that electroshock, like insulin treatment, is more effective when combined with psychotherapy. One drawback in the use of electroshock, besides not being anywhere near 100 per cent effective, is that patients who improve after its use seem to run a somewhat greater risk of succumbing to their disorder again than patients who improve spontaneously or after other kinds of treatment. But this is not a very serious shortcoming, considering the ease with which shock treatment can be administered. Many manic-depressive patients, at the first sign of the disorder's recurrence, go directly to their psychiatrist's office and begin a series of shock treatments. In this way they live with their psychosis by effectively controlling it.

Why should shock therapy have the effects it does? Nobody really knows. One possibility is that it reduces fear. We know that a rat's fear in avoidance conditioning (see page 167) and also in approach-avoidance conflicts (see page 413) can be reduced by electroshock treatment (Carson, 1957; Poschel, 1957). But obviously we need to know a lot more, particularly about the physiological mechanisms responsible for the known effects of electroshock treatment.

Chemotherapy. Chemicals have long been known to exert powerful influences on behavior. Narcotics like opium and codein are prescribed to reduce pain and fear. Sedatives are widely used to calm and relax patients who are upset. And alcohol is resorted to almost universally to ease the strain of conflicts and anxieties. But only recently have certain kinds of chemicals been used extensively in coping with behavior disorders. The much-publicized tranquilizing drugs have given a great impetus to **chemotherapy.**

The most famous of these are *reserpine* and *chlorpromazine*. Reserpine was isolated in 1952 from the root of an Indian plant (Rauwolfia) which Hindus had used for centuries as a sedative. It is still used in some parts of India to put children to sleep. Chlorpromazine is a recent product developed in a French laboratory.

Tranquilizers, as their name indicates, have the uncanny property of being able to calm, relax, and help dissipate anxieties without inducing sleep. Like all drugs, their effects may vary widely, depending on the individual and on the dosage. But their most dramatic effects have been on violent and agitated psychotics whose behavior and lucidity often improve spectacularly, to the point where they are easily manageable on the ward and sometimes can make a go of it in society.

Tranquilizers have altered the whole atmosphere of wards for disturbed patients: iron bars have come down; draperies have gone up. Patients now attend to their appearance. Female patients are given cosmetics and mirrors. Male patients can be given occupational therapy and be trusted with carpenter's tools—saws, chisels, and hammers. These are the very patients no one would have dreamed of giving knives and forks for fear they would harm themselves or assault others. Being a psychiatric nurse or ward attendant is no longer the harrowing experience it was. Rarely is it necessary to tie violent patients down in their beds or to force them into isolation rooms, as it was common to do. Ward personnel have been sharply reduced because patients no longer require close supervision and can do many things for themselves which were previously beyond their capacities. Probably the most impressive and encouraging fact of all is that many state institutions, for the first time in their histories, report more discharges than admissions. As the final report (1961) of the Joint Commission on Mental Illness, created by the United States Congress, stated, tranquilizers ". . . have delivered the greatest blow for patient freedom, in terms of nonrestraint, since Pinel struck off the chains in the Paris asylum 168 years ago."

So much for newly achieved successes. The whole picture is not so rosy. Many patients who have been released from psychiatric institutions are forced to return. Others suffer dangerous side effects, such as liver damage. Most important of all, the drugs do not, for the most part, bring about a cure. Patients, who have become more manageable, still have difficulties adjusting to the demands of society.

Nevertheless, the beneficial effects of tranquilizers far exceed their defects. It had always been practically impossible to persuade agitated and incoherent psychotics to discuss their problems. Now tranquilizers permit the use of psychotherapy with such patients. Tranquilizers also calm individuals who have serious personal difficulties and protect them from possible breakdowns. They are extremely effective in toning down the complaints of neurotics, particularly the anxious ones. Reserpine, for example, can lower the dangerously high blood pressure which many anxiety neurotics suffer from, although we should add, it also reduces their efficiency. And some of the milder tranquilizers (*meprobamate,*

a long-acting muscle relaxant) are effective in aiding fairly well-adjusted individuals to cope with some sudden difficult problems. The author has an acquaintance who has but one problem—a difficult mother. Whenever she comes for a visit, the atmosphere in his home becomes charged with tension. She disapproves of the way her grandchildren are being raised, and although she tries to hold her tongue she can't do so for long. Her son and daughter-in-law react immediately to her criticisms, and the result is a fiery argument which they all regret later. Being a practical person, the son has devised a way of solving the problem. On the day of his mother's visit, he and his wife take tranquilizers. They meet his mother at the door with a tranquilizer, which she obligingly consumes. Now everybody seems to be happy.

The ultimate benefits of tranquilizers are yet to be realized. We know already that disordered reactions can be modified by chemical means. Not every consequence of their use is wholly desirable, but new drugs that do not produce dangerous side effects will undoubtedly be synthesized in the future. Moreover, experimental techniques (see page 20) which allow objective evaluation of a drug's behavioral effects are available. For example, it has been found that reserpine knocks out an avoidance response based upon a visual stimulus but not one based on an auditory stimulus (John, Wenzel, & Tschirgi, 1958). Now the problem is to modify the chemical basis of the drug so that it can effectively eliminate a fear response to auditory stimuli. Similarly, the tendency of reserpine to reduce performance (see page 486) may be rectified by further modifying the drug itself or by synthesizing a new drug that will leave performance unimpaired. We are optimistic that this can be done, because neural transmission is apparently based on chemical changes at the synapse. Therefore, it should be possible to control behavior by controlling the chemical processes going on at the juncture of nerve cells. This is the idea that guides the researchers in psychopharmacology, that science which combines chemistry, physiology, and psychology.

PREVENTION AND CONTROL

In response to the question of what is needed most in the war against psychiatric affliction, many workers in behavior pathology would simply reply "research and then more research." There is no doubt we shall need a great deal more knowledge before we can mount a really large-scale attack against what is probably our greatest health problem. A single fact can dramatize how much more support our nation might give to this effort. In 1958 the total amount of financial support for research in behavior pathology supplied by the Federal government amounted to the cost of constructing and firing two Atlas missiles!

We desperately need research in many areas. The origins of various psychiatric disorders need to be better understood. If we know more about their early stages, our chances of preventing and controlling them would improve. If we were to discover, for example, that a particular disorder begins when a person fails to learn appropriate responses, we could set about modifying the influences in his environment so that he could learn different and more effective ones. Or if we were to discover that genetic factors increase a person's susceptibility to a certain psychiatric disturbance, we could supervise the circumstances of his life more closely and minimize his risks. Even if we were to learn that a disease is inherited directly, we would not have to abandon hope. Such problems are not necessarily insoluble.

Huntington's chorea, a disorder of the central nervous system that attacks 25,000 Americans of middle age annually, presents just such a problem. Initially the victim makes jerky, involuntary movements and shows signs of irritability, moodiness, memory impairment, and loss of motivation. Hallucinations and delusions of persecution are apt to follow, sometimes leading victims to commit crimes of violence. But the really terrible thing about this disease is that it is increasing at a faster rate than the general population, for it has been found to be transmitted according to a simple rule of heredity: roughly one-half the children of each case succumb to it. We know, for instance, that 1,000 American cases have descended from three people who emigrated from the same English village to this country in 1630. At present no cure is known. But there is hope. For one thing, we know that genes exert their control on physiological development by biochemical means (see page 101). Hence, by chemical intervention it should be possible to modify this rigid genetic determination. For another, it might be possible to distinguish from among children of parents who have the disorder, those who are destined to contract the disease themselves. This would at least enable their more fortunate siblings to marry and have children in peace.

There must be more and better research in all areas of treatment. For the simple truth is that the therapeutic techniques we have now are not good enough. Of course, we cannot abandon these techniques. We have nothing better. Moreover, research may point to methods by which they can be improved. But society must not be lulled into inactivity in the belief that any presently available therapeutic technique is good enough to cope with a specific psychiatric problem or with behavior problems in general.

The fruits of present-day research will be harvested in the future. Meanwhile we cannot turn our backs on psychiatric problems. Although much is being done with our limited fund of knowledge, still more can be accomplished in the fight against psychiatric ills.

One way in which the campaign could definitely be advanced is through increased public appreciation of the fact that practically all therapeutic techniques, including tranquilizers, are most effective when they are used in the early stages of a disorder. This makes early diagnosis extremely desirable. Everybody—particularly parents, teachers, ministers, and others with more than ordinary social influence—should be taught to recognize the early symptoms of behavior pathology. Too often quiet, detached children in school, and even very odd children, are ignored because they do not at the time present the teacher with behavior problems. In reality, these children may be in the early stages of a crippling neurotic disorder, perhaps even schizophrenia. No one wants to turn everybody into an amateur psychiatrist, but if teachers were alert to such problems and if school systems had the services of professional psychologists who could make early diagnoses, the chances that these children would be helped to overcome their difficulties would be much greater than they are now when the children are ignored and their disorders allowed to become more severe.

You can see that a more enlightened attitude toward behavior pathology generally would do much toward improving prevention and control. The person whose behavior is sometimes bizarre is too often hidden from society by relatives afraid of embarrassment. If people would learn to react to behavior disorders as realistically as they do to infectious diseases, everything would be so much better, especially for the patient. Patients discharged from psychiatric institutions would be more able to make satisfactory adjustments to society and less likely to return to institutions. It is a common and understandable reaction of former patients to feel alone and scared when they try to gain readmission to soci-

ety. They are afraid of rebuffs—rebuffs due to the general public's unwarranted fears and lack of understanding. Most of these patients need help from out-patient clinics and special recreation centers which can make the transition from the protected life of the institution to normal community life easier in many respects. It is generally believed that if more help and supervision were given these discharged patients, fewer of them would be forced back into psychiatric hospitals. Statistics compiled in New York State indicate that the number of those who have to return is as high as 30 per cent.

Antisocial and criminal behavior is another major area in which our efforts at prevention and control must be increased. Although some criminals are the products of "good" neighborhoods, cold statistics prove that our slums contribute disproportionately to the incidence of crime and juvenile delinquency. The slums must go and good schools and recreational facilities be provided. At the same time, however, what happens in any social environment, particularly one where there are children, has to be judged by what is done there to reinforce socially cooperative and responsible behavior. Stated otherwise, all facets of society, from the family to the school, must become more effective in training their members to acquire a conscience attuned to the demands of a democratic society.

Another important ingredient in the problem of crime and antisocial behavior is our penal system, including its prisons. One reason the penal system does not work as well as it might is that many of us misunderstand its function. What we need is not punishment for crime but instruments and techniques to modify the criminal behavior. The real problem is not to keep criminals in prison but to keep them out. More than 50 per cent of the inmates of state and Federal prisons are repeaters, clear proof that prison terms are not particularly effective in modifying criminal behavior. If anything, they perpetuate it. This is not surprising, considering the evidence from laboratory experimentation that punishment is *by itself* not effective in producing desirable behavior (see page 279).

Moreover, attempts to treat psychiatric problems in prison have not proved very successful. Psychotherapy is hindered by the intense hostility of almost all patients behind bars. Their hostility makes them instead eager disciples of the unofficial training in criminal behavior that goes on in most prisons. First offenders come in contact with hardened criminals anxious to teach them the techniques of a criminal career and the most cynical attitudes toward the law and every sort of moral code.

What is needed are institutions which provide genuine rehabilitation. Many people believe that it would be valuable to set up institutions where those persons who have not given up struggling against their antisocial tendencies could go voluntarily in the same way that sick people go to hospitals. Therapy is more likely to be successful in such a setting. However, as far as we can see into the future, custodial institutions for criminals who are not receptive to therapy are going to be needed. The hope is that this need will gradually decrease as effective programs of crime prevention increase.

The growing number of the aged in our society poses another severe psychiatric problem that we must do something about. Thanks to medical progress, more people than ever are reaching or living well past the Biblical "three score and ten." At the same time, many of our industries are turning away job applicants 40 and 45 years old, and often, even younger. We can see one consequence of this social dilemma in New York City, where one million of the city's eight million inhabitants are past 60, and where 50 per cent of the patients admitted to psychiatric institutions are also past that age. To many senior New Yorkers, then, longer life must be a burden rather than a boon.

Although most of the psychiatric problems of older people are simply the result of aging, a sizable percentage can be traced to the current social situation. For this reason, we must consider more carefully the question, At what age does a person become old? Our answer to it lies at the root of the problem confronting the elderly. We must realize that it is impossible, for two reasons, to set a precise year at which everyone becomes old. First, the effect age has on behavior depends on the form of behavior one is thinking of. Only rarely can a sprinter maintain his speed past his late twenties, but significant Supreme Court decisions have been written by justices in their seventies and older. Second, individual differences in this respect are tremendous. Prize fighters typically fade in their late twenties or early thirties, but Archie Moore successfully defended his light heavyweight crown several times after he had passed forty. And in the arts and sciences, as well as business and government, there are many individuals who remain highly productive well past the conventional retirement age of 65.

That the effects of age must be judged in relation to a specific job as well as to a specific individual, argues against the practice of a definite retirement age for all persons and for all jobs. But the trends in industry, government, and education are toward enforced retirement at 65, and no doubt this is an easy policy to administer and one that opens positions for younger men. Nevertheless, it works a hardship on elderly people who are still doing excellent work and wish to continue. Enforced retirement often leaves them in despair. When America was a rural society, there was something for most every able-bodied person to do, and many of the aged filled positions of respect. Today the old person is often pitied because he no longer has any opportunity to participate in useful and satisfying activities.

In some way our industrial society must plan more sensibly and humanely for its aged. If they lose neither their places in society nor their interest in life, they are less likely to be susceptible to psychiatric disabilities. What we need are better ways of measuring job efficiency without discriminating against older people and programs that will prepare men and women for interesting activities when they do retire. These are difficult problems, but they become more pressing each year as the proportion of the aged in the population rises.

We could cite other social problems intimately related to maintaining psychological health, but we do not have the space. Perhaps your instructor will suggest other topics. Although what we now know about behavior pathology is limited, we have not yet utilized our insights as fully as we might in the fight against psychiatric ills and their social consequences.

SUMMARY

Psychological ("mental") health can be defined as the presence of healthy reactions or the absence of pathological reactions. But since there is no general agreement about a positive definition of psychological health, a negative one is more widely used.

Behavior pathology exists when an individual's reactions are disordered. This means one or both of two things: the reactions are not justified by the external situation or they are ineffective in achieving desired results. There are three major categories of behavior disorders: neurosis, psychosis, and character disorders.

A neurotic is a person who admits to being unhappy, behaves irrationally, and exhibits certain symptoms (tension, phobia, compulsion). His behavior, which is characterized by a punishing circularity, fails to resolve his conflicts. The four diagnostic categories of neuroses can be ordered on a dimension ranging from high to low manifest anxiety: anxiety, phobic, obsessive-compulsive, and conversion reactions. In a psychosomatic reaction a psychological disturbance is combined with some organic disorder.

The psychoses represent the most extreme forms of pathological reactions. Psychotics have poor contact with reality, behave peculiarly, are a danger to themselves or others, and are often unable to care for themselves. Schizophrenia is the most common psychotic reaction and is characterized by poor contact with reality and disordered intellectual and affective responses. The four main types of schizophrenia are simple, paranoid, hebephrenic, and catatonic. Manic-depressive psychotics exhibit severe disturbances in mood ranging from overactive, manic reactions to underactive, depressed reactions. Involutional melancholia, which occurs during the change-of-life period, resembles the depressed reactions of the manic-depressive psychotics.

Organic psychoses are those directly attributable to damage to the central nervous system brought about by disease (e.g., Pick's Disease), injuries (e.g., brain damage), chemicals (e.g., Korsakow's syndrome), or aging (e.g., senile psychosis). Organic psychotics usually exhibit one or all of the following symptoms: intellectual impairment, mood swings, and defective social behavior.

Persons suffering from character disorders behave, with little evidence of anxiety, in an immature, self-centered manner oblivious to the needs of others and society.

The psychopath behaves without regard to social law, while the sociopath directs his hostility against society.

There are two major classes of psychological therapies, psychotherapy and somatotherapy. Psychotherapists attempt to modify their patients' behavior by communication, somatotherapists use physiological methods to bring about changes in behavior. The most commonly practiced forms of psychotherapy are psychoanalysis, client-centered therapy, group psychotherapy, and general psychotherapy. The main forms of somatotherapies are shock therapy and chemotherapy. The effectiveness of all forms of therapy is difficult to estimate because of inadequate methods of personality evaluation. There is general agreement that new and better techniques are needed.

To reduce the problem of behavior pathology the following are demanded: more and better research; more effective methods of diagnosing pathological reactions during their early stages; a sympathetic, as well as a better, understanding of behavior pathology by all members of society; elimination of conditions that breed antisocial behavior and the development of techniques to modify the behavior of criminals; and a more sensible, humane, and effective method of coping with the ever-increasing problems of the aged.

SUGGESTIONS FOR FURTHER READING

BRILL, A. A. (Ed.) *The basic writings of Sigmund Freud.* New York: Modern Library, 1938.

A compilation of some of Freud's major contributions to his theory of behavior. This volume contains his famous book, *The interpretation of dreams.*

BURTON, A., & HARRIS, R. E. *Clinical studies of personality.* New York: Harper, 1955.

Case studies illustrating different forms of disordered reactions.

CAMERON, N., & MAGARET, A. *Behavior pathology.* Boston: Houghton Mifflin, 1951.

A well-organized text that examines the nature, etiology, and treatment of pathological forms of behavior.

DOLLARD, J., AULD, F., & WHITE, A. M. *Steps in psychotherapy.* New York: Macmillan, 1953.

A detailed study of a patient undergoing psychotherapy.

DOLLARD, J., & MILLER, N. E. *Personality and psychotherapy.* New York: McGraw-Hill, 1950.

An analysis of personality and psychotherapy that emphasizes principles of learning.

LEHNER, G. F. J., & KUBE, E. *The dynamics of personal adjustment.* Englewood Cliffs, N.J.: Prentice-Hall, 1955.

A psychological analysis of problems of adjustment in everyday life.

ROGERS, C. R. *Client-centered therapy.* Boston: Houghton Mifflin, 1951.

An exposition, supplemented with case records, of client-centered therapy.

SHAFFER, L. F. & SHOBEN, E. J., Jr. *The psychology of adjustment.* (2nd ed.) Boston: Houghton Mifflin, 1956.

An analysis of human adjustment based upon both experimental and clinical evidence.

SUNDBERG, N. D., & TYLER, L. E. *Clinical psychology: research and practice.* New York: Appleton-Century-Crofts, 1962.

A general introduction to the concepts and methods of clinical psychology as well as to the training and work of the clinical psychologist.

WEINBERG, H., & HIRE, A. W. *Case book in abnormal psychology.* New York: Knopf, 1957.

Case studies of various kinds of personality disorders.

WHITE, R. W. *The abnormal personality.* (2nd ed.) New York: Ronald, 1956.

An extremely well-written textbook on behavior pathology.

SOCIAL BEHAVIOR

15

SOCIAL INFLUENCES ON BEHAVIOR

One point should be crystal-clear by now. An organism's environment exerts a powerful influence on its behavior. As we have progressed from our examination of simple reactions to simple physical stimuli, in the study of sensation, to our consideration of the complex responses to all kinds of stimuli, which are expressions of personality, we have repeatedly demonstrated the principle that behavior is controlled by stimuli. As you proceeded through the succession of topics, however, you should have noticed something of a shift in the meaning of the term *stimulus*. Initially a *stimulus* was defined entirely in terms of its physical properties. When the topic was visual or auditory thresholds, the *physical* intensity of the stimulus was its important feature. As later topics were taken up, stimuli were more frequently defined in terms of their

social properties. For example, a child's reactions to his mother depend more upon the relationship he has had with her than upon her weight or height.

The obvious importance of these social stimuli has led to the development of the broad field known as **social psychology.** On the simplest level, social psychology is concerned with how each of us responds to other people and to the environment which has been formed for us by others. This definition covers a wide range of behavior: nursing at your mother's breast; learning to read; dancing with a partner; belonging to a social organization; cooperating in a group venture; persuading others to believe as you do or being persuaded to think as they do, and so on. In fact, this definition of social psychology is so inclusive that it is difficult to think of any behavior that falls outside its scope. Shading your eyes from the sun's glare may seem to be an example of behavior that is not the concern of social psychology, but even it is a response you probably learned by imitation, and therefore a social response. Salivating to food may be another instance of nonsocial behavior, but again it is a response that has been affected by social custom, for each society trains its members to salivate only to certain kinds of foods. A fat, juicy grasshopper evokes salivary responses in most African Bushmen but in few Americans.

The difficulty we have in separating social psychology from what we have already discussed illustrates two important facts. First, social psychology does not deal with phenomena that are uniquely different from those that we have been reviewing in the preceding chapters. Second, social psychology does not require a method of investigation *fundamentally* different from those used elsewhere by psychologists. Every psychological experiment—whether designed to investigate sensory processes or social behavior—requires that the behavior of some organism in some environment be measured.

Now, various areas of psychology do, of course, differ in the special techniques their explorations require. In social psychology, for example, in order to investigate the important topic of how **attitudes** are formed and modified, one must create a situation in which an attitude can be measured objectively and quantitatively. One can do this by devising an **attitude test** and measuring a person's attitude by his responses. But such special techniques are outgrowths of, not departures from, the same fundamental method used in all psychological research.

The Scope of the Chapter

The range of social psychology is so vast that no satisfactory overview of the entire subject can be made in one chapter. And matters are made even more difficult by the fact that there is no sharp separation between social psychology and its allied disciplines, sociology and anthropology. Therefore, rather than attempt the impossible, we shall content ourselves with discussing a small sample of topics in this chapter. They are socialization, experimental studies with small groups, leadership, and attitudes. You will discover that these subjects are highly related, information from each contributing to the understanding of the others.

In the selection of these topics, we do not imply that they are superior to a number of others, including perhaps some your instructor may prefer. In any case, your brief exposure to social psychology can provide you, at best, with only a fleeting glimpse of some of its objectives and methods, its facts and theories. To obtain a fuller understanding of social behavior you will need to take a course entirely devoted to this fascinating subject.

SOCIALIZATION

What society does to a human being is in some ways like what a maze does to a rat. The structure of a maze shapes the rat's behavior first by limiting the kinds of responses he can make and then by reinforcing some and not reinforcing others. Society does the same thing. It limits the range of its members' behavior, encourages certain responses by reinforcing them, and discourages others by withholding rewards or by meting out punishment. We call this shaping process the **socialization** of the individual.

Socialization *cannot* be sharply distinguished from the learning that goes on during the development of personality (see page 455). Both socialization and development of personality shape the general behavior patterns of individuals, and both occur in a similar way. As we emphasized in our discussion, personality develops, for the most part, from specific training experiences (feeding, cleanliness training, etc.).

Socialization takes place more gradually and subtly. As a child matures he seems to be slowly transformed from a cute animal into a socialized being. But regardless of how it appears to take place, socialization actually results from many specific learning experiences in a variety of situations. More specifically, it depends upon the combined effects of the principles of learning and the structure of the social environment. We have already studied the principles of learning, so our task now is to describe briefly the social environment and to illustrate how it encourages socialization.

The socializing process can be examined from many different perspectives, but for our purposes we can analyze this process as it functions on three levels. At the uppermost level is the influence of the *culture* to which an individual belongs. **Culture** is an inclusive term for the general behavior patterns shared by the members of the same society. Next below this is the effect of his particular **social group,** an integral part of the culture and one that reinforces distinctive patterns of behavior. At the lowest level are the influences a group of two people, a **social dyad,** exert on each other.

Analysis of each social level contributes knowledge necessary for a complete understanding of social behavior. To discover why Americans behave differently from the French or Bantus, we make a cultural analysis. However, we know that the social behavior of individuals within the same culture differs, that a culture actually consists of many social groups or what is often called **subcultures** (rich and poor, young and old, men and women, educated and uneducated), and that the environment provided by these groups exerts its own special influences on social behavior. Therefore, to find out how the behavior of rich and poor or men and women differs, we make a social group analysis. Finally, since we know that the social behavior of one person with another depends on who

that other person is, to find out how a person's behavior changes when he is with his mother, a professor, his sweetheart, his best friend, a salesman, a prospective employer, or a child of three, we examine the influence of the social dyad.

An analysis of social behavior on any one level is incomplete. An overall cultural analysis will fail to include the variability in behavior from subgroup to subgroup. Similarly, an analysis of the influence of one person on another (of a tyrannical father upon his son) must leave out of account the general ways of acting which are common to all members of the same culture.

Culture

Your being a member of a culture means that you are bound to receive certain characteristic kinds of training. Cultural training includes a very wide range of activities, not the least of which is language as the instrument of communication. What you are doing right now, a kind of social behaving in which you and the writer are involved, would not be possible if we did not share a common language. Learning a language usually means more than learning how to understand, speak, read, and write it. It also involves the acquisition of many kinds of attitudes and values. American reactions to such words as *democracy, goodness, elections, fair play,* and *freedom* often differ greatly from the reactions of members of other societies.

You can see the impact of cultural influences on social behavior most clearly when you compare one culture with another. We become so accustomed to our own way of behaving that we believe it to be the "natural" way for all mankind. But it is just as "natural" for the Bushmen (Thomas, 1959) who live in the Kalahari Desert of Southwest Africa to avoid owning property and giving any evidence of doing so as it is for Americans to try to acquire property, and a good deal of it if possible. Living a marginal kind of existence, the Bushmen are constantly threatened by famine and drought. Their survival depends on a rigidly maintained cooperative attitude that allows no room for quarreling or fighting of any kind. The few possessions they do have are constantly rotated among various members of the tribe to make sure that no one starts an argument because he is jealous. It is also just as "natural" for the British to revere and abide by the principles of their unwritten constitution as it is for us to obey the laws of our written one. Moreover, among the Todas of India, it is natural for brothers to share a common wife, and for a ceremony to determine which brother shall be called the father of all future children. Since death does not automatically abrogate the ceremonial decision, children are born whose "fathers" have been dead for ten years (Mead, 1930).

There is nothing mysterious in the way that culture shapes behavior. Learning principles operate in social situations as they do in experimental ones. Parents teach their children what they in turn learned from their parents. German children are reinforced for being orderly and dutiful (Schaffner, 1948); Japanese children are trained to avoid shame (the contempt of others) by making rigidly prescribed social responses (Benedict, 1946). That learning principles operate in social situations also explains why a culture is so difficult to change. Attempts at modifying cultural patterns are usually met with resistance because they go against firmly established habits and strong motivations.

History offers many examples of governments failing in attempts to institute new cultural patterns by force. After it came to power in the revolution of 1918, the Soviet government had, on several occasions, to abandon sweeping programs of social change because they failed to conform to Russian traditions. The Communist leaders learned from experience to change their tactics, to avoid direct opposition to preexisting cultural patterns. They allowed more time for changes to take place and compromised their goals in order to conform more closely with Russian habits and traditions. Of course, their main technique in establishing a new social order was to break the chief link by which the old culture was transmitted. That link was, as everywhere, the education of the younger generation by the older. The Soviet government instituted sweeping changes in the educational system aimed at having the children introject Communist ideology instead of the traditions and values of the older social system. But even so, the Communists often underestimated the influence that parents had on their children at home. Other countries like China, Poland, India, and many of the new African nations are encountering similar problems when they try to break too rapidly with the traditions of the past.

In America, too, there are many examples of the resistance of cultural traditions to change. Many second- and third-generation families descended from immigrants cling stubbornly to the cultural patterns of their forebears. There are remnants of Italian, Jewish, Irish, German, and Chinese traditions in families that have been in America for several generations. There are even certain religious sects, such as the Mennonites in Pennsylvania, who live much as their ancestors did centuries ago in Europe. Ignoring their contemporary world so far as possible, they cultivate a religious life, dress in a distinctive way, and refuse to ride in automobiles. They even converse in their own special Pennsylvania Dutch tongue, High German mixed with English.

The persistence of cultural patterns does not mean, of course, that old customs are unmodifiable. Some do change, but ordinarily at a slow rate. Sometimes, however, powerful combinations of circumstances bring about fairly rapid social changes. The industrial revolution, with its new

FIGURE 15.1 Mennonites From Pennsylvania.

methods of production, has caused far-reaching upheavals in many social institutions. Among its other effects it has utterly altered the position of women in society. It has freed them from a great many household chores, which can now be done by machines, and it has opened to them numerous opportunities for suitable jobs, largely because machines have eliminated many of the tasks which only strong men could perform. In this way, women have been enabled to pursue careers outside the home. And moreover, the wealth of machine-produced goods money can buy has tempted them, often encouraged by their husbands, to enter the job market. By having jobs women have achieved greater economic independence and, along with this, greater social independence. The industrial revolution, with its exploitation of machine power, has had a most profound cultural influence in making women more independent and therefore in reducing the social differentiation between the sexes.

Laws can encourage cultural changes but do not automatically establish them. This point is vividly demonstrated by what has happened in some parts of the country since the Supreme Court decision outlawing segregation of Negroes and whites in public schools. Since the tradition of racial segregation is deeply entrenched in most parts of the South, the Supreme Court's decision could not eradicate it overnight. But it has mobilized cultural traditions in opposition to the segregation policy—traditions of obedience to the law and of support for free universal education.

The Supreme Court decision has set the stage for conflict between different cultural traditions. The behavioral effects of this conflict depend on the strengths of the competing values and the response tendencies they influence. Where the Federal government has not exerted much pressure on Southern communities to integrate, many of them have made little or no effort. The tendency to be law-abiding and of providing free public education have not been brought into active conflict with the tendency to continue racial segregation. However, where Southern communities have been compelled to face the choice of either integrating their schools or being in immediate defiance of the law, the relative strengths of the opposing response tendencies can be observed. In some places, the cultural tradition of racial segregation is stronger than the sum of all competing traditions. There, people have fought school integration even at the risk of being jailed. In others, integration may be repugnant but to break the law or to close the schools is even more offensive. And there are Southerners who have rejected the tradition of racial segregation and actively support school integration.

The reactions of different communities, as well as different individuals within the same community, to school integration show how social behavior can be the product of many different response tendencies operating simultaneously. Furthermore, these different tendencies have not always been based on broad ethical principles of the rights of individuals or equality of opportunity. Some communities have adopted integrated school systems because they knew they could not bear the cost of maintaining segregation by providing "private" schools for white children. Some individuals have given their support to integration because they realized they would suffer business losses if their community did not make a peaceful transition from a segregated school system to an integrated one. And some who have championed integration have reversed themselves when their friends began to ostracize them.

Regardless of what has brought about the changes, the Supreme Court's decision has had a profound effect on the social fabric of our Southern states. Certain social customs, particularly in the large cities, have been drastically changed. But it must be understood that the changes have not been directly instituted by the law. The law changes the patterns of reinforcement and these in turn determine behavior, what people actually do.

Social Groups

Every Presidential election makes clear the extent to which American society contains powerful subcultures. Campaign speeches are directed toward winning the support of "minority groups," such as farmers, laborers, businessmen, the retired, and those with particular religious, racial, and national backgrounds. In truth there are so many "minority groups" that no "majority group" can be actually said to exist.

Politicians direct their appeals to these groups because their members are known to behave alike, especially in their voting habits. This is not surprising, considering that they often share a common social environment and similar backgrounds.

Past elections have shown that a large majority of many distinguishable social groups tend to favor one or another of the candidates. Franklin Roosevelt and Harry Truman were loyally supported by large majorities of union laborers. Dwight Eisenhower was extremely popular with citizens in the suburban communities that mushroomed around our large cities following World War II. In 1960 huge majorities of Jews and Catholics voted for John Kennedy.

It is risky business to try to explain why people vote as they do. No election can be repeated almost exactly but with just enough experimental modification to test the validity of certain hypotheses. But there is strong reason to believe that membership in a social group can make people sufficiently similar psychologically to determine how they vote. And these social groups sometimes play decisive roles in certain elections. An analysis of past Presidential elections would suggest the following hypotheses. Franklin Roosevelt came to power during the most severe depression this country has ever experienced, when many millions of workers were out of jobs. His administration encouraged further unionization of labor and alleviated the distress caused by unemployment. Harry Truman inherited Roosevelt's political mantle as well as his prolabor attitudes. Both these men were perceived by workers as Presidents who would protect their economic security. Dwight Eisenhower held out to the citizens of the new suburban communities the best hope of raising their families in peace. Kennedy proved an appealing candidate to Catholics and Jews because he was a member of a minority religious faith and never before had such a person been elected to the Presidency. He was supported by members of these groups because some of them wanted a Catholic President, while others wanted to show that a Catholic *could* be President.

A person's vote is usually not based on only one consideration. Three main factors tend to affect how he votes: (1) party affiliation; (2) election issues; and (3) the candidate's personality (Campbell, Gurin, & Miller, 1954). Social group membership plays an important role in elections when it predisposes people to react to one or all of these factors in a common manner.

Social Class

A special kind of group is the *social class*. Although our democratic ideals tend to make us ignore social classes or at least to minimize the differences among them, we cannot sensibly maintain that they do not exist. However, it is difficult to define the particular social classes because many different ways of measuring them have been used. Sometimes a person's social class is measured by an objective index, such as income, education, or occupation. But it can also be measured by a subjective one, a person's evaluation of his own position in the social hierarchy.

In the 1940's, when a sample of people were asked what social class—upper, middle, lower—they belonged to, 6 per cent identified themselves as members of the upper class, 88 per cent thought they belonged to the middle class, and 6 per cent thought of themselves as lower class. These results were interpreted as demonstrating that American society is largely middle class. But obviously the designation *lower class* is not particularly flattering, and when a few years later (Centers, 1949) a sample of men were asked whether they belonged to the upper, middle, working, or lower class, the distribution of responses was quite different. The results from this sample were:

	PER CENT
Upper Class	3
Middle Class	43
Working Class	51
Lower Class	1
Don't know	1
Don't believe in classes	1

Obviously the number of people who think they belong to the middle class in the United States depends on what alternative classes they can identify with.

Another method of measuring social class is based upon the informal evaluations people make of each other. Particular informants in a community are selected and subjected to extensive interviews. The information they give serves to describe the social structure of the town. Sociological analysis (Warner, 1953) using this technique suggests that relatively small American communities varying in population from about 6,000 to 17,000 can be divided into three main classes, upper, middle, and lower, each of which may be further separated into an upper and lower section. Figure 15.2 shows the distribution of these classes in one New England city. Although the proportion of the population in each class may vary from town to town, its citizens are usually perceived by their fellows as belonging to one of these classes.

Typically members of the upper class are seen to occupy some elevated social position described by such phrases as "the 400," "the

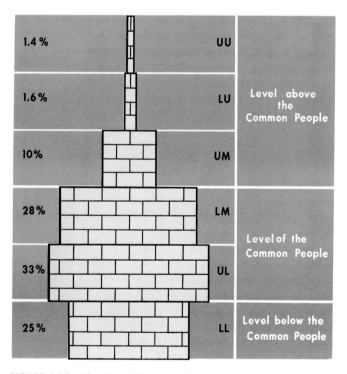

FIGURE 15.2 The Social Structure of a Small New England Community. These social classes were based upon interviews with selected informants who evaluated the social position of people in their town (After W. L. Warner. *American Life: Dream and reality.* Chicago: Univer. of Chicago Press, 1953. By permission of The University of Chicago Press.)

Figure labels: 1.4 % UU — Level above the Common People; 1.6 % LU; 10% UM; 28% LM — Level of the Common People; 33% UL; 25% LL — Level below the Common People

people with family and money," and "the elite" or "the fancy crowd." The main factor distinguishing the *upper-upper* and the *lower-upper* is the length of time their families have occupied their high-level social positions. The *upper-upper* are the old families, while the *lower-uppers* are the newcomers, the *nouveaux riches*. The people often described as the most "solid" citizens of the community are the members of the upper-middle class. They are usually members of the influential clubs and associations that give status and position in the community. They are sometimes described as "a notch or two below the fancy crowd" and "the strivers who are working hard to get into the 400."

The lower-middle class consists of small-business men, clerks, and highly skilled workers. They are hard-working and very proper. They, too, belong to clubs and organizations, but of the fraternal and patriotic sort that are not particularly exclusive. They are the "nobodies but nice" and "the top of the common people." Immediately below them on the social ladder are members of the upper-lower class, the semiskilled workmen and the small tradesmen. They, too, are respectable and honest but they are "the little people." The lowest rung of the ladder is occupied by the lower-lower class, whose members are looked down upon or pitied because they are perceived as having neither past nor future. They are among the latest of the immigrants to arrive or the completely unsuccessful native-born. This class is perceived by the members of the superior classes as neither respectable nor moral.

One of the characteristics of social stratification in the United States has always been that rigid boundaries do not separate one class from another. That is to say, there is some mobility between classes. This is a characteristic we have always prided ourselves on. Many of our great political leaders (Andrew Jackson, Abraham Lincoln) and industrial giants (Andrew Carnegie) have risen from low beginnings to high positions in our social hierarchy. As we all know, it is a point of national pride that, "every American boy can become President."

Most of us believe that American society is a great deal more mobile than the societies of Western Europe. But our belief has not been supported by data showing the amount of upward and downward occupational mobility in the United States and various European countries (Lipset & Bendix, 1959). When the percentage of sons of manual workers who moved up to nonmanual occupations was compared in the United States, Germany, Sweden, France, and Switzerland, it was found to be approximately the same for all countries, varying from a low of 31 per cent in Sweden to a high of 45 per cent in Switzerland. Similarly, the incidence of downward mobility (sons of nonmanual workers becoming manual laborers) was essentially equal. Interestingly, data from Japan suggest that it has a degree of occupational mobility comparable to the Western countries.

Another widely accepted belief that fails to be supported by the same study is that the commercial segment of our society is becoming less mobile (Lipset & Bendix, 1959), that whereas in our early history many of our business leaders came from the lower classes, today only the sons of the wealthy have an opportunity to become "captains of industry." When business leaders born during different periods of our history were compared as to origins, the majority of them were in fact found to have come from wealthy families, and *to have always come from wealthy families*.

In societies where *caste systems* exist, the boundaries between social classes are sharply defined and not to be crossed. In the Hindu society, for example, there are four castes, which from the top rung of the ladder to the bottom are: the *Brahmans* or priests, the *Kshatriyas* or rulers and warriors, the *Vaisyas* or farmers and trades-

TABLE 15.1 The Social Origins of Business Leaders Born at Different Times in American History (Data from S. M. Lipset & R. Bendix, *Social mobility in industrial society*. Berkeley: Univ. of California Press, 1959).

YEAR OF BIRTH	PER CENT OF BUSINESS LEADERS WHOSE FATHERS WERE:	
	Businessmen and gentry farmers	*Farmers and manual workers*
1785	65	12
1815	63	13
1845	69	11
1875	73	8
1905	74	7

men, and the *Sudras* or laborers. Below these but so much below that they cannot be considered on the same ladder are the *out*caste untouchables. An orthodox Hindu must not touch any untouchable or anything an untouchable touches. As a result the untouchables are segregated in the world's worst slums. Forbidden to use water from wells in fear that the wells would be "polluted," they can only use drain water.

According to Hindu religion a person's caste membership is determined by his behavior in a previous life. An untouchable might have been a Brahman who behaved wickedly, and if he accepts his fate and behaves properly, he might be elevated in his next incarnation.

Because the caste system is imbedded in a sacred formula, people are willing to accept their inevitable fate during their present lifetime. Nevertheless, changes are taking place even in this rigid social hierarchy. Gandhi, the great religious leader in India, who himself was a member of the Vaisyas caste (*Gandhi* means grocer) was instrumental in developing a more humane attitude toward untouchables. The economic revolution that has taken place in India has destroyed many of the occupa-

tional barriers of the caste system. A Brahman may be a taxi driver, while a Kshatriya could be a bookkeeper. Nevertheless, the social restrictions of the caste system persist and are very resistant to change. No matter what his job, a member of one caste is reluctant to have his children marry beneath their caste. Although it seems absurd to Americans, it would not be unusual in India for a taxi driver, who is a member of a high caste, to disapprove the marriage of his child into a wealthy merchant family of lower caste.

The important psychological question is whether social class membership influences behavior. There is no doubt that it does. Membership in a social class determines to some extent (1) the training a person received during his most formative years and (2) the rewards and punishments his present behavior will bring him.

In a rigid caste system a child is trained to accept his position. He does not acquire the strong motivations for upward mobility the child in a more mobile society acquires. Consequently his lower social status is not as much a source of frustration as it would be for the person who is allowed, and usually encouraged, to climb the social ladder.

In our society a "psychological price" is paid for the relative fluidity of its social structure. Frustration and discontent can be the consequences of social mobility. During World War II promotions were more rare in the Military Police (MP's) than in the Air Corps. Yet the MP's felt less frustrated about their chances for promotion (Stouffer, Suchman, De Vinney, Star, & Williams, 1949). Knowing that getting ahead was a slow process, they were happier with their lot than were the soldiers in the Air Corps. In a study of the relationship between social class and psychiatric disturbances (Hollingshead & Redlich, 1958), skilled workers who came from families of skilled workers had a lower incidence of symptoms of maladjustment than did skilled workers who had risen from the ranks of the unskilled. Striving to get ahead generated dissatisfaction. Somewhat similar results were obtained in the same study with "old" and "new" members of the upper class. The "new" members had a higher incidence of divorces, separations, and other signs of family disorganization.

You should not take this evidence to mean that social mobility is intrinsically bad. When adolescent boys who aspired to positions higher than their fathers' were compared with those who wanted positions of the same level or lower, it was found that the former group was psychologically healthier (Douvan & Adelson, 1958).

The psychological effects of social mobility obviously depend on a number of factors. Societies that allow for advancement encourage creative efforts that would be impossible in rigidly stratified societies, but at the same time they can generate severe frustrations and conflicts, and the pathological behavior patterns that often result from them (see page 395). Although the caste system avoids social frustration, it also prevents large numbers of people from utilizing their potential talents to benefit society as well as to better themselves. In this way, a caste system actually wastes manpower. A modern industrial society cannot afford so uneconomical a system.

In the United States class membership is an important variable in everyone's upbringing. Among other aspects of personality it influences the development of need achievement (see page 480). When senior high school students from middle- and working-class homes were compared in the performance of a task for which a ten-dollar bill was offered, no difference was found in the two groups' ability. However, when the only reward was knowing they did well, the performance of the middle-class children was much higher. Success strivings, success for the sake of success, characterized the behavior of the middle-class adolescents, whereas the achievement motivation of the working-class subjects depended more on material rewards (Douvan, 1956).

Of course, the belief that success and achievement are desirable pervades the entire society. But middle-class children are, on the average, more likely to learn the responses that lead to achievement than are lower-class children (Rosen, 1956). Not only do they value achievement but they are willing to take those steps that ensure success: to "sacrifice," "plan ahead," "be good," "work hard," and "persevere."

Class membership also exerts a strong influence on sexual behavior (Kinsey, Pomeroy, & Martin, 1948). In a comparison of sexual behavior patterns of 16-to-20-year-old males in the semiskilled labor class and in the professional class, a marked difference was noted. The semiskilled group had a low frequency of masturbation and a high frequency of premarital intercourse. The pattern was reversed for the professional group.

Of course, there is a good deal of variability in the behavior of members of the same social class. There are many reasons for this, one of the most important being differences in social environment within the same class. Middle-class suburban communities around New York City are subjected to quite different social pressures than middle-class communities in small Midwestern towns. Occupational differences also play a part. The middle-class businessman is expected to conform, but the middle-class college professor is often reinforced for nonconformity. And of particular importance are differences in individuals' perceptions of their positions on the social ladder. For example, although physicians are generally considered to be members of the upper or middle class, some consider themselves workers. As a result their political beliefs are less conservative than those of their professional colleagues.

The concept of **social role** can help us to understand the way group membership influences individual behavior. A *role* can be defined as a pattern of behavior that society encourages an individual in a particular social position to adopt. For example, one role each of us has assigned to him is his sex role. In the United States, the behavior of boys and girls becomes differentiated at a very early age, because they receive different patterns of reinforcement. "Tomboyish" and "sissyish" behavior are almost always discouraged, while appropriately masculine or feminine behavior is encouraged. Parents want their boys to be boys, even though boyishness may include troublesome, "Dennis the Menace" behavior. However, in some cooperative farms in Israel, boys and girls are treated in much the same way and consequently their behavior is more alike than it is in the United States.

Because we belong to many groups, we are forced to assume many roles, each requiring a different pattern of behavior. A young woman, for example, may be daughter, mother, wife, member of a social club, churchgoer, and just a young woman. She is expected to behave differently in each role, and she usually does this without too much difficulty, because distinctive stimuli which evoke the behavior appropriate to them are associated with each role. But sometimes conflicts do arise, as when she is with her husband, her mother, and her children, all at once and is expected to be the loving wife, the dutiful daughter, and the considerate mother. But even in this situation a basic adjustment problem does not usually arise if everyone recognizes that incompatible demands are being made upon her and that she may not be able to meet them all perfectly. But the conflict between roles can figuratively, and in the most extreme cases almost literally, tear a person apart. The most dramatic examples are the cases of multiple personality, where more than one personality or self-consistant set of traits can be distinctly distinguished in the same individual. A classical case in recent years was that of

Eve White (Thigpen & Cleckly, 1957), a real woman who became the basis of the movie, *The Three Faces of Eve*. Eve White was a sweet, retiring, conscientious young mother who could at times change suddenly into Eve Black, a flirtatious, happy-go-lucky girl, crazy about parties. Later during the course of treatment a new, more mature individual, Jane, emerged. The personalities of Eve White and Eve Black had their roots in different childhood experiences. Eve White was largely shaped by her mother's values; Eve Black seemed a product of identification with her father. These two personalities were exaggerations of the two quite different roles many women in early adulthood are expected to play: the dutiful and responsible mother and wife, on the one hand, and the attractive and flirtatious young lady, on the other. Most women can combine these two roles successfully as they progress, often reluctantly, toward greater maturity, although conflicts do arise in some cases. In Eve White's case the two could not be merged because of their pathological origin and the difficulties she had experienced in marriage. Although cases of multiple personality are rare, they nevertheless emphasize the fact that one personality contains many social roles.

The Social Dyad

The simplest, but often most influential, social relationship exists between two organisms, and is sometimes called a **social dyad.** This relationship is in some ways similar to the relationship between an organism and its inanimate environment. In order to illustrate this similarity, we shall refer to a Skinner box (inanimate environment) with an experimental subject (organism) inside. If we arranged the Skinner box to dispense some combination of rewards and punishments in *reaction* to the subject's behavior, his behavior would be shaped by this combination. In other words, an organism's behavior is controlled by the "design" of his inanimate environment. Now, let us assume that we could replace the scheduling mechanisms of the Skinner box with a living organism that would dispense the reinforcements, so that the reinforcements one animal would receive would be contingent upon the behavior of the other. And further, that we could arrange for a reciprocal relationship to develop between the two organisms in which the behavior of each would be reinforced by the action of the other. We would then have a social dyad, and it would be similar to the relationship between an organism and its environment. Let us see how some social dyads function.

One of the earlier attempts (Crawford, 1937) to demonstrate cooperative behavior in animals involved a pair of young female chimpanzee subjects. Each of them was first trained to pull unaided a weighted box toward herself by means of an attached rope. Reinforcement in the form of a piece of food, was placed on the box. The weight of the box was then increased so that one animal alone could not move it. It was baited with two portions of food and two ropes were attached to it and their ends placed in the experimental cage housing both animals. At first each chimpanzee pulled without reference to her partner's behavior. Only by chance were their efforts synchronized so that the box could be pulled forward. With some help from the experimenter who gave a signal, the animals learned to start pulling together. Later, this signal was eliminated and the animals truly began to cooperate. One partner usually watched the other and added her strength as soon as the other began pulling in the rope. Their synchronized efforts produced the reward, which they usually shared. The animals even cooperated when only one of them was hungry. The hungry one would "urge" her satiated partner to pull the rope and would usually succeed in persuading her eventually. They would then pull in the box together, and the hungry chimpanzee would be left free to consume the food all by herself.

A similar experiment was carried out with children as subjects (Azrin & Lindsley, 1956). Two children were placed at the opposite sides of a table. In front of them were three holes and a stylus. When both children placed their styli in the holes opposite each other, a red light flashed on the table and a single jelly bean fell into a container. Eight out of the ten teams of children who participated in the experiment arranged to divide the candy in some manner. In the other two teams one member at first took all the candy himself, but the other member soon refused to cooperate until a more equitable arrangement was worked out.

These two experiments show that cooperative behavior can be developed, maintained, and eliminated by manipulating the contingency between the cooperative response and the reinforcement. This does not mean, however, that cooperative behavior must always be based directly upon the satisfaction of a physiological drive such as hunger. Cooperation can function as a learned drive so that the cooperative behavior itself can be its own reinforcement (see page 163). Many self-denying people sacrifice their own personal comfort and well-being in order to help less fortunate people who need help.

The reinforcement of a social act, although a very important determinant of social behavior, is certainly not the only one. Another important determiner is the organism's capacity for *forming* social attachments. For example, dogs seem incapable of forming attachments to humans unless they have been given opportunities to do so when they were very young (Scott, 1960). At about three weeks of age, a puppy begins to attend to new stimuli in his environment. His first response to a stranger is to show fear and avoidance, but because he is poorly coordinated at this age, he is probably unable to run away, and if the stranger maintains contact with him, his fear and avoidance will extinguish and the puppy will develop an attachment for his new "master." The strength of this attachment will depend on the puppy's age at the time it was formed. Puppies raised together away from humans can be removed from their litter mates when they are about seven or eight weeks old and made into devoted pets, but puppies separated at 12 or 14 weeks or older never become completely satisfactory pets, since they exhibit a greater attachment to dogs than to humans. As one recent experiment concludes, "Unless socialization occurred before 14 weeks of age, withdrawal reactions from humans become so intense that normal relationships cannot thereafter be established" (Freedman, King, & Elliot, 1961, p. 1016). This finding agrees with the common observation that a dog raised too long in the impersonal environment of a kennel does not make a very good pet.

Similarly, individuals with character disorders (see page 517) are unable to form close permanent friendships even when they are involved with others in joint enterprises in which their own reinforcements depend on cooperative behavior.

It may be that social attachments are related to what has been called imprinting (see page 248). Possibly there are certain optimal periods in the early lives of mammals like dogs and humans during which they can acquire the ability to form strong social attachments. If this can be proven, the next step will be to discover those crucial experiences that an organism must have to acquire this social ability.

There are innumerable other dyadic social relationships which we could investigate, but we will not try to. We discuss only those we need to make our point, which is to suggest that most, if not all, such relationships have a common property. They are essentially reciprocal learning situations in which two individuals shape each other's behavior.

Too often one side or the other of this reciprocal relationship is ignored. For example, people often remark on the important influence a mother has upon her child's behavior. But fewer note the fact that a child also shapes his mother's behavior. His smiling, cooing, and laughter function as powerful positive reinforcers, while his crying functions as a negative reinforcer; it is aversive. If you observe a new mother's behavior over a period of time, you will probably conclude it is being changed as much as her child's.

To further illustrate our point, we will examine one human dyadic relationship in detail. This is the all-important relationship of marriage, in which most of us become involved sooner or later. It is such an important relationship that it can exert a positive or destructive influence on the psychological health of both husband and wife. We all recognize that the high divorce rate, now about 25 per cent, constitutes a grave social problem. Presumably, if we could reduce this figure by educating young people to understand the nature and causes of marital happiness and unhappiness, our entire society would benefit.

In 1938 a large-scale study (Terman, 1938) sought to analyze the psychological factors responsible for success or failure in marriage. The findings were based on the testimony of 792 couples who lived in the Los Angeles area. The strategy of the study was simple. The first step was to construct a questionnaire which would provide a reasonable measure of marital happiness. The next step was to try to discover by using this questionnaire the variables encountered *prior to* and *during* married life that were responsible for the success or failure of the marriage. In other words, the study sought to establish an $R = f(R)$ type relationship (see page 24), in which the dependent variable consisted of responses indicative of marital happiness, and the independent variables were certain events prior to and during the marriage reported by those questioned.

Of all the background factors, the item

that correlated most highly with marital happiness was happiness during childhood. As one conclusion to the study stated: "It is a favorable omen for the success of a marriage if husband and wife had a happy childhood. According to our data, no other item of information relating to background is more significant" (Terman, 1938).

Other background factors that proved to be positively correlated with marital happiness were:

1. Happiness of parents.
2. Lack of conflict with mother.
3. Firm, but not harsh, discipline during childhood and adolescence.
4. Strong attachment to mother.
5. Strong attachment to father.
6. Lack of conflict with father.
7. Parental frankness about sexual matters.
8. Infrequent and mild childhood punishment.
9. Premarital sexual attitudes free from disgust and aversion.

Of equal interest and importance are those background factors that proved ·to have little or no relationship to marital happiness. Some of these were the amount of religious training, amount of schooling, number of opposite-sex siblings, and adolescent popularity.

These findings also failed to support the commonly held belief that sexual adequacy is of paramount importance for marital happiness. Such factors as actual frequency of intercourse, preferred frequency of intercourse, duration of the sex act, desire for extramarital intercourse, wife's rhythm of sexual desire, birth-control practices, and complaints about the sexual behavior of the spouse were found not to be markedly related to marital happiness. Two sexual factors were positively—but far from perfectly—correlated with marital success. One was the ability of the wife to achieve orgasm. The marriages of wives who said they never achieved orgasm were rated as

less successful than those marriages in which the wives reported that they had always experienced an orgasm. The second important factor was the degree of similarity in the strength of the husband's and wife's sex drive. The relative and not the absolute strengths of the partners' sex drives were the important variables. As the *difference* in ardor between the husband and wife increased, the marital happiness scores decreased. To be specific, spouses whose sex drives were nearly equal, whether they were strong or weak, were more likely to have a happy marriage than those couples in which one partner had a strong sex drive and the other a weak one.

A summary of the study's findings on the importance of sexual compatibility stated the following conclusions:

Our data do not confirm the view so often heard that the key to happiness in marriage is nearly always to be found in sexual compatibility. They indicate, instead, that the influence of sexual factors is at most no greater than that of the combined personality and background factors, and that it is probably less. The problem is complicated by the fact that the testimony of the husband and the wife regarding their sexual compatibility is influenced by their psychological compatibility. Couples who are psychologically well mated are likely to show a surprising tolerance for the things that are not satisfactory in their sexual relationships. The psychologically ill-mated show no such tolerance but instead are prone to exaggeration in their reports on sexual maladjustment. The two sexual factors of genuine importance are the wife's orgasm adequacy and relative strength of sex drive in the two spouses (Terman, 1938, p. 376).

There is, perhaps, one serious flaw in this study. The two sets of responses may not be completely independent (see page 11). For a person's memory of his past life is usually colored by the state in which he finds himself at present, and a happily married person is more likely to remember his life before marriage as being happy than an unhappily married person. The obvious control for such a possible infiltration of bias into the study is to *test* people *before* marriage and *study their happiness after* marriage.

When this was done (Kelly, 1939; Burgess & Wallin, 1953), significant *but small* positive correlations were found resembling those of the California study. Thus one is forced to conclude that some people are better marital risks than others. What a person has experienced prior to marriage will influence his chances of achieving success.

But this cannot be the only variable, for the correlations between premarital and marital experience found in these studies were low. An important variable is obviously the kind of adjustment the husband and wife make *to each other.* A young man who is excessively dependent, egocentric, and immature would be rated a poor marital risk. But his potential for a happy marriage will be to a large extent determined by the wife he chooses. If he marries a girl who is psychologically similar to himself they may be headed for trouble. If, however, he weds a mature, understanding girl who needs a dependent husband, their chances of building a successful marriage are much increased. The key to predicting success in marriage is not to limit oneself to studying which individuals are good or bad risks. What is needed is some method of predicting the kinds of reciprocal influences that two people will exert on each other after they are married. In short, in trying to predict marital happiness we must seek to understand not merely the individual personalities of the prospective husband and wife, but the dyadic social relationship that will probably develop between them.

In evaluating these studies of marital happiness, one cannot afford to overlook the problem of sampling (see page 73). The studies described drew their samples from the white, urban, middle-class society.

The conclusions drawn from this study must therefore be restricted to a population of this kind. Perhaps the same factors (a happy childhood) are not equally important for members of different socioeconomic and racial groups. Another point to consider is that with the numerous changes, both social and technological, now occurring in our society, perhaps success in marriage is no longer related to the same constellation of factors as it was 10 to 25 years ago. Further research on this subject is obviously needed.

EXPERIMENTAL STUDIES WITH SMALL GROUPS

It is most difficult to investigate the specific influence on behavior of highly complex social entities like whole cultures or large social groups. Although there is no denying the importance of trying to unravel the numerous and various effects of society on individual behavior, some social psychologists believe that it may be more effective to analyze first the social influences on behavior in small groups.

Psychologists have used two principal techniques to investigate behavior in small groups. One is to observe behavior as it occurs in a natural group. The other is to create artificial groups in the laboratory and set up experimental situations designed to reveal fundamental social processes as they occur. The latter technique, known as **small group research,** has become very popular with social psychologists, because it has all the advantages of controlled observation made under controlled conditions. In short it is the experimental method.

In order to study social influences on behavior, one must devise some method of describing the interpersonal relationships which exist in the group. Groups vary greatly in the kinds of social contacts they afford their members. There has to be some way of specifying, and if possible, measuring these differences. To put it more technically, it is necessary to describe the fundamental **group structure.** This is a difficult task and, in spite of persistent efforts, social psychologists, sociologists, and anthropologists have been unable to devise any completely satisfactory method for accomplishing it. Nevertheless, progress has been made in describing *specific* group structures. Perhaps someday someone will develop a general technique that will allow all groups in all situations to be described in terms of their fundamental characteristics.

Communication Network

One characteristic of a group structure is its **communication network,** the channels through which each member of the group can communicate, so far as communication is possible, within the group. In one experiment (Leavitt, 1958), groups made up of five men each were organized in different ways (see Figure 15.3). In one group the members could only communicate with one person (Individual *C*). Such a group structure exists in supervisory systems where one person is responsible for the performance of several workers, and where each worker can communicate only with the supervisor. In another group (see Group 2 in Figure 15.3), every member could communicate with two other members. This group is less hierarchical than Group 1; no one individual occupies a central role in the communication network.

Which is the better group structure, 1 or 2? By now you should be suspicious of such a question and ask immediately, Better for what? Or, using the language of psychology, you should remark that the answer is going to depend on what measure of response is used.

One study compared the efficiency of both group structures in solving a relatively simple problem. All members of both groups were given five marbles, each of a

different color. In both groups all members had one marble of the same color. The task of each group was to discover which was the common color. The members did this by sending through the permitted channels messages describing the colors of their marbles, and with no great difficulty both groups discovered the common color (blue). The groups were given a series of such problems until they became very efficient at solving them. Then the problems were made more difficult. The marbles which had been simple colors like red, blue, and green were replaced by marbles of odd hues such as greenish blue. Since the same words are not always used to refer to such colors —a color may be called aquamarine or greenish blue or bluish green—it was entirely possible for members of the same group to be looking at the same color but to be using different words for it. Thus, before they could determine the common color, the group members had to eliminate the confusions arising from the different color names. The results showed that Group 2 adapted to these more difficult problems more rapidly than did Group 1. In short, for this task the structure of Group 2 proved superior.

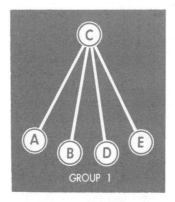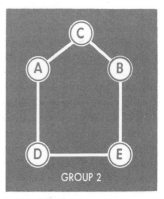

FIGURE 15.3 Two Different Communication Networks. Members of each group are designated by circles. The lines between them represent communication channels. In Group 1, C can communicate with each member but they can communicate only with him. In Group 2, each member can communicate with the two members closest to him (After Leavitt, 1958).

This is not the whole story. The problem of evaluating group structures is highly complex. Other research using the same communication networks suggests that in other problems, although Group 1 gets its work done more rapidly, the morale of its members suffers, since all but *C* are likely to become bored. In a commercial or industrial situation, the first kind of organization gets work done more rapidly, but because the workers occupying positions *B*, *A*, *E*, and *D* feel unimportant, there usually is a large labor turnover. An executive having to decide which of these two group structures is best for his business would have to decide first whether efficiency or morale is more important. Where it is easy to replace dissatisfied workers, he might decide to use the structure of Group 1. However, where much on-the-job training is required, or there is a shortage of available workers, he might decide on the other group structure, convinced, perhaps, that in the long run it will be more productive.

However, the structure of Group 1 does not automatically generate morale problems. Workers in unskilled factory jobs may expect and prefer to have only one immediate supervisor with whom they can communicate about their work. They may like to feel dependent and consider lack of responsibility a blessing. On the other hand, in an academic department of a university, a structure like that of Group 1 would very likely create severe morale problems, because college teachers generally prize individuality, independence, and a sense of responsibility. They would find it difficult to knuckle under to the autocratic structure of Group 1.

Sociometric Analysis

Groups have many features other than their communication networks. The pattern of interpersonal relationships is another important one. Consider the case of two groups of three students who are re-

quired to work together in the laboratory section of a science course. In one group the students like and respect each other; in the other group they all thoroughly dislike each other.

Sociometry is an inclusive name for formal methods of analyzing the interpersonal structure of groups (Moreno, 1934). If we wish to discover how each member of a group perceives his various colleagues, we may ask them to consider a hypothetical situation in which each member must choose the one he would most prefer to be associated with and the one he would prefer not to be associated with. Figure 15.4 shows how this sociometric analysis was applied to specific groups. Naval fliers in two flight squadrons were asked to choose a person whom they would like most as a flying partner and to reject anyone they would not want as a partner (Jenkins, 1948). The results are expressed in the two **sociograms,** schematic representations of interpersonal relationships, in Figure 15.4. In each sociogram the squares within the large rectangle represent the members of the flight squadron. The squares outside the rectangle represent members of other squadrons. *CO* stands for commanding officer and *XO,* the executive officer (assistant commander). Positive choices are indicated by white lines (member 7 in squadron *A* prefers to have the *CO* as his flying companion). Black lines indicate negative choices (member 7 in squadron *B* would reject his executive officer as his flying companion).

The interpersonal relationships within each squadron are strikingly different. From the number of positive choices they received, you can see that the two leaders in squadron *A,* the commanding and executive officers, are very popular. Whereas in squadron *B* the executive officer received a large number of rejections and the commanding officer received no positive votes. There are no cliques in squadron *A,* but in squadron *B* individuals 2, 3, 6, and 7 form a subgroup within the squadron. So do members 12, 13, 16, and 17. (In any group effort a faction, or clique, can function as a divisive force detracting from the group's overall efficiency.) In addition, all the positive choices in squadron *A* are within the squadron, and most of the negative choices are outside the squadron. In squadron *B*, on the other hand, several positive choices are individuals outside the group, and only a few positive choices, except for the two cliques, are individuals within the squadron.

The sociogram provides a neat summary of interpersonal relationships in a group. It can also direct attention to possible sources of difficulty within a group and suggest methods by which morale could be improved. For example, as you would guess from the sociograms, the morale of squadron *B* was much inferior to that of squadron *A,* and the difficulty seemed to center around the executive officer. An obvious way to improve morale would be to transfer him out of the squadron. Conceivably this might even improve the effectiveness of the commanding officer and help break up the clique composed of individuals 2, 3, 6, and 7, since all of them shared a dislike for the executive officer. However, if this move were not effective, it might be necessary to replace the commanding officer as well or to remove some of the members from each clique. Although the sociograms does not suggest any surefire cure, it is a reasonable starting point for any attempt to improve the situation.

Sociometric analysis has been applied to many groups—fraternities, groups of factory workers, boys in summer camp, girls in a reformatory, and others. In a study of college fraternities (Gardner & Thompson, 1956) it became quite obvious that an individual selects his companions for dif-

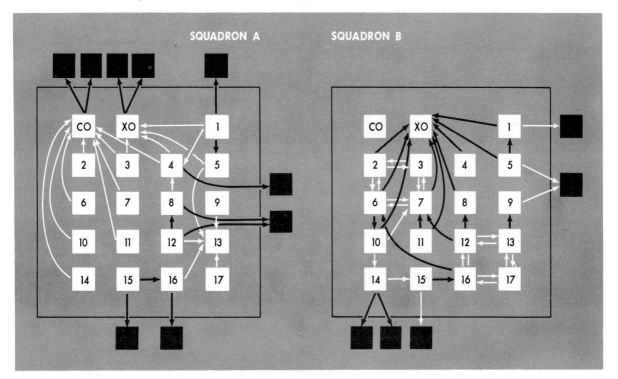

FIGURE 15.4 Sociograms of Two Flight Squadrons. Black squares outside of the large rectangles represent individuals who are not in the squadron. White lines between squares indicate positive choices; black lines, negative choices. CO is the commanding officer and XO is his executive officer (After Jenkins, 1948).

564

ferent reasons; he will, for example, choose different fraternity brothers, depending upon whether he wants to discuss a serious personal problem or wants a companion for double dating. And this must be taken into consideration in designing a sociometric questionnaire. In addition, quantitative descriptions more precise than the simple sociogram can provide are often needed. But for many purposes, such as measuring social status or the structure of a clique, sociometric questionnaires are available and useful.

Democratic and Autocratic Group Structures

Social scientists have always wanted to understand the psychological consequences of democratic and autocratic social structures. Because the problem seems so vast

one might easily conclude that it would not lend itself to experimental study. But investigations of small groups organized along democratic and autocratic lines have been attempted and their results are informative. One experiment (Coch & French, 1948), conducted in a pajama factory, shows that there are advantages to a management policy that allows members of a group to participate in making decisions that will effect their work. A new method of inspecting, folding, and packing pajamas was introduced with three groups of workers. One group was treated *autocratically*. They were told simply that a change was needed, and then shown how to use the new method. Another group was treated *democratically*. The reasons for the change were explained to them, and the members of the group were allowed to participate in planning how the new method would be introduced and executed. A third group participated indirectly, through the representation of two of its members, in planning the change with the management and then returned to inform their fellow workers of the new developments.

Figure 15.5 shows how productivity changed in the three groups after the new method was instituted. Before the change all the groups had been performing at essentially the same level. Following the change-over period the productivity of the group handled in an autocratic manner dropped sharply and remained below its previous level of performance. The democratically handled group showed a slight initial drop in production and then a gradual but definite rise to a level of productivity well above previous performance. The output of the group that participated through representatives also dropped at first and did not recover as rapidly as the output of the group whose members all participated. The group did, however, eventually reach a productivity level comparable to that of the democratically managed group. The effectiveness of the full

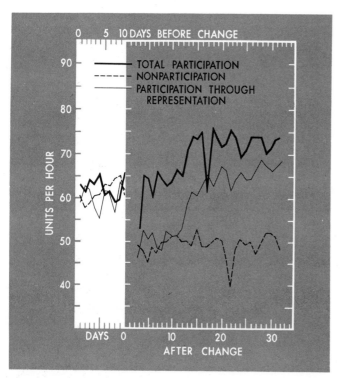

FIGURE 15.5 The Effect of Group Participation on Productivity. Allowing workers to participate in decisions concerning their work routine had beneficial effects on their output (After Coch & French, 1948).

participation procedure was again shown when it was adopted with the poorly performing, autocratic group. Their productivity shot up to a new high.

Besides increasing productivity, group participation improved morale. For instance, the labor turnover in the autocratic group was by far the largest. In a similar experiment (Lewin, Lippitt, & White, 1939), which we described earlier (see page 55), it was also found that a democratic atmosphere produced better morale than an autocratic atmosphere. There was less hostility, more cooperation, and greater friendliness among members of the democratic group. However, in that experiment the productivity of the democratic group was not consistently superior to the autocratic one.

We must, however,. be careful not to overgeneralize from these results. The experiments cited, and others that have reached similar conclusions, do not demonstrate that democratic organization is inherently superior in every respect to all other forms of group organization. To be precise, these studies merely show the advantages that inhere in certain democratic practices with *certain kinds of people in specific situations*. The experiments were carried out in a society where most of the members have learned to expect and value democratic practices like participation in group decisions. The results show that citizens in our democratic society are more strongly bound by a decision that they have had a share in making, but perhaps the results would have been different if the experiments had been performed in a totalitarian state. It is likely that at least part of the effectiveness of democratic methods depends upon training. Recent history provides all too clear evidence of the importance of such training. When democratic methods and institutions are suddenly introduced into a nation that has had no democratic tradition, as in the Congo in 1960, chaos usually results.

The final point is that even in a democracy there are situations in which a democratic group organization would be ineffective. The platoon sergeant in combat cannot risk group participation in the decisions that have to be made. The professor himself must decide what topics are most important for his students to study. The President at a cabinet meeting may seek advice but he cannot be bound by majority opinion. "The majority rules" is not a universal democratic principle, to be applied indiscriminately in all situations.

Decision-Making in Small Groups

Some members of large organizations, like corporations and universities, detest committee assignments because they believe that committees not only take time but waste time. This is the extreme view. No one denies that some committee work is useless, but any fair-minded person must recognize that committees can be highly productive and creative. The obvious psychological question is, What factors distinguish useless from useful committees? The answer, if it is to reflect more than personal prejudice, must be based on facts, and to obtain them requires investigation.

Some attempts to deal realistically with this problem have consisted of experimental studies of the kind of committee meetings where decisions must be reached. A situation was arranged so that the experimenters could observe the behavior of a committee without the members realizing it. Next a method of classifying the participants' behavior had to be devised. This was quite difficult to do. Initially the experimenters made up a list of 77 categories, but gradually they reduced it to the following 12:

1. Shows solidarity
2. Shows tension release
3. Shows agreement
4. Gives suggestion
5. Gives opinion
6. Gives information

7. Asks for information
8. Asks for opinion
9. Asks for suggestion
10. Shows disagreement
11. Shows tension
12. Shows antagonism

The manner in which these categories were assigned to specific reactions is illustrated by the following transcribed record (Bales, 1958, p. 439):

MEMBER 1: I wonder if we have the same facts about the problem? (*Asks for opinion*) Perhaps we should take some time in the beginning to find out. (*Gives suggestion*)

MEMBER 2: Yes. (*Agrees*) We may be able to fill in some gaps in our information. (*Gives opinion*) Let's go around the table and each tell what the report said in his case. (*Gives suggestion*)

MEMBER 3: Oh, let's get going. (*Shows antagonism*) We've all got the same facts. (*Gives opinion*)

MEMBER 2: (Blushes) (*Shows tension*)

Figure 15.6 shows the average results for a large number of committee meetings.

Note that the 12 response categories were grouped into four major categories: positive reactions, problem-solving attempts, questions, and negative reactions. The problem-solving attempts represented over 50 per cent of all reactions, with the "gives opinion" response the most common within this category. The next most common response was the positive reaction, constituting slightly over 25 per cent of the total responses. The remaining responses were divided among negative reactions and suggestions.

Figure 15.6 depicts the mean number of responses in each category for entire committee meetings. Responses do not, however, occur at the same rate. If meetings are broken down into three successive stages, a change is found in the frequency of different types of response as the meeting wears on. Information-giving responses are most frequent at the beginning of a meeting and then decrease. Rates of giving suggestions are low initially and reach their highest frequency during the last

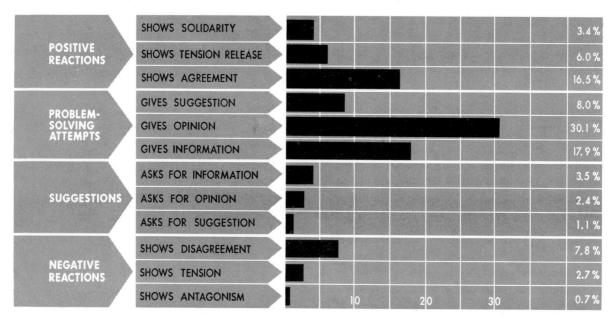

FIGURE 15.6 The Kinds of Responses Occurring in a Large Number of Committee Meetings. More than 50 per cent of all the responses were problem-solving attempts (After Bales, 1952).

third of the meeting. Positive and negative reactions also increase in frequency from beginning to end. Their rates of increase, however, differ. Negative reactions increase sharply from the first third to the second third and thereafter increase only slightly. In contrast, positive reactions increase slightly at the beginning but rise rapidly during the last third of the meeting. Evidently because committee decisions usually come near the end of meetings, negative reactions drop off then and positive ones rise sharply. Joking and laughter, indicating solidarity and tension release, help stabilize the interpersonal relationships that had been disturbed earlier by the friction engendered by openly expressed opposition.

In addition to describing the behavior of the entire committee, this method of analysis provides some insights into the behavior and function of its individual members. Some members develop specialized roles. One person may develop ideas (problem-solving attempts); another may express positive reactions. It is interesting to note, especially for the discussion of leadership to which we shall soon turn, that the group members who are rated "best liked" typically have higher than average scores for showing agreement and tension release. The man who advances the greatest number of ideas is not usually the best liked. In the particular experiments we are reviewing, the leading "idea man" at the end of the *first* committee meeting had an even chance to be rated best liked. This probability, however, dropped to about one in ten by the end of the fourth meeting. Why should this be so? One reason is that giving suggestions, although necessary to reaching a decision, often initiates negative reactions among fellow members. Whether this is due to competition among the members or to what may be called the vested interests of others is not known. In actual practice, whether in government, industry, or the armed serv-

ices, the leader often is not the man who originates new ideas but the person who can grasp them and help in their development while working for group effectiveness and minimizing interpersonal difficulties.

As a result of these studies, what recommendations can we make that might improve the effectiveness of committee work? The investigator (Bales, 1954) who conducted these experiments makes the following recommendations which, for the most part, are presented here in an abbreviated form:

1. Avoid appointing committees with more than seven members. Arrange for conditions that allow every member to communicate with every other member.
2. Avoid appointing committees of only two or three members if a power struggle is likely to develop.
3. Select members whose participation in group discussion is moderate in amount. High participators frequently compete with each other, while a group of low participators often runs out of ideas.
4. Do not assume that a good committee necessarily consists of one leader and several followers. Many different kinds of leadership can be exerted within the same group. Try to appoint both a task leader and a social leader who will support each other. The task leader will encourage the committee to get the work done while the social leader will create a pleasant atmosphere so that it will be done.
5. In dealing with each major problem an effective procedure is to try to have the group answer the following questions:
   a. What are the facts of the case?
   b. What are our reactions to them?
   c. How shall we go about solving the problem?
6. Solicit the opinions of other members, especially when disagreements crop up. When this is done it is often discovered that apparent disagreements are in reality due to misunderstanding.
7. When talking keep your eyes moving around the group rather than on one individual. Be alert to detect the nonverbal re-

568

actions that are going on. They will prove useful in comprehending how the committee's members are reacting to you.

8. When trouble begins to brew, it is best to return to the discussion of the facts.

9. Keep your ear to the ground. No recipe or set of rules can substitute for constant, sensitive, and sympathetic attention to what is going on in the relations between members. Do not get so engrossed in getting the job done that you lose track of what is the first prerequisite of success—keeping the committee in good operating condition (Bales, 1954, p. 50).

Of course, these principles need additional clarification. In fact, further evidence is needed to judge whether they are effective at all. But studies such as this show that it is possible to attack complex problems of social interaction with experimental methods. It seems certain that whatever knowledge and understanding we gain in the future will be based, in part, on these pioneering studies.

LEADERSHIP

One of the most obvious features of group behavior is the emergence of leaders. It is difficult to conceive how any group can function in any way, except chaotically, without leadership. A football team needs its quarterback, an army platoon, its sergeant, and a board of directors, its chairman.

One question that has always fascinated students of history as well as politicians, and even newspaper readers, is, What makes a person a national leader? What were the factors that made Churchill, Roosevelt, Stalin, and Hitler powerful leaders in this century, and Lincoln, Napoleon, and Caesar powerful leaders in the past? Two common-sense views seem to have emerged in response to this question. One is that a person assumes and exerts leadership by dint of his own strong personality. According to this view, in the final analysis World War II began as a consequence of Hitler's dynamic leadership over the German people, and its end was, in much the same way, a consequence of the skill and energy of Churchill, Roosevelt, and Stalin in leading their respective nations. The other view, which contradicts this "great-man theory" of history, is that leaders are created by the demands of a situation, often a critical one. The historical forces operating in the resurgent Germany of the 1930's, this view maintains, inexorably pushed someone like Hitler into the forefront. If Hitler had never been born, someone equally powerful would have assumed the leadership of Germany, and the historical results would have been much the same. Similarly the grave crisis that threatened the survival of Great Britain, the United States, and the U.S.S.R. created the kind of leadership that Churchill, Roosevelt, and Stalin gave to their respective countries.

Both the "man-makes-the-history" and the "history-makes-the-man" views are naive. It takes at least two elements to produce a leader: a man capable of being a leader and people to be led. If one is to understand the psychology of leadership, even superficially, he must resist the temptation to point arbitrarily to one of these two and assert that it is *the* factor that causes leadership. Instead, one must understand the contributions of each to leadership. Furthermore, to complete the analysis one has to consider the situation in which the group finds itself. A fraternity, for example, may shift from one leader to another, depending upon the situation. Its members may follow one leader when some campus political problem arises, but may choose another to lead in planning a social event or in winning an athletic competition.

Leadership can be defined as the act of controlling the behavior of a group that is seeking to achieve some goal. A leader can thus be evaluated in terms of how well he helps the group reach their goal. Specifically, the effective team captain in an athletic contest helps his team perform to the best of their ability; whereas the ineffective captain hinders his team's efforts. The good industrial manager is, in the long run, able to increase productivity, whereas the poor manager allows productivity to fall behind.

The Emergence of a Leader

In many situations the leader is designated by long-standing tradition, as when a member of the royal family ascends the throne. Sometimes a leader is appointed from outside the group in which he is to assume a particular function, like the governor general of colony or the teacher of a class. Because of the spread of democratic principles, it is becoming more common for leaders to be selected by the groups they will lead. Even in industrial organizations, where management once exercised complete control in appointing supervisors, workers have been given a voice in the selection of their own leaders.

The selection of a leader by members of a group can be considered an instrumental response designed to satisfy the motivation of the selectors. In a simple group effort, where success of that effort is the only concern, leaders are chosen for the effectiveness with which the group members believe they will contribute to reaching the goal. In one study (Leavitt, 1951) of five-man groups involved in solving a problem, the leader was perceived by the groups as the person who held the most important position in the communication network. His personal qualities appeared to be unimportant. Figure 15.7 shows the communication networks of the four groups. The lines connecting the members of each group represent the only channels of communication within the group. As you can see, in network 1 every

member communicated as often and received as many communications as every other member, but in network 4 all communications had to be processed through the central member. At the end of the experiment each subject was asked, "Did your group have a recognized leader?" The results show that the selection of the leader was based primarily on his favored position to receive and transmit information. In network 1, no dominant leader emerged, for there was no central member in the communication network. In network 4, the central member was perceived unanimously as the leader.

We know, however, that in most situations leaders are chosen for many reasons

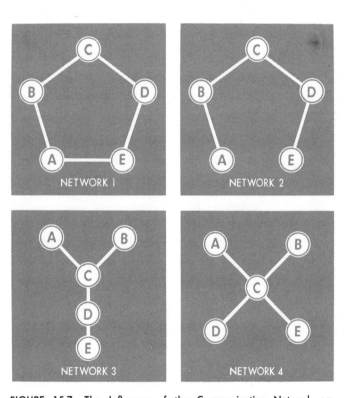

FIGURE 15.7 The Influence of the Communication Network on Leadership. In network 1, where each member could communicate only with his two neighbors, no leader was established. In the other networks the members occupying the C position, the most centrally located, were most frequently perceived as leaders by the other members. The percentage perceiving C as the leader increased successively from networks 2 to 4, with unanimous agreement among the members of network 4 (After Leavitt, 1951).

besides their ability to contribute toward achieving the goal. In some situations the ability to *set* goals is an important factor. This exerted an important influence in the 1960 Presidential election between John F. Kennedy and Richard Nixon. The leader of a group may also be selected on the basis of how well its members expect he will play the numerous roles which they believe he will be required to assume: organizer, executive, policy-maker, expert, representative of the group, peacemaker, friend, "father figure," and many others.

In the outcome, whether or not these roles are well played does not depend solely on the behavior of the leader. The behavior of the followers may be of equal or greater importance. As we have already indicated, leadership expresses a relationship between the leader and his followers. This point emerged in one study (Sanford, 1952) which discovered that individuals who are inclined to accept authority and dogma prefer strong leadership. In contrast, individuals who have a passionate devotion to democratic values prize fairness and understanding more than direction in their leaders. One need only compare the histories of the political leaders of the United States and Germany to realize the importance the followers have in setting the standards for their leaders. Americans resent leaders who are too authoritarian; Germans, for the most part, have turned away from leaders who were not sufficiently dogmatic.

The Personality and Behavior of Leaders

Although men who prove leaders in one situation are not always the same ones who lead in other situations, there does appear to be some degree of generality in the ability to lead. People who are leaders in some situations *tend* to be leaders in other situations; those who are followers in some situations *tend* to be followers in others. The question immediately arises, What are the traits that distinguish the leader from the follower? Numerous studies (Stogdill, 1948) have been designed to answer this question. At best such studies can only suggest an answer.

A summary of the results of a large number of experiments with small groups reported (Mann, 1959) that leaders tend to be, on the average, more intelligent and better adjusted than their followers. In addition they are more extroverted (oriented toward social life), more dominant, and more sensitive to the needs of others. However, these do not have to be the leader's dominant qualities *before* he assumes leadership. Being a leader demands extroverted, dominant, and socially sensitive behavior, and so these responses are reinforced and strengthened once a person becomes a leader. Thus we cannot conclude that traits that characterize leaders are always the reasons for their selection as leaders. They may develop from "on-the-job training."

Similarly, we cannot conclude that because leaders are found to be more intelligent, high intelligence will always increase a person's chances of becoming a leader. A leader may be handicapped by too great a discrepancy between his intellectual ability and that of the group he is to lead (Hollingworth, 1942). Consider the difficulty an extremely bright boy has in communicating with his less intelligent classmates.

A somewhat different investigation of the qualities of leadership was directed toward the leader's behavior at the time he is actually trying to lead. Specific instances of supervisory behavior were observed and sorted initially into more than 1800 categories. These were condensed into ten general categories, each indicating a somewhat different activity leaders engage in (Hemphill, 1950). These categories are:

1. *Initiation:* originating or resisting new ideas and practices.

2. *Representation:* representing, defending, and advancing the interests of the group.

3. *Fraternization:* being friendly with the members of the group.

4. *Organization:* planning and organizing the work and activities of the individual members.

5. *Domination:* restricting and curbing the behavior of individual members.

6. *Recognition:* expressing approval or disapproval of the activities of members.

7. *Emphasis on Production:* motivating the members to greater efforts.

8. *Integration:* increasing cooperation and reducing conflicts among members.

9. *Communication down:* providing information from higher levels of authority to the members of the group to inform them about the functioning of the organization of which the group is a part (e.g., a platoon sergeant describing to his platoon the plans of the company as formulated by the captain).

10. *Communication up:* obtaining information on what is going on in the group.

When a questionnaire, based upon these ten supervisory behavior patterns, was submitted to subordinates in a wide variety of job situations (e.g., in industry, in the armed forces, and in school systems), it was found that a supervisor was judged good when he rated high on each of the ten categories except *domination*.

By the method of factor analysis (see page 475), it was possible to reduce these ten supervisory behavior patterns to two basic ones: *consideration* and *initiating structure* (Halpin & Winer, 1957). *Consideration* is a summary term of the supervisor's behavior when he exerts himself to establish good interpersonal relations between himself and the other members of the group. *Initiating structure* refers to his efforts to get the group well organized. This involves planning the work of its various members, establishing lines of communication, and supervising the work.

How a leader rates along these two dimensions (consideration and initiating

structure) determines, to some extent, the group's response. A leader who rates high in consideration can create high morale in his group. A low rating in this dimension may be accompanied by poor morale, factionalism, and cliques (see Figure 15.4 on page 563). One study found (Fleishman, Harris, & Burtt, 1955) that foremen who show a high degree of consideration have records of relatively low absenteeism among their workers. There was also evidence that an unusual amount of activity in initiating structure increases both turnover rate and labor grievances. The interpretation seems to be that although workers desire instruction, they apparently want to make some decisions themselves.

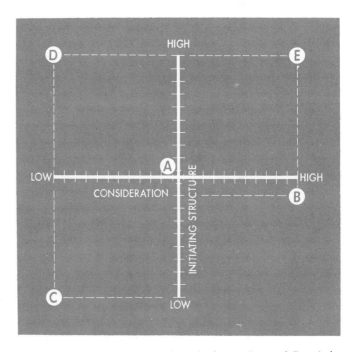

FIGURE 15.8 Representation of Leadership in Terms of Two Independent Axes: *Consideration* and *Initiating Structure.* Each circle represents one supervisor's score on both dimensions. Leader A is about average on both dimensions; leader B is high on *consideration* and average on *initiating structure;* and leader C is low on both. Leader D is an authoritarian leader, since he is high on *initiating structure* and somewhat low on *consideration.* Leader E is more democratic; he rates high on *consideration* as well as *initiating structure* (After R. M. Gagne & E. Fleishman. *Psychology and human performance.* New York: Holt, Rinehart, & Winston, 1959).

Naturally, the "best" behavior pattern for a leader depends upon the particular situation. But over a wide range of supervisory positions, from chairman of an academic department to aircraft commander, above-average scores in both dimensions appear to constitute the best combination for effective leadership (Halpin, 1957; Hemphill, 1957). Low scores in both tend to produce uncoordinated, chaotic group behavior. A leader who emphasizes only one of these factors, while ignoring the other, lowers group effectiveness.

One other related item must be added here. The effective leader is capable of delegating authority (Katz, Maccoby, & Morse, 1950). If he tries to do everything himself and is constantly checking on his workers, group efficiency is apparently lessened. This hints at an optimal level of the *initiating structure,* which should not be exceeded.

One of the difficulties many supervisors encounter is the irreconcilable demands made upon them by their superiors and by their subordinates. This point is illustrated in the responses privates, noncommissioned officers, and officers in the United States Army made to this statement in a questionnaire on leadership: "A noncom should not let the men of his squad forget that he is a noncom even when off duty." The following percentages of agreement with the statement were obtained: privates, 39 per cent; noncoms, 54 per cent; officers, 81 per cent (Stouffer, Suchman, De Vinney, Star, & Williams, 1949). It appears that if the noncom is too democratic, he may be reprimanded by his superiors, but if he is too aloof, he may antagonize his subordinates. This is a kind of conflict that is common among leaders in a democratic society. They are often required to lead without appearing to be leaders. In more authoritarian societies, leaders are not expected to be "the boss" and "a regular guy" at the same time.

ATTITUDES

If you stop to analyze your own social behavior, you will discover that your attitudes play a most important role in influencing it. Your attitude toward religion will probably determine what you do on Sunday morning. Your attitude toward members of the opposite sex will affect to some extent whom and when you marry, if at all. Your attitude toward the function of government will influence your political behavior. Your attitude about psychology, which probably has been crystallized by now, will determine whether you will take additional courses in the subject and whether you will consider it as a possible career.

There is no need to add to these examples, although we could go on endlessly. Our task now is to understand the psychology of attitudes. This requires first a definition of the term *attitude* and second a description of the basic method psychologists and sociologists use to measure attitudes.

The term **attitude** is applied to an individual's predisposition to respond in a characteristic way to some stimulus in his social environment. Basically, an attitude is a tendency to behave either positively or negatively toward any social cue whatever —an institution, a person, a situation, an idea, or a concept. For example, the concept of socialized medicine arouses widely different response tendencies, ranging from that of the ultra-conservative who almost froths at the mouth when it is mentioned, for he sees it as another sign of increasing government control of private enterprise, to that of the ardent socialist who embraces the concept energetically, for he believes it to be an element of that future Utopia he is anticipating, where the government looks after us all.

This definition of *attitude* highlights several problems. If an attitude is a tendency to respond, how does it differ from other response tendencies such as those leading to instrumental responses in conditioning situations? The answer is that basically there is no difference. Consider an instance of avoidance conditioning (see page 167). A child who is bitten by a dog fears dogs thereafter. Psychologists say that he exhibits a *response tendency* to avoid dogs. Or, in other words, he has formed a negative *attitude* toward dogs. Clearly the concepts of response tendency and attitude are similar. A response tendency refers to any predisposition to react in a certain way. An attitude is a predisposition to perform a social act that can be characterized by statements like: "I am against capital punishment"; or "Movies are a waste of time."

How does an attitude differ from a belief or an opinion? Actually, there is no basic psychological difference between these terms. Customarily we do think of attitudes as somewhat more general and less definite than beliefs, for *belief* usually implies the unequivocal acceptance or rejection of a specific proposition. Attitudes about religion, for example, can occupy any position on an extensive scale or dimension that ranges from very favorable to very unfavorable, but typically one either believes or does not believe in God. An opinion falls somewhere between an attitude and a belief. Like a belief, it is a response to a specific proposition but not necessarily an unequivocal one. For example, a person may say, "I really don't know, but my opinion is that it might be wise to get a new football coach."

Psychologically, attitudes, opinions, and beliefs are all similar in that they predispose a person to respond in a certain way. For convenience, we will generally use the term *attitude,* and not try to maintain the subtle, and not very important, distinctions among attitude, opinion, and belief.

If we know a person's attitude in a particular situation, we are in a position to make an informal guess as to how he will behave. But we cannot be sure our prediction will be correct, because a single predisposition is by no means always the only variable determining overt behavior. A person who actually believes that Negroes should enjoy equal rights may nevertheless exhibit certain prejudices to avoid clashing with the conventions of his social group. And as we know, attitudes and other predispositions can conflict with each other. In the 1960 Presidential election many people who believed that Kennedy would make a better President voted for Nixon because they had a negative attitude toward the Catholic Church. Others, with a higher opinion of Nixon's abilities, voted for Kennedy because their general evaluation of the Republican Party was unfavorable. Nevertheless, if we know a person's attitude toward something, we possess a useful clue in predicting at least something about his behavior. If we know a number of his attitudes, we have still more clues.

The discussion of attitudes will be arranged in terms of three related problem areas—measurement of attitudes, formation of attitudes, and changes in attitudes. The literature in these areas is so vast that we can only touch upon some of the major facts and ideas.

Measurement of Attitudes

The simplest way of obtaining information about a person's attitude is to ask a specific question like "Do you enjoy movies?" But the answer to this question does not measure the *degree* or *strength* of the attitude. Of two people who answered "yes," one might have a much stronger positive attitude toward movies than the other.

Psychologists whose aim is to develop more sensitive measures of an attitude have constructed *attitude scales* with this problem in mind. L. L. Thurstone (1887-1955), a psychologist who set standards of ingenuity and creativity difficult for other psychologists to match, pioneered in this effort. He constructed attitude scales by assembling a number of groups of statements on many subjects. Each statement embodied a particular attitude toward the subject, and the group included a wide range of attitudes. Examples of statements about the Chinese are: "The Chinese are no better and no worse than any other people"; "Chinese people have a refinement and depth of feeling that you don't find anywhere else"; "The Chinese are aptly described by the term 'yellow devils.'"

Judges rated a group of such statements by sorting them into piles according to the attitudes expressed. These piles were arranged on a scale from the most favorable to the least favorable and numbered from 1 to 11. The most favorable attitude was therefore at the bottom of the scale and numbered 1 and the least favorable was at the top and numbered 11.

The first question usually asked about this procedure is whether the judge's own attitude influences his ratings. Would not a judge who is favorably disposed toward Chinese rate statements differently than a judge who is not? Apparently not. Studies (Hinckley, 1932) have shown that judges who differ markedly in their own attitudes agree fairly well in their ratings.

After they had been sorted, each statement was analyzed statistically for its scale value and its degree of ambiguity. Its scale value is the median (see page 65) of all the rankings made by the judges. A high scale value would indicate an unfavorable attitude toward the Chinese, whereas a low scale value would indicate a favorable attitude. The three statements quoted above obtained scale values of 6.0, 1.4, and 11.0 respectively.

The median scale value of an item fails to convey a very important bit of information. Consider the case of two statements, both of which have an equivalent scale value of 9.5. In other words, half the judges placed each item in the tenth pile or above, while the other half placed each item in the ninth pile or below. But the range of placements for one statement might have extended from the first to the eleventh pile, while the range for the other statement might have run only from the seventh to the eleventh pile. Obviously, if this were so, the first statement would be more ambiguous than the second, for some judges would think it indicated a highly favorable opinion, but more would react to it as being highly unfavorable. In short, a wide divergence of opinion would have prevailed. In contrast, all the judges would have perceived the second statement to be unfavorable, although to different degrees. The first statement would be unsuitable for use in attitude testing because its meaning is ambiguous. The second statement would be good for this purpose because its meaning is clear.

After the statistical analysis for median scale value and degree of ambiguity had been completed, appropriate statements were selected for retention in the final attitude scale. They were chosen for their lack of ambiguity and because they covered the full range of median scale values. When the final scale is assembled the subject whose attitude is to be determined must indicate which of the statements he agrees with. His score is arrived at by obtaining the average (mean) of the median values of the statements he approves. Consequently it is important for the scale to include statements whose median values are distributed over the entire scale, not just located at the extremes. Otherwise, a person with a moderate view would not have any statements he could agree with.

The development of an attitude scale is not an end in itself, although this is the impression one sometimes gets from reading popular magazines with "do-it-yourself" testing sections. The purpose of a scale, whether it is a scale of length in physics or a scale of attitude in psychology, is to serve as a tool in gathering information. Only after we have succeeded in measuring attitudes can we go on and try to understand how those attitudes are formed and modified. One study (Thurstone, 1931), for example, tried to answer the question of whether a motion picture which offered a sympathetic and understanding portrayal of Chinese life could modify the audience's attitude toward the Chinese people. It should be obvious that this question could not be answered without some sort of an attitude scale. Using an attitude scale, the experimenter found that a definite shift in the audience's attitude occurred after they were exposed to the film. And when the members of the audience were tested 18 months later, the majority still retained the more favorable attitude.

Since the pioneering efforts of Thurstone, numerous statistical techniques have been devised that have improved the precision with which attitudes and opinions can be measured. There have also been developments in opinion measurement, many of which have been incorporated into the public opinion surveys that are so extensively publicized and eagerly studied before a Presidential election. Most of these improved techniques are too complicated to discuss here, but your instructor may find the time to outline the principles on which they are based. However, for you, the introductory student, it is more important to realize that attitudes and opinions are substantial psychological events that can be measured quantitatively. Keep this significant point in mind as we now turn to the important topic of how attitudes and opinions are formed and modified.

The Formation of Attitudes

The verbal expressions of attitudes possess some of the functional properties of instrumental responses. The little boy who parrots the political attitudes of his parents is more likely to be reinforced by them than the child who expresses opinions counter to theirs. It should, therefore, surprise no one that studies designed to investigate attitudes invariably show some similarity between the political attitudes of parents and their children (Hyman, 1959). According to the laws of learning, we expect responses that are reinforced to be learned, whether they are bar-pressing acts or expressions of attitude.

Of course, attitudes are not exactly like the conventional instrumental responses studied in the laboratory. Attitudes are being expressed constantly, in all sorts of ways, and in a wide variety of situations. You are expressing some of your political attitudes when you praise or criticize the actions of the President, when you argue for or against a particular political principle, when you get out and work for or against proposed legislation, and when you mark X or press a lever in the voting booth. It is, therefore, much more difficult to trace the development of an attitude than the development of a simple, experimentally isolated, instrumental response.

Nevertheless, the large number of studies directed toward understanding the variables that influence the formation of attitudes provide a partial picture of their development. But before discussing the growth of attitudes, we must emphasize that there is not just one pattern for the development of an attitude. Attitudes can grow gradually over the years by the accretion of individual responses that finally become integrated. For example, a girl might slowly develop a tolerant attitude toward members of minority groups as a result of numerous experiences. When very little she may have a Jewish playmate, even though she is only vaguely aware then of what a Jew is. Later on she may hear sermons in church espousing racial and religious tolerance. She may also learn during a family dinner conversation that both her parents, whom she admires, are opposed to bigotry. All these experiences, and many more, finally coalesce into clearly defined attitudes against racial and religious intolerance.

A single experience can· also serve as the foundation for an attitude. A single traumatic experience with a member of a different racial group can initiate a powerful racial prejudice. Or a child, eager to imitate someone else, may accept a completely ready-made attitude from one expression of it:

"Daddy, are you a Republican or Democrat?"

"I'm a Republican, son."

"Then I am a Republican, too!"

Between these two extremes of gradual accretion and a single experience lies the pattern probably most typical of attitude development. A single experience might initiate a weak attitude of limited scope, such as, "I sometimes get bored when people talk about baseball." Continued experiences, some more important than others,

would develop the attitude so that it became more organized and stronger: "All baseball fans are bores!"

There are many methods of organizing the variables that influence attitude formation. So far no one encompassing theory of attitude development has been offered which suggests—and demands—a particular arrangement of the major classes of relevant variables. We shall discuss briefly three groups of factors that have received the most attention from social psychologists. They are motivation and reinforcement, personality, and social environment. These variables cannot be investigated in isolation because they are highly interrelated. A person's motives, his drives and incentives, are an integral part of his personality. His personality determines what social environments he seeks out, what groups he belongs to. Group membership will in turn modify his motives. We are restricted, therefore, in discussing these sets of variables to reporting experiments highlighting their influence rather than showing how they alone determine the formation of attitudes.

Motivation and Reinforcement. Although some people like to believe that their attitudes are formed purely by intellectual judgments, the fact is that personal motives play an important role. When college students' attitudes toward allowing Communist Party members to speak publicly were analyzed, they were found to be related to the students' beliefs about the value freedom of speech had for them in achieving their *own* goals (Rosenberg, 1956). People adopt attitudes that could be useful to them in pursuing their personal goals; they reject attitudes that would frustrate them in attaining their incentives. Reinforcement and the anticipation of reinforcement are, as you can see, important variables in forming attitudes.

Attitudes can be a means of displacing aggression resulting from frustration. Among

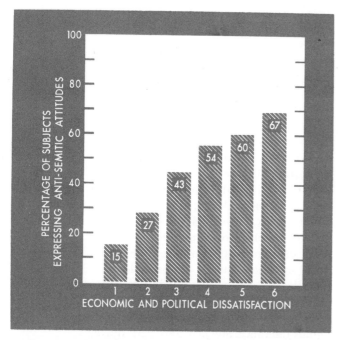

FIGURE 15.9 The Relationship Between Economic and Political Dissatisfaction and Anti-Semitic Attitudes. The greater the dissatisfaction, increasing on a scale of 1 to 6, the greater the per cent of subjects expressing anti-Semitic views (After Campbell, 1942).

subjects whose attitudes toward Jews were related to the degree of satisfaction they felt about their own economic situation and about the national situation, it was found that the greater the degree of personal dissatisfaction, the greater the amount of hostility (Campbell, 1947). Thus you can see how an attitude can function as an instrumental act that reinforces aggression.

Personality. Attitudes tend to fit the personalities of the individuals who adopt them. One study (Smith, Bruner, & White, 1956) showed that persons who tended to blame others when things went wrong were more likely to blame the Soviet Union for deteriorating Soviet-American relations. The writer is reminded of a paranoid patient (Kendler, 1947b) who harbored strong negative attitudes toward democracy, coupled with enormous admiration for dictators like Hitler and Mussolini. This authoritarian attitude was an expression of his personality difficulties. After his psychiatric condition improved his political attitudes underwent a complete change. He became more sympathetic to democratic processes and democratic leaders like Roosevelt.

Several studies (Titus & Hollander, 1957) have tried to show a link between personality structure and what is referred to as **ethnocentrism,** an attitude of extreme loyalty to one's own social group and the rejection of other social groups. Ethnocentric people, as you would guess, typically exhibit racial and religious intolerance. Although the results of all the studies are not entirely consistent, there is some suggestion that people with strong prejudices have somewhat different personality characteristics from unprejudiced people. The ethnocentric person is characterized by a tendency to be more authoritarian (dictatorial, rigid, inhibited, excessively conforming) and hostile than the average (Adorno, Frenkel-Brunswik, Levinson, & Sanford, 1950). It would be a mistake, however, to

believe that all intolerance is simply an expression of deep-seated personality difficulties. A person's social environment plays an important role.

The Social Environment. When racial prejudice was studied in South Africa (Pettigrew, 1958), it was found that an individual's group membership was an extremely important factor in determining his attitude. South African students who exhibited marked prejudice against the native Negro population were no more authoritarian than less prejudiced college students in the United States. And native-born white South Africans who were not any more authoritarian than whites who had emigrated to South Africa harbored more prejudice toward the black Africans. The influence on racial prejudice of the particular social group one is a member of is further evidenced by the finding that white Afrikaner-speaking students were much more prejudiced against Negroes than the English-speaking students, but the English-speaking students were much more prejudiced against South African Indians. Obviously differences in personality cannot account for these particular prejudices. Prejudice, like other habits, seems to be learned in the particular social environment in which one is raised.

Nevertheless, social environments do change, although gradually, and so do the attitudes of those who live in them. In 1932 (Katz & Braly, 1933) a sample of students at Princeton received a questionnaire which required them to describe the predominant traits of various ethnic groups. When they were tested again in 1950 (Gilbert, 1951) their attitudes toward Negroes and Jews had undergone considerable change. They now assigned fewer negative characteristics to these groups. Table 15.2 shows the change.

The influence of social environment on attitude is not limited to prejudices. One would expect the attitudes of members of

TABLE 15.2 A Comparison Between the Per Cents of a 1932 and a 1950 Sample of Princeton Undergraduates Who Attributed Certain Traits to Negroes and Jews (Katz & Braly, 1933; Gilbert, 1951)

TRAIT	PER CENT IN 1932	PER CENT IN 1950	DIFFERENCE IN PER CENT
Negroes			
Superstitious	84	41	—43
Lazy	75	31	—44
Happy-go-lucky	38	17	—21
Ignorant	38	24	—14
Musical	26	33	+ 7
Ostentatious	26	11	—15
Very religious	24	17	— 7
Stupid	22	10	—12
Jews			
Shrewd	79	47	—32
Mercenary	49	28	—21
Industrious	48	29	—19
Grasping	34	17	—17
Intelligent	29	37	+ 8
Ambitious	21	28	+ 7

different cultures toward their respective society to be quite different. Studies of these differences are difficult to do for they require some method of random sampling from large populations. In one cross-cultural comparison (McGranahan, 1946) between German and American youth, the young Germans expressed a stronger positive attitude toward authoritarian, as contrasted with democratic, social organizations. This finding agrees with the history of the two countries. However, we must avoid overgeneralizing from such limited data. The comparisons were not made between carefully selected representative samples of the entire German and American populations. Only the youth of one German town were compared with the youth of one American town. Although a study of this sort is extremely useful, we must recognize that a definitive conclusion about the general influences of cultural factors requires more information.

Our review of studies illustrating the effect social environment has upon attitude formation would be incomplete if we did not point out that very often the groups a person belongs to exert conflicting influences upon him. In a study (Newcomb, 1943), conducted in the 1930's, of the attitudes of students in a New England women's college noted for its liberal views and its relatively well-to-do students, it was discovered that students who were rather conservative in their freshman year became more and more liberal the longer they stayed in college. Evidently, social pressures from the family and college were operating in opposite directions. For most students, at least during their college days, college influences had the greater effect. Among the students, however, were some who for a number of reasons did not participate very much in college life. As a group they succumbed less to the "liberalizing influences" of the college.

Attitude Change

When you think of changing somebody's attitude, the term *persuasion* immediately comes to mind. Persuasion is usually associated with argument and debate and with one person trying to influence others to adopt some view or opinion that agrees with his own. If you think of persuasion in this limited sense, there is a danger that you will overlook its relationship to much of psychology. Fundamentally persuading a person to change his attitude is one facet of the general psychological problem of changing behavior. As such, persuasion—the technique of changing people's attitudes—is an extension of what has been studied in the area of sensation, conditioning, perception, and motivation.

There are two major ways to control behavior. The first is to intervene directly in the physiological system of an organism. This can be done by means of surgery or the administration of drugs or shock. Psychiatrists use this method, at times, to control the behavior of their patients. The second way to control behavior is to change an organism's environment. The large number of laws in the form of $R = f(S)$ demonstrate that by controlling the organism's environment we can alter his behavior. For the most part our discussion of persuasion will be restricted to the second method, mainly because it is more widely used.

In analyzing attitude change it is convenient to consider the process in terms of the persuader, his message, and his audience. The persuader is the person who, by his own action, desires to control the behavior of an individual or group. His message is the body of stimuli (exhortation, appeal, gesture, argument, etc.) with which he confronts his audience. The success of his persuasive technique may be measured by the modification he induces in the audience's behavior.

It is difficult to organize the facts of attitude change because they fail to fall neatly into any basic classificatory system. One must resort, therefore, to some arbitrary and conventional method of reporting them. One such method is to classify them according to the nature and size of the audience at which the persuader's message is directed. Thus we can discuss *mass persuasion, group persuasion,* and *individual persuasion.* Mass persuasion refers to the attempt to modify the behavior of an entire society—or at least a large segment of it. Nationwide advertising campaigns and TV political speeches aim at mass persuasion. The political speaker on his soapbox and the lecturer in a classroom illustrate group persuasion. The car salesman making his "pitch" to a customer and the boy struggling to make a date with a girl illustrate individual persuasion. In the final analysis, of course, all attempts at persuasion impinge upon an individual, whether he is alone or a member of a group, however large. The important point is that the techniques of persuasion are certain to be somewhat different, depending upon the size of the audience. And it is this that makes the above distinctions valuable. We will not, however, adhere rigidly to this classification. When, for example, findings from a study with small groups throw light upon a problem in mass persuasion they will be reported.

Mass Persuasion. The development of the techniques of mass communication comes at a period in history marked by conflict between democratic and Communist nations. Practically everyone in the world, whether he realizes it or not, is bombarded constantly by messages designed to mold his political attitudes, sometimes to modify them, sometimes to make them firmer and more resistant to attack. At the same time, Americans and Europeans are exposed to a constant barrage of advertisements aimed at controlling their buying behavior.

Obviously, then, there are tremendous investments in making mass persuasion as effective as possible. But is it effective? Undoubtedly the persuaders think so, but one can hardly put faith in the validity of their testimonials. What is needed is an objective evaluation based on facts. Of course, facts about changes in behavior of literally millions of people are hard to come by. However, there are a few practitioners of the art of mass persuasion who have been sufficiently curious about their own activities to try to determine whether or not they are effective. And there are always the observing social scientists whose aim it is to measure what others are likely to take for granted. The result of their combined efforts is that we do have some information on such varied topics as advertising, public relations, political attitudes, voting behavior, and propaganda. These topics will not be treated separately because findings in one area are highly relevant to understanding the others.

The advertising business, which now employs more than a million people and spends more than a billion dollars annually, is naturally interested in understanding mass persuasion. One of the first things an advertiser wants to know is how much attention value his message has. No matter how persuasive a message may be, it will be ineffective unless it first catches someone's attention. Are there rules that an advertiser can follow to insure that his audience will attend to his message? Translated into the language of experimental psychology and stated on the level of fundamentals, the question becomes, What are the laws of perceptual attention? This question was considered previously (see page 215), but it can now be reconsidered in a different context. In magazine advertising, the stimulus features of a visual display that command attention are its relative size, contrast, form, color, and novelty (Lucas & Britt, 1950).

Other factors may operate also, depending upon the medium used. Movement and repetition are particularly effective in gaining attention to such visual displays as TV advertisements and neon signs. The subject of the display has an important effect on its attention-getting potential. Advertising themes that emphasize sex or the quality of the product are very effective. Women are believed to respond more readily to the themes of personal attractiveness and health, whereas men are susceptible to appeals involving fear and novelty.

But getting somebody's attention is only the first step in persuading him to act. Most college men would attend to the message, "Buy *The Ladies' Home Journal*" embroidered on a bikini worn by a shapely model, but it is doubtful whether many would respond by buying the magazine. Unfortunately for advertisers, and fortunately for consumers, not nearly as much is known about influencing a person to make a purchase as is known about getting him to attend to a message.

However, there is general agreement among advertisers and students of mass persuasion that to be effective a message must agree with the motivation of the audience. The frequent use of beautiful women in advertisements for cosmetics and perfumes is a direct play upon the desire of most women to be physically attractive. By displaying his product or its name along with a striking example of beauty the advertiser hopes to link the two so that when a potential customer wonders how she can make herself attractive, she will buy the soap or perfume which she remembers was associated with the beautiful woman in the advertisement.

This technique may be psychologically sound, but there is no guarantee that it will increase sales. Other products are also paired with beauty in advertisements, and some campaigns are superior to others in persuasive power. Nevertheless, the cosmetic industry has had a tremendous growth over the years, probably due in in part to the success of its intensive advertising.

One reason that some advertising campaigns are unsuccessful, undoubtedly, is that many people have learned to distrust the claims they make. It is no secret that the primary aim of any advertising campaign is to sell a product rather than to describe it accurately. To defend themselves from the persuasive appeals of advertisers, consumers in most industrial countries support research and testing organizations where the true value of products can be objectively ascertained.

In spite of this increased sophistication on the part of the buying public, advertising campaigns that succeed in developing new ways of tapping powerful motivational systems continue to prove effective. To overcome consumers' suspicion of advertising appeals, humor and the lighter touch have been widely used. The message about the product is so disarming that the person who hears or reads it is not supposed to suspect that the advertiser is out to hook him.

Many advertising campaigns are successful because they recognize the basic motivations of a particular group of consumers. For many years Marlboro cigarettes based its advertising appeals on feminine daintiness. Their ads typically showed a well-groomed society woman smoking a Marlboro. Although this brand of cigarettes achieved a moderate degree of success, its strictly feminine advertising appeal failed to persuade the men, who after all, are the heaviest smokers. A new advertising campaign was initiated displaying unusually masculine-looking men (cowboys, soldiers, etc.), each with a tattoo on his hand and smoking a Marlboro. The change of appeal opened up a wider market for Marlboro cigarettes.

In another instance, a manufacturer of good quality candy that sold at a reasonable price wondered why his business was not more successful. He sought the advice of a psychologist, who suggested that he find out what motivates people to buy candy. This sounds like a psychological boondoggle. Don't people buy candy simply to *eat* it? Actually that is only one reason, for candy is also bought extensively as a gift. People who buy candy to give away usually want it to look expensive. One way a manufacturer can give this impression is to box his candy attractively. But the manufacturer in our story had, in his attempt to sell his candy at a reasonable price, used cheap, unimpressive boxes. By doing this he had cut himself off from the sizable market of gift buyers. His customers were the people who buy candy most often for themselves and their families. The psychologist recommended that the manufacturer package some of his candy in expensive, showy boxes and sell them for a higher price. Taking this advice, the manufacturer began to produce two lines, one expensive and the other moderate in price. The former appealed to the gift buyers and the latter to the consumers. Now that he was appealing to the entire candy-buying public the manufacturers' sales soared. The psychologist proved his point that successful advertising and other forms of merchandising depend upon knowing your potential customers' motives.

According to Freud, motives of which we are unaware often determine our behavior. Several psychoanalytically oriented psychologists have entered the field of advertising armed with a technique known as **motivational research.** If this term is somewhat vague, it is not to be wondered at, since the boundaries of motivational research itself are not well-defined. Some would cite as good examples the ideas and recommendations leading to increased sales of cigarettes and candy that we have already noted. Others would restrict the term to the uses of unconscious motivation in advertising appeals (see page 449). A few years ago one advertiser attempted to persuade fathers that they should purchase their daughter's first bottle of perfume rather than let it be given to her by some young boyfriend. The theory behind this appeal was that the libidinal attachment between father and daughter makes him particularly resent the encroachments of his young rivals, and therefore he would want to compete with them in any way he could. There is much argument about the effectiveness of an advertising campaign such as this. Our position is that Freudian theory is not formulated with sufficient clarity to lend itself to any straightforward application in advertising. Those who use it usually apply it inappropriately. For the present, then, we must be properly sceptical about enthusiastic claims for the effectiveness of advertising messages which appeal to the unconscious.

Another advertising technique that presumably exploits unconscious motivation is *subliminal advertising.* Several years ago the advertising world was rocked when newspapers reported that a command to eat popcorn, flashed on a movie screen for a tiny fraction of a second (actually, it was claimed, as briefly as 1/3000th of a second), increased purchases of popcorn enormously. This is far too brief an exposure to permit ordinary "reading." The adherents of this technique believed that in some manner the **subliminal stimuli** produced an unconscious motivation to purchase popcorn. When this idea was given careful scientific scrutiny, little if any evidence was found to support it. The original popcorn experiment must have been defective. There is really no sound evidence that subliminal advertising is effective (McConnell, Cutler, & McNeil, 1958).

Closely allied to advertising is the business of promoting positve attitudes toward organizations, individuals, and ideas. In the business and political community these efforts are sometimes referred to as **public relations.** Many years ago a railroad tycoon responded to severe criticism of his lack of regard for the public's rights with the short and simple statement, "The public be damned." Today, business executives with similar attitudes carefully avoid expressing them. The government has much more power to control business, and the public decides who shall govern. It has proved decidedly unprofitable for corporation and labor union executives to pursue for long a "public be damned" policy. Instead, organizations in the public eye try to improve their "public image." Much of the battle between capital and labor, for example, has been transferred to the arena of public relations, where representatives of both sides seek to gain the sympathy and support of the public during all phases of labor strife.

When examined closely there is no basic difference between persuading people to purchase an item and persuading them to think well of an organization or person. Both are directed at molding positive attitudes, one to buy something and the other, to refrain, at least, from adverse criticisms. Presumably, variables found to be effective in one of these efforts should be effective in the other.

One study designed to evaluate the effectiveness of a mass persuasion program showed that a person's motivation before the campaign had an influence upon his susceptibility to the persuasive message (Star & Hughes, 1950). This study was made during the latter part of the 1940's when an intensive public relations campaign was undertaken to establish a more favorable attitude toward the United Nations in a large Midwestern city. Before the program was begun, a survey was made to determine the attitudes toward the U.N. then prevailing. The results of this survey served as the reference point for evaluating the effectiveness of the campaign's efforts. The findings of the study indicated that the people who were already favorably disposed toward the U.N. were the ones who most welcomed further information about it. The people who were not informed about the U.N. were the least interested in getting information about it and were the ones whose attitudes were most resistant to change. All in all, the campaign failed to move the people who were either not interested in the organization or opposed to it. It is interesting to note that the people who actively participated in the campaign itself experienced the greatest changes in attitude. The lesson to be drawn from this study is that before you can change attitudes, you must arouse interest in your cause.

A somewhat similar conclusion was reached in a study evaluating the effectiveness of the persuasive techniques used in the 1940 Presidential campaigns of Franklin Roosevelt and Wendell Willkie. It was concluded that the people who gave the most attention to political appeals were the same people whose attitudes were most resistant to change. Democrats paid attention to Democratic messages and Republicans paid attention to Republican messages. When they were exposed to messages of the opposing party, they tended either to ignore or disbelieve them. The major contribution of these political messages seemed to be to reinforce prevailing attitudes (Lazarsfeld, Berelson, & Gaudet, 1948).

But not everyone's attitude has already been crystallized before the campaign begins. Some voters are "independent" and others are undecided, or perhaps, indecisive. How susceptible are these people to political messages? In one of the great political upsets in American history, Harry Truman unexpectedly won over Thomas Dewey in the Presidential election of 1948. Presumably, Truman was able, during the later part of the campaign, to win over to his side many previously undecided voters. In the last of the "whistle-stop campaigns," he traveled throughout the country, addressing crowds from the rear platform of a railroad train. One factor that worked to his advantage was that he was then President of the United States. Many people came to hear him simply because they wanted to see a real, live President. His engaging personality apparently appealed to a great many people in his audiences, and because they liked him they found themselves being persuaded by him and voting for him. The evidence is that people did not cast their votes for him because rational deliberation had led them to accept Truman's principles and logic. Other factors completely removed from the pros and cons of political issues led them to vote for Truman.

In the same election a study (Kitt & Gleicher, 1950) of how those persons voted who shifted their preference during the campaign, made it clear that their vote was influenced by the political affiliations of their friends. Individuals whose three closest friends were Republicans tended to shift toward the Republican ticket, and those whose three closest friends were Democrats tended to line up on that side. In other words, political attitudes can be modified by all of the pressures exerted by close friends.

All this suggests that a frontal assault on a strongly held opinion is not the most effective way of changing it. Because people usually try to be consistent, they find it difficult to consider, understand, and accept beliefs that are contrary to those they already hold. So they reject them or are simply not impressed by them. Perhaps the effective way to modify a strongly held opinion is to attack it obliquely. Consider the problem of an advertising agency in charge of the advertising program of a tea company. Their job is to devise a campaign aimed at increasing tea consumption. They know that more tea is not consumed because, in general, coffee is preferred. In their campaign, they might try to persuade coffee drinkers that tea is superior to coffee in such and such respects and should therefore be given a try. However, people with strong positive opinions about coffee are likely to ignore or disbelieve their message. Hence, they might try to base the appeal on the different taste of tea (e.g., "It is a change-of-pace drink"). This message would not contradict the coffee drinker's positive attitude toward coffee. Nor would it make the coffee drinker feel that he is being inconsistent if he drinks tea. Presumably, such an oblique appeal would be more effective in getting people to try tea, and particularly the tea that is being advertised whose name is now familiar to them.

Modifying attitudes is a facet of the more fundamental problem of breaking habits in general (see page 427). For a habit to be broken successfully, a new habit must replace the old one. The oblique method of modifying attitudes initially encourages the new attitude without forcing it to compete with the stronger existing one. The person is merely encouraged to drink tea without being forced to accept the idea that it is superior to coffee.

The importance of not arousing the existing attitude that one wants to change is illustrated by a study (Allyn & Festinger, 1961) in which two groups of high school students who were in favor of allowing teenagers to drive with few restrictions, heard the same lecture advocating that teenagers should drive only under strictly controlled conditions. Before the talk, one group was told what the speaker's topic would be and his point of view. This, of course, evoked the opinion they already held. The other group was given no advance information about either the subject of the talk or the speaker's view. They were instructed only to evaluate the speaker's personality. The results showed that the students who were forewarned about the topic and the lecturer's opinion, changed their attitude less than did the unprepared students. In changing an attitude, the direct approach is not necessarily the most effective one.

Without doubt, propaganda represents the most important area of mass persuasion, for it is in the field of propaganda that the free world and the Communist world are battling for the "minds" of all people. The relative effectiveness of the propaganda on both sides, and the techniques of mass persuasion, may well decide this historic struggle.

The term *propaganda* often seems a nasty one. It is usually associated with deceit, lies, boasting, and self-interest. We like to believe that the Voice of America and Radio Free Europe have as their aim the "education" of people behind the Iron Curtain, whereas Radio Moscow operates only to "propagandize" by spreading lies and distortions. We must realize, however, that the same distinction is made in Communist lands, with the roles reversed. To them, we are the purveyors of "propaganda" while they tell the "truth." The fact is that *truth* means something different to the two sides. In the last analysis both the free and Communist worlds are using techniques of mass persuasion in the hope of changing the attitudes, beliefs, and opinions of those who live in the other world or those who are still neutral. The term

propaganda is as good as any, and better than most, to describe efforts of this kind.

The principles governing effective propaganda have been summarized in a set of rules (Krech & Crutchfield, 1948). Four of these rules are given below:

1. *The message should meet the existing needs of the audience.* This simply re-emphasizes the importance of considering motives when you want to make an audience attend to a message and be persuaded by it. As we have already pointed out, a program designed to modify individuals' attitudes toward the United Nations was ineffective in reaching those who were not interested in the U.N.

A more striking example of the influence of needs upon the effectiveness of propaganda comes from a study of attitudes among the Japanese Americans who were sent to relocation centers during World War II (Festinger, 1957). Most of them resented being treated in this way, chiefly because they were forced to abandon their homes. Some developed a strong hatred of America, but others remained sympathetic to the American cause in spite of what they considered unjust treatment. Those who hated America refused to believe anything favorable about it. At the end of the war many of them chose to be repatriated to Japan, and a considerable number left this country believing that Japan had won the war. In contrast, although the Japanese who remained sympathetic to the American cause were shocked at the treatment they had received, they believed the whole episode was simply due to a mistaken policy. They were ready to accept favorable statements about the United States, evidence again that a message is more likely to be accepted if it is consistent with the motives of the person to whom it is directed.

2. *Messages that allow an audience to identify with people possessed of some prestige will be more effective than those that*

do not. Much advertising is based on this principle. The fact that Mickey Mantle or Willie Mays eats a certain breakfast food is supposed to prompt many little boys to do likewise. The same mechanism operates with adults in their acceptance of political opinions. Statements emanating from persons who are highly esteemed are more readily accepted than *exactly the same statements* credited to persons who are not thought well of. For example, the degree to which the following statement will be accepted depends upon who the reader believes said it: "I hold that a little rebellion, now and then, is a good thing, and as necessary in the political world as storms are in the physical."

When American readers were told that this statement was written by Thomas Jefferson, more of them agreed with it than did when it was attributed to Lenin, the father of the Russian Revolution. And the extent of their agreement, or disagreement, was found to correspond with how much, or how little, respect they had for the political philosophies of Jefferson and Lenin (Lorge, 1936).

3. *A message that is consistent with what a person already believes will be more readily accepted than one which is not.* This point has been touched on previously. In persuading a person to accept a new attitude, a message will be effective if it appears consistent with his old one. This way, the old attitude will serve as a kind of opening wedge for the new.

Communists exploit this principle. When they attempt to proselytize Christian groups, they depict Communism as consistent with early Christian ideals. When they proselytize antireligious groups, they represent religion as "the opiate of the people."

In one study (Ewing, 1942) subjects known to have a favorable attitude toward the Ford Motor Company were exposed to unfavorable propaganda about the company. One group was told explicitly that the message they would hear would be consistent with their attitudes toward Ford. The other group was warned that it would be inconsistent. The message had some effect in modifying the attitudes of the first group but not of the second. The propaganda seemed to be effective only when subjects thought it was consistent with the beliefs they already held.

4. *A message that clarifies an ambiguous subject or situation will be more effective than one concerning a situation already clearly defined.* If a propaganda message is aimed at clearing up an ambiguous situation, it has a good chance of being accepted. This is one reason why people are willing to accept tips on the stock market or on horse races or on what bait they should use to catch certain fish. These are ambiguous situations to them, for they do not understand clearly what will succeed and what will fail.

It has been said that propagandists fish in muddy waters and that if the waters are not muddy they should stir them up. This advice was followed all too well by the Nazis during World War II. By planting confusing rumors in countries which they planned to attack, they helped to make the civilian population ripe for Nazi propaganda. The Korean War was a decidedly ambiguous situation for many Americans; people were confused about its origin and purpose. For this reason, the propaganda against war was much more effective in this country than it was during World War II, where the situation was clearly defined.

Group Persuasion. Psychologists feel more at home with experiments on group persuasion than they do with attempts to discover how advertising and public relations programs and propaganda can influence large segments of a country's population. By exposing groups to messages that vary in some systematic manner, they can determine with precision the influence of many separate variables.

An illustration of the advantages of such methods is to be found in an experiment (Janis & Feshbach, 1953) which was designed to investigate the effectiveness of anxiety-inducing messages of different intensities. A group of high school students was given a questionnaire contrived to obtain information about their dental hygiene practices and about the amount of worrying they did over tooth decay and diseased gums. A week later they were divided into three experimental groups, each of which heard essentially the same illustrated lecture on dental hygiene but with a different slant on the information offered. The *strong-fear group* saw slides of decayed teeth and diseased gums and was admonished, "This can happen to you." The *moderate-fear group* was made aware of similar dangers, but these were expressed in a milder and more factual form. Finally, the *minimum-fear group* heard a message that rarely referred to the consequences of dental neglect. They were shown slides of healthy teeth and gums. Immediately after each lecture each group was given a second questionnaire to determine whether the particular form of anxiety message they received was effective in generating fear. All three were. The *strong-fear group* exhibited the greatest amount of worry about dental problems, followed by the *moderate-fear group* and the *minimum-fear group,* in that order.

The effectiveness of the dental hygiene lectures given under the different motivational conditions was evaluated in two ways: (1) whether the subject's behavior was modified in accordance with the dental hygiene recommendations made, and (2) how resistant this behavior was to a counterpropaganda message which urged the use of a toothbrush shaped differently from the one originally suggested. The results of both measures were essentially the same. The minimum-fear message was the most effective in modifying the group's dental hygiene procedures and in resisting the effects of the counterpropaganda. The strong-fear message was least effective.

The finding that a message's persuasiveness is inversely related to the amount of fear it generates is consistent with our previous analysis of fear and punishment (see page 279). Although punishment and fear are powerful motivators, they have side effects that can interfere with learning. A frightening appeal tends to encourage avoidance of the message (not listening to it). Or, if the message is learned, repression can occur, that is to say, instrumental forgetting takes place. Thus it is risky to base any educational campaign on strong fear, even when the topic is inherently fear-producing, like cancer, the dangers of smoking, or civil defense. Unless some reassurance is given that the danger is not as great as it appears and that there are effective ways of coping with it, the message that relies upon stirring up strong fear is not likely to be influential.

Fear, assuming it is not too strong, can be effectively used to change attitudes if it is *followed* by information about how to cope with it. This point was demonstrated in a study (Cohen, 1957) in which the sequence of fear-arousal message and information directed to reducing the fear was different for each of two groups. For one group the fear preceded the information; for the other group, the sequence was reversed. The fear-information group exhibited definite signs of attitude change, whereas the information-fear group did not. This is what you would expect from the principles of learning. The information designed to allay the fear could only operate as a reinforcement if the appropriate drive (fear) was present.

Perhaps the most common attempts at group persuasion are those that occur in the classroom. Much of what is called education consists of teachers attempting to mold the beliefs, opinions, and attitudes of their students. These attempts are no doubt successful with some students, perhaps all, if we are considering only attitudes about the subject matter of particular courses. However, often neither teachers nor institutions seem to have very much effect in modifying their students' values about life and society in general. (Whether or not this is one of the functions of a college is something that deserves debate!) There are, of course, exceptions to this sweeping statement. Many individual teachers through their enthusiasm and personal example do succeed in modifying drastically the value commitments of a few of their students. A student intent upon pursuing a business career and becoming wealthy may be so inspired by a professor of classics that his value system is altered sufficiently to make him decide to become a professor of classics. And there are cases in which a college community succeeds in modifying the attitudes of most of the students. One such case (Newcomb, 1943) is the small New England girls' college already mentioned (see page 578) where the students acquired values definitely at variance with the conservative attitudes in their homes. Such a value change is not likely to be produced by any one course. In this college, it seemed to emerge because the students identified with the college community at the time they were seeking independence from their families. Since the college community was liberal, the students who conformed to the standards of the new social environment were reinforced by becoming leaders and achieving prestige. The students whose attitudes were not markedly influenced by the college life were those who maintained their strong family ties and actively resisted the social pressures of the college community. One important factor operating here was that the college was in a small isolated community and was therefore relatively uninfluenced by other social forces. It is unlikely that a similar shift in students' attitudes could occur in an environment where strong conflicting social pressures exist, as in a metropolitan college where many students live at home.

Persuasion Directed at One Individual. The attempt to apply persuasion to one person rather than a group of people permits special techniques inapplicable elsewhere. Most important, the persuasive technique can be "tailor-made" to the individual. It would be difficult, if not impossible, to shape the behavior of a group of pigeons so that they would whirl around in a circle simultaneously (see page 291). While you were reinforcing the appropriate response in one pigeon you would probably be reinforcing an inappropriate response in another. By dealing only with one subject, the persuader can arrange his actions for maximum effectiveness.

In order to illustrate the effectiveness of individual persuasion we will deal extensively with two phenomena: one from the social psychology laboratory, the other from real life. The first is *conforming behavior,* the second, *brainwashing.*

Conforming Behavior

In social learning one learns what is acceptable behavior and what is not. He learns **conforming behavior.** A group he belongs to builds socially approved forms of behavior into him by reinforcing him when his behavior conforms to their standards and by withholding reinforcements or punishing him when it does not. In a broad sense of the term the group *persuades* the individual to adopt its standard of behavior. Or perhaps we can say, from the viewpoint of the individual, he is brought around to conform to group pressures.

An interesting and revealing series of experiments (Asch, 1955) have been concerned with how conformity is produced. The experimental technique used in these experiments is both simple and ingenious.

Seven to nine male college students are brought into the laboratory ostensibly to be subjects in an experiment on how perceptual judgments are formed. The experimenter tells them that they are to compare lines of different lengths. Two large white cards are then shown simultaneously to them. On one there is a single vertical line that serves as the standard against which their judgments are made; on the other are three vertical lines differing in length. Figure 15.10 shows two such cards. One of

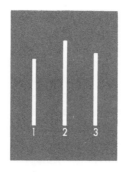

FIGURE 15.10 The Kind of Problem Used to Investigate the Effect of Majority Opinion on Individual Behavior. The subject is asked to indicate which of the three lines is the same length as the single line on the left. Before he answers, other subjects, who are instructed to give a wrong judgment, give their opinions (After Asch, 1955).

FIGURE 15.11 The Experimental Situation Used to Investigate Conforming Behavior. Six of the seven subjects have been instructed to give the wrong answer to a problem similar to the one in Figure 15.10. The experimental subject (sixth from the left) is exposed to the pressure of majority opinion when making his own judgment. In this instance he resisted it (William Vandivert for *Scientific American*).

the three lines on one card is the same length as the standard line on the other card. The problem for the subject is to identify this line.

The beginning of the experiment is uneventful. In the first two problems, each subject in turn announces his judgment and they find they all agree. With the third problem the experiment actually begins. For now all but one of the subjects deliberately choose a line that is *not* equal in length to the standard. These subjects are, in common parlance, "stooges." In an earlier session with the experimenter they were coached to give incorrect responses at certain points in the experiment. The only genuine subject in the experiment is the one who has not been coached and therefore has no idea that the procedure is rigged. The experiment obviously centers on him. He is subjected to two opposed forces: the evidence of his own senses and the group pressure embodied in the unanimous judgment different from his own. What does he do in this situation?

Many variables enter to determine whether he acts independently or yields to the example of the majority. One fact, however, stands out. Group pressure of this kind does have a considerable influence. Under ordinary circumstances subjects make an error less than 1 per cent of the time. However, when they have to buck the unanimous opinion of the majority they make errors 37 per cent of the time. There are, of course, striking individual differences. Some subjects "stick to their guns" and never agree with the majority; others knuckle down and conform on every problem.

The point of this experiment, however, is not merely to demonstrate that when people are confronted with social pressure they conform. It is also to investigate under controlled conditions the variables that influence the effectiveness of group pressure. This has been done in a large number of experiments employing procedures similar to the one just described. From these studies important conclusions about the factors that influence socially conforming behavior have been drawn. Some of the major findings will now be summarized under four headings: (1) stimulus variables; (2) group variables; (3) personality variables; and (4) cultural variables.

Stimulus Variables. As you would expect, a subject's resistance to majority opinion depends on how wrong the majority is. In an experiment like the one described before, the discrepancy between the standard line and the line chosen by the majority was varied until the difference was so glaring that no one expected a subject to yield to the pressure to conform. But even when the discrepancy amounted to seven inches, some subjects failed to behave independently and yielded to the majority opinion. Still, taking all the results into consideration, the effectiveness of group pressure was found to decrease with increasing discrepancies between the lengths of the standard line and the line chosen by the majority.

Several different experiments have suggested that the more ambiguous the situation, the more likely it is that the subject will submit to group pressure. For example, subjects who are required to make a judgment of stimuli from memory yield more readily than do those who have the stimuli immediately before them (Deutsch & Gerard, 1955). Also, attitudes have proved easier to shift than judgments of facts. Such results are consistent with the principle previously asserted, namely, that propaganda is most successful in ambiguous situations.

Group Variables. Four group variables which are important in their effect upon socially conforming behavior are: (1) the size of the group; (2) the group's unanimity; (3) the status or prestige of members of the group; and (4) the way individual and group judgments are reached.

In the experiment with the lines, the size of the group opposing the experimental subject was varied from 1 to 15 persons. Figure 15.12 shows the results. Exposed to the opinion of only one dissenting member, the subject's judgment was not appreciably different from those he made when he was alone. Two judges with opposing views produced appreciable pressure to conform; the proportion of the subjects' errors jumped to 14 per cent. The persuasive effect of three opposing judges increased the subjects' errors to 32 per cent. But further increases in the number of the opposition did not substantially increase the pressure to conform.

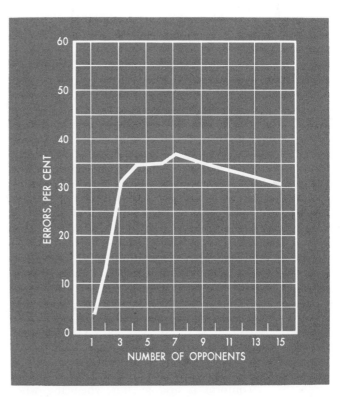

FIGURE 15.12 The Effect of the Size of the Group on the Conforming Behavior of an Individual. When the subject was confronted with a single dissenting opinion he made errors only about 4 per cent of the time. This was similar to his performance when he was alone. Pressure to conform, as measured by the per cent of errors, increased as the size of the group increased to three. Thereafter increases in the number of dissenters did not markedly influence the subject's behavior (After Asch, 1955).

In one problem, one of the opposing judges was instructed to estimate the length of the lines truthfully. This had a strong influence on the experimental subject. Although the rest of the group constituted a majority reporting opposing opinions, it had little persuasive effect on him. That is, with the support of one judge on his side, the accuracy of the experimental subject's judgments jumped from 63 to 90 per cent. The effectiveness of having a partner in resisting a majority is illustrated further by two other findings. When the partner suddenly switched back to the majority opinion, the errors of the experimental subject increased sharply. However, when the partner merely left the room, the subject was almost as effective in resisting majority opinion as when he had the partner supporting him. The knowledge that somebody else had resisted group pressure, even though he was no longer present, encouraged the experimental subject to do likewise. This is one important reason why totalitarian states cannot tolerate the slightest hint of opposition. Opposition creates more opposition.

The success of group pressure depends on who the members of the group are. The more prestige its members have, the more effective it will be in getting others to conform (Torrance, 1954). The more a person likes the members of a group, or the more he thinks they like him, the greater will be his susceptibility to group pressure (Jackson & Saltzstein, 1958).

When a person is required to express his opinion in front of a group, he is more likely to agree with them than he is when he is able to keep his opinion to himself (Deutsch & Gerard, 1955). The tendency to conform is also greater when the whole group has been instructed to come to a unanimous decision (Festinger & Thibaut, 1951), as a jury is. And finally, the greater the reward attached to unanimous opinions, the more likely it is that minority opinions will yield to that of the majority.

Personality Variables. An uncritical layman might suppose that people could be divided into two rigid groups: conformists or nonconformists. That is, he might think that some people always submit to group pressure and others never do. This view implies that situational factors are unimportant. Nothing could be further from the truth. The specific situation has been proved to have a great deal to do with the extent to which conforming is reinforcing. A theoretical physicist may be reinforced for dissenting in a matter of theory and reinforced for conforming in most social situations.

Nevertheless, there do seem to be some personality variables associated, although not perfectly, with tendencies to conform socially. Some studies suggest that the more conforming subjects tend to be more submissive and anxious than others (Crutchfield, 1955) and to have had parents who were relatively harsh (Mussen & Kagan, 1958). One cannot, however, conclude that nonconforming is psychologically healthy and conforming is not. Psychotics like schizophrenics and manic-depressives are notable nonconformists. Moreover, conformity and nonconformity are not two mutually exclusive behavior categories, but are points on a continuum. Although extreme behavior at either end may be associated with psychological difficulties, there is no reason to conclude that moderate amounts of conforming or nonconforming behavior, taken by themselves, are particularly symptomatic of anything.

Cultural Variables. These play an important role in social conformity. The fact that a culture has a distinctive character is evidence that a large segment of the population conforms to common standards of behavior. Nevertheless, it is probable that certain cultures reinforce conformity more strongly than others. Norwegian and French students were used as subjects in experiments, similar to the one we have described, in which the judgments of individuals were opposed by members of groups. The results of several studies (Milgram, 1961) showed consistently that the French were less conforming than the Norwegians. This result appears to agree with the history of the two peoples: Norwegians have been able to get along with a single constitution drafted in 1814, whereas the French are still trying to achieve political stability after having been through four Republics. Norwegian culture emphasizes cooperation and social responsibility, whereas individualism and dissent are strong French traditions.

Brainwashing

Brainwashing is a colorful but misleading term that has been applied to a technique of individual persuasion which received much publicity during the Korean War. After they had been in Chinese Communist prisons for a period of time, several Americans confessed publicly and untruthfully that the United States had used germ warfare. The press in Western nations described this example of psychological coercion as *brainwashing*. To many people this term implied a somewhat magical method of achieving total control over a person's behavior. As such it seemed to make more understandable the behavior of these American prisoners who sided with the enemy. Nowadays you may hear the proponents or opponents of fluoridation "brainwashing" the public, or even of children "brainwashing" their parents. If the term **brainwashing** is to preserve its original meaning, its usage should be restricted to those persuasive techniques used in Communist nations to effect dramatic attitudinal changes.

The public in the Western world first became aware of these techniques during the 1930's, when the USSR, under the control of Joseph Stalin, held a series of trials in which many Russian leaders openly confessed to being "counter-revolutionaries"

in the employ of "capitalist nations." They admitted that they had been intent upon overthrowing the Communist regime. It seemed incomprehensible that these confessions could be true for they came from persons who had dedicated their entire lives to the cause of Communism. A more reasonable interpretation was that Stalin, for political reasons, wished to get rid of them, and in some manner his henchmen were able to persuade their victims to publicly confess to crimes they did not commit. Later events, including speeches by Khrushchev, confirmed this hypothesis.

Although more is heard about the use of brainwashing with prisoners of war and with "imperialist spies," the official Chinese Communist program of *szu-hsiang kai-tsao* (variously translated "ideological remolding" or "ideological reform" and recently referred to as "thought reform") also exploits so-called brainwashing techniques on a mass scale. Some of the principal features of brainwashing are illustrated in the following account (Lifton, 1961) of the experiences reported by a European physician who, prior to the Communist revolution, had practiced medicine for twenty years in China. One of the few foreign physicians to remain in China after the Communists took over, he was able to carry on a rather lucrative practice which included several Communist officials.

One afternoon he was suddenly arrested in the street and sent to a detention house, or what was called a re-education center, where he spent the next three and one-half years.

In the beginning he was placed in a small bare cell with eight other prisoners, all of whom were Chinese. They were specially selected prisoners who were believed to have made progress toward ideological reform. The prison leader instructed the physician, who was identified by number only, to sit in the center of a circle. Each prisoner in turn shouted invectives at him, accusing him of being a "spy" in the employ of "imperialists" and urging him to "recognize" his "crimes" and "confess everything" to the government. The physician denied all the accusations. He had been, he said, a physician and nothing more. But his accusers were not to be denied. They persisted vehemently in their attempts to make him confess.

Later he was subjected to his first interrogation by a "judge," and was once again confronted with the accusation of having "committed crimes against the people." When he protested his innocence, he was told "the government never arrests an innocent man." He was then questioned about various activities and associations which the judge apparently considered among his crimes. The judge frequently resorted to thinly veiled threats and promises. He said that the government knew what crimes the physician had committed and the sooner he confessed, the sooner he would be released. After ten hours of constant interrogation, during which the prisoner gave much information but made no confession, the judge ordered that the prisoner's wrists be handcuffed behind him. He was given ten minutes to reconsider his refusal to confess. When he returned, still insisting that he did not commit any crimes, the judge became incensed and ordered that the prisoner's ankles be chained together.

He was then returned to his cell, where his cellmates tried for endless hours to persuade him to confess. The physician was subjected to frequent humiliations. Because he was chained he had to eat like a dog. No attention was paid to his personal hygiene, and only with 'another prisoner's help could he attend to his toilet needs.

At the end of the second day the physician was only interested in getting rid of the chains. He concocted a wild story, confessing all sorts of crimes against the state. But his interrogators were not interested in *any* confession. They wanted a confession that was consistent, and that the prisoner himself believed.

On the third night the prisoner changed his tactics. Before his accusers he tried to recall conversations that he had had with friends and associates during his entire 20 years in China. This encouraged his accusers, who took up most of the night reviewing these events, always demanding more and more detail. Now and then the prisoner was forced to take a short walk, which reminded him of his uncomfortable chains and which kept him awake. In his cell during the day he was required to dictate to another prisoner all he said the previous night. This program was continued without letup for several days and nights giving him no chance to sleep. He was constantly reminded that his present plight was his own doing and that if he did the right things he could escape from his chains; if he did not, he risked being shot. Overwhelmed by fatigue, confusion, and exhaustion, he stopped resisting.

A confession finally emerged from his detailed outpourings. Although distorted and exaggerated, it was related to real events in his past life. When he was required to report on others, he complied with a combination of truths, half-truths, and untruths, implicating former friends and associates in spying activities.

Three months after his arrest he seemed prepared to admit his "crimes." For example, the prisoner had been the friend and family physician of an American correspondent with whom he had occasionally discussed the military situation during the revolution. The prisoner recalled having reported to the correspondent that he had seen some Communist artillery. The judge insisted that the American correspondent was in truth a spy and that the prisoner was therefore supplying a spy with military information. The prisoner now recognized this as a "crime." In another instance the prisoner recalled having told an American military attaché that he was unable to get gasoline. Previously he had agreed that this constituted "economic intelligence." Now he was persuaded that he had been instructed by a third party to collect this information and to pass it on to the military attaché. The important point, psychologically, is that he had begun to have doubts about his own conception of truth and to see some "truth" in his captors' interpretation of his past behavior. What previously appeared to him as innocent acts now assumed the shape of crimes against the state.

Once he began to express things in this way—in his captors' words "from the people's standpoint"—some amelioration was made in the conditions of his imprisonment. His handcuffs and chains were removed. His ordeal, however, had not ended. He had to take an active part in his cell's re-education program, which usually occupied 10 to 16 hours of each day. Typically one prisoner read excerpts from some Communist book or newspaper that initiated group discussions. All the prisoners had to learn to express themselves correctly "from the people's standpoint" and to confess their past "crimes." At first the physician seemed to pay only lip service to "the people's standpoint," but gradually under these relentless conditions, he began to accept his fellow prisoners' and interrogator's judgments.

After more than a year of this re-education, the prisoner was subjected to a series of interrogations aimed at reconstructing his confession. Because the prisoner now had acquired a better understanding of "the people's standpoint," his confession seemed more real to the judge. But another 14 months of re-education were to follow, at the end of which there was another revision of his confession, which now became brief, logical, and factual. A few months later he was called in for a formal signing and reading of his confession before photographers and newsreel cameramen. A short time thereafter he was sentenced to three years for "espionage" and other "crimes," but was released because he had already been imprisoned for over three years. He was then expelled from China.

The process of brainwashing was not completely effective in this physician's case, if we judge it on the basis of whether he adhered to his new-found attitudes and beliefs. Eventually, he spontaneously expressed strong hostility toward Communism and Communists. But the turnabout took time and was not completely successful. He never completely escaped from the idea, for example, that there are really two kinds of truths: the truth of the Communist world and the truth of the free world. He remained confused about their relative merits, even though he eventually expressed his preference for the latter. But the brainwashing technique was effective in getting him to read a confession he actually believed in at the time. Such confessions produced a strong political impact in many Asian and European nations. And what is perhaps of even greater importance, those who elicited these confessions believed them also. The confessions reinforced their attitudes about those whom they saw as their enemies. And they helped persuade their fellow citizens to believe in the Communists' creed.

Not all prisoners subjected to this kind of brainwashing responded like the physician. Some came through their ordeal converted to the Communists' viewpoint. Others, particularly those who possessed strong, organized systems of belief in opposition to Communism, resisted the persuasive efforts of their captors. Still others, among them the physician, became confused. However, those three categories are not sharply distinguishable. Even among the converts and the resisters some doubts persisted about what was really true and false, and what was really right and wrong.

Techniques similar to the one described here were used with some Americans taken

594

prisoner during the Korean War. One group of psychologists (Farber, Harlow, & West, 1957) analyzed the Chinese indoctrination technique into three basic factors: debility, dependency, and dread. Another psychologist (McConnell, 1958) emphasized four factors: (1) persuasive appeals that coupled hope with fear; (2) isolation from groups who would support old attitudes; (3) reinforcement of the act of confessing, and (4) reinforcement of the act of informing on others. There is obviously overlapping among these classifications and techniques used with the European physician.

It is understandable that experimenters, and potential subjects, are reluctant to become involved in research on brainwashing. But evidence suggests that periods of inactivity and isolation can produce profound changes in behavior. Although the physician in the case just described was rarely physically isolated, he was to all intents and purposes isolated from the social world he previously inhabited. In attempts to brainwash American soldiers in the Korean War, Communists often placed them in physical isolation for long periods of time.

In several studies (Heron, 1957) college students who volunteered, for a 20-dollar daily wage, were required to lie on comfortable beds in isolated cubicles for 24 hours, except for the time they needed to eat and attend to their toilet needs. They wore translucent goggles that permitted them to see light but not objects, and had gloves and cuffs over their hands and forearms which minimized sensory stimulation. Few students could endure this treatment for more than two or three days and not one lasted more than one week. When their isolation was momentarily interrupted to test their intelligence, it was found that they were functioning at a lower level than normally. Some students reported hallucinations and immediately after their release from their "imprisonment" their perceptual ability seemed impaired. But these impairments disappeared after a while.

Results of experiments on sensory deprivation do not always produce the same dramatic findings as those just reported. But it seems reasonable to suggest that sensory isolation and monotony do encourage people to accept attitudes they previously did not hold. There are three possible reasons for this. After long periods of sensory deprivation, (1) an individual reacts to any form of stimulation, including a "propaganda" message, positively; (2) he is not as intellectually competent as previously; (3) the attitude change serves as an instrumental response to escape from an aversive environment.

Consistency Among Beliefs, Attitudes, and Opinions

In 1818 a New England farmer named William Miller reached the conclusion, after he had studied the Bible, that the world was going to come to an end in 1843. By the year 1831 many people had become interested in his prediction and a sizable number were convinced that it would come true. They formed an organization and started a newspaper for the purpose of proselytizing others. In 1842 a conference of Millerites passed a resolution stating that "God has revealed the time of the end of the world, and that time is 1843." As the time of the last judgment approached the Millerites became more and more convinced that they were right. Some farmers became so convinced that they did not bother to plow their fields. When the prediction failed to be confirmed the Millerites expressed disappointment. But soon thereafter a new date was set and they resumed their proselytizing with energy and enthusiasm.

Why the failure of the world to come to an end did not destroy the Millerites' belief is an interesting psychological question. Festinger, a social psychologist, answers this question at some length (Festinger, 1957; Festinger, Riecken, & Schachter,

1956). Man, who finds himself in many different situations, is motivated to maintain a consistent set of beliefs throughout them all. This tendency to remain consistent is one of the major factors controlling the crystallization of beliefs, attitudes, and opinions. When circumstances threaten to create inconsistency, or what Festinger prefers to call **cognitive dissonance,** man finds some way to reduce it. The Millerites had a choice between two alternative methods to reduce the cognitive dissonance by which they were confronted. They could deny their cherished belief. Or they could rationalize that they had made an error in computing the date and the predicted event was still coming. Now that they had found the error they knew the real date for the world's demise. Many found the second alternative more appealing, and before the Millerite movement finally collapsed, this sequence of prediction, disconfirmation, and rationalization was repeated several times.

A contemporary example of how dissonance may be reduced comes from a survey of smokers' beliefs concerning the medical evidence that there is a connection between smoking and lung cancer. A cigarette smoker who reads this evidence is confronted with cognitive dissonance. In order to reduce it he can do one of two things: he can stop smoking (or perhaps reduce the amount he smokes considerably) or he can deny that the evidence is valid. From this analysis you would expect that the more a person smokes, the less likely he is to believe the evidence that lung cancer may be caused by smoking. The data in Figure 15.13 provide confirmation of this expectation.

Other findings, many from experimental investigations, have supported the cognitive dissonance theory. In one study (Festinger & Carlsmith, 1959) three groups of students were required to perform a repetitive, dull chore. After completing it each subject was then instructed to tell a waiting fellow student that it was a pleasant, enjoyable task.

Each member of one group received a dollar for this bit of deception. Members of another group received 20 dollars to do the same thing. The third group, which served as a control, was not required to deceive fellow students. Afterwards an interview was held with each student to learn his attitude toward the monotonous assignment.

According to the cognitive dissonance theory, forcing a person to do something he does not believe in creates dissonance. This dissonance is greater among the "one-dollar" than among the "twenty-dollar" subjects. The subject receiving the large reward can rationalize his deception by claiming that he, and others too, if they had the chance, could not resist accepting so large a sum of money for so small a lie. But the one-dollar subject would find it

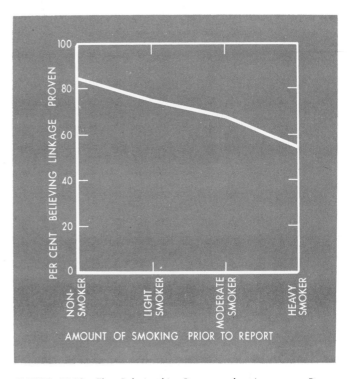

FIGURE 15.13 The Relationship Between the Amount a Person Smokes and His Belief That a Link Exists Between Smoking and Lung Cancer (After Data in the *Minneapolis Star and Tribune,* March 21, 1954, as reported by Festinger, 1957).

596

difficult to rationalize lying for such a paltry sum. He can, however, reduce his cognitive dissonance by modifying his attitude toward the boring task. He can make himself believe that really it was interesting. The results of the interview indicated that this analysis is correct. The one-dollar subjects had persuaded themselves that the task was relatively enjoyable whereas the "twenty-dollar" subjects had the same negative attitude toward the task that members of the control group had.

Some of the evidence previously cited in this chapter can also be incorporated into the cognitive dissonance theory. The effectiveness of brainwashing may be due, in part at least, to an attempt by the prisoner to reduce the dissonance he feels after his first confession has been wrung from him. The prisoner, reacting to his own confession, can either admit that it was cowardly of him to confess or that there is some truth in his confession. In many cases, prisoners choose the latter alternative. Cognitive dissonance theory is also consistent with the evidence that propaganda, political and advertising campaigns, and public relations programs tend to be more effective when they are consonant with the attitudes and beliefs of those to whom they are directed.

It was noted that such appeals are usually ineffective when they run sharply counter to a person's opinions. And last but not least, cognitive dissonance theory is compatible with many perceptual phenomena (see page 209 and 221) in which an ambiguous situation is interpreted in a consistent way.

The cognitive dissonance formulation, although stimulating and useful, needs elaboration. We need to know more about the conditions which lead people to abandon beliefs and those which prompt rationalization and disregard for the evidence. To be more specific, What was there about some Millerites that led them to reject their beliefs after the first disconfirmation? Or, why do some heavy smokers accept the evidence linking lung cancer to cigarette smoking? Perhaps the answer to these questions will come from studies of how people learn to be consistent. After all, children do not exhibit so great a need to maintain a consistent set of beliefs as do adults. It is quite possible that in the process of learning to be consistent some people learn to concentrate primarily on facts, while others become anchored to the beliefs themselves, feeling them to be of paramount importance.

SUMMARY

Behavior is shaped by the society in which a person lives. This shaping process is called socialization. Socialization can be examined at three levels: the culture, the social group, and the social dyad. At each level we find that the social environment determines the behavior that will be reinforced or punished.

Research with small groups has sought to unravel the social influences on behavior by observing them in well-controlled situations. The structure of a group determines how it will function.

There are three major variables in the study of leadership: the leader, the followers, and the situation. Leaders are often chosen for the effectiveness with which the group believes they will help achieve the group's goals. But other factors such as the ability to set goals and the personality desired by the followers enter into the selection of a leader. A factor analysis of leadership behavior suggests that it consists of two basic factors: consideration (establishing good interpersonal relationships) and initiating structure (organizing and planning the activities of the group).

Psychologists have developed methods of measuring attitudes. Motivation and reinforcement, personality, and the social environment are important variables in the formation and change of attitudes. Several lines of evidence support the idea that a direct attempt to persuade a person to give up his present attitude and accept a conflicting one is not as effective as one which de-emphasizes the inconsistency between the old and the new attitude. Propaganda messages are effective when they meet the existing needs of the audience, are approved by people with prestige, are consistent with presently held attitudes, and clarify an ambiguous situation. Messages which arouse strong fear are not effective in changing attitudes.

The experimental analysis of the tendency to conform to social pressures has revealed that many environmental, social, and personality variables are important. Clinical studies, buttressed by some experimental studies of sensory isolation, have suggested reasons (e.g., social isolation, fear, confusion, reinforcing confessions) for the effectiveness of brainwashing technique in producing marked changes in attitudes.

The cognitive dissonance theory, which postulates that individuals have a strong need to maintain a consistent set of beliefs, has been offered to explain many instances of social behavior.

SUGGESTIONS FOR FURTHER READING

ALLPORT, G. W. *The nature of prejudice*. Reading, Mass.: Addison-Wesley, 1954.
A review and integration of the literature on prejudice.

BENEDICT, R. *Patterns of culture*. Boston: Houghton Mifflin, 1934. (Published in a paperback edition in the Mentor Book series, New American Library of World Literature.)
A classic in the field of anthropology. The patterns of culture of different primitive societies are described.

CAMPBELL, A., CONVERSE, P. E., MILLER, W. E., & STOKES, D. E. *The American voter*. New York: Wiley, 1960.
The results of a large-scale survey designed to understand the variables influencing voting behavior.

FESTINGER, L. *A theory of cognitive dissonance*. New York: Harper & Row, 1957.
An exposition of one of the most influential theories in contemporary social psychology.

KATZ, D., CARTWRIGHT, D., ELDERVELD, S., & LEE, A. M. (Eds.) *Public opinion and propaganda*. New York: Holt, Rinehart, & Winston, 1954.

A collection of readings in the areas of persuasion, communication, and public opinion.

KLUCKHOHN, C. *Mirror for man*. New York: McGraw-Hill, 1949. (Published in a paperback edition in The Premier Books series, Fawcett Publications, 1957.)
A readable account of cultural differences, written by a famous social anthropologist.

KRECH, D., CRUTCHFIELD, R. S., & BALLACHY, E. L. *Individual in society: A textbook of social psychology*. New York: McGraw-Hill, 1962.
A well-organized text in social psychology that emphasizes the topics of attitudes, culture, and group behavior.

LIFTON, R. J. *Thought reform and the psychology of totalism*. New York: Norton, 1961.
An interesting book on brainwashing written by a psychiatrist.

LINDZEY, G. (Ed.) *Handbook of social psychology*. Reading, Mass.: Addison-Wesley, 1954. 2 vols.
A collection of detailed papers covering various aspects of social psychology.

Maccoby, E. E., Newcomb, T. M., & Hartley, E. L. *Readings in social psychology*. (3rd ed.) New York: Holt, Rinehart, & Winston, 1958.
A collection of interesting papers on various aspects of social psychology.

Newcomb, T. M. *Social psychology*. New York: Holt, Rinehart, & Winston, 1950.
A popular social psychology text.

Sherif, M., & Sherif, C. *An outline of social psychology*. (Rev. ed.) New York: Harper & Row, 1956.
An interesting text in social psychology.

Sprott, W. J. H. *Human groups*. Baltimore, Md.: Penguin Books, 1958.
A brief survey of group behavior.

APPLIED PSYCHOLOGY

VI

Americans are proud of their reputation for being practical. Inventors like Thomas Edison and Henry Ford, who were able to transform scientific principles into useful and serviceable creations, are accorded places of respect and honor unshared by most outstanding artists and scientists. Psychologists have not ignored the social demand that science be useful. It should be quite apparent by now that psychology has helped society to solve many of its problems.

Probably the most useful contribution has been the psychological test. By measuring an individual's performance in a test situation, it has been possible to predict his future behavior fairly precisely. There are many different kinds of psychological tests. No attempt will be made to review them all. The major concern will be to provide a fundamental understanding of the ideas responsible for developing, using, and interpreting psychological tests. The basic principles underlying these tests will be discussed in relation to intelligence, a topic that has probably been exposed to more publicity—and misunderstanding—than any other psychological concept.

Psychologists' practical contributions have not been limited to testing. The ways in which their findings have been applied are too numerous to mention, much less describe. Instead of attempting to cover a large number of applied psychology programs, three topics will be reviewed in depth. They are human engineering, the technology of learning, and vocational guidance. The first is concerned with establishing a better working relation between men and machines. The second is interested in exploiting some of the principles of learning in improving education. And the third is concerned with developing techniques so that people can make better decisions about the jobs for which they are best suited.

PSYCHOLOGICAL TESTING

16

THE VALUE OF PSYCHOLOGICAL TESTING

If a list were made of the most practical discoveries in psychology, psychological tests would be high on it, if not at the top. Today we have tests that measure many kinds of behavior, behavior occurring in schools, industry, business, the armed services, and elsewhere in our society. We have tests of finger dexterity that will help select workers who can make the precise movements needed in constructing delicate electronic equipment and watches; tests that will identify students who will probably do well in law school or medical school; tests that will pick out those who can become successful pilots, radar operators, and mechanics; and tests that will help people choose careers in which their chances of success will be high.

Knowing the tremendous number of psychological tests available, you will not be surprised to hear that the development,

printing, administration, and sale of psychological tests constitute a multimillion dollar business. As in any other business, the product varies in quality. Some tests are so good that if we tried to get along without them, we would be set back a long way. Others are literally not worth the paper they are printed on. Unfortunately, an untrained person cannot distinguish between a useful and useless test; he needs some knowledge of the principles underlying psychological tests to make this sort of discrimination.

The basic psychological principle underlying all psychological tests is simple: an individual's behavior in one situation (skillful work on the job) may be a function of the same individual's behavior in another situation (finger dexterity or manual coordination in the test situation). That is, $R = f(R)$ (see page 27). However, behavior in one particular situation is not necessarily related to behavior in any other situation that might be selected. You would not expect a person's ability to knit a sweater to correlate closely with his ability to fly a jet plane. To construct a useful test one must devise a situation (the test) which evokes behavior related to the performance (the criterion) one wishes to predict.

One very successful program of test construction was set up during World War II, when psychologists were called in to help select sailors who could be trained to become good radio-code operators. Radio code, as you may know, is a system of communication in which patterns of auditory signals, consisting of *dits* and *dahs*, represent the different letters of the alphabet (e.g., *A*, dit-dah; *B*, dah-dit-dit-dit).

Learning to receive and send radio code is an exacting task. If a group of newly inducted sailors is selected at random and sent to a radio-code school, about 40 per cent will fail. They just do not seem to have the skills necessary to function satisfactorily in this kind of work. Obviously, training 10,000 men in four to six weeks in order to get 6,000 radio-code operators would constitute a "double waste" of time and effort: the school would be wasting its time training 4,000 unsuccessful students, and the students would be wasting their time. They could have been somewhere else learning to serve the Navy in some way more suitable to their abilities.

In the interest of efficiency alone, only those students should be trained who can reasonably be expected to profit from training. But how can this be done? The principle, as we have already stated, is to devise a method of sampling the behavior which is predictive of later success in a radio-code school. The psychologists did this by constructing a test which belongs to the class of tests called **aptitude tests** because they measure an individual's *potential* for learning some skill or subject.

How the test should be constructed was suggested by the observation that learning to receive radio code is a two-stage process.

It involves, first, associating patterns of sound with their appropriate letters and, second, learning to identify the same signals transmitted at a much faster rate. Although some students can learn the correct associations when the stimuli are presented slowly, their discriminative capacity fails when the messages are speeded up. A half-hour test (Kurtz, 1944) was finally constructed in which students had first to learn to associate three letters with their appropriate sound patterns at a slow rate and then to identify them at faster rates.

In order to evaluate the effectiveness of the test, a study was designed to determine its **validity.** A large group of sailors was first given the test and then enrolled in radio-code school. When they finished the course, the correlation between their test scores and their final grades was ascertained. A high positive coefficient of correlation (see page 69) was obtained, indicating that the test had validity, that scores made on it actually did correlate with the *criterion* it sought to predict, ability to learn radio code.

Next, the **critical score,** below which a student would be rejected for radio-code school, was determined. Ideally, a critical score, or *cut-off point,* would guarantee success to every student who reached or surpassed it. It would also ensure that all students who scored below it, would have failed the course had they been given the opportunity to attend the school. Unfortunately, there is no such ideal cut-off point. In practice some individuals who score above the cut-off point fail in the course, and some who score below, pass when they are given the opportunity to attend the school.

Where a critical score is placed depends on many things. If the supply of potential trainees is unlimited and the training program, extremely expensive, the critical score can be very high. Under these circumstances the emphasis is on reducing the

false positives: individuals who score above the critical score but fail the course. However, if the supply of potential trainees is limited, the aim is to give each trainee who has a reasonable chance of succeeding the opportunity to enroll. Major attention here is on reducing the percentage of **false negatives:** individuals who obtain scores below the critical score but who would pass the course if given an opportunity.

Often during World War II, when the manpower pool for potential radio-code operators was large, it was possible to use a particularly high critical score for the radio-code aptitude test. Of all the students achieving or surpassing this critical score, only 6 per cent, on the average, failed the course. If you compare these results with the 40 per cent of unselected trainees who did not pass, you are bound to be impressed with the value of the test.

Another example of the value of aptitude tests is in the experience of the United States Air Force during World War II with a battery (group) of tests for selecting pilots (DuBois, 1947). From his performance on these tests, each pilot candidate was given a *stanine score,* which was based upon the *stan*dard deviation and ranged on a *nine*-point scale—hence the name *stanine.* Figure 16.1 shows the relationship between the pilots' scores and their success or failure in pilot training. As you can see, the higher the stanine, the fewer the failures in pilot training. Critical scores were set higher or lower depending upon conditions at the time, and occasionally whole groups taking the test were trained in order to test its validity. During the latter part of 1943 a stanine of 5 was selected as a critical score. Only 17 per cent of the candidates who received this score or higher failed pilot training. However, of the men who had received a stanine less than 5 and had been trained, 44 per cent failed. Obviously the battery of tests had definite value in selecting the better risks for pilot training.

One question that is frequently raised is whether or not these aptitude tests are "really fair" to those who score below the critical stanine. Even if you assume that these individuals would have turned out to be false negatives, and would have passed pilot training if they had been given the opportunity, the obvious answer to the charge of unfairness is that the desires of one such individual (or even a few) are less important than the efficiency and effectiveness of the armed services. The probability remains that an individual who scores above the critical score stands a better chance of succeeding than the man who scores below it. In other words, more pilots will be obtained from the group scoring above the critical stanine than from those scoring below it.

We have the same problem with students who "fail" medical aptitude tests. Some of these students might have become good physicians had they been given the opportunity. But medical education is ex-

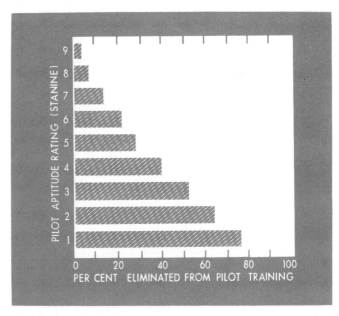

FIGURE 16.1 The Percentage of Failures in Pilot Training at Each Stanine Level. The higher the stanine level the lower the percentage of failures (After Du Bois, 1947).

604

tremely expensive, and for an accepted applicant to fail, after having taken the place of a man who might have passed with distinction, is serious indeed. From society's point of view, it is only reasonable to select those students who have the *best* chance of success.

The imperfections of a test should not hide the fact that it is superior to no test at all. No one today seriously proposes to do away with those aptitude tests that have demonstrated their validity simply because they may be imperfect. The best way to deal with the charge of injustice is to improve the tests and decrease the number of false negatives. Besides, these tests should be credited with saving many students, true negatives, from later, and perhaps bitterer, disappointments of failure. It is not a favor to a person to let him do an unwise thing just because he wants to.

APTITUDE AND ACHIEVEMENT TESTS AND HUMAN ABILITIES

Psychological tests assume many forms. You have already learned something about personality tests and attitude questionnaires. You have also seen that all psychological tests measure behavior in some standard situation. This is as true for aptitude and achievement tests as it is for personality tests and attitude questionnaires.

In order to understand the concepts of aptitude and achievement, you must grasp what is meant by the *more fundamental* concept of *ability*. No one questions the fact that individuals differ in ability to perform a variety of tasks. From the Little Leagues to the Major Leagues, baseball players range widely in ability to bat, field, and pitch. In schools, at every level from kindergarten to graduate school, students exhibit a range of abilities to acquire and

perform various intellectual skills. Individual differences among industrial workers are equally apparent. Figure 16.2 shows the productivity of three textile workers as indicated by their learning curves. Differences in productivity showed up very early and persisted over a relatively long period of time. At the end of 320 hours experience one worker was still improving, while the performances of the other two had stabilized at a much lower level.

Even in the most elementary forms of behavior such as visual and auditory discriminations, individuals exhibit differences in ability. Some people are able to make very fine pitch discriminations; others are unable to detect differences between sounds that are obvious to practically everyone else. Although some individuals can distinguish very fine differences in hue, others can distinguish differences between only a few hues, and a very few are totally insensitive to hue.

Since it is obvious that people differ, you will immediately want to ask why it is necessary to invoke the concept of abilities. Because, for one thing, an individual's performance in one task may be related to his performance in others, and his performance in a wide *variety* of tasks can often be accounted for in terms of a *few* basic abilities. When a large group of young men performed as subjects in 40 different motor tasks, their performances on the various tasks correlated to some degree (Hempel & Fleishman, 1955). Some who did well in certain tasks did well in certain other tasks, and some who did poorly in certain ones did poorly in others. By the method of factor analysis (see page 475), evidence was discovered in the widely differing performances for two basic sets of abilities: *athletic abilities* and *manipulative abilities*. The athletic abilities included *strength, flexibility, balance, gross body coordination,* and *energy mobilization.* The manipulative abilities included *manual dexterity, finger dexterity, arm-hand steadiness,* and *aiming.* Thus, as you can see, *ability* is a useful and economical term for some characteristic of behavior that determines performance in a variety of specific situations.

Another reason for using the concept of ability is that these basic ability factors can be predictive of future behavior. Knowing somebody's pattern of abilities makes it possible to predict how well he will be able to acquire certain skills. For example, if a teacher knows the particular ability of a child, which she calls his reading-readiness, she will be able to estimate whether or not he can profit from a certain kind of reading instruction.

With these examples in mind, we are in the position to say what we mean by ability. **Ability** *is a pattern of behavior tendencies responsible for skillful performance in a variety of related tasks.* Strength is a general ability that is evidenced in a variety of performances such as pushups, chinning, and weight lifting. Finger dexterity is an ability that determines performance in tasks demanding precise finger movements (watchmaking, manufacturing transistors, knitting).

A common misconception about tests of ability is that they somehow reveal the *innate* capacity of an individual. That is, the tests measure the genetic capability of an individual uncontaminated by environmental influences. The truth is that any test, whether it measures finger dexterity or reading ability, measures behavior and not its cause. When people differ in their responses, as they usually do, then one must restrict his conclusions to *how* they differ. *Why* they differ—that is, what combination of genetic and environmental factors produces the differences—must be answered by experimentation.

One group of psychologists hope eventually to demonstrate that all specific skills —from hitting baseballs to calculating equations—are due to a finite number of component basic abilities. If they can demonstrate this and identify the abilities required for every job, then they will be able to give every individual a test to find out his basic abilities and, with this information, fit him to the job he can perform most effectively.

Whether this dream can ever be turned into reality is an open question. It will be answered only when more is known about the origin of abilities and the degree to which they remain constant throughout the life span. If we discover that a finite

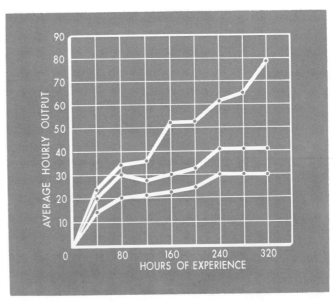

FIGURE 16.2 Learning Curves for Three Textile Workers. After 320 hours of experience, the most productive worker was still improving, but the productivity of the other two workers had levelled off (After McGehee, 1948).

set of abilities, sufficiently stable and the same in all cultures, can account for the variety of skills an individual exhibits at different stages of life, then perhaps the hope will be realized. If, however, we find that abilities are short-lived and sensitive to changes in experience, then the hope will prove illusory. But no matter what happens, no one can deny that in limited areas of behavior, the psychological technique of analyzing skills into component abilities is useful. Industry, education, and particularly the armed services have benefited immensely from the persistent attempts of psychologists to analyze groups of skills into more basic abilities.

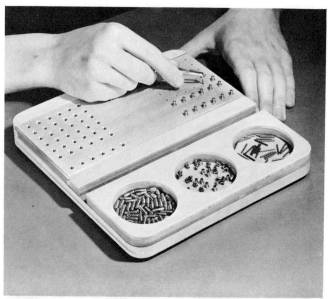

FIGURE 16.3 Two Tasks of the Small Parts Dexterity Test. The subject is timed while he fits the parts into the appropriate holes (The Psychological Corporation).

Perhaps the most common attempt to use measures of ability to predict behavior is aptitude testing. An **aptitude** is an individual's capacity to acquire some skill. Thus "musical aptitude" is measured in terms of those psychological abilities, such as habits and drives, sensory, motor, and intellectual abilities, an individual has which are conducive to acquiring proficiency in music. Again, we are not implying that aptitudes are necessarily inborn.

Aptitude is obviously related to ability. *Ability* is the more general term, *aptitude* represents one facet of it. An aptitude is the name for those behavior tendencies which when combined with appropriate training will result in a degree of proficiency in a particular skill. To say that a child has high musical aptitude is to say that he has those abilities that can help him become proficient in music with the proper training.

Years ago a person's job potential was measured by samples of his work. For example, at the turn of the century, when many immigrants from eastern Europe were coming to the United States, there was an oversupply of tailors. A garment factory advertising for tailors would be swamped by hundreds of applicants. Usually, a foreman—if he did not have a relative who wanted the job—would select about 20 candidates by appearance alone and let them work for a half-day without pay. He would then examine their work and hire the tailors who did the best work. There are many things wrong with this selection procedure, aside from the ethics of having these men do a great deal of work without pay. For example, a rejected applicant might have had the potential to become a far better tailor than the one selected. But this selection procedure served its purpose. Today, however, society is more concerned with saving human resources, and so a more objective and efficient method of personnel selection is needed. The aptitude test is one answer.

Some aptitude tests are constructed for a specific job. A psychologist associated with a company will construct an aptitude test that can predict performance on a specific task in that company's factory. He can ignore the question of the basic abilities that go into the successful performance of the job. But in huge organizations like the armed services, there are many different kinds of jobs; an attempt must be made not only to analyze the positions to be filled, but to determine the basic abilities of the personnel who might fill them.

An **achievement test** is slightly different from an aptitude test. It measures the degree of proficiency *already* attained in some specific skill. The work sample used to evaluate the proficiency of immigrant tailors is actually an example of an achievement test. Today achievement tests are not so casually devised. They are constructed with the same painstaking care as any other psychological test. They are given under carefully prescribed conditions and scored objectively.

Achievement tests serve two main functions. First, they are used to measure the effectiveness of training programs. If two methods of teaching arithmetic are to be compared, an achievement test is needed to evaluate them. It permits a comparison of the arithmetical achievement of pupils taught by the two methods. Second, achievement tests, like aptitude tests, are used to assess a person's capacity to do a job well. When skilled workers must be hired, it is useful to know the degree of mastery they have already achieved. Since the job they are to perform is identical to one they performed previously, their present capacity —that is, their achievement—is the best predictor of their future performance.

There are many different abilities that we could discuss, and many more aptitude and achievement tests. But rather than attempt a bird's eye survey of the field, we shall analyze one ability in some depth. And that ability is *intelligence*. We have chosen intelligence because it is the ability that psychologists have worked on most, and it is the ability that college students, one of the most intellectually gifted groups in society, find most interesting.

INTELLIGENCE

Intelligence may be defined in two ways. The first is simple, direct, but somewhat unsatisfactory. **Intelligence** *is what the intelligence test measures*. It is known as an operational definition (see page 9), for it specifies the operations performed by the psychologist when he measures what he calls intelligence. Since there are many different tests of intelligence, there are, according to this definition, many different kinds of intelligence. Therefore, when we speak of intellectual ability, we must specify the intelligence test used to measure it, since the scores on different intelligence tests do not correlate perfectly with each other.

For most students this simple operational definition of intelligence is not particularly satisfactory. It seems both arbitrary and circular. After all, what would prevent someone from defining intelligence as the ratio between the length and width of the big toe? Of course, if someone defined intelligence in that way, everyone would recognize immediately that the definition was useless and utterly without validity (see page 602). Presumably the ratio would not correlate with any significant form of behavior. However, this is not true of most tests of intelligence. We have abundant evidence that the Stanford-Binet intelligence test (see page 608), for example, has a positive correlation with scholastic achievement.

This simple operational definition has been offered in order to get away from the profusion, and confusion, of definitions of intelligence now current. "Intelligence is the ability to think abstractly," or "Intelligence is the power of understanding," or

"Intelligence is problem-solving efficiency." But what do these impressive sounding phrases, "think abstractly," "power of understanding," and "problem-solving efficiency," really mean? How do we decide whether one person is better able to think abstractly than another, or which of two individuals has the greater problem-solving ability? We understand each other better, the operationalists argue, if we define intelligence as what the test measures and let it go at that. This definition, although limited, is clear and to the point. And as you will see, when you get to know more about how intelligence tests are constructed and how they are used, and principally *what they correlate with*, this definition is not as arbitrary and circular as it appeared initially.

The second method of defining intelligence is to consider it as a theoretical construct (see page 29). According to this conception, intelligence is a basic ability underlying behavior in a wide variety of situations. In this sense the concept of intelligence is similar to the concepts of habit, drive, and personality. It can be inferred from performance, and its function, like all theoretical concepts, is to integrate and systematize knowledge and to predict new facts. Now that this kind of definition has been described, it would be nice if we could offer one. Unfortunately, we cannot, because psychologists do not yet have a satisfactory theory of intelligence. Nevertheless, some progress is being made, and later in this chapter some of the attempts to provide insights into the meaning of intelligence as a psychological process will be reported.

Intelligence Tests

The first intelligence test (see page 52) was designed to predict scholastic achievement. Since its development many tests of intelligence have been devised. All of them share with the original test the aim of predicting behavior, although nowadays, intelligence tests are used not only in predicting academic performance, but in predicting business, industrial, and military performance as well.

A test's ability to predict behavior rests heavily upon the statistical concept of the coefficient of correlation (see page 70). A coefficient of correlation used for predictive purposes has been compared to a three-legged stool. One leg is the predictor, which in the present case is the intelligence *test*. Another leg represents the *criterion*, the variable with which scores on a test will correlate if it is successful. School grades have been widely used as the criterion against which to validate intelligence tests. The third leg, one that is often overlooked, is the particular *population* of individuals used in obtaining the correlation between the test and the criterion.

In order to use any test sensibly and profitably, one must have precise information about each of the "three legs" on which its predictive power rests. Many misinterpretations and misunderstandings about intelligence have resulted from neglect of one or more of these factors. To make them seem more concrete to you, we shall take up each factor as it applies to a few of the best known and most widely used American tests of intelligence.

The Stanford-Binet Test. In 1916 Lewis Terman (1877-1956), a noted psychologist at Stanford University, made an English-language adaptation of the original French Binet-Simon intelligence test, which had been devised in the first place to identify children so low in intelligence that they could not profitably attend the schools of Paris (see page 51). Since 1916 there have been two revisions of the Stanford-Binet intelligence test, one in 1937 and one in 1960 (Terman & Merrill, 1937; 1960). Such revisions are necessary because some of the tests became obsolete. For example, one test used in the 1937 revision required the child to identify five of six objects represented in miniature. Among these objects were a telephone and a stove. In 1937, 69 per cent of 3-year-olds could pass this test. This figure dropped to 11 per cent during the 1950's because telephones and stoves had so changed in appearance that the children could not recognize the older models.

The central concept of the Stanford-Binet test is **mental age.** The mental age of a child is determined by his performance on a series of tests that are graded in difficulty so as to provide suitable tests for each age. For example, the *average* 9-year-old boy can tell you what is absurd about the following story: "I saw a well-dressed young man walking down the street with his hands in his pockets and twirling a brand new cane." But the *average* 7- or 8-year-old boy does not discover the absurdity. Similarly the average 7-year-old can answer questions like, "In what way are coal and wood alike?"—"a ship and an automobile?" Most younger children cannot do this.

By devising a number of tests that tap a variety of skills, arithmetical, memory, and vocabulary, a graded series of tests has been arranged according to age levels. The entire series of these tests (properly called *subtests*) constitutes the Stanford-Binet intelligence scale. It is primarily used with children ranging from 2 to 16 years of age. Any child taking this test can theoretically score at any mental age level regardless of his chronological age. A 4-year-old can make a score equal to the average 8-year-old's or an 8-year-old may score as low as the average 4-year-old's. An individual's mental age is determined by the subtests he passes. If his performance equals that of the average 8-year-old child, for example, his mental age is 8. Remember, the mental age is obtained independently of **chronological age,** which is his actual age in years.

A normal child's mental age increases as he grows older, at roughly the same rate

as his chronological age (CA). However, the MA of bright children, those above average in intelligence, increases faster than their CA. The MA of dull children, who are below average, increases at a slower rate than their CA. Figure 16.5 shows the change in MA as a function of CA for three different individuals. With differ-

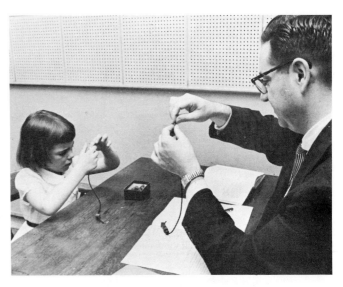

FIGURE 16.4 A Subtest from the Stanford-Binet Test. The child is required to reproduce the pattern of beads in the tester's string (New York University Testing and Advisement Center).

ences in rate of intellectual development like these, we come to the concept of the **intelligence quotient,** known everywhere by the initials IQ. If two children, one 4 years old and the other 6, both have a mental age of 6, the younger child is obviously brighter. As a simple way of expressing brightness in quantitative terms, the concept of IQ is extremely useful. The IQ is the ratio between an individual's mental age and his chronological age, multiplied by 100 to avoid the inconvenience of decimals. The formula is:

$$IQ = \frac{MA}{CA} \times 100$$

Thus the child of 5 with an MA of 5 has an IQ of 100. Any child whose MA equals

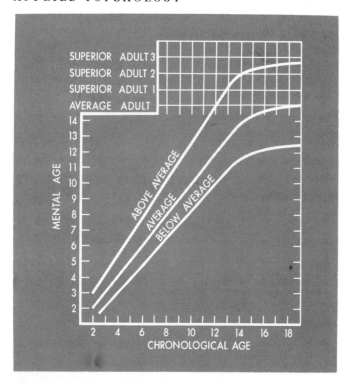

FIGURE 16.5 The Relation Between Mental Age and Chronological Age for Three Individuals of Different Intellectual Ability.

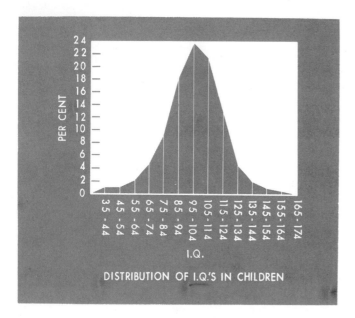

FIGURE 16.6 The Distribution of IQ's Obtained by the Standardization Group on the 1937 Revision of the Stanford-Binet Test (After L. M. Terman & M. A. Merrill. *Measuring intelligence.* Boston: Houghton Mifflin, 1937).

his CA has an IQ of 100 and is spoken of as average in intelligence. The child of 4 with an MA of 6 has an IQ of 150. The child of 8 with an MA of 6 has an IQ of 75.

Figure 16.6 shows the distribution of IQ's of approximately 3000 youngsters on the 1937 revision of the Stanford-Binet test. These subjects served as the **standardization group;** they constitute the reference population against which individual IQ scores on the Standard-Binet may be compared. For example, a child who obtains an IQ of 100 is considered average because his performance equals the average of the reference group. Similarly individuals who obtain IQ's of 50 and 160 are exceptional because a very small percentage of the standardization group got such scores.

You will note that the form of the distribution in Figure 16.6 is that of a normal curve (see page 64). The standard deviation of this particular distribution is 16. From our knowledge of the mathematical properties of the normal curve we know that 68 per cent of the standardization group received IQ's between 84 and 116, and 95 per cent of the group obtained IQ's between 68 and 132.

The constructors of the test restricted their standardized group to American-born white children to make it homogeneous in respect to language and general educational opportunity. The subjects, aged 2 to 18, who comprised the standardization group, were selected from 17 communities in 11 states with a proportion of rural and urban subjects similar to that of the whole United States.

The correlation between scores on the Stanford-Binet test and school grades is about +.50, permitting fairly good prediction. That the correlation is not higher is no fault of the test. Variables other than intelligence—neatness of work, promptness in completing homework, conduct—play a considerable role in determining how a child's scholastic performance is graded. Moreover, very bright children sometimes become bored because the instruction they receive is at a level much below their ability. They may develop into problem children in the classroom, and because they are not motivated to do their best and fail to pay attention to what bores them, receive mediocre and sometimes even low grades. At the other extreme, grades of polite, well-behaved students are often inflated because the teacher who is overworked or bored naturally rates these qualities high and mistakenly considers them signs of academic achievement. In fact, the imperfect correlation between scores on the Stanford-Binet test and school grades makes the test a useful diagnostic tool for evaluating poor performance in school. The child with a high IQ but a poor school performance has to be treated very differently from the child with a low IQ and a poor performance.

If it were possible to eliminate the influence of these nonintellectual factors upon grades, the correlation between intelligence test scores and school work would undoubtedly be higher. This expectation is supported by the fact that higher correlations are obtained between intelligence test scores and scores on objective tests of school achievement than are obtained between intelligence test scores and more subjective school grades. Furthermore, the degree to which intelligence tests are related to academic success depends upon the subject matter in which the grades are received. Intelligence test scores are more highly correlated, as you would expect, with science and English grades than with grades in domestic science and shop work (Thorndike & Hagen, 1955).

To make clearer the nature of intelligence tests in general and the Stanford-Binet test in particular, it may be useful to review the meaning of the "three-legged coefficient" as it applies to psychological tests. A test's correlation expresses the relationship between *test* scores and some *criterion* as these are found in a particular

population. All three components must be kept in mind if tests are to be properly interpreted and applied. To understand the Stanford-Binet test, you have to be familiar with all its subtests and with the exact methods of administering and scoring the test. To use it as a predictive instrument, you must know the criteria with which it is correlated and the makeup of the populations from which its correlations were obtained. For example, if you knew that a healthy five-year-old child from a middle-class home in a California city had an IQ of 70, you could predict fairly confidently that his performance in elementary school would be poor and his potential for scholastic achievement low. You would not, however, be justified in making the same prediction for a child who had recently been brought to the United States and whose knowledge of English was definitely limited compared to an American child of his age. Nor would it be proper for you to make a confident prediction for a child who happened to be ill on the day he was tested or for one whose hearing was defective. If the child who is taking the test cannot perform at his optimal level of ability or if he comes from a population markedly different from the one used in standardizing the test, it loses at least some and perhaps all its predictive power. For a prediction from an IQ score to be accurate, there must be some similarity between the conditions under which that score was obtained and the conditions under which the test was found to correlate significantly with a particular criterion.

Wechsler Adult Intelligence Scale. A test that is now used almost as much as the Stanford-Binet test is the Wechsler Adult Intelligence Scale, commonly abbreviated to WAIS (Wechsler, 1958). It was constructed by Dr. David Wechsler, of the Bellevue Hospital in New York City, to meet a long-felt need for an intelligence test designed for adults. Many items of the Stanford-

Binet are specially adapted for use with children and therefore inappropriate for adults. Moreover, its norms (the statistics that describe the performance of the standardization group) were obtained from children.

The WAIS test is organized differently than the Stanford-Binet. Whereas the latter is arranged by age level from younger to older, the WAIS consists of two sets of subtests: verbal and performance. They are:

VERBAL SUBTESTS

Information
General Comprehension
Digit Span
Arithmetical Reasoning
Similarities
Vocabulary

PERFORMANCE SUBTESTS

Picture Arrangement
Picture Completion
Block Design
Object Assembly
Digit Symbol

Figure 16.7 shows examples of the digit span, block design, and object assembly subtests. A verbal subtest, of course, emphasizes verbal skills, such as those required for both the vocabulary and similarities subtests. In the vocabulary test the subject must define words; in the similarities test he must identify similarities between words. Even the subtest of arithmetical reasoning requires some verbal skill, since the problems are expressed in words. In the performance subtests, however, the verbal elements are kept to a minimum. The object assembly test is similar to a jig-saw puzzle; in the block design test the subject must arrange blocks to match geometric designs.

One great advantage to the WAIS is that separate IQ measures can be obtained from the verbal and performance subtests. In this way, the tester can see that an immigrant, who did relatively well in the performance subtests and poorly in the verbal ones, probably had his verbal IQ depressed by a language handicap that has nothing to do with intelligence. Similarly, the IQ of a person who did poorly on the performance subtest may be depressed as a result of a physical handicap or lack of training in simple perceptual-motor skills. To this extent the test has a built-in warning device for identifying subjects who are not completely comparable to the members of the standardization group.

The WAIS also makes it possible to obtain what may be called an individual's IQ on the basis of a single subtest. These scores are particularly helpful to the clinical psychologist who is trying to diagnose a psychiatric patient. Some schizophrenics have great difficulty with the similarities test, whereas severely anxious neurotics, who sometimes give the impression of being schizophrenic, do not. Patients suffering from organic brain disturbances do poorly in several of the performance subtests but relatively well in the vocabulary test. Although performance on any one subtest is not sufficient evidence on which to base a psychiatric diagnosis, the trained clinician is helped in his task by studying his patient's pattern of performance on the various subtests of the entire WAIS.

The method of computing IQ scores for the WAIS is different from the method used for the Stanford-Binet test. Obtaining the IQ by dividing MA by CA is appropriate only for children, since performance on an intelligence test (see Figure 16.5) tends not to improve after 16 years of age. This means that if an adult's IQ were computed as a child's is on the Stanford-Binet, it would decrease with age, because the denominator (CA) would continue to rise while the numerator (MA) of the IQ formula would stay about the same.

The IQ scores of the WAIS are based on the statistics of the normal distribution. Wechsler took a distribution of scores on his test from a standardization group of

3. 4-8-5; 2-6-8
4. 9-2-6-4; 7-3-8-1
5. 3-5-6-9-1; 6-3-8-5-7
6. 2-9-6-8-1-4; 8-2-5-3-4-1
7. 3-9-1-4-6-8-2; 5-0-9-6-2-4-8
8. 2-7-4-1-9-6-5-3; 1-9-7-4-2-6-8-3
9. 5-8-2-5-9-3-1-4-7; 6-1-3-7-9-2-8-5-4

FIGURE 16.7 Examples of Three of the Subtests of the Wechsler Adult Intelligence Scale. In the Digit Span Test, the tester reads a series of numbers which the subject is required to repeat. His score is determined by the length of the series of digits he can recall. In the Object Assembly Test the subject is required to fit the parts together as rapidly as possible. In the Block Design Test he has to arrange the blocks to match a sample pattern (New York University Testing and Advisement Center).

over 2,000 persons ranging in age from 16 to over 75, and converted these scores so that the mean score was assigned an IQ of 100. He also chose to have one standard deviation equal 15. Thus a person who receives a score one standard deviation above the mean is assigned an IQ of 115; another who scores one standard deviation below the mean obtains an IQ of 85. Persons scoring two and three standard deviations above the mean are assigned IQ's of 130 and 145 respectively. By defining IQ in this way Wechsler related the distribution of IQ's directly to the characteristics of the normal curve (see page 64). Table 16.1 shows how the IQ scores from the WAIS are distributed. Knowing the characteristic distribution of a normal curve, we can see that 25 per cent of the population achieves WAIS IQ's of 110 and above, 10 per cent obtains IQ's of 119 and above, and only 1 per cent IQ's of 135 and above. By appropriate statistical manipulations Wechsler

TABLE 16.1 Distribution of IQ Scores on the Wechsler Adult Intelligence Scale (Wechsler, 1958).

IQ	% OF ADULTS
Above 130	2.2
120-129	6.7
110-119	16.1
90-109	50.0
80-89	16.1
70-79	6.7
Below 70	2.2

614

arranged to have the mean IQ at every age level equal 100 and its standard deviation equal 15. Thus a person's IQ as determined by the Wechsler test indicates how his performance compares with that of persons of his own age.

The WAIS is valid in several respects. It correlates well with achievement in schools of higher education (college, graduate school, professional school) and with performance in different jobs. Information about a person's score on the Wechsler test can be used for situations ranging from educational and vocational counseling to job assignment in business organizations.

The Army General Classification Test (AGCT). Both the Stanford-Binet and the Wechsler tests are **individual tests.** A trained examiner can administer them to only one person at a time. Since expert personnel are needed, and since testers often have to spend considerable time preparing a sub-

ject to perform at his optimal level, administering these tests is costly and time-consuming (the Stanford-Binet test usually takes not less than one hour, and often more than that). Obviously more efficient testing procedures that put less of a drain on relatively scarce trained testers are needed in certain situations. During 1917-18, when 1,750,000 recruits were drafted into the armed services of the United States, American psychologists realized that a rapid method of determining their intelligence would be of great value. They constructed two tests that could be administered easily to large groups and scored quickly. One test, the *Army Alpha,* was devised for use with draftees able to read and write English; the other test, the *Army Beta,* was designed for illiterates and the foreign-born who were not proficient in English.

These tests are effective in weeding out the intellectually deficient draftees incapable of learning any military skill. They were also useful in selecting draftees for specific army jobs, ranging from cooks to officers.

By the time World War II began psychologists had the advantage of long experience with group tests of intelligence, and were able to construct an extremely effective test known as the Army General Classification Test (AGCT). Constructed so that the average person would obtain a score of 100, it used multiple-choice questions, was machine-scored, and was prepared in four different forms to reduce the possibility that a person might have prior knowledge of some of the questions. From their scores on this test, the army classified men into five categories of intelligence, which were used in assigning them to different jobs (see Figure 16.9).

Figure 16.10 shows the effectiveness of the AGCT in predicting success in officer candidate school. It shows that if a soldier scored below 110 on the AGCT, his chances of receiving a commission after being ad-

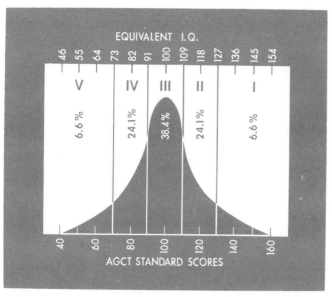

FIGURE 16.9 The Distribution of Scores on the AGCT. The AGCT scores are on the lower abscissa, and their equivalent IQ's are on the upper one. The Army divided the testees into five classifications in terms of their performance. Only those in the top two categories were permitted to go to officer candidate school.

ARMY ALPHA TEST

A. If 5½ tons of bark cost $33, what will 3½ cost? (   )

B. A train is harder to stop than an automobile because
(   ) it is longer, (   ) it is heavier, (   ) the brakes are not so good

C. If the two words of a pair mean the same or nearly the same thing, draw a line under *same*. If they mean the opposite or nearly the opposite, draw a line under *opposite*.

comprehensive	restricted	same	opposite
allure	attract	same	opposite
latent	hidden	same	opposite
deride	ridicule	same	opposite

D. If, when you have arranged the following words to make a sentence, the sentence is true, underline *true*; if it is false, underline *false*.

people enemies arrogant many make	true	false
never who heedless those stumble are	true	false
never man the show the deeds	true	false

E. The pitcher has an important place in—tennis   football   baseball   handball
Underline which

F. Dismal is to dark as cheerful is to—laugh   bright   house   gloomy

ARMY BETA TEST

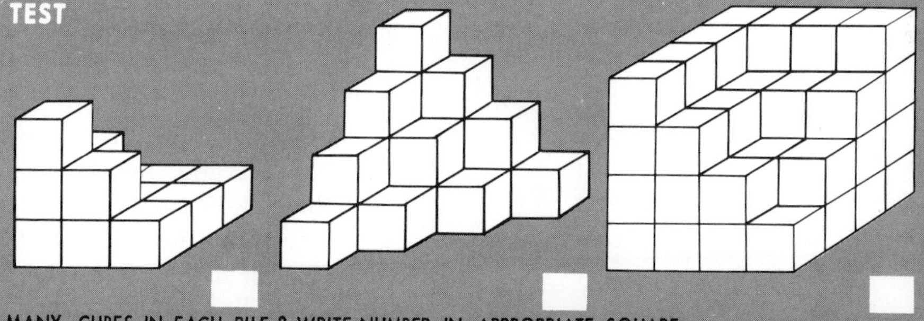

HOW MANY CUBES IN EACH PILE ? WRITE NUMBER IN APPROPRIATE SQUARE

WHICH IS THE SHORTEST WAY THROUGH THE MAZE ?

COMPLETE THE SERIES

FIGURE 16.8   Items From the Army Alpha and Beta Tests Used During World War I. The Alpha Test was used with all recruits but those with language handicaps. The Beta Test was used with illiterates and those who did not speak English.

mitted into officer candidate school were less than four out of ten. The critical score for admission to officer candidate school was set at 110. It was not set higher because the need for officers was greater than could be met from the population of those who, for example, obtained scores of 130 and above.

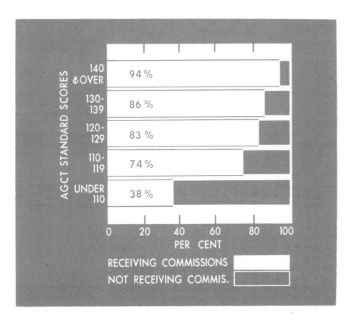

FIGURE 16.10 The Ability of the AGCT to Predict Success in Officer Candidate School During World War II. The histogram shows the per cent of officer candidates making a certain score on the AGCT who were graduated from officer candidate school and granted a commission (After Boring, 1945).

One cannot conclude that high intelligence scores are always positively related to job success. There are jobs which people of high intelligence do less effectively than people of lower intelligence. Highly intelligent people usually find simple, repetitive jobs too boring to hold their attention for long, or they may become dissatisfied with them for other reasons. During the Depression of the 1930's, when there was a very large labor market from which to choose, some organizations mistakenly selected the brightest people they could get to fill all their job vacancies. But one large retail

store soon dropped its policy of hiring college graduates as salesclerks. Their performance was relatively poor, their job turnover rate was high, and they had become the most active of all the sales personnel in attempting to form a union!

From the viewpoint of modern industrial society, which is so dependent on technical skills, it is an unfortunate waste of talent to put highly intelligent people to work on jobs that fail to tax their ability. Yet this frequently happens, as Figure 16.11 indicates. It shows the range of AGCT scores for a selected group of occupations. Although the median scores vary from occupation to occupation, there is an enormous amount of overlap between occupations. In every occupation there were some individuals who scored above 130 and others who scored below 100.

Although they are in many respects highly efficient, group tests of intelligence have certain limitations. For one thing, there is no guarantee that every individual who takes the test is at ease and can perform at his optimal level. For another, the possibility that a person will misunderstand the instructions is greater with a group test than it is with an individual test. These drawbacks can be minimized but not completely eliminated. In the army during World War II, a soldier was given the opportunity to take the AGCT a second time if he believed that his first score did not represent his ability fairly. Or, if there appeared to be a discrepancy between a soldier's score and the amount of schooling he had received or the quality of his performance in the army, he might have been required to take another test. This practice was not uncommon when a commanding officer believed that a soldier was a good prospect for officer candidate school despite his failure to score above the critical AGCT score. In almost all school systems today the use of group tests of intelligence is routine, and there too, if there is reason to believe that a particular score on one of these tests

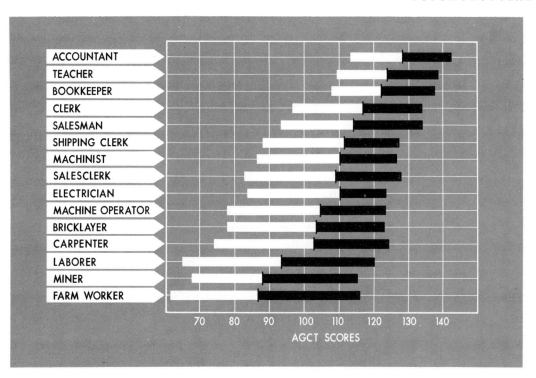

FIGURE 16.11 The Range of AGCT Scores for a Selected Group of Occupations. Each bar shows the range between the 10th and the 90th percentile of a sample of men in an occupation. The lowest and highest 10 per cent of AGCT scores for each occupation are not included. Scores below the median are shown in white; those above the median in black (After Anastasi & Foley, 1958).

does not represent a student's true ability, an individual test is given. So you can see that some of the possible errors that might result from group tests can be caught if appropriate checks are instituted.

The Nature of Intelligence

We can learn something about the nature of intelligence by looking at each of the empirical relationships involving intelligence test scores. That is to say, one way to understand intelligence is to know everything intelligence test scores are related to.

Up to this point we have noted only some of the criteria with which intelligence test scores correlate. There are many more which we could add, but we will have space for only some of them in connection with problems of particular importance.

The Stability of an Individual's IQ. One of the requirements of any good measuring instrument, whether it is a thermometer, a yardstick, or an intelligence test, is that it be reliable. The proof of reliability, applied to an instrument, is that if it is used repeatedly in taking the same measurement, the result will always be approximately the same. Provided you use a reliable tape measure, the width of your room will remain essentially the same each time you measure it. Some variation in the measurement may occur, especially if the tape measure has gradations as fine as 1/32 of an inch, but the variations will be relatively small.

How much variation is there in the IQ score of an individual who is tested repeatedly? The answer to this question depends on many factors, one of which is the particular test used. We shall discuss only those well-established tests (e.g., Stanford-Binet test) which are published in two alternate forms, so that when an individual is retested on a second form, especially within a short time after taking the first, any benefit he receives from practice on the first test will be minimized.

If the Stanford-Binet intelligence test is given twice to the same child under favorable conditions, his IQ will remain fairly constant. This does not mean that he will always obtain exactly the same IQ. An individual achieving an IQ of 110 on the first test will probably not get exactly 110 on his second test. It is naive as well as incorrect to consider a person's IQ as an exact, unchanging measure. A person getting an IQ of 110 is not *brighter* than a person getting an IQ of 109 in the same sense that a room 14 feet wide is *wider* than one 13 feet wide. If the two people were retested their relative positions might change, and this would not happen if the rooms were remeasured. It is much more sensible to think of an IQ as an approximate measure within a range. A person achieving an IQ of 110 will probably retest at an IQ somewhere between 105 and 115. And you must remember that the five-point spread on either side is the average amount of change. Some people vary more. However, 80 per cent of subjects' IQ's do not vary more than ten points, and in some cases of more extreme fluctuation factors extraneous to the subject's intelligence, such as his illness or errors in test administration, are probably responsible.

One variable that has an important influence on the stability of the obtained IQ is the length of time that elapses between successive tests (Sontag, Baker, & Nelson, 1958). The general rule is that the shorter the interval the more stable the obtained IQ. For example, the IQ's obtained at age 7 correlated with those obtained at age 8 at a value of +.91. However, when two

years separate the tests (age 7 and 9) the correlation drops to +.83. Three, four, and five-year intervals produce correlations of +.82, +.76, and +.73 respectively.

Another important factor is the age at which the child is first tested for his IQ. A test at age 3 correlates +.64 with one given at 7. A similar four-year interval between 8 and 12 years of age produces a much higher correlation of +.83. IQ's obtained between the ages of 2 and 4 should not be taken too seriously, since they are not *highly* predictive of intellectual performance several years later. Probably, one reason is that verbal skills are far from developed in the very young, yet it is precisely these skills that are so significant in the older child's intellectual performance. Another reason, although a hypothetical one, may be that the size and form of a child's brain continue to change until he is about 6 years of age (Todd, 1934). Nevertheless, IQ's at age 5 and later correlate highly with future intellectual performance. One study (Honzik, McFarlane, & Allen, 1948) showed that a test given at 8 or 9 correlated with one at age 14 or 15 almost as well as one given at 12 or 13 did. Although long intervals between testings do decrease the correlations between the two, the amount of any such decrease becomes less as the child grows older.

Intelligence and Age. The distinction in meaning between intelligence and brightness (or dullness) expressed in terms of IQ must be kept firmly in mind. A bright college boy is capable of learning much more difficult things than a bright kindergartner, even thought their IQ's are identical. The older boy certainly is more intelligent, but his intellectual ability is not proportionately greater than the child's when each is compared with his own age group. Given the same intelligence test, the WAIS, for example, the older boy will answer many more questions correctly, but when their IQ's are computed, taking scores on the test and age into consideration, they turn out to have the same IQ, that is, to be equally bright.

The difference between intelligence and IQ is brought home clearly when the performance on an intelligence test is compared for different age groups. Figure 16.12 shows this relationship between WAIS scores and age. The curve shows that intellectual ability, like physical ability, rises rapidly and reaches a peak somewhere between 20 and 30 years, after which it begins to decline. Relatively small at first, the decline becomes substantial after 40 until by age 65, people taking intelligence tests give 25 per cent fewer correct answers than do individuals between 20 and 30.

If these findings are to be interpreted correctly, certain facts must be kept in mind. The first is that these and similar data are derived from cross-sectional studies —studies comparing *different* individuals at different ages. They indicate that the mean performance of members of different age groups declines with age. There appears to be a physiological basis for this decline, for we know that during middle age the human brain starts losing cells. However, they do *not* indicate that the rate of decline is the same for each person or that every person's intellectual ability actually declines. Information of this sort can only be obtained from longitudinal studies in which the intelligence of the *same* individual is tested periodically during the entire span of his adult years, and such studies are difficult to carry out because they require contacts with willing subjects maintained over a long period of time. However, there is some recent evidence (Wechsler, 1958) to suggest that with a few people, intelligence test scores go on increasing until age 45 or 50. The best hypothesis to explain this apparent resistance to the ravages of time is that these people have "kept in practice." Scientists and other creative persons have often been known to make important discoveries, or formulate new theories, or do

some of their best work relatively late in their lives (although this is the exception, not the rule). The important point is that with increasing age such people can and do remain intellectually active.

The second fact to remember in interpreting Figure 16.12 is that the curve repre-

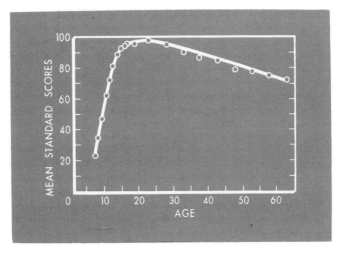

FIGURE 16.12 Changes in Intelligence Test Scores With Age (After Wechsler, 1958).

sents average performance on *all* subtests of an intelligence test. Not all abilities decline at the same rate, a contention supported by the two graphs in Figure 16.13. The graph on the left indicates that verbal tests resist the effects of age better than performance tests. The graph on the right compares the changes in performance due to age on three subtests: information, arithmetic, and block designs. Performance on the information test declines much less steeply than performance on the block designs.

The third fact to remember is one that emphasizes once again the distinction between intelligence and IQ, or brightness. When it is stated that the mean performance of a group of 60-year-olds is lower than that of a group of 30-year-olds, reference is being made to the total number of correct responses made on the same test. If you

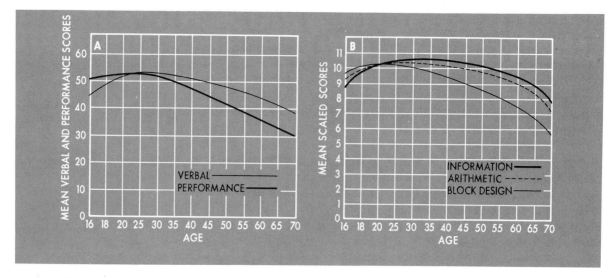

FIGURE 16.13 Change in Performance on Sections of the WAIS With Age. The graph on the left shows the comparative decline of verbal and performance subtests, while the graph on the right illustrates the variation of scores on different subtests (After Wechsler, 1958).

recall, however, Wechsler deliberately built his test so that the average IQ for every age group is 100. Therefore, a person's IQ at age 60 does not change simply because he answers fewer questions correctly than he did at 40. The practical advantage to be gained from this arrangement is that it allows comparison of an individual with members of his own age group.

Environmental Influences on Intelligence Test Performance. Perhaps the most common misconception concerning intelligence tests is that they measure innate capacity that is unmodifiable by experience. This belief is wrong on two counts. First, it distorts the meaning of heredity. What is inherited is not a capacity but genes which influence physiological development (see page 100). The structure of our nervous systems, just like the color of our eyes, is determined to some extent by genes. But at every stage of development environmental factors interact with these genetic influences and modify them. To pit hereditary and environmental

influences against each other is pointless, for they interact.

Second, the belief that heredity by itself governs performance on intelligence tests is inconsistent with the facts. Anyone who is familiar with the content of an intelligence test can see that environmental influences must play some role in performance on them. Consider the item on the Stanford-Binet that asks a child to identify a stove and refrigerator. Obviously, a child who lives in a shack without either gas or electricity has much less opportunity than another child to learn the names of these appliances, and a person who grew up in a small, isolated, impoverished town with a poor school system and no library did not have the same opportunity as a person who lived in a wealthy suburban community to learn the meaning of the words that appear in the vocabulary portion of most intelligence tests.

It is not necessary, however, to argue this point. Facts can be offered to prove it. Many studies have shown that intelligence test performance can be influenced by experience. They are of two kinds: those that show that an impoverished environment can lower IQ and those that show that a stimulating environment can raise it.

Intellectually Impoverished Environments. Psychologists have studied children who have been isolated from normal educational opportunities and cultural stimulation, children raised in isolated mountain communities, children living in houseboats along the Thames River in London, and children of gypsies. The results of these studies show consistently that the average IQ of these children is far below the national average. An obvious explanation might be that the children inherit the genetic inadequacy of their parents, who are of low intellectual caliber. But such an argument does not explain all the evidence. Not only is the average IQ of these children low, but it *declines with age*. The longer a child remains in an unstimulating environment, the lower his IQ becomes. If heredity were the only factor at work, you might expect his IQ to be low and to remain at the same level. That it declines is evidence that an impoverished environment can have a cumulative effect on an IQ. If this interpretation is correct, the average IQ in an isolated community should rise when the schooling is suddenly improved. This is exactly what happened in one mountain community. In a period of ten years after the school system had been improved, the average IQ of the children increased ten points (Wheeler, 1932).

Other evidence to support the idea that an unstimulating environment can depress the IQ comes from studies (Stoddard, 1943) showing a decline in IQ with continuing residence in orphanages, homes for juvenile delinquents, and institutions for the feebleminded. The environmental influence is not indicated by below-average IQ's to begin with, *but by their gradual decline with age*. In normal environments, IQ scores, regardless of whether they are above or below average, tend to remain stable over the years.

This evidence should not be taken to mean that all institutional environments have the effect of depressing the IQ. In fact, there is no inherent reason why institutional life cannot be made as stimulating as the average home environment. The truth is, however, that most state institutions operate on such lean budgets that they cannot provide the personnel and facilities required.

Intellectually Stimulating Environments. If impoverished environments can depress IQ's, stimulating environments can raise them. As you will see, however, there seem to be limits to the amount of increase that can be brought about. It seems easier to depress a child's IQ than to raise it.

Evidence on the effects of improved educational environments supports the belief that stimulating environments can improve IQ's. Studies (Wellman, 1945) of children going to good nursery schools show that they gain, on an average, 5 IQ points when compared to control children who do not go to nursery school. However, these studies have been criticized for their failure to control all relevant variables (McNemar, 1940; 1945). The average IQ of children tested in Hawaii was significantly higher in 1938 than in 1924 (Smith, 1942). During this time there was a marked improvement in educational opportunities, particularly for learning of English. Finally, there is the study (Lorge, 1945) of a group of children whose intelligence was measured when they were in the eighth grade and 20 years later. For subjects whose intelligence was initially equal, the later scores varied with the amount of schooling. Those who went to college had higher IQ's than those who did not. Presumably the more intellectually stimulating college life had an effect.

Improving the home environment seems also to have a beneficial effect on IQ. Several studies have sought to *estimate* the effect on a child's IQ of placement in a foster home. In one such study (Skodak & Skeels, 1949) the IQ's of children in foster homes were compared with those of their natural mothers. Normally the IQ's of children and their mothers are roughly equal. Hence, if IQ were not influenced by environmental factors, one could expect children raised in foster homes to have IQ's roughly equal to their natural mothers. However, the children in this study achieved IQ's of about 20 points higher, a difference attributed to the new and superior environment they enjoyed. Social agencies responsible for placing babies for adoption usually select homes that are psychologically stable and in the upper socioeconomic levels. We must emphasize that this study does not show that the IQ of the foster child was *raised*. These children were placed in the foster home during infancy, and their performance on their very first IQ test was considerably higher than their mothers'. Their IQ is simply higher than would have been expected had they been raised with their mothers. Other studies (Burks, 1923, Leahy, 1935) with foster children also suggest that beneficial effects accrue from stimulating home environments, although these studies fail to provide quantitative data on the size of the resulting change in IQ. One study suggested that placing young children in good foster homes, after they have spent time in an orphanage, increased their IQ's, on an average, by about ten points (Skodak, 1939).

Although we have shown that environmental factors can influence scores on intelligence tests, you must be careful not to overgeneralize for several reasons. First, many individuals who have been reared in extremely favorable environments turn out to have low IQ's. Apparently no amount of environmental stimulation can help them to improve their IQ's appreciably. Second,

many of the changes in IQ produced by transfer from a deprived environment to one more favorable should be considered as evidence of the meagerness of the environment from which the child came quite as much as of the stimulation of the improved environment to which he was transferred. Some children have such a stimulating environment at home that school has no discernable effect on their test performances. Third and last, the improvement in IQ that we have been discussing is usually very modest. This means simply that there seem to be definite limits beyond which no amount of stimulation or training can produce any additional improvement. This point was illustrated long ago by a case that has remained a classic (Itard, 1962).

In 1798 a savage boy who appeared to be about ten years of age was found living like an animal in the woods of southern France. He walked on all fours, ate like an animal, and made unintelligible noises. The most devoted effort was made to educate him. For a period of five years he received intensive training in reading and writing and made limited progress. Although he learned to say a few words and read a little, he never rose above the level of a mental defective. There is no way of knowing the relative contributions of heredity and environment to his intellectual inadequacy. But whatever they were, the handicaps produced by their combined effects could not be overcome by the more favorable environment.

Influences of Heredity on Intelligence Test Performance. That environmental factors can exert an influence on intelligence test performance is no reason for believing that factors of heredity cannot. Actually their influence is powerful.

Probably the clearest and most direct evidence in support of the determination of intelligence by genetic factors comes from an experiment using rats as subjects (Tryon, 1940). When you find out what was done you will see why the same study cannot be duplicated with humans.

Over one hundred rats were given a series of trials in a complicated maze in which there were many choice points. The measure of a rat's learning was the total number of errors he made, that is, the total number of times he entered the blind alleys. The smallest number of errors made by one rat was seven, the largest, 214. The distribution of these scores is shown in the upper graph of Figure 16.14. Those rats that made the fewest errors were considered *bright;* the ones that made the most errors were considered *dull.*

The experimenter then bred the brightest rats with each other and the dullest with each other. He repeated this for 18 generations, selecting bright and dull in each generation by the same method. By the seventh generation the distribution of error scores had become bimodal in shape. In subsequent generations the difference between the two strains did not increase. Figure 16.14 shows that selective breeding had produced two distinct populations; bright and dull rats. The difference between the two strains can be safely attributed to heredity, since the environments of the bright and dull rats were exactly alike. It can be concluded that in the typical laboratory environment genetic factors determine the intelligence of rats, intelligence being operationally defined in this experiment as the number of errors they made while learning the maze.

This is an ideal kind of experiment for reaching an unequivocal conclusion concerning the contribution of heredity to intelligence. Several reports of human families have been published which purport to show that high or low intellectual ability tends to run in particular families. Unlike the experiment with rats, these studies suffer from two major defects. First, the families involved cannot be considered selected strains. The selection of mates in these families was not strictly controlled as

it was in the animal study. The second defect is that the environments in which the bright and dull families lived differed tremendously. The families were dissimilar in respect to both socioeconomic level and opportunities for intellectual stimulation as provided by education, number of books in the home, and so forth.

If we wish to discover something about the genetic determination of human intel-

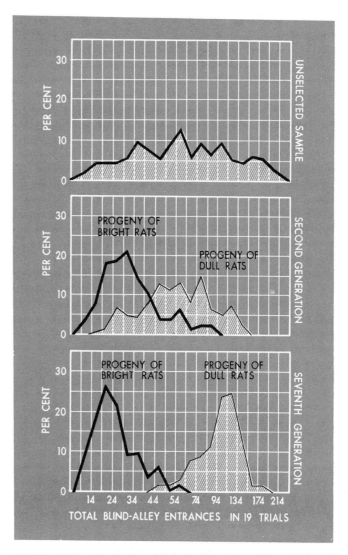

FIGURE 16.14. The Results of Selective Breeding of Maze-Dull and Maze-Bright Rats. By the seventh generation there were two distinct populations (After Tryon, 1940).

624

ligence the best we can do is to resort to indirect evidence. The most persuasive data come from studies of twins. As you undoubtedly know there are two kinds of twins, identical and fraternal. Identical twins, always the same sex, develop from one fertilized egg, and hence from precisely the same hereditary material. Fraternal twins, who are not always the same sex, develop from two different fertilized eggs. Genetically speaking, they are as different from each other as are ordinary siblings.

Table 16.2 shows the degree of resemblance in the heights of children of the same parents. It shows that identical twins re-

TABLE 16.2 Degree of Resemblance in Height of Children of the Same Parents (Newman, Freeman, & Holzinger, 1937).

PAIRS OF CHILDREN	NUMBER OF PAIRS	COEFFICIENT OF CORRELATION (r)
Ordinary siblings (like-sexed)	52	+.60
Fraternal twins (like-sexed)	52	+.64
Identical twins	50	+.93

semble each other in height much more closely than do fraternal twins, and that the degree of similarity between the heights of fraternal twins is about the same as that between ordinary siblings. This is evidence for the genetic determination of height. Otherwise, one would expect that like-sexed siblings born at different times might, perhaps because of different nutritional conditions, differ in height significantly more than would fraternal twins of the same sex.

Table 16.3 shows the resemblances between the IQ's of the same three kinds of siblings. Again we find the greatest resemblance between identical twins, although the correlation is somewhat less than that for height. In the case of intelligence, however, the fraternal twins are more alike than the ordinary siblings. Since there is

no genetic reason for this, it may be attributable to the greater similarity in the environments in which they grew up.

TABLE 16.3 Degree of Resemblance in IQ's of Children of the Same Parents (McNemar, 1942; Newman, Freeman, & Holzinger, 1937).

PAIRS OF CHILDREN	NUMBER OF PAIRS	COEFFICIENT OF CORRELATION (r)
Ordinary siblings	384	+.53
Fraternal twins (like-sexed)	52	+.63
Identical twins	50	+.88

Knowing that there is greater genetic similarity between identical twins than between fraternal twins, we may *reasonably* conclude that the greater correlation between the IQ's of the former is genetically determined. But cannot it be argued that the environments of identical twins are more alike than environments of fraternal twins? Because of their similar appearance they are often treated as a pair instead of as two independent children. This argument cannot be rejected, although there is evidence that would argue against this interpretation. An extensive search was undertaken to locate identical twins who had been separated from each other early in life (Newman, Freeman, & Holzinger, 1937). Nineteen pairs were located, and when they were brought together they were found to be strikingly similar in appearance, even when differences in grooming and dress were great. Figure 16.15 shows two 23-year-old identical twins who had been separated at two months of age. The twin on the left had lived in towns or cities all his life, finished high school when he was 18, and took some business courses while holding a job. His brother spent most of his time in a rural environment. He, too, completed high school at 18 and had one year of college, but dropped out because he had difficulty with mathematics. He became an assistant postmaster.

FIGURE 16.15 Identical Twins Reared Apart. These twins were separated when they were two months old. The twin on the left was raised in an urban environment, while the other one grew up in rural surroundings. When tested at 23 years of age, their IQ's differed by two points (Newman, 1929. Reprinted by special permission of the *Journal of Heredity*).

When tested these twins obtained IQ's that were only two points apart. The average difference in IQ for identical twins reared apart was found to be eight points, as against six points for those reared together. More important, the resemblance in intelligence of identical twins raised apart was higher (r = +.77) than for fraternal twins raised together (r = +.63).

These data are strong evidence for the role of heredity in determining the IQ's of the twins reared apart. That there is a lower correlation between the intelligence scores of identical twins reared apart than there is between those reared together (+.77 versus +.88) suggests that environmental factors also have an effect. This lower correlation for twins reared apart was largely due to four pairs of identical twins who were reared in highly contrasting environments. In one of these pairs, IQ differed by 24

points. Obviously, then, identical twins cannot be said to be predestined to have similar IQ's regardless of environmental factors.

The Nature-Nurture Controversy

Here, some students become dissatisfied, confused, or both. They wonder whether they are being asked to believe two contradictory things. First they are shown that environmental factors influence IQ scores. Then they are shown that genetic factors also play a role. They want to know which it is that determines IQ: heredity or environment—**nature** or **nurture,** as they are sometimes called. Since they are still asking this question, the basic point of the discussion has obviously not been made sufficiently clear.

Behavior on an intelligence test—or for that matter, any other sort of behavior—cannot be attributed solely to the influence of either hereditary or environmental variables. At every stage of development, prenatal and postnatal, genetic and environmental variables interact. For example, identical twins experience greater differences in environment during gestation than do fraternal twins. This is evidenced by the fact that at birth identical twins differ more in size, because both identical twins feed off the same blood supply and they often do not receive equal shares of nourishment. The imbalance can be sufficiently great to produce structural defects in one. In this way, a genetic similarity can be wiped out by an environmental difference.

Once you realize that the nature-nurture controversy cannot be resolved by attributing differences in IQ exclusively to either heredity or environment, your next question will be, "Is it possible to know how much each contributes to any person's IQ?" This question cannot be answered simply because it is not a single question, but contains instead a multiplicity of questions, each requiring a different answer. To illustrate, let us consider the cause of illiteracy, which is in this country highly related to low IQ. Does heredity contribute more than environment, or environment more than heredity? In India the answer would definitely be environment, for most of the illiteracy there can be traced to inadequate schooling. This means simply that most Indians have the genetic potential to read and write, but their environment often does not permit them to realize their potential. In the United States many cases of illiteracy can be traced to hereditary deficiencies. The opportunity to learn to read and write exists for practically everybody. Inability to read is due in the main to low intellectual aptitude brought about by defective heredity or prenatal or postnatal injuries.

Hence, when we consider whether environment or heredity plays a more important role in determining IQ, we are forced to limit our conclusions to *specific* comparisons in *specific* situations. For example, one form the question can take is whether genetic inheritance or socioeconomic level plays a more important role in determining an individual's IQ score. Assuming you know his socioeconomic level and the IQ of his identical twin who was reared apart from him, which of these two bits of knowledge is more useful in predicting the individual's IQ? Since there is a higher correlation between the person's IQ and that of his identical twin than there is between his IQ and his socioeconomic level, we can conclude that the genetic factor plays the greater role. Or, consider another question: Is heredity more important in determining a person's physique, his IQ, or his personality? The identical twin study obtained data relevant to this question. There was greater similarity, as indicated by correlation coefficients, between measures of physical characteristics than measures of IQ. But the twins' IQ scores correlated more highly than their scores on a group of personality tests. In this case, then we can conclude that physical characteristics are most influenced by heredity, intellectual factors, as measured by an IQ test, somewhat less, and personality, as measured by a group of personality tests, least of all.

The extreme caution and specificity that characterize all sensible statements about the influences of heredity and environment on behavior highlights the point that these do not operate as single variables. Since they represent broad classes of factors which require analysis into component parts, it is not possible to attribute test scores to one or the other. At this stage of our knowledge it would seem that the most appropriate summary of the facts indicates that heredity provides the potential for a person's IQ, and environment interacts with this potential to create the final product. The degree of stimulation provided by environment varies widely. At one extreme are environments completely barren of human influences, where "wild" children have been raised in forests without any apparent contacts with civilization. Although the genetic background of these children is unknown, all reported cases (except the fictitious Tarzan) have shown severe amounts of mental deficiency which could not be entirely eradicated by even the most careful subsequent training.

At the other extreme is the environment to which John Stuart Mill (1806-1873) was exposed. This noted English philosopher, describing the education he received from his father, a famous philosopher in his own right, wrote as follows:

... a considerable part of almost every day was employed in the instruction of his children: in the case of one of whom, myself, he exerted an amount of labour, care, and perseverance rarely, if ever, employed for a similar purpose, in endeavouring to give, according to his own conception, the highest order of intellectual education.

A man who, in his own practice, so vigorously acted up to the principle of losing no time, was likely to adhere to the same rule in the instruction of his pupil. I have no remembrance of the time when I began to learn Greek, I have been told that it was when I was three years old. My earliest recollection on the subject, is that of committing to memory what my father termed vocables, being lists of common Greek words, with their signification in English, which he wrote out for me on cards. Of grammar, until some years later, I learnt no more than the inflexions of the nouns and verbs, but after a course of vocables, proceeded at once to translation; and I faintly remember going through Aesop's *Fables,* the first Greek book which I read. The *Anabasis,* which I remember better, was the second. I learnt no Latin until my eighth year. At that time I had read, under my father's tuition, a number of Greek prose authors, among whom I remember the whole of Herodotus, and of Xenophon's *Cyropaedia* and *Memorials* of Socrates; some of the lives of the philosophers by Diogenes Laertius; part of Lucian, and Isocrates and Demonicum and Ad Nicoclem. I also read, in 1813, the first six dialogues (in the common arrangement) of Plato, from the *Euthyphron* to the *Theoctetus* inclusive: which last dialogue, I venture to think, would have been better omitted, as it was totally impossible I should understand it. But my father, in all his teaching, demanded of me not only the utmost that I could do, but much that I could by no possibility have done ...

The only thing besides Greek, that I learnt as a lesson in this part of my childhood, was arithmetic: this also my father taught me: it was the task of the evenings, and I remember its disagreeableness. But the lessons were only a part of the daily instruction I received. Much of it consisted in the books I read by myself, and my father's discourses to me, chiefly during our walks ... (Mill, 1924, pp. 4-5).

Although very few individuals could profit from such an early and intensive education, there is reason to believe that the capacities of many children, and particularly bright ones, have not been developed fully. In a society interested in getting people to function at their highest possible intellectual level, it is obviously desirable to provide stimulating environments for all.

Racial Differences in Intelligence. The question of whether there are racial differences in intelligence is for many people an emotionally laden one. Strong beliefs and attitudes are sometimes confused with factual answers. In order to understand what the facts are and what they mean, we must put aside preconceptions about racial differences.

The first task in any discussion is to clarify the chief terms involved in it. For the present topic there are two crucial terms: *intelligence* and *race*. The former can be defined by performance on intelligence tests. How can race be defined? There is no universally accepted answer to this question.

Definitions based on a single criterion, such as skin color, have limited value. The quality of skin color differs so much that it is very difficult to assign many individuals to a certain racial group on the basis of it alone. There are many dark "white" people and light "dark" people. And among the darker skinned people it is often impossible to distinguish South American Indians, Arabs, Asiatic Indians, or American Negroes solely on the basis of color.

In an effort to achieve clear demarcations between races, other criteria besides skin pigmentation have been proposed. These include shape of head, body build, texture of hair, eye color, amount of body hair, and shape of eyes. Many of these characteristics are independent of each other. Thus when a combination of physical characteristics are employed to define race, the resulting classification will depend on what characteristics have been arbitrarily selected. Skin pigmentation in combination with texture of hair will provide a different assortment of races than the combined characteristics of shape of head and body build.

Many geneticists have concluded that if we are going to talk about **race** we must define it in terms of clearly known genetic characteristics. In line with this view is the definition that ". . . a human race is a population which differs significantly from other human populations in regards to the frequency of one or more of the genes it possesses" (Boyd, 1950; p. 207). This method of defining a race obviously rests upon some technique of identifying different genes. Physical characteristics, like shape of head, are not particularly useful because their genetic mechanisms are not known, but the genetic mechanisms responsible for several different kinds of blood groupings are fully understood. Combined with other easily identified genetic characteristics, they

have served as the basis for a classification consisting of six races: Early European, European (Caucasoid), African (Negroid), Asiatic (Mongoloid), American Indian, and Australoid (Boyd, 1950).

We must not think that the divisions among these six races are absolutely sharp. They are defined in terms of frequency of certain genes (inferred from characteristics of the blood) *in a population, not in an individual.* For example, although the early European group, which is represented by their modern descendants, the Basques, have a relatively high incidence of one blood gene (the Rh negative type), this same gene is practically absent in the Mongoloid group. But, there are many Basques who do not possess this gene and some Asiatics who do.

It is not surprising that the examination of genetic characteristics of different populations fails to provide fixed lines of demarcation among them. Humans from all over the world are interfertile, that is, they can mate and have offspring. And in the numerous migrations that have occurred throughout the history of mankind this is what has happened. Europe has often been subject to migrations and invasions from Asia and North Africa, and many groups have invaded China only to disappear after centuries of interbreeding. Even in America, despite social and legal barriers, whites and Negroes have always interbred.

Another point that should be obvious, but is not, is that nationalities or religious groups do not represent unitary racial groups. There is no such thing as "the English race," "the Italian race," "the German race," or "the American white race." None of these groups possess genetic characteristics markedly different from the other.

Among religious groups, there is even less genetic homogeneity. Although many people conceive of the Jews as a racially distinct group, they are not. They have intermarried with other groups in spite of historical pressures against their doing so from within their own group and from outside it. The blood characteristics of the Yemenite Jews from Northern Africa, for example, are more similar to those of neighboring Arabs than they are to those of European Jews. Similarly the "Black Jews" from Cochin, India, show closer resemblance to their Hindu neighbors than to other Jews. The Jewish group with blood characteristics most distinctive from their neighbors are Ashkenazi Jews from Eastern Europe who lived in isolated communities possessing a language and culture markedly different from their neighbors. Nevertheless, their blood characteristics do not form a unique group.

Thus when the concept of race is used three points must be kept in mind: (1) there is no such thing as a race whose genetic characteristics are uniquely different from all other races; (2) the demarcation between races is not very sharp; and (3) national and religious groups are not racial groups.

Now we come to racial differences in intelligence. Because intelligence tests have been more extensively used in the United States than in other countries, the bulk of the work on racial differences in intelligence has been done here. The greater part of this work has been concerned with differences between Negroes and whites, and we shall limit our discussion to this topic. However, many of the general principles that emerge in the course of reviewing this work apply to all racial differences in IQ.

The first question we must answer is What are the facts about the average IQ of Negroes and whites? To be brief: in most comparisons whites earn a higher average IQ. Properly randomized groups of white children come up with what the tests were designed to give: a mean IQ of 100. In general, the average IQ of Negro children ranges from the low 80's to the middle 90's. But you know by now that averages ignore that very important characteristic

of a distribution of scores—the way in which the scores are dispersed about the measure of central tendency. Figure 16.16 shows the distribution of scores obtained in one study done in Kent County, Ontario, Canada (Tanser, 1939). As you see, there is a great deal of overlap between the Negro and white distributions. Eighteen per cent of the white children earned lower

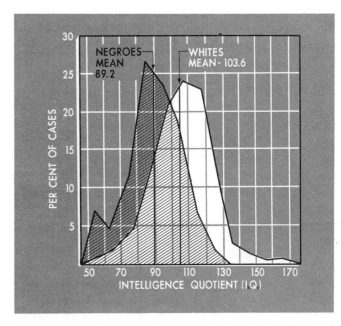

FIGURE 16.16 The Distribution of the IQ's of a Sample of White and Negro Children in Kent County, Ontario, Canada (After Tanser, 1939).

IQ's than did the average Negro child, while 22 per cent of the Negro children obtained higher IQ's than the average white child. Moreover, individual Negro children have obtained IQ's as high as 200. It is manifestly absurd to conclude in advance of testing that any specific white child is brighter than any specific Negro child. Neither skin color nor hair texture nor facial appearance nor a pattern of genetic blood characteristics is a guide to IQ.

A test score gives no indication of the cause of the behavior it measures. As you should know by now, the difference between test scores cannot be attributed solely to environment or to heredity, unless by some exceptional means one of these sets of variables has been kept constant, as with identical twins. Before the average difference in IQ repeatedly found between Negroes and whites can be interpreted as evidence of genetic differences, it has to be proved that no differences in environment have produced that effect. Can we assume that there are no environmental differences which could bring about the average difference in IQ between Negroes and whites? Apparently not. Negroes occupy a lower socioeconomic level than do whites, and IQ is highly correlated with this measure. A few studies have attempted to control this factor. One study (see Figure 16.16) was conducted is an environment in which racial discrimination was at a minimum, though some did exist. The schools were integrated and the socioeconomic status of the two groups was *almost* alike. However, there is another important set of variables that are difficult to measure, but most certainly play an important role. These variables are the difference in cultural tradition. They can exert strong pressures on children by shaping their social motivations. The Negro is short on European-American cultural traditions. His cultural history has been cloudy, his traditions, vague and weakened by the uncertainties of his social status. This should not surprise you, when you realize that some Negroes who were born slaves are still living. In the typical Negro home there has never been as much emphasis on formal education and intellectual pursuits as in homes of other cultural groups. That the pattern of success among Negroes has been largely in the fields of athletics and entertainment would of itself tend to steer the Negro child into relatively nonintellectual activities. So even if an investigator seeks to find equal environments, in which Negro and white children may be compared, he

will probably not succeed because he will be unable to control all the relevant factors.

Another approach to the problem, one where no attempt is made to equate the environments of Negroes and whites, is to discover whether improving the environment of Negroes tends to increase their IQ. A number of studies have demonstrated that the IQ's of Negro children whose parents have moved from the South to the North, where presumably they have better educational opportunities, do increase. In one of these studies (Lee, 1951), performed in the Philadelphia schools, it was found that the longer Southern-born Negroes stay in the Philadelphia schools, the higher their IQ's become. Children who entered the first grade received an average IQ of 86.5. The figure rose to 89.3 in the second grade and to 91.8 and 93.3 in the fourth and sixth grades, respectively. Southern-born Negro children who entered the Philadelphia schools later improved their IQ's but failed to catch up with those who moved to the North earlier, a finding that demonstrates once again the influence of early intellectual stimulation on IQ.

The importance of cultural influences on IQ is not something we surmise but is based soundly on fact. When an intelligence test was administered to university students in Ceylon, the Ceylonese greatly surpassed the norms of the American students in the verbal portion of the test, but fell far below them in the nonlanguage tests (Straus, 1951). A reasonable explanation of this is that in upper-class Ceylonese society, from which the university students came, the highest prestige attaches to "book learning" or verbal scholarship, while manual tasks are held in disdain. A similar situation prevails in the United States among Jewish children, who consistently perform much better on verbal tests than on performance tests. Traditional Jewish cultural values emphasize scholarly achievement. A study (Brown, 1944) carried out in Minneapolis with Jewish and Scandinavian children equated for socioeconomic status revealed that the Jewish children were superior on tests of verbal comprehension and information, whereas the Scandinavian children excelled in tests requiring spatial orientation and sensorimotor coordination. Another study (Levinson, 1959) showed that as Jewish children grow older, the discrepancy between their verbal and performance intelligence test scores becomes greater.

Are we justified, then, in drawing the conclusion that there is no genetic difference between the intelligence of Negroes and whites on the grounds that (1) environmental stimulation influences IQ scores, (2) the environments of Negroes and whites are not comparable, and (3) improvement in the surroundings of Negroes results in higher IQ's? Although the data reviewed suggest that equivalent environments might produce equal IQ's between these two groups, this has not been conclusively proven. The only valid conclusion that can be drawn from the evidence is a negative one, namely, *there is no definite proof that the obtained differences between the average Negro IQ and the average white IQ are due to genetic factors.* The conclusion that an innate difference has been demonstrated would be as false as the conclusion that those Northern Negroes who have a higher average IQ than the whites in some Southern communities are "racially superior."

The truth is that it is impossible, at the present time, to provide an unequivocal answer about any racial differences in intelligence. Environmental factors play a role in determining IQ scores, and there is no known way of equating the environments of different racial groups. If this question is to be answered in the future, one of two things must be done. Equal environments must be arranged for the two racial groups, or some physiological measure of intellectual potential (such as a physiochemical characteristic of the central nervous system) must be devised. It is difficult

to imagine how the first alternative can be realized in the near future. Perhaps the second possibility offers the best hope of some sort of answer to this question. But even if an answer were forthcoming, its interpretation would pose new problems. If racial differences did show up, they would have to be attributed to differences in the races at the present time. The history of races covers many thousands of years. Conceivably, two races might have been genetically equivalent in intelligence at one time, but because of different historical and environmental pressures the selective breeding that took place in one race instigated a higher reproductive rate among its brighter members than among its duller members. In this way, genetic differences among races could be found which earlier had been absent.

It is not the business of scientists to prescribe the ethical principles which should guide the policies of a nation, especially a democratic nation. What scientists can do is ascertain facts which have a bearing upon how social conventions should be judged by the members of the society. The argument that segregation is justified because of innate intellectual differences between Negroes and whites collapses upon close examination. If children were separated in classes and schools solely on the basis of the scores they earned on intelligence tests, racial segregation would disappear, because many Negro students have high IQ's and many whites have low IQ's.

The Genius and the Gifted

One unhappy error in the history of intelligence testing was made by psychologists who used the word *genius* to describe an individual who achieved a very high IQ (usually above 140). This has caused much confusion, because it implied that every individual with that high an IQ would become famous by dint of some world-shaking intellectual effort. And when this

632

did not happen—as it usually did not—the proud parents were disappointed and the "genius" perceived himself a failure.

It is much more sensible to describe the 1 per cent of children who score above 140 as *gifted,* reserving the term *genius* for individuals who are preeminently creative. The adjective *gifted,* then, implies high aptitude; *genius* implies very great and original achievement.

Psychologists have sought to discover, on the one hand, what makes gifted persons geniuses and, on the other, what happens to children whose very high IQ's prove that they are intellectually gifted. These are questions of obvious interest to college students, who prize and respect intellectual achievement, and of momentous practical significance. A nation can hardly be said to have a greater resource than her pool of gifted children. These children can be given the training that will permit them to realize their potential and make their maximum contribution to society, or stupidly—and today dangerously—they can be ignored, and their talents allowed to go to waste. But before we come to this problem we must first review what psychologists have discovered about the genius and the gifted, in order that the problem of training gifted children can be discussed in the light of facts.

The Psychology of Genius. Our folklore, all the way down to the comics, is filled with portrayals of the kind of person a genius is supposed to be. The genius is "crazy." He is stupid in everything but his one narrow specialty, he lacks common sense and is difficult to live with. He has spindly legs and his head is much too large. In short, he is a freak. Since these descriptions do not correspond with the facts, one wonders about how much rationalization is responsible for them.

The fact is that geniuses, whether artists, writers, or scientists, if not always easy to understand, are as easy to live with as most people. That does not mean, of course, that there are no "problem geniuses." Eugene O'Neill, the famous American playwright, was described by his second wife as self-centered, impetuous, unpredictable, and often rude. He was not averse to slapping her face. Vincent Van Gogh, the Dutch painter, went mad and finally killed himself. Edgar Allen Poe was an alcoholic, Fyodor Dostoyevski an obsessive gambler, and Samuel Taylor Coleridge, a drug addict. Henrik Ibsen, the Norwegian playwright, was a tyrant in his own family and so vain that he often fastened a mirror to his hat to admire himself as he sat in the park. But in contrast to these "characters" were Aristotle, Copernicus, and Dante, whose rational and agreeable behavior was completely at odds with what might be described as the "mad theory" of genius. Louis Pasteur, the medical genius, lived a simple, productive life dedicated to helping his fellow man. Darwin was described by one of his children as "affectionate and delightful." Sigmund Freud, although at times "difficult" if we listen to some of his colleagues, was much admired and loved by his children. And finally, Albert Einstein was a fine person—gentle, kind, considerate, well-liked by everybody. The conclusion is inescapable: a genius need not be mad, or even terribly odd.

What about the intellectual ability of the genius? Is it very great? If it were possible to measure the IQ's of geniuses, what scores would they achieve? In one attempt to answer these questions, historical data available for a group of 300 eminent persons whose fame was achieved through intellectual efforts was examined. The minimal IQ (in the interest of conservatism) that could reasonably account for their accomplishments was then estimated (Cox, 1926). For example, in Karl Pearson's biography (1914) of Francis Galton, the noted English anthropologist, psychologist, and geneticist, a well-documented description is given of Galton's early intellectual accomplishments. Francis learned to read at the age of two-and-a-half, and was able to write a letter before he was four. At the ripe old age of five he could read most English books and some French books. He knew his multiplication tables but had some difficulty with the 9's and 11's. He also could tell time and understood the rather complicated English monetary system.

Since the Stanford-Binet test includes items which test a child's vocabulary, mathematical ability, and knowledge of everyday skills, the information in Pearson's biography provides the basis for a fairly reliable estimate of what Galton's IQ would have been had he been tested as a child. The *minimum* IQ that could account for Galton's early achievement was estimated at 200, a score earned by only one child in every 50,000. Pearson was apparently so unaware of the significance of Galton's outstanding early performance that he could naively write, "I do not think we can say more than that Francis Galton was a normal child with rather more than average ability."

For the entire group of 300 geniuses the estimated *minimum* IQ's ranged from 100 to 200, with the mean at 155. This average is approximately three standard deviations above the mean of 100. An IQ of 155 or above occurs approximately once in every 800 cases. Most of the estimated minimum IQ's that fell between 100 and 120 were for individuals for whom there was little biographical data. Their true IQ's were almost certainly underestimated.

When the entire group of geniuses was divided into subgroups on the basis of professional affiliations, the philosophers were found to have the highest mean IQ (170) and the soldiers, the lowest (125). In between, in descending order, were literary figures and revolutionary statesmen (160), scientists (155), musicians (145), and artists (140).

You must realize, of course, that we cannot place the confidence in these estimates that we place in scores obtained from the best intelligence tests properly given. Many were based on information far short of what would have been desirable. Nevertheless, the data are sufficient to support the main conclusion of the study: namely, that a genius is a person who, if given an intelligence test in childhood, will be identified as gifted. The converse of this is not true; not every child who scores high on an intelligence test becomes eminent. Geniuses are not only characterized by exceptional intelligence, but "by persistence of motive and effort, confidence in their abilities and great strength or force of character" (Terman, 1940). We would expect this because, by definition, a genius is a person who creates something new. As an innovator he would have to be a radical nonconformist in his own field, to persist in his unusual way of doing things. Otherwise, he would not become a genius.

The study offers no consolation to those who believe, or hope, that geniuses "flower late." Oliver Goldsmith, the gifted English writer, was described as being dull in his childhood. Yet Goldsmith wrote clever verse when he was seven and read Horace and Ovid when he was eight. Sir Walter Scott is supposed to have been a dunce in school, but when he was seven years old his prose included words like *melancholy* and *exotic,* and at 13 he lay awake nights reading Shakespeare.

Another important common element in the lives of geniuses is that they are usually brought up in circumstances in which their extraordinary talents could achieve fruition. If they are not, luck often intervenes. At 15 Isaac Newton had already left school and was tending his mother's farm, apparently beginning a career as a farmer. A fortunate visit from an uncle who had attended Cambridge University opened up an opportunity for him to receive the education so necessary to his later formulation of the physical theories of gravitation and motion. Faraday left school at 13 and a year later became an apprentice bookbinder. While working on an encyclopedia he chanced to read the article on electricity. This fired his imagination and with the help of a friend, his career as a scientist began.

The Psychology of the Gifted. In studying the genius we look backwards for the roots of his greatness. In studying the gifted child we have to look into the future.

In the early 1920's Lewis Terman and his associates (1925) began a long-range study of a group of gifted children in California. At that time a school population of more than one-quarter million students was sifted for all those who had IQ's of 140 and above—a score that is obtained in the general population by only one person in about every 100. Fifteen hundred were discovered. They had an average IQ of 150, 80 of them with IQ's of 170 or higher.

The first popular misconception this study dispelled was that bright children tend to be weak and unhealthy. They are neither. The gifted child, in general, proves to be physically and medically superior to the average child. He is also better adjusted, as indicated by personality tests. His school work, as we would expect, is outstanding, and for the most part he excels not in one or two subjects but in all subjects. Marked unevenness in performance is the exception rather than the rule.

The major aim of the study was to observe the development of this group of gifted children as they matured. In order to do this, extensive surveys of their behavior and achievements were carried out in 1927-28, 1939-40, and 1951-52, the latest being when the gifted children, identified thirty years earlier, had reached the age of about 45. On each of the successive follow-ups much the same picture of the gifted person was obtained: in incidence of mortality, ill health, crime, psychiatric disturbances including alcoholism, and divorce, they were definitely below the general population of the same age. Their intellectual level, as measured by an adult intelligence test, remained far above average. In contrast to the results obtained from the general population, the scores of this gifted group tended to rise with age.

The educational and professional achievements of this group have been impressive. On the average they entered high school at age 13 and college at 17. Nearly 90 per cent attended college and 70 per cent graduated, percentages far above those for the general population. In college the gifted engaged more extensively in extra-curricular activities, received more honors from their fellow students, and many more graduated with distinction. Of those who graduated from college, approximately two-thirds of the men and one-half of the women went on to graduate work. Of 800 men who in 1950 averaged 40 years of age, 78 had earned a Ph.D. degree or its equivalent, 48 had M.D.'s, and 85 had law degrees. Of the same 800, 74 were teaching or had taught in a college or university, 51 had done basic research in physical sciences or engineering, and 104 were practicing engineers. This record is some 20 times better than the typical record for a group of 800 randomly selected men of the same age. The educational record of the gifted women is also impressive when compared with other women, but it failed to match the gifted men's achievement. Less than one-tenth as many gifted women, as compared to the gifted men, received a degree higher than a Master's degree.

Another indication of the achievement of the gifted group is their literary and scientific output. The same 800 men had by 1950 published 67 books, 1400 scientific, technical, and professional articles, and over 200 short stories and plays. Not counted in this quota are hundreds of newspaper stories, editorials, and articles and radio and TV scripts. The total record makes it unmistakably clear that a high IQ in childhood is positively correlated with outstanding achievement in later life. The correlation is not perfect, for some of the gifted men wound up in humble occupations like carpenter, gas station operator, house to house canvasser, and seaman—jobs that obviously failed to tax their intellectual talents.

Why did some of the gifted succeed and others fail? In order to answer this question a definition of success based primarily on "the extent to which a subject made use of his intellectual ability" was arrived at. Listing in *Who's Who* or *American Men of Science,* literary or scientific output, important managerial or administrative positions, and outstanding intellectual work were all considered indicative of success. Earned income, in which the gifted also excelled, was included but not given heavy weight. Each gifted man was given a rating of success and then assigned to one of three groups according to whether he fell in the upper 25 per cent, the middle 50 per cent, or the lowest 25 per cent. The highest and lowest one-fourths, or what were labelled the *A* and *C* groups, were then compared to discover factors which might have had something to do with their achievement or lack of it.

The difference between average IQ's of the most and least successful were negligible both in childhood and adulthood, since all were highly selected to begin with. The sources of success or failure had to be looked for in nonintellectual factors, the family backgrounds of the two groups, for example. Terman summarizes the difference in this respect as follows:

Nearly twice as many *A* parents as *C* parents had graduated from college, and a similar difference was found between the siblings of *A*'s and *C*'s. Fathers of the *A*'s were far more often in the professional classes. The important point here is that the educational tradition was stronger in the families of the *A* group. In line with this is the fact that the Jewish element is three times as large among the *A*'s as among the *C*'s. The Jewish child is under heavy pressure

to succeed, with the result that he accomplishes more per unit of intelligence than do children of other racial stock (Terman, 1940, pp. 300-301).

The *A*'s were better adjusted than the *C*'s, as ratings of their personality traits made by teachers and parents during their childhood indicated. These differences in personality are reflected in the different marital records of the two groups. The incidence of marital discord (separation or divorce) is only one-third as high in the *A* group as in the *C* group. There had been less marital discord between parents of the *A*'s than of the *C*'s, more of the *A*'s married, and finally, the *A*'s married more intelligent women.

Thus it becomes perfectly clear that achievement in this group of gifted persons is associated with psychological stability. It follows, therefore, that if gifted individuals are to exploit their intellectual talents to the fullest, their environments must be as supportive and as free from handicapping circumstances as possible. There is no evidence here that fighting obstacles is a prerequisite for achievement. Of course, this conclusion must be restricted to groups of gifted people like these. Although some of the achievements of the gifted group have been great, we cannot say that any one of them, at least by 1950, had arrived at the point in his career where he could be called a genius. However, the biographical data on historical geniuses that we have already reviewed are consistent with the findings of this study in failing to confirm the common belief that extraordinary achievement is associated necessarily with psychological disorders often bordering on the pathological. Although the contributions of some geniuses are no doubt influenced by their disordered personalities, pathological behavior cannot be listed as the prerequisite of genius.

Some readers, particularly the girls, will have noted the almost complete absence of references to the gifted women, except for a brief mention of their educational records. What happened to them? The fact is that although girls equal and often excel boys in grades from elementary school to college, only a small minority of them choose to compete with men in the professional and business world. For women in our society there is truly a conflict between behaving like women and pursuing careers. Although the writer knows of no formal inquiry into the validity of Dorothy Parker's line, "Men seldom make passes at girls who wear glasses," there is little doubt that some of its implications are true. Many men, some of whom have no objection to women wearing glasses, are reluctant to date girls who outrank them in intelligence, education, or income. The highly intelligent girl who openly exhibits her intelligence is no doubt limiting her appeal as a potential wife. It is not surprising, therefore, that gifted young women, like other members of their sex, tend to marry and dedicate their efforts to domestic roles. Those who do not marry often select "appropriate jobs" that do not conflict with their roles as women.

When the group of gifted women was surveyed during early middle age, approximately half were housewives with no outside employment. Many of these were highly successful in avocational fields such as writing, music, and art, or in community service. Among those employed, the majority had jobs consistent with their sex role, although some had attained eminence in the sciences, arts, and professions, and still others were extremely successful in business. And there were a few who were successful in combining a career with marriage and child-rearing. For the most part, however, the woman who is capable of high intellectual achievement usually gives up her professional ambitions to devote herself to her husband, children, and home. This dedication to domestic pursuits no doubt robs the sciences, arts, and professions of much creative talent.

Intellectual Talent and Society

There has been an unfortunate tendency in the United States, blessed as it is with vast natural resources, to overlook perhaps its greatest resource—the intellectual talents of its ablest children. However regrettable this may be, it is understandable. The democratic tradition of equality is strong in this country, and any educational program which might be suspected of trying to create an intellectual aristocracy encounters much resistance. One result has been the custom in past decades of placing most gifted children in classrooms where their progress is held back by less gifted classmates. Surprisingly enough, much more concern and effort has been directed, until very recently, toward helping retarded children than toward developing the gifted. Unfortunately, the policy of looking out for the hindmost on the assumption that the foremost will take care of himself has failed.

In recent years, there has been an ever-increasing realization that if the United States is to compete successfully with the Communist nations, we must make the most of every intellectual resource. Efforts must be made to identify every gifted child so that he may be given the opportunity to develop his talents to the fullest, not only in his own interest but in his nation's interest and that of the Free World. It is becoming more and more apparent that the shortage of trained personnel in such crucial fields as mathematics and science is not due to a shortage of potential. In the 1950's it was estimated, from the results of scholastic aptitude tests, that 15 per cent of American youth could match the aptitude exhibited by the average college graduate, and 7 per cent were as able as the average Ph.D. (Russell & Cronbach, 1958). This indicates that if every person capable of graduating from college in recent years had done so, the number of college graduates would have more than doubled. By the same logic, the number of Ph.D.'s would have increased about fortyfold. Obviously more of our youth must be attracted into specialized training.

If it is agreed that we need more "brains" to survive—and there can be no doubt that today's needs will be greatly surpassed in coming decades—what is to be done? There are several areas in which we must improve our effort, and in all of them the knowledge and "know-how" of psychologists can be of assistance.

The Identification of Talent. The history of psychological testing, with its hundreds of well-controlled studies, has repeatedly demonstrated that it is possible for us to identify many kinds of talent by means of psychological tests. These tests constitute standardized situations, so that they are similar for all the students who take them, regardless of their backgrounds. Thus, they provide objective measures of present performance and serve as grounds for predicting future performance. An intelligence test, like the Stanford-Binet test, has an amazing capacity to select those who will succeed in positions demanding high-level intellectual ability. The California study of the intellectually gifted demonstrates this point. However, intelligence test scores by themselves do not go as far as we need in identifying the intellectually talented. Additional tests should be constructed to identify special skills. At the present time the nation's most pressing needs are for mathematicians, scientists, and linguists, professions that probably require somewhat different abilities. If the search for talent is to be as effective as possible, general intelligence testing must be supplemented by other tests. Perhaps one of the most challenging problems confronting psychologists who seek to identify talent is to devise techniques that are capable of selecting the potentially *creative* person— the person who can make an original and

important artistic or scientific contribution. *Creativity* in this sense is related to the term *genius* in that it refers to exceptional achievement.

In the attempt to identify the potentially creative, we must first determine to what extent creative people possess psychological characteristics in common. In one study which tried to answer this question, the personalities of many outstanding artists and scientists were evaluated (MacKinnon, 1960). Although the results fail to prove that there is any single type of creative individual, there were underlying uniformities. As a group the creative individuals scored high on both theoretical and esthetic values on the Allport-Vernon-Lindzey test of values (see page 473). These values, it might be noted, are somewhat frowned upon by certain segments of our society. As a group the creative individuals were above-average in intelligence, but some had IQ's as low as 120.

As a group creative people are not all "grade-getters." Many have poor averages in school, possibly because their independent attitudes and ideas go counter to the tendency in many schools to encourage group work and conformity. The creative person follows his own interests and ignores pressures and the suggestions of his teachers and fellow students. Our educational system probably fails to detect many students with high creative potential because they are neither interested in nor adept at getting high grades.

It is quite obvious, then, that in order for society to exploit the potentially creative person, schools must become more alert in identifying and sustaining creative talent. And this task will require more than just selecting children with very high IQ's or those whose academic performance is exceptional.

The Training of Talent. Identifying talent is not enough. The intellectually talented must be trained if their potentialities are

638

to be realized. In order to do this two important conditions must be met. First, gifted children must be motivated to get ahead in their chosen directions. Second, they must be given an opportunity to learn.

In many ways the first problem is the more difficult. One principle of a democracy is that everybody be given an opportunity to develop his intellectual potential —if he wants to. That a sizable percentage of our talented high school students fail to enroll in college is an indication that many do not want to develop their potential. Moreover, of those who do go to college, about half fail to obtain degrees. If this situation is to change, the motivation of our young people will have to be modified, so that they will guide themselves, or accept guidance from their counselors, to select careers consistent with their intellectual abilities and to expend the large amount of time and energy required.

If we are to train many more scientists, mathematicians, and linguists, some fundamental values of large groups of Americans will also have to be modified. For generations the intellectual has been thought of as something of an "oddball" who is, at best, tolerated, and certainly not imitated, largely because intellectual careers have never been as economically rewarding as others. To some extent this condition has altered in the space age, but much cultural prejudice against intellectual careers remains. If talented youngsters are to be encouraged to imitate the intellectual, the prestige of the scholar and the teacher must be increased. This can be done in part by paying them wages that will attract talented youngsters to the professions, for they properly take such factors into account when deciding upon their future vocations. The social prestige of intellectual work must also be augmented in every way possible. Although it is probably too much to expect in this generation that the same promience be given to high school youngsters of outstanding intellectual achieve-

ment as is given to those who excel in making touchdowns, it would be healthier and a better guarantee of our own future if the discrepancy between the two could be reduced.

In addition, some resolution of the social conflict facing the gifted woman must be sought. This problem was highlighted when in 1961 Marlene Schmidt, an East German refugee who had been an engineer, won the title of Miss Universe in an American beauty contest. One newspaper from her Communist homeland bleated: "Farewell, Marlene; among us you were a respected engineer; in the West you have only your measurements." This comment reflected the fact that women in Communist countries, despite their late start, already play a more important role in the professions than they do in the United States. In the Soviet Union women hold 70 per cent of the teaching positions and constitute 75 per cent of the medical profession.

Whether women under optimal conditions might prove to be geniuses as often as men is a question that can be debated endlessly because facts are not yet available. But it must be recognized that the revolutionary developments in modern science and technology derive not only from the huge steps forward taken by a few geniuses, but equally from the less conspicuous efforts of hordes of the intellectually talented, and women, who may well possess half of our intellectual potential, are not contributing their share.

At the present time the attitude commonly held by both men and women that the female intellectual is somehow unglamorous may be robbing the country of much needed talent. The writer is neither so presumptuous nor so naive as to offer a neat solution for this terribly complex problem. The solution, if and when it comes, must fit in with the fundamental American values for the family and the home. But surely some feasible compromise can be made, so that the talented girl will be motivated to receive an appropriate education and be able to pursue an intellectual career. In some professions, like teaching or medicine, an arrangement making it easier for a woman to combine a career with marriage does not seem out of the question. Part-time work or a "leave of absence" during the period that the woman is raising a family are possible solutions. If some satisfactory answer is not worked out, we will be forced to limp along because of insufficient intellectual resources.

One Final Point. That we seem to have emphasized the need for more talent in science, mathematics, and languages does not mean that other intellectual areas, such as literature, art, and the law, that have at the moment less practical bearing on our strength in the cold war, should be ignored. Nor does it mean that such important segments of society as business need be stripped of outstanding talent. The important point is that, if our intellectual resources were fully utilized, there would be plenty to fill every need.

However efficient our tests for discovering exceptional talent may become, and however persuasive and successful our society is in motivating the gifted to pursue intellectual careers, both efforts will come to naught unless appropriate educational facilities are provided. Though our present educational facilities can turn out outstanding scholars in all areas of the arts, sciences, and professions, no one doubts that educational programs at every level might be improved. In 1961 a study of science instruction in elementary and junior high schools was made by the American Association for the Advancement of Science. Since the conclusion of the study was that there is "an urgent need for major improvement in the science instruction," several recommendations were made. One was, "Science should be a basic part of general education for all students at the elementary and junior high school." Chil-

dren are very curious about science, and if schools do not exploit this early interest, it is likely to extinguish. The attitudes they form toward science early in life often persist as long as they live. If our youngsters are taught ineffectively, they may turn away from science disillusioned. Good science education in the early grades not only contributes to the making of future scientists, but prepares the others to live with some understanding in a scientific and technological society.

Another recommendation from the same report was, "Science teaching should stress the spirit of discovery characteristic of science itself." Although adequate economic rewards for scientific work must be provided, evidence suggests that one of the most important drives in scientific creativity is "knowledge for knowledge's sake." The wages promised are often important in influencing the selection of a career, but the intrinsic motivation of satisfying curiosity is of utmost importance to the scientist. Consequently, when science is taught as a series of factual findings to be memorized, its spirit is seriously violated and its appeal may be destroyed. The curriculum in science must include concepts and theories as well as facts, and above all courses must be arranged so that the student *himself*, by his own observations and inferences, "discovers" important facts and principles.

Another recommendation was, "The preparation of instructional materials will require the combined efforts of scientists, classroom teachers, and specialists in learning and teacher preparation." Contemporary science is so complex that the ordinary classroom teacher can be aided immensely by teaching aids prepared by specialists. For it would be unfair to the classroom teacher and unfortunate for the nation if he were forced to bear the total responsibility for improving scientific education. There are many ways in which scientists, educators, and psychologists who are interested in the learning process, can help improve classroom instruction. And they have started to respond in a most promising way to the needs of the nation by helping plan new curricula, instructional aids, and novel departures from traditional forms of instruction (see page 655).

Improvement in education must not be restricted to the basic sciences. The teaching of mathematics, languages, literature, arts, history, and any subject can benefit from new ideas and new techniques. The debates going on everywhere around us about how poor—or how good—our educational system really is, tend to obscure the point—on which there is agreement—that there is much room for improvement. The tasks of designing new and imaginative educational procedures and of discovering objectively whether they will work require large investments of time and money. But no thoughtful person would dare set a limit on the vast returns that might accrue from this investment.

The Components of Intelligence

Intellectual Factors. For the most part what we have said about the nature of intelligence has kept close to "intelligence is what a properly standardized intelligence test measures." In spite of its apparent circularity this definition has proven useful. Nevertheless, it may not seem to you to provide a satisfactory statement of the nature of intelligence.

To arrive at a more fundamental statement, psychologists have analyzed intelligence test scores into their basic components by the method of factor analysis (see page 475). Charles Spearman (1863-1945), an eminent English psychologist, observed that when intelligence tests of many different kinds, both verbal and performance, were intercorrelated, the correlations were usually positive (Spearman, 1927). This suggested to him some fundamental intellectual factor, common to all kinds of intellectual behavior. He called this factor **general intelligence** which, abbreviated, became known widely as g. According to Spearman's theory such apparently different abilities as spelling, mathematical reasoning, remembering, and many others are in part determined by this basic g factor. Performance on any specific task is not, however, determined solely by general intelligence. In addition to the g factor there are **specific intelligences** or s's. Thus a person's performance in mathematics is the combined result of the amount of g factor he possesses and his specific mathematical ability. Likewise, his performance on a mechanical task may be attributed to the combined operation of a general intelligence factor and a specific variety of mechanical ability. As you can see, the contribution of the g factor varies, depending upon the specific task. It plays an important role in mathematical reasoning but a very minor role in mechanical manipulations.

Other psychologists, using various forms of factor analysis, take exception to Spearman's conclusion that there is a general intelligence factor. L. L. Thurstone (Thurstone & Thurstone, 1941) inferred from his analysis of 60 different kinds of intelligence tests that there are seven independent *primary factors* of intelligence. There are *number ability* (N), *word fluency* (W), *verbal meaning* (V), *memory* (M), *reasoning* (R), *spatial relations* (S), and *perceptual speed* (P). To understand a person's intellectual capabilities, therefore, a single global IQ is insufficient. Rather, a battery of tests that can provide measures of each primary factor is required (see Figure 16.17). More recently this view has been modified in the direction of Spearman's formulation. The current revision of The Primary Mental Abilities Test (Thurstone, 1963) concludes that in addition to primary factors, a "second-order," general factor of intelligence is at work.

Other factor analyses of intelligence have

VERBAL MEANING TEST

This is a test to see how well you know words. Find the word that means the same as the first word in the row.

SAFE *a.* secure *b.* loyal *c.* passive *d.* young *e.* cleft

NUMBER FACILITY TEST

This is a test to see how well you can work with numbers. Find the answer without using paper and pencil for figuring.

16 x 99 *a.* 154 *b.* 1,584 *c.* 1,614 *d.* 15,085 *e.* 150,084

REASONING TEST

This is a test to see how well you can follow a series of letters. Find the letter that follows the last letter in the row.

a m b a n b a o b a p b a 1. m 2. o 3. p 4. q 5. r

SPATIAL RELATIONS TEST

This is a test to see how well you can recognize figures and forms. Find the figure that is the same as the first figure in the row.

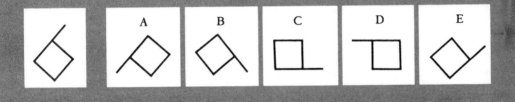

FIGURE 16.17 Examples of Sample Items from the Primary Abilities Tests for the Ninth to Twelfth Grades. These four factors appear to be the most critical for the performance in these grades (Reproduced with permission of Science Research Associates, Inc. Copyright 1962, Thelma Gwinn Thurstone).

been performed, and the results do not always agree with either Spearman's theory or Thurstone's. In some instances the analysts claim to have uncovered a somewhat different set of primary factors; in others they state that what one factor analyst takes to be a primary factor is really a complex of more elementary factors. This notion has been advanced concerning Thurstone's reasoning factor. It has also been suggested (Guilford, 1959b) that "creative thinking" is really different from "critical thinking," and that solving abstract problems requires skills that are different from those used in solving concrete problems.

It is not surprising that different factor analyses of intelligence do not result in exactly the same set of primary factors. Those who employ these techniques do not start with the same set of test items, nor do they test the same population of subjects. Moreover, there is reason to believe that the structure of intelligence does not remain constant throughout life, that it is affected by maturational events and different experiences. Intellectual behavior at one age might involve a set of primary factors quite different from the set needed at a later age. Similarly, the primary factors underlying intelligence in one culture might be in some respects different from those in another. Thus, the differences in the findings of Spearman, Thurstone, and others are to be expected. But in any case, you should not permit these discrepancies to hide the important basic similarity in all this work. All factor analytical studies support the idea that intellectual behavior in any situation results from a combination of several interacting factors. Even though Spearman assumes that a general factor exists, he finds it necessary to postulate that specific intellectual skills exist also. If this point is accepted, two procedures have to be undertaken in selecting personnel for any intellectual task. One must (1) assess the specific skills required for a particular job and (2) discover how these skills are distributed among the individuals available to fill the position.

Although factor analysis cannot claim to have provided a complete map of intelligence, it is, nevertheless, a useful start in that direction. It has reduced the complexity of the task by analyzing intellectual behavior into more manageable components. The true worth of factor analysis will be realized if and when we discover how primary intellectual factors are modified as the human organism matures and learns.

Intelligence and the Brain. Children who call their brightest classmate "The Brain" are acknowledging a widely accepted assumption, namely, that there is an intimate relationship between intelligence and the brain. The relationship, however, is not in every respect as close as people have sometimes believed or scientists have hoped. For example, intelligence is not correlated with the weight or size of the brain. Nor is it known to be highly correlated with any simple set of physiological characteristics of the brain, although there are suggestions that certain structural and chemical factors may be important (e.g., cell concen-

tration, fine runs of dendrite endings, blood supply).

One reason it is difficult to find a relationship between intelligence and the brain is that experience—or habit—plays such an important role in behavior. For example, accidental destruction of a sizable portion of an infant's frontal lobe will cause permanent intellectual loss, but a similar injury later in life may have no effect on intelligence whatever. In one case (Hebb, 1949) on record, a young man had one entire prefrontal lobe removed, yet he subsequently obtained an IQ of 160. In another case both prefrontal lobes of a patient were removed, representing a loss of around 15 per cent of the total weight of his cerebrum, yet afterwards his IQ was within normal range.

Thus it would seem that certain physiological structures are essential for intellectual development, but are not necessary for intellectual performance once the development has taken place. In order to understand this process more fully it will be necessary not only to discover how the brain is related to intelligence, but also how experience and learning modify both.

THE CHARACTERISTICS OF A USEFUL PSYCHOLOGICAL TEST

We made a decision at the beginning of the chapter to describe psychological tests by analyzing one kind intensively. This was the intelligence test. Now that we have done this, the reader may try to generalize from the principles that underlie intelligence testing to other forms of psychological tests. In order to assist his effort some of the basic characteristics of useful tests should be mentioned, at least briefly.

A useful test must be *standardized*. This means simply that uniform conditions for administering it and interpreting its results have been established. Giving a test under uniform conditions sounds easier to do than it actually is. It requires painstaking preparation to ensure that all examinees taking one particular test are confronted with exactly the same task. The whole point of standardization is to guarantee that the test will measure the particular ability it is designed to measure. Obviously, if a child's score on an intelligence test is influenced by his cuteness or his inattention, that test will not be very useful.

In order for a test to be interpreted sensibly, it must possess a set of **norms** so that the performance of one person can be compared with that of a large number of others. The norms provide the means for interpreting a test score. A test score by itself has no useful function. What would it mean if you knew merely that an experienced mechanic *A* was able to identify correctly the cause of motor failure in six out of ten instances that appeared in a test? If you knew, however, that in the same test situation over 95 per cent of inexperienced mechanics solved at least seven problems, then you would conclude that individual A is not a very good mechanic.

A useful test must be *reliable* (see page 49). If tomorrow a group of individuals should come up with entirely different scores on a test of visual acuity from the scores they made today, then the test would obviously not be measuring their visual acuity. Similarly a useful test must be *valid* (see page 470). It must be capable of predicting other forms of behavior. A watch manufacturer would see no reason for using a test of finger dexterity in his employment office, even though it was standardized with a good set of norms and was reliable, if it correlated zero with later performance as a watchmaker.

In conclusion, then, a useful test is one capable of predicting future behavior from present behavior. The better it can make that prediction, the more use it will have.

The emphasis on usefulness, which is the major concern of the applied scientist, should not make us lose sight of the importance of understanding the behavior that is sampled by a psychological test. Discovering how test performance is related to future behavior is only one part of the problem that in its entirety challenges the psychologists. What is also important is to understand the events, both in the experience and the physiology of an organism, that are responsible for his test performance.

SUMMARY

The basic principle underlying all psychological tests is that future behavior can be predicted from present performance, that is, $R = f(R)$. In order to do this successfully a test must be standardized, reliable, and valid.

Individuals differ in their abilities. Aptitude tests measure abilities in order to predict a person's capacity to acquire some skill. Achievement tests measure abilities in terms of skills already acquired. Some psychologists, with the techniques of factor analysis, are trying to discover a group of basic abilities that underlie all human skills.

Two of the most widely used individual tests of intelligence are the Stanford-Binet Test, for children, and the Wechsler Adult Intelligence Scale (WAIS), for adults. The Army General Classification Test (AGCT) is a a group test of intelligence that can be administered to a large number of individuals simultaneously. All of these tests are capable of predicting intellectual functioning in a wide variety of situations.

The intelligence quotient (IQ) of individuals for the most part tends to be stable. IQ's obtained below the age of four, however, are much less stable than those obtained later.

Intelligence increases rapidly during infancy and childhood, rises more slowly until a peak is reached somewhere between 20 and 30 years, and then begins to decline. The rate and amount of decline varies greatly among individuals, and some specific intellectual abilities are more resistant to the effect of aging than are others.

The fact that performance on an IQ test is influenced by environmental factors indicates that intelligence is not purely hereditary. It would seem that heredity provides the potential for a person's IQ, and his environment interacts with this potential to determine his actual IQ.

The question of whether races differ in their IQ's is obscured by the facts that the genetic characteristics of one race are not uniquely different from those of another race and that performance on IQ tests is influenced by environmental variables. When the IQ's of Negroes and whites have been compared, whites generally earn a higher average than Negroes, but there is much overlap between the IQ's of the groups. When Negroes have been placed in more stimulating environments, the differences between their IQ's and those of the whites have decreased.

A biographical analysis of geniuses has suggested that if they had been tested with IQ tests in their youth, they would have been identified as gifted. A developmental study of a group of gifted children shows that their level of achievement in later life is well above average. The failure of some gifted children to achieve success seems to be due to their psychological instability.

The United States is not making the best possible use of the intellectual talents of its ablest children. In order to correct this condition, a program must be instituted in which talented youngsters are identified, then given appropriate training and necessary social reinforcements to pursue a career that will utilize their abilities.

All attempts to factor analyze intelligence have shown that it consists of a combination of interacting factors. There is, however, no general agreement as to the specific number and kinds of primary factors.

SUGGESTIONS FOR FURTHER READING

ANASTASI, A. *Psychological testing.* (2nd ed.) New York: Macmillan, 1961.

A text in psychological testing that has an excellent treatment of intelligence.

CRONBACH, L. J. *Essentials of psychological testing.* (2nd ed.) New York: Harper & Row, 1960.

An excellent coverage of the broad field of psychological testing.

HOLLINGWORTH, L. S. *Children above 180 IQ.* New York: Harcourt, 1942.

An interesting account of the characteristics and problems of gifted children.

HUNT, J. McV. *Intelligence and experience.* New York: Ronald, 1961.

An analysis of intelligence that emphasizes the continuing interaction between an organism and his environment.

JENKINS, J. J., & PATERSON, D. G. *Studies in individual differences: The search for intelligence.* New York: Appleton-Century-Crofts, 1961.

A valuable anthology of historically important papers on intelligence and intelligence testing.

MASLAND, R. L., SARASON, S. B., & GLADWIN, T.

Mental subnormality. New York: Basic, 1958.
A survey of the causes and consequences of intellectual deficiency.

SUPER, D. E., & CRITES, J. O. *Appraising vocational fitness: By means of psychological tests.* (rev. ed.) New York: Harper & Row, 1962.
A discussion of psychological testing in vocational counseling.

TERMAN, L. M., & MERRILL, M. A. *The Stanford-Binet Intelligence scale.* Boston: Houghton-Mifflin, 1960.
A complete description, including the standardization of the Stanford-Binet Intelligence Scale.

THORNDIKE, R. L., & HAGEN, E. *Measurement and evaluation in psychology and education.* (2nd ed.) New York: Wiley, 1961.
A clearly written introduction to psychological testing. Some of the topics discussed are history of testing, reliability, validity, intelligence tests, aptitude and achievement tests, and projective tests.

TRAPP, E. P., & HIMELSTEIN, P. *Readings on the exceptional child: Research and theory.* New York: Appleton-Century-Crofts, 1962.
A collection of papers on the exceptional child. Some of the papers report experimental work on intellectually retarded and gifted children.

WECHSLER, D. *The measurement and appraisal of adult intelligence.* (4th ed.) Baltimore, Md.: Williams & Wilkens, 1958.
A complete description, including the standardization of the Wechsler Adult Intelligence Scale.

APPLIED PSYCHOLOGY

17

BASIC AND APPLIED RESEARCH

Modern technology is a distillation of the discoveries made by research, basic and applied. Even though a piece of research may have originated from man's persistent quest simply to understand better the world he lives in, its findings have usually been exploited for some practical purpose, good or evil. This is true in all sciences—physics, chemistry, biology, or psychology.

Although the scientific community is frequently spoken of as comprising basic (or pure) and applied scientists, this distinction does not always hold. The work of many researchers has both basic and practical significance simultaneously, as we have seen in many examples scattered throughout this book. Nevertheless, there are programs of psychological research and service that are concerned only with the solution of practical problems. The psychologists engaged in these efforts are usually referred to as **applied psychologists.**

Introductory textbooks in all the sciences —and the present book is no exception— are devoted largely to the exposition of fundamental knowledge. Nevertheless, a general review of psychology would be incomplete if it failed to make any reference to applied psychology. From the beginning, psychology—even more than the physical sciences in their youth—developed in a society that constantly demanded help from psychologists in solving many of its problems.

Psychologists have accepted these challenges by devising numerous techniques that apply psychological knowledge to many practical problems of everyday living. We have already hinted at the diversity of applied psychology in our discussion. We have such various examples of applied psychology as: the measurement of forms of behavior ranging from specific attitudes to general intelligence, from aptitudes to achievements, from the effects of drugs to the effects of different forms of training;

the diagnosis and treatment of pathological forms of behavior; the persuasion of individuals and groups to modify their attitudes; the selection of personnel in schools, industry and the armed services; the arrangement of groups to increase their efficiency and productivity. Many more illustrations can be added to this list. In fact, today, more than half of all psychologists are doing applied work in hospitals, clinics, government, schools, armed services, social welfare organizations, industry, and business. For convenience it is customary to classify applied psychologists into categories that apparently reflect the kind of work they do: industrial psychologists, school psychologists, clinical psychologists, personnel psychologists, and so on. These are broad categories and often, two psychologists with the same designation perform quite different tasks. One school psychologist will be primarily concerned with identifying and helping disturbed children while another will be concerned mainly with devising techniques to improve instruction.

Our aim, therefore, will not be to review the general areas of applied psychology, but to gain a feeling for it by discussing carefully human engineering, the technology of learning, and vocational guidance. We would have been equally justified in choosing any other fields, and your instructor may wish to supplement this selection by an account of what has been accomplished in some other area of applied psychology.

HUMAN ENGINEERING

Human engineering is a slick term and a misleading one. Offhand it sounds like a label for the attempt to remake man into an efficient machine. Actually it is quite the opposite. Human engineering tries to make machines conform to people's abilities.

We sometimes forget that machines always function in relation to man. If you ask a mechanic how convenient it is to repair most eight-cylinder engines in American cars, no doubt he will reply in a series of well-chosen phrases which can be summed up as a firm declarative statement that the car designers have completely ignored the problem of repairing these engines in the crowded spaces they occupy. And if you ask a basketball center how he likes low-slung automobiles, his remarks—unless acrobatics is his sideline—most likely will be equally pungent. At the same time there are examples of good human engineering to point to. A Coca-Cola bottle was made for the human hand. The new telephone handsets were manufactured after extensive measurements of the faces of thousands of persons, and after numerous experiments to determine the optimal weight and angle of the mouthpiece. From the mechanical point of view a variety of sizes and shapes and weights of phones would have functioned equally well as receivers and transmitters. But technical proficiency alone is not sufficient. Machines must be adapted to human use. This is the task of human engineering.

The concept of the **man-machine system** —that men and machines together operate as one system—is basic in human engineering. To devise a system that will function efficiently, it is necessary to investigate the capabilities and limitations of both components to see how they will interact.

In some very fundamental respects men and machines function alike. Both can *sense* physical changes. Often machines can sense changes to which humans are insensitive, such as in x-rays, ultrasonic sounds, and infrared rays, but human sensing devices are more remarkable in other ways. For example, our eye is amazingly sensitive to a wide range of light waves. It will be a long, long time before any machine receptor can duplicate all of its functions.

Both humans and machines can *process information* and arrive at a decision. Before a move is made in a chess game the position of a player and his opponent must be evaluated. A man can do this, but so can a computer. Although at present a top-notch chess player can beat the most talented computer, there is no guarantee that this superiority will be maintained. Not all human decisions are superior to those of machines, and today, many businesses are being revolutionized as computers are permitted to make decisions that were formerly left to highly paid executives. A computer can maintain an adequate inventory in a warehouse (e.g., for furniture or automobile parts) better than a person, because it has a superior capacity for storing (remembering), organizing, and making available on demand large numbers of facts. The fantastic amount of information that a computer can review and retrieve has convinced some researchers that if it is given the results of numerous laboratory tests, a computer is superior to a physician in making the correct medical diagnosis.

Finally, both machines and men can *respond*—they can do things. Both can paste labels on wine bottles. Machines, however, can do such repetitive tasks more rapidly and for longer periods of time without becoming fatigued. Compared to machines, man is both weak and slow. But so far no machine has been invented that can match the performance of a watch repairman in replacing flywheels in a variety of watches, or for that matter, in performing many similar tasks.

Human engineers, however, are not interested in acting as judges in a competition between men and machines. Their task is to devise ways in which men and machines can best work together toward a common purpose. Consider the problem of handling the mails in any large post office. Years ago this work was done entirely by human labor. Clerks read the addresses on letters, decided where they were to go, and tossed them into appropriate mailbags for different geographical regions. With the use of new electronic machines, the amount of mail a post office can handle has been increased tremendously. In one system letters are placed on a moving belt that takes them past a man who reads the addresses and then presses a key which stamps a code number on the envelope. The envelope continues on the belt until an electronic device reads the code number and triggers a mechanism that delivers the envelope to the appropriate mailbag. Jobs in this system are assigned on the basis of efficiency alone. The only task that is assigned to a man is actually the most difficult: reading and understanding innumerable different addresses written in innumerable different handwritings and containing innumerable abbreviations and misspellings. The skill that enables us to equate "Filadelfiy, Pensilvania" written in the halting, uncertain handwriting of a child, and "Philadelphia, Pa." inscribed in bold yet indistinguishable strokes by an adult, is truly amazing. No machine has been invented—yet—that can recognize the common factor beneath two such different physical stimulus patterns. Machines can read, but the printing must be standardized and free of ambiguity and irrelevance.

The Design of Displays

Most of the work in design that human engineers have done up to now has been to arrange information so that men can sense it easily and quickly. Human engineers call this designing displays. A simple but significant example of the kind of problem human engineers have dealt with is one that occurred during World War II. At the time the Japanese attacked Pearl Harbor, American planes bore as their insignia a white star in a blue circle. Although it was attractive and symbolic, this marking proved to be an ineffective display, because when it was seen from afar it lost its distinctiveness and looked simply like a round spot. The Japanese also used circles for identification on their planes, and although theirs were red, many American gunners, both on the ground and in the air, had trouble telling these two circles apart. In fact, during combat the circles seemed to them merely to be indistinguishable specks. As a result gunners sometimes withheld their fire from the enemy and at other times tragically fired on their countrymen. Obviously these errors were due not to equipment failure but to the difficulty men had in making correct sensory discriminations.

There were two possible ways of rectifying the situation. One was to give extensive training to gunners to improve their visual discrimination. But such training has its limits. A much more effective solution, and the one that was adopted, was to change the insignia so that it could be more easily identified, especially under difficult conditions. Groups of subjects were shown a variety of designs at different distances and under all sorts of conditions. From this simple experiment came a solution of the problem—the adoption of the insignia with the circle, star, and bar.

A much more complex task confronts human engineers who must design displays in the cockpits of airliners. Not so long ago cockpits were a mess of unrelated dials placed without regard to the needs of the pilot who had to keep an eye on all of them. A number of air disasters were undoubtedly caused by this haphazard arrangement of significant information.

It is not the sheer number of dials alone that makes a pilot's task difficult. Depending on how they are designed and displayed, the same number of dials can confront the pilot with either an impossible burden or a comparatively easy task.

A principle that human engineers stress is that no one sense modality should be "overloaded." This means if a lot of information has to be transmitted, it should

not all be sent through one sensory system. In airplane cockpit design, and in the design of most other machines, there has been an unfortunate tendency to overload the visual sense. The result is that the eyes have to take in too much important information, and some of it is sometimes missed or misread. An obvious way to avoid overloading the visual system is to utilize other sense modalities as well. A simple warning system, like one that indicates a malfunctioning engine, can make use of a buzzer. We also have evidence that a good

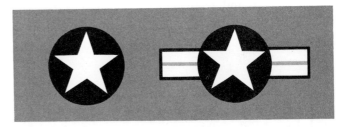

FIGURE 17.1 The Insignia Used on United States Warplanes at the Beginning of World War II and the One That Was Later Substituted. The blue circle with the white star was easily confused with the red circle of Japanese planes. The addition of a horizontal bar made the discrimination easier.

FIGURE 17.2 Cockpit View of American Airlines 707 Jet (American Airlines).

650

deal of information can be transmitted by tactual stimulation, a technique little used so far. But we must envisage the time when the tremendous demands placed upon astronauts by their complex equipment will force human engineers to utilize every possible sensory capacity.

Another principle of sound human engineering is to design displays so that the human operator can perceive the necessary information as quickly as possible with the least possible risk of error. For example, different kinds of dials have been found to vary in their ability to transmit information. Figure 17.3 shows five different types: round, semicircular, open-window dial with

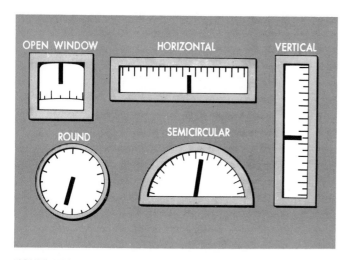

FIGURE 17.3 Five Dials Used in a Study of Errors in Dial Readings (After Sleight, 1948).

scale moving and pointer fixed, vertical dial with moving pointer, and horizontal dial with moving pointer. An experiment (Sleight, 1948) designed to evaluate the effectiveness of these five dials found that the open-window dial was read most accurately, while the vertical dial produced the largest number of errors. One obvious advantage of the open-window dial is that an operator need learn only one attending response, for the pointer always remains in the same place. In the other designs the operator

must first find the pointer and then take a reading.

Sometimes a display of information simpler than a dial is more satisfactory. In an automobile a speedometer is essential because there are times, as a driver nears the speed limit for example, when it is important for him to know exactly how fast he is going. But it is not important for him to know the exact oil pressure, only whether it is within normal range. For this purpose, then, a warning indicator such as a red light is superior to a dial. In fact, when automobiles did have dials to indicate oil pressure, drivers quickly learned to ignore them, because only rarely did anything go wrong with the pressure. As a result they didn't notice when something actually went wrong. Nowadays when a red light goes on it is noticed immediately. A new stimulus is perceived much more readily than a slight change in an old stimulus that you have learned to ignore.

Warning indicators, in combination with dials, can be effective transmitters of information. In 1958 one British airline pilot crashed during descent at night because he had misread his altimeter by 10,000 feet. In order to avoid a repetition of this accident, the airline modified its altimeter so that a flashing light went on automatically when the aircraft descended below 10,000 feet. Thus the same altimeter provided simultaneously two essential items of information: exact altitude and a warning when the plane was getting close to the ground. Some automobiles' speedometers operate in the same way. At a certain speed (60 miles per hour) a light goes on to attract the driver's attention, or the numbers in the open-window dial of the speedometer become red.

As we indicated before, human engineers are concerned with the effective arrangement of dials as well as with their individual design. Human operators typically have to attend to many dials, and so their arrangement greatly influences their perception of them. Figure 17.4 shows two different arrangements of nine dials. In both patterns the dials are located in the same relative positions, but are oriented differently. In the patterned display each dial is oriented so that it has a common normal position (at 12 o'clock in Figure 17.4). This makes it easy to detect any dial that is signalling some malfunctioning. Its pointer stands out from the others. It becomes the figure against a ground (see page 185). In an unpatterned display the operator must look at each dial separately to see if anything is going wrong (Woodson, 1954). To some of you the idea of patterning a dial display will seem so obvious that you will find it difficult to believe that it could have been so long ignored. But it was ignored, because the designers were mechanical engineers, and mechanical efficiency was the only criterion they gave serious thought in designing machines.

There is always a danger that when too much attention is centered on one display system something else will be ignored. To some extent this has happened in the design of airliners. The emphasis on displays *inside* of the plane has taken attention away from things that may be happening *outside* the plane. The unfortunate result is that mid-air collisions have become the nation's most pressing air safety problem. In 1956 a particularly tragic accident occurred on a fairly clear summer day in the empty air spaces over the Grand Canyon. Two airliners traveling in the same general direction on a converging course collided, resulting in the quick death of 128 people. Both pilots had failed to see the other plane because their vision of what was happening outside their own plane was severely limited. Their planes were described as providing only 15 per cent normal visibility. The dials believed necessary to monitor so complex an airliner had become so numerous that they left little space for the pilot to look outside. Although modern jetliners provide a somewhat wider

field of vision from the cockpit, pilots still have to function with vast blind spots behind and below them. Today, the ever-increasing speeds of jetliners leave pilots less and less time in which to avoid collisions once danger threatens. The pilots of two jet airliners approaching head on have only about ten seconds to avoid a collision after first noticing each other as small spots in the distance ahead. Even if human reaction time is fast enough, and often it is not, the giant plane's response may not be. What is obviously needed is an electronic device that can "see" further into the distance and give pilots more time to make the responses necessary to avoid mid-air collision.

FIGURE 17.4 The Difference Between a Patterned and an Unpatterned Dial Display. The normal range of each dial is indicated by the dark gray segment. You can easily see how a patterned display makes dial-checking easier (After Woodson, 1954).

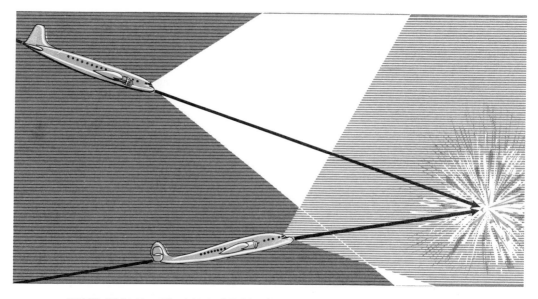

FIGURE 17.5 How Pilots' Limited Fields of Vision Can Cause a Midair collision. Although the planes are close together and traveling on converging courses, the pilots are prevented from seeing each other's planes because of restricted vision.

Decision Processes

Modern technology, with its increased need for brains and decreased need for brawn, demands much of human decision-making ability. And therefore one basic decision on many matters of great importance nowadays is whether or not men should assign some of their decision-making responsibilities to computers or keep it all themselves. In order to make our system of national defense sound, it has been decided that many important decisions, although certainly not those of very top importance, must be assigned to computers. Many of the decisions associated with allowing an astronaut to continue his space flight or making him return to earth are made by a computer after it has rapidly processed a vast amount of data. Similarly the decision to allow a rocket to continue in flight or be exploded in mid-air after leaving the launch pad is made by a computer and expressed by one of two lights flashing on. But other decisions, such as those of high-

level governmental policy, man is still considered more competent.

Much current research is aimed at understanding how men reach decisions between alternative courses of action and how their decision-making performance can be improved. We touched upon this question when we discussed problem solving (see page 355) and group pressures (see page 587). Although it is not feasible at present to lay down a set of principles applicable to every situation, we may cite two basic factors that must be considered in designing any effective man-machine system. The first is the limits of human decision-making capacity, and the second is how humans learn to make better decisions.

People who are forced to make too many or too complicated decisions sometimes become overtaxed. The control tower operator at a busy airport is an example. Responsible for the movements of any plane within a given range of the airport, he must decide where and when each airplane is to land and take off. The job demands the utmost vigilance and numerous life-and-death decisions, especially in bad weather or when the take-off and landing schedules become crowded. Before the optimal performance of control tower operators can be achieved, both under ordinary circumstances and in emergencies, we must know a great deal more about decision-making. Does a person's decision-making capacity deteriorate after it has been consistently taxed? How is it affected by stress? How many separate facts and ideas can a human operator consider? How much can training increase the efficiency of performance?

Relevant information is being gathered all the time, from a variety of sources. For the most part, however, the implications are limited to rather specific situations. We know, for example, that a man can be exceptionally effective in making appropriate decisions from information displayed on a radar screen. From the movements of little "blips" he is able to estimate course, velocity, and the time and point of intersection of ships or planes with considerable accuracy. He may also do a remarkably skillful job—one requiring intellectual effort—in keeping a helicopter in a fixed position above the water. It has been estimated that if a computer were to do the same task, it would have to solve twelve equations simultaneously. But how the decision processes involved in reading a radar screen and flying a helicopter are related to the decision processes in other tasks is far from clear. In short, we know that man can function like an amazingly intricate computer when he is making decisions based on inductive reasoning (inference), but we don't know much about how he does it. Therein lies the challenge—and afterwards the rewards of knowing.

The Design of Controls

Man can make many different kinds of responses. He can press buttons, move levers, turn hand cranks, and push pedals.

And he can talk. All of these responses, and any others you can think of, are mediated essentially by the contraction and relaxation of muscles attached to the skeleton. The problem for the human engineer is to understand these response capabilities and use them appropriately, or to substitute better controls in any man-machine system. In terms of sheer physical power, man is unable to compete with machines, although he is not as weak as is generally believed. With his legs and back muscles he can supply several hundred pounds of force— but for only a brief period of time. His arms can exert—also for a short spurt of time—a pull of over 50 pounds. A machine can do vastly more, and therefore, man-machine systems are arranged, whenever possible, for the machine to do the work, especially when great power is required.

Man as a source of power is much less important than man as a controller of power, the job he does by operating machines. And to do this well he must respond accurately. Several years ago when the Air Force was investigating the causes of some airplane accidents and near-accidents, they discovered that the shifting of pilots from one airplane to another with a different pattern of controls was an important contributing factor. The throttle, propeller, and gas-mixture levers located near the pilot's seat, were placed in a different sequence for three widely used planes. In one plane the sequence was throttle, propeller, and gas-mixture controls; in another the arrangement was propeller, throttle, and gas-mixture controls; while in the third the order was gas-mixture, throttle, and propeller controls. The reader who remembers the "lesson" of negative transfer (see page 311) will immediately recognize that shifting between these different arrangements would sometimes lead to an accident. A pilot trained in one type of plane might tend to pull the wrong control in another type of plane. Today, more care is taken to standardize the position of controls in order to avoid the potentially disastrous effects of negative transfer.

Because they must attend to visual displays constantly, some operators have to move controls without looking at them. Obviously, there is a chance that they may use the wrong lever.

In order to guard against this possibility controls are *coded* with distinctive "feels," making discriminations among them easier. To decide which shapes for controls are distinctive, a psychological investigation (Jenkins, 1947) sought to test how well blindfolded subjects could discriminate between 22 knobs of different shapes that might be used for controls in an airplane cockpit. Eleven of the shapes passed the stringent test of rarely being confused with the other shapes. They are shown in Figure 17.6.

Human Engineering and Man-Machine Systems

Most of the examples of human engineering that we have cited have been concerned with the improvement of one component in some existing man-machine system. If an altimeter is easily misread, an improved design is sought. If all the dials in a set cannot be read easily, more efficient patterns are tried out in laboratory tests. If man is unable to assimilate enough information to make a decision, a computer is

substituted. If men make errors in responding to a set of controls, different identification systems are experimentally tested until a better one is devised.

Not all human engineering is concerned simply with improving an already functioning man-machine system. A system may have to be built "from the ground up." This is happening today in our larger post offices. As we said, the invention of amazing new electronic equipment has revolutionized the handling of mail in huge bulk, making almost every former practice obsolete. The design of the control center of submarines has also been revolutionized. In old-style submarines a three-man crew cramped into the tightest of quarters operated the controls. Now, in atomic-powered submarines one man in a comfortable chair does the same job more easily despite its increased complexity.

Perhaps the most dramatic example of building an entirely new system from its very foundations is to be found in the brief history of man-machine systems that penetrate outer space and return. Any newspaper reader is at least dimly aware of the tremendous demand put upon human engineering before such feats could be accomplished. Through each stage of the system's development, the capabilities of both the man and the machine had to be studied with utmost care. The machines were constantly modified, because although

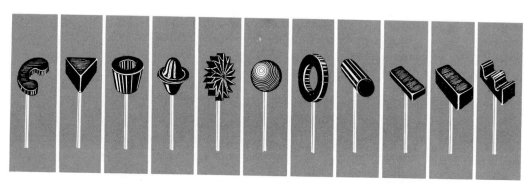

FIGURE 17.6 Eleven Shapes for Knobs Found to Provide Satisfactory Cues for Effective Tactual Discrimination (After Jenkins, 1947).

humans can be trained to perform more effectively, they cannot really be redesigned. Eyes must stay where they are, hands cannot be added, and intellectual power cannot be increased indefinitely. In short, every human capability has a limit. And man-machine systems like those used in space flight must be designed around these limitations and capabilities.

Much time and effort was saved in our space program because we knew a good deal beforehand about what man can do efficiently, safely, and easily, as well as what is difficult, dangerous, or impossible. But new information often had to be obtained, particularly about human performance during periods of weightlessness. At each point the answer to ignorance was experimentation.

The entire space program—like any good human engineering program—became a sequence of interrelated experiments designed to assist a man-machine system to achieve space flight.

THE TECHNOLOGY OF LEARNING

In this age of machines it is not surprising that a great deal of effort has been expended in exploiting technical devices for educational purposes. These devices are of many kinds ranging from the recently popularized teaching machines to the relatively old educational films. Our plan will be to review several kinds of instructional techniques that hold promise of improving the educational process.

Teaching Machines and Programmed Learning

Teaching machine is another slick label bandied about today without too much understanding. To many people it suggests a robot up in front of a class carrying out all the duties that were traditionally per-formed by teachers. It is not surprising that many people recoil from the idea of such a dehumanized arrangement. Of course, teachers also become uneasy and indignant because it seems not only to threaten them with technological unemployment but to equate the skills and ability of a machine with their own.

Actually, a teaching machine, or what is more accurately called an **auto-instructional device,** is a relatively simple mechanical instrument that confronts individual students with questions and items of information requiring responses. A teaching machine does not really teach at all. It merely arranges what some people believe to be optimal conditions under which learning may take place.

Hence, it is obviously not designed to replace a teacher, any more than a vacuum cleaner or an automatic dishwasher was planned to replace a housewife. Its purpose is to help the teacher do a better job than she is now doing—and do it with more students. Thus the argument that teaching machines will eliminate the personal relationship between teacher and student is either mistaken or false. Arguments like this are typical of reactions toward innovations in many professions. Since textbooks were first introduced, there have constantly been inventions designed to improve the effectiveness of education, and each new invention, from the textbook to the teaching machine, has met emotional opposition that was neither fair nor appropriate. Of course, some of the criticism directed at teaching machines is justified and doubtless will continue to be. But for the time being, the student would do well to maintain an objective attitude while he learns the facts.

Like most ostensibly new developments, teaching machines are not completely new. In 1925 Sidney L. Pressey designed a simple device about the size of a portable phonograph that presented multiple-choice questions on a drum that revolved. The student answered the question by pressing one of

FIGURE 17.7 An Early Teaching Machine. This machine was originally developed as a self-scoring machine for examinations but was also used as an auto-instructional device. The student read the question and pressed the button corresponding to what he believed the correct answer to be. When he pressed the appropriate button, the next question appeared. The machine recorded the number of errors made (Dr. S. W. Pressey).

four buttons, each representing a different answer. If the incorrect button was pressed, nothing happened. If the correct button was pressed, the drum rotated, bringing the next question into view, and indicating to the student that the response he had made was correct. Since the machine also kept a count of the student's errors, an objective evaluation of his performance was available.

Pressey's machine did not catch on for several reasons. First, it was perceived more as a testing device than a teaching machine. Second, and more important, in the 1920's no crisis threatened American education as it does today, when hordes of students are filling—and overfilling—our schools in ever-increasing numbers. Third, the original teaching machine did not grow out of a systematic approach to the psychology of learning as did the teaching machine which B. F. Skinner, a psychologist whose name has been frequently mentioned throughout this book, first espoused in the 1950's. Skinner had developed ingenious techniques of manipulating the behavior of animals which provided quantitative

measures of performance. The teaching machine allowed him to apply something like these techniques in the classroom. Thus, his teaching machine was not just a convenient mechanical device but an expression of a basic conception of behavior that had proved its worth. And finally, the success of technology in the age of atomic fission and space travel seems to have paved the way for more tolerant attitudes toward a technology of education.

One of Skinner's teaching machines, which is probably the best known of all auto-instructional devices, employs questions or statements printed on a disc mounted under the cover of the device. This is shown in Figure 17.8 by the dotted circle. Only one question or statement, appearing in the window marked Q, is visible at any one time. The answer is at A, immediately above the question but hidden from view. After the student has written his answer on an exposed frame of paper tape at $R1$, he raises the lever at the front of the machine, simultaneously exposing the correct answer at A and sliding his response under a transparent cover at $R2$ where it can no longer be changed. If the student's response is the same as the correct one exposed at A, he moves the lever horizontally. This punches a hole in the answer sheet and modifies the mechanism to skip this item when he runs through the same list again. The student then returns the lever to the starting position and a new item appears at Q. The student continues to work at his lesson until he has answered all the items correctly.

There are many other teaching machines, some of which are not machines at all but cleverly designed books or cardboard gadgets quite different in construction from the machine just described. These technical differences need not concern us. The important consideration is how the teaching machine facilitates learning. In order to get a better picture of this essential criterion of the machine's value let us examine some teaching machine lesson plans, or **programs,** as they are called.

Table 17.1 shows a set of items or frames from a program in high school physics. A student using a teaching machine with this program will write a word or phrase at *R*1 and then move the lever to uncover the appropriate answer at *A*. You can get the feel of how a student learns when he uses the teaching machine method if you cover the right-hand column with a card and uncover each answer only *after* you have answered the corresponding item. Although you may never have taken a course in physics, you should understand a good deal about the emission of light from an incandescent source by the time you finish this set of frames.

Programmed instruction is based upon the psychological principles of shaping (see page 291). The first principle of shaping, and programmed instruction, is to arrange the environment of an organism so that he will make the desired initial response voluntarily. Suppose you wanted to train a pigeon to whirl around like a top. The chance that a pigeon will turn slightly is so high to begin with that this response is bound to occur soon. As soon as the pigeon makes that move, you are in a position to shape his behavior by reinforcing that response. In the program on incandescent light the first response is also very likely to occur. Very few high school students eligible to enroll in a physics course do not know that the switch of a flashlight makes a connection between the battery and the bulb.

Once the initial response is made, the second principle of shaping comes into operation. That is the principle of immediate reinforcement. With this program its application is that the student knows immediately when his answer is correct. The results of the experimental psychology of learning are unequivocal in demonstrating that learning proceeds best when the correct response is immediately reinforced. And this principle is ignored, more often

than not, in traditional educational practices. It may be a full week before a student discovers whether he made a correct response to an item in his lab manual; and it may be while studying late at night that a student discovers whether his answer to a problem that puzzled him at lecture that day was correct. In contrast, programmed instruction is deliberately designed to give his correct answers immediate reinforcement.

The third principle of shaping, and programmed learning, is to proceed by small steps. Just as the pigeon is trained gradually to make a complete turn, so the high school physics student progresses gradually from his familiarity with a flashlight to an understanding of the relationship between heat and light. In order to ensure that the progress is gradual, successive items in the pro-

FIGURE 17.8 The Design of One of Skinner's Teaching Machines. The student is confronted with a question or statement at Q and writes his answer in at R₁. He raises the lever in the front exposing the correct answer at A and moving his answer under a transparent cover at R₂. If his answer is correct, he moves the lever to the right, to prevent the item from reappearing when he goes through the series again. When he returns the lever to its starting position, the next item appears.

TABLE 17.1 Part of a Program in High School Physics. The machine presents one item at a time. The student completes the item and then uncovers the corresponding word or phrase shown at the right (Skinner, 1958, with permission of *Science*).

SENTENCE TO BE COMPLETED	WORD TO BE SUPPLIED
1. The important parts of a flashlight are the battery and the bulb. When we "turn on" a flashlight, we close a switch which connects the battery with the ——.	bulb
2. When we turn on a flashlight, an electric current flows through the fine wire in the —— and causes it to grow hot.	bulb
3. When the hot wire glows brightly, we say that it gives off or sends out heat and ——.	light
4. The fine wire in the bulb is called a filament. The bulb "lights up" when the filament is heated by the passage of a(n) —— current.	electric
5. When a weak battery produces little current, the fine wire, or ——, does not get very hot.	filament
6. A filament which is *less* hot sends out or gives off —— light.	less
7. "Emit" means "send out." The amount of light sent out, or "emitted," by a filament depends on how —— the filament is.	hot
8. The higher the temperature of the filament the —— the light emitted by it.	brighter, stronger
9. If a flashlight battery is weak, the —— in the bulb may still glow, but with only a dull red color.	filament
10. The light from a very hot filament is colored yellow or white. The light from a filament which is not very hot is colored ——.	red
11. A blacksmith or other metal worker sometimes makes sure that a bar of iron is heated to a "cherry red" before hammering it into shape. He uses the —— of the light emitted by the bar to tell how hot it is.	color
12. Both the color and the amount of light depends on the —— of the emitting filament or bar.	temperature
13. An object which emits light because it is hot is called "incandescent." A flashlight bulb is an incandescent source of ——.	light
14. A neon tube emits lights but remains cool. It is, therefore, not an incandescent —— of light.	source
15. A candle flame is hot. It is a(n) —— source of light.	incandescent
16. The hot wick of a candle gives off small pieces of particles of carbon which burn in the flame. Before or while burning, the hot particles send out, or ——, light.	emit
17. A long candlewick produces a flame in which oxygen does not reach all the carbon particles. Without oxygen the particles cannot burn. Particles which do not burn rise above the flame as ——.	smoke

SENTENCE TO BE COMPLETED	WORD TO BE SUPPLIED

18. We can show that there are particles of carbon in a candle flame, even when it is not smoking, by holding a piece of metal in the flame. The metal cools some of the particles before they burn, and the unburned carbon —— collect on the metal as soot. **particles**

19. The particles of carbon in soot or smoke no longer emit light because they are —— than when they were in the flame. **cooler, colder**

20. The reddish part of a candle flame has the same color as the filament in a flashlight with a weak battery. We might guess that the yellow or white parts of a candle flame are —— than the reddish part. **hotter**

21. "Putting out" an incandescent electric light means turning off the current so that the filament grows too —— to emit light. **cold, cool**

22. Setting fire to the wick of an oil lamp is called —— the lamp. **lighting**

23. The sun is our principal —— of light, as well as of heat. **source**

24. The sun is not only very bright but very hot. It is a powerful —— source of light. **incandescent**

25. Light is a form of energy. In "emitting light" an object changes, or "converts," one form of —— into another. **energy**

26. The electrical energy supplied by the battery in a flashlight is converted to —— and ——. **heat, light; light, heat**

27. If we leave a flashlight on, all the energy stored in the battery will finally be changed or —— into heat and light. **converted**

28. The light from a candle flame comes from the —— released by chemical changes as the candle burns. **energy**

29. A nearly "dead" battery may make a flashlight bulb warm to the touch, but the filament may still not be hot enough to emit light—in order words, the filament will not be —— at that temperature. **incandescent**

30. Objects, such as a filament, carbon particles, or iron bars, become incandescent when heated to about 800 degrees Celsius. At that temperature they begin to —— ——. **emit light**

31. When raised to any temperature above 800 degrees Celsius, an object such as an iron bar will emit light. Although the bar may melt or vaporize, its particles will be —— no matter how hot they get. **incandescent**

32. About 800 degrees Celsius is the lower limit of the temperature at which particles emit light. There is no upper limit of the —— at which emission of light occurs. **temperature**

33. Sunlight is —— by very hot gases near the surface of the sun. **emitted**

34. Complex changes similar to an atomic explosion generate the great heat which explains the —— of light by the sun. **emission**

35. Below about —— degrees Celsius an object is not an incandescent source of light. **800**

gram are so constructed that a student's chance of making an error on any of them is slim. Note that the second item is slightly different from the first but it requires the same answer. The third item introduces the connection between heat and light in such a way that the correct answer is prompted by several cues. The words *flashlight* in the previous two items and *brightly*, which rhymes with the correct answer, tend to evoke the correct answer, *light*. In short, every possible technique is used to cue the correct response so that it will be emitted and reinforced immediately. The student is also prepared for the introduction of new technical terms. The technical word *filament* is preceded by the more familiar term *fine wire*. *Incandescent* has been introduced twice in earlier frames before it is called for as the correct answer to item 15. And when it is first called for it is part of a phrase used previously ("incandescent source of light"). If you run through the entire program in Table 17.1 again, you will see how the answer to each item, though it represents a step forward, emerges apparently spontaneously from the previous ones.

The fourth principle of shaping is a frank recognition of the fact that individuals differ widely in their learning ability. A large group of students at a classroom lecture are bound to differ in their rates of comprehending the material. Some students probably understand everything, and for these, the lecture may become a bore if it progresses too slowly. For perhaps a majority the lecture is paced at the proper rate. But there are slower students who, after missing a point or two, become completely "lost." In programmed learning each student progresses at his own rate. The slow student does not hold back the fast one, nor does the fast one set too rapid a pace for the slow one. Assuming the program is well made, each student advances only after he understands the previous point.

And fifth, in programmed learning as in shaping behavior, there is continuous feedback to the educator, indicating the success or failure of his program. Here again there is a clear difference between the program and the classroom lecture. Only a very candid lecturer will tell you how completely uncertain he often is as to how much of his lecture is being understood. But the writer long ago learned that the facial expressions of students are often misleading. The slouched, bored, sleepy looking young man may be absorbing everything, whereas the attentive, wide-eyed coed beside him, who seems to be exuding interest, may be comprehending nothing (or vice versa). By asking questions in class he can only gather information from a few students about what they may or may not be grasping. And to make the lecturer's problem more difficult, it is often impractical to interrupt a lecture with questions, especially in very large classes. Teaching machine records, which report the number of students missing each item, provide a constant source of information. It is easy to see which items are learned easily and which present difficulty and need to be changed. If a sizable number of students are having difficulty with one item, this means that there is something wrong with the program at this point that must be fixed. Perhaps the item is poorly expressed and confusing, or perhaps the leap from the previous item is too great. The item may have to be reworded or several intervening items may be introduced to make the transition more gradual.

Programming Techniques. When teaching machines were first introduced, greater attention was paid to the machine itself than to the program. Many different gadgets were put on the market, some of them, as we have said, not machines at all. However, it soon became apparent that the key to success in this movement did not lie in the instrument which exhibited the program, but rather in the quality of the program. Like textbooks and lectures, programs range from very poor to excellent.

One of the main objectives in constructing a program is to elicit the correct response at each step. Although errors will be made, it is one of the basic principles of Skinner's shaping technique that the correct response be, as nearly as possible, compelled to occur, so that it may benefit from immediate reinforcement. In a perfect program an alert student will make no errors. Therefore, the aim of the programmer is to devise methods to ensure the evocation of each correct response. One method of doing this is called *prompting.* Table 17.2 shows how pupils studying spelling may learn *manufacture* in six frames. These six frames illustrate what is called the *vanishing technique* of prompting. All the cues for spelling the word correctly are present at the beginning; in the first frame the pupil has merely to copy the correct

TABLE 17.2 A Set of Frames Designed to Teach a Third- or Fourth-Grade Pupil to Spell the Word *Manufacture* (Skinner, 1958, with permission of *Science*).

1. **Manufacture** means to make or build. *Chair factories manufacture chairs.* Copy the word here:

□ □ □ □ □ □ □ □ □ □ □

2. Part of the word is like part of the word **factory.** Both parts come from an old word meaning to *make* or *build.*

manu □ □ □ □ **ure**

3. Part of the word is like part of the word **manual.** Both parts come from an old word for *hand.* Many things used to be made by hand.

□ □ □ □ **facture**

4. The same letter goes in both spaces:

m □ **nuf** □ **cture**

5. The same letter goes in both spaces:

man □ **fact** □ **re**

6. **Chair factories**

□ □ □ □ □ □ □ □ □ □

chairs.

spelling. The external cues are then gradually withdrawn (they "vanish") until at the end the pupil has to generate the correct response himself. This kind of a prompt is known as a *formal prompt* because the correct response is triggered by some of its own cues.

Another kind of formal prompt uses the vanishing technique in reverse. When German is being taught by the paired-associates method (see page 306), the German word is projected on a screen and below it, its English equivalent badly out of focus. The subject attempts to supply the appropriate English equivalent. If he cannot, he presses a switch which gradually improves the focus until he is able to identify the correct answer. As learning progresses, less and less focusing is required because the subject becomes less dependent on external cues.

In evoking the correct response, the *thematic prompt* makes use of the student's previous learning. The correct response is elicited by this kind of prompt because it is based on strong verbal habits. In a programmed course in introductory psychology (Holland & Skinner, 1961), 174 out of 182 students answered *reflexes* to the frame, "A doctor taps your knee (patellar tendon) with a rubber hammer to test your ———." A similar percentage spontaneously gave the correct response to the frame, "Reinforcement, which consists of *presenting* stimuli (e.g., food) is called *positive* reinforcement; reinforcement which consists of *terminating* stimuli (e.g., painful stimuli) is called ——— reinforcement." The correct response, *negative,* is readily evoked because previously learned language habits encourage an opposite-type response. There are many techniques of prompting, and others will be invented. They all share the common aim of evoking correct responses so that the all-important reinforcement can occur immediately after each of them.

The problem of how best to prompt is not the only one facing programmers. Another is the size of the step. Both the programs illustrated in Figures 17.1 and 17.2 could be shortened by reducing the number of frames, but it would mean that the size of the steps between them would be increased. It might be argued that a program involving fewer steps would be better for brighter students. Conceivably the bright student may be bored if he is made to go through all the small steps believed necessary to teach a dull student. Of course, there must be an upper limit to the optimal number of steps. There is bound to be some point where the addition of more items does nothing to improve learning and may even hinder it. Skinner's principle is to employ that number of items which produces the smallest number of errors. The suggestion that bright students will become bored by this procedure has not been demonstrated, although it has been shown that sometimes large steps are as effective as small ones (Smith & Moore, 1962). We must admit, however, that up to now no studies using the same program for groups of students with widely different IQ's have been carried out. This is certain to be done soon.

Another problem facing programmers is to decide on the form of response the student is to make. In the programs we described the subject has to *construct* the response by writing his answer. Conceivably teaching machine equipment could be designed which would require the student to construct his answer by speaking it, leaving it for the machine to check whether it is right or wrong. In contrast to the construction method, written or spoken, is the *selection* technique. In programs using the *selection* technique the subject selects the answer from a group of alternatives, just as in true-false and multiple-choice tests.

The research done to determine which of the different modes of response is best, has failed to provide consistent answers (Silverman, 1960). The reason for this may be obvious, for you have already learned something about transfer of training (see page 311). It is likely that one relevant factor in

determining which mode of response is best is the criterion used in evaluating a program. Students who have had training in constructing responses might enjoy an advantage in tests requiring constructed responses. Similarly, a program using selected responses might prove more effective if the amount learned is evaluated by a test demanding the same kind of responses. Skinner, however, argues on principle in favor of constructed responses. The purpose of education, he believes, is to prepare students to *recall* ideas and information they need in all sorts of situations. Training in *selecting* an appropriate response will often be of no help if a student must recall it. And in most real-life situations *recall,* rather than *recognition,* is important.

In the long run, the issue of the relative merits of constructed and selected responses in programmed instruction will have to be resolved by studies in which the amount of transfer from the original learning will be measured. If Skinner is right, then the programs demanding constructed responses will produce better performance in situations that bear little resemblance to the conditions of training.

One basic question in programmed learning is, how are programs to be organized? The most popular method, known as **linear programming,** and illustrated in Tables 17.1 and 17.2, is favored by Skinner and his associates. The material is presented in a fixed sequence of small steps, each of which must be taken by every student. The rationale behind linear programming is that each step depends on those taken previously. Just as it is necessary for a pigeon to pass through every point of a circle as he is learning to turn around, it is necessary for a student to proceed through each step of a prearranged course of training.

Some psychologists (e.g., Crowder, 1959), taking exception to this position, believe that a program should be sufficiently flexible to handle different kinds of reactions to the same material. They have developed a **branching program** that utilizes multiple-choice items, where the student is given information in sizable chunks, and is then tested by a question which contains several alternate answers from which he must choose. If he makes a correct response, he is given a brief explanation of why his choice is correct, and he proceeds to the next frame. A wrong response directs him to a remedial frame where his error is pointed out, with an appropriate explanation and perhaps a chiding comment ("Come, come now"). An item with four alternatives could lead to four branches, since each error may require a different remedial frame. Although immediate reinforcement is also stressed by the technique, the explanation of the rights and wrongs of responses is considered an indispensable ingredient of education. The branching program, therefore, functions in imitation of a tutor, whereas the linear system functions like a psychologist shaping behavior.

It would require a very complicated machine to handle the many alternatives that develop when the branching technique is adopted in thorough-going form. This problem has been neatly solved by the **scrambled textbook** (e.g., Crowder, 1960). Although each student starts on page one, different students are sent scurrying to different pages scattered throughout the book, depending on the particular answers they choose. A correct answer may send one student to page 42, while an incorrect answer may send a student to page 19 or to page 157, depending upon the kind of mistake he has made. Ultimately every student "finishes" the book, but without having read the same number of pages or having read them in the same order. The more correct responses a student makes, the less work he has to do (see Figure 17.9).

An Evaluation of Teaching Machines and Programmed Learning. How effective is

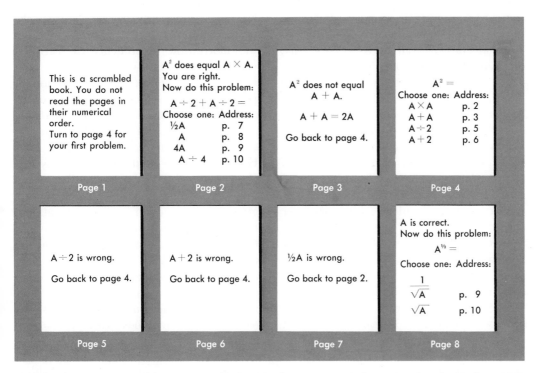

Page 1

This is a scrambled book. You do not read the pages in their numerical order.
Turn to page 4 for your first problem.

Page 2

A^2 does equal $A \times A$.
You are right.
Now do this problem:

$A \div 2 + A \div 2 =$
Choose one: Address:
½A	p. 7
A	p. 8
4A	p. 9
A ÷ 4	p. 10

Page 3

A^2 does not equal $A + A$.

$A + A = 2A$

Go back to page 4.

Page 4

$A^2 =$
Choose one: Address:
A × A	p. 2
A + A	p. 3
A ÷ 2	p. 5
A + 2	p. 6

Page 5

$A \div 2$ is wrong.

Go back to page 4.

Page 6

$A + 2$ is wrong.

Go back to page 4.

Page 7

½A is wrong.

Go back to page 2.

Page 8

A is correct.
Now do this problem:

$A^{1/2} =$

Choose one: Address:
$\dfrac{1}{\sqrt{A}}$	p. 9
$\sqrt{A}$	p. 10

FIGURE 17.9 Successive Pages in a Scrambled Textbook (From L. M. Stolurow, *Teaching by Machine*, 1961, p. 39, by permission of the publisher, Cooperative Research Division of the U. S. Office of Education, U. S. Department of Health, Education, and Welfare).

this new method of education? For three basic reasons no simple answer can be given. First, an overall answer is impossible because the effectiveness of the method may very well depend on the subject matter of the course and on the particular type of program used. It is reasonable to suppose that programmed learning is more effective with highly formalized subjects like logic and mathematics than it is with some of the social sciences. And there can be no doubt that some programs are better constructed than others. Second, the criteria used to evaluate the success of teaching machine programs determine how successful they are. A program in third-year arithmetic may prove very effective compared to mediocre conventional instruction, but not so effective compared to traditional educational methods that are *exceptionally* good. And lastly, not enough evidence is available for any final evaluation of the strengths and weaknesses of programmed learning.

All the same, new evidence and information are constantly trickling in and some of the reports are decidedly promising. In a private boys' school in New York City, for example, 74 students completed an algebra course in two weeks. Previously two months had been devoted to this course. At Hamilton College the time required for a course in logic was cut by one-third. At Harvard a group of students learned the equivalent of a first semester course in German in approximately half the normal time. In Roanoke, Virginia, a group of eighth graders completed a two-semester algebra course in half the usual time and worked only 50 minutes a day without homework. These results seemed so promising and the technique so simple that three public high schools in Roanoke gave it a tryout the following year. Each student was given a loose-leaf notebook of several hundred pages containing the program. As he answered each problem from the top to the bottom of a page, he moved a plastic slide that uncovered the correct answer. If his answer was incorrect he

had to review the problem, seeking to discover where he went wrong. Whenever he missed three or four problems in a row he either started the lessons over by himself or he sought help from the teacher. The teacher kept in touch with the progress of each student by checking the pages of the program he had finished.

Besides reports like these we have material ranging from masses of experimental data to testimonials of individuals and small groups who, with the help of programmed learning, have achieved mastery of some subject in a brief time. All these verdicts must be appraised, not with distrust, but with caution. The fact that programmed learning is found superior to conventional methods in particular *instances* does not warrant the conclusion that it is in *general* better than the whole armory of traditional methods of education. If we are to remain true to scientific tradition, we must entertain explanations other than the claim that programmed learning is inherently superior. Perhaps the novelty of programmed learning increases the motivation of students to learn. If teaching machines were commonly used everywhere, wouldn't the introduction of present-day traditional methods, flaunted as improvements, also improve performance? Another explanation that must be considered is that these early studies have been conducted, for the most part, by psychologists and educators who have been very deeply interested in developing programmed instruction as an educational tool. Although this interest is certainly not to be criticized, it is quite possible that the amount of energy and zeal expended in making the experimental programmed instruction effective has been much greater than that expended on behalf of the control (conventional) methods with which programmed learning has been compared. We must realize that comparing two methods of education is a complicated research effort.

The answer to the hypothesis that bias may have played a part in the research is more and better experiments. Various teaching-machine programs have to be compared with a variety of conventional methods using classroom learning and conventional textbooks. In order to examine all possibilities, various combinations of teaching machines and conventional methods must also be tested.

That investigations into the merits and limitations of programmed instruction must be sound and unbiased is not the only challenge the advocates of the new methods must meet. Not even the most ardent exponent of programmed learning is satisfied with the techniques developed so far. Everyone has come to realize that programming is an extremely difficult and time-consuming task. One first-year algebra course consists of 8,000 frames, not an atypical number. In fact, the longer people work at programming, the higher they set their estimates of the number of frames needed for ideal programs.

What are badly needed are some rules to guide the programmer in his laborious task. We have already discussed some of the rules of prompting. Another rule, known as the *ruleg system* (Homme & Glaser, 1959), is based on the assumption that most teaching involves the presentation of principles or abstractions (rules) and instances of these (examples). This system advocates the use of items that present principles followed by other items that illustrate each principle in a variety of examples. Despite the guidance such rules provide, programmers must still rely heavily on their own ingenuity and intuition. Just as there are good and poor classroom teachers, there seem to be good and poor programmers. But there is one important difference. Because constant feedback occurs in programming, and because the program can be changed more easily than the habits of a particular teacher, the likelihood is greater that a definable set of rules will be formulated and put into practice more easily in programmed instruction than in classroom teaching.

Programmed instruction has another advantage not shared by classroom teaching. Our knowledge, especially in science and mathematics, is forging ahead at such a rapid rate that classroom teachers often find their lesson plans quickly becoming obsolete. Programming allows the expert to contribute his special talents and knowledge in the construction of programs that may well be used by classes throughout the country.

Perhaps the greatest challenge that programmed instruction would like to meet is to provide convincing evidence that a subject is retained and transferred better than when it is taught by traditional methods. Educators have been too willing to use as their criterion of learning the scores or marks obtained on examinations taken at the end of a course, or at most, at the end of a year or so. This is understandable when you consider the difficulties involved in evaluating the effects of education after several years. But most education serves a long-term purpose. It is vastly more important to the individual and his society that a mathematics major, for example, should some day perform efficiently and creatively as a professional mathematician than that he achieve a high grade on a particular final examination. Although evidence suggests that scores do correlate with several long-range criteria, the ultimate evaluation of programmed instruction, or any form of learning, must come from knowledge of how well that learning has been understood, retained, and utilized. In order to appraise the most valuable consequences of programmed learning, one must first know that something more is learned than just the ability to complete the program and immediately thereafter pass an examination based upon it. A truly successful program is one in which students retain the knowledge they have acquired and are able to use it in (i.e. transfer it to) all sorts of exacting situations.

By now the reader will have concluded correctly that it is difficult to predict the future of programmed learning. The educated guess of most psychologists, including the writer, is that it is bound to help considerably in the solution of many of our educational problems in decades to come. Yet even informed guesses are not facts, and only the future will show how important programmed instruction will become. In any event, whether of major or of minor importance, programmed instruction will have had a salutary effect upon education by forcing society to re-evaluate the efficiency of its educational procedures and to seek to improve them.

Other Auto-Instructional Methods

It would be misleading to leave you with the impression that programmed learning constitutes the only technological development in education. While most educational research is now being put into teaching machines and programming, substantial efforts are being made to improve education by the use of films, television, and tape recorders.

Educational Films. Ever since "moving pictures" were invented, people have realized how important they should be for formal education, and through the years, a large number of training films have been produced to make learning easier and better. As with programmed instruction, we cannot offer a single appraisal of educational films. They vary in quality from excellent to poor, as the reader no doubt knows.

Educational films have one great psychological advantage. They can be extremely effective in providing clear pictures of stimulus situations to which responses have to be associated. A child studying geography can actually come close to seeing a country, instead of trying to imagine it for himself from an inadequate verbal description. There are several excellent films on psychology that allow the student to see many of the experimental phenomena reported in this book. For the purpose of training people to perform a variety of tasks—ranging from tying knots to repairing electronic gear—films can provide close-up views which actual demonstrations could provide for only a few lucky individuals. Films have the added advantage of being able to show how an object or a process looks at normal range and perceptual speed, enlarged, slowed down, or sped up to show continuous developments. And finally, techniques of film cartooning permit the simplification of complex stimuli, so that the audience can see the essentials of processes and principles.

Educational films also have their disadvantages. Since they exert no control whatever over a viewer's behavior, except through their inherent interest, their effectiveness may be dissipated because the audience responds in ways other than giving serious and thoughtful attention. In one army film designed to teach first aid for combat wounds, the gruesome pictures made many viewers turn away in horror and joke about them to relieve the tension. The purpose of a film presentation in a classroom is often defeated because a darkened room sets many students talking, wise-cracking, and kidding around.

If you consider the problem of how to evoke correct responses, you can see the advantage that programmed instruction has over training films. Programmed instruction has been intentionally designed to use an important principle of learning: the correct response must occur and be reinforced in the presence of the appropriate stimulus. Educational films, on the other hand, have been produced, for the most part, without a thought to this principle. Nevertheless, as we have pointed out, films are sometimes excellent vehicles for presenting the stimulus situation to which responses must be associated. Obviously, films should be incorporated into certain kinds of programmed instruction. No doubt this requires expensive equipment, but the benefits may well outweigh the cost.

Training by Television. The armed services

of the United States were prompt to recognize the educational potential in television. Today it is used as an aid to training in a variety of military situations. Although at first glance television instruction may seem to be essentially the same as training films, it has proved to be a much more flexible medium. Unlike training films, television instruction is not hampered by high production costs or excessive delays between the preparation of an instructional sequence and its use in the classroom. It can provide on-the-spot coverage of events that have educational significance (a rare surgical operation, demonstrations requiring bulky equipment that cannot be brought into the classroom).

One example of the value of television instruction is the procedure used in training soldiers to repair expensive missile-launching equipment. The size, weight, and complexity of the equipment, as well as its value, prevent it from being used in a classroom, much less in several classrooms simultaneously. However, missile training equipment can be brought into the television studio, together with an experienced repairman-instructor, and small groups of students can watch television receivers in separate classrooms. For the lesson, a defect in the operation of the equipment is deliberately introduced, and the television camera records all the symptoms, meter readings, and other information necessary for a diagnosis of the trouble. Through two-way intercommunication systems the students may request and receive additional information, and they may make suggestions to the television studio repairman about how he might repair the defect. All the trainees hear and see what is going on and profit from each other's failures and successes. In this way they receive first-hand information about the repair of the equipment without even being near it.

One of the advantages of television in the classroom is that it is economical of instructional personnel. At present there is a severe shortage of topnotch science teachers in our elementary and high school systems. To overcome this shortage schools are sharing special science teachers by means of closed-circuit television through which they can schedule lectures in sev-

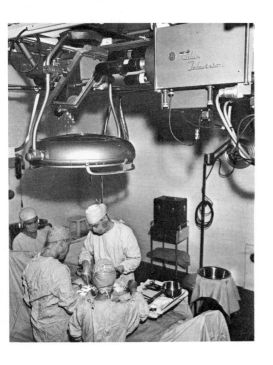

FIGURE 17.10 Two Examples of Training by Television (U. S. Army Photographer).

eral classrooms simultaneously. The same method is now used in nationwide educational television hook-ups, making it possible for professors with outstanding teaching reputations to be seen and heard by audiences of over a million persons.

Otherwise, television shares the virtues and faults of training films. It has an outstanding ability to display a stimulus situation, but it fails to guarantee that viewers will make correct responses. Television instruction can be made more effective if its advantages and disadvantages are considered. If this is done, the contributions of television to effective education will increase.

Language Laboratory. Many people who struggled to master a foreign language in their student days have distasteful memories of arduous drills, embarrassing mispronunciations, and irregular verbs. And to make their memories even more unpleasant, at the end of a two- or three-year college course they had nothing to show for their efforts but a poor reading knowledge and a still poorer speaking ability.

Today the picture is somewhat brighter for the language student who has the use of a language laboratory. Typically the facilities in a language laboratory consist of isolated booths where individual students can listen to tape recordings of correct pronunciations of foreign languages and can compare them with their own efforts. The idea underlying the language laboratory is that the easiest way to learn a language is to speak it and listen to it from the start—this is the method we all used in learning our native tongue.

Although language labs are based on the assumption that the aim in learning a language is to speak it, only two or three decades ago language training was handicapped by uncertainty as to its principal goal. The writer recalls that his own language teachers worked at cross-purposes. One was interested mainly in training students to read literature and made no effort

FIGURE 17.11 A Language Laboratory (William R. Simmons, photographer; New York University).

to teach them to converse in the new language. Another expended all her efforts in training the students to speak, as nearly as possible, like natives. And finally, there was a scholarly professor interested only in the culture and philosophy of the country whose language was being studied. The class discussions were all held in English because the ideas were too subtle to be expressed in a language whose nuances were largely unfamiliar to his students. Needless to say, a training program that is unclear about its purposes is doomed to failure.

Now, the U. S. Government's need for millions of Americans able to speak foreign languages has provided a sense of purpose and order to modern language instruction that it had not previously possessed. When the nature of the responses to be learned can be specified, the planning of instruction becomes simpler. The new emphasis on speaking the language does not mean that reading the literature or understanding the major philosophical ideas are neglected. These different kinds of knowledge and skill must be acquired in the proper order, and learning to speak a language is now seen as the right first step.

The language laboratory has several educational and psychological advantages over traditional training. Nevertheless, no one supposes that it is the only effective method of instruction. Having a good private tutor or spending a year in a foreign country are excellent ways of learning a new language, but they are obviously too costly for the majority of students. Language labs allow for mass instruction on an individualized basis. In a language lab the student can practice his pronunciation in a situation designed to allow him to make his own discriminations between the right and wrong ways of saying things. In a single lab period he receives more practice in speaking than he would normally get in a whole semester in a large class. And in the lab the student is spared listening to and sometimes unintentionally learning the imperfect pronunciation of his classmates. Instead he hears a variety of native speech patterns. When they get to Paris for the first time, many people who learned French in the classroom, are surprised to find that few (if any) Frenchmen speak the way their high school French teacher did. This does not bother the language lab student who has had an opportunity to listen to tapes of the voices of men, women, and children from all over France.

Language labs have other advantages. Slow and fast learners progress at their own rates. Self-consciousness, which is more of a problem in language training than in other subjects, is reduced markedly. Many students are very embarrassed when they mispronounce words; they think their fellow students are laughing at them. Their anxiety interferes with their performance, but off by themselves in a booth they lose their fear of embarrassment. The mike is not going to giggle at them as their classmates might. Their practice in speaking can go on in an unthreatening atmosphere.

Language labs, like all programmed instruction, require good programs if they are to be effective. However, the effects of different programming techniques in the language labs have not been investigated systematically. Methods of programming in languages have not attracted the interest of researchers whose specialty is the psychology of learning. But with the reawakened interest in all educational techniques stimulated by both the crisis in education and the programmed learning movement, this condition is going to change.

One subject for research that badly needs investigation is discrimination in language labs. One of their obvious advantages is that the student can hear proper speech and then compare it with his own. But often the arrangements are not optimal for making the comparison. Typically the student pronounces a word or phrase and then hears it pronounced correctly, or *vice versa*. This means that he is exposed only once to this particular comparison between his own speech and the correct pronunciation. It would seem a better arrangement to have the student's response recorded on tape alongside the correct response. Then repeated comparisons could be made and in the process better discrimination would be established. Some language labs provide facilities for doing this, but at present most of them do not.

A problem related to discrimination is the familiar one of reinforcement. In programmed learning the subject is reinforced when he makes the correct response. He can ascertain what the correct response is simply by reading the answer. In language training there is no such clear indication. The student has to make his own judgment as to whether or not his pronunciation is close enough to the correct one. Two students might pronounce the same phrase in exactly the same way and yet one of them would consider his response way off while the other would feel completely satisfied with it. Some method of providing several examples of appropriate and inappropriate responses would be advantageous; it would help the student decide on as objective grounds as possible whether or not he has reasonably mastered the proper pronunciation of the phrase. And if what is known about shaping behavior can be generalized to foreign language training, then the examples of "correct responses" should be lenient at first and then gradually sharpened and made more precise.

Concluding Remarks. Programmed instruction, training films, educational television, and language labs are not gimmicks that automatically insure effective instruction. If so conceived, they would be guaranteed to fail. Too often people are lulled into believing that a critical educational problem will quietly fade out when some dramatic new form of instruction is introduced. But a little knowledge of the psychology of learning effectively prevents you from believing that a device can by itself improve education. Devices are useful only if they are used to improve conditions of learning. This requires developing new methods, based upon quantitative research, in which the stimulus situation, the responses, reinforcements, and motivational conditions are all optimally ordered. Even at the start of the work psychologists can offer useful suggestions about how this can be done, but in the complex world of the classroom it is difficult to know beforehand just what effects any new method of instruction will have. This is why new educational practices will in the long run have to be subjected to the most rigorous kinds of experimental tests, including quantitative determinations of the influence of the principal variables that may affect learning.

VOCATIONAL GUIDANCE

It is a rare student who has not been bothered, perhaps tortured, by the question of what career he should pursue. It is even a rarer parent who has not worried about the same problem as he watched his offspring rapidly approach adulthood. Moreover, vocational choices are not simply individual or family matters. Any society which perceives them in that way will, of necessity, be making less than optimal use of its human resources. In the United States society tries to assist the individual who is selecting the vocation for which he is best fitted by means of vocational guidance.

Vocational guidance has been referred to as "the high art of helping boys and girls to plan their own actions wisely, in the full light of all the facts that can be mustered about themselves and about the world in which they will work and live." This description should dispel two common misconceptions about vocational guidance. The first is that guidance is an automatic process at the end of which the youth will be directed to become a "doctor or lawyer or Indian chief." Vocational guidance does not pretend to free the individual from making his own vocational decision, however difficult. But, properly conducted, it does provide him with information derived from the findings of experts on which a sound decision can be based. The second misconception is that vocational guidance is concerned only with the aptitudes and abilities of the individual student. Many more factors than these determine what is vocationally wise for an individual, some of these, conditions wholly outside of himself. This is particularly true in a highly industrialized society where new kinds of job opportunities are constantly created and where old ones disappear. No matter how much aptitude and enthusiasm a person may have for building horse-drawn carriages or steam locomotives, there would be little sense in encouraging him to pursue such a vocation. It is the responsibility of a vocational guidance counselor to keep abreast of occupational information, so that before anyone he is counseling makes a decision as to what career he will head toward, he not only has a fair estimate of his own capabilities, but also knows something about the financial and social potential of different professions and vocations.

Vocational Counseling

Vocational counseling shares with many other branches of psychology the goal of predicting future behavior from present performance. Although simple in conception, the actual task is most complicated. It demands reliable methods of measuring a person's aptitude, personality, and other forms of behavior that have been proved to be valid indicators of future job performance. Successful vocational guidance depends not only on predicting what jobs a person can do well, but also those that he will be happy in. Most of us know someone who so thoroughly dislikes his job that it darkens his very existence. More often than not such strong dissatisfaction interferes with his doing the job well. He is caught in a vicious circle, in which his dissatisaction results in poorer performance, which in turn creates greater dissatisfaction, and so on.

Job dissatisfaction, even of this intensity, is not rare. One study (Havemann & West, 1952) of college graduates discovered (see Figure 17.12) that 25 per cent of them wished they had studied something else in college. The amount of dissatisfaction they felt varied with their undergraduate major. The smallest proportion of dissatisfied graduates was found among those who had been premedical students, the greatest among the pharmacy majors. One reason for this is that dissatisfaction with one's job is not dependent simply upon how much a person enjoys his work. The amount of social prestige attached to a job is also important. About 50 per cent of a group of clerical and manual workers reported they were interested in their work, but, nevertheless, only one-third of these said

they would choose the same occupation if they were given another chance (Form, 1946). Most of them would have liked to enter occupations with higher social status.

Thus, in evaluating a client jobwise, a vocational guidance counselor must not only consider his capabilities and his interests, but also how much importance he attaches to social prestige, something that, as one might expect, is very difficult to estimate. There is little doubt that the task of the guidance counselor would be much easier, and his efforts probably considerably more effective, if there were some way of lessening the differences in prestige of various jobs.

Effective vocational guidance is usually a long-drawn-out process. The common notion that a student requires the services of a guidance counselor only during the later stages of his high school career is mistaken, because sound vocational decisions can come only after a student has had certain kinds of educational experiences, and in a great many instances it is too late to provide these at the end of high school. They must be planned for earlier. A boy at the end of his high school course may have good grades and the pattern of abilities suitable for a career in engineering but simply have not taken the courses needed for acceptance in engineering school. If his special talent had been discovered earlier, this deficiency could have been avoided. The following case history (Bennett, Seashore, & Wesman, 1951) is typical of many cases, and it illustrates how important testing and counseling programs can be at the earlier ages.

The student entered high school with a long history of below-average grades. He disliked reading and writing intensely, and failed to prepare the assignments that would have revealed his inadequacies in these skills. He had become convinced that intellectually he was below average. Tests showed that in reading proficiency he was in the lowest third of the class, but in four different types of reasoning ability he tested

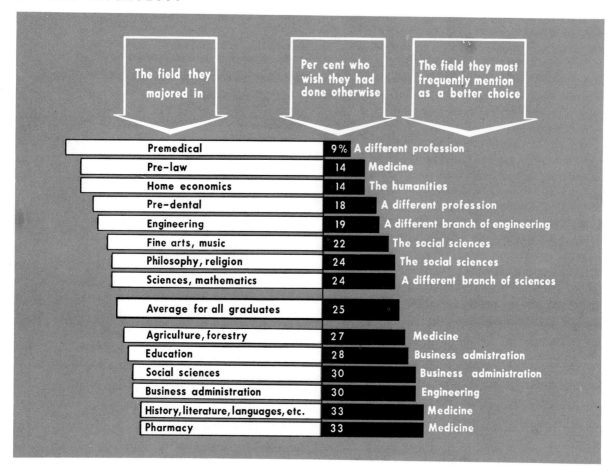

FIGURE 17.12   Job Dissatisfaction Among College Graduates (E. Havemann & P. S. West. *They went to college.* Harcourt, Brace, & World, 1952).

in the highest 5 per cent. The report of these tests delighted him and his teachers at once noted his new self-confidence and a changed attitude toward his work. With this more positive view of himself he began serious preparation for an engineering career and thereby avoided wasting his talents.

Education is vastly more effective when teachers are made aware of the potentialities of these students. Many a bright student goes unnoticed until the results of a testing program reveal his abilities. Once these are realized, many remedial measures can be instituted to get a student out of a rut and functioning in line with his talents and brightest prospects.

Vocational Guidance Programs

The manner in which a vocational guidance program is conducted depends upon who administers it. School systems and guidance clinics are the two organizations that do most of this work. Although schools usually counsel a much larger number of individuals, the procedures of the guidance clinic are somewhat less complex and we will therefore describe them to begin with.

A clinic, once a client has been referred to it, proceeds to interview and test him. This usually involves four basic steps.

Interviewing. A counselor, who is usually a psychologist, interviews the client to obtain from him the information needed to decide, at least in a preliminary way, upon the proper testing and counseling program. The interview typically touches upon such topics as the client's personal, educational, and vocational background, as well as upon his interests, aims, and aspirations. Just what form the interview will take depends upon the particular counselor who is giving it. Some of them prefer a rather standardized form of interview; others like to follow a more flexible approach. In either case, the counselor is probably going to develop some hypotheses about the nature of the client's vocational problem, and the information he gathers will both be of assistance in shaping his surmises and distinctly relevant to planning the next step in the counseling process.

Psychological Testing. The core of vocational guidance is the testing program. Although vocational guidance can, and perhaps still does, occur without any testing, its predictive aspects are surely crippled if no tests are used. Some clinics have a basic set of tests which they give to all their clients; others adapt the testing program to the particular requirements of different individuals. In either case the tests are given to obtain fundamental information about such things as the client's IQ, aptitudes, achievements, personality, and motivation. Tests of these kinds have already been described. In what is generally agreed to be the most difficult task facing the guidance counselor, assessing motivation, the Allport-Vernon-Lindzey Scale, which measures a person's values (see page 473), is extremely helpful. Two tests that have been constructed specifically to discover patterns of interests shared by members of

the same vocations and professions are the *Strong Vocational Interest Test* and the *Kuder Preference Record,* both of which are widely used in guidance counseling.

The Strong Vocational Interest Test (Strong, 1943) compares the interests of the client with those of individuals who have been notably successful in different occupations. The client simply registers his interest or lack of interest in a number of activities. The mechanics of the test are on the surface quite simple. Four hundred items are listed, including occupations, school subjects, amusements, hobbies, and peculiarities of people. The client responds to each by circling one of three letters, *L, I,* and *D,* indicating respectively *like, indifferent,* and *dislike.* In addition to these items there are others which require ranking certain activities in order of preference, expressing choices between two items, and finally self-ratings of abilities and personal characteristics. The person taking the test is scored according to the degree of resemblance between his answers and those of people who have been successful in various occupations. Thus, if a client gives answers that are in general like those of successful architects, he is recorded as scoring high in architect interest. If his answers are unlike those of a salesman he is put down as scoring low in salesman interest.

Two basic assumptions underlie this test. The first is that successful members of each occupation have similar patterns of interests. This has been found to be true in general. But the patterns of interest of different occupations are not always dissimilar. Occupational interests tend to run in groups. For example, mathematicians, physicists, engineers, and chemists show similar patterns of interests, but their interests are unlike those of salesmen. Because of this the scores obtained on the Strong Vocational Interest Test do not single out just one occupation as one for which the client has an appropriate pattern of interests, but several occupations for any one of which the client appears to have the necessary interests.

The second assumption underlying the Strong test is that interest patterns exhibited in college are indicative of later vocational interest and satisfaction. The results of a study of over 600 men who took the Strong Vocational Interest Test in college and then were examined 18 years later indicated the test had genuine predictive value (Strong, 1955). And there is evidence to suggest that the Strong test can predict success in a given occupation. A psychologist for an insurance corporation found that men scoring high in interest in salesmanship had a much greater chance of being a successful insurance salesman than men who exhibited a low interest (Bills, 1950).

The Kuder Preference Record (Kuder, 1958) is scored for a much wider range of interests than the Strong test. It assesses three interest areas. Like the Strong test, the subject's reaction can be scored in terms of specific occupations (minister, accountant). It can also be scored for various general interest patterns, such as outdoor, mechanical, computational, scientific, artistic, persuasive, literary, musical, social service, and clerical. And finally, the test measures personal interests, such as group

TABLE 17.3   Classification of Men's Occupations on Basis of Correlations of Interests on Strong Vocational Interest Test (Strong, 1943).

OCCUPATIONS COMPRISING EACH GROUP	GROUPS WITH WHICH CORRELATION WAS MOST SIGNIFICANT	
	Positive (similar interests)	*Negative* (dissimilar interests)
I. Artist, psychologist, architect, physician, dentist	II, VI	VII, IX
II. Mathematician, physicist, engineer, chemist	I, IV	IX
III. Production manager	IV	VI, X
IV. Aviator, farmer, carpenter, mathematics-physical science teacher, printer, policemen, forest service	II, III	VII, IX, X, XI
V. Y.M.C.A. secretary, Y.M.C.A. physical director, personnel manager, city school superintendent, minister, social science teacher		XI
VI. Musician	I	III, XI
VII. Certified public accountant	X	IV
VIII. Purchasing agent, office worker, accountant, banker		I, X
IX. Real estate salesman, life insurance salesman, sales manager	XI	I, II, IV
X. Lawyer, author-journalist, advertising man	VII	III, IV, VIII
XI. President of manufacturing concern	IX	IV, V, VI

activities, working with ideas, directing and influencing others, avoiding conflict, and interest in new experiences as compared with familiar ones. A person takes the Kuder test in much the same way he takes the Strong test. He indicates his likes and dislikes by selecting from three alternatives the one he likes most and the one he likes least.

There is no general agreement as to which of these two interest inventories is a superior instrument. The Strong Vocational Interest Test has somewhat better occupational norms. But the Kuder Preference Record has the advantage of providing a wider range of interest data, which some guidance counselors believe compensates for its limited norms. Despite the usefulness and general excellence of these tests, most guidance experts seek further information about their client's motivation and resort to personality tests and appropriate questioning during interviews.

Many aptitude and achievement tests are at the disposal of the guidance counselor. A test used by industrial concerns to select good mechanics or a test used to select entrants to medical school is obviously useful to him. But there are greater advantages in having a test which is not restricted to specific vocations. What he needs is a battery of tests that can get at those basic aptitudes which are related to potentiality in many different kinds of occupations.

One such test that is widely used is the Differential Aptitude Test (DAT) (Bennett, Seashore, & Wesman, 1959). The DAT was constructed by factor-analytic methods with the idea that it should be possible to identify a set of basic aptitudes in high school students. Its various subtests measure the following factors: verbal reasoning, numerical ability, abstract reasoning, spatial relations, mechanical ability, clerical speed, spelling, and sentence structure. As the names indicate, the DAT measures aptitudes which are obviously related to a wide variety of possible vocations. After a

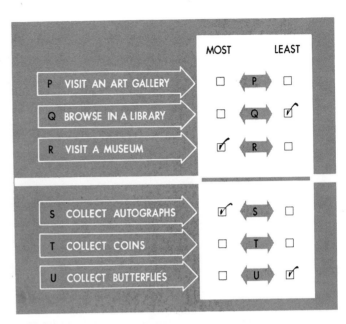

FIGURE 17.13 Two Items From the Kuder Preference Record. For each group of three alternatives the subject indicates which he likes most and which he likes least. In this case, choosing among P, Q, and R, the subject liked R most and Q least. He liked S most and U least when choosing among S, T, and U (Science Research Associates).

student has taken the DAT, his test profile is constructed showing his performance in terms of percentile ranks (see Figure 17.15). Each bar on the graph which is anchored to the median score shows the student's performance relative to other students of his grade. Scores obtained on the DAT during tenth grade have proved to be excellent predictors of performance on college entrance examinations (Seashore, 1954). Thus the DAT becomes a useful tool in counseling students fairly early in high school about their college plans as well as, for example, encouraging some who had not thought of doing so to consider going to college. Those who do plan to attend can be helped to select appropriate courses, and to make the increasingly important decision of which kind of college would be most suitable.

Conference between Client and Counselor.
After all the test results are in, they must

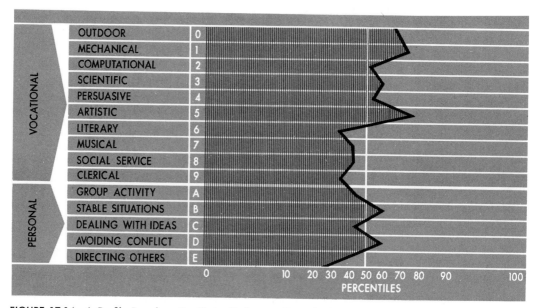

FIGURE 17.14 A Profile Based on the Kuder Preference Record. The percentile ranks obtained on the various personal and vocational interests indicate a subject's performance in relation to the standardization group. In this case, the subject had a *computational interest* stronger than 50 per cent of the group, an *artistic interest* stronger than 78 per cent of the group, and a *literary interest* stronger than 35 per cent of the group (Science Research Associates).

be interpreted in the light of evidence obtained from the interview and other sources. And to do this wisely and sensibly the counselor arranges one or more conferences with his client. The basic aim of these conferences is to help the client make a choice about his future vocation. But any occupational choice is a process that spans many years, and at any one moment such a decision can only be provisional. It would be foolhardy to think that at the end of any conference an irrevocable decision had been reached.

Instead, the aim of the conference depends upon the age of the client. The objective of a conference with a boy entering high school should be a decision on the course of study to be pursued. At some future date when more is known about his scholastic achievements in high school, decisions can be made about whether he should go to college or trade school, or go to work right away. Effective vocational

guidance involves a *series* of decisions, each dependent to some measure on preceding ones. There is always room for choice, although as the client grows older the range of choice becomes narrower and previous decisions become more difficult, and sometimes impossible, to reverse. In this light vocational guidance is perceived as an ongoing process that tries to take advantage of all available information including whatever (current scholastic performance, test performances, changes in economic conditions) is relevant to the client's vocational choice.

A very common case in vocational guidance is the student who is drifting aimlessly because he is unable to make any "fateful" decisions and, if allowed to continue, may find himself unprepared for any sort of vocation. Such a client must be treated by a counselor with methods that border on psychotherapy. If he can be persuaded that he has the talent to fill some kind of position, as most people do, and that any decision he has to reach now is not completely binding, then he may be freed from the doubts and fears immobilizing him. After this hurdle is cleared it is to be hoped that some achievement, some success in school or work, will turn up to make a definite decision much easier.

Other young people need the opposite type of influence from their counselor. They rush in making firm vocational decisions before they are required to, and before they are competent, in all sorts of respects, to do so. Usually such youngsters are responding to parental pressures or some felt personal difficulty. It is the task of a counselor to help them disengage themselves from hasty and unwise decisions, so that they will be free to make more judicious ones in the future.

Poor vocational choices are often made by talented children who come from low socioeconomic levels. They may not be motivated to think much about education and its values and are, therefore, willing to leave school at an early age. The possibility that they might pursue professional careers may appear too remote to be considered. In this case, it is the task of the counselor to inform the child and his family about possibilities that they might never have even entertained. It is also his responsibility to indicate how the economic problems associated with professional training might be solved, perhaps with outside financial assistance such as scholarships, etc.

Written Report. The next step, but not always the last one, in vocational guidance is to prepare a written report that summarizes the findings of the previous three steps and includes the counselor's own recommendation for future vocational guidance. Such reports, perhaps a succession of them, are essentials in any long-range counseling program for a client.

Guidance programs in school systems and colleges face special difficulties because they are required to service such large numbers of clients. Nevertheless, their procedures are similar to the ones in the typical clinic. The main difference is that in the school guidance program every possible attempt is made to use group procedures. The testing is often done in large groups. General problems of vocational guidance are discussed in lectures. Information about manpower needs and trends are made available to students in booklets that are distributed to them or placed in the school library. The hope of such a mass program has to be that not many students will require individual attention. And this is often the case. A student who wants to be a physician,

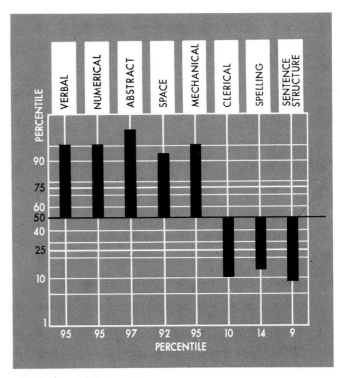

FIGURE 17.15 Differential Aptitude Test Profile. This profile was obtained by the subject in the case described on page 671. His scores in verbal reasoning, numerical ability, abstract ability, spatial relations, and mechanical ability were all above the 90th percentile, that is, his score exceeded more than 90 per cent of the members of the standardization group (After Bennett, Seashore, & Wesman, 1951, with permission of The Psychological Corporation).

has the abilities, personality, and motivation for such an exacting profession, has already selected the correct course of study, and is doing well in it, does not need much, if any, guidance. The problem for most school programs is to find time to provide individual counseling for those students who are badly in need of it. This need cannot be filled until more vocational guidance counselors have been trained. In 1960 it was estimated that only about half of the nation's high schools had as many as one half-time counselor, and yet this was supposed to be sufficient to serve the guidance needs of all their students.

The guidance problem, however, will not have been solved completely even when a sufficient supply of counselors becomes available. To a very considerable extent guidance is the responsibility of every teacher, especially if he has a conscience and realizes what his position might enable him to accomplish. Practically every high school and college teacher should be able to exert an influence on some students in the development of their vocational attitudes. The teacher must be aware of his influence so that he can exert it wisely and sensibly in the best interests of the student, instead of haphazardly, or worse, in the form of outright pressure. The teacher should also be on the lookout for the student who is not utilizing his talents to advantage, so that he can be helped to find his way to a guidance counselor.

Vocational Guidance and Social Needs

Vocational guidance programs are a typical American product, although other nations are beginning to imitate our methods. Initially vocational guidance was largely restricted to private clinics that dealt with "problem cases." When it was realized that vocational guidance was a social as well as an individual problem, programs were launched in the schools and in many communities and social welfare agencies set up their own clinics. In some rare cases there is duplication of effort between the clinics and the school programs. But at the moment our deficiencies are due to the fact that we have too little guidance rather than too much. The goal we must strive to attain is the optimal utilization of the talents of each individual within the framework of a highly industrialized, democratic society.

SUMMARY

Human engineering applies psychological knowledge and techniques to the design of man-machine systems so that together they can operate efficiently and effectively. In order to accomplish this it is necessary to understand the capabilities and limitations of both man and machine in relation to their abilities to sense, process information, and respond. With such information it becomes possible both to improve the performance of existing man-machine systems and to design superior ones.

Several auto-instructional devices have been designed to improve education. A teaching machine presents small amounts of information to which the student is required to respond. The most important feature of teaching machines are their programs, many of which can be arranged in book form. Linear programming is based upon the principles of shaping; the situation is arranged so that appropriate responses are emitted and reinforced immediately. Proceeding at his own pace the student in a series of "small steps" learns the subject matter of his course. Programming of the branching type resembles a series of multiple-choice questions. The student also proceeds at his own pace and is allowed, if capable, to make "big steps" forward. Training films, educational TV, and language laboratories are other examples of auto-instructional devices which are particularly suited for certain kinds of educational problems.

Vocational guidance is designed to assist young people in making wise decisions about the careers they seek to pursue. Like other areas of psychology it seeks to predict future behavior from present performance. It does this by interviews and psychological tests designed to measure abilities, personality, and motivation.

SUGGESTIONS FOR FURTHER READING

CHAPANIS, A., GARNER, W. R., & MORGAN, C. T. *Applied experimental psychology.* New York: Wiley, 1949.

An excellent text in applied experimental psychology that emphasizes human engineering.

DETERLINE, W. A. *An introduction to programmed instruction.* Englewood Cliffs, N.J.: Prentice-Hall, 1962.

An introductory presentation of the principles and potentialities of auto-instructional methodology.

FLEISHMAN, E. A. (Ed.) *Studies in personnel and industrial psychology.* Homewood, Ill.: R. D. Irwin, 1962.

A series of papers that reflect recent developments in personnel selection, leadership, industrial organization, engineering psychology, and other topics.

FRY, E. *Teaching machines and programmed learning.* New York: McGraw-Hill, 1962.

A detailed review of teaching machines and methods of programming.

GAGNÉ, R. M., & FLEISHMAN, E. A. *Psychology and human performance.* New York: Holt, Rinehart, & Winston, 1959.

An introductory psychology textbook that emphasizes industrial and business applications. The final four chapters offer an expanded treatment of personnel selection and training and human engineering.

GHISELLE, E. E., & BROWN, C. W. *Personnel and industrial psychology.* (2nd ed.) New York: McGraw-Hill, 1955.

A textbook that emphasizes aptitude testing in business and industry.

GOLDMAN, L. *Using tests in counseling.* New York: Appleton-Century-Crofts, 1961.

A well-organized book describing the use and misuses of psychological tests in vocational guidance.

GREEN, E. G. *The learning process and programmed instruction.* New York: Holt, Rinehart, & Winston, 1962.

An application of the principles of operant conditioning to programmed learning.

HOLLAND, J. G., & SKINNER, B. F. *The analysis of behavior: A program for self-instruction.* New York: McGraw-Hill, 1961.

A program in book form of B. F. Skinner's operant-conditioning view of behavior.

KARN, H. W., & GILMER, H. *Readings in industrial and business psychology.* (2nd ed.) New York: McGraw-Hill, 1962.

A collection of original papers representing current research and theory in industrial and business psychology.

LOFQUIST, L. H., & ENGLAND, G. N. *Problems in vocational counseling.* Dubuque, Iowa: Wm. C. Brown, 1961.

A brief book for the advanced student of vocational guidance. This book emphasizes research findings.

WEBB, W. B. *The profession of psychology.* New York: Holt, Rinehart, & Winston, 1962.

An excellent book for the student who is contemplating a career in psychology. Contains a series of chapters, written by experts, that describe the different work that psychologists do.

A FINAL COMMENT

When I started this book, it was my plan to convey a clear, frank picture of the science of behavior. I am in no position to offer an objective evaluation of how well I succeeded. I hope at least that reading this book has been an educational experience for you, as writing it has been for me. Attempting to organize the facts and principles of psychology has given me a clearer view of all of psychology. It might be helpful to share three of my impressions with you.

I am struck with the variety of ways in which the experimental method is being applied to all forms of behavior. Newer and better experimental methods are continually being developed. Scientific progress is closely tied to the quality of the techniques science has available to investigate its subject matter. And in psychology this progress is being aided by new equipment and clever experimental procedures.

It was disconcerting to me, as it no doubt was for you, to be forced to qualify so many of the principles of behavior that I set down. But one of the distinctive features of scientific knowledge is that it recognizes its limits. The unqualified common-sense notion that "practice makes perfect" is false in spite of its core of truth. By limiting its implications to situations where suitable conditions prevail, it becomes possible to transfer this unqualified statement into a true one: "Practice makes perfect when the organism is reinforced for making the appropriate response."

One point, repeatedly made, is that clear language is needed for discussing behavior sensibly. Clear language, however, rests upon our ability to break complex behavior down into some pattern of basic components. This is as true for everyday behavior as it is for responses observed in the laboratory. What response is occurring? What is the stimulus or perceptual pattern evoking it? Has the association between the two been previously reinforced? If so, what was the schedule of reinforcement? What are the competing responses? What is the motivation of the organism? And so forth. Unless we can become as analytical as this, behavior will remain a mystery. By reducing the complexity of behavior into a set of manageable variables, we are taking the first step toward understanding it. And as this book has shown, the systematic investigations of these variables have revealed underlying uniformities. As psychologists press forward with their research efforts, man's understanding of the principles governing his own behavior will continually increase.

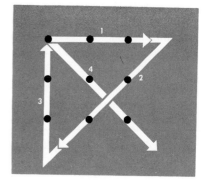

Solution to Figure 2.2.

GLOSSARY

Ability. A pattern of behavior tendencies responsible for skillful performance in a variety of related tasks.

Absolute Refractory Phase. The period after the transmission of a neural impulse when a nerve fiber is completely unresponsive to stimulation.

Absolute Stimulus Threshold. The weakest intensity of a stimulus that can be detected.

Accommodation. Adjustment of the curvature of the lens that regulates the focus of the image of an object on the retina.

Achievement Test. An examination that measures the degree of proficiency already attained in some specific skill or ability.

Acquisition Stage. The portion of a learning experiment in which an organism is acquiring a new mode of responding (e.g., the dog in the acquisition stage of classical conditioning is learning to salivate to a tone).

Activation. A dimension of activity against which behavioral and physiological events can be ranked. A high level of activation occurs during a rage when a persons' physiological system is responding at a relatively high level of activity. The term *arousal* is often used interchangeably with *activation*.

Adjustment. A general term that refers to an individual's ability to meet the demands of society and satisfy his own drives.

Afferent Nerves. Sensory nerves that connect receptors with the central nervous system.

Age Standard Method. The method, used initially by Alfred Binet, of measuring the intelligence of a child in relation to the average performance of different age groups (e.g., a four-year-old child might perform at a level equivalent to an average six-year-old).

Aggression. A general term describing behavior that is hostile, destructive, *or* hurtful.

Agnosia. A disorder in which a patient can see objects but cannot identify them by visual cues alone. The disorder results from damage to visual association neurons.

Alarm Reaction. The initial stage of the general adaptation syndrome. It involves a pattern of bodily changes in reaction to a stressor.

Albedo. The percentage reflected of the total light falling upon a surface.

Alcoholism. An excessive and compulsive consumption of alcohol.

All-or-None Law. The principle which states that a neuron responds completely or not at all.

Ambivalence. Simultaneous conflicting reactions toward a person or thing. According to psychoanalytic theory ambivalence can become so extreme that one can love and hate the same person.

Amnesia. A partial or complete loss of memory of some past experience that cannot be attributed to ordinary forgetting (e.g., soldiers forgetting their combat experiences).

681

Amplitude of the Response. The intensity or amount of a response (e.g., amplitude of the salivary response is measured by the amount of salivation). The amplitude of response is sometimes used to measure the course of learning. During the acquisition stage of classical conditioning the amplitude of the conditioned response increases.

Anal-Erotic Stage. The second stage of psychosexual development, in Freudian theory. Libidinal gratification is obtained from expulsion and retention of feces.

Anticipatory Error. An error in serial learning in which the subject makes a response before it is appropriate (e.g., he responds to the fifth item with the seventh item).

Anxiety. A vague fear. The stimulus which evokes anxiety is less specific than the one which evokes fear.

Anxiety Reaction. A neurotic reaction characterized by a chronically high level of tension and apprehension.

Apathy. A general term for listless and indifferent behavior; a common reaction to persistent and insurmountable frustration.

Aphasia. Disordered language behavior resulting from brain damage.

Appetitive Drive. A drive having incentives requiring approach and consummatory responses (e.g, hunger → food → eating). An appetitive drive is distinguished from an aversive drive.

Applied Psychologist. A psychologist who applies the facts, theories, and techniques of psychology to the solution of practical problems.

Approach-Approach Conflict. A conflict in which an organism has simultaneous approach tendencies toward mutually incompatible goals.

Approach-Avoidance Conflict. A conflict in which an organism is both attracted and repelled by the same goal.

Aptitude. An ability that is potentially related to the skillful performance of some task.

Aptitude Test. A test intended to measure an individual's aptitude.

Arousal. A dimension of activity against which behavioral and physiological events can be ranked. A person's level of arousal is low during sleep, when his physiological system is relatively inactive. The term *activation* is often used interchangeably with *arousal*.

Association Neuron. A neuron within the central nervous system that occupies a position between sensory and motor neurons.

Association Value. A method of measuring the "meaningfulness" of nonsense syllables. Subjects are instructed to respond to a nonsense syllable with any meaningful word it reminds them of. The association value of a nonsense syllable is determined by the percentage of subjects who respond with a meaningful association.

Associative Interference. The interference of an old association in the learning of a new association (e.g., the learning of *mef-zin* will be retarded if the subject has previously learned *mef-tep*).

Asthenic. A basic type of body build characterized by a tall, thin body. Kretchmer considered such physiques to be associated with introverted behavior and, in the extreme, with schizophrenic psychosis.

Athletic. A type of body build, characterized by broad shoulders, narrow waist, well-developed muscles, and considered by Kretchmer to be associated with aggressive and active behavior.

Attention. The focusing on certain features of a stimulus pattern while simultaneously ignoring others.

Attitude. A tendency to respond in a characteristic way to some social stimulus (e.g., idea, principle, subject).

Attitude Test. A psychological test to measure a person's attitude.

Autistic Child. A child who is pathologically withdrawn and behaves in a generally bizarre manner.

Auto-instructional Device. A device which a person can use to teach himself (e.g., teaching machines, programmed books).

Autonomic Nervous System. The portion of the peripheral nervous system that consists of the sympathetic and parasympathetic systems. The autonomic nervous system regulates the action of the endocrine glands and smooth muscles.

Aversive Drive. A drive that is reduced by escape from noxious stimulation. An aversive drive is distinguished from an appetitive drive.

Avoidance-Avoidance Conflict. Conflict in which an organism is repelled from both choices available to him.

Avoidance Conditioning. A form of instrumental conditioning in which the instrumental response prevents the occurrence of a noxious stimulus.

Axon. The fiber of the neuron through which neural impulses are transmitted away from the cell body to the synapse.

Backward Association. An association in which a response term evokes a stimulus term which immediately preceded it. For example, in paired-associate learning if a subject, after learning the association between *direct-proper,* responds to the word *proper* with *direct,* he has formed a backward association.

Backward Conditioning. The procedure in classical conditioning in which the conditioned stimulus *follows* the presentation of the unconditioned stimulus.

Basilar Membrane. A membrane within the cochlea to which the organ of Corti is attached.

Behavior. The observable responses of an organism (e.g., the contraction of a muscle, the pressing of a lever, speech).

Behavior Disorders. A general term to refer to all forms of disordered responses.

Behaviorism. A systematic position, vigorously expounded by John B. Watson, which maintained that the subject matter of psychology was behavior, not conscious experience.

Bel. A unit of measurement of sound intensity.

Bilateral Transfer. A specific case of cross education involving the transfer of a skill from one limb to its opposite member.

Binaural. Referring to two ears. A binaural cue for auditory space perception is one that results from the differences between the stimulation a sound produces in each ear.

Brain Stem. The portion of the central nervous system between the brain and spinal cord.

Brainwashing. A term used to describe coercive methods of persuasion characterized by the complete control of the individual who is being influenced.

Branching Programming. Programming that uses multiple-choice items and explanations of incorrect responses. The items covered by students depend on their previous responses. Scrambled textbooks are used to present the branching programs.

Brightness. A psychological dimension in which visual stimuli can be ordered along a light-dark continuum. The major physical correlate of brightness is light intensity.

Castration Complex. The fear a boy has, according to Freudian theory, that he will be emasculated by his father as punishment for his libidinal attachment to his mother during the later portion of the phallic stage. The castration complex helps resolve the Oedipus complex.

Catatonic Schizophrenia. A form of schizophrenia characterized by extreme motor disturbance, either muscular tension or stupor.

Central Nervous System. The nerves of the brain and spinal cord.

Cerebellum. A portion of the brain consisting of two hemispheres located in back of and above the medulla. Its function, primarily, is to coordinate motor activities and maintain bodily equilibrium.

Cerebral Cortex. The outer layer of the cerebrum.

Cerebrotonia. A dimension of temperament characterized by preoccupation, hypersensitivity, and reflection.

Cerebrum. The upper and anterior portion of the brain, consisting of two hemispheres.

Change-of-Cue Method. A technique of habit breaking in which the organism is removed from the situation evoking the undesirable response and placed in a different environment.

Character Disorder. A general term that refers to disordered reactions of conduct. Individuals with character disorders behave in socially unacceptible ways (e.g., stealing, embezzling).

Chromosomes. The structures within the nucleus of the cell that contain the genes.

Chronological Age (CA). The age of an individual from his birth.

Classical Conditioning. The experimental method used by Pavlov. A conditioned stimulus is paired with an unconditioned stimulus.

Client-Centered Therapy. A type of therapy in which the therapist gives little direction to the patient. The patient decides what problems he wants to discuss, and no attempt is made to trace the development of the client's personality from its very beginning. The therapist's main aim is to empathize with the patient, thus providing a suitable environment for the client to discover and solve his problems. Client-centered therapy is sometimes referred to as nondirective therapy.

Cochlea. A small structure which contains the receptors for hearing (organ of Corti).

Coefficient of Correlation. A statistical index which varies from $+1.00$ (perfect correspondence in the changes occurring in two variables) through 0.00 (no correspondence in the changes occurring in two variables) to -1.00 (perfect correspondence in the changes occurring in two variables with one variable changing in a direction opposite the other).

Cognitive Dissonance. The incompatibility between attitudes, beliefs, and opinions accepted by an individual. According to cognitive dissonance theory individuals are motivated to reduce this dissonance by modifying their attitudes, beliefs, and opinions in the direction of consistency.

Collective Unconscious. That part of the unconscious which Jung assumed to be inherited. The collective unconscious predisposes individuals to behave as they have throughout history.

Color Blindness. A visual defect that prevents a person from detecting differences in hue. The severity of the defect varies from complete color blindness, in sensitivity to any hue, to forms of color weakness, inability to discriminate between some hues (e.g., red and green) of the same brightness.

Communication Network. The pattern of communications existing between members of a group.

Compensation. Counterbalancing failure in one activity by excellence in another (e.g., the poor athlete becoming a good student).

Composition. The assortment of wave lengths in a beam of light is referred to as its composition.

Compulsion. A useless, stereotyped, and repetitive act that a person finds impossible to inhibit.

Concurrent Relationship. An empirical re lationship between an organism's response and an event which occurs simultaneously.

Conditioned Discrimination. The combin ing of acquisition and extinction proce dures to train an organism to respond to a conditioned stimulus and not to a general ized one. This is done by pairing the con ditioned and unconditioned stimuli and presenting the generalized stimulus alone.

Conditioned Response. The response which is evoked by the conditioned stimulus after conditioning has taken place.

Conditioned Stimulus. The stimulus which is paired with the unconditioned stimulus and subsequently acquires the capacity to evoke a response similar to the one made to the unconditioned stimulus (e.g., a tone which, after being paired with food, is capable of eliciting salivation).

Conditioning. An experimental procedure in which S-R associations can be formed, strengthened, and weakened. There are two major forms of conditioning: classical and instrumental.

Conduction Deafness. Deafness resulting from failure in the transmission of sound waves to the cochlea.

Cone. A photosensitive cell in the retina that functions as a receptor for color vision.

Confabulation. The tendency to improvise stories to compensate for lapses of memory. Confabulation is one of the dominant symptoms of Korsakow's syndrome.

Conflict. A state which results from the simultaneous arousal of incompatible re sponse tendencies.

Conformity. Behavior that is conventional, in agreement with social rules and customs.

Conscious. According to Freud, that por tion of the mind of which a person is at any given moment aware.

Constancy. *See* Perceptual Constancy.

Convergence. The turning inward of the eyes as an object is brought closer to the viewer.

Conversion Reaction. A neurotic reaction characterized by some physical symptom in the absence of any organic pathology.

Corpus Callosum. A large tract of fibers that unites the two cerebral hemispheres.

Correlation. The relationship between two variables. Variables are said to be corre lated when a change in one is accompanied by a change in the other. The degree of correlation is measured by the coefficient of correlation.

Cortex. The rind or outer layer. The cere bral cortex is the outer layer of the cere brum.

Criterion. A standard against which a psy chological test is evaluated (e.g., one cri terion for a medical aptitude test is per formance in medical school).

Critical Score. A cut-off score in an apti tude test. Those scoring above the critical score are accepted, those below rejected.

Cross Education. The positive transfer of a skill acquired by one part of the body to another part (e.g., knowing how to play ping-pong with your preferred hand will help you play it with your nonpreferred hand).

Culture. The general behavior pattern shared by members of the same society.

Cumulative Response Curve. The graphical representation of all the instrumental responses emitted during an operant conditioning session. The slope of the cumulative response curve indicates the rate of responding.

Decibel. One-tenth of a bel.

Decision Processes. The making of decisions between different courses of action. In many ways decision making is closely allied to problem solving.

Defense Mechanisms. A class of behavior patterns which, according to Freudian theory, function to control the violent impulses of the id. In more general psychological usage the concept refers to responses that enable an organism to avoid or escape fear-provoking stimuli.

Delayed Reaction Method. A type of experiment in which a subject is required to respond to a stimulus after it has been removed.

Delirium Tremens. A psychotic reaction exhibited by chronic alcoholics. It is characterized by extreme confusion, vivid hallucinations, and marked trembling.

Delusion. A false belief (e.g., a patient believing he is the President of the United States).

Dendrite. The fiber of the neuron through which neural impulses are transmitted from the synapse toward the cell body.

Dependent Variable. The observed changes resulting from the effects of the independent variables. The dependent variable in psychology is behavior, i.e., response variable.

Detour Problem. A problem which requires that the subject go away from the incentive initially in order to obtain it eventually.

Discriminative Stimulus. A cue that *evokes* and *maintains* a response.

Disordered Reaction. Behavior that is inappropriate to the external situation, or ineffective in achieving motivational satisfaction, or both.

Displacement. The transfer of behavior directed toward one object or person to another object or person (e.g., a child's displacement of his aggression from his father, whom he is afraid to strike, to his younger sibling).

Double Alternation Method. A type of experiment in which the subject is required to make a sequence of turns, such as right, right, left, left, and so on. The organism cannot solve the problem if he responds only to the cue from the last turn.

Double Approach-Avoidance Conflict. Conflict in which an organism is both attracted and repelled by each of two incompatible goals.

Drive. A condition or state of the organism which activates and directs his behavior.

Drive Stimulus. The cue resulting from a drive.

Duct Glands. Glands that secrete their chemicals through ducts (e.g., salivary gland).

Ductless Glands. *See* Endocrine Glands.

Ectomorphy. A dimension of physique characterized by delicacy of skin and sensitivity of the nervous system.

Educational Film. A film designed to teach.

Effectors. Muscles and glands.

Efferent Nerves. Nerves that connect the central nervous system with the reacting mechanisms (muscles and glands). They are sometimes called motor nerves.

Ego. That part of an individual's personality which, according to psychoanalytic theory, corresponds to the self and represents reason in reconciling the conflicting forces of the *id* and *superego*.

Electra Complex. The libidinal attachment that, Freud assumed, a daughter develops for her father, which is accompanied by a concomitant hostility toward her mother. The Electra complex occurs during the later portion of the phallic stage.

Electroencephalogram (EEG). A graphic record of the electrical activity of the brain.

Electroshock Treatment. *See* Shock Therapy.

Empirical Relationship. The statement of the relationship between dependent and independent variables. The three fundamental types of relationships in psychology are: $R = f(S)$, $R = f(O)$, and $R = f(R)$.

Encephalitis. Inflammation of the brain or its membranous covering. An attack of encephalitis sometimes produces psychopathic or sociopathic behavior.

End Brushes. The branching terminal fibers of the axon.

Endocrine Glands. Ductless glands that secrete hormones into the blood or lymph streams.

Endomorphy. A dimension of physique characterized by fat, particularly in the abdominal region.

Equal-Loudness Contours. A graphic method of representing tones of different frequency but equal loudness.

Escape Conditioning. A form of instrumental conditioning in which the instrumental response terminates a noxious stimulus.

Estrus. Periodic state of sexual receptivity in female mammals, during which fertilization can take place.

Ethnocentrism. The strong acceptance of the values of one's own culture and the rejection of the values of other cultures.

Exhaustion Method. A method of breaking a habit by forcing the organism to repeat the undesirable response until he becomes so fatigued that he can no longer make it, and a new response is substituted.

Explanation. The method in science by which understanding of an event is achieved. Low-level explanation consists of the specification of the variables determining an event. Higher-order explanation (i.e., theory) consists of general statements from which individual events can be logically predicted.

Extensional Meaning. The definition of word by its external referent. The extensional meaning of the word *chair* is the object chair.

Extraversion. A personality trait characterized by sociable and outgoing behavior. Kretchmer concluded that pyknics were extraverted.

Eyelid Conditioning. A form of classical conditioning in which lid closure becomes associated with a conditioned stimulus (e.g., when a weak light is paired with a puff of air to the subject's eye the light acquires the capacity to evoke lid closure).

Factual Meaning (Empirical Law). The statement of the relationship between two or more independently defined concepts (e.g., the number of reinforcements and the strength of the conditioned response).

False Negative. A person who scores below a critical score on an aptitude test but succeeds in performing the criterion task satisfactorily.

False Positive. A person who scores above a critical score on an aptitude test but fails to perform the criterion task satisfactorily.

Fantasy. A general term describing daydreaming, imagining, and reverie.

Feedback System. A self-regulating system which uses information from an event in the system to control related subsequent events (e.g., kinesthetic sensitivity and thermostatic control of room temperature).

Figure-Ground Perception. Perception of a stimulus or pattern of stimuli as a form that stands out against a formless background.

Fissure of Rolando. The central fissure in each cerebral hemisphere. It runs almost vertically, dividing the frontal lobe from the parietal lobe.

Fissure of Sylvius. The lateral fissure in each cerebral hemisphere. It runs diagonally, separating the temporal lobe below it from the frontal and parietal lobes above it.

Fixation. A stereotyped, repetitive form of behavior that is extremely resistant to change.

Fixed Interval Schedule. An interval reinforcement schedule in which the first response after a fixed, predetermined time interval is reinforced (e.g., after *every* five minutes).

Fixed Ratio Schedule. A ratio reinforcement schedule in which the response is reinforced after a fixed number of previous responses have been made (e.g., after *every* 30 responses).

Forgetting. A loss in retention of material previously learned.

Fovea. A centrally located, slightly indented portion of the retina containing only cones. It is the area that mediates the highest degree of visual acuity.

Free Association. A method used in psychoanalysis in which the patient is instructed to report to the analyst everything that comes into his awareness.

Free-Responding Conditioning. Instrumental conditioning in which an organism can make the instrumental response at all times. This term is used interchangeably with *operant conditioning.*

Frequency. One of the physical attributes of sound. It is measured in terms of cycles per second (c.p.s.).

Frequency Distribution. A distribution of scores, arranged in order of magnitude, showing the number of times each score occurs.

Frequency Polygon. A graphic representation of a frequency distribution, that uses a continuous line, the height of which indicates the frequency of the corresponding scores.

Frequency Theory. A theory of hearing which assumes that the sensation of pitch is a function of the frequency of neural impulses transmitted through the auditory nerve.

Frontal Lobe. The part of the cerebral hemisphere located in front of the fissure of Rolando.

Frustration. A state resulting from the blocking of goal achievement.

Frustration Situation. A situation containing an incentive for which an organism is motivated and an obstacle which blocks him from getting it.

Functional Disorder. A disordered reaction that is believed to be a learned response.

Functional Fixedness. The tendency to perceive things in terms of their familiar uses which makes it difficult to use them in an unfamiliar way (e.g., using a hammer as a weight).

Functionalism. An early school of psychology which, in opposition to Wundtian introspective psychology, proposed that the *function,* not the structure, of conscious experience should be studied. This viewpoint led many Functionalists to investigate behavior objectively and, thus, pave the way for the advent of behaviorism.

Functional Psychosis. A psychotic reaction believed to result from learning disordered reactions.

Galvanic Skin Response (GSR). A change in the electrical resistance of the skin. This response serves as a dependent variable in conditioning and is used in lie-detection tests.

General Adaptation Syndrome. A concept proposed by Hans Selye, referring to the sequence of physiological changes in an organism exposed to a stressful situation.

General Intelligence. A basic intellectual factor which some factor analysts believe operates in all intellectual problems.

Generalized Secondary Reinforcer. A secondary reinforcer that functions in a variety of situations.

General Psychotherapy. A term used to describe a psychotherapeutic approach which is eclectic in theory and uses a variety of techniques (e.g., reassurance, drugs, relaxation techniques, play therapy).

Genes. The agents responsible for hereditary transmission.

Genetics. The branch of biology concerned with hereditary transmission.

Genius. An individual who has demonstrated outstanding creativity by his original contributions (e.g., Einstein, Darwin).

Gestalt Psychology. A systematic position in psychology which emphasizes principles of organization exhibited in behavior and conscious experience.

Gifted. An individual who has achieved a high IQ (e.g., above 140).

Goal. A commodity or condition capable of reducing or eliminating a drive; an incentive.

Group Psychotherapy. A form of psychotherapy in which a group of patients meet together to discuss their problems, under the guidance of a therapist.

Group Structure. A general term referring to the nature of the social interactions between the members of a group.

Group Test. A psychological test that can be given to groups of individuals at the same time.

Habit. A theoretical construct referring to the tendency for a stimulus to evoke a response.

Habit Breaking. The elimination of habitual modes of behaving.

Habit Chaining. The integration of successive S-R associations to form a behavior sequence.

Habit Competition. The tendency for a stimulus to evoke incompatible habits (e.g., at the outset of conditioned discrimination the organism has a tendency to respond to both the positive stimulus and the negative stimulus).

Habit Conflict. Conflict between two behavior tendencies involving competing habits (e.g., a driver is conflicted about turning left or right at an intersection with which he is unfamiliar).

Hallucination. A sense impression for which there is no appropriate external stimulus (e.g., hearing church bells when none are ringing).

Halo Effect. The influence of one characteristic of an individual upon the rating of another characteristic (e.g., a pretty girl might receive a higher rating in intelligence than she deserves).

Hebephrenic Schizophrenia. A form of schizophrenia characterized by silly behavior and a poorly organized delusional system.

Hering Theory. A theory of color vision that assumes three visual systems involving opponent pairs: yellow-blue, red-green, and white-black.

Higher-Order Conditioning. A classical conditioning procedure in which a previously conditioned stimulus functions as an unconditioned stimulus to establish a new conditioned response. Higher-order conditioning demonstrates how a neutral stimulus can acquire reinforcing properties, that is, become a secondary reinforcing agent.

Histogram. A frequency distribution represented by vertical bars, the height of which indicates the frequency of the corresponding scores.

Historical Relationship. An empirical relationship in which an organism's response is related to a past event.

Homeostasis. The tendency of an organism to maintain a condition of physiological equilibrium.

Hormones. The chemical secretions of endocrine (ductless) glands.

Hue. The characteristic of visual sensations that results from stimulation of the eye by lights of different wave lengths.

Human Engineering. The branch of applied psychology that is concerned with increasing the efficiency of man-machine systems by designing machines suited to the men who run them.

Huntington's Chorea. A genetically determined disease of the central nervous system which sometimes leads to psychotic behavior.

Hypermania. A manic reaction of a severe degree.

Hypomania. A manic reaction of a mild degree.

Hypothalamus. The underside of the thalamus containing centers that influence many physiological drives, such as hunger and thirst.

Hysterical Motor Disturbance. A conversion reaction characterized by loss of muscular control (e.g., an uncontrollable and repetitive tic) in the absence of any organic pathology.

Hysterical Paralysis. A conversion reaction characterized by paralysis of some part of the body in the absence of any organic pathology.

Hysterical Sensory Disturbance. A conversion reaction in which the patient suffers from a sensory defect (e.g., blindness, deafness) without any apparent organic pathology.

Id. A term used in psychoanalytic theory to designate one of the three parts of the personality. It consists of the unconscious biological drives presumed to be pressing for satisfaction.

Illusion. A perception that fails to correspond with the actual stimulus.

Imprinting. Very rapid learning that occurs in some animals during a critical early stage in their development. It is believed by some investigators to lay the basis for future social development.

Incentive. A commodity or condition capable of reducing or eliminating a drive; a goal.

Incompatible Response Method. A method of habit breaking in which a new and more desirable response is substituted for an undesirable one.

Independent Variable. The variable controlled by the experimenter in order to determine its effect on the dependent variable. In psychology there are three main classes of independent variables: stimulus, organismic, and response.

Individual Test. A psychological test that can only be given to one individual at a time.

Inhibition. A theoretical construct that refers to the negative or retarding effect certain variables have upon conditioning.

Insight. A general term to describe the sudden solution of a problem.

Instinct. *See* Instinctive Behavior.

Instinctive Behavior. Behavior that is (1) complex, (2) rigidly patterned, (3) not learned, and (4) found in all members of the species.

Instrumental Conditioning. A form of conditioning in which the organism's response is instrumental in obtaining reinforcement. This form of conditioning is distinguished from classical conditioning.

Instrumental Response. A response that acts upon the environment (e.g., the bar-pressing behavior of the rat, the disk-pecking response of the pigeon).

Instrumental Reward Conditioning. Instrumental conditioning in which a positive reinforcer such as food or water serves as an incentive.

Insulin Shock Treatment. *See* Shock Therapy.

Intelligence. The term that refers to intellectual ability. It can be defined specifically as *what an intelligence test measures* or more generally as *an ability, or pattern of abilities, influencing intellectual functioning.*

Intelligence Quotient (IQ). A relative measure of a person's intelligence, with an IQ of 100 representing the performance of an average person. Originally IQ was measured as the ratio between mental age and chronological age:

$$IQ = \frac{MA}{CA} \times 100$$

Intensional Meaning. The verbal description of a word. The intensional meaning of the word *rouge* is *any cosmetic for coloring the skin pink or red.*

Intensity. A dimension representing the magnitude of a physical stimulus. The intensity of a light wave is measured by its energy level; the intensity of a sound wave, by its pressure.

Interposition. A stimulus cue for visual depth perception resulting from a near object obscuring a distant object in the same line of vision.

Intertrial Interval. The time interval between successive trials in a learning experiment.

Interval Reinforcement Schedule. A schedule of reinforcement in which the response is reinforced after a predetermined time interval.

Introspection. The observation and report of one's own inner experience. Introspection was the major method used by Wundt and other introspective psychologists in their investigation of psychological phenomena.

Introspectionism. The first school of psychology, founded by Wilhelm Wundt, who interpreted the task of psychology as the analysis of conscious experience into its basic elements, that is, the investigation of the structure of the mind.

Introversion. A personality trait characterized by introspection and shyness. Kretchmer believed that asthenics were introverted.

Intrusion Error. An inappropriately placed response in serial learning (e.g., responding with the fourth item in place of the third item).

Involutional Melancholia. A psychotic reaction similar to the depressed reaction of the manic-depressive. Involutional melancholia occurs during the "change-of-life" period, when marked changes in endocrine functioning are taking place.

Kinesthesis. Sensitivity to position and movement of the body which results from stimulation of receptors located in tendons, muscles, and joints.

Korsakow's Syndrome. A pattern of symptoms exhibited by chronic alcoholics, especially after delirium tremens. It is characterized by a loss of memory for recent events and by confabulation.

Language Laboratory. A laboratory in which students can listen to tape recordings of foreign languages and compare their own pronunciation with native speech patterns.

Latency of Response. The time interval between the onset of the stimulus and the occurrence of the response. Latency of a response is sometimes used to measure the course of learning. During the acquisition stage of classical conditioning the latency of the response to the conditioned stimulus decreases.

Latency Period. A stage of psychosexual development when, according to Freud, the sexual drives are dormant. This stage follows the phallic stage and lasts until puberty.

Leadership. The ability of an individual to control or direct the behavior of the members of a group.

Learned Drive. A drive acquired through learning, as distinguished from a physiological (primary) drive; a secondary drive.

Learning. Change in behavior resulting from practice.

Learning Set. A case of positive transfer in which an organism increases his speed of learning successive problems of the same general type. The organism learns-how-to-learn.

Libido. The central motivational concept within psychoanalytic theory. The libido represents a predetermined amount of psychological energy that drives man to seek pleasure, especially erotic pleasure. This energy becomes attached to different objects as an individual matures and has different experiences.

Linear Perspective. A stimulus cue for visual depth perception resulting from the apparent convergence of lines and decrease in size of objects as they are moved away from the viewer.

Linear Programming. Programming that consists of a fixed sequence of small "steps" each of which must be taken by every student.

Longitudinal Fissure. The deep groove that separates the two cerebral hemispheres.

Loudness. A characteristic of auditory sensations that can be measured on a scale from soft to loud. Loudness is primarily, but not exclusively, a function of sound intensity.

Manic-Depressive Psychosis. A psychotic reaction characterized by a disturbance in mood. The patient can be highly elated and active (manic) or despondent and inactive (depressed).

Manifest Anxiety. Overt apprehension and tension.

Man-Machine System. A system in which a man and a machine function together (e.g., typist and typewriter, programmer and computer).

Massed Practice. Continuous learning with little or no time interval between successive trials.

Maternal Overprotection. Excessive maternal care or control. Maternal overprotection prevents the child from learning to behave independently.

Maturation. Changes in behavior resulting from physiological development.

Mean. The sum of all the scores in a frequency distribution divided by the number of scores:

$$M = \frac{\Sigma X}{N}$$

Measure of Central Tendency. A value representing the center of a distribution. The three most common measures of central tendency are the mean, median, and mode.

Measure of Variability. A value representing the variability of scores within a distribution. The most widely used measure of variability is the standard deviation.

Median. The middlemost score in a frequency distribution.

Mediated Transfer. The transfer between two activities that results from intermediary events. A human organism can sometimes learn to make a new response to an old stimulus easily with the aid of mediated verbalizations.

Medulla. Structure located in the lower part of the brain stem. It regulates such vital functions as breathing and heart beat.

Mental Age (MA). A unit of measurement proposed by Binet for use in intelligence tests. The MA is that score which represents the average score of children of a designated age level (e.g., an MA of 8 is the average score obtained by a representative group of 8-year-olds, an MA of 9 is the average score obtained by a representative group of 9-year-olds, etc.). A bright child obtains an MA above his chronological age (CA), while a dull child gets an MA equivalent to that obtained by a lower age group.

Mental Health. *See* Psychological Health.

Mesomorphy. A dimension of physique characterized by muscularity and prominent bone structure.

Midbrain. A portion of the brain stem that contains centers influencing seeing and hearing.

Mode. The most frequent score in a frequency distribution.

Motion Parallax. A change in the direction of apparent movement of an object as a result of a change in the observer's position in space. Motion parallax is a stimulus cue for visual depth perception.

Motivational Conflict. Conflict between two behavior tendencies involving rival motivations (e.g., a child's conflict between buying a toy or candy).

Motivational Research. A technique in advertising which tries to base its appeals on consumers' motivations.

Motivational Sequence. A series of events that begins with the arousal of a drive and is followed by an instrumental response that obtains an incentive.

Motor Learning. Learning in which muscular movements predominate.

Motor Neuron. An efferent neuron that transmits neural impulses away from the central nervous system toward effectors (e.g., muscles and glands).

Motor Skill. A skill requiring muscular coordination. Because a motor skill involves kinesthetic feedback, it is often referred to as a sensorimotor skill.

Myelin. A white sheath covering some nerve fibers.

Nature. In the nature-nurture issue, nature refers to the hereditary component influencing behavior.

Negative Practice. A form of the exhaustion method of habit breaking, in which the undesirable habit is deliberately repeated for long periods of time.

Negative Reinforcer. A reinforcement which strengthens an association between a stimulus and response by its termination (e.g., shock in classical or instrumental conditioning).

Negative Transfer. The interfering effect of prior learning on present learning or performance.

Nerve. A bundle of nerve fibers.

Nerve Cells. Specialized cells that transmit neural impulses.

Nerve Deafness. Deafness due to the inability of the auditory nerve to transmit neural impulses to the temporal lobes.

Nerve Fibers. Thread-like extensions of a neuron through which neural impulses are transmitted.

Neural Impulses. Electrochemical energy changes which travel through nerve fibers.

Neuron. A single nerve cell consisting of the cell body and nerve fibers.

Neurosis. A disordered reaction that prevents a person from dealing effectively with conflicts and anxiety.

Noncontingent Reinforcement. Reinforcement that occurs independently of the behavior of the organism.

Nondirective Therapy. *See* Client-Centered Therapy.

Nonreinforcing. A term which describes an event that fails to reinforce.

Nonreversal Shift. An experimental procedure used in discrimination studies. The subject is required to shift his response to a previously irrelevant dimension (e.g., after choosing *white* and avoiding *black,* he is reinforced for ignoring color and selecting *large* or *small*).

Nonsense Syllable. A combination of letters, usually of two consonants with a vowel in between (e.g., *tav*), that does not form a word in the language of the person using it. Nonsense syllables were invented by Ebbinghaus and are used chiefly in experiments investigating memory.

Normal Probability Curve. The frequency polygon that represents the distribution of chance events.

Norm. The test scores of some specified group to which an individual's score can be compared.

Null Hypothesis. The assumption that the true difference between two statistics (e.g., two means) is zero. Sampling statistics are used to reject or retain the null hypothesis.

Nurture. In the nature-nurture issue, nurture refers to the environmental component influencing behavior.

Objective Psychology. The contemporary behavioristic point of view that accepts as a dependent variable in psychological research any behavior which is publicly observable or capable of being repeatedly recorded.

Obsession. A persistent, recurring thought.

Obsessive-Compulsive Reaction. A neurotic reaction characterized by persistent and ostensibly senseless repetition of some thought or act.

Occipital Lobe. The part of the cerebral hemisphere located at the back of each hemisphere.

Oedipus Complex. The sexual attachment a child develops for the parent of the opposite sex, which, according to Freud, normally occurs during the later portion of the phallic stage. The term *Oedipus complex* most commonly refers to the attachment between a son and his mother, and the term *Electra complex,* to the attachment between a daughter and her father.

Operant Conditioning. An instrumental conditioning situation in which the organism is free to respond at any time. This term is used interchangeably with *free-responding conditioning.*

Operational Definition. The definition of a concept in terms of the operations or manipulations performed by the scientist in investigating the concept.

Operational Meaning. *See* Operational Definition.

Oral-Erotic Stage. The first stage of psychosexual development, in Freudian theory. Libidinal satisfaction is obtained from the activities of the lips and mouth, as in sucking.

Organic Need. A condition resulting from a physiological imbalance.

Organic Psychosis. A psychotic reaction with a known physiological cause.

Organic Reaction. A disordered reaction that results from known physiological causes.

Organismic Variable. A distinctive physiological characteristic of an organism.

Organ of Corti. The structure in the basilar membrane of the cochlea. It contains the receptors for hearing.

Ossicles. A set of three small bones located behind the eardrum. They transmit auditory vibrations from the eardrum to the cochlea.

Overcompensation. Counterbalancing failure in an activity by achieving success in the *same* activity (e.g., the unathletic, fat boy becoming, through intensive training, an outstanding shot-putter and weightlifter).

Overlearning. Continued practice after some criterion of mastery has been achieved.

Paired-Associate Learning. The learning of pairs of syllables, digits, or words so that the first member of the pair, the stimulus term, evokes the second member, the response term.

Paradigmatic Associate. A response in a word-association test which bears some logical relationship to the stimulus word,

that is, is in the same grammatical class and has similar, contrasting, or related meaning (e.g., smart-dumb, flower-rose).

Paranoia. Behavior marked by extreme suspiciousness. In its severe form it is a psychotic reaction.

Paranoid Schizophrenia. A form of schizophrenia characterized primarily by some strong delusion (e.g., the patient feels he is being persecuted).

Parasympathetic Division. A division of the autonomic nervous system. Its function is to conserve the resources of the body.

Parietal Lobe. The part of the cerebral hemisphere situated between the fissure of Rolando and the occipital lobe.

Percentile Rank. The percentile rank of a given score in a distribution indicates the per cent of scores in the entire distribution which are lower. An individual who obtains a percentile rank of 83 in a test exceeds the scores obtained by 83 per cent of the people taking the test.

Perceptual Constancy. The tendency to perceive objects as relatively unchanged under widely different conditions of stimulation.

Perceptual Grouping. The tendency to perceive discrete stimuli in an organized manner (e.g., to perceive similar stimuli as belonging to the same group).

Perceptual Learning. The influence of experience on perception.

Perceptual Organization. The tendency to perceive complex forms of stimulation in some organized manner (e.g., figure-ground, grouping of similar stimuli).

Perceptual Satiation. The tendency for a perception to weaken after prolonged exposure.

Perceptual Set. The readiness to pay attention to certain features of a stimulus pattern.

Perceptual Tendency. A theoretical construct referring to the tendency of an organism to perceive his environment according to the principles of organization, emphasis, and consistency.

Peripheral Nervous System. That part of the nervous system lying outside of the brain and spinal cord. It includes both the nerves that connect the brain and spinal cord with receptors and effectors and the autonomic nervous system.

Perseverative Error. A response in serial learning which would have been correct earlier (e.g., responding to the fifth item with the second item).

Personality. The general pattern of behavior exhibited by an individual; a unified system of responding.

Personality Characteristic. A pattern of interrelated responses; a component of personality.

Personality Inventory. A questionnaire designed to measure various aspects of personality.

Personality Structure. The manner in which personality characteristics are organized and integrated.

Phallic Stage. In Freudian theory, a stage of development in which libidinal gratification is obtained from stimulation of the sex organ, and later a libidinal attachment develops for the parent of the opposite sex.

Phi-Phenomenon. Illusion of motion resulting from two stationary lines being exposed successively with a suitable time interval in between.

Phobia. An intense irrational fear.

Phobic Reaction. A neurotic reaction characterized by an excessive fear of some specific object or place in the absence of any real danger.

Photopic Vision. Vision mediated by cones.

Physiological Drive. A drive resulting from a condition of physiological imbalance (e.g., hunger). A primary drive.

Pick's Disease. An organic psychosis due principally to the degeneration of the cortical cells of the frontal lobes.

Pitch. A psychological characteristic of tones that can be ordered from low to high. It is primarily, but not exclusively, a function of frequency.

Place-Frequency Theory. A theory of hearing which assumes that the sensation of pitch is due both to the portion of the basilar membrane stimulated and the frequency of neural impulses in the auditory nerve.

Place Theory. A theory of hearing which assumes that the sensation of pitch depends on the portion of the basilar membrane that is set into motion.

Play Therapy. The use of play for therapeutic purposes with children.

Pons. The portion of the brain stem above the medulla that connects the cerebellum with the cerebral hemispheres.

Population. The total group from which a sample of scores is drawn.

Positive Reinforcer. A reinforcement which strengthens an association between a stimulus and a response by its presentation (e.g., food in classical or instrumental conditioning).

Positive Transfer. The facilitating effect prior learning has on present learning or performance.

Preconscious. According to psychoanalytic theory, the portion of the mind that is not in one's consciousness at present but which one can become aware of without great difficulty.

Primary Drive. A drive resulting from a condition of physiological imbalance; a physiological drive.

Primary Generalization. Stimulus generalization based upon the physical properties of the stimuli (e.g., a conditioned response to a light of 550 mμ will generalize to a light of 560 mμ).

Primary Reinforcement. A reinforcement, such as food or water, that reduces a physiological (i.e., primary) drive.

Primary Trait. A trait which has been found through factor analysis to be relatively independent of other primary traits.

Proactive Inhibition. The interfering effect previous learning can have upon the retention of material learned subsequently.

Probability Learning. A kind of learning experiment in which the subject must choose which of two events will occur. Unknown to the subject the events are randomly determined.

Program. The lesson plan for an auto-instructional device, or a similar plan which may be used independently. It consists of a sequence of items, or frames, designed to encourage learning.

Programmed Learning. Self-instruction based upon a program.

Projective Technique. A test which uses ambiguous material in order to allow the subject to express freely the basic structure of his personality.

Psychoanalysis. A method of psychotherapy, introduced by Freud, which attempts to make a person aware of his repressed conflicts and motives so that he may acquire healthier modes of responding.

Psychodrama. Spontaneous play acting used for therapeutic purposes.

Psychogenetics. The study of the hereditary basis of behavior.

Psychological Health. A general term for what is commonly called mental health. When defined negatively, it refers to the absence of disturbed behavior. Defined positively, the term refers to adjusted, productive behavior.

Psychological Test. An examination that provides a measure of a person's behavior. This measure is often used to predict his future behavior.

Psychopath. A person who behaves *without* regard to laws and customs; one who has a psychopathic personality.

Psychopathic Personality. A type of behavior disorder in which the individual behaves *without* regard to social laws and customs.

Psychophysical Relationship. A relationship between behavior and some physical characteristic of a stimulus; an $R = f(S)$ type of relationship.

Psychophysiological Relationship. A relationship between behavior and some physiological mechanism; an $R = f(O)$ type of relationship.

Psychosexual Stages. According to Freudian theory, human development occurs in stages, each of which is characterized by a particular mode of achieving libidinal satisfaction.

Psychosis. A disordered reaction involving peculiar and inappropriate reactions to the environment. The psychotic's contact with reality is poor. He is usually unable to care for himself or to get along in society and is therefore institutionalized.

Psychosomatic Reaction. Organic pathology believed to be based on a neurotic reaction.

Psychotherapy. The treatment of behavior disorders through communication between the therapist and the patient, or patients.

Public Relations. An enterprise designed to promote positive attitudes toward particular organizations, individuals, or ideas.

Punishment. The application of noxious stimulation.

Pyknic. A basic type of body build, characterized by a stocky, heavy-set torso. Kretchmer considered such physiques to be associated with extraverted behavior, and in the extreme, with manic-depressive psychosis.

Race. A group of human beings who share a genetic similarity that distinguishes them from other racial groups.

Random Sample. *See* Sample.

Range. A measure of variability that is computed by subtracting the lowest score from the highest score.

Rate of Responding. The measure of behavior used in operant conditioning (i.e., free-responding conditioning). The rate of responding equals the number of responses divided by some unit of time.

Rating Scale. A method by which an observer can record his judgment of a person's behavior along some dimension.

Rationalization. Assigning acceptable, but erroneous, interpretations to behavior in order to avoid the anxiety that the correct interpretation arouses.

Ratio Reinforcement Schedule. A schedule of reinforcement in which the response is reinforced after the subject has made a predetermined number of previous responses.

Reasoning. The spontaneous integration of two separate habits to solve a problem.

Recall. A method of measuring retention (or forgetting), in which the subject is instructed to reproduce what he previously learned.

Receptive Aphasia. Disturbance in the ability to understand language as a result of brain damage.

Receptors. Specialized cells that are sensitive to stimulation (e.g., rods and cones are the receptors for vision).

Reciprocal Innervation. The neural mechanism responsible for coordinated activity of antagonistic muscle groups. When one muscle contracts, the contraction of an antagonistic muscle is inhibited.

Regression. The reappearance of previously abandoned behavior patterns (e.g., a six-year-old child begins to suck his thumb again).

Reinforcement. An event like the presentation of food or the termination of shock, that increases the tendency for a stimulus to evoke a response.

Reinforcement Therapy. The use of verbal conditioning and shaping techniques to treat disordered reactions.

Reinforcing. Possessing the ability to reinforce, that is, increase the tendency for a stimulus to evoke a response.

Relative Refractory Phase. The period after the transmission of a neural impulse during which a nerve fiber is responsive only to stimulation *above* the threshold of excitation. It follows the absolute refractory phase.

Reminiscence. A sudden improvement in performance following a rest interval with no practice.

Remote Association. An association in serial learning formed between items that are not adjacent (e.g., between the second and fourth item in a list of nonsense syllables).

Repression. In psychoanalytic theory, the basic defense mechanism. It refers to the process that forces or keeps out of consciousness motives and memories that arouse anxiety. Although a person is unaware of repressed events, they influence behavior.

Resonance Theory. A theory of hearing that assumes the fibers of the basilar membrane operate as a set of resonators tuned to different frequencies.

Response. An instance of behavior measured either directly by physiological activity (e.g., secretion of a gland) or indirectly by its effect (e.g., depressing a bar).

Response-Produced Cue. A cue that results from an organism's response and which in turn becomes associated with subsequent behavior (e.g., a word in a sentence becomes a cue for subsequent words).

Response to Frustration. Behavior occurring in a frustration situation.

Response Variable. The behavior of an organism which can serve as the dependent or independent variable in a psychological experiment.

Retention. The amount of previously learned material that is remembered.

Reticular Activating System. A portion of the reticular formation that functions to arouse cortical activity.

Reticular Formation. A small collection of neurons in the brain stem which influences the activities of the cerebral cortex.

Retinal Disparity. The slight difference between the images an object projects on the retina of each eye.

Retroactive Inhibition. The interfering effect present learning can have upon the retention of previously learned material.

Reversal Learning. A discrimination problem in which an organism has to reverse his choice in order to obtain reinforcement (e.g., after learning to choose black in preference to white, he must choose white in preference to black).

Reversal Shift. An experimental procedure used in discrimination studies, in which the subject must make a response opposite to the one he has previously learned (e.g., after choosing *black,* he must select *white*).

Rhodopsin. A photochemical substance found in the rods of the eye. The concentration of rhodopsin in the eye increases during dark adaptation and is responsible for the increased sensitivity.

Rod. A photosensitive cell in the retina. It functions as the only receptor of light in dim illumination.

Rote Learning. A general term applied to the repetitive memorizing of verbal material, such as a list of nonsense syllables.

Sadism. Behavior directed at inflicting pain on another person.

Sample. A group of scores selected from a population of scores. A sample is considered random if each individual score has, in principle, the same chance of being selected as any other score in the population.

Sampling Distribution. The distribution of a given statistic calculated from successive samples drawn from the same population (e.g., a distribution of means from several samples).

Satiation. *See* Perceptual Satiation.

Saturation. A psychological characteristic of color sensation. It refers to the amount of hue a particular color has (e.g., pink and maroon are less saturated than fire-engine red).

Schedule of Reinforcement. The program governing the sequence of reinforcements and nonreinforcements of a response.

Schizophrenia. A psychotic reaction characterized by poor contact with reality and by disturbances in intellectual and affective behavior. Delusions and hallucinations are common among schizophrenics.

Scotopic Vision. Vision mediated by rods.

Scrambled Textbook. A programmed textbook in which the student does not proceed through consecutive pages but instead is instructed to turn to various pages, depending upon his answer to multiple-choice items.

Secondary Drive. A drive that is acquired through learning, as distinguished from a primary (i.e., physiological) drive; a learned drive.

Secondary Reinforcement. A previously neutral stimulus that acquires reinforcing properties. *See* Higher-Order Conditioning.

Self. The pattern of reactions a person has to himself.

Self-Esteem. The reaction a person has to his own competence.

Semantic Generalization. Generalization between stimulus events based on verbal habits (e.g., a conditioned response to the word *large* will generalize to the word *big*).

Senile Psychosis. A psychotic reaction due in part to the physiological changes correlated with old age.

Sensitivity. The capacity to respond to a given stimulus (e.g., a person with normal hearing is sensitive to sound waves; a deaf person is not).

Sensorimotor Skill. *See* Motor Skill.

Sensory-Motor Reflex. An unlearned stimulus-response connection in which a specific stimulus evokes a relatively simple, characteristic response (e.g., tapping the patellar tendon produces a knee jerk).

Sensory Neuron. An afferent neuron that transmits neural impulses away from receptors toward the central nervous system.

Serial Learning. The learning of a series of syllables, digits, or words in a predetermined order.

Set. The tendency or readiness to respond in a predetermined manner. *See* Perceptual Set.

Shaping. A method of modifying behavior by reinforcing successive approximations of the kind of behavior the experimenter desires.

Shock Therapy. The production of physiological convulsions for therapeutic purposes. Convulsions are produced by passing an electric current through the patient's head or by injecting large doses of insulin.

Sibling Rivalry. The competition between brothers and sisters for the affection and attention of parents.

Significant Results. Data that cannot reasonably be attributed to chance.

Simple Schizophrenia. A form of schizophrenia characterized by excessive withdrawal and disordered intellectual and emotional reactions.

Situational Test. A test using real-life situations similar to those in which the behavior that is to be predicted will occur.

Skeletal Muscles. Muscles that are attached to the skeleton by means of tendons.

Skinner Box. An apparatus designed by B. F. Skinner which is used to study instrumental conditioning. The organism makes a simple response (e.g., a rat presses a bar or a pigeon pecks a disk) to obtain reinforcement.

Small Group Research. Research done in social psychology with small groups of people.

Smooth Muscles. The type of muscles found in the visceral organs and in the walls of the blood vessels. The autonomic system controls their contractions.

Social Class. A social group that is defined in terms of its position in the social hierarchy.

Social Dyad. A social group of two people whose behavior influences each others.

Social Group. A portion of society that encourages particular modes of behavior (e.g., industrial workers form a different social group than do engineers).

Socialization. The process by which an individual's behavior is shaped in the direction of conforming to the standards of his society.

Social Psychology. An area of psychology concerned with social influences on individual behavior and group behavior.

Social Role. A pattern of behavior that an individual is reinforced for adopting because he is a member of a social group.

Sociogram. A diagram indicating the preferences and aversions among the members of a group. A sociogram is one method of depicting group structure.

Sociopath. A person whose hostility and aggression are directed *against* society; an individual with a sociopathic personality.

Sociopathic Personality. A type of behavior disorder in which the individual's behavior is directed *against* society.

Somatotherapy. The treatment of behavior by techniques that affect bodily processes (e.g., drugs, electric shock).

Somatotonia. A dimension of temperament characterized by activity and aggressiveness.

Somatotype. The measurement of body build in terms of three components: endomorphy, mesomorphy, and ectomorphy.

Spaced Practice. Learning that allows for time intervals between successive trials.

Specific Intelligence. An intellectual ability that operates in some but not all intellectual tasks.

Spectral Luminosity Function. The visibility curve for lights of different wave lengths. There are two spectral luminosity functions, one for photopic vision (cones), the other for scotopic vision (rods).

Spectrally Homogeneous Light. Light that consists of radiations of approximately the same wave length.

Spontaneous Recovery. The reappearance of an extinguished conditioned response after a time interval in which no practice occurred.

Stage of Exhaustion. The third and final stage of the general adaptation syndrome, during which the body's resources for coping with a stressor are exhausted.

Stage of Resistance. The second stage of the general adaptation syndrome during which the body's reaction to a stressor increases.

Standard Deviation. A statistical index of variability, the size of which is influenced by every score in the frequency distribution. The formula for computing the standard deviation is:

$$SD = \sqrt{\frac{\Sigma d^2}{N}}$$

where Σ = the sum of, d = deviation of a score from the mean, and N = the number of cases in the frequency distribution.

Standard Error of the Mean. The standard deviation of a sampling distribution of means.

Standardization Group. A sample of subjects that serves as a reference group against which specific scores on a psychological test can be compared.

State of Frustration. A theoretical concept referring to a condition that is produced in an organism by a frustrating situation.

Stimulus. Some property of the environment. Stimuli are one of the three classes of independent variables to which psychologists relate behavior. The term *stimulus* has been extended to events within the body (e.g., response-produced cues) that can become associated with a response.

Stimulus Generalization. The tendency for stimuli similar to the conditioned stimulus to evoke a conditioned response.

Stimulus-Induced Motivation. A drive condition which is evoked by environmental stimulation and is apparently independent of life-maintaining and life-reproducing physiological mechanisms.

Stimulus Variable. A characteristic of an organism's environment that influences its behavior.

Stress. A general term to describe difficult and tense situations and reactions to them. An analysis of the concept suggests that it contains three components: the stressful situation, the physiological changes produced by stress, and stressful behavior.

Stressor. A stress-provoking agent (e.g., physical injury, fear).

Subculture. One of the social groups that comprise a culture.

Subliminal Stimuli. Stimuli that are so faint or are presented so briefly that the observer is unaware of them.

Sublimation. The gratification of a frustrated drive through substitute activity. According to Freudian theory sublimation operates to make socially unacceptable drives acceptable.

Substitution Method. A method of breaking a habit by substituting a new response for the undesirable old one.

Superego. The part of personality which, according to Freud, corresponds most nearly to what is meant by conscience.

Suppression. The elimination of a response for a limited period of time.

Sympathetic Division. A division of the autonomic nervous system that acts to mobilize bodily resources during moments of stress.

Synapse. Where the end brushes of the axon of one neuron come into close proximity with the dendrite of another neuron. If the neural impulse in the axon is sufficiently strong it will activate a neural impulse in the dendrite of the adjacent neuron.

Syntagmatic Associate. A response in a word-association test that would be likely to occur in sequence with the stimulus word in a sentence (e.g., sit-up, brown-table).

Teaching Machine. A device used to present programmed educational material.

Temperament. The aspect of personality pertaining to mood and general level of activity.

Temporal Lobe. The part of the cerebral hemisphere located below the fissure of Sylvius.

Thalamus. A structure located in the upper part of the brain stem. One function of the thalamus is to relay neural impulses to various parts of the cerebral cortex.

Theoretical Construct. A concept that is *inferred* from observable events. The function of a theoretical construct is to integrate existing data and predict new events.

Theory. A group of principles from which the occurrence of individual events can be logically deduced. Theories function to integrate existing data and predict new events.

Theory of Disuse. A theory of retention that assumes forgetting results from the passage of time.

Threshold of Excitation. The amount of energy required to excite a nerve fiber.

Timbre. The unique characteristic of an auditory sensation generated by a complex tone. The timbre of the same note from a clarinet and an oboe differs because the composition of their sound waves differs.

Toleration Method. A method of habit breaking by gradual substitution of a desirable habit for an undesirable one.

Trait. A measurable and relatively stable characteristic of personality.

Tranquilizer. A drug that reduces anxiety and increases relaxation. *Reserpine, chlorpromazine,* and *meprobamate* are examples of tranquilizing drugs.

Transference. The tendency for a patient in psychoanalysis to respond to the analyst as he did to persons important in his childhood, like his father and mother. According to psychoanalytic theory, this makes it possible to uncover, and ultimately understand, the patient's repressed feelings.

Transfer of Training. The influence the learning of one task has upon the learning or performance of another task.

Transposition. A phenomenon in which an organism transfers his general reaction from one discrimination problem to a similar one (e.g., after learning to choose a medium gray in preference to a dark gray, the animal will choose a light gray in preference to a medium gray).

Trial. A unit of practice in learning experiments during which an organism is exposed to a specific stimulus situation.

Unconditioned Response. The response that is made to the unconditioned stimulus in classical conditioning (e.g., salivation is the response made to food).

Unconditioned Stimulus. The stimulus that elicits the unconditioned response in classical conditioning (e.g., food elicits salivation).

Unconscious. A concept introduced by Freud to refer to those "mental events" which a person is not aware of, even though they influence his behavior.

Validity. The validity of a test is determined by the correlation its scores have with some criterion (e.g., the validity of a medical aptitude test would be determined by the degree of correlation between scores obtained on it and performance in medical school).

Variable Interval Schedule. An interval reinforcement schedule in which the first response after a variable time interval is reinforced. The time interval is designated by the average length of these intervals (e.g., in a variable interval schedule of five minutes the response is reinforced once every five minutes on the average, with some intervals being as brief as a few seconds and others much longer than five minutes).

Variable Ratio Schedule. A ratio reinforcement schedule in which the response is reinforced after a varying number of responses have been made. The ratio is designated by the average number of responses that precede a reinforcement (e.g., a variable interval schedule of 30 responses would be one in which reinforcement occurs on the *average* after every 30 responses, but varies from one response to 100 or more responses).

Verbal Conditioning. The reinforcement of special classes of verbal responses (e.g., plural nouns, attitudes).

Verbal Learning. Learning in which language behavior predominates.

Viscerotonia. A dimension of temperament characterized by relaxation and sociability.

Visibility. The ability to detect the presence of light.

Visual Acuity. The ability to distinguish visual detail.

Vocational Guidance. The assistance and direction a counselor gives to a person in selecting a vocation.

Warm-up Effect. Rapid improvement in performance during a practice period immediately after a long rest interval.

Wave Length. The distance between corresponding positions in a wave form, such as the distance between two successive crests. Wave length, measured in millimicrons, is a unit of measurement for light.

Waxy Flexibility. A symptom exhibited by some catatonic schizophrenics. They maintain for many hours a position imposed on them.

Word-Association Test. A test in which a subject is instructed to listen to a given word and respond with the first word that occurs to him.

Work Inhibition. A negative process that operates to inhibit the performance of a motor skill.

Young-Helmholtz Theory. A theory of color vision which assumes that there are three basic color experiences (red, green, and blue) and three types of cones each of which is especially receptive to the wave lengths of one of the colors.

REFERENCES

Action for mental health. Final Report of the Joint Commission on Mental Illness and Health. New York: Basic Books, 1961.

ADAMSON, R. E. Functional fixedness as related to problem solving: a repetition of three experiments. *J. exp. Psychol.,* 1952, 44, 288-291.

ADELMAN, H. A., & ROSENBAUM, G. Extinction of instrumental behavior as a function of frustration at various distances from the goal. *J. exp. Psychol.,* 1954, 47, 429-432.

ADORNO, T. W., FRENKEL-BRUNSWIK, E., LEVINSON, D. J., & SANFORD, R. N. *The authoritarian personality.* New York: Harper & Row, 1950.

ALBERTS, E., & EHRENFREUND, D. Transposition in children as a function of age. *J. exp. Psychol.,* 1951, 41, 30-38.

ALLPORT, G. W. *The nature of prejudice.* Reading, Mass.: Addison-Wesley, 1954.

ALLPORT, G. W., VERNON, P. E., & LINDZEY, G. *A study of values: A scale for measuring the dominant interests in personality.* (3rd ed.) Boston: Houghton Mifflin, 1960.

ALLYN, J., & FESTINGER, L. The effectiveness of unanticipated persuasive communications. *J. abnorm. soc. Psychol.,* 1961, 62, 35-40.

American Association for the Advancement of Science. Science teaching in elementary and junior high schools. *Science,* 1961, 133, 2019-2024.

AMSEL, A., & ROUSSEL, J. Motivational properties of frustration: I. Effect on a running response of the addition of frustration to the motivational complex. *J. exp. Psychol.,* 1952, 43, 363-368.

ANASTASI, A. *Psychological testing.* (2nd ed.) New York: Macmillan, 1961.

ANREP, G. V. Pitch discrimination in the dog. *J. Physiol.,* 1920, 53, 367-385.

ASCH, S. E. Opinions and social pressure. *Scientific Amer.,* 1955, 193, No. 5, 31-35.

ASHLEY, W. R., HARPER, R. S., & RUNYON, D. L. The perceived size of coins in normal and hypnotically induced economic status. *Amer. J. Psychol.,* 1951, 64, 564-572.

ATHERTON, M. V., & WASHBURN, M. F. Mediate associations studied by the method of inhibiting associations: an instance of the effect of *Aufgabe. Amer. J. Psychol.,* 1912, 23, 101-109.

AZRIN, N. H., & LINDSLEY, O. R. The reinforcement of cooperation between children. *J. abnorm. soc. Psychol.,* 1956, 52, 100-102.

BAGBY, E. *The psychology of personality.* New York: Holt, Rinehart, & Winston, 1928.

BAILEY, C. J., & MILLER, N. E. The effect of sodium amytal on an approach-avoidance conflict in cats. *J. comp. physiol. Psychol.,* 1952, 45, 205-208.

BAIRD, J. C., GULICK, W. L., & SMITH, W. M. The effects of angle of regard upon the size of after-images. *Psychol. Rec.,* 1962, 12, 263-272.

BALES, R. F. In conference. *Harvard Bus. Rev.,* 1954, 32, 44-50.

BALES, R. F. Task roles and social roles in problem-solving groups. In E. E. Maccoby, T. M. Newcomb, & E. L. Hartley (Eds.), *Readings in social psychology.* (3rd ed.) New York: Holt, Rinehart, & Winston, 1958. Pp. 437-447.

BARKER, R. G., DEMBO, T., & LEWIN, K. Frustration and regression: an experiment with young children. *Univer. Iowa Stud. Child Welf.,* 1941, 18, No. 386.

BARTLEY, S. H. *Principles of perception.* New York: Harper & Row, 1958.

BARTOSHUK, A. K. Electromyographic gradients in goal-directed activity. *Canad. J. Psychol.,* 1955, 9, 21-28.

BAYER, E. Beiträge zur Zweikomponotentheorie des Hungers. *Z. Psychol.,* 1929, 112, 1-54.

BEACH, F. A. The neural basis of innate behavior: III. Comparison of learning ability and instinctive behavior in the rat. *J. comp. Psychol.,* 1939, 28, 225-262.

BEACH, F. A. Comparison of copulatory behavior of male rats raised in isolation, cohabitation, and segregation. *J. genet. Psychol.,* 1942, 60, 121-136.

BEACH, F. A. Effects of injury to the cerebral cortex upon sexually receptive behavior in the female rat. *Psychosom. Med.,* 1944, 6, 40-55.

BEACH, F. A. Evolutionary changes in the physiological control of mating behavior in mammals. *Psychol. Rev.,* 1947, 54, 297-315.

706

BEACH, F. A. *Hormones and behavior.* New York: Hoeber, 1948.

BECK, S. J. *Rorschach's test: II. A variety of personality pictures.* New York: Grune & Stratton, 1945.

BÉKÉSY, G. VON. Current status of theories of hearing. *Science,* 1956, 123, 779-783.

BÉKÉSY, G. VON. *Experiments in hearing.* New York: McGraw-Hill, 1960.

BELLAK, L. The concept of projection. *Psychiatry,* 1944, 7, 353-370.

BELLOWS, R. T. Time factors in water drinking in dogs. *Amer. J. Physiol.,* 1939, 125, 87-97.

BENEDICT, R. *Patterns of culture.* Boston: Houghton Mifflin, 1934.

BENEDICT, R. *The chrysanthemum and the sword.* Boston: Houghton Mifflin, 1946.

BENNETT, G. K., SEASHORE, H. H., & WESMAN, A. G. *Counseling from profiles: A casebook for the differential aptitude tests.* New York: The Psychological Corp., 1951.

BENNETT, G. K., SEASHORE, H. H., & WESMAN, A. G. *Manual for the differential aptitude tests.* (3rd ed.) New York: The Psychological Corp., 1959.

BERLYNE, D. E. The arousal and satiation of perceptual curiosity in the rat. *J. comp. physiol. Psychol.,* 1955, 48, 238-247.

BERLYNE, D. E. *Conflict arousal and curiosity.* New York: McGraw-Hill, 1960.

BERNSTEIN, B. B. Extinction as a function of frustration drive and frustration drive stimulus. *J. exp. Psychol.,* 1957, 54, 89-95.

BEST, C. H., & TAYLOR, N. B. *The living body.* (4th ed.) New York: Holt, Rinehart, & Winston, 1958.

BILLS, A. G. The influence of muscular tension on the efficiency of mental work. *Amer. J. Psychol.,* 1927, 38, 227-251.

BILLS, M. A. Field salesmen. In D. H. Fryer & E. R. Henry (Eds.), *Handbook of applied psychology.* New York: Holt, Rinehart, & Winston, 1950. Pp. 212-215.

BINDRA, D. *Motivation: A systematic reinterpretation.* New York: Ronald, 1958.

BIRCH, H. G. The relation of previous experience to insightful problem-solving. *J. comp. Psychol.,* 1945, 38, 367-383.

BIRCH, H. G. Sources of order in the maternal behavior of animals. *Amer. J. Orthopsychiat.,* 1956, 26, 279-284.

BIRCH, H. G., & RABINOWITZ, H. S. The negative effect of previous experience on productive thinking. *J. exp. Psychol.,* 1951, 41, 121-125.

BLOMMERS, P., & LINDQUIST, E. F. *Elementary statistical methods.* Boston: Houghton Mifflin, 1960.

BORING, E. G. (Ed.) *Psychology for the armed services.* Washington, D. C.: Combat Forces Press, 1945.

BORING, E. G., LANGFELD, H. S., & WELD, H. P. *Foundations of psychology.* New York: Wiley, 1948.

BORING, E. G. *A history of experimental psychology* (Rev. ed.) New York: Appleton-Century-Crofts, 1950.

BOYD, W. C. *Genetics and the races of man.* Boston: Little, Brown, 1950.

BRADY, J. V. Animal experimental evaluation of drug effects upon behavior. In *The effect of pharmacologic agents on the nervous system.* Proc. ass. res. nerv. ment. Dis. Vol. 37. Baltimore: Williams & Wilkins, 1959.

BRADY, J. V., PORTER, R. W., CONRAD, D. G., & MASON, J. W. Avoidance behavior and the development of gastroduodenal ulcers. *J. exp. anal. Behavior,* 1958, 1, 69-72.

BRILL, A. A. (Ed.) *The basic writings of Sigmund Freud.* New York: Modern Library, 1938.

BROOKS, C. McC. The role of the cerebral cortex and of various sense organs in the excitation and execution of mating activity in the rabbit. *Amer. J. Physiol.,* 1937, 120, 544-553.

BROWN, F. A. A comparative study of the intelligence of Jewish and Scandinavian kindergarten children. *J. genet. Psychol.,* 1944, 64, 67-92.

BROWN, J. S. Gradients of approach and avoidance responses and their relation to level of motivation. *J. comp. physiol. Psychol.,* 1948, 41, 450-465.

BROWN, J. S. Principles of intrapersonal conflict. *Conflict Resolution,* 1957, 1, 135-154.

BROWN, J. S. *The motivation of behavior.* New York: McGraw-Hill, 1961.

BROWN, R. W. *Words and things.* New York: Crowell-Collier, 1958.

BRUCE, R. W. Conditions of transfer of training. *J. exp. Psychol.,* 1933, 16, 343-361.

BRUNER, J. S., GOODNOW, J. J., & AUSTIN, G. A. *A study of thinking.* New York: Wiley, 1956.

BRUNER, J. S., & POSTMAN, L. On the perception of incongruity: a paradigm. *J. Pers.,* 1949, 18, 206-223.

BUCHWALD, A. M., & YAMAGUCHI, H. G. The effect of change in drive level on habit reversal. *J. exp. Psychol.,* 1955, 50, 265-268.

BUGELSKI, B. R. *The psychology of learning.* New York: Holt, Rinehart, & Winston, 1956.

BUGELSKI, R. Extinction with and without subgoal reinforcement. *J. comp. Psychol.*, 1938, 26, 121-133.

BUNCH, C. C. Age variations in auditory acuity. *Arch. Otolaryng.*, 1929, 9, 625-636.

BURCHARD, E. M. L. Physique and psychosis: an analysis of the postulated relationship between bodily constitution and mental disease syndrome. *Comp. psychol. Monogr.*, 1936, No. 13.

BURGESS, E. W., & WALLIN, P. *Engagement and marriage.* New York: Lippincott, 1953.

BURKS, B. S. The relative influence of nature and nurture upon mental development: a comparative study of foster parent-child resemblance. *27th Yearb. Nat. Soc. Stud. Educ.*, Part I, 1928. Pp. 219-316.

BURTON, A., & HARRIS, R. E. *Clinical studies on personality.* New York: Harper & Row, 1955.

BUSH, R. R., & ESTES, W. K. (Eds.) *Studies in mathematical learning theory.* Stanford, Calif.: Stanford Univer. Press, 1959.

BUSS, A. H. *The psychology of aggression.* New York: Wiley, 1961.

CAMERON, N. The development of paranoic thinking. *Psychol. Rev.*, 1943, 50, 219-233.

CAMERON, N., & MAGARET, A. *Behavior pathology.* Boston: Houghton Mifflin, 1951.

CAMPBELL, A. Factors associated with attitudes toward Jews. In T. M. Newcomb & E. L. Hartley (Eds.), *Readings in social psychology.* New York: Holt, Rinehart, & Winston, 1947.

CAMPBELL, A., CONVERSE, P. E., MILLER, W. E., & STOKES, D. E. *The American voter.* New York: Wiley, 1960.

CAMPBELL, A., GURIN, G., & MILLER, W. E. *The voter decides.* Evanston, Ill.: Row, Peterson, 1954.

CANNON, W. B. Hunger and thirst. In C. Murchison (Ed.), *A handbook of general experimental psychology.* Worcester, Mass.: Clark Univer. Press, 1934. Pp. 247-263.

CANTOR, G. M. Effects of three types of pretraining on discrimination learning in preschool children. *J. exp. Psychol.*, 1955, 49, 339-342.

CARMICHAEL, L. A further study of the development of behavior in vertebrates experimentally removed from the influence of environmental stimulation. *Psychol. Rev.*, 1927, 34, 34-47.

CARMICHAEL, L., HOGAN, H. P., & WALTER, A. A. An experimental study of the effect of language on the reproduction of visually perceived form. *J. exp. Psychol.*, 1932, 15, 73-86.

CARSON, R. C. The effect of electroconvulsive shock on a learned avoidance response. *J. comp. physiol. Psychol.*, 1957, 50, 125-129.

CATTELL, R. *Personality and motivation structure and measurement.* New York: Harcourt, Brace, & World, 1957.

CATTELL, R. B. *Description and measurement of personality.* New York: Harcourt, Brace, & World, 1946.

CENTERS, R. *The psychology of social classes.* Princeton, N. J.: Princeton Univer. Press, 1949.

CHAPANIS, A. How we see: a summary of basic principles. In *Human factors in undersea warfare.* Washington, D. C.: Natl Res. Council, 1949. Pp. 3-60.

CHAPANIS, A., GARNER, W. R., & MORGAN, C. T. *Applied experimental psychology.* New York: Wiley, 1949.

CHAPLIN, J. P., & KRAWIEC, T. S. *Systems and theories of psychology.* New York: Holt, Rinehart, & Winston, 1960.

CLARK, R., & POLISH, E. Avoidance conditioning and alcohol consumption in rhesus monkeys. *Science*, 1960, 132, 223-224.

COCH, L., & FRENCH, J. R. P., Jr. Overcoming resistance to change. *Human Relat.*, 1948, 1, 512-533.

COHEN, A. R. Need for cognition and order of communication as determinants of opinion change. In C. I. Hovland (Ed.), *The order of presentation in persuasion.* New Haven, Conn.: Yale Univer. Press, 1957.

COHEN, M. R., & NAGEL, E. *An introduction to logic and scientific method.* New York: Harcourt, Brace, & World, 1934.

COLBY, K. M. *An introduction to psychoanalytic research.* New York: Basic Books, 1960.

CONANT, J. B. *On understanding science.* New Haven, Conn.: Yale Univer. Press, 1947.

CONGER, J. J. The effects of alcohol on conflict behavior in the albino rat. *Quart. J. Stud. Alcohol*, 1951, 12, 1-29.

COOK, T. W. Studies in cross education: III. Kinaesthetic learning of an irregular pattern. *J. exp. Psychol.*, 1934, 17, 749-762.

COX, C. M. *Genetic studies of genius: II. The early mental traits of three hundred geniuses.* Stanford, Calif.: Stanford Univer. Press, 1926.

CRAWFORD, M. P. The cooperative solving of problems by young chimpanzees. *Comp. Psychol. Monogr.*, 1937, 14, No. 68.

CRISLER, G. Salivation is unnecessary for the establishment of the salivary conditioned reflex induced by morphine. *Amer. J. Physiol.*, 1940, 94, 553-556.

CRONBACH, L. J. Statistical methods applied to Rorschach scores: a review. *Psychol. Bull.*, 1949, 46, 393-429.

CRONBACH, L. J. *Essentials of psychological test-*

708

ing. (2nd ed.) New York: Harper & Row, 1960.

CROWDER, N. A. Automatic tutoring by means of intrinsic programming. In E. Galanter (Ed.), *Automatic teaching: The state of the art.* New York: Wiley, 1959. Pp. 109-116.

CROWDER, N. A. *The arithmetic of computers: An introduction to binary and octal mathematics.* Garden City, N. Y.: Doubleday, 1960.

CRUTCHFIELD, R. S. Conformity and character. *Amer. Psychologist,* 1955, 10, 191-198.

D'AMATO, M. R., & GUMENIK, W. E. Some effects of immediate versus randomly delayed shock on an instrumental response and cognitive processes. *J. abnorm. soc. Psychol.,* 1960, 60, 64-67.

DANIEL, R. S., & SMITH, K. U. The sea-approach behavior of the neonate loggerhead turtle (Caretta caretta). *J. comp. physiol. Psychol.,* 1947, 40, 413-420.

DANZIGER, K. The operation of an acquired drive in satiated rats. *Quart. J. exp. Psychol.,* 1951, 3, 119-132.

DAVIS, C. M. Self-selection of diet by newly weaned infants. *Amer. J. dis. Child.,* 1928, 36, 651-679.

DAVIS, K. B. *Factors in the life of twenty-two hundred women.* New York: Harper, 1929.

DEESE, J. *The psychology of learning.* (2nd ed.) New York: McGraw-Hill, 1958.

DEMBER, W. N. *Psychology of perception.* New York: Holt, Rinehart, & Winston, 1960.

DENNIS, W. *Readings in the history of psychology.* New York: Appleton-Century-Crofts, 1948.

DETERLINE, W. A. *An introduction to programmed instruction.* Englewood Cliffs, N.J.: Prentice-Hall, 1962.

DEUTSCH, M., & GERARD, H. B. A study of normative and informational social influences upon individual judgment. *J. abnorm. soc. Psychol.,* 1955, 51, 629-636.

DIETZE, D. The facilitating effect of words on discrimination and generalization. *J. exp. Psychol.,* 1955, 50, 255-260.

DIVEN, K. Certain determinants in the conditioning of anxiety reactions. *J. Psychol.,* 1937, 3, 291-308.

DOLLARD, J., AULD, F., & WHITE, A. M. *Steps in psychotherapy.* New York: Macmillan, 1953.

DOLLARD, J., DOOB, L. W., MILLER, N. E., MOWRER, O. H., SEARS, R. R., FORD, C. S., HOVLAND, C. I., & SOLLENBERGER, R. I. *Frustration and aggression.* New Haven, Conn.: Yale Univer. Press, 1939.

DOLLARD, J., & MILLER, N. E. *Personality and psychotherapy.* New York: McGraw-Hill, 1950.

DOUVAN, E. Social status and success strivings. *J. abnorm. soc. Psychol.,* 1956, 52, 219-223.

DOUVAN, E., & ADELSON, J. The psychodynamics of social mobility in adolescent boys. *J. abnorm. soc. Psychol.,* 1958, 56, 31-44.

DUBOIS, P. H. (Ed.) The classification program. *AAF Aviat. Psychol. Program Res. Rep.,* 1947, No. 2.

DUNLAP, K. *Habits: their making and unmaking.* New York: Liveright, 1932.

EBBINGHAUS, H. *Memory.* Trans. by H. A. Ruger & C. E. Bussenius. New York: Columbia Univer. Press, 1913.

EDWARDS, A. L. *Experimental design in psychological research.* (Rev. ed.) New York: Holt, Rinehart, & Winston, 1960.

EHRENFREUND, D. Effect of a secondary reinforcing agent in black-white discrimination. *J. comp. physiol. Psychol.,* 1949, 42, 1-5.

EISMAN, E., ASIMOW, A. M., & MALTZMAN, I. Habit strength as a function of drive in a brightness discrimination problem. *J. exp. Psychol.,* 1956, 52, 58-64.

ENGLISH, O. S., & PEARSON, G. H. J. *Emotional problems of living.* New York: Norton, 1945.

ERIKSEN, C. W., & KUETHE, J. L. Avoidance conditioning of verbal behavior without awareness: a paradigm of repression. *J. abnorm. soc. Psychol.,* 1956, 53, 203-209.

ERVIN, S. M. Changes with age in the verbal determinants of word-association. *Amer. J. Psychol.,* 1961, 74, 361-372.

ESTES, W. K. An experimental study of punishment. *Psychol Monogr,* 1944, 57, No. 263.

ESTES, W. K. The statistical approach to learning theory. In S. Koch (Ed.), *Psychology: A study of a science.* Vol. 2. New York: McGraw-Hill, 1959. Pp. 380-491.

ESTES, W. K., & STRAUGHAN, J. H. Analysis of a verbal conditioning situation in terms of statistical learning theory. *J. exp. Psychol.,* 1954, 47, 225-234.

EWERT, H. Eye movements during reading and recall. *J. gen. Psychol.,* 1933, 8, 65-84.

EWING, T. A study of certain factors involved in changes of opinion. *J. soc. Psychol.,* 1942, 16, 63-88.

EYSENCK, H. J. The effects of psychotherapy: an evaluation. *J. consult. Psychol.,* 1952, 16, 319-324.

FABING, H. On going berserk: a neurochemical inquiry. *Scientific Monthly,* 1956, 83, 232-237.

FARBER, I. E. Response fixation under anxiety and non-anxiety conditions. *J. exp. Psychol.,* 1948, 38, 111-131.

FARBER, I. E., HARLOW, H. F., & WEST, L. J. Brainwashing, conditioning, and DDD (debility, dependency, and dread). *Sociometry,* 1957, 20, 271-285.

FEIGL, H. Logical empiricism. In H. Feigl & W. Sellars (Eds.), *Readings in philosophical analysis.* New York: Appleton-Century-Crofts, 1949. Pp. 3-26.

FERSTER, C. B., & DE MYER, M. K. The development of performance in autistic children in an automatically controlled environment. *J. chron. Dis.,* 1961, 13, 312-345.

FERSTER, C. B., & SKINNER, B. F. *Schedules of reinforcement.* New York: Appleton-Century-Crofts, 1957.

FESTINGER, L. *A theory of cognitive dissonance.* New York: Harper & Row, 1957.

FESTINGER, L., & CARLSMITH, J. M. Cognitive consequences of forced compliance, *J. abnorm. soc. Psychol.,* 1959, 58, 203-210.

FESTINGER, L., RIECKEN, H. W., & SCHACHTER, S. *When prophecy fails.* Minneapolis: Univer. of Minnesota Press, 1956.

FESTINGER, L., & THIBAUT, J. Interpersonal communication in small groups. *J. abnorm. soc. Psychol.,* 1951, 46, 92-99.

FIELDS, P. E. Studies in concept formation: I. The development of the concept of triangularity by the white rat. *Comp. Psychol. Monogr.,* 1932, 9, No. 2.

FITTS, P. M., & JONES, R. E. Psychological aspects of instrument display: I. Analysis of 270 "pilot-error" experiences in reading and interpreting aircraft instruments. In H. W. Sinaiko (Ed.), *Selected papers on human factors in the design and use of control systems.* New York: Dover, 1961.

FLAVELL, J. H., & DRAGUNS, J. A microgenetic approach to perception and thought. *Psychol. Bull.,* 1957, 54, 197-217.

FLEISHMAN, E. A. (Ed.) *Studies in personnel and industrial psychology.* Homewood, Ill.: R. D. Irwin, 1962.

FLEISHMAN, E. A., HARRIS, E. F., & BURTT, H. E. *Leadership and supervision in industry.* Columbus, Ohio: Bureau of Educational Research, Ohio State Univer., 1955.

FOLEY, J. P., & MACMILLAN, Z. L. Mediated generalization and the interpretation of verbal behavior: V. "Free association" as related to differences in professional training. *J. exp. Psychol.,* 1943, 33, 299-310.

FORD, C. S., & BEACH, F. A. *Patterns of sexual behavior.* New York: Harper & Row, 1952.

FORM, W. H. Toward an occupational social psychology. *J. soc. Psychol.,* 1946, 24, 85-99.

FREEDMAN, D. G., KING, J. A., & ELLIOT, O. Critical period in the social development of dogs. *Science,* 1961, 133, 1016-1017.

FRENCH, J. D., & MAGOUN, H. W. Effects of chronic lesions in the central cephalic brain stem of monkeys. *Arch. Neur. Psychiatry,* 1952, 68, 591-604.

FREUD, S. *An outline of psychoanalysis.* New York: Norton, 1949.

FRY, E. *Teaching machines and programmed learning.* New York: McGraw-Hill, 1962.

FULLER, J. L. Behavior genetics. In P. R. Farnsworth & Q. McNemar (Eds.), *Ann. Rev. Psychol.* Vol. II. Palo Alto, Calif.: Annual Reviews, Inc., 1960. Pp. 41-70.

FULLER, J. L., & THOMPSON, W. R. *Behavior genetics.* New York: Wiley, 1960.

FUSTER, J. M. Effect of stimulation of brain stem on tachistoscopic perception. *Science,* 1958, 127, 150.

GAGNÉ, R. M., & BAKER, K. E. Stimulus predifferentiation as a factor in transfer of training. *J. exp. Psychol.,* 1950, 40, 439-451.

GAGNÉ, R. M., & FLEISHMAN, E. A. *Psychology and human performance.* New York: Holt, Rinehart, & Winston, 1959.

GARDNER, E. *Fundamentals of neurology.* (3rd ed.) Philadelphia: Saunders, 1958.

GARDNER, E. F., & THOMPSON, G. G. *Social relations and morale in small groups.* New York: Appleton-Century-Crofts, 1956.

GATES, A. I. Recitation as a factor in memorizing. *Arch. Psychol.,* 1917, 6, No. 40.

GELDARD, F. A. *The human senses.* New York: Wiley, 1953.

GELLER, I., DE MARCO, A. O., & SEIFTER, J. Delayed effects of nicotine on the timing behavior in the rat. *Science,* 1960, 131, 735-737.

GELLERMAN, L. W. The double alternation problem: III. The behavior of monkeys in a double alternation box-apparatus. *J. genet. Psychol.,* 1931, 39, 359-392.

GHISELLI, E. E., & BROWN, C. W. *Personnel and industrial psychology.* (2nd ed.) New York: McGraw-Hill, 1955.

GIBSON, J. J. *The perception of the visual world.* Boston: Houghton Mifflin, 1950.

GILBERT, G. M. Hermann Goering, amiable psychopath. *J. abnorm. soc. Psychol.,* 1948, 43, 211-229.

GILBERT, G. M. Stereotype persistence and change among college students. *J. abnorm. soc. Psychol.,* 1951, 46, 245-254.

GILBRETH, F. B. *Motion study.* New York: Van Nostrand, 1911.

GLUCKSBERG, S. The influence of strength of drive on functional fixedness and perceptual recognition. *J. exp. Psychol.,* 1962, 63, 36-41.

GOLDMAN, L. *Using tests in counseling.* New York: Appleton-Century-Crofts, 1961.

710

GOLDSTEIN, K. *Aftereffects of brain injuries in war.* New York: Grune & Stratton, 1942.

GOLDSTEIN, K., & KATZ, S. The psychopathology of Pick's Disease. *Arch. Neur. Psychiat.,* 1937, 38, 473-490.

GOODBEER, E. Factors inducing conflict in the choice behavior of children. Unpublished Master's thesis, Yale Univer., 1940.

GREEN, E. G. *The learning process and programmed instruction.* New York: Holt, Rinehart, & Winston, 1962.

GREENSPOON, J. The reinforcing effect of two spoken sounds on the frequency of two responses. *Amer. J. Psychol.,* 1955, 68, 409-416.

GRETHER, W. F. *Analysis of types of errors in reading of the conventional three-pointer altimeter.* Aero-Medical Laboratory, Air Material Command, Dayton, Ohio. Report MCREXD-694-14A, 16 March 1948.

GRICE, G. R. The relation of secondary reinforcement to delayed reward in visual discrimination. *J. exp. Psychol.,* 1948, 38, 1-16.

GRIFFIN, D. R., & GALAMBOS, R. The sensory basis of obstacle avoidance by flying bats. *J. exp. Zoology,* 1941, 86, 481-506.

GUILFORD, J. P. *Personality.* New York: McGraw-Hill, 1959. (a)

GUILFORD, J. P. Three faces of intellect. *Amer. Psychologist,* 1959, 14, 469-479. (b)

GUILFORD, J. P., & ZIMMERMAN, W. S. Fourteen dimensions of temperament. *Psychol. Monogr.,* 1957, 70, No. 417.

GUTHRIE, E. R. *The psychology of learning.* New York: Harper & Row, 1952.

GUTTMAN, N. Operant conditioning, extinction, and periodic reinforcement in relation to concentration of sucrose used as reinforcing agent. *J. exp. Psychol.,* 1953, 46, 213-224.

HALL, C. S. The inheritance of emotionality. *Sigma Xi Quart.,* 1938, 26, 17-27.

HALL, C. S. *A primer of Freudian psychology.* New York: New American Library (a Mentor Book), 1955.

HALL, C. S., & LINDZEY, G. *Theories of personality.* New York: Wiley, 1957.

HALL, J. F. *Psychology of motivation.* Chicago: Lippincott, 1961.

HALMOSH, A. F. Sur les modifications sanguines pendent l'emotion. *Encéphale,* 1953, 42, 250-273.

HALPIN, A. W. The leader behavior and effectiveness of aircraft commanders. In R. M. Stogdill & A. E. Coons (Eds.), *Leader behavior: Its description and measurement.* Columbus, Ohio: Bureau of Business Res., Ohio State Univer., 1957.

HALPIN, A. W., & WINER, B. J. A factorial study of the leader behavior descriptions. In R. M. Stogdill & A. E. Coons (Eds.), *Leader behavior: Its description and measurement.* Columbus, Ohio: Bureau of Business Res., Ohio State Univer., 1957.

HAMMOND, K. R., & HOUSEHOLDER, J. E. *Introduction to the statistical method.* New York: Knopf, 1962.

HARLOW, H. F. The formation of learning sets. *Psychol. Rev.,* 1949, 56, 51-65.

HARLOW, H. F. Functional organization of the brain in relation to men and behavior. *The biology of mental health and disease.* Milbank Memorial Fund. New York: Hoeber, 1952.

HARLOW, H. F. The nature of love. *Amer. Psychol.,* 1958, 13, 673-685.

HARLOW, H. F., BLAZEK, N. C., & McCLEARN, G. E. Manipulatory motivation in the infant rhesus monkey. *J. comp. physiol. Psychol.,* 1956, 49, 444-448.

HARTSHORNE, H., & MAY, M. A. *Studies in deceit.* New York: Macmillan, 1928.

HASKELL, R. I. A statistical study of the comparative results produced by teaching derivation in the ninth-grade Latin classes and in the ninth-grade English classes of non-Latin pupils in four Philadelphia high schools. Doctoral dissertation, Univer. of Pennsylvania, 1923.

HATHAWAY, S. R., & McKINLEY, J. C. *The Minnesota Multiphasic Personality Inventory.* (Rev. ed.) Minneapolis: Univer. of Minnesota Press, 1943.

HAVEMANN, E. *The age of psychology.* New York: Simon and Schuster, 1957.

HAVEMANN, E., & WEST, P. S. *They went to college.* New York: Harcourt, Brace, & World, 1952.

HAYES, C. *The ape in our house.* New York: Harper & Row, 1951.

HAYWARD, S. C. Modification of sexual behavior of the male albino rat. *J. comp. physiol. Psycol.,* 1957, 50, 70-73.

HEBB, D. O. *The organization of behavior.* New York: Wiley, 1949.

HEFFERLINE, R. F., KEENAN, B., & HANFORD, R. A. Escape and avoidance conditioning in human subjects without their observation of the response. *Science,* 1959, 130, 1338.

HEIDBREDER, E. *Seven psychologies.* New York: Appleton-Century-Crofts, 1933.

HEMPEL, W. E., & FLEISHMAN, E. A. A factor analysis of physical proficiency and manipulative skill. *J. appl. Psychol.,* 1955, 39, 12-16.

HEMPHILL, J. K. *Leader behavior description.*

Columbus, Ohio: Personnel Res. Board, Ohio State Univer., 1950.

HEMPHILL, J. K. Leader behavior associated with the administrative reputations of college departments. In R. M. Stogdill & A. E. Coons (Eds.), *Leader behavior: Its description and measurement.* Columbus, Ohio: Bureau of Business Res., Ohio State Univer., 1957.

HENDRICKSON, G., & SCHROEDER, W. H. Transfer of training to hit a submerged target. *J. educ. Psychol.,* 1941, 32, 205-213.

HENRY, W. E., & FARLEY, J. The validity of the thematic apperception test in the study of adolescent personality. *Psychol. Monogr.,* 1959, 73, No. 487.

HERNÁNDEZ-PEÓN, R., SCHERRER, H., & JOUVET, M. Modification of electric activity in cochlear nucleus during "attention" in unanesthetized cats. *Science,* 1956, 123, 331-332.

HERON, W. The pathology of boredom. *Scientific Amer.,* 1957, 199, No. 1, 52-56.

HERRICK, E. H., & HARRIS, J. O. Singing female canaries. *Science,* 1957, 125, 1299-1300.

HILGARD, E. R. The nature of the conditioned response: I. The case for and against stimulus substitution. *Psychol. Rev.,* 1936, 43, 366-385.

HILGARD, E. R. *Theories of learning.* (Rev. ed.) New York: Appleton-Century-Crofts, 1956.

HILGARD, E. R., & MARQUIS, D. G. *Conditioning and learning.* New York: Appleton-Century-Crofts, 1940.

HINCKLEY, E. D. The influence of individual opinion on construction of an attitude scale. *J. soc. Psychol.,* 1932, 3, 283-296.

HOLLAND, J. G., & SKINNER, B. F. *The analysis of behavior: A program for self-instruction.* New York: McGraw-Hill, 1961.

HOLLINGSHEAD, A. B., & REDLICH, F. C. *Social class and mental illness: A community study.* New York: Wiley, 1958.

HOLLINGWORTH, L. S. *Children above 180 IQ.* New York: World Book, 1942.

HOLWAY, A. H., & BORING, E. G. The moon illusion and the angle of regard. *Amer. J. Psychol.,* 1940, 53, 109-116.

HOLWAY, A. H., & BORING, E. G. Determinants of apparent visual size with distance variant. *Amer. J. Psychol.,* 1941, 54, 21-37.

HOMME, L., & GLASER, R. Relationship between the programmed textbook and teaching machines. In E. Galanter (Ed.), *Automatic teaching: The state of the art.* New York: Wiley, 1959. Pp. 103-108.

HONZIK, M. P., McFARLANE, J. W., & ALLEN, L. The stability of mental test performance between two and eighteen years. *J. exp. Educ.,* 1948, 17, 309-324.

HOVLAND, C. I. The generalization of conditioned responses: I. The sensory generalization of conditioned responses with varying frequencies of tone. *J. gen. Psychol.,* 1937, 17, 125-148. (a)

HOVLAND, C. I. The generalization of conditioned responses: III. Extinction, spontaneous recovery, and disinhibition of conditioned and of generalized responses. *J. exp. Psychol.,* 1937, 21, 47-62. (b)

HUDDART, J. An account of persons who could not distinguish colours. *Philos. Trans.,* 1777, 67, 260-265.

HULL, C. L. Quantitative aspects of the evolution of concepts. *Psychol. Monogr.,* 1920, 28, No. 123.

HULL, C. L. *Principles of behavior.* New York: Appleton-Century-Crofts, 1943.

HUNT, J. McV. *Intelligence and experience.* New York: Ronald, 1961.

HUNTER, W. S. The delayed reaction in animals and children. *Behav. Monogr.,* 1913, 2, 21-30.

HUNTER, W. S. The behavior of raccoons in a double alternation temporal maze. *J. genet. Psychol.,* 1928, 35, 374-388.

HUNTER, W. S., & NAGGE, J. W. The white rat and the double alternation temporal maze. *J. genet. Psychol.,* 1931, 39, 303-319.

HURVICH, L. M., & JAMESON, D. An opponent-process theory of color vision. *Psychol. Rev.,* 1957, 64, 384-404.

HUTT, P. J. Rate of bar pressing as a function of quality and quantity of reward. *J. comp. physiol. Psychol.,* 1954, 47, 235-239.

HYMAN, H. *Political socialization: A study in the psychology of political behavior.* New York: The Free Press of Glencoe, 1959.

INHELDER, B., & PIAGET, J. *The growth of logical thinking from childhood to adolescence.* New York: Basic Books, 1958.

ISAACS, W., THOMAS, J., & GOLDIAMOND, I. Application of operant conditioning to reinstate verbal behavior in psychotics. *J. speech hear. Dis.,* 1960, 25, 8-12.

ITARD, J.-M-C. *The wild boy of Aveyron.* New York: Appleton-Century-Crofts, 1962.

JACKSON, J. M., & SALTZSTEIN, H. D. The effect of person-group relationships on conformity processes. *J. abnorm. soc. Psychol.,* 1958, 57, 17-24.

JACOBSON, E. Electrophysiology of mental activities. *Amer. J. Psychol.,* 1932, 44, 677-694.

JAHODA, G. A note of Ashanti names and their relationship to personality. *British J. Psychol.,* 1954, 45, 192-195.

JAHODA, M. *Current concepts of positive mental health.* New York: Basic Books, 1958.

JAMES, W. *The principles of psychology.* New York: Dover, 1950.

JANIS, I. L., & FESHBACH, S. Effects of fear-arousing communications. *J. abnorm. soc. Psychol.,* 1953, 48, 78-92.

JASPER, H. H. Electroencephalography. In W. Penfield & T. Erickson (Eds.), *Epilepsy and cerebral localization.* Springfield, Ill.: Charles C. Thomas, 1941.

JAYNES, J. Imprinting: the interaction of learned and innate behavior: I. Development and generalization. *J. comp. physiol. Psychol.,* 1956, 49, 201-206.

JAYNES, J. Imprinting: the interaction of learned and innate behavior: II. The critical period. *J. comp. physiol. Psychol.,* 1957, 50, 6-10.

JENKINS, J. G., & DALLENBACH, K. M. Oblivescence during sleep and waking. *Amer. J. Psychol.,* 1924, 35, 605-612.

JENKINS, J. G. Nominating techniques as a method of evaluating air group morale. *J. Aviat. Med.,* 1948, 19, 12-19.

JENKINS, J. J., & HANRATTY, J. A. Drive intensity discrimination in the albino rat. *J. comp. physiol. Psychol.,* 1949, 42, 228-232.

JENKINS, J. J., & PATERSON, D. G. *Studies in individual differences: The search for intelligence.* New York: Appleton-Century-Crofts, 1961.

JENKINS, J. J., & RUSSELL, W. A. Systematic changes in word association norms. *J. abnorm. soc. Psychol.,* 1960, 60, 293-304.

JENKINS, W. O. The tactual discrimination of shapes for coding aircraft-type controls. In P. M. Fitts (Ed.), *Psychological research on equipment design.* Washington: U.S. Gov't. Printing Office, 1947. Pp. 199-205.

JOHN, E. R., WENZEL, B. M., & TSCHIRGI, R. D. Differential effects on various conditioned responses in cats caused by intraventricular and intramuscular injections of reserpine and other substances. *J. pharm. exp. Therapeutics,* 1958, 123, 193-205.

JOHNSON, D. M. *The psychology of thought and judgment.* New York: Harper & Row, 1955.

JONES, M. C. A laboratory study of fear: The case of Peter. *Ped. Sem.,* 1924, 31, 308-315.

JOST, H., & SONTAG, L. W. The genetic factor in autonomic nervous system functioning. *Psychosom. Med.,* 1944, 6, 308-310.

JUDD, D. B. Basic correlates of the visual stimulus. In S. S. Stevens (Ed.), *Handbook of experimental psychology.* New York: Wiley, 1951. Pp. 811-867.

JUDSON, A. J., & COFER, C. N. Reasoning as an associative process: I. "Direction" in a simple verbal problem. *Psychol. Rep.,* 1956, 2, 469-476.

JUDSON, A. J., COFER, C. N., & GELFAND, S. Reasoning as an associative process: II. "Direction" in problem solving as a function of prior reinforcement of relevant responses. *Psychol. Rep.,* 1956, 2, 501-507.

JUNG, C. G. *Studies in word-association.* Trans. by M. D. Eder. London: William Heinemann, 1918.

KALISH, H. I. Strength of fear as a function of the number of acquisition and extinction trials. *J. exp. Psychol.,* 1954, 47, 1-9.

KALLMAN, F. J. Heredity in health and mental disorder. New York: Norton, 1953.

KARN, H. W., & GILMER, H. *Readings in industrial and business psychology.* (2nd ed.) New York: McGraw-Hill, 1962.

KATZ, D., & BRALY, K. W. Racial stereotypes of 100 college students. *J. abnorm. soc. Psychol.,* 1933, 28, 280-290.

KATZ, D., CARTWRIGHT, D., ELDERSVELD, S., & LEE, A. McC. (Eds.) *Public opinion and propaganda.* New York: Holt, Rinehart, & Winston, 1954.

KATZ, D., MACCOBY, N., & MORSE, N. C. *Productivity, supervision and morale in an office situation.* Ann Arbor, Mich.: Survey Res. Center, Univer. of Michigan, 1950.

KATZ, S. E., & LANDIS, C. Psychologic and physiologic phenomena during a prolonged vigil. *Arch. Neurol. Psychiat.,* 1935, 34, 307-316.

KAUFMAN, E. L., & MILLER, N. E. Effect of number of reinforcements on strength of approach in an approach-avoidance conflict. *J. comp. physiol. Psychol.,* 1949, 42, 65-74.

KAUFMAN, L., & ROCK, I. The moon illusion. *Scientific Amer.,* 1962, 207, No. 1, 120-130.

KELLEHER, R. T. Discrimination learning as a function of reversal and nonreversal shifts. *J. exp. Psychol.,* 1956, 51, 379-384.

KELLEHER, R. T. Concept formation in chimpanzees. *Science,* 1958, 128, 777-778.

KELLER, F. S. *The definition of psychology.* New York: Appleton-Century-Crofts, 1937.

KELLER, F. S., & SCHOENFELD, W. N. *Principles of psychology.* New York: Appleton-Century-Crofts, 1950.

KELLY, E. L. Concerning the validity of Terman's weights for predicting marital happiness. *Psychol. Bull.,* 1939, 36, 202-203.

KELLY, E. L. Consistency of the adult personality. *Amer. Psychol.,* 1955, 10, 659-681.

KENDLER, H. H. A comparison of learning under motivated and satiated conditions in the white rat. *J. exp. Psychol.,* 1947, 37, 545-549. (*a*)

KENDLER, H. H. S. F., a case of homosexual panic. *J. abnorm. soc. Psychol.*, 1947, 42, 112-119. (*b*)

KENDLER, H. H., & KARASIK, A. D. Concept formation as a function of competition between response produced cues. *J. exp. Psychol.*, 1958, 55, 278-283.

KENDLER, H. H., & KENDLER, T. S. Vertical and horizontal processes in problem solving. *Psychol. Rev.*, 1962, 69, 1-16.

KENDLER, H. H., & LACHMAN, R. Habit reversal as a function of schedule of reinforcement and drive strength. *J. exp. Psychol.*, 1958, 55, 584-591.

KENDLER, H. H., PLISKOFF, S. S., D'AMATO, M. R., & KATZ, S. Nonreinforcements versus reinforcements as variables in the partial reinforcement effect. *J. exp. Psychol.*, 1957, 53, 269-276.

KENDLER, H. H., & VINEBERG, R. The acquisition of compound concepts as a function of previous training. *J. exp. Psychol.*, 1954, 48, 252-259.

KENDLER, T. S. An experimental investigation of transposition as a function of the difference between training and test stimuli. *J. exp. Psychol.*, 1950, 40, 552-562.

KENDLER, T. S., & KENDLER, H. H. Reversal and nonreversal shifts in kindergarten children. *J. exp. Psychol.*, 1959, 58, 56-60.

KENDLER, T. S., & KENDLER, H. H. Inferential behavior in children as a function of age and subgoal constancy. *J. exp. Psychol.*, 1962, 64, 460-466.

KENT, G. H., & ROSANOFF, A. J. A study of association in insanity. *Amer. J. Insanity*, 1910, 67, 37-96, 317-390.

KEYS, A., BROZEK, J., HENSCHEL, A., MICKELSEN, O., & TAYLOR, H. L. *The biology of human starvation.* Minneapolis: Univer. of Minnesota Press, 1950.

KIENTZLE, M. J. Properties of learning curves under varied distributions of practice. *J. exp. Psychol.*, 1946, 36, 187-211.

KIMBLE, G. A. An experimental test of a two-factor theory of inhibition, *J. exp. Psychol.*, 1949, 39, 15-23.

KIMBLE, G. A. *Hilgard and Marquis' conditioning and learning.* (2nd ed.) New York: Appleton-Century-Crofts, 1961.

KIMBLE, G. A. *Principles of general psychology.* New York: Ronald, 1957.

KIMBLE, G. A., & BILODEAU, E. A. Work and rest as variables in cyclical motor learning. *J. exp. Psychol.*, 1949, 39, 150-157.

KIMBLE, G. A., & KENDALL, J. W., Jr. A comparison of two methods of producing experimental extinction. *J. exp. Psychol.*, 1953, 45, 87-90.

KING, S. H., & HENRY, A. F. Aggression and cardiovascular reactions related to parental control over behavior. *J. abnorm. soc. Psychol.*, 1955, 50, 206-210.

KINSEY, A. C., POMEROY, W. B., & MARTIN, C. E. *Sexual behavior in the human male.* Philadelphia: Saunders, 1948.

KITT, A., & GLEICHER, D. B. Determinants of voting behavior: a progress report on the Elmira election study. *Publ. Opin. Quart.*, 1950, 14, 393-412.

KLUCKHOHN, C. *Mirror for man.* New York: McGraw-Hill, 1949.

KLÜVER, H., & BUCY, P. C. Preliminary analysis of functions of the temporal lobe in monkeys. *Arch. Neurol. & Psychiat.*, 1939, 42, 979-1000.

KOCH, S., & DANIEL, W. J. The effect of satiation on the behavior mediated by a habit of maximum strength. *J. exp. Psychol.*, 1945, 35 167-187.

KÖHLER, W. *The mentality of apes.* New York: Harcourt, Brace, 1925.

KÖHLER, W. *Gestalt psychology.* (2nd ed.) New York: Liveright, 1947.

KRASNER, L. Studies of the conditioning of verbal behavior. *Psychol. Bull.*, 1958, 55, 148-170.

KRECH, D., & CRUTCHFIELD, R. S. *Theory and practice of social psychology.* New York: McGraw-Hill, 1948.

KRECH, D., CRUTCHFIELD, R. S., & BALLACHY, E. L. *Individual in society: A textbook of social psychology.* New York: McGraw-Hill, 1962.

KRUEGER, W. C. F. The effect of overlearning on retention. *J. exp. Psychol.*, 1929, 12, 71-78.

KUDER, G. F. *Revised manual for the Kuder Preference Record.* Chicago: Science Research Associates, 1958.

KURTZ, A. L. *The prediction of code learning ability.* OSRD Report No. 4059. New York: The Psychological Corp., 1944.

LAMBERT, W. W., SOLOMON, R. L., & WATSON, P. D. Reinforcement and extinction as factors in size estimation. *J. exp. Psychol.*, 1949, 39, 637-641.

LAMBERT, W. W., & SOLOMON, R. L. Extinction of a running response as a function of block point from the goal. *J. comp. physiol. Psychol.*, 1952, 45, 269-279.

LASHLEY, K. S. *Brain mechanisms and intelligence.* Chicago: Univer. of Chicago Press, 1929.

LAWSON, R. *Learning and behavior.* New York: Macmillan, 1960.

714

LAZARSFELD, P. F., BERELSON, B. R., & GAUDET, H. *The people's choice.* New York: Duell, Sloan, & Pearce, 1944.

LAZARUS, R. S., & ERIKSEN, C. W. Effects of failure stress upon skilled performance. *J. exp. Psychol.,* 1952, 43, 100-105.

LEAHY, A. M. Nature-nurture and intelligence. *Genet. Psychol. Monogr.,* 1935, 17, 235-308.

LEAVITT, H. J. Some effects of certain communication patterns on group performance. *J. abnorm. soc. Psychol.,* 1951, 46, 38-50.

LEAVITT, H. J. *Managerial psychology.* Chicago: Univer. of Chicago Press, 1958.

LEE, E. S. Negro intelligence and selective migration: a Philadelphia test of the Klineberg hypothesis. *Amer. sociol. Rev.,* 1951, 16, 227-233.

LEEPER, R. W. The role of motivation in learning: a study of the phenomenon of differential motivational control of the utilization of habits. *J. genet. Psychol.,* 1935, 46, 3-40. (a)

LEEPER, R. W. A study of a neglected portion of the field of learning: the development of sensory organization. *J. genet. Psychol.,* 1935, 46, 41-75. (b)

LEHNER, G. F. J., & KUBE, E. *The dynamics of personal adjustment.* Englewood Cliffs, N.J.: Prentice-Hall, 1955.

LEHRMAN, D. S. On the organization of maternal behavior and the problem of instinct. In P.-P. Grasse (Ed.), *l'Instinct dans le Comportement des Animaux et de l'Homme.* Paris: Masson et Cⁱᵉ, Editeurs, 1956. Pp. 475-520.

LENNEBERG, E. H., & ROBERTS, J. M. The language of experience: a study in methodology. *Int. J. Am. Linguistics Suppl.,* 1956, 22 (Memoir 13).

LEVINE, S. Stimulation in infancy. *Scientific Amer.,* 1960, 202, No. 5, 80-86.

LEVINSON, B. M. Traditional Jewish cultural values and performance on the Wechsler tests. *J. educ. Psychol.,* 1959, 50, 177-181.

LEVY, D. M. *Maternal overprotection.* New York: Columbia Univer. Press, 1943.

LEWIN, K. *A dynamic theory of personality.* New York: McGraw-Hill, 1935.

LEWIN, K., LIPPITT, R., & WHITE, R. K. Patterns of aggressive behavior in experimentally created "social climates." *J. soc. Psychol.,* 1939, 10, 271-299.

LEWIS, D. J., & DUNCAN, C. P. Effect of different percentages of money reward on extinction of a lever-pulling response. *J. exp. Psychol.,* 1956, 52, 23-27.

LICHTEN, W., & LURIE, S. A new technique for the study of perceived size. *Amer. J. Psychol.,* 1950, 63, 280-282.

LIFTON, R. J. *Thought reform and the psychology of totalism.* New York: Norton, 1961.

LINDSLEY, O. R. Operant conditioning methods applied to research in chronic schizophrenia. *Psychiat. Res. Rep.,* 1956, 6, 118.

LINDZEY, G. (Ed.) *Handbook of social psychology.* Reading, Mass.: Addison-Wesley, 1954, 2 vols.

LIPSET, S. M., & BENDIX, R. *Social mobility in industrial society.* Berkeley: Univer. of California Press, 1959.

LIUBLINSKAYA, A. A. The development of children's speech and thought. In B. Simon (Ed), *Psychology in the Soviet Union.* Stanford, Calif.: Stanford Univer. Press, 1957. Pp. 197-204.

LOFQUIST, L. H., & ENGLAND, G. N. *Problems in vocational counseling.* Dubuque, Iowa: William C. Brown, 1961.

LORGE, I. Prestige, suggestion, and attitudes. *J. soc. Psychol.,* 1936, 7, 386-402.

LORGE, I. Influence of regularly interpolated time intervals on subsequent learning. *Teach. Coll. Contr. Educ.,* 1939, No. 438.

LORGE, I. Schooling makes a difference. *Teach. College. Rec.,* 1945, 46, 483-492.

LOUCKS, R. B. Studies of neural structures essential for learning: II. The conditioning of salivary and striped muscle responses to faradization of cortical sensory elements, and the action of sleep upon such mechanisms. *J. comp. Psychol.,* 1938, 25, 315-332.

LOUCKS, R. B., & GANTT, W. H. The conditioning of striped muscle responses based upon faradic stimulation of dorsal roots and dorsal columns of the spinal cord. *J. comp. Psychol.,* 1938, 25, 415-426.

LUCAS, D. B., & BRITT, S. H. *Advertising psychology and research.* New York: McGraw-Hill, 1950.

LUCHINS, A. S. Mechanization in problem solving: The effect of *einstellung. Psychol. Monogr.,* 1942, 54, No. 248.

LUCKHARDT, A. B., & CARLSON, A. J. Contributions to the physiology of the stomach: XVII. On the chemical control of the gastric hunger mechanism. *Amer. J. Physiol.,* 1915, 36, 37-46.

LUNDIN, R. W. *Personality: An experimental approach.* New York: Macmillan, 1961.

LYKKEN, D. T. A study of anxiety in the sociopathic personality. *J. abnorm. soc. Psychol.,* 1957, 55, 6-10.

MACCOBY, E. E., NEWCOMB, T. M., & HARTLEY, E. L. *Readings in social psychology.* (3rd ed.) New York: Holt, Rinehart, & Winston, 1958.

MACKINNON, D. W. What do we mean by talent

and how do we test for it? *The search for talent.* New York: College Entrance Examination Board, 1960.

McClelland, D. C. *Personality.* New York: Morrow, 1951.

McClelland, D. C. *Studies in motivation.* New York: Appleton-Century-Crofts, 1955.

McClelland, D. C., & Apicella, F. S. A functional classification of verbal reactions to experimentally induced failure. *J. abnorm. soc. Psychol.,* 1945, 40, 376-390.

McClelland, D. C., Atkinson, J. W., Clark, R. A., & Lowell, E. L. *The achievement motive.* New York: Appleton-Century-Crofts, 1953.

McConnell, J. V. *Battle for the mind.* Television film produced by the Univer. of Michigan, Ann Arbor, 1958.

McConnell, J. V., Cutler, R. L., & McNeil, E. B. Subliminal stimulation: an overview. *Amer. Psychologist,* 1958, 13, 229-242.

McGehee, W. Cutting training waste. *Pers. Psychol.,* 1948, 1, 331-340.

McGeoch, J. A. The influence of degree of learning upon retroactive inhibition. *Amer. J. Psychol.,* 1929, 41, 252-262.

McGeoch, J. A. The influence of associative value upon the difficulty of nonsense-syllable lists. *J. genet. Psychol.,* 1930, 37, 421-426.

McGeoch, J. A., & Irion, A. L. *Psychology of human learning.* (2nd ed.) New York: David McKay, 1952.

McGeoch, J. A., & McDonald, W. T. Meaningful relation and retroactive inhibition. *Amer. J. Psychol.,* 1931, 43, 579-588.

McGranahan, D. V. A comparison of social attitudes among American and German youth. *J. abnorm. soc. Psychol.,* 1946, 41, 245-257.

McNemar, Q. A critical examination of the University of Iowa studies of environmental influences upon the I.Q. *Psychol. Bull.,* 1940, 37, 63-92.

McNemar, Q. *The revision of the Stanford-Binet scale.* Boston: Houghton Mifflin, 1942.

McNemar, Q. Note on Wellman's re-analysis of I.Q. changes of orphanage preschool children. *J. genet. Psychol.,* 1945, 67, 215-219.

McNemar, Q. *Psychological statistics.* (3rd ed.) New York: Wiley, 1962.

Mahut, H. Breed differences in the dog's emotional behaviour. *Canad. J. Psychol.,* 1958, 12, 35-44.

Maier, N. R. F. *Frustration: The study of behavior without a goal.* New York: McGraw-Hill, 1949.

Maier, N. R. F., Glaser, N. M., & Klee, J. B. Studies of abnormal behavior in the rat: III. The development of behavior fixations through frustrations. *J. exp. Psychol.,* 1940, 26, 521-546.

Mandler, G., & Kessen, W. *The language of psychology.* New York: Wiley, 1959.

Mann, R. D. A review of the relationship between personality and performance in small groups. *Psychol. Bull.,* 1959, 56, 241-270.

Marx, M. H. *Psychological theory.* New York: Macmillan, 1951.

Masland, R. L., Sarason, S. B., & Gladwin, T. *Mental subnormality.* New York: Basic Books, 1958.

Maslow, A. H. Self-actualizing people: a study of psychological health. *Personality Symposia,* 1950, No. 1.

Matthews, S. A., & Detwiler, S. R. The reaction of amblystoma embryos following prolonged treatment with chloretone. *J. exp. Zool.,* 1926, 45, 279-292.

Max, L. W. Experimental study of the motor theory of consciousness: IV. Action current responses in the deaf during awakening, kinesthetic imagery and abstract thinking. *J. comp. Psychol.,* 1937, 24, 301-344.

Mead, M. Adolescence in primitive and in modern society. In V. F. Calverton & S. D. Schmalhausen (Eds.), *The new generation.* New York: Macauley, 1930.

Melzack, R. The perception of pain. *Scientific Amer.,* 1961, 204, 2, 41-49.

Menzies, R. Conditioned vasomotor responses in human subjects. *J. Psychol.,* 1937, 4, 75-120.

Milgram, S. Nationality and conformity. *Scientific Amer.,* 1961, 205, No. 6, 45-51.

Mill, J. S. *Autobiography.* London: Oxford Univer. Press, 1924.

Miller, G. A. *Language and communication.* New York: McGraw-Hill, 1951.

Miller, G. A., & Selfridge, J. A. Verbal context and the recall of meaningful material. *Amer. J. Psychol.,* 1950, 63, 176-185.

Miller, N. E. Experimental studies of conflict. In J. McV. Hunt (Ed.), *Personality and the behavior disorders.* Vol. 1. New York: Ronald, 1944. Pp. 431-465.

Miller, N. E. Studies of fear as an acquirable drive: I. Fear as motivation and fear-reduction as reinforcement in the learning of new responses *J. exp. Psychol.,* 1948, 38, 89-101. (a)

Miller, N. E. Theory and experiment relating psychoanalytic displacement to stimulus-response generalization. *J. abnorm. soc. Psychol.,* 1948, 43, 155-178. (b)

Miller, N. E. Learnable drives and rewards. In S. S. Stevens (Ed.), *Handbook of experimental*

716

psychology. New York: Wiley, 1951. Pp. 435-472.

MILLER, N. E. Experiments on motivation. *Science*, 1957, 126, 1271-1278.

MILLER, N. E. Liberalization of basic S-R concepts: Extension to conflict behavior, motivation and social learning. In S. Koch (Ed.), *Psychology: A study of a science.* Vol. 2. New York: McGraw-Hill, 1959. Pp. 196-292.

MILLER, N. E. Learning resistance to pain and fear: Effects of overlearning, exposure, and rewarded exposure in context. *J. exp. Psychol.,* 1960, 60, 137-145.

MILLER, N. E., & BUGELSKI, R. Minor studies of aggression: II. The influence of frustrations imposed by the in-group on attitudes expressed toward out-groups. *J. Psychol.,* 1948, 25, 437-442.

MILLER, N. E., & KRAELING, D. Displacement: greater generalization of approach than avoidance in a generalized approach-avoidance conflict. *J. exp. Psychol.,* 1952, 43, 217-221.

MINAMI, H., & DALLENBACH, K. M. The effect of activity upon learning and retention in the cockroach, *periplaneta americana. Amer. J. Psychol.,* 1946, 59, 1-58.

MISCHEL, W. Preference for delayed reinforcement and social responsibility. *J. abnorm. soc. Psychol.,* 1961, 62, 1-7.

MONTGOMERY, M. F. The role of salivary glands in the thirst mechanism. *Amer. J. Physiol.,* 1931, 96, 221-227.

MOON, P. *The scientific basis of illuminating engineering.* New York: McGraw-Hill, 1936.

MOON, L. E., & HARLOW, H. F. Analysis of oddity learning by rhesus monkey. *J. comp. physiol. Psychol.,* 1955, 48, 188-194.

MORENO, J. L. *Who shall survive?* Washington, D.C.: Nervous and Mental Disorders Publishing Co., 1934.

MORENO, J. L. *Psychodrama.* New York: Beacon House, 1946.

MORGAN, C. T., & STELLAR, E. *Physiological psychology.* (2nd ed.) New York: McGraw-Hill, 1950.

MORUZZI, G., & MAGOUN, H. W. Brain stem reticular formation and activation of the EEG. *EEG Clin. Neurophysiol.,* 1949, 1, 455-473.

MOWRER, O. H. An experimental analogue of "regression" with incidental observations on "reaction formation." *J. abnorm. soc. Psychol.,* 1940, 35, 56-87.

MOWRER, O. H. The psychologist looks at language. *Amer. Psychologist,* 1954, 9, 660-694.

MOWRER, O. H., & LAMOREAUX, R. R. Avoidance conditioning and signal duration: A study of secondary motivation and reward. *Psychol. Monogr.,* 1942, 54, No. 247.

MOWRER, O. H., & JONES, H. M. Extinction and behavior variability as functions of effortfulness of task. *J. exp. Psychol.,* 1943, 33, 369-386.

MUNN, N. L. *Handbook of psychological research on the rat.* Boston: Houghton Mifflin, 1950.

MUNN, N. L. *Psychology.* (3rd ed.) Boston: Houghton Mifflin, 1951.

MURDOCK, B. B., JR. "Backward" learning in paired associates. *J. exp. Psychol.,* 1956, 51, 213-215.

MURPHY, G. *Historical introduction to modern psychology.* (Rev. ed.) New York: Harcourt, Brace, & World, 1949.

MURRAY, E. J., & MILLER, N. E. Displacement: steeper gradient of generalization of avoidance than of approach with age of habit controlled. *J. exp. Psychol.,* 1952, 43, 222-226.

MURRAY, E. J., & BERKUN, M. M. Displacement as a function of conflict. *J. abnorm. soc. Psychol.,* 1955, 51, 47-56.

MURRAY, H. A. *Thematic apperception test.* Cambridge, Mass.: Harvard Univer. Press, 1943.

MUSSEN, P. H., & CONGER, J. J. *Child development and personality.* New York: Harper & Row, 1956.

MUSSEN, P. H., & KAGAN, J. Group conformity and perceptions of parents. *Child Develpm.,* 1958, 29, 57-60.

NACHMAN, M. The inheritance of saccharin preference. *J. comp. physiol. Psychol.,* 1959, 52, 451-457.

NAGEL, E. Methodological issues in psychoanalytic theory. In S. Hook (Ed.), *Psychoanalysis, scientific method and philosophy.* New York: New York Univer. Press, 1959.

NAGEL, E. *The structure of science.* New York: Harcourt, Brace, & World, 1961.

NEWCOMB, T. M. *Personality and social change: Attitude formation in a student community.* New York: Dryden Press, 1943.

NEWCOMB, T. M. *Social psychology.* New York: Holt, Rinehart, & Winston, 1950.

NEWMAN, H. H. Mental traits of identical twins reared apart. *J. Hered.,* 1929, 20, 153-166.

NEWMAN, H. H., FREEMAN, F. N., & HOLZINGER, K. J. *Twins: A study of heredity and environment.* Chicago: Univer. of Chicago Press, 1937.

NUNNALLY, J. C. *Tests and measurements: Assessment and prediction.* New York: McGraw-Hill, 1959.

Office of Strategic Services, Assessment Staff.

Assessment of men: Selection of personnel for the Office of Strategic Services. New York: Holt, Rinehart, & Winston, 1948.

OLDS, J. Satiation effects in self-stimulation of the brain. *J. comp. physiol. Psychol.,* 1958, 51, 675-678.

OLDS, J., & MILNER, P. Positive reinforcement produced by electrical stimulation of septal area and other regions of rat brain. *J. comp. physiol. Psychol.,* 1954, 47, 419-427.

ORBISON, W. D. Shape as a function of the vector field. *Amer. J. Psychol.,* 1939, 52, 31-45.

OSGOOD, C. E. *Method and theory in experimental psychology.* New York: Oxford Univer. Press, 1953.

OSTERBERG, G. Topography of the layer of rods and cones in the human retina. *Acta Ophthal. Suppl.,* 1935, 61, 1-102.

OVERTON, R. K., & BROWN, W. L. Unrecognized weakness and compensatory learning. *Amer. J. Psychol.,* 1957, 70, 126-127.

PAVLOV, I. P. *Conditioned reflexes.* Trans. by G. V. Anrep. London: Oxford Univer. Press, 1927.

PEARSON, K. *Life, letters, and labors of Galton: Birth 1822 to marriage 1853.* Cambridge, England: Cambridge Univer. Press, 1914.

PERIN, C. T. Behavior potentiality as a joint function of the amount of training and degree of hunger at the time of extinction. *J. exp. Psychol.,* 1942, 30, 93-113.

PERIN, C. T. The effect of delayed reinforcement upon the differentiation of bar responses in white rats. *J. exp. Psychol.,* 1943, 32, 95-109.

PETERSON, M. S., & JENKINS, J. J. Word association phenomena at the individual level: a pair of case studies. Technical Report No. 16, ONR Contract N8 ONR-r-662-16, Univer. of Minnesota, 1957.

PETTIGREW, T. F. Personality and sociocultural factors in intergroup attitudes, a cross national comparison. *J. Conflict Resolution,* 1958, 2, 29-42.

PIAGET, J. How children form mathematical concepts. *Scientific Amer.,* 1953, 189, No. 5, 74-79.

PITTES, J. E. Extinction during psychotherapy of GSR accompanying "embarrassing" statements. *J. abnorm. soc. Psychol.,* 1957, 54, 187-191.

POMEROY, D. S. Retention of a motor act as a function of interpolated activity. Unpublished master's thesis, State University of Iowa, 1944.

PORTER, L. W., & DUNCAN, C. P. Negative transfer in verbal learning. *J. exp. Psychol.,* 1953, 46, 61-64.

POSCHEL, B. H. Proactive and retroactive effects of electroconvulsive shock on approach-avoidance conflict. *J. comp. physiol. Psychol.,* 1957, 50, 392-396.

POSTMAN, L. Retention as a function of degree of overlearning. *Science,* 1962, 135, 666-667. (a)

POSTMAN, L. The temporal course of proactive inhibition for serial lists. *J. exp. Psychol.,* 1962, 63, 361-369. (b)

PRATT, C. C. *The logic of modern psychology.* New York: Macmillan, 1939.

PRUITT, W. O., JR. Animals in snow. *Scientific Amer.,* 1960, 202, No. 1, 60-68.

RATOOSH, P. On interposition as a cue for the perception of distance. *Proc. Nat. Acad. Sci.,* 1949, 35, p. 258.

RAZRAN, G. The observable unconscious and the inferable conscious in current Soviet psychophysiology: interoceptive conditioning, semantic conditioning, and the orienting reflex. *Psychol. Rev.* 1961, 68, 81-147.

RIBBLE, M. A. *The rights of infants.* New York: Columbia Univer. Press, 1943.

RICHMAN, J. (Ed.) *A general selection from the works of Sigmund Freud.* New York: Liveright, 1957.

RICHTER, C. P. Symposium: contributions of psychology to the understanding of problems of personality and behavior: IV. Biological foundations of personality differences. *Amer. J. Orthopsychiat.,* 1932, 2, 345-354.

RICHTER, C. P. The phenomenon of unexplained sudden death in animals and man. In H. Feifel (Ed.), *The meaning of death.* New York: McGraw-Hill, 1959.

RIESS, B. F. Genetic changes in semantic conditioning. *J. exp. Psychol.,* 1946, 36, 143-152.

RIESS, B. F. The isolation of factors of learning and native behavior in field and laboratory studies. *Ann. New York Acad. Sci.,* 1950, 51, 1093-1102.

RILEY, D. A. The nature of the effective stimulus in animal discrimination learning: transposition reconsidered. *Psychol. Rev.* 1958, 65, 1-7.

ROESSLER, R. L., & BROGDEN, W. J. Conditioned differentiation of vasoconstriction to subvocal stimuli. *Amer. J. Psychol.,* 1943, 56, 78-86.

ROGERS, C. R. *Counselling and psychotherapy.* Boston: Houghton Mifflin, 1942.

ROGERS, C. R. *Client-centered therapy.* Boston: Houghton Mifflin, 1951.

ROGERS, C. R. A theory of therapy, personality and interpersonal relationships, as developed in the client-centered framework. In S. Koch (Ed.), *Psychology: A study of a science.* Vol. 3. New York: McGraw-Hill, 1959.

RORSCHACH, H. *Psychodiagnostics.* Berne: Hans Huber, 1942.

ROSEN, B. C. The achievement syndrome: A psychocultural dimension of social stratification. *Amer. Soc. Rev.* 1956, 21, 203-211.

ROSENBERG, M. J. Cognitive structure and attitudinal affect. *J. abnorm. soc. Psychol.,* 1956, 53, 367-372.

ROTTER, J. B., & RAFFERTY, J. E. *Manual for the Rotter incomplete sentence blank, college form.* New York: The Psychological Corp., 1950.

ROWAN, W. *The riddle of migration.* Baltimore: Williams & Wilkens, 1931.

RUNDQUIST, E. A. Inheritance of spontaneous activity in rats. *J. comp. Psychol.,* 1933, 16, 415-438.

RUSSELL, R. W., & CRONBACH, L. J. Report of testimony at a Congressional hearing. *Amer. Psychologist,* 1958, 13, 217-223.

RUSSELL, W. A., & STORMS, L. H. Implicit verbal chaining in paired-associate learning. *J. exp. Psychol.,* 1955, 49, 287-293.

SALZINGER, K., & PISONI, S. Reinforcement of affect responses of schizophrenics during the clinical interview. *J. abnorm. soc. Psychol.,* 1958, 57, 84-90.

SALZMAN, L. An evaluation of shock therapy. *Amer. J. Psychiat.,* 1947, 102, 669-679.

SANFORD, F. H. Research on military leadership. In J. C. Flanagan (Ed.), *Psychology in the world emergency.* Pittsburgh: Univer. of Pittsburgh Press, 1952.

SAPHIR, W. Chronic hypochloremia simulating psychoneurosis. *J. Amer. med. Ass.,* 1945, 129, 510-512.

SARBIN, T. R. The concept of role-taking. *Sociometry,* 1943, 6, 273-285.

SAWREY, W. L., & WEISZ, J. D. An experimental method of producing gastric ulcers. *J. comp. physiol. Psychol.,* 1956, 49, 269-270.

SAWREY, W. L., CONGER, J. J., & TURRELL, E. S. An experimental investigation of the role of psychological factors in the production of gastric ulcers in rats. *J. comp. physiol. Psychol.,* 1956, 49, 457-461.

SCHACHTER, S. *The psychology of affiliation.* Stanford, Calif.: Stanford Univer. Press, 1959.

SCHAFFNER, B. *Fatherland.* New York: Columbia Univer. Press, 1948.

SCHMIDT, H. O. Test profiles as a diagnostic aid: The Minnesota Multiphasic Inventory. *J. appl. Psychol.,* 1945, 29, 115-131.

SCOTT, J. P. Comparative social psychology. In R. H. Waters, D. A. Rethlingshafer, & W. E. Caldwell (Eds.), *Principles of comparative psychology.* New York: McGraw-Hill, 1960.

SEARS, R. R., HOVLAND, C. I., & MILLER, N. E. Minor studies of aggression: I. Measurement of aggressive behavior. *J. Psychol.,* 1940, 9, 275-294.

SEARS, R. R., MACCOBY, E. E., & LEVIN, H. *Patterns of child rearing.* Evanston, Ill.: Row, Peterson, 1957.

SEARS, R. R., PINTLER, M. H., & SEARS, P. S. Effect of father separation on preschool children's doll play aggression. *Child Develpm.,* 1946, 17, 219-243.

SEASHORE, L. E., & WILLIAMS, M. C. An illusion of length. *Psychol. Rev.,* 1900, 7, 592-599.

SEASHORE, H. Tenth grade tests as predictors of twelfth grade scholarship and college entrance status. *J. counsel. Psychol.,* 1954, 1, 106-115.

SELYE, H. *The stress of life.* New York: McGraw-Hill, 1956.

SEM-JACOBSEN, C. W. Symposium. In H. H. Jasper, L. D. Proctor, R. S. Knighton, W. C. Noshay, & R. T. Costello (Eds.), *Reticular formation of the brain.* Boston: Little, Brown, 1958. Pp. 725-726.

SENDEN, M. V. *Space and sight.* Trans. by P Heath. New York: The Free Press of Glencoe, 1960.

SHAFFER, L. F., & SHOBEN, E. J., JR. *The psychology of adjustment.* (2nd ed.) Boston: Houghton Mifflin, 1956.

SHAW, F. J. Two determinants of selective forgetting. *J. abnorm. soc. Psychol.,* 1944, 39, 434-445.

SHEFFIELD, F. D., & ROBY, T. B. Reward value of a non-nutritive sweet taste. *J. comp. physiol. Psychol.,* 1950, 43, 471-481.

SHELDON, W. H., & STEVENS, S. S. *The varieties of temperament.* New York: Harper & Row, 1942.

SHELDON, W. H., STEVENS, S. S., & TUCKER, W. B. *The varieties of human physique.* New York: Harper & Row, 1940.

SHERIF, M., & SHERIF, C. *An outline of social psychology.* (Rev. ed.) New York: Harper & Row, 1956.

SIDMAN, M., & BOREN, J. J. The relative aversiveness of warning signal and shock in an avoidance situation. *J. abnorm. soc. Psychol.,* 1957, 55, 339-344.

SIEGEL, P. S., & FOSHEE, J. G. The law of primary reinforcement in children. *J. exp. Psychol.,* 1953, 45, 12-14.

SIIPOLA, E. M. A group study of some effects of preparatory set. *Psychol. Monogr.,* 1935, 46, No. 210.

SILVERMAN, R. E. *Automated teaching: A review of theory and research.* NAVTRADEV-

CEN 507-2. U. S. Naval Training Device Center, Port Washington, New York, June 8, 1960.

SIMON, C. W., & EMMONS, W. H. Responses to material presented during various levels of sleep. *J. exp. Psychol.,* 1956, 51, 89-97.

SKINNER, B. F. *The behavior of organisms.* New York: Appleton-Century-Crofts, 1938.

SKINNER, B. F. Are theories of learning necessary? *Psychol. Rev.,* 1950, 57, 193-216.

SKINNER, B. F. *Science and human behavior.* New York: Macmillan, 1953.

SKINNER, B. F. Teaching machines. *Science,* 1958, 128, 969-977.

SKINNER, B. F. *Cumulative record.* New York: Appleton-Century-Crofts, 1959.

SKODAK, M. Children in foster homes: A study of mental development. *Univer. of Iowa Stud. in Child Welf.,* 1939, 16, No. 11.

SKODAK, M., & SKEELS, H. M. A final follow-up of one hundred adopted children. *J. genet. Psychol.,* 1949, 75, 85-125.

SLEIGHT, R. B. The effect of instrument dial shape on legibility. *J. appl. Psychol.,* 1948, 32, 170-188.

SLOAN, L. L. Rate of dark adaptation and regional threshold gradient of the dark-adapted eye: physiologic and clinical studies. *Amer. J. Ophthal.,* 1947, 30, 705-720.

SLOTKIN, J. S. Culture and psychopathology. *J. abnorm. soc. Psychol.,* 1955, 51, 269-275.

SMITH, G. M. *A simplified guide to statistics.* (3rd ed.) New York: Holt, Rinehart, & Winston, 1962.

SMITH, M. B., BRUNER, J. S., & WHITE, R. W. *Opinions and personality.* New York: Wiley, 1956.

SMITH, O. A., JR., & GEIS, A. D. Comparative psychology in wildlife conservation. *Amer. Psychol.,* 1956, 11, 183-187.

SMITH, S. Language and non-verbal test performance of racial groups in Honolulu before and after a 14-year interval. *J. gen. Psychol.,* 1942, 26, 51-93.

SMITH, W., & MOORE, J. W. Size of step and achievement in programmed spelling. *Psychol. Rep.,* 1962, 10, 287-294.

SONTAG, L. W., BAKER, C. T., & NELSON, V. L. Mental growth and personality development: a longitudinal study. *Soc. for Res. in Child Develpm. Monogr.,* 1958, No. 23.

SPEARMAN, C. *Abilities of man.* New York: Macmillan, 1927.

SPENCE, K. W. The differential response in animals to stimuli varying in a single dimension. *Psychol. Rev.* 1937, 44, 430-444.

SPENCE, K. W. Learning and performance in eyelid conditioning as a function of the intensity of the UCS. *J. exp. Psychol.,* 1953, 45, 57-63.

SPENCE, K. W. *Behavior theory and conditioning.* New Haven, Conn.: Yale Univer. Press, 1956.

SPERRY, R. W. Cerebral organization and behavior. *Science,* 1961, 133, 1749-1757.

SPROTT, W. J. H. *Human groups.* Baltimore, Md.: Penguin Books, 1958.

STAATS, A. W., STAATS, C. K., & BIGGS, D. A. Meaning of verbal stimuli changed by conditioning. *Amer. J. Psychol.,* 1958, 71, 429-431.

STAATS, C. K., & STAATS, A. W. Meaning established by classical conditioning. *J. exp. Psychol.,* 1957, 54, 74-80.

STAATS, C. K., & STAATS, A. W. Effect of number of trials on the language conditioning of meaning. *Amer. Psychol.,* 1958, 13, 415 (Abstract).

STAGNER, R. *Psychology of personality.* (3rd ed.) New York: McGraw-Hill, 1961.

STAR, S. A., & HUGHES, H. McG. Report on an educational campaign: The Cincinnati plan for the United Nations. *Amer. J. Sociol.,* 1950, 55, 389-400.

STEINBERG, H., & SUMMERFIELD, A. Influence of a depressant drug on acquisition in rote learning. *Quart. J. exp. Psychol.,* 1957, 9, 138-145.

STELLAR, E. The physiology of motivation. *Psychol. Rev.,* 1954, 61, 5-22.

STEVENS, S. S. (Ed.) *Handbook of experimental psychology.* New York: Wiley, 1951.

STEVENS, S. S., & VOLKMANN, J. The relation of pitch to frequency: a revised scale. *Amer. J. Psychol.,* 1940, 53, 329-353.

STODDARD, G. *The meaning of intelligence.* New York: Macmillan, 1943.

STOGDILL, R. M. Personal factors associated with leadership: a survey of the literature. *J. Psychol.,* 1948, 25, 35-71.

STONE, C. P. The initial copulatory response of female rats reared in isolation from the age of 20 days to puberty. *J. comp. Psychol.,* 1926, 6, 73-83.

STOUFFER, S. A., SUCHMAN, E. A., DE VINNEY, L. C., STAR, S. A., & WILLIAMS, R. M., JR. *The American soldier.* Vol. I. *Adjustment during army life.* Princeton, N. J.: Princeton Univer. Press, 1949.

STRASSBURGER, R. C. Resistance to extinction of a conditioned operant as related to drive level at reinforcement. *J. exp. Psychol.,* 1950, 40, 473-487.

STRAUS, M. A. Mental ability and cultural needs: A psychocultural interpretation of the intelligence test performance of Ceylon University entrants. *Amer. sociol. Rev.,* 1951, 16, 371-375.

STRONG, E. K., JR. *Vocational interests of men and women.* Stanford, Calif.: Stanford Univer. Press, 1943.

STRONG, E. K., JR. *Vocational interests 18 years after college.* Minneapolis, Minn.: Univer. of Minnesota Press, 1955.

SUMMERFIELD, A., & STEINBERG, H. Reducing interference in forgetting. *Quart. J. exp. Psychol.,* 1957, 9, 146-154.

SUNDBERG, N. D., & TYLER, L. E. *Clinical psychology: An Introduction to research and practice.* New York: Appleton-Century-Crofts, 1962.

SUPA, M., COTZIN, M., & DALLENBACH, K. M. "Facial vision": The perception of obstacles by the blind. *Amer. J. Psychol.,* 1944, 57, 133-183.

TANSER, H. A. *The settlement of Negroes in Kent County, Ontario.* Chatham, Ontario: Shephard Publ. Co., 1939.

TEMPLETON, R. D., & QUIGLEY, J. P. The action of insulin on motility of the gastrointestinal tract. *Amer. J. Physiol.,* 1930, 91, 467-474.

TERMAN, L. M. (Ed.) *Genetic studies of genius.* Vol. 1. Stanford, Calif.: Stanford Univer. Press, 1925.

TERMAN, L. M. *Psychological factors in marital happiness.* New York: McGraw-Hill, 1938.

TERMAN, L. M. Psychological approaches to the biography of genius. *Science,* 1940, 92, 293-301.

TERMAN, L. M., & MERRILL, M. A. *Measuring intelligence.* Boston: Houghton Mifflin, 1937.

TERMAN, L. M., & MERRILL, M. A. *The Stanford-Binet Intelligence Scale.* Boston: Houghton Mifflin, 1960.

TEUBER, H. L. Review of Wepman's *Recovery from aphasia. J. abnorm. soc. Psychol.,* 1951, 46, 610-611.

THIGPEN, C. H., & CLECKLEY, H. M. *The three faces of Eve.* New York: McGraw-Hill, 1957.

THOMAS, E. M. *The harmless people.* New York: Knopf, 1959.

THOMPSON, R. Successive reversal of a position habit in an invertebrate. *Science,* 1957, 126, 163-164.

THOMSON, R. *The psychology of thinking.* Baltimore, Md.: Penguin Books, 1959.

THORNDIKE, E. L. Mental discipline in high school studies. *J. educ. Psychol.,* 1924, 15, 83-98.

THORNDIKE, R. L., & HAGEN, E. *Measurement and evaluation in psychology and education.* (2nd ed.) New York: Wiley, 1961.

THOULESS, R. H. Phenomenal regression to the real object. *Brit. J. Psychol.,* 1931, 21, 339-359.

THURSTONE, L. L. The measurement of change in social attitude. *J. soc. Psychol.,* 1931, 2, 230-235.

THURSTONE, L. L. *The dimensions of temperament.* Chicago: Univer. of Chicago Press, 1947.

THURSTONE, L. L., & THURSTONE, T. G. Factorial studies of intelligence. *Psychometric Monogr.,* 1941, No. 2.

THURSTONE, T. G. *Primary mental abilities for grades 9-12.* Chicago: Science Research Associates, 1962.

THURSTONE, T. G. *Examiner's manual: Primary mental abilities for grades 9-12.* Chicago: Science Research Associates, 1963.

TITUS, H. E., & HOLLANDER, E. P. The California F-scale in psychological research: 1950-55. *Psychol. Bull.,* 1957, 54, 47-64.

TODD, T. W. The growing-up pattern. *Progressive Educ.,* 1934, 11, 445-450.

TOTTEN, E. Eye movements during visual imagery. *Comp. Psychol. Monogr.,* 1935, 11, No. 3.

TOULMIN, S. *The philosophy of science.* London: Hutchinson Univer. Library, 1953.

TRAPP, E. P., & HIMELSTEIN, P. *Readings on the exceptional child: Research and theory.* New York: Appleton-Century-Crofts, 1962.

TRYON, R. C. Genetic differences in maze-learning ability in rats. *Thirty-ninth Yearb. nat. Soc. Stud. Educ.,* 1940, Part I. Pp. 111-119.

UNDERWOOD, B. J. Interference and forgetting. *Psychol. Rev.,* 1957, 64, 49-60.

UNDERWOOD, B. J. *Psychological research.* New York: Appleton-Century-Crofts, 1958.

UNDERWOOD, B. J., DUNCAN, C. P., TAYLOR, J. A., & COTTON, J. W. *Elementary statistics.* New York: Appleton-Century-Crofts, 1954.

UNDERWOOD, B. J., & RICHARDSON, J. The influence of meaningfulness, intra-list similarity, and serial position on retention. *J. exp. Psychol.,* 1956, 52, 119-126.

VERPLANCK, W. S. The control of the content of conversation: Reinforcement of statements of opinion. *J. abnorm. soc. Psychology,* 1955, 51, 668-676.

VINACKE, W. E. *The psychology of thinking.* New York: McGraw-Hill, 1952.

VON FRISCH, K. *Bees: their vision, chemical senses, and language.* Ithaca, N. Y.: Cornell Univer. Press, 1950.

WALKER, H. M., & LEV, J. *Elementary statistical methods.* (Rev. ed.) New York: Holt, Rinehart, & Winston, 1958.

WARD, L. B. Reminiscence and rote learning. *Psychol. Monogr.*, 1937, 49, No. 220.

WARNER, W. L. *American life*. Chicago: Univer. of Chicago Press, 1953.

WATSON, J. B., & RAYNOR, R. Conditioned emotional reactions. *J. exp. Psychol.*, 1920, 3, 1-14.

WEBB, W. B. *The profession of psychology*. New York: Holt, Rinehart, & Winston, 1962.

WECHSLER, D. *The measurement and appraisal of adult intelligence*. (4th ed.) Baltimore: Williams & Wilkins, 1958.

WEINBERG, H., & HIRE, A. W. *Case book in abnormal psychology*. New York: Knopf, 1957.

WEINER, M. Perceptual development in a distorted room: a phenomenological study. *Psychol. Monogr.*, 1956, 70, No. 423.

WEININGER, O. Physiological damage under emotional stress as a function of early experience. *Science*, 1954, 119, 285-286.

WELLMAN, B. L. *IQ* changes of preschool and nonpreschool groups during the preschool years: a summary of the literature. *J. Psychol.*, 1945, 20, 347-368.

WENDT, G. R. Two and one-half year retention of a conditioned response. *J. gen. Psychol.*, 1937, 17, 178-180.

WENGER, M. A., JONES, F. N., & JONES, M. H. *Physiological psychology*. New York: Holt, Rinehart, & Winston, 1956.

WERTHEIM, T. Ueber die indirekte Sehschaerfe. *Ztschr. f. Psychol.*, 1894, 7, 172-187.

WERTHEIMER, M. *Productive thinking*. (Rev. ed.) New York: Harper & Row, 1959.

WHEELER, L. R. The intelligence of east Tennessee mountain children. *J. educ. Psychol.*, 1932, 23, 351-370.

WHITE, R. W. *Lives in progress: A study of the natural growth of personality*. New York: Holt, Rinehart, & Winston, 1952.

WHITE, R. W. *The abnormal personality*. (2nd ed.) New York: Ronald, 1956.

WHITE, W. A. *Outline of psychiatry*. New York: Nervous and Mental Disease Publishing Co., 1932.

WHITING, J. W. M., & MOWRER, O. H. Habit progression and regression—a laboratory investigation of some factors relevant to human socialization. *J. comp. Psychol.*, 1943, 36, 229-253.

WHORF, B. L. *Language, thought and reality*. New York: Wiley, 1956.

WILDER, C. E. Selection of rachitic and antirachitic diets in the rat. *J. comp. Psychol.*, 1937, 24, 547-577.

WILENSKY, H. The performance of schizophrenic and normal individuals following frustration. *Psychol. Monogr.*, 1952, 66, No. 344.

WILLIAMS, C. D. The elimination of tantrum behavior by extinction procedures. *J. abnorm. soc. Psychol.*, 1959, 59, p. 269.

WILLIAMS, D. R., & TEITELBAUM, P. Control of drinking behavior by means of operant-conditioning technique. *Science*, 1956, 124, 1294-1295.

WILLIAMS, S. B., & WILLIAMS, E. W. Barrier-frustration and extinction in instrumental conditioning. *Amer. J. Psychol.*, 1943, 56, 247-261.

WOLFF, S., & WOLFF, H. G. *Human gastric function: An experimental study of a man and his stom*ach. (2nd ed.) New York: Oxford Univer. Press, 1947.

WOODSON, W. E. *Human engineering guide for equipment designers*. Berkeley, Calif.: Univer. of Calif. Press, 1954.

WOODWORTH, R. S. *Personal data sheet (psychoneurotic inventory)*. Chicago: C. H. Stoelting Co., 1919.

WOODWORTH, R. S. *Contemporary schools of psychology*. (Rev. ed.) New York: Ronald, 1948.

WOODWORTH, R. S., & SCHLOSBERG, H. *Experimental psychology*. (Rev. ed.) New York: Holt, Rinehart, & Winston, 1954.

WOODWORTH, R. S., & SELLS, S. B. An atmosphere effect in formal syllogistic reasoning. *J. exp. Psychol.*, 1935, 18, 451-460.

WORCHEL, P., & DALLENBACH, K. M. "Facial vision": perception of obstacles by the deaf-blind. *Amer. J. Psychol.*, 1947, 60, 502-553.

YAMAGUCHI, H. G. Drive (D) as a function of hours of hunger (h). *J. exp. Psychol.*, 1951, 42, 108-117.

YATES, A. J. The application of learning theory to the treatment of tics. *J. abnorm. soc. Psychol.*, 1958, 56, 175-182.

YERKES, R. M., & ELDER, J. H. Oestrus, receptivity, and mating in the chimpanzee. *Comp. Psychol. Monogr.*, 1936, 13, 1-39.

YOUNG, D. T. Auditory localization with acoustical transposition of the ears. *J. exp. Psychol.*, 1928, 11, 399-429.

YOUNG, O. G. Rate of learning in relation to spacing of practice periods in archery and badminton. *Res. Quart. Amer. Ass. Hlth. Educ.*, 1954, 25, 231-243.

YOUNG, P. T. Food preferences and the regulation of eating. *J. comp. Psychol.*, 1933, 15, 167-176.

YOUNG, P. T. Reversal of food preferences

722

through controlled pre-feeding. *J. gen. Psychol.*, 1940, 22, 33-66.

YOUNG, P. T. *Motivation and emotion: A survey of determinants of human and animal activity.* New York: Wiley, 1961.

ZANDER, A. F. A study of experimental frustration. *Psychol., Monogr.*, 1944, 56, No. 256.

ZEAMAN, D. Response latency as a function of the amount of reinforcement. *J. exp. Psychol.*, 1949, 39, 466-483.

ZEIGARNIK, B. Ueber das Behalten von erledigten und unerledigten handlungen. *Psychologische Forschung*, 1927, 9, 1-85.

ZELLER, A. F. An experimental analogue of repression: II. The effect of individual failure and success on memory measured by relearning. *J. exp. Psychol.*, 1950, 40, 411-422.

ZIMMERMAN, D. W. Durable secondary reinforcement: method and theory. *Psychol. Rev.*, 1957, 64, 373-383.

NAME INDEX

SUBJECT INDEX